Dear Prospective Doctor:

Students differ both in their needs and in their styles of learning. Some students may choose to pursue an MCAT preparatory *course* in addition to this book. For those who do, we recommend The Princeton Review.

The Princeton Review offers the most comprehensive MCAT preparatory course in the nation. Its instructors specialize in teaching MCAT science conceptually and in training students to use good test-taking strategies to succeed on the MCAT. These effective instructional methods result in an average MCAT score improvement of 10 points.

Students who take the Princeton Review MCAT course must be prepared for, and committed to, an intense preparatory experience. For weeks on end, they will eat, sleep, and breathe just one thing—*the MCAT*. Together with trained, highly skilled teachers who understand how the MCAT is designed and how its questions are built, the student will work through the most comprehensive and extensive course materials.

• Princeton Review students thoroughly review every aspect of physics, inorganic chemistry, organic chemistry, biology, and verbal reasoning, *precisely as it is tested on the MCAT.*

• Our students master dozens of techniques and strategies custom-designed to crack the most challenging MCAT questions.

• Our students receive thousands of exercises and drills on which to practice these techniques and solidify his/her grasp of the concepts.

• Our students sit for five full-length simulated MCAT tests, administered under conditions similar to those they will be confronted with on the day of the real test.

• Detailed score reports, individual review with teachers, and extra help are included in the *most* complete MCAT preparatory course available.

For those students who feel they would benefit from an MCAT course, The Princeton Review's course is clearly the best choice. It is for this reason that we chose to publish this book in association with The Princeton Review.

Wishing you much success in your medical endeavors,

James L. Flowers, MD

Ted Sil

Dr. James L. Flowers, M.D., M.P.H.   Dr. Theodore Silver, M.D., M.P.H.

For more information, call 800-2Review.

The Princeton Review®

Cracking the
MCAT®

2010–2011 Edition

James L. Flowers, M.D., M.P.H. and Theodore Silver, M.D.

PrincetonReview.com

Random House, Inc. New York

The Princeton Review, Inc.
2315 Broadway
New York, NY 10024
E-mail: editorialsupport@review.com

ISBN 978-0-375-42963-7
ISSN 2150-8747

Editor: Selena Coppock
Production Editor: Jennifer Graham
Production Coordinator: Sheena Paul

Printed in the United States of America.

10 9 8 7 6 5 4 3 2 1

2010–2011 Edition

Editorial
Robert Franek, VP Test Prep Books, Publisher
Seamus Mullarkey, Editorial Director
Laura Braswell, Senior Editor
Rebecca Lessem, Senior Editor
Heather Brady, Editor
Selena Coppock, Editor

Production Services
Scott Harris, Executive Director, Production Services
Kim Howie, Senior Graphic Designer
Ryan Tozzi, Production Manager

Production Editorial
Meave Shelton, Production Editor
Jennifer Graham, Production Editor
Kristen O'Toole, Production Editor

Research & Development
Ed Carroll, Agent for National Content Directors
Liz Rutzel, Project Editor

Random House Publishing Team
Tom Russell, Publisher
Nicole Benhabib, Publishing Manager
Ellen L. Reed, Production Manager
Alison Stoltzfus, Associate Managing Editor
Elham Shabahat, Publishing Assistant

Acknowledgments

The authors thank Daniel Silver, M.D., who, as contributing author, is largely responsible for Chapters 42 to 46.

The authors are especially beholden to Timothy McGarvey and Professor Lindy Harrison for their contributions bearing on Chapters 33 through 41.

The authors also wish to thank the following people: Jonathan Silver, Linda Tarleton, Robert Fang, Danielle Giliberti, Jason Hoffman, Emma Husain, John Katzman, Braken Kolle, Kevin Noland, Tessa Sundaram, Eric Wagner, and Sara Woodruff.

And many thanks to the MCAT experts who thoroughly reviewed and revised all of the content for the 2010–2011 edition: Judene Wright, Chris Pentzell, Matt Patterson, Kristen Brunson, Tom Watts, Bill Ewing, Bethany Blackwell, Jennifer Wooddell, and Jes Adams.

Special thanks to Adam Robinson, who conceived of and perfected the Joe Bloggs approach to standardized tests and many of the other successful techniques used by The Princeton Review.

Contents

...So Much More Online!

More Practice...

- 4 Full-length practice MCATs

- Score Reports

- Interactive, click-through learning

Information about Medical School

- Profiles for hundreds of schools help you find the school that is right for you

- Information about financial aid and scholarships

- 5-minute quizzes help you figure out which medical school is right for you

- Search medical schools by program or specialization

Register your book now!

- Go to PrincetonReview.com/cracking

- You'll see a Welcome page where you should register your book using the serial number. What's a serial number, you ask? Flip to the back of your book and you'll see a bunch of letters and numbers printed on the inside back cover. Type this into the window.

- Next you will see a Sign Up/Sign In page where you will type in your e-mail address (username) and choose a password.

- Now you're good to go!

CHAPTER 1

UNDERSTANDING THE MCAT AND THIS BOOK

1.1 THE MCAT

CREATION AND ADMINISTRATION OF THE TEST

The Medical College Admissions Test (MCAT) is produced, administered, and scored under the auspices of the Association of American Medical Colleges (AAMC). Contact information for the AAMC is as follows:

> Association of American Medical Colleges
> 2450 N Street, NW
> Washington, DC 20037-1126
> tel: (202) 828-0400 / fax: (202) 828-1125
> www.aamc.org
> e-mail: mcat@aamc.org

The exam is delivered by Thompson-Prometric testing centers, on behalf of the AAMC.

Registration for the MCAT is available online at the AAMC website: www.aamc.org/students/ mcat. The MCAT is administered on multiple days of the year in morning, afternoon, and weekend sessions. Information regarding deadlines, fees and testing locations is available on the MCAT website.

TEST DESIGN AND SCORING

In 2007, the AAMC adopted a CBT (computer-based test) format for the MCAT and reduced the number of questions on the test by nearly one-third. The test structure, content, and scoring system did not change.

The MCAT CBT, like the old exam, has four components:

(1)   Scientific Reasoning: The Physical Sciences

(2)   Verbal Reasoning

(3)   Writing Sample

(4)   Scientific Reasoning: The Biological Sciences

, The current test is structured as follows:

Test Section	Questions	Time
Tutorial (optional)		10 minutes
Non-Disclosure Agreement		5 minutes
Physical Sciences	52	70 minutes
Break (optional)		10 minutes
Verbal Reasoning	40	60 minutes
Break (optional)		10 minutes
Writing Sample	2	60 minutes
Break (optional)		10 minutes
Biological Sciences	52	70 minutes
Void Question		5 minutes
Survey		5 minutes
Total Test Content Time		4 hours, 20 minutes

Test takers should arrive at the test center at least one half hour before testing begins. The entire test day is approximately $5\frac{1}{2}$ hours long.

The test taker receives four scores, one for each component. The verbal reasoning component and the two scientific reasoning components (biological and physical sciences) are scored on a scale of 1 to 15 where 1 is low and 15 is high. The writing sample component is scored on a scale of J to T where J is low and T is high.

Scientific Reasoning: The Physical Sciences

The MCAT's physical sciences component contains a total of 52 questions and is structured, principally, on reading passages and corresponding questions. Each passage is followed by approximately four to seven multiple-choice questions that in some way pertain to (a) the passage or (b) matters tangentially related to it. Frequently, passages are accompanied by diagrams, graphs, and charts. These also form the bases of questions.

The physical sciences component will also contain some multiple-choice questions that do not pertain to passages. These stand apart from the passage-based questions.

Verbal Reasoning

The MCAT's verbal reasoning section contains a total of 40 questions and largely resembles the "reading comprehension" components of other standardized tests. As in the physical sciences section, each verbal reasoning passage is followed by five to seven multiple-choice questions.

Verbal reasoning questions test the student's ability to (a) recognize statements that paraphrase the passage's text, (b) draw logical inferences on the basis of information presented in the passage, (c) characterize themes on which the passage is built, and (d) follow the lines of reasoning on which the passage or any of its portions might rest.

Writing Sample

The MCAT's writing sample involves writing two essays, each one within thirty minutes. For each essay, the test taker is given a short statement that sets forth a philosophy or point of view. The test taker must then comment on the statement's meaning and application.

Scientific Reasoning: The Biological Sciences

The MCAT's fourth section, biological sciences, deals with biology and organic chemistry. The structure of this section is identical to that of the physical sciences section. There are a total of 52 questions, the majority of which are based on passages. Like physical science passages, biological science passages frequently include diagrams, graphs, and charts. In addition, like the physical sciences component, the biological sciences component contains some questions that do not pertain to passages.

THE CBT FORMAT

Unlike some computerized standardized tests, the MCAT CBT is *not* a computer-adaptive test (CAT). This means that the questions given on the MCAT CBT are predetermined; they are not selected based on the test taker's performance.

The MCAT CBT requires test takers to use basic mouse and keyboard commands to answer questions and navigate through the test. Test takers can also highlight sections of passages, cross off answer choices that the test taker has eliminated, and—in the writing sample—perform basic word processing functions such as cut, copy, and paste.

It is also possible to review and change answers within a section, as long as one is still working in that section. Test takers cannot return to a section once they have exited it.

Before the test begins, test takers have the option to view a brief tutorial which provides information on using the MCAT computer interface. For additional practice with a simulated interface, visit **PrincetonReview.com** or **www.e-mcat.com.**

Students are allowed to use scratch paper during the MCAT CBT; scratch paper is provided by the testing center.

1.2 USING THIS BOOK

Cracking the MCAT offers a thorough program of review and preparation for the MCAT candidate. With respect to the biological and physical sciences, it:

- Presents systematic reviews of all topics on which the MCAT draws;

- Provides drills to reinforce knowledge and mastery; and

- Presents simulated MCAT passages and questions resembling those on the MCAT.

With respect to verbal reasoning and the writing sample, this book

- Teaches you how to systematically approach MCAT questions and exercises, and

- Gives you repeated opportunities for self-testing with simulated passages, questions, and exercises.

ORGANIZATION

Chapters Relating to Science

Chapters 4–12 address substantive physics. **Chapters 13–22** concern inorganic (general) chemistry. **Chapters 23–32** relate to biology, and **chapters 33–41** pertain to organic chemistry. Each chapter features a first principal section called **Mastery Achieved**, a second entitled **Mastery Applied**, and a third called **Mastery Verified**.

Typically, the section entitled **Mastery Achieved** has a great many subsections. It reviews the material germane to the chapter's title primarily with text but also with questions, problems, and exercises that enable you to test and master the material as you work. Answers and explanations follow these questions directly so that, after arriving at an answer, you may immediately understand and correct any errors that were made.

The section entitled **Mastery Applied** provides a simulated MCAT passage relating to the subject of the chapter. Here you have the opportunity to apply your mastery to questions resembling those on the MCAT.

The section called **Mastery Verified** provides answers and explanations for the simulated MCAT passage.

Chapters Relating to Verbal Reasoning

Chapters 42–45 comprehensively prepare you for the MCAT's verbal reasoning section by revealing with repeated drills and practice (a) the manner in which passages are constructed, (b) the design on which questions are built, and (c) the logical and orderly system through which passages and questions should be addressed. **Chapter 45** provides nine simulated MCAT verbal reasoning sets (passages and questions) followed by answers and explanations.

Chapters Relating to the Writing Sample

Chapter 46 explains the nature of the MCAT's writing sample component and teaches you how to systematically construct the essays.

Chapter 47 presents you with six simulated MCAT writing exercises, each followed by a model response. Together with Chapter 46, it fully prepares you for the MCAT's writing sample component.

1.3 ADDITIONAL PREPARATION AND MATERIALS

AAMC MATERIALS

Many students will find that this book fully meets their needs for MCAT preparation. Some may also wish to buy practice tests or other materials from the AAMC. These materials are available for purchase at the AAMC website. Computerized practice tests can also be purchased from the AAMC at **www.e-mcat.com**.

COURSES

Students differ both in their needs and in their styles of learning. Some of you may want to pursue, in addition to this book, an MCAT preparatory course. Among the courses available, the authors recommend the course offered by The Princeton Review. To learn more, visit **PrincetonReview.com** or call 1-800-2Review.

CHAPTER 2

INSIGHTS INTO MCAT SCIENCE COMPONENTS

Before we move to a comprehensive review of MCAT-related science, let's briefly discuss the nature of MCAT science passages and questions and the way you should approach and prepare for MCAT science passages.

2.1 MCAT SCIENCE PASSAGES AND QUESTIONS

This book reviews *all* of the science tested on the MCAT—and then some. Understanding science means understanding that its principles, laws, and concepts apply to limitless numbers of situations and phenomena; the very purpose of learning science is to be able to apply it in unfamiliar contexts.

Many MCAT passages are deliberately designed to present you with information that seems, at first, to be entirely *foreign*—no matter how thorough the student's preparation. The MCAT's writers have unlimited contexts in which to set passages and problems. An MCAT passage might, for example, offer a relatively detailed description of the devices and mechanisms associated with the operation of an electrical power plant, or the physics of aeroflight. The passage might feature unfamiliar terms like "feed water," "bus structure," "yawing moment," "induced drag," and "angle of attack." It might present equations and charts concerning seemingly foreign phenomena, such as "lagging current," "corona," "the Reynolds number," "lift coefficient," "airscrew efficiency, " and "manifold pressure." The passages will often feature illustrations, graphs, and charts that might cause you to conclude that the passage and its questions are beyond your knowledge and ability. This is not true!

MCAT passages are deliberately designed to test your ability to see beyond unfamiliar subject matter and recognize that the *questions* asked are readily answerable with (a) a knowledge of basic science (as found in this book), (b) the capacity to interpret an illustration, graph, or table, and (c) the ability to read carefully and process unfamiliar scientific information.

ILLUSTRATION: THE BIOLOGICAL SCIENCES

No *premedical* student is expected to come to the MCAT with an understanding of the diseases and conditions that he will study as a *medical* student. Nevertheless, MCAT passages frequently concern medical syndromes and diseases, and there is no predicting what syndromes or diseases they might address.

Consider, for example, this excerpt from a simulated MCAT biological science passage:

Passage

Seizures involve uncontrolled and excessive activity of some or all of the central nervous system. Epilepsy is a disorder of the central nervous system in which the patient is prone to seizures. The disorder shows increased frequency among the families of afflicted individuals, but it does not show genotypes or heritability associated with classic Mendelian patterns.

Seizures can be categorized as focal or generalized. The generalized forms give rise to three recognized types: *petit mal*, *grand mal*, and *psychomotor*. Each type yields a fairly characteristic electroencephalogram, as shown in Figure 1. Figure 2 shows the alpha, beta, theta, and delta waves associated with a normal electroencephalogram.

An epileptic who is subject to grand mal seizures is thought to have an intrinsic, ongoing overexcitability of the affected neurons of the brain. The actual seizure might be generated by a variety of external stimuli. The seizure is probably brought to an end through feedback mechanisms in which inhibitory cerebral centers are stimulated.

Seizures do arise from conditions other than epilepsy. For example, excessive quantities of carbon dioxide in the blood (hypercapnia) are known to produce seizures, as do a variety of cerebral disorders, including brain tumor. Young children from infancy to approximately seven years of age are sometimes prone to experience seizures when body temperature is markedly elevated. The manifestation of such febrile seizures on one or more occasions during childhood does not in itself suggest a diagnosis of epilepsy.

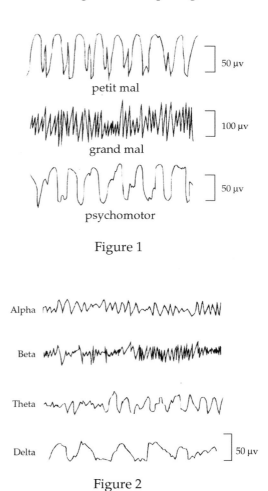

petit mal — 50 μv

grand mal — 100 μv

psychomotor — 50 μv

Figure 1

Alpha

Beta

Theta

Delta — 50 μv

Figure 2

The MCAT writers know very well that seizures and epilepsy do not belong to the premedical syllabus; they do not expect you to have any background in the subject, so the appearance of a passage that relates to epilepsy and associated electroencephalographic data should not make you anxious. The *questions* that follow the passage should be answerable with your knowledge of premedical biology (**Chapters 23–32**). Consider these questions (which could follow a passage like the one just presented):

1. According to the passage, which one of the following would most likely give rise to a seizure?

 A. Excessive feedback inhibition within cerebral circuitry

 B. Failure of blood constituents to move metabolic by–products from tissue to pulmonary alveoli

 C. Increased threshold of neuronal response within the brain and spinal cord

 D. Reduced number of action potentials within the brain and spinal cord

B is correct. The test writers know that in conceptual substance, this question is truly unrelated to the subject of seizures. You could answer this question by noting that according to the passage's last paragraph, "excessive quantities of carbon dioxide in the blood (hypercapnia) are known to produce seizures…" Once you have studied **Chapter 29**, you will know that elevated quantities of carbon dioxide in the blood result from a failure of blood constituents to carry metabolic waste products from the tissues to the pulmonary alveoli.

2. Which, among the following, is NOT characteristic of epilepsy?

 A. Increased excitability of central nervous system neurons

 B. Seizures induced by external stimuli

 C. Seizures of several identifiable patterns

 D. Identifiable homozygous and heterozygous states

D is correct. Like question 1, this question is answerable from (a) what is presented in the passage and (b) what you know through your study of basic biology. According to the passage, epilepsy "does not show genotypes or heritability associated with classic Mendelian patterns." The fundamental principles of inheritance (**Chapter 31**) dictate that the absence of classic Mendelian genotypes and inheritance means the absence of identifiable homozygous and heterozygous states.

3. Among the following, the voltage difference between electroencephalographic peaks and troughs is greatest for:

 A. grand mal seizures

 B. petit mal seizures

 C. psychomotor seizures

 D. normal theta waves

A is correct. You are not expected to be familiar with electroencephalograms, but you *are* expected to answer this question by examining Figures 1 and 2 calmly and logically. In Figure 1, the bracket to the right of the grand mal seizure wave is labeled 100 microvolts. All other waves in both Figures 1 and 2 are associated with a similarly sized bracket labeled 50 microvolts. Logic dictates that the peaks and troughs associated with the grand mal wave carry a greater voltage difference than those of any of the other waves mentioned in the passage.

4. A therapeutic agent with which of the following effects would most merit a trial for prevention of grand mal seizures?

   A. Increasing the threshold for action potential within the central nervous system
   B. Decreasing the threshold for action potential within the peripheral nervous system
   C. Increasing the axon length for neurons within the central nervous system
   D. Increasing the growth of connective tissue within the central nervous system

A is correct. The passage attributes grand mal seizures to an "intrinsic, ongoing overexcitability of the affected neurons of the brain." On the basis of a fundamental knowledge of nerve function (**Chapter 30**) you know that excitability pertains to the threshold potential, which, for any given cell, induces an action potential. In order to prevent grand mal seizures, one would therefore want to decrease excitability, which would, in turn, require an increase of neuronal threshold potential.

ILLUSTRATION: THE PHYSICAL SCIENCES

The MCAT's physical science passages frequently involve subject matter and phenomena that you may not be familiar with. As in the case of the biological passages, all of the *questions* are answerable on the basis of logical thought, careful reading, and a basic knowledge of the science taught in **Chapters 3–22**. Consider, for example, this excerpt from a simulated MCAT physical science passage:

Passage

In the operation of a turbojet, the heat and pressure associated with a working fluid is harnessed to produce physical movement. Heated gas under high pressure is allowed to escape through a nozzle, which causes a reduction in the gas's temperature and pressure, and a concomitant increase in rearward velocity and momentum. If, and only if, the initial pressure of the working fluid is no greater than twice that of the surrounding pressure, a converging nozzle is employed, as shown in Figure 1. Where the subscripts 1 and 2 refer to sections 1 and 2, respectively, of the nozzle, the mass flow, m, is given by the equation:

$$m = A_2 \rho \sqrt{2gJC_pT_t} \sqrt{\left(\frac{p_2}{p_1}\right)^{2/\gamma} - \left(\frac{p_2}{p_1}\right)^{(\gamma+1)/\gamma}}$$

$$v_2 = \sqrt{2gJC_pT_t} \sqrt{1 - \left(\frac{p_2}{p_1}\right)^{(\gamma-1)/\gamma}}$$

m = mass flow
A = cross-sectional area
ρ = density
g = specific constant
J = work equivalent of heat
T_t = total temperature
C_p = specific heat at constant pressure
γ = specific heats
p = static pressure
v = velocity

Maximum flow corresponds to the attainment of critical pressure, which is the pressure at which fluid in the nozzle's throat is equal to the local velocity of sound. For most combustible gases used in turbojets surrounded by air, critical pressure = approximately $(0.5p_1)$

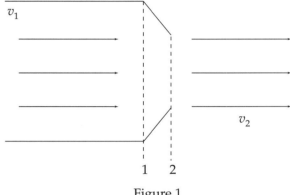

Figure 1

The usual premedical physics syllabus does *not* include any of the material just presented. Nevertheless, the questions that follow are answerable if you combine your knowledge of physical science with a logical and thorough reading of the passage.

1. If gas moving through the nozzle shown in Figure 1 undergoes ideal flow, which of the following is true?

   A. The velocity at section 1 is equal to pressure at section 1.
   B. The pressure at section 2 exceeds pressure at section 1.
   C. The velocity at section 1 exceeds velocity at section 2.
   D. The velocity at section 2 exceeds velocity at section 1.

D is correct. This question requires that you examine Figure 1 and consider it as you would any pipe or vessel of varying diameter. The laws of ideal flow (**Chapter 7**) say that for a fluid moving through a cylindrical vessel of varying size, increased diameter increases pressure and decreases velocity. Decreased diameter increases velocity and decreases pressure, and when you learn from the passage that the nozzle depicted in Figure 1 represents a vessel through which gas is flowing, you can conclude that the velocity at section 2 exceeds the velocity at section 1.

2. If, in Figure 1, the cross-sectional area of section 2 is increased by a factor of 3 and the density of the fluid is reduced by a factor of 4, mass flow will be:

   A. reduced by a factor of 0.75.
   B. reduced by a factor of 12.
   C. increased by a factor of 1.25.
   D. unchanged.

A is correct. The question tests your ability to apply algebraic logic to a seemingly complex equation. The equation plainly indicates that mass volume (m) is directly proportional to:

(cross-sectional area at section 2) × (density) = $A_2 \rho$

If A_2 is multiplied by 3 and ρ is divided by 4, then the overall quantity $A_2\rho$ is multiplied by a factor of $3/4 = 0.75$. Since m is proportional to $A_2\rho$ the value of m is reduced by a factor of 0.75.

3. The emission of the fluid jet involves the conversion of:

   A. work to power.
   B. power to work.
   C. kinetic energy to potential energy.
   D. potential energy to kinetic energy.

D is correct. After studying energy conversions (**Chapter 6**), you will be able to answer this question by noting the relevant information in the passage's first paragraph: "...the heat and pressure associated with a working fluid is harnessed to produce physical movement." The system is one in which potential energy (inherent in the heat and pressure of the gas) is converted to kinetic energy (inherent in the motion of the gas). Moreover, you will know that choices A and B are incorrect because work is never *converted* to power, or power to work.

4. Under which of the following conditions would a turbojet NOT employ a converging nozzle?

    A. When pressure and volume are inversely proportional

    B. When temperature and pressure are directly proportional

    C. When the working fluid is one and a half times the pressure of the ambient pressure

    D. When fluid pressure is three times the pressure of the ambient pressure

D is correct. Again, in the passage's first paragraph you read: "If, and only if, the initial pressure of the working fluid is no greater than twice that of the surrounding pressure, a converging nozzle is employed." It logically follows that if the pressure of the working fluid is more than twice that of the surroundings (ambient pressure), a converging nozzle is *not* used.

2.2 READING, MATHEMATICS, AND MEMORIZATION

READING THE PASSAGE

Success on the MCAT's science sections requires that you read scientific text efficiently. In each chapter, you will encounter a simulated MCAT exercise that appears under the subheading **Mastery Applied**, and as you go through the exercise, you will see that in most cases, the answer to a question derives partly from the passage and partly from your knowledge of basic science.

On the other hand, (1) MCAT passages are frequently arcane and complex, and (2) no set of questions will draw on *all* of the information presented in the associated passage. You should first approach an MCAT science passage without attempting to *fully* comprehend all of its subject matter, or the workings of its illustrations, graphs, and tables. Instead, you should examine the passage and take note of its subject matter and organization, then examine the questions and for each one, return to the passage to find the necessary information.

If you are accustomed to reading material carefully and thoroughly, start to break yourself of this habit because this will cost you time that you cannot afford. Reading with scrupulous attention to detail is undoubtedly an asset in *medical school*, but it may, at times, be a handicap on the MCAT.

MATHEMATICS AND MEMORIZATION

Success on the MCAT requires a working knowledge of algebra, geometry, and trigonometry.

The memorization of mathematical formulas plays a smaller role in answering MCAT questions than most students think. Our review of physics and inorganic chemistry involves many formulas and physical laws, but in each case we are careful to note which *aspects* of a formula or law require your attention.

For example, many of the mathematical formulas relevant to the MCAT are more important for the *proportions* they establish than for the equivalencies they create. Studying Coulomb's law (**Chapter 8**), you should recognize that force is (a) directly proportional to the charge of each object under consideration, and (b) inversely proportional to the square of the distance between the objects; this will serve you better than mechanically memorizing the formula. In connection with ideal gases (**Chapter 19**), if you understand that pressure and volume are inversely proportional and that temperature is directly proportional to each, you will fare better than one who has mechanically memorized $PV = nRT$ and the value of R (the ideal gas constant).

Throughout **Chapters 4–22**, we suggest you place greater and lesser degrees of emphasis on various aspects of formulas and equations, according to the degree to which they are represented on the MCAT.

CHAPTER 3

PHYSICS AND THE MCAT: CONCEPTUAL PREMISES

3.1 MASTERY ACHIEVED

MASTERING UNITS

SI Units

Modern science expresses measurements according to the International System of Units, (SI). SI recognizes seven basic units, each of which measures a fundamental quantity. Five of the seven units are significant for the MCAT student:

Measured Quantity	SI Unit	Symbol
1. Distance/Displacement	meter	m
2. Time	second	s
3. Mass	kilogram	kg
4. Current	ampere	A
5. Temperature	degrees kelvin	K

Table 3.1

SI also includes more complex units that are drawn from the basic ones. **Velocity**, for example, represents change in displacement over change in time and is expressed in meters per second (m/s). **Acceleration** represents change in velocity over change in time and is expressed in meters per second per second (m/s^2).

Some complex quantities are normally expressed in **derivative** units bearing their own names and symbols. For instance, the quantity of force is typically described as:

$$(\text{mass}) \times (\text{acceleration})$$

which can also be written as:

$$(\text{mass}) \times \frac{\left(\dfrac{\text{displacement}}{\text{unit of time}} \right)}{\text{unit of time}}$$

In basic units, force can be expressed in kg • m/s^2, but for convenience, it is normally measured in the derivative unit **newton** (**N**), where $1N = 1kg \bullet m/s^2$.

All derivative units that are significant to the MCAT are thoroughly discussed in the following chapters, so you need not memorize them now. However, for now, take a brief look at Table 3.2:

Measured Quantity	SI Unit and Symbol	Mathematical Derivation/Definition
1. Force	newton (N)	$1\text{ N} = 1\text{ kg} \bullet \text{m/s}^2$
2. Energy	joule (J)	$1\text{ J} = 1\text{ N} \bullet \text{m}$
3. Power	watt (W)	$1\text{ W} = 1\text{ J/s}$
4. Charge	coulomb (C)	$1\text{ C} = 1\text{ A} \bullet \text{s}$
5. Potential	volt (V)	$1\text{ V} = 1\text{ J/C}$
6. Resistance	ohm (Ω)	$1\text{ }\Omega = 1\text{ V/A}$
7. Capacitance	farad (F)	$1\text{ F} = 1\text{ C/V}$
8. Magnetic Field Strength	tesla (T)	$1\text{ T} = 1\text{ N/A} \bullet \text{m}$

Table 3.2

Dimensional Consistency

Calculations must be consistent with respect to the units involved. For example, if time is multiplied by acceleration using the units m/s^2, the result *must* be velocity, expressed in meters per second (m/s).

$$(\text{time}) \times (\text{acceleration}) = \text{velocity}$$

$$[(s) \bullet (m/s^2)] = [(m)(s)/s^2] = [\,(m)(s)/1 \bullet 1/(s)(s)] = (m)(s)/(s)(s) = m/s$$

If the result is in units other than m/s, then there is an error and you must redo your calculations. Similarly, if work is divided by displacement in SI units, the result must be force, expressed in newtons (N).

$$\text{work / displacement} = \text{force}$$

$$J/m = (N \bullet m)/m = N$$

A result in units other than newtons (N) indicates an error. As you can see, this is one simple way to determine a calculation error.

Please solve this problem:

- Power is measured in the SI unit of watts (W) and represents work/time. "Work" represents force × distance. Force represents mass × acceleration. Which of the following expresses the quantity of 1 watt in terms of the *five basic* SI units?

    A. $\text{kg} \bullet \text{m}^2/\text{s}$
    B. $\text{kg} \bullet \text{m}^2/\text{s}^3$
    C. $\text{kg}^2/\text{m}^3 \bullet \text{s}$
    D. $\text{kg}/\text{m}^3 \bullet \text{s}^3$

Problem solved:

B is correct. From Table 3.2 we can see that watts can be written as J/s. Joules can be broken down further to N•m, which can be broken down further to kg•m/s². Thus:

$$W = J / s = \frac{N \bullet m}{s} = \frac{kg \, \frac{m}{s^2} \bullet m}{s} = \frac{kg \bullet m^2}{s^3}$$

MASTERING GRAPHS

The Cartesian Coordinate System (CCS)

The MCAT candidate should understand graphs and the **cartesian coordinate system (CCS)**. In three dimensions, cartesian coordinates look like this:

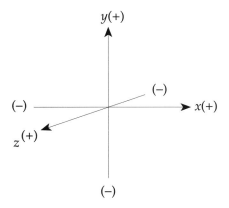

NOTE :
• Three perpendicular axes: x, y, and z.
• The arrow indicates the positive direction.

Figure 3.1a

MCAT graphs will almost always be two-dimensional, making use of the x- and y-axes only (not the z-axis). A plane defined by the x- and y-cartesian coordinates is called a **cartesian plane**.

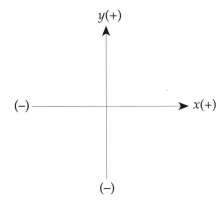

Cartesian Plane

Figure 3.1b

CCS on the MCAT

The MCAT will usually present **straight-line graphs,** as shown in Figure 3.2 (A) and (B), and **curvilinear graphs,** as shown in Figure 3.2 (C).

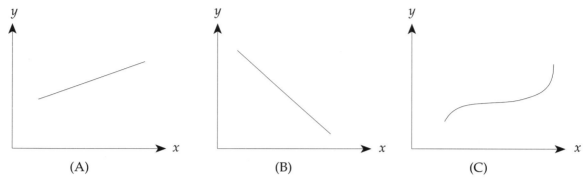

Figure 3.2

For any two-dimensional graph, you should be able to identify (1) the **coordinates**, (2) the **slope**, and (3) the **area under a curve**. As redrawn in Figure 3.3, graphs (A), (B), and (C) highlight these three features.

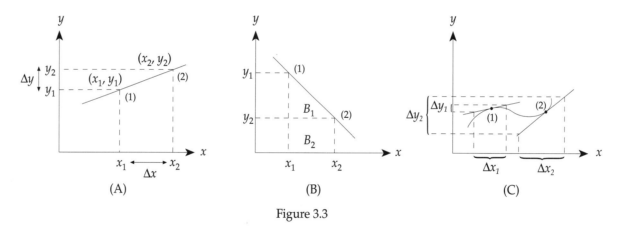

Figure 3.3

Coordinates

For any straight-line graph, coordinates describe a single point by identifying its location along each axis, vertical and horizontal. On Figure 3.3, graph (A), point 1 has coordinates x_1 and y_1, meaning it is located x_1 units "along" the x-axis and y_1 units "up" the y-axis.

Slope

For any straight-line segment on a linear graph, slope is equal to $\dfrac{\Delta Y}{\Delta X}$. For points 1 and 2 on the line:

$$\Delta Y = Y_2 - Y_1$$

and

$$\Delta X = X_2 - X_1$$

(The quantity $\Delta Y = Y_2 - Y_1$ is called the Y component of the line segment between points 1 and 2, and $\Delta X = X_2 - X_1$ is the X component of the line segment between points 1 and 2.) Note that the designation Y_1 and Y_2 for any Y-coordinate point is arbitrary and will yield the correct slope during calculations.

For a *straight-line* graph, the slope is equal at all positions and is found by reference to the values ΔY and ΔX for any two points. For graph (A), Figure 3.3, the slope at all points is equal to the slope of the line segment: point 1 – point 2. For graph (B), Figure 3.3, the slope at all points is equal to the slope of the line segment point 1 – point 2:

$$\frac{\Delta Y}{\Delta X} = \frac{Y_2 - Y_1}{X_2 - X_1}$$

The slope of graph (B) is *negative,* since $Y_2 < Y_1$ and $X_1 < X_2$. Confirm that the slope is negative by noting that the line on graph (B) runs downward to the right, which is characteristic of a negative slope. The line on graph (A) runs upward to the right, which is characteristic of a positive slope.

Any equation of the form $y = mx + b$ will generate a straight-line graph with slope = m and y intercept = b. Therefore, the equation $y = 3x + 5$ generates a straight line with slope = 3 and y intercept = 5.

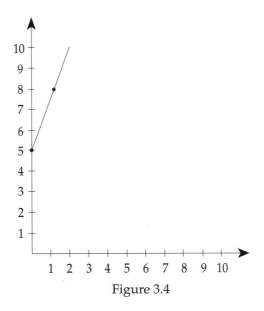

Figure 3.4

For a *curvilinear* graph, the slope at one point is *not* necessarily equal to the slope at any other point. For curvilinear graphs, therefore, the slope is equal to the slope of a line *tangent* to the curve at that point, measured by the value $\dfrac{\Delta Y}{\Delta X}$ for the tangent line.

On graph (C), Figure 3.3, the slope at point 1 differs from the slope at point 2. As shown, the slope at point $1 = \dfrac{\Delta Y_1}{\Delta X_1}$. The slope at point $2 = \dfrac{\Delta Y_2}{\Delta X_2}$.

Because slope represents the ratio:

Y component : X component

it frequently represents quantities that are derived directly from the quantities depicted on the x and y axes. For example, if a graph plots time (*x*-axis) versus displacement (*y*-axis), its slope is:

$$\frac{\Delta Y}{\Delta X} = \text{velocity}$$

If a graph plots time (*x*-axis) versus velocity (*y*-axis), its slope is:

$$\frac{\Delta Y}{\Delta X} = \text{acceleration}$$

Area Under a Curve

The *area under* a given portion of a curve may be found by visualizing the area in terms of familiar geometric figures. In graph (B) of Figure 3.3, for example, the area under the curve between points 1 and 2 can be determined by partitioning the area into a triangle (B_1) and a rectangle (B_2). The area of the triangle ($\frac{1}{2}$ base × height) is added to the area of the rectangle (side × side), and this sum represents the total area.

Like the slope, the area under the curve may represent a quantity derived from values plotted on the *x*- and *y*-axes. If, for example, a graph should plot velocity (*y*-axis) versus time (*x*-axis), the area under any segment of the curve represents displacement.

Please solve this problem:

- The slope of a curvilinear graph set forth on a cartesian plane is equal at any given point to:

  A. the slope of the graph at all other points.
  B. the area under the curvilinear graph at that point.
  C. the slope of a line tangent to the curvilinear graph at that point.
  D. infinity.

Problem solved:

C is correct. The question refers directly to section **3.1.2.2**, where it is explained that for a curvilinear graph, the slope at any point is equal to that of a hypothetical line tangent to the curve at that point.

REVIEW OF TRIGONOMETRY

Measuring Angles in Degrees and Radians

An angle (θ) may be described in degrees or in **radians**. A radian is the measure of a circle's radius as it is applied to the circle's circumference. That is, if a circle's radius is 2 centimeters, then one radian represents that portion of the circle corresponding to 2 centimeters of its circumference. Because the circumference of a circle = $2\pi r$, there are 2π radians in a circle. A radian is (a) that portion of the circle that corresponds in circumference to one radius and also (b) the arc subtended by that portion of a circle. Therefore, you can say that the full 360° of a circle is equivalent to 2π radians. Since π = approximately 3.14, 360° = approximately 6.28 radians. Conversion between degrees and radians is a matter of simple proportion.

Remembering that 360° = 2π radians = 6.28 radians enables you to (1) express an angle in degrees if you know its value in radians and (2) express an angle in radians if you know its value in degrees.

Please solve this problem:

- Express 267° in radians.

Problem solved:

1. $267° \times$ _____ = _____radians

2. $267° \times \dfrac{6.28 \text{ radians}}{360°}$ = _____radians (*radians in the numerator!*)

3. $267° \times \dfrac{6.28 \text{ radians}}{360°}$ = 4.66 radians

Pythagorean Theorem

The **Pythagorean theorem** describes the relationship among the three sides of any right triangle:

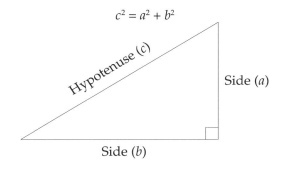

$$c^2 = a^2 + b^2$$

Hypotenuse (*c*)

Side (*a*)

Side (*b*)

Figure 3.5

Trigonometric Functions

The three trigonometric functions—**sine** (sin), **cosine** (cos), and **tangent** (tan)—relate to the right triangle according to the mnemonic device SOH CAH TOA.

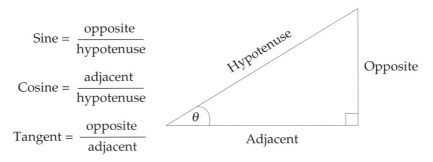

$$\text{Sine} = \frac{\text{opposite}}{\text{hypotenuse}}$$

$$\text{Cosine} = \frac{\text{adjacent}}{\text{hypotenuse}}$$

$$\text{Tangent} = \frac{\text{opposite}}{\text{adjacent}}$$

Figure 3.6

The three trigonometric functions relate graphically to the angles 90°, 180°, 270°, and 360°:

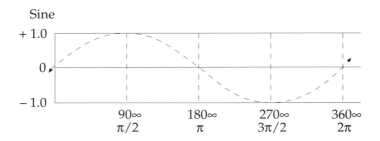

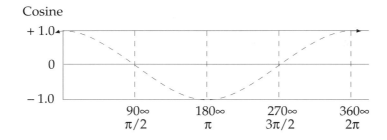

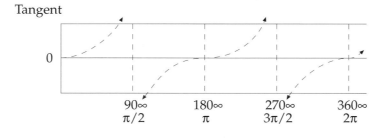

Figure 3.7

Be familiar with the terms **arcsin**, **arccos**, and **arctan**:

arcsin x means the angle whose sine = x

arccos x means the angle whose cosine = x

arctan x means the angle whose tangent = x.

For example:

the sine of 30° = 0.5, so arcsin 0.5 = 30°

the tangent of 45° = 1, so arctan 1 = 45°.

For any *small* angle (<15°) sine, cosine, and tangent may be *closely estimated* without reference to a table:

$\sin \theta \cong \theta$ (*expressed in radians!*)

$\tan \theta \cong \theta$ (*expressed in radians!*)

$\cos \theta \cong 1$ (*expressed in radians!*).

Three Right Triangles of Special Significance

Three right triangles have special importance for the MCAT and for trigonometry generally.

1. The 30°, 60°, 90° right triangle. Its sides always bear the ratio:

$$a : 2a : a\sqrt{3}$$

- The 2 multiple represents the hypotenuse.

- The $\sqrt{3}$ multiple represents the side opposite the 60° angle.

- a represents the side opposite the 30° angle.

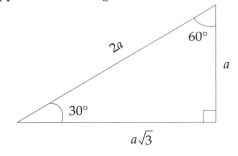

Figure 3.8

2. The 45°, 45°, 90° right triangle. Its sides always bear the ratio:

$$a: a: a\sqrt{2}$$

- The $\sqrt{2}$ multiple is associated with the hypotenuse.

- a is the length of each leg.

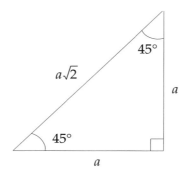

Figure 3.9

3. The right triangle with sides of 3:4:5. If, in any right triangle, the hypotenuse bears a ratio of 5:4 to any other side, then to the third side it bears the ratio 5:3. Similarly, if, in any right triangle, the hypotenuse bears a ratio of 5:3 to any other side, then to the third side it bears the ratio 5:4. If the legs of a right triangle bear a 3:4 ratio, then the hypotenuse will be 5.

Furthermore, the angle situated between the 3 and 5 sides is approximately 53°, and the angle situated between the 5 and 4 sides is approximately 37°.

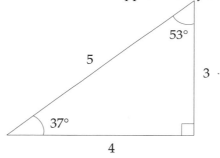

Figure 3.10

Of course, all three of these right triangles conform to the Pythagorean theorem.

1. $1^2 + \sqrt{3})^2 = 2^2$

2. $1^2 + 1^2 = (\sqrt{2})^2$

3. $3^2 + 4^2 = 5^2$

Familiarity with the ratios that apply to these three particular triangles will save you the time it would otherwise take to apply the Pythagorean theorem.

Please solve this problem:

- A right triangle has sides 4 centimeters, 8 centimeters, and $\sqrt{48}$ centimeters. What are the values of its angles?

Problem solved:

The triangle conforms to one of the three special right triangles recently discussed. Notice that two of the sides, 4 and 8, bear the ratio of 1:2:

$$4(1) = 4 \qquad 4(2) = 8$$

Therefore, the other side is equal to $4\sqrt{3}$.

A triangle with sides in the ratio of $1:2:\sqrt{3}$ always has angles of 30°, 60°, and 90°.

Please solve this problem:

- A right triangle has an angle equal to 45° and a hypotenuse with length equal to $\sqrt{18}$ meters. Find the lengths of the two remaining sides.

Problem solved:

Since all right triangles have one angle = 90° and this right triangle has one angle = 45°, the third angle must also = 45°, since $(180° - (90° + 45°)) = 45°$. Hence the problem involves a 45°, 45°, 90° right triangle. Its sides must bear the ratio $1:1:\sqrt{2}$, with the length of the hypotenuse being equal to ($a\sqrt{2}$), where a = the length of a side opposite one of the 45° angles.

Consider the number $\sqrt{18}$, and express it as $a\sqrt{2}$.

$$\sqrt{18} = a\sqrt{2}$$

$$a = \frac{\sqrt{18}}{\sqrt{2}}$$

$$a = \sqrt{9}$$

$$a = 3$$

$$\sqrt{18} = 3\sqrt{2}$$

In order for the triangle's sides to bear the ratio $1:1:\sqrt{2}$ the other two sides must be equal to $3(1) = 3$. The triangle's sides have lengths:

$$3 \text{ meters, } 3 \text{ meters, and } 3\sqrt{2} \text{ meters}$$

Please solve this problem:

- A right triangle has a hypotenuse with length of 2.5 centimeters and a leg with length of 2 centimeters. Find the length of the third side.

Problem solved:

Consider the two numbers 2.5 and 2. Do they reveal any of the ratios that pertain to the three special right triangles?

Examination reveals that:

$$(2.5)(2) = 5 \text{ and } (2)(2) = 4$$

The hypotenuse of 5 and side of 4 bear a ratio of 5:4. This must then be a 3:4:5 triangle, with each side multiplied by a coefficient of .5. The third side, therefore, must equal (3)(.5) cm = 1.5 cm.

Please solve this problem:

- A right triangle has two 45° angles. A side opposite one of them has a value of 13. What is the value of the hypotenuse?

Problem solved:

Among the three right triangles of special significance, one is the 45°, 45°, 90° right triangle for which the sides always bear the *ratio* $1:1:\sqrt{2}$. The two legs of a 45°, 45°, 90° right triangle are equal to each other, and the hypotenuse is equal to (leg) $\times (\sqrt{2})$. Since we deal here with a right triangle of which one angle is 45°, it must be a 45°, 45°, 90° right triangle. The length of the legs is 13, and the length of the hypotenuse therefore is $13\sqrt{2}$.

CHAPTER 4

TRANSLATIONAL MOTION

4.1 MASTERY ACHIEVED

VECTORS

Scalar Quantities versus Vector Quantities

A **scalar quantity** has magnitude but no direction. **Speed**, for example, is a scalar quantity. To state that an object travels at a speed of 450 m/s says nothing about the object's direction; it could be traveling north, south, east, west, or even along an irregular, nonlinear path.

Distance is also a scalar quantity. To state that an object has traveled 300 meters gives no information about its ultimate position relative to its starting point. If the object starts at a point P, moves 150 meters to the west, and returns 150 meters to the east, then it has covered a distance of 300 meters, although it has come to rest at its starting point P.

A **vector quantity** has magnitude and direction. It is symbolized by a line segment with an arrowed tip.

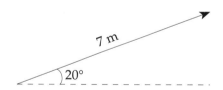

Length indicates magnitude, and orientation indicates direction. The figure above depicts a vector with a magnitude of 7 meters and a direction of 20° above the horizontal.

Velocity is a vector quantity. The designation "820 meters per second to the left" describes a velocity; it has both magnitude and direction. The designation "820 meters per second" does not; it describes only speed, a scalar quantity. **Displacement** is another vector quantity. To state that an object has moved "760 centimeters to the north" is to describe the object's displacement. Do not confuse distance and displacement. This will be revisited on page 35.

Note: Vector quantities in this book will be written in bold (for example, **v** for velocity). The magnitude of the vector can either be represented as

$$|\mathbf{v}|$$

or v.

Vector Addition and Subtraction

When asked to add one vector to another:

1. recognize that each vector may be freely "moved" about the page, as long as its length and orientation are not disturbed, and

2. place the tail of either vector at the head of the other.

The arrow that runs from the free tail to the free head represents the vector sum, also known as the *resultant* vector.

Please solve this problem:

- Draw a vector, **C** , that represents the sum of vectors **A** and **B** below.

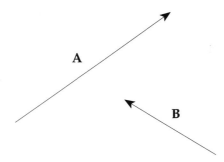

Problem solved:

Move the vectors so that the head of one touches the tail of the other (without changing either of their sizes or orientations).

For example, you might proceed by placing the head of **B** at the tail of **A**, like this:

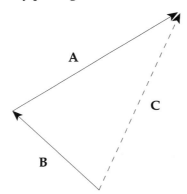

or by placing the head of **A** at the tail of **B**, like this:

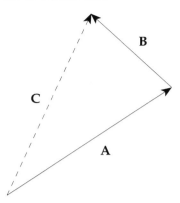

In either case, the resultant vector, **C**, has the same magnitude and direction.

When adding vectors, be sure to place the head of one at the tail of the other. Do not place them tail to tail or head to head: The line segment that follows from that method does not constitute the resultant vector.

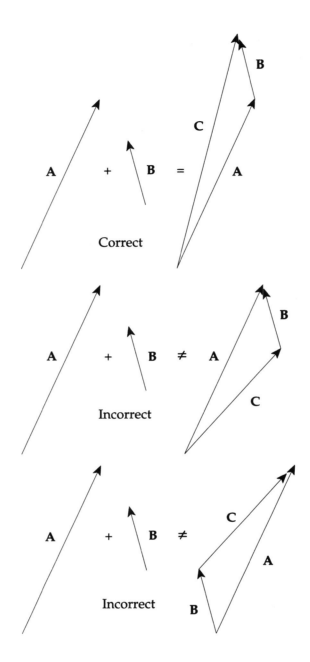

When asked to subtract one vector from another, add the opposite of one vector to the other vector:

$$A - B = A + (-B)$$

To find the opposite (–) of a vector, keep its magnitude, but reverse its orientation by 180°. For example, $\mathbf{V_1}$ and $\mathbf{V_2}$ are vectors:

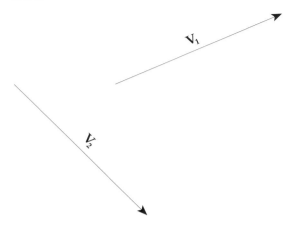

These are the vectors opposite to $\mathbf{V_1}$ and $\mathbf{V_2}$:

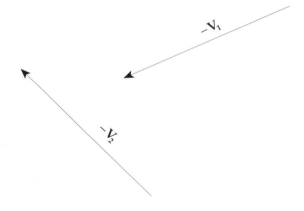

Please solve this problem:

- Draw a vector, **F**, that represents **D** minus **E**.

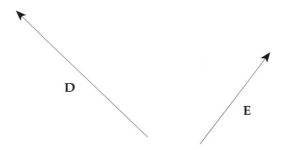

Problem solved:

Convert vector **E** to its opposite. Add −**E** to vector **D** by placing the head of one at the tail of the other.

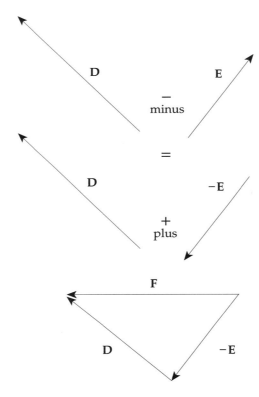

The diagram shows that the head of −**E** has been placed at the tail of **D**. The line segment linking the tail of −**E** to the head of **D** represents the resultant vector, **F**.

Vector Components

On the MCAT, you may be asked to resolve a vector into its x- and y-components.

Please solve this problem:

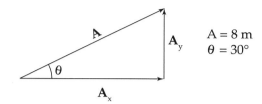

$A = 8$ m
$\theta = 30°$

Find A_x and A_y.

Problem solved:

1. Recognizing the trigonometric relationship $\cos 30° = \dfrac{A_x}{A}$

we can arrange the equation to read: $A_x = A \cos 30°$

2. Given that A = 8 m and $\cos 30° = \dfrac{\sqrt{3}}{2} \approx 0.87$, we can see that $A_x \approx 8 \bullet (0.87) \approx 7$ m.

3. Similarly:

$$\sin 30° = \frac{A_y}{A}$$
$$\text{since} \quad \sin 30° = 0.5$$
$$A_y = A \sin 30° = 8 \bullet (0.5) = 4 \text{ m}$$

Please solve this problem:

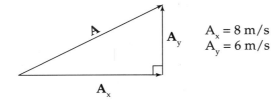

$A_x = 8 \text{ m/s}$
$A_y = 6 \text{ m/s}$

Find the magnitude of **A**.

Problem solved:

Using the Pythagoreon Theorem, we see that:

$$A^2 = A_x^2 + A_y^2$$

$$A = \sqrt{(8 \text{ m/s})^2 + (6 \text{ m/s})^2} = 10 \text{ m/s}$$

Other Types of Vector Components

Sometimes it may be useful to split vector components that are not vertical or horizontal.

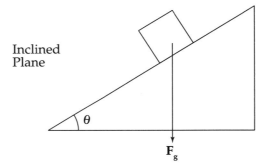

An example is the inclined plane as shown above (we will revisit this in the next chapter). It is common to split the force of gravity (a vector) into components parallel and perpendicular to the plane:

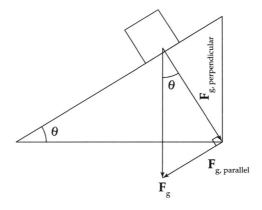

Note: It is also common to rename the parallel direction the x-direction and the perpendicular direction the y-direction.

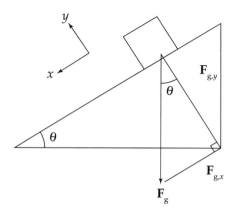

$$\mathbf{F}_{g,x} = \mathbf{F}_g \sin \theta$$
$$\mathbf{F}_{g,y} = \mathbf{F}_g \cos \theta$$

DISTANCE AND DISPLACEMENT

As we've said, **distance** is a scalar quantity. For any moving body, distance expresses the length of travel, regardless of direction. If an object, starting at point P, moves 500 km to the north, 600 km east, and then 300 km north:

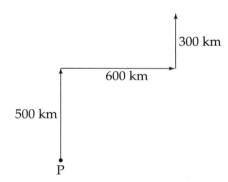

The object moves a distance of 500 km + 600 km + 300 km =1400 km.

Displacement is a vector quantity, represented by **d**. For any moving body, displacement describes net change in position, regardless of distance and path. Consider the displacement of the object as described above—**d is the vector that points from the starting point to the ending point:**

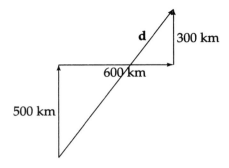

To find the magnitude of **d**, we use the Pythagorean Theorem:

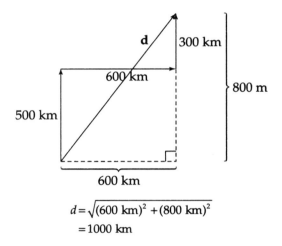

$$d = \sqrt{(600 \text{ km})^2 + (800 \text{ km})^2}$$
$$= 1000 \text{ km}$$

Please solve this problem:

- Which of the following statements correctly describes the motion of a body that travels a total *displacement* of 400 meters north?

    A. From its starting point, the body travels 200 meters due east and then 600 meters due west.
    B. From its starting point, the body travels 600 meters due west and then 200 meters due east.
    C. From its starting point, the body travels 200 meters due east and then 200 meters due west.
    D. From its starting point, the body travels 100 meters due east, 100 meters due west, and 400 meters due north.

Problem solved:

D is correct. The question requires that you understand displacement as a vector quantity. A vector takes into account the direction or the net distance between starting point and final resting point. The body described by choice D moves 100 meters east and then returns to its starting point by moving 100 meters west. It then moves 400 meters north to its final position. This is 400 meters north of its initial position, and thus its displacement is 400 meters north.

Displacement is completely independent of path.

Please solve this problem:

- A person makes one complete lap around a circular track with radius 50 m.

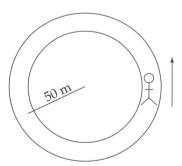

What is the person's displacement?

Problem solved:

Zero. Since the person begins and ends in the same position, there is no displacement. The distance, however, would be the circumference of the circle:

$$= 2\pi r$$
$$\approx 2(3)(50 \text{ m})$$
$$= 300 \text{ m}$$

Note: Distance is *not* the magnitude of displacement.

SPEED AND VELOCITY

Average Velocity and Average Speed

Average velocity is a vector, denoted by $\bar{\mathbf{v}}$.

It is defined as:

$$\bar{\mathbf{v}} = \frac{\mathbf{d}}{\Delta t}$$

[units: m/s]

where Δt is the change in time. It measures how quickly an object moves away from its starting point with direction.

Please solve this problem:

- A person makes one complete lap around a circular track of radius 50 m in 60 s.

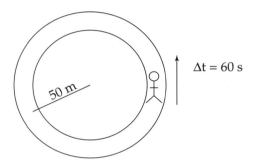

What is the magnitude of its average velocity?

Problem solved:

Zero. The person has zero displacement, so the average velocity is also zero.

Average speed is defined as $\frac{\text{total distance}}{\Delta t}$ [units: m/s]

In the previous example, average speed $\approx \frac{300 \text{ m}}{60 \text{ s}} = 5$ m/s

Note: Average speed is not the magnitude of average velocity.

(Instantaneous) Speed and Velocity

In basic terms, **speed** refers to how fast an object is moving. It is a scalar quantity, also measured in m/s. If an object's speed is constant, then:

$$\text{speed} = \frac{\text{distance}}{\Delta t}$$

Velocity, a vector, is speed with direction. If an object's velocity is constant, then $\mathbf{v} = \frac{\mathbf{d}}{\Delta t}$

Note: Speed *is* the magnitude of velocity.

ACCELERATION

Average Acceleration

Average Acceleration is a vector quantity denoted by $\bar{\mathbf{a}}$.

It is defined as:

$$\bar{\mathbf{a}} = \frac{\Delta \mathbf{v}}{\Delta t} = \frac{\mathbf{v}_f - \mathbf{v}_o}{\Delta t} \text{ [units: m/s}^2\text{]}$$

where *f* denotes final and *o* denotes initial. It measures how quickly an object's velocity changes. This includes both the magnitude and direction of velocity.

Please solve this problem:

- An object moving to the right increases its speed from 0 m/s to 40 m/s in 5 s. What is the magnitude of its average acceleration?

Problem solved:

Since the object is always moving to the right, we don't have to worry about the direction aspect of velocity.

$$\bar{a} = \frac{\Delta v}{\Delta t} = \frac{v_f - v_o}{\Delta t} = \frac{40 \text{ m/s} - 0 \text{ m/s}}{5 \text{ s}} = 8 \text{ m/s}^2$$

Please solve this problem:

- If the initial and final velocity vectors are as shown:

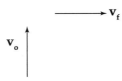

From the four choices below, find the direction of the average acceleration.

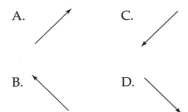

Problem solved:

The direction of $\bar{\mathbf{a}}$ is the same as the direction of $\mathbf{v}_f - \mathbf{v}_o$. Remembering how to subtract vectors,

$$\mathbf{v}_f - \mathbf{v}_o = \mathbf{v}_f + (-\mathbf{v}_o)$$

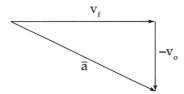

Choice D is the answer.

(Instantaneous) Acceleration

Acceleration, denoted by $\mathbf{a}$, is the rate of change of velocity. If acceleration is constant, then

$$\mathbf{a} = \frac{\Delta \text{ velocity}}{\Delta \text{ time}}.$$

Don't Confuse Velocity and Acceleration

The direction an object moves is the direction of its velocity. An object does not have to move in the direction of acceleration.

Case 1: **v** and **a** are in the same direction.

This physically corresponds to *speeding up.*

Case 2: **v** and **a** are in opposite directions.

The object is still moving to the right, but is *slowing down.*

Case 3: **v** and **a** are perpendicular.

This corresponds to a *change in direction.*

Note that any other orientation would correspond to both a change in direction and either speeding up or slowing down.

MOTION GRAPHS IN ONE DIMENSION

If an object is constrained to move in one dimension (e.g., along the *x*-axis), then it is convenient to drop vector notation.

d = displacement
v = velocity   can be + or −
a = acceleration

Position vs. Time

The figure below depicts the motion of an object moving along the *x*-axis.

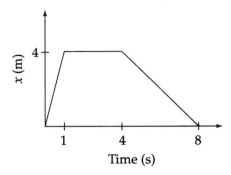

The object starts at the origin, moves to x = 4 m in 1 s, remains at x = 4 m for 3 s, and then returns to the origin in 4 s.

1. The displacement, *d*, of the object is 0 m since the object started and ended at the origin.

2. The distance traveled is 8 m (4 m during the first part, 0 m during the second part, 4 m during the third part).

3. The average velocity is 0 m/s (because *d* = 0).

4. The average speed is 1 m/s ($\frac{\text{distance}}{\Delta t} = \frac{8\text{ m}}{8\text{ s}}$).

5. The *slope* of each segment represents the velocity.

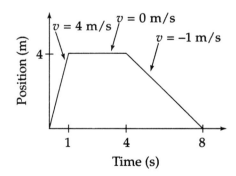

The corresponding Velocity vs. Time graph would look like this:

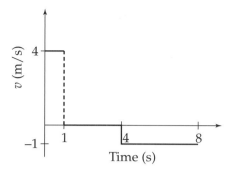

Note that acceleration on a Position vs. Time graph would be represented as curved:

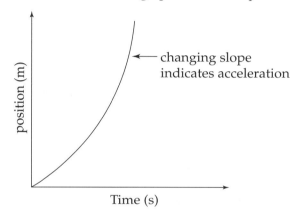

Velocity vs. Time

The figure below depicts the velocity of a particle moving along the *x*-axis as a function of time.

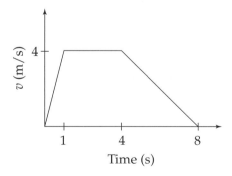

The object accelerates from rest for 1 s until it reaches a velocity of 4 m/s, then remains at 4 m/s for 3 s, and then slows down to rest in the remaining 4 s.

1. Since the entire graph is above the horizontal access, the object is *always moving forward*.

2. The slope of each segment represents the object's acceleration.

3. The area under the curve represents the object's displacement.

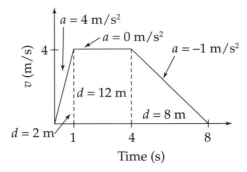

If a Velocity vs. Time graph crosses the horizontal axis, the object has changed direction.

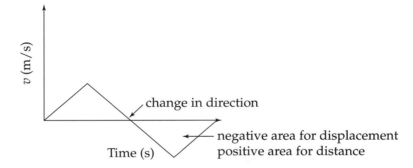

In addition, the area of the region between this section and the horizontal axis must be treated as negative when calculating displacement.

Please solve this problem:

- In the figure below, in which regions is the object speeding up?

    A. I only
    B. I and II
    C. I and III
    D. I and IV

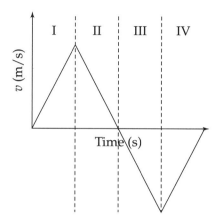

Problem solved:

As we learned earlier in the section "Don't Confuse Velocity and Acceleration," an object is speeding up if both velocity and acceleration point in the same direction. For motion along the x-axis, that means both positive or both negative.

The velocity is positive (above the axis) in regions I and II and negative (below the axis) in regions III and IV.

The acceleration (slope) is positive in regions I and IV and negative in regions II and III.

Thus, a and v are both positive in region I and both negative in region III. The correct answer is C.

UNIFORMLY ACCELERATED MOTION IN ONE DIMENSION

If an object moves with constant acceleration, it is said to be in *uniformly accelerated motion*. The equations that relate displacement (d), initial velocity (v_0), final velocity (v_f), acceleration (a), and time (t) are known as the **Big Five**.

The Big Five

$$1.\ d = \frac{1}{2}(v_0 + v_f)t \qquad \text{missing } a$$

$$2.\ v_f = v_0 + at \qquad \text{missing } d$$

$$3.\ d = v_0 t + \frac{1}{2}at^2 \qquad \text{missing } v_f$$

$$4.\ d = v_f t - \frac{1}{2}at^2 \qquad \text{missing } v_0$$

$$5.\ v_f^2 = v_0^2 + 2ad \qquad \text{missing } t$$

Note that d, v_o, v_f, and a are vectors that can be positive or negative.

There are five variables and five equations. Each equation contains four out of the five variables—in other words, each equation is missing one variable. Knowing which variable is missing is an extremely useful tool in solving problems.

How to Solve Problems:

Step 1. Identify the three variables you have been given.

Step 2. Identify the variable you are looking for.

Step 3. Identify the variable you don't care about (that is, that you don't know and you don't want).

Step 4. Choose the equation that is missing that variable.

Step 5. Calculate, and voilà!

Please solve this problem:

- An object starts from rest and accelerates uniformly at 5 m/s² and travels 40 m. What is its final speed?

Problem solved:

Step 1. We have been given $v_0 = 0$ ("starts from rest"), a = 5 m/s² and d = 40 m. (Note: in some cases, minus signs need to be incorporated. However, an object starting from rest will only move in a single direction, which we'll call "positive").

Step 2. We are looking for v_f. (Note: the question asks for speed and v_f is velocity, but speed is merely the magnitude of velocity.)

Step 3. We do not care about time (t).

Step 4. Choose Big Five #5.

Step 5. Calculate:

$$v_f^{\,2} = v_o^{\,2} + 2ad$$
$$= v_f^{\,2} = 0^2 + 2\,(5\text{ m/s}^2)\,(40\text{ m})$$
$$= v_f = \sqrt{400} = 20\text{ m/s}$$

Kinematics Proportions

The MCAT often asks kinematics questions that involve proportions. Most often, these involve situations where $v_o = 0$. Since a is a constant, Big Five #2, 3, and 5 reduce to:

Big Five # 2	$v_f \propto t$
Big Five # 3	$d \propto t^2$
Big Five # 5	$v_f^2 \propto d$

Please solve this problem:

- An object accelerates uniformly from rest for T seconds and travels D meters. How far will it travel in total after 2T seconds?

  A. $D/2$ meters
  B. $\sqrt{2}\ D$ meters
  C. $2D$ meters
  D. $4D$ meters

Problem solved:

Right away we can eliminate choice A since it doesn't make sense that object would travel a shorter distance in a longer amount of time. Looking at the proportions above, we see that Big Five #3 is relevant.

$$d \propto t^2$$

Since T doubles, T^2 will quadruple and therefore so will D. Choice D is the answer.

FREE FALL MOTION

Free fall motion describes an object falling from some height, h, to the ground. It is a form of uniformly accelerated motion along a straight line. The acceleration results from the earth's gravitational field. This acceleration is a constant for all objects near the surface of the earth: $g = 9.81$ m/s² (often approximated as 10 meters per second squared) and the direction is downward. When MCAT questions address free fall motion, they will usually instruct you to disregard rotation of the earth, air resistance, and differences in the magnitude of gravity exerted at different heights from the earth.

The acceleration due to gravity is positive (+) or negative (–), depending on perspective. One direction should be chosen as positive and the other negative for all vectors, and that convention should be maintained throughout the problem.

The Big Five can be customized for gravity. Big Five #1 is no longer useful since we always know acceleration, and Big Five #4 rarely comes up in any situation on the MCAT. In addition, it is useful to add the subscript "y" to d, v_o, and v_f to distinguish these quantities from those in the x-direction (which we'll need to do with Projectile Motion).

Big Five for Gravity:

2. $v_{fy} = v_{oy} + at$ missing d_y

3. $d_y = v_{oy}t + 1/2\,at^2$ missing v_{fy}

4. $v_{fy}^2 = v_{oy}^2 + 2ad_y$ missing t

Please solve this problem:

- If an object is dropped from a height of 80 meters above the earth, (a) how long does it take to reach the earth, and (b) what is the object's velocity at the instant prior to impact with the earth?

Problem solved:

Before we proceed with our usual steps, we should first choose the positive direction. Since the object only moves downward, it is reasonable to choose downward as the positive direction.

For part (a) we are given $v_{oy} = 0$, $d_y = 80$ m, and a = 10 m/s². We are looking for t. Since we don't care about v_{fy}, we should use Big Five #3.

$$d_y = v_{oy}t + 1/2\,at^2$$
$$80\text{ m} = 0 + 1/2\,(10\text{ m/s}^2)\,t^2$$

Solving for t, we see that $t = 4$ s.

For part (b) we are now free to choose either Big Five #2 or #5 (since we just solved for t).

Since Big Five #2 is easier:

$$v_{fy} = v_{oy} + at$$
$$v_{fy} = 0 + (10\text{ m/s}^2)\,(4\text{ s})$$
$$= 40\text{ m/s}$$

Please solve this problem:

- An object is projected upward at 20 m/s and hits the ground 6 s later. From what height was it thrown?

Problem solved:

The question, "From what height was it thrown?" implies the object was not initially on the ground. A diagram might look like this:

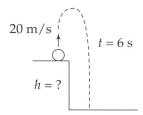

Choosing upward as positive, we know $v_{oy} = +20$ m/s, $t = 6$ s and $a = -10$ m/s². (If we had chosen downward as positive, then v_{oy} would be negative and a would be positive.) We do not care about v_{fy}, so we use Big Five #3.

$$d_y = v_{oy}t + 1/2\, at^2$$

$$d_y = (20 \text{ m/s})(6 \text{ s}) + 1/2\,(-10 \text{ m/s}^2)\,(6 \text{ s})^2$$

$$d_y = 120 \text{ m} - 180 \text{ m}$$

$$= -60 \text{ m}$$

d_y is negative only because we chose upward as positive. *h is merely the magnitude of d_y*, therefore $h = 60$ m.

Note that we do not need to know how high the object travels. Displacement, remember, is the vector that points from beginning to end (i.e., from cliff to ground).

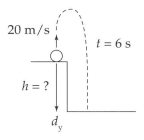

Useful Facts About Gravity

1. When an object moves upward, it slows down by approximately 10 m/s every second.

2. When an object moves downward, it speeds up by approximately 10 m/s every second.

3. An object projected upward from the ground will take the same amount of time to travel up as it will to travel back to the ground.

4. An object projected upward from the ground will land with the same speed as it was initially projected.

Please solve this problem:

- An object is projected upward at 50 m/s from the ground. (a) How long will it take to reach the top of its trajectory, (b) how long will it travel in total before hitting the ground, and (c) with what speed will it land?

Problem solved:

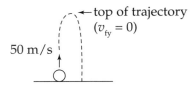

a) Since an object slows down 10 m/s every second on the way up, it will take 5 s to slow down from 50 m/s to 0. Thus, $t = 5$ s.

b) Since time up equals time down, the total time is 10 s.

c) Since the object will land with the same speed as initially projected, the final speed = 50 m/s.

PROJECTILE MOTION

Projectile motion generally refers to an object moving under the influence of gravity with a velocity that has both horizontal and vertical components.

The velocity is always tangent to the path of motion, while the acceleration always points downward.

Since the acceleration is only vertical, the horizontal component of velocity remains constant.

MCAT questions usually address idealized projectile motion and will instruct you to ignore the effects of friction and air resistance. You should learn to analyze projectile motion in idealized terms.

Initial Velocity

It is useful to separate the initial velocity into x- and y-components.

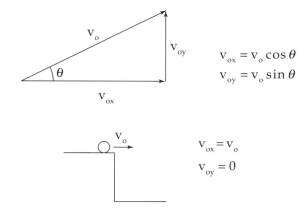

$$v_{ox} = v_o \cos \theta$$
$$v_{oy} = v_o \sin \theta$$

$$v_{ox} = v_o$$
$$v_{oy} = 0$$

Please solve this problem:

- An object is launched at 40 m/s at an angle of 60° above the horizontal. What will be its horizontal velocity 2 seconds later?

Problem solved:

Since horizontal velocity never changes, it is equal to

$$v_{ox} = v_o \cos \theta = (40 \text{ m/s}) \cos 60°$$

$$= (40 \text{ m/s}) (0.5) = 20 \text{ m/s}$$

Solving Problems

For projectile motion, the x- and y-motions should be separated.

y-equations	x-equation
2. $v_{fy} = v_{oy} + at$	$d_x = v_{ox} t$
3. $d_y = v_{oy} t + 1/2 \, at^2$	
5. $v_{fy}^2 = v_{oy}^2 + 2 a d_y$	

Note the x-equation is just "distance = speed x time."

Please solve this problem:

- An object is projected horizontally off a cliff of height 20 m at 15 m/s. How far from the base of the cliff does the object land?

Problem solved:

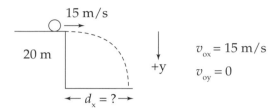

We are looking for d_x, but $d_x = v_{ox} t$ and we don't know t. Therefore, we first turn to the y-equations. Choosing downward as the positive direction, we know that $v_{oy} = 0$, $a = +10$ m/s² and $d_y = +20$ m.

Using Big Five #3, we see that:

$$d_y = v_{oy}t + 1/2\, at^2$$
$$20\text{ m} = 0 + 1/2(10\text{ m/s}^2)\, t^2$$

Solving for t, we get $t = 2$ s.

Plugging this into our x-equation:

$$d_x = v_{ox}t$$
$$d_x = (15\text{ m/s})(2\text{ s})$$
$$= 30\text{ m}$$

Note that the time it takes to hit the ground is exactly the same as if the object were dropped from rest from the same height.

Please solve this problem:

- An object is projected from the ground at 100 m/s at an angle of 30° above the horizontal. Find (a) how long it takes to reach the top of its trajectory, (b) how high it goes, and (c) how far away it lands.

Problem solved:

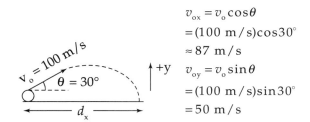

$$v_{ox} = v_o \cos\theta$$
$$= (100 \text{ m/s}) \cos 30°$$
$$\approx 87 \text{ m/s}$$
$$v_{oy} = v_o \sin\theta$$
$$= (100 \text{ m/s}) \sin 30°$$
$$= 50 \text{ m/s}$$

(a) To find the time up, we look to the y-equations (time is generally influenced by gravity, which is a "y-thing.") Calling up positive, we know that $v_{oy} = +50$ m/s, $v_{fy} = 0$ (we are calling the top the "final" position), and $a = -10$ m/s^2.

Using Big Five #2:

$$v_{fy} = v_{oy} + at$$
$$0 = 50 \text{ m/s} + (-10 \text{ m/s}^2)t$$
$$t = 5 \text{ s}$$

(b) To find the height, we can use either Big Five #3 or Big Five #5, given that we just solved for t. Using Big Five #3:

$$d_y = v_{oy}t + 1/2 \, at^2$$
$$d_y = (50 \text{ m/s})(5 \text{ s}) + 1/2 \, (-10 \text{ m/s}^2)(5 \text{ s})^2$$
$$= 250 \text{ m} - 125 \text{ m}$$
$$= 125 \text{ m}$$

(c) To find d_x, we first have to realize that the total time of flight is twice the time it took to reach the top of its trajectory (i.e., 10 m/s).

$$d_x = v_{ox}t$$
$$d_x = (87 \text{ m/s})(10 \text{ s}) = 870 \text{ m}$$

ACCELERATION AND CIRCULAR MOTION

Recall that acceleration is a vector quantity, and consider an object which moves in a circular path as shown below.

MOTION OF OBJECT

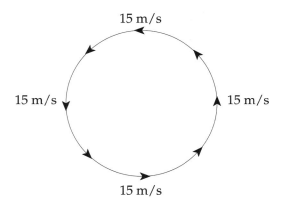

An object that travels at a constant velocity in a straight line experiences no acceleration. This object moves circularly at a constant rate of 15 meters per second. The object's speed is constant, but its direction is not. At every instant, direction is subjected to a change that produces the circular motion. If a body's velocity undergoes change in magnitude, direction, or both, it experiences acceleration. Therefore, *the continuous change in the object's direction signifies acceleration.*

The maintenance of circular motion requires an acceleration with constant magnitude directed *toward the center* of the circle. Such acceleration is termed **centripetal acceleration**. The circular motion that results is shown in the figure below.

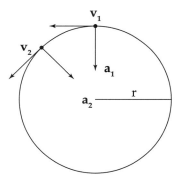

If, at any point, centripetal acceleration were suddenly to cease, the object would move off in a straight line tangent to its original circular path.

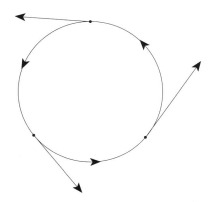

The magnitude of centripetal acceleration, $a_c = \dfrac{v^2}{r}$, where v = the speed and r = radius of the circle. For circular motion at constant speed, therefore, the following phenomena apply:

- at all moments, the object's velocity vector is tangent to the circular path;

- centripetal acceleration $(a_c) = \dfrac{v^2}{r}$; and

- $v = \dfrac{d}{t} = \dfrac{2\pi r}{T}; \; T = \dfrac{2\pi r}{v};$

where:

v = speed

T = period = time required for one complete revolution.

Please solve this problem:

- Assume that the objects shown in the three previous figures travel in a circle with radius of 30 meters. Determine (a) the magnitude of centripetal acceleration and (b) the period of its motion.

Problem solved:

You are asked to determine the values of a_c and T. As shown above:

$$a_c = \frac{v^2}{r} = \frac{(15 \text{ m / s})^2}{30 \text{ m}} 7.5 \text{ m / s}^2$$

$$T = \frac{2\pi\, r}{v} \approx \frac{2(3)(30 \text{ m})}{15 \text{ m / s}} = 12 \text{ s}$$

Please solve this problem:

- An object is moving in a circle with radius R and speed V. How many times greater must its acceleration be to travel with speed $2V$?

Problem solved:

Since $a_c = \dfrac{v^2}{r}$

and r is a constant, we see that $a_c \propto v^2$.

If v doubles, then a_c would need to quadruple to maintain circular motion.

4.2   MASTERY APPLIED: PRACTICE PASSAGE AND QUESTIONS

Passage

According to our present-day understanding of aeroballistics and associated aerodynamic force systems, the axis of a moving projectile is not expected to always point along the path of motion of its center of gravity. Rather, the axis is inclined at an angle—the *angle of yaw*—to the direction of motion. Consequently, a force, F, acts at a point P. The force acts in a direction that is inclined to the projectile's axis and its direction of motion.

As shown in Figure 1, **F** may be resolved into two components, drag **(D)** and lift **(L)**. The drag resists the projectile's forward motion and acts therefore in the direction opposite its velocity. The lift acts in the direction perpendicular to the projectile's motion. **F** also produces a torque around the projectile's center of gravity (point G). This causes a turning effect and gives rise to the "yawing moment."

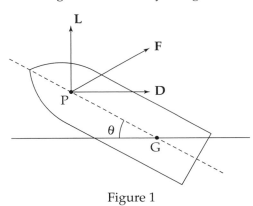

Figure 1

Every aeroballistic projectile has an associated nondimensional drag coefficient, f_R, which depends largely on its Mach number, M, which in turn is equal to $\dfrac{\text{velocity}}{\text{angle of yaw}}$. The drag coefficient also depends on the shape of the projectile and, in particular, on the degree to which the projectile's head is blunt or pointed. Figure 2 demonstrates, generally, the relationship of drag coefficient f_R to Mach number (M) (ignoring the effects of the Reynolds number

Re, the effects of which are significant only for very long projectiles with large surface areas).

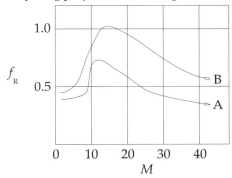

A: Projectile with slender pointed head
B: Projectile with blunt head

Figure 2

The drag coefficient tends also to increase with increasing angles of yaw according, to the formula $f_R = F_{Ro}\left(1 + \dfrac{\theta^2}{200}\right)$, where F_{Ro} is the zero yaw drag coefficient and θ is the angle of yaw.

Two other coefficients, the lift and yawing moment coefficients, show a variation with the Mach number similar to that seen in the case of the drag coefficient.

1. An ascending aeroballistic projectile is launched at an initial angle of θ, with an applied initial force F, and no continuing applied force. The vertical component of its initial velocity is 9,000 meters per second. Assuming the acceleration due to gravity is 10 meters per second squared, and ignoring the effects of air resistance, what magnitude will be associated with the vertical component of the projectile's velocity at time = t?

   A. 9,000 m/s
   B. 9,000 + (t^2) m/s
   C. 9,000 + 10(t) m/s
   D. 9,000 − 10(t) m/s

2. Accounting for air resistance, which of the following is true of an aeroballistic projectile when it reaches the highest point in its path, if it is launched from the earth at angle θ with an initial force F, and no continuing applied force?

   A. It has vertical acceleration of 0.
   B. It has vertical velocity of 0.
   C. It has horizontal acceleration of 0.
   D. It has horizontal velocity of 0.

3. The effect of lift is to:

   A. slow the projectile down.
   B. speed the projectile up.
   C. change the direction of the projectile.
   D. both change the speed and the direction of the projectile.

4. Two aeroballistic projectiles, A and B, differ in their angles of yaw, projectile A having one half that of projectile B. According to the passage which of the following will be true of projectile A?

   A. Its mass will be equal to the (mass of projectile B)^2.
   B. It will experience acceleration due to gravity of 0.5 meters per second squared.
   C. At equal velocities, projectile A's Mach number will be twice that of B's.
   D. Its velocity will be equal to (Mach number for projectile B) $\times$ 0.5.

5. According to Figure 2, for Mach numbers below 10, increased Mach numbers produce:

   A. increased coefficients of drag.
   B. increased angles of yaw.
   C. decreased coefficients of drag.
   D. decreased angles of yaw.

6. By extrapolation, the curves set forth on Figure 2 tend to indicate which one of the following trends?

   A. When the Mach number is less than 20, it has a negligible effect on the coefficient of drag.
   B. When the Mach number is greater than 20, it has a negligible effect on the coefficient of drag.
   C. When the Mach number exceeds 40, further increases tend to have relatively greater effects on the coefficient of drag.
   D. When the Mach number exceeds 40, further increases tend to have relatively smaller effects on the coefficient of drag.

7. According to the passage, which of the following is true of a projectile's yawing moment?

   A. It is nondimensional and therefore exerts little significance on the projectile's motion.
   B. It is never significantly affected by the Reynolds number.
   C. It tends to produce a turning motion that pivots on the projectile's center of gravity.
   D. It is unrelated to Mach number but depends heavily on the value of the lift coefficient.

4.3 MASTERY VERIFIED: ANSWERS AND EXPLANATIONS

1. **D is correct.** The problem bears little relation to the passage per se; it concerns projectile motion in general and, in particular, the formula $v_{fy} = v_{oy} + at$. We are told that the projectile is launched with an initial velocity whose vertical component is 9,000 meters per second. The only acceleration to which the projectile is subjected in the vertical direction is that of gravity (g) = 10 meters per second squared downward. Calling upward the positive direction:

$$v_{fy} = v_{oy} + at$$

$$v_{fy} = 9{,}000 \text{ m/s} + (-10 \text{ m/s}^2)(t) = 9{,}000 \text{ m/s} - 10t \text{ m/s}$$

2. **B is correct.** Again, the question bears little relation to the passage per se. Rather, it requires that you understand certain fundamental dynamics of projectile motion on the earth. A projectile launched with an initial applied force takes on a vertical and horizontal velocity. With or without air resistance, the projectile experiences a downward acceleration due to gravity (10 meters per second squared) and ultimately slows to a halt. At that point where vertical motion stops, the projectile has a velocity of zero (and then begins to descend with acceleration of negative (–) 10 meters per second squared). Because the reader is advised to account for air resistance, which does impart a negative acceleration in the horizontal direction, choice C is not correct. In the absence of air resistance, choice C would also be correct.

3. **C is correct.** Since lift is perpendicular to the direction of motion, the acceleration due to lift would also be perpendicular to the direction of motion. This type of accelerate indicates only a change of direction. The drag, however, influences the speed of the projectile.

4. **C is correct.** This question draws only on your ability to (a) use the formula provided in the passage and (b) understand the simple proportionality it establishes. You don't need to know anything about Mach number, just its *proportionality* to the angle of yaw.

$$\text{Mach number, } M = \frac{\text{velocity}}{\text{angle of yaw}}$$

Instead of succumbing to intimidation by these foreign terms, notice that Mach number (M) is directly proportional to velocity and inversely proportional to the angle of yaw. This means that when the angle of yaw is halved, Mach number is doubled.

5. **A is correct.** You must avoid being intimidated by Figure 2. Look at the curves on Figure 2. Each first slopes upward (positive slope), reaches a peak, and then slopes downward (negative slope). Note that for Mach number = 10, each curve is to the left of its peak. Now, observe each curve to the left of its peak: Rightward movement (increase) along the x-axis (Mach number) corresponds to upward movement (increase) in the y-axis (coefficient of drag).

6. **D is correct.** Observe each curve where Mach number = 40. Each shows a pronounced tendency to flatten. Extrapolation (reading beyond the values actually shown) indicates that the slope will tend to progress further toward a flat configuration and that additional positive movement along the x-axis (Mach number) will bring about progressively smaller changes on the y-axis (coefficient of drag).

7. **C is correct.** The question tests your ability to read relatively complex scientific matter while taking note of relatively simple statements. The passage refers to the drag coefficient as "nondimensional," but this question concerns the yawing moment. The conclusion of the passage's second paragraph states that component forces R and L impose "a turning effect around the projectile's center of gravity G, this giving rise to the *yawing moment*." Choice C represents a paraphrase of this statement.

CHAPTER 5

FORCES

5.1 MASTERY ACHIEVED

THE PHENOMENON OF FORCE AND NEWTON'S FIRST LAW

The definition of **force** as it pertains to the MCAT is simply a "push" or "pull." Force is a *vector* quantity: It has both direction and magnitude.

A body—in motion or at rest—retains its velocity indefinitely, unless it is acted on by some force. This principle underlies **Newton's First Law**:

> *An object initially at rest or in motion with a constant velocity will remain in its initial state unless acted upon by a nonzero net external force.*

Because a change in velocity indicates acceleration (**Chapter 4**), Newton's First Law implies that objects have a natural tendency *not* to accelerate (i.e., speed up, slow down, change direction, or a combination). That tendency is termed **inertia**, and Newton's first law is sometimes called **the Law of Inertia**.

NEWTON'S SECOND LAW

The converse of Newton's First Law implies that a net external force will produce acceleration. **Newton's Second Law** provides a quantitative relationship between a force and the **acceleration** it produces. The force is directly proportional to the object's **mass**, and the relationship may be expressed as:

net applied force = (object's mass) × (acceleration produced)

This is equivalent to:

$$\mathbf{F}_{net} = m\mathbf{a}$$

Mass is expressed by the SI unit **kilogram (kg)**, and acceleration is in **m/s²**. It follows that force, which represents mass × acceleration, is expressed in the unit: **kg × m/s²**. For convenience, 1 kg × m/s² is named 1 **newton (N)**. The magnitude of a force is usually expressed in newtons (N).

Net Force

An object might experience two or more forces simultaneously, and this results in a net force that is equal to the sum of those forces. Since force is a vector, net force is a **vector sum**. Newton's Second Law becomes

$$\mathbf{F}_{net} = \mathbf{F}_1 + \mathbf{F}_2 + \dots \, m\mathbf{a}$$

Please solve this problem:

- An object is subjected to a 40 N force westward and a 15 N force eastward. What net force does it experience?

Problem solved:

Since the two forces are exactly opposite in direction, the answer is derived easily with a drawing. An eastward force of 15 newtons added to a westward force of 40 newtons yields a westward force of 25 newtons.

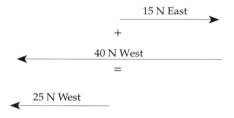

Please solve this problem:

- A 5 kg object is subjected to a 90 N force to the north and a 120 N force to the east. What is the magnitude of its acceleration?

Problem solved:

First, draw the forces.

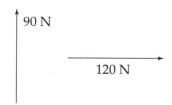

Next, connect the tip of one tail to the other in order to add them.

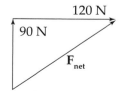

The arrow that points from the free tail to the free tip represents the net force.

To find the magnitude of $\mathbf{F}_{net}$, use the Pythagorean Theorem:

$$\mathbf{F}_{net} = \sqrt{(90 \text{ N})^2 + (120 \text{ N})^2}$$
$$= 150 \text{ N}$$

Newton's Second Law states that $\mathbf{F}_{net} = m\mathbf{a}$.

In terms of magnitude, $F_{net} = ma$.

Therefore, $a = \dfrac{F_{net}}{m} = \dfrac{150 \text{ N}}{5 \text{ kg}} = 30 \text{ m/s}^2$.

It is often useful to split forces into x- and y-components.

$F_{net,x}$ = sum of all x-components = ma_x.

$F_{net,y}$ = sum of all y-componnents = ma_y.

Please solve this problem:

- Using the figure below, find a_x and a_y.

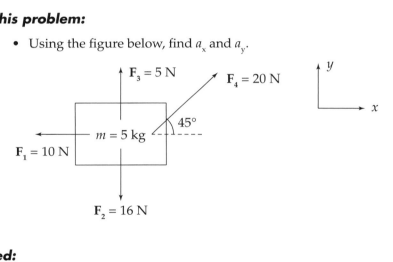

Problem solved:

First, split $\mathbf{F}_4$ into components:

$$F_{4,x} = F_4 \cos\theta$$
$$= (20 \text{ N})\cos 45°$$
$$\approx 14$$
$$F_{4y} = F_4 \sin\theta$$
$$= (20 \text{ N})\sin 45°$$
$$\approx 14 \text{ N}$$

x-direction $F_{net,x} = +14 \text{ N} - 10 \text{ N}$
$= +4 \text{ N}$

since $F_{net,x} = ma_x$
$4 \text{ N} = (5 \text{ kg})a_x$
$a_x = 0.8 \text{ m/s}^2$

y-direction $F_{net,y} = +5 \text{ N} + 14 \text{ N} - 16 \text{ N}$
$= 3 \text{ N}$

since $F_{net,y} = ma_y$
$3 \text{ N}(5 \text{ kg})a_y$
$a_y = 0.6 \text{ m/s}^2$

NET FORCE AND VELOCITY

Newton's Second Law tells us that an object will accelerate in the direction of the net force. In the previous chapter, we learned that an object does not have to move in the direction of acceleration. Now we can state:

An object does not have to move in the direction of the net force.

A basic example is gravity. The force of gravity acting on an object experiencing projectile motion is always downward, yet the projectile can move in a parabolic path.

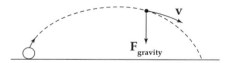

Case 1: **v** and **F** are in the same direction.

This physically corresponds to *speeding up.*

Case 2: **v** and **F** are in opposite directions.

This physically corresponds to *slowing down.*

Case 3: **v** and **F** are perpendicular.

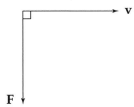

This corresponds to a *change in direction*.

NEWTON'S THIRD LAW

On the MCAT, net force requires an understanding of **Newton's Third Law**:

> *When one body exerts a force on another, the second body will exert an equal and opposite force on the first.*

Mathematically, $\mathbf{F}_{2\,\text{on}\,1} = -\mathbf{F}_{1\,\text{on}\,2}$

These forces are often referred to as an **Action-Reaction Pair** and this law has given rise to that familiar statement: "For every action there is an equal and opposite reaction."

Unfortunately, this popular version of Newton's Third Law can lead to confusion. Picture a block of wood resting on the floor. The block is not accelerating, therefore the net force on it must be zero. In other words, the downward force of gravity acting on the block must be equal and opposite to the force that the floor is exerting to support it.

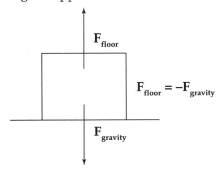

However, these two forces are *not* an action-reaction pair. With a true action-reaction, one force is exerted *by* the object and the other is exerted *on* the object. The forces above are, in fact, equal and opposite, but they both act *on* the block. They are actually two action-reaction pairs:

(1) the force that the earth exerts on the block (gravity) and the force that the block exerts on the earth, and

(2) the force the floor exerts on the block and the force that the block exerts on the earth.

Please solve this problem:

- A 1 kg block collides head-on with a 100 kg block. During the collision, which block feels the greater force?

Problem solved:

Newton's Third Law states that they each feel the same magnitude force. However, the *effect* of the force is different.

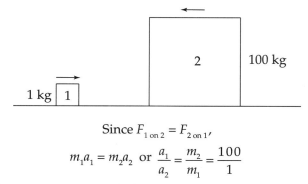

Since $F_{1 \text{ on } 2} = F_{2 \text{ on } 1}$,

$$m_1 a_1 = m_2 a_2 \quad \text{or} \quad \frac{a_1}{a_2} = \frac{m_2}{m_1} = \frac{100}{1}$$

The small block will experience 100 times the acceleration of the large block.

FORCES IN MECHANICS

Gravity: Distinguishing Between Mass and Weight; Weight as Force

The force of gravity due to the earth pulls objects toward it. For objects on or near the surface, we can write:

$$F_g = mg$$

where g is the acceleration due to gravity ($\approx 10 \text{ m/s}^2$). Note that this force exists even if the object is not actually accelerating.

$a = g$ | m

$F_g = mg$

m | $a = 0$

$F_g = mg$

The force of gravity acting on an object is also referred to as the object's **weight**. Remember that mass is an intrinsic property of an object, while weight depends on the pull of gravity.

Please solve this problem:

- An object on earth has a weight of 50 newtons. What is its mass?

Problem solved:

Weight is equal to the product:

$$\text{weight } (w) = F_g = mg$$

$$\text{Therefore, } m = \frac{w}{g}$$

$$m = \frac{50 \text{ N}}{10 \text{ m/s}^2}$$

$$m = 5 \text{ kg}$$

Please solve this problem:

- An object situated on Planet X has mass of 80 kilograms and weight of 320 newtons on Planet X. The object is dropped from 18 meters above the surface of Planet X. Find the time before the object strikes the surface of the planet, and find the object's velocity at the instant before impact with the planet's surface.

Problem solved:

To solve this problem, the student will need to understand Newton's Second Law, free fall, and the relationships among velocity, time, and acceleration.

First, determine the object's acceleration:

$$\mathbf{F}_{net} = m\mathbf{a}$$

Choosing downward as the positive direction:

$$320 \text{ N} = 80 \text{ kg } (a)$$

$$a = 4.0 \text{ m/s}^2$$

Knowing that the body accelerates at 4.0 meters per second squared, calculate t:

$$d = v_o t + \frac{1}{2} a t^2$$

$$18 \text{ m} = 0 + \frac{1}{2} (4)(t^2)$$

$$18 \text{ m} = 2t^2$$

$$\frac{18}{2} = t^2$$

$$t^2 = 9$$

$$t = 3 \text{ s}$$

Knowing that the object travels for 3 seconds with an acceleration of 4.0 meters per second squared, calculate its final velocity:

$$v_f = v_o + at$$

$$v_f = 0 + (4.0 \text{ m/s}^2)(3 \text{ s})$$

$$v_f = 12 \text{ m/s}$$

Newton's Law of Universal Gravitation

Not only does the earth attract objects, but all objects with mass attract all other objects with mass. **Newton's law of universal gravitation** states that any pair of objects will produce a mutually attractive gravitational force according to this equation:

$$F_g = G\frac{m_1 m_2}{r^2}$$

where:

F_g = force of gravity

m_1 = mass of object 1

m_2 = mass of object 2

r = distance between the centers of the masses of objects 1 and 2

G = universal gravitational constant = 6.67×10^{-11} N•m^2/kg^2

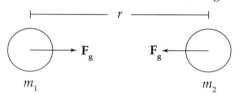

The MCAT will not require you to know the value of the universal gravitational constant, but some questions will require an understanding of the proportionalities in Newton's law of gravitation. Note that gravitational force is:

- directly proportional to the mass of each object, and

- inversely proportional to the square of the distance between the centers of mass of the objects.

Please solve this problem:

- An object with mass 36 kg and weight 360 N rests on the surface of the earth. If it is transported to an altitude of twice the earth's radius, what are its new mass and weight?

  A. $m = 36$ kg, $w = 90$ N
  B. $m = 9$ kg, $w = 90$ N
  C. $m = 36$ kg, $w = 40$ N
  D. $m = 4$ kg, $w = 40$ N

Problem solved:

Since mass is an intrinsic property of the object, it will not change. This eliminates choices B and D. The only variable changing in the gravitational formula is r. Therefore, $F_g \propto \dfrac{1}{r^2}$.

In addition, the term "altitude" refers to the distance to the *surface*, while r refers to the distance to the *center* of the earth.

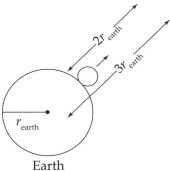

Earth

r has therefore tripled in size. Since $F_g \propto \dfrac{1}{r^2}$, F_g has become $\dfrac{1}{3^2}$ or $\dfrac{1}{9}$ times its previous value.

$$\frac{1}{9}(360 \text{ N}) = 40 \text{ N}$$

Choice C is the answer.

How does $F_g = mg$ relate to $F_g = \dfrac{Gm_1m_2}{r^2}$?

When an object is on or near the surface of the earth, $r \approx$ the radius of the earth. So:

$$m_{object}g = \frac{Gm_{earth}m_{object}}{R_{earth}^2}$$

Cancelling m_{object} from each side, we see that:

$$g = \frac{Gm_{earth}}{R_{earth}^2} \approx 10 \text{ m/s}^2.$$

On the surfaces of other planets or moons, g would be determined by the new mass and radius.

The Normal Force

When an object is in contact with a surface (i.e., a floor, a wall, an inclined plane), the surface exerts a pushing force on the object. This is referred to as the **Normal Force**, denoted by $\mathbf{F}_N$. The word "normal" refers to the fact that the direction of the force is always perpendicular to the surface.

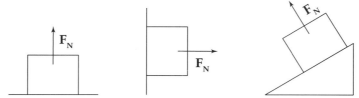

There is no explicit formula for the normal force. It can only be found using Newton's Second Law.

Please solve this problem:

- Find the normal force in all three cases:

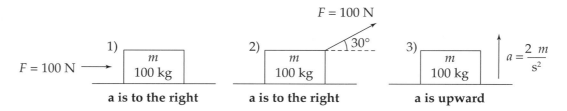

Problem solved:

1. Drawing all of the forces acting on the object:

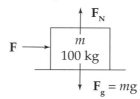

To find the normal force, we only need to look at Newton's Second Law in the y-direction.

$$F_{net,\ y} = ma_y$$

Calling upward positive, $F_N - F_g = mg$, since there is no acceleration in the y-direction. Therefore,

$$F_N = F_g$$

$$= mg$$

$$= (100 \text{ kg})(10 \text{ m/s}^2)$$

$$= 1000 \text{ N}$$

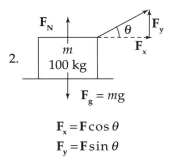

2.

$$F_x = F\cos\theta$$
$$F_y = F\sin\theta$$

First, we split **F** into components. Again, we are only concerned with the y-direction.

$$F_{net,\,y} = ma_y$$

Calling upward positive, we see that:

$$F_N + F\sin\theta - F_g = m \bullet 0$$

Therefore, $F_N = F_g - F\sin\theta$
$$= mg - F\sin\theta$$
$$= (100\text{ kg})(10\text{ m/s}^2) - (100\text{ N})\sin 30°$$
$$= 1000\text{ N} - 50\text{ N}$$
$$= 950\text{ N}$$

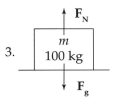

3.

Now, there is an upward acceleration.

$$F_{net,y} = ma_y$$
$$F_N - F_g = ma_y$$
$$F_N = F_g + ma_y$$
$$= mg + ma_y$$
$$= (100\text{ kg})(10\text{ m/s}^2) + (100\text{ kg})(2\text{ m/s}^2)$$
$$= 1000\text{ N} + 200\text{ N}$$
$$= 1200\text{ N}$$

Tension

Tension, denoted as $\mathbf{F_T}$, refers to the force exerted by ropes, strings, and cables. On the MCAT, it is always a *pulling* force.

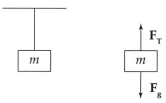

On the MCAT, all ropes, strings, and cables will be massless. As a result, if two different objects are connected by the same string, each object will experience the same magnitude of tension, but in opposite directions.

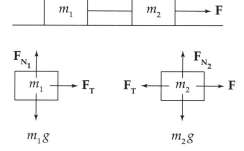

Please solve this problem:

- From the diagram above, $m_1 = 10$ kg, $m_2 = 20$ kg, and $F = 60$ N. Find (a) the acceleration of the blocks and (b) the tension in the string between them.

Problem solved:

The standard way of solving this problem is to examine each block separately. According to Newton's Second Law, the equation in the horizontal direction for block one is:

$$(1)\ F_T = m_1 a$$

For block two:

$$(2)\ F - F_T = m_2 a$$

Since the blocks move together, the acceleration is the same for each. Since they are connected by a single string, F_T is the same for each.

Plugging equation (1) into equation (2), we see:

$$F - m_1 a = m_2 a$$
$$F = m_1 a + m_2 a$$
$$F = (m_1 + m_2)a$$
$$a = \frac{F}{m_1 + m_2} = \frac{60 \text{ N}}{10 \text{ kg} + 20 \text{ kg}}$$
$$= 2 \text{ m/s}^2$$

To solve for F_T, we can plug the value of a into either equation (1) or (2).

(1) $F_T = m_1 a$

$F_T = (10 \text{ kg})(2 \text{ m/s}^2)$

$ = 20 \text{ N}$

Note: On the MCAT, you would be asked for *either* acceleration *or* tension, but not both. A quicker way of solving for acceleration would be to *treat the entire system as if it were one object.* What does this mean? Newton's Second Law tells us we only need to consider forces acting on the object *from the outside.* If the entire system is our "object," then the string is "inside." Therefore, tension need not be considered.

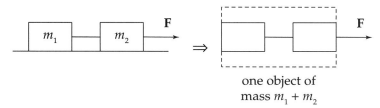

In the horizontal direction:

$$F_{net} = ma$$
$$F = (m_1 + m_2)a$$
$$a = \frac{F}{m_1 + m_2}$$

Which is the same result we achieved before.

This method could also be applied to pulley systems and to problems where two or more blocks are being pushed together along a surface.

Friction

Friction is a force that occurs between two bodies that are in contact with each other. You should think of friction as the force that causes two objects to resist moving or sliding "against" one another. It is due to the inherent roughness of all surfaces.

The classic illustration for friction is that of an object on a table. Any attempt to move the object across the tabletop requires an initial application of force, and any effort to maintain the object in motion across the tabletop requires a persistent application of force. The necessity for such forces arises from the force of friction, which must be overcome if motion is to be initiated and maintained.

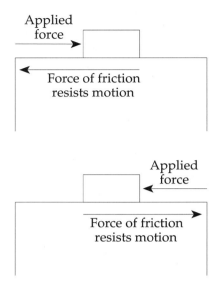

There are two types of friction: kinetic (sliding) and static (not sliding). They are denoted as $\mathbf{F}_{f,k}$, and $\mathbf{F}_{f,s}$, respectively. While they are similar, problem-solving on the MCAT involving the two types of friction can be very different.

KINETIC FRICTION

If two objects in contact move relative to one another (i.e., slide) the friction is kinetic. Kinetic friction always opposes the motion of each object.

The magnitude of $F_{f,k}$ is:

$$F_{f,k} = \mu_k F_N$$

where F_N is the normal force and μ_k is referred to as the coeffecient of kinetic friction. μ_k is an experimentally determined, unitless quantity that measures the roughness of the two surfaces in contact.

Please solve this problem:

- An object of mass 100 kg is moving along the floor. A force of 200 N is applied in the direction of motion. If $\mu_k = 0.3$, what is the object's acceleration?

Problem solved:

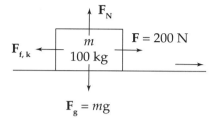

In the horizontal direction, we see that:

$$F_{net} = ma$$
$$F - F_{f,x} = ma$$
$$F - \mu_k F_N = ma$$

In the vertical direction:

$$F_{net} = ma$$
$$F_N - F_g = 0$$
$$F_N = F_g$$
$$= mg$$

Plugging this into the horizontal equation:

$$F - \mu_k mg = ma$$
$$200 \text{ N} - (0.3)(100 \text{ kg})(10 \text{ m/s}^2) = (100 \text{ kg})a$$
$$200 \text{ N} - 300 \text{ N} = (100 \text{ kg})c$$
$$a = \frac{-100 \text{ N}}{100 \text{ kg}} = -1 \text{ m/s}^2$$

Note that the object is slowing down and that the friction force is greater than the applied force. A greater applied force was, of course, needed to start the object moving in the first place, but once the object is moving, the value of kinetic friction remains constant regardless of whether the applied force changes.

STATIC FRICTION

If there is no relative motion between the objects in contact, the friction is static. Static friction always opposes the *intended* motion.

$$\mathbf{F}_{f,s} \longleftarrow \boxed{} \longrightarrow \mathbf{F}$$

no motion

If there were no friction, the applied force would accelerate the object to the right. Static friction prevents this from happening.

Unlike kinetic friction, static friction is defined with an *inequality* rather than an equation:

$$F_{f,s} \leq \mu_s F_N$$

where μ_s is the coefficient of static friction.

The quantity $\mu_s F_N$ is the maximum static friction ($F_{f,s,max}$). The applied force must overcome this to start the object moving.

Please solve this problem:

- An object of mass 100 kg is at rest on the floor. If $\mu_s = 0.4$, how much force is required to start the object moving?

Problem solved:

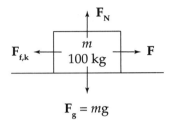

$$F_g = mg$$

To get the object moving:

$$F > F_{f,s,max}$$
$$F > \mu_s F_N$$
$$F > \mu_s mg$$
$$F > (0.4)(100 \text{ kg})(100 \text{ m/s}^2)$$
$$F > 400 \text{ N}$$

Warning: Static friction is not always equal to $\mu_s F_N$. In general, it is whatever it needs to be to make sure that the object does not move.

Please solve this problem:

- A 100 kg object rests on the floor. A horizontal force of 100 N is applied. If $\mu_s = 0.4$, what is the force of static friction?

    A. 0 N
    B. 100 N
    C. 300 N
    D. 400 N

Problem solved:

The "trap" answer would be $\mu_s F_N$, but remember this is the maximum static friction, not necessarily what static friction is in this particular case. However, we still need to calculafe $F_{f,s,max}$ in order to determine whether or not the object will move as the result of the applied force.

$$
\begin{aligned}
F_{f,s,max} &= \mu_s F_N \\
&= \mu_s mg \\
&= (0.4)(100 \text{ kg})(10 \text{ m/s}^2) \\
&= 400 \text{ N}
\end{aligned}
$$

This tells us that an applied force of more than 400 N is required to start the object moving. Since the applied force is only 100 N, the object is *not moving*.

If the object is not moving (or accelerating), we can apply Newton's Second Law.

$$
\begin{aligned}
F_{net} &= ma \\
F - F_{f,s} &= 0
\end{aligned}
$$

Therefore: $F_{f,s} = F = 100 \text{ N}$

In other words, static friction does whatever it takes to balance the applied force.

Note: μ_s is always larger than μ_k. Physically, this means that it takes more force to start an object moving than it does to keep an object moving with constant velocity.

MOTION ON AN INCLINED PLANE

An **inclined plane** is a surface raised at an angle above the horizontal.

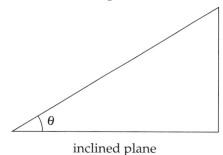

inclined plane

An object placed on an inclined plane is constrained to move along its surface. Therefore, it is convenient to create new coordinate axes parallel and perpendicular to the plane.

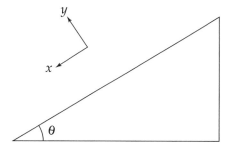

Note: You could also choose up the plane to be the positive x-direction.

Changing the coordinate axes means that we must split all forces into components that correspond to these axes.

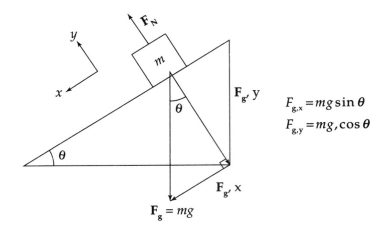

$$F_{g,x} = mg \sin \theta$$
$$F_{g,y} = mg, \cos \theta$$

The normal force is already in the y-direction, while gravity needs to be split into components.

Please solve this problem:

- A 10 kg object slides down a frictionless inclined plane raised 30 degrees above the horizontal. What is its acceleration?

Problem solved:

Looking at the diagram above and using Newton's Second Law in the new x-direction, we see that

$$F_{net} = ma$$
$$mg \sin \theta = ma$$
$$a = g \sin \theta$$
$$= (10 \text{ m/s}^2) \sin 30°$$
$$= 5 \text{ m/s}^2$$

Note that the acceleration is independent of mass.

Please solve this problem:

- What is the smallest angle of incline that would cause a 10 kg object, initially at rest, to start sliding down the inclined plane? Note that $\mu_s = 0$.

  A. 22°
  B. 45°
  C. 68°
  D. The block will never slide.

Problem solved:

First, a diagram:

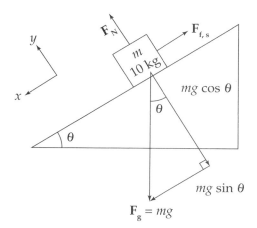

To make an object just start to move, the downward component of gravity must be slightly larger than the maximum static friction.

$$mg\sin\theta > F_{f,s,max}$$
$$mg\sin\theta > \mu_s F_N$$

To find the normal, we look at the y-direction:

$$F_{net} = ma$$
$$F_N - mg\cos\theta = 0$$
$$F_N = mg\cos\theta$$

Plugging this in above:

$$mg\sin\theta > \mu_s\, mg\cos\theta$$
$$\sin\theta > \mu_s\cos\theta$$
$$\tan\theta > \mu_s$$
$$\theta > \tan^{-1}(\mu_s)$$
$$\theta > \tan^{-1}(0.4)$$

Since we know $\tan^{-1}(0) = 0$ and $\tan^{-1}(1)$ is $45°$, $\tan^{-1}(0.4)$ must be in between $0°$ and $45°$. Choice A is the answer.

PULLEYS

Pulleys are often used to make lifting or moving objects easier by reducing the force needed and/or reducing the direction of force.

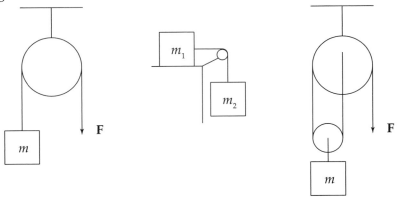

All pulleys on the MCAT will be massless and frictionless.

A single pulley changes the direction of the force. If two masses are connected by a string over a pulley, then each mass feels the same magnitude tension.

Please solve this problem:

- A block of mass 10 kg rests on a frictionless table and is connected via string and pulley to a 5 kg mass hanging off the edge of the table. What is the acceleration of the system?

Problem solved:

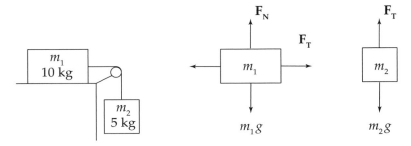

A diagram of each block's forces is shown above. Note that F_T is the same for both blocks.

Since each block experiences the same magnitude of acceleration, it is useful to choose the direction of motion to be positive for each block.

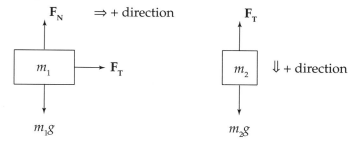

Using Newton's Second Law, we see that:

$$F_T = m_1 a \text{ and } m_2 g - F_T = m_2 a$$

Plugging the first equation into the second:

$$m_2 g - m_1 a = m_2 a$$
$$m_2 g = (m_1 + m_2)a$$
$$a = \frac{m_2 g}{m_1 + m_2}$$
$$= \frac{(5 \text{ kg})(10 \text{ m/s}^2)}{(5 \text{ kg} + 10 \text{ kg})}$$
$$\approx 3 \text{ m/s}^2$$

To find F_T, we would plug the value into either equation above. Note: As we saw earlier, a quicker way to solve this problem would be to treat the entire system as one object. Tension becomes an internal force and can be ignored.

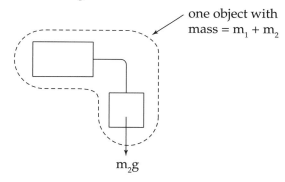

Now, we only need to concern ourselves with forces in the direction of acceleration ($m_2 g$) and opposite (none). Using Newton's Second Law:

$$F_{net} = ma$$
$$m_2 g = (m_1 + m_2)a$$
$$a = \frac{m_2 g}{m_1 + m_2}$$

Multiple pulleys are usually designed to reduce the force needed to move or lift an object.

Please solve this problem:

- In the diagram below, how much force is needed to lift the block?

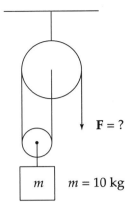

$F = ?$

m $m = 10$ kg

Problem solved:

In this problem, the upper pulley is fixed in place while the lower pulley moves with the mass. Treating the movable pulley and mass as an object:

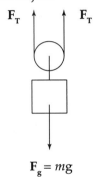

F_T F_T

$F_g = mg$

Even though it is one string lifting the pulley, the tension acts on each side of it, counting it as two forces. The minimum force required to lift the pulley-mass system is:

$$2F_T - mg = 0$$

$$F_T = \frac{1}{2}mg$$

Looking at the original diagram, we can see that F is equal to F_T (since it is all one string). Therefore:

$$F = F_T$$

$$= \frac{1}{2}mg$$

$$= \frac{1}{2}(10 \text{ kg})(10 \text{ m/s}^2)$$

$$= 50 \text{ N}$$

CENTRIPETAL FORCE

As we saw in Chapter 4, an object moving in a circle of radius r and speed v experiences acceleration toward the center of the circle, given by $a_c = \dfrac{v^2}{r}$. Newton's First Law tells us that objects naturally travel in straight lines. Therefore, a force is required to give an object this centripetal acceleration. We call this **centripetal force**.

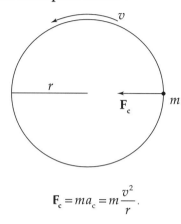

$$\mathbf{F}_c = ma_c = m\frac{v^2}{r}.$$

Note that this force is not a new force like gravity or friction, but rather it is the force *needed* to cause circular motion. What provides the centripetal force? Real forces, such as gravity, tension, etc.

Please solve this problem:

- If a satellite of mass M_s orbits the earth (mass = M_e) with radius r, what is its speed?

Problem solved:

Real forces provide centripetal force. In this case, the gravitational attraction between the satellite and the earth is providing it.

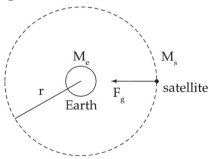

$$F_c = \frac{m_s v^2}{r}$$

$$F_g = \frac{m_s v^2}{r}$$

$$\frac{Gm_e m_s}{r^2} = \frac{m_s v^2}{r}$$

Solving for v, we get:

$$v = \sqrt{\frac{Gm_e}{r}}$$

Note that the mass of the satellite does not matter.

Please solve this problem:

- A ball of mass 5 kg moves in a vertical circle with a constant speed of 10 m/s while attached to a string of length 50 cm. (a) What is the maximum tension in the string? (b) What is the minimum speed with which the ball must travel to keep it in a circle?

Problem solved:

(a) The maximum tension occurs when the ball is at the bottom of the circle, since the string needs to both support its weight and to provide necessary centripetal force.

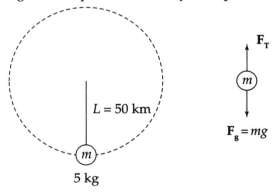

If we decide that toward the center is positive,

$$F_{net} = ma$$

$$F_T - mg = m\frac{v^2}{r}$$

$$F_T = mg + \frac{mv^2}{r}$$

$$= (5 \text{ kg})(10 \text{ m/s}^2) + \frac{(5 \text{ kg})(10 \text{ m/s}^2)}{0.5m}$$

$$= 1050 \text{ N}$$

(b) To find the minimum speed needed to make it around the circle, we look at the top of the circle.

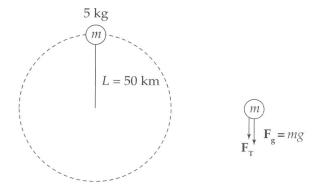

Now, $F_T + mg = m\dfrac{v^2}{L}$

The minimum speed corresponds to the minimum tension (zero). Therefore:

$$mg = m\frac{v_{\min}^2}{L}$$
$$V_{\min} = \sqrt{gL}$$
$$= \sqrt{(10\ \text{m}/\text{s}^2)(0.5\ \text{m})}$$
$$\approx 2.2\ \text{m}/\text{s}$$

CENTER OF MASS

Every object (whether it is regularly or irregularly shaped) has a **center of mass** (sometimes called the *center of gravity*).

The MCAT candidate should think of the center of gravity as the point at which an object's mass is concentrated. In day-to-day application, it is conceived as the object's "balancing point."

For any object whose mass is *uniformly distributed*, the center of mass is at the *geometric center*.

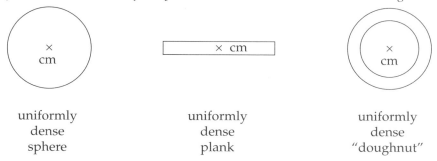

uniformly
dense
sphere

uniformly
dense
plank

uniformly
dense
"doughnut"

For a system of objects arranged along the *x*-axis:

the location of the center of mass, denoted by x_{cm} is:

$$x_{cm} = \frac{m_1 x_1 + m_2 x_2 + m_3 x_3 + \ldots}{m_1 + m_2 + m_3}$$

In most MCAT problems, a coordinate system is not given, therefore you must choose where the original should be. A useful method would be to choose the location referenced in the problem. If the question asks, "How far from the left is the center of mass?" choose the left as the origin.

Please solve this problem:

- A block of mass 2 kg and a block of mass 6 kg sit on the ends of a plank of length L, as shown. How far from the left end is the center of mass if (a) the plank is massless and (b) the plank has mass and is uniformly dense?

2 kg   6 kg

m_1 m_2

L

A. 1/4 L
B. 1/3 L
C. 2/3 L
D. 3/4 L

Problem solved:

(a) Conceptually, we can see that the center of mass will be closer to the heavier mass (i.e., where the balance point would be). This eliminates choices A and B. Choosing the left edge as the origin, we see that $x = 0$ and $x_2 = L$. Therefore:

$$x_{cm} = \frac{(2 \text{ kg}) \bullet 0 + (6 \text{ kg}) \bullet L}{2 \text{ kg} + 6 \text{ kg}}$$

$$= \frac{3}{4}L$$

Choice D.

(b) Even with the plank having mass, we can eliminate choices A and B. Since the mass of the plank was not given, we cannot use the formula. However, since the plank is uniformly dense, its center of mass is the actual center. This new mass would skew the answer to part (a) closer to the actual center.

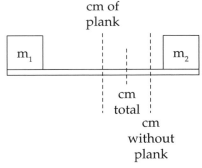

cm of
plank

m_1 m_2

cm
total

cm
without
plank

Therefore, $\frac{1}{2}L < x_{cm} < \frac{3}{4}L$, choice C, is the only choice that fits the criteria.

ROTATIONAL MOTION AND TORQUE

In translational mechanics, a force is required to produce acceleration (i.e., speeding up, slowing down, changing direction). Mass is the measure of inertia—the property that measures how difficult it is to accelerate an object.

In the rotational world, torque is required to produce rotational acceleration. The property that makes rotational acceleration difficult is called rotational inertia or the moment of inertia.

The moment of inertia, denoted by I and measured in $kg \cdot m^2$ increases with mass and with how far away the mass is from the axis of rotation.

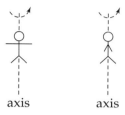

An example would be a figure skater spinning on ice. If the figure skater is spinning with his or her arms outstretched and then pulls them in, the moment of inertia would decrease. This makes the figure skater turn faster.

The MCAT does not emphasize rotational motion and provides most relevant information and equations in a given passage or problem.

A force that causes an object to turn or rotate provides a torque. Torque is denoted by τ and is measured in $N \cdot m$. Torque is a vector that will be either clockwise (cw) or counter-clockwise (ccw) on the MCAT.

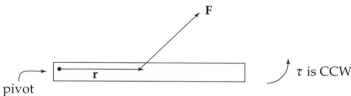

If an object is constrained to rotate around a fixed point, called the **pivot**, then a torque will only exist if a force is applied at a different point.

r is the vector that points from the pivot to the location of the applied force and θ is the angle between **r** and **F**. The equation for torque is:

$$\tau = rF \sin \theta$$

Note that torque increases as both **r** and **F** increase and is maximized when $\theta = 90°$. An alternative way of calculating torque is to split the force into components parallel and perpendicular to **r**.

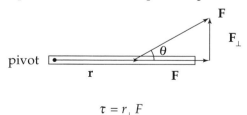

$$\tau = r_\perp F$$

Please solve this problem:

- A pendulum with mass 10 kg and string length 50 cm is pulled 30° from the vertical. Find the torque due to (a) tension and (b) gravity.

Problem solved:

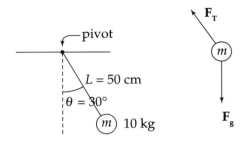

(a) Since the angle between **r** and $\mathbf{F}_T$ is 180°, $\tau_T = L \cdot F_T \sin 180° = 0$.

(b) The angle between **r** and $\mathbf{F}_g$ is 30°, so

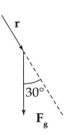

$$\tau_g = L \cdot F_g \sin 30° = L \cdot mg \sin 30°$$
$$= (0.5 \text{ m})(10 \text{ kg})(10 \text{ m/s}^2)(0.5)$$
$$= 25 \text{ N} \cdot m$$

Another way of calculating torque is to use the **lever arm**. The lever arm is the distance from the pivot to the **line of action**.

The line of action is created by extending the force as a line, infinite in both directions.

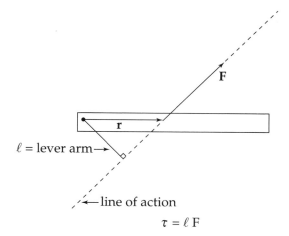

$$\tau = \ell\, F$$

Please solve this problem:

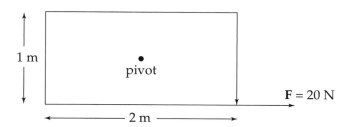

- Find the torque. τ.

Problem solved:

Using $\tau = rF\sin\theta$ would be difficult since θ isn't given. $\tau = lF$ would be easier.

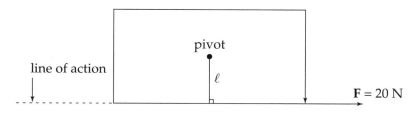

Since:

$$\tau = lF$$
$$l = \frac{1}{2}(1\text{ m}) = 0.5\text{ m},$$
$$\tau = (0.5\text{ m})(20\text{ N})$$
$$= 10\text{ N}\bullet\text{m}$$

STATICS: TRANSLATIONAL AND ROTATIONAL EQUILIBRIUM

You must be familiar with the concepts of:

- translational equilibrium and

- rotational equilibrium.

A body (or system of bodies) is in translational equilibrium if it experiences no net force in any direction. A body (or system of bodies) is in rotational equilibrium if it experiences no net torque.

Please solve this problem:

- Ropes 1, 2, and 3 are knotted together, as shown in the figure below. Rope 2 is fastened to a vertical wall, and rope 3 is fastened to a horizontal ceiling. A mass with a weight of 50 newtons hangs on rope 1. The angle between rope 3 and the ceiling is 60°. Find T_1, T_2, and T_3, the tension in each of the ropes. (Assume that the weight of the ropes is negligible.)

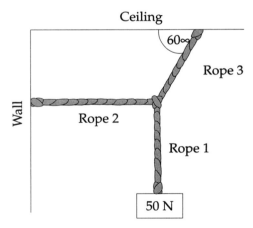

Problem solved:

Since the system is in equilibrium, the net force on the mass is equal to zero.

$$T_1 - F_g = 50 \text{ N}$$

You can also examine the forces acting on the knot.

Splitting T$_3$ into horizontal and vertical components, we see:

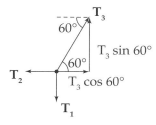

Horizontal: $T_2 = T_3 \cos 60°$

Vertical: $T_3 \sin 60° = T_1$

Starting with the vertical equation $T_3 = \dfrac{T_1}{\sin 60°} = \dfrac{50 \text{ N}}{.87} \approx 60 \text{ N}$

And therefore: $T_2 \approx (60 \text{ N}) \cos 60° \approx 30$]

Please solve this problem:

- If the plank is uniform with $m = 30$ kg, find m_2, such that the system is balanced.

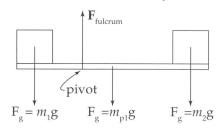

Problem solved:

While this problem can be solved using center of mass, using torque is easier. First, see the force diagram. Treating plank and blocks as one object, where m_{pl} is the mass of the plank:

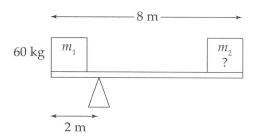

   While forces do balance, there are two unknown forces, which prevents us from finding m_2.
Knowing that the net torque also equals zero will help us solve this problem. The reason? Since
$\tau = rF\sin\theta\,(or\,\ell F)$, the torque due to the fulcrum force = 0 ($r = 0$). This leaves three nonzero torques,
only one of which is unknown.

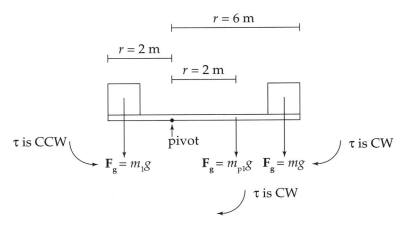

Setting the clockwise torques equal to the counterclockwise torque:

$$\tau_{cw} = \tau_{ccw}$$
$$(2m)m_{pl}g + (6m)m_2g = (2m)m_1g$$
$$(2m)(30\ kg)(10\ m/s^2) + (6m)m_2(10\ m/s^2) = (2m)(60\ kg)(10\ m/s^2)$$

Canceling $10\ m/s^2$ in each term:

$$30\ kg \bullet m + (6m)m_2 = 120\ kg \bullet m$$
$$m_2 = \frac{90\ kg \bullet m}{6m}$$
$$= 15\ kg$$

5.2 MASTERY APPLIED: PRACTICE PASSAGE AND QUESTIONS

Passage

Many of the muscles in the human body cause movement by exerting forces on tendons, which in turn exert forces on bones, which then act to m ove limbs, such as arms or legs. When nerve signals indicate to do so, muscles expand or contract (both of which are often termed "contraction" in the context of muscles), and it is this contraction that is ultimately responsible for the force.

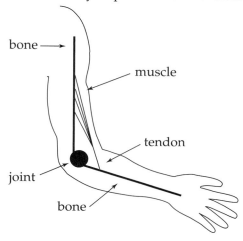

Figure 1

In Figure 1, a human arm is pictured, with the biceps muscle and associated parts indicated. When the biceps muscle contracts, it pulls up on the lower arm, which causes movement. The place where the tendon meets the bone is called the insertion point, and it is not precisely at the joint, but is slightly apart from it. The appearance of strong upper-arm muscles comes in part from large biceps, and indeed, the amount of force that a muscle can exert is proportional to the cross-sectional area of the muscle.

In the body, most muscles are grouped in agonist/antagonist pairs, such as the biceps and triceps in the arms. The former is responsible for rotating the lower arm toward the shoulder, while the latter is responsible for motion in the opposite direction. However, in each of the following questions, assume that the muscles mentioned in the questions or answers are the only muscles exerting any force.

1. Why is the insertion point for the biceps a distance away from the joint?
    A. The distance increases the center of mass of the biceps.
    B. The distance increases the force from the biceps.
    C. The distance increases the torque from the biceps.
    D. Evolutionary history; it is disadvantageous.

2. Imagine that a head of 5 kg is balanced on a rigid spinal column. If the center of mass of the head is 3 cm in front of the top of the spinal column and the anterior neck muscles balancing it are 5 cm behind the spinal column, how much vertical force do the anterior neck muscles need to exert to keep the head upright?
    A. 3 N
    B. 25 N
    C. 30 N
    D. 83 N

3. Why can the upper arm remain motionless when the biceps and tendon exert a force on the lower arm, even though these fibers are also connected to the upper arm?
    A. It feels no forces, since it is exerting a force on the lower arm, not vice-versa.
    B. It feels an opposing force from the torso, to which it is also attached.
    C. It feels a reaction force from the lower arm in the opposite direction.
    D. Its bones are rigid, holding it in place.

4. In a typical weight room, how much force from a weightlifter is required to lift a weight of 30 N at constant velocity?

   A. 0 N
   B. 15 N
   C. 30 N
   D. 60 N

5. Would muscles need to exert less force to accelerate a mass lying initially at rest on the surface of the moon than they would if it were on the surface of the earth, given that the acceleration due to gravity on the moon is approximately one-sixth that on the earth?

   A. Yes, both vertically and horizontally
   B. Yes, but only vertically
   C. Yes, but only horizontally
   D. No

6. Before an arm-wrestling bout, an unlucky challenger notices that his arm is only half a large as the champion's, measured from top to bottom when both arms are held out horizontally from their shoulders. If all other factors are the same and the sizes of the two arm wrestlers' arms are entirely determined by the size of their respective biceps, then given that the maximum force from the champion's arm is F, what is the maximum force from the challenger's arm?

   A. $\frac{1}{4}F$

   B. $\frac{1}{2}F$

   C. $2F$

   D. $4F$

7. A weightlifter is holding a weight in her right hand. Her upper arm is pointed downwards at an angle of 45° and her upper arm upwards at an angle of 45°, both with respect to the vertical. Her biceps and tendon are horizontal, and the tendon inserts a quarter of the way from the elbow joint to the weight. If the weight has a weight of mg, what is the tension force exerted by the tendon?

   A. $\frac{1}{2}mg$

   B. mg

   C. $2mg$

   D. $4mg$

5.3 MASTERY VERIFIED: ANSWERS AND EXPLANATIONS

1. **C is correct.** The equation for torque is $\tau = rF\sin\theta$. If the force were applied exactly at the pivot point (the joint), then r would equal zero, so there would be no torque. Putting some distance between the force and the pivot increases the torque from the muscle. A is wrong because the center of mass is a position; saying that it "increases" doesn't make sense. Its distance from an origin could increase, but this depends on the position of the origin, so A would be wrong even if it mentioned something about distance. B is wrong because there is no reason to think that the force depends on position. D is wrong because being able to provide torque to make an arm rotate is advantageous, not disadvantageous.

2. **C is correct.** For the head to remain upright, there must be no net torque. That is, the torque from the neck muscles must balance the torque from the weight of the head. As an equation, that means $r_1 mg\sin 90° = r_2 F\sin 90°$, where F is the neck force, r_1 is the distance between the spinal column and the center of mass of the head, and r_2 is the distance between the spinal column and the application of the neck force. Since $\sin(90°) = 1$, this becomes $F = \dfrac{r_1 mg}{r_2}$, which, when plugged into, becomes $F = \dfrac{(3)(5)(10)}{5} = 30$ N (where the distances have been left in centimeters, since the units cancel in the fraction).

3. **B is correct.** For an object to remain motionless, it must have zero acceleration. This means that it has zero net force. Thus, since the biceps pull on the upper arm as well as the lower, there must be some external force in the opposite direction and of equal magnitude. This can come from the torso, so B is correct. A is wrong because Newton's Third Law requires that an object exerting a force must also feel a force. C is wrong because the upper arm pulls on the lower via the biceps, so the reaction force must pull on the upper arm via the biceps; the reaction force isn't in the opposite direction as the biceps force, but rather, it is the biceps force. D is wrong because while the bones don't bend, they are attached via joints that allow for rotation (as in Figure 1), so movement is possible.

4. **C is correct.** Constant velocity occurs when an object feels zero net force, so a weightlifter would need to supply enough force to balance the gravitational force to keep the weight at constant velocity. The gravitational force is the weight, so the weightlifter would need to supply 30 N of force.

5. **A is correct.** The weight is definitely less, so lifting vertically would be easier. Eliminate both C and D. Since the weight is less, the normal force balancing the weight should also be less, so the maximum force of static friction should be less as well (since it is given by $f_{s,max} = \mu_s F_N$, so the maximum force of static friction is proportional to the normal force). The maximum force of static friction determines the force required to accelerate an object horizontally on a surface, so eliminate B, too.

6. **D is correct.** The challenger is measuring the diameter of his arm in comparison to the champion's ("measured from top to bottom"). Since $d = 2r$, the diameter is directly proportional to the radius, so the champion's arm has twice the radius of the challenger's. Since $A = \pi r^2$ for a circle, the area is proportional to the square of the radius, so the champion's arm has quadruple the area of the challenger's. The second paragraph of the passage indicates that maximum force from a muscle is directly proportional to cross-sectional area, so the champion can exert four times as much force as the challenger's can. If the champion's force is F, the challenger's must be $\frac{1}{4}F$.

7. **D is correct. If the weightlifter is holding the weight, not moving it, then the net torque must be zero. Thus, the torque from the tendon's tension force must balance the torque from the weight.** If L is the distance between the pivot (the elbow joint) and the weight, then the torques balance as follows: $(L)(mg)\sin 45° = (L/4)(T)\sin 45°$. (Both angles are 45° because the lower arm is at a 45° to the vertical, and the weight is a downward force, while the tension is horizontal, since the tendon is horizontal, and 45° with respect to the vertical is 45° with respect to the horizontal, too.) Solving the previous equation for T yields 4 mg. Note that one cannot simply solve this by setting the net force in the vertical direction to zero, because the joint of the elbow may exert a force of some sort as well, and we have no idea what its magnitude is. Considering torques allows us to neglect this force, since it is exerted at a position $r = 0$, but considering forces would force us to consider it.

CHAPTER 6

ENERGY, WORK, POWER, AND MOMENTUM

6.1 MASTERY ACHIEVED

WORK

The **work** done by a constant force, **F,** to move an object through a displacement, **d**, is given by:

$$W = Fd \cos \theta$$

where θ is the angle between **F** and **d**.

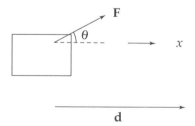

Loosely speaking, it is a measure of how much a force succeeds in moving an object in its own direction.

Because work is the product of force and displacement, it is expressed in the SI unit N • m, which is also called the **joule (J)**. **Torque** is also expressed in N • m, but is not expressed in joules. This is because torque is a vector quantity. Work is scalar, and the joule is a scalar unit:

$$1N \bullet m = 1\,J$$

Please solve this problem:

- If a 50 kilogram object is pushed to the right with a 30 newton force in the same direction for a distance of 1 kilometer along a frictionless surface, how much work is performed on the object?

Problem solved:

The mass of the object is irrelevant because the applied force is provided (and, in any event, the surface is frictionless). Also, since the object is moving in the direction of the applied force, $\theta = 0°$.

$$W = Fd\cos 0° = (30 \text{ N})(1{,}000 \text{ m})(1) = 30{,}000 \text{ N} \bullet \text{m} = 30{,}000 \text{ J}$$

As with torque, it is often useful to split the force into components:

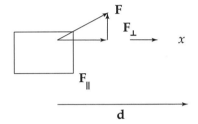

where $F_{\parallel}$ is the component in the direction of displacement and $F_{\perp}$ is the component perpendicular to displacement. We can treat these components as two separate forces acting on the object. Of the two, only $F_{\parallel}$ does work.

$$W = F_{\parallel}d$$

Please solve this problem:

- A 10 newton force is applied as shown to a 10 kilogram object. If the object is displaced by 10 meters to the right, then how much work has been done by the applied force?

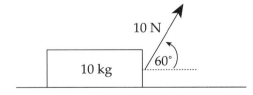

Problem solved:

The work equals only the force applied in the direction of displacement, which is 10 newtons times the cosine of 60°. Thus:

$$W = Fd \cos \theta \text{ or } (F \cos \theta)d$$

$$= (10)(10)(.5) = 50 \text{ J}$$

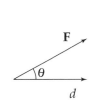

The Sign of Work

Work is a scalar that can be positive, zero, or negative depending on θ.

Case 1: $\theta \leq \theta < 90°$ Case 2: $\theta = 90°$ Case 3: $90° < \theta \leq 180°$

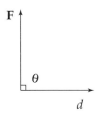 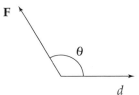

$\cos \theta$ is positive $\cos \theta$ is zero $\cos \theta$ is negative
$\Rightarrow W$ is positive $\Rightarrow W$ is zero $\Rightarrow W$ is negative

Please solve this problem:

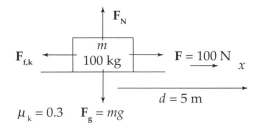

$\mu_k = 0.3$ $F_g = mg$

- Find the work done by F, $F_{f,k}$, F_g and F_N.

Problem solved:

F: since **F** is in the direction of **d**, $\theta = 0$

$$W_F = Fd \cos 0$$

$$= (100 \text{ N})(5 \text{ m})(1)$$

$$= 500 \text{ J}$$

$\mathbf{F}_{f,k}$: since $\mathbf{F}_{f,k}$ is opposite the direction of d, $\theta = 180°$

$$W_{F_{F,k}} = F_{F,k} \mathbf{d} \cos 180°$$
$$= \mu_k F_N \mathbf{d} \cos 180°$$
$$= \mu_k mg d \cos 180°$$
$$= (0.3)(100 \text{ kg})(10 \frac{m}{s^2})(5 \text{ m})(-1)$$
$$= -1500 \text{ J}$$

$\mathbf{F}_g$ and $\mathbf{F}_N$: since these forces are perpendicular to d, $\theta = 90°$

$$W_g = W_N = 0$$

Here are some useful facts about work:

- Kinetic friction always does negative work.

- Static friction always does zero work (on MCAT problems).

- All centripetal forces do zero work (since the force is directed toward the center and the direction of motion is tangent to the circle).

- The normal force often (but not always) does zero work (since objects often move parallel to the surface and the normal is always perpendicular to the surface).

Consider this example:

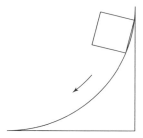

As the object slides down the curved ramp, the normal force continues to change. However, at all points the normal force is always perpendicular to the surface, while the direction of motion is always parallel.

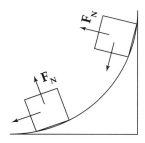

Therefore the work done by normal force is zero.

You do not always have to know the value of a force to calculate the work done.

Total Work

Since work is scalar, the total work acting on an object is merely the sum of the individual works.

For the example we did earlier (find the work done by $\mathbf{F}$, $\mathbf{F}_{f,k}$, $\mathbf{F}_g$ and $\mathbf{F}_N$),

$$W_{\text{TOTAL}} = W_F + W_{F_{f,k}} + W_g + W_N$$
$$= 500 \text{ J} + (-1500 \text{ J}) + 0 + 0$$
$$= -1000 \text{ J}$$

We will look at the physical significance of total work later in the chapter when we discuss the kinetic energy theorem.

Work Done by Changing Forces

The formulas

$$W = Fd \cos \theta$$

or:

$$W = F_{\parallel} d$$

are only valid for constant forces. If the force changes during the motion, other methods for finding work need to be employed.

One option is if a graph of Force vs. Position is given,

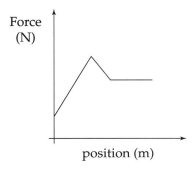

the work done can be calculated by finding the *area under the curve.*

Work Done by Gravity

Gravity, along with the Electrostatic Force and the Spring Force, are called **conservative forces**. One feature of conservative forces is that the work done is **path independent**.

Consider gravity:

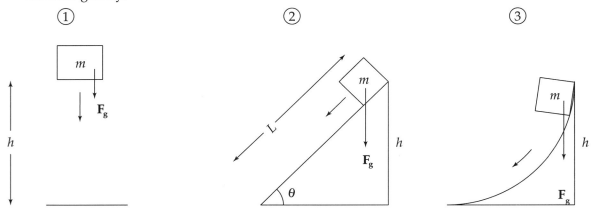

In case 1, the object is moving in the direction of $\mathbf{F}_g$. Therefore:

$$W_g = \mathbf{F}_g \cdot h \cdot \cos 0$$
$$= mgh$$

In case 2, the object is moving at an angle with respect to $\mathbf{F}_g$. Knowing that $mg \sin \theta$ is the component of gravity that points down the plane:

$$W_g = \mathbf{F}_\parallel \cdot d$$
$$= mg \sin \theta \cdot L$$
$$= mg(L \sin \theta)$$
$$= mgh$$

Note that this is the same answer as in case (1). The work done by gravity can be calculated merely by looking at the overall **vertical displacement**, rather than the particular path.

In case (3), we cannot even use $W = \mathbf{F}_\parallel d$ since the component of gravity down the plane changes. However, since gravity is a conservative force, we can say that $W_g = mgh$.

Please solve this problem:

- An object is moved along a path as shown:

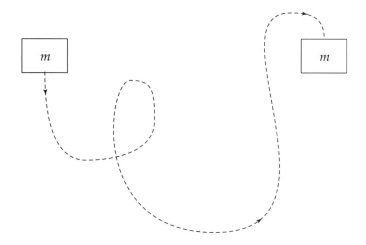

Find the work done by gravity.

Problem solved:

Since there was no vertical displacement, $W_g = 0$.

We will continue our discussion of conservative forces later in this chapter, under the heading "Potential Energy."

ENERGY

Energy is frequently described as the capacity to do work and is also measured in the SI unit joule (J). Energy may take a variety of forms, including kinetic energy, mechanical potential energy, chemical potential energy, heat energy, and light energy. You should comprehend the relationship between kinetic energy, potential energy, and work.

Kinetic Energy

Kinetic energy (KE) refers to the energy inherent in the movement of an object and can be determined by the formula:

$$KE = \frac{1}{2} mv^2$$

Observe the consistency of units associated with all forms of energy. The value mv^2 represents the multiplication:

$$(\text{kg})\left[(\text{m}/\text{s})(\text{m}/\text{s})\right] = \frac{\text{kg} \bullet \text{m}^2}{\text{s}^2} = \frac{\text{kg} \bullet \text{m}}{\text{s}^2} \bullet \frac{\text{m}}{1} = \text{N} \bullet \text{m} = \text{J}$$

Please solve this problem:

- A 40 kg object falls from a height. When its velocity reaches 20 meters per second, what kinetic energy does the object possess?

Problem solved:

Apply the formula:

$$KE = \frac{1}{2}\,mv^2 = 0.5(40 \text{ kg})(20 \text{ m/s})^2 = 8{,}000 \text{ J}$$

Work-Kinetic Energy Theorem

While energy can be considered as the capacity to do work, alternatively work can be considered as a *transfer of energy*.

One equation that connects work and energy is the Work-Kinetic Energy Theorem:

The total work done on an object equals the object's change in kinetic energy.

$$W_{\text{TOTAL}} = \triangle KE = KE_f - KE_O$$

Conceptually, this means that if a force does *positive work* on an object, the object *gains KE*. If a force does *negative work* on an object, the object *loses KE*.

Please solve this problem:

- How much work is required to stop a 1000 kg car moving at 20 m/s?

Problem solved:

We know that $W = Fd\cos\theta$, but no information has been given about F, d, or θ. We do not need to know what is actually stopping the car (is it friction? a wall?), but we can calculate the work done based on how much kinetic energy is being lost.

$$W_{\text{TOTAL}} = KE_f - KE_O$$
$$= \frac{1}{2}(1000 \text{ kg})(0)^2 - \frac{1}{2}(1000 \text{ kg})(20\,\frac{\text{m}}{\text{s}})^2$$
$$= -200{,}000 \text{ J}$$

We expect the answer to be negative since kinetic energy is being taken away from the car.

Potential Energy

Earlier we learned that the work done by conservative forces is path independent. In particular, we saw that the work done by gravity only depends on the initial and final height of the object.

Please solve this problem:

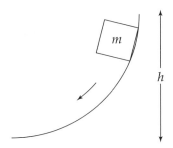

- The object above slides from rest down the friction-less ramp of height h. Find an expression for its final speed.

Problem solved:

We cannot solve this with kinematics since the Big Five require uniform acceleration. Instead, we can use the Work-Kinetic Energy Theorem:

$$W_{\text{TOTAL}} = KE_f - KE_0$$

Since the ramp is frictionless, the only forces acting on the object are gravity and the normal. As we saw earlier in this chapter, the work done by the normal force is zero. Therefore:

$$W_g = KE_f - KE_O$$

$$\Rightarrow mgh = \frac{1}{2}mv_f^2 - \frac{1}{2}mv_O^2$$

$$\Rightarrow mgh = \frac{1}{2}mv_f^2 - 0$$

$$\Rightarrow v_F = \sqrt{2gh}$$

Note that this is the same speed that an object would have if it were dropped from rest from height h.

Conceptually, gravity does work on the object, which gives it kinetic energy. An alternate way of looking at the situation is to consider **potential energy.**

The term potential energy, denoted PE, describes the energy inherent in the status or position of an object or system. A classic example is a stretched or compressed spring; the spring has the potential to perform work.

Gravity has the potential to do work on an object positioned above the ground. Therefore, we say that:

$$PE = mgh$$

For an object falling from height h, we can say that the potential energy of the system was converted into kinetic energy.

Note that the ground is an arbitrary point of reference—h can be measured from anywhere.

Please solve this problem:

- A body with a mass of 75 kilograms is situated at a height of 30 meters above the ground. What is its gravitational potential energy

  (a) relative to the ground;

  (b) relative to a point 30 m above the ground; and

  (c) relative to a point 60 m above the ground?

Problem solved:

Applying the formula for potential energy:

(a) $PE = mgh$, where h is 30 m:

$$= (75 \text{ kg})(10 \text{ m/s}^2)(30 \text{ m})$$
$$= 22{,}500 \text{ J}$$

(b) $PE = mgh$, where h is now 0:

$$= (75 \text{ kg})(10 \text{ m/s}^2)(0)$$
$$= 0$$

(c) $PE = mgh$, where h is now –30 m:

$$= (75 \text{ kg})(10 \text{ m/s}^2)(-30 \text{ m})$$
$$= -22{,}500 \text{ J}$$

The actual value of potential energy isn't important. How it changes is the important part, as we'll see in the next section. We can say that $W_g = -\Delta PE$.

Conservation of Mechanical Energy

The law of conservation of energy states:

The energy of an isolated system is constant.

This means that the energy in the universe may change form, but it cannot be destroyed or created. MCAT questions will sometimes draw on the candidate's ability to apply this principle to situations and systems involving the conversion of energy from one form to another.

Mechanical energy refers to the sum of kinetic energy and potential energy.

$$E = KE + PE$$

The Work-Kinetic Energy Theorem states that $W_{\text{TOTAL}} = \Delta KE$. If gravity is the only force doing work, then $W_g = \Delta KE$. In the last section, we learned that $W_g = -\Delta PE$. Therefore,

$$-\Delta PE = \Delta KE$$

or:

$$\Delta(KE + PE) = 0$$

or:

$$KE_0 + PE_0 = KE_f + PE_f$$

This is the Law of Conservation of Mechanical Energy.

Let's look at the example we solved in the last section:

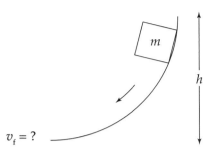

We used the Work-Kinetic Energy Theorem to solve for the final speed: Gravity did work on the object, which gave it kinetic energy.

Now we can solve using Conservation of Mechanical Energy:

$$KE_0 + PE_0 = KE_f + PE_f$$

Setting the ground as our reference point:

$$0 + mgh = \frac{1}{2}mv_f^2 + 0$$

Solving for v_f, we get $v_f = \sqrt{2gh}$.

Please solve this problem:

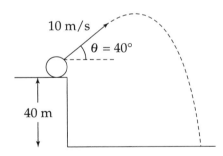

Find the final speed.

Problem solved:

While we could solve using kinematics, it would be very time-consuming. We'd have to find both the final x- and y-components of velocity and use the Pythagorean Theorem to find the total (not to mention that $40°$ is not one of our "nice" angles). Conservation of Mechanical Energy is much easier:

$$KE_0 + PE_0 = KE_f + PE_f$$

Setting the ground as our reference point:

$$\frac{1}{2}m(10\ \frac{m}{s})^2 + m(10\ \frac{m}{s^2})(40\ m) = \frac{1}{2}mv_f^2 + 0$$

Canceling m from each term:

$$50\ \frac{m^2}{s^2} + 400\ \frac{m^2}{s^2} = \frac{1}{2}v_f^2$$

$$\Rightarrow v_f = \sqrt{2(50\ \frac{m^2}{s^2} + 400\ \frac{m^2}{s^2})}$$

$$= 30\ \frac{m}{s}$$

Work as a Function of Kinetic Energy and Gravitational Potential Energy

On the MCAT, the only conservative forces encountered will be gravity, the electrostatic force, and the spring force. Each of these forces has a potential energy associated with it and, if only these forces do work, you may use Conservation of Energy.

But what if other forces do work (for example, friction and all applied forces)? Mechnical energy will *not* be conserved. Rather, the work done by non-conservative force will change the total energy. If **F** is the non-conservative force, then

$$KE_0 + PE_0 + W_F = KE_f + PE_f$$

or:

$$W_F = \Delta(KE + PE)$$

Please solve this problem:

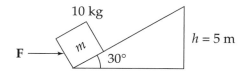

- What is the work required by **F** to push the block up a frictionless plane?

Problem solved:

The word "required" means that we are looking for the minimum work and hence, the minimum force. The long way would be to solve for **F**—the force that would make the object move up the plane without acceleration—and then use $W = Fd\cos\theta$. A shorter way would be to look at work and energy. Since the force will not be accelerating the block, the kinetic energy will remain constant. Therefore, the work done by **F** is only giving the block potential energy.

$$PE_0 + W_{f = PEf}$$

Setting the ground as our reference:

$$W_f = mgh$$

$$= (10 \text{ kg})(10 \text{ m/s}^2)(5 \text{ m})$$

$$= 500 \text{ J}$$

Note that this is the same as if the force were applied directly up the plane or if the force were lifting the object straight upward.

MECHANICAL ADVANTAGE

Recall, once again, that for a force acting in the direction of motion, $W = Fd$. Therefore, keeping work constant, applied force is inversely proportional to distance ($F \propto \dfrac{1}{2}$).

Various simple machines afford **mechanical advantage** by reducing the force required and, consequently, by increasing the distance required by a corresponding factor. Common machines tested on the MCAT are the pulley, the lever, and the inclined plane.

For example, if an 80-newton object is to be lifted a distance of 12 meters, the work required is equal to (80 N)(12 m) = 960 J. If the object were to be lifted directly upward without machinery, the applied force would be 80 newtons, and the displacement 12 meters. If, however, a simple machine is used, *the necessary force is reduced while the displacement is increased by a corresponding factor*.

On the MCAT, questions concerning mechanical advantage and simple machines draw on the candidate's understanding that using a machine does not reduce the work to be done; rather, it reduces the *force* (and increases the necessary displacement) and the application of inverse proportionality.

These phenomena are most easily illustrated with an inclined plane. Suppose the 80-newton object of the previous example was pushed upward along a frictionless plane inclined 30° to the horizontal to a vertical displacement of 12 meters, as shown in the figure below.

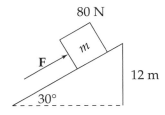

Simple trigonometry (**Chapter 3**) provides the length of the inclined plane (d):

$$\sin 30° = 12 \text{ m}/d$$

$$(d)(\sin 30°) = 12 \text{ m}$$

$$(d)(0.5) = 12 \text{ m}$$

$$d = 24 \text{ m}$$

Knowing that work of 960 joules will be done by moving an 80 newton object 40 meters up an inclined plane, calculate the force associated with the work thus performed:

$$W = Fd$$

$$960\,J = F(24\text{ m})$$

$$F = \frac{960\,J}{24\text{ m}} = 40\text{ N}$$

To lift an 80 newton object 12 meters from the ground along a plane inclined at 30° requires the application of 40 newtons. To lift this object without machinery would require the application of 80 newtons of force.

You should think of mechanical advantage as *a reduction in force and an increase in displacement.*

POWER

Power refers to the quantity of work performed over time:

$$P = \frac{W}{\Delta t} \text{ or } \frac{W}{t}$$

It is expressed in joules per second. In the SI system, 1 joule per second is renamed the **watt (W)**:

$$1\,J/s = 1\text{ W}$$

Please solve this problem:

- How much power is needed to lift an object with a mass of 75 kilograms straight upward to a height of 16 meters in 20 seconds at a constant speed?

Problem solved:

Since the object is not accelerating, the upward force necessary to lift it is merely equal to the object's weight. The object's mass is 75 kilograms, and its weight is:

$$F_g = weight = 75\text{ kg}(10\text{ m/s}^2) = 750\text{ N}$$

The lift will involve work of:

$$W = Fd = (750\text{ N})(16\text{ m}) = 12{,}000\text{ J}$$

If 12,000 joules of work are to be performed in 22 seconds, the associated power =

$$12{,}000\,J/20\text{ s} = 600\text{ W}$$

You should follow this analysis of the units associated with power:

(1) "watt" is equivalent to J/s,

(2) "joule" is equivalent to $N \bullet m$, and

(3) the watt is therefore equivalent to $N \bullet m/s$, which also represents the product: (force)(velocity).

For a constant force, an alternate formula for power is:

$$P = Fv \cos \theta$$

or:

$$F_{\parallel} v$$

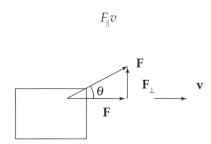

Please solve this problem:

- An engine that delivers power of 27,000 watts lifts an object straight upward against the force of earth's gravity with a constant velocity of 300 meters per second. Determine the mass of the object (and assume friction to be negligible).

Problem solved:

Since the force is acting in the same direction as the motion:

$$P = Fv$$

In this instance, power = 27,000 watts and velocity = 300 meters per second:

$$27,000 \text{ W} = F(300 \text{ m/s})$$

$$F = \frac{27,000}{300}$$

$$F = 90 \text{ N}$$

The force applied by the engine to keep the object moving upward at constant velocity = 90 newtons, which, if we assume no air resistance, means the object's weight = 90 newtons. This means its mass is:

$$m = \frac{w}{g} = \frac{90 \text{ N}}{10 \text{ m/s}^2} = 9 \text{ kg}$$

LINEAR MOMENTUM

For any object, linear momentum (**p**) equals (mass of body)(velocity):

$$\mathbf{p} = m\mathbf{v}$$

In terms of SI units, the product represents:

$$(\text{kg})(\text{m/s})$$

Momentum is therefore expressed in the SI unit kg • m/s.

Please solve this problem:

- If an object with a mass of 100 kilograms moves to the west with a velocity of 20 meters per second, what is its momentum?

Problem solved:

The magnitude of momentum can be found by:

$$\mathbf{p} = m\mathbf{v}$$

$$(100 \text{ kg})(20 \text{ m/s}) = 2,000 \text{ kg} \bullet \text{m/s}$$

Because momentum has direction, it is a vector quantity, so the momentum of the object is 2,000 kg • m/s west.

Impulse

Newton's Second Law tells us $\mathbf{F}_{net} = m\mathbf{a}$. If only one force, **F**, acts on the object, then $\mathbf{F} = m\mathbf{a}$.

Average acceleration is given by $\bar{a} = \dfrac{\Delta \mathbf{v}}{\Delta t}$.

Therefore, $\mathbf{F}_{av} = m\dfrac{\Delta \mathbf{v}}{\Delta t}$.

If the object's mass remains constant, then $\mathbf{F}_{av} \bullet \Delta t = \Delta(m\mathbf{v})$.

The product $\mathbf{F}_{av} \bullet \Delta t$ is called **impulse**, denoted by **J**. We see that impulse equals the change in momentum:

$$\mathbf{F}_{av} \bullet \Delta t = \Delta(m\mathbf{v})$$

or:

$$\mathbf{J} = \Delta \mathbf{p}$$

Impulse can be measured in:

$$N \bullet s$$

or:

$$\text{kg} \bullet \frac{\text{m}}{\text{s}}$$

Please solve this problem:

- A batter strikes a thrown ball ($m = 0.15$ kg) that was moving horizontally at 40 m/s. The ball leaves the bat moving at 40 m/s in the opposite direction. The bat was in contact with the ball for 15 ms. Find:

  (a) the baseball's change in momentum;

  (b) the impulse exerted by the batter;

  (c) the magnitude of the average force exerted by the bat on the ball.

Problem solved:

(a) Momentum, like velocity, is a vector. If we call the direction of the initial velocity of the ball positive, then:

$$p_O = mv_O = (0.15 \text{ kg})(40 \, \frac{\text{m}}{\text{s}})$$

$$=^+ 6 \text{ kg} \cdot \frac{\text{m}}{\text{s}}$$

$$p_f = mv_f = (0.15 \text{ kg})(-40 \, \frac{\text{m}}{\text{s}})$$

$$= -6 \text{ kg} \cdot \frac{\text{m}}{\text{s}}$$

and:

$$p_f = mv_f = (0.15 \text{ kg})(-40 \, \frac{\text{m}}{\text{s}})$$

$$= -6 \text{ kg} \cdot \frac{\text{m}}{\text{s}}$$

Therefore, the change in momentum is:

$$\Delta p = p_f - p_O = (-6 \text{ kg} \cdot \frac{\text{m}}{\text{s}}) - (6 \text{ kg} \cdot \frac{\text{m}}{\text{s}})$$

$$= -12 \text{ kg} \cdot \frac{\text{m}}{\text{s}}$$

Note that since direction matters, the answer is not zero.

(b) $\mathbf{J} = \Delta p = -12 \text{ kg} \cdot \frac{\text{m}}{\text{s}}$

or -12 N•S.

(c) Since, by definition,

$$\mathbf{J} = \mathbf{F}_{av}\Delta t$$

$$\mathbf{F}_{av} = \frac{\mathbf{J}}{\Delta t}$$

$$= \frac{-12 \ kg \ m/s}{15 \times 10^{-3} s}$$

$$= -800 \ N$$

it makes sense that the force should be negative since the bat is hitting the ball in the negative direction. The magnitude of the force is therefore 800 N.

Consider two scenarios:

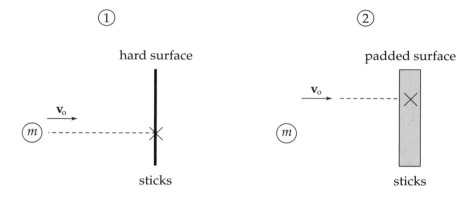

In both cases, the initial momentum is the same ($m\mathbf{v}_0$) and in both cases the final momentum is the same (zero). This means that average force and time are inversely proportional.

$$\mathbf{F}_{av} \propto \frac{1}{\Delta t}$$

Conceptually, the force exerted by the padded surface in case 2 will be less than the force exerted by the hard surface in case 1 because the time of collision is longer:

$$\downarrow \mathbf{F}_{av} \propto \frac{1}{\Delta t \uparrow}$$

For a changing force, an alternate way of calculating impulse is to look at a graph of force vs. time.

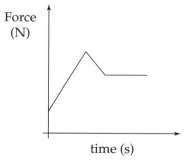

J = area under the curve (recall that work was the area under a force vs. position curve).

Conservation of Linear Momentum

If the two objects involved in a collision are free of net external forces (i.e., the net force that each object feels is the force due to the other object), then the *total* momentum of the system is *conserved*.

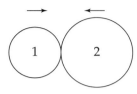

Newton's Third Law tells us that, during the collision,

$$\mathbf{F}_{2on1} = -\mathbf{F}_{1on2}$$

since

$$\mathbf{J} = \mathbf{F} \cdot \Delta t:$$
$$\mathbf{J}_{2on1} = -\mathbf{J}_{1on2}$$

and because

$$\mathbf{J} = \Delta p:$$
$$\Delta p_1 = -\Delta p_2.$$

or:

$$\Delta(p_1 + p_2) = 0$$

or:

$$p_{10} + p_{20} = p_{1F} + p_{2F}$$

$$\Rightarrow m_1 \mathbf{v}_{10} + m_2 \mathbf{v}_{20} = m_1 \mathbf{v}_{1f} + m_2 \mathbf{v}_{2F}$$

This is known as the **Law of Conservation of Momentum.**

Please solve this problem:

- For the figure below, the surface is frictionless.

Find the velocity of m_2.

Problem solved:

Choosing the positive direction to the right:

$$m_1 v_{10} + m_2 v_{20} = m_1 v_{1f} + m_2 v_{2f}$$
$$(2 \text{ kg})(6 \text{ m/s}) + (1 \text{ kg})(0) = (2 \text{ kg})(3 \text{ m/s}) + (1 \text{ kg})v_{2f}$$
$$v_{2f} = 6 \text{ m/s}$$

ELASTIC VS. INELASTIC COLLISIONS

For all collisions between objects free of net external forces, momentum is conserved. For some collisions, kinetic energy is also conserved. These collisions are called **elastic**.

Elastic collision: $\mathbf{p}_O = \mathbf{p}_f$ and $KE_O = KE_f$

If kinetic energy is *not* conserved, the collision is **inelastic**.

Inelastic collision: $\mathbf{p}_O = \mathbf{p}_{f \text{ and}}$ $KE_O \neq KE_f$

Please solve this problem:

- For the previous example, determine whether the collision is elastic or inelastic.

Problem solved:

We need to calculate the initial and final kinetic energies.

$$KE_O = \frac{1}{2}m_1 v_{10}{}^2 + \frac{1}{2}m_2 v_{20}{}^2$$
$$= \frac{1}{2}(2 \text{ kg})(6 \text{ }\frac{m}{s})^2 + \frac{1}{2}(1 \text{ kg})(0)^2$$
$$= 36 \text{ J}$$
$$KE_f = \frac{1}{2}m_1 v_{1f}{}^2 + \frac{1}{2}m_2 v_{2f}{}^2$$
$$= \frac{1}{2}(2 \text{ kg})(3 \text{ }\frac{m}{s})^2 + \frac{1}{2}(1 \text{ kg})(6 \text{ }\frac{m}{s})^2$$
$$= 9 \text{ J} + 18 \text{ J}$$
$$= 27 \text{ J}$$

Since $KE_O \neq KE_f$, the collision is inelastic.

Conceptually, kinetic energy is lost when the objects deform during collision. The energy is transferred to vibration and heat. Collisions between hard metal spheres and billiards are close to being elastic.

PERFECTLY INELASTIC COLLISIONS

A **perfectly inelastic** collision is one where kinetic energy is lost and the *objects stick and move together*.

Please solve this problem:

- The following collision is perfectly inelastic:

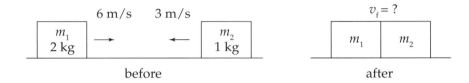

| before | after |

Find the final velocity of the objects.

Problem solved:

Since the objects move together after the collision, we can write:

$$m_1 v_{10} + m_2 v_{20} = (m_1 + m_2) \, v_f$$

Choosing the positive direction to the right:

$$(2 \text{ kg})(6 \text{ m/s}) + (1 \text{ kg})(-3 \text{ m/s}) = (2 \text{ kg} + 1 \text{ kg})v_f$$

$$12 \text{ kg m/s} - 3 \text{ kg m/s} = (3 \text{ kg})v_f$$

$$v_f = +3 \text{ m/s (to the right)}$$

COLLISIONS IN TWO DIMENSIONS

Remember that momentum is a vector. If it is conserved, then *each component of momentum is conserved.*

$$p_{ox} = p_{fx}$$
$$\text{and}$$
$$p_{oy} = p_{fy}$$

Examples:

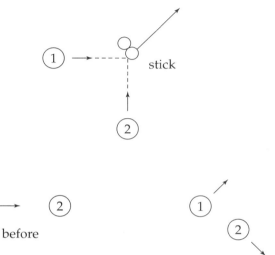

The MCAT rarely asks questions featuring two-dimensional equations that involve computation.

RECOIL OR EXPLOSIONS PROBLEMS

When two objects begin as one and then separate, total momentum is also conserved (provided there are no net external forces).

Please solve this problem:

- A woman of mass 60 kg stands at rest on a friction-less surface. If she throws a 2-kg ball horizontally at 10 m/s, with what speed will she move backward? Is this situation elastic?

Problem solved:

First, a picture:

$$v = ?$$

$m_b = 2 \text{ kg}$ $\quad m_p = 60 \text{ kg}$ $\qquad 10 \text{ m/s}$

$$v_b = v_p = 0$$

before $\qquad\qquad\qquad$ after

Since the surface is frictionless, we can use Conservation of Momentum. Choosing the positive direction to the right:

$$m_p v_{po} + m_b v_{bo} = m_p v_{pf} + m_b v_{bf}$$

$$0 + 0 = (60 \text{ kg})v_{pf} + (2 \text{ kg})(-10 \text{ m/s})$$

$$v_{pf} = +3 \text{ m/s}$$

To determine whether or not the situation is elastic, we look at the initial and final kinetic energies.

$$KE_O = \frac{1}{2}m_p v_{po}^2 + \frac{1}{2}m_b v_{bo}^2$$

$$= 0 + 0 = 0$$

$$KE_f = \frac{1}{2}m_p v_{pf}^2 + \frac{1}{2}m_b v_{bf}^2$$

$$= \frac{1}{2}(60 \text{ kg})(3 \frac{\text{m}}{\text{s}})^2 + \frac{1}{2}(2 \text{ kg})(-10 \frac{\text{m}}{\text{s}})^2$$

$$= 270 \text{ J} + 100 \text{ J}$$

$$= 370 \text{ J}$$

Since $KE_O \neq KE_f$, the situation is inelastic.

Note that $KE_f > KE_O$ means that the system gained kinetic energy, as opposed to a perfectly inelastic collision, where kinetic energy was lost.

6.2   MASTERY APPLIED: PRACTICE PASSAGE AND QUESTIONS

Passage

The modern bicycle reflects several centuries of progress in engineering and design. In the early 1880s, a bicycle nicknamed the "Ordinary" became popular. It featured an extraordinarily large front wheel and pedals situated relatively close to that wheel's axis of rotation, as shown in Figure 1.

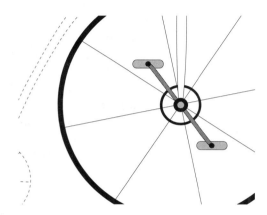

Figure 1

The construction of the Ordinary meant that each revolution of the rider's legs produced one revolution of the wheel, although the circumference of the rider's revolution was much less than that of the front wheel itself. Variations on the Ordinary were undertaken in order to afford the rider more mechanical advantage. One variation extended the lengths of the shafts on which the pedals were held so that the rider's legs would travel a circumference more nearly equal to that of the wheel, as shown in Figure 2.

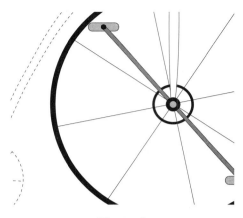

Figure 2

Advances in mechanical engineering led to a bicycle on which the pedals drove a toothed sprocket connected by a flexible chain to a toothed sprocket on the rear wheel. Lateral mobility of the chain at the rear aspect, within the control of the rider, provided the possibility of positioning the rear portion of the chain on relatively larger or smaller sprockets to adjust the mechanical advantage. The relatively larger sprockets on the rear afforded the rider a greater degree of mechanical advantage than did the relatively smaller ones.

More recent models provide multiple gears at the pedaling axis so that the mechanical advantage may be changed. On these vehicles, a rider will have difficulty propelling himself/herself uphill with the chain revolving about the largest front gear, since that requires a greater force. Moreover, the design of these multigeared machines prevents movement of the chain unless the bicycle is in motion.

Increased efficiency was also achieved by the advent of the pneumatic tire and by the subsequent narrowing of its gauge.

1. A bicycle rider with a mass of m_r rides a bicycle with a mass of m_b. He pedals d meters directly up a hill, inclined at an angle of θ to the horizontal. On reaching the top of the hill, he has achieved a true vertical *height* of h meters from the point at which he started. Where g = acceleration due to gravity, which of the following expressions describes the work the rider has performed in riding up the hill? (Assume friction to be negligible.)

   A. $(g)(h)(m_r + m_b)$
   B. $(m_r^2 + m_b^2)(\cos\theta)$
   C. $(d)(\cos\theta)(h^2)$
   D. $m_b gd$

2. If the rider described in question 1 turns around and coasts downward along the incline, what will be the normal force exerted on his bicycle?

   A. dgh
   B. $(\theta)^2 (g)^2 (m_r + gm_b)$
   C. $(\sin\theta)(gm_r + m_b)$
   D. $(\cos\theta)(gm_r + gm_b)$

3. Two riders, A and B, of equal mass, ride (separate) bicycles, also of equal mass. The bicycles are fitted with derailleurs that allow for adjustment of the mechanical advantage by lateral movement of the chain among several gears located on the rear axle. Rider A positions the chain on a smaller rear sprocket than does Rider B, and both riders travel the exact same path covering a displacement over the road of d. Which of the following is true? (Assume friction to be negligible.)

   A. Rider A performs less work on the pedals than does Rider B.
   B. Rider A performs more work on the pedals than does Rider B.
   C. Riders A and B perform equal quantities of work on the pedals.
   D. Neither Rider A nor Rider B performs any work on the pedals.

4. The engineer who designed the modified Ordinary, as shown in Figure 2, most probably attempted to achieve which objective?

   A. Reduce the amount of work performed by the rider
   B. Reduce the amount of force applied by the rider
   C. Increase the velocity attained by the rider for any given quantity of work performed
   D. Increase the acceleration attained by the rider for any given quantity of work performed

5. Rider A rides an old-fashioned Ordinary (shown in Figure 1) and Rider B rides a modified Ordinary (shown in Figure 2). The bicycles are of equal mass. Rider A attains a westward velocity of v_1 and Rider B attains a westward velocity of v_2, which is equal to $2(v_1)$. Assuming that Riders A and B are of equal mass, which of the following is true?

   A. Rider B achieves a momentum equal to one half that of Rider A.
   B. Rider B achieves a momentum twice that of Rider A.
   C. Rider B achieves a momentum equal to that of Rider A.
   D. The sum (momentum achieved by Rider A + momentum achieved by Rider B) remains constant, even if each rider changes her/his velocity.

6. An investigator wishes to know which of two innovations afforded the greater advance in efficiency: the introduction of narrow gauge tires or the availability of multiple sprockets. She conducts an experiment in which Subject 1 rides a bicycle with *wide* gauge tires and *no* multiple sprockets; Subject 2 rides a bicycle with *wide* gauge tires *and* multiple sprockets; and Subject 3 rides a bicycle with *narrow* gauge tires and *no* multiple sprockets. In relation to her experiment, which rider constitutes the control?

   A. Subject 1
   B. Subject 2
   C. Subject 3
   D. Subjects 1 and 2 together

7. In terms of mechanical advantage, the use on a modern bicycle of a relatively small sprocket on the axle attached to the pedals is roughly analogous to:

   A. the introduction of pneumatic tires.
   B. the use on a modern bicycle of a relatively small sprocket on the rear axle.
   C. creating a large wheel on the original Ordinary.
   D. increasing the size of the pedal shafts on the modifed Ordinary.

6.3 MASTERY VERIFIED: ANSWERS AND EXPLANATIONS

1. **A is correct.** The work performed is equal to *Fd*, but a variable representing *F* is not provided. The rider is, however, given the variables associated with the gravitational potential energy garnered in climbing the hill. The increase in potential gravitational energy, *mgh*, must be equal to the work the rider has performed. Therefore, the answer is one that reflects the formula *mgh*.

   In this instance, *m* is equal to the combined mass of rider and bicycle, $m_r + m_b$. The height = *h* and *g* = acceleration due to gravity. Therefore, the answer is

   $$(g) \times (h) \times (m_r + m_b)$$

   You should note that the answer is a formula with which you are familiar: *PE = mgh*. It has only been presented in an unfamiliar form. *You should become accustomed to questions that require you to work with abstract variables instead of numerical values.*

2. **D is correct.** The normal force (F_N) is the force exerted by the plane onto the bicycle. The normal force is equal to the weight of the object times the cosine of the angle of the plane from the horizontal. The combined weight of the bicycle and rider = $(g)(m_r + m_b)$, which, through the distributive property of multiplication, is equal to $(gm_r + gm_b)$. Simple trigonometry reveals that $F_N = (\cos \theta)(\text{combined weight}) = (\cos \theta)(gm_r + gm_b)$.

3. **C is correct.** Recall that mechanical advantage reduces force but not work. This concept yields the answer to the question.

4. **B is correct.** Like question 3, this question can be answered by understanding that mechanical advantage affects force but not work. The passage states that the extension of the pedal shafts was undertaken to afford mechanical advantage. Again, you have to look within the passage and questions for the familiar principles and phenomena.

5. **B is correct.** The bicycles do not collide, and there is no occasion here to consider conservation of momentum. The fact that the two bicycles differ in design is similarly irrelevant to the problem. Rather, you need only apply the formula:

   $$\text{momentum} = (m)(v)$$

   Remember that momentum is directly proportional to velocity. Since Rider B attains a velocity that has a magnitude twice that of Rider A on equivalent masses, a momentum that is twice that of Rider A is also achieved.

6. **A is correct.** The experimenter is testing the effects of two innovations: narrow gauge tires and multiple sprockets. In order to compare their effects as innovations, she must have, as a control, a device that offers *neither feature*. Subject 1 rides a bicycle that lacks both innovations.

7. **D is correct.** The question calls for careful reading. The passage indicates that the modified Ordinary was designed to afford the rider greater mechanical advantage. It also indicates, with reference to the modern bicycle, that "a rider will have difficulty propelling himself/herself uphill with the chain revolving about the largest front gear, since that requires a greater force." The reference to a greater force means that the large sprocket offers a relatively smaller degree of mechanical advantage. The small sprocket, therefore, must offer a greater degree of mechanical advantage, and so it is analogous to the lengthening of the shafts on the modified Ordinary.

CHAPTER 7

FLUIDS AND SOLIDS

7.1 MASTERY ACHIEVED

SOLIDS

Solids are distinct from fluids in that solids do not flow.

Density and Specific Gravity

For any solid, density is a measure of mass per volume and is expressed in the SI unit kilogram per cubic meter:

$$\frac{\text{kg}}{\text{m}^3}$$

The statement that "lead is heavier than cotton" lacks scientific meaning. Rather, lead is *more dense* than cotton: Any given volume of lead has greater mass (and hence weight) than the same volume of cotton. For any sample of solid, volume may be obtained, among other methods, by immersing the solid in liquid and observing the volume of liquid that is displaced.

Density can be treated as a *unit conversion ratio,* where mass is calculated on the basis of volume or volume on the basis of mass.

Please solve this problem:

- If a substance has a density of 9.3×10^4 kilograms per cubic meter, what volume is occupied by 88 kilograms of the substance?

Problem solved:

$$\text{density} = \frac{\text{mass}}{\text{volume}}$$

$$\text{volume} = \frac{\text{mass}}{\text{density}} = \frac{88 \text{ kg}}{9.3 \times 10^4 \text{ kg} / \text{m}^3} = 9.5 \times 10^{-4} \text{m}^3$$

The density of water is 1,000 kilograms per cubic meter. For any solid, the value known as **specific gravity** represents the ratio of density of the solid to density of water. A solid whose density is 2,000 kilograms per cubic meter—twice that of water—has a specific gravity of 2.

The same holds for fluids: A fluid whose density is 600 kilograms per cubic meter—0.60 times that of water—has a specific gravity of 0.60.

Because specific gravity reflects the division:

$$\frac{\left[\text{density}\left(\frac{kg}{m^3}\right)\right] \quad \text{Solid}}{\left[\text{density}\left(\frac{kg}{m^3}\right)\right] \quad H_2O}$$

the result is expressed without units. Specific gravity is a dimensionless quantity.

Please solve this problem:

- A container with total capacity of 1.0×10^{-3} cubic meters is half-filled with water so that the fluid level reaches the mark, 0.5×10^{-3} cubic meters. A solid object with mass of 0.2 kilograms is completely submerged in the water. The presence of the object causes the fluid level in the container to rise to 0.75×10^{-3} cubic meters. What is the density of the object? What is the specific gravity of the object?

Problem solved:

Density = mass/volume. The object's mass is 0.2 kilograms. Its volume is equal to the volume of liquid it displaces:

$$(0.75 \times 10^{-3} \text{ m}^3) - (0.50 \times 10^{-3} \text{ m}^3) = 0.25 \times 10^{-3} \text{ m}^3$$

Its density is calculated by:

$$\frac{0.2 \text{ kg}}{0.25 \times 10^{-3} \text{m}^3} = \frac{\left(0.2 \times 10^0\right) \text{kg}}{0.25 \times 10^{-3} \text{m}^3} = 0.8 \times 10^3 \frac{\text{kg}}{\text{m}^3} = 800 \text{ kg/m}^3$$

Thus, its specific gravity can be determined:

$$800/1{,}000 = 0.8$$

Tensile Stress, Tensile Strain, and Young's Modulus

The subjects of stress, strain, and the associated quantity Young's modulus pertain to the application of stretching and compressive forces to elongated solids. You should understand these phenomena only as they pertain to substances that obey Hooke's law; the MCAT does not address them in other contexts.

TENSILE STRESS

Tensile stress (T_{ss}) refers to a force that (a) is applied equally at both ends of a solid object and (b) tends to stretch *or* compress it. Consider stress as it relates to forces applied at either end of an elongated object, such as a bar, rod, or pole:

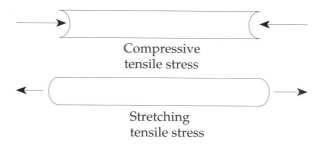

Figure 7.1

Tensile stress is measured in terms of applied force per cross-sectional area of solid. In the SI unit system, it represents the quantity N/m^2. For convenience, $1\ N/m^2$ is termed the **pascal (Pa)**:

$$1\ N/m^2 = 1\ Pa$$

Tensile stress (T_{ss}) is normally expressed in the unit Pa.

Consider a cylindrical rod with a radius of 3 centimeters (0.03 meters). The rod's cross-sectional area is calculated by:

$$\pi r^2 = (3.14)(0.03)^2 = 2.83 \times 10^{-3}\ m^2$$

If the rod is subjected to a 90-newton stretching force at each end, the stress it experiences is found by:

$$\frac{force}{cross\text{-}sectional\ area} = \frac{90\ N}{2.83 \times 10^{-3} m^2} = \frac{90 \times 10^0\ N}{2.83 \times 10^{-3} m^2} = 31.80 \times 10^3\ Pa$$

The same computation applies to both stretching and compressing forces applied to an object:

$$T_{ss} = F/A_c$$

Please solve this problem:

- A rectangular steel bar, the ends of which have two edges measuring 3 centimeters and 4 centimeters, respectively, is subjected at each end to a compressive force of 40 newtons. What tensile stress does the bar experience?

Problem solved:

Use the formula $T_{ss} = F/A_{cs}$.

Calculate the bar's cross-sectional area (A_{cs}):

$$(0.04\ m)(0.03\ m) = 0.0012\ m^2 = 1.2 \times 10^{-3}\ m^2$$

Since applied force is 40 newtons, T_{ss}, the tensile stress is:

$$\frac{force}{cross\text{-}sectional\ area} = \frac{40\ N}{1.2 \times 10^{-3} m^2} = \frac{40 \times 10^0\ N}{1.2 \times 10^{-3} m^2} = 33.33 \times 10^3\ Pa$$

In the previous illustrations, tensile stress was calculated without regard to the solid object's length. Note that calculation of tensile stress takes into account cross-sectional area (A_{cs}) but not length. Length *is* relevant to the calculation of tensile strain, however, as you will see below.

TENSILE STRAIN

Tensile strain (T_{sn}) refers to the degree to which tensile *stress* causes a solid object to undergo a change in length. It is measured as a function of change in length relative to the original length. If a solid object of length 2 meters undergoes tensile stress that stretches it and, as a result, actually lengthens it so that its new length is 2.01 meters, the object experiences tensile strain (T_{sn}) of:

$$\Delta L/L_o = \frac{2.01 \text{ m} - 2.0 \text{ m}}{2.0 \text{ m}} = \frac{.01 \text{ m}}{2.0 \text{ m}} = .005$$

Note that the result shows no units. Strain is a dimensionless quantity; it is expressed without units.

Compressive tensile stress is calculated in the same way.

Please solve this problem:

- A rectangular bar of length 34 meters is subjected to a compressive force at either end, and its length is reduced to 33.97 meters. What tensile strain has the object experienced?

Problem solved:

The object experiences tensile strain (T_{sn}) of:

$$\Delta L/L_o = \frac{34 \text{ m} - 33.97 \text{ m}}{34 \text{ m}} = \frac{0.03 \text{ m}}{34 \text{ m}} = .00088 = 8.8 \times 10^{-4}$$

Note that both cross-sectional area and the magnitude of applied force are irrelevant to the calculation of tensile strain. Observe that:

- the calculation of *stress* draws on applied force and cross-sectional area (A_{cs}), and

- the calculation of *strain* draws on change in length and original length.

Tensile stress and tensile strain are related by Young's modulus.

YOUNG'S MODULUS

For any solid that obeys Hooke's law, **Young's modulus** represents the ratio:

$$\frac{\text{tensile stress}}{\text{tensile strain}}$$

Every substance that obeys Hooke's law is associated with its own Young's modulus—a value that, *for that particular substance*, expresses the degree of strain that will be imposed by a given degree of stress. Because Young's modulus represents:

$$\frac{\text{stress}(\text{in Pa})}{\text{strain}(\text{no units})}$$

it gives rise to the fraction $\dfrac{\text{Pa}}{1}$ = Pa. Therefore, Young's modulus is expressed in pascals.

For any substance, knowledge of Young's modulus permits the algebraic calculation of stress, when strain is known, and of strain, when stress is known.

Consider an object composed of substance X, for which Young's modulus is 7.5×10^5 pascals. If it is subjected to a tensile stress of 50 pascals, it will undergo a degree of strain as calculated below:

$$\frac{50 \text{ Pa}}{\text{tensile strain}} = 7.5 \times 10^5 \text{ Pa}$$

$$(\text{tensile strain})(7.5 \times 10^5 \text{ Pa}) = 50 \text{ Pa}$$

$$(\text{tensile strain}) = \frac{50 \text{ Pa}}{7.5 \times 10^5 \text{ Pa}} = 6.67 \times 10^{-5}$$

(The problem does not specify whether the imposed stress was stretching or compressive; the math is the same in either case.)

Please solve this problem:

- A cylindrical rod measures 5 meters in length and 1.5 centimeters in radius. It obeys Hooke's law and has a Young's modulus of 5.2×10^6 pascals. What compressive force is necessary to reduce its length to 4.9981 meters?

Problem solved:

Note that you are asked to identify *force*, not stress. Since stress represents F/A_{cs}, force is ascertained by (1) the calculation of cross-sectional area by reference to the data and (2) the calculation of strain by reference to original and modified lengths, which allows for (3) the calculation of stress via Young's modulus, which then allows for (4) the calculation of force via the formula $T_{ss} = F/A_{cs}$.

Calculate cross-sectional area (A_{cs}):

$$A_{cs} = \pi r^2 = 3.14 \,(.015)^2 = .00071 \text{ m}^2 = 7.1 \times 10^{-4} \text{ m}^2$$

Calculate strain:

$$\text{strain} = \Delta L/L_o = \frac{5 \text{ m} - 4.9981 \text{ m}}{5 \text{ m}} = \frac{.0019 \text{ m}}{5 \text{ m}} = .00038 = 3.8 \times 10^{-4}$$

Calculate stress:

$$\frac{\text{stress}}{\text{strain}} = 5.2 \times 10^6 \text{ Pa}$$

$$\frac{\text{stress}}{3.8 \times 10^{-4}} = 5.2 \times 10^6 \text{ Pa}$$

$$\text{stress} = (5.2 \times 10^6 \text{ Pa}) \times (3.8 \times 10^{-4}) = 1.9 \times 10^3 \text{ Pa}$$

Calculate force by rearranging $T_{ss} = F/A_{cs}$:

$$F = (T_{ss})(A_{cs}) = (1.9 \times 10^3 \text{ Pa})(7.1 \times 10^{-4} \text{ m}^2)$$

$$F = 1.4 \text{ N}$$

Checking for dimensional consistency in the last calculation, note that:

$$\text{Pa} = \text{N/m}^2$$

and:

$$(\text{Pa})(\text{m}^2) = (\text{N/m}^2) \times (\text{m}^2) = \text{N}$$

FLUIDS

Density and Specific Gravity

Any substance that when poured into a container takes on the shape of that container can be considered a fluid.

Every fluid, like every solid, is associated with a specific gravity, which is represented by the ratio of the density of fluid to the density of water (which, as noted above, is $\frac{1,000 \text{ kg}}{\text{m}^3}$). A fluid whose density is three times that of water has a specific gravity of 3. A fluid whose density is 0.25 times that of water has a specific gravity of 0.25.

For any ordinary liquid (as for any ordinary solid), density is relatively constant under varying conditions of temperature and pressure. For gases, however, density is subject to change. The density of a gas must be described in terms of a given temperature and pressure.

Fluid Pressure

Pressure is a measure of force per unit area and is expressed in the SI unit N/m^2, which, as was discussed earlier, is called the pascal (Pa). Pressure, like stress, is expressed in pascals, and you should note that stress and pressure are related.

Fluid pressure refers to the pressure exerted by a fluid on a real or hypothetical body. Fluid exerts a pressure of P on an object submerged in it at depth d. Whether or not an object is in fact situated at depth d, the fluid pressure still exists at d; it represents the pressure that *would* be exerted on an object situated within the fluid at the given depth.

For any resting fluid that is not experiencing any external pressure, the fluid pressure at a specified depth is given by the formula:

$$P = (\text{density})(\text{acceleration due to gravity})(\text{depth below the surface of the fluid})$$

Depth is often conceived of as the height (h) of the fluid column above the point in question, and the formula just described is often expressed:

$$P = \rho(g)(h)$$

where:

ρ = fluid density

g = acceleration due to gravity

h = height of the fluid above the point in question.

The above pressure is referred to as **gauge pressure**. In real situations, the fluid within which pressure is to be measured will often be exposed to atmospheric pressure at its surface. When measuring the pressure at a depth "h" below the surface of such a fluid, atmospheric pressure is added directly as follows: $P = (ρ)(g)(h) +$ atmospheric pressure.

This new sum is called **absolute pressure**. It is the actual pressure to which a submerged object is exposed.

Pascal's principle says that *pressure applied to an enclosed fluid is transmitted undiminished to every portion of the fluid and the walls of the containing vessel.*

Accordingly, the following statement is also true: *Fluid pressure at any given depth in a resting fluid is unrelated to the shape of the container in which the fluid is situated.*

Observe the proportion in the formula for fluid pressure. Pressure is directly proportional to fluid density and to depth.

Please solve this problem:

- Fluid F has density d. At a given depth x, within a sample of fluid F, fluid pressure is 3,000 pascals. What is the fluid pressure at depth $2x$ in a sample of fluid E, whose density is $0.4d$?

Problem solved:

Because fluid pressure is directly proportional to fluid density and depth, the pressure at depth $2x$ in fluid E is calculated from:

$$P = 3{,}000 \text{ Pa} \times (0.4)d \times 2x = 0.8(3{,}000 \text{ Pa}) = 2{,}400 \text{ Pa}$$

Buoyancy

Buoyancy refers to a fluid's tendency to propel submerged or partially submerged substances toward the surface of that fluid. The buoyancy force then is an upward force exerted by a fluid on another body or fluid.

For any body immersed in fluid, the magnitude of buoyancy is calculated using **Archimedes' principle**:

Buoyancy (Fb) =

(volume of fluid displaced)(density of displaced fluid)(acceleration due to gravity)

$$F_b = (V)(ρ)(g)$$

Observe that the quantity just set forth is in fact equal to the *weight* of the fluid displaced, which is verified by examination for dimensional consistency:

$$(\text{m}^3)(\text{kg/m}^3)(\text{m/s}^2) = (\text{m}^4 \bullet \text{kg/m}^3 \bullet \text{s}^2) = (\text{kg} \bullet \text{m/s}^2) = \text{newton (N)}$$

Archimedes' principle may thus be restated:

$$\text{Buoyancy } (F_b) = \text{weight of fluid displaced}$$

Therefore, for any body immersed in a fluid, buoyancy represents a force with **upward direction** and a magnitude equal to the weight of the fluid displaced. In this connection, a fully **submerged** body will displace a volume of fluid equal to its own volume.

An object immersed in a fluid experiences a downward force equal to its own weight and an upward force equal to the force of buoyancy (F_b), as just described. Whether the object accelerates downward (sinks) or upward depends on the relative magnitudes of the downward and upward forces.

Please solve this problem:

- An object with density of 11.3×10^3 kilograms per cubic meter and mass of 57 kilograms is immersed in water and subjected to no horizontal or rotational forces.

  (1) What is the approximate net force experienced by the object?
  (2) Will it accelerate? If so, with what magnitude?

Problem solved:

(1) The only forces to which the object is subject are those of its own weight, and the upward force of buoyancy.

Calculate the object's weight:

$$w = 57 \text{ kg} \times 10 \text{ m/s}^2 = 570 \text{ N}$$

We wish next to calculate the magnitude of buoyancy (F_b), but that calculation requires that we figure out the volume of water that was displaced. Recalling that the volume of water displaced is equal to the volume of the solid itself, and noting that the solid has a density of 11.3×10^3 kilograms per cubic meter and a mass of 57 kilograms, we calculate the volume of the solid (and, therefore, the volume of the fluid the solid displaces):

$$\text{volume} = \frac{\text{mass}}{\text{density}}$$

$$\text{volume} = \frac{57 \text{kg}}{11.3 \times 10^3 \text{kg/m}^3}$$

$$\text{volume} = 5.0 \times 10^{-3} \text{ m}^3$$

Knowing now that the solid object displaces 5.0×10^{-3} cubic meters of water, and recalling that the density of water is 1,000 kilograms per cubic meter, we calculate F_b with Archimedes' principle:

$$F_b = (\text{volume})(\text{density of fluid})(g)$$

$$F_b = (5.0 \times 10^{-3} \text{ m}^3) \times (1 \times 10^3 \text{ kg/m}^3) \times (10 \times 10^0 \text{ m/s}^2) = 50 \text{ N}$$

The object experiences a downward force of 570 newtons and an upward force of 50 newtons. It experiences, therefore, a net force of 520 newtons downward.

(2)   The object will accelerate downward. Since its downward net force has a magnitude of 520 newtons, we apply the formula:

$$F = m$$

$$a = \frac{F}{m}$$

$$a = \frac{520 \text{ N}}{57 \text{ kg}} = \text{approx. } 9.1 \text{ m/s}^2$$

Flow and Ideal Flow

Flow (Q) refers to the quantity of fluid that passes a given point in a given period of time. It is expressed in units of $\frac{\text{volume}}{\text{time}}$, and in the SI system, the unit of flow is:

$$\frac{\text{m}^3}{\text{s}} \text{ or sometimes } \frac{\text{m}^3}{\text{min}}$$

Simple unit analysis discloses that the fraction $\frac{\text{volume}}{\text{time}}$ results from the computation:

$$(\text{area})(\text{velocity}) = (\text{m}^2)(\text{m/s}) \ \frac{\text{m}^3}{\text{s}}$$

and you should remember that for any fluid flowing through a vessel (pipe or tube):

Flow = (area of pipe or tube)(velocity of fluid)

The MCAT candidate should comprehend several phenomena associated with *ideal flow*:

- flow is constant at all points,

- has no viscosity,

- has no turbulence,

- has no drag (fluid friction), and

- flow = (velocity)(area).

THE BERNOULLI EQUATION AND POISEUILLE'S LAW

Laminar flow refers to flow in which whirlpools and eddies are absent; turbulent flow is flow in which such phenomena do occur.

The Bernoulli equation and Poiseuille's law are given below, but you will not be expected to have them memorized.

The **Bernoulli equation** describes a relationship among density, pressure, fluid velocity, and vessel height. For any fluid undergoing ideal flow:

$$P + \rho(g)(h) \; \frac{1}{2} \; \rho v^2 = \text{constant}$$

where:

P = pressure of fluid

ρ = density of fluid

h = height of vessel's center above a reference point

v = velocity of fluid

Poiseuille's law describes the relationship among flow, radius of the vessel, P, viscosity, and vessel length:

$$Q = \frac{\pi r^4 \left(P_1 - P_2\right)}{8(n)(L)}$$

where:

Q = flow

r = vessel radius

n = coefficient of viscosity

L = vessel length.

CALIBER (WIDTH) OF THE VESSEL

For an ideal fluid flowing through a vessel, or system of vessels, in which caliber varies, as shown below, areas of smaller caliber represent areas of greater velocity and reduced pressure.

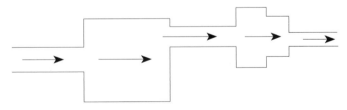

Figure 7.2

When a fluid flows through a system resembling that shown above, the *velocity* of the fluid is greatest in areas of smallest caliber and least in areas of greatest caliber. In contrast, the *pressure* experienced by the fluid is greatest in areas of widest caliber and least in areas of least caliber.

The fact that velocity is less with greater diameter of the vessel is consistent with the idea, as already discussed, that flow = (area) × (velocity).

For fluid flowing within a vessel system of variable caliber, velocity is inversely proportional to cross-sectional area.

Such a proportionality does not hold for pressure and vessel caliber. The relationship between those two parameters can be derived using $Q = Av$ and the Bernoulli equation. In relating pressure and caliber, one must remember that an increase in one corresponds to an increase in the other, but that the relationship is *not proportional*.

Please solve this problem:

- Fluid flows through a system of vessels of various calibers, as shown in Figure 7.3:

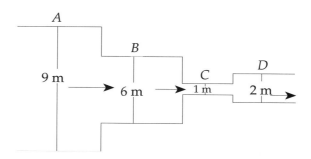

Figure 7.3

(1) In which section of the system is the fluid under the greatest pressure?
(2) Through which section of the system does the fluid travel at the greatest velocity?
(3) If the fluid's velocity is 0.5 meters per second through section B, (a) what is its velocity through section D? (b) what is its flow at section D? and (c) what is the flow through section A?

Problem solved:

(1) Where caliber is greatest, pressure is greatest; thus pressure is greatest at section A.

(2) Where caliber is least, velocity is greatest; thus velocity is greatest at section C.

(3)(a) Area and velocity are inversely proportional. Ascertain the ratio:

area of section B : area of section D

Noting that the formula for the area of a circle is πr^2, recognize that area of a circle is proportional to the square of the radius. The radius of section B is 3 meters, and the radius of section D is 1 meter. The two radii bear the ratio 3:1, which means that the ratio of their areas is:

$$3^2 : 1^2 = 9 : 1$$

Since velocity is inversely proportional to area, and the velocity in section B is 0.5 meters per second, the velocity in section D is:

$$(0.5 \text{ m/s}) \times 9 = 4.5 \text{ m/s}$$

(3)(b) Since flow equals the product of area and velocity, flow in section D equals:
$$(\pi r^2) \times (4.5 \text{ m/s}) = (3.14)(1 \text{ m}^2) \times 4.5 \text{ m/s} = 14.3 \text{ m}^3/\text{s}$$

(3)(c) Flow is equal at all points. Having calculated flow in section D at 14.3 cubic meters per second, we know that flow in all sections, including section A, is also 14.3 cubic meters per second.

7.2 MASTERY APPLIED: PRACTICE PASSAGE AND QUESTIONS

Passage

Tropical fish tanks require regular maintenance. The removal and replacement of a significant amount of water from the fish tank is one aspect of this maintenance. Considering the weight of the water, this can be quite a chore for large tanks. Traditionally, the removal has been accomplished with a siphon. The siphon, a long hose with an equal diameter throughout, is filled with water either by submerging it in the fish tank or by sucking water in from one end like a large straw. Once it is filled with water, one end is left in the fish tank and the water is allowed to drain through the siphon, as shown in Figure 1.

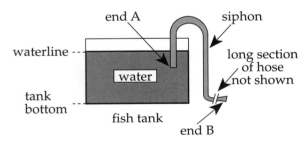

Figure 1
Traditional siphon

Because some fish enthusiasts find starting a siphon to be unpleasant, a commercial device (similar to Figure 2) has been proposed to simplify the process. This device is designed to attach to a faucet. The dotted lines represent the interior of the device. The large arrows represent the flow of water. When the faucet is turned on, in position 1, water flows through the device, draining the tank. The stop valve can then be closed and the tank refilled, as shown by position 2. (Assume ideal behavior for all fluids unless otherwise stated.)

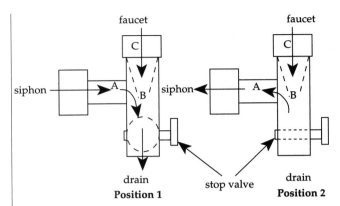

Figure 2
Commercial device

1. In order for the traditional siphon to remove water from the tank in Figure 1, end B must be positioned:

    A. anywhere below the level of the waterline.
    B. only below the level of end A.
    C. anywhere out of the water.
    D. only below the level of the tank bottom.

2. If the fish tank in Figure 1 were filled with a fluid having a higher density than water, then the velocity at end B of the heavier fluid would be:

    A. less than the velocity of water because a greater force would be required to accelerate the greater mass.
    B. equal to the velocity of water.
    C. greater than the velocity of water because greater pressure is created by the higher density fluid.
    D. greater than the velocity of water because the fluid with the greater mass has more potential energy to convert to kinetic energy.

3. If the siphon hose in Figure 1 were replaced with a hose of variable diameter, wider at some points and narrower at others, which of the following would be true of water undergoing ideal flow through the hose?

   A. The velocity would be relatively high at the widest portions of the hose.
   B. The pressure would be highest at the narrowest portions of the tube.
   C. Velocity and pressure would be constant at all portions of the tube.
   D. Flow would be constant at all portions of the tube.

4. Even when positioned above the fish tank, the commercial device in position 1 draws water from the fish tank because:

   A. low pressure is created at B.
   B. low pressure is created at C.
   C. high pressure is created at A.
   D. high pressure is created at B.

5. Which of the following choices is likely to have the greatest pressure?

   A. A in position 1
   B. A in position 2
   C. B in position 1
   D. C in position 2

6. Why does the commercial device narrow just before point B?

   A. To decrease pressure at point B
   B. To increase pressure at point B
   C. To increase flow rate at point B
   D. To decrease velocity at point B

7.3 MASTERY VERIFIED: ANSWERS AND EXPLANATIONS

1. **A is correct.** In order for the siphon to work, the pressure at end B must be greater than atmospheric pressure. If we pretend, for a moment, that end B is closed, then we just have an irregularly shaped container. Since we know that the pressure is unrelated to the shape of the container, we can find the pressure at any point by the equation:

$$P = \rho gh + \text{atmospheric pressure}$$

    where h is the distance below the surface. Now, when end B is opened, only atmospheric pressure opposes the movement of water out of the siphon. Thus, the siphon will work if, before the siphon is opened, the pressure, P, at end B is greater than atmospheric pressure. P will be greater than atmospheric pressure if h is not negative; h is positive below the waterline and negative above the waterline. End B must be held below the waterline.

2. **B is correct.** The velocity of an ideal fluid flowing from a container is:

$$v = \sqrt{2gh}$$

    Notice that the velocity is unrelated to the mass or density. When considered together, the reasons given in choices A, C, and D actually offset each other. Greater force is required to accelerate greater mass. However, just like with any falling object, the force accelerating the fluid is proportional to the mass and thus results in the same acceleration for any density of fluid. This is true for energy as well; both potential and kinetic energy are proportional to mass, and thus the greater potential energy of a heavier fluid is required to achieve a greater kinetic energy and the same velocity.

3. **D is correct.** As fluid flows through a tube of variable width, flow is constant *throughout*. That represents a cardinal rule of ideal flow. At wider areas, pressure will increase and velocity will decrease. At the narrower regions, pressure will decrease and velocity will increase. That is why choices A, B, and C are wrong. At all points in the hose, however, flow will proceed at a constant rate.

4. **A is correct.** Of the choices, only low pressure at B could draw water from the fish tank. High pressure at C creates high velocity at B. The high velocity creates low pressure, allowing water to come through the siphon, even at some heights above the waterline.

    If we relate Figure 2 to Figure 1, we see that the commercial device attaches to end B of Figure 1. Remember from the explanation to question 1 that end B must be greater than atmospheric pressure for water to leave the siphon. The commercial device simply lowers the pressure that the water at end B must overcome. Thus, for the siphon to work above the waterline, point B must be lower than atmospheric pressure.

    Notice that question 4 suggests that answer choice C to question 1 is incorrect. If you chose C for question 1, you should have gone back and changed your answer after reading question 4. You can and should use information in some questions to answer others on the MCAT.

5. **D is correct.** Position 2 is simply ideal fluid flow, represented by $Q = Av$. C has the largest cross-sectional area of all the choices and thus the lowest velocity. From Bernoulli's equation, $K = P + \frac{1}{2}\rho v^2 + \rho gh$, we see that the lowest velocity corresponds to the largest pressure. A and B at position 1 are both low pressure areas, as explained in the explanation to question 4.

6. **A is correct.** Again, as explained above, the device works by lowering pressure at point B. Pressure is lowered by increasing velocity. Flow rate remains unchanged unless we consider the flow rate before the tank water arrives compared to after it arrives. Answer choice A is the best answer.

   You should be aware that, on the MCAT, two apparently correct answers may arise, as they did in question 6. When faced with this dilemma, you should choose the simplest answer. In this case of question 6, choice C would be a trick answer; it refers to an exceptional situation, the seeming violation of the rule of constant flow in an ideal fluid. Since there is a straightforward answer that relies on a fundamental principle of physics, Bernoulli's equation, the straightforward answer is the better choice.

CHAPTER 8

ELECTROSTATICS

8.1   MASTERY ACHIEVED

ELECTRON MOBILITY: CONDUCTION AND INSULATION

The term **electron mobility** refers to the movement of electrons between and among the atoms or molecules within some sample of a given substance.

Substances (elements and compounds) vary in their degree of electron mobility. Among the elements, metals are characterized by relatively high electron mobility, and nonmetals are characterized by relatively low electron mobility.

Movement of electrical charge is attributable to the movement of electrons. Substances whose electrons are mobile tend, therefore, to conduct the movement of electrical charge and are termed **electrical conductors**. Substances whose electrons are *extremely* immobile tend to resist the conductance of electrical charge and are termed **insulators**.

Electron mobility is a matter of degree. Every substance has some degree of electrical mobility, and so every substance is, in a sense, a conductor. We identify some substances as conductors and others as insulators based on the degree to which they manifest electron mobility. Metals, for example, tend to show a high degree of electron mobility and are considered conductors. Rubber and glass, on the other hand, show an extremely low degree of electron mobility and are insulators.

CONTACT CHARGE AND INDUCTION

Contact Charge

Consider a body that acquires an electrical charge—meaning that through some process, its supply of electrons comes to be less than or greater than its total supply of protons. The phrase **contact charge** refers to the phenomenon in which such a charged body comes in contact with another body and imparts some or all of its charge to that second body. The first body is said to produce contact charge; it imparts its charge *to* the second body. The second body is said to experience contact charge; it acquires charge *from* the first body. As explained below, the phenomenon arises from this fundamental proposition: Bodies of like charge tend to repel one another, and bodies of opposite charge tend to attract one another. *Contact charge proceeds rapidly*—almost instantaneously: The moment one charged conductor comes in contact with another, the second conductor undergoes an immediate alteration in its own charge.

Because contact charge arises from electron mobility, only relatively good conductors will produce and experience it. Consider a negatively charged metal. Its supply of electrons exceeds its supply of protons:

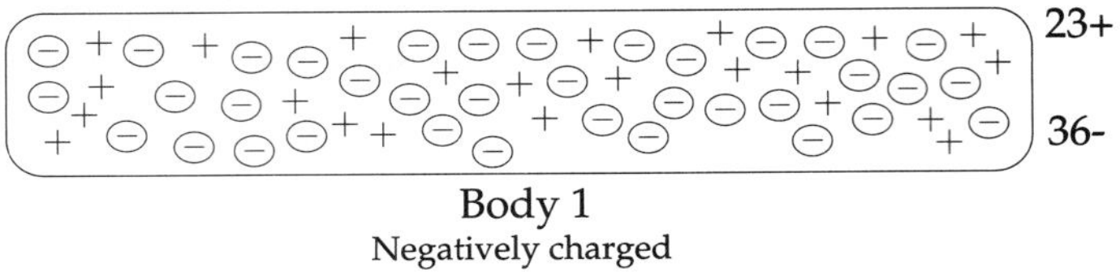

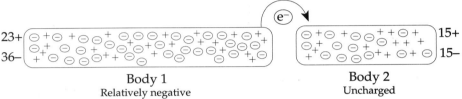

23+
36-

Body 1
Negatively charged

Figure 8.1

If this metal is placed in contact with another uncharged conductor (another metal, for example), the tendency of its excess electrons to repel one another will cause movement of electrons from it into the second metal:

23+
36–

Body 1
Relatively negative

15+
15–

Body 2
Uncharged

Figure 8.2

Now consider a body that is *positively* charged. Its supply of electrons is less than its supply of protons:

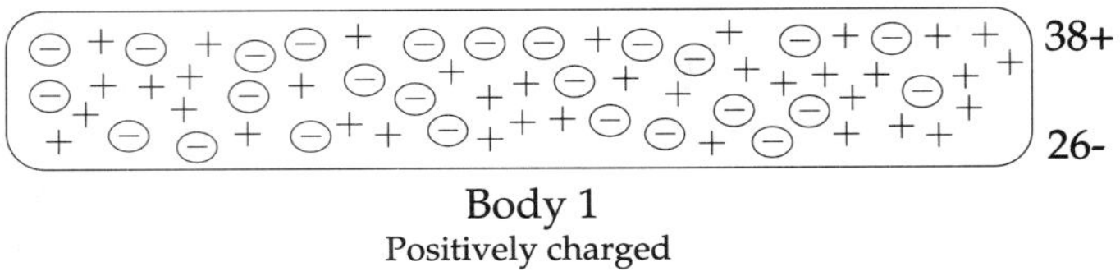

38+
26-

Body 1
Positively charged

Figure 8.3

If, as before, the body is placed in contact with an uncharged conductor, the overall positive charge of the first body and its attraction for a negative charge will cause electrons to move from the second body to the first body:

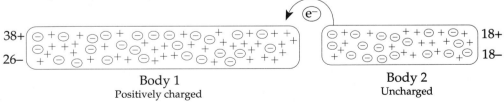

38+
26–

Body 1
Positively charged

18+
18–

Body 2
Uncharged

Figure 8.4

The movement of electrons from the second body to the first leaves the second body with a positive charge and the first body with less of a positive charge than it had initially.

If either of the second bodies had not been a good conductor, neither movement of charge nor contact charge would have occurred. That is, because the entire process requires mobility of electrons within both bodies, and because a poor conductor has relatively poor electron mobility, *a poor conductor will neither produce nor experience contact charge.*

Please solve this problem:

- A positively charged body is placed in contact with an uncharged body. Which of the following choices is (are) true?

  I. If either of the bodies is a poor conductor, each body will tend to maintain its initial charge status.
  II. If both bodies are good conductors, each body will tend to maintain its initial charge status.
  III. If both bodies are good conductors, protons will move from the uncharged body to the negatively charged body.

  A. I only
  B. II only
  C. I and III only
  D. I, II, and III

Problem solved:

A is correct. Contact charge between a charged and uncharged body involves the movement of electrons (not protons) from one body to the other and proceeds only if both bodies experience relatively good electron mobility; in other words, both bodies must be good conductors.

The phenomenon of contact charge arises not only between charged and uncharged bodies but between *two charged* bodies if their magnitudes of charge differ. Consider two negatively charged bodies, A and B:

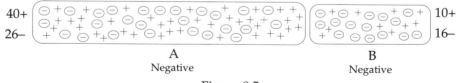

40+
26–

10+
16–

A
Negative

B
Negative

Figure 8.5

Since each body carries an excess of negative charge, both bodies have a tendency to repel electrons. But this tendency is greater for body A than for body B because body A carries the greater excess of electrons. Electrons will move from body A to body B; body B will undergo contact charge, and the magnitude of its negative charge will increase. Because both bodies began as charged entities, and because each will undergo alteration in its charge, each body produces and experiences contact charge.

In principle, a charged body that is placed in contact with a neutral body also experiences contact charge, since its charge is altered by emission or absorption of electrons. By convention, however, a charged body contacting a neutral body is said to **produce** contact charge, and the neutral body is said to **experience** it:

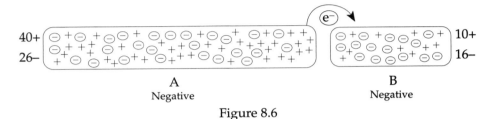

Figure 8.6

The same reasoning applies to (a) two positively charged bodies, if the magnitudes of their charges differ, and to (b) two bodies of opposite charge.

Please solve this problem:

- A negatively charged body, X, and a positively charged body, Y, come into contact. Each body is composed of a metallic substance that features a high degree of electron mobility. Which of the following choices is (are) true?

    I. Body Y will undergo a contact charge.
    II. Body X will undergo a contact charge.
    III. Electrons will move from body X to body Y.

    A. I only
    B. II only
    C. I and II only
    D. I, II, and III

Problem solved:

D is correct. The question concerns contact charge as applied to a negatively and a positively charged body. Both bodies are good conductors. Body X will impart electrons to body Y, which makes choice III correct. The negative charge on body X will be reduced in magnitude, as will the positive charge in body Y. Choices I and II are also accurate.

Induction

Charge induction refers ideally to the phenomenon in which a charged body is brought into proximity with a neutral conductor, whereupon the charged body *induces* uneven distribution of electrons within the conductor, making one end negatively charged relative to the other. One end of the conductor is then apposed to another conductor, thereby imparting or absorbing electrons according to the relative charge at that end. The second conductor is then removed, leaving a net charge on the first.

For example, suppose that a positively charged rod is placed near one end of a conductor as in Figure 8.7. The electrons in the conductor will move toward the positively charged body but be unable to leave the conductor due to the space between the two bodies.

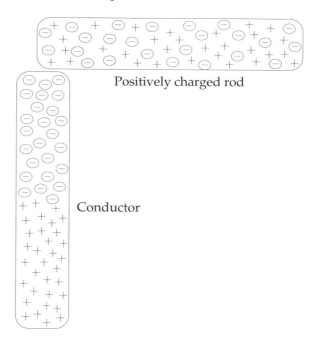

Figure 8.7

Consequently, the conductor, although neutral as an entire entity, is negatively charged at the end nearest the rod and positively charged at its other end. If the charged rod is removed from the vicinity of the conductor, the conductor will return to its normal state, with electrons evenly distributed.

If, while the positively charged rod remains near the conductor (now labeled A), another neutral conductor (labeled B) is touched to the opposite end of conductor A, electrons will be induced to move from conductor B to conductor A.

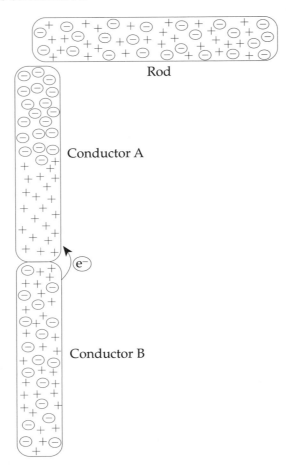

Figure 8.8

In absolute terms, then, conductor A will have an excess of electrons and conductor B will have an electron deficit: A will be negatively charged, and B will be positively charged. If all elements are then separated, the charged rod will remain charged, as it was before the process was initiated, but the two conductors, which are *initially neutral*, will now be *charged*: Conductor A will be *negatively* charged and conductor B will be *positively* charged.

Note that induction does not require that the two conductive elements be neutral at the outset; it requires that their charge *differ* from that of the rod.

Please solve this problem:

- A negatively charged object, A, is brought near the end of a conductive metal object, B, which has no charge. At its opposite end, object B is connected directly to another metal object, C. Object C is removed first, and then object A is removed. Which of the following statements is true at the end of this experiment?

    I.   Object A is negatively charged.
    II. Object A has no charge.
    III. Object B is negatively charged.

    A. I only
    B. II only
    C. I and III only
    D. I, II, and III

Problem solved:

A is correct. The question concerns charge by induction. Object A neither gains nor loses electrons throughout the process and so maintains its original negative charge. Some of the electrons in object B are repelled by the negative charge of object A and passed to object C. When object C is removed, object B is left positively charged.

CHARGE AND COULOMB'S LAW

Charge is expressed in the SI unit **coulomb (C)**. As already noted, like charges repel and unlike charges attract; these attractive and repulsive forces are called **Coulomb's forces**. **Coulomb's law** provides that the force with which two charged particles repel or attract each other is equal to:

$$F = \left(\frac{1}{4\pi\varepsilon_0}\right)\left(\frac{q_1 q_2}{r^2}\right)$$

where:

$$\varepsilon_0 = \text{permittivity constant}$$
$$q_1 = \text{charge on object 1}$$
$$q_2 = \text{charge on object 2}$$
$$r = \text{distance between the centers of charge.}$$

You should think of Coulomb's law as a law of *proportionality*, and, for all intents and purposes, ignore the fraction:

$$\left(\frac{1}{4\pi\varepsilon_0}\right)$$

since it operates only as a constant and hence contains no variables that you might need for problem solving. Thought of this way, Coulomb's law provides that for any two point charges:

$$F = k\frac{q_1 q_2}{r^2} \text{ where } k \text{ equals } \left(\frac{1}{4\pi\varepsilon_0}\right)$$

Observe that the force on each is directly proportional to the charge on each of the bodies and inversely proportional to the square of the distance between them. (Note also that in its mathematical operation, Coulomb's law is closely analogous to Newton's universal law of gravitation, which provides that for any two bodies, the attractive force is directly proportional to the mass of each body and inversely proportional to the square of the distance between their centers of mass.)

Please solve this problem:

- A particle with a charge of –4 C lies 3 centimeters from a particle with a charge of –3 C. The particles affect each other with a repulsive force, F_{r1}. Assume the distance between the particles is decreased to 0.75 centimeters, thus modifying the repulsive force, so that it acquires a new value, F_{r2}. Write an equation that expresses F_{r2} in terms of F_{r1}.

Problem solved:

The problem draws on the proportionalities associated with Coulomb's law. The repulsive (or attractive) force created by two point charges is inversely proportional to the square of the distance between them. In this instance, the distance has been *reduced* by a factor of $\frac{3}{0.75} = 4$, which means that the repulsive force is increased by a factor of $4^2 = 16$, so that

$$F_{r2} = 16\, F_{r1}$$

Please solve this problem:

- Two charged particles, A and B, separated by a distance, D, carry charges of +X coulombs and –Y coulombs, respectively. Another pair of charged particles, G and H, separated by a distance, 0.5 D, carry charges of +3X and +6Y, respectively. Write an equation that expresses the magnitude of the attractive force $F_{a(ab)}$ created by particles A and B in terms of the repulsive force $F_{r(gh)}$ created by particles G and H.

Problem solved:

As noted in the problem, particles A and B experience an attractive force, since their charges are of opposite sign, and particles G and H experience a repulsive force, since their charges are of like sign. The question concerns the relationship between the magnitude of these forces, and the answer lies in the proportionalities associated with Coulomb's law:

$$F = k\frac{q_1 q_2}{r^2}$$

In relation to the first pair of particles, the second pair of particles generates a numerator that is $(3) \times (6) = 18$ times as large. *Of itself*, that difference would create the relationship:

$$F_{a(ab)} = \left(\frac{1}{18}\right)\left(F_{r(gh)}\right)$$

However, the second pair of particles is separated by one half the distance that separates the first pair. Since the applicable force is inversely proportional to the square of the distance between the particles:

$$F_{a(ab)} = \left(\frac{1}{(2)^2}\right)\left(F_{r(gh)}\right) = \left(\frac{1}{4}\right)\left(F_{r(gh)}\right)$$

Combine the effects of numerator and denominator:

$$F_{a(ab)} = \left(\frac{1}{4}\right)\left(\frac{1}{18}\right)\left(F_{r(gh)}\right)$$

$$F_{a(ab)} = \left(\frac{F_{r(gh)}}{72}\right)$$

Please solve this problem:

- Two charged particles experience a repulsive force of 33 newtons. If the charge on one of the particles is tripled, and the distance between the particles is also tripled, what will be the magnitude of the repulsive force experienced by the two particles?

Problem solved:

According to Coulomb's law, tripling the magnitude of charge on one of the particles will triple the repulsive force between the particles. Tripling the distance between the particles reduces the force by a factor of $(3)^2 = 9$. Multiply the new force by $\frac{3}{9}$ or $\frac{1}{3}$:

$$33\text{N}\bullet\frac{1}{3}=\frac{33}{3}=11\text{ N}$$

ELECTROSTATIC FIELDS AND ELECTROSTATIC FIELD STRENGTH

A charged particle situated at any given location establishes an **electrostatic field**—a surrounding area of force that would exist between it and any other charged particle located somewhere in its vicinity, according to Coulomb's law, as previously discussed:

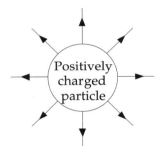

Figure 8.9

With reference to any point at a given distance from such a charged particle, electrostatic field generally refers to the hypothetical attractive or repulsive force that the charged body would exert on a particle carrying a (+1) coulomb charge, situated at that point. The phrase **electrostatic field strength** refers specifically to the *magnitude* of that force. It is expressed in **newtons per coulomb (N/C)**.

When calculating electrostatic field strength, you should calculate force in newtons (N), and then, recalling that the force was calculated on the basis of an imagined particle of charge (+1) C, express the electrostatic field strength in newtons per coulomb (N/C).

Consider a particle, X, with a charge of (–3) coulombs and a point, P, 2 centimeters (.02 meters) from it. The electrostatic field strength created by X at P is ascertained by imagining a particle with charge (+1) C at point P and calculating the force that would exist on the hypothetical particle due to X.

The magnitude of the force is given by Coulomb's law:

$$F = \left(\frac{1}{4\pi\varepsilon_0}\right)\left(\frac{(q_1)(q_2)}{r^2}\right)$$

Taking π as 3.14 and the permittivity constant as 8.85×10^{-12} $C^2/N \times m^2$, the value of the fraction $\left(\frac{1}{4\pi\varepsilon_0}\right)$ is approximately equal to $9 \times 10^9 \frac{N \cdot m^2}{C^2}$.

The total force that would act upon the hypothetical particle situated at point P is given as:

$$\left(9 \times 10^9 \frac{N \cdot m^2}{c^2}\right)\left(\frac{(-3)C \times (+1)C}{(.02m)^2}\right) = -6.75 \times 10^{13} N$$

The magnitude of the force is approximately 6.8×10^{13} newtons. Since magnitude is at issue, the (–) sign is unimportant.

Verification of dimensional consistency shows that:

$$\left(\frac{1}{C^2/N \cdot m^2}\right)\left(\frac{(C)(C)}{m^2}\right) = \left(\frac{1}{C^2}\right)\left(\frac{N \cdot m^2}{1}\right)\left(\frac{C^2}{m^2}\right) = \frac{N \cdot m^2}{m^2} = N$$

As such, the electrostatic field strength exerted by particle X at point P is 6.8×10^{13} newtons per coulomb.

The MCAT will probably not require you to compute electrostatic field strength, but it may require you to solve problems on the basis of mathematical relationships and, more particularly, by using the proportionalities inherent in Coulomb's law.

Please solve this problem:

- A particle, A, carries a charge of magnitude x coulombs. At a point, P_1, located y meters from particle A, particle A creates an electrostatic field strength of .008 newtons per coulomb.

  (a) What electrostatic field strength does particle A exert at point P_2, located $6y$ meters from particle A?

  (b) Among the following choices, the equation that properly expresses x in terms of y, π, and ε_0 is:

  A. $x = \dfrac{y(0.008)}{(\pi\varepsilon_0)}$

  B. $x = \dfrac{y^2(0.008)}{(\pi^2\varepsilon_0^2)}$

  C. $x = y^2(0.008)(4\pi\varepsilon_0)$

  D. $x = y(0.004)(2\pi\varepsilon_0^2)$

Problem solved:

The problem requires that you use the mathematical relationships inherent in Coulomb's law.

Part (a): The force between two charged particles is inversely proportional to the square of the distance between them. The ratio $6y:y$ is equivalent to the ratio 6:1. Since $(6)^2 = 36$, the electrostatic field strength at $P_2 = \dfrac{x}{36} = .008/36$ N/C $= 2.2 \times 10^{-4}$ N/C.

Part (b): C is correct. Using Coulomb's law:

$$F = \frac{1}{4\pi\varepsilon_0} \times \frac{(q_1)(q_2)}{r^2}$$

The problem allows for the replacement of F with 0.008 and q_1 with x, the value for which we are to solve. Since the question asks for electrostatic field strength, q_2 is thought of as $(+1)$ coulombs. The value for r is given as y. With the variables replaced, Coulomb's law gives us:

$$0.008 \text{ N} = \frac{1}{4\pi\varepsilon_0} \times \frac{(x)(1)}{y^2}$$

Solving for x is a matter of simple algebra:

$$0.008 \div \frac{1}{4\pi\varepsilon_0} = \frac{(x)(1)}{y^2}$$

$$\frac{(0.008)(4\pi\varepsilon_0)}{1} = \frac{(x)}{y^2}$$

$$x = y^2(0.008)(4\pi\varepsilon_0)$$

Since electrostatic field strength is expressed in the SI unit newtons per coulomb (N/C), the force experienced by any charged particle located at a position of known electrostatic field strength is:

(electrostatic field strength)(charge on particle), or

$$F_{es} = E_{fs}(q)$$

Please solve this problem:

- A positively charged particle situated at point P establishes an electrostatic field with strength = 6 newtons per coulomb at point P_1. What is the magnitude of force experienced by a particle with a charge of 0.0022 coulombs located at point P_1?

Problem solved:

The problem can be solved by using the equation:

$$F_{es} = \text{(electrostatic field strength)(charge on particle)}$$

$$F_{es} = E_{fs}\,(q)$$

$$F_{es} = (6 \text{ N/C}) \times (0.0022 \text{ C})$$

$$F_{es} = 0.0132 \text{ N}$$

8.2 MASTERY APPLIED: PRACTICE PASSAGE AND QUESTIONS

Passage

The human heartbeat is produced by a cyclic series of electrical events. An initiating impulse is issued approximately once every 0.83 seconds at the sinoatrial node, located in the right atrium, and conducted around both right and left atrial chambers more or less simultaneously. The impulse is then conducted to the atrioventricular node, to the transitional fibers, and to the "A-V" (**a**trio**v**entricular) bundle of myocardial fibers.

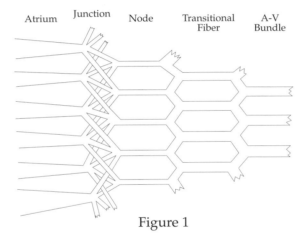

Figure 1

The conduction between atria and the atrioventricular bundle is a frequent site of pathologic difficulty, giving rise to cardiac arrhythmias, some of them life-threatening. A microanatomic depiction of the normal route through which the impulse travels from atria to ventricles is set forth schematically in Figure 1, and a macroscopic view of the associated structures is set forth schematically in Figure 2. The atrioventricular node produces a conduction *delay* so that the impulse does not travel too quickly from atria to ventricles; too rapid transmission might produce dangerous arrhythmias.

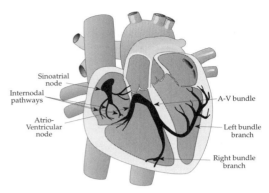

Figure 2

From the atrioventricular node, the impulse is conducted throughout both right and left ventricles. The conduction produces contraction of the two chambers, and this propels blood from the right ventricle into the pulmonary circulation and from the left ventricle into the systemic circulation.

Ideal function of cardiac muscle would require that the impulse originating at the sinoatrial node reach all portions of the ventricle simultaneously. Practically, however, the impulse reaches almost all portions of the ventricle within a very small span of time. The first muscle fiber within the ventricle receives the impulse only 0.06 seconds before the last fiber. The actual time during which the muscle remains contracted is approximately 0.30 seconds, and so the rapid spread of the impulse causes both ventricles to contract almost simultaneously.

This sort of synchronicity is important to the effectiveness of cardiac function. If the impulse were to travel through the ventricles slowly, the heart would lose a great deal of its effectiveness.

1. A researcher constructs an artificial heart in which heart muscle fibers are replaced by finely drawn threads of a conductive metal. She initiates a simulated cardiac cycle by imparting an electrical charge to the region of her model that is anatomically analogous to the sinoatrial node. In view of her model's construction, the impulse will be conducted by means of:

   A. induction produced by the insulating effects of the metal.
   B. contact charge produced by the electron mobility of the metal.
   C. electrostatic field force produced by charge at the simulated sinoatrial node.
   D. Coulomb's forces produced by separation of metal threads.

2. If, when first initiating an impulse, the sinoatrial node were regarded momentarily as a single charged particle, any charged particle in its vicinity would be subject to:

   I.   conduction.
   II. Coulomb's forces.
   III. an electrostatic field.

   A. I only
   B. II only
   C. I and II only
   D. II and III only

3. An experimenter notes that conduction through the atrioventricular node is delayed. Among the following choices, the hypothesis best supported by the observation is:

   A. the cardiac impulse does not move through the atrioventricular node via classic contact charge.
   B. the atrioventricular node is positively charged at the time the impulse reaches it.
   C. the muscle fibers of the atrioventricular node permit no electron mobility.
   D. the muscle fibers of the atrioventricular node feature extraordinarily high electron mobility.

4. An investigator measured the electrostatic force on a point charge at various distances from the SA node. Assuming the charge on the SA node was the same for each measurement, which of the following graphs would most accurately reflect the magnitude of the force experienced by these charges as a function of their distance from the SA node?

A.

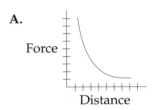

B.

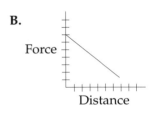

C.

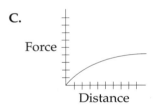

D.

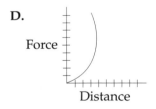

5. An experimenter determines that cardiac muscle is NOT composed of an insulating material. Which of the following conclusions about cardiac muscle most logically follows from this observation?

A. It will donate or receive protons if exposed to a charged body made of a conductive material.
B. It will neither donate nor receive electrons if exposed to a charged body made of a conductive material.
C. If no insulating substance exists between the heart muscle and the SA node, any charge on the SA node will cause a charge to conduct across the heart muscle.
D. It is metallic in nature.

6. Taken together with Figure 1, the passage indicates which of the following about the normal heart?

A. It sends an impulse from the A-V bundle to the transitional fibers.
B. It experiences a delay in conduction between the atria and the A-V bundle.
C. It cannot conduct an impulse through the atrioventricular node.
D. Its electrical impulses are directed from the ventricles toward the atria.

8.3 MASTERY VERIFIED: ANSWERS AND EXPLANATIONS

1. **B is correct.** The cardiac cycle depends on the movement of electrical impulses through a network of conductive substances; the movement of electrical charge is a function of contact charge, which is attributable to electron mobility.

2. **D is correct.** The sinoatrial node is hypothesized as the charged particle. Charged particles produce an electrostatic field, so any other charged particle within the field's vicinity will be subject to an attractive or repulsive Coulomb's force. Statement I refers to conduction, which is a process that requires contact between the bodies.

3. **A is correct.** The means of conduction is not classic contact charge, which is virtually immediate.

4. **A is correct.** The attractive or repulsive force between any two charged particles varies inversely with the square of the distance that separates them; such a relationship between variables is depicted in cartesian coordinates.

   Choices C and D are eliminated because they show force tending to *increase* with distance. Choice B depicts a *linear* relationship, not a proportional one. Only choice A shows force varying inversely with the square of distance.

5. **C is correct.** Any conducting material will conduct a charge, thus Choice A is incorrect because the movement of charge involves movement of electrons, not protons. Choice B is incorrect because a material that is not an insulator will receive and donate electrons if exposed to a charged conductor. Choice D states that metals are good conductors, but that is not to say that all good conductors are metals.

6. **B is correct.** It is clear that the impulse passes from the atria to the ventricles via the pathway just mentioned. Figure 1 serves only to confirm that which the text sets forth.

CHAPTER 9

CAPACITORS

9.1 MASTERY ACHIEVED

ELECTROSTATIC FIELD STRENGTH

The topic of **capacitors** on the MCAT refers generally to the electrostatic field and associated considerations of force and energy associated with two charged plates that are equal in area, of equal and opposite charge, and, relative to their own size, close to one another. Two such plates together constitute a capacitor and are represented in the diagram below as **A** (a positively charged plate) and **B** (a negatively charged plate).

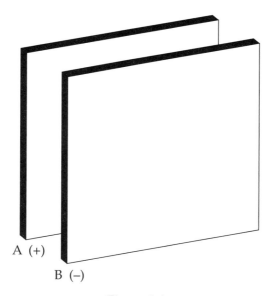

Figure 9.1

Although capacitors may be structured with nonrectangular plates, *MCAT questions require only an understanding of the dynamics of the capacitor with parallel plates.*

The strength of the electric field produced between such a pair of plates (equal in size and of equal and opposite charge) is equal to the quotient:

$$\text{Electric field strength} = \frac{\text{charge on one plate}}{(\varepsilon_0)(\text{area of plate})}$$

$$E = \frac{Q}{(\varepsilon_0)(A)}$$

where:

$$Q = \text{the magnitude of charge on either plate}$$
$$\varepsilon_0 = \text{permittivity constant}$$
$$(A) = \text{area of either plate}$$

Noting that charge is expressed in coulombs, area in square meters, and the permittivity constant in $\dfrac{C^2}{N \bullet m^2}$, a verification for dimensional consistency reveals that:

$$\frac{\text{charge}}{(\varepsilon_0)(\text{area})} = \frac{C}{\left(\dfrac{C^2}{N \bullet m^2}\right)(m^2)} = \left(\left(\frac{C}{m^2}\right) \times \frac{N \bullet m^2}{C^2}\right) = \frac{N}{C}$$

which constitutes a correct expression for electrostatic field strength as discussed in Chapter 8.

Note the proportionalities established by the formula just provided; for any two closely spaced plates of equal area and equal but opposite charge, the electrostatic field strength between them is proportional to the fraction:

$$\frac{\text{charge on either plate}}{\text{area of one plate}} = \frac{(Q)}{(A)}$$

As such, electrostatic field strength is directly proportional to the charge on either plate and inversely proportional to the area of either plate.

Please solve this problem:

- Two plates, A and B, each measuring 1.5 centimeters × 2 centimeters, are closely spaced, one carrying a charge of $(+)1 \times 10^{-5}$ coulombs, and the other, a charge of $(-)1 \times 10^{-5}$ coulombs. A separate pair of plates, C and D, each measuring 1.8 centimeters × 2 centimeters, are closely spaced, one carrying a charge of $+1.2 \times 10^{-5}$ coulombs, and the other, a charge of $(-) 1.2 \times 10^{-5}$ coulombs. Write an expression that describes the electrostatic field strength associated with the first pair of plates (E_1) in terms of that associated with the second (E_2).

Problem solved:

The charge on each plate in the first pair in relation to the charge on each plate in the second pair gives rise to the ratio $1 : 1.2 = \dfrac{5}{6}$. The area of each plate in the first pair in relation to the area of each plate in the second pair gives rise to the ratio $3.0 : 3.6 = \dfrac{5}{6}$. This second ratio is the ratio of the areas, which is inversely proportional to the electric field and, thus, should be inverted. The electric field strength associated with the first pair of plates in relation to that associated with the second creates the ratio $(5/6):(5/6)=1$.

The equation for the electrostatic field, E_1, in terms of E_2 is simply $E_1 = E_2$.

ELECTROSTATIC POTENTIAL

For any capacitor, **electrostatic potential** is equal to the product, (electrostatic field strength) × (separation of plates), or:

$$V = Ed$$

where:

V = electrostatic potential,

E = electrostatic field strength, and

d = distance between the plates.

Electrostatic potential is expressed in the unit joule per coulomb $\left(\dfrac{J}{C}\right)$, and one joule per coulomb is renamed one volt (V):

$$\frac{1J}{C} = 1\,V$$

With electrostatic field strength expressed in newtons per coulomb, and length expressed in meters, verification for dimensional consistency reveals that:

$$\text{(newtons per coulomb)} \times \text{(meter)} = m \bullet \frac{N}{C} = \frac{joules}{coulomb} = volt\ (V)$$

In addition, electrostatic potential for a capacitor refers to the potential energy that would be possessed by a massless particle with charge of magnitude 1 coulomb, situated on the plate of like charge.

Consider a capacitor and imagine a massless charge of (–1) coulomb situated on the positively charged plate. The hypothetical particle is attracted to the positively charged plate and held there with a force equal to the capacitor's electrostatic field strength. Suppose, as shown below, that the plates of a particular capacitor have such area and charge as to produce an electrostatic field strength of 800 $\frac{N}{C}$. Suppose further that the plates are separated by a distance of 1.5 centimeters (.015 meters), as shown below:

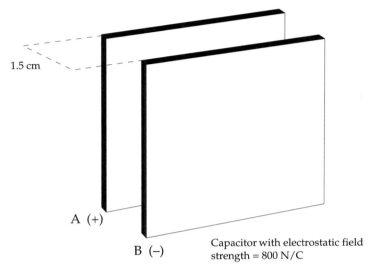

1.5 cm

A (+)

B (–)

Capacitor with electrostatic field
strength = 800 N/C

Figure 9.2

A massless particle with charge of (–1) coulomb situated on the positively charged plate will be held to the plate with a force of 800 newtons. To move the (–1) coulomb particle from the positive plate to the negative plate—*thereby opposing the force imposed by the electrostatic field*—one would have to perform work on the particle equal to:

$$800 \text{ N} \times (.015 \text{ m}) = 12 \text{ N} \bullet \text{m} = 12 \text{ J}$$

If the particle was moved across the capacitor and held to the *negatively* charged plate, its *tendency* to move back to the positively charged plate, through the ordinary operation of Coulomb's forces, as shown below, would represent potential energy equal to:

$$800 \text{ N} \times (.015 \text{ m}) = 12 \text{ N} \bullet \text{m} = 12 \text{ J}$$

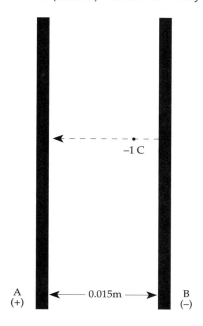

Figure 9.3

If, as just explained, we conceive of the capacitor in terms of the potential energy that would be possessed by a hypothetical particle with a (–1) coulomb charge, located on the *negatively* charged plate (the plate of like charge), we describe the capacitor as having electrostatic potential of 12 joules per coulomb $\left(\dfrac{12 \text{ J}}{\text{C}} \right)$.

Coulomb's forces **(Chapter 8)** dictate that the force with which the hypothetical particle would be repelled from the plate of like charge and attracted to the plate of opposite charge is proportional to the charge on the particle. If, then, the hypothetical particle carried a charge not of (–1) coulomb but of (–3) coulombs, the Coulomb's forces would be equal to (800 newtons) × (3) = 2,400 newtons. The potential energy possessed by such a particle, if located on the negatively charged plate, would be equal to 3 times 12 joules:

$$2400 \text{ N} \times (.015 \text{ m}) = 36 \text{ J}$$

If the hypothetical particle carried a charge of (–5.5) coulombs, Coulomb's force would be equal to (800 newtons) × (5.5) = 4,400 newtons. The potential energy possessed by such a particle, if located on the negatively charged plate, would be equal to 5.5 times 12 joules:

$$4,400 \text{ N} \times (.015 \text{ m}) = 66 \text{ J}$$

For this capacitor, however, the *ratio* of potential energy to charge remains:

$$\frac{36 \text{ J}}{3 \text{ C}} = \frac{66 \text{ J}}{5.5 \text{ C}} = \frac{12 \text{ J}}{\text{C}} = 12 \text{ volts}$$

You should be aware of the proportionalities inherent in the formula $V = Ed$. For a capacitor, electrical potential is directly proportional to electrostatic field strength and is also directly proportional to the distance between the plates.

Please solve this problem:

- A capacitor is composed of two plates separated by a distance d, each plate having an area A and carrying a charge of magnitude Q_1. The capacitor's electrostatic potential is V_1. If (1) the capacitor is replaced with another for which the area of each plate is doubled, (2) the distance between the plates is tripled, and (3) the charge between the plates is maintained at Q_1, what is the electrical potential, V_2, of the new capacitor, expressed in terms of V_1?

Problem solved:

Recall that (1) electrostatic field strength (E) is directly proportional to the charge on either plate (Q) and inversely proportional to the area of either plate (A), and (2) electrical potential (V) is directly proportional to electrostatic field strength (E) and also directly proportional to the distance between the plates (d). V is directly proportional to the fraction:

$$\frac{(Q)(d)}{A}$$

The doubling of (A) tends to reduce V by a factor of 2, and the tripling of d tends to increase V by a factor of 3. The alterations, therefore, multiply V by the fraction $\frac{3}{2}$ = 1.5, which means that:

$$V_2 = (1.5)(V_1)$$

CAPACITANCE

The term **capacitance** refers qualitatively to the degree to which a capacitor stores an electric charge *in relation to its electrostatic potential*. For any capacitor, capacitance (C) is proportional to the quotient:

$$\frac{\text{charge}}{\text{electrostatic potential}} = \frac{Q}{V}$$

As is indicated by the fraction $\frac{Q}{V}$, capacitance is expressed in coulombs per volt $\left(\frac{C}{V}\right)$, and one coulomb per volt is renamed a **farad**.

Consider the effect on capacitance of plate size:

- The area of the plates is inversely proportional to electric field strength (E).

- The electric field strength is directly proportional to electrostatic potential (V).

- The electrostatic potential is inversely proportional to capacitance (C); *increased size of the capacitor's plates is directly proportional to capacitance.* The relevant algebra is shown below:

C is proportional to $\frac{Q}{V}$.

V is proportional to $(E)(d)$.

E is proportional to $\frac{Q}{(\varepsilon_0)(A)}$.

C is plainly proportional to:

$$Q \div \frac{(d)(Q)}{(\varepsilon_0)(A)} = \frac{(Q)(\varepsilon_0)(A)}{(d)(Q)} = \frac{(\varepsilon_0)(A)}{d}$$

which is proportional to A.

Dielectric constant refers to the material situated between the capacitor's plates. No capacitor can maintain a charge on its plates unless the material or mixture of materials between them has some tendency to insulate. The dielectric constant (K) represents the degree to which a substance or common mixture of substances tends to reduce the electric field between the plates. Hence, *capacitance is directly proportional to the dielectric constant,* and the true quantitative definition of capacitance is:

$$C = \frac{(K)(\varepsilon_0)(A)}{d}$$

where:

K = dielectric constant of material between plates,

ε_0 = permittivity constant,

A = equal area of either plate, and

d = distance between plates.

The formula reveals that capacitance is:

- directly proportional to the dielectric constant,

- directly proportional to the area of the plates, and

- *inversely* proportional to the distance between the plates.

Because the dielectric constant of air is close to 1, and because some authors assume the material between the plates to be air, unless otherwise stated, it is sometimes written that:

$$C = \frac{(\varepsilon_0)(A)}{d}$$

CAPACITORS: ENERGY

Electrostatic potential represents considerations of potential energy, and a capacitor is said to store energy. It is not necessary to memorize the equations that quantify the energy of a capacitor (u). If any such equation is relevant to an MCAT question, it will be provided. But understand that capacitors do store energy and that the energy storage is related to the electrical potential difference between the plates.

Three common equations that describe the energy of a capacitor are below :

$$(\text{energy of a capacitor}) = \frac{(\text{charge})(\text{electrostatic potential})}{2}$$

(1) $u = \frac{1}{2}(Q)(V)$,

(2) $u = \frac{1}{2}CV^2$,

(3) $u = \frac{Q^2}{2C}$.

CAPACITORS: DIELECTRIC BREAKING POINT

One should appreciate the significance of a dielectric's **breaking point**. When the electrostatic field is raised to a sufficiently high level, discharge will occur: Electrons will move through the dielectric from the negatively charged plate to the positively charged plate. For any dielectric, the breaking point represents the electrostatic field at which discharge occurs.

9.2 MASTERY APPLIED: PRACTICE PASSAGE AND QUESTIONS

Passage

Modern understanding of electrostatics identifies lines of force that arise from two or more charged particles placed in some given position relative to one another. All such lines of force are ultimately traceable to Coulomb's forces.

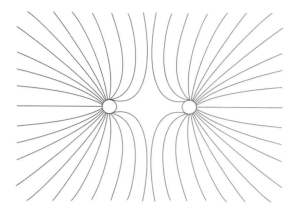

Figure 1

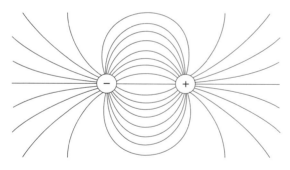

Figure 2

Figure 1 shows the lines associated with a repulsive force between two such particles with charges of equal magnitude. Figure 2 shows the lines associated with an attractive force between two such particles with charges of equal magnitude. Figure 3 shows the lines associated with an attractive force between two such particles with charge magnitudes differing by a factor of 4.

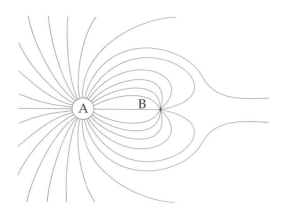

Figure 3

The potential difference between two points within an electric field may be defined to be the work in ergs, joules, or other applicable units that is required to move a charged particle of one coulomb from one point to the other. The work required is identical for all paths between the two points. That proposition is fundamental to the law of conservation of energy; if it were not so, the work *required* to move a particle from one position to the other might differ from the work *produced* by returning the particle to its original position.

1. If a particle with charge of (+) 3×10^{-7} coulombs is first situated on the negative plate of a 100-volt capacitor and then moved to the positive plate, the amount of work performed on it will be:

   A. 3.0×10^{-5} joules.
   B. 9.0×10^{-5} joules.
   C. 1.5×10^{-4} joules.
   D. 1.8×10^{-4} joules.

2. Assuming that the value of the permittivity constant, $\varepsilon_0 = 8.85 \times 10^{-12}$ C²/N • m², consider two parallel plates of equal area and equal but opposite charges. Each plate measures 10 centimeters × 9 centimeters, and the magnitude of charge on each is 9×10^{-4} coulomb. The electrostatic field strength produced by such a pair is most nearly equal to:

A. 0.1 newtons per coulomb.
B. 1.13×10^{10} newtons per coulomb.
C. 71.65×10^{5} newtons per coulomb.
D. 88.5×10^{12} newtons per coulomb.

3. Within an electrostatic field, the movement of a charged body from point A to point B requires work of 40 joules. The movement of the charged body back to point A from point B produces 38 joules of work. Which of the following best explains the finding?

A. The sign of the body's charge is positive.
B. The charged body acquired 78 joules of potential energy when it moved from point A to point B.
C. The charged body followed two different pathways in traveling between points A and B.
D. Two joules of energy were lost as heat.

4. Among the following, Figure 1 might depict:

I. the lines of force that arise between one body with charge (+) 1 coulomb and one body with charge (–) 1 coulomb.
II. the lines of force that arise between one body with charge (–) 1 coulomb and one body with charge (–) 1 coulomb.
III. the lines of force that arise between one body with charge (+) 1 coulomb and one body with charge (+) 1 coulomb.

A. I only
B. II only
C. I and II only
D. II and III only

5. Two charged bodies, A and B, are located near one another. Body A has charge of (+) 6×10^{-6} coulombs and body B has charge of (–) 2.4×10^{-5} coulombs. Among the following figures, the associated force lines are best represented by:

A.

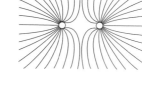

B.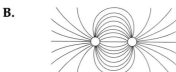

C.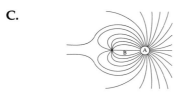

D.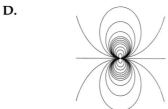

6. An investigator makes appropriate electrical connections between a capacitor and an electrical lifting device so that energy stored within the capacitor may be used to lift a 5-kilogram object. She hypothesizes that if the capacitor causes the machine to lift the object a total distance of 2 meters upward, it will, in the process, lose more than 100 joules of potential energy. Is the hypothesis plausible?

A. Yes, because the first law of thermodynamics is inapplicable to charged plates so long as they are spaced relatively close together.

B. Yes, because the operation of the machine itself will occasion the performance of work and the generation of heat.

C. No, because the gravitational potential energy of the object would then be greater than the potential energy expended.

D. No, because gravitational potential energy cannot be related mathematically to electrical potential energy.

9.3 MASTERY VERIFIED: ANSWERS AND EXPLANATIONS

1. **A is correct.** The designation "100-volt capacitor" signifies a capacitor in which a hypothetical particle with charge of magnitude 1 coulomb would acquire 100 joules of potential energy when moved from the plate with a charge of opposite sign to the plate with a charge of like sign.

   The question concerns a hypothetical particle with charge of (–) 3×10^{-7} coulombs. If situated on the positive plate, the repulsive force it experiences is far less than that which would be experienced by a hypothetical particle with charge of 1.0 coulombs. The difference is indeed a function of proportion:

   $$100 \text{ V} = \frac{100 \text{ J}}{\text{C}}$$

   $$100 \text{ J/C} \times 3 \times 10^{-7} \text{ C} = 300 \times 10^{-7} \text{ J} = 3.0 \times 10^{-5} \text{ J}$$

2. **B is correct.** Knowing that electrostatic field strength is equal to the fraction:

   $$\frac{Q}{(\varepsilon_0)(A)}$$

   calculate:

   $$\frac{9 \times 10^{-4}\text{C}}{\left(8.85 \times \dfrac{10^{-12}\text{C}^2}{\text{N} \bullet \text{m}^2}\right)\left(9 \times 10^{-3}\text{m}^2\right)} = \frac{90 \times 10^{-5}\text{C}}{79.65 \times \dfrac{10^{-15}\text{C}^2}{\text{N}}}$$

   $$= 1.13 \times \frac{10^{10}\text{N}}{\text{C}}$$

   In this case, all choices are expressed in newtons per coulomb, so there is no purpose in verification for dimensional consistency. Moreover, electrostatic field strength is expressed in $\dfrac{\text{N}}{\text{C}}$. If, however, you had forgotten the unit in which electrostatic field strength is expressed and one of the answer choices provided the correct numerical response but the incorrect unit (for instance, coulombs per farad), you could go through the following computations to determine the correct units:

   $$\frac{\text{C}}{\left(\dfrac{\text{C}^2}{\text{N} \bullet \text{m}^2}\right)(\text{m}^2)} = \frac{\text{C}}{\dfrac{\text{C}^2\text{m}^2}{\text{N} \bullet \text{m}^2}} = \frac{\text{C}}{\dfrac{\text{C}^2}{\text{N}}} = \text{C} \div \frac{\text{C}^2}{\text{N}}$$

   $$= \text{C} \times \frac{\text{N}}{\text{C}^2} = \frac{\text{C} \bullet \text{N}}{\text{C}^2} = \frac{\text{N}}{\text{C}}$$

3. **D is correct.** If the movement of a charged body between two points in an electrostatic field requires work, then the body is acquiring potential energy equal to the amount of work required *minus* any energy that's converted to other forms, *such as heat.* In no event can the body acquire potential energy greater than the work performed on it. When the charged body is allowed to move back to its original position, its potential energy might be harnessed to perform work. The maximum amount of work that might be performed is equal to the potential energy, which, in turn, is equal, at maximum, to the amount of work originally performed to move the object *from* its original position. If the work done by the object during its "return" trip is less than that done on the object during its initial movement, the explanation might be that the potential energy it acquired has been converted, in part, to heat, and not directed to the production of work.

4. **D is correct.** The lines in Figure 1 represent a *repulsive* force, so the two charged bodies that they relate to must be of like charge: They might both be positive or negative, but the charge of one cannot be negative and that of the other positive. The lines also reflect two bodies whose charges are of equal magnitude.

5. **C is correct.** The question refers to two bodies that exert an attractive force on one another; their charges are of opposite signs. The difference in magnitude is 4, since:

$$\frac{2.4 \times 10^{-5}}{6 \times 10^{-6}} = \frac{24 \times 10^{-6}}{6 \times 10^{-6}} = 4 \times 10^{0} = 4$$

One should search among the answer choices for a figure that closely resembles Figure 3.

6. **B is correct.** The investigator intends to apply the energy stored within a capacitor (the potential energy represented by its electrical potential) toward the performance of work. The lifting of a 5 kilogram body 2 meters upward imparts gravitational potential energy of:

$$(m)(g)(h) = (5 \text{ kg})(10 \text{ m/s}^2)(2 \text{ m}) = 100 \text{ joules}$$

which corresponds to 100 joules of potential energy. Since the operation of the machine itself will require the performance of work and hence the conversion of potential energy, it is plausible that the actual amount of potential energy lost by the capacitor will be greater than that acquired by the lifted object.

CHAPTER 10

ELECTROMAGNETISM

10.1 MASTERY ACHIEVED

ELECTRIC CIRCUITS

When two entities of different electrical potentials are connected by a conductor, an electric current will flow between them. The potential difference just described, which promotes the flow of a current, is called **electromotive force** (**emf**), or *E*. You should recognize that electromotive force is not a Newtonian force; electromotive force is measured in volts and not in newtons.

If an electrical device is interposed within the connection between potentials, then it will be made to operate. The arrangement of such a device along with an electromotive force and conductors is called an **electric circuit**. The two sources of diverse potential are termed positive and negative **poles**, or positive and negative **terminals**.

In an electrical circuit, electrons flow from the negative terminal, through the circuit, to the positive terminal. The role of the electromotive force (emf) is to take the electrons at the positive terminal and move them back to the negative terminal. Without the emf, the flow of electrons would stop.

As a matter of convention, the flow of current is defined as the "flow of positive charge." Current flow is *opposite* in direction to electron flow. Although there is no *actual* flow of positive charge, you should be familiar with the concept of current.

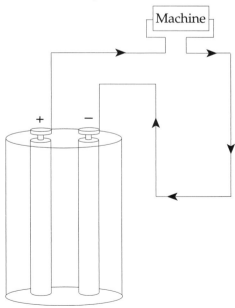

Figure 10.1

A battery may be described in terms of its voltage, which reflects the electrical potential difference between its cathode (+) and anode (–). In a 2-volt battery, for instance, the cathode and anode differ in electrical potential by a magnitude of 2 volts.

You should be familiar with this seemingly paradoxical concept: *Every conductor, even as it mediates and facilitates the flow of current, simultaneously resists it.* By analogy, you might imagine a crowded four-lane highway during rush hour, merging onto a one-lane bridge that conducts traffic across a river. The loss of three lanes impairs the traffic flow: The bridge produces a "resistance." Without the bridge, however, traffic could not traverse the river: The bridge "conducts" the traffic even as it resists it.

Current

The flow of a current is promoted by the potential difference between positive and negative poles; increased potential difference between positive and negative poles increases current flow. The flow of current is impaired by resistance, and increased resistance decreases current flow. The relationships just described constitute the essence of **Ohm's law**, which provides that when two entities of differing potential are connected by a conductor:

$$I = \frac{V}{R}$$

where:

I = current (amperes—A),

V = voltage (volts—V), and

R = resistance (ohms—Ω).

Problem solving on the MCAT often calls for algebraic manipulation of the Ohm's law equation, and you should be familiar with these relations:

$$R = \frac{V}{I} \qquad\qquad V = IR$$

Once again, note the *proportionalities* inherent in these equations. Current is directly proportional to voltage (electrical potential difference) and inversely proportional to resistance.

Please solve this problem:

- The cathode of a 12-volt battery is connected by a conductive wire to an electric motor, which is then connected by another wire to the battery's anode. The total resistance of the circuit—through the wire, motor, and battery—is 2 ohms. What is the magnitude of current traveling through the circuit?

Problem solved:

The problem requires the simple application of Ohm's law:

$$\frac{V}{R} = I \qquad\qquad \frac{12V}{2\Omega} = 6A$$

Please solve this problem:

- A piece of equipment requires for its operation a minimum current of 4,800 amperes. It draws electricity from an 1,800-volt source. What is the maximum resistance of the system under which the equipment will remain operational?

Problem solved:

This problem, like the preceding one, draws on Ohm's law:

$$4800 \text{ A} = \frac{1800 \text{ V}}{R} \qquad R(4800 \text{ A}) = 1800 \text{ V} \qquad R = \frac{1800 \text{ V}}{4800 \text{ A}} = 0.375 \ \Omega$$

If the resistance in the circuit exceeds 0.375 ohms, the current will fall below 4,800 amperes, and the equipment will not operate.

Note that the problem may be solved by initially applying the following form of the Ohm's law equation:

$$R = \frac{V}{I}$$

$$R = \frac{1800 \text{ V}}{4800 \text{ A}} = 0.375 \ \Omega$$

Please solve this problem:

- Consider a power source of 50 volts that drives equipment with a current of 40 amperes. What is the total resistance in the circuit through which the equipment operates?

Problem solved:

Once again, the problem involves the simple application of Ohm's law:

$$R = \frac{V}{I}$$

$$R = \frac{50 \text{ V}}{40 \text{ A}} = 1.25 \ \Omega$$

Please solve this problem:

- An electrical device is driven by a power source of voltage V. The circuit through which it operates has resistance R and carries a current of I. Assuming that the conductor in the circuit is modified so that the total resistance of the circuit is $3R$, and the power source is modified so that its voltage is $\frac{1}{2} V$, write an equation that expresses the resulting modified current, I_1, in terms of the original current I.

Problem solved:

The problem requires an appreciation of the proportionalities of Ohm's law. Current is directly proportional to voltage and inversely proportional to resistance. Since resistance is multiplied by a factor of 3, and voltage by a factor of $\frac{1}{2}$, the new current, I_1, comes from the original current, I, divided by a factor of 3 and multiplied by a factor of $\frac{1}{2}$:

$$I_1 = (I) \times \left(\frac{0.5}{3} \right)$$

$$I_1 = 0.167(I)$$

Electrical Circuits and Power

Power represents the quantity of work per unit time, and is expressed in the SI unit **watt** (**W**). One must be able to derive and manipulate **power, P,** using the electrical variables current, voltage, and resistance.

The power of electricity flowing through a circuit is equal to the product of current and voltage:

$$P = IV$$

If we know the resistance of the system, we can derive another expression for electrical power:

$$P = I(IR)$$

and

$$P = I^2R$$

Since Ohm's law can also be expressed as:

$$I = \frac{V}{R}$$

the following substitution can be made, giving a third expression for power:

$$P = \frac{V}{R}(V)$$

$$P = \frac{V^2}{R}$$

Please solve this problem:

- A 200-watt device is operated within a circuit that draws 1.60 amperes. What is the voltage of the power source?

Problem solved:

The problem is solved by the simple application of the equation that relates power, current, and voltage:

$$P = IV$$

$$V = \frac{P}{I}$$

$$\frac{200 \text{ W}}{1.60 \text{ A}} = 125 \text{ V}$$

Note that power does *not* represent one concept in the context of electricity and another in the context of force and motion. Power has the same meaning in *both* cases, and can therefore be expressed in both electrical and mechanical terms. If, for example, you are told that an electric motor lifts a 45-kilogram object a distance of 8 meters over a period of 2 seconds, you can determine the motor's power by:

$$P = \frac{\text{work}}{\text{time}} = \frac{\text{force} \times \text{distance}}{\text{time}} = \frac{(\text{mass} \times \text{acceleration}) \times \text{distance}}{\text{time}}$$

for vertical lifting.

Using $g = 10 \text{ m/s}^2$:

$$P = \frac{(45 \text{ kg} \times 10 \text{ m/s}^2)(8 \text{ m})}{2 \text{ s}} = 1800 \frac{(\text{kg} \bullet \text{m/s}^2)}{\text{s}} = 1800 \text{ N} \bullet \text{m/s}$$

$$P = 1800 \text{ J/S} = 1800 \text{ W}$$

If the current in the system is known to be 6 amperes, you can also determine the voltage of the circuit:

$$P = IV$$

$$1800 \text{ W} = (6 \text{ A}) \times (V)$$

$$V = \frac{1800 \text{ W}}{6 \text{ A}} = 300 \text{ V}$$

The circuit's resistance may be determined by applying Ohm's law, $R = \frac{V}{I}$, or by applying the formula $P = I^2R$. Using the first approach:

$$R = \frac{V}{I}$$

$$R = \frac{300 \text{ V}}{6 \text{ A}} = 50 \text{ } \Omega$$

Using the second approach:

$$P = I^2R, \text{ or } R = \frac{P}{I^2}$$

$$R = \frac{1800 \ W}{36 \ A^2} = 50 \ \Omega$$

Please solve this problem:

- An electric lifting device operates from a 3,000-volt power source, and the circuit through which it operates has total resistance of 1,200 ohms. If the lift is attached to a mass of 200,000 kilograms, during what time period will it raise the mass to a height of 8 meters? (Assume that no energy is lost to heat and that $g = 10 \ m/s^2$.)

Problem solved:

Solving this problem requires that you relate electrical terms and mechanical terms through their respective formulae for power. In mechanical terms, the time required to lift a given mass a specified distance depends upon the power of the lift, as specified by:

$$P = \frac{work}{t} = \frac{W}{t}$$

which can be rearranged to:

$$t = \frac{W}{P}$$

Power can be readily derived from the information provided in the problem by using the formula:

$$P = \frac{V^2}{R}$$

$$P = \frac{(3000 \ V)^2}{1200 \ \Omega} = 7500 \ W$$

which by definition:

$$= 7500 \ J/s$$

Work can also be derived from the information given by using:

$$W = (\text{force})(\text{distance})$$

$$= [(200,000 \ kg)(10 \ m/s^2)] \ [8 \ m]$$

$$= 1.6 \times 10^7 J$$

Substituting these results into our previously rearranged formula, we find that:

$$t = \frac{1.6 \times 10^7 \text{ J}}{7500 \text{ J/s}}$$

$$= 2133 \text{ s}$$

$$\approx 36 \text{ minutes}$$

Resistors

MCAT questions will require that you understand quantitative relationships that arise from the placement of **resistors** within electric circuits.

Resistors are objects that conduct electricity poorly. All conductors inherently *resist* current (electron) flow to some extent. Thus, all conductors are resistors, and all resistors are conductors. Whether an object is considered a "resistor" or a "conductor" is based on a matter of degree. That which conducts well is considered a conductor (even though it also resists) and that which conducts poorly is considered a resistor. Materials such as wood, rubber, and glass are all very poor conductors of electricity, and are thus termed resistors.

In any electric circuit, one should appreciate the difference between a group of resistors connected **in series** and a group connected **in parallel**. To state that a group of resistors is connected in series means that they are arranged sequentially, as shown in Figure 10.2:

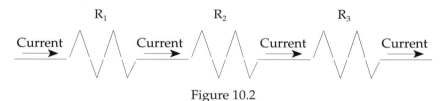

Figure 10.2

To state that a group of resistors is connected in parallel means that one end of each resistor is connected at a common junction and the opposite ends are attached to another common junction, as shown in Figure 10.3:

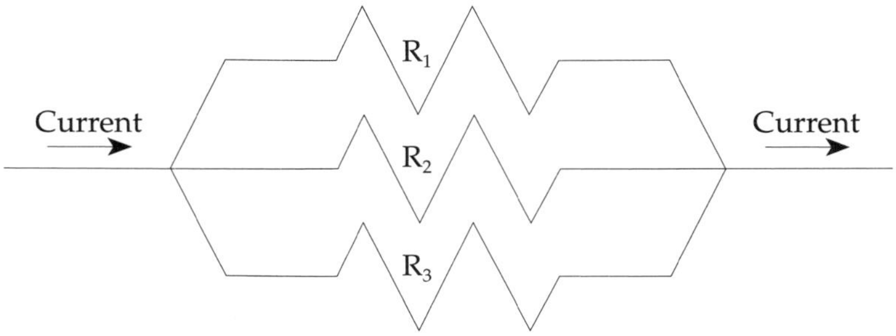

Figure 10.3

When two or more resistors are placed in series, the total resistance they offer is equal to the sum of the resistance of each.

The electric circuit shown in Figure 10.4 features two resistors connected in series, plus a light bulb. The resistors have resistances of 8 ohms and 2 ohms, respectively, and the light bulb has a resistance of an additional 1 ohm. The light bulb (like any device or mechanism driven by electricity) has resistance of its own. The light bulb is connected in series with the two resistors, and the circuit thus features three resistors connected in series.

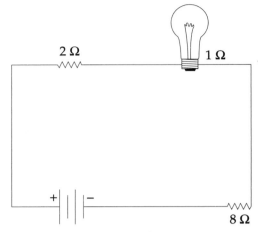

Figure 10.4

To ascertain the total resistance in the circuit (ignoring that of the conducting wire itself and the battery), simply sum the resistances of each of the resistors:

$$R_t = R_1 + R_2 + R_3 + \ldots$$

Thus, in this case:

$$8\,\Omega + 2\,\Omega + 1\,\Omega = 11\Omega$$

The mathematics are more complicated in cases where resistors are connected in parallel. When two or more resistors are connected in parallel, total resistance is equal to the reciprocal of the sum of reciprocals of individual resistances.

The electric circuit depicted in Figure 10.5 features a power source and a set of four parallel resistors. The resistors have resistances of 9 ohms, 7 ohms, 5 ohms, and 2 ohms, respectively.

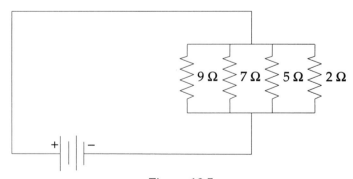

Figure 10.5

Total resistance, R_t, is calculated according to the formula:

$$\frac{1}{R_t} = \frac{1}{R_1} + \frac{1}{R_2} + \frac{1}{R_3} + \ldots$$

If one ignores all other resistance in the circuit (such as that of the conducting wire and power source, for example), the total resistance, R_t, is calculated from the individual resistances according to this equation:

$$\frac{1}{R_t} = \frac{1}{9\ \Omega} + \frac{1}{7\ \Omega} + \frac{1}{5\ \Omega} + \frac{1}{2\ \Omega}$$

You calculate the result by (1) taking the sum set forth on the right side of the equation, and then (2) taking the reciprocal of the result. The denominators 9, 7, 5, and 2 have a common denominator of 630. Hence, the sum:

$$\frac{1}{9\ \Omega} + \frac{1}{7\ \Omega} + \frac{1}{5\ \Omega} + \frac{1}{2\ \Omega}$$

is equivalent to:

$$\frac{70}{630\ \Omega} + \frac{90}{630\ \Omega} + \frac{126}{630\ \Omega} + \frac{315}{630\ \Omega} = \frac{601}{630\ \Omega}$$

R_t is found by taking the reciprocal of the sum:

$$R_t = \frac{1}{\dfrac{601}{630\ \Omega}}$$

$$R_t = 1.05\ \Omega$$

Notice that the total resistance is less than the smallest resistor in parallel. This will always be the case. The bridge example from earlier in the chapter explains this nicely. If another bridge is added across the river, then the overall resistance to traffic flow will be decreased.

Circuitry

The student should be able to calculate the total resistance of a circuit of complex organization by applying the following principle, which derives from the formulas just described: If, *within a single set of resistors connected in parallel* two or more resistors are connected *in series*, then one first takes the sums of the resistances aligned in series and then uses those sums in calculating the resistances arranged in parallel.

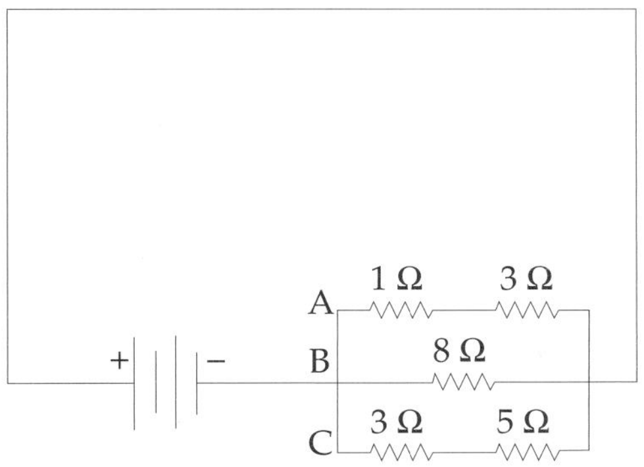

Figure 10.6

Referring to the circuit depicted in Figure 10.6, note that entities A and C each carry two resistors in series. That is, A carries a 1-ohm resistor and a 3-ohm resistor, and its total resistance is 4 ohms. C carries a 3-ohm resistor and a 5-ohm resistor, and its total resistance is 8 ohms. Thus, the set of five resistors can be interpreted more simply as three resistors connected in parallel, the first with resistance of 4 ohms, the second with 8 ohms, and the third with 8 ohms. The total resistance of the set can then be calculated according to the equation for resistances in parallel:

$$\frac{1}{R_t} = \frac{1}{R_1} + \frac{1}{R_2} + \frac{1}{R_3}$$

$$\frac{1}{R_t} = \frac{2}{8\ \Omega} + \frac{1}{8\ \Omega} + \frac{1}{8\ \Omega} = \frac{4}{8}\Omega$$

$$\frac{1}{R_t} = 0.5\ \Omega$$

Thus:

$$R_t = 2\Omega$$

Please solve this problem:

- The electric circuit depicted in Figure 10.7 presents a 220-volt power source that operates an article of equipment having 3 ohms of resistance. The circuit further features a 3-ohm resistor, a 2-ohm resistor, and the set of resistors connected in parallel, as shown. *Within* the set of resistors connected in parallel are resistors connected in series. Ignoring any resistance offered by the conducting wire itself or the power source, please find (a) the total resistance in the circuit, (b) the total current drawn by the device, and (c) the total power associated with the circuit.

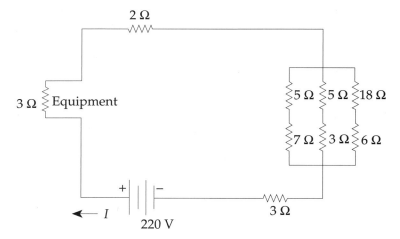

Figure 10.7

Problem solved:

(a) The total resistance within the circuit is the sum of the four resistors connected in series, including, as one resistor, the equipment itself, and as another resistor, the set of resistors connected in parallel. The resistors other than those connected in parallel have a total resistance of:

$$3\ \Omega + 2\ \Omega + 3\ \Omega = 8\ \Omega.$$

The set connected in parallel features three resisting entities, each composed of two resistors in series. Find the resistance of each of the parallel resisting entities by summing their respective resistances in series. The series on the right has a resistance of 6 ohms + 18 ohms = 24 ohms; the middle series, 5 ohms + 3 ohms = 8 ohms; and the series on the left, 5 ohms + 7 ohms = 12 ohms. The entire set, therefore, is equivalent to three parallel resistors of 24 ohms, 8 ohms, and 12 ohms, respectively.

To determine the total resistance of the parallel resistors, apply the equation:

$$\frac{1}{R_t} = \frac{1}{R_1} + \frac{1}{R_2} + \frac{1}{R_3}$$

$$\frac{1}{R_t} = \frac{1}{24\ \Omega} + \frac{1}{8\ \Omega} + \frac{1}{12\ \Omega}$$

Since 24 is the common denominator, the equation may be rewritten:

$$\frac{1}{R_t} = \frac{1}{24\ \Omega} + \frac{3}{24\ \Omega} + \frac{2}{24\ \Omega}$$

$$= \frac{6}{24\ \Omega}$$

$$\frac{1}{R_t} = \frac{1}{4\ \Omega}$$

The reciprocal of $\frac{1}{4}$ is 4, and therefore the total resistance of the set is equal to 4 ohms. Adding the 4 ohms to the 8 ohms of the circuit's other resistors, you can determine that the total resistance within the circuit is 12 ohms.

(b) Knowing now that the circuit's total resistance is 12 ohms, one can calculate the current of the circuit using Ohm's law:

$$I = \frac{V}{R}$$

$$I = \frac{220\ V}{12\ \Omega}$$

$$I = 18.33\ A$$

(c) Knowing that the circuit's resistance is 12 ohms, and its current 18.33 amperes, power can now be calculated using either of the equations $P = I^2R$ or $P = IV$.

The first equation gives us:
$$P = I^2R$$

$$P = (18.33 \text{ A})^2 \times (12 \text{ }\Omega)$$

$$P = 4{,}032 \text{ W}$$

The second equation gives us:
$$P = IV$$

$$P = (18.33 \text{ A}) \times (220 \text{ V})$$

$$P = 4{,}032 \text{ W}$$

Please solve this problem:

- The electric circuit depicted in Figure 10.8 presents a 450-volt power source that operates an article of equipment having 7 ohms of resistance. The circuit further features a 3-ohm resistor, and two sets of resistors connected in parallel, as shown. Within the second set of parallel resistors are two resistors connected in series. Ignoring any resistance offered by the conducting wire itself or the power source, please find (a) the total resistance in the circuit, (b) the total current drawn by the device, and (c) the total power associated with the circuit.

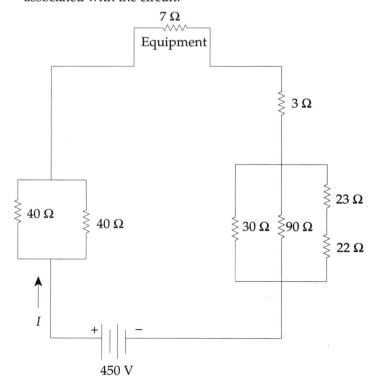

Figure 10.8

Problem solved:

(a) The circuit features two sets of parallel resistors. The total resistance of the circuit is equal to the sum of all resistors connected in series, which means the sum of (1) the first set of parallel resistors, (2) the equipment with resistance of 7 ohms, (3) the 3-ohm resistor, and (4) the second set of parallel resistors. Total resistance of the first set of parallel resistors is:

$$\frac{1}{R_t} = \frac{1}{40\ \Omega} + \frac{1}{40\ \Omega}$$

$$\frac{1}{R_t} = \frac{2}{40\ \Omega}$$

$$R_t = 20\ \Omega$$

Total resistance of the second set of parallel resistors is determined by first summing two resistors connected in series:

$$R = 22\ \Omega + 23\ \Omega$$

$$R = 45\ \Omega$$

The parallel set is thus equivalent to a set consisting of a 45-ohm resistor, a 90-ohm resistor, and a 30-ohm resistor. Total resistance of the set is:

$$\frac{1}{R_t} = \frac{1}{R_1} + \frac{1}{R_2} + \frac{1}{R_3}$$

$$\frac{1}{R_t} = \frac{1}{45\ \Omega} + \frac{1}{90\ \Omega} + \frac{1}{30\ \Omega}$$

The denominators 45, 90, and 30 have 90 as a common denominator; thus, the equation may be rewritten:

$$\frac{1}{R_t} = \frac{2}{90\ \Omega} + \frac{1}{90\ \Omega} + \frac{3}{90\ \Omega}$$

$$\frac{1}{R_t} = \frac{6}{90\ \Omega}$$

The fraction $\dfrac{6}{90\text{ ohms}}$ represents $\dfrac{1}{R_t}$, so the total resistance is equal to its reciprocal, $\dfrac{90}{6}$ ohms $= 15$ ohms.

Total resistance of the circuit is equal to 20 ohms + 7 ohms + 3 ohms + 15 ohms = 45 ohms.

(b) Knowing that the circuit's total resistance is 45 ohms, its current is calculated by reference to Ohm's law:

$$I = \frac{V}{R}$$

$$I = \frac{450\text{ V}}{45\ \Omega}$$

$$I = 10\text{ A}$$

(c) Knowing that the circuit's current is 10 amperes, the associated power is calculated according to the equation, $P = I^2R$, or $P = IV$.

The first equation generates the result:

$$P = I^2R$$

$$P = (10 \text{ A})^2 \times (45 \text{ } \Omega)$$

$$P = 4,500 \text{ W}$$

The second equation generates the result:

$$P = IV$$

$$P = (10 \text{ A}) \times (450 \text{ V})$$

$$P = 4,500 \text{ W}$$

VOLTAGE DROP

Over the course of an electric circuit, voltage drops progressively. A true evaluation of voltage drop between any two points in the circuit would have to take into account the resistance offered by the conducting wire itself. (MCAT questions, however, will not consider resistance within the conducting wire or power source unless the relevant information is provided to the test taker.)

As a current within a circuit moves across any individual resistor, however, the voltage drops according to Ohm's law:

$$V = IR$$

where:

V represents the voltage drop between any two points in the circuit,

I represents the circuit's current (which is constant throughout), and

R represents the resistance between the two points under consideration.

Consider the circuit described in the previous problem:

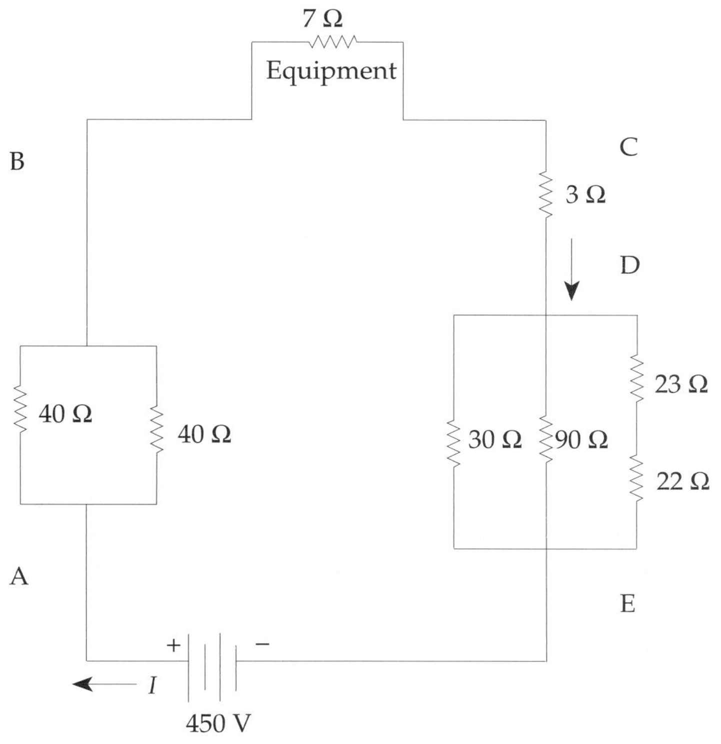

Figure 10.9

As calculated earlier, the current is 10 amperes. The voltage drop between points A and B, as shown in Figure 10.9, is calculated using Ohm's law equation, $V = IR$. The total resistance between points A and B is equal to the resistance offered by the parallel set of resistors that intervenes, which was calculated to be 20 ohms. Therefore, the voltage drop between points A and B =

$$IR = (10 \text{ A}) \times (20 \text{ } \Omega) = 200 \text{ V}$$

Similarly, the voltage drop between points B and C is:

$$V = (10 \text{ A}) \times (7 \text{ } \Omega) = 70 \text{ V}$$

The voltage drop between points C and D is equal to:

$$V = (10 \text{ A}) \times (3 \text{ } \Omega) = 30 \text{ V}$$

The voltage drop between points D and E is equal to:

$$V = IR$$

$$V = (10 \text{ A}) \times (15 \text{ } \Omega) = 150 \text{ V}$$

Note that the total of the voltage drops just calculated is equal, as it should be, to the total voltage drop across the entire circuit:

$$200 \text{ V} + 70 \text{ V} + 30 \text{ V} + 150 \text{ V} = 450 \text{ V}$$

which, as you can see, is the voltage drop across the positive and negative poles of the power source.

If you are asked to calculate the voltage drop between points A and D, you only need to sum the individual voltage drops between points: The total voltage drop interposed between points A and D is thus 200 volts + 70 volts + 30 volts = 300 volts. The remaining voltage drop between point D and the negative terminal is equal to 150 volts, for a total, once again, of 300 volts + 150 volts = 450 volts.

Please solve this problem:

- Consider the circuit shown in Figure 10.10 in which, as calculated earlier, the current is 18.33 amperes, and total resistance of the parallel resistors is 4 ohms. What is the voltage drop between (1) points A and B, (2) points A and C, (3) points B and C, (4) points C and D, and (5) points A and D?

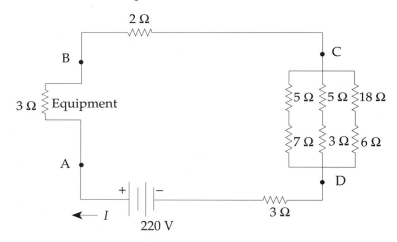

Figure 10.10

Problem solved:

Apply the principle just explained, recalling that voltage drop between any two points is a function of the product *IR*:

(1) The voltage drop between points A and B is equal to the product:

$$V = (18.33 \text{ A}) \times (3 \text{ }\Omega) = 55 \text{ V}$$

(2) The voltage drop between points A and C is determined in the same way. The total intervening resistance is 3 ohms + 2 ohms = 5 ohms. Therefore:

$$V = (18.33 \text{ A}) \times (5 \text{ }\Omega) = \text{approximately } 92 \text{ V}$$

(3) Since the total intervening resistance is 2 ohms:

$$V = (18.33\ \text{A}) \times (2\ \Omega) = \text{approximately } 37\ \text{V}$$

(4) Since the total intervening resistance is 4 ohms:

$$V = (18.33\ \text{A}) \times (4\ \Omega) = \text{approximately } 73\ \text{V}$$

(5) The voltage drop between points A and D is determined by adding the voltage drops A–B, B–C, and C–D, as calculated above:

$$55\ \text{V} + 37\ \text{V} + 73\ \text{V} = 165\ \Omega$$

Alternatively, the value might have been calculated by noting that the total intervening resistance between points A and D is 3 ohms + 2 ohms + 4 ohms = 9 ohms, and applying Ohm's law:

$$V = (18.33\ \text{A}) \times (9\ \Omega) = 165\ \text{V}$$

Note that if the 165-voltage drop between A and D, as just calculated, is added to the voltage drop between the negative terminal itself, and point D, where a 3-ohm resistor is interposed, the result is:

$$165\ \text{V} + [(18.33\ \text{A}) \times (3\ \Omega)] = 165\ \text{V} + 55\ \text{V} = 220\ \text{V}$$

which represents the voltage drop associated with the entire circuit.

MAGNETISM, MAGNETIC FIELDS, AND CURRENT

A moving charged particle creates its own magnetic field. Electrons moving through a wire constitute a stream of moving, charged particles in which the magnetic field created will be strongest near the wire and diminish with distance.

Magnetic field strength is given in units called **tesla (T)**, where T = N/A•m. The strength of the magnetic field, B, arising from a current in a wire has direction as well as strength inversely proportional to the distance from the wire.

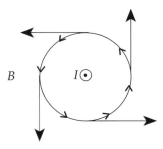

Figure 10.11

By convention, the dot at the center of Figure 10.11 indicates that a current is flowing *from* the page out *toward* the reader's face. If an "x" were placed at the center of the circle, it would signify a current flowing *from* the reader *toward* the page.

It is important to remember that the magnetic field generated by the current in the wire is continuous at all distances from the wire, so that it can be thought of as an infinite series of circles from the wire outward (see Figure 10.12).

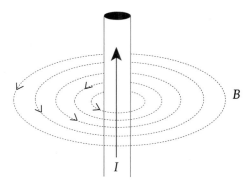

Figure 10.12

The reader should also be aware that there are two possible directions for the magnetic field, as shown in Figure 10.13.

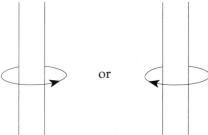

Figure 10.13

Imagine a current—a stream of positive charge—flowing through a conducting wire to the left, as shown in Figure 10.14.

Figure 10.14

Recall, for theoretical purposes only, that the movement of the current *truly* represents the flow of electrons in the opposite direction.

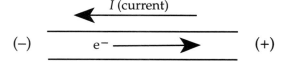

Figure 10.15

To identify the direction of the magnetic field, B, surrounding the wire, apply what is called the **right-hand rule**. This rule is applied by positioning the right hand so that the thumb points in the direction of the current in the wire. If the hand grasps the wire in this way, the bend of the fingers around the wire will indicate the direction of the induced field surrounding the wire.

Application of the right-hand rule is demonstrated in Figure 10.16 with respect to a current flowing to the left. The magnetic field occupies a path that corresponds to the circle suggested by the curve of the fingers:

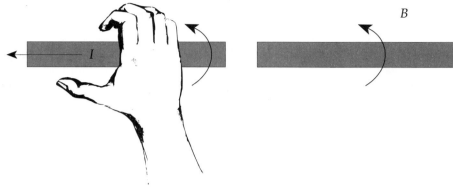

Figure 10.16

Please solve this problem:

- Consider a current moving through the conducting wire shown in Figure 10.17 and determine which of the illustrations that follows it correctly depicts the direction of the resulting magnetic field.

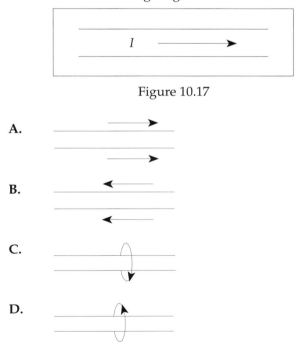

Figure 10.17

A.

B.

C.

D.

Problem solved:

C is correct. Use the right-hand rule. The illustration depicts a current moving through a conducting wire to the reader's right. With the right hand open and the fingers pointing upward, point the thumb to the right (the direction of current flow). Observe the bend of the fingers when a fist is made. The direction of the bending fingers describes the direction of the resulting magnetic field.

Although the total magnetic field is described by concentric circles, the magnetic field at any given point is described by a vector. As shown in Figure 10.18, each arrow represents a magnetic field vector that is *tangent to* the circle describing the field. The vectors point in a direction that corresponds to the orientation of the field at an exact point on the circle:

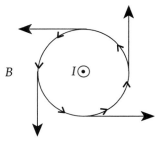

Figure 10.18

You should understand the interaction between a magnetic field and a moving or changing electrical field. When a charged particle moves through a magnetic field, the magnetic field exerts a force upon that particle. The magnitude of this force (F) is equal to the product of the charge of the particle (q), the velocity (v) of the particle, and the magnetic field strength (B).

$$F = qvB$$

The direction of the force is determined by another right-hand rule. Orient your right hand so that your fingers point in the direction of the magnetic field vectors and your thumb extends in the direction of current (opposite the direction of electron flow). The direction in which your palm is facing is the direction of the force on a positively charged particle. In the example below, since an electron is negatively charged and will experience a force opposite of that of a positively charged particle, you should have concluded that the electron will be deflected toward you—out of the page.

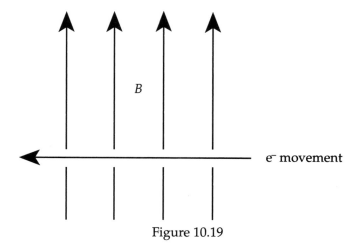

Figure 10.19

Please solve this problem:

- Consider an electron that moves upward, as shown in Figure 10.20. Assume that the particle passes through a magnetic field causing the electron to be deflected away from the reader—into the page. Characterize by illustration the direction of the magnetic field that the particle encounters.

e⁻ path

Figure 10.20

Problem solved:

Since you know the direction of deflection, you can place your right hand with your palm facing in this direction. Next, point your thumb in the direction of the current (opposite the direction of electron flow). Your fingers should be pointing to the left. This is the direction of the magnetic field.

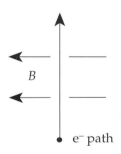

B

e⁻ path

Figure 10.21

10.2 MASTERY APPLIED: PRACTICE PASSAGE AND QUESTIONS

Passage

Electric current is produced by electromotive force (ε). The term *force*, in this context, however, does not carry its usual meaning and cannot be measured in newtons; rather, it is measured using the unit joule/coulomb (J/C).

In an ordinary battery, for instance, energy is stored as chemical energy. When the positive and negative terminals of the battery are connected across, some resistance of this chemical energy can be used to do work.

The chemical reaction that takes place inside a battery is often reversible. Any reversible process experiences an equilibrium state in which its course might be reversed through an alteration in the system's environment. A battery, for example, may be charged or discharged. A generator may be operated mechanically to produce electrical energy; alternatively, it can be driven backward to operate as a motor.

Kirchoff's second rule, also known as the **loop rule**, dictates that the sum of changes in potential associated with the completion of a full loop through an electric circuit equals zero.

All seats of electromagnetic force (emf) have internal resistance, r, which is to be distinguished from external resistance, R, imposed by a conventional resistor. Calculations of real emf must include the internal resistance. Figure 1 depicts an electric circuit, with internal resistance labeled r:

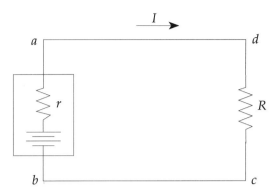

Figure 1

Accounting for r in the loop theorem, and beginning arbitrarily at point b of Figure 2:

$$\varepsilon - Ir - IR = 0$$

In Figure 2, the circuit of Figure 1 is represented as a straight line, with corresponding changes in potential plotted along a vertical line:

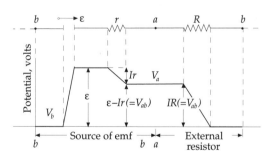

Figure 2

Experiment 1:

An investigator assembles an electrical circuit, attaching to it an electric motor, as shown below in Figure 3:

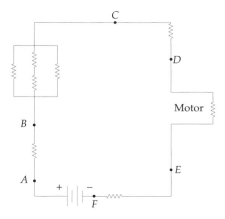

Figure 3

Measuring voltage drop across various sections of the circuits, she obtains the following plot (Figure 4):

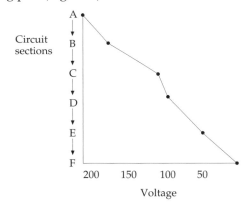

Figure 4

1. With reference to Figure 1, the magnetic field generated by the current between points a and d is oriented:

   A. around the conducting wire directed out of the page above the wire and into the page below the wire.

   B. around the conducting wire directed into the page above the wire and out of the page below the wire.

   C. parallel to the conducting wire and directed to the left.

   D. parallel to the conducting wire and directed to the right.

2. If, at a very small distance r from the conducting wire shown in Figure 1, the associated magnetic field has strength of B tesla, what is the strength of the magnetic field at a distance $2.5r$ from the conducting wire?

   A. $I^2 B^2 \pi$ tesla

   B. $(2.5\pi)B^2$ tesla

   C. $(2.5)B$ tesla

   D. $(0.4)B$ tesla

3. Which of the following conclusions is justifiable on the basis of the investigator's data as shown in Figure 4 as they relate to Figure 3?

   A. The current between points A and B is greater than the current between points B and C.

   B. The current between points A and B is less than the current between points B and C.

   C. The electric motor offers greater resistance than does the resistor situated between points C and D.

   D. The electric motor offers less resistance than does the resistor situated between points C and D.

4. According to Kirchoff's second rule, as described in the passage, which of the following would accurately represent the strength of a real electromotive force?

   A. $I(r + R)$
   B. $I/(r + R)$
   C. Eq
   D. $K(qq)/r^2$

5. With reference to Figure 3, which of the following choices best characterizes the set of resistors situated between points B and C?

   A. As a set, they are connected in parallel with the electric motor.
   B. As a set, they are connected in series with the electric motor.
   C. As a set, they are connected in series with one another.
   D. As a set, they must necessarily offer less resistance than any other resistive element in the circuit.

6. According to Figure 2, as it relates to Figure 1, the electrical potential at point a is:

   A. greater than that at point b.
   B. less than that at point b.
   C. greater than that at point b, only if electromotive force is constant.
   D. equal to zero.

7. The fact that a battery might undergo charge or discharge illustrates phenomena associated with:

   A. external resistance.
   B. internal resistance.
   C. loop theory.
   D. reversible equilibria.

10.3 MASTERY VERIFIED: ANSWERS AND EXPLANATIONS

1. **A is correct.** The solution requires the right-hand rule. Examining the segment of conducting wire between points A and D in Figure 1, the investigator sees that with reference to the page, the current is directed to the right. She should then extend her thumb to the right and direct her fingers upward (which means her palm will face her). The natural curve of her fingers will then suggest the circle followed by the magnetic field surrounding the wire. Her fingers point toward her as they go over the wire and away from her (into the page) as they pass under the wire.

2. **D is correct.** The question tests your ability to apply the proportional relationships associated with the equation that describes field strength, B. Strength is *inversely* proportional to r, the distance from the conducting wire. If at distance r, field strength equals B, then at a distance of 2.5r, the field strength will equal $\frac{1}{2.5}B$ or (0.4)B.

3. **C is correct.** Figure 4 describes the voltage drop between various sectors of the circuit. Voltage drop is determined by Ohm's law: $V = IR$. Since current (I) is identical between any two labeled points in the circuit, the greater the drop between any two points in the circuit, the greater the resistance between those points. The electric motor is positioned between points D and E, and the voltage drop between D and E, as shown in Figure 4, is approximately 50 volts (100 V – 50 V). The voltage drop between points C and D, on the other hand, is clearly less than that amount, as indicated by the markedly greater slope of the line segment corresponding to points C and D.

4. **A is correct.** Examine the equation associated with Kirchoff's second rule (as supplied in the passage) and rearrange it through simple algebra:

$$E - Ir - IR = 0$$

$$E = Ir + IR$$

$$E = I\,(r + R)$$

5. **B is correct.** The question tests your knowledge of the distinction between resistors connected in parallel and those connected in series. Although the set of resistors between points B and C is one of parallel resistors (with one segment consisting of two resistors connected in series), *the entire set as a unit* is connected in series with all other resisting elements of the circuit.

6. **A is correct.** Figure 2 relates electrical potential to various points within the circuit shown in Figure 1. Electrical potential is described by the vertical axis. Notice that the position associated with point a is higher than that associated with point b.

7. **D is correct.** The chemical reactions that take place within a battery are often reversible, and thus often susceptible to an equilibrium state, and the direction of a reaction may be altered by a change in environment. As an example, the author refers to the charge and discharge of a battery. The question, then, calls only for reading comprehension in a scientific context.

CHAPTER 11

WAVES, OSCILLATIONS, AND SIMPLE HARMONIC MOTION

11.1 MASTERY ACHIEVED

DYNAMICS OF THE WAVE

You should understand the characteristics of **transverse waves** and **longitudinal waves**. The accepted model for a transverse wave conforms to the traditional wavelike appearance that you are familiar with. It can be represented schematically, as in Figure 11.1.

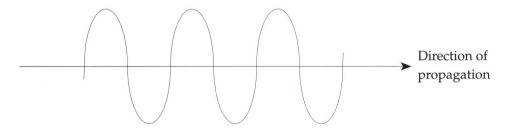

Figure 11.1

The arrow indicates that the wave is moving to the right. The medium through which the wave moves (whether it be a rope, string, or wire) does *not* move in the direction associated with the wave's movement. Rather, it **oscillates** cyclically, corresponding to the wave's movement.

If, for example, with respect to the diagram presented above, one imagines that the wave is propagated through a rope, the rope itself does *not* move rightward. Rather, it moves cyclically in vertical orientation, repeatedly creating crests and troughs, whose *locations within the medium move* rightward, without any rightward movement of the medium itself.

A transverse wave is said to have a **cycle**; its cycle is most easily understood in terms of the movement of its medium, as just described. The fact that the medium exhibits a rightward-moving series of peaks and troughs represents a repetition of events, and each such repetition describes a cycle. One such cycle is associated with the generation of one crest and one trough.

The transverse wave's cycle is expressed in terms of its **period**. The wave's period represents the time associated with one cycle, or the time in which a point in the medium experiences the cycle of crest-trough-crest. In other words, the time that intervenes between one crest and the next represents the wave's period.

Period expresses the ratio time per cycle (time/cycle), although, by convention, the reference to the cycle is taken for granted and so is omitted from the expression. Period is measured simply in units of time. The SI unit for period is the **second (s)**, and to state that a wave has a period of 4 seconds is to state that it undergoes one cycle in 4 seconds (4 seconds per cycle).

Frequency is the reciprocal of period. It expresses the number of cycles the wave undergoes in one second. If, for example, a wave undergoes 1 cycle in 4 seconds, then it undergoes 0.25 cycles in one second, and its frequency is 0.25 cycles per second. The phrase "cycles per second" is renamed **hertz (Hz)**, and the frequency of such a wave would most commonly be described as 0.25 Hz.

Please solve this problem:

- A transverse wave travels through a visible medium. An observer directs her attention to one point on the medium, and with the appearance of a given crest, which she numbers as the first, she marks the time as zero. Including the first crest, she notes that a total of 5 crests pass her view in a period of 8 seconds. Find the wave's (a) period and (b) frequency.

Problem solved:

Part (a): The appearance of 5 crests in a period of 8 seconds indicates that the wave has undergone 4 (not 5) cycles in 8 seconds. The first crest does not represent a cycle. Rather, the appearance of 2 crests represents a cycle, and the appearance of 5 crests represents 4 cycles, as shown below:

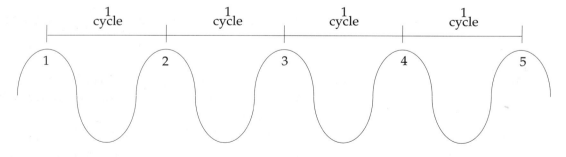

Figure 11.2

The wave undergoes 4 cycles in 8 seconds. The fraction $\dfrac{8 \text{ seconds}}{4 \text{ cycles}}$ is equivalent to the fraction $\dfrac{2 \text{ seconds}}{1 \text{ cycle}}$, and the period of the wave is 2 seconds.

Part (b): If you know that the wave's period is 2 seconds, you know that it undergoes 1 cycle in 2 seconds. To ask a wave's frequency is to ask how many cycles it undergoes in 1 second, which is to ask for the reciprocal of the period. The reciprocal of $\dfrac{2 \text{ seconds}}{1 \text{ cycle}}$ is $\dfrac{1 \text{ cycle}}{2 \text{ seconds}} = 0.5$ cycles/second. The wave's frequency, therefore, is 0.5 Hz.

Please solve this problem:

- A transverse wave travels through a visible medium. An observer directs her attention to one point on the medium, and with the appearance of a given trough, which she numbers as the first trough, she marks the time as zero. Including the first trough, she notes that a total of 13 troughs pass her view in a period of 60 seconds. Find the wave's (a) period and (b) frequency.

Problem solved:

The second of the 13 troughs that pass the observer's view represents the completion of 1 cycle, and the 13 troughs in total represent the completion of 12 cycles. The wave, therefore, undergoes 12 cycles in 60 seconds.

Part (a): The wave's period is derived from the fraction $\dfrac{60 \text{ seconds}}{12 \text{ cycles}} = 5$ seconds/cycle, which is conventionally expressed as 5 seconds.

Part (b): The wave's frequency is the reciprocal of its period. The reciprocal of $\dfrac{5}{1}$ is $\dfrac{1}{5} = 0.2$, and the frequency, therefore, is 0.2 Hz.

It follows that when a wave's period is less than 1 second, its frequency is greater than 1. If a given wave undergoes 1 cycle in 0.7 seconds, its frequency is approximately $\dfrac{1}{0.7}$ Hz = 1.43 Hz.

For any wave, **wavelength** represents the distance from one crest to the next (or from one trough to the next) and, generally, from one position within a single wave unit to the corresponding position of the next.

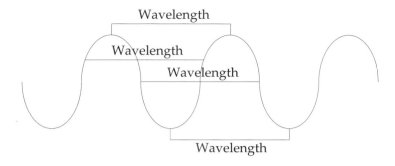

Figure 11.3

Wavelength is symbolized by the Greek letter **lambda** (λ) and is measured in meters. (More precisely, wavelength is a measure of meters per cycle; but by convention the reference to cycles is understood and omitted from the expression.)

With respect to any wave, **speed** refers to the rapidity (measured in units of distance per time) with which the wave moves through its medium. Since wavelength represents the distance from crest to crest, and frequency represents the time during which two crests (representing one cycle) pass a given point within the medium, the speed of any transverse wave is equivalent to the product:

$$v = (\text{frequency})(\text{wavelength}).$$

For any transverse wave, $v = f\lambda$.

Verification for dimensional consistency shows us that:

$$v = (\text{frequency})(\text{wavelength}) = \text{speed}$$

$$\left(\frac{\text{cycles}}{\text{second}}\right)\left(\frac{\text{meters}}{\text{cycle}}\right) = \frac{\text{meters}}{\text{second}}$$

Please solve this problem:

- A given transverse wave has a period of 4×10^{-5} seconds and a speed of 680 meters per second. Find (a) its frequency and (b) its wavelength.

Problem solved:

Part (a): The wave's period is 4×10^{-5} seconds, and its frequency is the reciprocal:

$$\frac{1}{4 \times 10^{-5}} = \frac{1 \times 10^{0}}{4 \times 10^{-5}}$$

$$= 0.25 \times 10^{-5}$$

$$= 2.5 \times 10^{4} \text{ Hz}$$

which means that it undergoes 25,000 cycles per second.

Part (b): Knowing that the wave's frequency is 25,000 Hz, and that its speed is 680 meters per second, calculate its wavelength by reference to the equation:

$$speed = (frequency)(wavelength)$$

$$wavelength = \frac{speed}{frequency} = \frac{680 \ m/s}{25,000 \ Hz}$$

$$\frac{680 \times 10^0}{2.5 \times 10^4} = 2.72 \times 10^{-2} m$$

With respect to any transverse wave, **amplitude** represents the wave height: the distance from the central portion of one wave unit to the crest or the distance between the central portion of the wave unit and the trough.

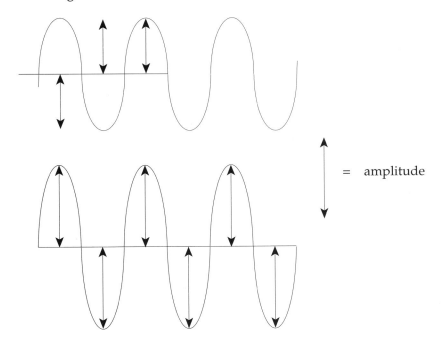

Figure 11.4

Longitudinal Compression Waves

A **longitudinal compression wave** is a wave that travels parallel to the plane in which its own medium oscillates, and gives rise cyclically to areas of increased and decreased density. The phenomenon is best visualized by reference to a cylindrical steel bar that is fixed at one end and free at the other. If the bar is struck at the free end, then at the point of impact it will momentarily compress—its density will increase. The compression will travel longitudinally through the bar, so that along its length, the bar experiences a moving area of increased density.

Since the overall mass of the bar does not change, each region of increased density must leave behind an area of reduced density (just as the peak of a transverse wave leaves a trough immediately behind). The area of reduced density is called an area of **rarefaction**, and for a longitudinal compression wave, the analogs to crest and trough are compression and rarefaction, respectively.

Figure 11.5 depicts a steel bar, with the six circles inside representing the molecules that comprise it. The six drawings show the bar in its initial state (1), a moment after it is struck at the left end (2), and successive moments thereafter (3)–(6).

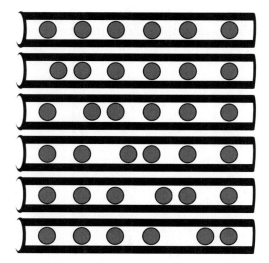

Figure 11.5

Observe the second of the six bars. The first two "molecules" have been compressed. The third bar shows that the area of compression is moving rightward, leaving behind it an area of rarefaction. The fourth through the sixth bars show that the area of increased density—the compression—is advancing to the right, with rarefaction appearing immediately to its left, and that areas still further to the left are recovering their normal density. Think of the longitudinal compression wave as being analogous to the transverse wave and showing a cyclic pattern of crests (compression) and troughs (rarefaction).

Figure 11.6 schematically depicts the analogy.

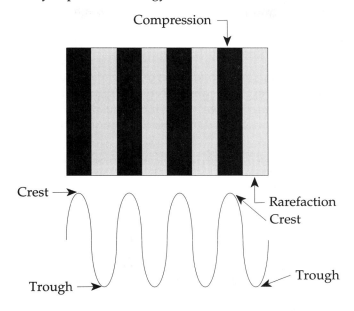

Figure 11.6

The longitudinal compression wave has the five essential features of a transverse wave: period, frequency, wavelength, speed, and amplitude. Do not invest effort in acquiring a true conceptual appreciation of those phenomena as they relate to longitudinal compression waves. Instead, in all contexts concerning period, frequency, wavelength, speed, and amplitude, visualize it as a transverse wave.

Please solve this problem:

- If a particular sound wave has a period of approximately 0.0286 seconds and speed of 1,190 meters per second, find (a) its frequency and (b) its wavelength.

Problem solved:

Part (a): Knowing that the wave has a period of 0.0286 seconds (meaning that it undergoes one cycle in 0.0286 seconds), identify its frequency by taking the reciprocal of that number:

$$\frac{1}{0.0286} = \text{approx. } 3.5 \times 10^1 \, \text{Hz}$$

$$\text{approx. } 3.5 \times 10^1 \, \text{Hz} = 35 \, \text{Hz}$$

Part (b): Knowing that the wave's frequency is 35 Hz (meaning that it undergoes 35 cycles in one second) and that its speed is 1,190 meters per second, its wavelength (which is in reality meters/cycle) is calculated by the equation:

$$(\text{speed}) = (\text{frequency}) \times (\text{wavelength})$$

$$\text{wavelength} = \frac{\text{speed}}{\text{frequency}} = \frac{1190 \, \text{m/s}}{35 \, \text{Hz}} = 34 \, \text{m}$$

SOUND WAVES

Sound travels as a longitudinal compression wave and may do so through a variety of media. Humans are most accustomed to receiving sound as it travels through air, but it may also travel through water, metals, wood, and other media.

The speed of sound depends on two features of its medium: **density** and **resistance to compression**. Increased density of the medium decreases speed. Increased resistance to compression increases speed. In general, then, a medium of relatively greater density tends to conduct sound more slowly, and a medium that is relatively more resistant to compression tends to conduct sound more quickly.

Please solve this problem:

- If sound travels through two media that are equal in their resistance to compression, then it will travel:

    A. more quickly through the medium of higher density.
    B. more quickly through the medium of lower density.
    C. at equal speed through the two media.
    D. more quickly or less quickly through the medium of higher density, depending on the mass of each medium.

Problem solved:

B is correct. Since the two media are equally resistant to compression, density is the only factor affecting speed. The higher the density of the medium, the slower the conduction.

Please solve this problem:

- If sound travels through two media, one more resistant to compression than the other, then it will travel:

    A. more quickly through the medium that is more resistant to compression.
    B. more quickly through the medium that is less resistant to compression.
    C. at equal speed through the two media.
    D. more quickly or less quickly through the medium that is more resistant to compression, depending on the densities of the two media.

Problem solved:

D is correct. The speed of sound is dependent not only on the medium's resistance to compression but also on its density.

Loudness and Intensity

Sound has both **loudness** and **intensity**. Loudness [β] is measured in the unit **decibel (dB)**, and intensity [I], in the unit **watts per square meter (W/m²)**.

At the threshold of human hearing, sound intensity is approximately 10^{-12} watts per square meter, and for any level of intensity, loudness is equal to the product:

$$10 \times \log \left[\frac{\text{Intensity}}{10^{-12} \text{W} / \text{m}^2} \right]$$

As noted, the value 10^{-12} watts per square meter represents the threshold of human hearing and is assigned the symbol I_o. Therefore, the conventional equation relating loudness to intensity is:

$$\beta = 10 \log \frac{I}{I_o}$$

where:

β = loudness (in decibels),

I = intensity in watts per square meter, and

I_o = threshold of human hearing = 10^{-12} watts per square meter.

One should understand that according to the above equation:

If any given intensity, I_1, corresponds to a particular loudness, β_1, then for any x >1, a new intensity I_2, which is equal to $(I_1)(10^x)$, corresponds to a new loudness, β_2, which is equal to $(\beta_1 + 10x)$.

With respect to the paragraph above, consider the variable x. Suppose, for example, one is told that a sound wave of intensity Z watts per square meter corresponds to a loudness of Y decibels. The relationship between loudness and intensity is such that:

Intensity		Loudness	
100 (Z) W/m²	corresponds to	Y + 20 dB	(x = 2)
1,000 (Z) W/m²	corresponds to	Y + 30 dB	(x = 3)
10,000 (Z) W/m²	corresponds to	Y + 40 dB	(x = 4)

Study the pattern just presented; it represents the context in which the equation $\beta = 10 \log \frac{I}{I_o}$ will most likely be tested on the MCAT.

Please solve this problem:

- A whistle has a loudness of 88 decibels. If its loudness is increased to 108 decibels, its intensity will be:

    A. multiplied by a factor of 200.
    B. multiplied by a factor of 100.
    C. increased by 200.
    D. increased by 100.

Problem solved:

B is correct. Again, for any $x > 1$, a new intensity I_2, which is equal to $(I_1)(10^x)$ corresponds to a new loudness, β_2, which is equal to $\beta_1 + 10x$. In this instance, loudness has been increased by 20, which is equal to $10(2)$. The x value, therefore, is 2. Intensity, therefore, is multiplied by 10^x, which, in this instance, is $10^2 = 100$.

Please solve this problem:

- An engine's sound has intensity of 8×10^{-12} W/m². If the intensity is increased to 8×10^{-9} W/m², the associated loudness, in decibels, will be:

    A. multiplied by a factor of 300.
    B. divided by a factor of 3,000.
    C. increased by 30.
    D. increased by 3,000.

Problem solved:

C is correct. The x value as used in this context is 3. When intensity is multiplied by 1,000, loudness is increased by $10x$, or 30.

Pitch and the Doppler Effect

Sound has **pitch**, which, in common terms, refers to how high or low it sounds. For any given sound wave, pitch corresponds to frequency; with respect to sound, the two words are virtually synonymous. Pitch, therefore, is described in the unit hertz (Hz), as is frequency. The higher the frequency, the higher the pitch; the lower the frequency, the lower the pitch. The range of human hearing is approximately 10 to 20,000 hertz. Because sound was historically conceived as a phenomenon significant to human beings, a frequency below 10 hertz (the lower limit of human hearing) is called **infrasonic**, and a frequency above 20,000 hertz (the upper limit of human hearing) is called **ultrasonic**.

The **Doppler effect** arises when a source of sound moves in relation to an observer (listener). From the observer's perspective, as a source of sound approaches, the wavelength shortens and the frequency increases. The apparent increased frequency causes the observer to hear an elevated pitch. From the observer's perspective, as the sound source recedes, the wavelength increases, the apparent frequency decreases, and the observer experiences a declining pitch.

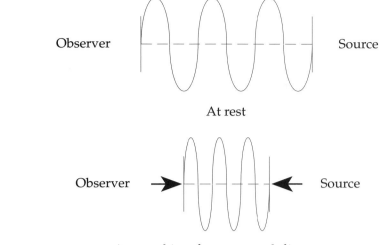

At rest

Approaching: λ compressed, *f* increases

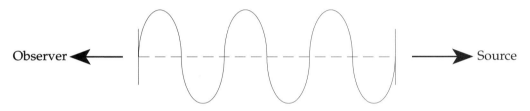

Receding: λ expanded, *f* decreases

Figure 11.7

The Doppler effect is expressed as:

$$f_o = f_s \left(\frac{v \pm v_o}{v \pm v_s} \right)$$

where:

f_o is the frequency perceived by the observer,

f_s is the frequency as actually emitted,

v is the speed of the wave in the given medium (usually air),

v_o is the velocity at which the observer moves, which is (+) if the observer moves toward the source and (–) if the observer moves away from it, and

v_s is the velocity at which the source moves, which is (–) if the source moves toward the observer and (+) if it moves away from the observer.

The (+) and (−) signs are assigned on the basis of the following. Any motion that tends to draw the source and the observer closer should make the fraction larger. If the observer moves toward the sound source, the sign associated with his movement—the sign between v and v_o—should be positive (+) because it will increase the size of the fraction's numerator and hence the size of the fraction. If the source moves toward the observer, the sign between v and v_s should be negative (−), and it will decrease the size of the denominator, raising the value of the fraction. Conversely, if the observer moves away from the source, the sign between v and v_o should be negative (−) because that will tend to decrease the numerator and reduce the value of the fraction. If the sound source moves away from the observer, the sign between v and v_s should be positive (+) because that will tend to raise the denominator and reduce the value of the fraction.

Please solve this problem:

- A sound source moves toward an observer at a rate of 80 meters per second. Assuming that the speed of sound in air is 340 meters per second and that the true frequency of the source's sound is 400 hertz, what frequency would the observer perceive?

Problem solved:

The problem concerns the Doppler effect as just explained. The observer is stationary, and the sound source is moving *toward* the observer. The numerator of the fraction is $v = $ (340 meters per second), and the denominator is (340 meters per second − 80 meters per second). The subtraction of 80 from 340 *increases* the size of the fraction, since the sound source is approaching the observer. The equation becomes:

$$f_o = (400\,\text{Hz}) \times \frac{340\,\text{m/s}}{340\,\text{m/s} - 80\,\text{m/s}}$$

$$f_o = (400\,\text{Hz}) \frac{340\ \text{m/s}}{260\ \text{m/s}}$$

$$f_o = 400\,\text{Hz}\,(1.3) = \text{approx. } 520\,\text{Hz}$$

Please solve this problem:

- A sound source emits a sound with frequency of 280 hertz. It moves away from a listener at a rate of 30 meters per second, but the listener moves toward the source at a rate of 70 meters per second. Assuming that the speed of sound in air is 340 meters per second, what frequency would the observer perceive?

Problem solved:

Both sound source and observer are in motion. The sound source moves away from the observer, which means the sign within the numerator will be positive (+), reducing the size of the fraction. The observer moves toward the sound source, which means the sign in the numerator will also be positive (+), increasing the size of the fraction:

$$f_o = (280\,\text{Hz}) \times \frac{340\,\text{m/s} + 70\,\text{m/s}}{340\,\text{m/s} + 30\,\text{m/s}}$$

$$f_o = (280\,\text{Hz})\frac{410\,\text{m/s}}{370\,\text{m/s}}$$

$$f_o = 280\,\text{Hz}\,(1.1) = \text{approx. } 310\,\text{Hz}$$

OSCILLATIONS AND SIMPLE HARMONIC MOTION

The phrase **simple harmonic motion** refers to a certain form of oscillatory motion classically illustrated by a swinging pendulum. Were it not for relevant forces of friction, the pendulum would oscillate endlessly. When the pendulum is at the rightmost position of its path, it is momentarily stationary, but the force of gravity draws it down to the bottommost position of its path, where velocity reaches a maximum. It continues, swinging leftward and upward, and reaches the uppermost position on the left side of its path, where velocity is again momentarily zero. The force of gravity, however, sends it downward once again, its velocity now increasing, until it reaches the bottommost position of its path, where velocity is again at a maximum. The pendulum then moves upward and to the right, and the oscillatory motion continues without end (ignoring, once again, applicable forces of friction).

Simple harmonic motion is by no means limited to the operation of a pendulum. One might envision an object affixed to the end of a spring that moves in a horizontal path rightward and leftward in response to the cyclic stretch, relaxation, and compression of the spring. Again, if forces of friction are ignored, the oscillatory motion continues without end. When the spring is fully compressed, the object is momentarily stationary. The force associated with the spring's compression causes the spring to move toward its relaxation point, the object being propelled with it.

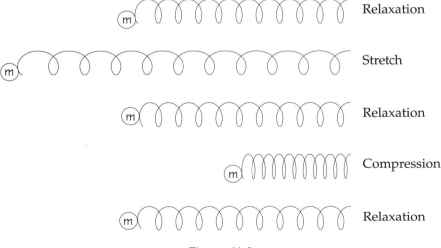

Figure 11.8

The mass attains a maximum velocity at the relaxation point (which is analogous to the bottommost point of a pendulum's path). As motion continues in the same direction, the spring begins to stretch, during which period the velocity decreases until the spring's motion ceases momentarily. The force associated with the stretching of the spring, however, causes the spring to move backward—again toward its relaxation point (just as gravity causes the pendulum to move downward from the uppermost position of its path). The attached object follows, and its velocity increases. The spring again reaches its relaxation point, at which time velocity is maximum. Motion continues, the spring compresses, and velocity decreases, until the spring reaches maximum compression.

Simple Harmonic Motion as a Wave

The oscillation of an object in simple harmonic motion has features analogous to those of a wave. An object in simple harmonic motion is said to have a period, frequency, and amplitude. The period represents the time taken to complete one full cycle. In the case of a pendulum, it might be measured as the time taken for the pendulum to complete its travel from rightward end to rightward end (which involves two passages through its bottommost position) or, alternatively, from its leftward end to its leftward end. If the time associated with one full cycle of the pendulum's travel is 2 seconds, its period is 2 seconds.

The same principle applies to the object attached to the end of a spring. The period of the associated simple harmonic motion is the time taken for the spring to complete one full cycle, which might be measured as the time taken for its travel from its point of maximum compression to return to its point of maximum compression. Alternatively, it might be expressed as the time taken for the spring to travel from its point of maximum stretch to return to its point of maximum stretch.

As in the case of a wave, the frequency associated with simple harmonic motion is the reciprocal of the period representing the number of oscillations (cycles) that occur in one second. If an object in simple harmonic motion has a period of 5 seconds (meaning, in fact, $\frac{5\,\text{seconds}}{1\,\text{cycle}}$), then its frequency is $\frac{1}{5} = 0.2$ cycles per second.

Simple Harmonic Motion: Force and Energy

Simple harmonic motion is associated with force. In the case of a pendulum, the associated force is the pendulum's weight. In the case of the object affixed to a spring, the associated force is the tension within the spring.

The force associated with any point in the oscillation of simple harmonic motion is a function of **displacement**, which refers to the distance from the point of maximum velocity, and the **spring constant**, which, while initially named in relation to a spring, applies whether or not the simple harmonic motion involves a true spring. The spring constant is expressed in the SI unit **newtons/meter (N/m)**. The equation from which force is derived is **Hooke's law**:

$$F = -k(x)$$

where:

   F = force,

   k = spring constant, and

   x = displacement.

For any instance of simple harmonic motion, you will be supplied with the spring constant because it will differ depending on the entity in motion. In the case of a pendulum, the spring constant is approximately equal to the fraction $\dfrac{\text{weight of pendulum}}{\text{length of pendulum}}$.

Hooke's law may only be applied to a spring or other object if the spring or other such object obeys Hooke's law. When a spring is the instrument of motion and it conforms to Hooke's law, it is actually called a **Hooke's law spring**. (MCAT problems will not ask you to solve problems in which Hooke's law is not obeyed, unless the relevant information is supplied.)

Please solve this problem:

- A Hooke's law spring has a spring constant of 2,500 newtons per meter. It is stretched to a position located 0.06 meters from its relaxation point. What is the force that acts to restore the spring to its relaxation point?

Problem solved:

The problem calls for the application of Hooke's law: $F = -(k)(x)$. The spring constant is given as 2.5×10^3 newtons per meter, and the displacement as 0.06 meters. The solution then requires simple algebra:

$$F = (-2500 \text{ N/m})(0.06 \text{ m}) = -150 \text{ N}$$

(The [–] sign in the Hooke's law formula indicates that force is opposite the direction of displacement. The force at issue is **restorative**; it tends to restore the moving object to the point at which it has no potential energy. The force of a swinging pendulum is downward as the pendulum moves upward. The force of a spring is toward the relaxation point as the spring moves away from it.)

Envision a pendulum at the rightward end of its path. It is raised, and relative to the bottommost position of its path, has a gravitational potential energy equal to the product of:

$$(\text{mass})(g)(\text{height}) = mgh$$

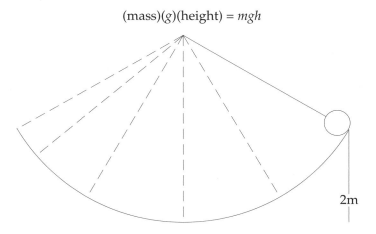

Figure 11.9

Imagine that the pendulum has a mass of 25 kilograms and that its height at the upward end of its motion is 2 meters, as shown. Its gravitational potential energy (relative to the bottommost position of its path) = (25 kg)(10 m/s²)(2 m) = 500 joules (J). The pendulum has the same gravitational potential energy, 500 joules, when it swings fully leftward and occupies a position at the left end of its path.

When the pendulum reaches the bottommost position of its path, all of its potential energy has been converted to kinetic energy; potential energy is zero, and kinetic energy is at a maximum. The mathematical corollary is that $(m)(g)(h)$ at the point of maximum potential energy is equal to $\frac{1}{2}mv^2$ at the point of maximum kinetic energy. Moreover, since the total sum (kinetic energy) + (potential energy) is unchanged at all points in the path, *the sum of $(m)(g)(h)$ and $\frac{1}{2}mv^2$ is constant throughout the path of simple harmonic motion.*

For simple harmonic motion, depending on some instrument other than a pendulum, the same principle applies, but the potential energy at issue will not necessarily be *gravitational* potential energy. Whatever the source and form of the simple harmonic motion, however, you must be aware that: (1) there is a perpetual conversion between potential and kinetic energy; (2) at the point of maximum velocity, kinetic energy is at a maximum and potential energy is at a minimum; (3) at the point of minimum velocity, potential energy is at a maximum, and kinetic energy is at a minimum, and (4) throughout the motion, the sum of potential energy and kinetic energy is constant.

Please solve this problem:

- A pendulum swings in simple harmonic motion and has a mass of 240 kilograms. Each time it passes the bottommost point in its path, it has speed of 8 meters per second. Ignoring all forces of friction, determine the maximum height it reaches on each side of its path.

Problem solved:

In the case of a swinging pendulum, the potential energy to be considered is gravitational potential energy = $(m)(g)(h)$. Kinetic energy, as always, = $\frac{1}{2}mv^2$. The sum: $(m)(g)(h) + \frac{1}{2}mv^2$ is constant throughout the path of simple harmonic motion. At the bottommost position, potential energy is zero, and the entire sum of potential and kinetic energy is attributable to kinetic energy alone:

$$\left(\frac{1}{2}mv^2\right) = \frac{1}{2} \times (240 \text{ kg}) \times (8^2) = 7{,}680 \text{ J}$$

At the uppermost portion of the pendulum's path, kinetic energy is zero and potential energy, therefore, must be equal to 7,680 J. Knowing that $(m)(g)(h) = 7{,}680$ joules, the student may solve for h:

$$(m)(g)(h) = 7{,}680 \text{ J} \qquad (240 \text{ kg}) \times (10 \text{ m/s}^2) \times (h) = 7{,}680$$

$$2{,}400\ (h) = 7680 \qquad h = \frac{7{,}680}{2{,}400} = 3.2 \qquad h = 3.2 \text{ meters}$$

11.2 MASTERY APPLIED: PRACTICE PASSAGE AND QUESTIONS

Passage

The superposition phenomenon involves the coincident use of one space by more than one wave. That is, more than one wave may travel and occupy the same space at the same time, each independent of the other.

Illustrations of the superposition principle are numerous, radio waves and sound waves furnishing good examples. Large numbers of radio broadcasting facilities commonly operate at the same time, and the "tuning" of a radio to one such station involves adjusting the receiver so that it receives only *one* of the many frequencies traveling through the surrounding space. Similarly, the perceived sound that emerges from an orchestra involves the contemporaneous travel through the air of a large number of longitudinal waves which the human ear is capable of perceiving as a cacophony, but which it may also resolve into the individual sounds of orchestral instruments.

The medium through which independent waves move is displaced according to the sum of the displacements that would be associated with each one of them independently. Indeed, the term "superposition" refers to the vector summation that accompanies the summed displacement. This superposition principle, however, does not always hold. It applies to waves in deformable media only when a relation of proportionality exists between the deformation and the restorative force. The relationship would then be manifest mathematically in a linear equation of the form $y = mx + b$. Hooke's law represents a linear equation, and it fails to operate when wave disturbance is sufficiently large as to distort the normal linear laws of mechanical action. Superposition applies to electromagnetic waves, for example, because the relations between electric and magnetic fields are linear.

1. One musical instrument sounds a frequency of 440 cycles per second and another simultaneously sounds a frequency of 600 cycles per second. Both instruments are located on a vehicle that travels toward a listener at a rate of 90 meters per second. Assuming the speed of sound through air is approximately 340 meters per second, which of the following numbers best approximates the factor by which each frequency is multiplied in order to yield the apparent frequency perceived by the listener?

   A. 0.2
   B. 0.8
   C. 9.0
   D. 1.36

2. An investigator discovers a particular wave that does not conform to the superposition principle. Which of the following choices would LEAST likely be true of such a wave?

   A. Amplitude and restorative force would bear a proportional relationship.
   B. Speed and wavelength would bear a directly proportional relationship.
   C. Frequency and period would bear an inversely proportional relationship.
   D. The wave would not obey Hooke's law.

3. Two longitudinal compression waves, 1 and 2, travel through the same space simultaneously. Wave 1 has a period of P_1 and a speed of S_1. Wave 2 has a period of P_2 and a speed of S_2. If the wavelengths of waves 1 and 2 are represented by WL_1 and WL_2, respectively, which of the following represents the ratio WL_2:WL_1?

   A. $S1S2$: $P1P2$

   B. S_2P_2:S_1P_1

   C. $\dfrac{S_2}{P_1}$: (P_2P_2)

   D. $\dfrac{P_2}{P_1}$: (S_1P_1)

4. An experimenter designs a pendulum according to a carefully devised set of specifications. In a variety of experimental trials, she demonstrates that when the pendulum swings and is raised above the lowest position of its path, the force tending to draw it downward is NOT proportional to its displacement. The investigator concludes that the pendulum she has designed does not conform to Hooke's law. Is her conclusion justified?

   A. No, because Hooke's law applies to simple harmonic motion involving a spring.
   B. No, because the conclusion cannot be drawn unless the investigator has calculated the pendulum's spring constant.
   C. Yes, because according to Hooke's law, restorative force and displacement are proportional.
   D. Yes, because the absence of the proportionality indicates the absence of a spring constant.

5. A laboratory worker experiments with a spring and mass that exhibit classic simple harmonic motion. For several positions relating to the path of motion, he records the tension in the spring and the corresponding displacement from the spring's relaxation point. On a Cartesian plane, he then plots his results, with force recorded on the y-axis and displacement on the x-axis. Which of the following descriptions would most likely characterize the resulting graph?

   A. The graph would be linear, with a slope of 1.
   B. The graph would be linear, with a slope of magnitude equal to the spring constant.
   C. The graph would be linear, with an x intercept equal to the spring constant.
   D. The graph would be nonlinear.

6. Which of the following choices best explains the fact that waves of electromagnetic radiation conform to the superposition principle?

   A. For waves of electromagnetic radiation, period and frequency are inversely proportional.
   B. Electromagnetic waves move at the speed of light.
   C. Magnetic and electric fields may occupy the same space simultaneously.
   D. Magnetic and electric fields bear a linear relationship.

11.3 MASTERY VERIFIED: ANSWERS AND EXPLANATIONS

1. **D is correct.** Although the question concerns two sound waves traveling simultaneously, the passage indicates that for most practical purposes, such waves may be treated separately. Each sound source moves toward the observer at a rate of 90 meters per second. The perceived frequencies will be greater than the true frequencies emitted by the instruments. The factor by which each frequency is multiplied to yield the apparent frequency is equal to the fractional component of the Doppler formula: $f_o = f_s \left(\dfrac{v \pm v_o}{v \pm v_s} \right)$.

   Since the observer does not move, the sum $(v + v_o)$ is equal to $v = 340$ meters per second. Since the sound source is moving toward the observer, frequency will increase, and the denominator must be reduced to reflect an increase in the overall size of the fraction. The sign employed in the denominator, therefore, must be (–), and the fraction becomes:

   $$\frac{340}{340-90} = \frac{340}{250} = 1.36 \, .$$

2. **A is correct.** The superposition principle applies only when there is a proportional relationship between deformation and restorative force. Choice A states that amplitude and restorative force are proportional. Such is said not to be the case of waves for which the superposition principle does not operate. Choices B and C are truths that apply to all waves with which one is expected to be familiar; but in relation to this question (which essentially asks for false statements), they are incorrect answers. Choice D might be true, since Hooke's law does manifest a relationship of proportion and is specifically cited by the author in that regard.

3. **B is correct.** The question tests only your mastery of (a) algebraic manipulation and (b) the relationships among period, speed, frequency, and wavelength.

   Recalling that period is the reciprocal of frequency, and that:

   $$(speed) = (wavelength)(frequency)$$

   then:

   $$(speed) = (wavelength) \, \frac{1}{period} \, .$$

   Solve for wavelength in terms of speed and period by multiplying each side of the equation by period.

   $$(speed)(period) = (wavelength)$$

   Wavelength is directly proportional to speed and frequency, so the ratio of WL_1 to WL_2 is simply $S_2P_2 : S_1P_1$.

4. **C is correct.** For any oscillatory motion that conforms to Hooke's law, restorative force and displacement are proportional. The question describes a swinging pendulum for which restorative force and displacement are *not* proportional. It is a simple logical deduction, therefore, that the pendulum does not conform to Hooke's law—for the reason as stated in choice C that "according to Hooke's law, restorative force and displacement are proportional."

5. **B is correct.** The passage characterizes a linear equation as one that takes the form $y = mx + b$. It further states that Hooke's law represents a linear equation. Since Hooke's law, $F = -(k)(x)$, represents such an equation, where $m = -k$ and x = displacement, the graph drawn by the laboratory worker will be linear.

   For any linear equation, the slope has a magnitude equal to m, which, in connection with Hooke's law, is $-k$, the spring constant. The graph drawn by this laboratory worker will be linear and will have a slope equal to the magnitude of the spring constant.

6. **D is correct.** In this case, the last sentence provides the answer in rather a straightforward fashion: "Superposition applies to electromagnetic waves, for example, because the relations between electric and magnetic fields are linear."

CHAPTER 12

LIGHT AND OPTICS

12.1 MASTERY ACHIEVED

GENERAL CHARACTERISTICS OF LIGHT

Wavelength and Speed

Visible light is a form of electromagnetic radiation that is normally conceived of as a wave. Electromagnetic radiation has the essential features associated with waves: period, frequency, wavelength, and speed. Electromagnetic radiation whose wavelength falls between 390×10^{-9} meters and 700×10^{-9} meters is visible light.

White light represents a mixture of all wavelengths within the spectrum of visible light. Here, variable wavelength corresponds to diversity of color. Wavelength of 390 nm corresponds roughly to the color violet, 500 nm to the color green, 600 nm to orange, and 700 nm to red. The term **infrared** light refers to electromagnetic radiation with wavelength somewhat above 700 nm, and the term **ultraviolet** light refers to electromagnetic radiation, falling somewhat below 390 nm.

When moving through space, electromagnetic radiation has a speed of approximately 3×10^8 meters per second, which is known as the **speed of light** and is assigned the symbol c. For any given wavelength of electromagnetic radiation or light, frequency is determined by the formula that relates speed and wavelength for waves in general:

$$\text{frequency} = \frac{\text{speed}}{\text{wavelength}}$$

For light:

$$\text{frequency} = \frac{3 \times 10^8 \, \text{m/s}}{\text{wavelength}}$$

The spectrum of visible light is depicted in Figure 12.1 in terms of wavelength and corresponding frequency.

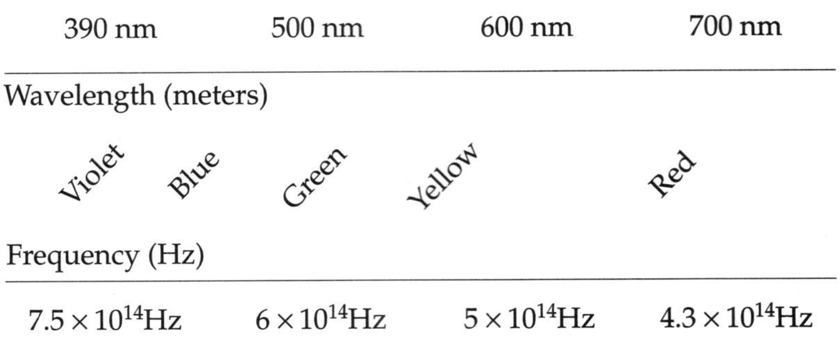

390 nm	500 nm	600 nm	700 nm

Wavelength (meters)

Violet   *Blue*   *Green*   *Yellow*   *Red*

Frequency (Hz)

7.5×10^{14} Hz	6×10^{14} Hz	5×10^{14} Hz	4.3×10^{14} Hz

Figure 12.1

The Index of Refraction

As noted previously, the speed of light through a vacuum is 3×10^8 meters per second. Its speed through some physical medium is reduced according to the medium's **refractive index**. The index of refraction is defined in terms of the degree to which it slows the travel of light. For any medium, it is equal to the fraction:

$$\frac{\text{speed of light in vacuum}}{\text{speed of light in medium}}$$

$$n = \frac{c}{v}$$

where:

n = refractive index of medium,

c = speed of light in vacuum (3×10^8 m/s), and

v = speed of light in medium.

Index of refraction is dimensionless (without units), as is evidenced by the fraction $\frac{c}{v}$, in which the units in the numerator and denominator both are (meters per second), and thus cancel out.

For any medium, the index of refraction varies slightly with the frequency of light that traverses it.

Please solve this problem:

- The speed of light through water is approximately 2.26×10^8 meters per second. Find the refractive index of water.

Problem solved:

The question requires algebraic application of the equation just presented:

$$n = \frac{c}{v} = \frac{3 \times 10^8 \, \text{m/s}}{2.26 \times 10^8 \, \text{m/s}} = \frac{3}{2.26} = \text{approx. } 1.33$$

Please solve this problem:

- The refractive index of fused quartz is approximately 1.46. At what speed does light travel through the substance?

Problem solved:

The problem once again relies on the equation that defines refractive index and, in this instance, provides refractive index, requiring one to calculate speed:

$$n = \frac{c}{v}$$

$$1.46 = \frac{3 \times 10^8 \, \text{m/s}}{v}$$

$$v = \frac{3 \times 10^8 \, \text{m/s}}{1.46 \times 10^0 \, \text{m/s}} = \text{approx. } 2.05 \times 10^8 \, \text{m/s}$$

In most contexts, light is conceived of as a wave, but within the field of optics, it is best depicted as a **ray**. The sections and subsections that follow deal with optics, so light will be referred to as a ray.

Refraction and Reflection

Refraction refers to the phenomenon in which a light ray, on passing from one medium to another, bends, as shown in Figure 12.2.

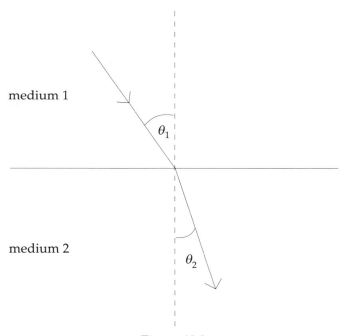

Figure 12.2

In Figure 12.2, the angles θ_1 and θ_2 represent the **angles of incidence** and **angles of refraction**, respectively.

Reflection refers to the phenomenon in which a light ray, while traveling through one medium, encounters another, and bounces, as shown below:

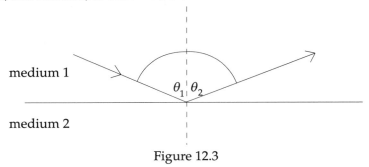

Figure 12.3

In Figure 12.3, θ_1 and θ_2 represent the angle of incidence and angle of reflection, respectively.

With respect to refraction, the angles of incidence and refraction are related by **Snell's law,** which provides that for each such angle, there is equality between the product:

$$\sin \theta \times \text{index of refraction}$$

Thus,

$$n_1 \sin \theta_1 = n_2 \sin \theta_2$$

where:

n_1 is the index of refraction for medium 1,

n_2 is the index of refraction for medium 2,

θ_1 is the angle of incidence, and

θ_2 is the angle of refraction.

With respect to reflection, the angles of incidence and reflection are equal.

The angles of incidence, refraction, and reflection are all measured by reference to an imaginary line oriented perpendicular to the medium interface.

Please solve this problem:

- A light ray travels through a first medium and, on encountering a second, is reflected so that it makes an angle of 75° with the interface between the two media. What is the associated angle of incidence?

Problem solved:

The 75° angle to which the problem refers is made between the reflected ray and the interface between the two media. It is not the angle of reflection. Rather the angle of reflection falls between the reflected ray and a line that runs perpendicular to the interface. The angle of reflection is complementary to the 75° angle mentioned in the problem:

$$90° - 75° = \text{angle of reflection} = 15°$$

Please solve this problem:

- A light ray traveling through a medium encounters a second medium, forming an angle of 60° with the interface between the two media. If the first medium has a refractive index of R_1 and the second, a refractive index of R_2, which of the following expressions best characterizes θ_2, the angle of refraction (sin 30° = 0.5; sin 60° = 0.867)?

  A. $\arccos (0.867) \times \dfrac{R_1}{R_2}$

  B. $\arccos (R_1)(R_2) (0.867)$

  C. $\arcsin (90 - 60) (R_2)$

  D. $\arcsin \dfrac{R_1}{2R_2}$

Problem solved:

D is correct. The 60° angle to which the problem refers does not constitute the angle of incidence, as it is formed by the media interface and the incident light ray. The angle of incidence is equal to the difference between that angle and 90°, as shown in Figure 12.4:

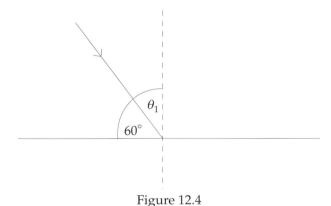

Figure 12.4

The angle of incidence, then, is 90° − 60° = 30°. The sin of 30° is 0.5. Using Snell's law:

$$n_1 \sin \theta_1 = n_2 \sin \theta_2 \quad R_1(0.5) = R_2 \sin \theta_2 \quad \frac{(0.5)(R_1)}{R_2} = \sin \theta_2$$

$$\left(\frac{1}{2}\right) \times \left[\frac{(R_1)}{R_2}\right] = \sin \theta_2 \quad \frac{(R_1)}{2(R_2)} = \sin \theta_2$$

$$\theta_2 = \arcsin \frac{(R_1)}{2(R_2)}$$

TOTAL INTERNAL REFLECTION AND THE CRITICAL ANGLE

Total internal reflection refers to a ray of light that travels through a medium and encounters a second medium with a lower index of refraction than the first. If the angle between the incident ray and the line perpendicular to the interface exceeds the **critical angle** (θ_{cr}), all of the incident light will be reflected back into the first medium.

Total internal reflection is depicted qualitatively in Figure 12.5, which shows three light rays, 1, 2, and 3, emanating from a source located within medium A, each approaching an interface with medium B. Ray 1 reaches the interface and is refracted. (If the angle of incidence were known, the angle of refraction could be calculated, as already demonstrated, through application of Snell's law.) Ray 2 strikes the interface and forms with the perpendicular an angle that is equal to the critical angle (θ_{cr}) for these two media. The consequent refraction causes the ray to run parallel to the interface and hence make a 90° angle with the perpendicular, as shown. Ray 3 strikes the interface at an angle that exceeds the critical angle, and the consequence is total internal reflection, as shown:

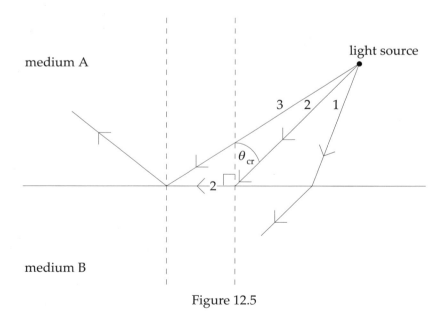

Figure 12.5

The quantitative aspects of total internal reflection pertain to the evaluation of the critical angle for any two interfaces, and are calculated with a modification of Snell's law, with the angle of refraction equal to 90° (its sin is set to 1):

$$\sin \theta_{cr} = \frac{n_b}{n_a}$$

where:

θ_{cr} is the critical angle that applies to the two media in question,

n_b is the index of refraction for the second medium, and

n_a is the index of refraction for the first medium.

MIRRORS: CONVEX AND CONCAVE

In the area of **optics**, a variety of fundamental tenets are associated with mirrors. Recall that mirrors may be **flat** or **spherical** and that spherical mirrors in turn may be **convex** or **concave**. A convex mirror is one whose exposed surface curves outward toward incoming light rays, and a concave mirror is one whose exposed surface curves inward toward incoming light rays, as shown in Figure 12.6:

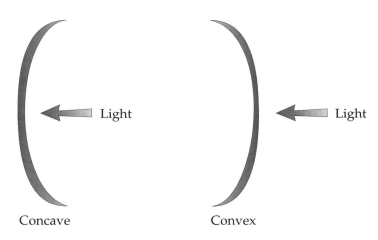

Figure 12.6

Focal Length of a Mirror

All spherical mirrors feature a **focal length,** at the end of which sits a **focal point**. The focal length is equal to one-half the mirror's radius of curvature:

$$f = \frac{1}{2}R_c$$

where:

f = focal length, and

R_c = mirror's radius of curvature.

For a convex mirror, the focal length extends into the mirror, and the focal point is said to be located behind it. For a concave mirror, the focal length is directed away from the mirror, and the focal point is said to be located in front of it. That is, with respect to an observer who faces the surface of a convex mirror, the side on which he stands is opposite to that on which the focal point is located. With respect to an observer who faces the surface of a concave mirror, the side on which he stands is the same as that on which the focal point is located.

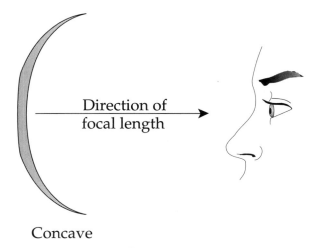

Concave

Figure 12.7

By convention, when the focal point is located behind a mirror, its associated focal length is given a negative (–) sign. When the focal point is located in front of a mirror, its associated focal length is assigned a positive (+) sign. Thus, for convex mirrors, focal length is negative; for concave mirrors, it is positive.

Please solve this problem:

- A concave mirror has a radius of curvature equal to 40 centimeters. Identify the location of its focal point in terms of distance and sign.

Problem solved:

The mirror is concave, and its focal point is located in front of the mirror, which gives it a positive sign. Absolute value of focal length is easily calculated with the above equation:

$$f = \frac{1}{2}R_c = \frac{40 \text{ cm}}{2} = 20 \text{ cm}$$

The focal length is +20 centimeters.

Please solve this problem:

- A convex mirror has a radius of curvature equal to 162 centimeters. Identify the location of its focal point in terms of distance and sign.

Problem solved:

The problem is analogous to the previous one, but involves a convex mirror. The focal length is directed into the mirror, and the focal point therefore carries a (–) sign. The absolute value of the focal length is equal to:

$$f = \frac{1}{2}R_c = \frac{162 \text{ cm}}{2} = 81 \text{ cm}$$

The focal point is located –81 centimeters from the mirror.

Conformation, Orientation, Location, and Magnification of Mirror Images

The location of a mirror's focal point is not necessarily the location of the image the mirror produces. Rather, the position of a mirror image produced by some object is determined by the **thin lens equation**, which, despite its name, applies to mirrors (as well as to lenses, which will be discussed in subsequent subsections):

$$\frac{1}{f} = \frac{1}{o} + \frac{1}{i}$$

where:

f is the mirror's focal length,

o is the distance of the object from the mirror, and

i is the distance of the image from the mirror.

Although a concave mirror has its focal point located in front of the mirror, it may produce images behind the mirror.

One should be familiar with the distinction between **real** and **virtual** images. A mirror image that is located behind a mirror—which means that it is visible in the mirror—is termed *virtual*. A mirror image that is located in front of the mirror—which means that it cannot be seen in the mirror but rather on a screen held in front of the mirror—is termed *real*. In addition, the signs (+) and (–) are assigned to the location of mirror images as they are assigned to the location of focal points: An image located behind a mirror carries a negative (–) sign, and an image located in front of a mirror carries a positive (+) sign.

Any virtual mirror image is **upright**, and any real image is **inverted**. The association of *real* with *inverted* and *virtual* with *upright* is somewhat counterintuitive, as one might expect that a real image should more accurately reproduce an object. For this reason, take special care not to be confused by terminology. Make these associations:

Mirror Image Location	Real/Virtual	Orientation	Sign
behind mirror	virtual	upright	(–)
in front of mirror	real	inverted	(+)

Table 12.1

Please solve this problem:

- A convex mirror has a radius of curvature equal to 80 centimeters, and an object is situated 20 centimeters in front of it. Identify the location of the resulting image in terms of distance and sign.

Problem solved:

First, determine the absolute value of the focal length according to the simple equation $f = \frac{1}{2}(Rc)$. The absolute value is 40 centimeters. The mirror is convex, and its focal point is located behind it. The focal length carries a negative (–) sign. Focal length = –40 centimeters. Next, apply the thin lens equation set forth above to locate the mirror image:

$$\frac{1}{f} = \frac{1}{o} + \frac{1}{i}$$

$$\frac{1}{-40 \text{ cm}} = \frac{1}{20 \text{ cm}} + \frac{1}{i}$$

$$\frac{-1}{40 \text{ cm}} - \frac{1}{20 \text{ cm}} = \frac{1}{i}$$

$$\frac{1}{i} = \frac{-1}{40 \text{ cm}} - \frac{2}{40 \text{ cm}}$$

$$\frac{1}{i} = \frac{-3}{40 \text{ cm}}$$

$$i = \frac{-40 \text{ cm}}{3} = \text{approx. } -13.33 \text{ cm}$$

The negative sign indicates that the image is behind the mirror and thus virtual and upright.

Spherical mirrors may produce **magnification,** and the size of an image may therefore vary from the size of the object that generates it. Magnification is a dimensionless quantity, and for any object and mirror, it is equal to the fraction:

$$- \frac{\text{distance of image from mirror}}{\text{distance of object from mirror}}$$

The distance is taken in terms of its absolute value, so the sign is ignored:

$$m = \frac{-i}{o}$$

where:

i = distance of image from mirror, and

o = distance of object from mirror.

Please solve this problem:

- A convex mirror has a radius of curvature equal to 60 centimeters, and a 20-centimeter object is positioned 15 centimeters in front of it. Determine the size of the image that results.

Problem solved:

First, calculate i, the distance of the image from the mirror. You make that calculation, as before, by first ascertaining the relevant focal length. Its absolute value is equal to $\frac{1}{2}(R_c) = \frac{60}{2} = 30$ cm. The mirror is convex, and the focal length carries a negative (–) sign; focal length = –30 cm. The value for i is then calculated by the thin lens equation:

$$\frac{1}{f} = \frac{1}{o} + \frac{1}{i}$$

$$\frac{1}{-30 \text{ cm}} = \frac{1}{15 \text{ cm}} + \frac{1}{i}$$

$$\frac{-1}{30 \text{ cm}} - \frac{1}{15 \text{ cm}} = \frac{1}{i}$$

$$\frac{-1}{30 \text{ cm}} - \frac{2}{30 \text{ cm}} = \frac{1}{i}$$

$$\frac{1}{i} = \frac{-3}{30 \text{ cm}}$$

$$i = \frac{-30 \text{ cm}}{3} = -10 \text{ cm}$$

The magnification is calculated by the equation:

$$m = \frac{-i}{o}$$

$$= \frac{10 \text{ cm}}{15 \text{ cm}} = 0.67$$

Since the object's true size is 20 centimeters, the mirror image will have size equal to:

$$(0.67)(20) = 13.4 \text{ cm}$$

A negative magnification would indicate an inverted image.

LENSES

Converging and Diverging Lenses

A **lens** is a structure with two refracting surfaces. **Thin lenses** are lenses for which the two refractory surfaces are so closely spaced as to render the intervening space optically negligible. All matters discussed in sections and subsections to follow concern thin lenses.

Lenses may be **converging** or **diverging;** each term refers to the effect of the given lens on light rays that pass through it. Converging lenses produce the convergence of rays toward the lens's central axis. Diverging lenses produce the divergence of rays away from the central axis. As shown in Figure 12.8, convergence corresponds to convexity, and divergence, to concavity. Lens A is convex and converging. Lens B is concave and diverging.

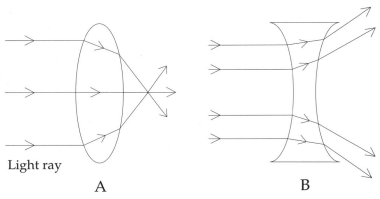

Figure 12.8

Like mirrors, every lens, converging or diverging, is associated with a **focal length**, the terminus of which represents the **focal point**. For a converging lens, the focal point is that point at which parallel rays traversing the lens will come together through refraction. For a diverging lens, the focal point represents that point at which parallel rays that have traversed the lens, and so have been subjected to divergence, will meet by hypothetical linear extension in the reverse direction.

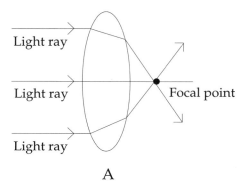

A

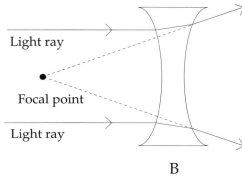

B

Figure 12.9

Light rays emanating from a common source diverge in all directions. If a lens is very close to the source, light rays will remain markedly divergent at the time they reach it. The closer the lens is to the source, the greater the divergence at the time the rays reach the lens. If a lens is removed some distance from a source, many of the rays that reach it will miss the path in which it stands. Moreover, those rays that do reach it will show a markedly reduced degree of divergence.

Figure 12.10 illustrates the point.

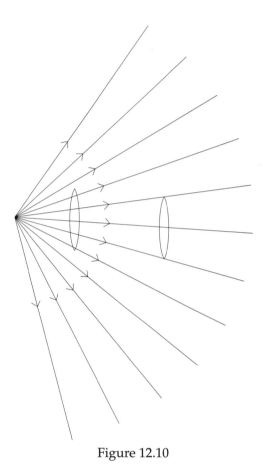

Figure 12.10

A source of light is shown at the left, emitting widely divergent rays. If a lens is positioned some small distance away from the source, many widely divergent light rays reach it. (The lens's tendency to refract the rays is not illustrated, so the status of the rays in the absence of the lens might be understood at a more distant position, where a second lens is positioned.) If a lens is placed at a considerable distance from the light source, most of the emitted rays miss its path. Those rays that do reach the lens show relatively small divergence and are considered parallel (although some divergence is evident).

The side from which light approaches a lens is considered the **front**. If an object is subjected to light, then the object itself constitutes a source of light. Consequently, when an object is viewed through a lens, the object serves as a source of light and is said to be at the front of the lens. Divergent lenses have their focal points located at the front, and convergent lenses, at the back.

Through the **lensmaker's equation**, the focal length of a lens is determined through (a) the refractive index that applies to the material of which the lens is made and (b) the radius of curvature associated with each side of the lens. For each side of a lens, radius of curvature represents the radius of a circle that would be completed if the curve were extended to suggest the circle of which it is a part, as shown in Figure 12.11.

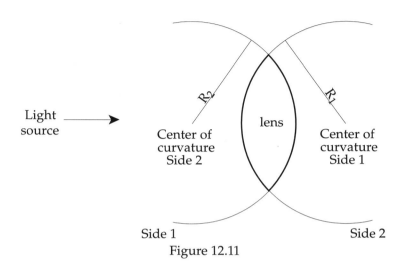

Figure 12.11

The designation "side 1" is assigned to the first of the lens surfaces to be struck by incident light (the "incoming side"), and the designation "side 2" is assigned to the second surface (the outgoing side). In the foregoing illustration, the light source is positioned to the left, which means that the left surface of the lens is side 1 and the right surface is side 2. Had the light source been positioned to the right, the right surface would be side 1 and the left surface, side 2. The lensmaker's equation provides that:

$$\frac{1}{f} = (n-1)\left(\frac{1}{R_1} - \frac{1}{R_2}\right)$$

where:

f is focal length,

n is refractive index of the lens material,

R_1 is the radius of curvature for side 1, and

R_2 is the radius of curvature for side 2.

Each radius of curvature R_1 and R_2 is associated with a sign, positive (+) or negative (–), in accordance with this rule: *With reference to the movement of light, the curved surface whose center of curvature is on the outgoing side has a positive (+) sign, and the side whose center of curvature is on the incoming side has a negative (–) sign.*

If, as shown in Figure 12.11, light travels from left to right through a convex lens, the left side is side 1, and side 1 has its center of curvature on the outgoing side—the right side. R_1, therefore, is positive (+). Side 2 has its center of curvature on the incoming side, and so R_2 is negative (–).

Please solve this problem:

- The left side of a convergent glass lens has a 20-centimeter radius of curvature, and the right side has a 5-centimeter radius of curvature. Assuming that the refractive index of glass is 1.5, find the focal length of the lens.

Problem solved:

If we imagine that light is incident from the right side, then side 1 is on the right, and $R_1 = 5$ centimeters. Side 2 is on the left, and $R_2 = 20$ centimeters. Since side 1 is on the right (and is convex), its center of curvature is on the left—the outgoing side—and it takes a positive sign, $R_1 = +5$ centimeters. R_2, then, with center of curvature on the incoming side, takes a negative (–) sign and is equal to –20 centimeters. Application of the lensmaker's equation yields:

$$\frac{1}{f} = (n-1)\left(\frac{1}{R_1} - \frac{1}{R_2}\right)$$

$$\frac{1}{f} = (1.5-1)\left(\frac{1}{5} - \frac{1}{-20}\right)$$

$$\frac{1}{f} = (0.5)\left(\frac{-4}{-20} - \frac{1}{-20}\right)$$

$$\frac{1}{f} = (0.5)\left(\frac{-5}{-20}\right)$$

$$\frac{1}{f} = (0.5)\frac{1}{4} \qquad \frac{1}{f} = \frac{1}{8}$$

$$f = 8.0 \text{ cm}$$

Conformation and Orientation of Images

Again, lenses are unlike mirrors because an image formed behind a lens is real and inverted. An image formed in front of a lens is virtual and upright.

You should memorize Table 12.2 so you are not confused about sign, focal point, and image orientation as they apply to mirrors, on the one hand, and lenses on the other.

	Type	Image	Focal Point
For Mirrors	concave	* in front: real, inverted	in front (+)
	convex	behind: virtual, upright	behind (–)

	Type	Image	Focal Point
For Lenses	diverging	in front: virtual, upright	in front (–)
	converging	* behind: real, inverted	behind (+)

Table 12.2

*For concave mirrors and converging lenses, objects placed within the focal distance will create a virtual, upright image.

It should be apparent that for mirrors and lenses alike, all real images are inverted and all virtual images are upright.

The location and magnification of an image produced by a lens are determined by the equations discussed in connection with mirrors. Keeping in mind the differences between lenses and mirrors as just discussed, you could locate a lens image by using the thin lens equation, $\frac{1}{f} = \frac{1}{o} + \frac{1}{i}$, and identify the magnification of an image by using the equation, $m = \frac{-i}{o}$.

Please solve this problem:

- A divergent glass lens has a focal length of 80 centimeters. A 40-centimeter object is held in front of it at a distance of 20 centimeters. Ascertain the location and size of the image, and determine whether it will be real, virtual, upright, or inverted.

Problem solved:

The absolute value of the lens's focal length is 80 centimeters; since the lens is divergent, the sign is negative (–). The focal length, therefore, is –80 centimeters. To locate the image, apply the equation:

$$\frac{1}{f} = \frac{1}{o} + \frac{1}{i}$$

$$\frac{-1}{80 \text{ cm}} = \frac{1}{20 \text{ cm}} + \frac{1}{i}$$

$$\frac{-1}{80 \text{ cm}} - \frac{1}{20 \text{ cm}} = \frac{1}{i}$$

$$\frac{-1}{80 \text{ cm}} - \frac{4}{80 \text{ cm}} = \frac{1}{i}$$

$$\frac{-5}{80 \text{ cm}} = \frac{1}{i}$$

$$i = \frac{-80}{5 \text{ cm}} = -16 \text{ cm}$$

The image is located at a position of –16 centimeters from the lens, which means it is 16 centimeters in front of the lens. Any image located in front of a lens is virtual and upright.

The size of the image is obtained by taking the product:

object size × magnification

Magnification is determined by the equation:

$$m = \frac{-i}{o} = \frac{-(-16) \text{ cm}}{20 \text{ cm}} = 0.8$$

$$(0.8) \times (40 \text{ cm}) = 32 \text{ cm}$$

Focal Power

Focal power, P, expresses the degree to which a lens imposes a convergence or divergence on the light rays that traverse it. The converging lens of relatively greater power produces greater convergence than does one of relatively lesser power; the diverging lens of relatively greater power produces greater divergence than does one of relatively lesser power.

Focal power is expressed in the unit **diopter**, and it is equal to the reciprocal of the focal length:

$$P = \frac{1}{f}$$

where:

P = focal power, and

f = focal length (expressed in meters).

Since the focal length associated with a diverging lens is negative (–), so is its power. Since the focal length associated with a converging lens is positive (+), so is its power.

- **Power of converging lens carries positive (+) sign**

- **Power of diverging lens carries negative (–) sign**

Please solve this problem:

- A lens brings parallel light rays to a focus, as shown below. Determine its focal power.

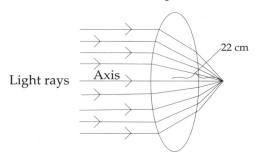

Figure 12.12

Problem solved:

The illustration reveals a convergent lens with a focal length of +22 centimeters. Expressed in meters, the focal length is +0.22 meters, and the focal power is:

$$\frac{1}{0.22}\text{diopters}$$

$$= \text{approx. } 4.5 \text{ diopters}$$

12.2 MASTERY APPLIED: PRACTICE PASSAGE AND QUESTIONS

Passage

The human eye mediates the sense of vision by focusing incoming light rays reflected from objects within the environment onto the retina. As indicated below, the necessary refractive power is attributable to several interfaces: between the air and the anterior surface of the cornea; between the posterior surface of the cornea and the aqueous humor; between the aqueous humor and the anterior surface of the lens; and between the posterior surface of the lens and the vitreous humor which, in turn, contacts the retina.

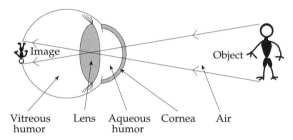

For optic analysis, all refractive components of the eye are summed algebraically to form a hypothetical construct called the *reduced eye*, in which the eye's refractory power is imagined to arise from a single lens located approximately 17 millimeters anterior to the retina and to have positive focal power of approximately 59 diopters in the absence of any effort to increase it by muscular activity. Of those 59 diopters, the eye's own lens proper provides only 15 diopters; the majority of refractory power arises from the anterior surface of the cornea.

The eye's lens proper is convex, and its principal importance lies in the adjustability of its focal power. Through muscular mechanisms, the individual may increase its convexity through a process known as *accommodation*. During childhood, for example, the individual may increase the lens's focal power from 15 diopters to 49 diopters. In middle and older age, the power of accommodation tends to diminish, and the average 55-year-old can perhaps accommodate to the extent of 2 diopters. A very aged individual will frequently lose power of accommodation entirely, a condition called *presbyopia*.

The lens is also susceptible to other deficiencies, among them a phenomenon termed *chromatic aberration*, illustrated below.

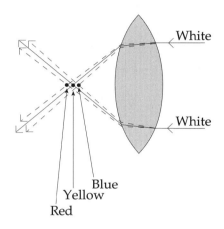

The condition arises from the fact that the lens's focal power varies slightly, depending on the color of the light passing through it.

Early investigators were at a loss to explain the fact that the individual with two eyes focused on an object sees a single image just as he does with one eye closed. The phenomenon of *fusion*, in which the individual sees one image with two eyes open, is mediated by centers within the brain.

1. Each choice in the figure below schematically represents light rays moving from an object toward a human eye. For which set of light rays would the human eye require the greatest degree of accommodation?

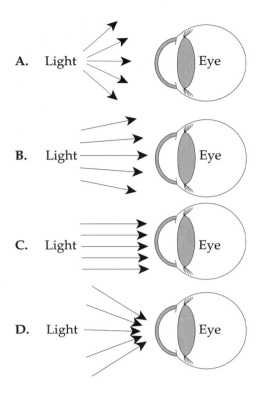

A.   Light
B.   Light
C.   Light
D.   Light

2. The image formed on the retina is most likely:

A. virtual and inverted.
B. virtual and upright.
C. real and inverted.
D. real and upright.

3. The condition of hypermetropia arises when the eye's refractory components have a focal point that falls behind the retina, as shown schematically below:

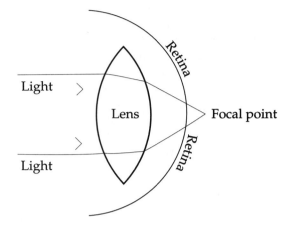

Among the following choices, the most effective corrective measure would probably be:

A. surgical adjustment of the retina's location so that it is moved forward.
B. obliteration of the eye's lens with laser technology.
C. a corrective lens with negative focal power.
D. a corrective lens with positive focal power.

4. A patient complains of blurred vision when viewing objects located in the distance, but reports visual clarity when viewing objects located close to his eye. A physician hypothesizes that the difficulty is attributable to a condition in which the right retina is located at an abnormally large distance from the anterior surface of the right eye. Which of the following findings would best confirm her hypothesis?

A. The patient reports improvement when a convex lens is placed in front of his right eye.

B. The patient reports improvement when a concave lens is placed in front of his right eye.

C. The patient reports improvement when he opens his eyes more widely.

D. The patient reports that he does not experience the symptom when either eye is closed and the other remains open.

5. Which of the following most probably explains the phenomenon of chromatic aberration?

A. The model of the "reduced eye" does not account for the fact of separate refractory components.

B. The eye cannot diffract white light into its component wavelengths.

C. The eye's refractory apparatus offers different focal power for different light wavelengths.

D. Different portions of the eye's retina vary in their degree of sensitivity to color.

12.3 MASTERY VERIFIED: ANSWERS AND EXPLANATIONS

1. **A is correct.** When the individual accommodates, he increases the convexity of his lens and so increases the degree to which his eye will produce convergence. The greater the divergence among incoming rays, the greater the eye's need to produce convergence in order that the rays be focused. The correct figure is the one that depicts the greatest degree of divergence among the incoming light rays.

2. **C is correct.** The image formed on the retina is a product of light traversing that which amounts to a converging lens. Any image formed behind a lens is real and inverted. (An image formed behind a mirror, on the other hand, is virtual and upright.) Moreover, all real images are inverted and all virtual images are upright. Choices A and D are clearly erroneous, for they refer to images that are virtual and inverted, and real and upright, respectively.

   If one chooses B, one may be working from some intuitive belief that the image formed on the retina should be upright, since human beings are not accustomed to seeing their surroundings in inverted terms. The fact that human beings do not perceive inverted images is a function of processing that occurs at the level of the brain—subsequent to the retina's receipt of an inverted image. As the passage indicates, the same is so for the phenomenon of fusion.

3. **D is correct.** As described and depicted in the question, hypermetropia indicates that the eye's refractory components give rise to a focal length that is too long to allow for focus on the retina. The theoretical solutions are to relocate the retina so that it is farther back (not farther forward as mentioned in choice A) or to decrease the combined focal length of the eye's refractory components. The latter solution would involve increasing the focal power of the sight system by (a) increasing the convexity of the eye's internal system or (b) supplementing the system with an artificial lens that is convex. Convex lenses have positive focal power.

4. **B is correct.** The patient is unable to focus objects in the distance, suggesting that as parallel light rays traverse the refractive components of his eye, they experience such convergence as produces a focal point anterior to the retina. Either one or both of his eyes has excessive focal power or his retina is located too far back.

   That the patient clearly sees objects located near to him tends to confirm the physician's hypothesis, since, as an object comes closer to a lens, the rays that emanate from it show increased divergence in relation to one another. For such rays, the focal point would be moved backward and might focus *on* the retina as they should.

   If the physician's hypothesis is correct—that in relation to the retina's location, parallel rays of light are focused too far forward—some improvement should accompany the placement of a concave lens in front of the eye. The lens would diverge the incoming light rays before they reached the eye, and would present the eye with rays that, in their divergence, resemble rays that come from objects situated close to it. If the placement of a concave lens brings improvement, the hypothesis is supported.

5. **C is correct.** The passage describes and illustrates chromatic aberration as a condition in which light may be focused at different points, depending on its color. Specifically, the passage states that, "The condition arises from the fact that the lens's focal power varies slightly depending on the color of the light passing through it." Variation of color is a function of variation of wavelength. As such, the statement in the passage becomes equivalent to: The condition arises from the fact that the lens's focal power varies slightly, depending on the wavelength of the light passing through it.

CHAPTER 13

ATOMS, ELEMENTS, AND THE PERIODIC TABLE

13.1 MASTERY ACHIEVED

ATOMIC MASS, ATOMIC WEIGHT, ISOTOPES, AND IONS

Atoms and Subatomic Particles

Chemistry is the study of matter. **Atoms** are the building blocks of all matter. Atoms are made up of **electrons**, **neutrons**, and **protons**. The center of an atom, called the atomic **nucleus**, contains protons and neutrons and is surrounded by a cloud of electrons. Some important properties of these three subatomic particles are summarized in Table 13.1.

PARTICLE	LOCATION	CHARGE	MASS	MCAT MASS
electron	outside nucleus	−1	$\frac{1}{1840}$ amu	zero
neutron	in nucleus	zero	$\frac{1856}{1840}$ amu	1 amu
proton	in nucleus	+1	$\frac{1853}{1840}$ amu	1 amu

Table 13.1

Amu stands for atomic mass unit. By convention, the most abundant isotope of carbon (carbon –12) is assigned a mass of exactly 12 atomic mass units, and the masses of all other atoms or subatomic particles are determined from this standard. Thus, 1 amu = 1.66×10^{-27} kg.

When representing an element by its one- or two-letter symbol, we can also include information about its numbers of electrons, neutrons, and protons:

$$^{N+Z}_{Z}X^{Z-E}$$

where N = number of neutrons,

Z = number of protons, and

E = number of electrons.

The number of protons is given in the subscript. This number is also known as the **atomic number (Z)** because the number of protons in an atom distinguishes one element from another. The number of protons plus the number of neutrons is given in the left superscript. Since the protons and neutrons are the major constituents of atomic mass (the electrons can be considered massless), this number is also known as the **mass number** (*A*). Unlike the atomic number, the mass number of the atoms of a particular element is not always the same. When two atoms of the same element differ in mass number (therefore, in their number of neutrons), these atoms are said to be **isotopes** of one another. Two isotopes of carbon are $^{12}_{6}C$ and $^{13}_{6}C$; the former contains six neutrons and the latter contains seven neutrons. Both contain six protons.

The right superscript of a chemical symbol is reserved for the number of protons minus the number of electrons. Since protons are positively charged and electrons are negatively charged, this difference tells us the net **charge** (*C*) on an atom. When the number of protons is equal to the number of electrons, the atom is neutral. All atoms in their elemental form are neutral. When the number of protons exceeds the number of electrons, the charge is positive, and we refer to the atom as being **electron deficient**. When the number of electrons exceeds the number of protons, the charge is negative, and we refer to the atom as **electron rich**. An electron-deficient atom has a positive charge and is referred to as a **cation**. An electron-rich atom has a negative charge and is referred to as an **anion**.

Please solve this problem:

- What is the charge on an aluminum atom that contains 10 total electrons?

Problem solved:

The charge on an aluminum atom that contains 10 total electrons is +3. We can determine this by referring to the periodic table (**Table 13.2**). The atomic number of aluminum is 13; therefore aluminum atoms contain 13 protons. This makes an aluminum atom with 10 electrons a cation, or an electron-deficient species. Its charge is 13 − 10 = +3.

Considering atomic number, mass number, and charge, we can also interpret an atomic symbol as:

$$^{A}_{Z}X^{C}$$

It is important to note that mass number is not equal to atomic weight. The **atomic weight** of an element is a weighted average of the mass numbers of all naturally occurring isotopes for that element. There are two isotopes that contribute to the atomic weight of chlorine: $^{35}_{17}Cl$ and $^{37}_{17}Cl$. In a sample of pure chlorine, approximately three-quarters of the atoms are the isotope with a mass number of 35, the remainder are the chlorine–37 isotope. By taking the weighted average, we can compute the atomic weight of chlorine as 35.453 atomic mass units.

Please solve this problem:

- A scientist is attempting to determine the accurate atomic mass of a sample of naturally occurring chlorine. Which of the following would introduce the most error into her measurements?

  A. Neglecting the mass of the electrons
  B. Neglecting the mass of the neutrons
  C. Neglecting the mass of the protons
  D. Neglecting the mass of the chlorine–36 isotope

Problem solved:

B is correct. We see from Table 13.1 that neutrons are slightly heavier than protons, which are substantially heavier than electrons. Neglecting the mass of the chlorine–36 isotope is an MCAT "trap" answer. While it appears to address the question at hand, it is factually incorrect, as the chlorine–36 isotope is not naturally occurring. You must be wary of such traps. If an MCAT answer sounds too complicated relative to the other three answer choices, or unrelated to the other three answer choices, it is probably wrong. In this case, you should recognize that choices A, B, and C all deal with subatomic particles while choice D does not.

THE PERIODIC TABLE

Mendeleev's Periodic Table

The first version of the periodic table of the elements was proposed in 1869 by the Russian scientist Dmitri Mendeleev. Since that time, the periodic table has become a permanent fixture in the science classrooms of the world. A periodic table is presented below. (As of 2003, laboratory synthesis has expanded the known elements so that there is an element with an atomic number as high as 118. However, for MCAT purposes, only the elements set forth on the classic periodic table [**Table 13.2**] are relevant.)

PERIODIC CHART OF THE ELEMENTS

1 H 1.0																	2 He 4.0
3 Li 6.9	4 Be 9.0											5 B 10.8	6 C 12.0	7 N 14.0	8 O 16.0	9 F 19.0	10 Ne 20.2
11 Na 23.0	12 Mg 24.3											13 Al 27.0	14 Si 28.1	15 P 31.0	16 S 32.1	17 Cl 35.5	18 Ar 39.9
19 K 39.1	20 Ca 40.1	21 Sc 45.0	22 Ti 47.9	23 V 50.9	24 Cr 52.0	25 Mn 54.9	26 Fe 55.8	27 Co 58.9	28 Ni 58.7	29 Cu 63.5	30 Zn 65.4	31 Ga 69.7	32 Ge 72.6	33 As 74.9	34 Se 79.0	35 Br 79.9	36 Kr 83.8
37 Rb 85.5	38 Sr 87.6	39 Y 88.9	40 Zr 91.2	41 Nb 92.9	42 Mo 95.9	43 Tc (98)	44 Ru 101.1	45 Rh 102.9	46 Pd 106.4	47 Ag 107.9	48 Cd 112.4	49 In 114.8	50 Sn 118.7	51 Sb 121.8	52 Te 127.6	53 I 126.9	54 Xe 131.3
55 Cs 132.9	56 Ba 137.3	57 La 138.9	72 Hf 178.5	73 Ta 180.9	74 W 183.9	75 Re 186.2	76 Os 190.2	77 Ir 192.2	78 Pt 195.1	79 Au 197.0	80 Hg 200.6	81 Tl 204.4	82 Pb 207.2	83 Bi 209.0	84 Po 209.0	85 At 210.0	86 Rn 222.0
87 Fr 223.0	88 Ra 226.0	89 Ac 227.0															

Lanthanum Series

Ce 140.1	59 Pr 140.9	60 Nd 144.2	61 Pm 145.0	62 Sm 150.4	63 Eu 152.0	64 Gd 157.3	65 Tb 158.9	66 Dy 162.5	67 Ho 164.9	68 Er 167.3	69 Tm 168.9	70 Yb 173.0	71 Lu 175.0

Actinium Series

Th 232.0	91 Pa 231.0	92 U 238.0	93 Np 237.0	94 Pu (244)	95 Am (243)	96 Cm (247)	97 Bk (247)	98 Cf (251)	99 Es (252)	100 Fm (258)	101 Md (258)	102 No (259)	103 Lr (260)

Table 13.2

Each element is represented by its one- or two-letter chemical symbol. Above each chemical symbol is the atomic number (number of protons) for that element. Below each chemical symbol is that element's atomic weight. There is no need for you to memorize the periodic table for the MCAT because both the Biological Sciences section and the Physical Sciences section of the exam will include a periodic table inside the front cover for your use. However, it may serve you well to be familiar with the location of the more popular elements: H, Li, C, N, O, F, Na, Mg, P, S, Cl, K, Ca, Fe, Cu, Br, Ag, and I.

Periods and Groups

Each horizontal row in the periodic table is called a **period**. The outermost electrons of every atom in a period have the same principal quantum number, or shell number. Each vertical column in the periodic table is called a **group**. Every member of a group has the same number of valence electrons and may be expected to have similar chemical properties to other members of the group. In addition to the designation of groups, we can designate blocks of the periodic table. The blocks are designated by the letter that corresponds to the subshell presently being filled. The two rows farthest to the left (and He) are designated the *s* block, the next ten rows the *d* block, the six rows farthest to the right are designated the *p* block, and the actinides and lanthanides are designated the *f* block.

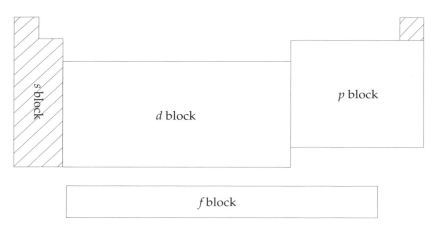

Figure 13.1

QUANTUM NUMBERS AND THE AUFBAU PRINCIPLE

Quantum numbers are used to designate the "address" of each electron within an individual atom. The first, or principal, quantum number refers to the **shell**. The second, or azimuthal, quantum number refers to the **subshell**. The third, or magnetic, quantum number refers to the **orbital**. And, the fourth, or spin, quantum number refers to the **electron spin**. Each of these four concepts is explored in detail below.

The Principal Quantum Number (Shell)

In the broadest sense, the address of an electron is given by the **shell** in which it resides. A shell is equivalent to a row in the periodic table. The principal quantum number is designated n and can take the value of any positive integer. The currently known elements require the use of $n = 1$ through $n = 7$. A low principal quantum number indicates electrons that are close to the nucleus. As n increases, the size of the shell also increases. Shells that are entirely filled with electrons are termed **core shells,** or **inner shells,** and the electrons within them are **core electrons**, also known as **inner shell electrons**. Shells that are only partially full are called **valence shells**. The electrons within these shells are called **valence electrons**. The valence electrons are the focus of most chemists; these electrons impart most of the atom's chemical properties.

The Azimuthal Quantum Number (Subshell)

Subordinate to n, the principal quantum number is the second quantum number, ℓ, which designates a **subshell** within a particular shell and can take any integral value from zero to $n - 1$. So if $n = 2$, then $\ell = 0$ or $\ell = 1$. Each value of ℓ corresponds to a particular subshell, so there are two subshells ($\ell = 1$ and $\ell = 0$) in the second ($n = 2$) shell. (There are n subshells in the nth shell.) At present, all known elements are accommodated by $\ell = 0, 1, 2,$ or 3. Subshells are so important in the study of chemistry that they are also labeled by a lettering system:

$$
\begin{array}{ccccc}
\ell & 0 & 1 & 2 & 3 \\
letter & s & p & d & f
\end{array}
$$

These letter designations also correspond to the blocks in the periodic table (**Table 13.2**).

The Magnetic Quantum Number (Orbital)

Subordinate to the azimuthal quantum number is the magnetic quantum number, m_ℓ, which designates an **orbital** within a particular subshell. An orbital is the region surrounding an atom's nucleus where an electron is most likely to be. The possible values of m_ℓ are any integral value from $-\ell$ to $+\ell$, including zero. Therefore, there are $2\ell + 1$ orbitals in the ℓ subshell.

For example, when $\ell = 1$, the values of m_ℓ are $-1, 0,$ and 1. Each value of m_ℓ corresponds to an orbital. From this, we can see that per shell, there is only one orbital in the s ($\ell = 0$) subshell:

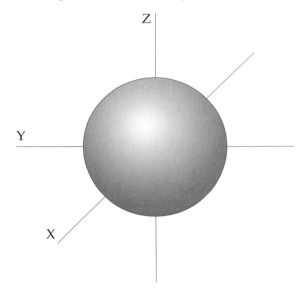

Figure 13.2

Three p ($\ell = 1$) orbitals:

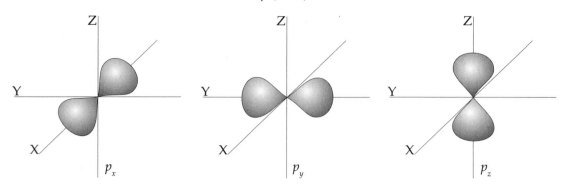

Figure 13.3

Five d ($\ell = 2$) orbitals:

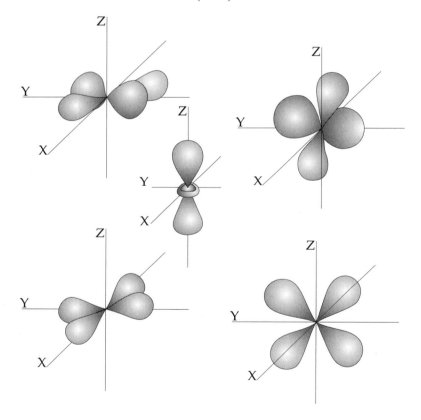

Figure 13.4

There are seven f ($\ell = 3$) orbitals, the shapes of which are similar to the shapes of the d orbitals. The f orbital shapes will not be important on the MCAT.

The Spin Quantum Number (Electron Spin State)

The first three quantum numbers are derived from theory. The fourth quantum number, m_s, is experimentally derived and designates the **spin** state of a particular electron within a particular orbital. There are two possible values of m_s: $+\frac{1}{2}$ and $-\frac{1}{2}$.

Tabular Summary of Quantum Numbers

Symbol and Name	Possible Values	Related Quantities
n shell	{positive integers}	
ℓ subshell	{0, 1, 2, ..., $n-1$}	n subshells per shell
m_ℓ orbital	{$-\ell$, ..., 0, ..., $+\ell$ }	$2\ell + 1$ orbitals per subshell, n^2 orbitals per shell
m_s electron spin	{$+\frac{1}{2}$, $-\frac{1}{2}$ }	2 electrons per orbital, $4\ell + 2$ electrons per subshell, $2n^2$ electrons per shell

Table 13.3

The Pauli Exclusion Principle and Hund's Rule

According to the **Pauli exclusion principle**, no electron in any one atom may have all four quantum numbers identical to another electron in the same atom. Electrons will always be added to the lowest available energy level (as defined by the four quantum numbers). While it is possible to have two electrons with the same n, ℓ, and m_ℓ, these two electrons must differ in m_s. Two electrons that differ only in spin quantum number are said to be spin paired. Spin-paired electrons share an orbital within a subshell of a particular shell in the same atom. **Hund's rule** states that no two electrons will become spin paired unless there are no empty orbitals at the energy level of the orbitals that are presently being filled. To illustrate this, consider the three $2p$ orbitals of carbon. Each of these orbitals has the same energy as the other two orbitals. When orbitals have identical energies, they are called **degenerate orbitals**. Applying Hund's rule, you should recognize that when filling the $2p$ subshell, one electron goes first into each of the three p orbitals; it is not until a fourth electron is placed into a p orbital that spin pairing would occur in the $2p$ subshell of carbon.

When an atom contains only electrons that are spin paired, that atom is **diamagnetic**. When an atom contains one or more electrons that are not spin paired, that atom is **paramagnetic**. You should recognize that an atom that contains an odd number of electrons is, by necessity, paramagnetic; however, an atom that contains an even number of electrons may be either diamagnetic or paramagnetic.

The Aufbau Principle and Electron Configuration

In order to determine the electron configuration of a particular atom, you need to understand the **aufbau principle**, or "building-up" principle. Electrons are placed into orbitals from lowest energy orbital to highest energy orbital. The aufbau principle is summarized by:

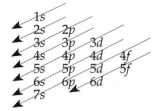

Figure 13.5

Orbitals are filled in the order $1s$, $2s$, $2p$, $3s$, $3p$, $4s$, $3d$, $4p$, $5s$, $4d$, $5p$, $6s$, $4f$, $5d$, $6p$, $7s$, $5f$, $6d$ as indicated by the arrows in the figure. In order to determine the lowest possible electron configuration for an atom, you should determine the number of electrons to be put into orbitals (equal to the atomic number for neutral atoms), and use Figure 13.6:

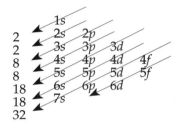

Figure 13.6

Consider vanadium (Z = 23). Its electron configuration must end somewhere in the fifth arrow (2 + 2 + 8 + 8 = 20 and 2 + 2 + 8 + 8 + 18 = 38). The electron configuration is therefore: $1s^22s^22p^63s^23p^64s^23d^3$ (and notice that the sum of the superscripts gives the electron total of the atom). You should be aware that the electron configuration just determined for vanadium is the **ground state** configuration. Any other configuration that contains 23 electrons and does not violate the filling rules (e.g., by putting more than 6 electrons in a p subshell) is an **excited state** electron configuration for vanadium. It is often an excited state configuration that is asked for when electron configuration questions are given on the MCAT.

Please solve this problem:

- Which of the following represents a possible electron configuration of a neutral magnesium atom?

    A. $1s^22s^22p^8$
    B. $1s^22s^22p^6$
    C. $2s^22p^63d^4$
    D. $1s^22s^12p^6$

Problem solved:

C is correct. First, any configurations that do not contain twelve electrons should be eliminated, since the atomic number of magnesium is twelve. This eliminates choices B and D. Next, configurations that violate filling rules should be eliminated. Choice A is an invalid configuration, since the *p* subshell can only contain six electrons. This leaves only choice C. While choice C is not the ground state electron configuration of magnesium, it is still a *possible* electron configuration for magnesium. Choice A is invalid. Choice B is the ground state electron configuration of neon or an **isoelectronic** ion to neon (that is, one that contains the same number of electrons as neon). For example, Mg^{+2}, Na^{+1}, F^{-1}, O^{-2}, and N^{-3} would all be isoelectronic to neon and each other. Choice D is a non-ground state electron configuration (excited state) of fluorine or an ion isoelectronic to fluorine.

Periodic Trends

There are five periodic trends that are governed by electron configuration: **electro-negativity**, **atomic radius**, **ionization energy**, **metallic character**, and **electron affinity**. Here is a mnemonic device that should help you remember this. Those trends that contain a word beginning with the letter "e" increase from left to right across the periodic table and from bottom to top; those trends that do not contain a word beginning with the letter "e" do the opposite and increase from right to left and from top to bottom. This is illustrated in Figure 13.7.

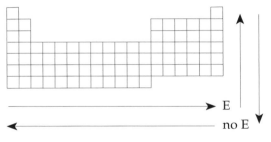

Figure 13.7

Electronegativity can be thought of as the affinity of a particular atom for electrons when that atom is engaged in a chemical bond. Electronegativity is not a directly measurable quantity. The most electronegative atom, fluorine, is assigned an electronegativity of 4.0. The most electropositive (therefore, least electronegative) atom, francium, is assigned an electronegativity of 0.7. Since the noble gases rarely form chemical bonds, they are not included in electronegativity tables. Any two atoms with an electronegativity difference equal to or *greater than 1.7* are said to **bond ionically**. Any two bound atoms with an electronegativity difference *less than 1.7,* but not equal to 0, are said to be involved in a **polar covalent bond**. A **nonpolar covalent bond** can only occur between atoms of nearly **identical electronegativity**—that is, this case can only occur when the two bound atoms are atoms of the same element. In an ionic, or polar covalent bond, the electrons forming the bond spend more time close to the atom with the greater electronegativity.

Atomic radius decreases from left to right within a period. While this may seem counter-intuitive, since the number of electrons within a shell increases from left to right within a period, it is due to the fact that there is an increasing number of protons in the nucleus while the amount of shielding exerted by the core shells remains constant. Therefore, the valence electrons are more strongly attracted to the nucleus and spend more time closer to it. As more shells are added, the electron cloud does get larger; therefore, atomic radius increases from the top of the periodic table to the bottom.

Ionization energy is that energy necessary to release the outermost electron from an atom. Ionization energy generally increases from left to right across a period. As atoms decrease in size (remember that shells *contract* as protons more strongly attract the valence electrons), the valence electrons become more strongly attracted to the nucleus, and more energy is required to liberate an electron.

Metallic character refers to the ease with which an atom loses valence electrons. Atoms with low ionization energies are strongly metallic. Conversely, as ionization energy increases, metallic character decreases.

Electron affinity is the tendency of an atom to gain an additional electron. An atom that would move closer to the electron configuration of a noble gas by gaining an electron is more likely to do so than an atom that would move away from the nearest noble gas electron configuration by picking up an electron.

Group Names

Certain columns within the periodic table are assigned group names, and there are two systems of naming the groups. The current system, used by contemporary chemists, is fairly straightforward; the older system, which is still at times used by MCAT writers, is slightly less straightforward. In the newer system, groups are numbered sequentially from 1 to 18 from left to right:

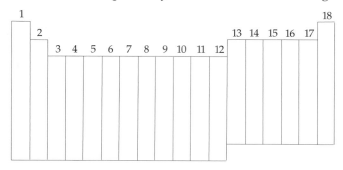

Figure 13.8

In the older (MCAT) system, the groups are numbered I through VIII and denoted as either "A" or "B." All "A" groups are in the *s* and *p* blocks, all "B" groups are in the *d* block:

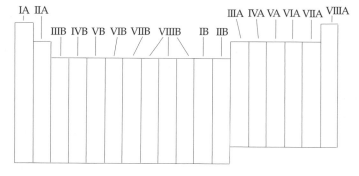

Figure 13.9

In addition to the system of group numbers, certain groups have common names. Group IA represents the **alkali metals**. Group IIA constitutes the **alkaline earth metals**. Group VIIA represents the **halogens**. Group VIIIA represents the **noble gases**. Groups IA, IIA, and IIIA–VIIIA are the **representative elements**, or **main block elements** (which include the noble gases and halogens). Groups IB–VIIIB are the **transition metals**. The **actinides,** with atomic numbers greater than 92, are called the **transuranium elements**. Elements of the same group generally share certain fundamental chemical properties.

THE ATOM IN MODERN PERSPECTIVE

With the advent of **quantum mechanics**, our understanding of the atom has changed dramatically. An important precursor to the field of quantum mechanics was the atomic theory of Max Planck. According to Planck, electrons are able to exist only at discrete energy levels. In fact, energy itself can occur only in discrete units. These discrete units of energy are called **quanta**. Planck theorized that electrons are able to move from one energy level to the next only when they are given enough energy to jump to that level; an electron cannot absorb an excess of energy that is not sufficient for a transition to a higher energy level. This is summarized by the equation:

$$\Delta E = hf$$

where ΔE is the difference in energy between two allowed energy levels for an electron, h is Planck's constant, and f is the frequency of the electromagnetic radiation used to increase the energy of the electron. Each allowable energy level is therefore separated by a quanta of energy, hf. Since (wavelength)(frequency) = velocity, and electromagnetic radiation travels at the speed of light (c), we can arrive at the equation $\mathbf{c} = \lambda f$, where λ is the wavelength of the electromagnetic radiation.

Substituting for f, the quantum equation becomes:

$$\Delta E = h\frac{c}{\lambda}$$

The Bohr Theory of the Atom and the Heisenberg Uncertainty Principle

Using the work of Planck, Niels Bohr theorized that if electrons are confined to discrete energy levels, then electrons must travel in spherical orbits around the nucleus at distances corresponding to these energy levels. This is known as the **Bohr theory of the atom**. While it has since been supplanted, it remains a convenient method for visualizing the atom.

Utilizing the Schrödinger wave equation, Werner Heisenberg determined that it is impossible to simultaneously determine both the position and the momentum of an electron. This is known as the **Heisenberg uncertainty principle**, and is mathematically stated:

$$\partial p \partial x \geq \frac{h}{4\pi}$$

where ∂p is the uncertainty in momentum and ∂x is the uncertainty in displacement (position). Heisenberg showed that an electron's location in space at any given time may be determined with certainty only at the expense of the determination of its momentum at that instant. Since it is theoretically impossible to determine both of these variables simultaneously, we cannot assume that electrons travel in spherical orbits. (Using simple geometry, both the position and momentum are absolutely determinable at all times for an electron traveling in a spherical orbit.) Application of the Heisenberg uncertainty principle and the Schrödinger wave equation gives rise to **probability density orbitals** (pictured in Figure 13.3 and Figure 13.4). These orbitals are usually pictured at the 90-percent confidence level, which is to say that "I am 90 percent sure that the electron is somewhere within this 'balloon' at any moment in time."

The de Broglie Hypothesis

In 1924, Louis de Broglie posited that any particle traveling with a momentum p should have a wavelength:

$$\lambda = \frac{h}{p}$$

Since $p = mv$, we may also write this equation as:

$$\lambda = \frac{h}{mv}$$

The significance of the **de Broglie hypothesis** is that not only do wave phenomena, like light, have particle characteristics but that the converse is true as well: Moving particles exhibit wave characteristics.

Nuclear Chemistry and Radioactivity

Atoms seek to have a balance between protons and neutrons in their nuclei. For relatively light nuclei, a neutron-to-proton ratio of one to one will tend to be stable. For heavier nuclei, a neutron-to-proton ratio as high as 1.5 to 1 may be needed to confer ideal stablity. If an isotope has too many neutrons relative to protons, it may seek either to shed some of those neutrons or to convert some of those neutrons to protons. Likewise, if an isotope has too many protons, it may seek either to shed a proton or convert a proton to a neutron. These and related processes are collectively known as **radioactive decay**.

THE IMPORTANT RADIOACTIVE DECAY PROCESSES

If an isotope is unstable simply because of its nuclear size, it will often seek to shed both neutrons and protons in the process of **alpha decay**. An alpha particle is a helium ion, $_2^4\alpha$ or $_2^4\text{He}^{2+}$. An example of alpha decay is:

$$_{84}^{210}\text{Po} \rightarrow {}_2^4\alpha + {}_{82}^{206}\text{Pb}$$

If an isotope has too many neutrons, it may seek to convert a neutron to a proton via **beta decay**. A beta particle is an electron and can be represented as $_{-1}^{0}\beta$ or as $_{-1}^{0}\text{e}$. An example of beta decay is:

$$_{82}^{210}\text{Po} \rightarrow {}_{-1}^{0}\beta + {}_{83}^{210}\text{Bi}$$

Notice that the resulting bismuth—210 isotope has the same mass as the lead—210, but the bismuth isotope has a higher atomic number: A neutron has been converted to a proton. If a relatively light isotope has too many protons, it may seek to convert a proton to a neutron via **positron emission**. A positron is an antimatter electron. It has the same mass as an electron, but a +1 charge. It can be represented as $_{+1}^{0}\beta$ or as $_{1}^{0}\text{e}$. An example of positron emission is:

$$_{20}^{39}\text{Ca} \rightarrow {}_{+1}^{0}\beta + {}_{19}^{39}\text{K}$$

Another method to eliminate an excess of protons (particularly for heavier nuclei) is **electron capture**. An example of electron capture is:

$$^{55}_{26}\text{Fe} + ^{0}_{-1}\text{e} \rightarrow ^{55}_{25}\text{Mn}$$

Associated with each of the above processes is the concomitant release of a photon, or **gamma particle**. A gamma particle is effectively massless and therefore does not affect the chemical symbol:

$$^{55}_{26}\text{Fe} + ^{0}_{-1}\text{e} \rightarrow ^{55}_{25}\text{Mn} + ^{0}_{0}\gamma$$

TABULAR SUMMARY OF RADIOACTIVE DECAY PROCESSES

Decay Type	Symbol	Change in Mass Number	Change in Atomic Number
alpha emission	$-\left(^{4}_{2}\alpha\right)$	-4	-2
beta emission	$-\left(^{0}_{-1}\beta\right)$	0	$+1$
positron emission	$-\left(^{0}_{+1}\beta\right)$	0	-1
electron capture	$+\left(^{0}_{-1}\text{e}\right)$	0	-1
gamma emission	$-\left(^{0}_{0}\gamma\right)$	0	0

Table 13.4

It should also be noted that of the particles involved in radioactive decay, gamma particles have the least mass and the highest energy; alpha particles have the greatest mass and the lowest energy.

NUCLEAR BINDING ENERGY, MASS DEFECT, AND EINSTEIN'S EQUATION

We have all heard this famous equation:

$$E = mc2$$

The only times that you will use this equation on the MCAT are in cases involving the computation of **nuclear binding energies** or cases of **mass defect**. It takes energy to break up a nucleus into its constituent protons and neutrons. This energy is the nuclear binding energy, E. It has also been observed that the mass of an atomic nucleus is less than the sum of the masses of the individual protons and neutrons of which it is constituted. This difference in mass is the mass defect, m. Einstein showed that these two quantities, energy and mass, are related by the square of the speed of light.

13.2 MASTERY APPLIED: PRACTICE PASSAGE AND QUESTIONS

Passage

Groups 3–12 in the periodic table are the transition elements. These elements are characterized by a partially filled outermost shell and a partially filled (or completely filled, in the case of group 12) next-to-outermost d subshell. All of these elements exhibit metallic properties.

The first ionization energy of an atom is that energy input required to remove a valence electron from a neutral atom. The second ionization energy is the energy input necessary to remove a second electron from the valence shell. Figure 1 depicts the first ionization energy of the fourth period transition elements.

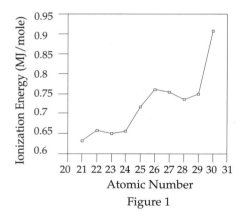

Figure 1

In general, transition elements react:

$$1s^2 2s^2 2p^6 3s^2 3p^6 3d^n 4s^2 \rightarrow 1s^2 2s^2 2p^6 3s^2 3p^6 3d^n$$

This is true not only of the first transition series, but also of the later transition series. The aufbau principle suggests that the $4s$ energy level is lower than the $3d$ energy level, so why would the $4s$ electrons be lost before the $3d$ electrons? An often- posited explanation for this is that the $3d$ energy level decreases in energy as it fills, such that at AN = 29, the energy levels invert. While this explains why copper and zinc would lose their $4s$ electrons before

losing their $3d$ electrons, it fails to address the other eight first transition series elements.

A more satisfactory explanation of this phenomenon is that what is important is not the relative energies of the $4s$ and the $3d$ levels taken individually as electrons are put in, but rather the relative energies of these levels as electrons are taken out to form cations. When this scenario is considered, it becomes clear that the $4s$ level is higher in energy than the $3d$ level relative to cation formation and that the $3d$ level is higher than the $4s$ level relative to anion formation.

1. Every element in the first period of transition elements except scandium (AN = 21) forms a +2 cation. Scandium most likely does not form this cation because:

    A. the two electrons removed are $4s$ electrons.
    B. removing two electrons from scandium would make it isoelectronic with potassium.
    C. the first ionization energy of scandium is low, the second ionization energy of scandium is high.
    D. the third ionization energy of scandium is low.

2. From the information given in Figure 1, which of the following is NOT true?

    A. Iron forms a +1 cation more easily than cobalt.
    B. Zinc is the least likely of the fourth period transition elements to form a +1 cation.
    C. Nickel forms a +1 cation more easily than iron.
    D. Cr^{+1} is favored by a d^5 valence shell configuration.

3. Ionization energy is expected to increase from left to right across a period. The most likely explanation for the discrepancies observed in Figure 1 is:

   A. electrons will fill empty orbitals before pairing.
   B. the $4s$ orbital is higher in energy than the $3d$ orbital for all the fourth period transition elements.
   C. the $4s$ orbital is higher in energy than the $3d$ orbital for the fourth period transition elements as they form ions.
   D. electrons will move from a paired orbital into an empty orbital even if the empty orbital is higher in energy.

4. The first ionization energy of potassium (K) is 0.4189 MJ/mol. The first ionization energy of barium (Ba) is 0.5029 MJ/mol. Therefore:

   A. barium is more metallic than potassium.
   B. potassium is more metallic than barium.
   C. barium has a greater electron affinity than potassium.
   D. potassium has a greater electron affinity than barium.

5. Would methane or ethane be expected to have the lower ionization energy?

   A. Methane, because a methyl cation is more stable than a primary cation.
   B. Methane, because a methyl anion is more stable than a primary anion.
   C. Ethane, because a primary cation is more stable than a methyl cation.
   D. Ethane, because a primary anion is more stable than a methyl anion.

6. The most common ions of iron are Fe^{2+} and Fe^{3+}. Are these ions diamagnetic or paramagnetic?

   A. Fe^{2+} is diamagnetic, Fe^{3+} is paramagnetic.
   B. Fe^{3+} is diamagnetic, Fe^{2+} is paramagnetic.
   C. Both ions are diamagnetic.
   D. Both ions are paramagnetic.

13.3 MASTERY VERIFIED: ANSWERS AND EXPLANATIONS

1. **D is correct.** Choices A and B represent true statements, however, these statements do not answer the question. Choice C is true, since the second ionization energy of any atom is higher than the first ionization energy. However, it fails to address why a +2 cation is not formed, since it would imply that a +1 cation is the most common ion for scandium. Choice D is the correct answer, since the most common cation formed from scandium is the +3 ion. Therefore, the +2 ion is not formed because if it was formed, it would be immediately transformed into the +3 ion, which corresponds to a noble gas configuration for scandium. The noble gas configuration is the most favored electron configuration for any atom that can assume it.

2. **A is correct.** According to Figure 1, iron (AN = 26) has a higher first ionization energy than cobalt (AN = 27); therefore, cobalt will form a +1 cation more easily than iron. Therefore, choice A is *false*. According to Figure 1, zinc has the highest first ionization energy. Therefore, zinc (AN = 30) is the least likely of the fourth period transition elements to form a +1 cation. Therefore, choice B is *true*. Nickel (AN = 28) has a lower first ionization energy than iron, thus it will more easily form a +1 cation. Therefore, choice C is *true*. Chromium (AN = 24) has a ground state elemental electron configuration of $1s^22s^22p^63s^23p^63d^54s^1$. When a single electron is removed from this atom to make the +1 cation, the electron configuration for the ion is $1s^22s^22p^63s^23p^63d^5$. Therefore choice D is also *true*.

3. **C is correct.** Choice A is true, however, it does not directly address the question. According to the passage, choice B is false—the 3d level drops below the 4s level for copper (AN = 29) and zinc (AN = 30). According to the passage, choice C is true—the energy levels that must be considered when taking an electron out of an atom are not necessarily equal in energy to the energy levels seen when that electron was being put into the atom via the aufbau principle. Choice D is false. Although it costs energy to pair electrons, electrons will not avoid pairing by inserting into higher energy levels; if they did, electrons would never pair!

4. **B is correct.** Metallic character has to do with the tendency of an atom to give up electrons. A low first ionization energy indicates a valence electron that can be easily lost. Electron affinity is the willingness of an atom to gain an electron. While it may seem straightforward to assume that an atom that is less willing to give up an electron must be more willing to take an electron, it is not quite so clear. By knowing the first ionization energy of an atom, we can say nothing about the electron affinity of that atom.

    Considering these facts, it is clear that neither choice C nor choice D can be the correct answer because we cannot determine electron affinity from an ionization energy measurement. It should also be clear that an atom with a lower ionization energy is more metallic. For this reason, choice B is a better answer than choice A.

5. **C is correct.** This question requires that you integrate your organic chemistry knowledge with your inorganic chemistry knowledge. The MCAT will frequently require you to do this.

    First, to eliminate choices B and D, we need only to consider the fact that we are removing electrons, thus making cations, not anions.

    From organic chemistry, we remember that a tertiary cation is more stable than a secondary cation, a secondary cation is more stable than a primary cation, and a primary cation is more stable than a methyl cation. Therefore, in deciding between choices A and C, it is clear that choice A is false, while choice C is true.

6. **D is correct.** Iron has an atomic number of 26. Therefore, Fe^{2+} has 24 electrons and Fe^{3+} has 23 electrons. An atom, or ion, with an odd number of electrons cannot be diamagnetic (all electrons paired). For this reason, choices B and C are thrown out, leaving choices A and D. Since we know that Fe^{3+} must be paramagnetic, the question reduces to: Is Fe^{2+} diamagnetic or paramagnetic?

Since iron is filling a *d* subshell, it has five orbitals to fill before it will electron pair. Fe^{2+} has six electrons past the nearest noble gas configuration. It is irrelevant whether two of these electrons are paired in the 4*s* orbital, or one electron is in the 4*s* orbital, or no electrons are in the 4*s* orbital. In any case, the remaining 4, 5, or 6 electrons, respectively, will not all pair in the 3*d* orbitals. Therefore, Fe^{2+} is paramagnetic, and the answer must be D.

CHAPTER 14

BONDING AND MOLECULAR FORMATION

14.1 MASTERY ACHIEVED

ATOMIC AND MOLECULAR INTERACTIONS: BONDING

Elements that form chemical bonds do so through an alteration of their electron configurations. This alteration occurs only if it leads to a more stable arrangement of electrons. As we saw in Chapter 13, noble gases represent the most stable electron configurations available to the main block (*s* and *p* block) elements. For this reason, the most stable ions, or other electron configurations, are isoelectronic with the noble gases.

Lewis Dot Structures and the Octet Rule

Lewis dot structures are often useful when considering the bonding requirements of individual atoms. However, you should be aware that Lewis structures begin to break down for atoms that violate the octet rule.

The **rule of eight**, or the **octet rule**, states that each atom would like to have a valence, or outer, shell configuration that matches that of the noble gases. For elements that are in the *p* block, this corresponds to a filled valence shell of eight electrons. G. N. Lewis devised a clever way of denoting the number of electrons in the valence shell of an atom by placing dots (one for each electron) around the chemical symbol for that atom. Thus, the Lewis dot structures for the second period elements are:

$$\text{Li}\cdot \quad \text{Be}\!:\ \quad \cdot\dot{\text{B}}\cdot \quad \cdot\dot{\text{C}}\cdot \quad \cdot\ddot{\text{N}}\cdot \quad :\ddot{\text{O}}\cdot \quad :\ddot{\text{F}}\cdot \quad :\ddot{\text{Ne}}\!:$$

Notice that it does not matter where we place the dots around the element, as long as those electrons that do not appear in the same subshell are not paired in the dot structure. The Lewis dot structure for beryllium (Be) shows the electrons paired because both of these electrons are in the *s* subshell. The Lewis dot structures for boron (B) and carbon (C) do not show paired electrons, since once the *p* subshell is made available, by the first electron entering it, the electrons have a tendency to "spread out" via a process known as **hybridization**. Hybridization will be discussed in greater detail in **Chapter 33**.

An octet may be achieved in the three ways outlined below:

1. A metal may lose electrons to form a cation that is isoelectronic with the previous noble gas. An example of this is the Mg^{2+} cation, which is isoelectronic with neon (Ne). The formation of this ion is given by the equation:

$$Mg\text{:} \longrightarrow Mg^{2+} + 2e^-$$

2. A nonmetal may gain electrons to form an anion that is isoelectronic to the next noble gas. An example of this is the F^{1-} anion, which is isoeletronic with neon. The formation of this ion is given by the equation:

$$\text{:}\ddot{F}\cdot + e^- \longrightarrow \text{:}\ddot{\ddot{F}}\text{:}^-$$

3. Atoms (typically two nonmetals) may share electrons with one another such that each atom effectively becomes isoelectronic with the next noble gas. Two examples of this are given below in the HF and NH_3 molecules.

Using the octet rule, we can see that fluorine would like to gain a single electron, while nitrogen would like to gain three electrons. As a result, the following dot structures can be constructed of these elements bonding with hydrogen:

$$H\overset{x}{\cdot}\ddot{\ddot{F}}\text{:} \qquad H\overset{x}{\cdot}\overset{\cdot\cdot}{N}\overset{x}{\cdot}H$$
$$\underset{H}{\overset{x\,\bullet}{}}$$

where the dots came originally from the fluorine or the nitrogen, and the x's came originally from the hydrogens.

Please solve this problem:

- An atom has the electron configuration $1s^22s^22p^63s^23p^64s^2$. This configuration could represent any of the following species EXCEPT:

A. $Ca\text{:}$

B. $Ti\text{:}^{2+}$

C. $Mn\text{:}^{5+}$

D. $K\cdot$

Problem solved:

D is correct. The electron configuration given is the ground state electron configuration for a calcium atom. This electron configuration also represents possible electron configurations for the dipositive titanium ion and the pentapositive manganese ion. In its ground state, the potassium atom (K) has only *one* electron in the 4s subshell; therefore, its electron configuration is $s^22s^22p^63s^23p^64s^1$.

Intramolecular Bonds: Ionic and Covalent

It is convenient to think of the interactions between atoms that allow them to form molecules as bonds. In the broadest sense, there are eight types of bonds, the most familiar of which are **covalent** and **ionic bonds**.

In an ionic bond, one atom receives an electron from another atom; the former atom becomes negatively charged, and the latter atom becomes positively charged. This is an ion–ion bond. An example of an ionic bond is the bond between Na and Cl to form sodium chloride:

$$Na\bullet \; + \; :\!\overset{\bullet\bullet}{\underset{\bullet\bullet}{Cl}}\!\bullet \;\; \longrightarrow \;\; Na^+ \; + \; :\!\overset{\bullet\bullet}{\underset{\bullet\bullet}{Cl}}\!:^-$$

In a covalent bond, an electron pair is shared between two atoms. The diagrams of HF and NH_3 on the previous page are examples of covalent bonding.

Electronegativity determines whether a bond will be ionic or covalent. If two atoms with identical electronegativities come together to form a bond, this bond will be a true covalent bond. If two atoms with a large difference in electronegativities come together to form a bond, this bond will be an ionic bond. For any two atoms with an electronegativity difference in excess of 1.7, the bond between these atoms is considered an ionic bond. In the case of a true covalent bond, the two electrons constituting the bond each spend an equal amount of time associated with each of the two atomic nuclei.

However, when the two atoms forming a covalent bond differ in electronegativity, the two electrons forming the bond will spend a larger amount of time associated with the more strongly electronegative atom than with the more electropositive atom. This is termed a **polar** covalent bond. When a polar covalent bond is formed, a **dipole** is also formed. The symbol for a dipole is an arrow with a perpendicular line through its tail. The head of the arrow is pointed in the direction of the more electronegative atom.

Consider the possibility of a polar covalent bond between hydrogen and chlorine. This bond could be written:

$$H \longmapsto\!\!\!\blacktriangleright Cl$$

This may also be represented in one of two ways:

$$\overset{\delta^+}{H} \qquad \overset{\delta^-}{Cl}$$

$$\big(H \quad Cl\big)$$

In the upper representation, $\delta+$ is used to show a partial positive charge on the hydrogen atom, and $\delta-$ is used to denote a partial negative charge on the chlorine atom. In the lower representation, the outline represents the shape of the electron cloud that is formed by the electrons in the bond.

Note that a dipole may be either **permanent** or **induced**. Consider the following set of diagrams:

$$F^- \qquad\qquad H-H$$

$$F^- \;\; \overset{\delta^+}{H}-\overset{\delta^-}{H}$$

Initially, the H_2 molecule has no net dipole—it is a purely covalent molecule. As a fluoride ion is brought closer to the hydrogen on the left, the electrons in the H_2 molecule are repelled by this negatively charged ion. The net result is an induced dipole in the H_2 molecule.

Please solve this problem:

- Which of the following molecules is expected to have the largest individual bond dipole moment?

    A. N_2
    B. CH_4
    C. NaH
    D. H_2O

Problem solved:

C is correct. The nitrogen molecule will not have an overall dipole moment, nor will it have a bond dipole moment. The two nitrogens are equivalent, and they share a pure covalent bond. Methane (CH_4) will not have an overall dipole moment due to the symmetry of the molecule; however, it will have an individual bond dipole in each of the C-H bonds. These dipoles result from the difference in electronegativity of carbon and hydrogen. It is important that you recognize that carbon is slightly more electronegative than hydrogen, so each dipole points in the direction of the carbon atom.

Sodium has an electronegativity of 0.93 on the Pauling scale (relative to fluorine, which has an electronegativity of 4.0). The electronegativity of hydrogen is 2.20. The difference in electronegativity between these two atoms is therefore 1.27. Recalling that we want an electronegativity difference of greater than 1.7 for an ionic bond, we can state that this is a polar covalent bond.

The electronegativity difference between hydrogen and oxygen is 1.24. This is close to the difference between sodium and hydrogen, but not quite as large. You will not be expected to know values of electronegativity for the MCAT, but you must recognize that electronegativity is a periodic trend that increases from bottom to top and from left to right. Also, be aware that when considering the electronegativity of hydrogen, you should imagine hydrogen as falling between boron and carbon in the periodic table. Using this scenario, without resorting to electronegativity values, we can see that Na—H is the most polar bond in the above question, since these elements (with hydrogen imagined between boron and carbon) are the farthest apart in the periodic table.

Intermolecular Bonds

Ions, dipoles, and induced dipoles can interact in six ways: **ion–ion, ion–dipole, ion–induced dipole, dipole–dipole, dipole–induced dipole,** and **induced dipole–induced dipole**. We have already discussed the strongest of these six interactions: the intramolecular ionic bond. The other five types of interaction are between separate molecules or are intermolecular. Each of these six interactions is summarized in Table 14.1. The interactions are organized from strongest to weakest.

Type of Interaction	Example
ion–ion	Na^+/Cl^-
ion–dipole	Na^+/H_2O
dipole–dipole	H_2O/H_2O
ion–induced dipole	Na^+/CCl_4
dipole–induced dipole	CH_3OH/CCl_4
induced dipole–induced dipole	CCl_4/CCl_4

Table 14.1

As can be seen from Table 14.1, even molecules that do not possess a permanent dipole have interatomic or intermolecular forces that are created by induced dipole-induced dipole interactions. These forces, also known as **London dispersion forces,** are the weakest intermolecular forces.

Please solve this problem:

- The sodium cation, Na$^+$, is more soluble in water than the silver cation, Ag^{2+}. The best explanation for this fact is:

  A. sodium has a greater electronegativity than silver.
  B. silver has a greater electronegativity than sodium.
  C. the sodium cation experiences ion–dipole interactions with the water.
  D. the silver cation is larger than the sodium cation.

Problem solved:

B is correct. Because silver is more electronegative than sodium, we expect sodium to maintain itself as a "naked" cation (not accepting electron density from the water). This leads to a large ion–dipole interaction between the sodium and the water. Choice C is true; however, it does not provide the complete explanation of the problem at hand, since the silver cation also experiences ion–dipole interactions with water.

Water is a polar molecule; as such, it will dissolve polar entities (the more polar, the better). The extremely low electronegativity of sodium makes the sodium cation a better "positive charge" than the silver cation.

In terms of choice D, we must remember that our periodic trend was in terms of atomic radius, *not* ionic radius.

Hydrogen Bonding

So far, we have discussed seven types of bonding. The eighth, and final, type is **hydrogen bonding**.

A hydrogen bond consists of two components: a hydrogen atom attached to an electronegative atom X and a second electronegative atom Y that contains a lone electron pair. Since the hydrogen that is attached to X is participating in a net dipole with X, the hydrogen possesses a net partial positive charge. The electrons that form the bond between the hydrogen and the electronegative atom spend a majority of time associated with the electronegative atom:

$$\overset{\delta^+}{H} - \overset{\delta^-}{X}$$

When the electron-rich Y comes into the vicinity of this electron-poor hydrogen, it is willing to donate a portion of its lone electron pair to the hydrogen. The hydrogen accepts the electron density from Y because the hydrogen is electron-deficient. Atom Y is willing to donate a portion of its electron density to the hydrogen because it can, in effect, give up only a small portion of this electron density while gaining the stability of an additional bond:

$$Y\text{:} \longrightarrow \overset{\delta^+}{H} - \overset{\delta^-}{X} \Longrightarrow Y \cdots H - X$$

Hydrogen bonds vary in strength, from nearly the strength of a covalent or ionic bond to the strength of only a very weak bond (approximately the strength of dipole–induced dipole bonds). The high strength of hydrogen bonds in water accounts for the peculiar chemical properties of water.

On the MCAT, the term *hydrogen bond* is generally restricted to situations in which hydrogen interacts, as shown above, with nitrogen (N), fluorine (F) or oxygen (O). Hydrogen bonding, and the degree of hydrogen bonding that occurs within a given substance, tends to prevent its molecules from undergoing physical separation, and thus tends to increase its boiling point (see **Chapter 20**).

Please solve this problem:

- The boiling point of water is 373 K. The boiling point of ethanol (C_2H_5OH) is 351.5 K. The difference in boiling points observed is most likely accounted for by the fact that:

  A. water is involved in hydrogen bonding, ethanol is not.
  B. both are involved in hydrogen bonding, but the hydrogen bonds in water are stronger.
  C. ethanol has a higher molecular weight than water and therefore is expected to have a lower boiling point.
  D. ethanol has a higher molecular weight than water and therefore is expected to have a higher boiling point.

Problem solved:

B is correct. Both molecules can form hydrogen bonds with themselves, since they both contain a hydrogen attached to an electronegative oxygen atom, and they both contain an electronegative oxygen with lone pairs to donate to the hydrogen. The hydrogen bonds in water are much stronger than the hydrogen bonds in ethanol, which makes the boiling point of water higher than the boiling point of ethanol. Choice D is a true statement, but it does not solve the problem that has been presented.

MULTIPLE BONDS, RESONANCE, AND POLYATOMIC IONS

Multiple Bonds

When an atom is in need of more than one electron, it may form multiple covalent bonds with another atom. When two atoms share a single pair of electrons, as was discussed above, they form a **single bond**. When two atoms share two pairs of electrons, they form a **double bond**. The sharing of three pairs of electrons creates a **triple bond**.

Examples of double and triple bonds are:

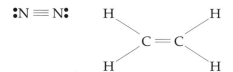

Understand the implications of single, double, and triple bonds for bond *length* and bond *strength*. As to any two given atoms, a triple bond is shorter and stronger than a double bond, and a double bond is shorter and stronger than a single bond. Among the three kinds of bonds, a single bond is the longest and weakest.

Please solve this problem:

- Which of the following gases is expected to have the strongest intramolecular bond(s)?

   A. H_2
   B. N_2
   C. O_2
   D. F_2

Problem solved:

B is correct. If we consider the Lewis dot structures of each of these molecules, we see:

$$ H - H \qquad :N \equiv N: \qquad \ddot{O} = \ddot{O} \qquad :\ddot{F} - \ddot{F}: $$

Both hydrogen gas and fluorine gas have single bonds. Oxygen gas has a double bond. Nitrogen gas has a triple bond.

Polyatomic Ions

Just as an atom may bond with more than one other atom in order to form a neutral molecule, an atom may also bond with more than one other atom to form an ion. Consider the molecule $NaNO_3$. The molecular structure might first be thought of as:

$$
\begin{array}{c}
O \\
\parallel \\
N \\
\diagup \quad \diagdown \\
O \qquad\quad O - Na
\end{array}
$$

However, considering the criterion for the formation of an ionic bond (an electronegativity difference of 1.7 or larger), we can see that sodium is expected to form an ionic bond, not a covalent bond, with oxygen. Therefore, the corrected molecular structure is:

$$
\begin{array}{c}
O \\
\parallel \\
N \\
\diagup \quad \diagdown \\
O \qquad\quad O^- \; Na^+
\end{array}
$$

where a negative charge is left on one of the oxygen atoms. The resultant molecule is composed of (a) a sodium cation bound to (b) the polyatomic anion, NO_3^-.

The names and formulas of some of the more important polyatomic ions are given in Table 14.2.

Name	Formula
ammonium	NH_4^+
nitrate	NO_3^-
carbonate	CO_3^{2-}
sulfate	SO_4^{2-}
phosphate	PO_4^{3-}

Table 14.2

Resonance

The depiction of the polyatomic nitrate ion (NO_3^-) is not entirely accurate. Since all three of the ion's oxygen atoms are equivalent, there is no reason that the ion should choose to locate its double bond at one of them and to leave the other two with single bonds. The nitrate ion (and many other species) exists as an intermediate among three separate structures in which the double bond between the nitrogen (N) and oxygen (O) atoms is *delocalized*. In other words, the nitrogen atom is not truly double bonded to one of the oxygen atoms and single bonded to the other two. Rather, the double bond "bounces around" among the three oxygen atoms so that the true NO_3^- species represents an intermediate or average among three structures depicted thus:

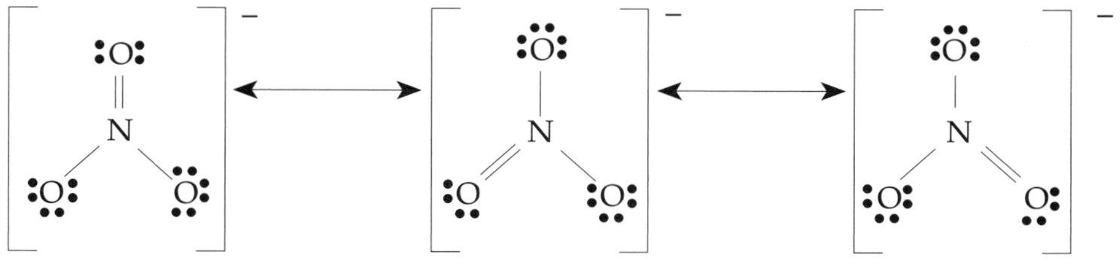

The three structures depicted above are called **resonance forms**, and we say that the NO_3^- ion represents a **resonance structure** for which there are three resonance forms. We conceive of the molecule as resonating ("bouncing around") among the three forms so that the molecule on average is structured thus:

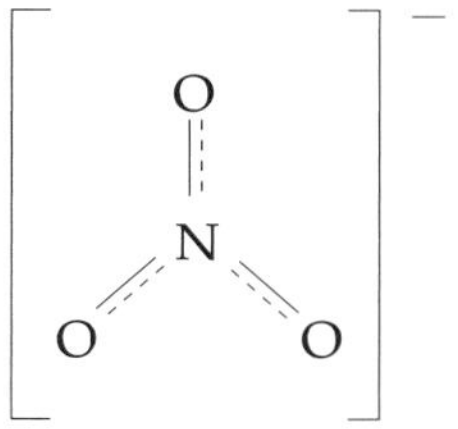

Resonance affects a species' chemical properties by providing added stability, making it, for example, less prone to undergo chemical reaction. This stabilizing influence is called **resonance stabilization**.

Please solve this problem:

- How many resonance structures exist for the phosphate ion (PO_4^{3-})?

  A. 1
  B. 2
  C. 3
  D. 4

Problem solved:

D is correct. We can envision a structure with a central phosphorus atom and four attached oxygen atoms. Since the phosphate ion has a net charge of –3, only one of these oxygens will have a double bond to phosphorus in any resonance structure, and each of the other three oxygens will form a single bond with phosphorus. Since there are four different oxygen atoms that could form the double bond, we have four resonance structures.

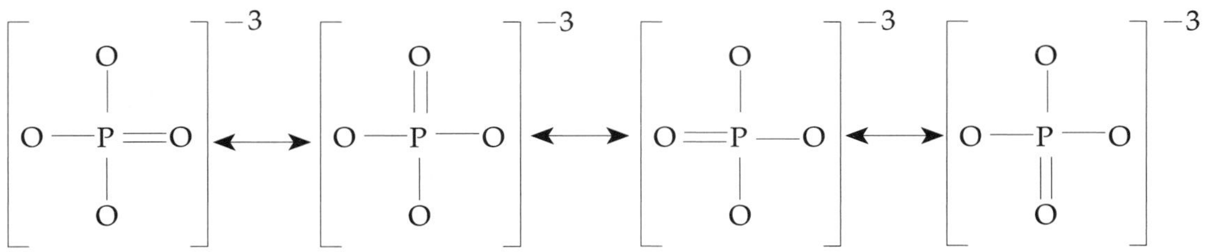

THE FORMATION OF MOLECULES

Stoichiometry Within Molecules

As we saw in earlier, nitrogen will form one bond with each of three or four hydrogens, while fluorine will form only one bond with only one hydrogen. The resulting molecular formulas are NH_3 and HF. The subscript number is known as a **stoichiometric number**. The stoichiometric number 3 on the H in the NH_3 molecule indicates that there are three hydrogens for each nitrogen in this molecule. In this case, there are also three hydrogens **bonded** to each nitrogen; however, the subscript 3 does not tell us this: stoichiometric numbers give only the **ratios** between constituent atoms, *not* information on bonding.

For example, the molecular formula of glucose is $C_6H_{12}O_6$, which tells us that there are six carbons, twelve hydrogens, and six oxygens in a molecule of glucose; it also tells us that there are two hydrogen atoms and one oxygen atom for every carbon atom in a molecule of glucose. But this formula tells us nothing about how these elements are arranged to form glucose.

Please solve this problem:

- The chemical formula for aluminum sulfate is:

    A. Al_3SO_4.
    B. $Al_2(SO_4)_3$.
    C. $Al_3(SO_4)_2$.
    D. $AlSO_4$.

Problem solved:

B is correct. Since aluminum is a group 13 element, it has a valence state of 3^+. From Table 14.2, we know that the complex ion, sulfate, has a charge of 2^-. From this, we can see that we need two aluminum ions ($3^+ \times 2 = 6^+$) for every three sulfate ions ($2^- \times 3 = 6^-$).

Molecular Geometry and the VSEPR Model

After we have drawn a Lewis dot structure for a molecule, we can determine the geometric shape of the molecule based on the valence properties of the central atom. A central atom can possess from one to six electron pairs. In turn, each of these electron pairs will be either a bonding pair (involved in a bond between two atoms) or a nonbonding pair (lone pair). Once the total number of pairs is known, and the status (bonding or nonbonding) of each pair has been determined, we employ **Valence Shell Electron Pair Repulsion** (**VSEPR**) to determine the geometry of the molecule. VSEPR allows geometry to be determined by considering the repulsive forces between electron pairs in the central atom of a molecule. These repulsive forces cause the attached atoms, or ligands, to fill a three-dimensional space in which they are as far away from one another as possible. Accounting for both lone pairs and bonding pairs of electrons, we can see that there are three separate repulsive forces: **lone pair–lone pair**, **lone pair–bonding pair**, and **bonding pair–bonding pair**. Since a portion of the electron energy in a bonding pair is used to stabilize the bond, and none of the electron density in a lone pair is used for bonding purposes, lone pair–lone pair interactions create the strongest repulsive forces while bonding pair–bonding pair repulsions create the weakest ones. The variety of geometric shapes available to molecules with a single central atom are summarized in Table 14.3.

Total Pairs	Bonding Pairs	Lone Pairs	Shape	Example
1	1	0	linear	H_2
2	2	0	linear	CaH_2
3	3	0	trigonal planar	BH_3
4	4	0	tetrahedral	CH_4
4	3	1	trigonal pyramidal	NH_3
4	2	2	bent	H_2O
4	1	3	linear	HF
5	5	0	trigonal bipyramidal	SbF_5
5	4	1	seesaw	SeF_4
5	3	2	T-shaped	IF_3
5	2	3	linear	XeF_2
6	6	0	octahedral	SF_6
6	5	1	square pyramidal	BrF_5

Table 14.3

Each of the representative molecules in Table 14.3 is graphically depicted in Figure 14.1:

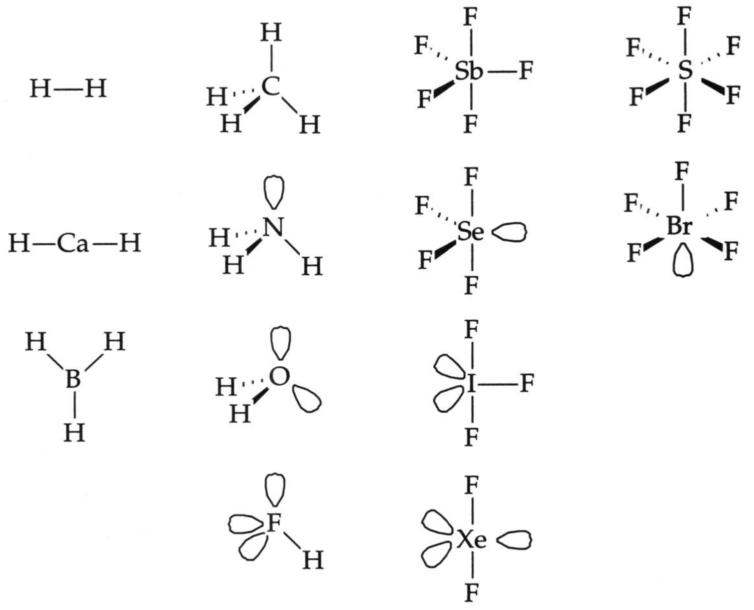

Figure 14.1

○ = lone pair of electrons

'·... = bond extending into the page

╱ = bond extending out of the page

—— = bond in the plane of the page

Please solve this problem:

- The predicted molecular shape of MnBr$_3$ is:

    A. linear.
    B. trigonal planar.
    C. seesaw.
    D. T-shaped.

Problem solved:

D is correct. From the periodic table, we see that manganese has seven valence electrons. Since three of these electrons will be allocated to bonding with the three bromine atoms, we have three bonding pairs and four nonbonding electrons, or two lone pairs. This gives us a total of five electron pairs: three bonding pairs and two lone pairs. From Table 14.3, we see that this coincides with a T-shaped geometry.

14.2 MASTERY APPLIED: PRACTICE PASSAGE AND QUESTIONS

Passage

For years, the newspaper business has been plagued by the problem of ink that smudges. Millions of dollars have been spent to develop a high-speed ink that will not smudge. Recent advances in this area have come from the arena of bonding phenomena. The Dayton Tinker Corporation has invented an ink that does not smudge. In this new process, a positively charged dye is chemically bound to a negatively charged paper.

Traditional newspaper inks never dried to the paper. These inks consisted of an oil mixed with carbon black (soot). While the oil would eventually be absorbed by the paper, the soot remained unattached to the paper.

Paper is mostly composed of cellulose, a sugar. Sugars contain many alcohol groups and are susceptible to hydrogen bonding. The negatively charged paper used in conjunction with the new smudgeless inks is a simple modification of the normal cellulose paper, where protons are removed from the various alcohol groups, creating a negative charge.

1. The bonding responsible for the smudgeless ink is:
   A. pure covalent.
   B. polar covalent.
   C. ionic.
   D. ion-dipole.

2. Carbon black is the carbon residue that remains after the complete burning of carbon-containing compounds; it is composed entirely of carbon. The bonds between individual carbon atoms in carbon black are MOST likely:
   A. nonpolar covalent.
   B. polar covalent.
   C. ionic.
   D. dipole-dipole.

3. The bonding between carbon black and newsprint is most likely:
   A. ion-dipole.
   B. dipole-dipole.
   C. dipole-induced dipole.
   D. induced dipole-induced dipole.

4. Suppose a new ink is developed that involves a polar covalent bond between the ink and the paper. This ink is expected to:
   A. adhere to the paper more strongly than both the traditional ink and the smudgeless ink.
   B. adhere to the paper more strongly than the traditional ink but less strongly than the smudgeless ink.
   C. adhere to the paper more strongly than the traditional ink, but it cannot be predicted whether it will be held more or less strongly than the smudgeless ink.
   D. adhere to the paper less strongly than both the traditional ink and the smudgeless ink.

5. The oil used in traditional newspaper inks is a nonpolar substance. The oil is preferred over water as a solvent for the carbon black because:

   A. the oil is nonpolar while carbon black is polar.
   B. the oil is nonpolar while carbon black is nonpolar.
   C. the oil is nonpolar while the paper is polar.
   D. the oil is nonpolar while the paper is nonpolar.

6. Colored smudgeless inks have also been developed. These inks are susceptible to fading after two days of exposure to sunlight. This is most likely due to:

   A. a change in the chemical composition of the oil holding the ink to the paper.
   B. a change in the bond between the ink and the paper.
   C. a change in the chemical bonding within the ink.
   D. a change in the chemical bonding within the paper.

14.3 MASTERY VERIFIED: ANSWERS AND EXPLANATIONS

1. **C is correct.** As stated in the passage, a negatively charged ink is bound to a positively charged paper. While this could also result in the formation of a polar covalent bond, we do not have enough information to choose polar covalent in preference to ionic, so ionic is the best answer.

2. **A is correct.** In the question, we are told to consider carbon black as consisting entirely of carbon. A material that is composed of a single element cannot have polar covalent or ionic bonds. Such a material also cannot contain a permanent dipole. Therefore, by process of elimination, choice A is correct.

3. **C is correct.** From question 2, we know that carbon black does not contain ions or dipoles; this eliminates choices A and B. From the passage, we know that the paper has many alcohol groups, which means that it possesses many dipoles. Since a dipole can induce a dipole in another material, we choose choice C and eliminate choice D.

4. **C is correct.** A polar covalent bond is definitely stronger than the dipole-induced dipole bond of the traditional ink. We cannot say for sure whether this polar covalent bond will be weaker or stronger than the ionic bond in smudgeless ink.

5. **B is correct.** This question refers to the common statement "like dissolves like." Since carbon black is nonpolar, it is more likely to dissolve in a substance that is also nonpolar. The paper is polar, but this has little to do with the choice of oils.

6. **C is correct.** When the color of these inks fades, it is due to a change in the chemical bonds within the ink. These bonds impart the color to the ink, therefore it must be these bonds that change to effect a change in color. Choice A is incorrect, since this inking process does not involve an oil. This can be deduced from our knowledge that oils are nonpolar and the smudgeless inks are charged. Therefore, an oil would not be a good solvent for smudgeless ink. Choice B is incorrect, as a change in the bonds between the ink and the paper might cause the ink to smudge, not fade. Choice D is incorrect. A change in the internal structure of the paper may lead to brittleness and cracking, but it will not lead to a change in the color of the ink.

CHAPTER 15

CHEMICAL REACTIONS I: FUNDAMENTAL PHENOMENA

15.1 MASTERY ACHIEVED

REACTION CLASSES

In broad terms, there are five types of chemical reactions:

- synthesis,

- decomposition (analysis),

- single replacement,

- double replacement (ion exchange), and

- oxidation-reduction.

Oxidation-reduction, or redox reactions, which may take the form of any of the four other classes, are addressed later in this chapter; the other types of reactions are discussed below.

Synthesis

A **synthesis reaction** is the direct combination of two or more compounds, or elements, to form a new chemical compound. The general form of a synthesis reaction is:

$$A + B \rightarrow AB$$

Examples of synthesis reactions include the reaction between hydrogen and oxygen gases to form water:

$$2H_2(g) + O_2(g) \rightarrow 2H_2O(l)$$

and the reaction between barium oxide and water to form barium hydroxide:

$$BaO(s) + H_2O(l) \rightarrow Ba(OH)_2(aq)$$

Please solve this problem:

- All of the following are examples of synthesis reactions EXCEPT:

    A. $2Na(s) + Cl_2(g) \rightarrow 2NaCl(s)$

    B. $4FeO(s) + O_2(g) \rightarrow 2Fe_2O_3(s)$

    C. $FeCl_3(s) + 3Na(s) \rightarrow Fe(s) + 3NaCl(s)$

    D. $H2O(l) + O_2(g) \rightarrow H_2O_2(aq)$

Problem solved:

C is correct. The reaction given in choice C is an example of a single replacement reaction.

Decomposition

A **decomposition reaction**, or analysis reaction, is the opposite of a synthesis reaction. In a decomposition, two or more compounds, or elements, are formed from a single chemical compound. The general form of a decomposition reaction is:

$$AB \rightarrow A + B$$

Examples of decomposition reactions include the electrolysis of water to form hydrogen and oxygen gases:

$$2H_2O(l) \rightarrow 2H_2(g) + O_2(g)$$

and the decomposition of aluminum trichloride to form aluminum metal and chlorine gas:

$$2AlCl_3(s) \rightarrow 2Al(s) + 3Cl_2(g)$$

Please solve this problem:

- All of the following are examples of unbalanced decomposition reactions EXCEPT:

    A. $Fe_2O_3(s) \rightarrow FeO(s) + O_2(g)$

    B. $FeO(s) \rightarrow Fe(s) + O_2(g)$

    C. $HIO_3(aq) + O_2(g) \rightarrow HIO_4(aq)$

    D. $HIO_4(aq) + HIO_3(aq) \rightarrow O_2(g)$

Problem solved:

C is correct. The reaction given in choice C is an example of a synthesis reaction.

Single Replacement

In a **single replacement reaction**, an element reacts with a compound to form a new compound and a different element. The general form of a single replacement reaction is:

$$AB \rightarrow AX + B$$

Examples of single replacement reactions include the reaction between copper metal and sulfuric acid to form hydrogen gas and copper(II) sulfate:

$$Cu(s) + H_2SO_4(aq) \rightarrow CuSO_4(aq) + H_2(g)$$

and the replacement of bromine by chlorine in sodium bromide:

$$2NaBr(aq) + Cl_2(g) \rightarrow 2NaCl(aq) + Br_2(l)$$

(All of the single replacement reactions just described represent **oxidation reduction reactions**.)

Please solve this problem:

- All of the following are examples of single replacement reactions EXCEPT:

    A. $Na(s) + KCl(s) \rightarrow NaCl(s) + K(s)$

    B. $3NaOH(aq) + FeBr_3(aq) \rightarrow 3NaBr(aq) + Fe(OH)_3(s)$

    C. $2Mn(s) + 10HCl(aq) \rightarrow 2MnCl_5(s) + 5H_2(g)$

    D. $16NaCl(s) + S_8(s) \rightarrow 8Na_2S(aq) + 8Cl_2(g)$

Problem solved:

B is correct. The reaction given in choice B is an example of a double replacement reaction.

Double Replacement

In a **double replacement reaction**, two compounds exchange ions with one another. The result is the formation of two new chemical compounds. The general form of a double replacement reaction is:

$$AX + BY \rightarrow AY + BX$$

An example of double replacement reactions include the neutralization reaction between sodium hydroxide and hydrochloric acid:

$$NaOH(aq) + HCl(aq) \rightarrow NaCl(aq) + H_2O(l)$$

(This particular reaction also represents an acid–base reaction **[Chapter 21]**.) Another example is the reaction between silver nitrate and sodium chloride to form silver chloride and sodium nitrate:

$$AgNO_3(aq) + NaCl(aq) \rightarrow NaNO_3(aq) + AgCl(s)$$

BALANCED EQUATIONS AND LIMITING REAGENTS

Balancing Equations

The subscript 3 in NH_3 is termed a **stoichiometric number**. When we want chemicals to react with one another, stoichiometry must be considered. In this case, we cannot change the stoichiometric numbers that designate atomic ratios within molecules, so we must rely on stoichiometric coefficients. A **stoichiometric coefficient** is a determinant of the molar ratio between two or more separate molecules in a **balanced reaction**.

The mass of the reactants in a chemical equation must equal the mass of the products. We can use stoichiometric coefficients to check this mass balance. Consider the reaction of nitrogen gas (N_2) and hydrogen gas (H_2) that produces ammonia (NH_3). This reaction, when run in an industrial setting, is known as the **Haber process,** and the unbalanced reaction is:

$$N_2 + H_2 \rightleftharpoons NH_3$$

We can see that this reaction is unbalanced (does not obey the law of conservation of matter) because there are two atoms of nitrogen on the left, but only one atom of nitrogen on the right. Similarly, there are two hydrogen atoms on the left, but there are three hydrogen atoms on the right. In order to balance this equation, we must ensure that there are equal numbers of nitrogen atoms on each side of the equation and equal numbers of hydrogen atoms on each side of the equation. If we consider the ratio of N_2 to NH_3, there is a ratio of two to one in nitrogen atoms. If we consider the ratio of H_2 to NH_3, there is a ratio of two to three hydrogen atoms. These two ratios indicate that in order for the atoms to balance on each side, we must invert each ratio.

$$\begin{array}{c} N_2 + H_2 \rightleftharpoons NH_3 \\ 1 \qquad\qquad 2 \\ 3 \quad 2 \end{array}$$

Once we have written these ratios, it is clear that since the stoichiometric coefficient prescribed for ammonia in each case is 2, we are finished balancing the equation:

$$N_2 + 3H_2 \rightleftharpoons 2NH_3$$

We can now say that if one mole of nitrogen gas is allowed to react with three moles of hydrogen gas, the product will be two moles of ammonia. It is important to remember that stoichiometric coefficients are measured in terms of moles or atoms, not grams!

Please solve this problem:

- Iron (III) hydroxide may be formed via a reaction between sodium hydroxide and iron (III) bromide. In the balanced equation, what is the ratio of $Fe(OH)_3$ to NaBr?

   A. 1:1
   B. 1:2
   C. 1:3
   D. 3:1

Problem solved:

C is correct. To solve this problem, we must balance the equation:

$$FeBr_3 + NaOH \rightarrow Fe(OH)_3 + NaBr$$

In the unbalanced reaction, there is one iron on each side—iron is balanced. Next, we can balance bromine. There are three bromines on the left, but only one on the right. To balance Br, we get:

$$FeBr_3 + NaOH \rightarrow Fe(OH)_3 + 3NaBr$$

Next, we can balance sodium:

$$FeBr_3 + 3NaOH \rightarrow Fe(OH)_3 + 3NaBr$$

Checking for a balance of oxygen and hydrogen, we can see that this equation is now balanced. From the balanced equation, we can see that the ratio of $Fe(OH)_3$ to $NaBr$ is 1:3.

Limiting Reagents

Once we have a chemically balanced reaction, we need to concern ourselves with the amounts of reagents that are available to perform the desired reaction. Often, one will add an excess of one reagent relative to the other reagent(s). The reagent that is present in the smallest quantity (based on equivalents) is termed the **limiting reagent**—it limits the extent of the reaction. Consider again the Haber process. If 28 grams of nitrogen gas are allowed to react with 4 grams of hydrogen gas to produce ammonia, which is the limiting reagent?

First, convert all gram masses into moles:

$$\frac{28 \text{ g N}_2}{28 \text{ g / mole}} = 1 \text{ mole N}_2$$

$$\frac{4 \text{ g H}_2}{2 \text{ g / mole}} = 2 \text{ mole H}_2$$

Divide each molar quantity by the appropriate stoichiometric coefficient to arrive at a number of "equivalents." An **equivalent** is the amount of each substance that is needed in the balanced reaction.

$$\frac{1 \text{ mole N}_2}{1 \text{ mole/equivalent}} = 1 \text{ equivalent N}_2$$

$$\frac{2 \text{ mole H}_2}{3 \text{ mole/equivalent}} = 0.667 \text{ equivalents H}_2$$

Since there are fewer equivalents of hydrogen gas than equivalents of nitrogen, hydrogen is the limiting reagent—it will be entirely consumed first. There is an excess of 0.333 equivalents of nitrogen gas, so at the end of the reaction (when all of the hydrogen gas has been consumed), 0.333 moles (or 9.333 grams) of nitrogen gas will remain unreacted.

To calculate the amount of ammonia produced, we multiply the number of equivalents of the limiting reagent by the stoichiometric coefficient of ammonia.

$$0.667 \text{ equivalents} \times \frac{2 \text{ mole NH}_3}{\text{equivalent}} = 1.333 \text{ mole NH}_3$$

or:

$$1.333 \text{ mole NH}_3 \times \frac{17 \text{ grams}}{\text{mole}} = 22.667 \text{ grams NH}_3$$

We can verify this result by checking for mass balance. We put in 28 grams of nitrogen and 4 grams of hydrogen, therefore our reagents had a mass of 32 grams. We produced 22.667 grams of ammonia and left 9.333 grams of nitrogen unreacted, therefore our post-reaction mass is also 32 grams, and we have a mass balance.

Please solve this problem:

- To form calcium hydroxide and sodium carbonate, 100 grams of calcium carbonate are allowed to react with 100 grams of sodium hydroxide in 100 grams of water. In this reaction, the limiting reagent is:

  A. calcium carbonate.
  B. sodium hydroxide.
  C. water.
  D. sodium.

Problem solved:

A is correct. To solve this problem, first write the balanced equation:

$$CaCO_3 + 2NaOH \rightarrow Ca(OH)_2 + Na_2CO_3$$

Because water does not appear in the balanced equation, we can eliminate choice C.

Determine the number of moles of each reagent that are available for the reaction by dividing the masses in grams by their respective molecular weights:

$CaCO_3$:	100 g ÷ 100 g/mol = 1 mol
NaOH:	100 g ÷ 40 g/mol = 2.5 mol

Next, we must find the number of equivalents of each reactant that are available:

$CaCO_3$:	1 mol ÷ 1 mol/equivalent = 1 equivalent
NaOH:	2.5 mol ÷ 2 mol/equivalent = 1.25 equivalents

Since $CaCO_3$ is available in the least number of equivalents, $CaCO_3$ is the limiting reagent.

OXIDATION-REDUCTION REACTIONS

Oxidation Numbers

The **oxidation number** of an atom indicates the number of electrons that this atom would have either gained or lost in the formation of the molecule of which it is a part if the molecule were assumed to be entirely composed of ions. *Positive* oxidation numbers indicate a *loss* of electrons. *Negative* oxidation numbers indicate a *gain* of electrons. For a neutral molecule, all oxidation numbers must add up to zero. When the oxidation numbers do not add up to zero, the result is a charged molecule or a complex ion.

Most atoms have more than one possible oxidation number. For the transition metals (*d* block), oxidation numbers are easiest to determine from the oxidation numbers of the other elements to which the transition metal is bound. Fortunately, certain elements have only one oxidation number:

- All group IA elements have an oxidation number of +1.

- All group IIA elements have an oxidation number of +2.

- All group IIIB elements have an oxidation number of +3.

- Fluorine always has an oxidation number of –1.

- Oxygen almost always has an oxidation number of –2 (oxygen has a –1 oxidation state in peroxides, e.g., H_2O_2).

- Hydrogen has an oxidation number of either +1 or –1. Use this rule of thumb: +1 when bonded to nonmetals, –1 when bonded to metals.

In a molecule with one of these elements, you can figure out the oxidation numbers of other atoms by summing to get zero (or the overall charge on the molecule).

Consider $K_2Cr_2O_7$. Since we know that oxygen has an oxidation number of –2 and potassium, being a group IA element, has an oxidation number of +1, we can solve for the oxidation number of chromium:

K	2 ×	+1	=	+2
O	7 ×	–2	=	–14
Cr	2 ×	__	=	+12 (since the sum must be zero)

The oxidation state of chromium in $K_2Cr_2O_7$ is +6.

Please solve this problem:

- What is the oxidation number of iodine in periodic acid (HIO_4)?

    A. −5
    B. −1
    C. +5
    D. +7

Problem solved:

D is correct. Since we know oxygen has an oxidation number of −2 and hydrogen has an oxidation number of +1, we can solve for the oxidation number of iodine:

H	1	×	+1	=	+1
O	4	×	−2	=	−8
I	1	×	__	=	+7 (since the sum must be zero)

The oxidation state of iodine in HIO_4 is +7.

Redox Reactions

Sometimes the oxidation state of an atom changes during a reaction. When this occurs, the reaction is termed an **oxidation-reduction reaction**, or a **redox reaction**. If the oxidation number of an atom increases during a reaction, it is said to be **oxidized**. If the oxidation number of an atom decreases during the reaction, it is said to be **reduced**. An increase in oxidation number indicates a loss of electrons. A decrease in oxidation number indicates a gain of electrons. Oxidation always occurs in tandem with reduction—the total number of electrons does not change; rather, the electrons are redistributed among the participating atoms.

An atom that undergoes a loss of electrons is being **oxidized**. Because this atom must also then be causing another atom's reduction, the oxidized atom is called the **reducing agent**, or **reductant**. Conversely, an atom that undergoes a gain of electrons is being **reduced**. Since this atom is also causing another atom to be oxidized, this atom is called the **oxidizing agent**, or **oxidant**.

Consider the following redox reaction:

$$Cu(NO_3)_2(aq) + Zn(s) \rightarrow Zn(NO_3)_2(aq) + Cu(s)$$

In this reaction, we can see that copper undergoes a change in oxidation state from +2 to 0, while zinc undergoes a change in oxidation state from 0 to +2. Therefore, copper is reduced (gains electrons) and zinc is oxidized (loses electrons). For this reaction, we can write two **half reactions**:

The half reaction for the reduction of copper is:

$$Cu^{2+} + 2e^- \rightarrow Cu^0$$

and the half reaction for the oxidation of zinc is:

$$Zn^0 \rightarrow Zn^{2+} + 2e^-$$

In this case, each half reaction is a two electron transfer:

$$Cu^{2+} + Zn^0 + 2e^- \rightarrow Cu^0 + Zn^{2+} + 2e^-$$

or:

$$Cu^{2+} + Zn^0 \rightarrow Cu^0 + Zn^{2+}$$

The reaction is balanced as written.

Consider the oxidation-reduction reaction between potassium dichromate and hydrogen iodide:

$$K_2Cr_2O_7 + HI \rightarrow KI + CrI_3 + I_2 + H_2O$$

In order to balance this reaction, we must first determine which atoms have been oxidized and which have been reduced. We do this by assigning oxidation numbers to each atom:

K_2	Cr_2	O_7	+	H	I	→	K	I	+	Cr	I_3	+	I_2	+	H_2	O
+1	+6	−2		+1	−1		+1	−1		+3	−1		0		+1	−2

We can see that chromium is reduced from a +6 oxidation state to a +3 oxidation state, and that some of the iodine is oxidized from a −1 oxidation state to a 0 oxidation state. Therefore the two half reactions for this equation are:

$$Cr^{6+} + 3e^- \rightarrow Cr^{3+}$$

and:

$$2I^{1-} \rightarrow I_2 + 2e^-$$

These two half reactions are not balanced in terms of electrons—balancing the electrons is our first step:

$$2 \times (Cr^{6+} + 3e^- \rightarrow Cr^{3+})$$

$$3 \times (2I^{1-} \rightarrow I_2 + 2e^-)$$

$$\overline{\phantom{2Cr^{6+} + 6I^{1-} + 6e^- \rightarrow 2Cr^{3+}}}$$

$$2Cr^{6+} + 6I^{1-} + 6e^- \rightarrow 2Cr^{3+} + 3I_2 + 6e^-$$

or:

$$2Cr^{6+} + 6I^{1-} \rightarrow 2Cr^{3+} + 3I_2$$

Therefore, the minimum number of chromium atoms on each side of the balanced equation is two, and the minimum number of iodine atoms on each side of the balanced equation is six. Using this, we get:

$$K_2Cr_2O_7 + 6HI \rightarrow KI + 2CrI_3 + 3I_2 + H_2O$$

Balancing for potassium, this becomes:

$$K_2Cr_2O_7 + 6HI \rightarrow 2KI + 2CrI_3 + 3I_2 + H_2O$$

Balancing for oxygen, this becomes:

$$K_2Cr_2O_7 + 6HI \rightarrow 2KI + 2CrI_3 + 3I_2 + 7H_2O$$

And, finally, balancing for hydrogen, we get the completely balanced equation:

$$K_2Cr_2O_7 + 14HI \rightarrow 2KI + 2CrI_3 + 3I_2 + 7H_2O$$

Although the MCAT will not directly ask you to balance such equations (given the multiple choice nature of the test), it is definitely to your benefit to be able to balance complex redox equations.

Please solve this problem:

- What is the ratio of copper to nitric acid (HNO_3) in the redox reaction between these substances to form copper (II) nitrate, water, and nitric oxide?

  A. 1:4
  B. 3:8
  C. 8:3
  D. 4:1

Problem solved:

B is correct. To solve this problem, we must balance the reaction:

$$Cu + HNO_3 \rightarrow Cu(NO_3)_2 + H_2O + NO$$

The oxidation half reaction is:

$$Cu \rightarrow Cu^{2+} + 2e^-$$

The reduction half reaction is:

$$N + 3e^- \rightarrow N^{2+}$$

Balancing for electrons, we get:

$$3Cu + ?HNO_3 \rightarrow 3Cu(NO_3)_2 + H_2O + 2NO$$

The question mark is inserted to show that since not all of the N^{5+} is reduced, we do not know with certainty what this stoichiometric coefficient is simply from an electron balance. In order to determine this value, we need to balance nitrogen. There are $6 + 2 = 8$ nitrogens on the right, so there need to be 8 nitrogens on the left:

$$3Cu + 8HNO_3 \rightarrow 3Cu(NO_3)_2 + H_2O + 2NO$$

At this point, even though we are not finished balancing the equation, we can see that the ratio of copper to nitric acid is 3:8.

To check, we can complete the balancing using either hydrogen or oxygen:

$$3Cu + 8HNO_3 \rightarrow 3Cu(NO_3)_2 + 4H_2O + 2NO$$

REACTION KINETICS: RATE, RATE LAWS, AND CATALYSIS

Kinetics: The Study of Reaction Rates

Kinetics is the study of the rates of chemical reactions. The field of kinetics focuses on both the speed at which a reaction occurs and the mechanism by which it occurs.

The amounts of products formed, or the equilibrium amounts of products and reactants (**Chapter 18**), are not accounted for by kinetics. The thermodynamics of an overall reaction (**Chapter 17**) also have no bearing on the rate of reaction. Likewise, the stoichiometry of the balanced equation of the reaction is irrelevant to kinetics.

Reaction Mechanisms

A chemical reaction involves the breaking of existing chemical bonds and the formation of new chemical bonds. Breaking a chemical bond requires the input of energy, while the formation of a chemical bond involves the release of energy. Many different factors contribute to the strength of a chemical bond (**Chapter 14**). The breaking or making of bonds may be accomplished in a variety of ways; this results in many different reaction paths from reactants to products. A **reaction mechanism** is the pathway by which reactants are converted to products. Each reaction has available to it a number of different mechanistic pathways. Each mechanism will have different steps, different rates, and different combinations of possible products. The particular mechanism that prevails, or predominates (since often a reaction will proceed simultaneously along competitive pathways) depends on the conditions of the reactions. The reaction conditions include concentrations, pressure, temperature, and the absence or presence of a catalyst.

Each mechanism is comprised of a series of steps, called **elementary processes**. Consider the overall reaction:

$$2AB + C \rightleftharpoons A_2C + B_2$$

One possible mechanism for this reaction is:

Step 1:	$AB \rightarrow A + B$
Step 2:	$A + C \rightarrow AC$
Step 3:	$AC + A \rightarrow A_2C$
Step 4:	$B + B \rightarrow B_2$

Another possible mechanism for this reaction is:

Step 1:	$AB + C \rightleftharpoons ABC$
Step 2:	$ABC \rightleftharpoons AC + B$
Step 3:	$AB \rightarrow A + B$
Step 4:	$AC + A \rightarrow A_2C$
Step 5:	$B + B \rightarrow B_2$

Elementary processes are distinguished by the number of reactant molecules involved in that particular step. A step involving only one reactant molecule, such as step 1 in the first mechanism or steps 2 or 3 in the second mechanism above, is called a **unimolecular process**. A step involving two reactant molecules, such as steps 2, 3, or 4 in the first mechanism or steps 1, 4, or 5 in the second mechanism above, is called a **bimolecular process**. Elementary processes involving more than two reactant molecules are rare: therefore, most mechanistic steps are either unimolecular or bimolecular.

For each elementary process, or step, in a mechanism, there is an energy barrier that must be overcome in order for that step to proceed. This energy barrier is termed the **activation energy** for that step. The higher the activation energy of a step, the less likely that step is to occur and, therefore, the slower that step will be. For any mechanism, the step with the highest activation energy is the slowest step. The slowest step in a series of steps will limit the overall progression from reactants to products, so this step is termed the **rate-determining step**. Because steps are dependent on reaction conditions, the rate-determining step under a given set of reaction conditions may change as reaction conditions change.

Another important feature of elementary processes is **microscopic reversibility**. While an overall chemical reaction may not be considered to be reversible, given the order and combination of mechanistic steps, *all* elementary processes are reversible. The reversibility of elementary processes is termed the principle of microscopic reversibility. This principle states that for every forward process, the reverse process also occurs in *exactly* the reverse manner.

If $AB \rightarrow A + B$ then $A + B \rightarrow AB$ by reversing the path.

During the elementary processes of a mechanism, products may be formed and later consumed. An example of this is product ABC of step 1 of the second mechanism above. Such a substance is termed an **intermediate**. An intermediate is a detectable substance that is neither reactant nor product and that is formed and then consumed within a mechanistic pathway. The detection of such intermediates is often crucial in determining the mechanism of a reaction.

An intermediate should not be confused with a **transition state**. The latter is a high-energy species found at the peak of the reaction curve. Intermediates are found in the troughs of reaction curves. This is discussed in greater detail when reaction diagrams are presented.

Please solve this problem:

- All the following affect reaction kinetics EXCEPT:

    A. catalysts.
    B. temperature.
    C. microscopic reversibility.
    D. stoichiometry.

Problem solved:

D is correct. Kinetics is *not* concerned with the stoichiometry of the reaction under investigation. Kinetics is affected by catalysts and other reaction conditions, such as temperature and pressure. Kinetics is concerned with the mechanism of reactions. Mechanisms of reactions are comprised of steps, or elementary processes, which are all reversible.

Reaction Rates

The rate of a chemical reaction is the answer to the question "How much does this reaction move from reactants to products in a given amount of time?" We can express this quantity either as the amount of product formed in a given amount of time or as the amount of reactant consumed in a given amount of time.

Consider the general reaction:

$$aA + bB \rightarrow cC + dD$$

The rate at which the reaction proceeds can be measured as the rate at which reactant A or reactant B is consumed, or as the rate at which reactant C or reactant D is formed:

$$\text{Rate of Reaction} = \frac{-\Delta[A]}{a\Delta t} = \frac{-\Delta[B]}{b\Delta t} = \frac{\Delta[C]}{c\Delta t} = \frac{\Delta[D]}{d\Delta t}$$

To see this more clearly (especially when stoichiometry applies to the rate expression), consider the following example:

$$N_2O_4(g) \rightarrow 2NO_2(g)$$

The rate of this reaction is given by:

$$\text{Rate of Reaction} = \frac{-\Delta[N_2O_4]}{\Delta t} = \frac{\Delta[NO_2]}{2\Delta t}$$

We can see that for every 1 mole of N_2O_4 consumed, 2 moles of NO_2 are produced.

Please solve this problem:

- The rate of the reaction $2NO(g) + O_2(g) \rightarrow 2NO_2(g)$ is given by:

  A. $\dfrac{\Delta[NO]}{2\Delta t}$

  B. $\dfrac{\Delta[O_2]}{\Delta t}$

  C. $\dfrac{\Delta[NO_2]}{2\Delta t}$

  D. $\dfrac{\Delta[N_2]}{\Delta t}$

Problem solved:

C is correct. The rate of reaction is given by either the rate of disappearance of reactants in a given time or the rate of formation of products in a given time. Choices A and B would be rate of reaction expressions for the reverse reaction. Choice D is nonsense.

The Effect of Concentration: The Rate Law

Concentration has a marked effect on the rate of reaction. In general, a reaction will slow down as time passes because reactants are being consumed. As the concentration of reactants decreases, there are fewer collisions between reactant molecules.

The quantitative implication of reaction rate decreasing as concentration of reactants decreases is that rate is proportional to reactant concentration. Considering the general reaction:

$$aA + bB \rightarrow cC + dD$$

the **rate law** is given by:

$$Rate = k[A]^x[B]^y$$

where [A] and [B] are the concentrations of A and B, respectively. The value of x is the *order of the reaction with respect to A* and the value of y is the *order of the reaction with respect to B*. The **overall order** of this reaction is given by the sum of x and y. The values of x and y must be experimentally determined. The values of x and y bear *no* relationship to the stoichiometric numbers a and b.

For instance, it has been experimentally determined that the rate law expression for:

$$3NO(g) \rightarrow N_2O(g) + NO_2(g)$$

is given by:

$$Rate = k[NO]^2$$

The final quantity in the above general rate law expression, k, is the **specific rate constant** (or sometimes just the **rate constant**) for the reaction at a particular temperature. Note that if the temperature of the reaction is changed, a new k must be calculated. The following are the important points to remember about rate constant, k:

- The value of k is unique to each reaction at a given temperature.

- The value of k will change if the temperature is changed.

- The value of k does *not* change with time.

- The value of k is not dependent on the concentrations of either reactants or products.

- The value of k *must* be determined experimentally.

- The units of k depend on the overall order of the reaction.

Since k must be determined experimentally, a common method for doing so is the **method of initial rates**. As stated above, k does not change with time; therefore, the value of k found from the initial concentration conditions will hold at any later time during the course of the reaction.

Please solve this problem:

- All of the following factors do not affect the specific rate constant, k, EXCEPT:

    A. temperature.
    B. time.
    C. initial concentration of reactants.
    D. volume of reaction system.

Problem solved:

A is correct. Be careful of the double negative questions on the MCAT. You should rephrase this question: "Which of the following affects k?" Then, the answer is clearly "temperature."

The Effect of Temperature: The Arrhenius Equation

A change in the temperature of a reaction will lead to a change in the value of the rate constant, k. The average kinetic energy of the molecules in a reaction system is proportional to the temperature (in Kelvin) of the system **(Chapter 20)**. This is because kinetic energy provides the movement for collisions to occur. It is also necessary to provide sufficient energy during the collision such that the activation energy for the reaction, or reaction step, is available for reaction.

From experimental evidence, Svante Arrhenius was able to develop the mathematical relationship between activation energy, absolute temperature (Kelvin), and the rate constant at that temperature. The result is the **Arrhenius equation**:

$$k = Ae^{-\frac{E_a}{RT}}$$

which, in terms of log, base 10, may be written:

$$\log k = \log A - \frac{E_a}{2.303\ RT}$$

This equation is used to determine the rate constant, k_2, at a temperature, T_2, when the rate constant, k_1, is known at temperature T_1. In this case, the Arrhenius equation becomes:

$$\log \frac{k_2}{k_1} = \frac{E_a}{2.303\ R}\left(\frac{T_2 - T_1}{T_1 T_2}\right)$$

If you are expected to use the Arrhenius equation on the MCAT, it will be provided. The important points to remember here are that the rate constant of a reaction is different for different temperatures, and the magnitude of the change in the rate constant is directly proportional to the activation energy of the reaction—the larger the activation energy, the greater the change in rate constant for the same temperature change.

Please solve this problem:

- As temperature is increased:

    A. k increases for all reactions.
    B. k increases for some reactions.
    C. k decreases for some reactions.
    D. k decreases for all reactions.

Problem solved:

A is correct. Given the Arrhenius equation:

$$\log \frac{k_2}{k_1} = \frac{E_a}{2.303\ R}\left(\frac{T_2 - T_1}{T_1 T_2}\right)$$

because temperature is measured in Kelvin, the temperature term must always be positive when temperature increases ($T_2 > T_1$). By definition, activation energy, E_a, is always positive, as is the gas constant, R. Therefore, for increasing temperature, the right side of the Arrhenius equation is always positive. We can now reduce the Arrhenius equation to:

$$\log K = P$$

where $K = k_2/k_1$ and P is meant to designate the positive value of the right side of the equation. Solving for K:

$$K = 10^P$$

By definition, 10^P is always greater than 1. Therefore, K must always be greater than 1, implying that the numerator (k_2) must always be greater than the denominator (k_1).

The Effect of Catalysts

Catalysts are substances that are added to reaction systems either to *increase or decrease* the rate of reaction. While catalysts are usually thought of as speeding up a reaction, it *must* be recognized that a catalyst may also *slow down* a reaction. A catalyst that's used to slow down a reaction is called an **inhibitory catalyst**, or **inhibitor**. The following discussion will focus on catalysts that speed up reactions. You should be aware that an inhibitor will have the reverse effect on a reaction.

A catalyst that increases the rate of reaction acts by allowing the reaction to occur via an alternative pathway. This alternative pathway serves to lower the overall activation energy of the reaction system. Although a catalyst may react with reactants or intermediates along the path of the reaction, it does not appear in the balanced equation for the reaction. If a catalyst does react with a reactant or an intermediate, it is regenerated in subsequent steps. If what might appear at first to be a catalyst is not regenerated, it is not a catalyst but a reactant.

- A catalyst is neither consumed nor produced during the course of a reaction.

Catalysts may be classified into two categories: **homogeneous catalysts** and **heterogeneous catalysts**. A homogeneous catalyst exists in the same phase as the reactants. An example of a homogeneous catalyst is an acid or a base added catalytically to an organic reaction. **Enzymes** are proteins that act as homogeneous catalysts for specific biochemical reactions.

A heterogeneous, or **contact catalyst,** exists in a different phase than the reactants. Heterogeneous catalysts are usually solids that operate by supplying a surface upon which the reaction may occur. An example of a contact catalyst is "poisoned palladium" (palladium with added graphite), which is often used as a hydrogenation catalyst in organic chemistry.

The most important thing to remember about catalysts is that they operate by altering the activation energy of a reaction. Catalysts have no effect on the equilibrium concentrations of reactants and products **(Chapter 18)**.

Please solve this problem:

- A catalyst does NOT:

    A. affect the mechanism of a reaction.
    B. affect the activation energy of a reaction.
    C. affect the concentration of products at equilibrium.
    D. affect the elementary processes of a reaction.

Problem solved:

C is correct. Catalysts operate by altering the activation energy of a reaction. This alteration in activation energy is achieved by providing an alternative mechanism—via altered elementary processes. Catalysts do not affect equilibrium.

15.2 MASTERY APPLIED: PRACTICE PASSAGE AND QUESTIONS

Passage

The rate of chemical reactions involving gas phase reactants, gas phase products, or both is easily measured by a change in pressure as the reaction proceeds.

In a reaction involving gas phase reactants, the partial pressures of the reactant gases were varied while the initial reaction rate was recorded. The results for this reaction at 1099°C are tabulated in Table 1. The stoichiometry of this reaction is:

$$2AB(g) + 2C(g) \rightarrow A_2(g) + 2BC(g)$$

Trial #	P_C (torr)	P_{AB} (torr)	Initial Rate (torr/s)
1	200	400	0.160
2	300	400	0.240
3	400	400	0.320
4	400	200	0.040
5	400	300	0.135

Table 1

1. What is the rate law for this reaction?

    A. Rate = $k[AB]^3[C]$
    B. Rate = $k[AB]^2[C]^2$
    C. Rate = $k[AB]^2[C]$
    D. Rate = $k[AB]^3$

2. What is the rate constant, k, in s^{-1} torr^{-3}, for this reaction?

    A. 1.25×10^{11}
    B. 5.00×10^3
    C. 2.32×10^{-4}
    D. 1.25×10^{-11}

3. If the total pressure in the container were increased by reducing the volume, the rate of the reaction would:

    A. increase.
    B. decrease.
    C. remain the same.
    D. not be predictable.

4. If the total pressure in the container were increased by adding a nonreactive gas, the rate of the forward reaction would:

    A. increase.
    B. decrease.
    C. remain the same.
    D. not be predictable.

5. If a sixth trial of the reaction is conducted with $P_{AB} = 500$ torr and $P_C = 100$ torr, the initial rate is expected to be:

    A. 0.006 torr/s
    B. 0.062 torr/s
    C. 0.156 torr/s
    D. 0.625 torr/s

6. If an inhibitory catalyst were added to the reaction system:

    A. the equilibrium concentration of $A_2(g)$ would increase.
    B. the equilibrium concentration of $A_2(g)$ would decrease.
    C. the activation energy would increase.
    D. the activation energy would decrease.

15.3 MASTERY VERIFIED: ANSWERS AND EXPLANATIONS

1. **A is correct.** Comparing trial 1 to trial 3, we can see that when P_C is doubled and P_{AB} is held constant, the rate is doubled. Therefore, we can say,

$$\text{rate} \propto P_C \text{ and } P_C \propto [C], \text{ therefore rate} \propto [C]$$

Comparing trial 4 to trial 3, we can see that when P_{AB} is doubled and P_C is held constant, the rate is increased by a factor of 8 (2^3). Therefore, we can say,

$$\text{rate} \propto P_{AB}^3 \propto [AB]^3$$

The rate law says that:

$$\text{rate} = k[AB]^3[C]$$

2. **D is correct.** To solve this problem, we can use our answer from question 1 and plug in numbers for [AB] and [C] from any of the five trials. Using trial 1:

$$\text{rate} = 0.160 = k[400]^3[200] = k(1.28 \times 10^{10})$$

$$\text{Therefore, } k = 0.160 \div (1.28 \times 10^{10}) = 1.25 \times 10^{-11}$$

3. **A is correct.** If the total pressure of the container is increased by decreasing the volume, the frequency of collisions between reactant molecules will increase. The more often the reactant molecules collide, the more likely they are to collide in the proper orientation for a successful reaction. Therefore, as pressure is increased, the rate of the reaction is also increased.

4. **C is correct.** Adding a nonreactive gas would not change the partial pressures of the reacting gases and would not affect the rate of reaction.

5. **C is correct.** Using the rate law derived from question 1 and the rate constant obtained from question 2:

$$\text{rate} = (1.25 \times 10^{-11})[500]^3[100] = 0.156$$

6. **C is correct.** A catalyst acts by affecting the activation energy of a reaction. An inhibitory catalyst increases the activation energy of a reaction by forcing the reaction to take a mechanistic pathway that is less energetically favorable than the pathway available in the absence of the catalyst. Catalysts do *not* affect equilibrium concentrations of reactants or products.

CHAPTER 16

CHEMICAL REACTIONS II: EQUILIBRIUM DYNAMICS

16.1 MASTERY ACHIEVED

EQUILIBRIUM

When appropriate reactants are placed together, they react to form products. The reactants must collide with each other in the correct orientation and with sufficient energy to break old bonds and to form new bonds. Once products are formed, they, too, can collide with one another in the correct orientation and with sufficient energy to reform the reactant molecules.

As a reaction progresses, a time is reached at which the rate of formation of products from reactants is equal to the rate of formation of reactants from products. From this time forward, in the absence of outside influence, there is no net change in the concentrations of products relative to the concentrations of reactants. The reaction system is not static: Reactants are still forming products, and products are still re-forming reactants. It is the *ratio* of products to reactants that is static. This state is called **chemical equilibrium**.

Depending on the starting conditions of the reaction system or the activities performed upon it prior to equilibrium, the absolute concentrations of reactants and products may vary while the relative concentrations—expressed as the ratio of products to reactants—remain constant.

To summarize the equilibrium condition:

- Equilibrium is a *dynamic condition*—forward and reverse reactions occur simultaneously and at the same rate.

- Equilibrium is *independent of the path taken to reach equilibrium*—the ratio of products to reactants will not change as long as temperature and, in some cases, pressure and volume do not change.

Please solve this problem:

- Equilibrium is:

    A. a static condition in which the concentration of the reactants is equal to the concentration of the products.
    B. a dynamic condition in which the concentration of the reactants is equal to the concentration of the products.
    C. a static condition in which the rate of formation of the reactants is equal to the rate of formation of the products.
    D. a dynamic condition in which the rate of formation of the reactants is equal to the rate of formation of the products.

Problem solved:

D is correct. This is the definition of chemical equilibrium.

EQUILIBRIUM CONSTANTS

The Equilibrium Constants (K_{eq}, K_c, K_p)

The equilibrium constant, K_{eq}, is the ratio of product concentrations to reactant concentrations that exists at equilibrium. For the general reaction:

$$aA + bB \rightarrow cC + dD$$

the equilibrium constant is given by:

$$K_{eq} = \frac{[C]^c [D]^d}{[A]^a [B]^b}$$

The concentrations are the equilibrium concentrations (not the initial concentrations), and they are usually measured in molarity (M). Pure liquids and pure solids do not appear in the equilibrium equation; these are assumed to have a concentration of 1 M. If all reactants and products are gases, the partial pressures of the gases can be used in place of molarity. When this is done, however, the value of K_{eq} for gases is different from the value of K_{eq} that would have been calculated using molar concentrations. The relationship between these two quantities is:

$$K_p = K_c(RT)^{\Delta n}$$

where K_p is the equilibrium constant calculated from the partial pressures (in atmospheres), K_c is the equilibrium constant calculated from the molar concentrations, R is the gas constant (0.082 L•atm/mol•K), T is the absolute temperature, and Δn is the change in the total number of moles of gas from the reactants to the products.

All K_{eq}'s on the MCAT are K_c's, unless otherwise noted.

The magnitude of K_{eq} is independent of the amounts of reactants and products, but it is *not independent* of changes in temperature and, in some cases, pressure or volume. A change in one of these factors does not *necessarily* correspond to the change in K_{eq}. For example, some reactions will have a *decrease* in K_{eq} with an *increase* in temperature.

When the system is at equilibrium, the value of the equilibrium constant tells us the relative amounts of reactants and products. If K_{eq} is much larger than 1, then the ratio of product concentrations to reactant concentrations is high. If K_{eq} is close to 1, the relative concentrations of products and reactants are similar. And, if K_{eq} is much smaller than 1, then the ratio of product to reactant concentrations is low.

In summary:

- If $K_{eq} \gg 1$, then products are favored over reactants.

- If $K_{eq} \approx 1$, then neither reactants nor products is favored.

- If $K_{eq} \ll 1$, then reactants are favored over products.

Please solve this problem:

- Consider the following unbalanced reaction: $CuSO_4 + Fe_2O_3 \rightleftharpoons CuO + Fe_2(SO_4)_3$. The equilibrium concentrations are: $[CuSO_4] = 1.2\ M$, $[Fe_2O_3] = 0.4\ M$, $[CuO] = 1.5\ M$, and $[Fe_2(SO_4)_3] = 0.5\ M$. The resulting equilibrium:

    A. favors reactants.
    B. favors products.
    C. favors neither reactants nor products.
    D. cannot be determined from the information given.

Problem solved:

B is correct. To solve this problem, we must first balance the equation:

$$3\ CuSO_4 + Fe_2O_3 \rightleftharpoons 3\ CuO + Fe_2(SO_4)_3$$

We then see that the equilibrium constant is given by:

$$K_{eq} = \frac{\left[CuO\right]^3 \left[Fe_2(SO_4)_3\right]^1}{\left[CuSO_4\right]^3 \left[Fe_2O_3\right]^1} = \frac{\left[1.5\right]^3 \left[0.5\right]^1}{\left[1.2\right]^3 \left[0.4\right]^1} = \text{approximately } 2.44$$

Since this value is greater than 1, the equilibrium favors products.

The Reaction Quotient

The reaction quotient, Q, is related to the equilibrium constant, K_{eq}. While K_{eq} gives the ratio of products to reactants at equilibrium, the reaction quotient gives the same ratio at all times other than at equilibrium. The value of the reaction quotient at equilibrium is equal to K_{eq}. If the equation for the reaction is:

$$a A + b B \rightleftharpoons c C + d D$$

Then the equation for the reaction quotient is:

$$Q = \frac{(C)^c (D)^d}{(A)^a (B)^b}$$

Parentheses are used instead of brackets to designate concentrations other than equilibrium concentrations.

The reaction quotient can be calculated for any concentrations of reactants and products. The relationship between Q and K_{eq} is described in Table 16.1:

Relationship	Interpretation	Change as Reaction Approaches Equilibrium
$Q > K_{eq}$	Products in excess	Decrease in products, increase in reactants
$Q = K_{eq}$	At equilibrium	No change
$Q < K_{eq}$	Reactants in excess	Decrease in reactants, increase in products

Table 16.1

Please solve this problem:

- At high temperatures, $K_{eq} = 1 \times 10^{-13}$ for $2\,HF\,(g) \rightleftharpoons H_2\,(g) + F_2\,(g)$. At a certain time, the following concentrations were detected: $[HF] = 0.5\,M$, $[H_2] = 1 \times 10^{-6}\,M$, $[F_2] = 1 \times 10^{-4}\,M$. In order to reach equilibrium:

  A. HF must react to form more hydrogen and fluorine gases.
  B. hydrogen and fluorine gases must react to produce more HF.
  C. nothing needs to happen—the reaction is at equilibrium.
  D. the temperature of the reaction should be lowered.

Problem solved:

B is correct. To solve this problem, we must first determine Q.

$$Q = \frac{(H_2)(F_2)}{(HF)^2} = \frac{\left(1 \times 10^{-6}\right)^1 \left(1 \times 10^{-4}\right)}{(0.5)^2} = \frac{1 \times 10^{-10}}{0.25} = 4 \times 10^{-10}$$

Since we were told that $K_{eq} = 1 \times 10^{-13}$, we know that $Q > K_{eq}$. When this is the case, the products are in excess. Therefore, to reach equilibrium, H_2 and F_2 need to react to form HF.

Modifications in the Equilibrium Constant

The equilibrium constant of a chemical reaction system is affected by changes in the chemical equation.

For the general reaction:

$$aA + bB \rightarrow cC + dD$$

the equilibrium constant is given by:

$$K_{eq} = \frac{[C]^c [D]^d}{[A]^a [B]^b}$$

For the reaction:

$$cC + dD \rightarrow aA + bB$$

$$K_{eq}' = 1/K_{eq}$$

The equilibrium constant of a multistep reaction may be determined from the equilibrium constants of the individual steps. Consider the following two-step reaction:

$$aA + bB \rightarrow cC + dD \qquad K_{eq} = K_1$$

$$cC + dD \rightarrow eE + fF \qquad K_{eq} = K_2$$

The equilibrium constant of the reaction:

$$aA + bB \rightarrow eE + fF$$

is given by:

$$K_{eq}'' = K_1 K_2$$

Please solve this problem:

- The equilibria $H_2SO_4 \rightleftharpoons H^+ + HSO_4^-$ and $HSO_4^- \rightleftharpoons H^+ + SO_4^{-2}$ have equilibrium constants of 2.4×10^2 and 5.0×10^{-5}, respectively. The equilibrium constant for the dissociation of H_2SO_4 is:

  A. 5.0×10^{-5}
  B. 1.2×10^{-2}
  C. 2.4×10^2
  D. 4.8×10^6

Problem solved:

B is correct. The equilibrium constant of a two-step reaction is equal to the product of the equilibrium constants of each step:

$$K_{eq} = K_1 K_2 = (2.4 \times 10^2)(5.0 \times 10^{-5}) = 1.2 \times 10^{-2}$$

LE CHATELIER'S PRINCIPLE

Basic Le Chatelier

Once a reaction is at equilibrium, a variety of factors may cause a shift away from equilibrium. The addition or removal of either a reactant or a product will affect the concentration of that substance, but it will not affect the value of K_{eq}. Therefore, when a product or reactant is added or removed, the system will seek ways in which to reestablish the equilibrium condition. The tendency of a system to return to a condition of chemical equilibrium is **Le Chatelier's principle**. A statement of Le Chatelier's principle is:

- When a system at equilibrium is subjected to a stress, the equilibrium will shift in a direction that tends to alleviate the effect of that stress.

Consider the general reaction:

$$A + B \rightleftharpoons C + D$$

which is originally at equilibrium.

The addition of more A to the system will have the effect of producing more C and D. Therefore, the addition of A will also have the effect of reducing the equilibrium concentration of B, since C and D are made from both A and B:

$$A + [A + B \rightleftharpoons C + D]$$

leads to:

$$\uparrow A + \downarrow B \rightleftharpoons \uparrow C + \uparrow D$$

Likewise, an increase in the concentration of B would have a similar result:

$$\downarrow A + \uparrow B \rightleftharpoons \uparrow C + \uparrow D$$

The addition of more A and more B will drive the equilibrium to the right:

$$\uparrow A + \uparrow B \rightleftharpoons \uparrow\uparrow C + \uparrow\uparrow D$$

The addition of more C to the system increases production of A and B. Therefore, the addition of C will also reduce the equilibrium concentration of D, since A and B are made from both C and D:

$$C + [A + B \rightleftharpoons C + D]$$

leads to:

$$\uparrow A + \uparrow B \rightleftharpoons \uparrow C + \downarrow D$$

Increasing the concentration of D will have a similar result:

$$\uparrow A + \uparrow B \rightleftharpoons \downarrow C + \uparrow D$$

Adding more C and D will drive the equilibrium to the left:

$$\uparrow\uparrow A + \uparrow\uparrow B \rightleftharpoons \uparrow C + \uparrow D$$

The above scenarios all consider the addition of a substance to the reaction system. The scenarios work in exactly the opposite fashion when a substance is removed from the system.

Remove A:	$\downarrow A + \uparrow B \rightleftharpoons \downarrow C + \downarrow D$
Remove B:	$\uparrow A + \downarrow B \rightleftharpoons \downarrow C + \downarrow D$
Remove A and B:	$\downarrow A + \downarrow B \rightleftharpoons \downarrow\downarrow C + \downarrow\downarrow D$
Remove C:	$\downarrow A + \downarrow B \rightleftharpoons \downarrow C + \uparrow D$
Remove D:	$\downarrow A + \downarrow B \rightleftharpoons \uparrow C + \downarrow D$
Remove C and D:	$\downarrow\downarrow A + \downarrow\downarrow B \rightleftharpoons \downarrow C + \downarrow D$

Please solve this problem:

- In the aldol cycloaddition reaction of isobutyraldehyde with methyl vinyl ketone to form 4,4-dimethyl-2-cyclohexen-1-one and water, water is removed using a Dean-Stark trap to:

    A. decrease the yield of 4,4-dimethyl-2-cyclohexen-1-one.

    B. increase the yield of 4,4-dimethyl-2-cyclohexen-1-one.

    C. increase the yield of isobutyraldehyde.

    D. increase the yield of methyl vinyl ketone.

Problem solved:

B is correct. In order to answer this problem, one needs only to understand simple applications of Le Chatelier's principle. It is unimportant to this problem that you understand any of the chemistry involved—although this is not always the case.

Recognizing the Effect of a Change in pH

For an aqueous solution, an increase in pH means a lowering of H^+ concentration and a raising of OH^- concentration. A decrease in the pH of an aqueous solution means a higher H^+ concentration and a lower OH^- concentration.

Consider the general acid dissociation reaction:

$$HA \rightleftharpoons H^+ + A^-$$

The effect of *increasing* the H^+ concentration within this system is to (a) lower the pH and (b) drive the reaction to the left, thereby decreasing the concentration of the conjugate base A^-.

$$\uparrow HA \rightleftharpoons \uparrow H^+ + \downarrow A^-$$

The effect of *decreasing* the H^+ concentration within this system is to (a) raise the pH and (b) drive the equilibrium to the right, thereby increasing the concentration of the conjugate base A^-.

$$\downarrow HA \rightleftharpoons \downarrow H^+ + \uparrow A^-$$

Please solve this problem:

- The equilibrium constant of the reaction CH_3CO_2H $\rightleftharpoons H^+ + CH_3CO_2^-$ is 1.76×10^{-5}. NaOH is added until a pH of 10 is achieved. The equilibrium concentration of $CH_3CO_2^-$ has done the following:

    A. increased.
    B. remained unchanged.
    C. decreased.
    D. The effect of the addition of NaOH is impossible to predict from the given information.

Problem solved:

A is correct. A change to pH = 10 is an increase in pH. (This is discussed in detail in **Chapter 21**.) Regardless of what reactant is added, if the pH of the solution increases, the H^+ concentration decreases. Using Le Chatelier's principle, if $[H^+]$ decreases, $[CH_3CO_2H]$ must also decrease and $[CH_3CO_2^-]$ must increase.

EFFECTS OF PRESSURE, VOLUME, AND TEMPERATURE ON EQUILIBRIUM

Effects of Pressure and Volume

For a gaseous mixture at equilibrium, the overall pressure within a container can be changed either by adding more gas to the container or by decreasing the volume of the container.

The effects of adding a gas that is already a reactant or product in the reaction can be predicted by simply following Le Chatelier's principle as described earlier in this chapter. However, if the gas added to the mixture is a nonreactive gas, then the pressure will increase without changing the equilibrium concentrations. Since the equilibrium state can be represented by partial pressures of the products over the reactants, and the addition of a nonreactive gas does not change the partial pressures of either the products or the reactants, the equilibrium is unaffected.

To predict changes in equilibrium resulting from pressure changes due to a change in volume, Le Chatelier's principle can be used as follows:

- If volume is decreased, then pressure is increased. The reaction will be pushed in the direction resulting in lower moles of gas.

- If volume is increased, then pressure is decreased, and the reaction will shift in the direction with more moles of gas.

So when using Le Chatelier's principle to predict changes in equilibrium that result from change in pressure due to change in volume, pressure can be thought of as a variable on the side of the balanced reaction equation with the greater number of gaseous molecules.

If both sides contain an equal number of gaseous moles, then there is no change in equilibrium when pressure is changed.

Please solve this problem:

- The **Haber process** is the industrial method for the production of ammonia: $3\,H_2(g) + N_2(g) \rightarrow 2\,NH_3(g)$. If the pressure in a vessel containing hydrogen gas and nitrogen gas is increased, how is the Haber process affected?

  A. It is favored.
  B. It is disfavored.
  C. It is unaffected.
  D. It is impossible to tell from the information given.

Problem solved:

A is correct. To solve this problem, we must first determine the total number of moles of gas on both the reactant side and the product side of this reaction. Since the number of moles of gas on the reactant side is 4, and the number of moles of gas on the product side is 2, pressure moves the reaction to the right to compensate.

Effects of Temperature

The effects of temperature on the equilibrium of a system are more complicated than the effects of pressure. To determine the effects of temperature, one must first determine whether a reaction is endothermic or exothermic. These terms are discussed in greater detail in **Chapter 17**. For now, it is sufficient to define an endothermic reaction as a reaction that *consumes* heat and an exothermic reaction as a reaction that *gives off* heat. Stating this in Le Chatelier terms:

- An endothermic reaction requires heat as a reactant.

- An exothermic reaction produces heat as a product.

EFFECTS OF TEMPERATURE ON AN ENDOTHERMIC REACTION

Consider the following equilibrium, where the forward reaction is endothermic:

$$J + K \rightleftharpoons L + M$$

Because the forward reaction is endothermic, this equilibrium can be rewritten as:

$$J + K + heat \rightleftharpoons L + M$$

If the temperature of this system is raised, products are favored:

$$\downarrow J + \downarrow K + \uparrow heat \rightleftharpoons \uparrow L + \uparrow M$$

Likewise, if the temperature of this system is lowered, reactants are favored:

$$\uparrow J + \uparrow K + \downarrow heat \rightleftharpoons \downarrow L + \downarrow M$$

Please solve this problem:

- The production of hydrogen and oxygen gases from water is an example of an endothermic reaction. As the temperature of this reaction is increased:

  A. more water is formed.
  B. less hydrogen gas is produced.
  C. more hydrogen gas is produced.
  D. the equilibrium is unaffected.

Problem solved:

C is correct. If the temperature of an endothermic forward reaction is raised, products are favored.

EFFECTS OF TEMPERATURE ON AN EXOTHERMIC REACTION

Consider the following equilibrium, where the forward reaction is exothermic:

$$R + S \rightleftharpoons U + V$$

We can rewrite this equilibrium as:

$$R + S \rightleftharpoons U + V + heat$$

If the temperature of this system is raised, reactants are favored:

$$\uparrow R + \uparrow S \rightleftharpoons \downarrow U + \downarrow V + \uparrow heat$$

If the temperature of this system is lowered, products are favored:

$$\downarrow R + \downarrow S \rightleftharpoons \uparrow U + \uparrow V + \downarrow heat$$

Please solve this problem:

- The formation of ATP from ADP and inorganic phosphate is an endothermic reaction: $ADP(aq) + P_i(aq) + H^+(aq) \rightarrow ATP(aq) + H_2O(l)$. As body temperature increases, ADP production from ATP:

  A. decreases.
  B. increases.
  C. remains constant.
  D. cannot be determined from the information provided.

Problem solved:

A is correct. To solve this problem, we must recognize that the equilibrium, given the endothermic nature of the forward reaction, may be written:

$$ADP(aq) + P_i(aq) + H^+(aq) + heat \rightleftharpoons ATP(aq) + H_2O(l)$$

Therefore, if the temperature is increased,

$$\downarrow ADP(aq) + \downarrow P_i(aq) + \downarrow H^+(aq) + \uparrow heat \rightleftharpoons \uparrow ATP(aq) + \uparrow H_2O(l)$$

16.2 MASTERY APPLIED: PRACTICE PASSAGE AND QUESTIONS

Passage

The equilibrium constant for the dissolution of one substance into another substance, typically water, is termed the *solubility product constant* and is designated K_{sp}. Since pure solids do not appear in equilibrium expressions, K_{sp} has no denominator. For the dissociation:

$$A_aB_b(s) \rightleftharpoons aA^+(aq) + bB^-(aq)$$

the solubility product constant is given by:

$$K_{sp} = [A^+]^a[B^-]^b$$

The solubility of a material is given by its equilibrium concentration in solution. The solubility of A_aB_b can therefore be determined from K_{sp}.

The solubility product constants for selected materials are given in Table 1.

Compound	K_{sp} (at 25°C)
CdS	1.0×10^{-28}
AgI	1.5×10^{-16}
Al(OH)$_3$	2.0×10^{-32}
CuI	5.1×10^{-12}
AgCl	1.6×10^{-10}
BaSO$_4$	1.5×10^{-9}
CaCO$_3$	8.7×10^{-9}
BaCO$_3$	1.6×10^{-9}
PbSO$_4$	1.3×10^{-8}
CaSO$_4$	6.1×10^{-5}
CuSO$_4$	1.9×10^{0}

Table 1

1. Which of the following is the most soluble compound?

   A. $PbSO_4$
   B. $CaCO_3$
   C. CdS
   D. $AgCl$

2. The solubility of $BaSO_4$ is:

   A. 7.5×10^{-10}.
   B. 1.5×10^{-9}.
   C. 7.7×10^{-5}.
   D. 3.9×10^{-5}.

3. The chelator EDTA is sometimes used to treat cases of lead poisoning. EDTA forms a soluble complex with lead(II), which is excreted in the urine:

   $$Pb\text{-}EDTA2^- \rightleftharpoons Pb2+ + EDTA4-$$

   The equilibrium constant for this reaction is 5.0×10^{-19}. What is the blood concentration of Pb^{2+} after EDTA treatment if [Pb-EDTA^{2-}] = 2.0×10^{-4} M and [EDTA^{4-}] = 2.5×10^{-2} M?

   A. 4.0×10^{-21}.
   B. 2.5×10^{-20}.
   C. 6.3×10^{-17}.
   D. 1.6×10^{-16}.

4. A solution contains Ba^{2+}, Ca^{2+}, Cu^{2+}, and Pb^{2+}. When sulfuric acid is added, the first substance to precipitate will be:

   A. $BaSO_4$.
   B. $CaSO_4$.
   C. $CuSO_4$.
   D. $PbSO_4$.

5. The K_{sp} for silver(I) chloride at 100°C is 2.15×10^{-8}. The dissolution of silver(I) chloride:

   A. is exothermic.
   B. is endothermic.
   C. is neither endothermic nor exothermic.
   D. cannot be determined from the information provided.

6. The chloride ion is infinitely soluble in water. If the solubility product constants for $BaCl_2$, $CuCl_2$, $HgCl_2$, and $PbCl_2$ are 35.8, 73.0, 6.57, and 1.00, respectively, the least soluble cation is:

   A. Ba^{2+}.
   B. Cu^{2+}.
   C. Hg^{2+}.
   D. Pb^{2+}.

16.3 MASTERY VERIFIED: ANSWERS AND EXPLANATIONS

1. **A is correct.** Since each compound dissociates into two ions, the most soluble compound is the one with the highest K_{sp}: lead(II) sulfate.

2. **D is correct.** Solubility, x, is found from:

$$K_{sp} = [Ba^{2+}][SO_4^{2-}] = [x][x] = x^2$$

From the table, $K_{sp} = 1.5 \times 10^{-9}$. Thus:

$$x = \sqrt{1.5 \times 10^{-9}} = \sqrt{15 \times 10^{-10}} = \sqrt{15} \times \sqrt{10^{-10}} = 3.9 \times 10^{-5}$$

3. **A is correct.** We solve this problem using the expression for K_{eq}:

$$K_{eq} = \frac{\left[EDTA^{4-}\right]\left[Pb^{2+}\right]}{\left[Pb-EDTA^{2-}\right]}$$

Rearranging,

$$\left[Pb^{2+}\right] = \frac{\left[Pb-EDTA^{2-}\right]K_{eq}}{\left[EDTA^{4-}\right]} = \frac{\left(2.0 \times 10^{-4}\right)\left(5.0 \times 10^{-19}\right)}{\left(2.5 \times 10^{-2}\right)} = 4.0 \times 10^{-21}$$

4. **A is correct.** The first substance to precipitate will be the one with the lowest solubility. The substance with the lowest solubility is the substance with the lowest K_{sp}. The substance with the lowest K_{sp} is $BaSO_4$.

5. **B is correct.** The K_{sp} of silver(I) chloride at 25°C is x. At a higher temperature (100°C), the K_{sp} is increased, and more products are formed in the equilibrium:

$$AgCl \rightleftharpoons Ag^+ + Cl^-$$

When accounting for temperature, the equilibrium must be:

$$AgCl + heat \rightleftharpoons Ag^+ + Cl^- \text{ (endothermic)}$$

Thus:

$$\downarrow AgCl + \uparrow heat \rightleftharpoons \uparrow Ag^+ + \uparrow Cl^-$$

6. **D is correct.** $PbCl_2$ has the lowest K_{sp}, and is therefore the least soluble.

CHAPTER 17

CHEMICAL REACTIONS III: THERMODYNAMICS

17.1 MASTERY ACHIEVED

THERMODYNAMICS OF CHEMICAL REACTIONS: IN THEORY

Basic Definitions and Concepts of Thermodynamics

Thermodynamics is the study of heat and its interconversions with other energy forms. The **system (sys)** is the object under investigation. The **surroundings (surr)** are everything outside the system. The **universe (univ)** is the sum of the system and the surroundings.

An **open** system is a system that allows for the exchange of matter and energy between the surroundings and the system. A **closed** system allows for the exchange of energy only, meaning that mass is conserved within the system. An **isolated** system does not allow for the exchange of anything (matter or energy) between the system and the surroundings. In order for a system to be considered an isolated system it must be a closed system that is in neither mechanical nor thermal contact with the surroundings. While thermodynamics usually focuses on the system, changes in the thermodynamic properties of the surroundings must also be considered.

A variety of functions is used to determine the thermodynamic characteristics of a system. The **state** of a system is characterized by definite values of each of these functions. A **state function** is determined only by the current state of the system, not by the path taken to achieve this state. A **nonstate function** is path-dependent. Common thermodynamic state functions are **pressure, temperature, volume, internal energy, enthalpy, entropy,** and **free energy**. Common thermodynamic nonstate functions include **work** and **heat**. While nonstate functions may be interrelated, state functions are much more codependent. Once two or three state functions have been set or determined, the remaining state functions are also set, or may be determined without further measurement.

The **path** that a system takes to reach a given state may be given by a single step or by multiple steps. A **reversible path** is a continuous path that may be reversed at any point to restore the original values of the nonstate functions. An **irreversible path** is characterized by an inability to reverse the direction of the path with the achievement of the original nonstate function values.

The **energy** of a system is a state function that may take many different forms: **mechanical kinetic, mechanical potential, heat, electrical, light, sound, magnetic, chemical**, and others.

Please solve this problem:

- All of the following are thermodynamic state functions EXCEPT:

  A. internal energy.
  B. work.
  C. entropy.
  D. enthalpy.

Problem solved:

B is correct. A state function is determined by the current state of the system, not by the path taken to get to this state. The work performed by, or performed on, a system is dependent on the path.

There are two principal ways by which a system can gain or lose energy: by heat transfer or by work (the two common thermodynamic nonstate functions). Heat transfer occurs only when there is a temperature difference, or gradient, between the two objects (in chemical thermodynamics, these two items are typically the system and the surroundings, but they could be two items within the system itself). In the case of a system with a temperature higher than its surroundings, energy, in the form of heat, is transferred from the system to the surroundings. In the case of a system with a temperature lower than the surroundings, heat is transferred from the surroundings into the system. In the former process, convention dictates that the heat (Q_{sys}) takes a negative value. In the latter process, Q_{sys} takes a positive value. This also implies that Q_{surr} takes a positive value in the former process and a negative value in the latter process (since energy is conserved in the universe).

We can also denote heat as either Q_{rev} or Q_{irr}, where **rev** indicates a reversible process, and **irr** indicates an irreversible process. The heat of a reversible process (Q_{rev}) is always greater than the heat of an irreversible process (Q_{irr}).

Thermodynamic work principally takes the form of mechanical work (as in the lifting of an object) or of electrical work (as in a car battery). Work done by the system is negative (less energy is available to the system). Work done by the surroundings upon the system is positive (more energy is available to the system). There are many types of work, but we will focus here on the mechanical work done by expanding gases, which may be represented by the equation:

$$W = P\Delta V$$

where W is work, P is the pressure of the system, and ΔV is the internal volume change undergone by the system. As was the case for heat, the work performed by a reversible process is always greater than the work performed by an irreversible process.

Please solve this problem:

- Which of the following statements is true for any given change in state?

    I. The heat of an irreversible process is greater than the heat of a reversible process.
    II. The work performed on a system in a reversible process is greater than the work performed on a system in an irreversible process.
    III. The work performed by a system in a reversible process is greater than the work performed by a system in an irreversible process.

    A. I only
    B. II only
    C. III only
    D. II and III only

Problem solved:

D is correct. Both II and III are true, and I is false. The heat (whether given off or gained) in a reversible process is greater than the heat (whether given off or gained) in an irreversible process. Likewise, the work performed in a reversible process is greater than the work performed in an irreversible process, regardless of whether the system is performing work on the surroundings or the surroundings are performing work on the system.

A system's internal energy describes the total of energy stored within it. It is a state function, and represents the total kinetic energy of its molecules and the potential energy of the atoms that comprise the molecules. Measuring a given system's energy in absolute terms would require that we compare the energy within it to the energy it would embody if temperature were reduced to absolute zero. Since absolute zero is not experimentally achievable, internal energy cannot be expressed in absolute numbers.

Rather, we express internal energy in relative terms; we measure a system's change (ΔU) in internal energy before and after some process that affects it.

In that regard, science offers two closely related formulas, differing only as to the sign (+ or −) that precedes the term W (work). They are:

$$\Delta U = Q - W$$

where U is change in the system's internal energy, Q is heat gained by the system, and W is work performed by the system.

$$U = Q + W$$

where U is change in the system's internal energy, Q is heat gained by the system, and W is work performed on the system.

Please solve this problem:

- All of the following are thermodynamic state functions EXCEPT:

    A. heat.
    B. temperature.
    C. pressure.
    D. volume.

Problem solved:

A is correct. Three of the variables of the ideal gas law—pressure, volume, and temperature ($PV = nRT$)—are thermodynamic state functions.

Entropy

Entropy is a measure of the disorder of a system. As disorder increases, so does entropy. As a result, the entropy of a substance in the gaseous state is greater than the entropy of the same substance in the liquid state. Likewise, the entropy of a substance in the liquid state is greater than the entropy of that substance in the solid state.

- Entropy increases as temperature increases.

- Entropy increases in a reaction if that reaction produces more product molecules than it contained reactant molecules.

- Entropy increases when pure liquids and/or pure solids form solutions.

- The entropy of the universe, S_{univ}, always increases.

Please solve this problem:

- All of the following are properties of entropy EXCEPT:

    A. the entropy of the universe increases.
    B. the entropy gained by a system is not equal to the entropy lost by the surroundings.
    C. entropy is an energy term, as are all thermodynamic state functions.
    D. entropy increases with increasing temperature.

Problem solved:

C is correct. Not all thermodynamic state functions are energy terms; examples include entropy, volume, and pressure. Conversely, not all energy terms are state functions; examples of energy terms that are not state functions include work and heat. Choice A is true: The entropy of the universe must increase. Choice B is true: If the entropy gained by a system were equal to the entropy lost by the surroundings (and vice versa), the entropy of the universe (system + surroundings) would remain a constant. Choice D is true.

Enthalpy, Endothermic Reactions, and Exothermic Reactions

Enthalpy (*H*) is a measure of the heat released when pressure is held constant. By definition, the change in enthalpy of a system at constant pressure is given by the equation:

$$\Delta H_{sys} = Q_{sys,\,p}$$

where ΔH_{sys} is the change in enthalpy of the system, and $Q_{sys,p}$ is the heat absorbed by the system under conditions of constant pressure. As was the case for U, it is not possible to measure or calculate the absolute value of H. ΔH is related to ΔU by the equation:

$$\Delta H = \Delta U + \Delta(PV)$$

- A reaction is **endothermic** when ΔH_{sys} is positive.

- A reaction is **exothermic** when ΔH_{sys} is negative.

Please solve this problem:

- All of the following are properties of enthalpy EXCEPT:
    - A. a positive change in enthalpy indicates that heat is absorbed by the system.
    - B. a negative change in enthalpy indicates that heat is lost to the surroundings.
    - C. the change in enthalpy of a system is equal to the change in its internal energy
    - D. a reaction with a negative change in enthalpy is exothermic, a reaction with a positive change in enthalpy is endothermic.

Problem solved:

C is correct. The change in enthalpy is equal to the change in internal energy of a system only when the work done by a change in pressure and volume is zero.

Heats of Formation, Heats of Reaction, and Hess's Law

The **heat of formation** (ΔH_f) of a substance is the enthalpy required for the formation of one mole of that substance from its elements. The standard heat of formation (ΔH_f°) is the change in enthalpy for such a process under standard conditions. Standard thermodynamic conditions are defined as a temperature of 298.15 Kelvin (25°C) at a pressure of 1 atm. This should not be confused with **STP (standard temperature and pressure)**, where temperature is defined as 273.15 Kelvin (0°C). The ΔH_f° of all elements in their naturally occurring state is defined as zero.

The **heat of reaction** (ΔH°) is given by the sum of the heats of formation of the products minus the sum of the heats of formation of the reactants.

- An **endothermic** reaction has a positive ΔH°.

- An **exothermic** reaction has a negative ΔH°.

Consider the following reaction:

$$H_2(g) + \frac{1}{2}\,O_2(g) \rightarrow H_2O(g) \qquad \Delta H^\circ = -241.8 \text{ kJ}$$

The heat of formation is taken, by definition, to be zero for both H_2 and O_2, since these are the natural elemental forms of the elements H and O, respectively. Therefore, since the heat of reaction is equal to the heats of formation of the products minus the heats of formation of the reactants, we can say that the heat of formation of $H_2O(g)$ is equal to –241.8 kilojoules.

Note that the heat of formation of *liquid* water is not the same as the heat of formation of *gaseous* water:

$$H_2(g) + \frac{1}{2}\,O_2(g) \rightarrow H_2O(g) \rightarrow H_2O(\ell) \quad \Delta H^\circ = -285.8 \text{ kJ}$$

The extra 44 kilojoules of enthalpy given off is the result of a transition from the more energetic gaseous form to the less energetic liquid form. This energy is known as the **enthalpy of liquefaction**, or the **enthalpy of condensation**. Some heats of formation are given in Table 17.1.

Compound	ΔH_f (kJ/mol)	Compound	ΔH_f (kJ/mol)
$NH_3(g)$	−46.11	$CH_4(g)$	74.85
$NH_3(aq)$	−80.29	$C_2H_2(g)$	26.73
$PCl_5(g)$	−374.9	$C_2H_4(g)$	52.26
$PCl_5(s)$	−443.5	$C_2H_6(g)$	84.86
$C(g)$	716.68	$C_3H_8(g)$	−103.85
$H^+(aq)$	0	$C_4H_{10}(g)$	−126.15
$CO(g)$	−110.53	$C_5H_{12}(g)$	−146.11
$CO_2(g)$	−393.51	$C_6H_{14}(g)$	−198.7
$CO_2(aq)$	−413.80	α-D-glucose(s)	−1,274
$CO_3{}^{2-}(aq)$	−677.14	β-D-glucose(s)	−1,268
$HCO_3{}^-(aq)$	−691.99	β-D-fructose(s)	−1,266
$H_2CO_3(aq)$	−699.65	sucrose(s)	−2,222

Heats of Formation for Various Compounds
Table 17.1

Heats of reaction for complex reactions are determined via the use of **Hess's law of constant heat summation**. Consider the following reaction:

$$CO_2(g) + 4\ H_2(g) \rightarrow CH_4(g) + 2\ H_2O(\ell)$$

One method to determine the heat of reaction involves the heats of formation of each reactant and of each product.

For reactants:

- The heat of formation of H_2 is, by definition, zero.

- The heat of formation of $CO_2(g)$ is:

$$C(s) + O_2(g) \rightarrow CO_2(g) \qquad \Delta H_f^\circ = -393.5\ \text{kJ/mol}$$

- Therefore, the heat of formation of the reactants is −393.5 kilojoules.

For products:

- The heat of formation of $CH_4(g)$ is:

$$C(s) + 2\ H_2(g) \rightarrow CH_4(g) \qquad \Delta H_f^\circ = -74.85\ \text{kJ/mol}$$

- The heat of formation of $H_2O(\ell)$ is −285.8 kJ/mol, as given above.

- Therefore, the heat of formation of the products is:

$$-74.85 + 2(-285.8) = -646.45 \text{ kJ}$$

- Thus, the heat of reaction is:

$$-646.45 - (-393.5) = -252.95 \text{ kJ}$$

Please solve this problem:

- The complete combustion of n-butane is given by:

$$C_4H_{10}(g) + \frac{13}{2} O_2(g) \rightarrow 4 \ CO_2(g) + 5 \ H_2O(g)$$

The heat of this reaction is:

A. +2,657 kilojoules
B. +509.15 kilojoules
C. −509.15 kilojoules
D. −2,657 kilojoules

Problem solved:

D is correct. Remember that this is a combustion reaction, which we would expect to be *exothermic*. Also recall that exothermic reactions have *negative* heats of reaction. Therefore, you should have been able to eliminate choices A and B by inspection.

The heat of reaction is given by:

$$\Delta H^\circ_{rxn} = \Delta H^\circ_{f \, (products)} - \Delta H^\circ_{f \, (reactants)}$$

The heat of formation of the products is given by:

$$\Delta H^\circ_{f \, CO_2(g)} \times mol_{CO_2(g)} = (-393.5 \text{ kJ/mol})(4 \text{ mol}) = -1,574 \text{ kJ}$$
$$\Delta H^\circ_{f \, H_2O(g)} \times mol_{H_2O(g)} = (-241.8 \text{ kJ/mol})(5 \text{ mol}) = -1,209 \text{ kJ}$$
$$\Delta H^\circ_P = -2,783 \text{ kJ}$$

The heat of formation of the reactants is given by:

$$\Delta H^\circ_{f \, C_4H_{10}(g)} \times mol_{C_4H_{10}(g)} = (-126.15 \text{ kJ/mol})(1 \text{ mol}) = -126.15 \text{ kJ}$$
$$\Delta H^\circ_{f \, O_2(g)} = 0 \text{ kJ} = 0 \text{ kJ}$$
$$\Delta H^\circ_{f \, (reactants)} = -126.15 \text{ kJ}$$

Therefore, the total heat of reaction is (−2,783 kilojoules) − (−126.15 kilojoules) = −2,657 kilojoules, which is choice D. Choice C could be arrived at by neglecting to multiply the molar heats of formation in Table 17.1 by the stoichiometric coefficients in the balanced equation.

Gibbs Free-Energy and Reaction Spontaneity

The **free energy** of a system (or **Gibbs free-energy** of a system) at constant temperature is given by the equation:

$$\Delta G = \Delta H - T\Delta S$$

where all thermodynamic quantities refer to the system, and T is given in kelvin.

The Gibbs free-energy of a system is a measure of the energy available to the system for the performance of useful work. The absolute value of G cannot be calculated, or measured. As was the case for U and H, we refer to the change in G (ΔG) between two states of the system. Taking a closer look at the equation defining the Gibbs function, we see that ΔG may take either a positive or a negative value, depending upon the signs and magnitudes of ΔH and ΔS.

• When ΔG of a reaction is negative, the reaction is spontaneous in the forward direction.

• When ΔG of a reaction is positive, the reaction is nonspontaneous in the forward direction.

• When ΔG of a reaction is equal to zero, the reaction is at equilibrium.

A reaction with a positive ΔG is termed an **endergonic** reaction. A reaction with a negative ΔG is termed an **exergonic** reaction. Recall that it is ΔH that determines endothermicity versus exothermicity. All of the possible relationships between ΔG and ΔH, T, and ΔS are shown in Table 17.2.

ΔH	$-$	T	ΔS	ΔG
+		low	+	+
+		high	+	−
+		low	−	+
+		high	−	+
−		low	+	−
−		high	+	−
−		low	−	−
−		high	−	+

Free-energy Changes

Table 17.2

From these observations it should be clear that only those endothermic reactions that occur at a high temperature with an increase in entropy will occur spontaneously. On the other hand, an exothermic reaction that occurs at high temperature with a decrease in entropy will not be spontaneous. The probability of obtaining a negative entropy at high temperature is not large (recall that a gas possesses more entropy than a liquid and a liquid possesses more entropy than a solid).

Please solve this problem:

- Which of the following statements would serve as useful rules of thumb?

    I.   Exothermic reactions at high temperatures will be exergonic.
    II. Exothermic reactions at low temperatures will be exergonic.
    III. Endothermic reactions at low temperatures will be endergonic.
    IV. Endothermic reactions at high temperatures will be endergonic.

    A. I and III only
    B. II and III only
    C. II and IV only
    D. I and IV only

Problem solved:

B is correct. This question is best answered by referring to Table 17.2. You must know the relationships between ΔG, ΔH, ΔS, and T to avoid missing easy questions on the MCAT.

The Three Laws of Thermodynamics

There are three laws of thermodynamics. The first law states that for any isolated system (as defined earlier in this chapter) energy is constant. This law is simply a restatement of the general **principle of conservation of energy**. If we take our system to be the universe, we can state that energy is neither created nor destroyed within our system. In this regard, an isolated system may be thought of as a miniuniverse. The equation given earlier for the internal energy of a system:

$$\Delta U = Q + W$$

is a mathematical statement of the **first law of thermodynamics** where W is work done ON the system.

The **second law of thermodynamics** introduces the concept of entropy. This law states that no cyclic process in which the heat absorbed is completely converted into useful work is possible. This is not to say that natural processes that convert heat entirely into work cannot exist, but no process may exist in which a system is cycled from its point of origin to other points and back to its point of origin, with the heat produced being converted entirely to useful work.

The second law of thermodynamics points directly to the asymmetrical nature of all natural processes. While the first law provides for the conservation of energy, the second law cleaves the first law in half, asserting that even if a forward process converts all of the heat produced into useful work, the reverse process will not do so; similarly, even if a forward process does not convert all of the heat produced into useful work, this does not preempt the reverse process from doing so. In other words, the entropy of the universe is constantly increasing.

The **third law of thermodynamics** is perhaps the least useful thermodynamic law for the MCAT. This law, in effect, states that absolute zero is unattainable. While you should appreciate the significance of this statement, it probably won't be very useful on the MCAT.

Please solve this problem:

- According to the laws of thermodynamics:
  - A. absolute zero exists and is attainable.
  - B. entropy is conserved in the universe.
  - C. energy is conserved in the universe.
  - D. entropy is a thermodynamic state function.

Problem solved:

C is correct. Choice A is false: the third law of thermodynamics posits the existence of absolute zero; however, it also states that the attainment of absolute zero in a finite number of steps is an impossibility. Choice B is false: The second law of thermodynamics shows that the change in entropy of a forward process cannot be equal to the change in entropy of the reverse reaction. If these two quantities were equal, a system could be cycled from one state to another and back without heat loss. If such a cycling were possible, the construction of a perpetual motion machine would also be possible. Choice C is directly provided for by the first law of thermodynamics. While choice D is true, it is not provided for by any of the three laws of thermodynamics.

THERMODYNAMICS OF CHEMICAL REACTIONS: IN OPERATION

Reaction Diagrams, ΔH, ΔG, and Activation Energy

Drawn with a vertical **energy coordinate** and a horizontal **reaction coordinate,** reaction diagrams depict the relationship between the energy of the reaction system (energy coordinate) and the progress of the reaction (reaction coordinate). The energy coordinate may depict enthalpy (ΔH) or Gibbs free-energy (ΔG).

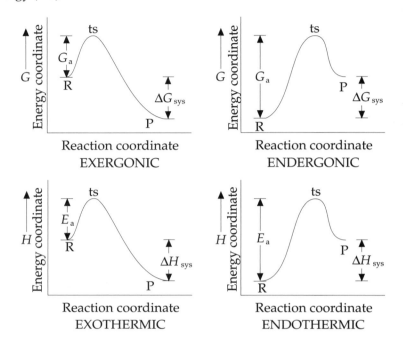

Figure 17.1

In the case of an endergonic or an exergonic reaction, the vertical distance between the energy of the reactants and the energy of the products is a measure of ΔG_{sys}. For exothermic or endothermic reactions, the vertical distance between the energy of the reactants and the energy of the products is a measure of ΔH_{sys}. Additionally, the vertical distance between the reactants and the highest vertical point on the curve is significant. In the case of a graph of free energy versus reaction coordinate, this vertical distance is a measure of the **free energy of activation**, or how much free energy is required to activate, or start, the reaction. In the case of a graph of enthalpy versus reaction coordinate, this vertical distance is a measure of the **enthalpy of activation**, or how much heat is required to activate the reaction. For the MCAT, enthalpy of activation is the activation energy, E_a.

The **transition state** (**ts**) of a system is the highest energy state that the system achieves during the course of its reaction. At this state, some of the bonds of the reactants are partially broken (elongated), and some of the new bonds that will be in the products have begun to form.

In the case of the exothermic reaction depicted, the transition state is less than halfway along the reaction coordinate. The transition state for the endothermic reaction is more than halfway along the reaction coordinate, which is generally the case. This observation leads us to two conclusions: (1) For exothermic processes, the transition state resembles the reactants more than it resembles the products and (2) for endothermic reactions, the transition state resembles the products more than it does the reactants.

Considering a reversible reaction, we can imagine the reaction diagram for the reverse reaction to be simply the mirror image of the reaction diagram for the forward reaction. From this it is clear that the activation energy is higher in the endothermic direction than in the exothermic direction; thus, the transition state in the endothermic direction is more similar to the products than the reactants, while the transition state in the exothermic direction is more similar to the reactants than the products. These are useful concepts to keep in mind when dealing with reaction diagrams.

For the MCAT, you should also be familiar with reaction diagrams of multistep processes. Represented below are typical reaction diagrams for exothermic S_N2 (one-step) and S_N1 (two-step) reactions. (Organic nucleophilic substitution reactions are discussed in detail in **Chapter 36**.)

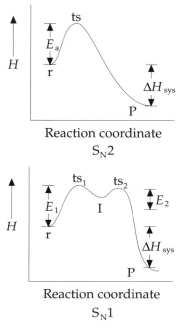

Figure 17.2

The S_N2 reaction diagram is provided merely as a comparison to the S_N1 diagram. The S_N1 diagram has two separate activation energies, labeled E_1 and E_2. The first activation energy is the enthalpy change that is accompanied by a movement from the reactants to the first transition state (ts_1). The second activation energy is the enthalpy change that is accompanied by movement from the reaction intermediate (I) to the second transition state (ts_2). An intermediate in a reaction pathway is an unstable species that has a relatively short lifetime in the reaction mixture compared to the products and the reactants. In terms of a reaction diagram, a trough in the pathway is indicative of an intermediate. The number of steps in an overall reaction is equal to the number of troughs plus one, or alternatively, to the number of peaks (or transition states).

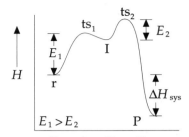

Reaction Coordinate

Figure 17.3

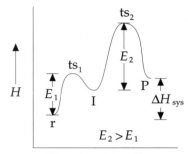

Reaction Coordinate

Figure 17.4

The slowest step in a multistep reaction is the **rate-determining step**, which is the step in the reaction diagram that has the greatest *individual* activation energy. The rate-determining step is *not* determined by the step with the highest-energy transition state. In Figure 17.3, you will notice that the second step has the highest-energy transition state, but that the first step has the highest activation energy. For this system, the rate-determining step is the first step. In Figure 17.4, you will notice that the second step has the highest-energy transition state *and* the highest activation energy. For this system, the rate-determining step is the second step.

Please solve this problem:

- The rate-determining step in a reaction sequence is:

    A. the step with the highest activation energy.
    B. the step with the highest energy transition state.
    C. the step which involves the limiting reagent.
    D. all of the above.

Problem solved:

A is correct. Choices B and C are commonly misinterpreted. As explained above, the rate-determining step is the step with the highest individual activation energy. While this may also coincide with the step having the highest-energy transition state, it need not do so. The rate-determining step is the kinetically slowest overall step in a reaction sequence. While the speed of a given step may be affected by the amount of reactants available for the performance of this step, the limiting reagent has little to do with kinetics. The limiting reagent is simply the reagent that gets used up first because there is less of it, not because of the speed of a step that consumes it.

Kinetics and Thermodynamic Reaction Energetics

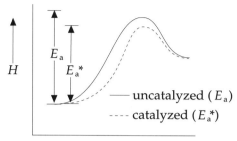

Figure 17.5

Catalysts (**Chapter 15**) alter a reaction's pathway. Catalysts cannot alter the reactants nor can they alter the products; therefore, they must alter the transition state(s). A catalyst is employed to reduce the activation energy of a reaction (or a step in a multistep reaction). Therefore, it should be clear that catalysts affect E_a, but they do not affect the ultimate changes in state functions between reactants and products (e.g., ΔH, ΔG). In the reaction diagram depicted in Figure 17.5, the solid line represents the uncatalyzed reaction pathway while the dashed line represents the catalyzed reaction pathway.

Please solve this problem:

- A catalyst causes:

  A. a shift in the equilibrium of a reaction.
  B. a decrease in activation energy of a reaction.
  C. an increase in ΔG.
  D. an decrease in ΔH.

Problem solved:

B is correct. A catalyst affects only the activation energy of a system. A catalyst does not cause the equilibrium of a reaction to shift toward products. The equilibrium mixture of products and reactants in a catalyzed reaction will be identical to the equilibrium mixture of products and reactants in the uncatalyzed reaction. A catalyst affects neither the energy states of the products nor the energy states of the reactants. As a result, a catalyst alters neither ΔG nor ΔG.

Reactions at Equilibrium

A reaction may be characterized by its equilibrium constant, K_{eq} (see **Chapter 16**). For a reaction, the change in Gibbs free-energy (ΔG) is:

$$\Delta G = \Delta G° + RTlnQ$$

where ΔG is the change in Gibbs free-energy of the reaction at a constant temperature and a constant pressure. $\Delta G°$ is the standard free energy change of the reaction at 298 Kelvin and 1 atm.

R is the universal gas constant, T is the temperature at which the reaction is occurring, and Q is given by:

$$Q = \frac{(C)^c (D)^d}{(A)^a (B)^b}$$

For the general reaction:

$$aA + bB \leftrightarrow cC + dD$$

where (A), (B), (C), and (D) represent the molar concentrations of the respective chemicals at any point in the reaction.

Recall from **Chapter 16** that the equilibrium constant of a reaction is temperature dependent and must be calculated for each temperature.

By definition, $\Delta G = 0$ at equilibrium, giving:

$$\Delta G° = -RTlnK_{eq}$$

From this, we can see that if $\Delta G°$ is negative, then K_{eq} is larger than l; therefore, products are favored. Likewise, if $\Delta G°$ is positive, then K_{eq} is smaller than l, and reactants are favored. In summary:

- If $\Delta G > 0$, then reactants are favored over products.

- If $\Delta G = 0$, then neither reactants nor products are favored.

- If $\Delta G < 0$, then product formation is favored.

Please solve this problem:

- The reaction ATP + H_2O → ADP + phosphate is run at 25°C under atmospheric conditions. Its free energy, $\Delta G°$, is –30 kilojoules per mole.

    A. The reaction is spontaneous under these conditions because $\Delta G°$ is negative.
    B. The reaction is nonspontaneous under these conditions because $\Delta G°$ is negative.
    C. The reaction is at equilibrium under these conditions because $\Delta G = 0$.
    D. It cannot be said whether this reaction is spontaneous or nonspontaneous under these conditions without knowing the equilibrium constant, K_{eq}.

Problem solved:

A is correct. Since $\Delta G°$ is negative, the reaction is spontaneous.

17.2 MASTERY APPLIED: PRACTICE PASSAGE AND QUESTIONS

Passage

ATP hydrolysis is an important biochemical reaction. The function of ATP is to store energy from food for later use. ATP's ability to store energy is due to its ability to lose a phosphate group by hydrolysis, forming ADP:

$$ATP + H_2O \rightarrow ADP + phosphate$$

Since this reaction is exergonic, it can drive endergonic reactions that might not otherwise occur. At 37°C (body temperature), the thermodynamic values for ATP hydrolysis are $\Delta G = -30$ kJ/mol, $\Delta H = -20$ kJ/mol, and $\Delta S = +34$J/K • mol.

The energy-liberating process in anaerobic organisms is glycolysis. For glycolysis at body temperature, $\Delta G = -218$ kJ/mol and $\Delta H = -120$ kJ/mol. Glycolysis is coupled with the conversion of two ADP molecules into two ATP molecules via the equation:

$$Glucose + 2 \text{ ADP} + 2 \text{ phosphate} \rightarrow$$
$$2 \text{ lactate} + 2 \text{ ATP} + 2 \text{ H}_2\text{O}$$

The biosynthesis of sucrose from fructose and glucose has $\Delta G = +23$ kJ/mol. The formation of a peptide bond, which is essential for the production of proteins, directly consumes 17 kilojoules per mole. However, this latter process is an indirect one that also entails the consumption of three ATP molecules for each peptide bond formed. A moderately small protein contains 150 peptide bonds, a medium-size protein contains four hundred peptide bonds, and a large protein may contain several thousand peptide bonds.

1. The hydrolysis of ATP is:
   A. exergonic and endothermic.
   B. exergonic and exothermic.
   C. endergonic and endothermic.
   D. endergonic and exothermic.

2. The ΔG of the reaction of glucose with ADP and inorganic phosphate to produce lactate, ATP, and water is:
   A. −278 kilojoules per mole.
   B. −218 kilojoules per mole.
   C. −188 kilojoules per mole.
   D. −158 kilojoules per mole.

3. The energy from a mole of ATP molecules hydrolyzed to a mole of ADP molecules is sufficient for the synthesis of how many molecules of sucrose from fructose and glucose?
   A. 7.85×10^{23}
   B. 6.02×10^{23}
   C. 7.85×10^{21}
   D. 6.02×10^{21}

4. The synthesis of a medium-size protein requires:
   A. 400 ATP molecules.
   B. 627 ATP molecules.
   C. 1,200 ATP molecules.
   D. 1,427 ATP molecules.

5. If the complete aerobic respiration of one glucose molecule produces 38 ATP molecules, and the Gibbs free-energy of combustion of glucose is −2,880 kilojoules per mole, what is the amount of heat lost in the transformation of one mole of glucose to thirty-eight moles of ATP?
   A. −1,740 kilojoules
   B. 0 kilojoules
   C. 1,740 kilojoules
   D. 2,842 kilojoules

6. The synthesis of proteins from amino acids and the synthesis of carbohydrates from simple sugars both involve the breakage of relatively stronger bonds followed by the formation of relatively weaker ones. Both processes are endergonic, which is likely the result of:

    A. an overall endothermic process accompanied by a decrease in entropy.
    B. an overall endothermic process accompanied by an increase in entropy.
    C. an overall exothermic process accompanied by a decrease in entropy.
    D. an overall exothermic process accompanied by an increase in entropy.

7. Based on the information in the passage, the process of glycolysis:

    A. results in a decrease in entropy.
    B. results in an increase in entropy.
    C. results in an increase in enthalpy.
    D. results in an increase in Gibbs free-energy.

17.3 MASTERY VERIFIED: ANSWERS AND EXPLANATIONS

1. **B is correct.** From the information in the passage, we see that both ΔG and ΔH are negative. Therefore, by definition, this reaction is both exergonic and exothermic.

2. **D is correct.** In this case, we can add the ΔGs:

$$\Delta G_{total} = \Delta G_{glucose} - 2(\Delta G_{ATP}) = -218 \text{ kJ/mol} - [(2)(-30 \text{ kJ/mol})] = -158 \text{ kJ/mol}$$

    From the answer choices, we can see that the assumption of additivity will be valid. We know that since ΔG_{ATP} is negative, ΔG_{ADP} must be positive. For this reason, we can eliminate choice A (which assumes a negative ΔG_{ADP}) and choice B (which assumes $\Delta G_{ADP} = 0$). This leaves only choices C and D. By assuming that $\Delta G_{ADP} = \Delta G_{ATP}$, we can see that choice C has failed to account for the stoichiometric coefficient 2. Therefore, we can eliminate choice C, and we are left with choice D.

3. **A is correct.** To solve this problem, we must first recall that Avogadro's number allows us to convert between moles and molecules, and that its value is 6.02×10^{23}. Then we must use the information in the passage that the energy from a mole of ATP molecules is equal to -30 kilojoules and that the energy required to form a sucrose molecule is $+23$ kilojoules per mole. Since the energy available in an ATP molecule is larger than the energy required to form a sucrose molecule, we can see that our answer must be larger than Avogadro's number. The only choice that fits this criterion is choice A.

4. **D is correct.** From the passage, we see that the production of a peptide bond requires the input of $+17$ kilojoules per mole and three additional ATP molecules. Since the passage also tells us that the synthesis of a medium-size protein requires the formation of four hundred peptide bonds, we need at least twelve hundred ATPs per protein molecule plus the number of ATPs that are necessary to supply the other 17 kilojoules per mole for each bond. Choice D is the only choice larger than twelve hundred.

5. **C is correct.** Thirty-eight moles of ATP will store 38 moles $\times$ 30 kilojoules per mole, or 1,140 kilojoules of the energy that is released from the glucose. Since the glucose releases 2,880 kilojoules, the amount of this energy that is stored (and therefore is the amount lost) is 2,880 $-$ 1,140 = 1,740 kilojoules.

6. **A is correct.** We are told that both processes involve the breakage of relatively stronger bonds followed by the formation of relatively weaker ones. Consequently, the energy released when the bonds are broken exceeds the energy consumed when the new bonds are formed. Overall, both processes are <u>endo</u>thermic, which eliminate choices C and D. Since both processes involve the formation of larger, more ordered molecules from smaller, less ordered ones, entropy (<u>dis</u>order) must decrease. That eliminates choice B.

7. **B is correct.** From the thermodynamic data given in the passage, we can see that the change in Gibbs free-energy associated with this process is negative: Gibbs free-energy is decreased. This eliminates choice D.

    Since this process occurs at 37°C, we do not have the necessary high-temperature conditions for an exergonic, endothermic reaction (Table 17.2). Therefore, since the reaction is exergonic, it is also exothermic. This eliminates choice C. Since this reaction involves the fragmentation of a large molecule (glucose) into smaller molecules (lactate), we have a condition of increasing entropy. Therefore, we are able to pick choice B over choice A.

CHAPTER 18

SOLUTIONS AND SOLUBILITY

18.1 MASTERY ACHIEVED

SOLUTIONS IN QUALITATIVE TERMS

Basic Definitions

A **solution** is a homogeneous mixture of two or more chemical compounds. Solutions may contain materials in any phase (gas, liquid, or solid) mixed with materials in any phase. While gaseous and solid solutions are common, this chapter will focus on solutions in which the liquids are mixed or liquid is a solvent.

The **solvent** of a solution is the substance into which other chemicals are dissolved. The **solute** of a solution is the compound that is dissolved in the solvent. Sometimes, it is not clear which compound is dissolved; in such cases, the solvent is the compound that is present in the largest quantity, and all other compounds present are considered solutes.

In the pure liquid state, forces exist that stabilize the liquid. In order for a solute to dissolve in a liquid, it must possess similar forces as the solvent. Therefore, substances with similar intermolecular forces will tend to form solutions with one another: like dissolves like. Solutes that have strong attractive forces for a solvent are more soluble in that solvent than solutes with weaker attractive forces for that solvent. Even if the intermolecular forces between solvent molecules are greater than the attractive forces between solvent and solute, dissolution is still possible.

The process of **solvation** occurs when a solute is added to a solvent. As the solute is added, the solvent molecules separate from one another to make room for the solute molecules and then surround the solute molecules. Solvation depends on the intermolecular forces **(Chapter 14)** present between the solvent molecules and the solute molecules.

Hydration is the term for the solvation process when the solvent is water. Substances that are water soluble have a high charge density, form hydrogen bonds, or have a large dipole moment. Chemicals with large dipole moments are said to be **polar**.

Please solve this problem:

- Of the following compounds, the LEAST water soluble is:

    A. CH_3OH.
    B. CH_3CH_2OH.
    C. $CH_3(CH_2)_4CH_2OH$.
    D. $CH_3(CH_2)_6CH_2OH$.

Problem solved:

D is correct. Polar molecules are water soluble. In each of the four choices, the only polar group is the –OH functionality. As methylene groups (–CH$_2$–) are added, the dipole moment of the molecule will decrease. Therefore, the molecule with the smallest dipole moment is **1-octanol**.

Thermodynamics of Solutions

Solvation is controlled by two different thermodynamic properties: the tendency of a system to seek a minimum energy state and the tendency of a system to maximize entropy. **Heat of solution** is the enthalpy change that occurs when a solute dissolves in a solvent. Heat of solution may be either positive (energy absorbed) or negative (energy released). As with other thermodynamic systems, a **positive heat of solution** indicates an **endothermic solvation,** and a **negative heat of solution** indicates an **exothermic solvation.**

An exothermic solvation will result from the dissolution of a solute that has a greater affinity for solvent molecules than for other solute molecules. An endothermic solvation will result from the dissolution of a solute that has a lower affinity for solvent molecules than for other solute molecules. Stated another way, a solution that has a negative heat of solution is lower in enthalpy than the pure solute and the pure solvent. A solution that has a positive heat of solution is a solution that is higher in enthalpy than the pure states of the solute and the solvent.

Exothermic solvation (–ΔH) tends to promote spontaneity, and endothermic solvation tends to oppose spontaneity. On the other hand, increased entropy (+ΔS) tends to promote spontaneity, and decreased entropy (–ΔS) tends to oppose spontaneity.

Solvation is like other chemical processes in that spontaneity depends, finally, on the balance between these two tendencies—on whether or not the overall Gibbs free-energy is negative (exergonic; spontaneous) or positive (endergonic; nonspontaneous).

An endothermic process *will* occur spontaneously if it involves an increase in entropy that overcomes the +ΔH. If ΔS is sufficiently positive to make the overall quantity (ΔH – TΔS) *negative*, ΔG will be negative, and solvation will be a spontaneous process.

Please solve this problem:

- A substance that has a positive enthalpy of solution will also exhibit:

  A. an endothermic heat of dilution and an increased solubility with increasing temperature.
  B. an endothermic heat of dilution and a decreased solubility with increasing temperature.
  C. an exothermic heat of dilution and an increased solubility with increasing temperature.
  D. an exothermic heat of dilution and a decreased solubility with increasing temperature.

Problem solved:

A is correct. Since we are told that the enthalpy of solution is positive, we know that this is an endothermic process. An endothermic enthalpy of solution implies an endothermic heat of dilution. This eliminates choices C and D. An endothermic process is favored by an increase in temperature, while an exothermic process is favored by a decrease in temperature. Therefore, since we are dealing with an endothermic process, solubility will increase with increasing temperature.

Relative Concentrations

A solution is **saturated** when no more solute molecules will dissolve in the quantity of solvent available. A solution may become **supersaturated** under certain conditions. A supersaturated solution is an unstable system in which more solute molecules have been dissolved than would be possible under normal conditions. This state may have been achieved by preparing the solution at a higher temperature (for an endothermic heat of solution) and then slowly cooling it. A supersaturated solution will eventually stabilize by precipitating out the excess dissolved solute molecules.

A **concentrated solution** is one in which there is a relative abundance of solute molecules. A **dilute solution** is one in which there is only a relatively small number of solvent molecules. The terms "concentrated" and "dilute" can qualitatively describe the amount of solute in a solution. There are other quantitative expressions for solution concentration such as molarity, normality, molality, and mole fraction.

Please solve this problem:

- A supersaturated solution of sodium thiosulfate is used as a hand warmer. Squeezing a seed crystal of solid sodium thiosulfate into the supersaturated solution causes precipitation of excess solute and the release of heat because:

  A. the enthalpy of solution is negative, and solvation is an exothermic process.
  B. the enthalpy of solution is positive, and solvation is an exothermic process.
  C. the enthalpy of solution is negative, and solvation is an endothermic process.
  D. the enthalpy of solution is positive, and solvation is an endothermic process.

Problem solved:

D is correct. Choices A and C can be eliminated immediately, since a positive enthalpy of solution is an endothermic process and a negative enthalpy of solution is an exothermic process.

We are also told that heat is given off when excess sodium thiosulfate solute precipitates from solution. For a supersaturated solution, equilibrium is reached by precipitation of the excess dissolved solute, and heat is given off when the solute falls out of solution. From this, we conclude that heat must have been absorbed during solvation. Therefore, the enthalpy of solution must be positive, and the process of solvation must be endothermic.

Qualitative Solubility

Solubility is the ability of a solute to dissolve in a solvent. The solubility of gases in a liquid solvent is determined using **Henry's law**:

$$p = k_H C$$

where C is solubility, k is the Henry's law constant for the gas under consideration, and p is the gas pressure, or **partial pressure** of the particular gaseous solute over the solution. Note that the solubility of a gas is directly proportional to the pressure of that gas above the solution: As pressure is increased, solubility is also increased.

The heat of solution for gases in liquid solvents is almost always negative: As temperature is increased, gas solubility is decreased (think Le Chatelier's principle for exothermic reactions).

Liquids are said to be **miscible** in other liquids when they are soluble in all proportions. Liquids that do not dissolve in one another are **immiscible**.

Solids that may be dissolved in a liquid solvent to attain a concentration greater than 0.05 M (molarity) are **soluble** in that liquid. Solids that cannot be dissolved in a liquid solvent to attain a concentration greater than 0.01 M are **insoluble** in that liquid. Solids that are soluble between 0.01 M and 0.05 M are **slightly**, or **moderately, soluble**.

Some general solubility rules for aqueous solutions can be stated as follows:

- All alkali and ammonium (NH_4^+) compounds are soluble. The alkali metals are included in Group IA (Li^+, Na^+, K^+, Rb^+, Cs^+).

- All acetates (CH_3COO^-), chlorates (ClO_3^-), nitrates (NO_3^-), and perchlorates (ClO_4^-) are soluble.

- Pb^{n+}, Hg^{n+}, and Ag^{n+} salts are insoluble, *unless* they are paired with one of the anions from the previous rule.

Please solve this problem:

- Which of the following is LEAST likely to be water soluble?

    A. Na_2CO_3
    B. $CrPO_4$
    C. K_3PO_4
    D. $AgNO_3$

Problem solved:

B is correct. Both Na_2CO_3 and K_3PO_4 contain alkali metals and are water soluble. $AgNO_3$, though a silver salt, is a nitrate, which are always soluble. $CrPO_4$, like most phosphates, is insoluble in aqueous solutions.

Solubility: pH and Temperature

The solubility of a substance is affected by several factors, including temperature, common ions, and pH.

As discussed earlier, for a system with an endothermic heat of solution, solubility will generally increase with increasing temperature and decrease with decreasing temperature. For a system with an exothermic heat of solution, solubility will typically decrease with increasing temperature and increase with decreasing temperature. Recall the discussion in Chapter 16 regarding the way that temperature affects equilibrium. The same ideas are at play here.

If a basic or acidic ion is produced in a dissolution process, a change in pH will affect the solubility of this solute. This point will be addressed in greater detail in **Chapter 21**. For now, let us say that a solute that dissociates into an acidic ion will have enhanced solubility in a solution with a high pH (basic), and diminished solubility in a solution with a low pH (acidic). A solute that dissociates into a basic ion will have enhanced solubility in a solution with a low pH (acidic) and diminished solubility in a solution with a high pH (basic).

Please solve this problem:

- If the pH of an aqueous solution of $NaHCO_3$ is increased, the solubility of $NaHCO_3$ will:

   A. increase.
   B. decrease.
   C. remain unchanged because sodium bicarbonate does not contain an acidic ion.
   D. remain unchanged because sodium bicarbonate does not contain a basic ion.

Problem solved:

B is correct. Consider the equilibrium reaction:

$$NaHCO_3(s) \rightleftharpoons Na^+(aq) + HCO_3^-(aq)$$

The bicarbonate ion (HCO_3^-) is a basic ion. In the aqueous solution, the following equilibrium reaction is also occurring:

$$H^+(aq) + HCO_3^-(aq) \rightleftharpoons H_2CO_3(aq)$$

When the pH of this solution is increased, the H^+ concentration is decreased. Therefore,

$$\downarrow H^+ + \uparrow HCO_3^- \rightleftharpoons \downarrow H_2CO_3$$

which leads to:

$$\uparrow NaHCO_3 \rightleftharpoons \downarrow Na^+ + \uparrow HCO_3^-$$

A decrease in $[H^+]$ shifts the second equilibrium reaction to the left, which causes the formation of a greater amount of bicarbonate ion. The increased bicarbonate concentration then causes a shift in the first equilibrium reaction to the left, which indicates decreased solubility of sodium bicarbonate.

SOLUTIONS IN QUANTITATIVE TERMS: CONCENTRATION

In order to determine the quantitative properties of solutions, you must first understand the various ways in which concentration may be expressed. Each of these methods for the expression of concentration is used at different times and for different reasons. You must be familiar with each concentration term.

Molarity

The most common quantitative measure of concentration is **molarity** (M).

Molarity is defined as:

$$M = \frac{\text{moles of solute}}{\text{liters of solution}}$$

Please solve this problem:

- The molarity of a 750 milliliters aqueous solution containing 270 grams of glucose ($C_6H_{12}O_6$) is:

  A. 0.36 M
  B. 1.0 M
  C. 2.0 M
  D. 3.6 M

Problem solved:

C is correct. Molarity is defined as moles of solute per liter of solution. The number of liters of solution is 0.750 liters. In order to find the number of moles of solute, we must convert grams to moles using the molecular weight of glucose. The molecular weight of glucose is 180 grams per moles. Therefore, the number of moles of glucose, n, is given by:

$$n = 270 \text{ g} \div 180 \text{ g/mol} = 1.5 \text{ mol}$$

Therefore, molarity is:

$$M = \frac{n}{V} = \frac{1.5 \text{ mol}}{0.750 \text{ L}} = 2 \ M$$

Normality

Normality is used almost exclusively when referring to acids and bases, where one is concerned about the number of moles of H^+ or OH^- ions that a compound contains.

$$N = \frac{\text{moles of potential } H^+ \text{ or } OH^-}{\text{liters of solution}}$$

Please solve this problem:

- The normality in acid of a 500 milliliters aqueous solution of 1 M sulfuric acid (H_2SO_4) is:

  A. 1 N
  B. 2 N
  C. 3 N
  D. 8 N

Problem solved:

B is correct. The normality of a solution is equal to the number of potential acid particles (H^+) per liter of solution. Since there are two H^+ particles per sulfuric acid molecule, the normality of the solution is 2.

Molality

Molality is normally not used unless we are concerned with a colligative property. Molality is symbolized by m, and is defined as:

$$m = \frac{\text{moles of solute}}{\text{kilograms of solvent}}$$

Note that while both molarity and normality are expressed in terms of volume (liters of solution) in the denominator, molality is expressed in terms of mass (kilograms of solvent). For dilute aqueous solutions, however, molality and molarity are nearly identical, as the density of water is approximately 1 kilogram per liter.

Please solve this problem:

- The molality of a 300 milliliters water containing 33.3 grams of calcium chloride is:

  A. $1\ m$
  B. $2\ m$
  C. $3\ m$
  D. $4\ m$

Problem solved:

A is correct. The molality is given by:

$$m = \frac{\text{moles of solute}}{\text{kilograms of solvent}}$$

$$\frac{0.3\ \text{mol CaCl}_2}{0.3\ \text{kg H}_2\text{O}} = 1\ m$$

(Note that the density of water is roughly 1 kilogram per liter. Therefore, 0.3 liters of water has a mass of 0.3 kilograms.)

Mole Fraction

The **mole fraction** of a solution is usually of interest only in problems involving gases, or problems concerned with vapor pressure. Mole fraction (X_s, where s is the substance under consideration) is defined as:

$$X_s = \frac{\text{moles of solute (s)}}{\text{total moles of solution}}$$

Please solve this problem:

- An air sample contains 77 percent nitrogen, 16 percent oxygen, and 7 percent carbon dioxide by weight. The mole fraction of oxygen in the air is:

    A. 0.147
    B. 0.160
    C. 0.172
    D. 0.512

Problem solved:

A is correct. To solve this problem, we must first convert the weight percentages to moles. For convenience, assume that this air sample had a mass of 100 grams. As such, there are 77 grams of nitrogen, 16 grams of oxygen, and 7 grams of carbon dioxide. Converting to moles:

$$N_2: \quad \frac{77 \text{ g}}{28 \text{ g/mol}} = 2.75 \text{ mol } N_2$$

$$O_2: \quad \frac{16 \text{ g}}{32 \text{ g/mol}} = 0.50 \text{ mol } O_2$$

$$CO_2: \quad \frac{7 \text{ g}}{44 \text{ g/mol}} = 0.16 \text{ mol } CO_2$$

You can add the moles together to get 3.41. From this, the mole fraction of oxygen gas is given by:

$$X_{O_2} = \frac{0.50 \text{ mol } O_2}{3.41 \text{ total moles}} = 0.147$$

A number worth committing to memory, useful in quick calculations of mole fractions in water, is the molarity of water itself: **55 M**. Say we wanted to calculate the mole fraction of Cl^- ions with a 1 L solution of 0.01 M NaCl in water. Knowing that water is 55 M, we can say that there are approximately 55 moles water in the solution.

$$X_{Cl} = \frac{mol Cl^-}{mol Na^+ + mol Cl^- + mol H_2O}$$

$$X_{Cl} = \frac{0.01}{0.01 + 0.01 + 55} \sim \frac{100 \times 10^{-4}}{55} \sim 2 \times 10^{-4}$$

SOLUBILITY AND SATURATION: K_{sp}

In **Chapter 16**, we discussed the equilibrium ⇌ constant, K_{eq}. For the general reaction:

$$aA + bB \rightleftharpoons cC + dD$$

the equilibrium constant is given by:

$$K_{eq} = \frac{[C]^c [D]^d}{[A]^a [B]^b}$$

The solubility product constant, K_{sp}, is the equilibrium constant that results when a solid is in equilibrium with its solution:

$$A_aB_b(s) \rightleftharpoons aA(aq) + bB(aq)$$

(Assuming A_aB_b is an ionic solute, A is the cation and B is the anion.)

Recall that pure liquids and pure solids do not appear in equilibrium expressions. Since A_aB_b is a pure solid, it does not affect the equilibrium constant, which then reduces to:

$$K_{eq} = K_{sp} = [A]^a[B]^b$$

Note that K_{sp} will never have a denominator.

K_{sp} is the solubility product constant for a substance; it is *not* the solubility of that substance. Solubility is the amount of substance (expressed in grams) that may be dissolved in a unit volume of solution. Solubility may be calculated from a known value of K_{sp}, or vice versa.

For example, assume that it is known that the solubility of A_2B is 1×10^{-2} moles per liter of solution. We may now calculate K_{sp}.

From the equilibrium expression:

$$A_2B(s) \rightleftharpoons 2A^+(aq) + B^{2-}(aq)$$

we see that for every one A_2B that is dissolved, two A^+ and one B^{2-} go into solution.

$$A_2B(s) \rightleftharpoons 2A^+(aq) + B^{2-}(aq)$$
$$x \qquad\quad 2x \qquad\quad x$$

Knowing that solubility, x, is 1×10^{-2} M, and employing the equilibrium expression for this reaction:

$$K_{sp} = [A]^2[B] = [2x]^2[x] = [4x^2][x] = 4x^3 = (4)(1 \times 10^{-2})^3 = 4 \times 10^{-6}$$

Similarly, if K_{sp} is known, solubility may be determined.

Please solve this problem:

- The K_{sp} of aluminum hydroxide is 3.7×10^{-15} at 25°C. The solubility of aluminum hydroxide at this temperature is:

  A. 9.3×10^{-16} M
  B. 3.7×10^{-15} M
  C. 6.1×10^{-8} M
  D. 1.1×10^{-4} M

Problem solved:

D is correct. The equilibrium expression for aluminum hydroxide is given by:

$$Al(OH)_3 \rightleftharpoons Al^{3+} + 3OH^-$$
$$ x \qquad x \qquad 3x$$

Therefore, the solubility product constant, K_{sp}, is given by:

$$K_{sp} = [Al^{3+}][OH^-]^3 = [x][3x]^3 = 27x^4$$

Since we are told that $K_{sp} = 3.7 \times 10^{-15}$, this becomes:

$$27x^4 = 3.7 \times 10^{-15}$$

or:

$$x = \text{approx. } 1.1 \times 10^{-4} M$$

COLLIGATIVE PROPERTIES

Definitions

A **colligative property** is a property that depends only on the number of particles present in solution and **not** on the identity of those particles. Colligative properties are only valid for aqueous solutions when the total concentration of particles (molality) is equal to or less than $0.5 \ m$. The four most important colligative properties for the MCAT are discussed in the following sections.

When a substance is solvated, it can either enter the solution through simple solvation or dissociation.

Most covalently bonded molecules are simply solvated by water, that is, they don't dissociate into two or more parts. Examples of molecules that are simply solvated include methanol, ethanol, glucose, and fructose.

Ionic compounds dissociate upon dissolving in water. Solutes that dissociate into constituent ions are **electrolytes**. **Strong electrolytes** dissociate completely or nearly completely, while **weak electrolytes** dissociate only slightly. Examples of strong electrolytes include salts of the alkali metals (Group IA) and of ammonium, some salts of the alkaline earth metals, all nitrates, chlorates, perchlorates, and acetates. Examples of weak electrolytes include weak acids and bases **(Chapter 21)**, such as carbonic acid, phosphoric acid, acetic acid, and ammonia.

The number of species which a substance dissociates into when solvated is known as its Van 't Hoff factor, normally signified by the letter i. A binary salt, like NaCl, dissociates into two ions, and therefore $i_{NaCl} = 2$. A compound like $CaCl_2$, which dissociates into three ions, has $i_{CaCl2} = 3$. Species that undergo simple solvation without dissociation have $i = 1$.

There are cases where both covalent and ionic materials can form larger, more organized structures in solution (micelles, ion or metal clusters, etc.) but these are generally unimportant for the MCAT.

Please solve this problem:

- Which of the following would be expected to exhibit the highest change in the colligative properties of a dilute aqueous solution, given equal concentrations of each?

  A. Glucose
  B. Sodium chloride
  C. Potassium phosphate
  D. Silver(II) iodide

Problem solved:

C is correct. Glucose will not dissociate in water; therefore, it consists of only one particle. Sodium chloride dissociates into two particles. Silver(II) nitrate dissociates into three particles. Potassium phosphate dissociates into four particles. The compound that dissociates into the largest number of particles will have the greatest effect on the colligative properties of water. Therefore, the answer is potassium phosphate.

Vapor Pressure

The **vapor pressure** of a pure liquid is the partial pressure exerted by its vapor at the liquid-gas interface when the liquid and vapor are at equilibrium. A high vapor pressure indicates a volatile liquid. A low vapor pressure indicates a nonvolatile liquid. When the pressure exerted by a liquid (the vapor pressure) is equal to the external pressure above that liquid, the liquid will boil. When a solute is added to a liquid, solute particles reduce the tendency of solvent particles to escape into the vapor phase. It is this momentary escape into the gas phase by the individual liquid molecules that is responsible for the vapor pressure of the liquid.

The vapor pressure of a pure liquid is lowered by the addition of a nonvolatile solution. This effect is quantified by **Raoult's law**:

$$p_i = X_i p_i^{\circ}$$

where p_i is the **vapor pressure of the solvent i above the solution i**, X_i is the **mole fraction of the solvent i**, and p_i° is the **vapor pressure of the pure solvent i**.

Please solve this problem:

- The vapor pressure of pure water is 0.3 atm at 300 Kelvin. Calculate the vapor pressure above a solution prepared from 360 grams of water and 90 grams of glucose ($C_6H_{12}O_6$) at 300 Kelvin.

  A. 0.32 atm
  B. 0.30 atm
  C. 0.29 atm
  D. 0.26 atm

Problem solved:

C is correct. To solve this problem, we must use Raoult's law:

$$p_{H_2O} = X_{H_2O} p_{H_2O}^\circ$$

where:

$$p_{H_2O}^\circ = 0.3 \text{ atm}$$

and:

$$X_{H_2O} = \frac{(360 \text{ g H}_2\text{O})\left(\dfrac{1 \text{ mol}}{18 \text{ g}}\right)}{(360 \text{ g H}_2\text{O})\left(\dfrac{1 \text{ mol}}{18 \text{ g}}\right) + (90 \text{ g C}_6\text{H}_{12}\text{O}_6)\left(\dfrac{1 \text{ mol}}{180 \text{ g}}\right)}$$

$$X_{H_2O} = \frac{20 \text{ mol}}{20 \text{ mol} + 0.5 \text{ mol}} = \frac{20}{20.5} = 0.976$$

Therefore,

$$p_{H_2O} = X_{H_2O} p_{H_2O}^\circ = (0.976)(0.3 \text{ atm}) = 0.29 \text{ atm}$$

Boiling Point Elevation

The boiling point of a pure liquid is elevated by the addition of a nonvolatile solute; this follows from the effect of solute on vapor pressure. The boiling point of a substance is defined as the temperature at which the vapor pressure of the substance is equal to atmospheric pressure. Since vapor pressure is lowered by the addition of nonvolatile solute, the solution will require a greater temperature before its vapor pressure is equal to atmospheric pressure. The **boiling point elevation** that is observed in a solution is given by:

$$\Delta T_b = K_b i m$$

where ΔT_b is the boiling point elevation (boiling point of the solution minus boiling point of the pure solvent), K_b is the **boiling point elevation constant** (which is a constant for each solvent, $K_b(H_2O) = 0.52°C/m$), i is the Van 't Hoff factor for the solute, and m is the **molality of the solute**.

Please solve this problem:

- The normal boiling point of pure water is 373.15 Kelvin. Calculate the boiling point of a solution prepared from 360 grams of water and 106 grams of sodium carbonate (Na_2CO_3), $K_b = 0.52°C/m$.

  A. 368.82 Kelvin
  B. 373.15 Kelvin
  C. 375.93 Kelvin
  D. 377.48 Kelvin

SOLUTIONS AND SOLUBILITY ■ 341

Problem solved:

D is correct. To solve this problem, we must first determine the molality of the sodium carbonate solution. The molecular mass of Na_2CO_3 is 106 g/mol, which means that there is 1 mole of Na_2CO_3 in 0.360 kg of water. By estimating 360 g of water as (1/3) kg:

$$\frac{1\,mol\,Na_2CO_3}{1/3\,kg\,H_2O} = 3m$$

Na_2CO_3 dissociates into 3 ions, 2 Na^+ and 1 CO_3^{2-}, so $i = 3$.

Using the boiling point elevation equation:

$$\Delta T_b = K_b i m$$

$$\Delta T_b = (0.52)(3)(3),\ or \sim 4.5\ K$$

Since the boiling point is elevated, the boiling point of this solution is equal to:

$$373.15\ K + 4.5\ K = 377.55\ K$$

D is the closest answer.

Freezing Point Depression

The freezing point of a pure liquid is depressed by the addition of a solute. At the freezing point of a liquid the substance orders and crystallizes. This crystallization is hindered by solutes creating disorder in the system. To cope there must be a stronger driving force for crystallization, meaning a lower temperature. The **freezing point depression** that is observed in a solution is given by:

$$\Delta T_f = K_f i m$$

where ΔT_f is the **freezing point depression** (freezing point of the pure solvent minus freezing point of the solution), K_f is the **freezing point depression constant** (which is a constant for each solvent, $K_f(H_2O) = 1.86°C/m$), i is, again, the Van 't Hoff factor, and m is the **molality of the solute**.

Please solve this problem:

- The normal freezing point of pure water is 273.15 Kelvin. Calculate the freezing point of a solution prepared from 1800 grams of water and 106 grams of sodium carbonate (Na_2CO_3), $K_f = 1.86°\ C/m$.

  A. 270.04 Kelvin
  B. 272.12 Kelvin
  C. 273.15 Kelvin
  D. 276.26 Kelvin

Problem solved:

A is correct. As before, $i = 3$, so now we must determine the molality of the sodium carbonate solution. If we round the mass of the solute to 2 kg, we can say that m = 0.5.

$$\frac{(3)(106 \text{ g Na}_2\text{CO}_3)\left(\dfrac{1 \text{ mol Na}_2\text{CO}_3}{106 \text{ g Na}_2\text{CO}_3}\right)}{1.800 \text{ kg H}_2\text{O}} = 1.67 \text{ m}$$

Using the freezing point depression equation, round:

$$\Delta T_f = K_f m \sim (1.86)(3)(0.5) \sim 3 \text{ K}$$

Since the freezing point is depressed, the freezing point of this solution is equal to:

$$273.15 \text{ K} - 3 \text{ K} = 270.15 \text{ K}$$

Osmotic Pressure

Osmosis is the spontaneous process by which solvent molecules (but not solute molecules) pass through a semipermeable membrane along a concentration gradient. **Osmotic pressure** is the excess hydrostatic pressure created on the more concentrated side of a semipermeable membrane due to osmosis. Because a greater concentration of solvent molecules is initially present on the dilute side of the membrane, more solvent molecules will collide with the membrane per unit time on this side. Therefore, more solvent molecules will pass from the dilute side to the concentrated side than from the concentrated side to the dilute side. This process will continue until equilibrium is reached. The pressure exerted on the membrane when equilibrium is reached is the osmotic pressure. The osmotic pressure of a solution is increased by the addition of solute.

Osmotic pressure is given by the equation:

$$\pi = \frac{n}{V} RT$$

where π is the osmotic pressure, n is the number of moles of particles dissolved, R is the gas constant, T is the absolute temperature, and V is the volume of the solution. Since

$$iM = \frac{n}{V}$$

we can rewrite the equation for osmotic pressure as:

$$\pi = iMRT$$

Please solve this problem:

- Calculate the osmotic pressure of a 0.1 *M* solution of barium hydroxide at 300 K, $R = 0.0821$ L•atm/mol•K.

    A. 0.25 atm
    B. 2.46 atm
    C. 4.93 atm
    D. 7.39 atm

Problem solved:

D is correct. We note that barium hydroxide dissociates into three components. By rounding the ideal gas constant to 0.1 and using the equation for osmotic pressure, we get:

$$3(0.1 \text{ } M)(0.1 \text{ L•atm/mol•K})(300 \text{ K}) = 9 \text{ atm}$$

9 atm is certainly closer to 7.39 than it is to any of the other answer choices, but it's not as close as we might like it to be. Does it make sense? Remember, we rounded 0.0821 to 0.1, so we expect our answer to be larger than the more precise answer. With this in mind, and no other choices in the vicinity, we can safely say that choice D is correct.

Hints on Colligative Properties Questions

Colligative properties questions will, in general, come in two forms: (1) questions dealing with *equimolar* solutions, and (2) questions dealing with solutions in which *equal masses* of solute are utilized. Depending on which type of question it is, it's possible to simplify answer choices based on which factor of the colligative properties questions you're being asked to examine.

Questions about equimolar solutions are asking for the comparison of Van 't Hoff factors. Equimolar, aqueous solutions have identical molalities, so solute with the largest *i* will produce the largest colligative change.

Questions in which equal masses of solute are utilized are often more concerned with the calculation of *m*. Small, low MW salts will have the most moles in a given mass, and hence give larger *m* and a larger colligative change. Of course it's always important, in this case, to examine *i*. If the value of *i* is much larger in one salt compared to the rest, this may outweigh the differences in mass, but in general, when equal masses of solute are added to a solution, the lightest one gives the largest colligative change.

18.2 MASTERY APPLIED: PRACTICE PASSAGE AND QUESTIONS

Passage

Colligative properties are properties of a substance that depend only upon the number of particles involved, not upon the chemical nature of these substances. Colligative properties, such as boiling point elevation, freezing point depression, and osmotic pressure, may be used to determine the molecular weight of an unknown chemical compound.

Boiling point elevation is given by the equation:

$$\Delta T_b = K_b i m$$

where ΔT_b is the observed elevation in boiling point, K_b is the boiling point elevation constant for the solvent (tabulated in Table 1), and m is the molality of the solution. For a substance that does not dissociate in solution ($i = 1$), finding the molality can help us find the molecular mass of the solute. Once the number of moles has been determined, calculation of the molecular weight is easily accomplished: (mass of unknown added to solution) ÷ (moles of unknown).

The equation for freezing point depression takes a form similar to that for boiling point elevation:

$$\Delta T_f = K_f i m$$

where ΔT_f is the observed depression in freezing point, K_f is the freezing point depression constant for the solvent, and m is the molality of the solution. Molecular weight of an unknown is found in a manner analogous to that employed for boiling point elevation data.

Solvent	Normal Boiling Point (°C)	K_b(°C/m)	Normal Freezing Point (°C)	K_f(°C/m)
benzene	80.1	2.53	5.5	4.90
water	100.0	0.52	0	1.86
acetic acid	117.9	3.07	16.6	3.90
phenol	181.8	3.56	43.0	7.40

Table 1

1. The smallest boiling point elevation is demonstrated by a 0.1 *m* solution of:

   A. sodium chloride in water.
   B. glucose in benzene.
   C. glucose in phenol.
   D. glucose in acetic acid.

2. The solution with the lowest freezing point is:

   A. 50 grams sodium chloride in 1 kilogram water.
   B. 360 grams glucose in 1 kilogram water.
   C. 50 grams sodium chloride in 1 kilogram phenol.
   D. 360 grams glucose in 1 kilogram phenol.

3. A solution is prepared from 100 grams of an unknown material and 1 kilograms water. This solution has a boiling point of 101.8°C at 1 atm. The identity of the unknown material is most likely:

   A. NaCl
   B. $Ba(OH)_2$
   C. NH_4NO_3
   D. $C_6H_{12}O_6$

4. Two solutions containing equal molal quantities of an unknown material are prepared using water and acetic acid as solvents. The aqueous solution has a freezing point of –4.65°C. The acetic acid solution has a freezing point of 9.58°C. The best explanation for this difference is that:

   A. the unknown material dissociated equally in the two solvents.
   B. the unknown material dissociated to a greater extent in water than in acetic acid.
   C. the unknown material dissociated to a greater extent in acetic acid than in water.
   D. the unknown material aggregated in water but not in acetic acid.

5. An aqueous solution has a boiling point of 101.3°C at 1 atm. This solution is cooled to the freezing point. The freezing point is measured as –3.9°C. The discrepancy between the boiling point elevation and freezing point depression is most likely due to:

   A. the difference in K_b and K_f for water.
   B. the difference in the volume of water at 100°C versus 0°C.
   C. the difference in solubility of the solute at 100°C versus 0°C.
   D. the difference in the solvation process for the solute at 100°C versus 0°C.

18.3 MASTERY VERIFIED: ANSWERS AND EXPLANATIONS

1. **A is correct.** To solve this problem, compare the Van 't Hoff factors of the salts in question. For choices B, C, and D, $i = 1$. For choice A, each sodium chloride unit will dissociate into two particles in solution, so $i = 2$.

   We must multiply the molalities of the solutions by their Van 't Hoff factor and boiling point elevation constants of the respective solvents:
   - **A.** $(2)(0.1\ m)(0.52°C/m) = 0.104°C$
   - **B.** $(0.1\ m)(2.53°C/m) = 0.253°C$
   - **C.** $(0.1\ m)(3.56°C/m) = 0.356°C$
   - **D.** $(0.1\ m)(3.07°C/m) = 0.307°C$

   The smallest boiling point elevation is given by the solution in choice A.

2. **B is correct.** To solve this problem, we must make sure that we solve for freezing point, *not* for freezing point depression.

   A. $\Delta T_f = (1.86°C/m)\dfrac{(50\ g)(2\ particle)}{(58.5\ g/mol)} = 3.18°C \qquad \Delta T_f = 0°C - 3.18°C = -3.18°C$

   B. $\Delta T_f = (1.86°C/m)\dfrac{(360\ g)(1\ particle)}{(180\ g/mol)} = 3.72°C \qquad \Delta T_f = 0°C - 3.72°C = -3.72°C$

   C. $\Delta T_f = (7.40°C/m)\dfrac{(50\ g)(2\ particle)}{(58.5\ g/mol)} = 12.64°C \qquad \Delta T_f = 43°C - 12.64°C = 30.26°C$

   D. $\Delta T_f = (7.40°C/m)\dfrac{(360\ g)(1\ particle)}{(180\ g/mol)} = 14.80°C \qquad \Delta T_f = 43°C - 14.80°C = 28.20°C$

   From the above calculations, we see that the solution in choice B provides the lowest freezing point.

3. **A is correct.** From the problem, we see that the solution has a boiling point elevation of $1.8°C$.

   $$\Delta T_f = 1.8°C = K_b(i)m$$

   Since two of the answers have $i = 2$, let's assume this and calculate m.

   $$1.8°C = .5 \times 2 \times m$$

   $$1.8 = m$$

   The molecular weight is then found by

   $$100\ g\ /\ 1.8\ mol \sim 55\ g/mol$$

   Since NaCl weights 58.5 g/mol, 55 isn't far off. (Remember, the MCAT isn't about splitting hairs. An answer this close will generally be the correct one.) And certainly it rules out NH_4NO_3 (MW = 80). $Ba(OH)_2$ (MW = 171) is far too heavy to be the correct answer even with $i = 3$, and $C_6H_{12}O_6$ is even heavier, with a smaller i.

4. **B is correct.** A freezing point depression of 4.65°C in water corresponds to a solution that has a molality given by:

$$4.65°C \div 1.86°C/m = 2.5 \ m \text{ ions}$$

A freezing point of 9.58°C in acetic acid gives a freezing point depression of

$$16.6°C - 9.58°C = 7.02°C$$

A freezing point depression of 7.02°C in acetic acid corresponds to a solution that has a molality of:

$$7.02°C \div 3.90°C/m = 1.8 \ m \text{ ions}$$

Therefore, the molality of ions of the substance in water is higher than the molality of this substance in acetic acid.

5. **C is correct.** At the boiling point, the molality of the solution is:

$$1.3°C \div 0.52°C/m \sim 2.5 \ m \text{ ions}$$

The logic in the rounding is that 1.25 / .5 = 2.5, so if each side is a little larger, we can safely say that the answer is very close to 2.5.

At the freezing point, the molality of the solution is:

$$3.9°C \div 1.86°C/m \sim 2 \ m \text{ ions}$$

Therefore, the molality of the solution is higher at the boiling point than at the freezing point, and we can say that uneven dissociation at low and high temperature is to blame.

CHAPTER 19

GASES

19.1 MASTERY ACHIEVED

THE GAS PHASE AND ASSOCIATED PHENOMENA

Temperature

Temperature is a function of the **average translational kinetic energy** of the molecule in a system. As the molecular kinetic energy of a system increases, the temperature increases. As the molecular kinetic energy of a system decreases, the temperature decreases. A temperature scale may be either **absolute** or **relative**. The absolute temperature scale you must be familiar with is **Kelvin (K)**. The **Celsius** scale (°C) and the **Fahrenheit** scale (°F) are examples of relative scales. A relative temperature scale chooses two points of known energy and assigns them fixed and convenient values. The Celsius scale fixes the temperature of the freezing point of water at 1 atm as 0°C, and the temperature of the boiling point of water at 1 atm as 100°C. The Fahrenheit scale fixes the temperature of the freezing point of water at 1 atm as 32°F, and the temperature of the boiling point of water at 1 atm as 212°F. The MCAT does not use the Fahrenheit scale, so you don't need to concern yourself with conversions from Celsius to Fahrenheit.

Absolute zero (0 K) is the lowest possible temperature. At this temperature, virtually all movement has ceased. The third law of thermodynamics shows that absolute zero is unattainable **(Chapter 17)**, but it can still be determined with great accuracy. The Kelvin temperature scale is based on the Celsius scale in that one degree Kelvin is equivalent in magnitude to one degree Celsius. Absolute zero on the Celsius scale is –273.15°C; therefore, the conversion from Celsius to Kelvin is given by:

$$K = °C + 273.15$$

It is important to notice that this relationship (a temperature increase of 1 Kelvin is equivalent to a temperature increase of 1°C) can give rise to traps on the MCAT. Also note that in the questions that follow, the Kelvin-to-Celsius conversion is rounded to K = °C + 273.

Please solve this problem:

- The rate at which heat is radiated by an object is given by the **Stefan-Boltzmann law**: $H = Ae\sigma T^4$, where A is surface area, T is temperature of the substance, emissivity (e) is material specific and ranges from 1 for a black body radiator to 0 for a perfect reflector, and σ is 5.6×10^{-8} W/m²K⁴. The rate of heat radiated by a substance at –233°C would be equal to the rate of heat radiated by the same substance at –253°C times:

  A. 0.719
  B. 2
  C. 16
  D. 20

Problem solved:

C is correct. The key to answering this problem is to realize that the temperature has changed from –253°C to –233°C, but everything else (A, e, and σ) remains constant. Therefore, if we take –253°C as state 1 and –233°C as state 2, we have the following relationship:

$$\frac{H_2}{H_1} = \frac{Ae\sigma T_2^4}{Ae\sigma T_1^4} = \frac{T_2^4}{T_1^4}$$

or:

$$H_2 = \left(\frac{T_2^4}{T_1^4}\right) H_1$$

This reduces the question to "What is the ratio of T_2^4 to T_1^4"? If you leave the temperatures in terms of °C, you will find:

$$\frac{T_2^4}{T_1^4} = \frac{(-233)^4}{(-253)^4} = \frac{2.947 \times 10^9}{4.097 \times 10^9} = 0.719$$

But this is a trap. Convert the temperatures to the Kelvin scale (as the units of σ make necessary). $T_1 = 20$ K and $T_2 = 40$ K, or:

$$\frac{T_2^4}{T_1^4} = \frac{(40)^4}{(20)^4} = \frac{(2)^4 \times (20)^4}{(20)^4} = 2^4 = 16$$

Pressure

The **pressure** exerted by a gas is a measure of the **force per unit area** of the total of all the collisions that the moving gas particles have with the walls of their container:

$$P = \frac{F}{A}$$

Pressure depends on the number of **collisions** with the walls, the **velocity** of the colliding gas molecules, and the **mass** of the colliding gas molecules. As each of these factors increase, the pressure increases. The number of collisions with the walls will increase if there is a greater number of molecules or if the same number of molecules are confined to a smaller volume. The velocity of the colliding gas molecules will increase as temperature (average kinetic energy) increases.

Pressure is measured in the SI units of **pascals (Pa)**.

$$P = \frac{F}{A} = \frac{N}{m^2} = Pa$$

Pressure may also be measured in **atmospheres (atm)**, **millimeters of mercury (mmHg)**, or **torr**.

$$1 \text{ atm} = 760 \text{ mmHg} = 760 \text{ torr} = 1.013 \times 105 \text{ Pa}$$

STP

Standard temperature and pressure (STP) is defined as 0°C and 760 torr. This is a reference point for the comparison of one gas to another. One mole of an ideal gas at STP occupies a volume of 22.4 liters (or 0.0224 cubic meters in SI units). It should be noted that gas STP differs from the standard state for thermodynamic functions. The temperature at STP for a gas is 0°C; the temperature of the standard thermodynamic state is 25°C. Both are defined at a pressure of 760 torr, or 1 atm.

KINETIC MOLECULAR THEORY

The **kinetic molecular theory** of gases regards a gas as a collection of point masses in constant chaotic independent motion. There are five basic premises of kinetic molecular theory:

1. Gases are composed of molecules, or particles, which are in **rapid, random translational motion** (straight-line motion). Because these particles have mass and velocity, they possess kinetic energy given by $KE = \frac{1}{2}mv^2$.

2. The particles undergo collisions with the walls of their container and with one another. These collisions are perfectly elastic: There is no loss of kinetic energy during any collision.

3. At any instant in time, the particles are separated by a distance much greater than the size of the particles themselves. Thus, the space occupied by the particles is negligible with regard to the size of the container.

4. There are no attractive or repulsive forces between the particles.

5. The average kinetic energy of the particles is directly proportional to the absolute temperature of the particles. From the **Maxwell-Boltzmann distribution**: $KE = \frac{3}{2}nRT$, where n = moles of gas particles, R = the Universal Gas Constant, and T = temperature of the gas.

The first statement says that any particle that possesses both mass and velocity will have a kinetic energy given by $KE = \frac{1}{2}mv^2$.

The second statement says that all collisions are elastic. In practice, perfectly elastic collisions are extremely rare.

The third states that there is no excluded volume. That is, none of the volume of the container is excluded from use by any one gas molecule at any moment in time. This, of course, is not true. The only way this could be true is if only one gas molecule was present in a given volume or if the gas particles were truly point masses.

The fourth states that all other gas particles do not influence each other except in collisions. However, as we have seen **(Chapter 14)**, all molecules will exert either repulsive or attractive forces upon one another (**London dispersion forces**).

The fifth is a statement of the Maxwell-Boltzmann distribution, which is a special case of the equipartition theorem of classical physics. When quantum effects become important, the equipartition theorem, and thus the Maxwell-Boltzmann distribution, fails.

Ideal behavior of gases relies upon the above five premises, so they will be considered valid throughout the next section (The Gas Laws). Deviations from ideality, which are caused by the failure of one or more of the five premises of the kinetic molecular theory, are treated in detail in the section after The Gas Laws (Deviations From Ideality).

THE GAS LAWS

Boyle's Law

Boyle's law for ideal gases states that under conditions of constant temperature and with a constant number of moles of gas, the product of pressure and volume is a constant:

$$PV = \text{constant}$$

or:

$$P_1V_1 = P_2V_2$$

The subscript 1 refers to initial conditions, and the subscript 2 refers to conditions after either a change in volume or a change in pressure. The important relationship to understand from this law is that pressure and volume are inversely proportional:

$$P \propto \frac{1}{V}$$

$$V \propto \frac{1}{P}$$

Please solve this problem:

- A fixed quantity of gas at a temperature of 200°C has a volume of 2 liters and pressure of 2 atm. If the volume is increased to 6 liters, the pressure is:

   A. increased by a factor of 9.
   B. increased by a factor of 3.
   C. decreased by a factor of 3.
   D. decreased by a factor of 9.

Problem solved:

C is correct. Using Boyle's law:

$$P_2 = \left(\frac{V_1}{V_2}\right)P_1 = \left(\frac{2}{6}\right)P_1 = \frac{P_1}{3}$$

Therefore, P_2 is decreased by a factor of three.

Charles's Law

Charles's law establishes the relationship between volume and temperature (Kelvin) for ideal gases under conditions of constant pressure and a constant number of moles of gas:

$$\frac{V}{T} = \text{constant}$$

or:

$$V = (\text{constant})(T)$$

$$\text{or: } \frac{V_1}{T_1} = \frac{V_2}{T_2}$$

$$\text{or: } V_1 T_2 = V_2 T_1$$

The important relationship to remember from this law is that temperature and volume are directly proportional:

$$V \propto T$$
$$T \propto V$$

Please solve this problem:

- A fixed quantity of gas at a constant pressure of 10 atm and a temperature of 500 Kelvin is heated. If the temperature is increased to 750 Kelvin, the gas will occupy a volume that is:

  A. twice the original volume.
  B. one and a half times the original volume.
  C. equal to the original volume.
  D. two-thirds of the original volume.

Problem solved:

B is correct. Using Charles's law:

$$V_2 = \left(\frac{T_2}{T_1}\right)V_1 = \left(\frac{750}{500}\right)V_1 = \left(\frac{1.5T_1}{T_1}\right)V_1 = 1.5V_1$$

Therefore, V_2 is increased by a factor of one and a half.

Gay-Lussac's Law

Gay-Lussac's law includes Charles's law and the relationship between pressure and temperature under conditions of constant volume and a constant number of moles of gas:

$$\frac{P}{T} = constant$$

or:

$$P = (constant)(T)$$

$$\text{or: } \frac{P_1}{T_1} = \frac{P_2}{T_2}$$

$$\text{or: } P_1 T_2 = P_2 T_1$$

The important relationship to understand from this law is that temperature is directly proportional to pressure and that pressure is, therefore, also directly proportional to temperature:

$$P \propto T$$

$$T \propto P$$

Please solve this problem:

- A fixed quantity of gas at a constant volume and a temperature of 500 Kelvin has a pressure of 5 atm. If the temperature is increased to 750 Kelvin, the gas will develop a pressure of:

  A. 10 atm
  B. 7.5 atm
  C. 5 atm
  D. 3.33 atm

Problem solved:

B is correct. Using Gay-Lussac's law:

$$P_2 = \left(\frac{T_2}{T_1}\right)P_1 = \left(\frac{750}{500}\right)P_1 = \left(\frac{1.5T_1}{T_1}\right)P_1 = 1.5P_1 = 1.5(5 \text{ atm}) = 7.5 \text{ atm}$$

Therefore, P_2 is increased by a factor of $1\frac{1}{2}$ to 7.5 atm.

The Combined Gas Law

The **combined gas law** unites the relationships found in Boyle's law, Charles's law, and Gay-Lussac's law, for conditions where the number of moles of gas is constant, as:

$$\frac{PV}{T} = constant$$

$$\text{or: } PV = (constant)(T)$$

$$\text{or: } \frac{P_1 V_1}{T_1} = \frac{P_2 V_2}{T_2}$$

$$\text{or: } P_1 V_1 T_2 = P_2 V_2 T_1$$

Please solve this problem:

- A gas has an initial volume of 5 liters at a temperature of 400 Kelvin. If the volume of the same amount of gas is 15 liters at 800 Kelvin, the pressure is:

  A. increased by a factor of 6.

  B. increased by a factor of $1\frac{1}{2}$.

  C. decreased by $\frac{1}{3}$.

  D. decreased by $\frac{5}{6}$.

Problem solved:

C is correct. Using the combined gas law:

$$\frac{P_1 V_1}{T_1} = \frac{P_2 V_2}{T_2}$$

which becomes:

$$P_2 = \frac{P_1 V_1 T_2}{V_2 T_1} = \left(\frac{V_1}{V_2}\right)\left(\frac{T_2}{T_1}\right) P_1 = \left(\frac{5}{15}\right)\left(\frac{800}{400}\right) P_1 = \left(\frac{1}{3}\right)(2) P_1 = \frac{2}{3} P_1$$

Therefore, since the volume change decreases the pressure by a factor of 3, and the temperature increases the pressure by a factor of 2, the overall effect is a decrease in pressure of $\frac{1}{3}$.

Avogadro's Hypothesis

Avogadro's hypothesis establishes the relationship between the number of moles (n) of gas and volume for ideal gases under conditions of constant pressure and constant temperature:

$$\frac{V}{n} = \text{constant}$$

or:

$$V = (\text{constant})(n)$$

$$\text{or: } \frac{V_1}{n_1} = \frac{V_2}{n_2}$$

$$\text{or: } V_1 n_2 = V_2 n_1$$

The important relationship to extract from this hypothesis is that volume is directly proportional to number of moles of gas, and that number of moles of gas is, therefore, also directly proportional to volume:

$$V \propto n$$
$$n \propto V$$

This hypothesis also asserts that under identical pressure and temperature conditions, the volume taken up by one mole of a gas is equal to the volume taken up by one mole of any other gas.

Please solve this problem:

- Initially, a balloon at STP has a volume of 2.24 liters. If the gas in the balloon is allowed to escape until the balloon has a volume of one-tenth the original volume, the total number of moles of gas in the balloon (still at STP) is:

  A. 0.01 mole
  B. 0.1 mole
  C. 1 mole
  D. not determinable from the information provided.

Problem solved:

A is correct. From Avogadro's hypothesis, since $n \propto V$, when V decreases by a factor of 10, n must also decrease by a factor of 10. We now know:

$$n_2 = \frac{n_1}{10}$$

But how much was n_1? We can get this from the information that the balloon is at STP. From earlier, one mole of gas occupies a volume of 22.4 liters at STP. Again, using Avogadro's hypothesis:

$$\frac{V_1}{n_1} = \frac{V_{STP}}{n_{STP}} \text{, therefore, } n_1 = \frac{V_1 n_{STP}}{V_{STP}} = \frac{(2.24)(1)}{(22.4)} = 0.1 \text{ mol}$$

Plugging this back into our first equation:

$$n_2 = \frac{n_1}{10} = \frac{0.1 \text{ mol}}{10} = 0.01 \text{ mol}$$

The Ideal Gas Law and the Gas Constant

Avogadro's hypothesis may be incorporated into the combined gas law to give the following relationship:

$$\frac{PV}{nT} = \text{constant}$$

Since it holds for any ideal gas, this constant is called the **universal gas constant** and is symbolized by R. Thus,

$$\frac{PV}{nT} = R$$

or:

$$PV = nRT$$

In SI units, the value of R is given by:

$$R = \frac{PV}{nT} = \frac{(\text{Pa})(\text{m}^3)}{(\text{mol})(\text{K})} = \frac{\left(\frac{\text{N}}{\text{m}^2}\right)(\text{m}^3)}{(\text{mol})(\text{K})} = \frac{(\text{N} \bullet \text{m})}{(\text{mol})(\text{K})} = \frac{\text{J}}{(\text{mol})(\text{K})}$$

If we consider conditions of STP, we can numerically solve for R:

$$R = \frac{PV}{nT} = \frac{\left(1.01325 \times 10^5 \text{Pa}\right)\left(0.0022414 \text{m}^3\right)}{(1\text{mol})(273.15\text{K})} = 8.314 \frac{\text{J}}{(\text{mol})(\text{K})}$$

You don't need to memorize the value of the universal gas constant; it will be provided on the MCAT.

Under conditions of low pressure and high temperature, the ideal gas law holds for most gases. Deviations from the ideal occur at low temperatures and at high pressures (conditions that tend to favor the formation of a liquid phase from the gas phase), and these deviations are the subject of the next section.

Please solve this problem:

- A sample of gas has a volume of 100 milliliters at 35°C and 740 torr. The gas constant, R, is 0.0821 L • atm/mol • K. The volume of the same quantity of gas at STP is:

    A. 114 milliliters
    B. 106 milliliters
    C. 100 milliliters
    D. 86 milliliters

Problem solved:

D is correct. First we must convert all units into the units given for R:

$$V = 100 \text{ ml} = 0.100 \text{ L}$$

$$T = 35°C = 308 \text{ K}$$

$$P = 740 \text{ torr} = 0.974 \text{ atm}$$

Then, using the ideal gas law to solve for the initial number of moles:

$$n = \frac{PV}{RT} = \frac{(0.974 \text{ atm})(0.100 \text{ L})}{(0.0821 \text{L} \bullet \text{atm}/\text{mol} \bullet \text{K})(308 \text{ K})} = 0.00385 \text{ mole}$$

Finally, we solve for the final volume using the STP values of $P = 1$ atm and $T = 273$ K:

$$V_{\text{STP}} = \frac{nRT_{\text{STP}}}{P_{\text{STP}}} = \frac{(0.00385 \text{ mol})(0.0821\text{L} \bullet \text{atm}/\text{mol} \bullet \text{K})(273 \text{ K})}{1 \text{ atm}} = 0.086 \text{ L} = 86 \text{ ml}$$

As an alternative to performing all these calculations (which would have to be done on the MCAT without a calculator), we could instead set the ideal gas law for the initial conditions equal to the ideal gas law for the final conditions:

$$\frac{P_1 V_1}{nRT_1} = \frac{P_2 V_2}{nRT_2}$$

Rearrange to solve for V_2:

$$V_2 = \frac{P_1 nRT_2 V_1}{P_2 nRT_1} = \left(\frac{P_1}{P_2}\right)\left(\frac{n}{n}\right)\left(\frac{R}{R}\right)\left(\frac{T_2}{T_1}\right)V_1$$

Eliminate the unity terms:

$$V_2 = \left(\frac{P_1}{P_2}\right)\left(\frac{T_2}{T_1}\right)V_1$$

We must then recognize that since P_1 is 740 torr and P_2 is 760 torr, the ratio of P_1 to P_2 must be less than unity. Similarly, since T_2 is 273 Kelvin and T_1 is 308 Kelvin, the ratio of T_2 to T_1 must also be less than unity, therefore $V_2 < V_1$, and the answer must be D.

DEVIATIONS FROM IDEALITY

Deviations in Pressure

As temperature is decreased in a gas, the individual gas particles have decreasing kinetic energy (as seen in premise 5 of the kinetic molecular theory). As a result, the velocity of the particles is decreased, which leads to a higher probability of inelastic collisions (violation of premise 2). Molecules that are moving at a slower velocity are also more likely to feel the attractive or repulsive forces of other gas molecules in the container (violation of premise 4). Any, or all, of these factors will lead to the measurement of an actual pressure that is less than the pressure calculated from the ideal gas law. *The actual pressure exerted by a gas is always less than or equal to the pressure calculated by the ideal gas law.*

Deviations in Volume

As the pressure of a gas is increased, the volume occupied by the individual gas particles themselves becomes more important. As pressure goes up, the volume in which gas particles move goes down. Therefore, the average separation between any two gas molecules must also decrease (violation of premise 3). Individual gas molecules now occupy a more significant amount of the total volume. Thus, there is an **excluded volume**, which is the volume occupied by the gas molecules themselves. The actual volume of the gas is equal to the volume of the container plus the excluded volume. *The actual volume occupied by a gas is always greater than or equal to the volume calculated by the ideal gas law.*

Van der Waals's Equation

The results of the above two sections are summarized by the **van der Waals's equation**:

$$\left(P + \frac{an^2}{V^2}\right)(V - nb) = nRT$$

It is not important to memorize this equation, but you should be familiar with the form. The $\frac{an^2}{V^2}$ term is a correction factor for the presence of intermolecular forces, and the nb term is a correction factor that accounts for the excluded volume. The constants a and b are specific to individual gases. Employing the van der Waals's equation, we see that the relationship between ideal pressure (P_I) and actual pressure (P_A) is given by:

$$P_I = P_A + \frac{an^2}{V^2}$$

and that the relationship between ideal volume (V_I) and actual volume (V_A) is given by:

$$V_I = V_A - nb$$

Please solve this problem:

- When a gas deviates from ideal gas values, the pressure and volume measured will be related to the values calculated from the ideal gas law by which of the following?

  A. Both measured values will be higher than the calculated values.
  B. The measured pressure will be higher and the measured volume will be lower.
  C. The measured pressure will be lower and the measured volume will be higher.
  D. Both measured values will be lower than the calculated values.

Problem solved:

C is correct. This is a simple application of the van der Waals's equation. If you did not answer this question correctly, you should reread this section (Deviations From Ideality).

MIXTURES OF GASES

Dalton's Law

The key to understanding gaseous mixtures is to assume that each individual gas behaves as if no other gases are present. In terms of number of moles (n), it is obvious that the presence of other gases does not affect this value. In terms of temperature, each individual gas will have an average kinetic energy that is directly proportional to the temperature: Each gas will have the same distribution of energies as every other gas, and these will be independent of the presence of the other gases. Since we can assume that, under ideal conditions, all gas molecules occupy no volume, the presence of other gases in a container with a gas will not affect the volume of the container that is available to this gas. Pressure is affected by the presence of other gases. Since pressure is a measure of the force of gas particle collisions against the walls of the container, it stands to reason that each gas of a mixture will contribute only part of the total pressure on the container walls (since all gases collide with the walls).

Dalton's law of partial pressures sets forth the relationship between the total pressure exerted by the mixture and that part of the pressure that is due to a given gas in the mixture. This law states that the pressure exerted by a mixture of gases behaving ideally is equal to the sum of the pressures exerted by the individual gases:

$$P_T = P_A - P_B$$

where P_T is the total pressure exerted by a mixture of gas A and gas B, P_A is the pressure that gas A would exert alone under the same conditions in the same volume, and P_B is the pressure that gas B would exert alone. Putting this relationship into the ideal gas law yields:

$$P_T = \frac{(n_A + n_B)RT}{V}$$

where n_A and n_B are the number of moles of gas A and gas B, respectively. Put another way, the partial pressure exerted by gas A is equal to the product of the total pressure exerted by the mixture and the mole fraction of gas A that is present in the mixture:

$$P_A = X_A - P_T$$

where X_A is the mole fraction of gas A, which is given by:

$$X_A = \frac{n_A}{n_T} = \frac{n_A}{n_A + n_B}$$

Vapor pressure is a special case of Dalton's law that applies to gases in contact with a liquid. In this case, some molecules of the liquid will escape into gas phase and contribute to the total gas pressure. The partial pressure so exerted by the liquid (by molecules that have escaped into the gas phase) is the vapor pressure of the liquid. The vapor pressure of a liquid is dependent on its temperature.

Please solve this problem:

- The vapor pressure of water at 296 Kelvin is 0.0275 atm. The value of the gas constant is 0.0821 L • atm/ mol • K. If 500 milliliters of oxygen is collected over a bath of water at a temperature of 296 Kelvin and a pressure of 0.5135 atm, the weight of the oxygen collected will be:

  A. 32.00 grams.
  B. 3.2 grams.
  C. 0.32 grams.
  D. 0.032 grams.

Problem solved:

C is correct. To solve this problem, we must realize that the ideal gas law may also be written:

$$PV = \left(\frac{m}{MW}\right)RT$$

since moles, n, is equal to mass (in grams) divided by molecular weight (in grams per moles). We must also realize that the term P in the above equation refers to the partial pressure of oxygen, which is given by Dalton's law of partial pressures:

$$P_T = P_A + P_B$$

Taking A as oxygen and B as the water vapor, we can solve for P_A:

$$P_{O_2} = P_T - P_{H_2O} = 0.5135 - 0.0275 = 0486 \text{ atm}$$

Plugging this and the other known values into the ideal gas law, we get:

$$m = \frac{PV(MW)}{RT} = \frac{(.486 \text{ atm})(.5 \text{ L})(32 \text{ g/mol})}{(0.0821 \text{ L} \bullet \text{atm/mol} \bullet \text{K})(296 \text{ K})} = 0.32 \text{ g}$$

Alternatively, if we had realized that the temperature given is approximately STP temperature and that the given pressure is approximately one-half of STP pressure, we could reason that our volume is approximately twice STP volume. Twice STP volume for one mole of gas is 44.8 liters. Using Avogadro's hypothesis, we could solve:

$$n_{O_2} = \left(\frac{V_{O_2}}{2V_{STP}}\right)n_{STP} = \left(\frac{.486 \text{ L}}{44.8 \text{ L}}\right)(1 \text{ mol}) \approx 0.01 \text{ mol}$$

From this, our approximate O_2 mass must be closest to 0.32 grams—therefore the answer is C.

Raoult's Law

Raoult's law describes a relationship similar to Dalton's law, observed in certain **ideal solutions**. Raoult's law asserts that the vapor pressure exerted by a component of a liquid mixture is equal to the product of the vapor pressure of the pure component and the mole fraction of that component in the *liquid* phase:

$$P_{A(K)} = X_{A(\ell)}P^*_{A(K)}$$

where $P_{A(K)}$ is the vapor pressure exerted by liquid component A, $X_{A(\ell)}$ is the mole fraction of A in the liquid phase, and $P^*_{A(K)}$ is the vapor pressure of pure A. In the case of a nonvolatile solute dissolved in a solvent, the vapor pressure of the solution can be calculated from:

$$P_{soln} = X_{solv}P^*_{solv}$$

where:

P_{soln} = vapor pressure of solution,

X_{soln} = mol fraction of solvent, and

P^*_{solv} = vapor pressure of pure solvent.

Please solve this problem:

- The vapor pressure of water at 300 Kelvin is 0.3 atm. Calculate the vapor pressure above a solution prepared from 360 grams of water and 180 grams of glucose. $C_6H_{12}O_6$.

A. 0.315 atm
B. 0.300 atm
C. 0.286 atm
D. 0.235 atm

Problem solved:

C is correct. To solve this problem, we must first convert all terms given in grams to moles:

$$\text{moles } H_2O = \frac{360\,g}{18\,g/mol} = 20\,mol$$

$$\text{moles glucose} = \frac{180\ g}{180\,g/mol} = 1\ mol$$

Then we apply Raoult's law:

$$P_{soln} = X_{H_2O}P^*_{H_2O} = \left(\frac{20\,mol}{20\,mol + 1\,mol}\right)(0.300\,atm) = \left(\frac{20}{21}\right)(0.300\,atm) = 0.286\,atm$$

DIFFUSION AND EFFUSION OF GASES: GRAHAM'S LAW OF DIFFUSION

Diffusion is the movement of a gas through space, while **effusion** is the movement of a gas under pressure through a small hole. An example of effusion is the escape of air through the walls of a balloon along the pressure gradient as the balloon slowly deflates. The mathematics of diffusion and effusion are the same. Remember that premise 1 of the kinetic molecular theory provided for gas molecules with an average kinetic energy of $KE = \frac{1}{2}mv^2$. Rewriting to solve for velocity, we get:

$$v = \sqrt{\frac{2KE}{m}}$$

from which come the two proportionalities:

$$v \propto (KE)^{1/2}$$

$$v \propto \left(\frac{1}{m}\right)^{1/2}$$

Remembering that kinetic energy is directly proportional to absolute temperature, which is premise 5 of the kinetic molecular theory, we can also write:

$$v \propto T^{1/2}$$

Any two gases at the same temperature will have identical average kinetic energies:

$$KE_1 = KE_2$$

or:

$$\frac{1}{2}m_1 v_1^2 = \frac{1}{2}m_2 v_2^2$$

Therefore:

$$\frac{v_1^2}{v_2^2} = \frac{m_2}{m_1}$$

$$\frac{v_1}{v_2} = \sqrt{\frac{m_2}{m_1}}$$

The above relation is an expression of **Graham's law of diffusion**. According to Graham's law, for any two gas molecules of unequal mass at an identical temperature, the lighter molecule will have a higher velocity (or rate of diffusion) than the heavier molecule.

Please solve this problem:

- An oxygen molecule at 500 Kelvin has:

   A. sixteen times the velocity of a hydrogen molecule at 500 Kelvin.
   B. one-sixteenth the velocity of a hydrogen molecule at 500 Kelvin.
   C. four times the velocity of a hydrogen molecule at 500 Kelvin.
   D. one-fourth the velocity of a hydrogen molecule at 500 Kelvin.

Problem solved:

D is correct. Using Graham's law of diffusion:

$$\frac{v_{O_2}}{v_{H_2}} = \sqrt{\frac{m_{H_2}}{m_{O_2}}} = \sqrt{\frac{2\,\text{g/mol}}{32\,\text{g/mol}}} = \sqrt{\frac{1}{16}} = \frac{1}{4}$$

19.2 MASTERY APPLIED: PRACTICE PASSAGE AND QUESTIONS

Passage

Since an ideal gas is not subjected to intermolecular forces, an ideal gas will never liquefy. Any real gas, however, will liquefy if subjected to a sufficiently high pressure and a significantly low temperature. A necessary condition of liquefaction is that the kinetic energy of the molecules be reduced enough that the attractive forces between molecules predominate. Because the relationship of kinetic energy, given by the Maxwell-Boltzmann distribution:

$$KE = \frac{3}{2}nRT,$$

depends only upon temperature and not pressure, there is, for any gas, a critical temperature above which the gas will not liquefy, regardless of the pressure applied. The pressure necessary to liquefy a gas at its critical temperature is called the critical pressure.

The critical temperature of a gas depends on its intermolecular forces. A gas with high intermolecular forces will liquefy more easily and, thus, will have a higher critical temperature. In general, polar gases may be expected to have higher critical temperatures than nonpolar gases. Among nonpolar gases, higher molecular weight gases will be expected to have higher critical temperatures than lower molecular weight gases, as shown in Table 1.

Gas	Critical Temperature (K)	Critical Pressure (atm)	Critical Volume (ml/mol)
H_2O	647	217.7	56
NH_3	406	111.5	72
HCl	324	81.6	81
CO_2	304	72.9	94.0
O_2	155	49.7	73
Ar	151	48.0	75.3
N_2	126	33.5	90.1
H_2	33	12.8	65
He	5	2.3	57.8

Table 1

If liquefaction occurs at precisely the critical temperature, there is no surface between the gas phase and the liquid phase during the liquefaction process. The absence of this visible phase separation (the meniscus) is indicative of a liquid volume, after the liquefaction, that is equal to the gaseous volume prior to the liquefaction. This volume is the critical volume.

1. When liquefaction occurs at the critical point of a substance, the absence of a meniscus is most likely due to:
    A. the gas phase and the liquid phase having equal densities.
    B. the gas phase having a density higher than that of the liquid phase.
    C. the absence of a gas phase.
    D. the absence of a liquid phase.

2. According to the passage:
    A. helium would be correctly predicted to have a critical temperature lower than that of hydrogen.
    B. hydrogen would be correctly predicted to have a critical temperature lower than that of helium.
    C. helium would be incorrectly predicted to have a critical temperature lower than that of hydrogen.
    D. hydrogen would be incorrectly predicted to have a critical temperature lower than that of helium.

3. The universal gas constant is 0.0821 L·atm/mol·K. From Table 1, which of the following is behaving most ideally at its critical point?
    A. Ar
    B. N_2
    C. H_2
    D. He

4. The critical temperature of dimethyl ether is 126.9°C while that of ethanol is 243°C. This could be due to all of the following EXCEPT:

   A. dimethyl ether experiences lesser intermolecular forces than ethanol.
   B. ethanol tends to ionize in the gaseous state.
   C. dimethyl ether does not experience hydrogen bonding.
   D. ethanol has a higher boiling point than dimethyl ether.

5. Which of the following could NOT be converted to a liquid at room temperature?

   A. H_2O
   B. CO_2
   C. H_2
   D. It cannot be determined from the information given.

6. An unknown gas with a molecular weight of 30 grams per moles is determined to be nonpolar. Its critical temperature is most likely:

   A. 165 Kelvin.
   B. 140 Kelvin.
   C. 115 Kelvin.
   D. 90 Kelvin.

19.3 MASTERY VERIFIED: ANSWERS AND EXPLANATIONS

1. **A is correct.** Based on information in the last paragraph of the passage, the gas phase prior to liquefaction and the liquid phase after liquefaction occupy equal volumes. Since mass is conserved in the liquefaction process, and density is given by:

$$\rho = \frac{m}{V}$$

the densities must also be equal. If choice B were true, there would still be a meniscus between the phases, but the gas would be on the bottom of the container rather than the liquid. Choices C and D are incorrect since during any liquefaction process, there must be both gas and liquid present until the process is complete.

2. **D is correct.** According to the passage, nonpolar molecules are expected to show a linear relationship between molecular weight and critical temperature. Helium has a molecular weight of 4 grams per moles. Hydrogen gas has a molecular weight of 2 grams per moles. From this, we would predict that helium would have the higher critical temperature. This eliminates choices A and C, which predict a higher critical temperature for hydrogen. From Table 1, we see that a lower critical temperature is observed for helium than is observed for hydrogen. Although we would have predicted that hydrogen would have had the lower critical temperature from the passage, Table 1 clearly shows this to be incorrect; therefore, the answer is D.

3. **D is correct.** We answer this question by using the information in Table 1 and the ideal gas law in the form:

$$\frac{PV}{nT} = R$$

The table gives us values for T, P, and V/n for each gas. Solving for R for each gas (after converting the volumes from milliliters to liters):

$$R_{Ar} = \frac{(48.0 \text{ atm})(0.0753 \text{ L/mol})}{(151 \text{ K})} = 0.0239 \text{ L} \cdot \text{atm/mol} \cdot \text{K}$$

$$R_{N_2} = \frac{(33.5 \text{ atm})(0.0901 \text{ L/mol})}{(126 \text{ K})} = 0.0240 \text{ L} \cdot \text{atm/mol} \cdot \text{K}$$

$$R_{H_2} = \frac{(12.8 \text{ atm})(0.0635 \text{ L/mol})}{(33 \text{ K})} = 0.0246 \text{ L} \cdot \text{atm/mol} \cdot \text{K}$$

$$R_{He} = \frac{(2.3 \text{ atm})(0.0578 \text{ L/mol})}{(5 \text{ K})} = 0.0266 \text{ L} \cdot \text{atm/mol} \cdot \text{K}$$

Since we know that $R = 0.0821$ L · atm/mol · K, the gas behaving most ideally is that gas with a calculated value of R closest to this ideal value, which is helium.

4. **B is correct.** Dimethyl ether does not experience hydrogen bonding with itself, so it has lesser intermolecular interactions than ethanol, which will hydrogen bond with other molecules of ethanol. Therefore, choices A and C are true. Ethanol has a higher boiling point than dimethyl ether because of these hydrogen bonds. As pointed out in question 2, the passage suggests that materials with higher boiling points will also have higher critical temperatures. Therefore choice D is true. Choice B is false; substances do not tend to ionize simply by passing from one phase to another.

5. **C is correct.** Room temperature is approximately 295 Kelvin. Referring to Table 1, we see that the critical temperatures of water and carbon dioxide are both above room temperature, whereas the critical temperature of hydrogen gas is below room temperature. The definition of critical temperature is that temperature above which a liquid will not form, regardless of the pressure applied. As we know, water is a liquid at room temperature and atmospheric pressure: Choice A is obviously incorrect. Carbon dioxide (dry ice) does not have a liquid phase at room temperature (under atmospheric pressure conditions). However, since room temperature is below the critical temperature of carbon dioxide, there is a pressure at which carbon dioxide would become a liquid, with a temperature of 295 Kelvin. Since room temperature is well above the critical temperature of hydrogen gas, it is clear that hydrogen gas cannot be a liquid at room temperature; hydrogen gas cannot become a liquid above 33 Kelvin.

6. **B is correct.** From the passage, nonpolar gases will tend to show a direct relationship between molecular weight and critical temperature. Since our unknown gas has a molecular weight of 30 grams per moles, we would expect it to have a critical temperature between the nonpolar gas O_2 (MW = 32 g/mol) and the nonpolar gas N_2 (MW = 28 g/mol). Choice B is the only answer choice between 153 Kelvin and 126 Kelvin, the critical temperatures of oxygen gas and nitrogen gas, respectively.

CHAPTER 20

PHASE CHANGES

20.1 MASTERY ACHIEVED

CHANGING PHASES: SOLID, LIQUID, GAS

Phases and Their Dependence on Temperature and Pressure

Within a system, all matter that has a particular set of properties is said to be in a **phase**. On the MCAT, you need only to concern yourself with single component systems when considering phases. The phases available to a system are the **gas** phase (g), the **liquid** phase (ℓ), and the **solid** phase (s). In certain cases, a pure substance may adopt more than one crystalline structure in the solid phase; for example, diamond and graphite are two different solid phases of carbon.

In MCAT terms:

- The gas phase of a material is characterized by the ability of the material to take the shape of the container that holds it and the ability of the material to expand to fill the available volume.

- The liquid phase of a material is characterized by the ability of the material to conform to the shape of the container that holds it, but an inability of the material to expand to fill the available volume.

- The solid phase of a material is characterized by an inability of the material to conform to the shape of the container that holds it and an inability of the material to expand to fill the available volume.

Whether a substance exists in the solid, liquid, or gas phase depends primarily on temperature and pressure. As temperature is increased under conditions of constant pressure, a substance will move from the solid phase to the liquid phase. As temperature is further increased, the substance will move from the liquid phase to the gas phase, following Charles's law **(Chapter 19)**: As temperature is increased, volume is increased.

To summarize:

- Under conditions of high temperature and/or low pressure, the gas phase will be favored over the liquid phase, and the liquid phase will be favored over the solid phase.

- Under conditions of low temperature and/or high pressure, the solid phase will be favored over the liquid phase, and the liquid phase will be favored over the gas phase.

Please solve this problem:

- A substance exists in the gas phase at room temperature at atmospheric conditions. If the pressure is doubled and the temperature is halved, the substance will do the following:

  A. Remain in the gas phase.
  B. Become a liquid.
  C. Become a solid.
  D. It is impossible to tell the final phase of the material from the information given.

Problem solved:

D is correct. Unless we know the pressures and temperatures of the phase changes of this substance, we cannot say with certainty in which phase the substance will be. An increase in pressure and a reduction in temperature favor the formation of a liquid or solid phase. However, the question is whether we have increased the pressure and lowered the temperature enough to cause a phase change to occur. We cannot tell.

The Available Phase Changes

The change in phase that occurs when a solid becomes a liquid is called **melting**. The opposite of melting is **freezing**.

When a liquid becomes a gas, this process is called **boiling**, or **vaporization**. The opposite of boiling is **condensing**.

Under appropriate conditions, such as carbon dioxide (dry ice) at room temperature and atmospheric pressure, it is possible for a substance to skip the liquid phase altogether. Such a process—the direct conversion of a solid to a gas—is called **sublimation**. The direct conversion from a gas phase to a solid phase, without an intervening liquid phase, is **deposition**.

Please solve this problem:

- The opposite of sublimation is:

  A. freezing.
  B. vaporization.
  C. deposition.
  D. condensation.

Problem solved:

C is correct. Sublimation is the process whereby a solid is transformed directly into a gas, without an intervening liquid phase. Deposition is the process whereby a gas is transformed directly into a solid, without an intervening liquid phase.

THE THERMODYNAMICS OF PHASE CHANGES

There are six possible phase changes: **melting, vaporization, sublimation, deposition, condensation**, and **freezing**. The first three changes involve a change from a lower energy state to a higher energy state; the second three involve a change from a higher energy state to a lower energy state.

Since energy is always conserved, the transition from a phase or state that contains more energy to a phase or state that contains less energy must involve the release of energy; it must be **exothermic**. Deposition, condensation, and freezing are all exothermic processes.

Conversely, a transition from a phase or state that contains less energy to a phase or state that contains more energy requires the input of energy. Such a process is **endothermic**. Melting, vaporization, and sublimation are endothermic processes.

Associated with each phase change is an increase or decrease in enthalpy. The enthalpy of the phase change from solid to liquid is termed the **heat of fusion**. The heat of fusion, ΔH_{fus}, of any substance at constant temperature and pressure normally takes a positive value, since melting (fusion) is an endothermic process, and any endothermic process will have a positive value of ΔH. Since energy is conserved in forward and reverse processes, the negative of the heat of fusion is the enthalpy change associated with freezing.

The enthalpy change associated with the phase change from liquid to gas is called the **heat of vaporization**. The heat of vaporization, ΔH_{vap}, of any substance at constant temperature and pressure normally takes a positive value, since vaporization is an endothermic process, and any endothermic process will have a positive value of ΔH. The negative of the heat of vaporization is the enthalpy change associated with condensation.

The enthalpy change associated with the phase change from a solid directly to a gas is called the **heat of sublimation** (ΔH_{sub}). As was the case for heat of fusion and heat of vaporization, heat of sublimation at constant temperature and pressure normally takes a positive value for any substance, since sublimation is an endothermic process. The negative of the heat of sublimation is the enthalpy change associated with deposition.

Please solve this problem:

- The heat of fusion is:

   A. positive, because melting is an exothermic process.
   B. positive, because melting is an endothermic process.
   C. negative, because melting is an exothermic process.
   D. negative, because melting is an endothermic process.

Problem solved:

B is correct. Heat of fusion refers to the heat that must be supplied to a substance to make it melt. When heat must be supplied to a reaction, that reaction is termed endothermic.

Had this question asked about the process of solidification, heat would have been given off, leading to a negative ΔH, or an exothermic process.

CALCULATING WITH HEAT: AT AND AWAY FROM PHASE CHANGES

Comparing Heat During and Away from a Phase Change

During a phase change, there is no change in temperature. For example, when solid water is heated from –5°C to +5°C, the temperature of the system changes until the melting point of water is reached (0°C). At this point, even though heat is being supplied, the temperature of the water does not change. All the energy being supplied to the system is used to convert the solid water into liquid water. It is not until the phase change is complete that the temperature begins to rise again. In this regard, energy added to a system at a time other than at a phase change will induce a change in temperature in the system. Energy added to a system during a phase change will *not* induce a change in temperature. Molecular kinetic energy is directly related to temperature (**Chapter 19**). Therefore, when temperature is increased, molecular kinetic energy is also increased. When a system gains energy without an increase in temperature, the system must be gaining potential energy.

- When a system is not undergoing a phase change, the heat added to that system adds to the kinetic energy of the molecules of that system.

- When a system is undergoing a phase change, the heat added to that system adds to the potential energy of the molecules of that system.

The converse of these two postulates is also true:

- When a system is not undergoing a phase change, the heat released by that system diminishes the kinetic energy of the molecules of that system.

- When a system is undergoing a phase change, the heat released by that system diminishes the potential energy of the molecules of that system.

Please solve this problem:

- As water is cooled slowly from 5°C to –5°C, it will undergo a phase change from the liquid state to the solid state, and:

   A. the kinetic energy of the water molecules will increase, and the potential energy will decrease.
   B. the kinetic energy of the water molecules will decrease, and the potential energy will increase.
   C. both the kinetic energy and the potential energy of the water molecules will increase.
   D. both the kinetic energy and the potential energy of the water molecules will decrease.

Problem solved:

D is correct. As the temperature is lowered, the molecules of that system will contain less kinetic energy. Recall that kinetic energy is directly proportional to temperature. The phase change from a liquid to a solid is an exothermic process; heat is given off. When energy is given off in the form of heat, there must be less potential energy in the system, since energy is conserved.

Heat Away from a Phase Change

When a system is not undergoing a phase change, the heat absorbed by the system is given by:

$$q = mc\Delta T$$

where:

q is the heat absorbed,

m is the mass of the substance under consideration,

c is the specific heat capacity of the substance in this particular phase, and

ΔT is the change in temperature observed.

We are familiar with all these variables, except specific heat capacity, c.

Specific heat is the heat capacity of a substance per unit mass. As can be seen from the above equation, specific heat has the units of energy per mass per temperature:

$$c = \frac{q}{\Delta T} = \frac{J}{kg \bullet K} \text{ or } \frac{J}{kg \bullet {}^\circ C} \text{ or } \frac{cal}{g \bullet {}^\circ C} \text{ or } \frac{kcal}{kg \bullet {}^\circ C}$$

Calories (cal) are a unit of energy. One calorie is defined as the amount of heat energy that must be supplied to one gram of liquid water at 25°C to raise the temperature of the water 1°C. Therefore, the specific heat of liquid water is defined as 1 cal/g • °C.

(With respect to food and nutrition, the common term *calorie* refers to 1,000 calories [1 Kcal]. When we say that a certain food item contains "100 Calories," we refer to *100,000 times* the energy required to raise one gram of water by 1°C.)

Please solve this problem:

- The specific heat of liquid water is 4.18 J/°C • g. The heat required to raise the temperature of 10 grams of liquid water from a temperature of 20°C to 50°C is:

  A. 125.4 joules
  B. 836.0 joules
  C. 1254.0 joules
  D. 2090.0 joules

Problem solved:

C is correct. Employing the formula:

$$q = mc\Delta T$$

where:

$$m = 10 \text{ g}$$

$$c = 4.18 \text{ J/}^\circ C \bullet g$$

$$\Delta T = 50^\circ C - 20^\circ C = 30^\circ C$$

$$q = (10 \text{ g})(4.18 \text{ J/}^\circ C \bullet g)(30^\circ C) = 1254 \text{ J}$$

Heat During a Phase Change

To calculate the heat of a phase change, we only need to know how much material is undergoing the change and the magnitude of the change of enthalpy that is associated with this change for this substance. As stated earlier in the chapter, each substance has a heat of fusion, heat of vaporization, and heat of sublimation. The opposite of each of these is heat of freezing, heat of condensation, and heat of deposition, respectively. The formula for calculating the amount of heat that is either absorbed (fusion, vaporization, or sublimation) or given off (freezing, condensation, or deposition) is given by:

$$q = m\Delta H$$

where q is the heat, m is the mass, and ΔH is the enthalpy of the phase change in the units of energy per mass. The uses of this equation are summarized in Table 20.1.

Phase Change	Formula
melting (solid to liquid)	$q = m\Delta H_{fus}$
vaporizing (liquid to gas)	$q = m\Delta H_{vap}$
subliming (solid to gas)	$q = m\Delta H_{sub}$
freezing (liquid to solid)	$q = m(-\Delta H_{fus})$
condensing (gas to liquid)	$q = m(-\Delta H_{vap})$
depositing (gas to solid)	$q = m(-\Delta H_{sub})$

Table 20.1

Please solve this problem:

- How much heat must be supplied to slowly lower the temperature of 1 gram of water from 120°C to −10°C? (Assume that the water is initially in the gas phase, passes through the liquid phase, and ends up in the solid phase. The specific heat of gaseous water is 1.87 J/°C • g. The specific heat of liquid water is 4.18 J/°C • g. The specific heat of solid water is 2.03 J/°C • g. The heat of fusion of water is 333.8 J/g. The heat of vaporization of water is 2259 J/g.)

   A. 0 joules
   B. 476.4 joules
   C. 2592.8 joules
   D. 3068.5 joules

Problem solved:

A is correct. You should be careful not to fall for traps like this on the MCAT. No heat must be *supplied* in order for this process to take place: Heat must be *removed*! Had the question been "How much heat must be removed…," the answer would have been D, based on the following:

120°C to 100°C:	$q = mc\Delta T$	=	(1 g)(1.87 J/°C • g)(20°C)	=	37.4 J
at 100°C:	$q = m\Delta H_{vap}$	=	(1 g)(2259 J/g)	=	2259.0 J
100°C to 0°C:	$q = mc\Delta T$	=	(1 g)(4.18 J/°C • g)(100°C)	=	418.0 J
at 0°C:	$q = m\Delta H_{fus}$	=	(1 g)(333.8 J/g)	=	333.8 J
0°C to -10°C:	$q = mc\Delta T$	=	(1 g)(2.03 J/°C • g)(10°C)	=	20.3 J
Therefore, total q is given by:	q_{total}			=	3068.5 J

THE PHASE CHANGE DIAGRAM

The phase changes of a substance may be represented graphically in a variety of ways, two of which will be used on the MCAT. The first of these is the **phase change diagram**, shown below. The second is the phase diagram, or P-T diagram, which is covered in the next section.

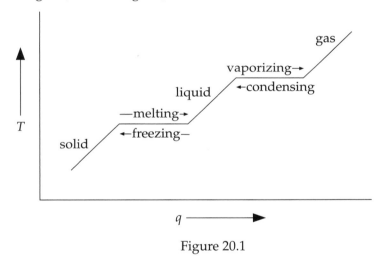

Figure 20.1

The phase change diagram is useful for graphical depiction of many things. The horizontal lines denote the amount of heat energy that is added or released during a change in phase. Horizontal components of the graph are given by the formula:

$$q = m\Delta H$$

Therefore, the length of such a line divided by the mass under consideration gives a value for ΔH.

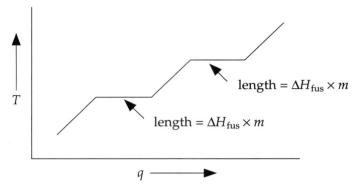

length = $\Delta H_{fus} \times m$

length = $\Delta H_{fus} \times m$

Figure 20.2

Nonhorizontal components of the phase change diagram represent the thermodynamics of a system that is not undergoing a phase change; these portions of the graph are given by the equation:

$$q = mc\Delta T$$

Since the slope of a line is defined as:

$$slope = \frac{\Delta Y}{\Delta X} = \frac{rise}{run}$$

we can see that since $X = q$ and $Y = T$, the slope of the line is given by:

$$slope = \frac{\Delta T}{\Delta q}$$

Rearranging the equation for heat, we get:

$$\frac{q}{\Delta T} = mc, \text{ or}$$

$$\frac{1}{slope} = mc, \text{ since } mc = C$$

$$slope = \frac{1}{C}$$

where C is the heat capacity for the exact amount of substance being considered.

Therefore, from a phase change diagram, we can calculate the heat capacity of each phase.

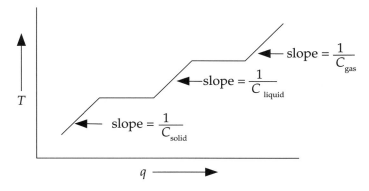

Figure 20.3

You should be aware that each phase change diagram is calculated for a specific constant pressure. If pressure is changed, the phase change diagram must also be changed.

Please solve this problem:

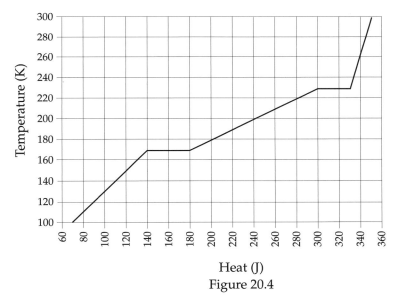

Heat (J)
Figure 20.4

- Referring to the phase change diagram (Figure 20.4), which was derived experimentally from a 5-gram sample of an unknown substance, the heat of fusion of this substance and specific heat capacity of the liquid phase are:

    A. $\Delta H_{fus} = 40$ J/g and $C_{liquid} = 0.4$ J/K • g
    B. $\Delta H_{fus} = 40$ J/g and $C_{liquid} = 0.5$ J/K • g
    C. $\Delta H_{fus} = 8$ J/g and $C_{liquid} = 0.4$ J/K • g
    D. $\Delta H_{fus} = 8$ J/g and $C_{liquid} = 0.5$ J/K • g

Problem solved:

C is correct. The distance of the phase transition from a solid to a liquid gives us the heat of fusion: length of horizontal line = $(\Delta H_{fus})(m)$. Therefore,

$$\Delta H_{fus} = \frac{\text{length of line}}{m} = \frac{(180 \text{ J} - 140 \text{ J})}{5 \text{ g}} = \frac{40 \text{ J}}{5 \text{ g}} = 8 \text{ J/g}$$

The slope of the line representing the liquid phase will tell us the heat capacity of the liquid:

$$c = \frac{1}{m(\text{slope})}$$

where:

$$\text{slope} = \frac{\Delta T}{\Delta q} = \frac{(230 \text{ K} - 170 \text{ K})}{(300 \text{ J} - 180 \text{ J})} = \frac{60 \text{ K}}{120 \text{ J}} = 0.5 \text{ K/J}$$

Therefore,

$$c = \frac{1}{(0.5 \text{ K/J})(5 \text{ g})} = \frac{1}{2.5 \text{ K} \cdot \text{g/J}} = 0.4 \text{ J/K} \cdot \text{g}$$

THE PHASE DIAGRAM: P-T DIAGRAM

A second way to depict phase changes graphically is in a **phase diagram**. The usual axes for such a diagram are pressure and temperature. For this reason, phase diagrams are often referred to as **P-T diagrams**. A typical phase diagram is depicted below:

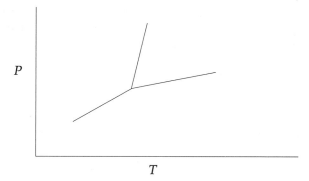

Figure 20.5

Under conditions of sufficiently high temperature or sufficiently low pressure, we would expect to find any substance in the gas phase. Therefore, the region to the far right bottom of a phase diagram represents the gas phase.

Under conditions of sufficiently low temperature or sufficiently high pressure, we would expect to find any substance in the solid phase, so the region to the far left top of a phase diagram represents the solid phase.

Liquids exist under conditions of moderate temperature or moderate pressure, so the middle region of a phase diagram represents the liquid phase.

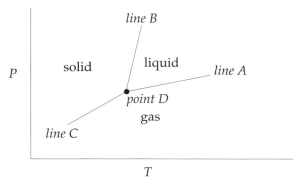

Figure 20.6

The lines in a phase diagram represent the boundaries between two phases. Above *line A*, the substance is in the liquid phase. Below *line A*, the substance is in the gas phase. Along *line A*, the liquid and the gas phases are in equilibrium.

To the left of *line B*, the substance is in the solid phase. To the right of *line B*, the substance is in the liquid phase. Along *line B*, the solid and the liquid phases are in equilibrium.

Above *line C*, the substance is in the solid phase. Below *line C*, the substance is in the gas phase. Along *line C*, the solid and the gas phases are in equilibrium.

Point D lies at the point at which all three phases are in equilibrium. This point is referred to as the **triple point**. There is no way to get back to this point after a decrease in temperature, other than by increasing the temperature. Likewise, there is no way to return to this point after a decrease in pressure, other than by raising the pressure.

Please solve this problem:

- A phase diagram is most likely constructed experimentally by:

    A. changing both temperature and pressure simultaneously from one data point to the next.
    B. changing temperature slowly at several constant pressure readings.
    C. changing pressure slowly at several constant temperature readings.
    D. changing one variable—either temperature or pressure—while holding the other variable constant.

Problem solved:

B is correct. While choice D makes sense in theory, in practice, it is much easier to vary temperature at a constant pressure than to vary pressure at a constant temperature. This is particularly true in the gas phase, where a gas will cool via an effect (known as the Joule-Thomson effect) as pressure is released.

While it is not important for you to understand the Joule-Thomson effect for the MCAT, it is important that you understand basic experimental design. Common sense dictates that it is easier to control temperature than pressure. For example, the air coming out of a balloon feels cooler than the surrounding air, even if the balloon has had plenty of time to equilibrate its internal gas temperature to the surrounding air temperature.

The Phase Diagram of Water

For a typical substance, the phase boundary between the liquid and the solid phases has a positive slope; for water, the opposite is true. For a typical substance, the solid phase is denser than the liquid phase; for water the opposite is true.

The significance of a solid/liquid phase boundary with a negative slope is that as pressure is increased, the freezing point is depressed. In a typical substance, the freezing point is increased with increasing pressure. Two phase diagrams are shown below:

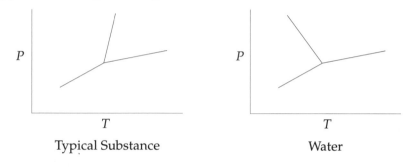

Typical Substance   Water

Figure 20.7

Please solve this problem:

- As the pressure on a sample of water is increased, the melting point of the water:

    A. decreases, as is expected for "normal" substances.
    B. decreases, contrary to what is expected for "normal" substances.
    C. increases, as is expected for "normal" substances.
    D. increases, contrary to what is expected for "normal" substances.

Problem solved:

B is correct. From our knowledge of phase diagrams, we can see that the solid/liquid phase boundary line depicts melting point versus pressure. From our phase diagrams of water and "normal" substances above, we can see that as the pressure in a sample of water is increased, the melting point decreases; whereas, for "normal" substances, the opposite is true: As pressure increases, melting point increases.

In a typical substance, the solid phase expands upon melting. In water, the solid phase contracts on melting. In other words, for most materials, the solid phase is more dense than the liquid phase. In water, the liquid phase is more dense than the solid phase.

Substances with More Than One Solid Form

Certain substances exist in more than one solid form. Examples include the graphite and diamond forms of carbon and the S_4 and S_8 forms of sulfur. The phase diagram of sulfur is given below:

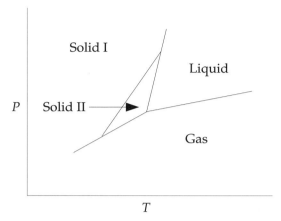

Figure 20.8

THE TRIPLE POINT AND CRITICAL POINT

As mentioned previously, the **triple point** of a substance is the point, defined by a specific temperature and a specific pressure, at which all three phases of the substance exist at equilibrium. A slight decrease in temperature from the triple point will often lead to entrance into the solid phase. A slight increase in temperature will lead to entrance into the gas phase. A small increase in pressure will lead to the formation of the liquid or solid phase. A slight decrease in pressure will lead to entrance into the gas phase.

If the triple point of a substance occurs at a pressure greater than 1 atm (atmospheric pressure), the substance will sublimate under atmospheric conditions and an appropriate change in temperature. Such is the case for carbon dioxide, which has a triple point at 216.8 Kelvin and 5.11 atm.

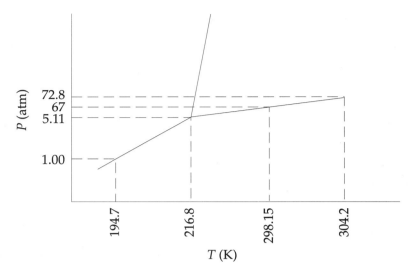

(NOTE: Axes are not drawn to scale.)

Figure 20.9

The triple point should not be confused with the **critical point**. The triple point is where all **three** phases exist in equilibrium. The critical point of a substance is the temperature above which there is no phase boundary between the liquid and the gas phases **(Chapter 19)**. The minimum pressure that is required to convert the gas to its liquid at the critical temperature is the critical pressure of that substance. The critical values of carbon dioxide are given on the above graph (T_c = 304.2 K, P_c = 72.8 atm).

Note that in a phase diagram, the liquid/gas phase boundary cannot be extrapolated above the critical temperature. By definition, there is no way to distinguish between these two phases above this temperature.

Please solve this problem:

- A substance has a triple point at 300 Kelvin and 760 torr. Under conditions of atmospheric pressure at sea level, this substance:

  A. is a liquid at room temperature.
  B. is a solid at room temperature.
  C. is a gas at room temperature.
  D. sublimates at room temperature.

Problem solved:

B is correct. Since room temperature is 298 Kelvin, this represents a decrease in temperature from the triple point. As pointed out above, if pressure is held constant, a decrease in temperature from the triple point of a substance will lead to the formation of a solid phase. Since 760 torr is atmospheric pressure at sea level, there is no change in pressure from the triple point pressure to atmospheric pressure.

20.2 MASTERY APPLIED: PRACTICE PASSAGE AND QUESTIONS

Passage

Campers and military personnel routinely carry freeze-dried foods because these foods are lightweight. Additionally, bacteria cannot grow or reproduce in the total absence of moisture that is afforded by freeze-dried items. Freeze-dried foods may be quickly reconstituted simply by adding water to them. The technique of freeze-drying can be applied to almost any substance that contains water. Biologists often freeze-dry tissue cultures in order to preserve them for later research.

Freeze-drying takes advantage of the phase properties of water. In the process of freeze-drying, a sample is first cooled to a temperature below the freezing point of water such that all of the water solidifies. Next, the sample is placed in a chamber to which a vacuum pump is attached. The pump serves to lower the pressure in the chamber below the vapor pressure of ice, such that all of the ice sublimates. Once the water is in the gaseous state, it is evacuated from the chamber by the vacuum pump.

This process has many advantages over traditional drying methods, which rely on boiling off the unwanted water. The heat necessary to remove all the water from a sample usually results in damage to the sample itself, especially with regard to most flavor agents in foods. The majority of the chemicals responsible for the flavor of food are esters, which decompose at high temperatures.

The triple point of water exists at a temperature of 0.01°C and a pressure of 0.006 atm. The critical temperature and pressure of water are 374.2°C and 218 atm, respectively. The triple point of carbon dioxide exists at a temperature of 216.8 Kelvin and a pressure of 5.11 atm. The critical temperature and pressure of carbon dioxide are 31.1°C and 72.8 atm, respectively. The sublimation point of carbon dioxide at 1 atm is 195 Kelvin.

1. A liquid that is surrounded by a gaseous medium, such as the atmosphere, will boil when:
   A. the density of the liquid is equal to the density of the surrounding gas.
   B. the heat capacity of the liquid is equal to the heat capacity of the surrounding gas.
   C. the vapor pressure of the liquid is equal to the pressure of the surrounding gas.
   D. the kinetic energy of the molecules of the liquid is equal to the kinetic energy of the molecules of the surrounding gas.

2. The strongest reason for the difference in triple points of carbon dioxide and water is:
   A. carbon dioxide has a higher molecular weight than water.
   B. carbon dioxide is a linear molecule, water is bent.
   C. carbon dioxide participates in hydrogen bonds with water molecules in the air, which cause it to sublimate.
   D. carbon dioxide cannot form hydrogen bonds with itself, unlike water.

3. A mixture of 0.5 moles of carbon dioxide vapor and 0.5 moles of water vapor are held in a 35-liter container at atmospheric pressure. The temperature of the container is:
   A. 426 Kelvin.
   B. 373 Kelvin.
   C. 293 Kelvin.
   D. 273 Kelvin.

4. If the same mixture is confined to a volume of 12 liters, at a temperature of 150 Kelvin, then:

   A. the water will liquefy and the carbon dioxide will remain a gas.
   B. the water will solidify and the carbon dioxide will liquefy.
   C. the water will solidify and the carbon dioxide will remain a gas.
   D. both will solidify.

5. A refrigerator freezer removes heat from the air inside the refrigerator. This heat is absorbed in the phase transition from liquid to gas of the refrigerant. A compressor is then employed to reconvert the gas to a liquid so that it may be recirculated. The boiling and freezing points of the refrigerant relate in what way to the boiling and freezing points of water?

   A. The boiling point of water is lower than the boiling point of the refrigerant.
   B. The freezing point of water is higher than the boiling point of the refrigerant.
   C. The boiling point of water is lower than the freezing point of the refrigerant.
   D. The freezing point of water is lower than the freezing point of the refrigerant.

6. Which of the following statements is true?

   A. Sublimation occurs when the critical pressure is greater than atmospheric pressure.
   B. Sublimation occurs when the triple point pressure is greater than atmospheric pressure.
   C. Deposition occurs when the critical pressure is lower than atmospheric pressure.
   D. Deposition occurs when the triple point pressure is lower than atmospheric pressure.

20.3 MASTERY VERIFIED: ANSWERS AND EXPLANATIONS

1. **C is correct.** When the vapor pressure of a liquid is equal in pressure to the pressure of the surrounding gas, the liquid will boil. When the density of a liquid is equal to the density of its own gas phase, it is at or above the critical point and cannot distinguish between the gas and liquid phases, so the term "boil" becomes meaningless. If the surrounding gas is a substance other than that which we wish to boil, we cannot directly compare the two substances' densities for any meaningful information about the boiling point of the liquid.

    Heat capacity is the ability of a substance, in a particular phase, to absorb heat. The heat capacity of a liquid can be equal to the heat capacity of the same substance, or another substance, in the gas phase. Again, comparing heat capacities tells us nothing about the boiling point of the liquid.

    If the kinetic energy of the molecules of the liquid were equal to the kinetic energy of the molecules of the surrounding gas, we could only conclude that the two phases are at the same temperature. We cannot say anything about whether or not the liquid will boil unless we know what the liquid and the temperature are.

2. **D is correct.** Choices A and B are true, but they do not offer an explanation of the difference in triple points of carbon dioxide and water. The strength of hydrogen bonds in water is responsible for the peculiarities of water, including its high freezing temperature and low triple point pressure.

3. **A is correct.** Employing the ideal gas law:

    $$T = \frac{PV}{nR} = \frac{(1 \text{ atm})(35 \text{ L})}{(1 \text{ mol})(0.082 \text{ L} \cdot \text{atm}/\text{mol} \cdot \text{K})} = \frac{35}{0.082} \text{K} = 426 \text{ K}$$

    Choice B is the boiling point of water under atmospheric conditions. Since we know that the water is in the gas phase at atmospheric pressure, we must have a temperature higher than 373 Kelvin.

4. **D is correct.** In order to solve this problem, we must first compute the pressure in the vessel:

    $$P = \frac{nRT}{V} = \frac{(1 \text{ mol})(0.082 \text{ L} \cdot \text{atm}/\text{mol} \cdot \text{K})(150 \text{ K})}{12 \text{ L}} = 1.02 \text{ atm}$$

    From this and the phase transition points of water and carbon dioxide, we can determine the phase of each. This eliminates choice A:

    $$H_2O: T_b = 373 \text{ K}$$
    $$T_f = 273 \text{ K}$$

    The temperature of the vessel is below the freezing point of water; therefore, water is a solid under these conditions:

    $$CO_2: T_s = 195 \text{ K}$$

    Since carbon dioxide sublimates at this temperature at 1 atm, freezing point is meaningless, and the liquid phase is not an option. This eliminates choice B.

    The temperature of the vessel is below the sublimation point of carbon dioxide; carbon dioxide must also exist in the solid phase. This eliminates choice C, leaving only choice D.

5. **B is correct.** For the freezer compartment of a refrigerator to work, it must cool the air in the freezer to a temperature below the freezing point of water.

    If the freezing point of water was lower than the freezing point of the refrigerant, we would freeze our refrigerant before we froze any water. This would be a problem, since we want the refrigerant to alternate between the liquid and gas phases, so that it can continue to circulate through our system. We must be concerned with only the boiling point of the refrigerant and the freezing point of water.

    If the freezing point of water were lower than the boiling point of the refrigerant, we might still have been able to cool the air in the refrigerator, but we would have been unable to make ice.

6. **B is correct.** Choice B is the definition of the conditions that are necessary for sublimation to occur. While this may lead one to believe that choice D is also true, having a triple point pressure that is lower than atmospheric pressure is not sufficient to cause deposition.

CHAPTER 21

ACID-BASE CHEMISTRY

21.1 MASTERY ACHIEVED

BASIC CONCEPTS AND DEFINITIONS

Ionization of Water, pH, and pOH

Under any conditions of hydrogen ion concentration (pH), water is subject to the ionizing equilibrium:

$$H_2O(l) \rightleftharpoons H^+(aq) + OH^-(aq)$$

This is called the autoionization of water. The equilibrium expression for the autoionization of water is:

$$K_w = [H^+][OH^-] = 1 \times 10^{-14}$$

From this expression and the equilibrium equation, we can see that, in the absence of outside influence, the concentration of hydrogen ions must be equal to the concentration of hydroxide ions. Therefore, $[H^+] = [OH^-] = 1 \times 10^{-7} M$. Although the ion product constant for water, K_w, was obtained for pure water, it is valid for any aqueous solutions at 25°C.

This is one of the most important relationships in all chemistry, since it establishes the inverse relationship between $[H^+]$ and $[OH^-]$ for all dilute (< 1 M) aqueous solutions.

To summarize:

- When $[H^+] = [OH^-]$, a solution is neutral.

- When $[H^+] > [OH^-]$, a solution is acidic.

- When $[H^+] < [OH^-]$, a solution is basic.

- $[H^+][OH^-] = 1 \times 10^{-14}$

The pH scale provides a convenient method of expressing the relative acidity (or basicity) of dilute aqueous solutions. The pH of a solution is defined as:

$$\boxed{pH = -\log[H^+]}$$

Likewise, the pOH of a solution is defined as:

$$\boxed{pOH = -\log[OH^-]}$$

Since we know that the autoionization constant of water is 10^{-14}, we can say:

$$K_w = [H^+][OH^-]$$

or:

$$-\log(K_w) = (-\log[H^+]) + (-\log[OH^-]) = -\log(1 \times 10^{-14})$$

or:

$$pH + pOH = 14$$

Therefore, once we have determined the pH (or pOH) of a solution, the pOH (or pH) is given as 14 − pH (or pOH). The pH of a solution with a pOH of 8.2 is 14 − 8.2 = 5.8.

Restating the basic definitions of neutrality, acidity, and basicity in terms of pH and pOH:

- When pH = 7 (pOH = 7), a solution is neutral.

- When pH < 7 (pOH > 7), a solution is acidic.

- When pH > 7 (pOH < 7), a solution is basic.

- pH + pOH = 14

To summarize, as pH increases, $[H^+]$ decreases, and as pOH increases, $[OH^-]$ decreases.

When attacking questions about the relationship between $[H^+]$ and pH, or $[OH^-]$ and pOH, it is important to remember the following: *logs are exponents!*

In order to determine, say, the pH of a system in which $[H^+] = 1 \times 10^{-2}$ we must look to the exponent. Since logs are exponents, $\log[10^{-2}] = -2$, and the −log of 10^{-2} is 2. If $[H^+] = 1 \times 10^{-10}$ then we know that pH = 10. The same is true for determining pOH from $[OH^-]$.

The scenario is slightly more complicated when the concentrations of $[H^+]$ and $[OH^-]$ have preexponential factors other than 1, but these situations can be handled by trying to put boundaries on the possible values of pH. If $[H^+] = 6.7 \times 10^{-8}$ we can no longer say that pH = 8. However, since 6.7×10^{-8} is *between* 10^{-8} and 10^{-7} we know that the pH must fall somewhere between 8 and 7. This should make intuitive sense. Since $(6.7 \times 10^{-8}) > 10^{-8}$ we know there is more H^+ in solution than at pH = 8, and hence a lower pH value. In the majority of cases on the MCAT, narrowing the answer down to between 2 integers, as we just did, will allow you to unequivocally choose the correct answer of the four choices.

In the unlikely case that there are two answer choices between the two integers you've used to bound your possible pH value, it is useful to keep in mind that $10^{0.5}$ (the square root of 10) is approximately 3.17. That means that 3.17×10^{-5} can be written as $(10^{0.5} \times 10^{-5}) = 10^{(-5 + 0.5)} = 10^{-4.5}$. The pH of a solution whose $[H^+]$ is (3.17×10^{-5}) is − (−5 + 0.5) or −(−4.5) = 4.5. Similarly, if a solution has $[H^+]$ of (3.17×10^{-6}), its pH = 5.5. If a solution has $[H^+]$ of (3.17×10^{-9}), pH = 8.5.

Recognizing the significance of 3.17 as the close equivalent of $10^{0.5}$, we conclude that for any $[H^+] = n \times 10^{-x}$.

If:	Then:
$n = 1$	$pH = x$
$n = 3.17$	$pH = x - \dfrac{1}{2}$
n is between 1 and 3.17 $(1 < n < 3.17)$	pH is less than x and greater than $x - \dfrac{1}{2}$. $(x - \dfrac{1}{2} < pH < x)$
n is between 3.17 and 10 $(3.17 < n < 10)$	pH is less than $x - \dfrac{1}{2}$ and greater than $x-1$. $(x - \dfrac{1}{2} > pH > x -1)$

Please solve this problem:

- A solution in which $[H^+] = 5.9 \times 10^{-4}$ is closest to which of the following pH values?

  A. 1.6
  B. 2.8
  C. 3.2
  D. 4.2

Problem solved:

C is correct. From examination of the exponent in the $[H^+]$ we know that the pH must be between 4 and 3. Since we only have one answer choice in this range, we know at this point the answer must be C.

Please solve this problem:

- Among the following, the pH of a solution with $[H^+]$ of 2.7×10^{-7} is closest to:

  A. 2.7.
  B. 6.2.
  C. 6.6.
  D. 7.6.

Problem solved:

C is correct. We know that the answer must be between 6 and 7, but unfortunately, in this case, we have 2 possible answers in this range. If $[H^+] = 2.7 \times 10^{-7}$ we see that the preexponential is less than 3.17. As such we know that the pH must be *above* 6.5. Think: If $[H^+] = 3.17 \times 10^{-7}$ means pH = 6.5, then a *smaller* H^+ concentration must mean a *higher* pH!

Definition of Acid and Base

BROAD CONCEPTUAL TERMS

In broad terms, acidity and basicity refer to the hydrogen ion concentration of an aqueous solution. An acid is a substance that when added to water *increases its hydrogen ion concentration* (decreases its pH). A base is a substance that when added to water *decreases its hydrogen ion concentration* (increases its pH). Because aqueous solutions maintain an equilibrium characterized by $K_w = [H^+] \times [OH^-] = 1 \times 10^{-14}$, it is also true that when added to water (a) an acid *decreases the hydroxide ion concentration* (increases pOH), and (b) a base *increases the hydroxide ion concentration* (decreases pOH).

Beyond the broad conceptual meaning of acid and base just described, there exist specialized definitions that might arise on the MCAT. They are (a) the Arrhenius definition, (b) the Bronsted-Lowry definition, and (c) the Lewis definition.

ARRHENIUS DEFINITION OF ACID AND BASE

An **Arrhenius acid** is a substance that, in aqueous solution, produces H^+ (and a corresponding anion), thereby increasing the solution's H^+ concentration (decreasing its pH). Due to the constant mathematical relationship between $[H^+]$ and $[OH^-]$ in aqueous solution ($[H^+] \times [OH^-] = 1 \times 10^{-14}$), the increased H^+ concentration also produces a decreased concentration of OH^-. An **Arrhenius base** is a substance that contains one or more hydroxyl groups that, in aqueous solution, produces OH^- (and some corresponding cation), thereby increasing the solution's OH^- concentration (decreasing its pOH). The increased OH^- concentration also produces a decreased H^+ concentration (increased pH) due, once again, to the constant mathematical relationship between $[H^+]$ and $[OH^-]$ in aqueous solution ($[H^+] \times [OH^-] = 1 \times 10^{-14}$).

In Arrhenius terms, the dissociation of hydrogen chloride gas in water is described thus:

$$HCl(g) \xrightarrow{H_2O} H^+(aq) + Cl^-(aq)$$

Hydrogen chloride is an Arrhenius acid because its dissociation in water increases the solution's H^+ concentration. At the same time, it decreases the solution's OH^- concentration because in aqueous solution, any increase in H^+ concentration also produces a decrease in OH^- concentration.

In Arrhenius terms, the dissociation of sodium hydroxide in water is described thus:

$$NaOH \xrightarrow{H_2O} Na^+(aq) + OH^-(aq)$$

Sodium hydroxide is an Arrhenius base because its dissociation in water increases the solution's OH^- concentration, and consequently it decreases the solution's H^+ concentration.

Bronsted-Lowry Definitions of Acid and Base

According to the **Bronsted-Lowry** definitions, an acid is a **proton donor** and a base is a **proton acceptor**. The Bronsted-Lowry conception of acid and base reflects the hydronium ion, H_3O^+, produced when a hydrogen ion interacts with a water molecule:

$$H^+ + H_2O = H_3O^+$$

Let us now consider again the dissolution of hydrogen chloride gas in water, this time as a Bronsted-Lowry phenomenon:

$$HCl(g) + H_2O(l) \rightarrow H_3O^+ (aq) + Cl^- (aq)$$

In Bronsted-Lowry terms, the HCl molecule is an acid because it *donates a proton to* the H_2O molecule. The H_2O molecule is a base because it *accepts a proton from* the HCl molecule.

Consider in Bronsted-Lowry terms the reaction between ammonia (NH_3) and water:

$$NH_3 (aq) + H_2O(l) \rightarrow NH_4^+(aq) + OH^- (aq)$$

In Bronsted-Lowry terms, the NH_3 molecule is a base because it accepts a proton from the H_2O molecule. The H_2O molecule is an acid because it *donates a proton to* the NH_3 molecule. Note that in Arrhenius terms, water is neither an acid nor a base. In Bronsted-Lowry terms, it might be either an acid *or* a base.

Conjugate Acid-Base Pairs

The Bronsted-Lowry conception of acids and bases also creates the notion of **conjugate acid-base pairs**. The Bronsted-Lowry conception first recognizes that (in theory) the two processes described above are reversible:

$$HCl(g) + H_2O(l) \rightleftharpoons H_3O^+ (aq) + Cl^- (aq)$$
$$NH_3 (aq) + H_2O(l) \rightleftharpoons NH_4^+(aq) + OH^- (aq)$$

This means that the possessing of the donated proton (H_3O^+ in the first case, and NH_4^+ in the second) is also capable of "giving it back." In the process that reverses the dissociation of HCl, H_3O^+ donates a proton "back" to Cl^-, and Cl^- accepts it:

$$H_3O^+ (aq) + Cl^- (aq) \rightarrow HCl(g) + H_2O(aq)$$

In this reverse process, therefore, H_3O^+ is a Bronsted-Lowry acid and Cl^- is a Bronsted-Lowry base.

Consider, similarly, the process that reverses the reaction of NH_3 with H_2O:

$$NH_4^+ (aq) + OH^- (aq) \rightarrow NH_3 (aq) + H_2O(l)$$

NH_4^+ serves as a Bronsted-Lowry acid (donating a proton to the OH^- ion) and the OH^- ion serves as a Bronsted-Lowry base, accepting a proton from the NH_4^+ ion.

Mindful of the dynamic just described, we say that in the dissociation of HCl in water:

(a)   HCl is an acid, with Cl^- as its conjugate base.

(b) H_2O is a base, and H_3O^+ is its conjugate acid.

Similarly, in the reaction between NH_3 and H_2O, we say that:

(a) NH_3 is a base, with NH_4^+ as its conjugate acid.

(b) H_2O is an acid, with OH^- as its conjugate base.

An acid and its conjugate base differ by the presence or absence of a proton. A conjugate base is the species that remains after the associated acid has donated its proton. Consequently, the relationship between an acid and its conjugate base is described, generically, with this equation:

$$HA + H_2O \rightarrow A^- + H_3O^+$$

$$\underset{\text{acid}}{} \qquad \underset{\text{conjugate base}}{}$$

Consider the reaction between nitrous acid (HNO_2) and water:

$$HNO_2 + H_2O \rightleftharpoons NO_2^- + H_3O^+$$

$$\underset{\text{acid}}{} \qquad \underset{\text{conjugate base}}{}$$

HNO_2 represents HA, the acid, and NO_2^- represents A^-, its conjugate base. Water, in this case, is accepting the donated proton, and therefore is a base. H_3O^+ is its conjugate acid.

Reciprocally, a base and its conjugate acid also differ by the presence or absence of a proton. A conjugate acid is the species that remains after the associated base has accepted a proton. Consequently, the relationship between a base and its conjugate acid is generically described with this equation:

$$B + H_2O \rightarrow HB^+ + OH^-$$

$$\underset{\text{base}}{} \qquad \underset{\text{conjugate acid}}{}$$

Consider the reaction between the base pyridine (C_5H_5N) and water:

$$C_5H_5N + H_2O \rightleftharpoons C_5H_5NH^+ + OH^-$$

$$\underset{\text{base}}{} \qquad \underset{\text{conjugate acid}}{}$$

C_5H_5N represents the base, B, and $C_5H_5NH^+$ represents HB^+, its conjugate acid. Water, in this case, is donating the proton, and is therefore the acid. OH^- is its conjugate base.

Please solve this problem:

- In the dissociation of perchloric acid ($HClO_4$) in water, which of the following is the conjugate base?

   A. OH^-
   B. ClO_4^-
   C. H^+
   D. H_3O^+

Problem solved:

B is correct. For any Bronsted-Lowry acid (HA), find the conjugate base by stripping one proton from the acid to yield A^-. Stripped of one proton, $HClO_4$ produces the conjugate base ClO_4^-:

$$HClO_4 + H_2O \rightleftharpoons ClO_4^- + H_3O^+$$

$$\underbrace{}_{\text{acid}} \qquad \underbrace{}_{\text{conjugate base}}$$

Lewis Definition of Acid and Base

A substance can "accept" a proton (and thus constitutes a Bronsted-Lowry base) only if it carries an unshared pair of electrons; the unshared pair binds the proton. In order for a species to donate a proton, it must accept the electron pair donated by the base. The **Lewis definitions** of acid and base describe an acid as an "electron pair acceptor" and a base as an electron pair donor.

The Lewis conception of acid and base is broader than the Bronsted-Lowry definition. Any substance that qualifies as an acid or a base in the Bronsted-Lowry sense qualifies also in the Lewis sense. Yet, there are some substances that qualify as Lewis acids and bases that do not qualify as Bronsted-Lowry acids and bases.

Amines and phosphines, with their lone pairs, are frequently used on the MCAT as prototypical Lewis bases. Trivalent boron or aluminum compounds are frequently used as Lewis acids because of their vacant p-orbital. A typical purely Lewis acid/base reaction is shown below. The amine donates an electron pair to an electron deficient borane.

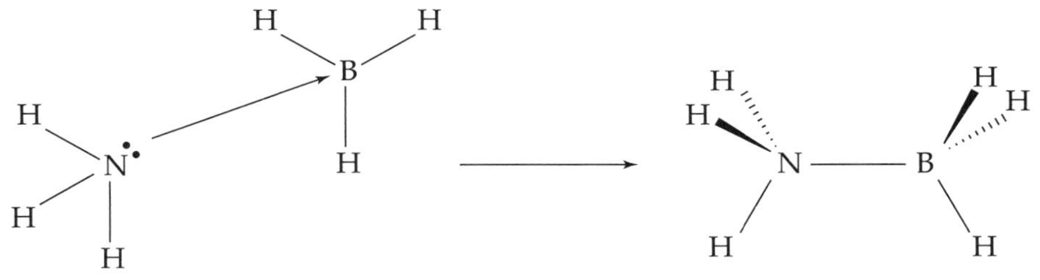

Lewis bases are sometimes referred to as "ligands" when used in conjunction with transition metals, as they donate electron pairs to form bonds.

Acids and Bases: Strong and Weak

THE GENERAL MEANING OF "STRONG" AND "WEAK"

Acids and bases may be categorized as strong or weak. A **strong acid** is one that *fully* tends to undergo its forward dissociation in aqueous solution so that it dramatically increases H^+ concentration (and dramatically decreases OH^- concentration). Put otherwise, a strong acid is one for which the dissociation equilibrium lies entirely to the right:

$$\underset{\text{acid}}{HA} + H_2O \rightarrow \underset{\text{conjugate base}}{A^-} + H_3O^+$$

The reverse reaction does not occur to any appreciable degree, and the resulting solution contains no appreciable amount of the original acid.

Strong acids likely to arise on the MCAT are *hydrochloric acid* (HCl), *hydrobromic acid* (HBr), *hydroiodic acid* (HI), *nitric acid* (HNO_3), *perchloric acid* ($HClO_4$), and *sulfuric acid* (H_2SO_4). Similarly, **strong bases** are those for which the dissociation reaction lies entirely to the right so that OH^- concentration dramatically increases (and H^+ concentration dramatically decreases).

$$\underset{\text{base}}{B} + H_2O \rightarrow \underset{\text{conjugate acid}}{HB^+} + OH^-$$

The reverse reaction does not occur to any appreciable degree, and the resulting solution contains no significant quantity of the original base. Rather, the base is completely converted to OH^- and its conjugate acid. Strong bases likely to arise on the MCAT are *lithium hydroxide* (LiOH), *sodium hydroxide* (NaOH), *potassium hydroxide* (KOH), *rubidium hydroxide* (RbOH), *amide ion* (NH_2^-), and *hydride ion* (H^-).

Please solve this problem:

- 12.8 g of HI is dissolved in 1 L of water. What is the resulting pH?

    A. 0.5
    B. 1
    C. 2.3
    D. -1

Problem solved:

B is correct. HI is a strong acid, and as such we expect total dissociation into H^+ and I^-. In order to find the concentration of H^+ we must calculate how much HI was added to the water in moles. The molecular weight of HI is 128 g/mol (I = 127, H = 1), which means that 12.8 g is 0.1 mol HI, all of which dissociates, giving the same amount of H^+. Since we have 1 L of solution, $[H^+] = .1 = 1 \times 10^{-1}$ mol/L. Finally, $-\log[10^{-1}] = 1$.

Weak acids and **weak bases** *dissociate partially* izJAn aqueous solution; the process is truly reversible and comes to an equilibrium in which the resulting solution contains in appreciable quantities both (a) the original acid or base and (b) its conjugate.

The relative strengths of weak acids and weak bases can vary widely. Some weak acids dissociate appreciably, while others dissociate barely at all.

A useful relation regarding the strengths of acids and bases is seen in comparing their conjugates. The two equations below are acid dissociation equilibria.

$$HBr + H_2O \rightleftharpoons Br^- + H_3O^+$$

$$HF + H_2O \rightleftharpoons F^- + H_3O^+$$

It should be recognized that HBr is on the list of strong acids, and as such the reaction in the forward reaction is complete, and the reverse reaction essentially nonexistent. HF, on the other hand, is a weak acid. This means that the dissociation isn't complete, and one direction (forward or reverse) doesn't *completely* dominate the other. As HF attempts to lose H^+, its conjugate, the weak base F^-, "pushes back" or attempts to become protonated, and doesn't allow for the complete dissociation of HF in solution.

This tells us something very useful. A strong acid, such as those found on the strong acid list, have conjugate bases with negligible basicity. They don't push back. Their conjugates are stable as anions in solution, and show no tendency to accept protons. The same is true for strong bases; their conjugates show only negligible acidity.

Weak acids are weak because their conjugates have real basicity. They seek to accept protons to some degree, and hence do not allow for complete dissociation of the acid. Within the set of weak acids, a stronger acid will spend more time dissociated, owing to the relatively weak basic properties of its conjugate. A weaker acid, on the other hand, will spend more time protonated, owing to the more basic properties of its conjugate.

This allows us to make the following important generalizations, which will be quantified in the next section.

• The stronger an acid or base is, the weaker its conjugate will be.

• The weaker an acid or base is, the stronger its conjugate will be.

Since a relatively non-basic conjugate is the sign of a strong acid, we explain how electron withdrawing groups on acids tend to make them more acidic. For example, which of the following is a stronger acid: acetic acid or trifluoroacetic acid?

acetic acid   trifluoroacetic acid

The inclusion of the electron withdrawing fluorine atoms on trifluoroacetic acid means that its conjugate base, CF_3COO^-, will be stabilized relative to acetate (CH_3COO^-) because fluorine serves to pull excess negative charge into the molecule and spread it out. A stable base is not looking to be protonated as much as a less stable one, and is therefore less basic. A less basic conjugate means a stronger acid (TFA wins!).

ACID-BASE EQUILIBRIA AND EQUILIBRIUM CONSTANTS

For the ionization of an acid in water, the equilibrium is generally described thus:

$$HA + H_2O \rightleftharpoons H_3O^+ + A^-$$

Recalling that pure liquids (such as water) do not appear in the equilibrium expression, the equilibrium constant may be rewritten as an **acid ionization constant**, K_a, expression:

$$K_a = \frac{[H_3O^+][A^-]}{[HA]}$$

Likewise, for the ionization of a base in water, the equilibrium is:

$$B + H_2O \rightarrow HB^+ + OH^-$$

Once again, since water does not appear in the equilibrium expression, the equilibrium constant may be rewritten as a **base ionization constant**, K_b, expression:

$$K_b = \frac{[HB^+][OH^-]}{[B]}$$

As the strength of an acid increases, the concentration of the acid, [HA], becomes negligible, and the acid ionization constant, K_a, approaches infinity. Similarly, as the strength of a base increases, the concentration of unionized base, [B], becomes negligible, and the base ionization constant, K_b, approaches infinity. In other words:

- Large values of K_a or K_b imply strong acids or bases.

- Small values of K_a or K_b imply weak acids or bases.

Rather than reporting acid or base strengths in exponents, strengths are generally given as pK_a or pK_b. As the similarity in nomenclature to pH might suggest, these values are simply $-\log K_a$ and $-\log K_b$ respectively. As is the case with [H$^+$] and pH, pK_a and pK_b have an inverse relationship with K_a and K_b. The following relations can then be summarized:

- Strong acids and bases have small values of pK_a and pK_b.

- Weak acids and bases have large values of pK_a and pK_b.

For *any* conjugate acid/base pair in a dilute aqueous solution:

$$K_a K_b = K_w$$

and:

$$pK_a + pK_b = 14$$

for any conjugate acid/base pair in a dilute aqueous solution.

This mathematically confirms the previous discussion on the relative strengths of acids or bases and their conjugates. An acid with a large pK_a (weak) will have a conjugate base with a small pK_b (strong) since their sum must be 14.

Please solve this problem:

- CN⁻ is a frequently used nucleophile in organic syntheses. Its K_b was measured to be 2.1×10^{-5}. What is the pK_a of hydrogen cyanide (HCN)?

   A. 9.2
   B. 8.3
   C. 4.7
   D. 6.3

Problem solved:

A is correct. First, we must realize that CN⁻ is conjugate to HCN. So, 14 minus the pK_b of CN⁻ will give us the pK_a of HCN. If $K_b = 2.1 \times 10^{-5}$ then pK_b must be between 4 and 5 (recall how we determined pH from [H⁺]). As such, the pK_a of HCN must be between 9 and 10. Choice A is the only possible answer.

Knowledge of an acid's K_a or base's K_b will allow us to calculate the pH of a solution in which they're dissolved.

Please solve this problem:

- What is the pH of a 0.10 M aqueous solution of HCN ($pK_a = 9.22$)?

   A. 3.16
   B. 5.11
   C. 7.16
   D. 9.16

Problem solved:

B is correct. To solve this problem, we must consider the equilibrium:

$$HCN \rightleftharpoons H^+ + CN^-$$

using the pK_a given for HCN. Since we start with 0.10 M HCN, and we dissociate some amount, which we will call x, into H⁺ and CN⁻, we can write the following relation:

$$K_a = \frac{[H^+][CN^-]}{[HCN]} = \frac{[x][x]}{[0.10 - x]} = 10^{-pk_a} = 10^{-9.22}$$

Given the small value of K_a, it is safe to consider x as negligible compared to 0.10, so the acid ionization constant expression simplifies to:

$$K_a = 10^{-9.22} = \frac{x^2}{0.10}$$

or:

$$x^2 = 10^{-10.22}$$

from which:

$$x = [H^+] = 10^{-5.11}$$

Therefore,

$$pH = -\log [H^+] = -\log [10^{-5.11}] = 5.11$$

HENDERSON-HASSELBALCH EQUATION

By taking the log of both sides of the equation for pK_a (below) and rearranging the terms, one can come to a very useful relation. The second equation is known as the Henderson-Hasselbalch (HH) equation:

$$K_a = \frac{[H^+][A^-]}{[HA]}$$

$$pH = pK_a + \log\frac{[A^-]}{[HA]}$$

Or, similarly, for basic systems:

$$pOH = pK_b + \log\frac{[BH^+]}{[B]}$$

The HH equation is useful in that it allows us to gauge ratios of acid and conjugate base of a system depending on what the pH is. It will be *very* useful in the coming sections on titrations, buffers, and indicators.

TITRATION

A Mixture of an Acid and a Base

When a strong acid and a base or a strong base and an acid are placed in the same container, a neutralization reaction occurs:

$$HA + BOH \rightarrow H_2O + B^+ + A^-$$

This reaction will continue to produce water and salt until either the acid (HA) or the base (BOH) is consumed. When there is an excess of acid in solution, the base will be entirely consumed in the neutralization reaction, and the solution will be acidic. When there is an excess of base in solution, the acid will be entirely consumed, and the solution will be basic. When the quantity of acid is equal to the quantity of base, the solution is completely neutralized and has a pH of 7. Neutralization reactions are always exothermic.

Please solve this problem:

- What is the pH of a 100 milliliter aqueous solution prepared with 0.10 moles HCl and 0.07 moles NaOH?

    A. 0.52
    B. 4.52
    C. 8.52
    D. 12.52

Problem solved:

A is correct. To solve this problem, we must recognize that we have an excess of 0.03 moles of the strong acid HCl. Choices C and D can be immediately eliminated, since an excess of acid would not result in a basic pH. Therefore, the hydrogen ion concentration is given by:

$$[H^+] = 0.03 \text{ mol} \div 0.100 \text{ L} = 0.3 \ M$$

Therefore,

$$pH = -\log [H^+] = -\log [0.3] = -\log [3 \times 10^{-1}]$$

$$0 < pH < 1$$

Acid-Base Titrations

In the section on the previous page, we only considered a mixture of a fixed amount of acid with a fixed amount of base. A **titration** is the gradual addition of a base to an acid or the gradual addition of an acid to a base. (Base to acid is the usual manner in which MCAT questions are phrased.)

As base is added to acid, the pH of the solution rises until all the acid has been consumed and excess base is present. A typical acid-base titration curve is shown in Figure 21.1.

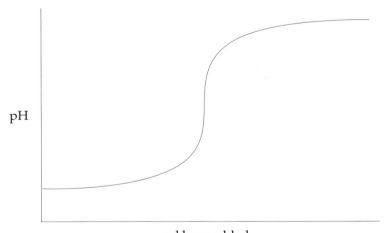

ml base added

Figure 21.1

Equivalence Point: Titration of a Strong Acid

In a titration, the point at which the acid has been neutralized by base is referred to as the **equivalence point**. This point is indicated on Figure 21.2.

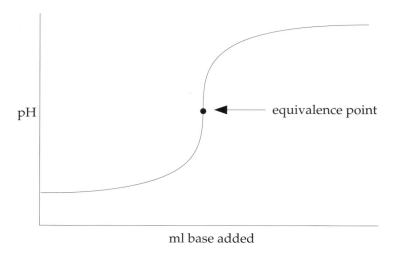

Figure 21.2

The equivalence point of a titration curve is the point at which exactly one equivalent of base has been added for one equivalent of acid. At any point in a titration curve prior to the equivalence point, the pH may be calculated from the concentration of acid. At any point after the equivalence point, the pH is determined by the excess base present.

In the case of a titration of a strong acid with a strong base, or vice versa, it is important to note that the **pH at the equivalence point is 7**. Remember, the conjugates of strong acids and bases have no basic or acidic properties, respectively. They are essentially spectator ions, e.g., Cl^- from HCl, or Na^+ from NaOH. When all of the H^+ and OH^- has been neutralized to H_2O and all that remain are the spectator conjugates, there is nothing affecting the pH and it will be neutral (7).

Please solve this problem:

- A 500 mL solution of 1M HCl is titrated with a concentrated 10 M solution of NaOH. Roughly, what will be the total volume at the equivalence point?

    A. 50 mL
    B. 510 mL
    C. 550 mL
    D. 1 L

Problem solved:

C is correct. Choice A can be eliminated immediately, as there are more than 50 mL present before the start of the titration. After this we need to determine how many moles of H^+ are in the HCl solution, and how many mL of the 10 M NaOH solution will be needed to give us this number of moles. The HCl solution has a concentration of 1 mol/L. Since there is half a liter, we knew there is half a mol (0.5 mol). The NaOH solution is much more concentrated. There are 10 mol NaOH in each L, which puts 1 mol in each 100 mL. This means that there are 0.5 mol in each 50 mL. Therefore, this 50 mL, in addition to the 500 original mL, leaves us with roughly 550 mL.

Titration of a Weak Acid

The titration of a weak acid with a strong base is different from the case where both the solution and titrant are strong. For one, since the acid we're titrating is weak, the initial pH will be larger relative to titrations of strong acids.

The more important difference, though, is the pH at which the equivalence point of the titration is reached. Remember, the pH at the equivalence point of a strong acid/strong base titration is always 7. When the solution being titrated isn't strong, this is no longer the case. Below is an example of a titration curve of a weak acid (acetic acid, CH_3COOH) being titrated with a strong base (NaOH).

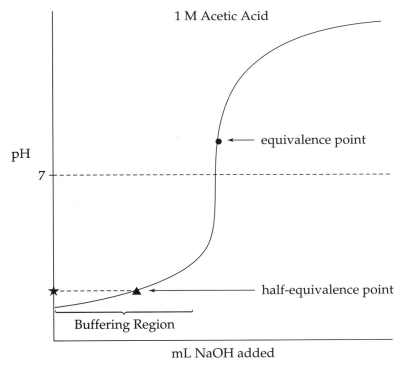

Figure 21.3

As should be noted, the equivalence point here isn't 7, in fact, it's *above* 7. Why is this the case? To answer this question we need to remember what the equivalence point is, and more importantly, the differences between strong and weak acids.

The equivalence point is where 1 equivalent of base has been added, or where all the acetic acid has been neutralized in the following reaction.

$$NaOH + CH_3COOH \rightarrow H_2O + Na^+ + CH_3COO^-$$

Left in solution, then, will be sodium ions and acetate ions. Sodium ions are spectator ions, but acetate ions are the conjugate base of a weak acid. This means that they have basic properties, and in solution will cause the pH to go above 7.

What does this mean for a titration of a weak base with a strong acid? Once all the weak base is neutralized, at the equivalence point, the remaining species in solution will be the conjugate of the strong acid (a spectator), and the conjugate of the weak base (with acidic properties). The pH at this equivalence point will be below 7, thanks to the conjugate of the initial weak base.

In summary:

- The equivalence point of a strong acid with a strong base will be pH = 7.

- The equivalence point of a weak acid titrated with a strong base will be pH > 7.

- The equivalence point of a weak base titrated with a strong acid will be pH < 7.

Also marked on the titration curve above is the half-equivalence point. As the name suggests, this is a point on the curve where the amount of base added is *exactly half* of the base needed to reach the equivalence point. This is important because if all of the weak acid has been neutralized at the equivalence point, exactly half of the acid will be neutralized at the half-equivalence point. This means $[A^-] = [HA]$.

Now, look back at the HH equation. Since $[A^-] = [HA]$ at the half equivalence point, we can say that $pH = pK_a$, since log 1 = 0.

- The pH at the half-equivalence point in a weak acid/strong base titration gives the pK_a of the weak acid.

This is a way to determine the pK_a of a weak acid or base system through titration. The equivalence point tells the initial concentration of the acid. The half-equivalence point gives its pK_a.

The last region of note on the titration curve above is the area labeled "buffering region." This is called such because in this region the pH changes only gradually with the addition of base. This is the case because the concentration of base, at this point, is low compared to the concentration of acid, and allows the acid to "buffer" the solution. This will be discussed more fully in the upcoming discussion of buffers. What is important to note now is that the *half-equivalence point is always within the buffering region*. If you have found the pH of one, you have the general pH of the other.

For comparison, below is the titration curve of a weak base (NH_3) being titrated with a strong acid (HCl).

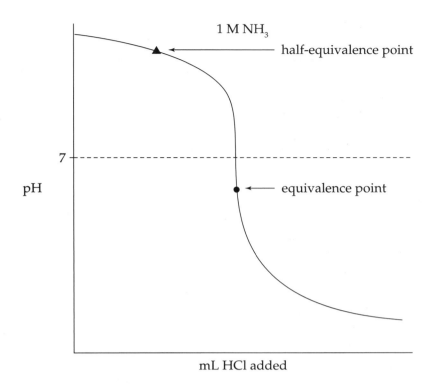

Figure 21.4

As expected, the equivalence point is below pH = 7. The meaning of the half-equivalence point, though, is a little different. We *cannot* say that the pH at the half-equivalence point is the pK_b of NH_3. Remember the HH equation for bases uses pOH, not pH. However, it is true in this case that at the half-equivalence point $[NH_3] = [NH_4^+]$. Using this relationship in the acid HH equation, we see that the pH at the half-equivalence point is the pK_a of NH_4^+, which allows us to find the pK_b of its conjugate (NH_3) because $14 - pK_a = pK_b$.

Please solve this problem:

- The half-equivalence point in titration of 750 mL unknown, monoprotic acid with 1 M KOH is found to fall at pH = 3.2. If there is 1 L of total solution at the equivalence point, what is the pH at this point?

  A. 6.2
  B. 7
  C. 8.3
  D. 11.2

Problem solved:

C is correct. Both A and B can be eliminated immediately since the titration of a weak acid with a strong base will give an equivalence point with pH > 7. From there, the fact that the half-equivalence point falls at pH = 3.2 tells us that the pK_a of the unknown acid is 3.2. This means that the pK_b of its conjugate is 10.8. We can find the concentration of the weak acid by taking note that 250 mL of base (1 M) was added to reach the equivalence point, meaning there must have been 0.25 moles of acid. So the concentration of the conjugate base of the initial acid is 0.25 M. Since this is conjugate base, we must use the following equation for K_b:

$$K_b = \frac{[BH][OH^-]}{[B^-]}$$

$$10^{-10.8} = \frac{[x][x]}{[0.25-x]}$$

Neglecting x in the denominator we find that $x^2 = 0.25 \times 10^{-10.8} = 2.5 \times 10^{-11.8}$. Since the square root of 2.5 is just over 1 we can simply and say $x \sim 10^{-5.9}$. As such pOH $\sim$ 5.9 and pH $\sim$ 8.1, so C is the closest answer.

Indicators and the End Point

It is often convenient to use a chemical that changes color when the equivalence point of a titration is reached. Such a chemical is called an **indicator**. The point at which the titration is stopped (because the indicator has changed color) is called the **end point**.

Generally speaking, an indicator changes color because of color differences between its protonated and deprotonated form. Phenolphthalein is a weakly acidic molecule, often used as an indicator because its protonated, neutral form is colorless, while its deprotonated, anionic form is pink. The equilibrium is shown below with the protonated form on the left and deprotonated on the right.

$$Phn(H) + B^- \rightleftharpoons Phn^- + BH$$
$$\text{clear} \qquad\qquad \text{pink}$$

According to the HH equation, if the pH of the solution equals the pK_a of phenolphthalein, then [Phn(H)] = [Phn⁻]. If the solution is more basic than this, pH > pK_a, then the deprotonated form of phenolphthalein will prevail and the solution will be pink. If pH < pK_a then, with the excess H⁺ in solution, the protonated form of phenolphthalein will dominate and the solution will be colorless. Other indicators work identically around their respective pK_as: **If pH < pK_a, then the acid (protonated) form dominates; if pH > pK_a, the base (deprotonated) form dominates.**

Since color change occurs in pHs around the pK_a of the indicator, it is optimal to match the pK_a of the indicator to the pH of interest. In the case of monitoring the equivalence point of a titration, matching the indicator's pK_a to the equivalence point will provide proof that an equivalence point has been reached. In titration, it's optimal if the pK_a of the indicator falls in the same numerical range as the pH levels seen in the gray box (Figure 21.5).

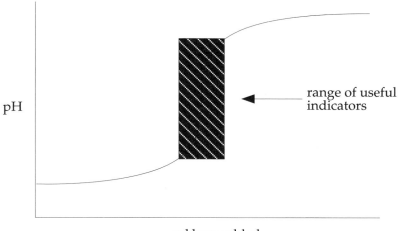

Figure 21.5

Polyprotic Acids

A **polyprotic acid** is an acid that contains more than one acidic proton. Sulfuric acid (H_2SO_4) is an example of a **diprotic acid**. Phosphoric acid (H_3PO_4) is an example of a **triprotic acid**. When dealing with polyprotic acids, it is important to remember that each proton will have a different K_a, and, therefore, each proton will be titrated separately. An example of a titration curve for a triprotic acid is shown in Figure 21.6.

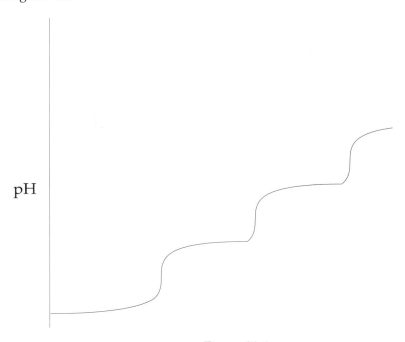

Figure 21.6

Note that since there are three acidic protons to be titrated, there are three equivalence points in the titration curve. The first equivalence point corresponds to the equilibrium:

$$H_3A \rightleftharpoons H^+ + H_2A^-$$

the acid ionization constant expression for which is:

$$K_{a1} = \frac{[H^+][H_2A^-]}{[H_3A]}$$

The second equivalence point corresponds to the equilibrium:

$$H_2A^- \rightleftharpoons H^+ + HA^{2-}$$

the acid ionization constant expression for which is:

$$K_{a2} = \frac{[H^+][HA^{2-}]}{[H_2A^-]}$$

And the third equivalence point corresponds to the equilibrium:

$$HA^{2-} \rightleftharpoons H^+ + A^{3-}$$

the acid ionization constant expression for which is:

$$K_{a3} = \frac{[H^+][A^{3-}]}{[HA^{2-}]}$$

Please solve this problem:

- The two pK_as of sulfurous acid (H_2SO_3) are 1.81 and 6.91, respectively. The predominant species at pH = 9 is:

    A. H_2SO_3.
    B. HSO_3^-.
    C. SO_3^{2-}.
    D. H^+.

Problem solved:

C is correct. At a pH of 9, the hydrogen ion concentration is 1×10^{-9}. It is not likely that a concentration of this magnitude is indicative of a *predominant* species, so choice D is eliminated. At a pH of 1.81, the titration of the first acidic proton is halfway complete, and at a pH of 9, there is not likely to be a measurable quantity of H_2SO_3 left. Therefore, choice A is eliminated. At a pH of 6.91, the titration of the second acidic proton is halfway complete; at this point, $[HSO_3^-] = [SO_3^{2-}]$. Therefore, for any pH greater than 6.91, $[SO_3^{2-}] > [HSO_3^-]$, eliminate choice B, which leaves only choice C.

BUFFERS

A **buffer** is composed of a weak acid and its conjugate base salt, or a weak base and its conjugate acid salt. A buffer is designed to resist a change in pH when an external acid or base is added to the solution. The acid component of a buffer system neutralizes added base, while the base component of a buffer system neutralizes added acid.

Buffers are generally made by mixing equal parts of a weak acid (or base) and its conjugate. For example, an acetic acid/acetate buffer would likely be comprised of equal moles acetic acid and sodium acetate. Since the acid [HA] and the conjugate base [A⁻] are equimolar in solution, we know from HH that the pH of the solution will be the pK_a of acetic acid (4.75). The acetic acid equilibrium, shown below, is what maintains this general pH:

$$CH_3COOH + H_2O \rightleftharpoons CH_3COO^- + H_3O^+$$

As long as the two sides, acid and acetate, are roughly equal in concentration, the pH will remain 4.75. However, if a small amount of a strong acid is added, it will protonate the acetate, causing a slight imbalance in the ratio. Say, for example, if we had a 1 L of a 1 M acetate buffer solution (1 mol CH_3COOH/ 1 mol CH_3COO^-), and we added 0.01 moles HCl, what would be the resultant pH?

To solve this question we must think of what happens when 0.01 moles of HCl are added. HCl, a strong acid, is going to protonate any base in its vicinity. The most basic species available is acetate, so 0.01 moles of acetate ion will be protonated into 0.01 moles of acetic acid. Our new HH equation looks like this:

$$pH = 4.75 + \log \frac{0.99}{1.01}$$

So, as expected with the addition of a strong acid, the pH decreases, *but not by much*. If 0.01 moles of HCl were added to 1 L of neutral water, in the absence of a buffer we'd expect the pH to drop to 2 (since $0.01 = 10^{-2}$ and $-\log 10^{-2} = 2$); however, in the presence of a buffer the change is only a fraction of this.

This effect only works when the amount of new acid or base added is small in comparison to the concentration of the buffer. Addition of large amounts of acid or base would change the HH equation above substantially. Also, a buffer will be more able to resist changes in pH in either direction near its pK_a. So, when choosing a buffer (or answering MCAT questions about choosing a buffer):

• The more concentrated the buffer, the more effective it will be.

• The pK_a of the buffer should be chosen to match the pH that is to be buffered.

The flat, initial portion of a titration curve is called the "buffering region" because the phenomena described here is exactly what's happening. In the buffering region the amount of titrant is small in comparison to the initial solution being titrated. Here, the addition of the strong acid or base causes relatively little change in the overall pH, and, as mentioned, the half-equivalence point (where pH = pK_a, the most effective region for a buffer), is in the middle of it.

Please solve this problem:

- All of the following acid-base pairs are examples of buffers EXCEPT:

  A. HF/NaF.
  B. H_2CO_3/NaHCO$_3$.
  C. CH_3CO_2H/NaCH$_3CO_2$.
  D. HCl/NaCl.

Problem solved:

D is correct. A buffer system is a mixture of a weak acid and its conjugate base salt, or a weak base and its conjugate acid salt. All of the choices give examples of weak acids and their conjugate base salts *except* choice D. HCl is a strong acid. Given the instability of excess charge on the spatially small F$^-$ ion and the capacity of fluorine to engage in hydrogen bonds, HF is *not* a strong acid. Compare the hydrohalogen acids:

HF: $pK_a = 3.14$

HCl: $pK_a = -6$

HBr: $pK_a = -9$

HI: $pK_a = -9.5$

21.2 MASTERY APPLIED: PRACTICE PASSAGE AND QUESTIONS

Passage

The suitability of a buffer made of components of a polyprotic system can be estimated from a distribution curve, which shows the variation in the percentage of each species with pH.

For the general triprotic system, the equilibria are:

$$H_3A \rightleftharpoons H^+ + H_2A^-$$

$$H_2A^- \rightleftharpoons H^+ + HA^{2-}$$

$$HA^{2-} \rightleftharpoons H^+ + A^{3-}$$

The ionization constant expressions are:

$$K_{a1} = \frac{[H^+][H_2A^-]}{[H_3A]} \text{ and}$$

$$K_{b1} = \frac{[H_3A][OH^-]}{[H_2A^-]}$$

$$K_{a2} = \frac{[H^+][HA^{2-}]}{[H_2A^-]} \text{ and}$$

$$K_{b2} = \frac{[H_2A^-][OH^-]}{[HA^{2-}]}$$

$$K_{a3} = \frac{[H^+][A^{3-}]}{[HA^{2-}]} \text{ and } K_{b3} = \frac{[HA^{2-}][OH^-]}{[A^{3-}]}$$

And the distribution curve is:

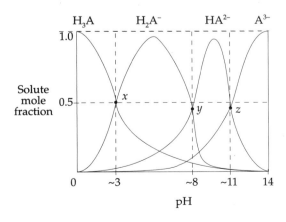

1. A buffer pair for a pH of 11 is:
   A. H_3A/H_2A^-.
   B. H_3A/HA^{2-}.
   C. H_2A^-/HA^{2-}.
   D. HA^{2-}/A^{3-}.

2. The K_b of H_2A^- is approximately:
   A. 1×10^{-4}.
   B. 1×10^{-6}.
   C. 1×10^{-11}.
   D. 1×10^{-13}.

3. Point x represents:
   A. the pH of the end point of the titration of H_3A with base.
   B. halfway to the equivalence point of the titration of H_3A with base.
   C. the pH of the equivalence point of the titration of H_3A with base.
   D. the pH of the equivalence point of the titration of H_2A^- with acid.

4. To monitor the titration of H_2A^- with a strong base, the best indicator to use is one that changes color in the range:
   A. 6.8 to 7.8.
   B. 7.8 to 8.8.
   C. 8.8 to 9.8.
   D. 10.8 to 11.8.

5. What is the predominant species when the hydrogen ion concentration is 3.17×10^{-12} ?
   A. H_3A
   B. H_2A^-
   C. HA^{2-}
   D. A^{3-}

6. Benzoic acid has a pKa of 4.19. Ranked in order of acidity:

   A. benzoic acid > H_3A > H_2A^- > HA^{2-} > A^{3-}.

   B. H_3A > benzoic acid > H_2A^- > HA^{2-} > A^{3-}.

   C. H_3A > H_2A^- > benzoic acid > HA^{2-} > A^{3-}.

   D. H_3A > H_2A^- > HA^{2-} > benzoic acid > A^{3-}.

7. When 1,000 milliliters of 0.1 M H_2A^- is mixed with 500 milliliters of 0.1 M H_3A. The resulting pH is:

   A. 9.65.

   B. 7.65.

   C. 5.65.

   D. 3.3.

   _____

21.3 MASTERY VERIFIED: ANSWERS AND EXPLANATIONS

1. **D is correct.** The answer is taken directly from the distribution curve. At pH = 11, the two predominant species are HA^{2-} and A^{3-}.

2. **C is correct.** The pK_a of H_2A (the conjugate acid of H_2A^-)is approximately 3 (from the graph). Using the relationship $pK_w = pK_a + pK_b$, where $pK_w = 11$, we see that $pK_b = 6$. Therefore, $K_b = 1 \times 10^{-11}$.

3. **B is correct.** Point x represents the point at which $[H_3A] = [H_2A^-]$. Using the Henderson-Hasselbalch equation:

$$pH = pK_a + \log \frac{[A^-]}{[HA]}$$

we see that the log term reduces to zero (log 1 = 0), and we are left with pH = pK_a. The point at which this is true is halfway to the equivalence point.

4. **C is correct.** By definition, the equivalence point is where all the acid is neutralized. In this case, it is where all H_2A^- has turned to HA^{2-}. From the graph, we see that HA^{2-} is 100 percent at about 9.5. Thus, choice C is the best answer. Note that in reality, there exists a negligible amount of H_2A^- at the equivalence point.

5. **D is correct.** When $[H^+] = 3.17 \times 10^{-12}$, pH = 11.5. The predominant species at pH = 11.5 is A^{3-}, as seen from the distribution curve.

6. **B is correct.** From the distribution curve data: $pK_{a1} = 3$, $pK_{a2} = 8$, and $pK_{a3} = 11$. Therefore, benzoic acid, with a pK_a of 4.19, is less acidic than H_3A, but more acidic than H_2A^-.

7. **D is correct.** To solve this problem, we must use the Henderson-Hasselbalch equation:

$$pH = pK_a + \log \frac{[A^-]}{[HA]}$$

We also can quickly calculate the final concentrations of H_3A and H_2A^-:

$$[H_3A] = \frac{0.05 \text{ mol}}{(1.000 \text{ L} + 0.500 \text{ L})} = 0.0333 \ M$$

$$[H_3A^-] = \frac{0.1 \text{ mol}}{(1.000 \text{ L} + 0.500 \text{ L})} = 0.0667 \ M$$

Thus:

$$pH_a = pK_a + \log \frac{[H_2A^-]}{[H_3A]}$$

$$= 3 + \log 2$$
$$= 3 + .3$$
$$pH = 3.3$$

CHAPTER 22

ELECTROCHEMISTRY

22.1 MASTERY ACHIEVED

REVIEW OF REDOX

The Half Reaction

As was discussed in **Chapter 15**, an **oxidation** cannot happen without a concomitant **reduction**. In this regard, we may consider an **oxidation–reduction reaction** (**redox**) as consisting of two **half reactions**: a half reaction representing an oxidation and a half reaction representing a reduction.

Oxidation is a loss of electrons. Reduction is a gain of electrons. Since an electron carries a charge of negative one, a single electron oxidation will increase the oxidation state by $-(-1)$, or $+1$. Similarly, a single electron reduction will decrease the oxidation state by $+(-1)$, or -1.

An oxidation half reaction takes the form:

$$M^{c+} \rightarrow M^{(c+n)+} + ne^-$$

For example:

$$Fe^{2+} \rightarrow Fe^{3+} + e^-$$

A reduction half reaction takes the form:

$$M^{c+} + ne^- \rightarrow M^{(c-n)+}$$

For example:

$$Al^{3+} + 3e^- \rightarrow Al^0$$

An **oxidizing agent**, or oxidant, is an agent that oxidizes. An oxidizing agent oxidizes another species by accepting electrons from that species. By accepting these electrons, the oxidizing agent is reduced.

A **reducing agent**, or reductant, is an agent that reduces. A reducing agent reduces another species by giving up electrons to that species. By giving up these electrons, the reducing agent is oxidized.

Please solve this problem:

- In the reaction $2Li + 2H_2O \rightarrow 2LiOH + H_2$:

    A. Li^+ is the oxidizing agent, and H^+ is the reducing agent.
    B. H^+ is the oxidizing agent, and Li is the reducing agent.
    C. Li^+ is the oxidizing agent, and H_2 is the reducing agent.
    D. H_2 is the oxidizing agent, and Li^+ is the reducing agent.

Problem solved:

B is correct. The half reactions for this redox equation are:

$$2Li \rightarrow 2Li^{+1} + 2e^-$$

$$2H^+ + 2e^- \rightarrow H_2$$

From these, we see that lithium metal is oxidized to lithium(I), and two protons are reduced to hydrogen gas. Therefore, H^+ is the oxidizing agent (the agent that caused the oxidation of lithium), and lithium is the reducing agent (the agent that caused the reduction of H^+).

Redox Couples

As we have previously stated, a redox reaction consists of a pair of half reactions: one oxidation reaction and one reduction reaction. These half reactions are reversible. The direction in which a given half reaction proceeds is determined by the half reaction with which it is allowed to react.

For instance, consider the half reaction:

$$Cu^{2+} + 2e^- \rightarrow Cu^0$$

If zinc metal is coupled with Cu^{2+}, the zinc metal is oxidized, and the copper(II) is reduced, since zinc(II) is a weaker oxidizing agent than Cu^{2+}:

$$Zn^0 + Cu^{2+} \rightarrow Zn^{2+} + Cu^0$$

However, iron(III) is a stronger oxidizing agent than copper(II). When copper metal is placed in a solution of Fe^{3+}, the copper metal is oxidized, and the iron(III) is reduced:

$$2Fe^{3+} + Cu^0 \rightarrow 2Fe^{2+} + Cu^{2+}$$

Given the reversibility of half reactions, it is often convenient to refer to **redox couples**, which consist of an oxidized form and a reduced form of a given species. The three redox couples referred to above are: Cu^{2+}/Cu, Zn^{2+}/Zn, and Fe^{3+}/Fe^{2+}. Note that redox couples are written oxidized form/reduced form. In many ways, redox couples are analogous to acid/conjugate base or base/conjugate acid pairs **(Chapter 21)**.

Please solve this problem:

- The redox couples involved in the reaction
$3Cu + 8HNO_3 \rightarrow 3Cu(NO_3)_2 + 4H_2O + NO$ are:

  A. Cu/Cu^{2+}, N^{5+}/N^{2+}.
  B. Cu^{2+}/Cu, N^{5+}/N^{2+}.
  C. Cu/Cu^{2+}, N^{5+}/N^{2+}.
  D. Cu^{2+}/Cu, N^{2+}/N^{5+}.

Problem solved:

B is correct. Redox couples must always be written as **oxidized form/reduced form**, so you should have been able to eliminate choices A, C, and D by inspection. Choice B is the only answer choice with both the copper couple and the nitrogen couple written in the correct form.

ELECTROCHEMISTRY DEFINITIONS

An **electrode** is the interface in an electrochemical cell at which the electron transfer in a redox reaction occurs. This does not imply, however, that the electrode is either oxidized or reduced. An **inert electrode** does **not** take part in the reaction; it simply facilitates the **electron transfer** process, or provides a site for deposition of a reacting chemical. An **active electrode does** take part in the redox reaction. As a result, an active electrode is either used up or augmented during the reaction. In redox reactions, there must be a minimum of two electrodes. The **anode** is the electrode at which **oxidation** occurs. The **cathode** is the electrode at which **reduction** occurs. One can remember these relationships through use of the simple vowel-vowel, consonant-consonant mnemonic:

$$\underline{c}athode = \underline{r}eduction; \qquad \underline{a}node = \underline{o}xidation$$

At the anode, electrons are transferred into the circuit. At the cathode, electrons are taken from the circuit. The circuit is a metal wire or other substance that connects the electrodes to one another and allows the transfer of electrons. Consequently, electrons flow from anode to cathode. By convention, the **current** (I), is considered positive, and is said to move *from cathode to anode*.

Please solve this problem:

- The definition of a cathode is:

  A. the negative electrode in an electrochemical cell.
  B. the positive electrode in an electrochemical cell.
  C. the electrode at which oxidation occurs in an electrochemical cell.
  D. the electrode at which reduction occurs in an electrochemical cell.

Problem solved:

D is correct. Choice C is the definition of an anode. As we will see below, the cathode is the positive electrode in certain circumstances (galvanic cells) and the negative electrode in other circumstances (electrolytic cells).

REDUCTION POTENTIAL, VOLTAGE, AND SPONTANEITY

Reduction Potentials and Oxidation Potentials

In order to determine the direction in which an oxidation-reduction equilibrium will run, we must have a means of quantifying half reactions. The most common method for quantification is the **reduction potential**. The sign and magnitude of a reduction potential tell how easily a species is reduced. The reduction potentials of some common species are given in Table 22.1.

Reduction	$E°$ (volts)	$\Delta G°$ (kJ)
$Li^+ + e^- \longrightarrow Li(s)$	−3.05	294.3
$K^+ + e^- \longrightarrow K(s)$	−2.93	282.7
$H_2(g) + 2e^- \longrightarrow 2H^-$	−2.25	434.3
$Al^{3+} + 3e^- \longrightarrow Al(s)$	−1.66	480.6
$Cr^{3+} + e^- \longrightarrow Cr^{2+}$	−0.41	39.6
$Pb^{2+} + 2e^- \longrightarrow Pb(s)$	−0.13	25.1
$2H^+ + 2e^- \longrightarrow H_2(g)$	0.00	0.0
$Cu^{2+} + 2e^- \longrightarrow Cu(s)$	+ 0.34	−65.6
$Cu^+ + e^- \longrightarrow Cu(s)$	+0.52	−50.2
$I_2 + 2e^- \longrightarrow 2I^-$	+0.54	−104.2
$Fe^{3+} + e^- \longrightarrow Fe^{2+}$	+0.77	−74.3
$Ag^+ + e^- \longrightarrow Ag(s)$	+0.80	−77.2
$Br_2 + 2e^- \longrightarrow 2Br^-$	+1.09	−210.4
$O_2(g) + 4H^+ + 4e^- \longrightarrow 2H_2O$	+1.23	−474.8
$Cr_2O_7^{2-} + 14H^+ + 6e^- \longrightarrow 2Cr^{3+} + 7H_2O$	+1.33	−770.1
$Cl_2 + 2e^- \longrightarrow 2Cl^-$	+1.36	−262.5
$MnO_4^- + 8H^+ + 5e^- \longrightarrow Mn^{2+} + 4H_2O$	+1.49	−718.9
$MnO_2 + 4H^+ + 2e^- \longrightarrow Mn^{2+} + 4H_2O$	+1.61	−310.7
$F_2 + 2e^- \longrightarrow 2F^-$	+2.87	−553.9

Reduction Potentials of Common Species
Table 22.1

Table 22.1 gives data in terms of both **voltage** ($E°$) and **standard Gibbs free-energy** ($G°$). Recall **(Chapter 17)** that a negative $\Delta G°$ denotes a spontaneous reaction. Therefore, a positive $E°$ also denotes a spontaneous reaction. Those reactions in the above table with a negative $\Delta G°$ (or positive $E°$) are expected to proceed to the right. Those reactions with a positive $\Delta G°$ (or negative $E°$) are expected to be nonspontaneous, or to proceed to the left.

Please solve this problem:

- Using the data in Table 22.1, the most easily oxidized species given below is:

   A. Mn^{2+}.
   B. Fe^{2+}.
   C. Al.
   D. Li.

Problem solved:

D is correct. Note the following four reduction potentials:

Reduction	$E°$ (volts)
$Li^+ + e^- \longrightarrow Li(s)$	−3.05
$Al^{3+} + 3e^- \longrightarrow Al(s)$	−1.66
$Fe^{3+} + e^- \longrightarrow Fe^{2+}$	+0.77
$MnO_4^- + 8H^+ + 5e^- \longrightarrow Mn^{2+} + 4H_2O$	+1.49

Table 22.2

In a reduction potential table, reductions will always be listed from the most negative $E°$ to the most positive $E°$. All you have to recognize is that the substances on the left of the reaction are being reduced, and the substances on the right are being oxidized. Using the four-item table above, in order from most easily reduced to least easily reduced, we see that $Mn^{7+} > Fe^{3+} > Al^{3+} > Li^+$. Likewise, the most easily oxidized substance to the least easily oxidized substance is $Li > Al > Fe^{2+} > Mn^{2+}$. Therefore, in a table of reduction potentials, the most easily reduced species may be found on the bottom left, and the least easily reduced species may be found on the top left. Similarly, the most easily oxidized species is found on the top right, and the least easily oxidized species is found on the bottom right.

Note that while it is customary to report **reduction potentials**, we also could have reported the above data as **oxidation potentials**. Table 22.3 shows the oxidation potentials for the four half reactions of the halogens given in Table 22.1.

Oxidation	$E°$ (volts)	$\Delta G°$ (kJ)
$2I^- \longrightarrow I_2 + 2e^-$	−0.54	+104.2
$2Br^- \longrightarrow Br_2 + 2e^-$	−1.09	+210.4
$2Cl^- \longrightarrow Cl_2 + 2e^-$	−1.36	+262.5
$2F^- \longrightarrow F_2 + 2e^-$	−2.87	+553.9

Oxidation Potentials for Halogens
Table 22.3

Note that while the half reaction for the reduction of F_2 is spontaneous (negative $\Delta G°$, positive $E°$), the half reaction for the oxidation of F^- is nonspontaneous (positive $\Delta G°$, negative $E°$). It should be clear that oxidation half reactions are simply the reverse of the corresponding reduction half reactions. It should also be clear that the oxidation potential of a half reaction is simply the negative of the reduction potential for that half reaction.

Please solve this problem:

- Using the data from Table 22.3, the strongest oxidizing agent within the halogen family is:

    A. F_2.
    B. F^-.
    C. I^-.
    D. I_2.

Problem solved:

A is correct. Remember that an oxidizing agent is reduced. This changes the problem to, "Which member of the halogen family is most easily reduced?" To have reduction potentials, we need to reverse the direction of the reactions given in Table 22.3, as well as reverse the sign of $E°$. The most positive $E°$ indicates the most easily reduced species, which is F_2.

The Electromotive Force

A **standard potential**, or **electromotive force (emf)**, is represented by $E°$. In a redox reaction, there is a movement of electrons from the substance being oxidized to the substance being reduced. This current arises from a **voltage**, which can be measured. In order to predict the efficacy of a redox pair, it is easier to refer to a table such as Table 22.1 than to perform an experiment. But since the reactions given in the table are half reactions, we must have a standard half reaction (or half cell) to which we may compare these half reactions. For electrochemistry, the **standard conditions** are: **1 molar** in any solute (for instance, Cu^{2+}); **1 atm** for any gas; and **25°C**. The **standard half cell** is the **hydrogen electrode**:

$$2H^+(aq, 1\ M) + 2e^- \rightarrow H_2(g, 1\ atm)$$

By definition, the electromotive force of the hydrogen half cell is taken as $E° = 0$ V.

Once a half reaction has been compared to the hydrogen half cell under standard conditions, its behavior, relative to each other half reaction that has also been compared to the hydrogen half cell, may be predicted. Table 22.1 is a tabulation of such comparisons to the hydrogen half cell.

Since electromotive force will be altered by changes in **concentration** (for solutes), **pressure** (for gases), and **temperature**, all electromotive forces recorded at nonstandard conditions are represented by E. For electromotive forces at nonstandard conditions, the temperature and concentration (or pressure) must also be given.

Much like Hess's law **(Chapter 17)** allowed the summation of enthalpies of formation, the electromotive forces of half reactions may also be summed to produce a **cell emf**.

$$Pb^{2+} + 2e^- \rightarrow Pb(s) \qquad\qquad E° = -0.13$$

$$2I^- \rightarrow I_2 + 2e^- \qquad\qquad E° = -0.54$$

$$Pb^{2+} + 2I^- \rightarrow Pb(s) + I_2 \qquad E° = -0.67$$

Note: The most common error made on the MCAT is the multiplication of half reaction electromotive forces by stoichiometric coefficients.

Never multiply an electromotive force by a stoichiometric coefficient! Electromotive forces are independent of the total amount of material present and depend only on concentration.

For example, consider the following balanced redox reaction:

$$14H^+ + Cr_2O_7^{2-} + 6Fe^{2+} \rightarrow 2Cr^{3+} + 6Fe^{3+} + 7H_2O$$

This reaction comes from the half reactions:

$$Cr_2O_7^{2-} + 14H^+ + 6e^- \rightarrow 2Cr^{3+} + 7H_2O \qquad\qquad E° = +1.33$$

and:

$$6 \times (Fe^{2+} \rightarrow Fe^{3+} + e^-) \qquad\qquad E° = -0.77$$

The total electromotive force for this reaction is $E° = +0.56$, **not** –3.26. By incorrectly using stoichiometric coefficients in this example, not only would you predict the wrong numerical answer for this redox equation, but you would also incorrectly predict that this reaction is nonspontaneous.

Please solve this problem:

- Using the data from Table 22.1, the electromotive force for the redox reaction between manganese(II) oxide (MnO), potassium dichromate ($K_2Cr_2O_7$), and nitric acid (HNO_3) in water to produce chromium(III) nitrate ($Cr(NO_3)_3$), permanganic acid ($HMnO_4$), and potassium oxide (K_2O) is:

    A. –0.16 V.
    B. –2.29 V.
    C. –2.82 V.
    D. –15.59 V.

Problem solved:

A is correct. The balanced equation for this reaction is:

$$6MnO + 5K_2Cr_2O_7 + 30HNO_3 \rightarrow 10Cr(NO_3)_3 + 6HMnO_4 + 5K_2O + 12H_2O$$

To solve this problem, you must recognize those species that undergo a change in oxidation state. Manganese changes from a +2 oxidation state to a +7 oxidation state, and chromium changes from a +6 oxidation state to a +3 oxidation state. All other species remain unchanged in oxidation state. Therefore, manganese is oxidized and chromium is reduced. Using Table 22.1, we see:

Reduction/Oxidation	$E°$(volts)
$Cr_2O_7^{2-} + 14H^+ + 6e^- \longrightarrow 2Cr^{3+} + 7H_2O$	+1.33
$Mn^{2+} + 4H_2O \longrightarrow MnO_4^- + 8H^+ + 5e^-$	–1.49
Total	–0.16

Table 22.4

Cell Diagrams

A **cell diagram** is the standard way to represent the half reactions in a redox reaction. By convention, the anode is given on the left, and the cathode is given on the right:

$$Fe^{2+}(aq), Fe^{3+}(aq) \parallel Cr_2O_7^{2-}(aq), Cr^{3+}(aq)$$

In a cell reaction, if the conditions are other than standard, the state (gas, liquid, solid, aqueous) and the concentration may be shown in parenthesis:

$$Fe^{2+}(aq, 0.5\ M), Fe^{3+}(aq, 0.5\ M) \parallel Cr_2O_7^{2-}(aq, 0.9\ M), Cr^{3+}(aq, 0.9\ M)$$

For an electrode, convention assigns a symbol to each species. A comma (,) separates species in different phases. Two vertical lines ($\parallel$) represent the salt bridge connecting two electrodes. Salt bridges are discussed in detail later in this chapter.

The order of listing reactants and products in a cell diagram is:

oxidation reactant | oxidation product | reduction reactant | reduction product.

Please solve this problem:

- The cell diagram for the reaction:

$$6MnO + 5K_2Cr_2O_7 + 30HNO_3 \rightarrow 10Cr(NO_3)_3 + 6HMnO_4 + 5K_2O + 12H_2O$$

  is given by:

  A. $Cr^{6+}(aq), Cr^{3+}(aq) \parallel Mn^{2+}(aq), Mn^{7+}(aq)$.
  B. $Cr^{3+}(aq), Cr^{6+}(aq) \parallel Mn^{2+}(aq), Mn^{7+}(aq)$.
  C. $Mn^{2+}(aq), Mn^{7+}(aq) \parallel Cr^{6+}(aq), Cr^{3+}(aq)$.
  D. $Mn^{7+}(aq), Mn^{2+}(aq) \parallel Cr^{6+}(aq), Cr^{3+}(aq)$.

Problem solved:

C is correct. This is the same redox reaction referred to in the problem in the previous section. In that section, we saw that manganese is oxidized from +2 to +7 and chromium is reduced from +6 to +3. Using the rules for writing cell diagrams (oxidation reactant | oxidation product || reduction reactant | reduction product), the correct answer must be C. Choices B and D are incorrect, since choice B depicts two oxidations and choice D depicts two reductions. Choice A would be correct if it were reversed.

GALVANIC CELLS

A **galvanic**, or **voltaic**, cell was first used to demonstrate the validity of the electron transfer occurring in a redox reaction. Consider the reaction of dichromate with iodine:

$$14H^+ + Cr_2O_7^{2-} + 6I^- \rightarrow 2Cr^{3+} + 3I_2 + 7H_2O$$

This reaction was chosen because it is easy to follow visually. Initially, a solution containing the dichromate ion will be orange. After the reduction to chromate, the solution will be green. Likewise, a solution containing iodide (I^-) will be colorless; however, a solution containing I_2 will be yellow-brown.

If a solution of potassium iodide is poured into an orange-colored potassium dichromate solution (which also contains sulfuric acid, H_2SO_4, as a proton source), the reaction mixture becomes green. The color of the iodine is masked by the green of the chromium(III). While simple chemical tests will indicate that the green color is indeed due to chromium(III) and that iodine (I_2) is also present in the resultant solution, we do not have direct proof of an electron exchange process. A galvanic cell provides such a direct proof.

Suppose that instead of mixing our two solutions, we connect them via a platinum wire connected to a **galvanometer** (to detect current), as shown below. Platinum is chosen, since it will not react with either of our initial solutions. The galvanometer will indicate a flow of electrons from one solution to the other.

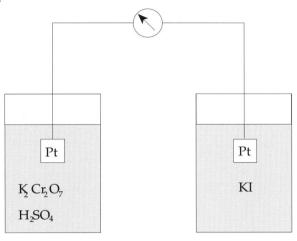

Figure 22.1

Please solve this problem:

- In the above diagram, there is no flow of electrons. Why?

Problem solved:

Initially, electrons flow from one solution to the other. A salt bridge is necessary to sustain the flow of electrons. In the solution containing the iodide, some of the iodide ions contact the platinum wire and electrons flow to the wire, thus forming oxidized iodine:

$$2I^- - 2e^- \rightarrow I_2$$

These electrons are then transferred through the wire to the solution containing the dichromate ion. Some of the dichromate ions accept these electrons and are reduced to chromate ions:

$$Cr_2O_7^{2-} + 14H^+ + 6e^- \rightarrow 2Cr^{3+} + 7H_2O$$

However, this process cannot continue. A consumption of the iodide ions in the oxidation vessel will leave an excess of positively charged potassium ions in this vessel. This build-up of positive charge will prevent the further release of electrons from the remaining iodide ions. Eliminating this excess positive charge is done by using a salt bridge.

A **salt bridge** is a link between the oxidation and reduction vessels that allows for the passage of the counter ions in each of the vessels. These counter ions must not be reactive under the conditions of either half reaction, and they should be highly soluble in the solution medium. A complete galvanic cell for the redox reaction of iodide and dichromate is depicted on the next page.

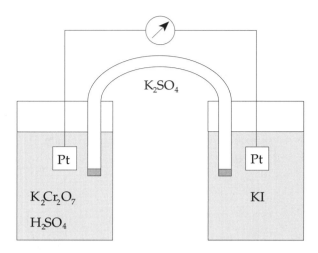

Figure 22.2

The salt bridge consists of an aqueous solution of potassium sulfate held into a U-tube by plugs of glass wool. As the iodide is oxidized at the anode, the build-up of positive charge is alleviated by the flow of potassium ions through the salt bridge to the cathodic vessel. Similarly, we recognize that a consumption of protons in the cathode reaction leaves an excess of negatively charged sulfate ions from the equilibria:

$$H_2SO_4 \rightleftharpoons H^+ + HSO_4^-$$

$$HSO_4^- \rightleftharpoons H^+ + SO_4^{2-}$$

To alleviate this build-up of negative charge in the cathodic vessel, sulfate flows through the salt bridge to the anodic vessel. The flow of the potassium ions and the sulfate ion maintain a charge balance in the reaction vessels and allow the redox reactions to proceed, thereby producing a measurable current in the galvanometer.

Because of the need for platinum electrodes in this galvanic cell, the cell diagram is slightly more complicated than those described earlier:

$$(Pt) \mid I^-, I_2 \parallel Cr_2O_7^{2-}, H^+, Cr^{3+} \mid (Pt)$$

In a cell diagram, the presence of an inert conductor (required when no solid metal is present) may be indicated by parentheses, as in the above example. A galvanic cell is a spontaneous redox cell. That is, a galvanic cell may be employed to produce a current (which results from the voltage) for the performance of useful work.

In a galvanic cell:

- the redox reaction is spontaneous,
- the cell creates an electron flow,
- oxidation occurs at the anode,
- reduction occurs at the cathode,
- the cathode is the positive electrode,
- the anode is the negative electrode, and
- electrons flow from the anode to the cathode.

Please solve this problem:

- The redox reaction which occurs in a galvanic cell:

    A. is nonspontaneous, requiring an electric current from anode to cathode.

    B. is spontaneous, creating an electric current from anode to cathode.

    C. is nonspontaneous, requiring an electric current from cathode to anode.

    D. is spontaneous, creating an electric current from cathode to anode.

Problem solved:

D is correct. By definition, an electrochemical cell is galvanic if the redox reaction is spontaneous. This definition eliminates choices A and C. To decide between choices B and D, one must remember that current flows in the opposite direction of electron flow: A galvanic cell creates a flow of electrons from the anode to the cathode and a current flow from cathode to anode.

ELECTROLYTIC CELLS

We saw in the section before this that a galvanic cell uses a spontaneous redox reaction to produce an electrical current. In an **electrolytic cell**, we are concerned with driving nonspontaneous redox reactions by supplying an electrical current.

Electroplating is an important application of electrolysis. This technique is often employed to improve the appearance and durability of metal objects. For example, a thin film of chromium is applied over steel automobile bumpers to improve appearance and to retard corrosion of the underlying steel. Silver plating is common on eating utensils. The typical apparatus for electroplating a fork is shown below:

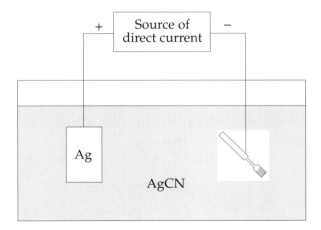

Figure 22.3

In this example, a direct current is supplied to the system from an external source. The silver bar is the anode and the fork is the cathode. At the anode, the silver is oxidized to furnish Ag^+ ions to the solution. At the cathode, the Ag^+ ions in solution are reduced to silver metal, which adheres to the surface of the fork. The half reactions are:

$$\text{Anode:} \quad Ag(s) - e^- \rightarrow Ag^+$$
$$\text{Cathode:} \quad Ag^+ + e^- \rightarrow Ag(s)$$

The purpose of the **external current source** is to supply electrons to the cathode for the reduction process. The oxidation process at the anode then supplies electrons to the external current source, so the process may continue. As time passes, silver metal from the anode is transferred to the cathode. You should note that electron flow in an electrolytic cell is confined to the wires attaching the anode and cathode to the external current source. Electrons do not flow through the electrolytic medium.

In an electrolytic cell:

- the redox reaction is nonspontaneous,*

- the cell requires an electron flow,*

- oxidation occurs at the anode,

- reduction occurs at the cathode,

- the anode is the positive electrode,*

- the cathode is the negative electrode,*

- electrons flow from the anode to the cathode, and

- current flows from the cathode to the anode.

* Items marked with asterisks differ from the case of a galvanic cell.

Please solve this problem:

- The electrolysis of brine (concentrated aqueous sodium chloride) is important for the production of hydrogen gas, chlorine gas, and sodium hydroxide. The overall reaction within the electrolytic system is:

$$2H_2O + 2NaCl \rightarrow H_2 + Cl_2 + 2NaOH$$

The half reaction occurring at the cathode is:

A. $2Cl^- - 2e^- \rightarrow Cl_2$
B. $2Na^+ + 2e^- \rightarrow 2Na$
C. $2H_2O \rightarrow 2H_2 + O_2$
D. $2H_2O + 2e^- \rightarrow H_2 + 2OH^-$

Problem solved:

D is correct. Inspection of the choices leads to the immediate elimination of both choices B and C. Choice B is eliminated since no sodium metal is produced in the electrolysis of brine. Choice C is eliminated since no oxygen gas is produced in the electrolysis of brine. Choice A represents an oxidation, and choice D represents a reduction. Choice D must be correct, since, by definition, oxidation occurs at the anode, and reduction occurs at the cathode, regardless of the type of cell.

A COMPARISON OF GALVANIC AND ELECTROLYTIC CELLS

Table 22.5, shown below, summarizes the similarities and differences between electrolytic and galvanic cells:

	Galvanic	Electrolytic
type of redox reaction	spontaneous	nonspontaneous
electron flow	created	supplied
site of oxidation	anode	anode
site of reduction	cathode	cathode
positive electrode	cathode	anode
negative electrode	anode	cathode
flow of electrons	anode to cathode	anode to cathode
flow of current	cathode to anode	cathode to anode

Table 22.5

CONCENTRATION CELLS

A **concentration cell** is a galvanic cell in which the cathodic half reaction and the anodic half reaction are the same reaction but opposite directions. It is possible to sustain such a cell by differing the concentrations between the two electrode vessels. Below is an example of a concentration cell employing differing concentrations of silver(I) with silver electrodes is shown below:

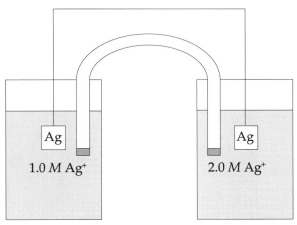

Figure 22.4

In this cell, the redox couple in each case is Ag^+/Ag. Since the vessel on the right contains a higher concentration of Ag^+, it is the more positive electrode, and is, therefore, the cathode. Since this is an example of a galvanic cell, we see that the half reaction for the right vessel will be:

$$Ag^+ + e^- \rightarrow Ag(s)$$

while the half reaction for the left vessel (anode) will be:

$$Ag(s) \rightarrow Ag^+ + e^-$$

The cell diagram for this cell is given by:

$$Ag(s) \mid Ag^+ (aq, 0.10 \ M) \parallel Ag^+ (aq, 2.0 \ M) \mid Ag(s)$$

Please solve this problem:

- A concentration cell is formed between a one liter aqueous solution containing 125 grams $Cu(NO_3)_2$ and a one liter aqueous solution containing 100 grams $CuSO_4$. Using Le Chatelier's principle, predict which solution will be the anode.

  A. The copper(II) nitrate solution
  B. The copper(II) sulfate solution
  C. These two solutions will not form a concentration cell.
  D. These solutions will form a concentration cell, but it cannot be determined which will be the anode.

Problem solved:

B is correct. To solve this problem, we must first determine the molarity of Cu^{2+} ions in each solution:

$$125 \text{ g } Cu(NO_3)_2 \div 187.5 \text{ g/mol} = 0.667 \text{ mol} \div 1 \text{ L} = 0.667 \ M$$

$$100 \text{ g } CuSO_4 \div 159.5 \text{ g/mol} = 0.627 \text{ mol} \div 1 \text{ L} = 0.627 \ M$$

Since the concentration of Cu^{2+} is higher in the copper(II) nitrate solution, Le Chatelier's principle indicates that this solution will tend to remove Cu^{2+} by reduction, while the copper(II) sulfate solution will tend to form Cu^{2+} by oxidation. Since oxidation always occurs at the anode, the copper(II) sulfate solution is the anode.

EFFECT OF CONCENTRATION ON POTENTIALS: THE NERNST EQUATION

In a quick comparison of $E°$ values and $\Delta G°$ values from Table 22.1, we can see that the relationship between these two quantities is given by:

$$\Delta G° = -nFE°$$

where:

n = moles of electrons, and

F = Faraday's constant = 96,485 C/mole.

For nonstandard conditions:

$$\Delta G = -nFE$$

Also from **Chapter 17**, ΔG is given by:

$$\Delta G = \Delta G° + RTlnQ$$

where Q is the reaction coefficient.

Substituting for ΔG and $\Delta G°$, and then dividing by $-nF$ we arrive at:

$$E = E° - \frac{RT}{nF}\ln Q$$

Using the relationship between natural log (ln) and log base ten (log), we see that:

$$E = E° - 2.303\frac{RT}{nF}\log Q$$

This is the **Nernst equation**.

The Nernst equation is used to calculate E at conditions other than standard, since R and F are constants, and Q, T, and n can be determined.

The Nernst equation can also be used to calculate the equilibrium constant, K_{eq}, for electrochemical systems at equilibrium under standard conditions. For a system under standard conditions, T is 298 K, and by definition, $E = 0$ at equilibrium. Therefore, the Nernst equation reduces to:

$$E° = (2.303)\frac{RT}{nF}\log K_{eq} = \frac{(2.303)(8.314)(298)}{n(96,485)}\log K_{eq} = \frac{0.0592}{n}\log K_{eq}$$

Please solve this problem:

- Using the problem from **22.1.7**, the value of E is:

  A. −0.795 V.
  B. −0.795 mV.
  C. +0.795 mV.
  D. +0.795 V.

Problem solved:

C is correct. Using the Nernst equation:

$$E = E^\circ - (2.303)\frac{RT}{nF}\log Q = E^\circ - \frac{0.0591}{n}\log Q$$

$E^\circ = 0$ (since the half reactions are the same)

$n = 2$ (since the half reaction involves a two-electron transfer)

$$Q = \frac{\left[Cu^{2+}(anode)\right]}{\left[Cu^{2+}(cathode)\right]} = \frac{0.627}{0.667} = 0.940$$

$$\log Q = \log(0.940) = -0.0269$$

$$E = E^\circ - \frac{0.0591}{n}\log Q$$

$$= 0 - \left(\frac{0.0591}{2}\right)(-0.0269) = 7.95 \times 10^{-4}\,V$$

$$= 0.795\ mV$$

22.2 MASTERY APPLIED: PRACTICE PASSAGE AND QUESTIONS

Passage

Electricity may be generated in an electrochemical cell, termed a **galvanic**, or **voltaic cell**. Such a cell uses a spontaneous oxidation-reduction reaction. The total **electromotive force (emf)** available from the cell is the sum of the electromotive force of the oxidation half reaction and the electromotive force of the reduction half reaction.

Cell emf is related to the Gibbs free energy change of the cell by:

$$\Delta G° = -nFE°$$

where n is the number of moles of electrons transferred in the reaction, and

$$F = 96,500 \text{ C/mole.}$$

Therefore, like ΔG, cell emf is a measure of the spontaneity of the oxidation-reduction reaction occurring within a cell. Examples of standard reduction potentials (emfs) are given in Table 1.

Reduction	$E°$(volts)	$\Delta G°$ (kJ)
$Li^+ (aq) + e^- \rightarrow Li(s)$	−3.05	294.3
$K^+ (aq) + e^- \rightarrow K(s)$	−2.93	282.7
$H_2 (g) + 2e^- \rightarrow 2H^- (aq)$	−2.25	434.3
$Al^{3+}(aq) + 3e^- \rightarrow Al(s)$	−1.66	480.6
$Cr^{3+}(aq) + e^- \rightarrow Cr^{2+}(aq)$	−0.41	39.6
$Pb^{2+} (aq) + 2e^- \rightarrow Pb(s)$	−0.13	25.1
$2H^+ (aq) + 2e^- \rightarrow H_2 (g)$	0.00	00.0
$Cu^{2+} (aq) + 2e^- \rightarrow Cu(s)$	+0.34	−65.5
$Cu^+ (aq) + e^- \rightarrow Cu(s)$	+0.52	−50.2
$I_2 (aq) + 2e^- \rightarrow 2I^- (aq)$	+0.54	−104.2
$Fe^{3+} (aq) + e^- \rightarrow Fe^{2+}(aq)$	+0.77	−74.3
$Ag^+ (aq) + e^- \rightarrow Ag(s)$	+0.80	−77.2

Standard Reduction Potentials
Table 1

The electrochemical cell in which zinc metal reacts with aqueous copper(II) ions is termed the Daniell cell. The reaction in a Daniell cell is given by:

$$Zn(s) + Cu^{2+}(aq) \rightarrow Zn^{2+}(aq) + Cu(s)$$

The emf of a Daniell cell is +1.10 V.

Another example of the use of electrochemical cells is the nickel-cadmium (or NiCad) rechargeable battery. The half reactions associated with this system are:

Anode:

$$Cd(s) + 2OH^-(aq) \rightarrow Cd(OH)_2(s) + 2e^-$$

$$E° = +0.761 \text{ V}$$

Cathode:

$$NiO_2(s) + 2H_2O(l) + 2e^- \rightarrow Ni(OH)_2(s) + 2OH^- (aq)$$

$$E° = +0.490 \text{ V}$$

1. Which of the following is the strongest reducing agent?

   A. $K(s)$
   B. $Cr^{2+}(aq)$
   C. $H_2(g)$
   D. $Fe^{2+}(aq)$

2. Which of the following cells would produce the galvanic cell with the largest emf?

   A. $Al \mid Al^{3+} \parallel Li^+ \mid Li$
   B. $K \mid K^+ \parallel Al^{3+} \mid Al$
   C. $Ag \mid Ag^+ \parallel Li^+ \mid Li$
   D. $Cr^{2+}, Cr^{3+} \parallel Fe^{3+}, Fe^{2+}$

3. What is the emf of the reduction of $Zn^{2+}(aq)$ to zinc metal?

   A. −1.10 V
   B. −0.76 V
   C. −0.58 V
   D. +0.76 V

4. How much voltage is supplied by a NiCad battery after it is 75 percent discharged?

   A. 1.251 V
   B. 0.938 V
   C. 0.413 V
   D. 0.313 V

5. NiCad batteries can be recharged by being run as electrolytic cells. During the recharging process, the reaction at the anode is:

   A. $Cd + 2OH^- \rightarrow Cd(OH)_2 + 2e^-$.

   B. $NiO_2 + 2H_2O + 2e^- \rightarrow Ni(OH)_2 + 2OH^-$.

   C. $Cd(OH)_2 + 2e^- \rightarrow Cd + 2OH^-$.

   D. $Ni(OH)_2 + 2OH^- \rightarrow NiO_2 + 2H_2O + 2e^-$

22.3 MASTERY VERIFIED: ANSWERS AND EXPLANATIONS

1. **A is correct.** The strongest reducing agent is the species that is most easily oxidized. The most easily oxidized species is the product of the least favorable reduction. The least favorable reduction of the four answer choices is the reduction of K^+ to form solid potassium. Therefore, the most easily oxidized species is $K(s)$.

2. **B is correct.** Using the data from the table in the passage, we can calculate the cell emfs for each cell diagram. Cell diagrams are written: oxidation reactant | oxidation product || reduction reactant | reduction product. So, to find cell emf, we must reverse the sign of the emf listed in the table for the oxidation half reaction, and add it to the emf listed in the table for the reduction half reaction.

    choice A: $(+1.66) + (-3.05) = -1.39$ V

    choice B: $(+2.93) + (-1.66) = +1.27$ V

    choice C: $(-0.80) + (-3.05) = -3.85$ V

    choice D: $(+0.41) + (+0.77) = +1.18$ V

    The question asked for the **galvanic** cell with the largest emf. Choices A and C are not galvanic cells. The emf of the cell given in choice B is larger than the emf of the cell given in choice D, so the correct answer is choice B.

3. **B is correct.** From the emf given for the Daniell cell and the emf of the reduction of Cu^{2+}, we can immediately find the emf for the oxidation of $Zn(s)$:

    $$1.10 - 0.34 = +0.76$$

    The question asks for the emf of the reduction of Zn^{2+}, so we reverse the sign:

    $$-0.76 \text{ V}$$

4. **A is correct.** A cell's voltage remains constant, or almost constant, until just before it dies. A battery that has 25 percent of its life left, will have a voltage that is very close to its standard potential.

5. **D is correct.** A galvanic cell runs in reverse in an electrolytic cell. For any cell, the reaction at the anode is oxidation. Thus choices B and C are wrong. The reaction in either choice takes place at the anode in the galvanic cell and, thus, does not occur in the electrolytic cell.

CHAPTER 23

EUKARYOTIC CELLS

23.1 MASTERY ACHIEVED

THE CELL MEMBRANE

The word *eukaryotic* refers to a cell that has a well-defined nucleus bound by a nuclear membrane, with a variety of organelles located outside the nuclear membrane. Eukaryotic cells include (1) animal cells and (2) plant cells. (**Prokaryotic** cells, on the other hand, are those that lack (a) well-defined *membrane-bound* nuclei and (b) a full complement of the organelles, which will be discussed below. Prokaryotes include bacteria and fungi.)

Familiarize yourself with the principal features of the eukaryotic cell, which are:

- a **cell wall** (*not* found in animal cells);

- a **cell membrane**;

- the **cytoplasm**, in which organelles are housed;

- a **nucleus**, separated from the remainder of the cell by a **nuclear membrane**.

The cell wall, composed largely of carbohydrates, is found on the cells of many organisms, including plants, yeasts, and bacteria. Cell walls, however, are *not* found on animal cells.

Where present, the cell wall is the outermost structure of the cell. All cells, regardless of whether or not they have a cell wall, possess a cell membrane, composed primarily of protein and phospholipid.

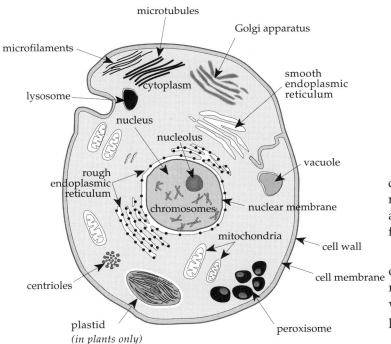

Prototypical Eukaryotic Cell

Figure 23.1

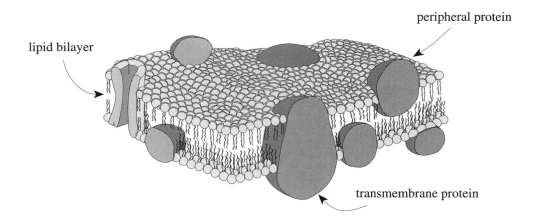

Fluid Mosaic Model of the Cell Membrane

(Space between the two layers exaggerated for conceptual clarity)
Figure 23.2

Associated with the membrane are proteins. Those proteins that are embedded in one of the two surfaces of the membrane are called **peripheral proteins**. Those that penetrate completely through the membrane are called **transmembrane proteins**.

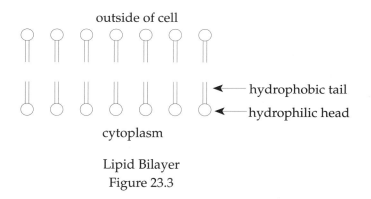

Lipid Bilayer
Figure 23.3

Please solve this problem:

- The phospholipid bilayer features:

    A. lipid-soluble components.
    B. water-soluble components.
    C. both A and B.
    D. neither A nor B.

Problem solved:

C is correct. The cell membrane is composed primarily of protein and phospholipid. The phospholipid molecules have lipid-soluble and water-soluble components.

Please solve this problem:

- The hydrophobic moieties of the cell membrane's phospholipid molecules are oriented:
    - A. toward the inner portion of the membrane.
    - B. toward the external environment surrounding the membrane.
    - C. both A and B.
    - D. neither A nor B.

Problem solved:

A is correct. The hydrophobic tails of each phospholipid molecule within the cell membrane are oriented so that they face one another, and have no significant contact with the intracellular or extracellular environments. The cell's internal and external environments are water rich and therefore tend to repel the hydrophobic moieties.

Please solve this problem:

- The typical animal cell contains all of the following EXCEPT:
    - A. a cell wall.
    - B. a mitochondrion.
    - C. microtubules.
    - D. a discrete nucleus.

Problem solved:

A is correct. Animal cells do not have cell walls. The outermost layer of an animal cell is the cell membrane, which is composed of protein and phospholipid.

Regulation of the Cell's Internal Environment

The cell membrane is permeable to some substances and impermeable to others. For that reason, it is termed **semipermeable**. Furthermore, the membrane's permeability is subject to *modification*. Under some circumstances, it might be permeable to a given substance, and under others, it might be impermeable to that same substance. For that reason, it is termed **selectively permeable**. Since the cell membrane's permeability by and large determines which substances enter the cell and which do not, the membrane is said to regulate the cell's internal environment.

SIMPLE DIFFUSION, OSMOSIS, HYPERTONICITY—AND THE CELL MEMBRANE

Put the cell membrane out of your mind for a bit and imagine a vessel filled with pure water. Imagine also that the vessel is divided into right and left halves by a membrane freely permeable to Solute X. Suppose now that Solute X is added to the vessel's right side but not to its left side.

Momentarily, the concentration of Solute X will be higher on the right than the left. Between the right and left sides of the vessel, Solute X will experience a concentration gradient (a difference in its concentration). The concentration gradient, however, will not endure. Rather, Solute X molecules will move naturally across the membrane from right to left until their concentration is uniform throughout the vessel. In other words, the solute will move "down" its concentration gradient (from an area of higher concentration to an area of lower concentration) until concentration is equalized.

The process just described is termed simple diffusion, which refers to this general phenomenon: In a given system of fluid, solute and solvent particles tend ("want") to disperse themselves so that solute concentration is uniform throughout the system. A variety of factors may prevent them from fully equalizing concentration, but they have a natural tendency ("desire") to do so. If circumstances do allow solute particles to move freely throughout the system, then they will in fact move down their concentration gradient and thus distribute themselves in uniform concentration.

Imagine now another water-filled vessel with a membrane that separates its right and left sides. This time, suppose that (1) the vessel is expandable (like a balloon), (2) the membrane is freely permeable to water, and (3) the membrane is impermeable to Solute X.

Suppose now that Solute X is added to the vessel's right side (but not to its left side). The system will "want" to equilibrate concentration, but the membrane will not allow Solute X to cross. Yet, since the membrane is permeable to water, water will tend to move via simple diffusion from the vessel's left side to its right side in an "effort" to equalize the concentration of Solute X.

When simple diffusion causes water (and not solute) to move across a membrane, we invoke the word osmosis. Osmosis refers to simple diffusion in which water (not solute) moves across a membrane in an "effort" to equalize concentration. Osmotic pressure refers to the tendency of water to move across a membrane (via osmosis) in an effort to equilibrate concentration. In the illustration just cited, the addition of Solute X to the vessel's right side created an osmotic pressure tending to move water from left to right across the membrane.

When one solution (or one portion of a solution) has a higher concentration than another, the region of higher concentration is said to be hypertonic (or hyperosmotic) to the region of lower concentration. The region of lower concentration is said to be hypotonic (or hypoosmotic) to the one of higher concentration. Consider again the expandable (balloon-like) vessel described above. When Solute X was first added to its right side, the right side became hypertonic to the left (and the left became hypotonic to the right). By osmosis, water moved from the hypotonic region to the hypertonic region.

The cell membrane is freely permeable to many solutes, including, for example, (a) most lipid-soluble substances, (b) small uncharged molecules such as oxygen and carbon dioxide, and (c) water. If any such solute should temporarily be in differing concentration inside and outside the cell (meaning that one side of the cell is hypertonic to the other) then, via simple diffusion, solute molecules will move across the cell membrane (inward or outward, as the situation may require) to "even out" the concentration. By simple diffusion, they will move across the membrane, down their concentration gradient, until concentrations are equal inside and outside the cell.

If a concentration gradient should develop across the cell membrane as to some solute to which the membrane is not permeable, then via osmosis, water will tend to move from hypotonic area to hypertonic area, once again, in an "effort" to equalize concentration.

Simple diffusion (including osmosis) does not require the expenditure of energy. The process is passive (and on that basis is distinct from active transport discussed in the next section).

Please solve this problem:

- Which of the following is NOT true of cell membranes?

    A. They regulate the cell's internal environment.
    B. They can alter their permeability to certain substances.
    C. They are universally permeable.
    D. They can mediate diffusion.

Problem solved:

C is correct. The cell membrane helps the cell maintain homeostasis by regulating the movement of substances into and out of the cell. A is a restatement of this fact. B and D describe ways in which this is accomplished. Answer choice C is untrue.

Please solve this problem:

- Simple diffusion occurs because:

    A. within a given solution, solute and solvent molecules tend to distribute themselves in uniform concentration.
    B. cells expend energy to make it occur.
    C. cell membranes are permeable only to certain substances.
    D. the cell membrane regulates the cell's internal environment.

Problem solved:

A is correct. As noted in the text, simple diffusion does not require the expenditure of energy by the cell. It proceeds from the tendency of solute and solvent molecules to disperse themselves evenly by moving down their concentration gradients. Answer choice C is true, but it does not answer the question.

Please solve this problem:

Table 23.1 lists the approximate ion concentrations found in the axonal cytoplasm and in the blood of the squid.

Ion	Axonal cytoplasm concentration (mmol/L)	Blood concentration (mmol/L)
K^+	397	20
Na^+	50	437
Cl^-	40	556
Ca^{++}	0.4	10

Table 23.1

- Assuming that the axonal cell membrane is permeable only to potassium (K^+), sodium (Na^+), and calcium (Ca^{++}), and that no cellular energy is available for transport, which of the following ion movements presented is most consistent with the data set forth in the table?

    A. Potassium flows out of the blood into the axonal cytoplasm.
    B. Sodium does not flow in either direction across the axonal cell membrane.
    C. Chloride flows from the blood into the axonal cytoplasm.
    D. Calcium flows from the blood into the axonal cytoplasm.

Problem solved:

D is correct. Calcium's relative concentrations—0.4 mmol/L in the axonal cytoplasm, 10 mmol/L in the blood—indicate that it will flow from the blood into the axonal cytoplasm. Answer choice A is incorrect because it suggests that potassium would move from a region of lower concentration (20 mmol/L in the blood) to one of higher concentration (397 mmol/L in the axonal cytoplasm). This movement would require the expenditure of energy; it cannot occur passively. Answer choice B is incorrect because sodium's relative concentrations (50 mmol/L in the axoplasm, 437 mmol/L in the blood) dictate that sodium flow from the blood into the axonal cytoplasm. Answer choice C is wrong because the question establishes that the axon cell membrane is not permeable to chloride.

Please solve this problem:

- If two solutions, X and Y, are separated by a membrane, and X has higher solute concentration than does Y, it may be concluded that:

    A. X is hypotonic to Y.
    B. Y is hypotonic to X.
    C. solvent will move from X to Y.
    D. solute will move from Y to X.

Problem solved:

B is correct. The question depends upon the meaning of the term *hypotonic*, which describes a solution with a solute concentration less than that of some other solution. Since solution X has a higher solute concentration, Y is hypotonic to X. Such movement (if any) would depend on the permeability properties of the membrane interposed between the two solutions. In any event, it could not be expected that solvent should move from the hypertonic to the hypotonic region nor that solute should move from the hypotonic to the hypertonic region. The natural tendencies would dictate just the opposite.

Please solve this problem:

- Which of the following correctly characterizes osmotic pressure?

  A. It tends to move solute from a hypotonic to a hypertonic region.
  B. It tends to move solute from a hypertonic to a hypotonic region.
  C. It tends to move solvent from a hypotonic to a hypertonic region.
  D. It tends to move solvent from a hypertonic to a hypotonic region.

Problem solved:

C is correct. Osmotic pressure tends to promote the movement of solvent from regions of greater concentration to regions of lower concentration. In other words, it is the driving force that causes water to move down its concentration gradient. Answer choices A and B are incorrect because they refer to the movement of solute, not solvent. Note that a solute does tend to move from hypertonic to hypotonic regions, but the term *osmotic pressure* is generally reserved for the tendency of concentration gradients to promote the movement of solvent.

Please solve this problem:

- Which of the following describes a form of passive diffusion?

  A. Semipermeability
  B. Osmosis
  C. Hypertonicity
  D. Hypotonicity

Problem solved:

B is correct. Osmosis refers, in essence, to the passive diffusion of solvent. Generally, passive diffusion is the process by which solute or solvent moves down its concentration gradient. Osmosis is the specialized term applied to the passive movement of solvent.

FACILITATED DIFFUSION AND ACTIVE TRANSPORT OF IONS AND MOLECULES

Passive diffusion is one of several processes by which substances cross the cell membrane. Two others are (1) **facilitated diffusion** and (2) **active transport**. Facilitated diffusion refers to the movement, *down* their concentration gradients, of certain lipid insoluble substances, these having little ability to cross the lipid bilayer without mediation by a specialized device. Facilitated diffusion proceeds via **ion channels** or **pores** within the cell membrane's protein components. The ion channels "facilitate" the movement across the membrane of lipid insoluble substances.

Like passive diffusion, facilitated diffusion (1) proceeds without the expenditure of energy and (2) promotes the movement of solutes *down* their concentration gradient (from areas of higher concentration to areas of lower concentration).

Active transport is a process by which substances cross the cell membrane *against* their concentration gradients (from areas of *lower* concentration to areas of *higher* concentration). In that way, it differs fundamentally from passive diffusion and facilitated transport. And for that same reason, it differs also in this fundamental way: *It requires the expenditure of energy.*

Bear in mind, then, the principal distinctions among passive diffusion, facilitated diffusion, and active transport:

(1)   Passive diffusion pertains to the movement of lipid-soluble particles (and certain small uncharged molecules to which the cell membrane is freely permeable). Movement proceeds down the concentration gradient and, for that reason, requires no expenditure of energy.

(2)   Facilitated diffusion pertains to the movement of lipid-insoluble substances and is mediated by ion channels within the membrane's protein components. Movement proceeds down the concentration gradient and, for that reason, requires no expenditure of energy.

(3)   Active transport pertains to movement against concentration gradient and, for that reason requires the expenditure of energy.

(In what is called "primary" active transport, the necessary energy arises indirectly from the hydrolysis of ATP. The ATP hydrolysis creates a chemical gradient across the membrane, and the potential energy inherent in the chemical gradient then drives the active transport.)

Please solve this problem:

- The sodium-potassium pump, also called $Na^+ - K^+$ ATPase, is a means by which the cell maintains a relatively fixed internal concentration of sodium and potassium ions. The pump continuously forces sodium ions out of the cell and draws potassium ions inward. In a typical $Na^+ - K^+$ ATPase, the cell moves three sodium ions outward for every two potassium ions drawn inward. A transmembrane protein facilitates this "ion exchange." Based on your knowledge of equilibria, would you speculate that the sodium-potassium pump represents active transport? Assuming that the cell membrane is permeable to both sodium and potassium ions, predict the ion flow that would follow if the pump were to suddenly cease operation.

Problem solved:

The problem asks that the student apply his or her understanding of transmembrane flow and equilibrium as it relates to intracellular and extracellular ion concentrations. In order to continuously expel sodium and take in potassium, the cell must expend energy, since the activity contravenes prevailing concentration gradients. The pump itself produces and maintains the concentration gradients against which it operates: one in which the sodium concentration is higher on the outside of the cell than on the inside and the other in which the potassium concentration is higher on the inside of the cell than on the outside. The process demands energy, which is supplied by ATP. The pump defies the natural tendency for solute concentrations to equilibrate. If it were to cease operating, the natural tendencies would manifest. Sodium would flow passively down its concentration gradient and enter the cell. Potassium would flow passively down its concentration gradient and exit the cell.

ENDOCYTOSIS: PINOCYTOSIS AND PHAGOCYTOSIS

Endocytosis is a process by which cells can ingest particles larger than an ion or a molecule. In this process, a small region of the lipid bilayer, located near the target particle, **invaginates**, surrounding the target. The invaginating portion of the lipid bilayer eventually pinches off to create a **vesicle**, which harbors the particle within the cell's interior. Endocytosis of liquids or small particles is termed **pinocytosis**, whereas endocytosis of larger particles, like bacteria or foreign matter, is termed **phagocytosis**. **Receptor-mediated endocytosis** involves the ingestion of specific particles after they bind to specific protein receptors on the membrane.

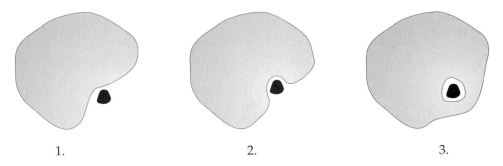

1.   2.   3.

Endocytosis of Particle by Cell

Figure 23.4

Please solve this problem:

- Which of the following is a form of endocytosis?

  A. Pinocytosis
  B. Expulsion
  C. Phagocytosis
  D. A and C

Problem solved:

D is correct. Phagocytosis describes the endocytosis of large particles, whereas pinocytosis describes the endocytosis of liquids or smaller particles.

Please solve this problem:

- Which among the following does NOT play a role in the process of endocytosis?

    A. Vesicle formation
    B. Pinching off of the membrane
    C. Ion channel
    D. Invagination

Problem solved:

C is correct. An ion channel is an entity associated with facilitated transport, not endocytosis. Endocytosis involves invagination, vesicle formation, and pinching off of the membrane. The process is largely mediated by proteins within the cell membrane.

CELLULAR ADHESIONS

While cells can be viewed as discrete living entities, those of the human body are organized into tissues. **Cellular adhesions** join cells together in various ways. In general, there are three types of cellular adhesions: tight junctions, gap junctions, and desmosomes.

Tight junctions link together portions of adjacent cell membranes to form a barrier. At a tight junction, there is no intercellular space. For example, tight junctions maintain the structural integrity of the small intestine's inner surface. There, they form the barrier that prevents the intestinal contents from leaking out between cells.

Gap junctions link together the cytoplasms of adjacent cells, and small particles, such as ions, can flow through them freely. They consist of protein channels that form a bridge between the two cells. Gap junctions are important in heart muscle contraction; they allow the heart's electrical signals to be passed quickly from cell to cell.

Desmosomes are composed of plaquelike proteins embedded in the cell membrane to which the cytoskeleton is attached. Desmosomes are responsible for the structural integrity of most tissues in the human body.

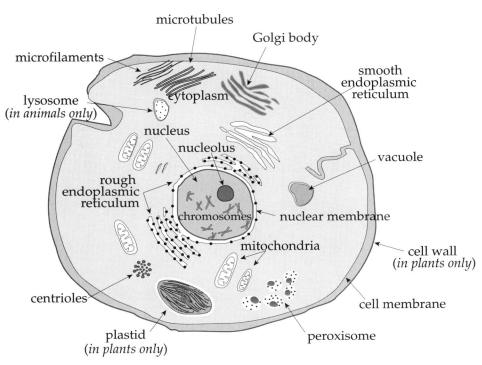

Prototypical Eukaryotic Cell
Figure 23.5

Eukaryotic Cell Organelles

THE CELL MEMBRANE, ENDOPLASMIC RETICULUM, AND GOLGI APPARATUS

You should be familiar with the structure and function of the principal organelles of the eukaryotic cell.

The **endomembrane system** of the cell consists of the outer membrane, located at the cell periphery; the **endoplasmic reticulum**, found throughout the cell cytoplasm; and the **nuclear membrane**, which encloses the cell nucleus. The network of channels that comprises the endoplasmic reticulum (ER) is of two types: **rough endoplasmic reticulum** (rough ER) and **smooth endoplasmic reticulum** (smooth ER). The rough ER is found in close association with **ribosomes**, which function in protein synthesis. *The rough ER constitutes a principal site of cellular protein synthesis,* and its ribosomes are intimately involved in that process. The smooth ER is devoid of ribosomes; smooth ER does not participate in protein synthesis but is involved in lipid synthesis and drug detoxification.

The **Golgi apparatus** is a specialized derivative of the endoplasmic reticulum, consisting of a series of flattened **sacs** rather than channels. It is responsible for packaging and transporting proteins to the cell surface, where they are either expelled into the extracellular space or incorporated into the cell membrane. This transport is accomplished through **vesicles**, which pinch off from the Golgi and migrate to the cell surface. They then fuse with the cell membrane and release their contents through the process of **exocytosis**. The Golgi apparatus is also thought to modify some proteins before expelling them from the cell.

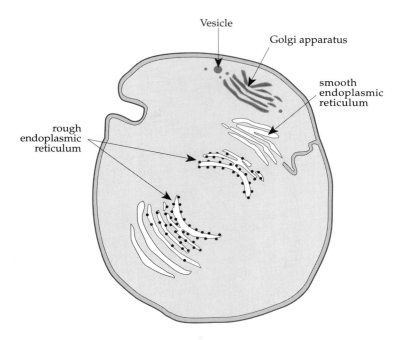

Vesicles, Golgi Apparatus, and Endoplasmic Reticulum

Figure 23.6

Please solve this problem:

- Among the following, which site is most closely associated with protein synthesis in the eukaryotic cell?

   A. The smooth endoplasmic reticulum
   B. The rough endoplasmic reticulum
   C. The nuclear membrane
   D. The Golgi apparatus

Problem solved:

   B is correct. The question asks the student to associate protein synthesis with the appropriate cellular organelle. Protein synthesis occurs on ribosomes, which may exist associated with endoplasmic reticulum, thus forming rough endoplasmic reticulum. (They may also float freely in the cytoplasm.)

Please solve this problem:

- Which among the following is a true statement regarding the Golgi apparatus?

    A. It functions in secretion.
    B. It functions in protein synthesis.
    C. It is a derivative of the nuclear membrane.
    D. It carries ribosomes on its surface.

Problem solved:

A is correct. The Golgi apparatus is a derivative of the endoplasmic reticulum. It does not carry ribosomes. (Ribosomes, if attached to an organelle, are attached to endoplasmic reticulum to form rough endoplasmic reticulum.) The Golgi apparatus forms vesicles that contain secretory proteins, which are then expelled from the cell via exocytosis.

PEROXISOMES, LYSOSOMES, VACUOLES, MITOCHONDRIA, AND PLASTIDS

Cellular organelles include the enzyme containing entities called **peroxisomes** and **lysosomes**. Peroxisomes contain catalase, an enzyme relevant to the processing of hydrogen peroxide. Lysosomes harbor hydrolytic enzymes that digest foreign particles and senescent (aged) organelles. [In plant cells, lysosomes house certain toxins, including alkaloids (primary amines).] **Vacuoles** constitute spaces or vacancies within the cytoplasm. Often they are fluid-filled. In protozoans, they function to expel wastes or excess fluid.

Mitochondria are double-membraned organelles that mediate the synthesis of ATP (adenosine triphosphate), the molecule associated with energy storage, and commonly termed the cell's "energy currency." The **inner mitochondrial membrane** is folded into convolutions called **cristae**. The interior of the inner mitochondrial membrane is termed the **matrix**. The Krebs cycle and oxidative phosphorylation occur within the mitochondria. These processes produce the bulk of the ATP generated in **aerobic** (oxygen-using) organisms. **Glycolysis** is a precursor step to these processes and produces some quantity of ATP. It does not occur in the mitochondria (which means that some ATP is in fact produced *outside* the mitochondria). Indeed, **anaerobic** organisms, which lack mitochondria, can and do conduct glycolysis, but conduct neither the Krebs cycle nor oxidative phosphorylation. Processes that depend on the mitochondria are aerobic; glycolysis is not. You will address cellular respiration and mitochondrial structure and function in greater detail when studying the chapter pertaining to cellular energy.

Plastids, found almost solely in plant cells, contain **pigment** and function in **photosynthesis** as well as in other cellular processes. The most abundant of the plastids are **chloroplasts**, which contain the green pigment **chlorophyll**.

Please solve this problem:

- Autolysis refers to the process by which the cell digests its own structures. Cell death allows the release of material normally sequestered within membrane-bound enclosures. The release of these materials brings on autolysis. Which of the following organelles most likely releases the substances that mediate autolysis?

    A. Plastid
    B. Mitochondrion
    C. Lysosome
    D. Vacuole

Problem solved:

C is correct. The question calls on the test taker to identify a cellular organelle that harbors degradative enzymes. You should recall that lysosomes contain hydrolytic enzymes that, among other things, digest senescent cellular components. Plastids are found in plant cells and do not function in autolysis. Mitochondria function in ATP production. Vacuoles are spaces in the cell cytoplasm that may contain, among other materials, water, food, or wastes.

Please solve this problem:

- Which of the following organelles plays the most direct role in the maintenance of concentration gradients across the cell membrane?
    - A. Vesicle
    - B. Mitochondrion
    - C. Golgi apparatus
    - D. Smooth endoplasmic reticulum

Problem solved:

B is correct. Maintaining a concentration gradient requires the expenditure of energy. ATP, which serves as the source of energy for this and other active processes, is synthesized in the mitochondria

CHROMOSOMES AND THE NUCLEOLUS

Chromosomes, composed of DNA (deoxyribonucleic acid) and proteins, bear the cell's genetic material and reside within the nucleus. Also located in the nucleus is a suborganelle called the **nucleolus.** It is the site of formation of ribosomal ribonucleic acid (rRNA), which functions in the translation of the genetic code. (Later chapters will discuss rRNA more fully.)

CILIA AND FLAGELLA

Cilia and **flagella** are associated with cellular locomotion, but depending on the cell site, they may serve other functions as well. In the human airway, cilia serve to propel foreign particles toward the throat, from which such particles can be expelled or swallowed. In the paramecium, cilia and flagella serve as means of locomotion. The flagellum comprises the tail of a sperm cell and confers motility so that the sperm may reach and fertilize the ovum. Both cilia and flagella are composed of a structured arrangement of **microtubules.**

MICROTUBULES, MICROFILAMENTS, AND CENTRIOLES

Microtubules, as just noted, are the structural basis of cilia and flagella. They are also the main component of **centrioles.** The centriole functions during cell division, assisting in the formation of the **mitotic spindle.** Microtubules are also found in the cytoplasm, where they serve as a quasiskeletal structure for the cell itself (**cytoskeleton**). Microtubules are principally formed of a protein termed **tubulin. Microfilaments,** also found in the cytoplasm, serve as a second element of the cytoskeleton. Microfilaments are composed of the protein **actin.** They also function in cellular movement.

Please solve this problem:

- All of the following structures contain microtubules EXCEPT:

    A. the cytoskeleton.
    B. the mitotic spindle.
    C. cilia.
    D. the nucleolus.

Problem solved:

D is correct. You should be mindful of the multiple functions performed by microtubules and be aware that they are largely composed of the protein tubulin. Single or in groups, microtubules provide the cell and some cell components with form and rigidity. They form the structural basis of the cytoskeleton, cilia, flagella, and the mitotic spindle (which functions during cell division). The nucleolus does not contain microtubules.

Please solve this problem:

- Microtubules and microfilaments are composed primarily of:

    A. phospholipid.
    B. carbohydrate.
    C. protein.
    D. lipopolysaccharide.

Problem solved:

C is correct. Microtubules are composed of the protein tubulin, and microfilaments of the protein actin.

Please solve this problem:

- In chronic obstructive pulmonary disease (COPD), the patient suffers, among other difficulties, an inability to expel mucosal secretion from the airway. Which cellular component is most likely dysfunctional?

    A. The nucleolus
    B. The cilia
    C. The centriole
    D. The mitotic spindle

Problem solved:

B is correct. Cilia may participate in cellular locomotion and, depending on the site of the cells on which they are located, other functions as well. In the human airway, they serve to remove secretions and thus to keep the airway free of obstruction. The nucleolus is located in the nucleus and is the site of the formation of rRNA; the centriole functions in the formation of the mitotic spindle. Neither serves to mediate the expulsion of secretions from the human airway.

23.2 MASTERY APPLIED: PRACTICE PASSAGE AND QUESTIONS

Passage

Two principal organelles of eukaryotic cells are mitochondria and chloroplasts. Mitochondria are found in nearly all eukaryotic cells, and chloroplasts are found in higher plant cells. Both organelles are double-membraned structures that enable the cell to synthesize ATP by way of a series of biochemical reactions. In mitochondria the energy source is food molecules; in chloroplasts the source is radiant energy from the sun.

The evolutionary origins of these organelles are not precisely known. The *endosymbiont theory* maintains that primitive prokaryotic organisms engulfed aerobic bacteria and entered into a symbiotic relationship with them. The high oxygen content of the atmosphere enabled the aerobic bacteria to provide the anaerobic organisms with energy. In turn, the primitive organism provided the bacteria with shelter and protection. Chloroplasts, according to this theory, are descendants of cyanobacteria. The following are two evolutionary biologists' views on the symbiotic theory. One argues in favor of the theory; the other argues against it.

Biologist 1

The symbiotic theory explains why mitochondria and chloroplasts show so many similarities to prokaryotic organisms today. Like free-living prokaryotes, these organelles possess their own DNA and reproduce by binary fission. Furthermore, these organelles are of similar size and shape as prokaryotes. The respiratory apparatus of the cell is located only in the mitochondria; without the mitochondria, the cell could not conduct respiration. Many bacteria also have respiratory capabilities strikingly similar in their mechanism to those of mitochondria.

Biologist 2

Eukaryotes could not have evolved by way of symbiotic arrangement between a prokaryotic anaerobe and an aerobic bacterium. Mitochondria and chloroplasts differ significantly from present-day bacteria. Not only is the quantity of their DNA quite small compared to that of bacteria, but all of the molecules required for their structure must be produced and imported from the rest of the cell.

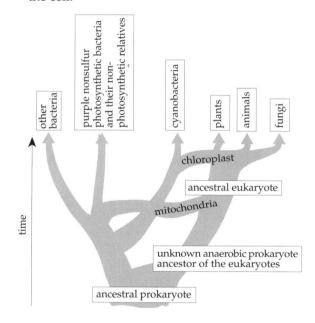

Figure 1

1. If Biologist 1 is correct, then the relationship that ancestral organisms had with aerobic bacteria is an example of:

   A. commensalism.
   B. parasitism.
   C. mutualism.
   D. socialism.

2. Which of the following observations provides the LEAST support for the viewpoint of Biologist 1?

   A. An amoeba exists that does not possess mitochondria but instead harbors aerobic bacteria in a symbiotic relationship.
   B. Some present-day eukaryotic cells contain cyanobacteria.
   C. Chloroplasts carry out photosynthesis in the same manner as cyanobacteria.
   D. Different eukaryotic cells share a number of different organelles that do not occur in prokaryotes.

3. Which of the following processes would be undertaken by a cell in the process of engulfing a bacterium in a symbiotic relationship?

   I. Pinocytosis
   II. Phagocytosis
   III. Endocytosis

   A. II only
   B. III only
   C. I and II only
   D. II and III only

4. Among the following, which explanation would best reconcile the differences in perspectives taken by Biologists 1 and 2?

   A. Mitochondria and chloroplasts represent only two of many different organelles and compartmentalized structures that reside in eukaryotic cells.
   B. Mitochondria and chloroplasts both contain a double membrane, which differs in its molecular makeup from the membrane that surrounds the nucleus.
   C. Mitochondria and chloroplasts may have originated as symbiotic organisms that evolved to become gradually more dependent on their hosts.
   D. Mitochondria and chloroplasts are shown to contain circular DNA, and while bacteria contains comparatively more DNA, its DNA is also circular.

5. A eukaryotic cell that had its mitochondria removed would be capable of carrying out:

   A. only glycolysis, which is an anaerobic process.
   B. only glycolysis, which is an aerobic process.
   C. only glycolysis and the Krebs cycle.
   D. only the Krebs cycle and oxidative phosphorylation, which are both aerobic.

6. Biologist 2 argues against the symbiotic theory based on which of the following criteria?

   A. Mitochondria and chloroplasts evolved from the ingestion of two different bacterial types.
   B. Mitochondria and chloroplasts rely on different energy sources to produce ATP.
   C. Mitochondria and chloroplasts do not contain DNA whereas bacteria do.
   D. Mitochondria and chloroplasts are not entirely self-sufficient organelles.

23.3 MASTERY VERIFIED: ANSWERS AND EXPLANATIONS

1. **C is correct.** The passage states that both members of the symbiotic relationship enjoyed a benefit. Hence the correct answer choice must denote a mutually beneficial relationship. Mutualism describes just such a symbiotic relationship. Two organisms living in mutualistic alliance confer some gain on each other. Commensalism defines a symbiotic relationship in which one member benefits and the other experiences neither benefit nor harm. Parasitism defines a symbiotic relationship in which one member benefits and the other is harmed. Socialism does not constitute a type of symbiosis.

2. **D is correct.** That eukaryotic cells share a variety of organelles represents a true statement, but tends neither to support nor refute the viewpoint at issue. The statement in choice A furnishes evidence of the symbiotic relationship in which Biologist 1 believes. The statement set forth in choice B also supports Biologist 1's thesis: It provides evidence that eukaryotic cells can form a symbiotic relationship with cyanobacteria, consistent with the biologist's view on the origin of chloroplasts. If chloroplasts did arise from cyanobacteria, similarities in their structure and/or function would be expected. Choice C, therefore, also lends support to the thesis.

3. **D is correct.** Pinocytosis, a form of endocytosis, involves cellular ingestion of liquid or small particles. Since the question refers to the ingestion of an entire bacterium, item I is not an accurate statement. Phagocytosis pertains to the ingestion of a foreign particle(s), which might include a bacterium, so item II is true. Phagocytosis is, in fact, a type of endocytosis, and so item III is true as well.

4. **C is correct.** The statement in choice C addresses the apparent discrepancies noted by Biologists 1 and 2. Choice A sets forth a true statement that does not, however, tend to reconcile the conflicting views. Choice B also makes a true statement, but also fails to harmonize the differences between the theories. Choice D, too, offers a true statement. Indeed, it tends to support the view of Biologist 1, but fails to make any point that would bridge the conceptual gap between Biologists 1 and 2.

5. **A is correct.** Glycolysis, an anaerobic process, occurs in the cellular cytoplasm. In the absence of mitochondria, the cell would still be able to conduct glycolysis. Glycolysis is not an aerobic process, which renders choice B incorrect. Although glycolysis can occur in a cell that lacks mitochondria, the Krebs cycle cannot. The Krebs cycle takes place within the mitochondria. Choice C, therefore, is incorrect. Both the Krebs cycle and oxidative phosphorylation are aerobic processes that occur in the mitochondria. If the mitochondria are absent, these processes cannot occur. Choice D is wrong.

6. **D is correct.** The statement forms a part of Biologist 2's argument. Although choice A makes a correct statement, it does not provide a correct answer because it fails to advance Biologist 2's viewpoint. Neither does it represent the criteria upon which she based her conclusion. Choice B also sets forth a true statement, but it neither advances the argument nor represents criteria on which the argument is based. Choice C sets forth a false statement. Both bacteria and the two organelles in question contain DNA. True *or* false, the statement plays no role in Biologist 2's argument.

CHAPTER 24

THE GENETIC MATERIAL: DEOXYRIBONUCLEIC ACID

24.1 MASTERY ACHIEVED

CHROMOSOMES AND GENES

Within the nucleus of a eukaryotic cell are the chromosomes, which are composed of **deoxyribonucleic acid** (**DNA**). A full complement of the organism's chromosomes are present in all of its **somatic** cells (meaning all cells other than the gametes, spermatozoa, and ova discussed in **Chapter 25**). Human chromosomes and those of other higher order eukaryotes generally exist in *pairs* and because of this, the organism is termed *diploid* or 2n. Every human somatic cell has forty-six chromosomes (2n=46), or twenty-three *pairs* of chromosomes. One such pair constitutes the **sex** chromosomes and is a **hemizygous** pair. The remaining twenty-two pairs (sometimes called **autosomes**) are **homologous**, and so we say:

Within the human somatic cell nucleus are forty-six chromosomes organized into twenty-two pairs of homologous chromosomes (or autosomes) and one pair of hemizygous (sex) chromosomes.

The phenomenon of paired chromosomes follows from the fact that eukaryotic organisms generally arise by sexual reproduction, each individual having two parents. For example, chromosome 1 in humans is the largest chromosome, and since humans are diploid, each somatic cell has two copies of chromosome 1. One copy came from an individual's mother and the other came from an individual's father. The same is true for the other chromosomes. Of the forty-six human chromosomes, therefore, twenty-three derive from the father and twenty-three from the mother.

It is important to remember that prokaryotic cells (bacterium) have a genome also, but they have a different structure. In prokaryotic cells, the genome is also composed of double stranded DNA, but there is only one highly coiled, circular chromosome, which is not enclosed in a membrane or nucleus.

Please solve this problem:

- Within a normal human somatic cell nucleus, there are:

  A. twenty-three pairs of genes embodied within the chromosomes.
  B. twenty-three chromosomes composed of deoxyribonucleic acid.
  C. forty-six genes embodied within chromosomes.
  D. forty-six chromosomes composed of deoxyribonucleic acid.

Problem solved:

D is correct. Every normal human somatic cell (meaning cells other than the gametes) has forty-six chromosomes (twenty-three pairs) in the nucleus. Of the twenty-three pairs, twenty-two are said to be homologous. The remaining pair, the sex chromosomes, is said to be hemizygous. Chromosomes are composed of deoxyribonucleic acid (DNA), so in that single regard, choice B is correct. It is incorrect however, because it refers to a total of twenty-three chromosomes when in fact the total is forty-six. Choices A and C are incorrect because the word "gene" does not mean "chromosome." On any chromosome, there are huge numbers of genes.

STRUCTURAL ARRANGEMENT OF CHROMOSOMES AND DNA IN THE EUKARYOTIC CELL

DNA molecules are very long. They fit within the eukaryotic cell nucleus only because they are wrapped and coiled. More specifically, they wrap themselves in a complicated arrangement around packaging proteins called **histones**. Near the time of cell division, the chromosomes wrap around their histones in a highly condensed form that makes the histones visible as discrete units that resemble beads on a string. The visible units of histone are called **nucleosomes**.

Please solve this problem:

- Histones allow for:

    A. mixing of genetic information between and among gene segments.
    B. proper reproduction of chromosomes.
    C. enzyme synthesis within the nucleus.
    D. efficient packaging of the nucleolus.

Problem solved:

B is correct. The cells of complex organisms, such as those of humans, have very long chromosomes. In order for the chromosomes to physically fit within the nucleus and to undergo accurate reproduction, they must be packed efficiently.

Please solve this problem:

- Histones are composed of:

    A. ribonucleic acid.
    B. nitrogen and phosphate.
    C. base pairs.
    D. protein.

Problem solved:

D is correct. Histones are proteins around which deoxyribonucleic acid is wrapped in its complex packaging structure. Histones are the protein component of the chromosome.

Please solve this problem:

- *Nucleosome* refers to:

  A. visible units of nucleotide bases.
  B. visible units of histone protein.
  C. functional units of the nucleolus.
  D. functional units of nuclear membrane.

Problem solved:

B is correct. Just prior to cell division, the eukaryotic cell's chromosomes wrap themselves tightly around their associated histone proteins. At that point, the histones are visible as beadlike units called nucleosomes. Choices A, C, and D make inaccurate statements (and might tempt you only because they share with the word *nucleosome* the root *nucle*).

COMPOSITION AND ARRANGEMENT OF DNA: DEOXYRIBOSE, PHOSPHATE GROUPS, AND NUCLEOTIDE BASE PAIRS

The Basic Picture: Double Helix

Picture an ordinary ladder; horizontal rungs run between two long, parallel upright sides.

A Ladder

Figure 24.1

Now, imagine that someone twists the ladder so that the two upright sides become spirally shaped, each one winding around the other.

A Twisted Ladder

Figure 24.2

You have just conceived a rudimentary picture of the DNA molecule; it looks like a *twisted ladder*. It has two spirally shaped **strands,** with rungs running between them.

Recall now that another word for spirally shaped object is **helix**. For example, the groove that runs up the shaft of a corkscrew is a helix. That means that each of the DNA molecule's two strands constitutes a helix. Since the molecule embodies two such helices, each one wound around the other, we say:

The DNA molecule is a double-stranded molecule in which the two strands form a double helix.

Chemistry of the Double Helix: Deoxyribose, Phosphate Groups, and Nucleotide Base Pairs

In your mind, unwind the double helix and picture it again as a ladder. Each of the two strands comprises a series of **2' deoxy-D-ribose** molecules (often called deoxyribose) bound to one another by **phosphodiester bonds**. In other words, the backbone strands of DNA are made of alternating units of deoxyribose and phosphate, so that in a schematic diagram, they look like this:

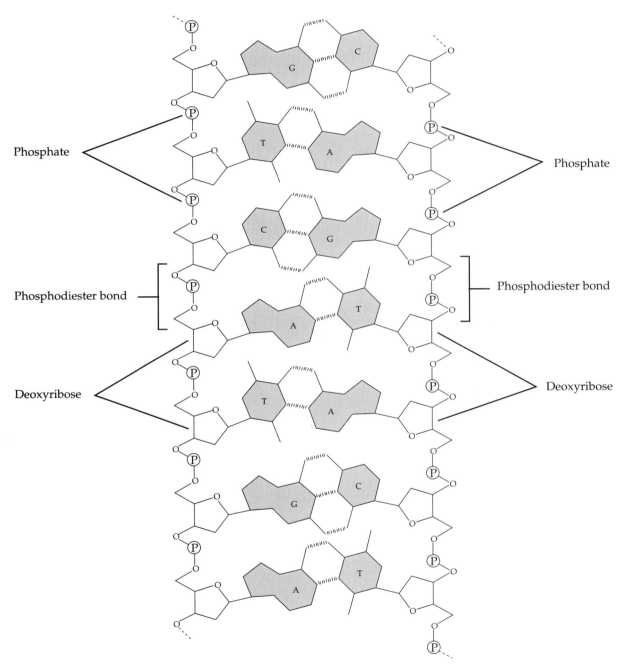

Deoxyribose-Phosphate "Backbone" of DNA Molecule

Figure 24.3

Deoxyribose is a sugar or carbohydrate, and the DNA molecule's deoxyribose phosphate entity is sometimes called its **sugar-phosphate backbone**.

Running between opposing units on each strand (analogous to the ladder's "rungs") are pairs of nitrogenous heterocyclic bases, one base attached to each strand. Each base, attached to a sugar and phosphate group, is a **nucleotide,** sometimes called a "base."

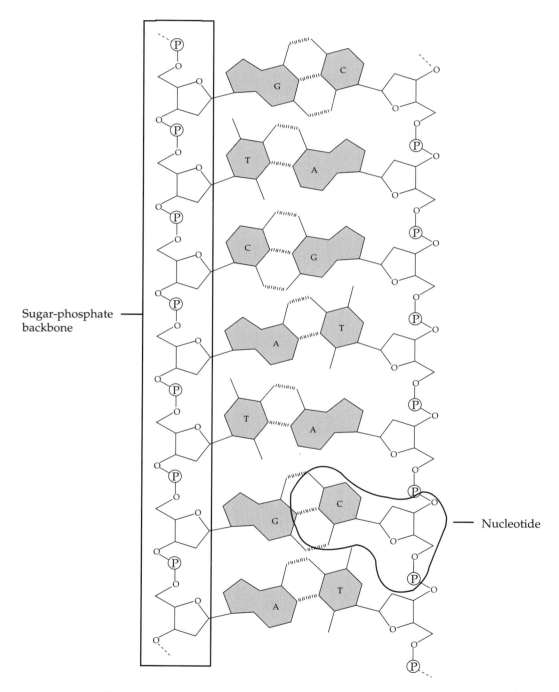

Deoxyribose-Phosphate Strands Joined by Nucleotides ("Bases")

Figure 24.4

The DNA molecule features four different nitrogenous bases. Two are **purines** and two are **pyrimidines**. In alphabetical order, the four nucleotides found in DNA are:

(1) adenine (A)   — a purine

(2) cytosine (C)   — a pyrimidine

(3) guanine (G)   — a purine

(4) thymine (T)   — a pyrimidine

A useful way to remember the purines and pyrimidines is the following:

Pure silver (silver is Ag on the periodic table): the **pur**ines are **A**denine and **G**uanine

You **CUT** a "pye": the pyrimidines are **C**ytosine, **U**racil (in RNA), and **T**hymine

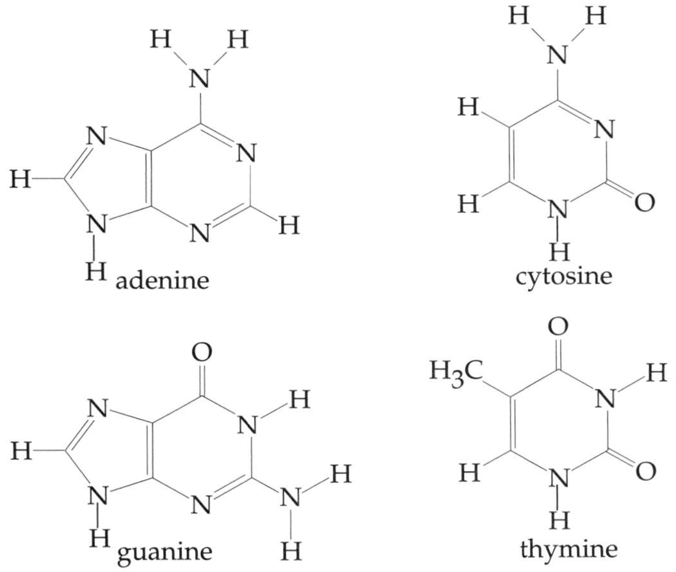

DNA Bases: Adenine, Cytosine, Guanine, Thymine

Figure 24.5

Please solve this problem:

- On one strand of a DNA molecule, units of the sugar-phosphate backbone are bound together by:

    A. dipole–dipole interactions.
    B. hydrogen bonds.
    C. phosphodiester bonds.
    D. noncovalent bonds.

Problem solved:

C is correct. The DNA strand backbone is made of alternating units of deoxyribose and phosphate, bound together by a phosphodiester bond. Phosphodiester bonds are covalent (D is incorrect) and are not an example of dipole–dipole interactions (A is incorrect). Hydrogen bonds do function in holding nucleotide base pairs together (as explained immediately below), but they do not serve directly in the structure of the sugar-phosphate backbone (B is incorrect).

Base-Pairing between Purines and Pyrimidines

On each strand of the DNA molecule, a nitrogenous base (either purine or a pyrimidine) is bound to each deoxyribose-phosphate unit. Across the rungs of the ladder, nucleotides pair according to this simple rule: Each purine pairs with (or is complementary to) a pyrimidine:

the purine **adenine (A)** *pairs with* the pyrimidine **thymine (T)**, and

the purine **guanine (G)** *pairs with* the pyrimidine **cytosine (C)**.

These are the rules of base-pairing (or nucleotide pairing) and you'll easily remember them by (a) listing the four nucleotides in alphabetical order, and (b) remembering that the one at the top of the list pairs with the one at the bottom, while the two in the middle of the list pair with each other. The rules of base-pairing arise partly from **steric hindrance**, or size restrictions regarding the structure of the different bases and the spaces available to them. Since the purines are composed of two rings and the pyrimidines have just one ring (see Figure 24.5), the complementary bases across the rungs of the ladder must always have one of each for the backbone to be parallel. If a purine paired with a purine, the backbone of the DNA would have to kink outwards to accommodate four rings; if a purimidine paired with a purimidine, the DNA backbond would have to kink inwards.

A small sequence of a DNA molecule (untwisted in our minds) might, therefore look like this:

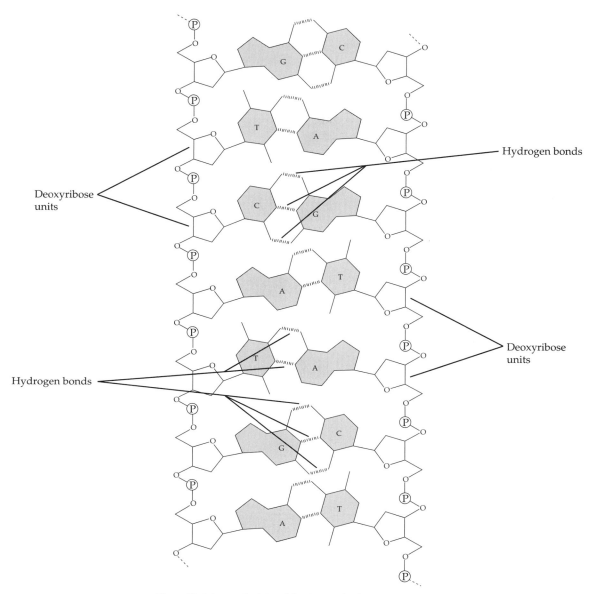

Base-Pairing of a Double-Stranded DNA Molecule

Figure 24.6

Each base pair is joined by hydrogen bonds (represented in Figure 24.6 by the hatched lines between nucleotide pairs). When adenine and thymine pair, *two* hydrogen bonds form to join them. When guanine and cytosine pair, *three* hydrogen bonds form to join them. Hydrogen bonds do not offer the strength of true covalent bonds, but by their large number, they impart considerable support to the DNA molecule (just as they produce a high degree of surface tension for an aggregation of water molecules).

The backbone of every strand of a DNA molecule is the same: It is made of deoxyribose units joined by phosphodiester bonds. DNA molecules can differ from each other in the ordering of the nitrogenous bases bound to the strands (and, consequently, the ordering of nucleotide pairs). For example, if a DNA molecule had the nucleotide sequence:

(5') - T   A   G   T   G - (3')

according to the base-pairing rules discussed above, the other deoxyribose-phosphate strand of that same DNA molecule would carry a complementary nucleotide sequence:

(3') - A   T   C   A   C - (5')

Because any two deoxyribose-phosphate strands might differ in their order of nucleotides, we say that the portion of the DNA molecule that presents its sequence of nucleotides (the ladder's rungs) constitutes its **variable region**. The DNA molecule's deoxyribose-phosphate component (the sides or backbone of the ladder) is not variable.

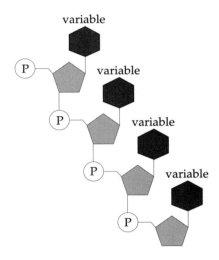

One Strand of a DNA Molecule (with Molecular Detail Removed):
The Nucleotide Sequence Represents the Variable Region

Figure 24.7

Please solve this problem:

- Adenine and guanine are:

    A. purines.
    B. pyrimidines.
    C. histones.
    D. nucleosomes.

Problem solved:

A is correct. Adenine and guanine are nitrogenous bases that belong to the purine category. The purimidines are C, U, and T (B is incorrect). Histones are protein components of the chromosome that play a role in structure and packing (C is incorrect). Nucleosomes represent discrete packaging units within the chromosome. They are not *functional* units (D is incorrect).

Please solve this problem:

- Which of the following represents a correct base pairing within a DNA molecule?

    A. Adenine – guanine
    B. Adenine – cytosine
    C. Cytosine – thymine
    D. Thymine – adenine

Problem solved:

D is correct. In the formation of base pairs, a purine always bonds with a pyrimidine. More specifically, in the DNA molecule, adenine bonds to thymine (via two hydrogen bonds) and cytosine bonds to guanine (via three hydrogen bonds).

Please solve this problem:

- Matched bases within a base pair are linked by:

    A. nonpolar covalent bonds.
    B. polar covalent bonds.
    C. hydrogen bonds.
    D. ionic bonds.

Problem solved:

C is correct. Within the DNA molecule, matched bases are linked by hydrogen bonds. Although these are not as strong as any of the other bonds listed in the answer choices, their large number affords the DNA molecule significant structural integrity and support.

Please solve this problem:

- Which of the following is true of DNA in a double helix?

    A. It is devoid of carbohydrate.
    B. It consists of two complementary strands.
    C. It is composed of phospholipid.
    D. It is single-stranded.

Problem solved:

B is correct. DNA in a double helix is a double-stranded molecule (B is correct and D is incorrect). Each strand is complementary to the other. DNA contains deoxyribose, which is a sugar or carbohydrate (A is incorrect). DNA is not composed of phospholipid, which is the main component in cell membranes.

As just noted, each strand of a double-stranded DNA molecule is the *complement* of the other. Because of the rules of base-pairing, the sequence of bases arranged on one strand dictates the sequence of matching bases situated on the complementary strand. Hence, a region of one DNA strand that reads:

(5') -   G   C   A   A   C   - (3')

will correspond to a complementary strand bearing the sequence:

(3') -   C   G   T   T   G   - (5')

Please solve this problem:

- If one strand of a DNA molecule shows the base sequence (5') - A G A T - (3'), its complementary strand will show the sequence:

    A. (3') - CCTA - (5')
    B. (3') - AAGA - (5')
    C. (3') - TCTA - (5')
    D. (3') - CTTG - (5')

Problem solved:

C is correct. According to the DNA base-pairing rules, adenine (a purine) pairs with thymine (a pyrimidine) and cytosine (a pyrimidine) pairs with guanine (a purine). Therefore, the sequence adenine-guanine-adenine-thymine pairs with the sequence thymine-cytosine-thymine-adenine.

Please solve this problem:

- The variable region of a DNA molecule carries:

    A. deoxyribose.
    B. purines and pyrimidines.
    C. histones.
    D. nucleosomes.

Problem solved:

B is correct. The backbone of DNA (deoxyribose and phosphate) is invariable (A is incorrect). The variability in DNA sequences is due to the order of the nitrogenous bases (B is correct), or the order of nucleotides. Recall that histones and nucleosomes have to do with chromosomal packing and organization (C and D are incorrect).

ORIENTATION OF DEOXYRIBOSE STRANDS: ANTIPARALLELISM

Look again at Figure 24.6 and examine the strand on the right. Each of the deoxyribose units is a five-membered ring. Each ring contains (a) one oxygen atom and (b) four carbon atoms, and is bound to a fifth carbon atom off the ring.

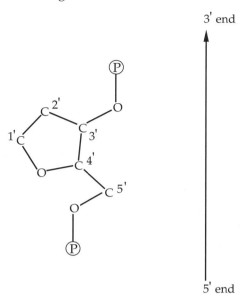

A Deoxyribose Unit from the Right Side of Figure 24.6

Figure 24.8

As shown in Figure 24.8, the carbon atoms associated with the deoxyribose unit are numbered 1'–5'. The carbon bound to the nucleotide unit is number 1'. Then, moving clockwise, the next three carbon atoms are numbered 2' to 4'. The carbon atom located off the ring is number 5'. Notice that for the backbone on the right of Figure 24.6, on each deoxyribose unit, carbon number 3' is located on the upward side of the ring and is bound by a phosphodiester bond to carbon number 5' of the next deoxyribose unit above it.

The deoxyribose units in the backbone on the left of Figure 24.6 have the same structure (a five-membered ring with one oxygen atom and four carbon atoms, and a fifth carbon outside the ring; the carbons are numbered the same way). However, the deoxyribose sugars on the left are upside down compared to the deoxyribose sugars on the right. On each deoxyribose unit, carbon 3' is located on the downward side of the ring and is bound by a phosphodiester bond to carbon 5' of the next deoxyribose unit below it.

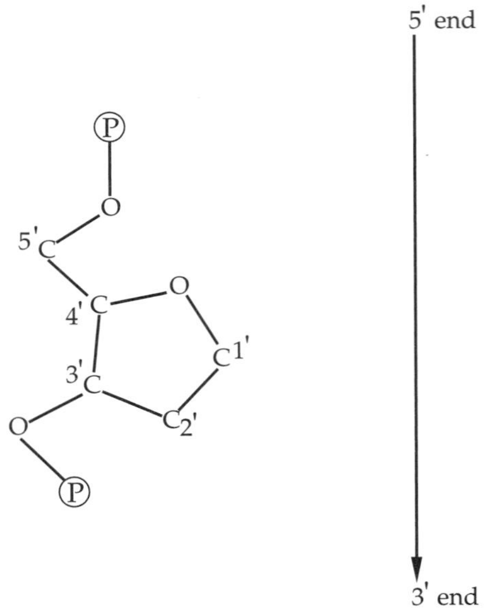

A Deoxyribose Unit from the Left Side of Figure 24.6

Figure 24.9

The orientation of the deoxyribose is how we name the direction of a DNA strand. For example, since carbon 3' is above carbon 5' in the backbone on the right of Figure 24.6, we say that the bottom of this diagram is the 5' end of the DNA and the top of the diagram is the 3' end of the DNA. The strand runs in the 5' to 3' direction *from its lower end to its upper end*. The opposite is true of the backbone on the left (Figure 24.9): the 5' end is at the top and the 3' end is at the bottom. The strand runs in the 5' to 3' *from its upper to its lower ends*. For this reason, we say the two complementary strands on a DNA molecule show **antiparallel orientation:** One strand runs in the 5' to 3' from downward to upward, and the other runs in the 5' to 3' from upward to downward.

Please solve this problem:

- Which of the following properly describes the anti-parallel structure of a DNA molecule?

    A. Base-pairing rules require that purines pair with pyrimidines and pyrimidines with purines.
    B. Complementary strands show opposite orientation in terms of their 3' and 5' carbon ends.
    C. Each complementary strand has a 3' carbon at its bottom end and a 5' carbon at its top end.
    D. Complementary strands will not bond unless bases are matched purine to purine and pyrimidine to pyrimidine.

Problem solved:

B is correct. Antiparallelism refers to the orientation of the two sugar-phosphate backbones with respect to each other in a DNA molecule. Specifically, it refers to how the backbone is oriented with respect to its 3' and 5' carbon ends. The 3' end of one strand is associated with the 5' end of the complement. Choice A makes a true statement, but it is not relevant to the concept of antiparallelism. Both choice C and D are false statements.

CHROMOSOMAL REPLICATION

Cells must duplicate their genome (or chromosomes) prior to mitosis. The replication of a chromosome requires the replication of DNA. DNA replication (also called DNA synthesis) occurs in the S phase of the cell cycle (see Chapter 25).

DNA Replication

DNA replication begins at the Origin of Replication (or Ori), a specific sequence of nucleotides that are the signal to start DNA synthesis. First, the DNA strands must be unwound; this is facilitated by **helicase** enzymes. The hydrogen bonds that join base pairs rupture, and the molecule's two strands are separated. The two deoxyribose-phosphate strands do not fully separate before daughter strands begin to form. Rather, they partially diverge at what is called a **replication bubble**, which has two **replication forks** (Figure 24.10).

Each strand, sometimes called a parent strand, then serves as a **template** for the production of a new daughter strand complementary to it. Synthesis of the new strand is accomplished by a family of enzymes called **DNA polymerases**, which read the template strand and synthesize a new complementary daughter strand. In order to begin synthesis, DNA polymerases require a primer. This is accomplished by an enzyme named **primase**, which lays down short RNA primers so DNA polymerases can begin.

DNA polymerases are one-way enzymes; they read the DNA template in the 3' to 5' direction and synthesize DNA in the 5' to 3' direction (that is to say, DNA polymerases make the 5' end of the new DNA strand first, and add new nucleotides onto the 3' end of a strand). Nucleotides (composed of phosphate-deoxyribose-nitrogenous base) are aligned along the template according to the base-pairing rules discussed earlier. Then, deoxyribose units are joined by phosphodiester bonds, paired nucleotides are joined by hydrogen bonds, and for each template there results a new double-stranded molecule. Because each of the newly formed molecules contains half of the original DNA molecule, replication is said to be **semiconservative**.

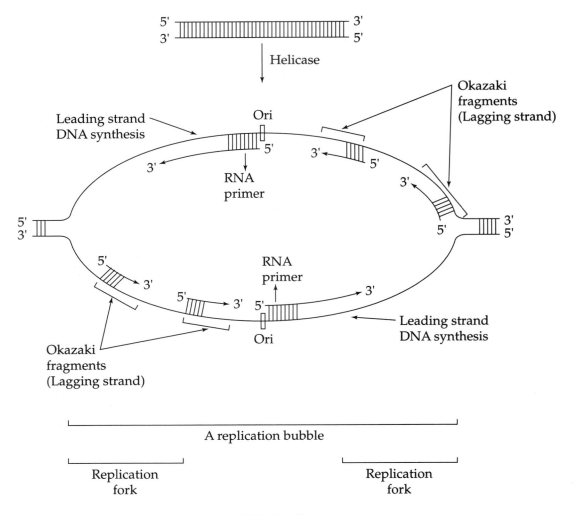

DNA Replication

Figure 24.10

The Polarity Problem and Its Solution

There are three directional concepts to keep in mind:

(1) Recall that the DNA molecule's two deoxyribose-phosphate strands lie in antiparallel orientation. As depicted in Figure 24.10, the top strand runs in the 5' to 3' direction from left to right, and the bottom strand runs in the 5' to 3' direction from right to left (this is the convention when drawing double stranded DNA).

(2) The replication forks at either end of the replication bubble open in opposite directions; the fork on the left will continue opening to the left and the fork on the right will continue opening to the right.

(3) DNA polymerases synthesize DNA in one direction only: 5' to 3'. As mentioned above, a newly growing nucleotide chain does NOT take on new nucleotide units at its 5' end, but rather at its 3' end. DNA polymerases will add nucleotide units only to the 3' end of the growing chain. In other words, when a DNA template strand causes the synthesis of a new nucleotide chain, the new chain grows in the **5' to 3' direction** (meaning that the growth "front" is at the 3' end of the newly

developing chain). On the top strand in Figure 24.10, DNA polymerases will read from right to left because they must read the template from 3' to 5'. On the bottom strand of Figure 24.10, DNA polymerases will read from left to right.

These three directional concepts lead to the difference between leading strand synthesis and lagging strand synthesis. Return to Figure 24.10: For DNA synthesis from the top strand template and to the left of the Ori, there are no issues; the replication fork is opening to the left and DNA synthesis is happening in this direction also. For DNA synthesis from the bottom strand template and to the right of the Ori, the same is true. The replication fork is opening to the right and DNA synthesis via DNA polymerases is happening in the same direction. We call these two the **leading strands**. For leading strand synthesis, the 3' of the new strand (the end of that is being added onto by DNA polymerases) is leading into the replication fork.

This is not the case for the other two strands (top template to the right of the Ori, and bottom template to the left of the Ori). For these two strands, the cell faces a **polarity problem**: the replication fork is opening one direction and DNA can only be synthesized in the opposite direction. These strands are presenting the 5' end of the new daughter strand to the replication fork but DNA polymerases cannot add nucleotides to this end. For example, the replication fork on the right of Figure 24.10 is opening to the right. However, synthesis from the top strand template must occur from right to left.

The only way around this is to synthesize the new DNA in fragments. Primase lays down a short primer and DNA polymerases create a new fragment of DNA by reading away from the replication fork (still synthesizing in the 5' to 3' direction). As the fork opens, another primer is laid down and another fragment is synthesized. These fragments are called **Okazaki fragments** and constitute the **lagging strand**. The production of a nucleotide chain via Okazaki fragments is called **semidiscontinuous** synthesis and this mechanism of synthesis solves the polarity problem. Fragments are then joined, by DNA ligase to generate a continuous DNA strand.

In summary, DNA replication occurs in the following steps:

(1) The Ori is recognized on the DNA strand.

(2) The DNA strands are separated via helicase.

(3) A replication bubble is formed, with two replication forks.

(4) RNA primers are laid down by primase.

(5) DNA polymerases read the template strand (in the 3' to 5' direction) and synthesizes a new complementary strand (in the 5' to 3' direction). This can occur in a continuous way (as in the leading strand) or via a semidiscontinuous mechanism (as in the lagging strand).

(6) Okazaki fragments of the lagging strand are joined by DNA ligase.

(7) The RNA primers are removed and replaced with DNA (this is done by DNA polymerases).

Please solve this problem:

- DNA polymerases catalyze:

 A. addition of a nucleotide residue at the 3' end of a growing chain of nucleotide residues.
 B. addition of a nucleotide residue at the 5' end of a growing chain of nucleotide residues.
 C. the synthesis of purines.
 D. the synthesis of pyrimidines.

Problem solved:

A is correct. Notice that choices A and B are opposites. DNA polymerases catalyze the polymerization of DNA subunits by adding to the growing chain of nucleotide residues one at a time. The chain is elongated in the 5' to 3' direction, meaning that each new nucleotide unit is added to the 3' end of the growing chain (A is correct and B is incorrect). Choices C and D are wrong because the synthesis of purines and pyrimidines (the nucleotides themselves) is not a part of DNA polymerization and is not catalyzed by DNA polymerases.

Please solve this problem:

- The need for semidiscontinuous synthesis of one DNA daughter strand arises because of the:

 A. pairing phenomena associated with purines and pyrimidines.
 B. antiparallel orientation of the two parent strands.
 C. hydrogen bonding between nucleotide base pairs.
 D. ability of DNA polymerases to add nucleotides to the 3' end or 5' end of a growing DNA polymer.

Problem solved:

B is correct. The two strands of a DNA molecule are oriented in antiparallel fashion. Because of this, at a given replication fork, one of the daughter strands will be synthesized in the same direction as the fork opening (the leading strand). The other must be made in fragments since the fork is opening one way and DNA replication must occur in the opposite direction. That is the essence of semidiscontinuous synthesis, and it is necessitated by the antiparallel orientation of the parental DNA strands (coupled with the _inability_ of DNA polymerases to add nucleotide units to the 5' end of a growing chain). Options A and B are not relevant to the question and option D is a false statement; DNA polymerases will add nucleotides only to the 3' end of a growing DNA polymer.

Conventional Expression of Nucleotide Sequence: 5' to 3' Direction

When we describe a DNA nucleotide sequence, convention dictates that we order the nucleotides from the molecule's 5' end to its 3' end. Consider again the DNA nucleotide sequence described earlier in the chapter, this time with its 5' and 3' ends identified.

(5') - T   A   G   T   G   - (3')

We previously stated that the complementary strand would appear thus:

(3') - A   T   C   A   C   - (5')

Conceptually, that is correct; thymine pairs with adenine and guanine pairs with cytosine. However, the complementary sequence shown above is shown with its 3' end on the left and its 5' end on the right. If we wish to describe the daughter strand in *conventional fashion,* ordering its nucleotide units in the 5' to 3' direction, we would turn it around and write it like this:

(5') - C   A   C   T   A   - (3')

Please solve this problem:

- With regard to DNA replication, the term *template* refers to the:

  A. role of enzymes in unwinding the molecule to be replicated.
  B. role of the parent strand in directing formation of a new complementary strand.
  C. elongation of a growing DNA strand.
  D. phosphodiester bonding that secures the sugar phosphate backbone of a new DNA molecule.

Problem solved:

B is correct. The process of chromosomal reproduction involves DNA replication. Each strand of the molecule to be replicated is called a parent strand and serves as a template that directs the production of a complementary daughter strand. Regarding choice D, phosphodiester bonds do secure the sugar-phosphate backbone, but this is not relevant to the definition of the template. Regarding choice A, enzymes do unwind the DNA molecule to be reproduced, but this is also not relevant to the definition of the template.

Please solve this problem:

- Synthesis of a daughter DNA strand is facilitated most directly by:

  A. a phospholipid-protein backbone.
  B. a cleaving enzyme.
  C. a helicase enzyme.
  D. a polymerase enzyme.

Problem solved:

D is correct. DNA polymerases synthesize the daughter DNA strands by reading the parental templates. Phospholipids are not part of DNA structure, although phosphodiester bonds do join adjacent nucleotide units (A is incorrect). DNA replication does not involve a cleaving enzyme (B is incorrect) and helicase enzymes facilitate the unwinding of the original DNA molecule to be replicated (C is incorrect).

Please solve this problem:

- With respect to chromosomal replication, a replication *fork* represents:

    A. the creation of Ozaki fragments that oppose the synthesis of nucleotide chains in the 5' to 3' direction.

    B. divergence of two parent strands, each of which then serves as a template for the creation of a new daughter strand.

    C. a catalytic addition of nucleotide units to the 5' end of a newly developing daughter strand.

    D. the joining of two parent strands to create a single new daughter strand.

Problem solved:

B is correct. The replication fork is the area at which two parent DNA strands separate (diverge), each one then to serve as a template from which a new daughter strand is created. On the newly growing strand, a new nucleotide is added to the 3' end of the growing chain; chain synthesis is catalyzed by DNA polymerases, which do not add nucleotides to the growing chain's 5' end (A and C are incorrect).

Please solve this problem:

- Okazaki fragments:

    A. facilitate semidiscontinuous synthesis on the lagging strand.

    B. are synthesized in the 3' to 5' direction.

    C. cannot be incorporated into newly forming daughter strands.

    D. contain neither purines nor pyrimidines.

Problem solved:

A is correct. On the leading daughter strand (the one that presents its 3' end to the replication fork) nucleotide chain synthesis and overall assembly proceed in the same direction. On the lagging daughter strand (the one that presents its 5' end to the replication fork), small fragments of nucleotide chains are synthesized to facilitate semidiscontinuous synthesis as is stated in choice A. Choice B is wrong because Okazaki fragments are synthesized in the 5' to 3' direction; DNA polymerases will have it no other way. Choice C is wrong because Okazaki fragments are incorporated into the newly forming daughter strand; such is the essence of semidiscontinuous synthesis. Choice D is wrong because an Okazaki fragment is a small chain of nucleotides, and every nucleotide contains either a purine or pyrimidine.

Please solve this problem:

- In conventional fashion, describe the nucleotide sequence of a daughter strand that follows from a template bearing this nucleotide sequence: (5') -T A G C G G T T A - (3').

Problem solved:

The base-pairing rules are clear. Thymine pairs with adenine, and guanine pairs with cytosine. The resulting complement is: (3') - A T C G C C A A T - (5'). Expressed in conventional fashion, from 5' end to 3' end, however, the sequence is expressed: (5') - T A A C C G C T A - (3') or, simply, T A A C C G C T A.

FROM DNA TO RNA: TRANSCRIPTION

RNA vs. DNA

Chromosomes serve their critical function within the cell (and the organism) by mediating the synthesis of **ribonucleic acid (RNA)**. Both DNA and RNA are nucleic acids, polymers composed of nucleotide monomers. However, there are some differences between them:

Characteristic	DNA	RNA
Sugar in the backbone	Deoxyribose (no OH on the 2' carbon of ribose)	Ribose (has an OH on the 2' carbon of ribose)
Pyrimidines	Cytosine and thymine	Cytosine and uracil
Strandedness	Usually double-stranded (except in some viruses)	Usually single-stranded
Stability	More stable	Less stable
Lifespan in the cell	Permanent	Transient

Table 24.1

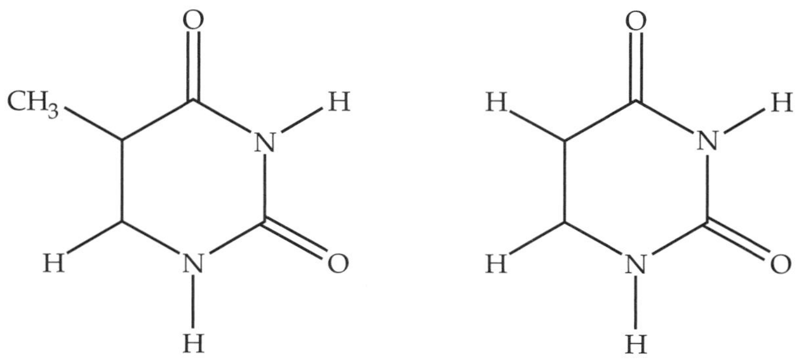

In RNA, Uracil (right) is Substituted for Thymine (left)

Figure 24.11

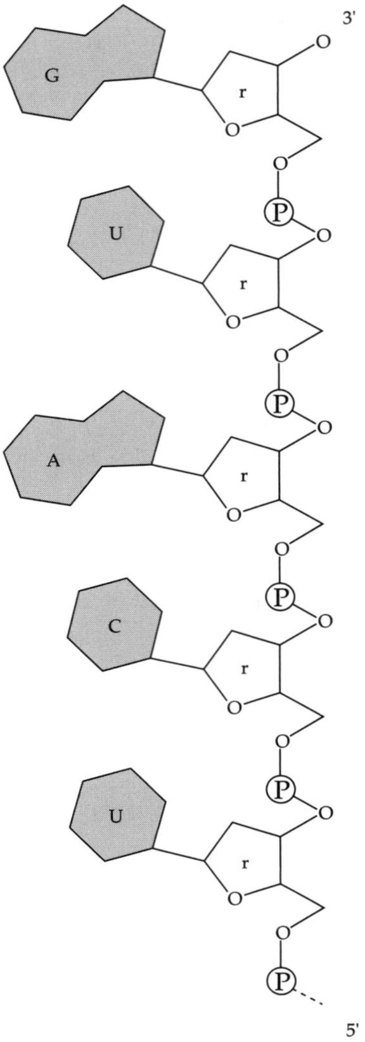

Portion of an RNA Molecule

Figure 24.12

RNA, therefore, is a nucleic acid composed of a sugar-phosphate backbone in which the sugar component is ribose. Bound to each ribose unit of the backbone is one of the four nitrogenous bases:

(1) adenine (A) a purine,

(2) cytosine (C) a pyrimidine,

(3) guanine (G) a purine, or

(4) uracil (U) a pyrimidine.

There are three common forms of RNA, each differing from the other in their function(s). Beyond the three well-recognized types, there are additional forms of RNA that serve enzymatic roles. The three predominant types of RNA are:

(1) ribosomal RNA (rRNA),

(2) transfer RNA (tRNA), and

(3) messenger RNA (mRNA).

In the synthesis of either of the three types of RNA, DNA serves as a template, and the process is termed **transcription**. Transcription is similar (but not identical) to DNA replication. Both DNA replication and transcription begin with separating the DNA molecule's two strands. In DNA replication, *both* strands serve as templates for the synthesis of a new DNA strand. In transcription, *one* of the strands serves as a template for the synthesis of an RNA molecule. The same base pairing rules apply to DNA replication and transcription, except in DNA replication thymine is used, and in transcription, uracil is used. For example, if some portion of a DNA template carries the nucleotide sequence:

(5') -　　T　　G　　A　　C　　A　　- (3')

then the complementary sequence of the newly formed RNA molecule would be:

(3') -　　A　　C　　U　　G　　U　　- (5')

or, expressed in conventional 5' to 3' direction:

(5') -　　U　　G　　U　　C　　A　　- (3')

Because RNA is a single-stranded molecule, it results from the reading of only one DNA strand; between the two strands of DNA, only one serves as template for RNA synthesis. The other one is complementary to the template, just like the RNA will be complementary to the template. Because of this, the DNA strands are given names: The one that serves as a template and is actually read and transcribed is called the template, the **non-coding strand** or the **anti-sense** strand. The other strand that does *not* serve as template is called the **coding strand** or **sense strand**.

Those labels seem paradoxical at first. Why should the strand that does *not* serve as template be called the *coding strand* and the one that *does* serve as template be termed the *non-coding* strand? The explanation relates to the phenomena of base pairing and complementary sequencing. Suppose the DNA strand that does not serve as template has the nucleotide sequence (5') - A T C A G A T - (3'). The complementary DNA strand—the one that serves as template—will have the sequence (5') - A T C T G A T - (3'), written in the conventional fashion. Transcription of the template strand will generate an RNA polymer with the nucleotide sequence (5') -A U C A G A U - (3'). If you compare the sequence of the non-template DNA (5' - A T C A G A T - 3') and the sequence of the RNA transcript (5' - A U C A G A U - 3'), you will notice that except for the fact that uracil replaces thymine, the nucleotide sequences are the same. This is because both the non-template strand and the RNA transcript are complementary to the template strand. The strand that did not serve as template is called the coding strand because its sequence is analogous to that of the new RNA molecule. The DNA strand that did serve as template is called the anti-coding strand; its nucleotide sequence is complementary to that of the new RNA molecule.

Recall that DNA polymerases generated the new daughter strands in DNA replication. In transcription, formation of an RNA polymer is catalyzed by enzymes called **RNA polymerases.** These two enzymes are similar in their mechanism of action; both DNA polymerases and RNA polymerases add nucleotides to the 3' end of the growing chain. Therefore, the template DNA is read in the 3' to 5' direction and the new nucleic acid molecule is synthesized in the 5' to 3' direction.

Please solve this problem:

- Among the similarities between DNA and RNA are that both molecules:

    A. include the pyrimidine thymine.
    B. include the sugar deoxyribose.
    C. are ordinarily double-stranded.
    D. are formed from DNA templates.

Problem solved:

D is correct. Choices A, B, and C all make false statements because they reflect where RNA and DNA *differ*. DNA includes the pyrimidine thymine, but RNA includes the pyrimidine uracil instead (A is incorrect). DNA has the sugar deoxyribose in the backbone, but RNA contains ribose instead (B is incorrect). DNA is ordinarily double-stranded, but RNA is ordinarily single-stranded (C is incorrect). Both DNA and RNA *are* formed from DNA templates. In DNA replication, each parent strand serves as a template for the formation of a new daughter strand. In RNA synthesis (transcription), one DNA strand serves as template for an RNA molecule.

Please solve this problem:

- What is the nucleotide sequence for an mRNA molecule transcribed from a DNA template with this nucleotide sequence: (5') - T A G C G G C T T A - (3')?

Problem solved:

Like any RNA molecule, messenger RNA has a nucleotide sequence complementary to that of the DNA template from which it is transcribed. According to the base-pairing rules, cytosine on the DNA template codes for a unit of guanine on the newly forming RNA molecule. Guanine on the DNA template codes for cytosine on the RNA polymer. Thymine on DNA codes for adenine on RNA. Adenine on DNA codes for uracil on RNA. Consequently, this template:

(5') - T A G C G G C T T A - (3')

codes for this RNA transcript:

(3') - A U C G C C G A A U - (5').

Expressed in conventional fashion (5' end to 3' end), the RNA polymer shows the sequence:

(5') - U A A G C C G C U A - (3')

Please solve this problem:

- If the process of transcription creates an RNA polymer with nucleotide sequence (5') - G A U U G G C A A C - (3'), the coding strand of DNA (*expressed in the conventional 5' to 3' direction*) has the nucleotide sequence:

    A. (5') - G A T T G G C A A C - (3').
    B. (5') - C A A C G G T T A G - (3').
    C. (5') - G A U U G G C A A C - (3').
    D. (5') - C A A C G G U U A G - (3').

Problem solved:

A is correct. An RNA molecule is complementary to the non-coding template strand of DNA, and is identical (except for the thymine/uracil switch) to the coding DNA strand. Therefore, for the RNA sequence in this question, the coding DNA strand (written in the conventional way) is (5') - G A T T G G C A A C - (3') and the non-coding template is (5') - G T T G C C A A T C - (3').

Please solve this problem:

- Transcription differs from DNA replication in that transcription:

  A. involves chain elongation in the 5' to 3' direction.
  B. does not involve base-pairing between cytosine and guanine residues.
  C. does not involve base-pairing between purine and pyrimidine residues.
  D. produces a single-stranded end product.

Problem solved:

D is correct. Transcription is the process whereby a DNA template, derived from a double-stranded DNA molecule, produces a single-stranded RNA molecule. Base-pairing rules are analogous (but not identical) to those of DNA replication. The purines adenine and guanine pair with the pyrimidines, cytosine and uracil, which makes choices B and C incorrect. In both DNA replication and transcription, polymer (chain) elongation proceeds in the 5' to 3' direction (A is incorrect). The product of transcription is a molecule of RNA, which is single-stranded. The product of DNA replication is a new molecule of DNA, which is double-stranded. Choice D, therefore, describes a difference between the two processes.

Prokaryotic Transcription in Detail

Transcription occurs in four steps: (1) **template recognition**, (2) **initiation**, (3) **elongation**, and (4) **termination**. This process was first studied and understood in bacteria or **prokaryotic cells** (see Chapter 27). The details of prokaryotic transcription are described below. At the end of this section, transcription in prokaryotic and eukaryotic cells will be compared.

DETAILS OF TEMPLATE RECOGNITION

RNA polymerase in prokaryotes is an elaborate enzyme complex that has four subunits: two alpha subunits, a beta subunit and a beta' subunit ($\alpha_2\beta\beta'$); this is the **core enzyme**. The core enzyme can synthesize RNA but cannot initiate transcription. The binding of RNA polymerase to the DNA template is mediated by an additional subunit, the sigma factor. The sigma factor can be recruited to the core enzyme and can leave the core enzyme.

RNA polymerase binds DNA at the **promoter sequence** or **promoter site**. The promoter is a particular sequence of nucleotide pairs that are part of the DNA molecule itself. The promoter determines which DNA strand is the template, where transcription starts and the direction of transcription.

To describe the location of the promoter on the DNA molecule, we must introduce the terms **upstream** and **downstream**. With respect to transcription, one strand (the anti-coding or anti-sense strand) serves as template and the other (the coding strand) does not. When transcription is discussed, by convention, we refer to sites on the DNA molecule according to the coding strand—

the one that does not serve as template. More specifically, we refer to the coding strand in terms of "upstream" and "downstream" directions. The upstream direction points toward the 5' end of the coding strand and the downstream direction points toward its 3' end.

In many bacteria, the promoter occupies a site that begins approximately forty base pairs upstream of the start site and ends at the start site; the start site is where RNA synthesis begins. In order words, the promoter site is a sequence approximately forty base pairs in length. Different bacteria differ as to the base pairs that constitute the promoter, yet a single RNA polymerase, common to many different bacteria, recognizes all of these different promoters. It appears that recognition is achieved via certain relatively small segments of the promoter sequence that have significant commonality among a great many bacteria. In what we might call a prototypical bacterial gene, the promoter carries:

(1) The sequence TATAAT (called the **Pribnow box**) at or near the –10 position (meaning ten nucleotides upstream of the start site).

(2) The sequence TTGACA at or near the –35 position (meaning thirty-five nucleotides upstream of the start site).

These two sequences are called **consensus sequences** because in a figurative sense, many diverse species of bacteria have achieved some "consensus" on what nucleotide sequences they will present at the –10 and –35 locations of their promoter sites. It is important to remember that consensus sequences are not rules, but rather trends. Indeed, even within a given organism, different genes might differ slightly as to the sequences they present at the –10 and –35 locations of their promoter sites. Overall, it is true that most bacteria present sequences very similar to the –10 TATAAT and –35 TTGACA prototypes in most promoters.

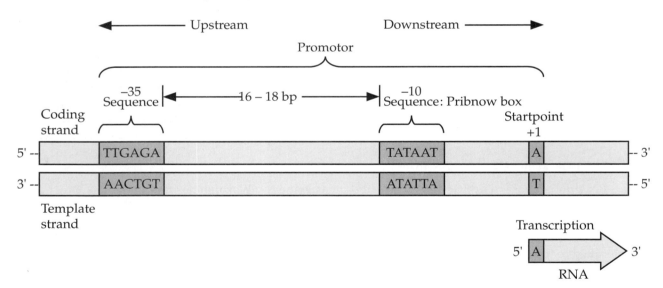

Upstream and Downstream Directions on DNA Molecule Are Identified with Reference to the 5' and 3' Ends of the Coding (Non-template) Strand

Figure 24.13

The binding of RNA polymerase to the promoter site causes the DNA double helix to unwind locally, over a length of approximately fifteen to eighteen base pairs. The two DNA strands are thus exposed. With RNA polymerase bound to the promoter, the coding (non-template) and anti-coding (template) strands are identified. Template recognition is complete, and initiation begins.

Consider the portion of a DNA molecule that undergoes transcription, particularly the whole length of the molecule that is truly involved from promoter site to terminator. That whole length of molecule, including the promoter site, the sequences that are transcribed, and the terminator (see below) are called the **transcription unit**.

Please solve this problem:

- The phrase "consensus sequence" refers to the fact that:

    A. prokaryotes and eukaryotes produce mRNA via the process of transcription, even though prokaryotic RNA is double-stranded.
    B. in prokaryotes, one subunit of RNA polymerase is detachable, even though it is essential to chain elongation.
    C. prokaryotes tend to show significant commonality in some of the nucleotide presented at their DNA promoter sites.
    D. the Pribnow box is absent in most prokaryotic cells.

Problem solved:

C is correct. A single RNA polymerase common to many bacteria recognizes a great many dissimilar bacterial promoter sites. That is because even though the bacterial promoter sites differ along much of their length, they tend to show high commonality at certain critical sites: the –35 site and –10 Pribnow box (C is correct and D is incorrect). Regarding choice B, it is true that the sigma factor constitutes a detachable subunit of prokaryotic RNA, but while the subunit is not necessary to chain elongation, it *is* necessary for initiation. Regarding choice A, it is true that both prokaryotes and eukaryotes produce mRNA via the process of transcription, but mRNA is single-stranded in both classes of cell.

Details of Initiation

At the beginning of initiation, two nucleotide units approach the template at the **start site**, which is the last position of the promoter site, and the place at which transcription truly begins. Nucleotides that arrive at the template are **ribonucleoside triphosphates (NTPs)**.

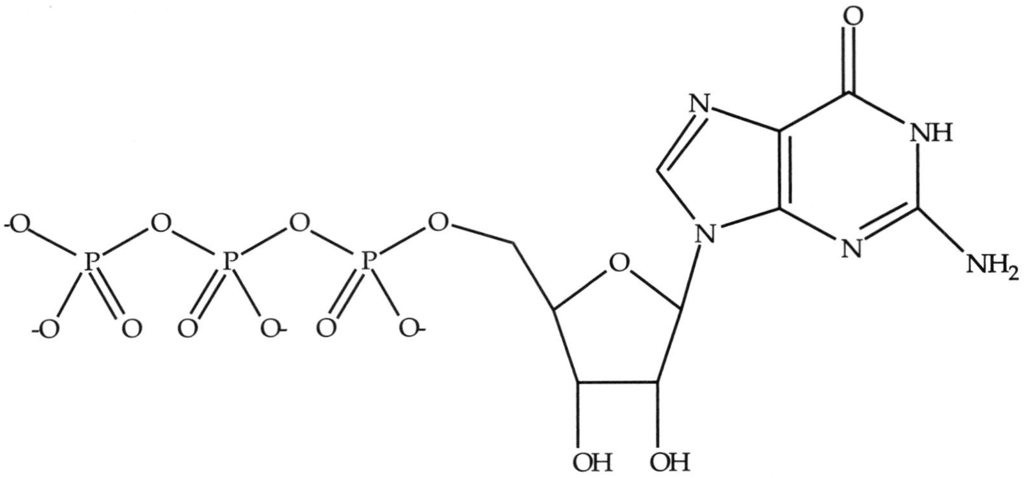

Guanosine Triphosphate, A Ribonucleoside Triphosphate Carrying the
Guanine Nucleotide Residue

Figure 24.14

In bacteria, the start site is usually marked by a purine, more often adenine than guanine. It is important to remember that the start site marks the beginning of transcription and is downstream of the promoter. The start site is NOT the same thing as the start codon, which starts translation.

The two ribonucleoside triphosphate molecules (NTPs) that approach the template locate themselves opposite their complementary nucleotides on the DNA template. Each forms a hydrogen bond between its nucleotide unit and the complementary nucleotide unit on the template strand. The result is a **DNA-RNA hybrid**, meaning a segment of DNA template that is hydrogen bound, temporarily, to the complementary bases on the growing RNA polymer.

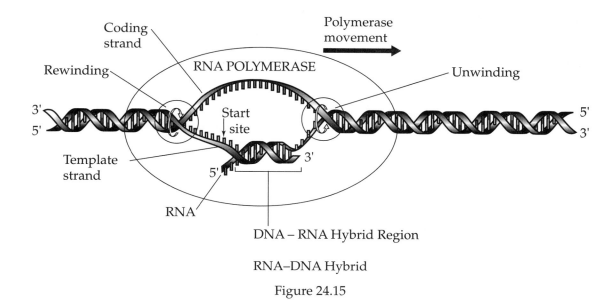

RNA–DNA Hybrid

Figure 24.15

RNA polymerase then catalyzes the creation of a phosphodiester bond between the 5' end of the second nucleotide and the 3' end of the first. This causes the release of pyrophosphate (PPi). The polymerase then moves along the template, adding additional nucleotides to the growing chain of RNA, continuing to form phosphodiester bonds between the 5' end of each newly added nucleotide and the 3' end of the growing chain; the chain begins to grow in the 5' to 3' direction. When the chain is about nine nucleotides long, the sigma factor detaches from the polymerase. At that point, initiation is complete.

Please solve this problem:

- The initiation phase of transcription is complete when:

   A. RNA polymerase loses its sigma factor.
   B. DNA and RNA form a hybrid.
   C. a first RNA nucleotide residue is hydrogen bonded to its counterpart on a DNA molecule.
   D. a first phosphodiester bond is formed between two nucleotide residues on a newly forming RNA polymer.

Problem solved:

A is correct. All of the events mentioned in choices B, C, and D belong to the initiation phase of transcription, but the one mentioned in choice A marks the end of initiation. Initiation begins after template recognition and involves these processes in this order:

(1) two ribonucleoside triphosphates (or nucleotides) approach the DNA template;

(2) temporary hydrogen bonds form between RNA nucleotide residues and DNA nucleotide residues to form a DNA-RNA hybrid;

(3) RNA polymerase catalyzes the formation of a phosphodiester bond between the two nucleotide residues, and pyrophosphate is released;

(4) additional ribonucleoside triphosphates are added to the growing chain, and additional phosphodiester bonds are formed;

(5) when the growing chain is about nine nucleotide residues in length, the sigma factor detaches from RNA polymerase, and *initiation is complete.*

Please solve this problem:

- During transcription, which of the following events is earliest to occur?

    A. Local disassembly of a DNA's double helical structure
    B. Binding of enzyme to a DNA molecule
    C. Location of ribonucleoside triphosphates at the start site
    D. Phosphodiester bond formation

Problem solved:

B is correct. Transcription involves these events occurring in this order:

(1) binding of RNA polymerase to a promoter site located on the DNA molecule;

(2) local unwinding of the DNA double helix;

(3) positioning of two nucleotide units, bound within ribonucleoside triphosphates at the start site, according to the base-pairing rules discussed in earlier sections; and

(4) the formation of a phosphodiester bond between the 3' end of the first nucleotide residue and the 5' end of the second.

The first to occur, therefore, is mentioned in choice B—the binding of enzyme (RNA polymerase) to a site on the DNA molecule.

DETAILS OF ELONGATION

After the sigma factor detaches from RNA polymerase, the **elongation phase** begins. The polymerase continues to move along the template, from its 3' end toward its 5' end, unwinding small segments of the DNA double helix. The region of unwinding is sometimes called the **transcription bubble**. At each open region, RNA polymerase catalyzes the addition of new RNA nucleotides complementary to the DNA nucleotides that are exposed. As in the initiation phase, the nucleotides arrive at the template bound as NTP molecules. It is important to remember that chain growth occurs in the 5' to 3' direction, just like in DNA replication (see above). In other words, the 5′ end of RNA is made first and 3′ end is made last; the 5' phosphate of each newly added nucleotide is bound to the 3' hydroxyl end of the growing chain.

Pairing between an incoming RNA nucleotide and its DNA complement on the template involves (as in initiation) the formation of hydrogen bonds between base pairs. Consequently, there is an RNA-DNA hybrid within the transcription bubble. Although the DNA double helix is unwound within the bubble, there is a winding between the DNA and RNA components of the DNA-RNA hybrid. The hydrogen bonds that create the hybrid are not permanent, since the single-stranded RNA molecule is released from the DNA template as elongation proceeds. It is currently thought that the RNA-DNA hybrid is about 12 base pairs in length.

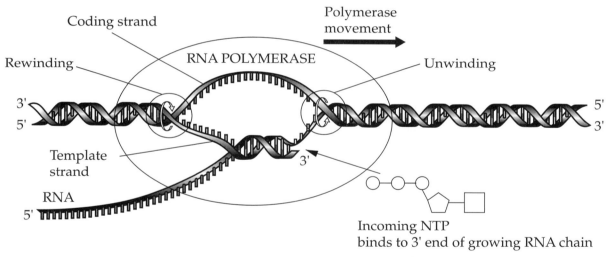

Prokaryotic Transcription: The Elongation Phase

Figure 24.16

Please solve this problem:

- Which of the following events does not occur during the elongation phase of transcription?

    A. Movement of DNA polymerase along a DNA template
    B. Elongation of an RNA polymer in the 5' to 3' direction
    C. Addition of nucleotides to the 3' end of a growing RNA polymer
    D. Pairing of purines with pyrimidines

Problem solved:

A is correct. All of the events mentioned in choices B, C, and D occur in connection with the elongation phase of transcription. RNA chain elongation occurs in the 5' to 3' direction (choice B). Nucleotide units are added to the 3' end of the growing polymer (choice C). As in DNA replication, purines pair with pyrimidines and pyrimidines pair with purines (choice D). The polymerization of RNA is catalyzed not by DNA polymerase, but by RNA polymerase. Choice A describes an event that does occurs in DNA replication, not transcription.

DETAILS OF TERMINATION

Elongation continues until RNA polymerase reaches a particular nucleotide sequence on the DNA template called a **terminator**, and termination begins.

Many bacterial RNA molecules show a region near their 3' ends that contains large numbers of guanine-cytosine sequences followed by several uracil residues (G C G C G C G C G C GC...U U U U U U U). Recall that guanine pairs with cytosine and that cytosine pairs with guanine. A length of RNA that is rich in GC sequences is able to "fold in" on itself and form a loop that base-pairs within itself. The creation of such a loop, called the **hairpin loop**, seems to pull the RNA polymer away from the DNA template and cause RNA polymerase to slow or pause in the process of RNA synthesis.

Recall that uracil and adenine form two hydrogen bonds between them when they are base-paired, and that guanine and cytosine form three hydrogen bonds. When the hairpin loop separates itself from the DNA template, it leaves a downstream RNA-DNA hybrid that is rich in uracil-adenine pairings. Since the bond between adenine and uracil is relatively weak (compared to the G-C bond), the RNA-DNA hybrid breaks apart with relative ease. The combination of a hairpin loop and ruptured uracil-adenine RNA-DNA hybrid is one means by which RNA synthesis terminates in bacteria.

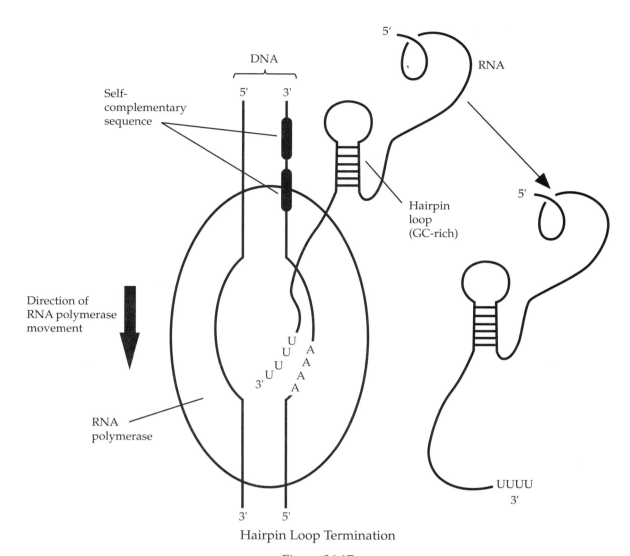

Hairpin Loop Termination

Figure 24.17

Some bacterial transcription units do not have the GC-rich and U-rich regions that characterize hairpin loop termination. The synthesis of such RNA is terminated by combined action of a termination sequence on the transcribed DNA, and an ATP-dependent enzyme called the **rho factor.** The rho factor gains access to the transcription bubble and, signaled somehow by the termination sequence, causes the RNA-DNA hybrid to unwind.

When transcription termination is complete, RNA polymerase (and the rho factor, if present) are released from the nucleic acids. DNA resumes its fully wound double helical state. Finally, the newly formed RNA polymer is released from the DNA molecule.

Please solve this problem:

- Which of the following events does not take place within the transcription bubble?

  A. Unwinding of the DNA double helix
  B. Rewinding of the DNA double helix
  C. Formation of a DNA-RNA hybrid
  D. Reattachment of the sigma factor to create a holoenzyme

Problem solved:

D is correct. All of the events mentioned in choices A, B, and C occur within the transcription bubble. All three belong to the elongation phase of the transcription process. RNA polymerase causes both the unwinding and the rewinding of the double helix (choices A and B). The DNA-RNA hybrid (thought to be about twelve base pairs in length) arises temporarily by the formation of hydrogen bonds between nucleotide residues on the DNA template and the newly growing RNA chain. The RNA polymerase sigma factor detaches at the end of initiation, but it does *not* reattach during elongation. It reattaches after termination of transcription, when RNA polymerase is released from the DNA template.

Please solve this problem:

- If the prokaryotic transcription process ends via hairpin loop, it is most likely that:

  A. the rho factor will be absent from the termination process.
  B. cytosine residues will be absent from all regions near the 3' end of the newly formed RNA molecule.
  C. guanine residues will be absent from any region near the 3' end of the newly formed RNA molecule.
  D. uracil residues will be absent from all regions near the 3' end of the newly formed RNA molecule.

Problem solved:

A is correct. The hairpin loop and the rho factor generally represent two *alternative* means by which prokaryotic transcription terminates. If termination proceeds via the hairpin loop, then it does not normally proceed via the rho factor. Choices B, C, and D, on the other hand, describe conditions that do attend hairpin loop termination. The hairpin loop is formed when large numbers of guanine and cytosine residues located at the 3' end of the newly forming RNA polymer fold in on themselves. A run of uracil residues usually follows, causing the new polymer to pull away from its DNA template and RNA polymerase to pause in the process of RNA synthesis.

Prokaryotic vs. Eukaryotic Transcription

The word prokaryote is largely synonymous with bacterium (Chapter 27). Prokaryotic cells have no nucleus. The genome of the prokaryotic cell (one supercoiled double-stranded DNA chromosome) is found in the cytoplasm, in a region called the nucleoid. In all discussions that follow, "prokaryote," "prokaryotic cell," and "bacterium" are synonymous.

Eukaryotic cells (Chapter 23) have membrane-bound organelles, such as nuclei, mitochondria, peroxisomes, lysosomes, endoplasmic reticulum, and the Golgi apparatus. The genome of eukaryotic cells (multiple linear chromosomes that are composed of DNA wound around histone proteins) is housed in the nucleus of the cell, surrounded by the nuclear envelope. Humans, animals, plants and fungi (including unicellular yeast cells) are all eukaryotic.

There are several differences in how prokaryotic and eukaryotic cells perform transcription. These will be described below.

CELLULAR SITE OF TRANSCRIPTION

The first important difference between transcription in bacteria and transcription in eukaryotes pertains to cellular site of transcription.

In the bacterium, transcription occurs in the cytoplasm because this is where the DNA template is found. In eukaryotes, transcription occurs in the nucleus (note that the synthesis of rRNA occurs, more specifically, within the nucleolus).

RNA POLYMERASE

The second important difference between transcription in bacteria and transcription in eukaryotes pertains to multiple types of RNA polymerase.

In the bacterium, a single form of RNA polymerase mediates synthesis of all types of RNA— mRNA, rRNA, and tRNA. Eukaryotes, on the other hand, show no fewer than three different RNA polymerases: RNA Polymerase I synthesizes rRNA, RNA Polymerase II makes mRNA, and RNA Polymerase III synthesizes tRNA.

NATURE AND COMPLEXITY OF PROMOTERS

A third important difference between transcription in bacteria and transcription in eukaryotes pertains to the nature and complexity of promoters.

In bacteria, promoters on the DNA molecule show considerable commonality within a given cell and significant commonality across diverse bacterial species. Bacterial promoters are located upstream of the transcription start site, and the prototypical TATAAT and TTGACA "consensus sequences" are generally found at the −10 and −35 positions upstream of the start site.

In eukaryotic cells, promoters are highly varied, longer, and more complex than those of bacteria. Eukaryotic promoters may be located on upstream and downstream sides of the start site. Moreover, a given promoter may have components located on upstream and downstream sides from the start site. Furthermore, the efficacy of many eukaryotic promoters is modulated by **control sequences** located upstream or downstream from the start site.

There is one common promoter element in eukaryotic cells: For most genes transcribed by RNA polymerase II, there appears to be a consensus sequence—TATAAAA—called the **TATA box**, located about thirty base pairs upstream of the start site.

TRANSCRIPTION FACTORS

The fourth important difference between transcription in bacteria and transcription in eukaryotes pertains to transcription factors.

In bacterial transcription, the binding of RNA polymerase to the DNA promoter site is a relatively simple affair: It is mediated by the sigma factor, which detaches from RNA polymerase at the end of initiation.

In eukaryotic cells, the binding of RNA polymerase to a promoter site is preceded by interactions among and between the DNA promoter site and several **transcription factors**. Transcription factors are proteins that bind with the DNA promoter site and interact with one another in such a fashion that facilitates the subsequent binding of the polymerase enzyme to the promoter.

Additional interactions with additional proteins then allow RNA polymerase to initiate RNA synthesis. Because transcription factors are proteins, it is frequently said that in eukaryotic cells, the binding of RNA polymerase to DNA promoter is preceded by **protein–protein interactions** (meaning the interactions among and between transcription factors as just described).

RNA PROCESSING: THE PRIMARY TRANSCRIPT, INTRONS, AND EXONS

The fifth important difference between transcription in bacteria and transcription in eukaryotes pertains to RNA processing.

When a bacterial gene completes transcription, the resulting RNA molecule is functional. In the case of mRNA, it is ready to be translated. In fact, in prokaryotic cells, transcription and translation can occur simultaneously: As soon as the 5' end of the transcript is made (remember, this end of the RNA is made first since RNA synthesis occurs 5' to 3'), it is bound by ribosomes, which read the transcript 5' to 3' to make a peptide (see "From mRNA to Protein: Translation" on page 488).

In eukaryotic cells, on the other hand, the mRNA molecule freshly produced by transcription is not functional or ready to use. It is called the **primary transcript** or **hnRNA (heterogeneous nuclear RNA)**, and is a precursor to a functional RNA molecule. The primary transcript needs to undergo three steps of **RNA processing** (splicing, 5' end modification and 3' end modification) and must be translocated before it can be used.

The primary transcript contains introns and exons. Introns are segments of the transcript that are not expressed in protein synthesis, but function to partition the RNA molecule into many functional segments. Exons are the segments of the transcript that are expressed in protein synthesis. The first step of RNA processing is **splicing**, which is accomplished by the splicosome. The splicosome excises or removes introns and joins together exons.

Each exon represents a functional and translatable unit of mRNA. With introns systematically and strategically excised, individual exons might be joined and combined in a variety of ways to produce a much larger number of expressible RNA messengers (and a larger variety of polypeptide products) than would be possible if each exon were to function by itself. Introns facilitate variable combinations of exons, called **alternative splicing**, and thus increase the eukaryotic genome's functional diversity.

A eukaryotic mRNA molecule, in functional form, does not have a 5' end. Rather, after transcription but before the RNA leaves the nucleus to enter the cytoplasm, its 5' end binds to a guanine residue by an (otherwise) unusual 5' to 5' linkage. The guanine unit then undergoes methylation, and the resulting methylated guanine residue becomes the molecule's **5' cap**.

At the 3' end, the RNA molecule acquires (once again, after transcription but before it leaves the nucleus) a long run of adenine residues, typically 100 to 200 nucleotides in length. These adenine units are termed the RNA molecule's **poly A tail**.

Finally, before the eukaryotic transcript can be translated, it must be translocated from the nucleus to the cytoplasm.

Please solve this problem:

- Which of the following is true of eukaryotic but not prokaryotic transcription?
    - **A.** The process occurs in the cytoplasm.
    - **B.** The process is mediated by a single form of RNA polymerase.
    - **C.** Promoters may be located upstream or downstream from the start site.
    - **D.** Enzyme binding to the promoter site is mediated by the sigma factor.

Problem solved:

C is correct. Relative to prokaryotic promoter sites, eukaryotic promoters are more complex and diverse in their nature and location; the promoter might be located upstream and/or downstream from the start site. In prokaryotes, the promoter is located upstream from the start site. Choices A, B, and D make statements that are true of prokaryotic transcription, but not of eukaryotic transcription. In prokaryotes transcription occurs in the cytoplasm, and in eukaryotes it occurs in the nucleus (A is incorrect). Prokaryotes have only one RNA polymerase, and eukaryotes have many (B is incorrect). Binding of RNA polymerase to the DNA promoter is mediated by the sigma factor in prokaryotes; in eukaryotes, the binding process involves complicated protein–protein interactions among a variety of transcription factors (D is incorrect).

Please solve this problem:

- The 5' cap is:
    - **A.** composed of adenine residues located at the 3' end of eukaryotic RNA.
    - **B.** a methylated guanine unit found in eukaryotic RNA.
    - **C.** found in the hairpin loop of prokaryotic RNA.
    - **D.** positioned after the mRNA molecule leaves the nucleus.

Problem solved:

B is correct. Addition of the 5' cap, a methylated guanine, is part of RNA processing in eukaryotes and occurs before the transcript leaves the nucleus (D is incorrect). Choice A is wrong because it describes the poly A tail, which is a different type of eukaryotic RNA processing. Choice C is wrong because it refers to prokaryotic RNA, which often features the hairpin loop.

Please solve this problem:

- An intron is NOT normally:
    - A. part of a functional mRNA molecule.
    - B. present in the primary transcript of eukaryotic transcription.
    - C. composed of purine and pyrimidine residues.
    - D. excised from eukaryotic mRNA within the cellular nucleus.

Problem solved:

A is correct. Before leaving the nucleus to enter the cytosol, eukaryotic primary transcripts undergo processing, including splicing out of introns and joining exons (D is incorrect). Introns do not normally form a part of a functional mRNA molecule, but are present in the eukaryotic primary transcript (A is correct and B is incorrect). Like all components of the primary transcript, they are composed of nucleotide (purine and pyrimidine) residues, which makes choice C incorrect.

FROM mRNA TO PROTEIN: TRANSLATION

DNA exerts its ultimate governance over a cell (and organism) by specifying the proteins it will produce. This occurs via the process of protein synthesis. The first part of protein synthesis is **transcription**, where the DNA template is read to make a molecule of RNA. There are three major types of mature RNA: mRNA, tRNA, and rRNA, and all three have important roles in protein synthesis. The second part of protein synthesis is **translation**: using the ribosome (including rRNA), tRNAs coupled to amino acids, and the mRNA transcript to make a peptide chain.

A Summary of Translation

Generally speaking, translation is a process in which mRNA issues orders that are read by the ribosome and carried out by molecules of tRNA coupled to amino acids. Translation is generally a process in which:

(1) the ribosome recognizes some portion of the mRNA molecule and binds it;

(2) the ribosome reads the mRNA molecule, three nucleotides at a time (these three nucleotides are called a **codon**);

(3) when read by the ribosome, each codon on the mRNA orders that some particular amino acid be brought *to* the ribosome;

(4) molecules of tRNA within the cytosol bring amino acids to the ribosome, as instructed by mRNA; and

(5) amino acids brought to the ribosome, one by one, in a sequence ordered by the mRNA molecule, form peptide bonds to form a polypeptide.

Prokaryotic Translation in Detail

We will examine translation as we examined transcription: first by detailing the process in prokaryotes and then by describing the ways in which it differs in prokaryotes versus eukaryotes.

THE RIBOSOME, tRNA, AND AMINO ACID ACTIVATION

Because translation involves ribosomes and tRNA, we first look at the nature of these complexes, and then at the thermodynamics tied to the bonding of tRNA with amino acid, a process called amino acid activation.

A prokaryotic ribosome embodies two **subunits**, a large one and a small one, sometimes called the **50S** and **30S** subunits, respectively. The "S" represents the unit "Svedberg" and denotes sedimentation rate; higher value indicates a higher sedimentation rate and larger mass. Each subunit is a complex of rRNA, enzymes, and structural protein. The ribosome also features three tRNA binding sites called the **A site** (or aminoacyl-tRNA site), the **P site** (or peptidyl-tRNA site), and the **E site** (or exit-tRNA site). In both prokaryotes and eukaryotes, many ribosomes synthesizing the same protein simultaneously associate with one another to form a **polyribosome**.

tRNA, or transfer RNA, is a single stranded molecule of RNA. Because there are regions where the tRNA molecule is complementary to itself, tRNAs fold into a cloverleaf structure that is composed of stems (areas of internal complementarity) and loops. tRNAs have two functional sites, the **anticodon** and the **amino acid acceptor site**.

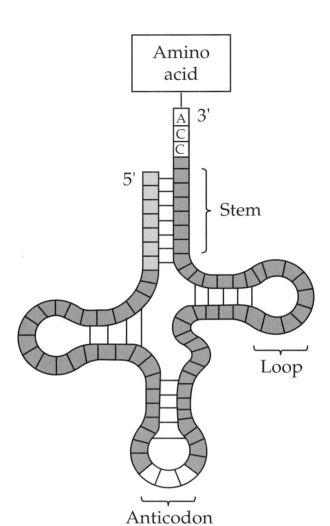

Transfer RNA (tRNA)

Figure 24.18

The tRNA anticodon is a sequence of three nucleotides. Since the anticodon is three nucleotides in length and since there are four nucleotide options for each site (A, C, G, or U), there are 64 different anticodons (this comes from 4 x 4 x 4). Like any set of nucleotides, those of the tRNA anticodon have complements according to the base-pairing rules described in earlier sections. The anticodon on tRNA is complementary to the codon on the mRNA transcript. By convention, a tRNA anticodon is written not in the 5' to 3' direction (like mRNA and DNA), but in the 3' to 5' direction. For example, the tRNA molecule with the anticodon (3') - C G G - (5') is complementary to the codon (5') - G C C - (3') on the mRNA transcript.

The tRNA molecule's amino acid acceptor site is a site at which the molecule binds (accepts) an amino acid. A given tRNA molecule with its particular anticodon has a binding site for one particular amino acid. However, since there are 64 anticodons and only 20 amino acids, there might be *more* than one tRNA molecule specific to a given amino acid. For example, the anticodon (3') - C G G - (5') is specific to alanine; it binds alanine and only alanine. On the other hand, the anticodons (3') - C G A - (5'), (3') - C G U - (5'), and (3') - C G C - (5') are also specific to alanine. They, too, bind alanine and only alanine.

The amino acid acceptor site of any tRNA molecule is the same as that of any other, which raises this question: On what basis does tRNA recognize the amino acid to which it is specific? For each amino acid, there exists (at least) one enzyme called an **aminoacyl-tRNA synthetase**. The synthetase enzyme recognizes both the tRNA carrier and the amino acid to which it is specific. Recognition between tRNA and amino acid, therefore, is mediated not by tRNA, but by the relevant aminoacyl-tRNA synthetase.

tRNA molecules are named according to the amino acid they are specific for. For example, a tRNA for methionine would be written tRNA^{Met}. When a tRNA and an amino acid are bound together, it produces an **aminoacyl-tRNA**. Aminoacyl-tRNA molecules are conventionally named with a prefix and superscript that designate the bound amino acid. For example, when the tRNA specific to methionine (tRNA^{Met}) binds methionine, it produces an aminoacyl-tRNA conventionally called methionyl-tRNA^{Met} or Met-tRNA^{Met}.

The binding of an amino acid to its tRNA to produce the corresponding aminoacyl-tRNA is called **amino acid activation**. The word "activation" arises from thermodynamic phenomena related to the binding process. The reaction in which an amino acid is bound to its tRNA is endergonic (meaning ΔG is positive). It involves the cleavage of two high-energy phosphate bonds (ATP $\rightarrow$ AMP + 2P$_i$), and the reaction is summarized thus:

$$\text{Amino Acid} + \text{ATP} + \text{tRNA} \rightarrow \text{Aminoacyl-tRNA} + \text{AMP} + \text{PP}_i$$

Subsequent cleavage of the pyrophosphate (PPi) by pyrophosphatase drives the equilibrium forcefully to the right. The ester linkage between the amino acid and the tRNA is a relatively high-energy bond, and for that reason, the amino acid is said to be activated; the energy stored within this bond is later used to drive peptide bond formation.

The principal functions of tRNA are to bind amino acids, bring them to the ribosome, line them up according to an order dictated by the mRNA codons, and facilitate the formation of peptide bonds to form proteins. Transfer RNA, therefore, mediates the process of translation.

DETAILS OF THE INITIATION PHASE

Translation proceeds according to three phases: (1) an **initiation phase**, (2) an **elongation phase**, and (3) a **termination phase**. These are best described, first, for prokaryotic cells.

Translation involves reading the mRNA transcript from 5' to 3' and making a peptide chain (from N-terminus to C-terminus). However, only part of the mRNA transcript is protein-coding. The 5' end of the mRNA is called the 5' untranslated region (or 5' UTR) and the 3' end of the mRNA is called the 3' untranslated region (or 3' UTR). The 5' UTR contains upstream regulatory sequences that are essential for initiation; the 3' UTR contains downstream regulatory sequences that help with termination.

Initiation of translation occurs in many steps. First, the small (30S) ribosomal subunit binds near the 5' end of the mRNA, due to regulatory sequences in the 5' UTR. It scans along the mRNA until it finds the first AUG codon; this is called the **start codon**. Next, a tRNA molecule (with the anticodon UAC and bound to the amino acid N-formylmethionine, a modified form of methionine) interacts with the AUG codon on the mRNA. These three molecules together (small ribosomal subunit, fMet-tRNA^{Met}, and a molecule of mRNA) are called the **initiation complex**. Finally, the large (50S) ribosomal subunit is recruited to the initiation complex, positioning the mRNA molecule within a groove that lies between the large and small ribosomal subunits and positioning the fMet-tRNA^{Met} in the P site.

The large (50S) and small (30S) subunits, now joined, make what is called a **70S ribosome**, on which the next phases of translation take place. (Although 50 + 30 does not equal 70, the 30S ribosome and 50S ribosome together make a 70S ribosome. When two entities of different sedimentation rates are joined, the sedimentation rate of the resulting entity is not necessarily equal to the sum of the individual rates.)

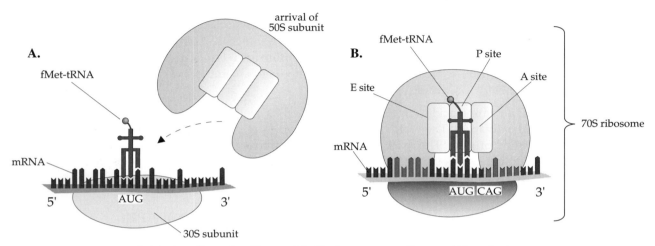

Initiation Complex Formed in Prokaryotes at Onset of Translation

Figure 24.19

Assembling the initiation complex and then the 70S ribosome is powered by the hydrolysis of one phosphate from a GTP molecule (note that the phosphate bonds in GTP are high energy bonds similar to those in ATP). Since it also required the hydrolysis of two high energy bonds to join fMet to tRNAf^Met (see above), the total energy requirement for initiation is three high energy bonds. With the mRNA molecule situated between the small and large subunits, the stage is set for the elongation phase.

Please solve this problem:

- Among the following, which represents the earliest event associated with the initiation phase of translation in prokaryotes?

    A. Formation of a 70S ribosome
    B. Joining of the large ribosomal subunit to a molecule of mRNA
    C. Binding of N-formyl-methionyl tRNA to the start codon
    D. Binding of N-formyl-methionyl tRNA to the 50S subunit

Problem solved:

C is correct. In summary, the steps of translation initiation are:
(1) The 30S subunit binds the 5' end of the mRNA transcript.
(2) The UAC anticodon of fMET-tRNA^{Met} recognizes and binds the AUG start codon on a molecule of mRNA.
(3) The large ribosomal subunit joins the initiation complex to form the 70S ribosome.

DETAILS OF THE ELONGATION PHASE

During the elongation phase, the ribosome reads the mRNA codons, tRNA molecules bearing appropriate anticodons bring amino acids to the ribosome, and peptide bonds form between the adjacent amino acids to form a polypeptide. The amino acid sequence of the polypeptide is dictated by the mRNA codons.

In more detailed terms, elongation involves this series of events:
(1) A mRNA codon is exposed at the A site of the ribosome.
(2) An aminoacyl-tRNA, whose anticodon is complementary to the codon, arrives at the A site and forms hydrogen bonds with the codon. This step requires the hydrolysis of one phosphate from GTP.
(3) The enzyme peptidyl transferase transfers the amino acid in the P site from its tRNA carrier to the amino terminus of the aminoacyl-tRNA in the A site. A peptide bond is formed between the two amino acids. The bond between the amino acid and the tRNA in the P site is broken.
(4) The ribosome moves, or translocates, a distance of three nucleotides along the mRNA molecule in the 5' to 3' direction. Translocation moves the growing polypeptide anchored to a tRNA molecule to the P site of the ribosome, the old tRNA to the E site and exposes the next mRNA codon at the A site. This step requires the hydrolysis of one GTP.

These steps repeat and the polypeptide chain grows, one amino acid at a time. The E site always contains a tRNA that has lost its amino acid to the growing peptide chain. This tRNA exits the ribosome and is recycled to the cytoplasm where it can be joined with another amino acid. The P site always contains a tRNA hydrogen bonded to the mRNA transcript, and this anchors the peptide chain to the ribosome. The A site is always where the next aminoacyl-tRNA arrives.

Overall, then, it costs four high-energy phosphate bonds to add an amino acid to fMet: Two high energy bonds are required by aminoacyl-tRNA synthetase to join the tRNA with its amino acid, one phosphate bond is required to bring the aminoacyl-tRNA into the A site of the ribosome and a final phosphate bond is required to translocate the ribosome so the next codon can be read.

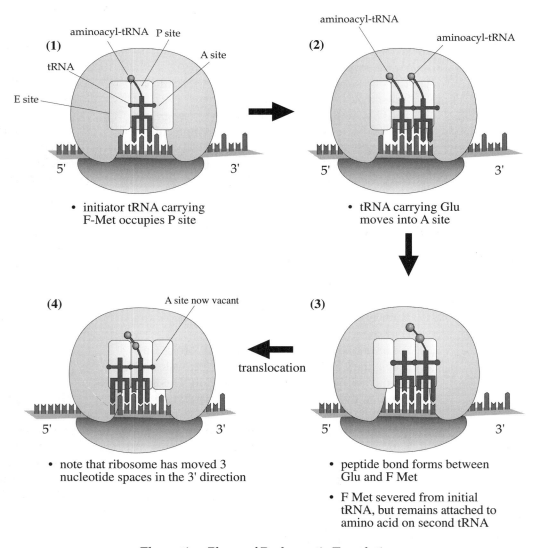

Elongation Phase of Prokaryotic Translation

Figure 24.20

Please solve this problem:

- On a molecule of tRNA, the anticodon represents the means by which:

    A. the small and large ribosomal units recognize one another.

    B. an mRNA codon locates itself at the ribosome's A site.

    C. a tRNA molecule recognizes the amino acid to which it is specific.

    D. an aminoacyl tRNA recognizes an mRNA codon.

Problem solved:

D is correct. An anticodon is a sequence of three nucleotide residues exposed at the surface of a tRNA molecule. During the process of translation, aminoacyl-tRNA molecules (tRNAs bound to their specific amino acids) recognize complementary sequences on the mRNA site exposed at the ribosomal A site. This is how the message originally on a DNA sequence makes its way to the process of protein synthesis. The other three answer options have little to do with the anticodon on a tRNA molecule and are not relevant to the question. Joining of the small and large ribosomal subunits is the final step of translation initiation (A is incorrect). The mRNA codon is located in the A site after translocation of the ribosome (B is incorrect). Aminoacyl-tRNA synthetases join tRNAs and the amino acids they are specific for; this recognition is not accomplished by the tRNA itself (C is incorrect).

Please solve this problem:

- During the process of translation, translocation serves directly to:

    A. promote the formation of aminoacyl-tRNA.

    B. allow for recognition between a tRNA molecule and the amino acid to which it is specific.

    C. expose a new mRNA codon at the ribosomal A site.

    D. supply energy for peptide bond formation.

Problem solved:

C is correct. During translocation, the growing polypeptide chain moves from ribosomal A site to ribosomal P site, which exposes a new mRNA codon at the A site. The processes and phenomena mentioned in choices A, B, and D have no direct relationship to translocation. Choices A and B refer to how aminoacyl-tRNA synthetases join tRNA molecules and the amino acids to which they are specific. While translocation requires the hydrolysis of a high energy phosphate bond, this does not power peptide bond formation (D is incorrect).

DETAILS OF THE TERMINATION PHASE

Translation elongation stops when a stop codon appears in the ribosomal A site. There are three stop codons (UAG, UGA, UAA) which can be remembered using the three phrases "You (U) Are Gone, U Go Away, U Are Away." Stop codons do not code for tRNA molecules. Rather, their arrival at the A site causes **release factors** (proteins) to stop the elongation process and to release the newly formed polypeptide from the ribosome. The ribosome dissociates into large and small subunits ready to begin the process of translation anew. The termination of translation does not require hydrolysis of any high energy bonds.

To summarize the energetics of translation: The first amino acid requires the hydrolysis of three high energy bonds, each amino acid after this requires the hydrolysis of four high energy bonds, and termination (which does not add an amino acid to the peptide chain) has no energy requirement. Overall, then, proteins cost $4n$-1 high energy bonds to make, where n is the number of amino acids in the peptide chain. For example, if a peptide chain has 100 amino acids in it, it will cost the cell 399 high energy bonds to synthesize (in other words, its synthesis will require the hydrolysis of 399 high energy phosphate bonds).

Please solve this problem:

- Among the following, a "codon" is best described as:
    A. a series of three mRNA nucleotide units recognized by complementary tRNA nucleotide units.
    B. a series of three tRNA nucleotide units recognized by complementary mRNA nucleotide units.
    C. a DNA template from which an mRNA molecule is synthesized.
    D. a group of polymerase enzymes that catalyze the elongation of nucleic acids.

Problem solved:

A is correct. A codon is a series of three nucleotide units that are located on an mRNA molecule and are recognized by complementary nucleotide units on a tRNA molecule. The word *codon* is also used to describe a series of three nucleotides that causes protein synthesis to stop when a protein molecule is fully formed. That codon is called a *stop* codon. The other three answer options are not relevant: Answer choice B describes an anticodon, option C describes the DNA template for transcription, and option D describes DNA or RNA polymerases.

Please solve this problem:

- No tRNA molecule contains the nucleotide:
    A. adenine.
    B. cytosine.
    C. guanine
    D. thymine.

Problem solved:

D is correct. Nucleotides found in DNA molecules are the purines adenine and cytosine, and the pyrimidines guanine and thymine. Nucleotides found in RNA (mRNA, tRNA, and rRNA) are the purines adenine and cytosine, and the pyrimidines guanine and uracil. Thymine does not appear in RNA molecules.

Please solve this problem:

- Which of the following happens in the A site of the ribosome during translation?

    A. N-formylmethionyl tRNA binds to the ribosome to create an initiation complex.
    B. DNA strands code for the synthesis of mRNA molecules.
    C. mRNA codons are exposed and joined by complementary tRNA molecules.
    D. peptide bonds are broken and amino acids separate.

Problem solved:

C is correct. During initiation, the ribosome assembles so that the fMet-tRNA is in the P site, not the A site (A is incorrect). While option B is a true statement and describes the process of transcription, it has nothing to do with the A site of the ribosome (B is incorrect). Option C describes processes that occur at the A site and is the best answer. Option D describes peptide hydrolysis and is the opposite of protein synthesis.

Prokaryotic vs. Eukaryotic Translation

For MCAT purposes, you should know a few critical differences between translation as it occurs in the prokaryote and eukaryote.

RIBOSOMES

The first important difference between translation in prokaryotes and translation in eukaryotes pertains to ribosomes.

Bacterial ribosomes comprise 30S and 50S subunits. Together, they make a 70S ribosome.

The eukaryotic ribosome comprises a 40S and 60S subunit which, together, make an 80S ribosome. Eukaryotic ribosomes are synthesized in the nucleolus, a suborganelle located within the nucleus of a eukaryotic cell. The nucleolus is the site of rRNA synthesis via transcription and is also where ribosomes are assembled from rRNA and proteins that have been imported to the nucleolus from the cytoplasm. It is important for the MCAT that you associate the nucleolus with synthesis of ribosomal RNA and ribosomes themselves.

Because prokaryotic ribosomes are different from eukaryotic ribosomes, many antibiotic drugs have been developed that target the prokaryotic ribosome. Taking advantage of differences in cell biology between prokaryotes and eukaryotes is an important theme in drug and therapeutic development.

SOURCE OF MRNA

The second important difference between translation in prokaryotes and translation in eukaryotes pertains to the source of mRNA.

Prokaryotes have no nucleus, and therefore no nuclear membrane. Transcription (mRNA synthesis) and translation (peptide synthesis) both occur in the cytoplasm.

Eukaryotic transcription occurs in the nucleus, and after processing, the mRNA must move through nuclear pores from the nucleus to the cytoplasm. All the translational machinery in a eukaryotic cell is housed in the cytoplasm.

THE 5'UTR

The third important difference between translation in prokaryotes and translation in eukaryotes pertains to the structure of the 5' untranslated region (or 5'UTR).

Similar to the promoter used to initiate transcription, the 5'UTR can contain consensus sequences that are conserved between organisms and between genes. A common 5'UTR in prokaryotes is called the **Shine-Dalgarno sequence.** It is typically found 10 nucleotides upstream (or towards the 5' end) of the start codon. A common 5'UTR in eukaryotes is called the **Kozak sequence**. It is typically found only a few nucleotides upstream of the start codon. In both prokaryotes and eukaryotes, the 5'UTR functions generally in assembly of the translation initiation complex.

THE FIRST AMINO ACID

The fourth important difference between translation in prokaryotes and translation in eukaryotes pertains to the first amino acid.

In prokaryotes, N-formylmethionyl tRNA (or fMet-tRNA) is the first amino acid brought to the ribosome. In eukaryotes, the first amino acid is methionine itself, not N-formylmethionine. Note that methionine can be found within peptide chains as well; just because it is the first amino acid in proteins does not mean this is the only place it can be found.

TIMING OF TRANSLATION AND TRANSCRIPTION

The fifth important difference between translation in prokaryotes and translation in eukaryotes pertains to timing.

In prokaryotes, mRNA is made 5' to 3' via transcription. Once the 5' end of the transcript has been made by RNA polymerase, it can start to undergo translation. In prokaryotes, translation and transcription occur simultaneously; RNA polymerase can be building the 3' end of the mRNA as ribosomes are already reading the 5' end of the mRNA.

In eukaryotes, such synchrony is impossible because the two processes occur in different cellular compartments. Transcription takes place in the nucleus and translation in the cytoplasm. Also, mRNA processing must take place between transcription and translation in eukaryotes.

Please solve this problem:

- Which of the following statements is true of prokaryotic but not eukaryotic translation?

  A. The process occurs in the cytosol.
  B. The process is mediated by tRNA.
  C. The process occurs simultaneously with transcription.
  D. The initiation phase begins with the binding of the small ribosomal subunit to the mRNA.

Problem solved:

C is correct. Prokaryotes (bacteria) have no nucleus. Transcription and translation take place simultaneously in the cytosol. In eukaryotic cells, transcription and RNA processing occurs in the nucleus, and translation occurs in the cytosol. The two processes do not occur simultaneously in the eukaryotic cell. Choices A, B, and D make true statements about the translation process as it occurs in both prokaryotes and eukaryotes.

DNA, TRANSCRIPTION, AND TRANSLATION IN PERSPECTIVE

The Genetic Code and Its Degeneracy

Now we know that the two sequential processes leading from a DNA molecule to protein are (1) transcription, in which a DNA template is read to produce a molecule of mRNA, and (2) translation, in which an mRNA template is read to generate a peptide with tRNA and the ribosomes (made, substantially, of rRNA) playing critical roles. In summary, DNA issues a "message" to mRNA, and mRNA "carries" the message to tRNA and the ribosomes.

Now, in biochemical terms, let us ask and answer this question: What is the form of this "message" that is delivered by DNA to mRNA and carried by mRNA to tRNA and the ribosomes? The message is individual sequences of nucleotide residues, each sequence consisting of three residues. Consider some tiny portion of a DNA strand that carries the nucleotide sequence:

$$(5') - \quad C \quad G \quad G \quad - (3')$$

When transcribed, it produces on the resulting mRNA molecule the sequence:

$$(5') - \quad C \quad C \quad G \quad - (3')$$

When the mRNA molecule undergoes translation, the (5') - C C G - (3') codon is presented at the ribosome's A site, where it is joined by the tRNA molecule that carries the anticodon:

$$(3') - \quad G \quad G \quad C \quad - (5')$$

(Recall that DNA and mRNA sequences are conventionally written in the 5' to 3' direction, whereas the tRNA anticodon is conventionally written in the 3' to 5' direction.)

The tRNA molecule that bears the (3') - G G C - (5') anticodon binds the amino acid alanine. At the ribosome's A site, alanyl tRNA^{Ala} recognizes the mRNA codon (5') - C C G - (3'), which was produced during transcription from a DNA template. Each three-membered nucleotide sequence on the mRNA transcript is called a codon. Each mRNA codon is specific to only one tRNA anticodon, which is specific for one amino acid. The association between each mRNA codon and the amino acid for which it codes is called the **genetic code**.

FIRST BASE IN THE CODON	SECOND BASE IN THE CODON				THIRD BASE IN THE CODON
	U	C	A	G	
U	Phenylalanine	Serine	Tyrosine	Cysteine	U
	Phenylalanine	Serine	Tyrosine	Cysteine	C
	Leucine	Serine	Termination	Termination	A
	Leucine	Serine	Termination	Tryptophan	G
C	Leucine	Proline	Histidine	Arginine	U
	Leucine	Proline	Histidine	Arginine	C
	Leucine	Proline	Glutamine	Arginine	A
	Leucine	Proline	Glutamine	Arginine	G
A	Isoleucine	Threonine	Asparagine	Serine	U
	Isoleucine	Threonine	Asparagine	Serine	C
	Isoleucine	Threonine	Lysine	Arginine	A
	Methionine	Threonine	Lysine	Arginine	G
G	Valine	Alanine	Aspartic acid	Glycine	U
	Valine	Alanine	Aspartic acid	Glycine	C
	Valine	Alanine	Glutamic acid	Glycine	A
	Valine	Alanine	Glutamic acid	Glycine	G

The Genetic Code

Figure 24.21

We stated before that each tRNA anticodon is specific to one and only one amino acid, but that for any given amino acid, there might be more than one tRNA anticodon. This phenomenon leads to the frequently made statement that *the genetic code is **degenerate***. The word "degenerate" does not suggest that the genetic code harbors any defect (moral or otherwise). Rather it means that the code does not represent a 1-to-1 codon–amino acid radio; any given amino acid might be coded for by more than one mRNA codon (but no mRNA codon codes for more than one amino acid). For example, all of the codons —(5') - U C U - (3'), —(5') - U C C - (3'), (5') - U C A - (3'), (5') - U C G - (3')—are specific to the amino acid serine, and each of those codons is specific *only* to the amino acid serine.

Please solve this problem:

- A codon is a nucleotide sequence situated on a molecule of:

    A. DNA.
    B. mRNA.
    C. tRNA.
    D. rRNA.

Problem solved:

B is correct. The genetic code refers, conceptually, to the fact that a sequence of three nucleotide residues on a DNA template produces, through transcription, a complementary sequence on an mRNA strand. On the mRNA strand, the sequence is called a codon and forms a part of the genetic code. The codon is complementary to the anticodon on tRNA.

Please solve this problem:

- The genetic code allows for the possibility that:

    A. one codon is specific to more than one amino acid.
    B. more than one codon is specific to a single amino acid.
    C. some amino acids do not correspond to codons.
    D. some anticodons correspond to no codons.

Problem solved:

B is correct. The genetic code is degenerate, which means that any given amino acid might correspond to more than one mRNA codon. For example, the two codons (5') - UUU - (3') and (5') - UUC - (3') code for phenylalanine. Choices A, C, and D make false statements. Any given mRNA codon cannot specify more than one amino acid (choice A). All amino acids correspond to at least one codon (choice C), and all anticodons (which appear on tRNA molecules) have corresponding codons.

Return to the Transcription Unit

Now that we have reviewed all of protein synthesis, let's return to the transcription unit. Recall that the transcription unit is the portion of a DNA molecule that undergoes transcription, from promoter site to terminator. A simple transcription unit might look like this:

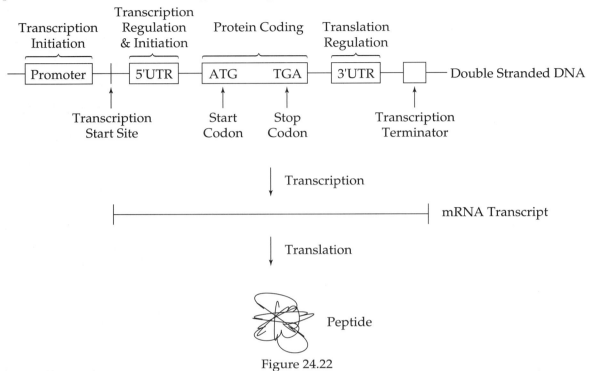

Figure 24.22

Notice that transcription is initiated at the promoter, starts at the start site (downstream from the promoter), and ends at the terminator. The protein coding region is within the mRNA transcript, but is not the entire mRNA transcript; mRNA also contains regulatory regions at the 5' and 3' ends (the 5'UTR and 3'UTR). Translation is initiated at the 5'UTR, starts at the start codon (ATG on the DNA coding strand or AUG on the mRNA transcript), and ends at one of the stop codons (UAG, UGA, UAA).

DNA Replication vs. Transcription vs. Translation

It is important to remember the similarities and differences between DNA replication, transcription and translation. In summary:

	DNA Replication	Transcription	Translation
Signal to get ready	Ori	Promoter	5' UTR *Shine-Dalgarno in prokaryotes Kozak sequence in eukaryotes*
Signal to start	Ori	Start site	AUG start condon
Key enzyme	DNA polymerase	RNA polymerase	Ribosome (made of rRNA and peptides)
Other enzymes	Helicase Primase Ligase	Splicosome (eukaryotes only)	Aminoacyl tRNA synthetases
Template molecule	DNA	DNA	mRNA
Read direction	3' to 5' on the DNA template	3' to 5' on the DNA template	5' to 3' on the RNA template
Molecule synthesized	DNA	RNA *mRNA in prokaryotes hnRNA in eukaryotes*	Peptides
Build direction	5' to 3'	5' to 3'	N-terminus to C-terminus
Prokaryotic location	Cytoplasm	Cytoplasm	Cytoplasm
Eukaryotic location	Nucleus	Nucleus	Cytoplasm
Signal to stop	When the replication bubbles or newly synthesized strands meet and are ligated together	Terminator	Stop codon (UAG, UGA, UAA)

Table 24.2

24.2 MASTERY APPLIED: PRACTICE PASSAGE AND QUESTIONS

Passage

Chromosome abnormalities in an embryo can result in either spontaneous abortions (miscarriages) or serious disorders, such as trisomy 21 (Down's syndrome) and the fragile X syndrome. Chromosomal abnormalities may be due either to a structural defect or a numeric defect. A standard technique for examining human chromosomes employs phytohemagglutinin, which is derived from the red bean. Added to a small quantity of anticoagulated blood, it engenders agglutination and stimulates the division of lymphocytes. Microtubule inhibitors can then be employed to halt mitosis, and metaphase chromosomes can be observed for any alterations in number and/or structure.

Another common technique used to examine chromosomes is Giemsa banding (G-banding). Trypsin is added to chromosome preparations and the chromosomes are then stained with Giemsa to produce a pattern of light and dark bands. Each chromosome can be identified by its unique banding pattern. This banding method results in the resolution of approximately 350–550 bands per haploid set of chromosomes. A single band represents about 5×10^6 to 10×10^6 base pairs of DNA. Each band represents a range of genes, from a few to many. A gene may involve 10^3 base pairs to more than 2×10^6 base pairs. Improvements to the Giemsa technique now permit observation of chromosomes in early metaphase. The advantage of this is that chromosomes in early metaphase are more extended than those in late metaphase, which allows the band resolution to be more refined. The improved technique is associated with the definition of over more than 850 bands.

Banding reveals the substructure of a chromosome and allows each chromosome to be identified unequivocally. Chromosomes are defined by their size, band pattern, and morphology (shape and structural charac-

teristics); this last criterion includes the positioning of their centromere (see Figure 1). The centromere is the point of constriction of the metaphase chromosome, and its position is constant for a specific chromosome. The centromere divides the chromosome into two arms. Metacentric chromosomes have their centromeres positioned near the center of the two arms, while submetacentric chromosomes have centromeres located in between the two arms, somewhat more distant from the center. Acrocentric chromosomes have centromeres positioned near one end of the two arms; often these chromosomes show satellites positioned above a thin stalk. Another useful piece of information is the number of chromosomes present. Once chromosomes have been sorted according to the criteria listed above, they are arranged in a karyotype, a sequential ordering of metaphase chromosomes based on length and position of centromere.

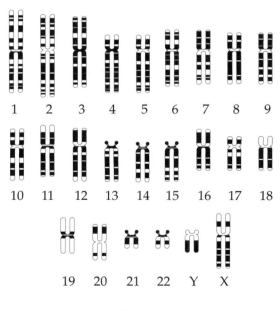

Figure 1

1. Which of the following reveals a chromosomal abnormality resulting from a numerical defect?

   I. A karyotype showing a total of forty-six chromosomes.
   II. A karyotype showing a total of twenty-two sets of autosomes.
   III. A karyotype showing a total of sixty-nine chromosomes.

   A. II only
   B. III only
   C. I and III only
   D. II and III only

2. The inhibitor used to arrest mitosis prevented the occurrence of which stages of cell division?

   A. Metaphase and prophase
   B. Anaphase and telophase
   C. Telophase, anaphase, and prophase
   D. Metaphase, anaphase, prophase, and telophase

3. Microtubules form which of the following structures during mitosis?

   A. The centrosomes
   B. The kinetochore
   C. The mitotic spindle
   D. The chromosomes

4. A geneticist in the process of assembling the karyotype of a cell based on stained metaphase chromosomes would assess all of the following characteristics EXCEPT:

   A. the number of chromosomes present.
   B. the individual sizes of the chromosomes.
   C. the comparative condensed states of a chromosome.
   D. the location of centromeres on the chromosomes.

5. Should chromosome banding of a mitotic chromosome be expected to identify sections of chromosomes that have been exchanged between chromosomes?

   A. Yes, because banding allows each specific chromosome to be identified unequivocally.
   B. Yes, because banding patterns vary from individual to individual.
   C. No, because banding does not reveal the substructure of a given chromosome.
   D. No, because banding only reveals the size and number of chromosomes.

6. The improved staining technique mentioned in the passage takes advantage of which of the following mitotic events?

   A. Chromosomes begin to condense during prophase and are still incompletely condensed at early metaphase.
   B. Chromosomes begin to condense during metaphase, and at early metaphase have not yet condensed.
   C. Chromosomes have not yet begun to condense at early metaphase or metaphase.
   D. Chromosomes do not condense until after anaphase, when cytokinesis is completed.

7. Research has shown that chromosomal abnormalities are found in fifty percent of spontaneously aborted fetuses, compared to a five-percent rate in stillborns. These data indicate that:

   A. chromosomal aberrations are spontaneously eliminated in fifty-five percent of conceptions.
   B. loss of chromosomally abnormal zygotes typically occurs early in gestation.
   C. ninety-five percent of stillborns will have chromosomal abnormalities.
   D. viability of offspring decreases as gestation proceeds.

24.3 MASTERY VERIFIED: ANSWERS AND EXPLANATIONS

1. **B is correct.** Human cells feature a total of forty-six chromosomes in their nuclei. Statement I does not relate to a numeric chromosomal abnormality. Human cells do not normally have a total of sixty-nine chromosomes as indicated in statement III. A genotype of sixty-nine chromosomes, however, indicates triploidy, a numeric chromosomal aberration. Humans have a total of twenty-two sets of autosomes and one set of sex chromosomes (XX for a female, XY for a male). Statement II therefore does not substantiate a numerical chromosomal abnormality. The correct answer option includes statement III and excludes the other two.

2. **B is correct.** The microtubule inhibitor used to inhibit mitosis yielded metaphase chromosomes. The stages of mitosis are, in sequential order, prophase, metaphase, anaphase, and telophase. Halting the cell division at metaphase circumvented anaphase and telophase, which would have followed metaphase.

3. **C is correct.** The mitotic spindle forms between the cell division stages of prophase and metaphase; it consists of microtubules and other components. The spindle spans the cell. The centrosomes are the two poles from which the microtubules emanate, not microtubules themselves, as choice A suggests. Similarly, in choice B, the centrioles are located at the two poles from which the microtubules emanate but are not microtubules. (Centrioles are at the center of the centrosomes.) Choice D is wrong because the chromosomes are composed only of DNA and protein.

4. **C is correct.** As described in the passage, karyotype is determined by four characteristics: the number of chromosomes present, their individual sizes, the location of their centromeres, and the banding pattern of individual chromosomes.

5. **A is correct.** A change in chromosome content would be detected using the method described. In choice B, variations from individual to individual, even if verifiable, would not address the question of a translocation between one individual's chromosomes. Choices C and D are incorrect because banding reveals the substructure of a given chromosome; it also reveals more than the size and number of chromosomes.

6. **A is correct.** Duplicated chromosomes begin to condense during prophase; by early metaphase they are still slightly extended compared to their status at metaphase. Chromosomes begin to condense at prophase, which precedes early metaphase and metaphase.

7. **B is correct.** The data suggest that embryos with chromosomal abnormalities are spontaneously rejected early in development rather than later in development. Choice A is incorrect because chromosomal aberrations are permanent. Choice C is nonsensical and is calculated to cause the student to account for the remaining ninety-five percent of stillborns whose conditions are not described. Organisms that are not viable tend to be rejected early in gestation rather than later in gestation. Choice D, therefore, is incorrect.

CHAPTER 25

PERPETUATION OF THE SPECIES—THE BIOLOGY OF REPRODUCTION

25.1 MASTERY ACHIEVED

HOMOLOGY, DIPLOIDY, AND HAPLOIDY

To understand the reproduction of cells and multicellular organisms, you must understand the terms **homology**, **diploidy**, and **haploidy** (also called **monoploidy**). In the human, all cells other than the **germ cells** (i.e., sperm and ova) contain forty-six chromosomes, or twenty-three homologous pairs. **Diploidy** is the state in which every chromosome of a cell has a homologue. The diploid state is also designated "2N."

If one chromosome were removed from each of the twenty-three pairs in a diploid human cell, the cell would be left with twenty-three chromosomes in total. Each of the twenty-three chromosomes would lack a homologous counterpart, and the cell would be termed **"haploid."** For any organism the number of chromosomes in a haploid cell is one half the number of chromosomes in a diploid cell. The haploid condition is designated "1N."

Please solve this problem:

- If a cell is diploid, then:

    A. it has one half the DNA content associated with a chromosome in the haploid state.
    B. each of its chromosomes has a homologous counterpart.
    C. it contains two nuclei.
    D. its nucleus contains single-stranded DNA.

Problem solved:

B is correct. The diploid state describes a cell in which all chromosomes possess homologous pairs. The haploid state describes a cell whose chromosomes do not have homologues. Regardless of whether a cell is diploid or haploid, its chromosomes are composed of double-stranded DNA; choices A and D are incorrect. Choice C is incorrect as well; the diploid cell does not contain two nuclei.

Please solve this problem:

- If, for a given organism, the diploid number is 24, the haploid number is:

    A. 48.
    B. 18.
    C. 12.
    D. 9.

Problem solved:

C is correct. A haploid cell has one half the number of chromosomes found in a diploid cell. A haploid cell's chromosomes do not have homologous counterparts. A diploid human cell has 46 chromosomes, or twenty-three homologous pairs. A haploid human cell (such as a sperm cell or an ovum) contains a total of twenty-three chromosomes.

CELLULAR REPRODUCTION

Cells reproduce through the process of **mitosis**. The period of the cell's life cycle between mitotic divisions is called **interphase**. Interphase has three subphases: (1) the G_1 phase, also called the **gap phase**; (2) the **S phase**, also called the **synthesis phase**; and (3) the G_2 phase, also called the **growth phase**. During the S phase the cell reproduces its genome in preparation for division. Mitosis involves **nuclear division**. **Cytoplasmic division** is also called **cytokinesis**.

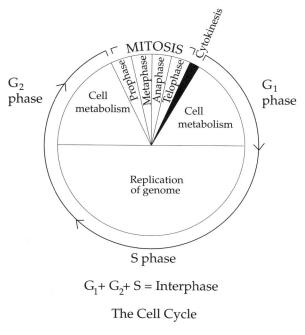

$$G_1 + G_2 + S = \text{Interphase}$$

The Cell Cycle

Figure 25.1

Please solve this problem:

- The cell-cycle phase associated with the replication of the cell's genome is:

  A. the S phase of interphase.
  B. mitosis.
  C. the G_2 period of interphase.
  D. cytokinesis.

Problem solved:

A is correct. The cell's genome is replicated during the S phase of the cell cycle. The G_2 portion of interphase represents the second gap phase. Mitosis involves nuclear division. Cytokinesis refers to the division of the cytoplasm (as opposed to the division of the nucleus).

Replication of the Genome

During the S phase of interphase, all twenty-three pairs of the cell's chromosomes replicate. When replication is complete, each chromosome has a duplicate. Each pair of duplicates is joined at a **centromere**.

Although in some sense (and by some older authorities) each duplicate pair might be considered two chromosomes, modern usage calls on us to consider the duplicated unit, still joined at its centromere, as *one* chromosome. Don't let this semantic problem confuse you (as it confuses most students).

Before a chromosome duplicates itself, it is, of course, one chromosome. Even after it duplicates itself (and the DNA quantity is doubled), the duplicated unit is still considered (these days) to be one chromosome—for as long as the duplicated entity is still joined by a centromere.

Each member of the pair, instead of constituting a "chromosome," is termed a "**sister chromatid.**"

Mindful of all that, we can say this: During the S phase of interphase, all twenty-three pairs of the cell's chromosomes replicate. Even after replication, however, for as long as duplicated pairs are joined at their centromeres, modern convention calls on us to say that the cell still has only twenty-three pairs of chromosomes, each chromosome comprising a pair of sister chromatids. Each pair of sister chromatids (joined at a centromere) represents what *will* become two separate chromosomes.

Please solve this problem:

- Sister chromatids are:

 A. homologous to one another.
 B. identical to one another.
 C. unrelated to one another.
 D. produced during the G_1 phase of the cell cycle.

Problem solved:

B is correct. Sister chromatids are produced through DNA replication and are therefore identical to one another. They are produced during the S phase, not the G_1 phase; choice D is incorrect.

Mitosis

Interphase is followed by mitosis, a process that is customarily divided into four phases—**prophase**, **metaphase**, **anaphase**, and **telophase**—and results in division of the nucleus. Mitosis is followed by the division of the cytoplasm, called cytokinesis.

During prophase, the chromosomes condense to the point that they are visible under the light microscope as an X-shaped structure. The **nucleolus** slowly disappears. Centrioles move to opposite poles of the cell. Star-shaped fibers, called **aster fibers,** form around the centrioles. Microtubules give rise to a mitotic spindle, which spans the cell from pole to pole. The nuclear membrane begins to dissolve.

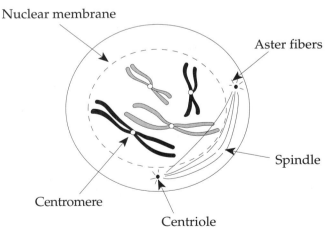

The Cell at Prophase of Mitosis

Figure 25.2

The beginning of metaphase is termed **early metaphase** (or **prometaphase**) and is marked by complete dissolution of the nuclear membrane. **Kinetochore fibers** associated with the centromeres interact with the mitotic spindle, producing movement of chromosomes. At metaphase proper, the chromosomes align on the **metaphase plate** so that centromeres lie in a plane along an axis at the cell's midpoint. The kinetochore fibers help to align and maintain the chromosomes on the metaphase plate.

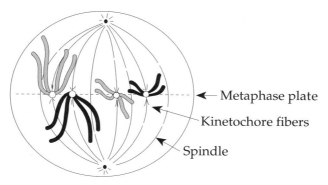

← Metaphase plate

← Kinetochore fibers

← Spindle

The Cell at Metaphase of Mitosis

Figure 25.3

During anaphase, sister chromatids separate (as a result of the splitting of the centromere) and move toward opposite poles of the cell along the path marked by the spindle apparatus. With the separation of sister chromatids, each chromatid is called a **daughter chromosome**.

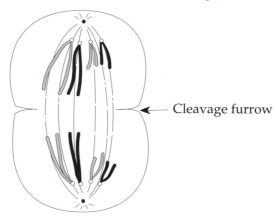

← Cleavage furrow

The Cell at Anaphase of Mitosis

Figure 25.4

At telophase, the daughter chromosomes are positioned at opposite poles of the cell, and the kinetochore fibers disappear. A nuclear membrane forms around each set of daughter chromosomes. The chromosomes decondense and are no longer visable by light microscopy. Nucleoli then reappear; mitosis and nuclear division are complete.

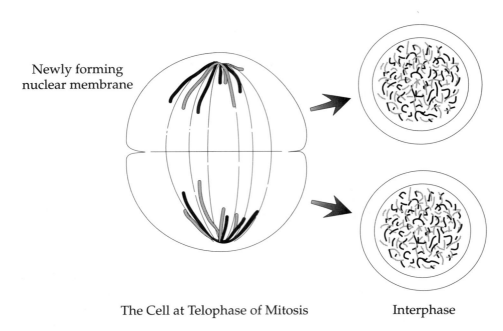

Newly forming
nuclear membrane

The Cell at Telophase of Mitosis   Interphase

Figure 25.5

Cytokinesis begins during the last part of anaphase or the early part of telophase. A **cleavage furrow** forms along the equator of the cell. The furrow deepens until it ultimately divides the cell, forming two daughter cells. Each daughter cell possesses a diploid number of chromosomes. The daughter cells then enter the interphase period of the cell cycle.

Please solve this problem:

- Development of a cleavage furrow occurs during:

    A. interphase.
    B. prophase.
    C. metaphase.
    D. cytokinesis.

Problem solved:

D is correct. The cleavage furrow develops around the periphery of the cell toward late anaphase or early telophase. However, the development of the cleavage furrow is the beginning of cytokinesis, which makes choice D the best answer. It initiates the division of the parent cell into two daughter cells. The daughter cells normally receive approximately equal amounts of cytoplasm and an equal inventory of organelles.

Please solve this problem:

- Which of the following stages involve(s) a change in chromosome density?

  A. Prophase alone
  B. Interphase alone
  C. Prophase and telophase
  D. Anaphase and telophase

Problem solved:

C is correct. At prophase, the chromosomes condense and become visible under the light microscope. At telophase, the process is reversed: Chromosomes decondense and disappear.

REDUCTION DIVISION: MEIOSIS

Reduction division refers to the generation of haploid daughter cells by a diploid parent cell. Reduction division is accomplished by meiosis and is the basis of **gametogenesis** (as discussed below). Like mitosis, meiosis involves nuclear division and cytokinesis. Nuclear division in meiosis embodies four stages bearing the same names as those in mitosis: prophase, metaphase, anaphase, and telophase. Meiosis, however, involves *two* divisions (or two cycles) instead of one. The first meiotic division/cycle consists of prophase I, metaphase I, anaphase I, and telophase I; the second meiotic division/cycle entails prophase II, metaphase II, anaphase II, and telophase II.

The First Meiotic Division

The first phase of the first meiotic division is termed prophase I. Prophase I follows interphase, during which the cell duplicates its chromosomes. As in mitosis, chromosomes condense during prophase I, the nucleolus begins to disassemble and disappear, and centrioles move to opposite poles of the cell. Aster fibers form around the centrioles. The mitotic spindle forms and spans the cell from pole to pole. The nuclear membrane begins to break down.

Prophase I differs from mitotic prophase in that *homologous pairs* of duplicated chromosomes align in proximity to one another, forming **tetrads**. The association of homologous pairs of duplicated chromosomes to form the tetrad is termed **synapsis**.

The proximity between homologous chromosomes during synapsis frequently leads chromatids from one homologue to physically bind with chromatids from the other homologue. The site at which binding occurs is called the **chiasma, or synaptonemal membrane**. Chromatids may break at the chiasma. When this happens, the resulting segments may change places with one another in a process called **crossing over**. Crossing over produces a physical exchange of chromatid segments between sections of homologous chromatids. The process causes each chromatid to lose a component of its own DNA and to acquire in its place a corresponding section of DNA from its homologue. Crossing over, therefore, is a form of **genetic recombination** that is specific to meiosis.

Chiasma

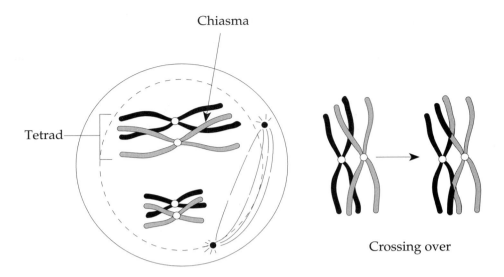

Tetrad

Crossing over

Synapsis and Crossing Over During Meiosis I

Figure 25.6

*Mei*otic metaphase I differs from *mit*otic metaphase in that *pairs* of homologous chromosomes (instead of *single* chromosomes) align on the spindle apparatus. That is, tetrads (composed of four chromatids) align along the spindles. By comparison, in mitotic metaphase a double-stranded chromosome composed of *two* sister chromatids aligns on the metaphase plate.

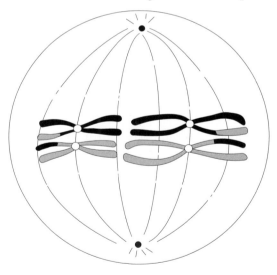

Alignment of Chromosome Pairs on Metaphase Plate
During Metaphase I of Meiosis

Figure 25.7

In meiotic anaphase I, homologous chromosome pairs separate and move to opposite poles of the cell. *Centromeres, however, do not split.* The two chromatids belonging to a chromosome remain attached. Each pole of the cell, therefore, contains one chromosome from each pair of homologous chromosomes.

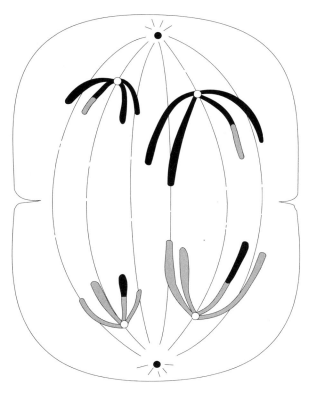

The Cell at Anaphase of Meiosis I

Figure 25.8

At meiotic telophase I, the chromosomes form two clusters at either end of the cell. The cell cytoplasm divides, leaving two daughter cells, each with genetic material from *only one* member of each pair of homologous chromosomes.

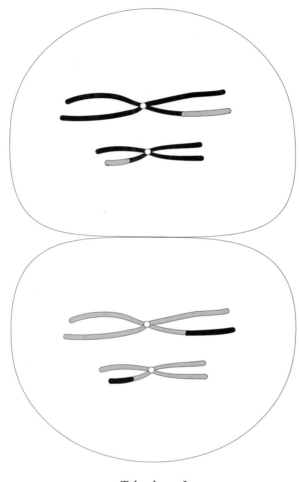

Telophase I

Figure 25.9

Please solve this problem:

- Which of the following is associated with meiotic prophase I but not with mitotic prophase?

  A. Spindle formation
  B. Movement of centrioles to opposite cellular poles
  C. Condensed chromosomes
  D. Tetrad formation

Problem solved:

D is correct. During mitotic prophase, chromosomes consisting of two sister chromatids align along the spindle fibers, without associating with their homologues. During meiotic prophase I, each chromosome aligns along the spindle fibers at the metaphase plate in association with its homologue, forming the four-chromatid tetrad. The formation of tetrads and the subsequent separation of homologous pairs without the splitting of centromeres ideally provides each daughter cell with the genetic information from only one homologue of each chromosomal pair. (As discussed earlier however, meiotic prophase I normally gives rise to crossing over. For that reason, each daughter cell does *not*, in fact, inherit homologues identical to those of the parent cell.)

Spindle formation, condensed chromosomes, and the existence of sister chromatids are found during both mitotic and meiotic prophases.

Please solve this problem:

- Which of the following most completely characterizes the process of crossing over?

    A. Genetic material is exchanged between homologous chromosomes during synapsis.
    B. Duplicated chromosomes pair with their duplicated homologues.
    C. A chiasma is formed.
    D. A nuclear division during which each daughter cell receives the genetic material from only one chromosome of each homologous pair.

Problem solved:

A is correct. Crossing over is associated with the process of synapsis, which occurs during meiotic prophase. Homologous chromosomes associate and exchange portions of their DNA. The result is an exchange of the genetic material and, consequently, genetic recombination. Choice B characterizes tetrad formation, a prelude to crossing over, and choice D characterizes the first meiotic division. The chiasma (choice C) is the site at which crossing over begins. Thus choice C does not characterize the process fully.

Please solve this problem:

- Which of the following correctly distinguishes mitosis from the first division of meiosis?

    A. After the first meiotic division, each daughter cell possesses a full complement of genetic material; after mitosis, they do not.
    B. After mitosis, each daughter cell possesses a full complement of genetic material; after the first meiotic division, they do not.
    C. After mitosis, each daughter cell possesses duplicated chromosomes; after meiosis, they do not.
    D. After the first meiotic division, each daughter cell possesses chromosomes that are organized into tetrads; after mitosis, they do not.

Problem solved:

B is correct. The daughter cells produced by the first meiotic division do not have a full complement of genetic material. Because homologues separate while their centromeres remain intact, each daughter cell receives only *one* member of each homologous chromosomal pair. The absence of the other member of the homologous pair means that each daughter receives half of the full parental genome.

Each of the daughter cells produced by mitosis, on the other hand, receives one copy of each member of each chromosome; it receives the full parental genome. Choices A and C are wrong because they reverse the truth. Choice D is incorrect as well; during meiosis, tetrads separate during anaphase I. The tetrad does not exist within the daughter cells.

The Second Meiotic Division

Each daughter cell that arises from the first meiotic division has half of the full complement of chromosomes, but it has two copies of that half. The two copies of each chromosome are joined by a centromere. During the second meiotic division, each daughter cell undergoes prophase II, metaphase II, anaphase II, and telophase II in much the same manner as a cell that undergoes mitosis. At anaphase II, centromeres divide, and the two chromatids are pulled to opposite poles of the cell. Cytokinesis follows, and two daughter cells result, each of which has one of the four chromatids from each original tetrad. Because the process just described occurs in each of the two daughter cells produced in the first meiotic division, a total of four daughter cells are produced. Each of the four daughter cells produced by meiosis is haploid.

MITOSIS AND MEIOSIS: THE FUNDAMENTAL DIFFERENCES

Mitosis generates two diploid daughters and meiosis generates four haploid daughters. The difference in ploidy and number of daughter cells arises from an initial difference in the alignment of chromosomes on the spindle apparatus and in the subsequent separation of chromosomes to form new daughter nuclei. In mitosis, chromosomes align without pairing with their homologues. Centromeres then divide, and each daughter is provided with one copy of *all* chromosomes. In the first meiotic division, chromosomes align on the spindle apparatus in association with their homologues. Centromeres do not then divide. Rather, homologues separate, and each daughter cell is provided with two copies of one half of the original genome. That is, each receives two copies of only one member of each homologous pair.

Each daughter then undergoes the second meiotic division, in which centromeres divide. Each daughter produces two new daughters (for a total of four daughters). Each daughter cell has one copy of one member of each homologous pair.

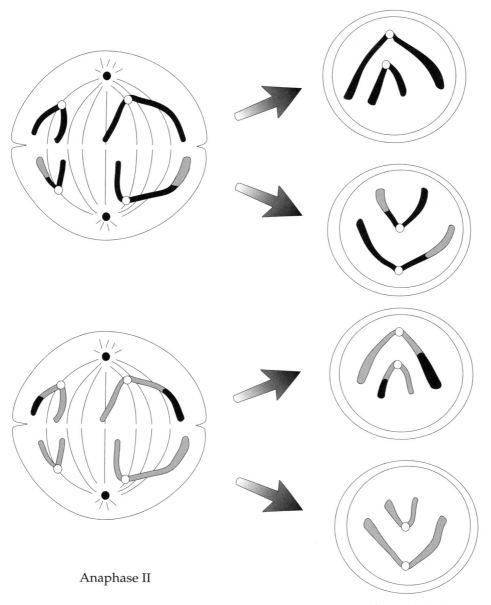

Anaphase II

After telophase II and cytokinesis

Anaphase II through Telophase II and Cytokinesis

Figure 25.10

GAMETOGENESIS: REPRODUCTION OF THE SEX CELLS

Gametogenesis refers to the generation of **gametes** through meiosis. More specifically, **spermatogenesis** denotes formation of the **sperm cell**, which is the male gamete, and **oogenesis** the formation of the **ovum**, which is the female gamete. Spermatogenesis occurs in the **seminiferous tubules** of the **testes** (the **male gonads**), and oogenesis in the **ovaries** (the **female gonads**). Ova and sperm are haploid cells, and their fusion at fertilization forms the diploid **zygote**. The zygote gives rise to a new diploid organism.

Spermatogenesis

Within the seminiferous tubules of the testes reside relatively undifferentiated diploid cells called **spermatogonia**.

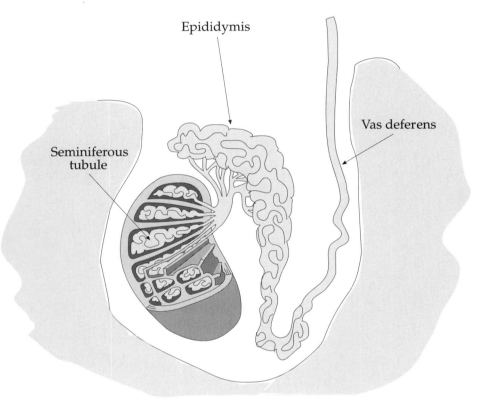

Testis

Figure 25.11

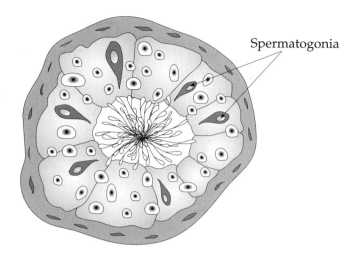

Cross-section View of a Seminiferous Tubule

Figure 25.12

Some spermatogonia multiply, enlarge, and undergo genomic replication to produce a large number of primary spermatocytes, each of which then undergoes a first meiotic cycle to yield two secondary spermatocytes. Each secondary spermatocyte then undergoes a second meiotic cycle to produce two haploid spermatids. Each primary spermatocyte, therefore, produces four haploid spermatids.

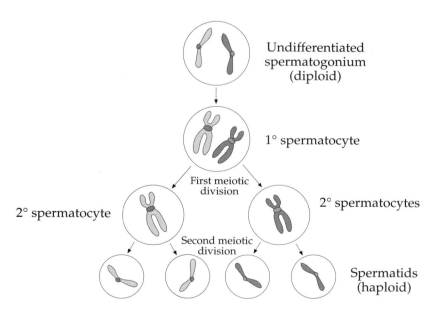

Spermatogenesis

Figure 25.13

Spermatids are immature sperm cells that travel to the **epididymis**, a coiled tube that serves as the site of maturation and storage for sperm. There, spermatids differentiate into mature sperm that will bear, among other structures, a **flagellum** for motility and an **acrosome** filled with degradative enzymes that facilitate penetration of the ovum during fertilization.

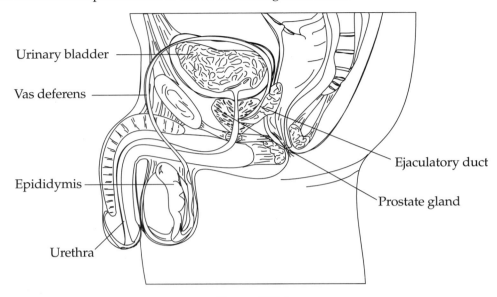

Figure 25.14

From the epididymis, the mature sperm enters first the **vas deferens**, then the **ejaculatory duct**, and finally the **urethra**, which runs through the **penis** to the outside of the body.

Please solve this problem:

- Which of the following correctly orders the structures through which sperm cells travel?

    A. Epididymis, vas deferens, ejaculatory duct, seminiferous tubule, urethra
    B. Vas deferens, epididymis, ejaculatory duct, seminiferous tubule, urethra
    C. Seminiferous tubule, epididymis, vas deferens, ejaculatory duct, urethra
    D. Ejaculatory duct, seminiferous tubule, vas deferens, epididymis, urethra

Problem solved:

C is correct. Newly formed spermatozoa travel first through the seminiferous tubule, then through the epididymis, then through the vas deferens, the ejaculatory duct, and the urethra. A flagellum affords a sperm cell the motility it needs to reach the ovum, and acrosomal enzymes assist it in penetrating the ovum during fertilization.

Please solve this problem:

- Which of the following describes an entity that is haploid?

    A. Spermatogonium
    B. Embryo
    C. Spermatid
    D. Zygote

Problem solved:

C is correct. Spermatogenesis begins with the spermatogonium, a diploid cell. After it enlarges and undergoes replication of its genome, it becomes a primary spermatocyte in which chromosomes have doubled, but are *still joined at a centromere*. According to current terminology, therefore, each primary spermatocyte is said to have twenty-three chromosomal pairs (not forty-six pairs), with each member of each pair being joined at a centromere to a sister chromatid. Like its progenitor the spermatogonium, the primary spermatocyte is diploid, with each chromosome (consisting of two sister chromatids) having a homologue (each of which also consists of two sister chromatids). The primary spermatocyte undergoes a first and second meiotic cycle to generate four spermatids, which are haploid cells. The spermatids mature to become spermatozoa (haploid gametes). The fusion of a spermatozoan with an ovum (a haploid gamete) produces a zygote, which is diploid.

Oogenesis

Oogenesis produces a single mature haploid ovum. The process begins in the ovary, where a diploid **oogonium** begins meiosis to produce a **primary oocyte**. The primary oocyte undergoes a first meiotic division. Unlike the first meiotic division that accompanies spermatogenesis, this division divides cytoplasm unequally between the progeny, producing one larger and one smaller daughter cell. The larger one is called a **secondary oocyte**, and the smaller a **polar body**. The secondary oocyte undergoes a second meiotic division. The polar body may or may not divide; if it does, it produces two new polar bodies, each haploid. The secondary oocyte produces two daughter cells, which are also haploid. When the secondary oocyte undergoes the second meiotic division, it again allocates cytoplasm unequally, producing one small haploid polar body and one haploid **ootid.** The ootid then matures to become a large haploid ovum. The point of this is the conservation of cytoplasm; almost all the cytoplasm from the original oogonium ends up in the secondary oocyte. The net products of oogenesis, then, are two or three small haploid polar bodies, which degenerate, and one large haploid ovum.

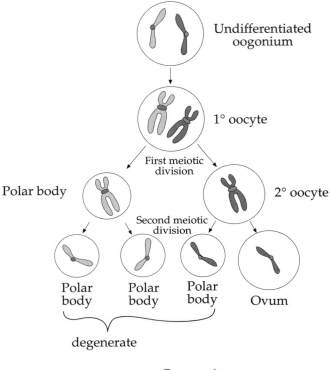

Oogenesis
Figure 25.15

Please solve this problem:

- Which of the following correctly orders the cell types that arise during oogenesis?

  A. Secondary oocyte, primary oocyte, oogonia, ovum

  B. Primary oocyte, secondary oocyte, oogonia, ovum

  C. Ovum, primary oocyte, secondary oocyte, oogonia

  D. Oogonia, primary oocyte, secondary oocyte, ovum

Problem solved:

D is correct. The undifferentiated oogonium becomes the primary oocyte, which produces secondary oocytes and then the ovum. In the course of oogenesis, as many as three polar bodies are generated.

Please solve this problem:

- Which of the following does NOT apply to a polar body?

    A. It is small in relation to an ovum.
    B. It arises as a by-product of oogenesis.
    C. It is diploid.
    D. It degenerates.

Problem solved:

C is correct. Meiosis generates four haploid cells from one diploid cell. In the case of oogenesis, the first meiotic division allocates cytoplasm unequally, yielding two progeny of unequal size. The smaller of the two is a polar body. The larger progeny, a secondary oocyte, undergoes a second meiotic division that yields a relatively large ovum and a relatively small polar body, both haploid. The polar bodies degenerate. Choices A, B, and D make true statements. Choice C does not.

Please solve this problem:

- Which of the following correctly distinguishes spermatogenesis from oogenesis?

    A. Spermatogenesis yields haploid cells; oogenesis does not.
    B. Spermatogenesis produces four functional gametes; oogenesis does not.
    C. Spermatogenesis produces a gamete; oogenesis does not.
    D. Spermatogenesis occurs in the gonads; oogenesis does not.

Problem solved:

B is correct. Spermatogenesis and oogenesis both lead to the production of gametes. Each occurs in the gonads: Oogenesis occurs in the ovaries (the female gonads) and spermatogenesis occurs in the testes (the male gonads). Both processes produce haploid gametes. Spermatogenesis produces four functional haploid gametes; oogenesis, however, produces only one functional haploid gamete and as many as three polar bodies, which degenerate. The disparate products of oogenesis result from unequal allocation of cytoplasm during the first and second meiotic divisions of the oocyte.

OVULATION, FERTILIZATION, AND IMPLANTATION

The mature ovum is surrounded by supporting cells. Together, the ovum and supporting cells compose a **follicle**. During **ovulation** (as it usually occurs) a given follicle in one of the two ovaries ruptures, releasing the ovum, which then enters the **fallopian tube**. The fallopian tube connects the ovaries and the **uterus**, and is normally the site of fertilization.

The ovum is surrounded by an outer and an inner membrane, termed the **corona radiata** and **zona pellucida**, respectively. During **fertilization,** the sperm releases *degradative enzymes* from its *acrosome*, located at its head. These degrade the corona radiata and zona pellucida. Fertilization is complete when sperm and ovum nuclei have fused to form the zygote, a single diploid cell. The zygote travels to the uterus, where it implants in the **endometrial tissue** in a process known as **implantation**.

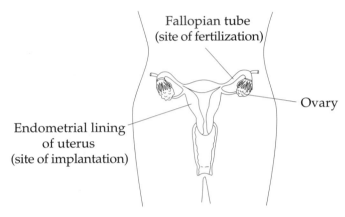

Sites of Fertilization and Implantation
in the Female Reproductive System

Figure 25.16

The **placenta**, a complex mix of embryonic and maternal tissue, develops at the site of implantation. The placenta is the site of the transfer of nutrients from mother to fetus as well as waste products from fetus to mother.

Please solve this problem:

- Which of the following is a false statement?

    A. The site of fertilization is the uterus.
    B. The site of implantation is the uterine wall.
    C. The placenta functions to exchange wastes and nutrients between the embryo and the mother.
    D. Enzymes derived from the acrosome of the sperm facilitate the sperm's penetration of the zona pellucida and corona radiata.

Problem solved:

A is correct. Fertilization occurs in the fallopian tube. The penetration of the ovum's outer layers is facilitated by degradative enzymes, which are stored in the acrosome of the sperm. The resulting zygote implants in the uterine wall. The placenta forms from a combination of maternal and embryonic tissue and exchanges nutrients and waste products between the embryo and the mother.

25.2 MASTERY APPLIED: PRACTICE PASSAGE AND QUESTIONS

Passage

The process of fertilization allows the transmission of genes to the offspring, which are contributed by both parents. Fusion of the genetic material of the sperm and egg—the male and female gametes, respectively—initiates a series of reactions in the egg cytoplasm that marks the beginning of the development of a new organism. Crucial to the success of fertilization is a species-specific recognition between sperm and egg. The egg governs the entry of sperm. Only one sperm can ultimately fertilize the egg.

A mature sperm cell possesses a haploid nucleus containing tightly compressed DNA, a flagellum for propulsion, and an acrosomal vesicle containing enzymes that facilitate entry of the nucleus into the egg. A modified lysosome, the acrosomal vesicle is derived from the Golgi apparatus. Enzymes within it digest proteins and complex sugars, enabling the sperm to penetrate the outer layers of the egg.

In sea urchins (the best-studied animal model of fertilization), globular actin molecules lie between the nucleus and the acrosomal vesicle in sperm. These molecules are proteins that polymerize to project a fingerlike process in early fertilization during the acrosome reaction.

The egg also contains a haploid nucleus and is much larger than a sperm cell. Unlike sperm, the egg has vast reserves of cytoplasm containing proteins, ribosomes, tRNA, mRNA, and morphogenic factors needed to facilitate the development of a new organism. The morphogenic factors govern the differentiation of cells.

The plasma membrane surrounds the egg cytoplasm. During fertilization, the plasma membrane regulates the flow of ions and is capable of fusing with the sperm plasma membrane. Directly above the plasma membrane is the vitelline envelope—a glycoprotein membrane critical to species-specific binding of sperm. In mammals, it is thickened and called the *zona pellucida*. Mammals also have the *corona radiata*, a layer of ovarian follicular cells responsible for providing nutrients to the egg at the time of ovulation. Sea urchin eggs contain an outer layer of jelly that the acrosomal enzymes must penetrate to reach the inner membrane layers.

An investigator wished to determine the location of a sperm protein called *bindin* during fertilization in order to observe when it promotes species-specific binding between sperm and egg. He conducted two experiments using the Mediterranean sea urchin, *Toxopneustes lividus*.

The first experiment was conducted as follows:

Step 1:

Rabbit anti-bindin (an antibody) was produced by injecting purified sea urchin bindin into rabbits.

Step 2:

The rabbit anti-bindin was then bound to sea urchin sperm that had undergone the acrosomal reaction.

Step 3:

Unbound antibody was washed off, and the sperm were exposed to swine antibodies that were capable of binding to rabbit antibodies. The swine antibodies were covalently linked to peroxidase enzymes, allowing peroxidase to be deposited wherever bindin occurred.

The peroxidase enzymes were able to produce an electron-dense precipitate upon reaction with diaminobenzidine (DAB) and hydrogen peroxide (H_2O_2). The precipitate indicates the location of bindin on the sperm.

Results:

The precipitate was found to be localized on the surface of the entire acrosomal process. (See Figure 1.)

A second experiment was performed in the same manner as the first except that in Step 2, the sperm had not yet undergone the acrosome reaction. No bindin was detected on the sperm surface in this trial.

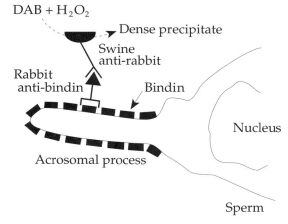

Figure 1

1. A frog egg would contain all of the following EXCEPT:

   A. morphogenic factors.
   B. a vitelline membrane.
   C. a plasma membrane.
   D. the corona radiata.

2. In the sea urchin egg, cortical granules that lie beneath the plasma membrane are homologous to the acrosomal vesicle of sperm. Which of the following characteristic(s) most likely apply (applies) to both structures?

   I. Both are derived from the Golgi apparatus.
   II. Both contain large stores of mRNA and tRNA.
   III. Both contain proteolytic enzymes.

   A. I only
   B. III only
   C. I and II only
   D. I and III only

3. Which of the following undergoes cleavage?

   A. A diploid cell in the S phase of its cell cycle
   B. A haploid cell at the onset of gametogenesis
   C. A diploid zygote just after fertilization
   D. A haploid gamete just after implantation

4. On the basis of the results of Experiments I and II, the researcher would be most justified in concluding that:

   A. bindin is virtually identical in function to egg cortical granules.
   B. bindin promotes species-specific binding of egg and sperm after the acrosomal reaction.
   C. rabbit anti-bindin caused bindin to localize on the acrosomal process.
   D. rabbit anti-bindin caused the sperm in Experiment I to undergo the acrosomal reaction.

5. Under normal conditions in humans, the egg is fertilized in which of the following reproductive structures?

   A. The ovary
   B. The fallopian tubes
   C. The uterus
   D. The corpus luteum

6. Which of the following statements is (are) true with regard to Experiment II?

   I. Rabbit anti-bindin did not bind to bindin.
   II. Diaminobenzidine and hydrogen peroxide did not react with peroxidases to yield a precipitate.
   III. Swine anti-rabbit did not bind to rabbit anti-bindin.

   A. I only
   B. II only
   C. I and III only
   D. I, II, and III

25.3 MASTERY VERIFIED: ANSWERS AND EXPLANATIONS

1. **D is correct.** The corona radiata only exists in mammalian eggs; it is not present in amphibian eggs. Choice A is incorrect; the passage states that morphogenic factors in eggs provide for differentiation of cells during development of the organism. Choice B is incorrect as well: The vitelline membrane of the egg, located above the plasma membrane, allows for species-specific binding of sperm. Choice C is wrong because the plasma membrane is common to all eggs; it encloses the cytoplasm.

2. **D is correct.** The passage states that the acrosomal vesicle derives from the Golgi apparatus. Since cortical granules are homologous to the acrosomal vesicle, they, too, must derive from the Golgi apparatus. Statement I is accurate. According to the passage, only the egg contains mRNA and tRNA stores. Furthermore, these are located in the cytoplasm, not in the cortical granules. Statement II is inaccurate. The passage states that the acrosomal vesicle contains enzymes that break down proteins (proteolytic enzymes). Since cortical granules are homologous to (similar to) acrosomes, they, too, should contain proteolytic enzymes. Statement III is accurate.

3. **C is correct.** Fertilization produces the zygote and triggers cleavage, a series of rapid and successive cell divisions that take place without an increase in size of the initial zygote. Choice A is incorrect because the S phase is the period during which DNA is replicated in the nucleus of the cell. Choice B, too, is incorrect. Gametogenesis entails a series of cell divisions that ultimately generate the gametes—the egg and sperm. Choice D is wrong because haploid gametes do not implant.

4. **B is correct.** The passage states that bindin is responsible for mediating species-specific recognition of egg and sperm; the experiments showed that bindin was localized only on the acrosomal process. Choice A is incorrect because egg cortical granules are similar—but not identical—to the acrosomal vesicle, which contains proteolytic enzymes. Choice C is wrong as well. Rabbit anti-bindin's only function is to attach to any bindin that is present. Presumably it does not affect bindin's location. Choice D is wrong because rabbit anti-bindin only serves to attach to any bindin present on sperm. It does not determine whether the acrosomal reaction will proceed.

5. **B is correct.** The fallopian tubes are the site of fertilization of the egg by a sperm. Choice A is incorrect; the ovary releases the egg at the time of ovulation. Choice C is wrong because the egg has already been fertilized when it implants in the uterus. Choice D, too, is wrong. The corpus luteum is the remains of the follicle from which the egg is released at the time of ovulation.

6. **D is correct.** Because bindin was not present on sperm in Experiment II, rabbit anti-bindin failed to bind to it. Statement I is accurate. Statements II and III are accurate as well. When unbound, rabbit anti-bindin was washed off during Step 3, all of the rabbit anti-bindin was removed, since no bindin was available for attachment. When swine antibodies were then introduced, no rabbit anti-bindin remained for them to bind. Because the swine antibodies could not bind rabbit anti-bindin at binding sites, they did not deposit peroxidases, which would have reacted with DAB and H_2O_2 to form precipitate. (The diagram also indicates this sequence: If bindin is removed from the acrosomal process, then no reactions that would occur subsequently are possible.)

CHAPTER 26

THE DEVELOPING ORGANISM

26.1 MASTERY ACHIEVED

EMBRYOLOGY IN OVERVIEW

This chapter will enable the student to identify and order the developmental stages and processes the early embryo passes through. In sequential order these are **zygote**, **cleavage**, **morulation, blastulation, gastrulation, germ layer formation**, and **neurulation**. The student will also learn to define and relate terms associated with these stages, including **morphogenesis, induction, differentiation, and determination**. Finally, the student will learn to associate a mature organ or tissue with the embryonic germ layer from which it is derived.

DEVELOPMENTAL STAGES OF THE EARLY EMBRYO

Transitional States from Zygote through Gastrula

The developmental process begins with the fertilized zygote, which is produced from the fusion of the **female gamete** (the **ovum**) and the **male gamete** (the **sperm**). Both gametes are **haploid**; their fusion yields a **diploid** zygote. Once the zygote is formed, it enters into a series of rapid cell divisions called **cleavage**. Each mitotic division that occurs during cleavage doubles the cell count, but the organism does not increase in size initially. When the developing organism consists of approximately thirty-two cells, it is called a **morula**. Cleavage continues, and the morula takes the shape of a hollow ball, called a **blastula** (the **blastocoel** is its fluid-filled center). The blastula, still hollow, next invaginates during **gastrulation** to form the **gastrula**. Invagination marks the beginning of morphogenesis, or "the genesis of form."

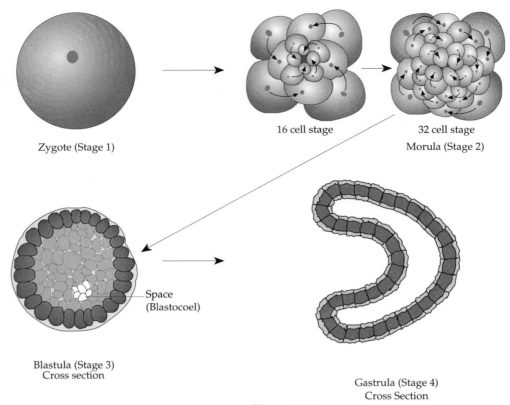

Figure 26.1

Please solve this problem:

- After a period of cleavage, what is the developing organism first called?

    A. Morula
    B. Gastrula
    C. Zygote
    D. Gamete

Problem solved:

A is correct. Cleavage is a series of rapid mitotic divisions that begin after fertilization of the ovum by a sperm cell. Each division produces a doubling of the number of cells present, but does not increase the volume of the initial zygote. During cleavage, the developing organism is called first the morula and then the blastula. The blastula contains hundreds of cells surrounding a hollow, fluid-filled center.

Derivation of Ectoderm, Endoderm, and Mesoderm

Through morphogenesis, the invaginated gastrula generates three distinct **germ cell layers**, called the **ectoderm** (the outer cell layer), **endoderm** (the inner cell layer), and **mesoderm** (the middle cell layer). The creation of these organized layers is directed by the developing embryo's genes.

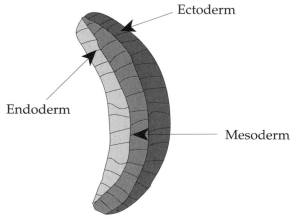

Figure 26.2

Please solve this problem:

- The outermost germ cell layer is the:

    A. epiderm.
    B. mesoderm.
    C. endoderm.
    D. ectoderm.

Problem solved:

D is correct. Germ cell layer formation creates *three* layers; the outermost is the ectoderm. "Epiderm" is not a germ cell layer.

Please solve this problem:

- Ectoderm, endoderm, and mesoderm develop as a result of:

    A. maternal intervention.
    B. programming within the genome.
    C. random orientation.
    D. sex-linked determination.

Problem solved:

B is correct. The formation of the three germ cell layers is genetically coded.

Neural Plate Formation

Once gastrulation is complete and the three germ cell layers have been established, **neurulation** occurs. A portion of the mesoderm forms a tubelike structure called the **notochord**. The notochord induces a thickening of the ectoderm directly above it. The thickened ectoderm forms the **neural plate**. Invagination causes it to assume a tubular shape and form the **neural tube**, a precursor to the brain, the spinal cord, and certain components of the eye, including the retina and optic nerve.

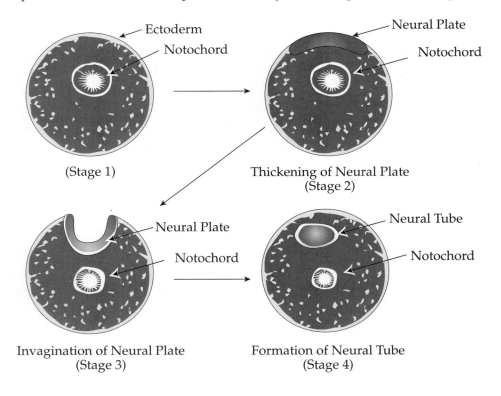

Stages of Neurulation

Figure 26.3

Please solve this problem:

- Neurulation occurs just after:

    A. morulation.
    B. gastrulation.
    C. fertilization.
    D. morphogenesis.

Problem solved:

B is correct. Neurulation, the formation of the neural tube, occurs just after gastrulation. Remember, morphogenesis is not a formal stage in development. It's part of gastrulation.

Please solve this problem:

- The invagination of the neural plate directly produces:

    A. the notochord.
    B. the brain.
    C. the neural tube.
    D. the spinal column.

Problem solved:

C is correct. Neurulation involves formation of the notochord. This causes the development of the neural plate, which, upon invagination, becomes the neural tube. The neural tube *ultimately* gives rise to the brain and spinal cord.

Please solve this problem:

- Trace the development of an embryo from zygote through neurula.

Problem solved:

The question tests your mastery of the sequential stages of embryological development. The zygote undergoes cleavage to become first a morula (a cluster of thirty-two cells), then a blastula (a fluid-filled ball of hundreds of cells), then a gastrula (formed through invagination of the blastula), and then a neurula, at which stage the neural tube is formed through invagination of the neural plate.

REQUIRED TERMINOLOGY

Induction, Determination, and Differentiation

Neurulation illustrates the process of **induction**, whereby development of one region of tissue is influenced by the tissues that surround it. The notochord releases chemical factors, called *inducers*, which activate certain genes in the ectodermal tissue. The products of the activated genes cause the tissue to undergo the process of neurulation. Induction is a common mechanism in development; it does not only occur during neurulation.

Differentiation is the process whereby a cell becomes more specialized. The cells of the gastrula become *differentiated* when the three germ layers are formed. It is thereafter possible to distinguish a mesodermal cell from an ectodermal cell, for example. It is no longer possible, however, for a mesodermal cell to *become* an ectodermal cell, at least under normal conditions. A mesodermal cell is now **determined** to become part of an organ that develops from the mesoderm. As development continues, a particular mesodermal cell will become determined to develop into one mesodermal organ and not another. Determination is the process whereby the number of possible tissue types a cell could conceivably become is progressively limited.

Differentiation and determination are closely related concepts. As a cell becomes more differentiated, its fate becomes more determined. A heart muscle cell can be *differentiated* from a stomach chief cell. Sometime during the process of development, the heart muscle cell was *determined* to become a heart muscle cell; it was no longer possible that the cell's progeny would be part of the stomach. (Cancer cells appear to be able to reverse the differentiation process.)

Please solve this problem:

- Induction may result in all of the following EXCEPT:

    A. cell movement.
    B. cell genome modification.
    C. cell proliferation.
    D. cellular differentiation.

Problem solved:

B is correct. In a developing organism, induction refers to the influence that one set of cells has on another nearby set. This influence can produce cell movement or determine the development of a cell group, but it cannot alter the genome.

GERM-LAYER ORIGINS OF ORGANS

The germ layers formed during gastrulation constitute the source of all organs and tissues of the body. The endoderm gives rise to the inner linings of the esophagus, the stomach, and the small and large intestines. It also gives rise to organs that are anatomic outgrowths of the digestive tract, such as the pancreas, the gall bladder, and the liver. The endoderm also gives rise to the inner linings of the respiratory tract. The ectoderm is the source of the epidermis, the eye, and the nervous system. The mesoderm is the origin of the connective tissue, the heart, blood cells (red and white, including those of the lymphatic system), the urogenital system as well as parts of many other internal organs.

Please solve this problem:

- The lining of the digestive tract and the lungs as well as the liver and the pancreas are formed from which germ cell layer?

Problem solved:

All of these develop from the endoderm.

Please solve this problem:

- All of the following structures arise from the ectoderm EXCEPT:

    A. the outer layer of the skin.
    B. the nervous system.
    C. the excretory system.
    D. the structures of the eye.

Problem solved:

C is correct. The outer layer of the skin, the nervous system, and the structures of the eye derive from ectoderm. The excretory system derives from mesoderm.

Please solve this problem:

- The retina develops from the same germ cell layer as does the:

    A. brain.
    B. trachea.
    C. heart.
    D. pancreas.

Problem solved:

A is correct. The eye, the epidermis, and all the structures of the central nervous system develop from ectoderm as does the retina, being part of the eye, and the brain.

Please solve this problem:

- Which of the following structures derives from the same germ cell layer as the heart?

    A. Liver
    B. Spinal cord
    C. Bone
    D. Retina

Problem solved:

C is correct. The heart derives from the mesoderm as do all structures other than (a) eye, epidermis, and nervous tissues (which develop from ectoderm) and (b) the inner linings of digestive organs and the respiratory tract, as well as the accessory organs to the digestive system (all of which derive from the endoderm). Heart and bone (among many other tissues and organs) derive from mesoderm.

Please solve this problem:

- Which of the following does NOT derive from the mesoderm?

    A. Arteries and arterioles
    B. Veins, venules, and capillaries
    C. Muscles and associated connective tissues
    D. Inner linings of the lungs

Problem solved:

D is correct. The structures named in choices A, B, and C derive from the mesoderm. Once again, all tissues and organs derive from the mesoderm except (a) the ectodermal structures: epidermis, eye, and nervous tissue, and (b) the endodermal structures: inner linings of the digestive tract and the respiratory tract, and the accessory digestive organs.

26.2 MASTERY APPLIED: PRACTICE PASSAGE AND QUESTIONS

Passage

The developing embryo arises from a series of mitotic divisions by the zygote. The gene content of each cell is identical throughout development, but as development proceeds, the genetic material's potential expression becomes increasingly restricted. Determination refers to the process that limits the number of cell types that an embryonic cell might become. Two separate mechanisms lead to determination in a developing embryo's cells. The first is cytoplasmic segregation. Egg cytoplasm contains determinative molecules; during cleavage, the zygote's cytoplasm is segregated into cells with unequal biochemical content. The second mechanism is embryonic induction, in which the interaction of cells (or tissues) with one another affects the development of one or both groups of cells. Differentiated cells express certain genes of their genome while other genes in their genome remain unexpressed. The differentiated cell takes on the characteristics of a specific cell type.

In order to test the reversibility of determination, the following experiment was conducted. The egg cell of a *Rana pipiens* (leopard frog) was selected. (The leopard frog is a diploid organism.) The egg nucleus was removed and the enucleated egg was then pricked with a sterile glass needle to initiate parthenogenetic activation. (Parthenogenesis is the production of offspring without fertilization.) A nucleus from a donor *Rana pipiens* cell was then introduced into the enucleated oocyte using a micropipette. Results of the experiment are shown in Figure 1. Most blastula nuclei, when transplanted, were able to orchestrate the development of a fully formed tadpole. When the experiment was repeated using nuclei from cells derived from increasingly later stages of development, a pronounced decrease in the number of fully formed tadpoles was observed.

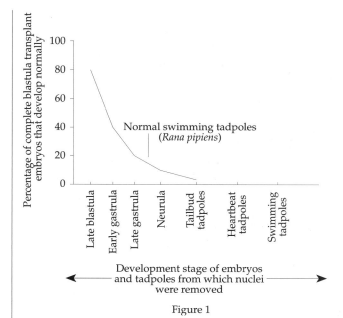

Figure 1

1. The nervous tissue, eye, and epidermis all derive from:

   A. the ectoderm.
   B. the mesoderm.
   C. the endoderm.
   D. the mesenchyme.

2. The decreasing percentage of viable tadpoles produced from nuclear transplants after the early gastrula stage (Figure 1) can most likely be explained by:

   A. a decrease in the genetic content of the transplanted nucleus.
   B. a shift in function of donor nuclei from regulation to temporary dormancy.
   C. an increase in nuclear instability due to decreasing levels of cell regulation.
   D. a decrease in genomic potential for expression due to increasing determination and differentiation.

3. A researcher interested in observing all of the mechanisms involved in determination would most benefit by observing cells in which of the following stages?

   A. The fertilization stage only
   B. The neurulation stage onward
   C. The gastrulation stage only
   D. The cleavage stage onward

4. According to the information in the passage, cleavage results in:

   A. unequal distribution of nuclei to daughter cells.
   B. unequal distribution of determinative factors to daughter cells.
   C. reduced gene content in daughter cells.
   D. increased size compared to that of the initial zygote.

5. Pricking the cell with a sterile needle in the experiment served the same purpose as:

   I. fusion of the egg nucleus by a sperm nucleus.
   II. penetration of the egg by a sperm.
   III. attachment of sperm cells to receptors located on the egg's outer layer

   A. I only
   B. II only
   C. III only
   D. I and II only

26.3 MASTERY VERIFIED: ANSWERS AND EXPLANATIONS

1. **A is correct.** The ectoderm, one of the three germ cell layers formed after gastrulation, gives rise to all three structures listed. The mesoderm, another of the germ cell layers, gives rise to such organs as the connective tissue (bone, muscle, and cartilage); the urinary system; the urogenital system; the heart, blood vessels, and blood cells of the circulatory system; and the inner linings of body cavities. The endoderm, the third germ cell layer, generates the inner linings of (a) the digestive tract (including the pancreas, gall bladder, and liver) and (b) the respiratory tract. Mesenchyme are migrating embryonic cells associated with morphogenic changes of cell clusters.

2. **D is correct.** As development progresses, cells undergo differentiation. Differentiation restricts the cell's ability to express all of its genomic potential. Differentiated cells cannot direct the development of a complete organism. Gene content does not change during development; genes are not lost. (The cell's ability to *express* certain of its genes is limited.) Choice A, therefore, is incorrect. Choice B is incorrect because cell nuclei do not become temporarily dormant during later stages of development. Instead they become more limited in the number of genes that they can express. Choice C is incorrect in both its implications: Cell nuclei do not become unstable, and a cell is not subject to reduced regulation as development progresses.

3. **D is correct.** The cleavage stage marks the unequal distribution of cytoplasmic determinants into cells. This stage and those that follow create the developmental pathways that lead to determination and differentiation. Once the germ cell layers are produced, embryonic induction may be observed. Choice A is incorrect because fertilization precedes determination of any sort. Choice B is incorrect as well. Neurulation and subsequent stages would provide information about embryonic induction mechanisms but would not reveal the role played by egg cytoplasmic determinants from the cleavage stage forward. The three germ layers are formed during gastrulation, which sets the stage for subsequent cell and tissue interactions. The researcher would have to observe subsequent stages. Furthermore, the researcher would once again be deprived of information concerning the influence of egg cytoplasm determinants. For these reasons, choice C is not correct.

4. **B is correct.** The passage states that determinative factors in the egg cytoplasm are unequally distributed during cleavage. Mitosis gives rise to daughter cells bearing the same ploidy as that of the egg cell. The passage does not imply otherwise, so choice C is not correct. Cleavage involves a series of rapid cell divisions. The total amount of cytoplasm of the original zygote remains the same and the resulting mass of cells is the same size as was the zygote. The passage does not suggest otherwise, so choice D is incorrect. All viable cells possess a nucleus, so choice A is incorrect.

5. **B is correct.** Only statement II is an accurate statement. The needle prick was a substitute for the penetration of the egg by a sperm cell. The penetration initiates a series of fertilization reactions in the egg, such as the release of cortical granules. In this experiment, the egg nucleus was removed and replaced with a donor cell nucleus. The needle prick would not be an adequate substitute for the insertion of genomic material. For these reasons, statement I is not an accurate statement. Attachment of sperm cells to the receptor sites available on the outer egg surface does not cause cell division; statement III, therefore, is not an accurate statement.

CHAPTER 27

MICROBIOLOGY: BACTERIA, VIRUSES, AND FUNGI

27.1 MASTERY ACHIEVED

BACTERIA

Identifying Features

Bacteria are single-celled organisms that typically contain an outer **cell wall**, a **cell membrane**, and a single **circular-shaped chromosome** in the cytoplasm. Since a bacterium is a **prokaryotic** organism, it lacks a nucleus and generally shows a more primitive organization than that of a eukaryotic cell. Bacteria lack membrane-bound organelles, such as the endoplasmic reticulum, mitochondria, the nuclear membrane, and Golgi bodies.

Cell wall

Cell membrane

Chromosome

Bacterium with its Chromosome

Figure 27.1

Differences in the composition of the bacterial cell wall allow the classification of bacterial species as **Gram positive** or **Gram negative**. A species is Gram positive if it retains Gram's dye, and Gram negative if it does not.

You should be familiar with three types of bacteria, categorized by shape: **bacilli**, **cocci**, and **spirilla**. Bacilli are rod-shaped. There is an enormous variety of bacilli. They cause, among other diseases, tuberculosis, leprosy, plague, and cholera. Cocci are ovoid or round-shaped. Again, there are a great many types of cocci. The illnesses they produce include gonorrhea, pneumonia, and scarlet fever. Spirilla, the third bacteria category, have a helical or spiral shape. Among other diseases, they cause rat-bite fever.

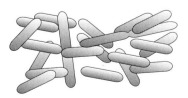

Bacilli

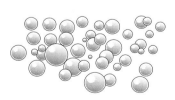

Cocci

Spirilla

Figure 27.2

Please solve this problem:

- Bacilli are:

    A. bacteria with a round or ovoid shape.
    B. bacteria with a rodlike shape.
    C. viruses with a spiral shape.
    D. fungi with a spiral shape.

Problem solved:

B is correct. Bacilli are rod-shaped bacteria.

Please solve this problem:

- Cocci are:

    A. bacteria with a round or ovoid shape.
    B. bacteria with a rodlike shape.
    C. bacteria with a spiral shape.
    D. fungi with a spiral shape.

Problem solved:

A is correct. Cocci are bacteria with a round or ovoid shape.

Please solve this problem:

- Spirilla are:

    A. bacteria with a round or ovoid shape.
    B. bacteria with a rod shape.
    C. bacteria with a spiral shape.
    D. fungi with a spiral shape.

Problem solved:

C is correct. Spirilla are spiral-shaped bacteria.

Bacterial Reproduction

The growth cycle of a bacterium is typically rapid. A bacterium replicates its DNA and divides into two daughter cells of approximately equal size. This process is termed **binary fission**. Because each instance of division produces two bacteria, *bacterial population growth is exponential,* and if population size is plotted against time, the resulting curve will be *logarithmic.* Consider a single bacterium and call it "generation 1." Suppose it divides, and the two resulting bacterium represent "generation 2." After a total of six divisions, the population of "generation 7" will be $2^{(7-1)} = 2^6 = 64$ bacteria.

A bacterium may acquire a different genome from that of its parents through one of three recombinant processes. These are (1) **transformation**, (2) **conjugation**, and (3) **transduction**. You should be able to recognize the mechanism by which each event transpires. Transformation involves the addition and incorporation of genetic material, usually pieces of DNA from lysed bacteria, into a bacterium's genome from its surroundings. The genetic material it receives may be prokaryotic or eukaryotic. In relation to its genetic content, the recipient bacterium cell is said to be **transformed**. Conjugation is, in some rudimentary ways, analogous to mating in animals.

A **plasmid**, called the **F (fertility) factor**, facilitates the transfer of DNA from one bacterium to another. The third recombinant mechanism is transduction, in which a *virus* transfers DNA from one bacterium to another.

Please solve this problem:

- Which of the following recombinant processes is dependent on the F factor plasmid?

    A. Transduction
    B. Binary fission
    C. Conjugation
    D. Crossing over

Problem solved:

C is correct. Conjugation involves the direct transfer of genetic material from one bacterium to another. The transfer is mediated by a plasmid called the F factor.

Please solve this problem:

- Which of the following recombinant processes is carried out by a virus?

    A. Transduction
    B. Binary fission
    C. Conjugation
    D. Transformation

Problem solved:

A is correct. Transduction involves the transfer of genetic material from one bacterium to another, with a virus acting as the carrier.

Please solve this problem:

- Which of the following does NOT constitute a recombinant process among bacteria?

    A. Transduction
    B. Binary fission
    C. Conjugation
    D. Transformation

Problem solved:

B is correct. The three recombinant processes observed among bacteria are transduction, conjugation, and transformation.

Please solve this problem:

- Which of the following represents the incorporation of genetic material into a bacterial genome that is not necessarily from a bacterium?

  A. Binary fission
  B. Translocation
  C. Conjugation
  D. Transformation

Problem solved:

D is correct. Transformation is a recombinant process in which a bacterium acquires genetic material that is not necessarily a bacterium. The cell from which the material derives might, indeed, be prokaryotic or eukaryotic.

VIRUSES

Identifying Features

There is some debate as to whether or not viruses are alive. They lack all organelles as well as most features normally associated with cells. Viruses have just two primitive cellular attributes: (1) an outer coat, or **capsid**, made of protein, and (2) a **core** of **nucleic acid**, contained within the coat. The nucleic acid may be DNA or RNA, depending on the virus. On that basis, viruses may be broadly classified as **RNA viruses** or **DNA viruses**.

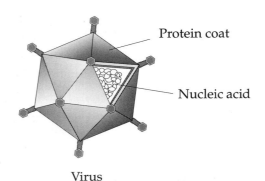

Virus
Figure 27.3

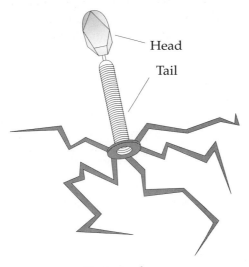

Bacteriophage
Figure 27.4

You should be familiar, in particular, with the **bacteriophage**, a type of virus that, in addition to the capsid and nucleic acid core, possesses a **tail fiber**. The bacteriophage infects bacteria; the tail fiber facilitates infection by allowing the virus to attach itself to the bacterial **host**, and to inject its genome *into* the host.

Viral Reproduction

In viral reproduction, the virus first binds itself to its host (the cell to be infected). **Receptors** found on the host's cell membrane facilitate the attachment of viral protein coat molecules. Viruses are **host-specific organisms**, meaning that in selecting their hosts, they depend on the presence of receptors to which they attach. Most viruses are capable of infecting only a few species.

After the virus attaches to its host, it delivers its contents into the host's cytoplasm. At this point, two general processes might take place. If the virus is **lytic**, it will then appropriate the cell's reproductive machinery to make copies of its own nucleic acids and proteins. The proteins and nucleic acid combine to form new viral particles, which then leave the cell, often by *lysing*, or bursting, the cell. If the virus is **lysogenic**, its nucleic acid becomes incorporated into the host's genome. At this point, the virus is called a **prophage** or a **provirus**, depending on whether or not the virus infects a bacterium (in which case it is a prophage) or a eukaryotic cell (in which case it is a provirus). The viral DNA is then replicated along with the host's genome. Under certain conditions, the viral DNA emerges from the host's genome and resumes the lytic life cycle.

Please solve this problem:

- Most viruses are very host-specific because:

    A. the viral capsid is composed of protein.
    B. a virus has no cellular organelles.
    C. viral nucleic acid might be DNA or RNA, depending on the virus.
    D. the attachment to the host involves the host's cell surface receptors.

Problem solved:

D is correct. To state that a virus is host-specific is to state that any one virus will infect only a limited number of host cell types. Whether or not the virus will infect a given host is determined by the host's cell membrane receptors. If a given host has the receptors that will allow a given virus to attach, then viral infection by that virus is possible. Host cell receptors, therefore, create the specificity. Choices A, B, and C are accurate statements, but they do not answer the question.

Please solve this problem:

- Which of the following precedes the replication of viral nucleic acid?

    A. Attachment to host cell receptors
    B. Replication of capsid protein
    C. Host cell lysis
    D. Assembly of viral progeny

Problem solved:

A is correct. The question requires that the student understand the sequence associated with viral reproduction: attachment, delivery of genome, replication of nucleic acid and capsid protein, assembly of new viruses, and lysis of the host. In terms of the processes listed in choices A–D, the appropriate order is A, B, D, C. Replication of viral nucleic acid occurs after A but either before or simultaneously with B.

Please solve this problem:

- Which of the following would be the most unlikely to occur after a virus has reproduced and its progeny have left the host cell?

  A. New infection by progeny virus of new host cells
  B. Reproduction of the original host cell itself
  C. Symptomatic disease in the organism to which the original host cell belonged
  D. Death of the organism to which the original host cell belonged

Problem solved:

B is correct. In the final stage of viral reproduction, the host cell often undergoes *lysis* (bursting); it is destroyed. It cannot undergo reproduction thereafter. Choices A, C, and D refer to processes that represent possibilities. The newly produced viruses might go on to infect new host cells and, moreover, if infection is repeated and widespread (as it often is), the virus might cause symptomatic disease (like the common cold) or death (from, for example, poliomyelitis).

Please solve this problem:

- Which of the following distinguishes a bacteriophage from other viruses?

  A. The presence of mitochondria
  B. The presence of a protein capsid
  C. The presence of RNA in the nucleic acid core
  D. The presence of a tail fiber

Problem solved:

D is correct. The bacteriophage possesses the two structures that characterize the prototypical virus—a protein capsid and a nucleic acid core—and then a third, the tail fiber, which facilitates attachment to a bacterial cell. (Viruses that lack a tail fiber nonetheless attach themselves to their target hosts. They make direct attachment between the capsid and host cell membrane receptors.)

FUNGI

Identifying Features

Fungi are primarily haploid organisms whose cells are eukaryotic. They contain a cell wall, composed largely of **chitin**, and organelles. A fungus can be **unicellular** or **multicellular**. Yeasts, for example, are unicellular fungi. **Molds**, **mushrooms**, and **mildews** are multicellular fungi. The fungal nucleus is surrounded by a **nuclear membrane**. The principal distinguishing feature of many multicellular fungi is the *absence of a partition between what would otherwise be separate cells*. In a sense, such multicellular fungi are simply composed of a large number of cells enclosed within one cell wall. Viewed another way, the organism can be thought of as a single cell with multiple nuclei. When viewed this way, fungi can be considered **multinucleate**.

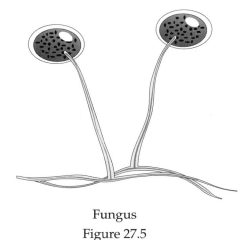

Fungus
Figure 27.5

Please solve this problem:

- Which one of the following does NOT possess a cell wall?

  A. A bacterium
  B. A plant cell
  C. A fungal cell
  D. A virus

Problem solved:

D is correct. Bacteria, plant cells, and fungi do possess cell walls. Viruses do not; they are contained within a protein capsid. Indeed, the cell walls of bacteria promote the categorization of species according to Gram staining. Some bacteria are Gram positive and others are Gram negative. A plant cell's cell wall is composed of cellulose, whose thickness and rigidity protect the cell against osmotic swelling and injury. Fungi possess cell walls that are in most cases extremely rigid and are composed primarily of chitin (which also comprises the exoskeletons of many insects).

Please solve this problem:

- Which among the following possesses such organelles as the endoplasmic reticulum, Golgi bodies, mitochondria, and a nuclear membrane?
  A. Viruses
  B. Prokaryotic cells
  C. Bacteria
  D. Fungi

Problem solved:

D is correct. Fungi possess membrane-bound nuclei and other organelles ordinarily associated with eukaryotic cells. Prokaryotic cells possess neither a membrane-bound nucleus nor the organelles associated with eukaryotic cells. Bacteria (choice C) *are* prokaryotic cells. As noted in the text, there is still a debate as to whether viruses (choice A) are in fact alive. They do not possess any organelles.

Fungal Reproduction

Fungi may reproduce either sexually or asexually. Asexual fungal reproduction occurs through **budding, fission,** or **spore formation**. (The term *spore* is also significant to *sexual* reproduction as explained below.) In budding, which occurs, for example, among yeasts, a cell or a body of cells separates from the parent organism, grows, and becomes a new organism unto itself. In fission, a single fungal cell divides to produce two new daughter cells. In sporulation, which occurs, for example, in bread mold, the fungus produces spores and releases them from stemlike structures called **hyphae**. Sporulation permits a yet undeveloped organism to survive hostile environmental conditions, like drought or extreme heat. A spore is metabolically inactive, encased in a thick protective wall, but under appropriate conditions, it germinates and forms a new haploid fungus. Note that all forms of asexual reproduction produce progeny whose *genome is identical* to that of the parent organism.

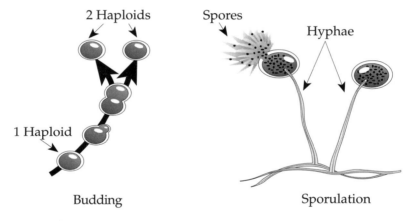

Asexual Reproduction Among Fungi Showing
Budding and Spore Formation

Figure 27.6

Sexual reproduction among fungi involves the fusion of haploid gametes from two parent fungi. The parents are usually of opposite sexual type; one type is designated (+) and the other (–). (The terms "male" and "female" are not used for the sexual reproduction of fungi.) Gametes arise from the hyphae of each parent. The haploid gametes fuse and form a diploid zygote. The zygote stage of a fungal life cycle, therefore, is diploid. The zygote undergoes meiosis (not mitosis) to produce haploid **spores**. (These are not the same "spores" that give rise to asexual reproduction as discussed above.) These, in turn, germinate and produce new haploid organisms. Note that the newly formed organisms are normally not genetically identical to either parent, their genomes having arisen from the combination of parental genes followed by meiosis.

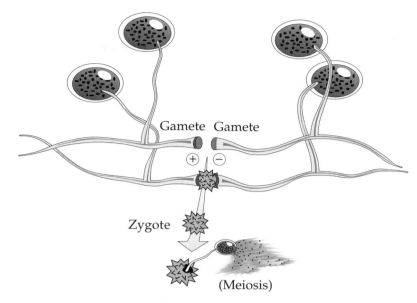

Sexual Reproduction of Fungi

Figure 27.7

Please solve this problem:

- Which of the following are NOT associated with asexual reproduction among fungi?

    A. Spores
    B. Zygotes
    C. Buds
    D. Hyphae

Problem solved:

B is correct. With respect to fungi, zygotes form only in association with *sexual* reproduction. They are diploid and arise through the fusion of haploid gametes. The term *spore* (choice A) refers both to sexual and asexual reproductive processes. In the asexual process, spores derive from hyphae (choice D). Although hyphae also produce the gametes that precede sexual reproduction, hyphae are associated also with asexual reproduction as just described. For that reason, choice D is wrong. In sexual reproduction, haploid spores ultimately derive from the meiotic division of a diploid zygote.

Please solve this problem:

- Among the following processes, which one can give rise to progeny that are not genetically identical to the parent(s)?

    A. Sexual reproduction
    B. Asexual spore formation
    C. Budding
    D. Fission

Problem solved:

A is correct. Choices B, C, and D are forms of asexual reproduction. Although spore formation is also a form of sexual reproduction, the answer stipulates "asexual." Asexual reproduction produces offspring with identical genomes to those of the parent. Sexual reproduction in fungi, which combines processes of fusion and meiosis, produces a haploid organism whose genome derives from the two parents but is not usually identical to either one.

NUTRITION IN MICROORGANISMS

Autotrophs versus Heterotrophs

Microorganisms, such as those discussed above, obtain nutrients through a variety of processes and mechanisms. All organisms may be classified as **autotrophic** or **heterotrophic.** Autotrophs capture their own energy through photosynthesis, which exploits the radiant energy of the sun, or, as in the case of chemoautotrophs, through chemical means. Heterotrophs cannot obtain their energy from the sun or chemical bonds and thus must rely on other organisms for nutrition.

Heterotrophs may or may not possess digestive systems. A heterotroph that *does* digest can be further subcategorized as a **herbivore**, a **carnivore**, or an **omnivore.** Herbivores obtain their nutrition from plants only. Carnivores obtain their nutrition from animals only, and omnivores obtain nutrition from plants *and* animals.

Heterotrophic microorganisms do *not* possess digestive systems. Such microorganisms may be classified in several categories. **Parasites** obtain nutrition directly from the body of a living organism *to the detriment of that organism.* (This is not to say that all parasites lack digestive systems. Many parasites, large and small, have well-developed digestive systems.) **Saprophytes** absorb nutrients from the remains of dead organisms. Some heterotrophic microorganisms are *neither* parasitic nor saprophytic. There are those, for example, that derive nutrition from living organisms *without* harming them.

Saprophytic organisms facilitate the release and recycling of numerous substances, promoting their availability to other organisms whose survival depends on them. These substances include carbon and nitrogen as well as the mineral components of a variety of organic compounds.

Please solve this problem:

- An organism that lacks a digestive system and obtains nutrients from other living organisms while harming the organism is:

  A. autotrophic.
  B. saprophytic.
  C. carnivorous.
  D. parasitic.

Problem solved:

D is correct. If an organism cannot synthesize its own nutrients, it is a heterotroph. If it lacks a digestive system, it is not a herbivore, carnivore, or omnivore. It is either a parasite or a saprophyte. If it feeds on the remains of deceased organisms, it is a saprophyte. If it feeds on living organisms and harms them in the process, it is a parasite.

Please solve this problem:

- An organism that captures its own energy is called:

    A. autotrophic.
    B. heterotrophic.
    C. saprophytic.
    D. omnivorous.

Problem solved:

A is correct. If an organism synthesizes its own energy, it is autotrophic. The term *heterotroph* (choice B) refers to those organisms that do not synthesize their own energy, and the terms *saprophytic* (choice C) and *omnivorous* (choice D) are subcategories within the classification heterotroph.

Please solve this problem:

- Which of the following is characteristic of saprophytic organisms?

    A. They obtain energy through photosynthesis.
    B. They recycle biological substances.
    C. They obtain nutrients from living organisms.
    D. They harm other living organisms.

Problem solved:

B is correct. Saprophytes are heterotrophs that (a) lack a digestive system and (b) absorb nutrients from the remains of dead organisms. Saprophytes often recycle a variety of substances that are useful to other organisms within their ecosystem.

Bacterial Metabolism

AEROBES VERSUS ANAEROBES

Bacteria use many different nutritional strategies. Some bacteria are autotrophs while others are heterotrophs. Some heterotrophs are saprophytes, some are parasites, and some are neither (deriving nutrition from living organisms *without harming them*). Regardless of their status as autotrophs, heterotrophs, parasites, or saprophytes, all must convert energy into a form that is usable by the cell. The process by which that conversion occurs is **cellular respiration**.

For some bacteria, respiration requires oxygen; for others, it does not. Respiration that requires oxygen is called **aerobic**. Respiration that does not require oxygen is called **anaerobic**. Anaerobic bacteria may be called **obligate anaerobes** or **facultative anaerobes**. Obligate anaerobes are unable to live in the presence of oxygen. Some facultative anaerobes will use oxygen in their respiratory process if it is available, but will conduct anaerobic respiration in its absence. Other anaerobes, **tolerant anaerobes**, always conduct anaerobic respiration but are indifferent to the presence of oxygen.

Please solve this problem:

- Which of the following characterizes anaerobic respiration?

  A. It is a respiratory process that cannot operate in the presence of oxygen.
  B. It is a respiratory process that can operate in the absence of oxygen.
  C. It is dependent on the remains of other organisms.
  D. It is dependent on living organisms and harms them.

Problem solved:

B is correct. Anaerobic respiration does not require oxygen, but oxygen does not, on the other hand, render it inoperative. Choice A, therefore, is incorrect. It is true that obligate anaerobic organisms cannot survive in the presence of oxygen, but that is not because anaerobic respiration requires an anaerobic environment. Choices C and D refer to nutritional mechanisms, not to respiratory mechanisms; neither has any direct bearing on anaerobic respiration.

Please solve this problem:

- Which of the following classes of bacteria can survive in the presence or absence of oxygen?

  A. Aerobes
  B. Obligate anaerobes
  C. Facultative anaerobes
  D. Saprophytes

Problem solved:

C is correct. The term *facultative anaerobe* only specifies bacteria that can survive whether or not oxygen is present; it does not say anything definitive about the organism's respiratory processes. Choice A is wrong because aerobes must have oxygen, and choice B is wrong because obligate anaerobes die in the presence of oxygen. In choice D, the term *saprophyte* refers to nutrition, not respiration.

NITROGEN-FIXING BACTERIA

Mutualism is a relationship between two organisms in which each confers a benefit on the other. For example, one specialized form of bacteria enters into a mutualistic relationship with the root nodules of certain legumes (such as pea plants). These **nitrogen-fixing bacteria** convert nitrogen into a form that can be used by the legume. The legume benefits from the association by being provided with nitrogen in a form it can readily utilize to synthesize protein. Meanwhile, the legume provides nutrition for the bacteria.

Please solve this problem:

- Nitrogen-fixing bacteria are classified as:

    A. saprophytes.
    B. parasites.
    C. autotrophs.
    D. heterotrophs.

Problem solved:

D is correct. Nitrogen-fixing bacteria are heterotrophs; they cannot synthesize their own food and must obtain their nutrients from other organisms. Choice A is incorrect because saprophytes derive their nutrients from dead organisms. Choice B is also incorrect. Although parasites absorb nutrients directly from the body of their host, they harm the host in doing so. Choice C is incorrect because the autotrophs conduct photosynthesis or obtain their energy from inorganic chemical bonds. Nitrogen-fixing bacteria do not.

27.2 MASTERY APPLIED: PRACTICE PASSAGE AND QUESTIONS

Passage

Viral population growth varies depending on the nature of the virus itself and of the host it infects. Some viruses that infect bacteria have growth cycles that are measured in minutes, whereas some viruses that infect human cells have growth cycles measured in hours.

Figure 1 depicts a growth curve for an infecting virus.

At the onset of viral infection of a host cell, the virus actually disappears: The virus particle is undetectable within the infected cell. This stage of the viral growth cycle is the *eclipse period*. Although the viral particle vanishes during the eclipse period, its nucleic acid is present and active. After the passage of some time, new viral nucleic acid molecules accumulate within the cell to a detectable level. The *latent period* is the interval between the onset of infection and the first extracellular appearance of the virus. Viral-related changes to cell morphology and function occur near the end of the latent period, which is known as the cytopathic effect (CPE). The cytopathic effect sometimes culminates in the rupture and death of affected cells. Some viruses can replicate without producing CPE in the host cell.

Table I outlines the various stages associated with the viral growth cycle. The virus first attaches to receptor proteins located on the periphery of the host cell. It gains entrance to the host cell by one of several mechanisms. Once inside the cell, the virus may then appropriate the host cell's machinery to replicate itself

Viral gene expression begins with mRNA synthesis. mRNA is then translated by host cell ribosomes into viral proteins. These early proteins are enzymes required for viral genome replication. As the replication of the viral genome continues, the cell synthesizes late mRNA. The late mRNA is translated into structural capsid proteins to enclose new viral particles. Progeny viral particles are assembled, enclosing nucleic acid within a capsid protein. The release of new viruses is accomplished either by the rupture of the cell membrane (the route taken by unenveloped viruses) or by budding out through an envagination of the cell membrane. Those that are shed by budding are enveloped viruses. They are enclosed in a lipoprotein envelope derived from the host's cell membrane.

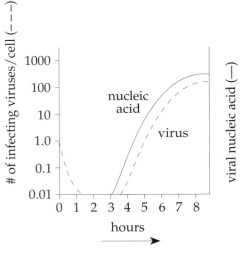

Figure 1

Early events	Parent virus attaches and penetrates host cell
	Parent virus genome is removed from protein coat
Middle events	Host cell synthesizes early viral proteins
	Host cell replicates viral genome
	Host cell synthesizes late viral proteins
Late events	New viruses assembled
	New viruses emerge from host cell

Table 1

1. An important early protein that is most likely translated from mRNA is:

   A. a protease.
   B. a polymerase.
   C. an antibody.
   D. a peptidase.

2. Which of the following is (are) possible templates for the synthesis of viral mRNA?

      I. Viral DNA
     II. Viral RNA
    III. Cellular DNA

   A. I only
   B. II only
   C. III only
   D. I and II only

3. Researchers find that a test-tube mixture containing only purified viral RNA and purified protein yields correctly assembled viruses. Among the following, the LEAST reasonable conclusion is that:

   A. specificity of viral assembly lies within the RNA and protein.
   B. enzymatic activity is not required for correct viral assembly.
   C. viral particles are capable of spontaneously disassembling.
   D. energy is not required for viral particles to assemble.

4. As characterized in the passage, the eclipse period for the viral growth curve represented in Figure 1 occurs during the period:

   A. 0 to 1.5 hours.
   B. 1.5 to 2.5 hours.
   C. 1.5 to 3.5 hours.
   D. 3.5 to 5.5 hours.

5. Which of the following is NOT true of the cytopathic effect?

   A. It affects all host cells within which viral replication takes place.
   B. It is associated with changes in a cell's shape and function.
   C. It culminates in cell lysis and cell death.
   D. It occurs at approximately the same time as the first extracellular appearance of the virus.

6. The latent period coincides with which of the following events listed in Table 1?

   A. Early events only
   B. Early and middle events only
   C. Middle and late events only
   D. Early, middle, and late events

27.3 MASTERY VERIFIED: ANSWERS AND EXPLANATIONS

1. **B is correct.** The passage states that protein created early in the virus growth cycle is used in the replication of viral nucleic acid. Polymerases are required for nucleic acid synthesis. Choice A is incorrect because a protease degrades protein. Choice C is incorrect because an antibody, although a protein, functions in the immune system of higher organisms and plays no role in the synthesis of nucleic acid. Choice D is incorrect because peptidases hydrolyze peptide bonds and thus degrade proteins. They are not involved in nucleic acid synthesis.

2. **D is correct.** Viruses contain, as their nucleic acid, either RNA or DNA. Viral reproduction requires the replication of the viral genome. An RNA virus appropriates a host cell's synthetic machinery and uses it to synthesize mRNA from *its own* RNA. (In some RNA viruses called "positive sense" RNA viruses, mRNA actually *is* the genome.) A DNA virus uses host cell machinery to synthesize mRNA from *its own* viral DNA. Items I and II, therefore, are accurate statements. Item III is not.

3. **C is correct.** The question asks the student to find the conclusion that is *least* justified by the data. The observation that viral particles spontaneously assemble under the circumstances described should not lead the observer to conclude that disassembly is also spontaneous. Choice A is a plausible conclusion; the viral particles assembled themselves without exogenous instruction or molecular intervention. Choice B represents a reasonable conclusion. Despite the absence of an energy source in the test-tube mixture, the viral particles assembled themselves properly. Choice D is a sensible inference since the experimental conditions did not provide an energy source.

4. **C is correct.** During the eclipse period, the virus is not detectable within the host. Figure 1 shows no virus between 1.5 and 3.5 hours after infection.

5. **A is correct.** The question requires only that the student carefully read the passage. At the end of its third paragraph, it is stated that "some viruses can replicate without producing CPE in the host cell." Choices B, C, and D are statements that, according to the passage, are true.

6. **D is correct.** The passage identifies the latent period as that between the onset of infection and the appearance of extracellular viruses. According to Table 1, early, middle, and late events all occur during that period.

CHAPTER 28

PRINCIPAL BIOCHEMICAL PATHWAYS OF THE CELL

28.1 MASTERY ACHIEVED

ENZYMATIC FACILITATION OF CELLULAR REACTIONS

A cell's survival is dependent on the biochemical reactions it conducts. Most of these reactions would not proceed at a rate consistent with survival were it not for the availability of **catalysts**. In a biochemical context, **enzymes** catalyze reactions; the cell's survival depends on its enzymes.

Whether a reaction is ultimately exothermic or endothermic, it requires energy at the outset. This energy is called the **activation energy**. Like all catalysts, *enzymes reduce a reaction's activation energy*. In so doing, they increase reaction rate. Like any catalyst, an enzyme itself undergoes *no net change* during the course of the reaction it catalyzes. An enzyme emerges from a chemical reaction unaltered in quantity and condition. Indeed, a single enzyme molecule will typically catalyze the same reaction over and over again.

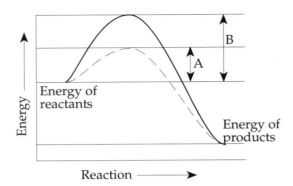

A = activation energy with enzyme

B = activation energy without enzyme

– – – catalyzed reaction

——— uncatalyzed reaction

Comparative Energies of Activation of a
Reaction, Catalyzed and Uncatalyzed

Figure 28.1

Although an enzyme increases the rate at which a given reaction occurs, it does not affect the **equilibrium concentrations** of the reactants or products.

Please solve this problem:

- A catalyst:

  A. increases activation energy.
  B. decreases activation energy.
  C. promotes exothermicity.
  D. decreases free energy.

Problem solved:

B is correct. All catalysts (including enzymes) serve to reduce activation energy. They do not promote exothermicity or endothermicity, and they have no effect on free energy.

Please solve this problem:

- After an enzyme has catalyzed a reaction several times, the quantity of the enzyme within that cell will have:

  A. decreased.
  B. increased.
  C. remained unchanged.
  D. increased, decreased, or remained unchanged, depending on the reaction.

Problem solved:

C is correct. Enzyme concentration undergoes no net change during the course of the reaction it catalyzes. Enzymes are "recycled"; an enzyme molecule will catalyze a reaction over and over again.

Mechanism of Enzymatic Action

The first step in the functioning of an enzyme is the formation of a transient **enzyme-substrate complex**.

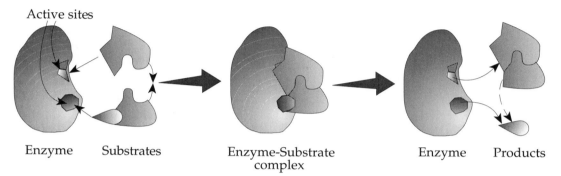

Lock and Key Theory of Enzymatic Activity

Figure 28.2

Each enzyme associates with its substrate at an **active site**, meaning a site on the enzyme's surface that is physically structured to accommodate the substrate molecule. The enzyme's active sites draw substrate molecules close together, allowing the substrates to interact. Substrates normally react when they are incorporated into an enzyme-substrate complex. Therefore, while an enzyme-substrate complex is formed from enzyme and substrates, its dissociation liberates enzyme and product(s).

Substrate A + Substrate B + Enzyme → Enzyme-Substrate Complex → Enzyme + Product(s)

Enzyme specificity refers to the fact that an enzyme is usually specific to one reaction. An enzyme functions because of the relationship of its physical conformation to the substrates on which it acts. Generally, the active site is structurally unreceptive to any molecules except those substrates to which the enzyme is specific, and so only reactions involving those substrates will be catalyzed. An early theory proposed to explain this specificity was called the **lock and key** hypothesis, which states that the enzyme's shape accomodated precisely the shape of the substrate. This hypothesis has been elaborated upon in the **induced fit** hypothesis, which states that the enzyme's shape compels the substrate to take on the shape of the reaction's transition state. This hypothesis is now the prevailing model for enzyme activity.

Limitations of Enzymatic Activity

Most enzymes are proteins. Any condition that affects the stability of a protein molecule, therefore, potentially affects an enzyme's stability and its ability to function. Such conditions include pH and temperature. A given enzyme will only function *within particular ranges of pH and temperature*.

An enzyme will only function within a very small pH range. For most enzymes, this pH is between 6.5 and 8.0 (which is the normal physiological pH range), but there are enzymes whose optimum pH falls outside this range. For example, pepsin, the proteolytic enzyme that operates in the stomach, works best in the pH range of the stomach, which is approximately 1.5 to 2.5. Similarly, most enzymes work best at physiological temperatures (around 37°C). Below this temperature, enzymatic activity slows, but the structure of the enzyme remains intact. Above this temperature, the enzyme's three-dimensional structure begins to break down. Since, as we discussed, the enzyme's shape is critical to its proper function, enzymatic activity falls off dramatically at temperatures exceeding 37°C by a significant amount. This breakdown in the enzyme's shape is called **denaturation,** and it occurs under conditions that disrupt hydrogen bonds, which function in maintaining the protein molecule's secondary and tertiary structures. Denaturation also explains the drop-off in enzymatic activity that occurs at pHs outside an enzyme's optimum range. If favorable pH and temperature conditions are restored, the enzyme will usually renature, or return to its functional conformation.

The rate of a catalyzed reaction depends on both the concentration of substrate and the concentration of enzymes. When substrate is first added to a reaction system, only a few molecules will be required to catalyze the reaction. In other words, only a few enzyme molecules are involved in enzyme-substrate complexes (ES); most remain as free enzyme molecules (E). As the concentration of substrate is increased, the proportion of ES will increase while the proportion of free E decreases. With continued addition of substrate, eventually all of the enzymes in the system will be involved in ES complexes; the addition of more substrate will not increase the overall rate of the reaction, since there is no more available enzyme to accomodate the additional substrate. At this point, the only way to increase the overall rate of reaction (assuming that external conditions, e.g., temperature, remain constant) is to add more enzyme to the system.

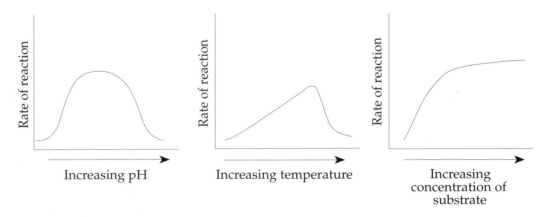

Factors That Affect Enzyme Function
Figure 28.3

For their activity, certain enzymes require the availability of **cofactors** or **coenzymes**. Cofactors are inorganic substances, such as Fe^{2+} or Cu^{2+} ions. Coenzymes are organic substances, such as vitamins.

Please solve this problem:

- All of the following are true of enzymes EXCEPT:

  A. they increase the rate at which a reaction will take place.
  B. they lower the activation energy of a reaction.
  C. most are proteins.
  D. they increase the equilibrium concentration of product.

Problem solved:

D is correct. Choices A, B, and C are true statements. Enzymes (like all catalysts) increase reaction rate by lowering activation energy. They do not, however, alter equilibrium concentrations of the product or reactant.

Please solve this problem:

- Among the following choices, which would most likely happen to an enzyme exposed to a temperature of 150°C?

  A. Saturation
  B. Desaturation
  C. Denaturation
  D. Excessive activity

Problem solved:

C is correct. Every enzyme operates best within a relatively narrow range of temperature. This is the principal reason that changes in human body temperature threaten health. If body temperature exceeds the upper or lower limits of various enzymes, then death or severe cell injury may result. In particular, excessively high temperatures disrupt the enzyme molecule's three-dimensional structure. This process is called denaturation.

Enzyme Inhibition

Enzymes exert control over the cell's activities by determining which reactions occur and which do not. Enzymes themselves are controlled by a process called **feedback inhibition,** where an enzyme's activity may be inhibited by accumulation of product. Some reaction products are toxic in high concentrations; feedback inhibition prevents the cell from producing an excessive quantity of product. Also, accumulating too much product can be a waste of energy.

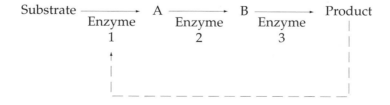

Feedback Inhibition of Enzyme Action

Figure 28.4

Competitive inhibition occurs when two molecules, one of which is the substrate and one of which is called the **inhibitor**, compete for an enzyme's active site. If bound to the enzyme, the substrate will participate in the reaction, but the inhibitor will not. Assuming that substrate concentration does not change, then for the time during which the inhibitor is bound to the enzyme, the enzyme is essentially nonfunctional. By effectively diluting the concentration of enzyme in a reaction system, it suppresses the rate of reaction.

Please solve this problem:

- The saturation point of an enzyme is reached when:

    A. the concentration of end products of the reaction exceeds the cell's need.
    B. all available active sites on enzyme molecules are occupied by substrate molecules.
    C. an enzyme-substrate complex is formed from reactants and enzyme.
    D. the enzyme experiences feedback inhibition.

Problem solved:

B is correct. The saturation point is that point at which the concentration of substrate is sufficiently high that all available enzyme molecules are in use; the active sites are saturated, and no additional substrate will increase the reaction rate.

Please solve this problem:

- If, during a particular enzymatic reaction, product concentration becomes excessively high, which of the following processes would most likely reduce enzymatic activity?

    A. Saturation
    B. Denaturation
    C. Competitive inhibition
    D. Feedback inhibition

Problem solved:

D is correct. Feedback inhibition refers to a phenomenon in which the accumulation of product inhibits the activity of the enzyme. This mechanism prevents the cell from accumulating excess product.

ENERGY PRODUCTION IN THE CELL

ATP

Most cellular processes rely on energy that is stored in the cell until it is needed and available for conversion to a usable form. **Adenosine triphosphate (ATP)** is the form in which most cells store their energy just before use. ATP is dubbed the cell's "energy currency." In a molecule of ATP, adenine (a nitrogenous base) is linked to ribose (a sugar), which is also linked to a chain of three phosphate (PO_4) groups. The bonds that link the two phosphate groups farthest from the adenosine moiety are **high-energy bonds**. Their disruption releases more energy than does disruption of other bonds in the molecule. (Remember that no bond releases energy when broken. The energy from disruption actually comes from the subsequent formation of bonds that are more stable.)

Although removal of both the second and third phosphate groups yield about the same amount of free energy under standard conditions, it is the third phosphate group that is removed most often in physiological systems. The liberated energy is then used to drive otherwise unfavorable processes.

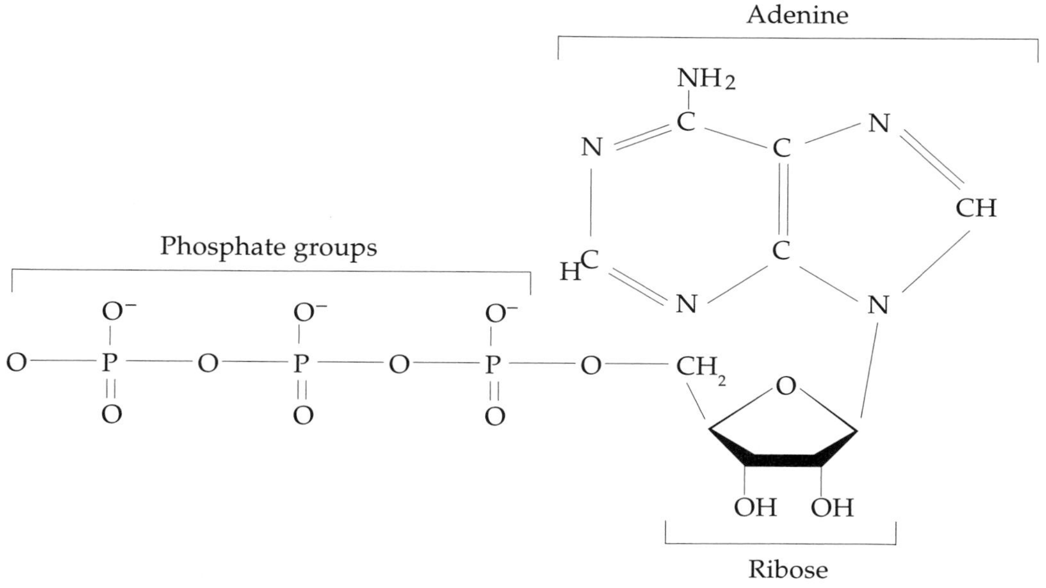

Adenosine Triphosphate (ATP)

Figure 28.5

The energy required to synthesize ATP is derived from glucose molecules stored in the cell. Glucose is a six-carbon monosaccharide. The chemical bonds within the molecule are broken by a series of reactions. The energy released by the formation of more stable bonds is an energy source for ATP production.

Anaerobic Processes

ATP is produced **anaerobically** via the process of **glycolysis**. Depending on the cell type and its oxygen supply, glycolysis might be followed, in turn, by

(a) **fermentation**, another anaerobic process, which facilitates the continuity of glycolysis, or

(b) certain **aerobic** processes that produce yet additional ATP.

GLYCOLYSIS

Glycolysis is a series of enzymatic reactions that breaks down a glucose molecule to yield two molecules of pyruvate (a three-carbon molecule). This process requires an initial input of two ATP molecules, but it leads to the production of four ATP molecules, for a net gain of two ATP molecules. Glycolysis also generates two molecules of NADH, which constitute the reduced form of two NAD^+ molecules. In this reduced form, NADH stores energy that will ultimately generate additional ATP if oxygen is present.

In net chemical terms, glycolysis (which involves a number of steps and substeps) may be represented as such:

$$1 \text{ Glucose} + 2 \text{ ADP} + 2 \text{ P}_i + 2 \text{ NAD}^+ \rightarrow 2 \text{ pyruvate} + 2 \text{ ATP} + 2 \text{ NADH} + 2 \text{ H}_2\text{O} + 2\text{H}^+$$

Note that:

• Glycolysis occurs in the cell's cytoplasm, where the substrates and enzymes necessary for its several steps are available.

• Glycolysis is an anaerobic process that occurs in both aerobic and anaerobic cells.

• For each molecule of glucose that undergoes glycolysis, the cell enjoys a net gain of (a) 2 ATP molecules (from two ADP molecules and two phosphate ions) and (b) 2 NADH molecules (from 2 NAD^+ molecules, 2 hydrogen ions, and 4 electrons). In net terms, those two components of the process might be summarized as such:

(a) $2 \text{ ADP} + 2 \text{ P}_i \rightarrow 2\text{ATP}$ (b) $2 \text{ NAD}^+ + 2 \text{ H}^+ + 4\text{e}^- \rightarrow 2 \text{ NADH}$

Glycolysis represents a primitive process that arose very early in the evolution of life. All cells harbor the enzymes necessary to conduct this anaerobic process, and some prokaryotes depend on it as their sole means of producing ATP. (Such cells, therefore, constitute obligate or tolerant anaerobes.) Eukaryotes, including animal cells, depend on aerobic respiration (to be discussed shortly) but will resort to glycolysis (as a kind of "emergency process") when oxygen is in short supply.

Please solve this problem:

• Which one of the following does NOT accurately characterize glycolysis as it occurs in animal cells?

   A. One molecule of glucose is converted to one molecule of pyruvate.
   B. Two ATP molecules are required for initiation and four ATP molecules are ultimately produced.
   C. It is an anaerobic process that occurs in both aerobes and anaerobes.
   D. It occurs in the cytoplasm, where the required enzymes and molecules are present.

Problem solved:

A is correct. Glycolysis is an anaerobic process and occurs in the cytoplasm of both aerobic and anaerobic organisms. Moreover, it requires, for its initiation, two molecules of ATP, and produces 4 ATP for a net yield of 2 ATP. Choices B, C, and D, therefore, are true statements. Choice A is false because for each molecule of glucose that enters the glycolytic pathway, *two* molecules of pyruvic acid are produced.

UNDER ANAEROBIC CONDITIONS GLYCOLYSIS IS FOLLOWED BY FERMENTATION

If oxygen is unavailable, or for a cell that cannot conduct aerobic respiration, the pyruvate produced through glycolysis undergoes fermentation. Fermentation is an anaerobic process in which some organic molecule accepts (is reduced by) the hydrogen atoms produced during glycolysis. In most animal cells, the hydrogen acceptor is pyruvate itself, the very molecule produced by glycolysis. Pyruvate is converted to lactate, and NAD^+ is regenerated from NADH.

$$\text{pyruvate} + \text{NADH} + H^+ \rightarrow \text{lactate} + NAD^+$$

(In humans undergoing vigorous exercise, the cardiovascular system may be unable to supply actively metabolizing muscle with enough oxygen to sustain aerobic cellular respiration. There results a so-called "oxygen debt," and the affected muscle cells conduct glycolysis, anaerobically, in order to sustain some degree of ATP production. Glycolysis is followed by fermentation, which produces lactate. Lactate, and the decreased pH it produces, likely causes the pain associated with muscle fatigue.)

For each of the two pyruvate molecules produced via glycolysis, fermentation (a) yields one molecule of lactate and (b) regenerates one molecule of NAD^+ from NADH. (For each molecule of glucose undergoing glycolysis, therefore, fermentation produces two molecules of lactate and regenerates two molecules of NAD^+.)

Fermentation occasions no net production of ATP molecules. Yet under anaerobic conditions, fermentation is essential to the continuity of glycolysis; without it, glycolysis would grind to a halt. That is because NAD^+, which is essential to glycolysis, is a relatively limited chemical resource within the cell. Fermentation serves to regenerate NAD^+—to prevent its depletion—so that glycolysis may continue.

$$1 \text{ glucose} + 2 \text{ ADP} + 2 P_i + \mathbf{2\ NAD^+} \rightarrow 2 \text{ pyruvate} + 2 \text{ ATP} + 2 \text{ NADH} + 2 H_2O + 2 H^+$$

Glycolysis

$$2 \text{ pyruvate} + 2 \text{ NADH} + 2 H^+ \rightarrow 2 \text{ lactate} + \mathbf{2\ NAD^+}$$

Fermentation

$$1 \text{ glucose} + 2 \text{ ADP} + 2 P_i + \mathbf{2\ NAD^+} \rightarrow 2 \text{ pyruvate} + 2 \text{ ATP} + 2 \text{ NADH} + 2 H_2O + 2 H^+$$

Glycolysis

(In yeasts, the hydrogen acceptor that mediates fermentation is not pyruvate, but rather acetaldehyde, which is produced when pyruvate loses a terminal CO_2 group. The acetaldehyde molecule accepts the hydrogen produced via glycolysis, producing NAD^+ and ethyl alcohol. For that reason, fermentation in yeasts is among the processes long exploited by humankind to produce alcoholic beverages.)

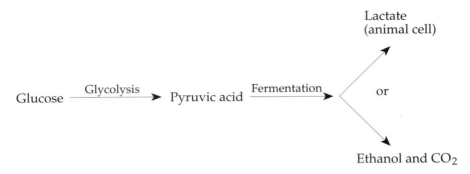

Anaerobic Pathways

Figure 28.6

Please solve this problem:

- Which of the following statements best characterizes glycolysis?

    A. It is an aerobic process that yields lactic acid.
    B. It is an aerobic process that yields ethyl alcohol.
    C. It is an anaerobic process that produces a net yield of two ATP molecules.
    D. It is an anaerobic process that produces a net yield of four ATP molecules.

Problem solved:

C is correct. Glycolysis involves the degradation of a six-carbon molecule (glucose) into two three-carbon molecules (pyruvate). The process requires an input of two ATP molecules and produces four ATP molecules, for a net yield of two ATP molecules. Glycolysis occurs in the absence of oxygen, that is, anaerobically.

Please solve this problem:

- Which of the following best characterizes fermentation?

    A. It is an aerobic process that yields lactic acid.
    B. It is an aerobic process that yields ethyl alcohol.
    C. It is an anaerobic process that produces no ATP.
    D. It is an anaerobic process that produces four ATP molecules.

Problem solved:

C is correct. Under anaerobic conditions, fermentation follows glycolysis. Through fermentation, pyruvic acid is converted to either (a) lactic acid or (b) ethyl alcohol and carbon dioxide. Fermentation does not produce ATP.

Please solve this problem:

- Which of the following substances most likely causes the pain associated with muscle fatigue?

    A. Lactate
    B. Pyruvate
    C. Carbon dioxide
    D. Ethyl alcohol

Problem solved:

A is correct. A rapidly exercising muscle may require more oxygen than is delivered to it. The result is that it experiences oxygen deprivation and cannot carry on the aerobic processes that would otherwise follow glycolysis. The pyruvate produced during glycolysis instead undergoes fermentation and is converted to lactate, which probably causes muscle fatigue.

Aerobic Processes

When adequate oxygen is available, aerobic organisms do not conduct fermentation. Rather, following glycolysis, they direct pyruvate toward aerobic respiratory processes, where they use molecular oxygen as a final oxidizing agent—a final electron acceptor. In terms of harvesting energy from glucose (measured in terms of ATP production), aerobic respiration is far more efficient than glycolysis followed by fermentation. Glycolysis and fermentation, as already noted, yield a net production of 2 ATP molecules per molecule of glucose. In aerobic respiration, on the other hand, a molecule of glucose produces between thirty and thirty-two molecules of ATP.

Aerobic respiration involves several phases. These are: glycolysis (which is anaerobic) and the **Krebs cycle, electron transport**, and **oxidative phosphorylation** (which require oxygen and are aerobic). When the cell conducts aerobic respiration, the pyruvic acid molecules formed during glycolysis enter the mitochondria (where all aerobic reactions occur). In the mitochondria, each pyruvic acid molecule is converted to acetyl CoA in preparation for the Krebs cycle.

THE KREBS CYCLE

The **Krebs cycle** (also called the **citric acid cycle** or the **tricarboxylic acid cycle**) represents eight reactions designed to harness the energy released from the stepwise oxidation of pyruvate. Students should know the fundamental principles of the Krebs cycle and be able to identify the processes and molecules associated with its critical steps.

Pyruvate produced during glycolysis is channeled to the Krebs cycle via the multienzyme complex pyruvate dehydrogenase, located in the mitochondrial matrix. In a reaction known as oxidative decarboxylation, pyruvate dehydrogenase catalyzes the release of carbon dioxide from pyruvate, and the resulting molecule is oxidized (two electrons are transferred to NAD^+ to produce NADH). The acetyl group that is produced is then combined with coenzyme A to yield acetyl CoA.

$$pyruvate + CoA + NAD^+ \rightarrow acetyl\ CoA + CO_2 + NADH$$

Acetyl CoA, a two-carbon molecule, enters the Krebs cycle and reacts with the four-carbon oxaloacetate molecule to produce the six-carbon citrate molecule (citric acid).

$$acetyl\ CoA + oxaloacetate \rightarrow citrate$$

Citrate then undergoes a series of oxidation–reduction reactions that lead to the removal of two carbon groups as CO_2 and the reduction of four **electron carrier molecules.** Specifically, three molecules of NAD^+ and one FAD molecule are reduced, as shown in the following reactions:

$$NAD^+ + 2e^- + 2H^+ \rightarrow NADH + H^+ \text{ and}$$
$$FAD^+ + 2e^- + 2H^+ \rightarrow FADH_2$$

(Customarily, when writing NADH, the "+ H^+" is omitted.) These reduced electron carriers store energy and are oxidized in a later stage of aerobic respiration, thereby releasing their energy into a process that generates ATP.

In essence, the Krebs cycle begins with a molecule of citric acid formed from the combination of a molecule of acetyl CoA and a molecule of oxaloacetate. The removal of two carbons from the six-carbon citrate regenerates the four-carbon oxaloacetate, which can then recombine with another molecule of acetyl CoA to initiate another turn of the cycle. The energy released during the oxidation–reduction reactions is used to produce NADH and $FADH_2$ by reduction from the electron acceptors NAD^+ and FAD.

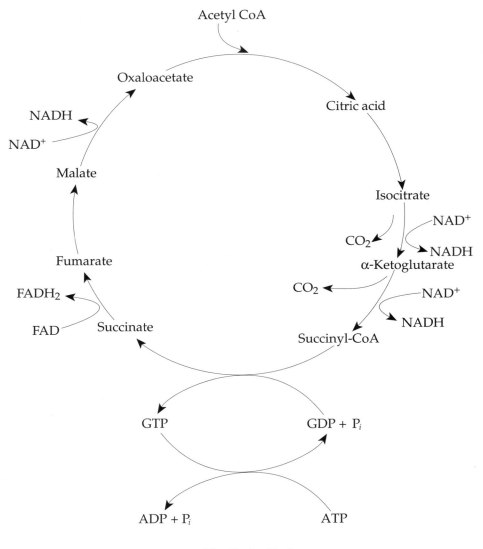

The Krebs Cycle
Figure 28.7

PRODUCTS GENERATED

In addition to the reduced electron carriers, one molecule of GTP (guanosine triphosphate) is produced from GDP (guanosine diphosphate) and inorganic phosphate during each turn of the Krebs cycle. GTP's phosphate bond is essentially equivalent in energy to ATP's, as evidenced by the fact that most of the GTP transfers its third γ phosphate group to ADP to produce ATP. (Under some circumstances, some cells use GTP directly as an energy currency; they do not require that it be used first to form ATP.)

Each turn of the Krebs cycle, therefore, oxidizes citric acid in a stepwise fashion and stores the liberated energy in the following forms:

(a) three molecules of NADH,

(b) one molecule of $FADH_2$, and

(c) one molecule of GTP.

Two molecules of CO_2 are also produced, regenerating the four-carbon oxaloacetate molecule for the next turn of the cycle.

Note that glycolysis generates *two* molecules of pyruvic acid, and in the presence of sufficient oxygen, each will generate a molecule of acetyl CoA. Therefore, one molecule of glucose generates two turns of the Krebs cycle, producing:

(a) four molecules of CO_2,

(b) six molecules of NADH,

(c) two molecules of $FADH_2$, and

(d) two molecules of GTP.

Please solve this problem:

- Which of the following does NOT represent an energy-rich molecule that contributes, ultimately, to the energy housed within an ATP molecule?

  A. NADH
  B. $FADH_2$
  C. CO_2
  D. GTP

Problem solved:

C is correct. As evidenced by its two oxygen atoms and one carbon atom, carbon dioxide (like water) represents a highly oxidized compound. Within the realm of biochemical systems, neither water nor carbon dioxide contains significant amounts of chemical energy. Indeed, H_2O and CO_2 are the end-products of physiologic oxidative processes in which chemical energy is drawn from high-energy molecules to produce both highly oxidized compounds that are low in energy and high-energy molecules that store the energy in a form that is more readily usable by the cell.

The oxidation of glucose—beginning with glycolysis, followed by the aerobic processes of (1) the Krebs cycle and (2) electron transport coupled to oxidative phosphorylation (discussed in the next four sections) produces as its end-products (1) stored energy (within ATP molecules) and (2) the low-energy compounds carbon dioxide and water. The end of the Krebs cycle constitutes an intermediate stage of aerobic cellular respiration. Much of the energy drawn from glucose then inheres in the reduced electron carriers NADH and $FADH_2$. Choice D is correct because each turn of the Krebs cycle produces, also, a molecule of GTP from GDP and inorganic phosphate. The GTP, in turn, regenerates GDP and inorganic phosphate, releasing energy that produces a molecule of ATP from ADP and inorganic phosphate, as shown at the bottom of Figure 28.7.

ELECTRON TRANSPORT

The inner mitochondrial membrane contains an array of molecules, collectively called the electron transport chain (formerly the "cytochrome carrier system"), many of which contain iron. The process of electron transport begins with the NADH and $FADH_2$ molecules produced by the Krebs cycle. These reduced electron carriers pass electrons to flavomononucleotide (FMN) and then to coenzyme Q (CoQ); the coenzymes NAD^+ and FAD are thus regenerated. The electrons are then passed from CoQ along the electron transport chain. With each transfer from one carrier molecule to the next, the electrons are passed to molecules whose centers of positive charge have a progressively increased tendency to attract them. That means that each transfer involves the processes of oxidation and reduction; the donor molecule is oxidized (loses electrons) and the recipient molecule is reduced (gains electrons). With each transfer, energy is released. The process of oxidative phosphorylation ultimately directs this energy to the production of ATP.

Once the electrons pass down the electron transport chain, they combine with protons and oxygen (the ultimate electron acceptor) to form H_2O according to this chemical dynamic:

$$2e^- + 2\,H^+ + \frac{1}{2}\,O_2 \rightarrow H_2O.$$

Please solve this problem:

- In the electron transport chain, oxygen serves to:

   A. generate CO_2 from carbon derived from cytochrome carrier molecules.
   B. serve as the ultimate reducing agent for the storage of energy.
   C. mediate the movement of electrons from NADH and $FADH_2$ to the cytochrome carrier molecules.
   D. accept electrons donated by NADH and $FADH_2$.

Problem solved:

D is correct. The cytochrome carrier system "passes electrons" from one oxidizing agent to the next, releasing energy with each pass. The ultimate oxidizing agent (electron acceptor) is oxygen, which, when combined with the electrons (and free-floating protons) forms water.

Please solve this problem:

- The electron transport chain serves to:

  A. oxidize water and carbon dioxide so that the energy they contain can be released for use by the cell.
  B. liberate energy through a series of oxidation –reduction reactions.
  C. move energy from glucose to NADH and $FADH_2$.
  D. move energy from GTP to ATP.

Problem solved:

B is correct. The electron transport chain is composed of a series of molecules that pass electrons from one to the other, the donor being oxidized and the recipient being reduced. Energy is liberated through this process.

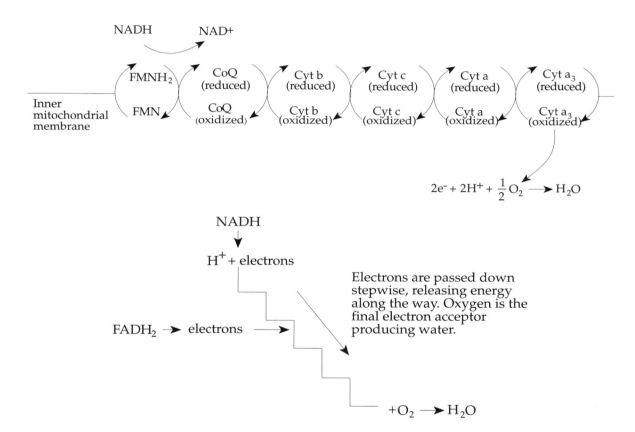

The Cytochrome Carrier System

Figure 28.8

OXIDATIVE PHOSPHORYLATION

The electron transport process releases energy. Certain complexes in the electron transport chain then use that energy to *pump hydrogen ions (H⁺) outward from the mitochondrial matrix into the space between the outer and inner membranes.* That creates an electrochemical gradient; the concentration of a positive charge and of hydrogen ions in the intermembrane space exceeds that within the matrix.

Any electrochemical gradient represents *potential energy* (as discussed in **Chapter 23**) because a membrane "wants" charge and concentration to be equalized on each of its sides (in the same sense that a ball sitting atop a hill "wants" to roll downward). *Creation* of an electrochemical gradient requires energy (just as rolling a ball up a hill requires energy). The energy invested in creating an electrochemical gradient is then "stored" or "housed" within the fact of the gradient itself.

At this stage of aerobic cellular respiration, therefore, the potential energy originally housed within the glucose molecule's chemical bonds now sits within the electrochemical gradient tied to the uneven distribution of protons between the mitchondrial matrix and the intermembrane space. Then, in an "effort" to eliminate the gradient between matrix and intermembrane space, protons move through channels, across the inner mitochondrial membrane, from intermembrane space to matrix. That movement releases energy (as does a ball rolling down a hill).

The channels through which the protons move are composed of the enzyme **ATP synthetase,** which is located at the inner mitochondrial membrane. As the movement proceeds, the enzyme catalyzes a reaction in which the released energy is used to form ATP from ADP and inorganic phosphate. That process—in which ATP synthetase catalyzes the formation of ATP—is called **oxidative phosphorylation**. As a result, oxidative phosphorylation, the energy formerly housed in the electrochemical gradient within the mitochondrion (which before *that* was housed within the glucose molecule's chemical bonds)—"finds itself" sitting in the high-energy phosphate bonds of newly formed ATP molecules.

COUPLING OF ELECTRON TRANSPORT AND OXIDATIVE PHOSPHORYLATION

We have just described electron transport and oxidative phosphorylation as though they were two separate processes, transport occurring first and phosphorylation thereafter. Although sometimes it is intellectually convenient to think of them that way, it is, unfortunately, inaccurate. The two processes are in fact **coupled**, meaning that they occur as two adjoined components of a single process.

Imagine a little toy airplane with a single propeller that "winds up" by attachment to a rubber band. When a child winds the propeller, the tension produced in the rubber band represents potential energy (energy invested by the child who wound it). When the child removes his hand from the propeller:

(1) the potential energy inherent in the wound rubber band is released;

(2) the release of the energy produces mechanical energy and the propeller turns;

(3) the turning propeller creates friction with the surrounding air, from which comes the force that drives the plane forward;

(4) the forward motion through the air creates negative pressure over the little wings' curved surfaces;

(5) the negative pressure creates lift; and

(6) the plane flies.

We might think of the six phenomena just listed as a series of discrete events, one leading to the next, like a line of falling dominos. Yet, the truth is that they all happen at the same time; when the child lets go of the wound propeller, the plane flies.

By making a somewhat crude analogy to the toy airplane, realize that electron transport and oxidative phosphorylation are not *separate* processes. Rather, they happen as one—together—and for that reason, we say they are "coupled."

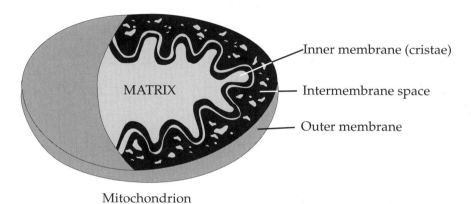

Mitochondrion

Structure of the Mitochondrion

Figure 28.9

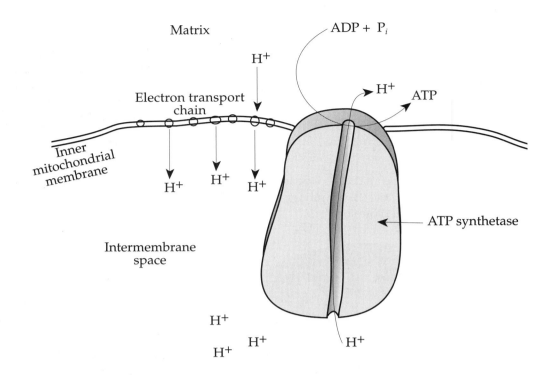

Oxidative Phosphorylation via ATP Synthetase

Figure 28.10

Please solve this problem:

- The movement of hydrogen ions from the mitochondrial matrix to the intermembrane space serves to:

   A. provide the energy gradient necessary to initiate and perpetuate the sequential delivery of electrons from one cytochrome carrier to the next.

   B. establish an electrochemical gradient that promotes the passive transport of protons and a concomitant conversion of potential energy to chemical energy.

   C. provide an environment in which electrons may be accepted by oxygen and free-floating protons and thereby regenerate water molecules disrupted during the Krebs cycle.

   D. promote the synthesis of enzymes necessary to generate ATP molecules from ADP and inorganic phosphate.

Problem solved:

B is correct. The electron transport chain uses some of the energy liberated through oxidation-reduction reactions to pump protons from the matrix into the intermembrane space. This gradient stores potential energy. The protons flow down their gradient, through ATP synthetase complexes, and back into the matrix. ATP synthetase converts the potential energy of the gradient into chemical energy when it catalyzes the synthesis of ATP from ADP and inorganic phosphate.

Please solve this problem:

- Oxidative phosphorylation occurs:

    A. in the mitochondrial cytoplasm before electron transport.
    B. on the nuclear membrane before electron transport.
    C. on the inner mitochondrial membrane contemporaneous with electron transport.
    D. in the cytoplasm after electron transport.

Problem solved:

C is correct. As noted in the text, the process of oxidative phosphorylation refers to the formation of ATP from ADP and inorganic phosphate. It is driven by the release of potential energy, which is stored in the electrochemical gradient created by the movement of hydrogen ions from the mitochondrial matrix into the intermembrane space. That movement of hydrogen ions is fueled by energy derived from electron transport. Oxidative phosphorylation is coupled with electron transport, and it occurs on the inner mitochondrial membrane through the action of ATP synthetase. Choices A, B, and D inaccurately describe the site at which oxidative phosphorylation occurs and do not reflect the concept that electron transport and oxidative phosphorylation are coupled.

Quantitative Comparison of ATP Production: Aerobic and Anaerobic Respiration

Under anaerobic conditions, glycolysis yields (net) only 2 ATP molecules per molecule of glucose. Without oxygen, the 2 NADH molecules that arise through glycolysis produce no additional ATP (but rather are recycled via fermentation to regenerate NAD^+).

Under aerobic conditions, however, one glucose molecule yields:

- via glycolysis, two molecules of ATP in the cytosol;

- via glycolysis, two molecules of NADH in the cytosol, these being termed **cytosolic NADH** ($NADH_{cyt}$);

- via the Krebs cycle two molecules of ATP in the mitochondrion via the Krebs cycle;

- via the Krebs cycle, eight molecules of NADH in the mitochondrion, these being called the **mitochondrial NADH** ($NADH_{mit}$); and

- via the Krebs cycle, two molecules of $FADH_2$ in the mitochondrion, these being called **mitochondrial FADH$_2$** ($FADH_{mit}$).

THE ELECTRON CARRIERS AND ATP PRODUCTION

As already noted, the movement of electrons from the reduced electron carriers ($NADH_{mit}$), ($FADH_{mit}$), and ($NADH_{cyt}$) through the electron transport chain and then to oxygen, releases energy which, in turn, moves protons from the mitochondrial matrix to the intermembrane space, thus creating an electrochemical proton gradient. Energy released from each molecule of mitochondrial NADH is thought to pump a sufficient quantity of protons ultimately to generate (by oxidative phosphorylation) 2.5 ATP molecules. One molecule of mitochondrial $FADH_2$ and one molecule of cytosolic NADH are each thought to pump a sufficient quantity of protons ultimately to generate (by oxidative phosphorylation) 1.5 ATP molecules.

Under aerobic conditions, therefore, the complete oxidation of one molecule of glucose produces:

- Two molecules of ATP via glycolysis   = **2 ATP**

- Two molecules of cytosolic NADH   = 2 molecules $NADH_{cyt}$ x 1.5 ATP = **3 ATP**
  by glycolysis

- Two molecules of pyruvate, each   x 2 pyruvate = 2 molecules $NADH_{mit}$ x 2.5 ATP = **5 ATP**
  of which yields 1 molecule of
  mitochondrial NADH

- One molecule of citrate, each of   x 2 pyruvate = 6 molecules $NADH_{mit}$ x 2.5 ATP = **15 ATP**
  which, in turn, produces 3 molecules
  of mitochondrial NADH

- One molecule of mitochondrial   x 2 pyruvate = 2 molecules $FADH_{2mit}$ x 1.5 ATP = **3 ATP**
  $FADH_2$

- One molecule of ATP via the   x 2 pyruvate   = **2 ATP**
  conversion of GTP to GDP
                                                                              _____

                                                                              30 ATP

Please solve this problem:

- With regard to cellular respiration, which of the following statements is true?

    A. Glycolysis requires two ATP molecules and produces two ATP molecules, yielding a net production of zero ATP molecules.
    B. The Krebs cycle produces three molecules of NADH for each molecule of glucose that is degraded.
    C. Carbon dioxide is formed during the Krebs cycle.
    D. Electrons and hydrogen ions are passed along a chain of electron transport molecules in a process that requires the input of energy.

Problem solved:

C is correct. During the Krebs cycle, two carbon dioxide molecules are released. Choice A is false because glycolysis offers a net yield of two ATP molecules, requiring two at initiation and generating four by completion. Choice B is similarly false. The Krebs cycle produces three molecules of NADH per molecule of acetyl CoA that enters the cycle. However, two molecules of acetyl CoA enter the cycle per molecule of glucose degraded (each arising from a molecule of pyruvate). Choice D is false because it describes electron transport as a process that requires the input of energy. The process liberates energy; it is an oxidative process, with oxygen serving as the electron acceptor.

Please solve this problem:

- In comparison to anaerobic respiration, aerobic respiration yields:

    A. greater quantities of ATP, because the presence of oxygen, a strong oxidizing agent, facilitates greater oxidation of the glucose molecule.
    B. greater quantities of ATP, because aerobic processes avoid the accumulation of lactic acid.
    C. lesser quantities of ATP, because oxygen has such a strong affinity for electrons that it obstructs the electron transport system.
    D. lesser quantities of ATP, because iron within the cytochrome carrier system competes for active sites on the ATP, synthetase molecule.

Problem solved:

A is correct. As noted in the text, aerobic respiration makes more efficient use of the glucose molecule than anaerobic resipiration. When glycolysis is complete, fermentation reoxidizes NADH, converting it to NAD^+, a process that does not produce ATP. In aerobic respiration, however, NADH and $FADH_2$ donate their electrons into the electron transport system, which converts some of the stored energy into a gradient that is used to produce more ATP. In order to do this, however, there must be a final electron acceptor, or else the electrons would accumulate. Oxygen fulfills this role.

Please solve this problem:

- Which of the following statements most likely represents the reason that oxidative phosphorylation occurs on the inner mitochondrial membrane?

    A. ATP synthetase is located on the membrane.
    B. The enzymes that catalyze the glycolytic pathway are located on the membrane.
    C. The membrane permits active transport of protons.
    D. The membrane permits passive diffusion of protons.

Problem solved:

A is correct. ATP synthetase is located in the inner mitochondrial membrane. Were that not stated in the text, you might infer it, since such an enzyme is necessary to ATP synthesis. Choices B, C, and D make inaccurate statements.

28.2 MASTERY APPLIED: PRACTICE PASSAGES AND QUESTIONS

Passage I

The smooth endoplasmic reticulum of the cells of the liver and other tissues is the site of numerous enzymes that metabolize drugs. Forming a significant class of such enzymes are the mixed function oxidases (MFO), also called monooxygenases. To function effectively, MFO enzymes require a reducing agent and molecular oxygen. A typical reaction involving a monooxygenase results in the consumption of one molecule of oxygen per substrate molecule. One of the oxygen atoms is incorporated into the product while the other is incorporated into water.

Homogenization and fractionation of the cell yield microsomes. Microsomes are vesicles that retain the morphological and functional traits of the intact endoplasmic reticulum. Two important microsomal enzymes that catalyze the oxidation-reduction reaction mentioned above are the flavoprotein, NADPH-cytochrome P-450 reductase, and the hemoprotein, cytochrome P-450. Cytochrome P-450 serves as the terminal oxidase in the reaction. An overview of the oxidative cycle involved in microsomal drug oxidation is presented in Figure 1.

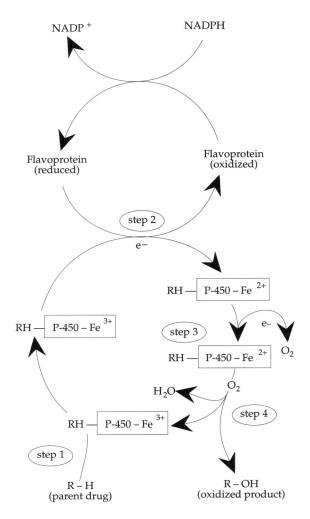

Cytochrome P-450 Cycle in Drug Oxidations

Figure 1

1. Drugs are metabolized largely in the:

    A. peroxisomes of all cells.
    B. cell membrane of liver cells.
    C. endoplasmic reticulum of liver cells.
    D. mitochondria of most cells.

2. Cytochrome P-450 reduction constitutes the rate-limiting step in hepatic drug oxidations. If the concentration of cytochrome P-450 reductase is higher than that of the other enzymes involved in the reaction, what is a possible explanation for cytochrome P-450 reduction being the rate-limiting step?

A. Cytochrome P-450 reductase is a poor reducing agent.
B. Cytochrome P-450 reductase is a poor oxidizing agent.
C. The reduction of cytochrome P-450 has a higher energy of activation than the other steps in the reaction.
D. The reduction of cytochrome P-450 has a lower energy of activation than the other steps in the reaction.

3. Which of the following choices is a cellular process with a biochemical reaction similar to the cytochrome P-450 cycle?

A. Oxidative phosphorylation/electron transport
B. Glycolysis
C. Conversion of glucose to pyruvic acid
D. Anaerobic respiration

4. Which of the following choices is a reducing agent employed in the cytochrome P-450 cycle (Figure 1)?

A. Water
B. Molecular oxygen
C. NADPH
D. NADP

5. Which of the following statements accurately describes the orientation of phospholipids found in the lipophilic membranes of the endoplasmic reticulum?

A. The hydrophilic tail faces the interior of the bilayer sheet while the hydrophobic head is positioned facing the cytoplasm.
B. The hydrophilic tail faces the cytoplasm while the hydrophobic head is positioned toward the interior of the bilayer sheet.
C. The hydrophobic tail faces the cytoplasm while the hydrophilic head is positioned toward the interior of the bilayer sheet.
D. The hydrophobic tail faces the interior of the bilayer sheet while the hydrophilic head is positioned facing the cytoplasm.

6. Among many of the drugs and substrates processed by the cytochrome P-450 cycle, high lipid-solubility constitutes the only common property. The best explanation for this phenomenon is that:

A. substrate specificity is high for this enzyme complex.
B. substrate specificity is low for this enzyme complex.
C. the energy of activation is decreased for this reaction.
D. the energy of activation is increased for this reaction.

Passage II

Cholesterol is a sterol, which is a kind of lipid. Located primarily in eukaryotic cell membranes, it regulates membrane fluidity. An amphipathic molecule, cholesterol's hydrophobic moiety is a fatty acid chain and hydrocarbon chain of sphingosine; its hydrophilic moiety consists of a hydroxyl group. Cholesterol is also a precursor to steroid hormones, such as progesterone, testosterone, estradiol, and cortisol. It is synthesized from acetyl CoA. Its metabolism must be carefully regulated, however. High serum levels of cholesterol can result in disease and death, particularly by contributing to the deposition of plaque in arteries throughout the body.

A lack of LDL (low-density lipoprotein) receptors leads to hypercholesterolemia and atherosclerosis. Low-density lipoproteins comprise the major carriers of cholesterol in the blood. In familial hypercholesterolemia, cholesterol is deposited in various tissues as a result of high plasma concentrations of LDL cholesterol. The molecular defect associated with familial hypercholesterolemia is the lack of, or defect in, functional receptors for LDL. Affected individuals who are homozygous for the condition are virtually devoid of receptors for LDL, while heterozygous individuals possess approximately one half the normal number of receptors. Both conditions impair entry of LDL into the liver and other cells, leading to increased plasma levels of LDL.

A precursor of cholesterol is 3-hydroxy-3-methylglutarate (HMG). Two preparations are used to treat hypercholesterolemia: Drug A and Drug B (Figure 2). Both drugs contain molecular groups that are structural analogs of HMG, and both act by inhibiting HMG-CoA reductase, which is a rate-limiting enzyme in the production of cholesterol. The enzyme is synthesized in greater quantities when cholesterol supplies are low and in lesser quantities when cholesterol supply is high. Inhibition of *de novo* cholesterol synthesis leads to a reduction of intracellular supply of cholesterol (Figure 1).

As a result, the cell increases production of cell-surface LDL receptors that can bind and internalize circulating LDL particles. Increased catabolism of LDL and reduced cholesterol synthesis result in a decrease in plasma cholesterol level.

Both therapeutic preparations are most effective in individuals who are heterozygous for familial hypercholesterolemia (see Figure 2). Patients who are homozygous for the condition lack the LDL receptors entirely, limiting the benefit they can derive from these agents.

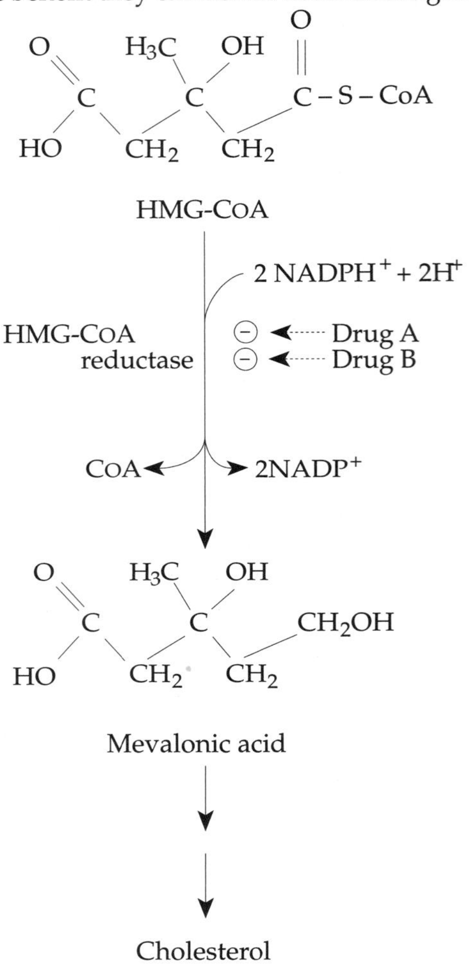

Figure 1

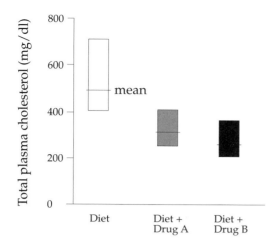

Figure 2

1. High LDL levels are likely to accumulate in the blood plasma when:
   A. receptors for LDL are sparse or non-functional.
   B. catabolism of LDL is increased.
   C. HMG-CoA reductase activity is enhanced.
   D. drugs A and B are administered.

2. Bile salt constitutes a principal breakdown product of cholesterol. Synthesized in the liver and stored in the gall bladder, it is:
   A. an enzyme that is released into the small intestine.
   B. an emulsifier that is released into the stomach.
   C. an enzyme that promotes hydrolysis by lipases.
   D. an emulsifier that aids in food absorption.

3. Figure 1 indicates that during the conversion of HMG-CoA to mevalonic acid, NADPH molecules undergo:
   A. oxidation to yield NADP$^+$.
   B. oxidation to yield HMG-CoA.
   C. reduction to yield NADP$^+$.
   D. reduction to yield HMG-CoA.

4. The molecule targeted for inhibition by the two therapeutic preparations described in the passage exhibits all of the following characteristics EXCEPT:
   A. it increases the activation energy required for a given reaction to occur.
   B. it functions optimally within a narrow pH range.
   C. it is subject to denaturation at high temperatures.
   D. it is not consumed in a reaction.

5. According to Figure 2, which experimental treatment(s) is (are) associated with the widest range of values for total blood plasma cholesterol?
   A. Diet
   B. Diet plus Drug A
   C. Diet plus Drug B
   D. No variation in range of values among the variables is apparent

6. An increase in dietary cholesterol would most likely have which of the following effects?
   A. LDL particles would cease to carry cholesterol in the blood.
   B. Synthesis of HMG-CoA reductase in the liver would be increased.
   C. Synthesis of HMG-CoA reductase in the liver would be reduced.
   D. Synthesis of steroid hormones would be decreased.

7. The initial precursor for cholesterol synthesis is also a direct participant in which of the following processes?
   A. Glycolysis
   B. Fermentation
   C. The Krebs cycle
   D. Oxidative phosphorylation

28.3 MASTERY VERIFIED: ANSWERS AND EXPLANATIONS

Passage I

1. **C is correct.** The passage states that drugs are metabolized primarily in the smooth endoplasmic reticulum of liver cells, among others: "The smooth endoplasmic reticulum of the cells of the liver and other tissues is the site of numerous enzymes that metabolize drugs." Choice A is not correct because peroxisomes, which contain the enzyme catalase, serve in the metabolism of hydrogen peroxide. Choice B is wrong, too. The cell membrane regulates the flow of material into and out of the cell. It is not associated with drug metabolism. Choice D is false. The mitochondria function in cellular respiration and the passage does not indicate otherwise.

2. **C is correct.** By definition, the rate-limiting step of a reaction is the one with the highest energy of activation. Choices A and B are nonsensical because an enzyme is never an oxidizing or reducing agent.

3. **A is correct.** Both pathways rely on oxidation-reduction reactions. The cytochrome P-450 cycle serves in drug metabolism, whereas oxidative phosphorylation (coupled with the electron transport chain) promotes ATP production. Choices B, C, and D refer to a single process: anaerobic respiration. None describes a process that closely resembles the cytochrome P-450 cycle.

4. **C is correct.** Regardless of the seeming complexity of Figure 1, a quick examination reveals that flavoprotein is reduced as NADPH is converted to NADP. NADPH, therefore, serves as the reducing agent.

5. **D is correct.** The phospholipid molecule of the membrane contains a hydrophobic moiety, the tail, and a hydrophilic moiety, the head. The hydrophobic tail faces the interior of the bilayer sheet, and the hydrophilic head faces the cytoplasm.

6. **B is correct.** Enzymes are ordinarily highly specific with respect to substrate. This trait explains why, in most cases, a given enzyme will catalyze only a very specific reaction. In this case, however, the same enzyme system will act on a variety of substrates, which suggests that enzyme specificity is low. Enzymes always serve to reduce (not increase) activation energy, but that fact is not relevant to the question. Choices C and D, therefore, are incorrect.

Passage II

1. **A is correct.** The passage states that deficiencies in LDL receptors impair the movement of LDL into tissue cells and out of the bloodstream. Choice B is contrary to information provided in the third paragraph: Catabolism of LDL inside cells is dependent on removing the LDL from the blood and internalizing it in the cell. Increased catabolism would *reduce* the quantity of circulating LDL in the blood, not increase it. Choice C is incorrect because HMG-CoA reductase is involved in the production of cholesterol from precursors within the cell. Enhancing its activity would likely result in greater manufacture of cholesterol, while blood-borne LDL-cholesterol molecules are not taken up by the cells. Choice D is likewise incorrect. The passage states that both therapeutic preparations increase production of LDL receptors, which then bind to LDL particles, removing them from the blood.

2. **D is correct.** The answer draws on the student's knowledge of bile and its function. It has little connection to the passage. On the basis of the question itself, you can be reasonably sure that bile is not an enzyme because it is not a *protein*. Bile is an emulsifier but is not released into the stomach. It is released into the small intestine.

3. **A is correct.** Oxidation–reduction reactions always occur together. The NADPH is serving as an electron donor, which results in the reduction of HMG-CoA. As a result of losing those electrons to HMG-CoA, NADPH is oxidized to NADP⁺.

4. **A is correct.** According to the passage, the molecule inhibited by both preparations is HMG-CoA reductase. The suffix "ase" ordinarily signifies an enzyme. All properties associated with an enzyme therefore apply. Since the question turns on the word "except," any false statement is correct. Enzymes *reduce* the activation energy; they do not increase it. Choices B, C, and D make statements that accurately describe enzyme properties.

5. **A is correct.** The total plasma cholesterol values for diet range from 400 mg/dl to approximately 700 mg/dl, compared to a range of roughly (a) 250 mg/dl to 400 mg/dl for diet plus Drug A, (b) 200 mg/dl to 350 mg/dl for diet plus Drug B. The widest range, then, is associated with diet alone.

6. **C is correct.** The availability of increased amounts of dietary cholesterol would tend to increase levels of cholesterol in the plasma and in the cells that normally take it in *from* the plasma. The pathways and mechanisms normally responsible for cholesterol synthesis would thus tend to be less active. HMG-CoA reductase catalyzes a reaction necessary for the synthesis of cholesterol. As stated in the passage, it is normally a rate-limiting enzyme. When plasma and cells have an increased supply of cholesterol, synthesis of the enzyme is reduced.

7. **C is correct.** The passage states that the initial precursor for cholesterol synthesis is acetyl CoA. Acetyl CoA also participates in the Krebs cycle: It combines with oxaloacetate to form citrate.

CHAPTER 29

HUMAN PHYSIOLOGY I: GAS EXCHANGE, CIRCULATION, DIGESTION, AND MUSCULOSKELETAL FUNCTION

29.1 MASTERY ACHIEVED

GAS EXCHANGE AND THE RESPIRATORY SYSTEM

The term **respiration** has two distinct but related meanings. Cellular respiration refers to the *oxidation of nutrients* to liberate energy, and respiration refers to the overall process of *gas exchange* in the organism. In human beings, gas exchange involves the intake of oxygen and its delivery to the cells, and the removal of carbon dioxide from the cells and its delivery to the environment.

Inspiration

REGULATION OF BREATHING

Although respiration is under some voluntary control, it is *normally an involuntary behavior*. In higher organisms, respiration is controlled by the **medulla oblongata**, a relatively primitive component of the brain. Signals that initiate each cycle of breathing arise from the part of the medulla oblongata known as the **respiratory center**.

The **diaphragm** is the major muscle of respiration. The **phrenic nerve** carries signals from the medulla oblongata to the diaphragm, and the diaphragm is thus stimulated to contract. Contraction of the diaphragm initiates **inspiration**, the process of breathing in.

NEGATIVE PRESSURE

The diaphragm is a large, dome-shaped muscle located between the **thorax** and the **abdomen**. When it is relaxed its dome arches upward. When it contracts, it flattens with its center drawn downward. Contraction causes the space between the lungs and diaphragm to increase, creating a *negative pressure differential* between the lungs and the diaphragm. The lungs respond to this by expanding, creating a negative pressure differential between the interior of the lungs and the outside air. This negative pressure differential is equilibrated by the inflow of air, which we experience as "drawing a breath." As the diaphragm contracts, so do the **intercostal muscles**, which are accessory muscles of respiration. Contraction of the intercostal muscles further expands the chest cavity, augmenting the pressure differential created by the contracting diaphragm.

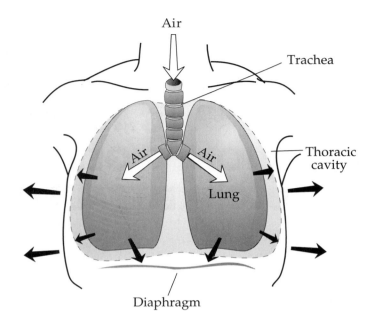

Expansion of Thoracic Cavity Creating Negative Pressure Outside Lungs,
Expansion of Lungs, and Influx of Air

Figure 29.1

The **elasticity** of the lung causes it to resist expansion. The negative pressure created by contraction of the diaphragm and accessory muscles must be sufficient to overcome the lung's natural tendency to collapse (as can be seen when a lung is punctured). With the lungs expanded and filled with air, inspiration is complete.

Expiration

Expiration occurs when the respiratory center *ceases* to send its signal to the diaphragm. The diaphragm relaxes and the lungs shrink, much like an emptying balloon. Air is forced from the lungs through the respiratory tract and out into the environment. Because expiration occurs when the diaphragm relaxes, it is normally a passive process, that is, no energy is required.

Please solve this problem:

- The phrenic nerve carries its signal:

    A. from the cerebral cortex to the lungs.
    B. from the lungs to the cerebral cortex.
    C. from the medulla oblongata to the diaphragm.
    D. from the diaphragm to the lungs.

Problem solved:

C is correct. The signal that initiates inspiration originates in the respiratory center of the medulla oblongata and is sent to the diaphragm via the phrenic nerve.

Please solve this problem:

- Expansion of the lungs occurs in response to:

    A. elimination of elasticity within the lungs.
    B. relaxation of the diaphragm.
    C. negative pressure within the esophagus.
    D. negative pressure between the diaphragm and the lungs.

Problem solved:

D is correct. Contraction of the diaphragm increases the space between the lungs and the diaphragm, thus creating a negative pressure in the pleural cavity around the lungs. This negative pressure causes the lungs to expand and consequently produces a negative pressure within the lungs themselves. That negative pressure is equilibrated by air flowing inward through the respiratory tract.

Structural Features of the Respiratory Tract

TRACHEA, BRONCHI, BRONCHIOLES, AND ALVEOLI

Air travels to the lungs through the **respiratory tract**. Air enters the respiratory tract through the nose and mouth, both of which serve to *warm and moisten* air as it enters the body. Mucus and the hairs lining the **nares** (nostrils) trap large particles that might be present in incoming air. After air enters through the nose, it passes through the **nasopharynx**, then the **oropharynx**.

Air travels through the oropharynx and the **larynx** and into the **trachea**. The trachea is a mucous-membrane–lined tubular structure whose lumen (i.e., the airway) is kept open by the **cartilaginous rings** that are embedded in its wall.

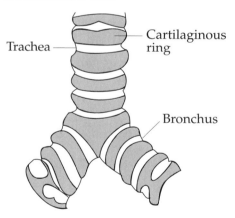

Section of Respiratory Tract

Figure 29.2

The trachea branches into a **left** and a **right bronchus**, which, like the trachea, are tubular structures kept open by a set of cartilaginous rings. The left and right bronchi themselves branch, giving rise to bronchi of progressively smaller size. Ultimately, the passages are called **bronchioles**. At the end of the bronchioles are minute air sacs called **alveoli**.

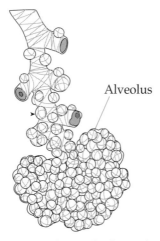

Terminal Bronchioles with
Alveoli

Figure 29.3

Very small foreign particles that reach the respiratory tract may be trapped by mucus. From there they are removed by the perpetual beating of **cilia**—the hairlike structures on the cells that coat the airway. Small particles sometimes escape this defense and enter the alveoli, where they are **phagocytized** (ingested and digested) by **macrophages** (phagocytic cells).

The most important function of the respiratory tract is to convey air to the alveoli, *delivering oxygen to* the blood and *removing carbon dioxide from* the blood (for expulsion from the body).

Each alveolus is surrounded by a rich network of **pulmonary capillaries**. The blood that enters these capillaries is higher in carbon dioxide and lower in oxygen because this blood has returned from systemic circulation, where it took carbon dioxide from the cells and delivered oxygen to the cells.

Ordinary air contains about twenty percent oxygen; its carbon dioxide content is less than one percent. Alveolar air contains relatively less oxygen and more carbon dioxide due to the mixing of atmospheric oxygen with residual air remaining in the alveoli and respiratory tract after each episode of expiration.

Please solve this problem:

- The cartilaginous rings that surround the trachea and bronchi serve to:
    - **A.** keep the airway open.
    - **B.** create the negative pressure generated by the contraction of the diaphragm.
    - **C.** maintain the movement of cilia within the airway.
    - **D.** facilitate the transmission of respiratory signals from the medulla oblongata.

Problem solved:

A is correct. The horseshoe-shaped cartilaginous rings that surround the trachea and bronchi hold the airway open (patent). You might think of a vacuum cleaner hose, which maintains its patency through the rigidity of stiff rings that support its otherwise collapsible walls.

Both the **pulmonary capillary wall** and the **alveolar wall** are permeable to carbon dioxide and oxygen. Like any substances in solution separated by a permeable membrane, carbon dioxide and oxygen move by passive diffusion down their respective concentration gradients until the concentrations are equalized. Oxygen passes from the alveolus, where its concentration is relatively higher, to the surrounding capillary blood, where its concentration is relatively lower. Carbon dioxide moves from the capillary blood, where its concentration is relatively higher, to the alveolus, where its concentration is relatively lower.

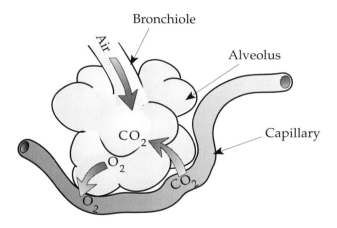

Gas Exchange at the
Alveolar–Capillary Interface

Figure 29.4

This kind of ongoing gas exchange requires continual maintenance of the concentration gradients that drive it. This is achieved by (a) the inspiratory and expiratory processes and (b) the systemic and pulmonary circulations. Inspiration and expiration draw carbon dioxide out of the alveoli while replenishing them with oxygen. Blood circulates continuously throughout the body, delivering oxygen to the cells and removing carbon dioxide from them.

Please solve this problem:

- Outgoing air from the body follows which one of the following pathways?

    A. Bronchi, bronchioles, trachea, alveoli
    B. Bronchioles, bronchi, trachea, alveoli
    C. Alveoli, bronchioles, bronchi, trachea
    D. Trachea, bronchi, bronchioles, alveoli

Problem solved:

C is correct. Incoming air travels through the trachea, the bronchi, the bronchioles, and the alveoli; outgoing air follows the reverse pathway out of the body.

Please solve this problem:

- Inspiration and expiration are necessary for the maintenance of gas exchange between an alveolus and a pulmonary capillary because:

   A. the phrenic nerve sends signals directly to the alveoli.
   B. gas exchange is dependent on the equality of gas concentrations across the alveolar membrane.
   C. the concentration gradients would disappear without them.
   D. body cells would cease to metabolize in their absence.

Problem solved:

C is correct. With respect to alveolar air, gas exchange across the alveolar membrane tends to increase the carbon dioxide concentration and decrease the oxygen concentration. In order to maintain the concentration gradient that drives the gas exchange, carbon dioxide must be expelled from the lungs and oxygen must be drawn inward. Expiration serves the first purpose, and inspiration, the second.

SURFACE TENSION OF ALVEOLI AND THE ROLE OF SURFACTANT

Surface tension results from the force of attraction among molecules in a liquid. If this liquid comes in contact with a substance with which it cannot establish intermolecular bonds, surface tension results, compelling both substances to minimize contact with each other. The polar water molecules that line the alveoli are in contact with air, a nonpolar substance. The resulting surface tension would normally cause the water to coalesce into a drop (because the shape with the smallest surface-to-volume ratio is a sphere), collapsing the alveoli in the process if there were no means to alleviate the surface tension.

In humans and other higher organisms, surface tension is relieved through the use of a **surfactant**. A surfactant has both a polar and a nonpolar end; a good example of one is a phospholipid. In the alveoli, the polar end of the surfactant dissolves into the water and the nonpolar end dissolves into the air, thereby separating the two from each other and eliminating the surface tension. Surfactant may be absent from premature newborns, in which case the alveoli remain collapsed. This is called **infant respiratory distress syndrome**.

Please solve this problem:

- A decreased concentration of surfactant leads to:

   A. a decrease in surface area for alveolar gas exchange.
   B. an inability to inspire air.
   C. a decrease in pulmonary elastic recoil.
   D. an inability of the phrenic nerve to transmit signals to the diaphragm.

Problem solved:

A is correct. If alveoli collapse, then the surface area for gas exchange decreases. Alveoli are more likely to collapse when surfactant is not present in sufficient quantities.

Gas Exchange at the Alveolar Surface

THE BIOCHEMISTRY OF THE BLOOD GASES

When carbon dioxide produced by metabolizing cells enters the bloodstream, it readily combines with water to form **carbonic acid** (H_2CO_3) in the presence of carbonic anhydrase, found in red blood cells:

$$CO_2 + H2O \rightleftharpoons H_2CO_3$$

While still in the red blood cells, carbonic acid dissociates into hydrogen ions and bicarbonate ions (HCO_3^-):

$$H_2CO_3 \rightleftharpoons H+ + HCO_3^-$$

Some carbon dioxide also combines directly with hemoglobin (HbO_2), producing **carboxyhemoglobin** ($HbCO_2$) and oxygen:

$$CO_2 + HbCO_2 \rightleftharpoons + HbCO_2 + O_2$$

When blood reaches the alveolar capillary bed, the chemical processes just described tend to move in the *reverse direction* in accordance with Le Chatelier's principle. *Molecular carbon dioxide* is regenerated and passively diffuses across the capillary wall into the alveolar space.

Please solve this problem:

- Vigorous exercise would tend to:

  A. reduce blood pH.
  B. increase blood pH.
  C. decrease blood carbon dioxide concentration.
  D. increase blood oxygen concentration.

Problem solved:

A is correct. Increased metabolic activity of any tissue or organ produces increased quantities of carbon dioxide, which is carried away from the tissues by the blood. The gas combines with water to form carbonic acid, which then dissociates into protons and bicarbonate ions. An increase in proton concentration is the same as a decrease in pH.

REGULATORY CONTROL OF BLOOD GAS LEVELS

The respiratory center in the medulla oblongata monitors several factors pertaining to the blood. These include its oxygen and carbon dioxide concentrations and pH. When the blood's oxygen concentration is low, its carbon dioxide concentration tends to be high, or its pH is low, the respiratory center induces the phrenic nerve to increase the respiratory rate. Among the factors just listed, the respiratory center is *most* sensitive to carbon dioxide concentration.

To summarize:

- Respiratory rate *increases* in response to *decreased oxygen* concentration in the blood *increased carbon dioxide* concentration in the blood and *decreased blood pH*.

- Among these factors, respiratory rate is most sensitive to *carbon dioxide* concentration.

The homeostatic mechanisms just described also operate inversely. Respiratory rate decreases in response to increased blood oxygen concentration, decreased blood carbon dioxide concentration, and increased blood pH (decreased blood acidity).

Please solve this problem:

- Decreased blood pH will:

    A. increase respiratory rate, and it accompanies an increased delivery of oxygen to the alveoli.

    B. increase respiratory rate, and it accompanies an increased level of carbon dioxide in the blood.

    C. decrease respiratory rate, and it accompanies reduced synthesis of carbonic acid.

    D. decrease respiratory rate, and it accompanies increased synthesis of hemoglobin.

Problem solved:

B is correct. Decreased blood pH may arise from an increased level of carbon dioxide in the blood. High carbon dioxide concentration promotes the formation of carbonic acid, which dissociates into hydrogen ions and bicarbonate ions, reducing blood pH. The respiratory center of the medulla oblongata responds by increasing respiratory rate. The respiratory center is most sensitive, however, to blood carbon dioxide levels. An increased carbon dioxide concentration raises respiratory rate, and decreased carbon dioxide concentration reduces respiratory rate.

THE BICARBONATE BUFFER SYSTEM

Human blood normally exhibits slight *basicity*, its pH falling between 7.35 (in the veins) and 7.4 (in the arteries). *Any* significant alteration in blood pH constitutes an extreme hazard to survival, and several physiologic **buffer systems** act to maintain blood pH very precisely within its normal range. The equilibrium dynamic among CO_2, H_2CO_3, H^+, and HCO_3^- creates the all-important **bicarbonate buffer system** whose components, in the blood's aqueous solution, are:

(1) CO_2;

(2) H_2CO_3, a weak acid;

(3) H^+; and

(4) bicarbonate salts (such as NaH_2CO_3).

Within the blood, these four equilibria are to some degree in constant operation:

(1) $CO_2 + H_2O \leftrightarrow H_2CO_3$;

(2) $H_2CO_3 \leftrightarrow H^+ + HCO_3^-$;

(3) $Na^+ + HCO_3^- \leftrightarrow NaHCO_3$;

(4) $Na^+ + OH^- + H_2CO_3 \leftrightarrow NaHCO_3 + H_2O$.

Since H_2CO_3 is a weak acid, it dissociates only slightly, and equilibrium 2 produces a relatively low concentration of hydrogen ion. The addition to the blood of a strong acid, such as HCl, drives equilibrium 2 leftward and tends to "eat up" the excess hydrogen ions by producing more H_2CO_3:

$$HCl \rightarrow \mathbf{H^+} + Cl^-$$

$$\mathbf{H_2CO_3} \leftarrow \mathbf{H^+} + HCO_3$$

The increased H_2CO_3 concentration then drives equilibrium 1 leftward, raising the concentration of CO_2:

$$CO_2 + H_2O \leftrightarrow H_2CO_3$$

Increased CO_2 concentration then causes the medulla's respiratory center to raise the respiratory rate, and excess CO_2 is discharged through the lungs.

On the other hand, addition to the blood of a strong base, such as NaOH, increases OH^- concentration, and drives equilibrium 4 rightward. That decreases the concentration of H_2CO_3 [and concomitantly increases the concentration of bicarbonate salt—in this case sodium bicarbonate $(NaHCO_3)$]:

$$NaOH \rightarrow Na^+ + OH^-$$

$$Na^+ + OH^- + H_2CO_3 \leftrightarrow NaHCO_3 + H_2O$$

The decreased H_2CO_3 concentration drives equilibrium 2 rightward and thus decreases the concentration of CO_2:

$$CO_2 + H_2O \leftrightarrow H_2CO_3$$

The decreased CO_2 concentration causes the medulla's respiratory center to reduce the respiratory rate, and the lungs decrease their discharge of CO_2

BLOOD FLOW

The Heart and Circulation in Overview

The heart is responsible for pumping blood throughout the body. Its muscular tissue is called **myocardium**. In humans, the heart is four-chambered, with two chambers on the left and two on the right. The two upper chambers, left and right, are the **atria**, and the lower chambers, left and right, are the **ventricles**. Hence, the heart has a left atrium and a left ventricle, and a right atrium and a right ventricle. Each atrium/ventricle pair is connected by a valve through which blood flows.

Systemic Circulation

ARTERIAL CIRCULATION

All components of the **arterial circulation** carry blood *away* from the heart. Blood first exits the left ventricle and enters the large **artery** called the aorta.

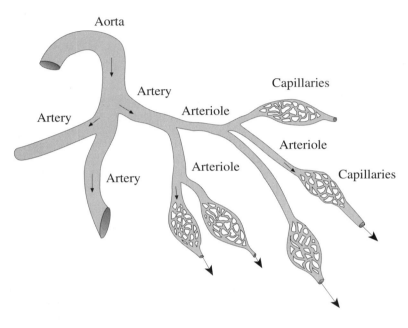

The Arteriole Tree

Figure 29.5

The aorta branches into arteries of progressively smaller size. These arteries continue to branch as they spread out to reach the body's tissues, becoming the very small **arterioles**. Arterioles continue branching to become millions of microscopic **capillaries**.

CAPILLARY BED EXCHANGE

Capillaries are found in every living part of the body and serve many functions. The most important is bringing *oxygen and nutrients* to all the cells of the body, simultaneously removing waste and the end products of respiration. The capillaries serve also as **thermoregulators**. Skin capillaries alter their diameter in response to changes in body temperature. In cold weather, when the body must conserve heat, capillaries constrict to reduce blood flow, thus reducing loss of heat into the environment. When the body becomes too warm, skin capillaries dilate, allowing blood to reach the body surface, and so facilitating the radiative loss of heat.

VENOUS CIRCULATION

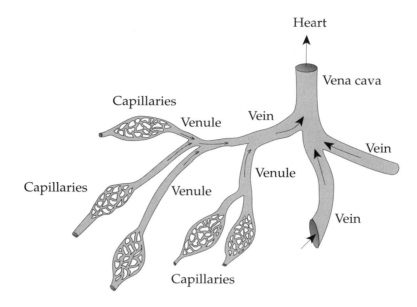

Venous Circulation

Figure 29.6

All components of the **venous circulation** carry blood toward the heart. From the **capillaries,** vessels *converge*, joining together into progressively larger vessels called **venules**, which converge to form **veins**. Veins continue to converge until they form two large veins called the **superior vena cava** and the **inferior vena cava**, each of which delivers blood directly to the heart's *right atrium*.

Please solve this problem:

- Outline the route of blood through the circulation, beginning with a capillary. Refer to the size of the operative vessels and the direction of flow.

Problem solved:

From any capillary, blood flows toward the heart in vessels of increasing size. It enters venules, then veins, and finally one of the two venae cavae, which empty blood into the heart's right atrium. Blood leaves the heart from the left ventricle via the aorta, which, by branching, forms arteries, arterioles, and capillaries.

The Heart Valves

Like many pumps, the heart has **valves,** which are essential to its function. The valves are situated *between the atrium and ventricle on each side* of the heart. Valves are also located at the *outlets of the right and left ventricles*, where the right ventricle delivers blood to the **pulmonary artery** and the left ventricle delivers blood into the aorta. The heart has four valves:

- **tricuspid valve**, located between the right atrium and right ventricle;

- **pulmonic valve**, located between the right ventricle and pulmonary artery;

- **mitral (bicuspid) valve**, located between the left atrium and left ventricle; and

- **aortic valve**, located between the left ventricle and aorta.

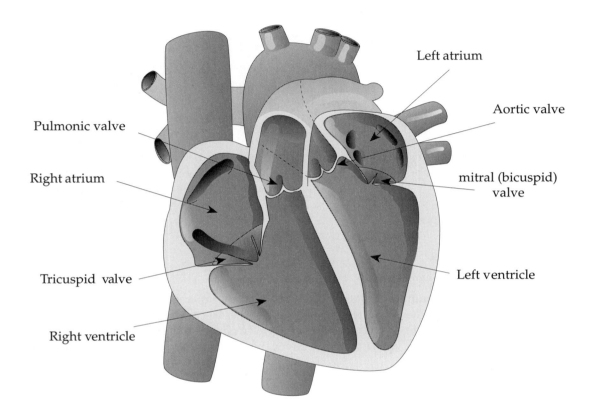

The Valves of the Heart

Figure 29.7

Heart valves operate via flexible **leaflets**, or **cusps**, which open when pressure is applied in the forward direction and close when pressure is applied in the backward direction. Healthy heart valves are *unidirectional.* When pressure in forward and backward directions is equal, the valve assumes its **native position**—closed.

The terms *tricuspid* and *bicuspid* are used both as names of particular valves and descriptively. The tricuspid, pulmonic, and aortic valves are *tricuspid*. The mitral, or bicuspid, valve is the only *bicuspid* valve in the human heart.

The heart valves serve two functions. First, by preventing backflow, they assure that *blood travels only in the forward direction*. Second, they facilitate the generation of the pressure necessary to propel blood through the circulation.

Please solve this problem:

- Which of the following correctly describes the order in which blood travels through the chambers of the heart?
    - A. Right ventricle, left ventricle, right atrium, left atrium
    - B. Right ventricle, right atrium, left ventricle, left atrium
    - C. Left atrium, right atrium, left ventricle, right ventricle
    - D. Left atrium, left ventricle, right atrium, right ventricle

Problem solved:

D is correct. You might answer by naming any of the cardiac chambers first, as long as you then list the remaining three chambers in appropriate order. Choice D selects the left atrium as starting point and then correctly orders the remaining three chambers; left ventricle, right atrium, right ventricle. Choices A, B, and C are incorrect, *not* because of the point they name as the beginning, but because of the order they describe. If, for example, the right ventricle is named as the beginning of the circulatory system, it must be followed with left atrium, left ventricle, and right atrium.

Pulmonary Circulation

Deoxygenated blood moves from the right ventricle through the right and left pulmonary arteries toward the right and left lungs to enter the pulmonary circulation (a network of capillaries that surrounds the pulmonary alveoli). Coursing through the pulmonary circulation, blood discharges carbon dioxide *to* the lungs and acquires oxygen *from* the lungs. Oxygenated blood then moves from the left and right sides of the pulmonary circulation, away from the lungs, via the two right and two left pulmonary veins to enter the left atrium.

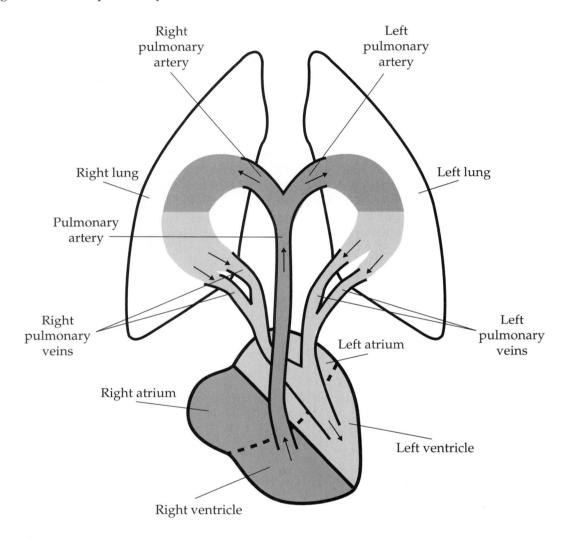

Flow of Deoxygenated Blood from Right Ventricle to
Pulmonary Circulation via Right and Left Pulmonary Arteries

and

Return of Oxygenated Blood from Pulmonary Circulation to
Left Atrium via Right and Left Pulmonary Veins

Figure 29.8

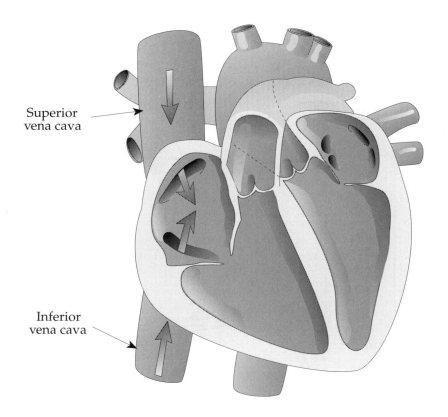

Superior and Inferior Vena Cavae

Figure 29.9

   Blood entering the right side of the heart via the superior and inferior venae cavae arrives at the right atrium. The right atrium delivers this blood to the right ventricle through the tricuspid valve, which closes when the ventricle contracts. Ventricular contraction propels blood through the pulmonary valve into the **pulmonary trunk**, which almost immediately divides into the left and right pulmonary arteries. These bring blood to the left and right lungs, respectively. Blood traveling toward the lungs is relatively deoxygenated and is relatively rich in carbon dioxide.

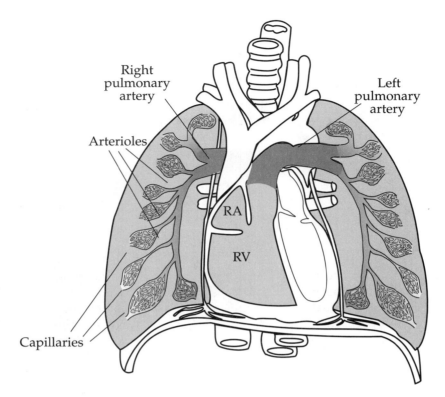

Pulmonary Circulation

Figure 29.10

At each lung, the pulmonary artery branches repeatedly, leading into capillary beds that flood the tissues and surround the alveoli with blood. The blood arriving in the capillary beds has low oxygen and high carbon dioxide concentrations relative to the alveolar air. At the alveoli, carbon dioxide is removed from capillary blood in exchange for oxygen. From the capillaries, the vessels come together and form venules, small veins, larger veins, and, ultimately, two left pulmonary veins and two right pulmonary veins. These veins return oxygenated blood to the left atrium. After passing through the mitral valve into the left ventricle, blood is moved into the systemic circulation.

Please solve this problem:

- Which of the following is true regarding human circulation?

    A. Pulmonary and systemic circulations comprise one continuous circulation.
    B. The systemic circulation delivers blood to the entire body with the exception of the lungs.
    C. Pulmonary circulation branches off the systemic circulation in the right side of the heart, where it then travels to the lungs.
    D. The pulmonary and systemic circulations are parallel but separate and nonintersecting.

Problem solved:

A is correct. Pulmonary and systemic circulations constitute two components of a continuous loop. Choice B confuses the fact that the pulmonary circulation travels to the lungs with the fact that systemic circulation eventually feeds capillary beds throughout the body. Although not explicitly stated, the student can infer that the lungs have two separate capillary beds. In the pulmonary circulation, capillaries bring deoxygenated blood to the alveoli for gas exchange, and in the systemic circulation, capillary beds bring oxygenated blood to the alveoli to provide the lung tissues with oxygen. Choices C and D contradict the notion of a continuous circulation.

The Heart as a Pump

Contraction is the means by which the heart serves as a pump. The myocardium, like any muscle, is **contractile**; it undergoes continuous cycles of precisely coordinated phases of contraction and relaxation.

In Stage 1A (Figure 29.11), all four cardiac chambers are relaxed. This creates relatively low pressure within each chamber, allowing the blood from the systemic circulation to rush into the right atrium, via the superior and inferior venae cava, and into the left atrium, from the four pulmonary veins returning from the lungs. Most of this blood flows directly into the ventricles through the open atrioventricular valves. In the next stage (1B), the two atria simultaneously contract, forcing blood into both ventricles. In Stage 2, the two atria are relaxed, and the two ventricles, now filled with blood, contract. **Ventricular contraction** opens the aortic and pulmonary valves. From the left, blood rushes into the systemic circulation. On the right, it enters the pulmonary circulation and moves toward the lungs for oxygenation.

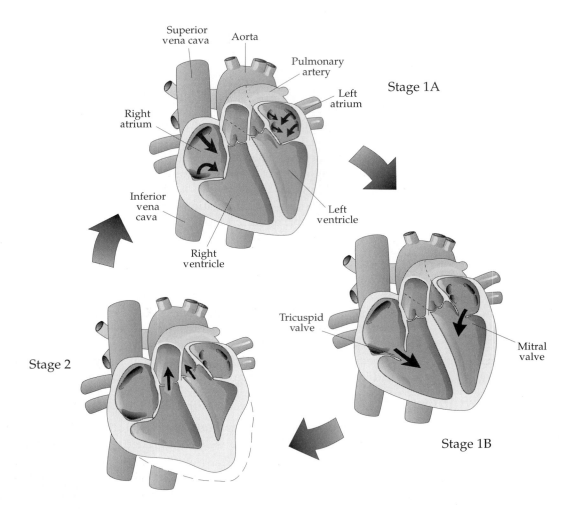

Blood Flow During Stages of Heart Contraction

Figure 29.11

Stages 1A and 1B together are called **diastole**, while stage 2 is called **systole**. In diastole, the atria are first relaxed and then contracted. The ventricles remain relaxed throughout diastole. In systole, the two ventricles contract.

THE PULSE

The force of propulsion of the blood as it enters the aorta from the left ventricle is transmitted throughout the body and can be felt in the periphery as the arterial **pulse**. The **radial pulse** is commonly measured by a clinician to obtain the heart rate, although numerous other pulses can be found in arteries throughout the body.

THE HEART AND ITS PACEMAKER

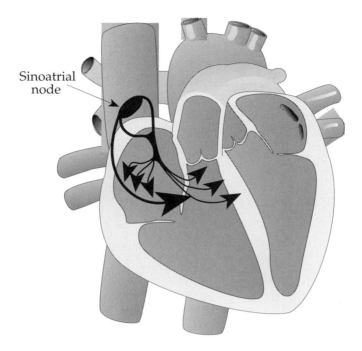

Sinoatrial node

The Pacemaker of the Heart

Figure 29.12

In the upper region of the right atrium, just below the opening of the superior vena cava, there lies a very small mass of muscular tissue termed the **sinoatrial node**, also called the **SA node** and **Sinus node**. The SA node is *intrinsically rhythmic*; it is self-excitable. If it were severed from its nerve supply, it would nonetheless, on its own, emit about 120 excitatory impulses every minute, causing the musculature of the right atrium to contract. Essentially, the sinus node tends to intrinsically produce rhythmic excitation of the right atrium at a rate of 120 impulses per minute.

The sinus node constitutes the heart's normal and **natural pacemaker**. Its regular, rhythmic emission of contractile signals initiates the process of electrical conduction throughout the heart and produces the heart's "beat"—the regular, rhythmic, organized contraction of all four cardiac chambers.

Because the sinus node receives a nerve supply (from both sympathetic and parasympathetic systems), it does not normally emit excitatory signals at its intrinsic rate of 120 impulses/minute. Rather, under normal circumstances, the **vagus nerve** (a component of the parasympathetic nervous system) slows the rate of the sinus node *so that it emits, in most persons under resting conditions, only fifty to seventy-five impulses per minute (thereby producing the normal heart rate of fifty to seventy-five beats per minute.*

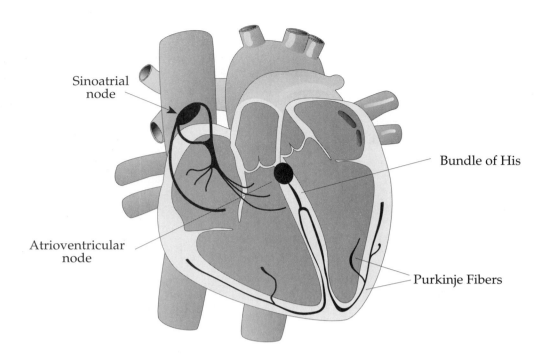

Electrical Conduction of the Heart

Figure 29.13

The pacemaker signal from the SA node is conducted electrically through the walls of the atria to the **atrioventricular node** (**AV node**), located near the intersection of the four heart chambers. From the AV node, the signal passes along the **septum** between the ventricles by way of another specialized set of myocardial fibers called the **bundle of His**. From the bundle of His, the signal moves through the **Purkinje fibers** and spreads throughout the ventricular walls.

Composition of the Blood

Blood cells are broadly divided into two types: **red cells** and **white cells**. Blood also contains **platelets**, which are cell fragments of a white cell type called **a megakaryocyte**. Blood is also composed of a host of proteins, such as **albumin** and **immunoglobulins,** and ions.

Red cells, or **erythrocytes**, carry oxygen and carbon dioxide. White blood cells, or **leukocytes**, mediate the immune system. Included among leukocytes are the **lymphocytes**. Platelets are essential in helping the blood to clot when a vessel has been injured. All blood cells arise from precursor cells within the **bone marrow**.

Several terms are commonly used in discussion of blood composition. **Hematocrit** represents the percentage of whole blood volume occupied by red cells, and it is typically measured by **centrifugation** of a blood sample. **Plasma** refers to the blood stripped of its cells. **Serum** refers to plasma stripped of the proteins that precipitate when clotting occurs; it is **defibrinated** plasma.

Capillary Exchange

Blood flowing through a capillary is exposed to two types of pressure: **hydrostatic** and **oncotic**. Oncotic pressure is a specific form of osmotic pressure across capillary walls due to the presence of proteins in the blood. From within the capillary lumen, hydrostatic pressure tends to push fluid out of the capillary, while oncotic pressure exerts an opposite force, keeping fluids within the capillary. The interaction of the two forces across the capillary membrane produces a number of phenomena associated with blood flow through the capillary bed.

At the proximal, or arterial, end of a capillary in the systemic circulation, hydrostatic pressure exceeds oncotic pressure within the lumen, and fluids are therefore propelled across the vessel's wall into the surrounding interstitial fluid. At the distal, or venous, portion of the capillary, oncotic pressure prevails, and ninety-nine percent of the fluid previously forced outward is drawn back into the capillary. The remaining one percent of the fluid pushed outward at the arterial end remains in the interstitium (surrounding tissue) and is ultimately returned to the systemic circulation via the lymphatic system.

Please solve this problem:

- Edema, an abnormal increase in fluid content in the interstitial spaces surrounding capillary beds, is manifested clinically as swelling. Describe the mechanisms that might produce edema.

Problem solved:

Edema is caused by disruption of the hydrostatic/oncotic pressure dynamics and/or compromise of the vessel membrane integrity. Either condition can arise in both capillaries and lymph vessels. When lymph vessels are affected, normal drainage of tissue fluid is disturbed. An increase in hydrostatic pressure forces fluid out of capillaries; the capillaries then fail to reabsorb the fluid in adequate amounts. Increased hydrostatic pressure within lymph vessels, as might be caused by a distal blockage, exerts a similar effect, and prevents normal lymphatic drainage. Backward-directed increases in venous pressure (seen in right-sided heart failure), venous blockage (in thrombophlebitis, for example), or valvular insufficiency (as in varicose veins) all increase capillary hydrostatic pressure. Excessive renal retention of salt and water can also increase fluid volume and capillary hydrostatic pressure, producing edema.

Diminished capillary oncotic pressure reduces the blood's tendency to draw fluid back from the interstitium into the capillary. Insufficient plasma concentrations of albumin (called hypoalbuminemia) reduces the blood's ability to draw water inward across the capillary membrane, and edema results. Hypoalbuminemia might be caused, for example, by liver failure or malnutrition. Finally, disruption of capillary wall integrity, precipitating loss of plasma proteins, reduces the ability of the vessels to hold and resorb fluid, causing edema. Such breakdown is seen, for example, in allergies and burns.

THE LYMPHATIC SYSTEM

The **lymphatic vessels,** often called the **lymphatics**, constitute another body-wide vessel system, called the **lymphatic system**. Lymphatic vessels carry fluid called **lymph**. The lymphatics create an alternative/accessory route by which fluid remaining in the interstitium makes its way back to the venous system and then to the heart's right atrium.

Lymphatics begin body-wide as microscopic vessels that coalesce sequentially (like capillaries) to form vessels of progressively increasing size. Ultimately, they coalesce and converge to form two large **lymphatic ducts** (the **thoracic duct** and the **right lymphatic duct)** that return lymph to the venous circulation by emptying into large veins at the neck and upper chest. (From the lower body parts and from the left side of the upper body parts, lymph empties ultimately into the thoracic duct, which, in turn, empties into the venous system at the junction of the left internal jugular and subclavian veins. From the right side of the upper body parts, lymph empties into the right lymphatic duct, which, in turn, empties into the venous system at the junction of the right internal jugular and subclavian veins.)

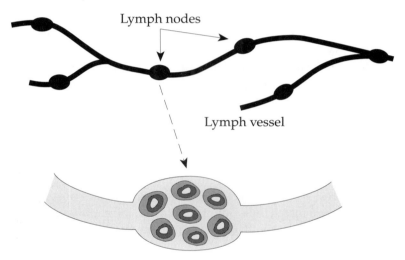

Figure 29.14

Lymph Nodes

Numerous **lymph nodes** are found along each lymph vessel. These nodes contain a concentration of *lymphocytes*, which fight infection. Lymphocytes also circulate freely in the blood stream. Infection in one part of the body causes swelling of regional lymph nodes as lymphocytes in the nodes multiply to combat the infection.

Other Lymphatic Organs

The **spleen** and **thymus** are also components of the lymphatic system. The spleen, located under the stomach, functions much like a large lymph node, except that the spleen acts as a lymphatic filter for blood while lymph nodes filter the lymph fluid. In addition, the spleen destroys senescent (aged) erythrocytes.

Found in the middle of the upper chest, the thymus is a small lymphoid organ that is especially active between birth and puberty. **T-lymphocytes** mature in the thymus, which degenerates during adolescence and adulthood, becoming largely nonfunctional.

Lymphocytes

Lymphocytes are a class of white blood cell (leukocyte). They are broadly divided into two classes: **T lymphocytes (T cells)** and **B lymphocytes (B cells)**. T cells are the basis of **cell-mediated immunity**. They have their origins in the bone marrow but mature in the thymus. Several subtypes of T cells have been identified, including **helper**, **suppressor**, and **killer T cells**. B cells also originate in the bone marrow. They participate in humoral immunity by producing antibodies, which belong to a class of proteins called immunoglobulins. The humoral immune system is mobilized when an antigen, a foreign particle or a portion of an invading organism, triggers the production of antibodies by specialized B cells known as plasma cells. The antibodies bind to antigens and mark them for destruction by other immune cells.

Please solve this problem:

- Which of the following is a true statement?
    A. Killer T cells kill B cells as a mechanism of regulating immune function.
    B. Leukocytes include lymphocytes and other cell types.
    C. T cells and B cells reside in the marrow, where immunoglobulins proliferate.
    D. T cells provide humoral immunity, and B cells provide cell-mediated immunity.

Problem solved:

B is correct. Lymphocytes are a subclass of leukocyte. Choice A is incorrect because the normal function of killer T cells is directed against foreign substances, not against other immune cells. Both T cells and B cells have their origins in the bone marrow, but once they mature they do not normally reside there, as choice C incorrectly suggests. (T cells mature in the thymus.) The reverse of choice D is true—correctly stated, B cells provide humoral immunity and T cells are the source of cell-mediated immunity.

THE DIGESTIVE SYSTEM

Macronutrients (which are found in both liquid and solid foods) can be grouped into three types: **carbohydrate**, **protein**, and **fat**. In order to be of use to the body, these foods must be broken down into smaller particles that can be absorbed from the lumen of the digestive tract into the blood stream. Digestion is of two types: **mechanical** and **chemical**. Mechanical digestion begins with the shredding and grinding of food into small pieces by chewing (mastication). It continues with vigorous churning in the stomach. Chemical digestion occurs by means of enzymes produced by several different organs associated with the alimentary canal. Enzymes break down food into absorbable molecules.

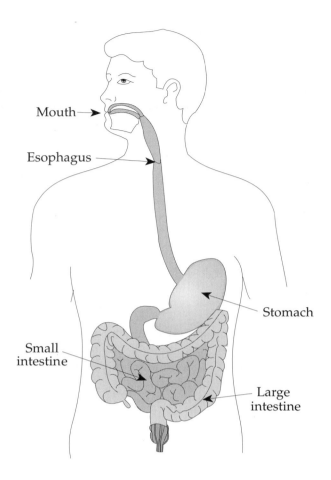

Mouth

Esophagus

Stomach

Small
intestine

Large
intestine

The Gastrointestinal Tract

Figure 29.15

Figure 29.15 identifies the basic organs of the human digestive tract. Food enters through the mouth, goes down the **esophagus** into the **stomach**, and then passes through the **small intestine** and the **large intestine**.

Enzymes and Organs

THE MOUTH: INGESTION

As food is chewed, it mixes with saliva, which contains the digestive enzyme **salivary amylase**. Salivary amylase initiates (but does not complete) the digestion of starch (a carbohydrate), hydrolyzing glycosidic bonds to produce component sugars.

THE ESOPHAGUS: PERISTALSIS

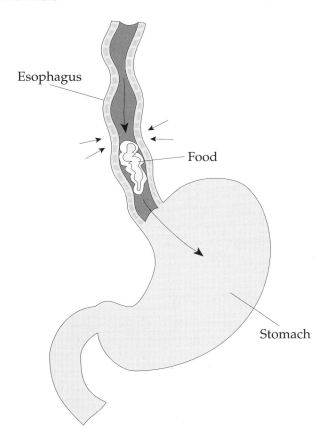

Peristalsis

Figure 29.16

The esophagus has no enzymatic function but serves as a conduit for food from the mouth to the stomach. It is a muscular structure with separate sets of muscle fibers arranged circumferentially and longitudinally. Transit through the esophagus results from a highly coordinated series of contractions, involving both circular and longitudinal muscles, known as **peristalsis**. This process squeezes a bolus of chewed food downward to the stomach. Peristalsis continues throughout the gastrointestinal tract.

THE STOMACH: ACIDIFICATION

Among the stomach's most striking features is its relatively *low pH*. Specialized cells, called parietal cells, in the lining of the stomach secrete **hydrochloric acid (HCl)** into the stomach's lumen. The **vagus nerve** stimulates the production and secretion of HCl. The acidity of the stomach is essential to the functioning of the gastric enzyme **pepsin**. Secreted by **chief cells** in the stomach wall, pepsin initiates the chemical breakdown of proteins. Once food has been churned and digested by pepsin, it passes through the **pyloric sphincter** into the first section of the small intestine, the **duodenum**.

Please solve this problem:

- What are the primary digestive functions of the mouth, esophagus, and stomach? What enzymes, if any, are associated with each?

Problem solved:

The mouth performs mastication—the mechanical breakdown of food with the teeth. Further, it secretes amylase-containing saliva, which begins the digestion of starch. The esophagus transports food from the mouth to the stomach through the synchronized muscular contractions called *peristalsis*. The stomach initiates protein digestion (and performs some mechanical digestion as well). The parietal cells within the walls of the stomach secrete hydrochloric acid, rendering the lumen highly acidic (the pH is normally between 1.5 and 2.5). The chief cells of the stomach secrete pepsinogen, which is converted to its active form—pepsin—by hydrochloric acid. Pepsin breaks down proteins.

THE SMALL INTESTINE: PANCREATIC ENZYMES

In the small intestine, the liquid food mixture, or **chyme**, is processed by enzymes that act on protein, carbohydrate, and fat. Unlike pepsin, which is produced by the organ into which it is released, the enzymes of the small intestine are synthesized in a separate organ—the **pancreas**. **Pancreatic enzymes** are delivered directly to the duodenum via the **pancreatic duct**.

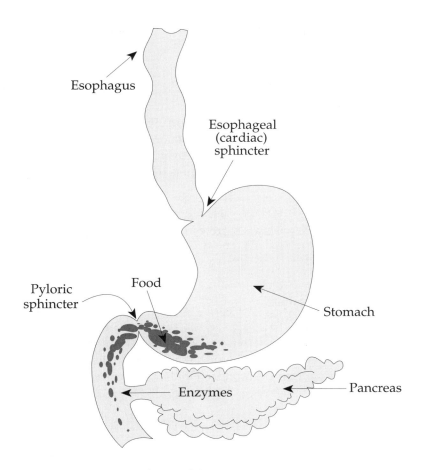

Release of the Pancreatic Enzymes

Figure 29.17

Some pancreatic enzymes are secreted into the small intestine in an inactive form. These inactive precursors are called **zymogens**. To be *activated*, zymogens normally must be cleaved by an enzyme. For example, among the zymogens released into the intestine is **trypsinogen**. The pancreatic enzyme trypsinogen is activated by an enzyme in the duodenum called **enterokinase** (also called **enteropeptidase**). The activation process produces **trypsin**, an active protein-degrading enzyme. Trypsin cleaves a number of other zymogens into their active forms.

Students should be familiar with the names and targets of a number of digestive enzymes. **Pancreatic amylase**, chemically identical to salivary amylase, continues the digestion of carbohydrates, which was initiated in the mouth. **Pancreatic lipase** serves in the enzymatic breakdown of fats (lipids). Trypsin and **chymotrypsin** are the two most important proteolytic, or protein-digesting, enzymes in the gastrointestinal tract. These two enzymes break peptide bonds, reducing large proteins into small chains composed of only a few amino acids.

Food particles are broken down by digestive enzymes into smaller subunits, which enter the blood stream by being absorbed across the wall of the small intestine into regional capillaries. From the small intestine, blood travels directly to the liver, where further processing occurs.

Please solve this problem:

- Characterize a zymogen.

Problem solved:

A zymogen is a digestive enzyme's inactive precursor. It prevents the exposure of non-target material, that is, the pancreas itself, to the digestive function of an active enzyme (or, in some cases, modification by acid). Cleavage by another enzyme activates a zymogen. The pancreatic enzyme trypsinogen, for example, is a zymogen; its active form is trypsin.

Please solve this problem:

- Pancreatic enzymes are secreted into the:

    A. pancreas.
    B. liver.
    C. stomach.
    D. small intestine.

Problem solved:

D is correct. The question asks you to distinguish the origin of the pancreatic enzymes from their site of action. Pancreatic enzymes are produced in the pancreas and secreted through the pancreatic duct into the duodenum of the small intestine.

THE LIVER AND BILE

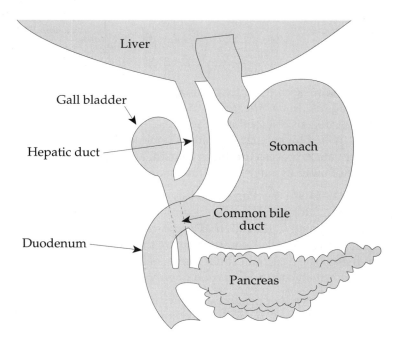

Release of Bile from the Gall Bladder

Figure 29.18

Also active in the duodenum is **bile**, which is produced in the **liver** and stored in the **gall bladder**. Bile is a complex mixture of water, electrolytes, cholesterol, bilirubin, steroid hormones, and several other substances. Unlike pancreatic secretions, bile contains no enzymes, but instead acts as an **emulsifier,** helping to separate large globules of *fat molecules* into smaller globules in order to increase the surface area available for the action of **lipase**. Bile enters the midsection of the duodenum via the **common bile duct**.

Bile production is only one of the important functions of the liver. The liver also plays a significant role in carbohydrate metabolism (for example, converting glucose to a storage form, **glycogen**), converts amino acids to **keto acids** and **urea**, and processes toxins. Another of its functions is the degradation of senescent (aged) erythrocytes.

Please solve this problem:

- Which one of the following statements is true?

    A. The gall bladder produces bile, which emulsifies fats.
    B. The gall bladder produces bile, which enzymatically degrades fats.
    C. Bile has no enzymatic activity in the digestive system.
    D. Bile enters the gall bladder for storage via the common bile duct.

Problem solved:

C is correct. Bile emulsifies fats—it reduces large globules of fats into smaller globules in order to prepare them for digestion by lipase. Choices A and B mistake the gall bladder for the liver, which is the site of bile production. Choice B also wrongly describes the role of bile as that of enzymatic degradation. Bile emulsifies fat. Choice D is incorrect because the *common bile duct* conducts bile into the duodenum from the gall bladder; it is the *cystic duct* that carries bile to the gall bladder for storage.

THE LARGE INTESTINE: RESORPTION

The soft, watery mixture of indigestible and nonabsorbable food remnants reaching the end of the small intestine finally arrives at the **large intestine**, or **colon**, by passing through the **ileocecal valve**. The most important function of the large intestine is the *resorption of large amounts of water* from its lumen.

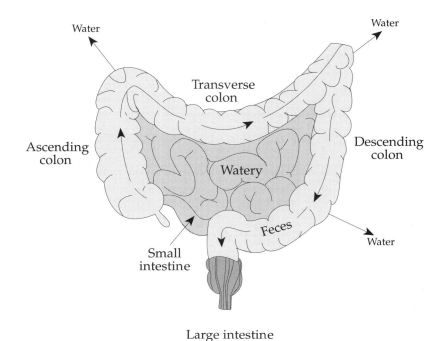

Large intestine

Figure 29.19

Several liters of water per day are delivered to the upper digestive tract. The water comes from what the individual has imbibed and from the fluid that carried enzymes from the pancreas (and other secretory organs) into the gastrointestinal tract. Failure to resorb adequate quantities of this water would lead to **dehydration** through water loss, as occurs when one has diarrhea. Normal feces consists of undigested food particles, other body waste products, and only a small amount of water.

THE MUSCULOSKELETAL SYSTEM

The musculoskeletal system, as its name implies, is comprised of the skeleton and the muscles of the body. While the skeleton includes the cartilage and teeth, its main constituent is bone.

Bone

Bone serves several important functions. As the major component of the skeleton, bone provides an *anchor for muscular contraction*. Bones also provide structural support and protection for organs and nerves. Red blood cells and platelets are formed in bone **marrow**. In addition, bone serves as a storage depot for calcium, phosphate, and other ions of biological significance. Bone takes up and releases such substances in response to changing needs and conditions. It serves to maintain a variety of ion concentrations within acceptable limits.

Basic Composition of Bone

Bone is a *dynamic connective tissue* composed principally of **matrix** and cells.

Bone matrix is composed of *organic* and *inorganic* substances in approximately a 1:1 ratio. The principal *inorganic constituents of bone are calcium and phosphorous,* which together form a crystalline compound called **hydroxyapatite**. Significant amounts of noncrystalline calcium phosphate are also present. Other minerals in the matrix include bicarbonate, citrate, magnesium, potassium, and sodium.

The organic component of matrix is mostly **Type I collagen** and amorphous **ground substance**. The ground substance consists largely of **glycosaminoglycans** and **proteins**. Hydroxyapatite and collagen create the characteristic hardness and resistance of bone.

Bone is a living tissue with three different cell types: **osteoblasts**, **osteocytes**, and **osteoclasts**. Osteoblasts are located on the inner surfaces of bone tissue, while osteocytes occupy minute spaces (**lacunae**) within the bony matrix. Osteoblasts synthesize Type I collagen and other organic components of the matrix. Osteocytes, which are simply osteoblasts with greatly reduced synthetic capacity, are responsible for maintaining the matrix. While the osteocyte and the osteoblast build and nourish bone, the osteoclast (also known as a **multinucleated giant cell**) promotes ongoing *breakdown, resorption, and remodeling* of bone.

Please solve this problem:

- Chemical removal of either the mineral or the organic substance of bone leaves the bone in its original shape but alters its mechanical properties. What changes would be produced by the removal of the mineral component? The organic component?

Problem solved:

The mineral composition of bone is largely a crystalline substance called hydroxyapatite. Dissolution of the mineral component would make the bone softer and more flexible. Collagen, composed of protein chains, can be correctly presumed to impart some flexibility to bone. The removal of the organic component of the bone matrix results in an inflexible, hard, brittle substance, subject to destruction under force.

Gross Morphology of Bone: Compact and Spongy

Gross examination of cut bone reveals two distinct bone morphologies. The outer, dense portion is called **compact bone**. The inner spongy-looking area is called **spongy bone** due to its many small, *marrow-filled cavities.*

Bone marrow is of two types: **red** and **yellow**. In addition to the bone cell types described above, other cell species inhabit the marrow. Red marrow is the site of red blood cell and platelet production and some immune cell development and maturation. Yellow marrow is filled with **adipocytes** (fat cells).

In a newborn, all marrow is red. In a mature adult, red marrow is confined primarily to flat bones, such as ribs, clavicles, pelvic bones, and skull bones. Under stress of blood loss or poor oxygen supply, however, yellow marrow may be transformed into red marrow to increase red blood cell production.

Despite differences in their gross appearances, compact bone and spongy bone are similarly constituted. Each consists of matrix and cells.

HISTOLOGY OF BONE: HAVERSIAN SYSTEMS

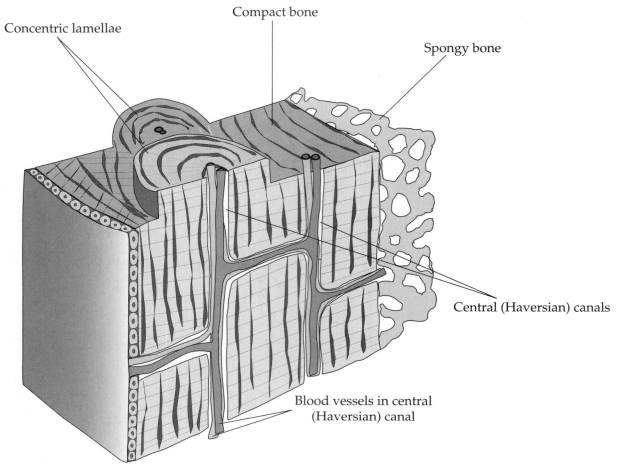

Haversian System; Osteon

Figure 29.20

On microscopic examination, a cross section of compact bone shows several sets of concentric **lamellae** (rings). Each set of concentric lamellae, running parallel to the bone's long axis, is a **Haversian system**, or **osteon**. Haversian systems exist to distribute nutrients throughout compact bone. Many Haversian systems together give compact bone its strength.

At the center of each Haversian system is a canal known as a **Haversian canal**. A Haversian canal runs the length of a Haversian system. This canal carries blood vessels and nerves, and is filled with loose connective tissue. Shallow indentations mark the surfaces of the lamellae.

In spongy bone, thin segments of bone, known as **spicules**, surround the many small marrow spaces. Because of their thinness, the spicules within spongy bone are able to absorb nutrients directly from the marrow contained within their cavities, and so do not require Haversian systems for nutrient delivery.

Please solve this problem:

- In what ways are compact bone and spongy bone similar? Dissimilar?

Problem solved:

Compact bone and spongy bone are similar in a number of ways: They have the same chemical and structural composition, both are composed of matrix and bone cells, and both are hard and resistant to bending or compression. The essential difference between compact bone and spongy bone is the manner in which the components are arranged. Compact bone is so densely arranged that the canals of the Haversian systems are required to convey nutrients to its cells. In contrast, the hard substance of spongy bone is laid out in a thin, bubble-like form that precludes the need for special nutrient delivery channels.

Associated Structures: Joints, Ligaments, and Tendons

Joints allow for motion and flexibility and may be grouped into three classes: **fibrous**, **cartilaginous**, and **synovial**. Fibrous joints are composed of collagen fibers and are designed to allow minimal movement. Synovial joints allow for the great range and extent of movement seen in the body.

The synovial joint consists of the approximated ends of two bones, covered with a common **synovial capsule** made of fibrous tissue. This capsule encloses a sac of **synovial fluid** between the bones. The ends of the bones, nearly in contact, are covered with smooth, tough **articular cartilage**. The synovial fluid contained in the joint space acts as a lubricant, which, with the underlying articular cartilage, allows smooth movement of the joint, protecting the bones from damage that might otherwise result from friction. Examples of synovial joints are those of the knees, hips, shoulders, and fingers.

Ligaments keep bones attached across joints. **Tendons** attach muscles to bones.

Muscle

On the basis of microscopic structure, muscle may be divided into three types: **skeletal**, **cardiac**, and **smooth**.

SKELETAL MUSCLE

A skeletal muscle that traverses a joint will be among those responsible for bending that joint. Consider the illustration below, which shows a muscle group, the **biceps brachii**, traversing the elbow joint.

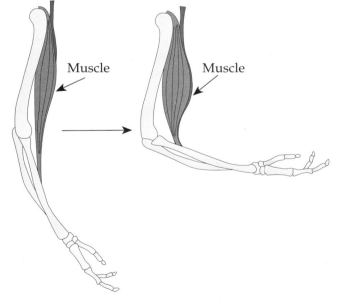

Biceps Brachii Flexes Elbow Joint

Figure 29.21

The biceps brachii attaches to the upper end of the forearm and the shoulder, crossing the elbow joint. Contraction of this muscle causes the elbow joint to bend. If the biceps muscle existed alone, as shown in the schematic diagram, the individual would be able to flex (bend) the elbow joint but would have no ability to straighten it (without application of some external force).

The two illustrations below demonstrate the manner in which the elbow joint is straightened.

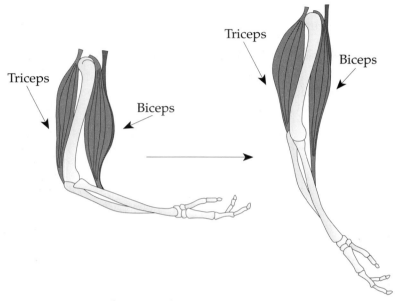

Flexion and Extension at the Elbow Joint

Figure 29.22

Active straightening of the elbow joint is possible, however, because of the action of the triceps, shown in Figure 29.22. When muscles such as the biceps and triceps pull in opposite directions across a joint, they are said to be **antagonistic** to one another.

MUSCLE FIBER

A skeletal muscle cell is a long, multinucleated cell in which many striations are visible. Because of their length, skeletal muscle cells are commonly referred to as muscle "fibers" or **myofibers**. A group or bundle of skeletal muscle fibers (cells) is referred to as a **fascicle**.

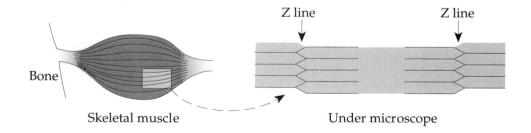

Skeletal Muscle

Figure 29.23

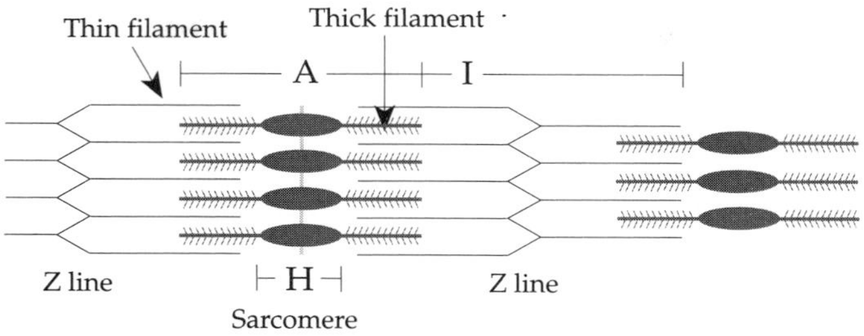

Functional Unit of the Muscle Fiber

Figure 29.24

A single **sarcomere** is a segment of muscle fiber between two Z lines, as shown in Figure 29.24. A sarcomere is composed of a series of **thick and thin filaments** arranged parallel to each other. Each **thin filament** is anchored at one end to a Z line. The **thick filaments** have no connection to the Z lines. Thin and thick filaments interdigitate in the very regular manner depicted in the figure.

Filaments are composed of proteins. Thin filaments are composed of the protein **actin,** and thick filaments, of the protein **myosin.** Contraction of muscle is achieved by the *sliding of actin and myosin filaments*, each over the other, bringing the Z lines closer together.

Various sectors of the sarcomere have been named. The length of a myosin (thick) filament corresponds to the **A band**. Because the filament itself does not contract, the A band has a fixed length equal to that of the myosin strands. A given length of thin filament that does not overlap with any thick filament is called the **I band**. In the middle of the sarcomere, containing only myosin filaments with no overlapping actin filaments, is the **H zone**.

SKELETAL MUSCLE CONTRACTION: INTERACTION OF ACTIN AND MYOSIN AS "SLIDING FILAMENTS"

In order for a muscle to contract, its thin and thick filaments must physically interact. For that reason, regularly spaced **crossbridges** extend from the myosin filaments to the actin filaments. Through the physical interaction of actin and myosin, made possible by the crossbridges, contraction is thought to occur according to a **sliding filament** mechanism, in which:

(1) the myosin head binds to the actin filament at a **myosin binding site,** and

(2) the myosin heads interact with the actin filaments in such a way as to draw them inward so that Z lines come closer together and the sarcomere shortens.

The shortening of a sarcomere means that the myofiber to which it belongs shortens as well. The shortening of *many* sarcomeres within a myofiber means that the myofiber undergoes significant reduction in length—and *that* amounts to contraction.

Understanding how and why actin and myosin should, at a given moment, "decide" to interact in this way and contract a muscle fiber requires that you understand some additional underlying facts and phenomena.

PRELUDE TO CONTRACTION: RESTING POTENTIAL, DEPOLARIZATION, AND ACTION POTENTIAL

All human cell membranes operate an energy-dependent sodium-potassium pump (Na^+-K^+ ATPase) that continuously pumps potassium ions into the cell and sodium ions outward. The pump does not move these two cations in one-to-one numerical correspondence. Rather, for every two potassium ions moved inward, three sodium ions move outward. The result is an electrochemical gradient across the cell membrane in which:

(1) Na^+ concentration is higher outside the cell than inside,

(2) K^+ concentration is higher inside the cell than outside, and

(3) *the cell's interior cell is electrically negative relative to its exterior.*

The fact that the cell's interior is electrically negative relative to its exterior creates the phrase **membrane resting potential,** which refers to the existence of a charge gradient across the cell membrane and, more specifically, to the fact that the gradient is one in which the *inside is negative relative to the outside.*

Some circumstances (that we will not now detail) *sometimes* cause *some* cells to suddenly experience at some small area of membrane a dramatic increase in permeability to sodium. When that happens, sodium ions rush inward in an "effort" to eliminate the sodium *concentration* gradient normally maintained by the sodium potassium pump. In some such cases, the inward rush of sodium ions is *so* great as to produce, at the small affected, area *reversal* of charge potential across the membrane so that the inside becomes *positive* relative to the outside. When that happens, we say that a portion of the cell membrane has been **depolarized,** meaning that its charge gradient has reversed itself so that—in that limited area—the interior is positive relative to the exterior.

DEPOLARIZATION IN NERVE AND MUSCLE CELLS: ACTION POTENTIAL AND REPOLARIZATION

If, in a muscle cell (or a nerve cell), depolarization at some small area of membrane occurs to some critical **threshold** degree, there occurs the first phrase of an **action potential,** meaning that a "wave" of depolarization spreads rapidly and extensively along the entirety of the cell membrane so that the whole of the cell is depolarized. The occurrence of an action potential means that an *entire cell* reverses its normal charge gradient and that its *inside* becomes positive relative to its outside.

After the wholesale depolarization just described, the cell suddenly loses its increased permeability to sodium and temporarily experiences an increased permeability to *potassium.* Potassium ions then rush outward in an "effort" to eliminate their concentration gradient across the membrane. The original resting potential is restored; the cell's interior becomes negative relative to its exterior. At that point, the cell is said to be **repolarized.** The phrase *action potential* is often used to designate the combination of the two sequential events: (1) rapid depolarization followed by (2) repolarization.

After repolarization occurs (and the original resting potential is restored), ion permeabilities return to their usual levels and the sodium-potassium pump resumes its activity, pumping sodium ions outward and potassium ions inward (in a ratio of 3:2).

The phenomena of depolarization and action potential are fundamental to the operation of muscle (and nerve) cells. When a muscle cell undergoes an action potential, there follows a series of events that cause actin and myosin to interact as the "sliding filaments" earlier described. Understanding those events means first recalling some additional facts about muscle cells.

Troponin and Tropomyosin

Within the myofiber's sarcomeres, actin molecules are intimately associated with two "regulatory" proteins called (1) **tropomyosin** and (2) **the troponin complex**. In a resting muscle, tropomyosin molecules "mask," or "cover," those sites on the actin molecule with which myosin heads are prone to interact. Tropomyosin and the troponin complex are intimately associated not only with the actin molecule but also with each other. Troponin has a tendency to bind calcium ions, *if they are present*, and when it does, it undergoes a change in its shape and position in such a way that causes the *tropomyosin* molecule to "uncover" the actin sites with which myosin is prone to interact. *Therefore, if the myofiber's troponin complex is exposed to calcium ions, the actin and myosin interact at their crossbridges, the sarcomere shortens, and the fiber contracts.*

The Sarcolemma, the Sarcoplasmic Reticulum, and Calcium Ion Release

Within a myofiber (muscle cell), the:

(1) cell membrane is called the **sarcolemma**;

(2) cytoplasm is called the **sarcoplasm;**

(3) endoplasmic reticulum is called the **sarcoplasmic reticulum,** which *stores calcium ions in a muscle* (Ca^{2+}); and

(4) sarcolemma and sarcoplasmic reticulum are roughly continuous with each other.

Muscle contraction proceeds from the following series of events:

(A) A motor neuron that innvervates the myofiber undergoes depolarization and an action potential, causing the motor neuron to release the neurotransmitter **acetylcholine**. (See **Chapter 30**.)

(B) The acetylcholine binds to receptors on the sarcolemma, which, as noted, is continuous with the sarcoplasmic reticulum.

(C) Acetylcholine causes depolarization of both sarcolemma and sarcoplasmic reticulum.

(D) The depolarization, if sufficient in magnitude, triggers an action potential, and the entire sarcolemma depolarizes.

(E) The action potential *causes calcium ions to move from the sarcoplasmic reticulum to the sarcoplasmic space, surrounding the fiber's actin and myosin filaments.*

(F) The calcium ions bind to troponin.

(G) The binding of calcium ions to troponin causes tropomyosin to undergo change in shape and position.

(H) The sites at which actin interacts with myosin are "uncovered." Myosin heads are thus able to contact actin filaments.

(I) Actin and myosin interact as "sliding filaments."

In order for the whole of a muscle fiber to undergo these processes synchronously, its action potential is carried deep into the fiber by a series of invaginations in the sarcolemma called **T tubules**. When contraction is over, calcium ions are pumped back from the sarcoplasm to the sarcoplasmic reticulum.

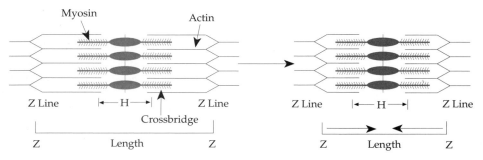

Shortening of Sarcomere During Contraction

Figure 29.25

Please solve this problem:

- In simple terms, list the order of events in muscle contraction, beginning with a nerve impulse to the muscle.

Problem solved:

A nerve impulse arrives at the neuromuscular junction, causing the release of acetylcholine, the neurotransmitter involved in muscle contraction. Depolarization of muscle cell membranes is carried throughout the fiber by the T tubules. The depolarization causes a release of calcium ions, which bind to troponin on the actin filaments. This causes a conformational change that uncovers myosin binding sites on the actin filaments. Myosin crossbridges are then able to attach to the actin and flex, pulling the actin fiber along the myosin fiber. This causes the simultaneous shortening of sarcomeres all along the muscle cell.

ENERGY REQUIREMENTS FOR MUSCULAR FUNCTION

Muscular function requires energy to maintain:

(1) the resting potential that allows for depolarization and action, potential

(2) the dynamic interaction of myosin and actin that underlies the physical shortening of the sarcomere, and

(3) the return of calcium ions from the sarcoplasm to the sarcoplasmic reticulum after contraction is complete.

The myofiber, like most human cells under most conditions, derives its energy most directly by dephosphorylation of ATP into ADP and inorganic phosphate. The muscle cell stores only very small amounts of ATP. In order to sustain its activity, therefore, it must somehow regenerate ATP from ADP and inorganic phosphate, and for that, it needs other energy sources.

Myofibers store (relatively small) amounts of **phosphocreatinine,** which, like ATP and GTP, embodies a high-energy phosphate bond. Dephosphorylation of phosphocreatinine, therefore, releases energy, which the myofiber uses to regenerate ATP from ADP and inorganic phosphate. Yet, the total amount of ATP and phosphocreatinine normally stored within a muscle cell is sufficient to maintain meaningful contraction for only five or ten seconds. For contractile activity that lasts longer, the cell must resort to yet another source of ATP generation.

Muscle cells store glycogen, which it readily breaks down to its component glucose units. Glucose then undergoes glycolysis to produce ATP and pyruvate, which, in the presence of an adequate oxygen supply, gives rise, in turn, to the Krebs cycle, electron transport, and oxidative phosphorylation (see **Chapter 28**). Where oxygen supply is inadequate to sustain the aerobic processes just mentioned, muscle cells resort to anaerobic processes alone (glycolysis and fermentation) and, on that basis, might sustain contraction for as long as a minute; the end-products of anaerobic respiration accumulate to such a degree as to bring the process to a halt.

Cardiac Muscle and Smooth Muscle

Cardiac muscle operates involuntarily (with the sinoatrial node acting as the initiator of its rhythmic contractions. Its microscopic structure is similar (but *not* identical) to that of skeletal muscle. It shows the striations attributable to actin and myosin molecules, and individual fibers (cells) contract largely according to the same chemistry and mechanisms on which skeletal muscle operates.

Examined by microscope, myocardium differs from skeletal muscle most notably in the appearance of dark lines called **intercalated discs,** which represent attachment points between adjacent muscle cells. The attachments are specialized in character and are called **gap junctions**. Gap junctions between cardiac muscle fibers allow a nearly unimpeded flow of ions from one fiber to the next, so that the action potential created in one cardiac cell is easily and readily propagated to the next. For that reason, the whole of the cardiac muscle mass, the **myocardium,** is termed a **syncytium** in which rapid intercellular transmission of action potentials promotes a particularly organized and synchronous mode of contraction.

Smooth muscle is under involuntary control. It is the operative muscle of such diverse organs and systems as the blood vessels, stomach, intestines, skin, glands, and ducts. Its cells are mononucleate, elongated, and nonstriated. The absence of striations relates to the arrangement of actin and myosin filaments, which is not as regular in smooth muscle fibers as in skeletal and cardiac cells.

Smooth muscle contracts according to a mechanism that resembles those of skeletal and cardiac muscle. Contraction is triggered by an action potential that releases calcium ions from the sarcoplasmic reticulum. Yet, tropomyosin and the troponin complex are absent. Calcium ions induce contraction by some device different than that which operates in the sarcomeres of skeletal and cardiac muscle. In smooth muscle cells, calcium ions bind to a calcium-binding protein, called **calmodulin.** The calcium-calmodulin complex then interacts with a protein called **myosin light chain kinase** (MLCK), which, in turn, directly phosphorylates the myosin head. Phosphorylation of the myosin head then allows myosin to form a cross bridge with actin, whereupon contraction occurs.

Like cardiac muscle, adjoining smooth muscle cells feature gap junctions so that the action potential is readily and rapidly transmitted from one cell to the next.

Please solve this problem:

- Identify the muscle type that characterizes these organs or structures: wall of the right ventricle, wall of the gall bladder, wall of a large artery in the quadriceps, the quadriceps, the diaphragm, and the iris of the eye.

Problem solved:

The wall of the right ventricle and the other cardiac chambers are the only sites at which cardiac muscle is found. The walls of the gall bladder, of arteries throughout the body, and in the iris are all composed of smooth muscle fibers. The quadriceps and the diaphragm are both composed of skeletal muscle.

29.2 MASTERY APPLIED: PRACTICE PASSAGE AND QUESTIONS

Passage

Bone is a dynamic organ composed of cells, matrix, and minerals. Osteoclasts, osteoblasts, and osteocytes, together with the matrix, comprise healthy bone. Bone continuously remodels itself along lines of stress (areas that bear weight). Normal bone repair in humans begins when osteoclasts resorb old bone in order to provide space for new bone. Osteoblasts, meanwhile, lay down new bone in the area. Under normal conditions, these two processes occur at the same rate, maintaining the strength of bone.

As the result of aging, however, bone remodeling can be disrupted. Dissolved bone can be diverted to the serum, causing more bone to be lost during remodeling than is replaced. The new, incompletely remodeled bone is then vulnerable to fracture. Osteoporosis results from reduced bone mass (osteopenia) while the bone matrix remains normally mineralized.

Adequate serum levels of calcium are crucial to maintaining healthy bone. Underabsorption of calcium by the GI tract threatens normal bone metabolism and leads to reduced bone mass. Low levels of serum calcium activate a biofeedback system involving calcium, vitamin D, and parathyroid hormone. The activated system causes bone destruction in order to release calcium into the blood stream. Figure 1 depicts the regulatory activity of parathyroid hormone.

Other conditions that adversely affect bone include hyperparathyroidism, renal failure, and vitamin D deficiency. Drugs implicated in the development of osteoporosis include corticosteroids, which reduce bone mass, and phenytoin, which alters the metabolism of vitamin D in the liver.

Another structural defect arising from an abnormality of bone turnover is Paget's disease. Affected bones become softened and enlarged, and those bearing weight become curved. In pagetic bone, there is a pronounced increase in bone, resorption, compounded by a secondary burst of new bone formation. Both processes are accelerated, producing bone that is both very dense and structurally inferior. Viewed through a microscope, pagetic bone shows a chaotic architecture that bears little structural resemblance to the honeycombed appearance of healthy bone. Furthermore, osteoclasts typically contain fifty to one hundred nuclei per cell in pagetic bone compared to four or five in osteoclasts from normal bone. These pagetic osteoclasts are also oversized and more numerous compared to those in healthy bone.

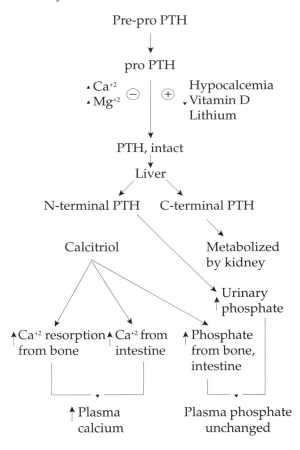

Figure 1

1. Which of the following applies to osteoclasts?

   I.   They are multinucleated cells.
   II. They are a type of bone cell.
   III. They deposit new bone during
        bone remodeling.

   A. II only
   B. I and II only
   C. II and III only
   D. I, II, and III

2. Hydroxyapatite and collagen are the
   principal components of:

   A. hard bone matrix.
   B. Haversian canals.
   C. cartilage matrix.
   D. lacunae.

3. The most appropriate pharmaceutical to
   administer to a patient with osteoporosis
   would be one that:

   A. inhibits the effects of osteoblasts.
   B. increases the production of osteo-
      clasts.
   C. decreases both bone resorption and
      bone formation.
   D. decreases bone resorption without
      affecting bone formation.

4. In Paget's disease, affected bone undergoes increased vascularization. All of the
   following could be possible effects on the
   body EXCEPT:

   A. pagetic bone can pose a risk of serious
      bleeding if it breaks.
   B. pagetic bone can exert an extra strain
      on cardiac tissue.
   C. increased warmth can be detected
      directly over the site of pagetic bone.
   D. decreased hemoglobin concentra-
      tions can occur in areas of nonpagetic
      bone.

5. Which of the following is a pathophysi-
   ological process associated with osteopenia?

   A. Decreased rate of bone resorption
   B. Decreased gastrointestinal absorp-
      tion of calcium
   C. Increased production of osteoblasts
   D. Increased rate of bone formation

29.3 MASTERY VERIFIED: ANSWERS AND EXPLANATIONS

1. **B is correct.** The fifth paragraph states that osteoclasts contain more than one nucleus per cell. Statement I is accurate. The first paragraph states that bone cells include osteoblasts, osteocytes, and osteoclasts, so statement II is accurate as well. The first paragraph also states that osteoclasts resorb old bone, making statement III inaccurate.

2. **A is correct.** Osteoblasts secrete bone matrix, containing mostly collagen. The bone matrix then becomes hardened when hydroxyapatite is deposited at the site. Choice B is incorrect because Haversian canals are found at the center of Haversian systems within compact bone. Blood vessels and nerves run through the Haversian canal. Choice C is incorrect as well: Cartilage matrix is composed of collagen and proteoglycans. Choice D is incorrect because lacunae are small cavities or wells. Cartilage cells (chondrocytes) and bone cells (osteocytes) reside in the lacunae.

3. **D is correct.** An agent that decreases bone resorption without affecting bone formation would constitute the ideal drug. The imbalance of bone remodeling processes would be compensated by such a pharmacological approach. Choice A is incorrect because osteoblasts build bone. Inhibiting their effects would worsen the condition rather than remedy it. Choice B is incorrect as well. Osteoclasts degrade bone. Increasing their numbers would likewise worsen the condition. Choice C is wrong because although a drug that decreases bone resorption would improve the osteoporotic condition, decreasing bone formation as well would worsen osteoporosis.

4. **D is correct.** The hemoglobin content of red blood cells remains the same throughout the body. Blood supply may increase at sites of pagetic bone, but it is not possible for a variation in blood supply to affect the hemoglobin content of blood. Choice A is correct because it is possible that increased blood vessels in the pagetic bone are supplying the site with blood. Therefore, it is reasonable to predict that a break at this site poses the risk of excessive bleeding. Choice B is also correct: It is possible that the increased need for blood by pagetic bone makes the heart work harder to supply blood to the site. This might exacerbate cardiac pathology. Choice C is correct because it is possible for the large volume of blood that supplies pagetic bone to cause an increase of heat at the diseased site.

5. **B is correct.** The passage states that absorption of calcium is critical to proper bone formation. If calcium is inadequately absorbed, bone formation (and mass) will be adversely affected. Choice A is incorrect because a decreased rate of bone resorption would not deplete bone mass (however, an increased rate would). Choice C is incorrect as well: Increased osteoblast production means increased bone formation. Choice D is incorrect because an increased rate of bone formation would *build* bone; it would have an effect opposite that associated with osteopenia.

CHAPTER 30

HUMAN PHYSIOLOGY II: THE RENAL, ENDOCRINE, AND NERVOUS SYSTEMS, AND THE SENSORY ORGANS AND SKIN

30.1 MASTERY ACHIEVED

THE RENAL SYSTEM

In humans, the **kidneys** are the main organs of excretion. Together with the **ureters**, **bladder**, and **urethra,** they form the urinary system. The kidneys play four important roles in helping to maintain body homeostasis:

(1) Excretion of hydrophilic waste; note that the liver is responsible for excreting hydrophobic or large waste products which cannot be filtered by the kidney.

(2) Maintain constant solute concentration.

(3) Maintain constant pH (approximately 7.4).

(4) Maintain constant fluid volume, which is important for blood pressure and cardiac output.

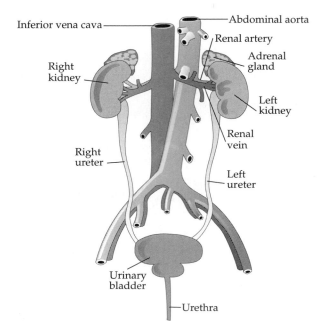

Gross Anatomy of the Urinary System

Figure 30.1

Gross and Microscopic Structure of the Kidney

On gross examination, the kidney consists of two portions: an outer portion, called the **renal cortex**, and an inner portion, called the **renal medulla**. The medulla is composed of wedge-shaped tissue structures called the **renal pyramids** (also called the medullary pyramids). A hollow **renal pelvis** makes up the innermost portion of the kidney, around which the medulla and cortex are wrapped. The pelvis, located in the kidney's hilus, is actually an extension and expansion of the ureter, which leads to the **urinary bladder**.

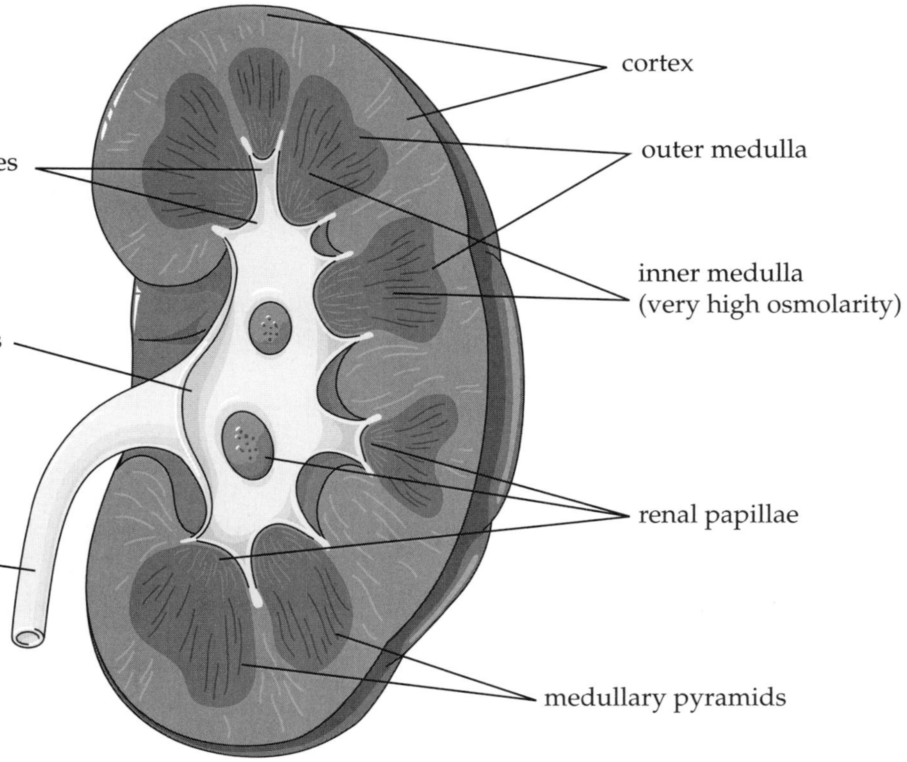

Internal Anatomy of the Kidney

Figure 30.2

The basic structural and functional unit of the kidney is the **nephron**. Each nephron consists of a **renal corpuscle**, continuous with a long "urinary pipeline," or **renal tubule;** the renal tubule is a hollow tube surrounded by epithelium cells. Each kidney consists of more than a million nephrons (see Figure 30.3). This discussion of renal function will focus on a single, representative nephron.

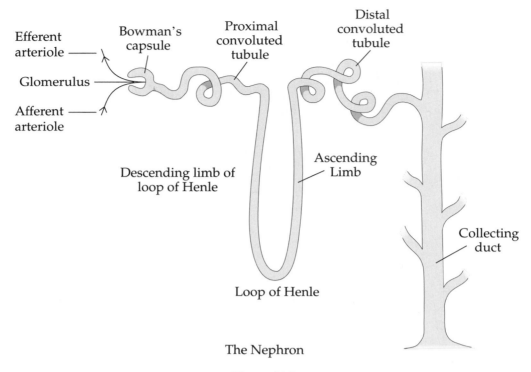

The Nephron

Figure 30.3

The renal corpuscle is comprised of three elements: a tuft of capillaries, called the **glomerulus**, a glomerular basement membrane, and a surrounding **Bowman's capsule**. Bowman's capsule is a double-walled cup formed as an enlargement of the **proximal** end of the renal tubule. This area of the nephron functions in blood filtration.

After Bowman's capsule, the renal tubule follows a twisting course, conventionally partitioned into five major segments: the proximal convoluted tubule, the descending loop of Henle, the ascending loop of Henle, the distal convoluted tubule and the collecting duct.

The first segment of the tubule, situated immediately beyond Bowman's capsule, is called the **proximal convoluted tubule** (PCT) because it is most proximal (closest) to the beginning, or glomerular, tip of the nephron. Both the renal corpuscle and the proximal convoluted tubule are situated in the cortex of the kidney.

After making a characteristic series of twists and turns, the tubule straightens out in the second segment, or **descending limb of the loop of Henle**, and extends into the pyramids of the renal medulla, the kidney's midsection. There, the loop of Henle makes a 180° hairpin turn and passes into the third segment, the **ascending limb of the loop of Henle**, which, running approximately parallel to the descending limb, courses back up into the cortex.

In the cortex, the renal tubule begins a second set of twists and turns that constitute its fourth segment, the **distal convoluted tubule**. Each distal convoluted tubule then empties into the fifth segment, a larger **collecting duct**, which courses back down into the medullary pyramids. A single collecting duct carries fluid away from numerous distal convoluted tubules.

Many nearby collecting ducts merge to form one **papillary duct**. Papillary ducts then empty into the funnel-shaped sections of the **renal pelvis** called the **calyces** (singular: calyx). From the renal pelvis, the ureter carries the urine away from the kidney to the **urinary bladder**, where it is stored until it passes from the body in **micturition** (urination).

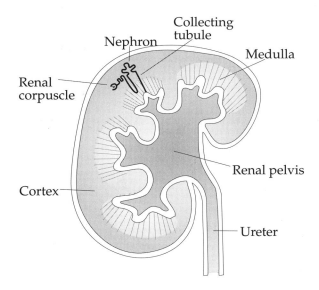

The Kidney Showing Position of a Nephron

Figure 30.4

Please solve this problem:

- Urine passes directly to the outside of the body through which of the following structures?

    A. The urethra
    B. The ureter
    C. The collecting duct
    D. The renal tubule

Problem solved:

A is correct. The urethra passes from the bladder to the outside of the body; it is from here that urine is excreted. A ureter passes from each kidney to the bladder (B is incorrect). Collecting ducts channel urine to the renal pyramids, which are still far from the point of excretion from the body (C is incorrect). The renal tubule refers to the portion of the nephron beginning immediately distal to the renal corpuscle (D is incorrect).

Filtrate Transit Through the Nephron

FILTRATION AT THE GLOMERULUS

The blood to be filtered by the kidney is delivered via the **renal artery**, which branches off the abdominal aorta (see Figure 30.1). The artery branches into **afferent** ("approaching") **arterioles**, which travel to individual renal corpuscles, where they branch profusely to form the **glomerular capillaries** inside a Bowman's capsule.

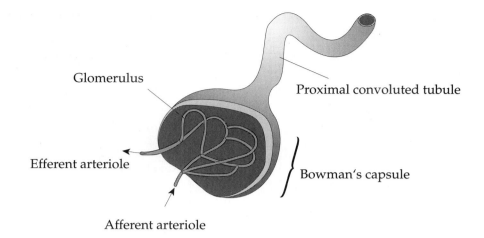

Glomerulus

Proximal convoluted tubule

Efferent arteriole

Bowman's capsule

Afferent arteriole

A Renal Corpuscle

Figure 30.5

The inner wall (or **visceral layer**) of Bowman's capsule is porous and permeable to plasma and other small blood constituents. The exterior wall of the capsule (**parietal layer**) is neither porous nor permeable. The space enclosed by the two walls—the **Bowman's space**—is the origin of the renal tubule. As blood goes through the glomerulus, certain components (water, amino acids, glucose, ions, urea and other small molecules) pass from the glomerulus, across the basement membrane, through the porous visceral layer of Bowman's capsule and into Bowman's space. This fluid is now called **filtrate** and after much modification, will eventually become urine. The blood reaching the glomerular capillaries via the afferent arterioles has the same composition of sugars, amino acids, ions, and water as the filtrate inside of Bowman's capsule. However, in a healthy kidney, blood cells, platelets and macromolecules such as blood proteins do not pass into Bowman's space.

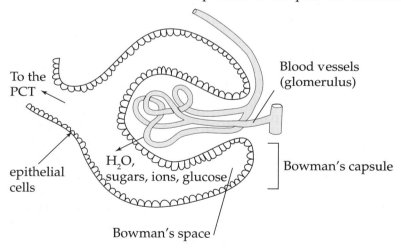

To the PCT

Blood vessels (glomerulus)

H_2O, sugars, ions, glucose

Bowman's capsule

epithelial cells

Bowman's space

Filtration of Blood at the Glomerulus

Figure 30.6

Filtration occurs across the glomerular capillary walls into Bowman's capsule. Because the efferent arterioles are narrower than the afferent ones, and because the efferent arterioles can constrict, a high blood pressure (about 60 mm Hg) can be created in the capillaries of the glomerulus. This pressure forces fluid to leave the capillaries, and the low pressure and permeable inner wall of Bowman's capsule provides an outlet.

The filtered blood leaves the glomerulus via the **efferent** ("exiting") **arterioles**, which eventually fuse with the renal vein.

Please solve this problem:

- Which of the following laboratory findings would most likely indicate disease?

    A. The absence of large proteins in the urine
    B. The absence of white blood cells in the urine
    C. The presence of red blood cells in the urine
    D. The presence of hydroxide ions in the urine

Problem solved:

C is correct. Blood coursing through the glomerular capillaries is filtered through the capillary walls into Bowman's capsule. As noted in the text, the filtrate contains a great many constituents of blood, but it does not contain blood cells. The presence of red blood cells in the urine **(hematuria)** is abnormal and a possible indication of disease. The urine does not normally contain large proteins or white blood cells; it does contain hydroxide ions.

Please solve this problem:

- Which of the following is an INCORRECT statement?

    A. Glomeruli are continuous with the proximal convoluted tubule.
    B. The proximal convoluted tubule is continuous with the distal convoluted tubule.
    C. The ureter empties into the bladder.
    D. Distal portions of each nephron coalesce to ultimately form a structure that is continuous with the ureter.

Problem solved:

A is correct. The glomerulus is a capillary bed, which, together with Bowman's capsule, constitutes the renal corpuscle. The glomerulus is not *continuous* with Bowman's capsule. Rather, certain blood constituents pass *through the walls* of the glomerular capillaries to reach Bowman's capsule. Bowman's capsule *is* continuous with the proximal convoluted tubule, which is continuous with the descending limb of the loop of Henle, which is continuous with the ascending limb of the loop of Henle, which is continuous with the distal convoluted tubule, which is continuous with the collecting duct. The collecting ducts coalesce to form papillary ducts, which, in turn, ultimately join to form the renal pelvis. The renal pelvis is continuous with the ureter, and the ureter empties into the bladder.

Please solve this problem:

- Which of the following choices correctly characterizes the glomerulus?

  A. It is composed primarily of nervous tissue.
  B. It is composed primarily of blood vessels.
  C. There is one per kidney.
  D. It is situated distal to Bowman's capsule.

Problem solved:

B is correct. The glomerulus is a tuft of capillaries, and capillaries are blood vessels. Blood is filtered through the glomerulus into Bowman's capsule, which means that the glomerulus is *proximal* (not distal) to Bowman's capsule. There is one glomerulus associated with each nephron, which means that there are many glomeruli (not one) associated with each kidney.

THE PROXIMAL CONVOLUTED TUBULE

A greater volume of blood is filtered at the kidney each minute than a person excretes as urine in a day. Therefore, the kidney *reabsorbs* water, ions, and other useful substances from the glomerular filtrate. Some of this reabsorption occurs along the entire length of a nephron, but most reabsorption happens at the proximal convoluted tubule, where 75 percent of the filtrate is reabsorbed. Also, certain waste molecules can be added to the filtrate, a process called **secretion**.

THE DESCENDING LOOP OF HENLE

Filtrate within the tubule is affected by the kidney insertitium, the fluid environment through which the tubule passes. The salt concentration of the interstitial fluid in the kidney is precisely regulated so there is a concentration gradient between the cortical and medullary regions of the kidney. The salt concentration of the cortical interstitial fluid—around the renal corpuscles, proximal convoluted tubules, and upper portion of the loop of Henle—is relatively low. The interstitial salt concentration increases at deeper levels within the medulla.

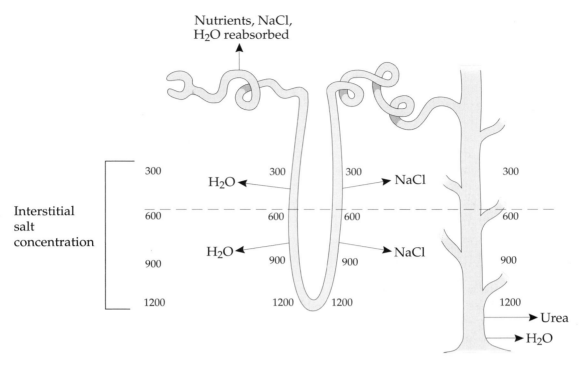

Fluid Transport Through the Loop of Henle

Figure 30.7

As filtrate travels through the descending loop of Henle, it encounters increasingly higher salt concentrations in the surrounding interstitial environment. To maintain osmotic equilibrium across a membrane, fluid and/or solutes must cross the membrane. Because the wall of the descending limb of the loop of Henle is permeable to water but nearly impermeable to solutes, water passes out of the loop of Henle to equalize concentrations inside the renal tubule with those outside the tubule. Therefore, large amounts of water are reabsorbed back into the body in the descending loop of Henle.

THE ASCENDING LOOP OF HENLE

Like the descending loop of Henle, the ascending loop also traverses the concentration gradient of the surrounding interstitial fluid; the dynamics are reversed, however. The concentration gradient decreases as the tubule extends into the relatively dilute interstitial environment of the cortex. As in the descending loop, the osmotic differential across the cells of the tubule walls will equalize the intratubal pressure with the pressure of the interstitial environment. Unlike the descending limb, however, the ascending limb is impermeable to water but becomes permeable to sodium. As the filtrate travels through the ascending tubule, it becomes dilute once again;

sodium is reabsorbed first by passive diffusion and then by active transport across tubule walls into the interstitial environment. Passage through the loop of Henle has restored the filtrate's solute concentration at the cortical portion of the ascending limb to levels nearly equal to those of the pre-loop filtrate at the cortical portion of the descending limb.

On first examination, the loop of Henle may appear to have no function, as it seems to produce no change in solute concentration. However, the ascending limb contains a *reduced volume* of filtrate. The water that diffused out of the tubule walls of the loop's descending limb has been essentially trapped within the surrounding interstitial space and will be eventually reabsorbed into blood vessels, known as the **vasa recta**, which are continuous with the renal vein. The water is thus withheld from excretion in the urine. If there were no *tubular reabsorption* mechanism, the large volume of glomerular filtrate passing into Bowman's capsule each day would swiftly lead to dehydration. By allowing for one-way diffusion of water out of the nephron, the limbs of the loop of Henle afford the body a mechanism for conservation of water.

The tubular reabsorption mechanism functions properly only if the concentration gradient around the loop of Henle is maintained. **Active transport** of salt from the filtrate of the ascending limb of the loop of Henle plays a role in maintaining that gradient. Consequently, the filtrate concentrations in the corresponding cortical segments of the descending and ascending limbs of the loop of Henle are not equal. The concentration of filtrate in the cortical portion of the ascending limb is, in fact, somewhat lower than that in the adjacent cortical portion of the descending limb, and is markedly hypoosmotic to blood plasma.

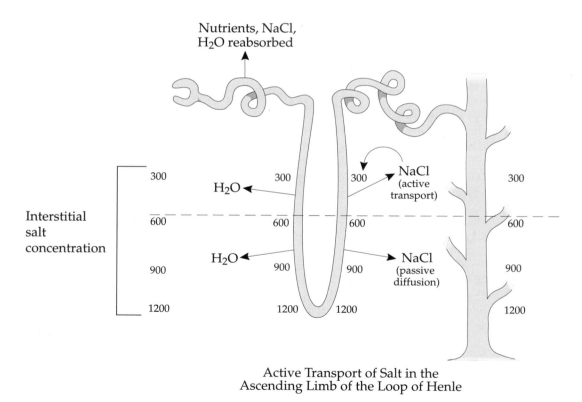

Active Transport of Salt in the
Ascending Limb of the Loop of Henle

Figure 30.8

THE DISTAL TUBULE

The distal convoluted tubule and the collecting duct are the site of additional reabsorption and secretion. These are areas of fine tuning the filtrate concentrations before the filtrate is lost as urine.

Please solve this problem:

- The kidney maintains a concentration gradient in its interstitial fluid, with the concentration of sodium and other ions increasing several fold from the cortex to the medulla. Discuss this gradient in relation to the composition of filtrate in the descending loop of Henle.

Problem solved:

Water will diffuse across a membrane to equalize ionic concentrations on both sides of the membrane. In the descending limb of the loop of Henle, the filtrate encounters a progressively increasing concentration of solute across the tubular membrane as it travels toward the medulla. Thus, water from the filtrate diffuses across the loop membrane into this surrounding interstitial fluid, which increases the concentration of tubular ions and dilutes the interstitial fluid. Despite this diluting effect of reabsorbed filtrate water, other mechanisms work to maintain the interstitial concentration gradient. Hence, the process of tubular filtrate concentration continues as it passes through the increasingly concentrated environment of the medulla near the hairpin loop.

Please solve this problem:

- Which of the following choices properly characterizes fluid in the distal convoluted tubule?

    A. Its concentration of protein is markedly higher than that of the proximal convoluted tubule.
    B. Its chlorine concentration is markedly lower than that of the proximal convoluted tubule.
    C. Its sodium concentration is markedly lower than that of the proximal convoluted tubule.
    D. Its volume is markedly less than that of the proximal convoluted tubule.

Problem solved:

D is correct. As described in the text, the passage of filtrate through the loop of Henle and its limbs allows for the conservation of water. That is, a net movement of water occurs *from* the tubule outward into the interstitium. Although the tubular fluid experiences little change in its concentrations of solutes as it passes from descending to ascending limbs, it undergoes a pronounced diminution in volume. Protein molecules are not normally filtered through the glomerulus into the tubular fluid. Protein concentration within the tubular fluid should be very nearly zero at all portions of the nephron. The presence of protein in the urine **(proteinuria)** is a classic sign of kidney disease.

Hormonal Regulation of Water Retention

From the cortical end of the ascending limb of the loop of Henle (also called the distal end, because it is farthest from the glomerulus), filtrate passes into the distal convoluted tubule and, from there, into a collecting duct. A significant amount of water reabsorption can occur in each of these latter segments. As filtrate flows from the proximal (cortical) end of the collecting duct down toward a papillary duct of the renal pelvis, it encounters the same increasing interstitial salt concentration as it did in the descending limb of the loop of Henle. Again, a concentration gradient exists across the tubule walls, but because the collecting duct is impermeable to salt, the filtrate does not receive any solutes from the surrounding environment.

The permeability of the collecting tubule to water, however, can be regulated depending on the body's need to conserve or eliminate water. This regulation is accomplished by antidiuretic hormone (ADH) or vasopressin, a peptide hormone synthesized in the hypothalamus and secreted by the posterior pituitary. When dehydration stimulates release of ADH from the posterior pituitary, where it is stored, it increases the collecting duct's permeability to water; water moves outward from duct to interstitium and is conserved. When the body is adequately hydrated, ADH secretion is diminished, reducing the permeability of the collecting duct, thereby trapping the water within the tubule and producing an increased volume of more dilute urine.

Please solve this problem:

- A woman preparing to undergo a sonogram drinks six 8-ounce glasses of water before the procedure. What will likely be the effect of her water intake on blood levels of ADH, a hormone released by her posterior pituitary?

Problem solved:

ADH increases the collecting duct's permeability to water, promoting water conservation. In this case, the patient is overhydrated. In order to reestablish homeostasis, she must excrete a relatively large volume of urine, so the posterior pituitary reduces its secretion of ADH.

Please solve this problem:

- Which of the following choices does NOT accompany increased secretion of ADH?

    A. Decreased urine volume
    B. A more dilute urine
    C. Increased movement of water from collecting ducts to interstitium
    D. Water conservation

Problem solved:

B is correct. ADH increases the collecting duct's permeability to water, causing (a) movement of water from the collecting duct to the interstitium; (b) the production of a concentrated urine, relatively low in volume; and (c) the concomitant conservation of water. ADH concentrates the urine; it does not dilute it.

Please solve this problem:

- In the condition known as diabetes insipidus, ADH secretion is impaired. Among the following, which symptom will the patient most likely experience?

  A. Increased thirst
  B. Decreased thirst
  C. Low urine output
  D. High content of protein in the urine

Problem solved:

A is correct. The absence of ADH will decrease the permeability of the collecting duct to water. Water will not move from the collecting duct to the interstitium, even in the face of relative dehydration. The patient will excrete relatively high volumes of dilute urine and will thus experience a tendency toward high salt concentrations and low volume of body fluids. If the patient's thirst mechanism is intact (as it ordinarily is in diabetes insipidus), she/he will experience increased thirst and will compensate by drinking. In the absence of kidney disease, the urine will not contain protein; that is, in the healthy kidney, protein is not filtered out of the glomerulus.

THE ENDOCRINE SYSTEM

Endocrine vs. Exocrine Glands

The **endocrine system** controls body homeostatis over hours and days by promoting communication among various tissues and organs through the secretion of **hormones**. Hormones are secreted by **endocrine organs**, more commonly called **endocrine glands**. Hormones usually act at considerable distances from the sites of their release. They are released from an endocrine gland into the **bloodstream**, by which they are carried to their **target cells**. In contrast, **exocrine organs**, secrete their products into the external environment (including the lumen of the gut) via ducts. These secretions can be mucus-based or serous (watery secretions that usually contain enzymes). Some example of exocrine organs are the salivary glands, mammary glands, pancreatic acinar cells, or sweat glands.

Most endocrine hormones act slowly and for longer periods (i.e., minutes to years) to maintain the body in relative homeostasis. Their secretion is modulated by changes in bodily needs and conditions. Because they are secreted directly into the bloodstream, endocrine hormones come into contact with nearly every cell of the body. Despite that fact, a given hormone may not have any effect on a given cell type. Most hormones affect a cell only if the cell has a **receptor** that binds them, either on the surface of the cell or inside the cell. A hormone's target cells, then, are those cells that have receptors for it. A given cell type might be the target of one hormone, many hormones, or no hormones, depending on the number and kind of receptors it possesses.

Please solve this problem:

- Which one of the following choices is NOT characteristic of an endocrine gland?

   A. It secretes enzymes that act on distant organs or cells.
   B. It helps to maintain homeostasis.
   C. It secretes hormones that exert their effects at a distant site.
   D. It secretes hormones that are transported through the bloodstream to reach their sites of action.

Problem solved:

A is correct. Endocrine glands secrete hormones into the bloodstream, while exocrine glands secrete their products to the external environment via ducts. Endocrine glands function in the maintenance of homeostasis—their hormones affect target cells and organs, in response to changes in internal and external bodily environments. Generally, hormones act at sites remote from the points at which they are released, and they reach their sites of action via the bloodstream.

Please solve this problem:

- Which of the following findings would justify an investigator in classifying the adrenal glands as an endocrine organ?

   A. They are associated with the kidneys.
   B. They receive a large blood supply.
   C. They secrete a substance that can be used clinically as an anti-inflammatory agent.
   D. They secrete a substance that travels through the blood and affects the degree protein catabolism in response to variable conditions.

Problem solved:

D is correct. An endocrine organ is one that secretes hormones, which travel in the blood to their target sites, and control homeostasis. If the adrenal glands secrete a substance that travels through the blood to modulate protein catabolism, it secretes a hormone and is an endocrine organ.

Types of Hormones

Hormones can be generally grouped into one of three classes: peptide hormones, steroid hormones, or amino acid derivatives. These chemical classes of hormones are made differently, travel in the blood differently, function at the target cell differently, and affect the target cell differently. Below is a summary table of the key features of peptide versus steroid hormones. Most amino acid derivatives act like peptide hormones (for example, epinephrine), but some can act like steroid hormones (for example, thyroid hormone).

	Peptide Hormone	Steroid Hormone
Chemical Class	Hydrophilic	Hydrophobic
Synthesis	Made in ER, Golgi	Made from cholesterol in SER
Storage	Stored in vesicles	Secreted right away; no storage
Blood travel	Dissolve in the plasma (because they are hydrophilic)	Travel in the blood bound to proteins (because they are hydrophobic)
Receptor binding	Bind to receptors on surface of the target cell; because they are hydrophillic, they cannot diffuse across the plasma membrane	Diffuse across the plasma membrane and bind to receptors in the cytoplasm of the target cell
Effect on target	Induce second messenger cascades that result in modifying the existing enzymes and proteins	Go to nucleus and alter transcription; change amount and types of proteins in the target cell
Length of effect	Rapid but short-lived	Slow but long-lasting

Key Features of Peptides vs. Steroid Hormones

Table 30.1

Principal Endocrine Organs

There are eight major endocrine glands in humans: the pancreas, the adrenal glands, the thyroid gland, the parathyroid glands, the ovaries, the testes, the hypothalamus, and the pituitary gland. This is not an exhaustive list; there are other organs (such as the thymus, heart, and kidney) that can also be classified as endocrine glands, but these will not be focused on here. In this section, we will focus on the eight major endocrine glands, discussing the hormones they release and how this affects human physiology and homeostasis.

THE PANCREAS

The **pancreas** is both an endocrine gland and an exocrine gland. It is an exocrine organ because it secretes digestive enzymes and bicarbonate into the lumen of the duodenum (see Chapter 29). Exocrine secretions of the pancreas come from acinar cells and empty via ducts into the gastrointestinal tract. The pancreas is as an endocrine organ because it secretes hormones, three of which are **insulin, glucagon,** and **somatostatin**. All three are secreted by pancreatic **islet cells** located in the **islets of Langerhans**. Insulin (secreted by the β cells) and glucagon (secreted by the α cells) regulate glucose transport, storage, and metabolism. Somatostatin (secreted by the ∂ cells) inhibits many digestive processes.

Glucose in our body comes from two major sources. First, polysaccharides that we eat are chemically broken down and then absorbed by the gastrointestinal tract. Second, glucose can be produced by the liver and released into the blood. In the absence of insulin, all body cells—except those of the brain and liver—are relatively impermeable to glucose. Glucose in the blood tends to remain in the blood when insulin secretion is low. When insulin secretion is high, however, circulating glucose is taken up by cells throughout the body, lowering blood glucose levels. The cells that receive the glucose either store it or metabolize it to produce ATP. It is important to note that the brain takes up glucose from the blood whether or not insulin is secreted. When the liver takes up glucose, it converts large quantities of it to **glycogen**, a long carbohydrate polymer that serves as a storage form of glucose.

Overall, insulin has four main functions in the human body. These are:

(1) increasing cellular uptake of glucose,

(2) promoting formation of glycogen from glucose in the liver,

(3) reducing glucose concentration in the blood, and

(4) increasing protein and triglyceride synthesis.

In many respects, **glucagon** has effects that are opposite to the those of insulin; glucagon promotes the breakdown of glycogen in the liver through a process termed **glycogenolysis**. The breakdown of glycogen produces glucose, which is, in turn, released into the blood. Glucagon also promotes the manufacture of glucose in the liver through a process called **gluconeogenesis**. Gluconeogenesis involves the synthesis of glucose—not from glycogen, but from lactate, amino acids, and triglycerides. This newly formed glucose is also released into the blood. The most easily detectable effect of glucagon, therefore, is to increase the blood's glucose levels. Glucagon also increases lipolysis (lipid breakdown). It is important to note that glucagon does not decrease cellular uptake of glucose.

In the service of homeostasis, a high blood glucose level normally stimulates the secretion of insulin. The insulin causes the body cells to take up glucose, thus lowering the blood glucose level. A low blood glucose level tends to decrease insulin secretion and raise glucagon secretion. The increased glucagon secretion causes the release of glucose from the liver and raises the blood glucose level.

Hyperglycemia refers to excessively high levels of glucose in the blood and is typically due to diminished insulin secretion or activity. **Hypoglycemia** refers to excessively low levels of glucose in the blood and may result from elevated levels of insulin or insufficient glucagon levels in the body.

Please solve this problem:

- Which of the following is a pair of hormones secreted by the pancreas?

    A. Glycogen and glucose
    B. Insulin and glycogen
    C. Insulin and glucagon
    D. Amylase and lipase

Problem solved:

C is correct. Insulin and glucagon are two of the hormones secreted by the endocrine cells of the pancreas into the blood. In contrast, the exocrine cells of the pancreas secrete digestive enzymes, including amylase and lipase, directly into the digestive tract via ducts (D is incorrect). Glycogen is the storage form of glucose found predominantly in the liver (A and B are incorrect.)

Please solve this problem:

- If a patient were to lose consciousness because his/her blood levels of glucose were low and his/her brain was receiving an inadequate supply of fuel, which of the following would be the best treatment?

    A. Administration of insulin
    B. Administration of glucagon
    C. Administration of glycogen
    D. Administration of oxygen

Problem solved:

B is correct. The patient has fallen unconscious because his/her brain has no source of glucose, which is required to produce the high-energy molecule ATP. In order to supply the brain with glucose, the physician must raise the glucose levels of the blood. Administration of glucagon will cause the liver to release glucose into the blood, making it available to the brain. Insulin administration would worsen the patient's condition (A is incorrect), since insulin tends to promote the uptake of glucose cells, thus lowering blood glucose levels even further. Note that the condition described in the question often arises in diabetics who have received too much exogenous insulin.

Please solve this problem:

- Among the following choices, which is most likely to produce hyperglycemia?

    A. A hepatic condition in which gluconeogenesis is impaired
    B. A hepatic condition in which glucagon fails to exert its effects
    C. A pancreatic condition in which glucagon is not secreted
    D. A pancreatic condition in which insulin is not secreted

Problem solved:

D is correct. Hyperglycemia refers to excessive quantities of glucose in the blood. It can be caused by either excessive secretion of glucagon or impaired secretion of insulin (in most cases, it is produced by impaired secretion of insulin, as in diabetes mellitus Type I). If gluconeogenesis were impaired, one potential source for blood glucose would be eliminated, and blood glucose levels would be reduced (A is incorrect). The same is true for choices B and C; suppression of glucagon function, by whatever means, would inhibit gluconeogenesis and glycogenolysis, thereby reducing blood glucose levels.

THE ADRENAL GLANDS

An **adrenal gland** sits on each kidney; humans have a left and a right adrenal gland. Each gland has two distinct regions that are developmentally and functionally distinct. The two regions are related more in name than in function, and are termed the **adrenal cortex** and the **adrenal medulla**.

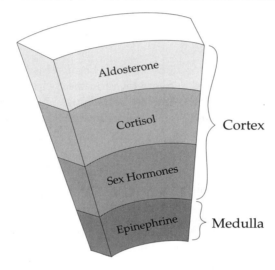

The Adrenal Gland

Figure 30.9

THE ADRENAL CORTEX

The **adrenal cortex** is the outer portion of the adrenal gland. It produces a class of endocrine hormones called **corticosteroids**, which are subdivided into three groups: the **mineralocorticoids,** the **glucocorticoids**, and the **sex hormones**.

The mineralocorticoids affect levels of the minerals sodium and potassium in the body. The main mineralocorticoid secreted by the adrenal cortex is the steroid hormone **aldosterone**, which acts primarily at the distal convoluted tubule of the kidney to promote sodium–potassium exchange. Aldosterone increases the activity of sodium–potassium pumps, which remove three sodium ions from the renal filtrate for every two potassium ions they transport into the filtrate. In promoting an uneven exchange of sodium and potassium at the distal tubule, aldosterone increases the interstitial concentration of solutes, and so tends to promote the movement of water from tubule to interstitium. The ultimate effects of aldosterone are to:

(1) increase urinary excretion of potassium,

(2) increase interstitial sodium concentration, and

(3) increase water conservation (as an effect secondary to the increase of interstitial sodium concentration).

As a result, it is not surprising that aldosterone secretion is stimulated by high levels of extracellular potassium, low levels of extracellular sodium, and low fluid levels (blood volume).

The glucocorticoids affect plasma glucose concentrations. They have a wide range of effects on many organ systems. One such effect is similar to that of glucagon: They increase blood glucose levels, especially in response to environmental stressors. The glucocorticoids also strengthen cardiac muscle contractions, increase water retention, and have anti-inflammatory and anti-allergic activities. The main glucocorticoid secreted by the adrenal cortex is the steroid hormone **cortisol**. Cortisol is released as part of the long-term stress response and affects most tissues in the body. It increases plasma glucose levels (mainly via increasing gluconeogenesis), and inhibits immune activity. Cortisol release is controlled by the hypothalamus and the anterior pituitary (see page 658), and cortisol causes negative feedback to both these areas of the brain.

Finally, the adrenal cortex secretes low levels of the sex steroids, mostly the androgens (the sex hormones that are dominant in men). The adrenal cortex is the main source of androgens in women (since women have no testes) and plays a role in sex drive.

THE ADRENAL MEDULLA

The adrenal medulla secretes **catecholamines**, mostly **epinephrine** (also known as **adrenaline**). Epinephrine is an amino acid derivative that acts like a peptide hormone. Receptors for norepinephrine and epinephrine are widely distributed throughout the body. It is normally released in very small quantities and is largely reserved for stressful situations in which the body prepares for the so-called "fight or flight" response. Nerve impulses arriving at the adrenal medulla stimulate catecholamine release. There are several types of catecholamine receptors; each type differs in the nature of its response to catecholamine binding. In general, epinephrine increases heart rate, raises blood pressure, and increases alertness.

THE THYROID

The **thyroid** is a flat gland located in the neck, in front of the larynx. It synthesizes and secretes two hormones: calcitonin and the thyroid hormones.

Thyroid hormones include **thyroxine** (also known as thyroid hormone, T4) or its analog, **triiodothyronine** (thyroid hormone, T3). Most cells of the body have receptors for thyroxine and triiodothyronine. Both of these hormones are synthesized in the follicles of the thyroid gland from the amino acid tyrosine. Although thyroid hormones are amino acid derivatives, they are hydrophobic, travel in the plasma bound to plasma proteins, and affect target cells by binding receptors in the nucleus. Overall, thyroid hormones are lipophilic, not hydrophilic.

Thyroxine contains four atoms of iodine, while triiodothyronine contains three atoms of iodine. Thyroid hormones produce a generalized increase in metabolism throughout the body; they stimulate increased oxygen demand and heat production as well as growth and development. The release of thyroid hormones is controlled by the hypothalamus and anterior pituitary (see page 658).

Hypothyroidism refers to an inadequate production of thyroid hormone. The hypothyroid patient tends to be overweight and slowed down in physical (and sometimes mental) activities. Although rare in areas where modern medicine is available, **cretinism** arises from a deficiency of thyroid hormone in the first six months of life.

Thyroid hormones require iodine. Insufficient dietary iodine intake produces a decrease in thyroid hormone production. A feedback mechanism stimulates the thyroid to increase its function, and as a result, the thyroid undergoes excessive growth (hypertrophy), producing the condition known as **goiter**. Goiter manifests as a large prominence in the anterior aspect of the neck. The prominence is the overgrown thyroid itself.

The peptide hormone **calcitonin** is produced in the **parafollicular cells** of the thyroid. Although its importance in the body is not fully understood, calcitonin administered therapeutically reduces blood calcium concentration and inhibits the normal process of bone resorption.

THE PARATHYROID GLANDS

The **parathyroids** are a set of four small glands located on the posterior aspect of the thyroid gland. The peptide hormone **parathyroid hormone (PTH, also known as parathormone)** exerts effects opposite to those of calcitonin. It is secreted in response to low blood levels of calcium, and through actions on various organs, it increases levels of blood calcium. It acts to:

(1) increase bone resorption and consequent calcium release,

(2) increase intestinal calcium uptake, and

(3) promote calcium re-uptake at the kidney.

THE OVARIES

The ovaries are the site of oogenesis in women; they brush up against the Fallopian tubes, which are connected to the uterus. The ovaries are responsible for the synthesis of the female sex steroid estrogen and progesterone. Production of both these sex steroids is linked closely to the menstrual cycle.

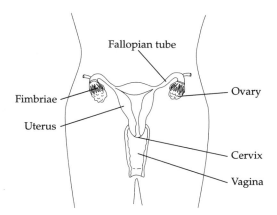

The Female Reproductive Organs

Figure 30.10

INTRODUCTION TO THE MENSTRUAL CYCLE

The **menstrual cycle** is a series of hormonally induced events that prepare the woman's body for pregnancy. Typically, the cycle takes twenty-eight days to complete, with the first day of menstrual bleeding conventionally recognized as Day 1 of the cycle. The menstrual cycle can be described with respect to changes that occur in the follicles of the ovaries (the ovarian cycle), or with respect to changes in the endometrial lining of the uterus (the uterine cycle).

THE OVARIAN CYCLE

The first phase of the ovarian cycle is known as the **follicular phase**, owing its name to the rapid growth of the **ovarian follicle**. During this phase, the anterior pituitary gland secretes two hormones that stimulate the growth of one follicle containing several ova, only one of which fully matures. The two follicular hormones are **follicle-stimulating hormone (FSH)** and **luteinizing hormone (LH)**. The follicle itself is secretory, releasing the hormone **estrogen** as it develops. The follicular phase ranges from seven to twenty-one days. Increased ovarian estrogen release prevents maturation of more than one follicle at a time.

At the end of the follicular stage (around Day 14), there is a surge in LH secretion from the anterior pituitary. This surge causes the release of the ovum from the enlarged follicle, and it is swept into the Fallopian tube by the fimbriae. There, the ovum waits for fertilization by sperm. The release of the ovum from the follicle is known as **ovulation**.

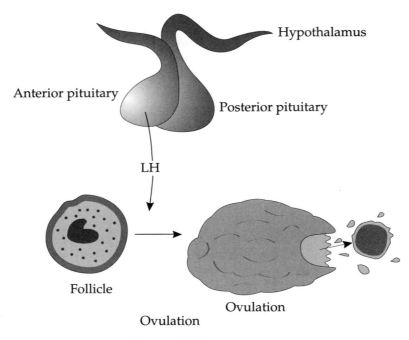

Figure 30.11

The final stage in the ovarian cycle is the **luteal phase**, typically Day 14 to Day 28. After ovulation, the part of the ruptured follicle that remains in the ovary is referred to as the **corpus luteum**. The corpus luteum secretes estrogen and progesterone.

THE UTERINE CYCLE

The first phase of the uterine cycle is **menses**, or shedding of the uterine lining. This typically lasts between four and seven days and occurs at the same time as the early follicular phase in the ovary. Next, the **proliferative phase** occurs until day 14. During this time, estrogen from the ovaries induces the proliferation of the endometrium. Finally, the **secretory phase** lasts for the final 14 days of the menstrual cycle. During this time, progesterone from the corpus luteum promotes the rapid thickening and vascularization of the uterine lining in preparation for the implantation of a fertilized ovum.

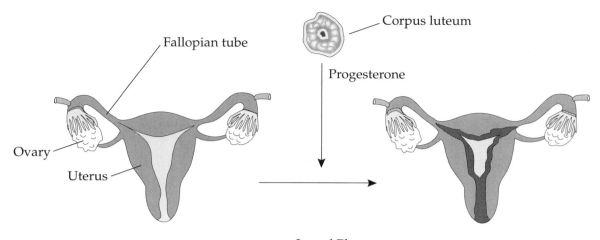

Luteal Phase

Figure 30.12

If the mature ovum is not fertilized, it will not implant into the uterine lining. At approximately thirteen days after ovulation (Day 27 of the cycle), the corpus luteum in the ovary degenerates and ceases to secrete estrogen and progesterone. With progesterone no longer available to maintain the thickened uterine lining, the lining begins to slough off the uterine wall. This causes severing of the newly formed vasculature and the bleeding that is characteristic of human menstruation. After an average of five days, the shedding of the uterine lining is complete, and a new proliferative phase begins.

If the ovum is fertilized (which would occur on or about Day 14 or around the time of ovulation), the developing placenta begins to secrete **human chorionic gonadotropin (hCG).** hCG prevents the corpus luteum from degenerating, allowing it to continue secreting progesterone. This maintains the integrity of the uterine lining and allows the pregnancy to continue. Before the end of the first trimester of pregnancy, the placenta begins to secrete estrogen and progesterone and the corpus luteum degenerates. These hormones are secreted at continuously increasing levels throughout pregnancy.

Please solve this problem:

- • Follicle-stimulating hormone (FSH) is secreted by:

    A. the hypothalamus.
    B. the follicular cells.
    C. the ovaries.
    D. the anterior pituitary gland.

Problem solved:

D is correct. Follicle-stimulating hormone (FSH) is secreted by the anterior pituitary gland. Together with luteinizing hormone (LH), also secreted by the anterior pituitary, FSH stimulates follicular development, ultimately producing an ovum.

Please solve this problem:

- The luteal surge causes:

    A. sudden shedding of the uterine lining.
    B. release of the ovum into the oviduct.
    C. implantation of a fertilized ovum in the uterus.
    D. the second meiotic division of a secondary oocyte.

Problem solved:

B is correct. The phrase *luteal surge* refers to a sudden increase in the secretion of luteinizing hormone (LH) from the anterior pituitary; this event is associated with the release of an ovum (a haploid cell produced by the first meiotic division of the primary oocyte) into the oviduct (the fallopian tube).

Please solve this problem:

- Which of the following correctly characterizes the corpus luteum?

    A. It secretes estrogen and progesterone.
    B. It undergoes meiosis.
    C. It is located in the uterine lining.
    D. It is nonsecretory.

Problem solved:

A is correct. The corpus luteum is the remnant of the ruptured follicle left in the ovary after ovulation occurs. Its cells secrete estrogen and progesterone. The secretion of progesterone promotes growth of the uterus and prepares it for implantation of a zygote.

Please solve this problem:

- Name the hormones that control the female menstrual cycle, and describe their functions.

Problem solved:

FSH and LH are peptide hormones secreted from the anterior pituitary during the follicular phase to cause follicular development in the ovary. A surge of LH causes ovulation.

Estrogen is secreted by the follicular cells during the follicular phase and promotes proliferation of the endometrium.

Estrogen and progesterone are secreted from the corpus luteum during the luteal phase. They cause further development of the endometrium, in preparation for zygote implantation.

Human chorionic gonadotropin (hCG) is secreted from the developing placenta upon fertilization and implantation. It stimulates the corpus luteum to continue progesterone and estrogen secretion. In the absence of implantation and the consequent absence of placental hCG, the corpus luteum degenerates, and its hormonal secretion terminates. Without progesterone, the endometrial lining deteriorates. Menstrual bleeding follows. Also, in response to the post-luteal fall in circulating levels of estrogen and progesterone, FSH production rises, initiating a new proliferative phase.

THE TESTES

Each **testis** contains specialized reproductive organs called **seminiferous tubules**, which contain **spermatogonia**, the precursors of spermatozoa formation. The interstitial cells, situated among the twisted seminiferous tubules, secrete **testosterone** under the stimulus of pituitary LH (also called **interstitial cell stimulating hormone, ICSH,** in mature males). This predominantly male sex hormone does not become plentiful until puberty. Like the other endocrine hormones, testosterone is secreted into the bloodstream and comes into contact with all parts of the body.

Testosterone serves diverse functions. In the testes, its principal role is to promote **spermatogenesis**, the division of spermatogonia within the seminiferous tubules to produce haploid spermatozoa (see **Chapter 25**). Testosterone also promotes the development of secondary sex characteristics, which, in adolescent males, include deepening of the voice; growth of facial, axillary, and pubic hair; and enlargement of the penis and scrotum.

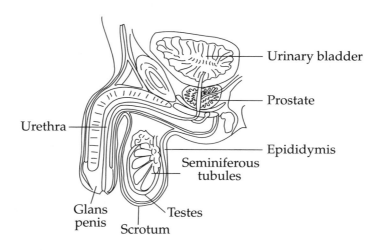

Male Reproductive System

Figure 30.13

Please solve this problem:

- Which of the following would most likely result from impaired secretion of testosterone in the mature male?

    A. Degeneration of the testes
    B. Sudden and pronounced feminization
    C. Absence of gamete production
    D. Increased metabolic rate

Problem solved:

C is correct. Testosterone promotes spermatogenesis in the seminiferous tubules, leading to production of spermatozoa, or the male gametes. If testosterone secretion is impaired, the gametes will not be produced. Sudden and pronounced feminization does not accompany impaired testosterone secretion in a mature male. (A degree of feminization may be achieved in the mature male by exogenous administration of female sex hormones.) The testes do not degenerate in the absence of testosterone. The metabolic rate bears no direct connection to testosterone secretion.

THE HYPOTHALAMUS

The hypothalamus is a portion of the diencephalon of the forebrain. It releases several hormones that control secretions from the pituitary gland. The hypothalamus provides neural input and central control of the endocrine glands outside of the brain. The hypothalamus serves as a high-level coordinating and regulating center for both the endocrine system and the autonomic nervous system. It integrates a variety of information from the **cerebral cortex** and **limbic systems,** and regulates output from the pituitary glands.

THE PITUITARY GLAND

The **pituitary gland** is a small structure on the underside of the brain; like the hypothalamus, it is part of the diencephalon of the forebrain. The pituitary gland has two halves. The front half is called the **anterior pituitary** and the back half is called the **posterior pituitary**.

THE ANTERIOR PITUITARY

The anterior pituitary secretes six peptide hormones. Four of them play a key role in controlling other endocrine secretions; these **tropic hormones** act as chemical switches, stimulating or inhibiting other endocrine glands:

(1) **Thyroid-stimulating hormone (TSH)**: Stimulates the thyroid gland to secrete thyroid hormone.

(2) **Adrenocorticotropic hormone (ACTH)**: Stimulates the adrenal cortex to secrete cortisol.

(3) **Luteinizing Hormone (LH)**: Stimulates the gonads (ovaries or testes) to promote sex hormone secretion and gamete production.

(4) **Follicle Stimulating Hormone (FSH)**: Stimulates the gonads (ovaries or testes) to promote sex hormone secretion and gamete production.

In addition to hormones that regulate the release of other hormones at a distant gland, the anterior pituitary secrets two other hormones that interact directly with certain target organs:

(5) **Growth hormone (GH)**: Influences the development of skeletal muscle, bone, and organs in infants and children. Without growth hormone, children fail to develop normally. GH is also known as **somatotropin (STH).**

(6) **Prolactin**: Directly targets the female breasts, where it stimulates breast development and milk production.

THE POSTERIOR PITUITARY

The posterior pituitary secretes two peptide hormones. These hormones are not synthesized in the posterior pituitary; they are made in neural soma in the hypothalamus and transported via vesicles down axons to the posterior pituitary. They are stored in the posterior pituitary, from which they are released directly into the bloodstream as needed. The two hormones secreted by the posterior pituitary are:

(1) **Antidiuretic hormone (ADH)**: Discussed previously, in connection with the kidney. It is also known as **vasopressin**.

(2) **Oxytocin**: Released at childbirth (parturition), causing the uterus to contract and push the fetus through the birth canal.

Please solve this problem:

- Which of the following would most likely be observed in a patient who secretes excessive quantities of thyroid hormone?

  A. Decreased cellular uptake of oxygen
  B. Decreased cellular uptake of glucose
  C. Increased cellular production of carbon dioxide and water
  D. Increased blood pH

Problem solved:

C is correct. Thyroid hormone acts to increase metabolic rate—to increase the rate at which cells burn fuel. The patient who secretes excessive quantities of thyroid hormone is hypermetabolic, burning fuel at a greater rate than normal. The burning of fuel produces carbon dioxide and water, since in aerobic respiration, oxygen serves as the ultimate oxidizing agent (electron acceptor). The increased metabolic rate would likely be associated with an increase—not a decrease—in uptake of oxygen and glucose. Hyperthyroidism does not ordinarily affect blood pH. Any tendency it might have to do so, however, would bring about a decrease, not an increase, in pH. The increased production of carbon dioxide would promote increased formation of carbonic acid, which, on dissociation, reduces pH (increases hydrogen ion concentration).

Please solve this problem:

- A tumor that secretes aldosterone would most likely lead to:

  A. an increased concentration of potassium in the urine.
  B. an increased concentration of potassium in the blood.
  C. an increased urinary output.
  D. a decreased metabolic rate.

Problem solved:

A is correct. Tumors commonly secrete hormones—often in an unpredictable and uncontrollable fashion. These hormones produce effects normally associated with the particular hormones. Aldosterone promotes an exchange of sodium and potassium ions between the distal tubular filtrate and the surrounding interstitium: Potassium moves into the tubular filtrate, to be excreted in the urine, and sodium moves out of the tubule, producing increased sodium concentration in the interstitium and a relative increase in the amount of water reabsorbed from the tubules. Aldosterone (a) increases urinary potassium concentration, (b) decreases extracellular potassium concentration, (c) decreases urinary sodium concentration, (d) increases extracellular sodium concentration, (e) decreases the volume of urine, and (f) increases body fluid volume.

Please solve this problem:

- A decrease in parathyroid hormone secretion will lead to:

    A. depletion of bone.
    B. an increased sodium concentration in the blood.
    C. a decreased calcium concentration in the blood.
    D. a decreased metabolic rate.

Problem solved:

C is correct. Parathyroid hormone increases calcium concentration in the blood by promoting (a) resorption of bone (which releases calcium into the blood), (b) calcium absorption in the digestive tract, and (c) calcium reabsorption in the kidney. A deficiency of parathyroid hormone will lead to a decreased calcium concentration in the blood.

Please solve this problem:

- The adrenal medulla releases:

    A. insulin and glucagon.
    B. epinephrine and norepinephrine.
    C. glucocorticoids, mineral corticoids, anabolic hormones, and sex hormones.
    D. aldosterone.

Problem solved:

B is correct. Functionally, the adrenal medulla and the adrenal cortex are two separate endocrine glands; anatomically they are adjoined. The cortex (not the medulla) secretes corticosteroids, which include the mineralocorticoids (aldosterone, for example), the glucocorticoids (cortisol, for example), the anabolic hormones, and the sex hormones. The adrenal medulla releases epinephrine (adrenaline) and norepinephrine (noradrenaline). Insulin and glucagon are secreted by the pancreas, not the adrenal gland.

Regulation of the Endocrine System

Hormone release is controlled via three mechanisms. First, the hypothalamus and the pituitary gland (both anterior and posterior) are the higher regulatory organs of the endocrine system; many of the hormones they secrete control other endocrine glands. Therefore, many functions of the endocrine system depend on instructions from the brain.

In addition, hormones can regulate other hormones and many endocrine secretions are part of a pathway that is master regulated. Hormones that control the release of other hormones are called **trophic hormones**. For example, cortisol release (also discussed below) is controlled by corticotropin-releasing hormone (CRH) release from the hypothalamus and adrenocorticotropic hormone (ACTH) release from the anterior pituitary. Thyroid hormone levels are controlled by thyrotropin-releasing hormone (TRH) from the hypothalamus and thyroid stimulating hormone (TSH) from the anterior pituitary. Release of the sex hormone (androgens, estrogens, and progesterone) from the gonads (testes and ovaries) is controlled by gonadotropin-releasing hormone (GnRH) from the hypothalamus and the gonadotropins (luteinizing hormone, LH, and follicle stimulating hormone, FSH) from the anterior pituitary. CRH, ACTH, TRH, TSH, GnRH, LH and FSH are all trophic hormones and are only some examples of the tropic hormone cascades in the human body.

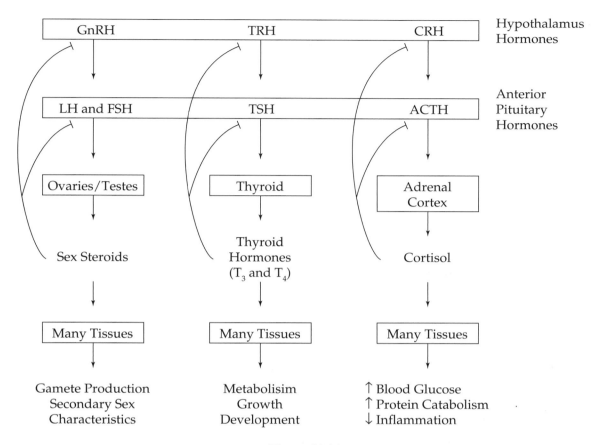

Figure 30.14

Finally, hormone levels are controlled by feedback regulation, especially negative feedback. There are two major divisions of feedback regulation:

(1) *A change in physiological status in response to a hormone can feed back to the endocrine gland to stop hormone secretion.* In other words, the physiological end point can shut off the signal that was trying to achieve it. For example, the hormone calcitonin is released from the thyroid when serum concentrations of calcium (Ca^{2+}) are above normal. Calcitonin inhibits osteoclasts (the cells that destroy bone by dissolving calcium phosphate crystals) and decreases calcium reabsorption in the kidney. This results in lower serum $[Ca^{2+}]$; the falling serum calcium levels feed back to the cells in the thyroid, which release calcitonin and calcitonin secretion drops. In this case, the physiological end point (decreased serum calcium levels) inhibited the release of a hormone (calcitonin) trying to achieve it. Parathyroid hormone (PTH) released from the parathyroid gland and insulin released from the pancreas are also regulated via this simple endocrine reflex; PTH is secreted when serum calcium levels are low; it causes an increase in blood calcium levels and this causes inhibition of PTH release. Insulin is secreted in response to high blood glucose levels; insulin causes glucose uptake and metabolism, and the resultant decrease in blood glucose inhibits insulin release.

(2) *Hormones can cause feedback regulation to the higher regulatory organs (hypothalamus and pituitary gland) that are controlling their release.* As discussed above, the hypothalamus and the pituitary gland are master regulators of the endocrine system. When they are controlling the release of a hormone, the hormone can feed back to these areas of the brain. For example, stress is the stimulus that causes corticotropin-releasing hormone (CRH) release from the hypothalamus, which causes adrenocorticotropic hormone (ACTH) release from the anterior pituitary. ACTH regulates the

release of cortisol from the adrenal cortex, and cortisol mediates the long-term stress response by increasing blood glucose levels, increasing protein catabolism, and inhibiting inflammation. Cortisol also feeds back to the brain to inhibit release of CRH and ACTH.

Overall, feedback loops are complex and intricate and sometimes depend on concentration thresholds.

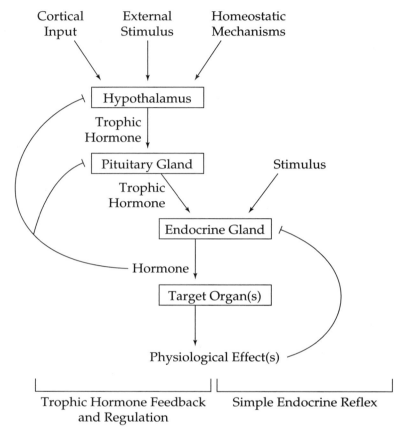

Figure 30.15

Please solve this problem:

- The hypothalamus affects secretion of corticosteroids by releasing:

  A. enzymes that catalyze secretory reactions in the adrenal cortex.
  B. catecholamines.
  C. thyroid-releasing hormone.
  D. corticotropin-releasing hormone (CRH).

Problem solved:

D is correct. Corticosteroids are released from the adrenal cortex, which is stimulated by adrenocorticotropic hormone (ACTH) released from the anterior pituitary. The anterior pituitary releases ACTH in response to the release of CRH from the hypothalamus.

THE NERVOUS SYSTEM

Cell Biology and the Nervous System: The Neuron

Nerves, ganglia, and the brain are composed of clusters of nerve cells, or neurons. In this section, we will review the cell biology of the neuron, and then discuss how these cells transmit electrochemical signals called action potentials. The we will discuss how a specialized cell structure called the myelin sheath affects action potential propagation. Finally, we will discuss how a neuron communicates with other neurons or its target tissue via a chemical signal.

NEURON STRUCTURE AND FUNCTION

The **neuron,** or nerve cell, is the fundamental cellular unit of the nervous system. In addition to the organelles normally found in eukaryotic cells, the neuron contains a number of unique organelles specialized for the transmission of electrical impulses. Cytoplasmic extensions of the cell, called **dendrites,** act like antennae, or sensors: They receive stimuli. A single, elongated cytoplasmic extension, known as the **axon** (or nerve fiber), is specialized to transmit signals. The distal end of the axon bears small extensions called **synaptic terminals,** which contain **synaptic vesicles.** The synaptic vesicles store **neurotransmitters,** the molecules that transmit chemical signals from one neuron to the next. In some situations, a neurotransmitter will exert an excitatory effect on a neuron, while in others, it will have an inhibitory effect.

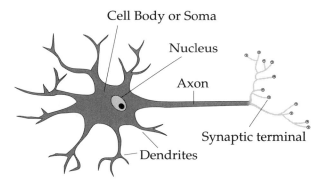

Specialized Features of the Neuron

Figure 30.16

Please solve this problem:

- If two neurons communicate in series, then the signal from one neuron reaches the other neuron via:

  A. direct contact between synaptic terminals.
  B. direct contact between axons of the first neuron and dendrites of the second neuron.
  C. release of a chemical by the first neuron and its receipt by the second neuron.
  D. direct contact between each neuron and an interneuron.

Problem solved:

C is correct. One neuron relays its message to the next by releasing a chemical messenger, called a neurotransmitter, from synaptic vesicles. Direct contact is not a means of communication between two neutrons. Rather, the neurotransmitter is released from the axon's synaptic terminal into the synaptic space, and binds to receptors on the plasma membrane of the second neuron.

NEURONAL RESTING POTENTIAL

Like all human cells, neurons express and constantly operate an energy-dependent sodium-potassium pump (Na^+–K^+ ATPase) that moves two potassium ions into the cell and three sodium ions out of the cell, across the plasma membrane. Across the neuronal membrane, then, there exists an imbalance of ion concentrations and an imbalance of charge. As in other cells:

(1) Na^+ concentration is higher outside the cell than inside.

(2) K^+ concentration is higher inside the cell than outside.

(3)   The cell's interior cell is electrically negative relative to its exterior.

In an ordinary motor neuron, the imbalance of charge (or the charge gradient) gives the neuronal interior a charge of (approximately) –70 millivolts (mV) relative to the exterior. For that reason, we say that such a neuron's **resting potential** is (approximately) –70 millivolts.

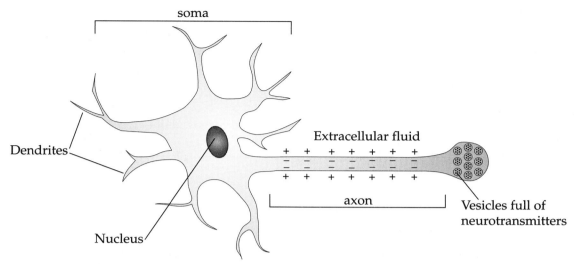

soma

Dendrites

Nucleus

Extracellular fluid

+ + + + + + +
− − − − − − −
+ + + + + + +

axon

Vesicles full of
neurotransmitters

The Interior of a Resting Neuron Is Negative Relative to its Exterior

Figure 30.17

Please solve this problem:

• A resting neuron may have which of the following
  electrical potentials across its membrane?

A. 0 mV
B. +50 mV
C. +20 mV
D. −70 mV

Problem solved:

D is correct. The relative excess of positive charges outside the cell compared to the inside (as a result of the action of the sodium–potassium pump) gives rise to a negative electrical potential across the membrane (as measured from the inside of the cell).

Please solve this problem:

- Which of the following correctly characterizes a neuron's resting potential?

  A. It is maintained by passive diffusion.
  B. It is maintained by an ATP-dependent mechanism.
  C. It creates a relative negative charge outside the neuronal membrane.
  D. It is attributable to a transmembrane calcium imbalance.

Problem solved:

B is correct. The neuron's resting potential is maintained by an uneven distribution of cations across the membrane. The uneven distribution is not a stable situation, since passive diffusion tends to eliminate electrical and chemical gradients. Rather, the cell must expend energy to maintain it, which requires ATP. This is an example of primary active transport.

Initiating an Action Potential

When a neuron is in its resting, unexcited state, its membrane is largely impermeable to sodium and somewhat permeable to potassium due to the presence of **potassium leak channels.** If some electrical, chemical, or mechanical event causes the dendritic membrane to increase its sodium permeability, sodium ions flow down their gradient and into the cell.

Since sodium ions are positively charged, their inward movement tends also to eliminate the membrane's charge gradient, and the cell's interior thus begins to lose its relative negativity. As the electrical potential within the cell rises from its resting potential of –70 mV *toward* zero, it crosses at some point "along the way" a critical **threshold** (perhaps –50 mV). When the internal charge reaches the threshold potential, the all-important **voltage-gated sodium channels** open.

VOLTAGE-GATED SODIUM CHANNELS AND DEPOLARIZATION

Voltage-gated sodium channels are membrane channels, composed of a protein complex. The word *voltage-gated* refers to the fact that they open and close in response to changes in membrane potential. Voltage-gated sodium channels have three conformations:

(1) Closed: In this conformation, the channel does not allow sodium into the cell.

(2) Open: In this conformation, the channel is activated and open wide, which allows sodium into the cell. The channel opens when the plasma membrane reaches the threshold potential of –50mV.

(3) Inactivated: When the cell has depolarized to +35mV, the voltage-gated sodium channels inactivate. In this conformation, they do not allow sodium into the cell but they are also unable to open. The channel must be reset to the closed conformation before they can open again, which occurs during the absolute refractory period.

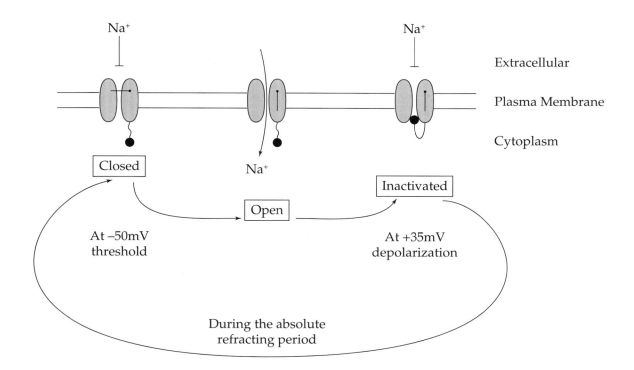

The Voltage-Gated Sodium Channel
Figure 30.18

When the voltage-gated sodium channels are wide open, sodium ions pour into the cell, rapidly raising the potential of the interior above zero to approximately +35 mV. This reversal of membrane potential from –70 mV to +35 mV (due to the influx of sodium ions through the voltage-gated sodium channels) constitutes the first part of an **action potential**.

The depolarization just described occurs at one small portion of the dendritic membrane. Yet the whole of the neuronal membrane, from dendrite through distal axon, houses voltage-gated sodium channels. When depolarization occurs at some small area of the dendrite, the electrical positivity at that small area causes nearby sodium channels to open as well. Sodium rushes into an adjacent portion of the cell, and that portion of the cell depolarizes as well. The positive charge in that portion causes the sodium channels in the next nearby region to open wide, and so that region, too, undergoes depolarization. The whole process propagates itself rapidly down the neuron from dendrite to axon, and in this way, the whole neuron fires an action potential.

It is frequently said that neurons discharge according to an "all-or-nothing" rule, meaning that neurons do not have the capacity to fire with variable intensity. A neuron has no option to fire strongly or weakly. In other words, it cannot depolarize more or less. Neurons either fire an action potential (from –70mV to +35mV) or they do not. Whether or not a neuron generates an action potential depends on whether the initial increase in sodium permeability at the dendrite (however it is caused) produces sufficient change in the membrane potential to reach the threshold. If it does not, then the voltage-gated sodium channels remain closed and no dramatic depolarization occurs. If membrane potential does rise to threshold level (–50mV), the sodium channels open and dramatic depolarization occurs at a small site and rapidly propagates itself along the whole neuron.

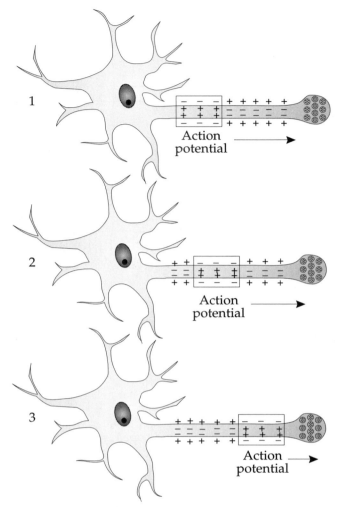

Propagation of a Nerve Impulse Along the Axon

Figure 30.19

VOLTAGE-GATED POTASSIUM CHANNELS AND REPOLARIZATION

At the peak of an action potential (when the cell potential is +35mV), the voltage-gated sodium channels become inactivated. At just about the same moment (or a little before), **voltage-gated potassium channels** open up. With the potassium channels open, potassium ions rush out of the cell along their concentration gradient (created initially by the sodium-potassium ATPase pump).

By moving outward across the neuronal cell membrane, positively charged potassium ions reduce electrical potential within the cell. The cell's interior once again becomes negative and is then said to be **repolarized**. When the potential of the cell reaches –70mV once again, the voltage-gated potassium channels close. However, there is a delay between when these channels should close and when they actually close. Because the voltage-gated potassium channels stay open a little too long, too many potassium ions flow out of the cell and the potential drops to approximately –90mV. During this time, the cell is said to be **hyperpolarized**. After the voltage-gated potassium channels close, the sodium-potassium ATPase and the potassium leak channels steadily bring the membrane back to the resting potential of –70mV.

The phrase "action potential" is used to designate combination of the two sequential events:

(1) Depolarization (–70mV to +35mV) due to sodium inflow, and

(2) Repolarization (+35mV to –70mV) due to potassium outflow.

Once the cell is repolarized, therefore, the action potential is complete. All voltage-gated channels are closed (or are in the process of resetting to the closed conformation) and the ever faithful sodium-potassium pump ($Na^+ – K^+$ ATPase) resumes its function. In a ratio of 3:2, sodium ions move outward and potassium ions move inward. The resting neuron thus recovers and maintains its resting potential and is susceptible, also, to yet another action potential.

THE REFRACTORY PERIODS

At the peak of its action potential, when the cell is fully depolarized, the neuron is wholly unsusceptible to additional stimulation. This continues as the cell is repolarizing. This phenomenon, called the **absolute refractory period,** arises because so many of the neuron's sodium channels are inactivated and cannot reopen until they are reset (or undergo a conformational switch from inactive form to the closed conformation).

Just after the cell passes the –70mV threshold and is hyperpolarized due to the delay of the voltage-gated potassium channels, the cell *is* susceptible to another action potential but requires a stimulus stronger than the one normally needed by a resting cell. This phenomenon, called the **relative refractory period**, arises because the potential of the cell is below that of a resting cell.

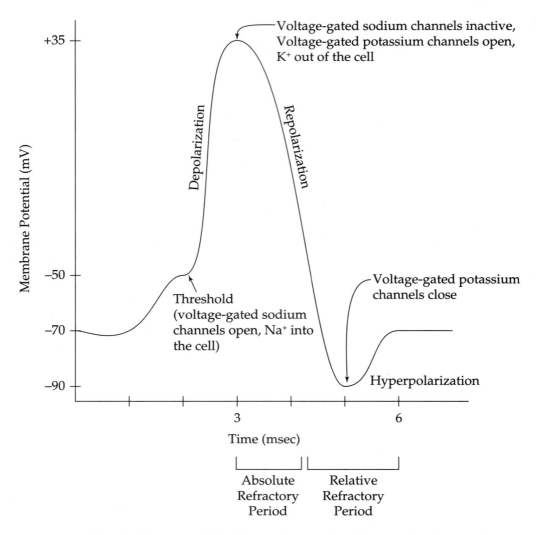

Principal Stages and Ion Flows Associated with an Action Potential
Figure 30.20

Please solve this problem:

- Depolarization of the neuron starts with:
  A. active pumping of sodium inward across the neuronal cell membrane.
  B. a change in the neuronal membrane's potassium permeability.
  C. a change in the neuronal membrane's sodium permeability.
  D. a change in the neuronal membrane's calcium permeability.

Problem solved:

C is correct. Depolarization begins when voltage-gated sodium channels open, allowing sodium to rush into the cell down its gradient.

Please solve this problem:

- Repolarization of the neuron is caused by:
  A. active pumping of sodium inward across the neuronal cell membrane.
  B. a change in the neuronal membrane's potassium permeability.
  C. a change in the neuronal membrane's sodium permeability.
  D. a change in the neuronal membrane's calcium permeability.

Problem solved:

B is correct. Repolarization occurs when potassium voltage-gated potassium channels open in response to the change in membrane potential caused by sodium influx. The loss of positive charge from the interior of the cell reestablishes the resting membrane potential.

SALTATORY CONDUCTION: THE MYELIN SHEATH

Certain neurons can conduct an impulse faster and more efficiently due to the **myelination** of their axons. **Schwann cells** encase long, discrete sections of the axons of neurons in the peripheral nervous system by wrapping layers of their plasma membranes around the axon, creating **myelin sheaths**. A similar function is served by **oligodendrocytes** in the central nervous system. Small areas of the axon remain unmyelinated at regular intervals along the axon's length. These unsheathed areas are called the **nodes of Ranvier**. The highly insulating properties of the myelin serve to block transmission of the depolarizing nerve impulse where myelin sheaths cover the axon, leaving the exposed nodes of Ranvier as the only sites available for electrical propagation along the axon. It is not necessary, then, for depolarization to occur along the entire membrane, a process that would consume a relatively long period of time. Myelin insulation significantly accelerates the transmission of the impulse as depolarization jumps from one node of Ranvier to the next (**saltatory conduction**), effectively skipping across the long, insulated portions of the axon.

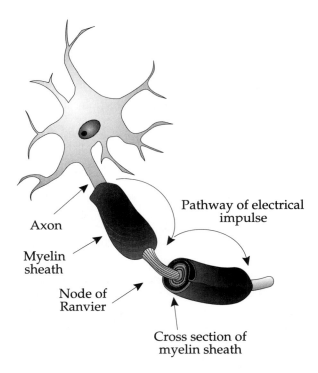

Myelinated Axon Showing Cross Section of Schwann Cell Layers

Figure 30.21

Please solve this problem:

- Nodes of Ranvier are:

    A. exposed areas of axon that permit saltatory conduction.
    B. segments of axon that are encased in Schwann cells.
    C. insulated regions of a myelinated axon.
    D. sections of axon that contain a double membrane.

Problem solved:

A is correct. The insulating properties of the myelin sheaths allow the nerve impulse to jump from one exposed node of Ranvier to the next, permitting more efficient and rapid propagation of the impulse.

Please solve this problem:

- The myelin sheath can be composed of:

  A. a low molecular weight salt.
  B. a high molecular weight salt.
  C. the plasma membranes of Schwann cells.
  D. interneurons.

Problem solved:

C is correct. The myelin sheath of the neurons in the PNS is composed of multiple wrapped layers of Schwann cells. It facilitates saltatory conduction, wherein an impulse jumps from one node of Ranvier to the next. The propagation along a myelinated neuron is much faster than that along an unmyelinated neuron.

IMPULSE TRANSMISSION AT THE SYNAPSE

When the action potential impulse arrives at the end of the axon, it triggers **voltage-gated calcium channels** to open; Ca^{2+} flows into the cell, binds with regulatory proteins and causes exocytosis of neurotransmitter-containing synaptic vesicles: The vesicles fuse with the plasma membrane and neurotransmitter molecules are released from the cell.

The neuron that releases the neurotransmitters is called the **presynaptic neuron** and the neurotransmitters are released from the terminal end of the axonal membrane, called the **presynaptic membrane**. Neurotransmitters are released from the synaptic vesicles into the **synaptic cleft**—the space between the presynaptic membrane and the **postsynaptic membrane**. At the **synapse**, the distance between the two cells is minute enough to permit rapid diffusion of neurotransmitter from the first neuron to either a second neuron or a tissue such as a muscle, gland, or organ. Synaptic transmission is the way in which a neuron can communicate with another cell.

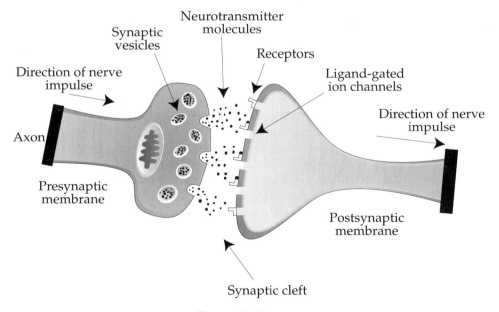

Figure 30.22

After neurotransmitters diffuse across the synaptic cleft, they bind to receptors on the postsynaptic membrane. The receptors on the plasma membrane of the postsynaptic cell are specific to the neurotransmitter. Each postsynaptic neuron can receive signals from many presynaptic neurons, each releasing a different neurotransmitter. For this reason, postsynaptic neurons express receptors for many types of neurotransmitters. However, it is important to remember that each neuron will release only one type of neurotransmitter from its presynaptic axon terminus.

Most postsynaptic receptors are **ligand-gated ion channels**, with specific neurotransmitters serving as ligands. Binding of the neurotransmitter to receptors at the postsynaptic membrane induces a conformational change in the receptors that open ion channels within the membrane. The resulting influx or efflux of ions produces the electrical change that acts as a signal to the neuron. Relatively weak stimuli produce relatively weak signals: Those signals that are below threshold level produce only small, localized depolarizations in the postsynaptic neuron (the "none" of the all-or-none reaction). A signal of sufficient strength to reach threshold level will initiate an action potential (the "all" of the all-or-none reaction).

The nervous system contains more than thirty different chemicals that act as neurotransmitters; you must be familiar with two of them:

(1) Acetylcholine triggers skeletal muscle contraction and is degraded by the enzyme **acetylcholinesterase**.

(2) **Epinephrine** (also called adrenaline) increases heart rate and blood pressure and decreases metabolic activity, such as that of the smooth muscle of the digestive system. Epinephrine is oxidized and methylated to inactive metabolites by **monoamine oxidase (MAO)** and **catechol-O-methyl transferase (COMT)**, respectively.

Please solve this problem:

- Which of the following statements does NOT accurately describe events associated with the neural impulse?

    A. Ligand-gated channels open upon binding of postsynaptic receptors with the appropriate neurotransmitter.
    B. Voltage-gated channels for potassium open in the course of an action potential, permitting influx of potassium into the neuron.
    C. Voltage-gated channels for potassium open during repolarization, permitting efflux of potassium from the neuron.
    D. Both ligand-gated channels and voltage-gated channels are required for successful transmission of a nerve impulse from one neuron to the next.

Problem solved:

B is correct. Voltage-gated *sodium* channels open during an action potential to allow influx of sodium ions down their concentration gradient. Each of the remaining options is an accurate statement of events occurring during neural transmission.

Please solve this problem:

- Acetylcholine serves as neurotransmitter at autonomic ganglia. What is the effect of acetylcholine on the postsynaptic membrane?

    A. It induces a change that ultimately renders the postsynaptic neuron more permeable to sodium.
    B. It renders the neuron more permeable to epinephrine and norepinephrine.
    C. It induces the production of synaptic knobs.
    D. It induces the production of synaptic vesicles.

Problem solved:

A is correct. When a neurotransmitter (like acetylcholine) crosses the synaptic cleft and reaches the postsynaptic neuron, it can initiate depolarization of the postsynaptic neuron (unless its stimulus is subthreshold). As a result, the postsynaptic neuron increases its permeability to sodium.

Please solve this problem:

- Which of the following would explain the failure of a neurotransmitter to elicit an action potential in a postsynaptic neuron?

    A. The postsynaptic neuron has receptors specific to the neurotransmitter.
    B. The neurotransmitter produces a subthreshold response.
    C. The postsynaptic neuron has been facilitated.
    D. The postsynaptic neuron is an interneuron.

Problem solved:

B is correct. Neuronal response to a stimulus is all or none. If a stimulus fails to reach a threshold, the neuron will not fire. Inadequate quantities of neurotransmitter or the prior inhibition of the neuron may prevent neurotransmitter from initiating depolarization. Facilitation of the neuron would tend to reduce the stimulus necessary to bring about depolarization. That the postsynaptic neuron should be an interneuron does not affect the dynamics just described. Interneurons, like other types of neurons, respond to stimuli in an all-or-none fashion.

The Central and Peripheral Nervous Systems

INTRODUCTION

The human nervous system is comprised of two principal divisions: the **central nervous system (CNS)** and the **peripheral nervous system (PNS)**.

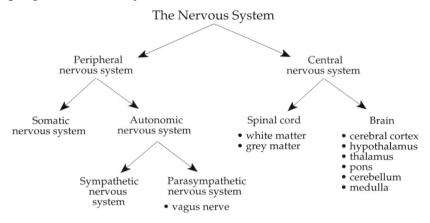

The Divisions and Subdivisions
of the Nervous System

Figure 30.23

The central nervous system consists of all neurons and neuronal connections within, among, and between the brain and spinal cord. The peripheral nervous system consists of all neurons and neuronal connections lying outside the brain and spinal cord. You should understand, however, that the dichotomy between the central and peripheral nervous systems is somewhat artificial. In fact, the two systems are fully connected.

CLASSIFICATION OF NERVE CELL TYPES

When humans register a stimulus (whether consciously or not), information is sent to the CNS, where it is processed, and then from the CNS back to the site of the body that responds to the stimulus. This requires the interaction of several different types of neurons and cells:

(1) **Sensory receptor cells** register a given stimulus, such as a smell or a sound, and gather information.

(2) **Sensory neurons** (also called **afferent neurons**) receive information from the sensory receptors and send it to the central nervous system; in some cases (such as olfactory transduction), the receptor is a modified part of the sensory neuron itself.

(3) In the CNS, one or more **interneurons** receive and process the information. Interneurons are also called **associative neurons** and generally function in relaying signals from neuron to neuron.

(4) **Motor neurons** (also called **effector** or **efferent neurons**) convey signals from the CNS to the target muscle, organ, or gland.

Overall, it is important to remember that **afferent nerves** transmit nerve impulses to the CNS, and **efferent nerves** conduct impulses from the CNS to the muscles or glands.

THE CENTRAL NERVOUS SYSTEM

During embryonic development, the anterior section of the **neural tube** gives rise to the brain, and the posterior portion forms the spinal cord. The brain and spinal cord are connected and communicate with each other. Together, they form the central nervous system (CNS). Both components of the CNS are protected by:

(1) layers of connective tissue (the **meninges**),

(2) bone (the spine and the skull), and

(3) circulating **cerebrospinal fluid (CSF)** that acts as a liquid shock absorber.

THE BRAIN

The embryonic precursors of adult brain structures are the **hindbrain**, the **midbrain**, and the **forebrain**. The hindbrain becomes the **cerebellum**, the **pons**, and the **medulla**. The midbrain gives rise to structures that govern visual and auditory reflexes and coordinate information on posture and muscle tone. The forebrain gives rise to diencephalon (which includes the thalamus, the hypothalamus, and the pituitary gland) and the telencephalon (which includes the cerebrum, the limbic system and the basal nuclei).

The **cerebrum** (not to be confused with the cerebellum) is composed of **two hemispheres** divided by a **longitudinal fissure**. The two hemispheres are connected by a thick bundle of axons called the **corpus callosum**. The cerebrum is the largest portion of the human brain. The cerebral cortex is readily observable as an outer layer of **gray matter** overlying the cerebrum. The gray matter of the cerebral cortex contains neuronal cell bodies (or soma) that conduct the highest of intellectual functions. It integrates and interprets sensory signals of all kinds. The size of the cerebral cortex in humans is unparalleled by that of any other species. This quantity of cortical material correlates with the highly developed functions of language and cognition that distinguish humans from other species. The cerebral cortex also governs voluntary motor activity. The cerebral cortex is divided into four pairs of lobes: frontal, parietal, temporal, and occipital.

Situated on the underside of the brain is the hypothalamus, which maintains homeostasis through hormonal regulation. Posterior to the hypothalamus is the thalamus, which relays information between the spinal cord and the cerebral cortex. The pons serves to connect the spinal cord and medulla with upper regions of the brain. The medulla is connected to the pons above and to the spinal cord below.

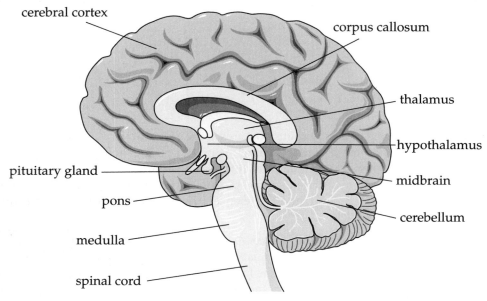

Figure 30.24

Each area of the CNS is responsible for certain functions. These are summarized below:

Structure	Subdivision (if applicable)	Function
Spinal cord	n/a	• simple spinal reflexes (example: deep tension reflex) • control of primitive processes (examples: walking, urination, sex organ function)
Medulla	Hindbrain	• controls autonomic processes like blood pressure, heart beat, respiratory rate, vomiting
Pons	Hindbrain	• some autonomic control • also controls anti-gravity posture and balance
Cerebellum	Hindbrain	• integrating center • coordination of complex movement, balance, and posture
Midbrain	n/a	• integration of visual and auditory information • wakefulness
Thalamus	Forebrain diencephalon	• somatic/conscious sensation

Hypothalamus	Forebrain diencephalon	• homeostasis (example: temperature) • primitive emotions (example: hunger, rage, sex drive)
Pituitary	Forebrain diencephalon	• homeostasis via hormone release • controlled by the hypothalamus • 2 peptide hormones from the posterior pituitary • 6 peptide hormones from the anterior pituitary
Basal nuclei	Forebrain telencephalon	• regulate body movement
Limbic System	Forebrain telencephalon	• emotion
Cerebral cortex (in general)	Forebrain telencephalon	• intelligence, communication, memory, planning, reading, voluntary movement, abstract thought • left side controls speech and motor function on the right side of the body; is dominant in most people • right side controls visual spatial reasoning and music, and motor function on the left side of the body
Frontal lobes	Forebrain telencephalon	• voluntary movement • complex reasoning skills • problem solving
Parietal lobes	Forebrain telencephalon	• general sensation (examples: touch, temperature, pressure) • gustation (taste)
Temporal lobes	Forebrain telencephalon	• auditory and olfactory sensation • short-term memory
Occipital lobes	Forebrain telencephalon	• visual sensation and processing
Corpus callosum	n/a	• connects the left and right cerebral hemispheres

Functions of the Central Nervous System

Table 30.2

Please solve this problem:

- A patient who shows loss of balance and the inability to perform tasks that call for rapid and refined coordination of musculature most likely suffers from dysfunction at which of the following sites?

  A. Cerebellum
  B. Corpus callosum
  C. Medulla
  D. Hypothalamus

Problem solved:

A is correct. The cerebellum controls such functions as balance and the ability to perform tasks that call for rapid and refined coordination of musculature. (Sewing and piano playing are examples of such activities).

Please solve this problem:

- A patient who shows loss of ability to think abstractly most likely has a lesion affecting the:

  A. cerebral cortex.
  B. hypothalamus.
  C. thalamus.
  D. spinal cord.

Problem solved:

A is correct. The processes of abstract thought are most closely associated with the cerebral cortex. A grossly observable loss in that regard is almost certainly associated with a lesion of the cerebral cortex.

Please solve this problem:

- In humans, appetite and body temperature are controlled by the:

  A. cerebellum.
  B. cerebrum.
  C. medulla.
  D. hypothalamus.

Problem solved:

D is correct. The hypothalamus maintains homeostasis, adjusting body temperature, fluid balance, and appetite. It governs autonomic functions and links the endocrine and nervous systems. The cerebellum governs posture, muscle tone, and equilibrium. The cerebrum controls complex integrative processes, such as learning, memory, and reasoning. The medulla regulates blood pressure, heart beat, and respiration, and controls reflex activity, such as sneezing.

THE SPINAL CORD AND THE SIMPLE REFLEX ARC

The spinal cord governs simple motor reflexes. It relays information from other sites of the body to the brain and from the brain to other sites of the body. The interior of the spinal cord contains **gray matter,** which is composed of cell bodies of spinal cord neurons. The exterior is composed of **white matter**, or **myelinated spinal cord axons**. White matter derives its name from the pale appearance of **myelin**, which insulates the axons.

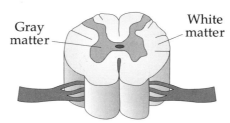

Gray matter

White matter

Cross Section of a Spinal Cord
Showing White and Gray Matter

Figure 30.25

Please solve this problem:

- Gray matter refers to:

  A. the substance of the cerebral cortex.
  B. the substance of the spinal cord.
  C. neuronal axons within the central nervous system.
  D. neuronal cell bodies within the central nervous system.

Problem solved:

D is correct. As it happens, the cell bodies of most neurons within the central nervous system have a grayish appearance on gross inspection. Within the brain and the spinal cord alike, the gray matter generally refers to the cell bodies of the enormous numbers of neurons that are situated there. White matter refers to the myelinated axons of these neurons.

A **simple reflex arc**—like the Achilles reflex or a patellar reflex (knee-jerk response)—requires two neurons. In the course of either one of the simple reflex arcs mentioned, a tap on the tendon stretches the attached muscle fibers. Specialized endings of affector (or sensory) neurons, called **stretch receptors**, are wrapped around individual muscle fibers and register the tap-induced fiber stretch. The sensory neuron synapses with the dendrites of a motor neuron, which then sends an axonal impulse to the muscle fiber bundle. The motor neuron's impulse causes the release of the neurotransmitter **acetylcholine** at the site where the neuron synapses with the muscle (the **neuromuscular junction**). The acetylcholine release begins the series of steps culminating in muscle fiber contraction.

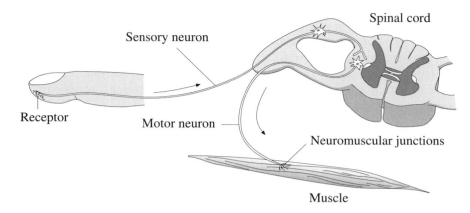

Anatomical Basis of Simple Reflex Arc

Figure 30.26

Please solve this problem:

- Cite the components involved in the Achilles reflex and describe their respective functions.

Problem solved:

A simple reflex arc is a monosynaptic reflex requiring sensory receptors, a sensory neuron, and a motor neuron. Tapping on a muscle's tendon with a mallet will cause its fibers to stretch. The stretch of the fibers is registered by sensory neuron stretch receptors located on the muscle. The neuron transmits the stretch signal to the central nervous system (spinal cord), where it synapses with a motor neuron. The motor neuron then transmits its signal back to the muscle, releasing acetylcholine at the neuromuscular junction and causing the muscle to contract.

Please solve this problem:

- Which of the following is not normally a component of a simple reflex arc?

    A. An efferent neuron
    B. An afferent neuron
    C. An interneuron
    D. The peripheral nervous system

Problem solved:

C is correct. A simple reflex arc involves one afferent neuron (with specialized receptors at its dendritic end), and one efferent neuron, which synapses with the afferent neuron in the spinal cord. It does not involve any interneurons (or associative neurons). Since the important parts of this pathway lie outside the brain and spinal cord, the simple reflex arc is said to belong to the peripheral nervous system.

THE PERIPHERAL NERVOUS SYSTEM

The peripheral nervous system (PNS) conveys information to and from the central nervous system (CNS). It is divided into the **somatic nervous system** and the **autonomic nervous system**.

The afferent neurons of the somatic nervous system receive information from sensory receptors for pain, touch, temperature, and proprioception (awareness of body position in space, and the relative location of body parts to each other). The efferent neurons innervate skeletal muscle by releasing the neurotransmitter acetylcholine. The somatic nervous system governs voluntary activities that we can consciously control.

The autonomic nervous system controls involuntary actions, such as those of the digestive, respiratory, circulatory, and excretory systems. The autonomic nervous system has two subdivisions: **the parasympathetic nervous system** and the **sympathetic nervous system**. Many organs are innervated by both of these systems, which exert opposing effects. Cardiac muscle, smooth muscle, and the endocrine glands are innervated by the autonomic nervous system.

In the autonomic nervous system, there are two efferent (or motor) neurons that work together to send instructions from the CNS to the organs, glands and muscle (cardiac and smooth only) of the body. The first (the **preganglionic neuron**) has its cell body in the brainstem or the spinal cord. It synapses with the postganglionic neuron and releases acetylcholine. The postganglionic neuron can release acetylcholine or norepinephrine to control the effector tissue. Note that a **ganglion** is a cluster of nerve cell bodies in the PNS.

The sympathetic nervous system prepares the body for the "fight or flight" response, for example, in times of crisis. When activated, it increases heart rate and blood pressure, and temporarily inhibits the **vegetative functions**, like gastrointestinal motility and digestive secretion. In contrast, the parasympathetic nervous system decreases the heart rate and increases digestive activity. The **vagus nerve** is part of the parasympathetic nervous system. It sends parasympathetic innervation to the thoracic and abdominal regions. One of the major effects of vagus nerve innervation is slowing down the heart rate, below the rate that is automatically generated by the SA node.

A summary of the two branches of the autonomic nervous system is below:

	Sympathetic	Parasympathetic
Functions		
General	Fight and flight, mobilize energy	Rest and digest; store energy
Heart rate	Increased	Decreased
Pupils	Dilate	Constrict
Vision	Favors far vision	Favors near vision
GI tract	Inhibit mobility	Stimulate mobility
Bladder	Inhibit	Stimulate
Bronchial smooth muscle	Relaxed, therefore open to facilitate deep breathing	Constricted, therefore closed to facilitate shallow breathing
Structure		
Origin of pre-ganglionic neuron	Thoracic and lumbar spinal cord	Brainstem and sacral spinal cord
Length of pre-ganglionic neuron	Short	Long
Neurotransmitter released by the pre-ganglionic ntm	Acetylcholine	Acetylcholine
Length of post-ganglionic neuron	Long	Short
Neurotransmitter released by the post-ganglionic ntm	Norepinephrine (in most cases)	Acetycholine

The Two Branches of the Autonomic Nervous System

Table 30.3

Please solve this problem:

- Which of the following statements is false?

    A. The parasympathetic and sympathetic nervous systems are subdivisions of the autonomic nervous system.
    B. The somatic and the autonomic nervous systems are subdivisions of the sympathetic nervous system.
    C. The spinal cord and the brain are constituents of the central nervous system.
    D. The peripheral and the central nervous systems constitute the two broad divisions of the nervous system.

Problem solved:

B is correct. The somatic and autonomic nervous systems are subdivisions of the peripheral nervous system. The other three statements characterizing the subdivisions of the nervous system are accurate.

Please solve this problem:

- The vagus nerve is a principal component of the parasympathetic nervous system. Excessive activity of the vagus nerve would most likely produce:

    A. high heart rate and blood pressure.
    B. an impaired cough and gag reflex.
    C. failure of the stomach to secrete hydrochloric acid.
    D. abdominal cramping and diarrhea.

Problem solved:

D is correct. The parasympathetic and sympathetic nervous systems are components of the autonomic nervous system. The sympathetic system mediates the "fight or flight" response, tending to increase heart rate and blood pressure. The parasympathetic system controls such functions as coughing, gagging, digestion, and parturition. Hyperactivity of the vagus nerve would be expected to enhance motility of the digestive tract, producing abdominal cramping and diarrhea. Choices B and C describe what would be expected with deficient activity of the vagus nerve.

Please solve this problem:

- A given neuron emanates from the spinal cord and synapses directly with a skeletal muscle cell. Which of the following correctly characterizes the neuron?

    A. It is an efferent neuron.
    B. It is an afferent neuron.
    C. It belongs to the sympathetic nervous system.
    D. It belongs to the parasympathetic nervous system.

Problem solved:

A is correct. If a neuron conducts its impulse from the central nervous system to the periphery (a skeletal muscle, for example), it is an efferent, or effector, neuron. An afferent neuron conducts its impulse toward the central nervous system. Because the neuron lies, for the most part, outside the brain and spinal cord, it is a part of the peripheral nervous system, not the central nervous system. It belongs to the somatic, and not to the autonomic, nervous system because it controls the movement of voluntary (skeletal) muscle. Therefore, it belongs to neither the sympathetic nor the parasympathetic system, both of which are components of the autonomic nervous system.

THE SENSORY ORGANS

Humans can respond to five types of stimuli: **tactile (touch)**, **olfactory (smell)**, **gustatory (taste)**, **auditory (hearing)**, and **visual**. Sensory receptors provide the organism with crucial information about its environment. The sensory receptors convey information to the organism in the form of action potentials that carry the information to the central nervous system. There are several types of sensory receptors:

(1) **Mechanoreceptors** respond to mechanical disturbances. These include **stretch receptors**, **tactile receptors**, **proprioceptors** (which provide cues to changes in pressure or tension in muscles), and **auditory receptors**.

(2) **Chemoreceptors** respond to particular chemicals, and register taste and smell. For example, the hairlike projections of the **taste receptors**, located in the taste buds, are sensitive to molecules in the mouth. The four basic types of gustatory receptors register sourness, sweetness, saltiness, and bitterness. **Olfactory receptors** are also chemoreceptors. They are located in the olfactory epithelium of the nasal cavity and detect airborne chemicals. Olfactory receptors allow us to smell things.

(3) **Thermoreceptors** are stimulated by changes in temperature.

(4) **Electromagnetic receptors** are stimulated by electromagnetic waves. In humans, the only examples are the **photoreceptors**: the rods and cones in the eye. Rods are more sensitive to dim light and are responsible for night vision. Cones require abundant light and are responsible for color and high-acuity vision.

(5) **Nociceptors** are pain receptors. They are stimulated by tissue injury.

The Vestibular and Auditory Systems

The ear serves two distinct functions: (1) maintenance of postural equilibrium and (2) reception of sound. There are three basic divisions of the ear—inner, external, and middle. The **inner ear** is the location of the **vestibular apparatus**, which interprets positional information required for maintaining equilibrium. The vestibular apparatus consists of a membranous **labyrinth** situated within the three **semicircular canals**. The semicircular canals are oriented perpendicularly to one another. Movement of the head causes movement of fluid within the labyrinths and displacement of specialized hair cells (the **crista**) located in the **ampulla** at the base of the semicircular canals. The direction and degree of head movement determine the angle and extent of fluid-mediated hair cell displacement, initiating sensory impulses conveyed via the **vestibular nerve** to centers in the cerebellum, midbrain, and cerebrum, where directional movement and position are interpreted.

The auditory system involves all three divisions of the ear. The external (or outer) ear is composed of the **pinna,** which funnels sound waves into the **ear canal**. At the middle ear, sound waves cause vibrations in the **tympanic membrane**, setting into motion the three auditory bones— the **malleus, incus,** and **stapes**. The arrangement of these bones is like that of levers, so that movement of the malleus is amplified by the incus, and movement of the incus is amplified by the stapes. Movement of the stapes is transmitted across the **oval window** into the inner ear, setting up vibrations in the fluid of the **cochlea**, which causes bending of **auditory hair cells** in the **organ of Corti**. The **cochlear nerve** and the vestibular nerve form the two branches of the **acoustic nerve** (**8th cranial nerve**).

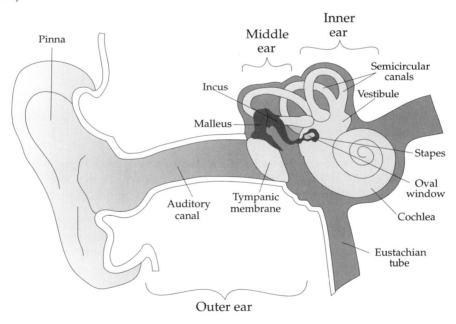

The Structure of the Ear

Figure 30.27

The Visual System

The transmission of light through the human eye follows the following pathway: Light enters the **cornea**, traverses the **aqueous humor**, passes through the **pupil**, and proceeds through the **lens** and the **vitreous humor** until it reaches the light receptors of the **retina**. Electrical signals are then transmitted via the **optic nerve** to visual centers in the brain.

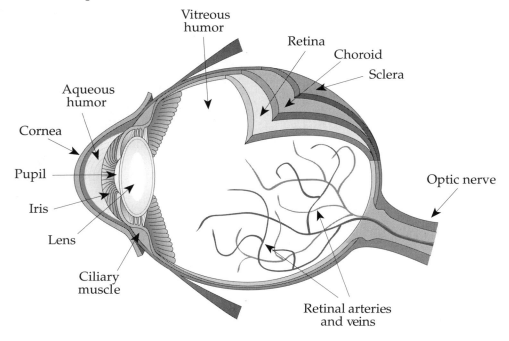

The Structure of the Eye

Figure 30.28

The lens is a transparent structure that focuses light rays on the retina. **Myopia** (nearsightedness) occurs when the lens focuses light from a distant object in front of the retina. **Hyperopia** (farsightedness) occurs when light from a nearby object is focused behind the retina.

The retina senses light rays with two types of photoreceptors located in its outer layer: (1) **rods**, which are specialized to register dim light, and (2) **cones**, which are specialized to register bright light as well as color. Both rods and cones contain pigments, allowing them to absorb energy from light rays. The pigment that mediates rod reception is **rhodopsin**. Cones are subdivided into three types: red-absorbing, blue-absorbing, and green-absorbing. Light reception in cones is mediated by **opsin**, which is similar to rhodopsin.

The **iris**, the colored part of the eye, contains muscles that dilate and constrict to regulate the amount of light that reaches the **retina**. The **ciliary muscle** changes the shape of the lens as the eye shifts its focus from distant to nearby objects.

THE SKIN

Constituting the largest organ in the body, the skin (1) maintains body temperature, (2) registers information from the environment, and (3) provides a barrier against infection. The skin is composed of three layers: the **epidermis**, the **dermis**, and the **subcutaneous** tissue.

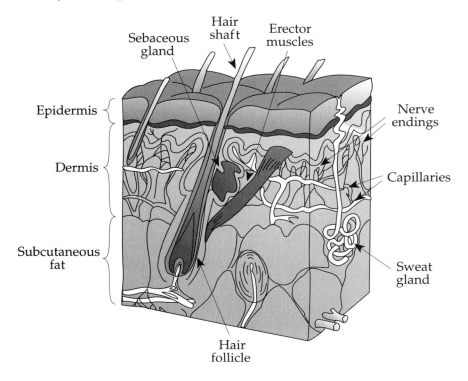

Diagram of Human Skin Showing
Three Dermal Layers

Figure 30.29

The epidermis is composed of stratified squamous epithelium and has a layered, flat cell structure. The external layer of the epidermis is the **stratum corneum**, composed of many layers of dead cells containing the protein **keratin**. The stratum corneum is waterproof and provides resistance to invasion of the body by microorganisms. The stratum corneum continuously renews itself by sloughing off cells, which are replaced by keratinized epithelial cells from deeper layers. Below the stratum corneum, the **stratum germinativum** is where skin cells replicate through mitosis and where keratin is produced. Cells from the germinativum layer migrate upward to the surface, away from the capillary beds that nourish the skin. As they lose contact with capillaries, the cells die and form the layers of the corneum.

The dermis directly underlies the stratum germinativum of the epidermis, and contains the blood vessels, nerve endings, sebaceous glands (which secrete oils), and sweat glands. The sweat glands secrete water and ions in response to high temperatures and sympathetic stimulation, serving to maintain a stable body temperature and optimal balance of sodium and chloride ions in the body. Subcutaneous tissue contains primarily **adipose** (or fat) tissue.

The subcutaneous tissue is also called hypodermis. It is a protective, insulating layer of fat, or adipose tissue.

30.2 MASTERY APPLIED: PRACTICE PASSAGE AND QUESTIONS

Passage

Schizophrenia refers to a group of mental disorders characterized by a disturbance of the thinking processes. The traditional animal model for schizophrenia has been a simple rodent model of amphetamine-induced excitation. When dopamine antagonists such as haloperidol and chlorpromazide (agents that counter the actions of the neurotransmitter dopamine by blocking dopamine receptors) are administered, symptoms of amphetamine-induced excitation in the rodents diminish according to a dose-response relationship. This appears to support the dopamine theory of schizophrenia, which postulates that excessive amounts of dopamine cause the disorder.

While excess dopamine plays a part in the expression of schizophrenia, it does not cause the disorder. Schizophrenia involves numerous neurotransmitter systems. In fact, the frontal cortex systems of schizophrenics are actually hypoactive for dopamine—not hyperactive, as originally proposed. The underactive cortex exerts a reduced modulating influence on the limbic system, producing an increase in dopamine activity in the midbrain.

The N-methyl-D-aspartate (NMDA) subgroup of glutamate receptors is emerging as an important component in the etiology of schizophrenia. The receptor complex modulates calcium channels and contains recognition sites for glutamate, spermidine, and zinc, which act as agonists (exerting excitatory effects) or antagonists (blocking excitatory effects). Glutamate has excitatory effects; in excess, it is toxic and destroys brain tissue.

Glutamate, dopamine, norepinephrine, and serotonin all play a role in the normal function of the brain's frontal cortex. The frontal cortex governs proper functioning of the glutamate pathways descending to the limbic system. The glutamate system, in turn, influences release of dopamine through *tonic leak*, a process in which neurons constantly release a low level of dopamine. Tonic leak maintains dopamine receptors at a normal sensitivity level.

Research with the glutamate antagonist phencyclidine (PCP) (see Figure 1) shows that phencyclidine leads to hypoactivity of the frontal cortex. This causes reduced outflow of glutamate, less NMDA receptor stimulation, decreased tonic signal, and reduced tonic leak. The net result is hypersensitivity to action potentials at the receptor level. Because dopamine is simultaneously associated with hypoactivity at the frontal cortex and hyperactivity at the receptor level, this phenomenon is explained by the *simultaneous dopamine activity/underactivity model.*

A drug that blocks only dopamine would block hyperactivity at the receptor level but would not address the frontal cortex dopamine deficit seen in the phencyclidine model. Serotonin antagonist drugs, such as risperidone and clozapine, correct this problem by blocking serotonin receptors. This has the effect of increasing dopamine activity in the frontal cortex: the dopamine increase restores glutamate levels, allowing a rise in tonic level and producing a reduction in receptor sensitivity. By this mechanism, schizophrenia can be treated with a pure serotonin blocker.

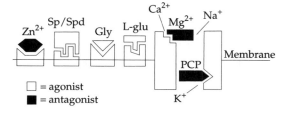

Key:

Sp/Spd = spermidine
Gly = glycine
L-glu = glutamate

Figure 1

1. Which one of the following does NOT occur during an action potential?

   A. Sodium flows into the interior of the neuron.
   B. The neuron becomes depolarized.
   C. The interior of the neuron becomes positive relative to its exterior.
   D. Calcium flows out of the neuron.

2. A physician whose treatment strategy is based on the simultaneous overactivity/underactivity model of schizophrenia would most likely prescribe which of the following therapeutics for patients?

   A. A dopamine antagonist
   B. A serotonin blocker
   C. Haloperidol
   D. Chlorpromazine

3. A researcher testing the dopamine hypothesis of schizophrenia constructs a graph of data points comparing symptoms of amphetamine-induced excitation with dosage of dopamine antagonists administered to the rats. Which of the following graphs would most nearly match the results?

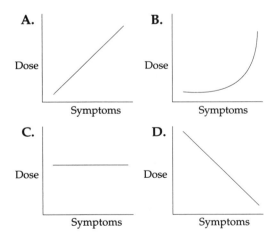

4. The glutamate antagonist phencyclidine has the effect of:

   A. impeding the release of neurotransmitter from synaptic vesicles of neurons.
   B. overstimulating the dendrites of neurons.
   C. blocking the neurotransmitter pathway across the synapse.
   D. accelerating saltatory conduction along the axon of neurons.

5. As a result of tonic leak:

   A. dopamine levels fluctuate from zero to very high across a twenty-four-hour period.
   B. normal neuron sensitivity to neurotransmitter is maintained.
   C. dopamine has toxic effects and destroys tissue.
   D. the glutamate system is maintained at normal functioning.

6. Traditional antipsychotics often produce side effects that require additional medicine that is anticholinergic in nature. The therapeutics given to counter the side effects target which of the following neurotransmitters?

   A. Acetylcholine
   B. Serotonin
   C. Thyroid hormone
   D. Norepinephrine

7. Based on Figure 1, the hallucinogen phencyclidine exerts its effect by:

   A. blocking the outer portion of the NMDA receptor channel.
   B. producing a conformational change in the exterior portion of the receptor channel.
   C. entering and then blocking the open NMDA receptor channel.
   D. competing with the binding of zinc at the zinc receptor site.

30.3   MASTERY VERIFIED: ANSWERS AND EXPLANATIONS

1. **D is correct.** The relevant ion flows associated with an action potential are the influx of sodium and the efflux of potassium, not calcium efflux. Choices A, B, and C are all true statements: During an action potential, a neuron's membrane becomes permeable to the influx of sodium down its concentration gradient and undergoes a depolarization. (The cell's interior undergoes a change in potential relative to the exterior from approximately –70 mV to approximately +50 mV.)

2. **B is correct.** A serotonin blocker increases dopamine activity in the frontal cortex, as outlined in the simultaneous overactivity/underactivity theory described in the passage. Choice A is not correct: A dopamine antagonist would be the therapy of choice according to the dopamine theory of schizophrenia; it does not address the problem of frontal cortex dopamine underactivity, however. Choices C and D are dopamine antagonists, the therapy of choice for the dopamine theory.

3. **D is correct.** The passage states that a dose-dependent relationship exists between a dopamine antagonist and the amphetamine-induced symptoms observed in rodents. Thus, the answer choice can be narrowed down to one that shows a set of data points that rise or fall in uniform increments. The passage also states that the symptoms diminish according to a dose-response relationship. The correct answer must therefore depict an inverse relationship. The graph in choice D shows a uniform inverse relationship between symptom level and dose level. As dose increases, symptoms decrease. Choice A correctly depicts a dose-dependent relationship. However, it does not show an *inverse* relationship. According to this graph, as dose increases, so do symptoms. Therefore, choice A is incorrect. Neither choice B nor choice C shows an inverse relationship. Both are incorrect.

4. **B is correct.** Phencyclidine causes hypersensitivity to action potentials at the receptor level. As such, the dendrites will be more readily stimulated to undergo an action potential. Choice A is incorrect. Phencyclidine causes hypersensitivity of neurons to action potentials; choice A implies the opposite. Choice C is wrong as well. Phencyclidine causes hypersensitivity of neurons to action potentials, and choice C indicates the opposite. Choice D, too, is wrong. The passage states that hypersensitivity of neurons to action potentials is due to increased sensitivity of receptors to dopamine. Neurotransmitter receptors are located on the dendrites of the neuron, not along the axon.

5. **B is correct.** Tonic leak preserves normal sensitivity of neurons to neurotransmitters. Choice A is incorrect: Tonic leak produces a constant low level of dopamine. Choice C is also incorrect: The passage states that high levels of glutamate have toxic effects and damage tissue, while tonic leak refers to low levels of dopamine release. According to the passage, the glutamate system governs the rate of tonic leak, and choice D indicates the opposite.

6. **A is correct.** Anticholinergic drugs oppose the effects of the neurotransmitter acetylcholine. Choice B is incorrect: Although serotonin is a neurotransmitter, it is not affected by anticholinergics. Choice C is incorrect because thyroid hormone is not a neurotransmitter, and anticholinergics do not act upon thyroid hormone. Choice D is wrong as well, since norepinephrine is not acted upon by an anticholinergic.

7. **C is correct.** Figure 1 shows that PCP is able to enter the NMDA receptor channel and then block the channel inside the passageway. Choice A is incorrect: Figure 1 indicates that PCP blocks the inner portion of the NMDA receptor channel, not the outer portion, where magnesium binds. Choice B is incorrect as well. Figure 1 does not indicate that a conformational change occurs at the NMDA receptor channel. Choice D, too, is wrong. According to Figure 1, zinc does not compete with PCP at the zinc receptor site: PCP acts on the receptor channel.

CHAPTER 31

MECHANISMS OF HEREDITY

31.1 MASTERY ACHIEVED

GENES, LOCI, AND ALLELES

The Gene

For MCAT purposes, a gene is a sequence of DNA on a chromosome, which codes for a gene product. There are three gene products:

(1) rRNA, made via transcription,

(2) tRNA, made via transcription, and

(3) polypeptide, made via transcription and translation. The polypeptide for which a gene codes might represent a discrete functional protein or one subunit of a protein, which is functional when all of its subunits are fully assembled. As a general rule, one gene codes for one polypeptide, but remember there may be different forms of the polypeptide in eukaryotes due to alternative splicing (see **Chapter 24**). In most eukaryotic organisms, most genes code for peptides.

Most DNA in a chromosome does not constitute genes; much of the DNA housed within a chromosome serves to regulate the function of other DNA sequences that do code directly for polypeptides. In eukaryotes, there are also non-protein-coding DNA sequences called introns (see **Chapter 24**). Moreover, some chromosomal DNA sequences serve no (presently) known function at all; according to current understanding, only about one percent of the DNA found on a given human chromosome directly codes for polypeptide formation. In other words, all genes contain chromosomal DNA sequences, but not all chromosomal DNA sequences constitute genes. For the rest of this chapter, keep these three important points in mind:

(1) Genes are composed of DNA on chromosomes and can code for one of three final gene products: rRNA, tRNA, or a polypeptide.

(2) The proteins formed via transcription and translation are encoded by DNA on the chromosomes.

(3) An organism's genetic traits are traceable, largely due to the proteins formed by its cells via the processes of transcription and translation.

Please solve this problem:

- In biochemical terms, genes are embodied most directly and immediately in subunits of:

  A. protein.
  B. carbohydrate.
  C. lipopolysaccharide.
  D. nucleic acid.

Problem solved:

D is correct. A gene is composed of units of chromosomal DNA (deoxyribonucleic acid), a nucleic acid. Via the mechanism of transcription followed by translation (**Chapter 24**), genes exert their influence over cellular structure and function by directing, from their "headquarters" in the nucleus, the synthesis of proteins that serve as enzymes and structural components of the cell.

Genetic Loci and Alleles

That area on a chromosome on which a gene is physically located is called a **genetic locus**; the locus of a gene is its address on the chromosome and in the genome.

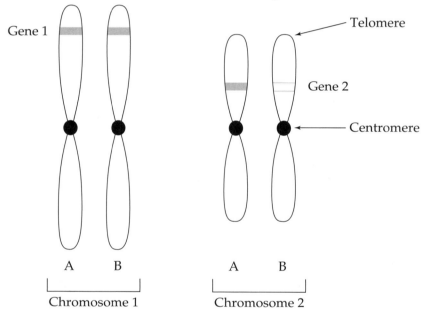

Two Genes, Located at Two Different Loci on Two Different Chromosomes

Figure 31.1

Recall (from **Chapters 24 and 25**) that in diploid organisms, chromosomes ordinarily exist in homologous pairs, with each parent contributing one chromosome to each pair. Homologous chromosomes are the same size and contain the same genes at the same location. However, they may not code for the same versions of each gene. At any given genetic locus, the two chromosomes of a given homologous pair might be:

(a) *identical* in DNA sequence and code for the same form of the gene (shown on Chromosome 1 in Figure 31.1), or

(b) *different* in DNA sequence and code for different versions of the same gene (shown on Chromosome 2 in Figure 31.1).

Different forms or versions of a gene are called **alleles**. Alleles can have different DNA sequences and a given gene can have numerous alleles. However, since humans are diploid, their genome can at most contain two alleles of a given single-copy gene. Some humans contain only one allele of some genes, if both their homologous chromosomes contain the same allele.

Figure 31.1 shows two chromosomes, 1 and 2. For each chromosome, two copies are shown (A and B), as would be present in a diploid organism. The individual that has these chromosomes in their genome would have received or inherited one Chromosome 1 and one Chromosome 2 from their mother and one Chromosome 1 and one Chromosome 2 from their father. The two homologous pairs of Chromosome 1 are the same size and code for the same genes in the same location. The same is true of Chromosome 2.

For Gene 1 on Chromosome 1, the same form of the gene is shown (grey). The DNA sequences of these two copies of Gene 1 are identical and the gene codes for the same gene product. The individual would be called **homozygous** at this locus. In contrast, this individual contains two different alleles of Gene 2 on Chromosome 2 (one grey and one white). These two forms of Gene 2 code for different versions of the gene product and have different DNA sequences. Since this individual expresses two different alleles at this locus, they would be called **heterozygous** for Gene 2. The full complement of alleles possessed by an organism represents its **genotype**.

Please solve this problem:

- Among the following, "allele" is best described as representing:

  A. corresponding regions on homologous chromosomes at which variance may occur as to actual DNA composition.
  B. a length of nucleic acid that codes for a single enzyme that catalyzes the processes of transcription and translation.
  C. a segment of DNA that expresses itself only in the absence of a corresponding segment on a homologous chromosome.
  D. a genetic locus.

Problem solved:

A is correct. In the somatic cells of sexually reproducing eukaryotic organisms, chromosomes exist in homologous pairs. The human nucleus, for example, harbors twenty-two pairs of autosomes and one pair of sex chromosomes, for a total of forty-six chromosomes housed within twenty-three pairs. The two members of each chromosomal pair are "homologous" but not identical. At corresponding locations (genetic loci), the two chromosomes of a homologous pair may or may not be identical. Each of the diverse (two or more) variants of DNA sequence possibly allocated to each locus constitutes an allele.

Please solve this problem:

- One's overall genotype refers to the:
    - **A.** traits and attributes overtly manifest in his/her cellular structure and function.
    - **B.** extent and degree to which his/her alleles create observable traits.
    - **C.** totality of the alleles present on all his/her chromosomes.
    - **D.** degree of identity as to the alleles carried on homologous chromosomal pairs.

Problem solved:

C is correct. As noted in the text, the full complement of alleles possessed by an organism represents its genotype. Alleles vary in the manner and extent to which they express themselves as observable traits, or phenotypes (which is what is described in choices A and B). Phenotype depends on the alleles of genes, but does not define it. It is also true that any given genetic locus on a pair of homologous chromosomes (or for any gene) alleles may be identical or variable (choice D). That truth, however, does not explain the *meaning* of "allele."

SOURCE OF THE GENOTYPE

The alleles carried on the chromosomes of an organism produced via sexual reproduction derive from those carried on the chromosomes of its parents. Human reproduction, for example, follows from the fusion of the two gametes, ova and spermatozoa. Recall from **Chapter 25** that gametes differ from ordinary somatic cells in that they are haploid, not diploid. They contain not twenty-three *pairs* of homologous chromosomes (as do ordinary somatic cells) but twenty-three chromosomes *in total*, unpaired—one *member* from each pair that was present in the diploid parent cell that underwent meiosis.

Fusion of haploid sperm and haploid ovum forms a *diploid* cell (called the zygote) from which a new diploid individual develops. The zygote undergoes mitosis and each daughter cell will have twenty-three *pairs* of chromosomes. At each genetic locus, then, the offspring takes *one allele from its mother* and *one allele from its father*. The offspring's genotype thus reflects the combination of parental alleles.

Distribution of Parental Alleles: The Laws of Segregation and Independent Assortment

Tied to the meiotic process is the **law of segregation.** Recall from **Chapter 25** that homologous chromosomes line up on the metaphase plate, across from each other, in meiotic metaphase I. During anaphase I, homologous pairs of chromosomes separate so that each of the two daughters takes one member of each homologous pair. For every genetic locus on every chromosome of the diploid parent cell, the gamete obtains one allele. Because the homologous chromosomes are separated into separate daughter cells at the end of meiosis I, the cell is haploid from this point onward.

Related to the law of segregation is the **law of independent assortment**, which reflects the phenomenon that at anaphase I, each homologous pair separates independently to the manner in which any other homologous pair separates. Examine Figure 31.2. For simplicity, it shows a cell with four pairs of homologous chromosomes (instead of twenty-three pairs) and the chromosomes are drawn with only one chromatid per chromosome (in other words, the chromosomes are drawn as they would look if they were condensed before DNA replication in the S phase). For each pair, there is a dark-colored chromosome and a light-colored chromosome.

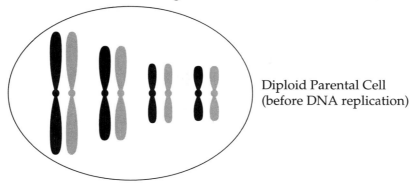

Diploid Parental Cell
(before DNA replication)

Hypothetical Parental Cell with Four Pairs of Homologous Chromosomes

Figure 31.2

When homologous pairs separate at anaphase, it is possible that one daughter cell will receive all the dark-colored chromosomes and the other daughter cell will receive all the light-colored chromosomes. However, it is important to remember that this is just one possibility out of many. In other words, there is no rhyme or reason to the way in which two homologous chromosomes allocate themselves between daughter cells. On one occasion of meiosis in this organism, the chromosomes may align themselves on the spindle apparatus and separate according to this pattern:

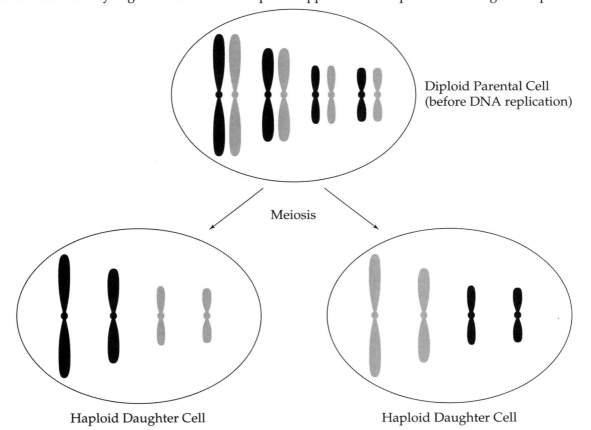

Diploid Parental Cell
(before DNA replication)

Meiosis

Haploid Daughter Cell

Haploid Daughter Cell

One Possible Manner of Chromosomal Assortment During Meiosis I

Figure 31.3

On the next occasion of meiosis, in this same organism, the chromosomes may align themselves on the spindle apparatus and separate according to this pattern:

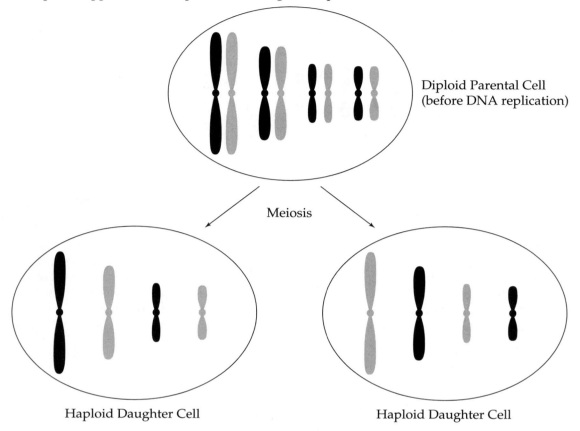

Diploid Parental Cell
(before DNA replication)

Meiosis

Haploid Daughter Cell   Haploid Daughter Cell

A Second Possible Manner of Chromosomal Assortment During Meiosis I

Figure 31.4

On yet a third occasion of meiosis in this same organism, the chromosomes may align themselves on the spindle apparatus and separate according to this pattern:

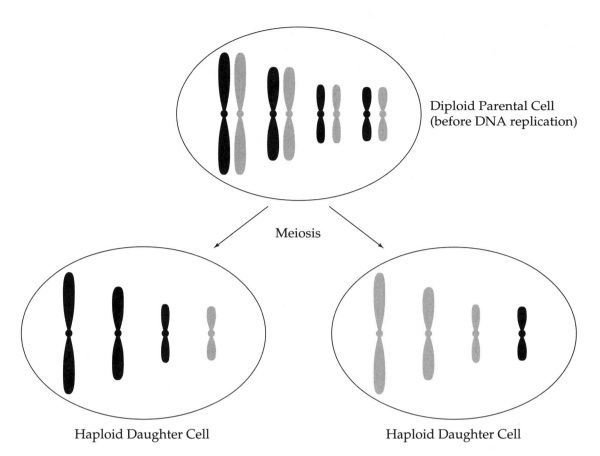

Diploid Parental Cell
(before DNA replication)

Meiosis

Haploid Daughter Cell   Haploid Daughter Cell

A Third Possible Manner of Chromosomal Assortment During Meiosis I

Figure 31.5

Owing to independent assortment, the number of different genotypes that might occur in the gametes produced by a single organism is enormous. In the lifetime of a single human being, for example, the chance that any two meiotic events would create the same two gametes is negligible. For that reason, any two parents have the capacity to create an *enormous* number of genotypically different offspring.

GENOTYPE AND PHENOTYPE

The ultimate significance of genotype lies in the **traits** it produces, meaning the features, attributes, or characteristics that it does (or does not) impart to the organism. Height, color-blindness, and lactose intolerance all constitute "traits." When we discuss an organism's traits, we refer to its **phenotype**. For example, we might say that one individual's phenotype is blue eye color and that another's phenotype is green eye color; eye color is a trait and blue and green are phenotypes that would be associated with different alleles in the genotype. An organism's phenotype is governed by its genotype—by its overall inventory of alleles. More specifically, phenotype comes about according to the way in which combined alleles interact to produce traits.

Consider hypothetical Trait X and two parents—a father who is positive for Trait X and a mother who is negative for Trait X. Depending on the nature of the two inherited alleles and the way in which they interact, the offspring might manifest:

(a) Trait X fully,

(b) Trait X not at all, or

(c) Trait X in some intermediate, attenuated, or hybrid form.

The dynamics through which an individual's genotype creates its phenotype are intimately tied to the phenomena of homozygous and heterozygous genotypic states.

Please solve this problem:

- Which of the following correctly characterizes the relationship between genotype and phenotype?
  - **A.** Genotype is a function of phenotype.
  - **B.** Phenotype is a function of genotype.
  - **C.** Genotype and phenotype are functions of one another.
  - **D.** Genotype and phenotype are related in some individuals, but not in others.

Problem solved:

B is correct. As noted in the text, phenotype is governed by genotype and genotype *creates* phenotype, meaning phenotype is a function of genotype. Choice C might be tempting at first glance because so much of biology involves complex relationships among and between various factors and phenomena, each affecting the other. Nonetheless, choice C is wrong. One's phenotype—his/her complement of traits—does *not* affect his/her genotype (choices A and C are incorrect). It's the other way around; genotype affects phenotype. Furthermore, it does so in all individuals (which is why choice D is wrong).

Homozygous and Heterozygous Genotypes

With respect to a given genetic locus, an individual's two alleles might be identical, meaning that the two alleles inherited from its two parental gametes were identical. Such an individual is **homozygous** with reference to that genetic locus. *The essence of the word* homozygous *refers to an organism whose two alleles for a given locus, or gene, are identical.*

On the other hand, if, for some genetic locus, an organism carries two different alleles on corresponding sites of homologous chromosomes, it is said to be **heterozygous**. The phenomena of homozygous and heterozygous genotypes give phenotypic effect to dominant and recessive alleles.

Please solve this problem:

- If a given individual is heterozygous at a particular gene, then, at that genetic locus, the individual has:

  A. two different alleles.
  B. two identical alleles.
  C. two alleles derived from a single parent.
  D. one allele from one parent and no allele from the other.

Problem solved:

A is correct. A sexually reproduced diploid organism gets one of each of its chromosomes from each of its parents. For every gene at every locus on the autosomes, one allele will be inherited from the father and one from the mother (C is incorrect). If an organism receives two identical alleles for a given locus, it is homozygous (B is incorrect). If an organism receives two different alleles from its parents, it is heterozygous (A is correct). Option D appears to describe an impossible phenomenon, given that half the chromosomes come from an organism's mother and half from the father. However, it is important to note that this is possible, and refers to phenomena that occur only with respect to the sex chromosomes.

Dominant and Recessive Alleles

Consider a hypothetical trait, Trait T. Assume that Trait T appears when the organism manufactures Protein T and does not appear when the organism fails to manufacture Protein T. Finally, suppose that the production or failure to produce Protein T is governed by a particular allele that exists in two forms:

(1) A form (T) that codes for Protein T, and

(2) A form (t) that does not code for Protein T.

Imagine that a particular individual is homozygous for the allele that *does* produce Protein T. We designate her genotype as TT, meaning that at the relevant homologous pair, both chromosomes do code for the production of Protein T. The cells of this individual will manufacture Protein T and she will, therefore, manifest Trait T; her genotype is TT, and her phenotype for trait T is positive.

Imagine another individual who is homozygous for the allele that does *not* code for Protein T. We designate his genotype as tt, meaning that at the relevant homologous pair, both chromosomes fail to code for Protein T. This individual will fail to produce protein T and fail to manifest Trait T. His genotype is tt and his phenotype for trait T is negative.

Now, imagine an individual who is heterozygous for the allele under discussion. We designate the genotype as Tt (or tT), meaning that at the relevant chromosomal pair, one chromosome carries the allele that *does* code for Protein T and the other carries the allele that does *not* code for Protein T. Since one of the two alleles codes for Protein T, this individual will produce Protein T and will consequently manifest Trait T. His genotype is Tt (or tT) and the phenotype for trait T is positive.

Regarding Trait T, we may say that if the individual carries one allele that codes for Protein T (The T allele) and one that does not (the t allele), he/she will manifest Trait T. This means the T allele is **dominant** over the t allele. In the heterozygous individual (genotype Tt), the T allele (positive for the trait) expresses itself in the phenotype and the t allele (negative for the trait) does not. Meanwhile, we say that the t allele is **recessive**. In the presence of the T allele, it does not express itself; it "recedes." The t allele expresses itself (negative for Trait T) only when present on both alleles—only when the individual is homozygous for that allele (tt).

When two alleles interact in the way just described, we say that they exhibit **classical dominance** (or, sometimes, classical **Mendelian** dominance). The essential features and phenomena associated with classical dominance are as follows:

(1) Dominant alleles are denoted by a capital letter and recessive traits are denoted by a lower-case letter.

(2) When an individual is either homozygous for the dominant allele (such as TT) or heterozygous (such as Tt), they express the dominant phenotype (such as T positive).

(3) When an individual is homozygous for the recessive allele (such as tt), they express the recessive trait (such as T negative).

Please solve this problem:

- If, in a given population, the alternative traits of curly hair (H) and straight hair (h) exhibit classic dominance, which of the following genotypes would NOT create a phenotype for curly hair?

  A. HH
  B. Hh
  C. hH
  D. hh

Problem solved:

D is correct. Choice D shows a genotype that features two recessive alleles (hh) and will produce a phenotype for the recessive trait (straight hair). All other choices show genotypes that carry, on at least one chromosome, the dominant allele (H). Choice A depicts a genotype that is homozygous for curly hair. Choices B and C depict equivalent heterozygous genotypes, both of which will create a phenotype for the dominant curly hair trait.

CLASSICAL DOMINANCE, THE PUNNETT SQUARE, AND GENETIC PROBABILITIES

The **Punnett square** can be a useful tool to identify the genotypic combinations that follow from a mating (or **cross**) between two individuals of known genotype, and to find the probability of any one genotype in the offspring.

Consider the trait of eye color and assume that it manifests via classical dominance; the dominant B allele codes for brown eyes and the recessive b allele codes for blue eyes. If a mating occurs between a heterozygous individual and a homozygous recessive individual, the Punnett sequence would look like this:

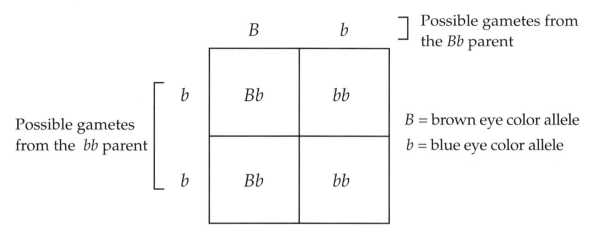

The Punnett Square for a Cross Between a Heterozygous Individual
and a Homozygous Recessive Individual

Figure 31.6

The heterozygous parent can make two different gametes; half the gametes from this individual will contain the B allele and the other half will contain the b allele. These two possibilities are at the top of the Punnett square. The homozygous recessive individual will make gametes that all contain the b allele; these are along the left side of the Punnett square. To fill in the square, you write the combination of alleles you would get by combining the gametes from each of the two parents.

For the offspring, the Punnett square shows two possible genotypes: Bb and bb. Further, it shows, in ideal statistical terms:

(1) fifty percent of offspring will have a Bb genotype and fifty percent will have a bb genotype.

(2) fifty percent of offspring will be brown-eyed (or have the B dominant phenotype) and fifty percent will be blue-eyed (or have the recessive b phenotype).

Although Punnett squares are useful to understand the biology behind genetic crosses, they can sometimes be time-consuming or error prone. Another way to answer monohybrid genetic cross questions (those that involve only one gene) is to know a few probability rules. They are:

Parental Cross	Genotypic Ratio of Offspring	Phenotypic Ratio of Offspring
AA × aa	100% Aa	100% dominant A phenotype
AA × Aa	50% AA 50% Aa	100% dominant A phenotype
Aa × aa	50% Aa 50% aa	50% dominant A phenotype 50% recessive a phenotype
Aa × Aa	25% AA 50% Aa 25% aa This is also called a 1:2:1 ratio	75% dominant A phenotype 25% recessive A phenotype

Table 31.1

It is also useful to know some probability rules for two common dihybrid genetic crosses (those that involve two genes). They are:

Parental Cross	Genotypic Ratio of Offspring	Phenotypic Ratio of Offspring
AaBb × aabb*	25% AaBb 25% Aabb 25% aaBb 25% aabb	25% A and B phenotypes 25% A and b phenotypes 25% a and B phenotypes 25% a and b phenotypes
AaBb × AaBb	n/a**	A 9:3:3:1 ratio of: 9 offspring have the A and B phenotypes 3 offspring have the A and b phenotypes 3 offspring have the a and B phenotypes 1 offspring have the a and b phenotypes

Table 31.2

*This cross can also be called a **testcross**, because one of the individuals is homozygous recessive.

** It is too complicated to predict the genotypic ratios in a heterozygous dihybrid cross. Instead, you would break the cross down into the two separate genes, calculate the probabilities associated with each, and then multiply these two numbers, since you want to include the results from gene 1 *and* gene 2 in your final answer.

Please solve this problem:

- If Trait Z exhibits classic dominance, and one parent is heterozygous and the other is homozygous recessive, then:

    A. approximately 25 percent of offspring will express the dominant phenotype.
    B. approximately 25 percent of offspring will express the recessive phenotype.
    C. approximately 50 percent of offspring will express the recessive phenotype.
    D. 100 percent of offspring will express the dominant phenotype.

Problem solved:

C is correct. The parental cross is Zz × zz (testcrossing a monohybrid heterozygote). This cross will result in 50 percent of offspring with the Z phenotype (genotype Zz) and 50 percent of offspring with the z phenotype (zz genotype). Because this is a testcross, all the offspring receive recessive alleles from the testcross parent (zz in this case). This allows both alleles of the other parent to show themselves in the offspring.

Please solve this problem:

- A woman heterozygous for brown eyes (blue are recessive) and brown hair (blond is recessive) mates with a man with the same genotype. What is the probability they will have a son with brown hair and brown eyes who is able to have blue-eyed children himself?

    A. ⅜
    B. ³⁄₁₆
    C. ⁹⁄₁₆
    D. ⁹⁄₃₂

Problem solved:

B is correct. If we let E = brown eyes and e = blue eyes, and H = brown hair and h = blond hair, the parental cross is EeHh x EeHh (notice that assigning letters to genes is usually arbitrary; pick a scheme that you will remember, and it is always a good idea to write these down). Let's start with the eye color locus: If the son has brown eyes, he must have one E allele. If he is able to have blue-eyed children, he must also have one e allele. Therefore, we want to find the probability of the son being Ee given the parental cross Ee x Ee for this locus. This is ½ (see the probability rules above or draw out a Punnett square to confirm this if you are not sure). Next, let's analyze the hair color locus. If the son has brown hair, he must have an H allele. Since this is the only information we are given, we need to calculate the probability of the son being H- (the second allele could be anything) given the parental cross Hh x Hh. This is ¾. Finally, we need to calculate the probability that the child is a male; this is ½. Since we want the offspring to be a male *and* have brown hair *and* have brown eyes (but the ability to have blue-eyed children), the rules of probabilities say we need to multiply our three results. Therefore, the overall probability will be ½ x ¾ x ½ = ³⁄₁₆. Note that if the question had asked for the probability of the offspring having brown hair *or* brown eyes, we would have added our results, not multiplied them.

Incomplete Dominance and Co-Dominance

Alternative alleles do not always (or even usually) interact to exhibit classic dominance. For some traits, alleles interact to produce an intermediate phenotype or a blended phenotype. In this case, we say that the trait exhibits **incomplete dominance**. For example, if flower color in plants exhibits incomplete dominance, and plants with an RR genotype have red flowers, and plants with an rr genotype have white flowers, plants with an Rr genotype would have pink flowers.

In other cases, two different alleles for the same locus might express themselves not as an intermediate phenotype, but as two distinct phenotypes both present in a single individual. Alleles for the human blood groups (which determine your blood type) exhibit this form of interaction, known as **co-dominance**.

Human blood is commonly typed as A, B, or O, and either positive or negative. Blood type is determined by the expression of antigens on the surface of red blood cells (also called erythrocytes). An antigen is a molecule that is recognized by an antibody.

706 ■ CRACKING THE MCAT

The blood group (A, B, AB, or O) is governed by three alleles designated I^A, I^B, and i at one locus:

- The I^A allele codes for an enzyme that adds the sugar galactosamine to the lipids on the surface of red blood cells. People with this allele express antigen A on their erythrocytes.

- The I^B allele codes for an enzyme that adds the sugar galactose to the lipids on the surface of red blood cells. People with this allele express antigen B on their erythrocytes.

- The i allele codes for a protein that does not add any sugar to the surface of red blood cells.

An individual of genotype:

(1) $I^A I^A$ or I^Ai shows the addition of galactosamine to the surface lipids of the red blood cells (or expresses antigen A); this person has blood type A.

(2) $I^B I^B$ or I^Bi shows the addition of galactose to the surface lipids of the red blood cells (or expresses antigen B); this person has blood type B.

(3) $I^A I^B$ shows the addition of *both* galactose and galactosamine to the surface lipids of the red blood cells (or expresses both antigens A and B); this person has blood type AB.

(4) i i shows the addition of no sugar to the surface lipids of the red blood cells (expresses neither antigen A nor antigen B); this person has type O blood.

Note that the alleles I^A and I^B exhibit co-dominance. The individual who carries both alleles exhibits the trait tied to each. Neither allele is recessive in relation to the other. At the same time, however, the i allele, which does not code for the addition of any sugar on the red blood cell surface, *is* recessive in relation to both the I^A and I^B alleles. Only the genotype ii produces that phenotype.

Positive or negative blood type is determined by a separate gene called the Rh factor or antigen D, which exhibits classical dominance. If an individual expresses antigen D, they have positive blood. If they do not express antigen D, they have negative blood.

Please solve this problem:

- If an individual has blood type A, it can be concluded that:

    A. his genotype at the relevant locus is $I^A I^A$.
    B. his genotype at the relevant locus is I^Ai.
    C. he carries either one or two I^A alleles.
    D. he carries at least one i allele.

Problem solved:

C is correct. The trait for human blood type (A, B, or O) exhibits co-dominance. Among the three alleles extant within the population (I^A, I^B, and i), any one individual carries two (since humans are diploid organisms). Blood type A can be due to one of two genotypes, either $I^A I^A$ or I^A i. While choices A, B, and D are possible for an individual with blood type A, they are not guaranteed. The only statement that must be true is choice C.

GENETIC ALTERATION AND DIVERSITY

Genes generally undergo alteration via two mechanisms: recombination and mutation.

Recombination

Genetic recombination generally refers to a process in which genetic information on one chromosome is moved to a:

(a) chromosome that belongs to some other cell, or a

(b) different chromosome within the same cell (often a homologous chromosome).

The human immunodeficiency virus (HIV), for example, transfers a segment of its genome to a human chromosome, and the human cell thereby undergoes (severely pathologic) genetic recombination.

During the synapsis phase of the first meiotic division, homologous chromosomes joined on the spindle apparatus undergo breakage and an exchange of genetic information. A physical "piece" breaks from each chromosome of the pair and "crosses over" to become integrated into its counterpart. This process is called **crossing over**, and represents another instance of genetic recombination; genetic information moves from one chromosome to another.

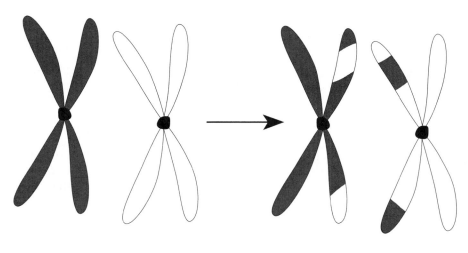

Homologous pair
before crossing over

Homologous pair
after crossing over

Crossing Over

Figure 31.8

Mutation

Mutation refers to the actual alteration of the DNA sequence on the chromosome. Often, mutation produces effects deleterious to the organism's function, adaptability, and survival. *Much more rarely*, it leads to improvement in the organism's adaptability. In some cases, mutation confers on the organism neither an advantage nor disadvantage.

Mutations in the cells destined to produce gametes (the **germ-line** cells) potentially affect the genome of the offspring. Mutation of germ-line cells, therefore, is critical to the genetic variability that underlies evolution and natural selection. Mutation of a somatic (non-gametic) cell is less significant to the *evolutionary* process but may have serious consequences for the affected individual. Mutation of a single somatic cell, for example, may be the first event in the genesis of cancer. There are two common types of mutations: **Point mutations** are when one nucleotide unit is substituted for another, and **frameshift mutations** occur when one or more nucleotides are added or deleted (note that the addition or deletion of a multiple of three nucleotides does not cause a frameshift mutation; see below).

Please solve this problem:

- Which of the following, if it occurs in a young human adult of reproductive age, is LEAST likely to contribute to the process of evolution?

  A. Damage to a somatic cell
  B. Crossing over
  C. Mutagenic ultraviolet exposure to a ootid
  D. Spontaneous mutation in a spermatogonia

Problem solved:

A is correct. Critical to the process of evolution is the phenomenon of genetic alteration and variation that affects offspring. Damage to a somatic (non–gamete-producing) cell may affect the individual who suffers the mutation, but it will not normally affect the genetic constitution of his or her offspring. Damage to a gamete-producing cell, or damage during meiosis (answer choices B, C, and D) will change DNA of potential offspring and contribute to the process of evolution.

POINT MUTATIONS

When a gene undergoes substitution of one DNA nucleotide unit for another it is said to experience a **point mutation.** If by some mechanism, for example, the DNA triplet TGA should become TGG, the gene on which the alteration occurs has undergone a point mutation.

A point mutation changes the mRNA codon that follows from transcription of the affected DNA triplet. Because the genetic code is degenerate, the altered mRNA codon might or might not code for the same amino acid as did the original codon. Consider a point mutation that causes an mRNA codon to change from CCU to CCA. Refer to Figure 24.21 and note that CCU and CCA both code for the amino acid proline. The point mutation that produces *that* particular change does not affect the amino acid that is added during translation and therefore would not affect gene function. Such a mutation is termed **silent**.

Suppose, on the other hand, that a given point mutation causes an mRNA codon to change from ACG to ACU. In this case, an alanine residue will be replaced by a threonine residue. The mutation would probably affect gene function and is called a **missense** mutation. Missense mutations tend to be more serious if they occur at an important location of the protein, such as at the active site of an enzyme. Sometimes, when missense mutations occur in the backbone or scaffolding region of a protein, they can have little to no effect on protein function. If the mutation causes the conversion of an mRNA codon to a stop codon, we call it a **nonsense mutation**.

FRAMESHIFT MUTATIONS

Frameshift mutations result from the insertion or deletion of one or more nucleotide units, in anything but multiples of three, along a given chromosomal strand. Such an alteration ultimately means that during translation of the resultant mRNA molecule, the ribosome reads three-base sequences in inappropriate groupings—according to a distorted **reading frame**. The genetic code loses its meaning, and the relevant genetic message is garbled. (Imagine, for example, that one writes in plain English a message beginning with these eight 3-letter words:

THE BIG DOG SAT AND ATE ITS PIE.

Suppose that we subject the message to a frameshift mutation by deleting the "G" at the end of the word "DOG." To a reader who believes that all words are three letters in length, the message will be much distorted:

THE BID OGS ATA NDA TEI TSP IE.

Please solve this problem:

- Refer to the genetic code. If a DNA triplet that codes for the mRNA codon CGC undergoes a point mutation, after which the triplet codes for the mRNA codon CGU, the result, in terms of polypeptide synthesis, will be:

  A. the replacement of a valine residue with a leucine residue.
  B. the replacement of a histidine residue with a glutamine residue.
  C. the shifting of the reading frame in which RNA polymerase and the ribosome assess mRNA codons.
  D. none.

Problem solved:

D is correct. A point mutation refers to a change within a portion of DNA such that a nucleotide residue is substituted for another nucleotide residue. If the substitution occurs within a triplet that actually transcribes an mRNA codon, then the resulting mRNA codon will be altered as well. Because the genetic code is degenerate, the alteration in the mRNA codon might or might not affect polypeptide synthesis. According to the genetic code (shown in **Chapter 24**) both mRNA codons CGC and CGU code for the amino acid arginine. Consequently, the point mutation will not change the amino acid inserted into the growing polypeptide chain.

SEX DETERMINATION AND SEX-LINKED TRAITS

Sex Determination

The human somatic cell has twenty-two pairs of homologous chromosomes, the **autosomes**, plus one pair of **sex chromosomes**. In females, the two sex chromosomes are X and X. In males, they are X and Y.

Consider the meiotic processes of spermatogenesis and oogenesis (**Chapter 25**). At anaphase of the first meiotic division, all chromosomal pairs separate, including the sex chromosomes. In the case of oogenesis, the secondary oocyte and first polar body both take an X chromosome (since the parent diploid cell has no Y chromosome to donate). Consequently, all mature ova carry an X chromosome; none carry a Y chromosome. In the case of spermatogenesis, one secondary spermatocyte takes the X chromosome and the other takes the Y chromosome. Consequently, half of the mature spermatozoa carry an X chromosome and half carry a Y chromosome.

Sex is determined when the spermatozoon fertilizes the ovum. If the ovum is fertilized by an X-bearing spermatozoon, the zygote takes an X chromosome from the ovum and an X chromosome from the spermatozoon; the offspring's genotype is **XX** (female). If the ovum is fertilized by a Y-bearing spermatozoon, the zygote takes an X chromosome from the ovum and a Y chromosome from the spermatozoon; the offspring's genotype is **XY** (male).

Since fifty percent of spermatozoon carry a Y chromosome and fifty percent carry an X chromosome, there is a fifty percent chance of a zygote being male and a fifty percent change of the zygote being female.

Sex-Linked Traits and Sex-Linked Inheritance

In the human population, most traits are carried by the autosomes (the twenty-two pairs of chromosomes that are not X or Y). In addition, some traits are carried by the mitochondrial genome, some are carried by the X chromosomes, and some are carried by the Y chromosome.

Autosomal traits can be recessive (the affected individual needs two copies of the affected allele to show the trait) or dominant (one copy of the affected allele is enough to show the trait). Autosomal traits affect males and females with equal frequency.

Mitochondrial traits are passed onto offspring from the mother and only the mother. This is because spermatozoon pass only twenty-three nuclear chromosomes to the zygote. The ovum also donates twenty-three nuclear chromosomes and all the other cellular components, including organelles. Since there is a very small and separate genome in the matrix of the mitochondria, all individuals inherit their mitochondrial genome (and any associated traits) from their mother. These traits are not recessive or dominant, since there is only one copy of the mitochondrial genome; they are either present or absent.

Y-linked traits are very rare. They never affect females (since females have no Y chromosome) and are passed from father to son. Similar to mitochondrial traits, there is no issue of dominance with these traits. Males have only one copy of the Y chromosome, so the trait is either present or absent.

There are also some traits that are carried on the X chromosome. These traits are termed **sex-linked** (or sometimes **X-linked**), and can be dominant or recessive. Two very common recessive X-linked traits are red/green color blindness and hemophilia.

Let us recall the dynamics of classic dominance (from earlier in this chapter) and apply them to the gene for red/green color blindness. The dominant CB allele is associated with the normal phenotype (no red/green color blindness) and the recessive cb allele is associated with color blindness. Recognize that:

(1) Any male who carries the color-blind gene ($X^{cb} Y$) will be color-blind. Even though the gene is recessive, the male has no second X chromosome to dominate it. The recessive gene is free to express itself and will do so.

More generally, a male who carries a sex-linked recessive gene will be positive for the relevant phenotype.

(2) A female who carries the color-blind gene on both X chromosomes ($X^{cb} X^{cb}$) will be color-blind. The gene is recessive, but if it is carried on two X chromosomes, the genotype has no allele that will dominate it. The recessive gene will express itself.

More generally, a female who is homozygous for a sex-linked recessive trait will be positive for the relevant phenotype.

(3) A female who carries the color-blind gene on one of her X chromosomes but not on the other ($X^{CB}X^{cb}$) will not be color-blind. The gene is recessive; the X chromosome that carries

the dominant allele (CB) will prevent the recessive allele (cb) from expressing itself. Females with this genotype are called **carriers** of the trait.

More generally, a female who is heterozygous for a recessive sex-linked gene will be negative for the relevant phenotype.

Because a sex-linked trait is carried on the X chromosome, and because a male receives a Y chromosome from his father (not an X chromosome), it follows that a sex-linked trait cannot pass from a male to a male. Rather, a male who carries a sex-linked recessive gene has always inherited it from his mother.

Because a male passes his X chromosome to his daughters, it follows that any male who carries a sex-linked recessive gene will pass it to all of his daughters. The daughter will not be positive for the trait, however, unless she is homozygous for the gene and she has also inherited the affected allele from her mother.

Because a female passes one of her two X chromosomes to each of her offspring, it follows that any female who carries a sex-linked recessive allele will pass it to fifty percent of her offspring, regardless of their sex. All of her sons who inherit the affected allele will be positive for the phenotype. Her daughters who inherit the affected allele will not be positive for the trait, unless they also inherit the allele from their father and are homozygous.

Pedigrees

Pedigrees are diagrams that show the genetic information of a family tree. They can be used to determine the mode of inheritance of a trait and to figure out the probability of individuals being affected by a trait or a disease.

On a pedigree, squares are males and circles are females. A diamond shape is used when the sex of an individual is not yet known (i.e., the child is not yet born). Individuals with a shaded symbol are affected by the trait or disease being studied; individuals with white symbols are not. When two people mate, a horizontal line is drawn between them, and their children are drawn below this.

In order to work with pedigrees, you need to understand a common assumption that is made: Since the traits being studied are usually rare in the human population, we assume that any non-family members have a homozygous normal genotype. A non-family member is an individual with no genetic information above them (i.e., you do not know the genotype or phenotype of their parents or grandparents or siblings). These individuals are marrying or mating into the family being studied.

There are six common modes of inheritance. They are summarized here:

Inheritance Pattern	Identification	Unaffected Genotypes	Affected Genotypes
Autosomal recessive	• can skip generations • # of affected males ~# of affected females • unaffected parents can have affected offspring	AA Aa	aa
Autosomal dominant	• does not skip generations • # of affected males ~# of affected females • an unaffected parent passes the trait to either all or half of offspring	aa	AA Aa
Y- Linked	• affects male only; females never have the trait • affected father has all affected sons • unaffected father cannot have an affected son	XY^a	XY^A
Mitochondrial	• material inheritance • every human gets their mitochondrial genome from their mother; sperm contribute only nuclear chromosomes • affected female has all affected children • affected male cannot pass the trait onto his children • unaffected female cannot have affected children	a	A
X-linked recessive	• can skip generations • tends to affect males more than females • unaffected females can have affected sons • affected female has all affected sons, but can have both affected and unaffected daughters	X^{A}X^A X^{A}X^a X^{A}Y	X^{a}X^a X^{a}Y
X-linked dominant	• hardest to identify • does not skip generations • usually affects males more than females • affected fathers have all affected daughters • affected moms can have unaffected sons, and give the trait equally to sons and daughters	X^{a}X^a X^{a}Y	X^{A}X^A X^{A}X^a X^{A}Y

Table 31.3

If you see a pedigree on the MCAT, a good strategy is to first determine the mode of inheritance. To do this, follow this three-step approach:

1. Check for Y-linked and mitochondrial inheritance. Both of these have very distinct patterns that you should spot easily.

2. Does the trait skip generations? That is, can you find a pattern such as "affected grandma, unaffected dad, affected son"? If so, the trait is probably recessive. If not, it is likely dominant.

3. What is the ratio of affected males and affected females in this family? If there are approximately equal numbers, it suggests the trait is autosomal. If there are more males affected, the trait is likely X-linked. It is very rare for a trait to affect females more than males on the MCAT.

This three-step approach is a good set of guidelines to use when working with pedigrees. Beware, however, that pedigrees can be very tricky and you may need to also use the identification tips listed in the table above.

When you are working with pedigrees, focus on the individual the question is asking you about, but be aware that you will probably have to work backward into their parental generation (sometimes you may need to go as far back as their grandparents), or work forward and look at their offspring. There are lots of strategies you can use to determine the genotype of an individual. To start with, determine their phenotype (i.e., are they white or shaded in?). This will usually allow you to fill in at least one of their alleles. Next, look at the parents of the individual. Does this give you any information about what alleles this individual inherited from their parents? Finally, look at the children of this individual to see if you can fill in the blanks.

For example, if you have a pedigree that is tracing an X-linked recessive trait and you are working with a female that is not shaded in, this individual must have the dominant normal allele to have a normal phenotype (X^A). If this female is breeding into the family, you can assume she is X^AX^A. If she is part of the family and has all normal sons, it is possible (but not assured) that she is X^AX^A; remember, it is possible that she hasn't had enough offspring for you to see her other X chromosome in the next generation. If she has sons that are affected by the X-linked recessive trait, she must be a carrier of the X^a chromosome, and her genotype is X^AX^a. If her parents are X^AX^A and X^AY, she must be X^AX^A. If her father is affected by the trait, he must be X^aY and she must be heterozygous (X^AX^a), since she gets an X chromosome from her father. Any or all of these strategies can help you determine the genotype of individuals on pedigrees.

The final tool you will need to work with pedigrees is an understanding of genetic probabilities, as discussed in the beginning of this chapter. Armed with these tools, you should be able to tackle pedigrees both large and small.

31.2   MASTERY APPLIED: PRACTICE PASSAGE AND QUESTIONS

Passage

Autosomal dominant (AD) inheritance is one of four basic patterns of Mendelian inheritance reflecting the types and combinations of alleles, or alternative forms of a gene, at a given site on a chromosome. A Mendelian disease is one in which a single mutant gene has a large phenotypic effect and is transmitted in a vertical pattern, being passed from one generation to the next vertically on a pedigree.

Of the four thousand traits delineated by scientists as following Mendelian inheritance, fifty-four percent are autosomal dominant, thirty-six percent are autosomal recessive, and ten percent are X-linked dominant or recessive. Of these traits, approximately three thousand have been linked to human disease. The Punnett square below illustrates the classical pattern of transmission of an autosomal dominant mutant trait from parents to offspring, where one heterozygous parent expresses the trait while one homozygous recessive parent does not express it.

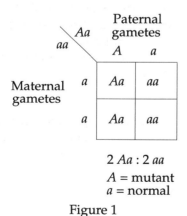

2 *Aa* : 2 *aa*

A = mutant
a = normal

Figure 1

1. The Punnett square presented in the passage indicates that:
    A. the parents produced four offspring.
    B. on average, mating of heterozygous parents yields a 50:50 ratio of heterozygous and homozygous offspring.
    C. on average, mating of a heterozygous and a homozygous parent yields equal numbers of heterozygous and homozygous recessive offspring.
    D. the probable outcome of heterozygous–homozygous matings is determined by the paternal chromosomal make-up.

2. Which of the following is true regarding the pedigree shown below?

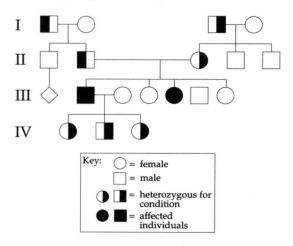

Pedigree of an Autosomal Recessive Trait

A. The trait illustrated in the pedigree is autosomal and sex-linked because both affected offspring and heterozygotes have affected or heterozygous fathers, and only generation III involves a carrier mother.

B. The pedigree is incorrect because genotype for the trait should skip generations in autosomal recessive inheritance.

C. Phenotypic expression of autosomal recessive traits in offspring requires that both parents be heterozygous, or that one parent is heterozygous and the other is homozygous recessive.

D. Phenotypic expression of autosomal recessive traits in parents must result in affected offspring.

3. A researcher discovers that a particular human disease state is attributable to a single sex-linked recessive allele. She names the allele Z-3. In the course of her research, she studies an urban population and finds that the incidence of the disease is greater in men than in women. The most sensible explanation for the relatively high incidence of the disease in men is that:

A. allele Z-3 is carried on the Y chromosome in males and on the X chromosome in females.

B. the Y chromosome carries no allele that will suppress expression of allele Z-3.

C. independent assortment of homologous chromosomes occurs during oogenesis but not during spermatogenesis.

D. allele Z-3 passes only from fathers to sons and not from mothers to sons.

4. According to the law of independent assortment:

A. homologous chromosomes enter the same gamete during meiosis.

B. homologous chromosomes become separated into different gametes during meiosis.

C. the gene for each trait in an organism will segregate independent of those for other traits in the organism during meiosis.

D. alternative alleles for a trait enter the same gamete during meiosis.

5. Achondroplasia, a common cause of dwarfism, is an example of an autosomal dominant condition, which arises through mutation eighty percent of the time. The disorder is characterized by decreased cartilage production at the bone growth plates. Increased paternal age may increase the rate of this mutation. All of the following are true statements with regard to mutations EXCEPT:

A. a mutation can arise spontaneously.

B. a mutation involves a change in the nucleotide sequence of DNA.

C. a mutation can alter the production of a specific protein.

D. a mutation is always inherited by offspring.

6. Among the following phenotypes, a trait included in the subcategory that comprises ten percent of Mendelian inheritance is:

A. eye color.
B. height.
C. color blindness.
D. sickle cell anemia.

31.3 MASTERY VERIFIED: ANSWERS AND EXPLANATIONS

1. **C is correct.** A Punnett square is used to determine the average or expected outcome of matings. They do not predict *actual* outcomes of individual pairings, which are subject to random variability of pairing of individual gametes. Choice A is not correct. A Punnett square describes the statistical probability of the outcome of a mating between two individuals. It does not predict the number of offspring. Choice B is incorrect as well. The Punnett square in Figure 1 indicates nothing about the mating of heterozygous parents. Choice D, too, is wrong. Although the offspring ratio (fifty percent [*Aa*], fifty percent [*aa*]) looks like the paternal gametes (*Aa*), the maternal gametes (*aa*) play an equal part in determining the genotypes of the offspring.

2. **C is correct.** Phenotypic expression of a recessive trait requires contribution of a recessive gene from each parent. Choice A is not correct. A gene can, by definition, be autosomal or sex-linked, but cannot be both. Choice B is incorrect. Expression of an autosomal recessive trait does not have to skip generations. Choice D is wrong as well. Heterozygous parents contribute either one or zero recessive genes each to a zygote. Using probability, one-quarter of offspring of such parents will be affected (homozygous for the abnormal gene) and one-quarter will be homozygous for the normal gene.

3. **B is correct.** We are told that the Z-3 allele is sex-linked. That means it is carried on the X chromosome, which makes choices A and D wrong. Since a father does not impart an X chromosome to his male offspring, he cannot pass to a son an allele that is located on the X chromosome. Choice C makes an inaccurate statement. Independent assortment is a "law" that applies to both spermatogenesis and oogenesis. The explanation for the researcher's observation pertains to the nature of sex-linked recessive alleles. In a female who is heterozygous for a sex-linked allele, one X chromosome carries the allele and the other carries an alternate allele. Since the disease-causing allele is recessive, the alternative allele dominates it, and the phenotype is not expressed. However, a male who carries the allele on his X chromosome has no second X chromosome to mask its expression. The Y chromosome does not do for the male what the second X chromosome does for the female. Although the sex-linked allele is recessive, it expresses itself in the male because his genome carries no alternative allele that will dominate it.

4. **C is correct.** This is an accurate statement of this law. D is not true, as described in the preceding chapter.

5. **D is correct.** Choices A, B, and C accurately characterize mutations.

6. **C is correct.** According to the passage, ten percent of traits that follow Mendelian inheritance are X-linked (sex-linked). Therefore, the correct answer must describe a sex-linked trait. Color blindness is a sex-linked trait. Choices A, B, and D are incorrect, since none lists a sex-linked trait.

CHAPTER 32

POPULATIONS, EVOLUTION, AND ECOLOGY

32.1 MASTERY ACHIEVED

GENE POOL, MUTATION, AND GENETIC VARIABILITY

A **gene pool** constitutes the total possible assortment of genes found in the population of a species. Each member of a population possesses an overall genotype (and therefore phenotype) that differs in some aspect from the other members of a population. The differences among the members' genotypes is an expression of the genetic variability present in the population. Genetic variability is predominantly the result of random **mutation**—the spontaneous addition, transfer, rearrangement, or deletion of one or several nucleotides in a section of DNA. The mutation may confer an advantage or a disadvantage on the organism with regard to its survival and ability to reproduce. If the mutation is heritable, the organism's progeny may also possess the advantageous or disadvantageous trait.

THE DYNAMICS OF EVOLUTION

Evolution is a change in the genetic makeup of a given population. The term applies to **populations** over time; a single individual is not capable of evolving. Evolution acts upon the population's gene pool. Advantageous mutations become incorporated into the gene pool, while those that confer serious disadvantage generally do not remain in the gene pool. Organisms placed at a serious disadvantage will usually not survive long enough to reproduce. Mutations producing deleterious effects of a subtler nature, however, tend to persist in the gene pool over time. At some future time, a change in circumstances may then cause the gene to provide some advantage, after which the gene will become more prevalent in the population.

Environment and Alteration of a Gene Pool

A new environment usually poses new challenges to the survival of an organism. Consequently, those organisms whose genes confer traits advantageous to their survival and reproduction in the new environment tend to proliferate at the expense of other organisms in the population. Over time, the gene pool of the population will shift, with the frequency of advantageous genes increasing and that of deleterious genes decreasing.

An example is the mutant sickle cell allele, which produces an altered form of hemoglobin designated HbS. The aberrant hemoglobin has the tendency to cause the red blood cell in which they are housed to sickle. The sickled cells will often clump and clog smaller blood vessels. Homozygous individuals for HbS normally do not survive to adulthood. Heterozygous individuals, whose genotype for hemoglobin consists of one allele for HbS and one allele for HbA (normal hemoglobin), are disadvantaged by the sickling of those red blood cells harboring HbS, but are also able to produce normal hemoglobin and a certain percentage of normal-shaped red blood cells.

Significantly, the allele for HbS also confers increased resistance to a virulent form of malaria caused by the protozoon *Plasmodium*. In environments where the likelihood of infection from the virulent form of malaria is high—such as in areas of Africa, Southern Asia, and India—the frequency of the HbS allele in the gene pool can rise as high as forty percent in the population. Alternatively, in environments that do not pose the risk of malarial infection (where possession of the allele conferring malarial resistance does not confer an advantage)—such as in North America—the frequency of the HbS allele is reduced in the population to as low as 4 percent.

Darwinian Fitness

According to Charles Darwin, *fitness* refers to the ability of an organism's genotype to persevere in subsequent generations. There is competition among organisms in a population; therefore not all previously existing and newly mutated alleles can be perpetuated in the finite gene pool of a population. Those alleles that persist in the gene pool (those that have been "selected" by the environment) will supplant alternative forms of the gene. An organism that is able to survive to reproductive age is able to pass on to its progeny whatever trait or traits that assisted in its survival. A given organism's fitness depends on the interplay between its environment and its phenotype, and is judged ultimately by its ability to survive to reproductive age.

Please solve this problem:

- Describe fitness as it applies to the Darwinian concept of evolution.

Problem solved:

Fitness, as it applies to Darwinian evolution, is the ability of a gene to persist in the gene pool through successive generations. An organism that can survive and reproduce, passing on its genotype to its offspring, embodies Darwin's concept of evolution. Differential reproduction rates dictate that all available alleles for a gene will not be inherited at equal rates from generation to generation. The factor that determines which genes persevere is natural selection. An organism possessing alleles for a trait that confers an advantage will more likely survive and, therefore, may reproduce more often than an organism that possesses an alternate form of the gene that does not confer advantage.

Please solve this problem:

- Which one of the following is essential to the process of evolution?

    A. Mutation
    B. Death of some mutant offspring before reproductive age
    C. Unchanging gene pool
    D. Physical separation of two populations of the same species

Problem solved:

A is correct. The process of evolution depends on ongoing random mutation within a population. Those mutations that favor survival are promoted simply because the individuals that possess them are more likely to survive to reproductive age and to pass them on. The process of mutation does not require that some mutant offspring die before reproductive age (although this is a common event). Evolution is the alteration in gene pool composition in a given population of a species. It may proceed in the absence of any physical separation between two populations of the species.

Please solve this problem:

- Environmental changes might produce evolution by:
  - A. inducing rapid and direct genetic change in response to the stresses imposed on the environment.
  - B. revealing the selective advantage conferred by a particular gene that is possessed by some but not all members of a population.
  - C. halting the process of random mutation.
  - D. producing mutations unfavorable to the altered environment.

Problem solved:

B is correct. Within the gene pool of a population, some genes have neither an advantageous nor a disadvantageous effect on the individual. Under some environmental change, however, such a gene might prove to be advantageous, and so confer a selective advantage on those individuals who possess it. Such individuals will be more likely to survive to reproductive age; as such, over some generations, the composition of the gene pool will change.

Please solve this problem:

- Jean Baptiste de Lamarck posited that an individual could pass on to its offspring a trait acquired in its lifetime. How does Lamarck's theory of evolution compare to the theory of evolution according to Darwin?

Problem solved:

Lamarck incorrectly theorized that an acquired trait, developed at some point during the organism's lifetime, was heritable in the same manner that a gene arising through mutation would be heritable. Additionally, Lamarck's theory of evolution embraced a direction of evolution that entailed a continual quest (and reward) for self-improvement by the organism that is absent in evolution. According to Darwin's theory of evolution, only traits that are coded for by the genes in the gametes can be transferred to offspring. Furthermore, the advantage that a trait confers to an organism depends primarily on the environment in which the organism finds itself.

Speciation

Reproductive Isolation

Speciation—one type of **divergent evolution**—refers to the evolution of a new species of plant or animal from a preexisting, or parent, species. The two populations evolve separately over time until what had originally been a common gene pool has evolved into two distinct gene pools. **Reproductive isolation** is insularity of a gene pool from genetic mixing, and it occurs when two species capable of interbreeding are prevented from doing so. Their reproductive isolation can take the form of temporal isolation (e.g., breeding that is confined to a specific time of day, season, or year), ecological isolation (e.g., different habitat requirements for two species within the same geographical area), or behavioral isolation (e.g., courtship behavior that is species-specific), among others. Often more than one form of reproductive isolation exists as a barrier to the mixing of genes between species.

Please solve this problem:

- Which of the following describes an instance of reproductive isolation?

    A. A rattlesnake becomes separated from other rattlesnakes and therefore cannot mate.
    B. Two distinct populations of the same species show subtle differences in traits and genotypes.
    C. Two populations of frogs share a common ancestor but will no longer interbreed because their mating seasons do not overlap.
    D. Each species of flycatcher, a bird, is associated with its own characteristic song.

Problem solved:

C is correct. Reproductive isolation requires two things: (1) that two populations once interbred, and (2) that they no longer do. Only choice C provides evidence that both of these criteria are met.

Adaptive Radiation

When a given species population has undergone a sufficient change in genotype to render it reproductively isolated from other populations of its parent species, it has evolved into a new species. This form of speciation is called **adaptive radiation** and is associated with reduced competition and an alteration of the organism's original **niche**. An organism's niche represents the organism's "environment" in its broadest sense, encompassing an organism's habitat, food sources, territory, range, and mating behavior.

One method by which adaptive radiation arises is through geographical separation, such as the migration of glaciers or the development of a land bridge or a mountain range. A population that migrates to and colonizes new territory will be subject to a different set of criteria for selection of its genotype—criteria that are based on the conditions of the new environment. Ultimately, those organisms able to survive and procreate in the new environment will belong to a gene pool that is reproductively isolated from the gene pool to which they originally belonged before their migration. This form of adaptive radiation is called **allopatric speciation**.

The other form of adaptive radiation is **sympatric speciation**, which occurs in the absence of geographical isolation: It occurs in a geographical area shared by the parent and the new species. Two closely related populations of one species can diverge, such that their differences allow them to exploit different niches within the same environment. Because adaptive radiation involves the creation of one or more species from a parent species, it acts to increase biological diversity.

Please solve this problem:

- Define the term *adaptive radiation*. Describe two mechanisms that give rise to this form of evolution. Does adaptive radiation increase or decrease biological diversity?

Problem solved:

Adaptive radiation is a form of evolution characterized by the creation of one or more new species that arise from a preexisting ancestral species. A key requirement for adaptive radiation is the reproductive isolation of a population of a species. One mechanism giving rise to adaptive radiation is geographical separation, such as what occurs with the development of a land bridge, the movement of a glacier, or the appearance of a mountain range. Another mechanism leading to adaptive radiation is the divergence of two gene pools of populations inhabiting the same geographical region. Speciation can occur in this case when two populations are able to exploit different niches in the same environment. Either mechanism of adaptive radiation increases biological diversity by increasing the number of species that exist.

Please solve this problem:

- Adaptive radiation results in all of the following EXCEPT:

  A. reduced competition.
  B. overall increase in the number of species.
  C. change of an organism's original niche.
  D. convergence of species.

Problem solved:

D is correct. Choice D is the only choice that fails to describe an effect of adaptive radiation. Adaptive radiation entails a divergence of species, ultimately increasing biological diversity.

Please solve this problem:

- Which of the following is associated with both al-lopatric and sympatric speciation?

    A. Gross geographic separation
    B. Occupation of a new niche
    C. Increased competition among original and newly developed species
    D. Decreased exploitation of resources

Problem solved:

B is correct. Both allopatric and sympatric speciation involve the occupation of a new niche by one or several populations, which in time gives rise to new species. Choice A describes allopatric speciation only. Choices C and D are false for both allopatric and sympatric speciation; both will decrease competition among species and will increase the efficiency of exploitation of resources.

PREDICTION OF GENE FREQUENCY IN A POPULATION

The Hardy-Weinberg Law

Consider a gene that embodies only two alleles: one recessive and one dominant. Contrary to intuitive belief, as a population mates, reproduces, and expands over time, the dominant allele does not "naturally" *replace* the recessive ones. The population does not undergo by some natural process a decline in the numerical occurrence of recessive genes or an increase in the numerical occurrence of dominant ones.

Rather, according to a precept called the **Hardy-Weinberg law**, the occurrence of dominant and recessive alleles within a population remains constant over time. The Hardy-Weinberg law is a (very useful) theoretical construct premised on these assumptions:

(1) population size is very large,

(2) mating is random,

(3) mutation does not occur,

(4) the population takes in no genes from other populations, and

(5) selection does not occur.

In mathematical terms, the Hardy-Weinberg law proceeds from the statistical notion of **frequency**. When we refer to the frequency of a given allele within a population, we mean the fractional contribution that allele makes to the total population of both alleles. Consider four dogs and a trait for which

— 1 dog is homozygous dominant (TT),

— 2 dogs are homozygous recessive (tt) (tt), and

— 1 dog is heterozygous (Tt).

Simple counting tells us that the total number of alleles in this little population is 8: 3 T alleles and 5 t alleles. The frequency of the dominant (T) allele is $\frac{5}{8}$ = 0.625. The frequency of the recessive (t) allele is $\frac{3}{8}$ = 0.375. The two numbers 0.625 and 0.375 yield the sum of 1 or 100 percent. That simple little fact represents the Hardy-Weinberg law's starting point.

With reference to a population and a single gene for which there exist only two alleles, the Hardy-Weinberg law assigns the letter p to the frequency of the dominant allele, and the letter q to the frequency of the recessive allele. Consider the discussion above, and you can easily recognize that:

$$p + q = 1$$

Algebraic manipulation of that simple principle readily leads to these mathematical truths:

$$p + q = 1$$
$$(p + q)^2 = 1^2$$
$$p^2 + 2pq + q^2 = 1$$

p^2 represents the frequency of homozygous dominant genotype,

q^2 represents the frequency of homozygous recessive genotype, and

$2pq$ represents the frequency of heterozygous genotype.

Suppose that as to a trait (T) that manifests classic Mendelian inheritance, a population of 1 million individuals embodies 160,000 individuals homozygous for the recessive genotype (recognizable, of course, by their phenotype). According to the Hardy-Weinberg law, q^2 = 160,000/1 million = 16% = 0.16. Now, if q^2 = 0.16, then q = 0.4, which means that the frequency of the recessive allele within the population is 0.4. Since $p + 1 = 1$, the frequency of the dominant allele within the population is (1 − 0.4) = 0.6. Furthermore, we can calculate the frequency within the population of all genotypes:

frequency of heterozygous genotype = $2pq$ = 2(0.4 × 0.6) = 0.48   = 48%

frequency of homozygous dominant genotype = p^2 = $(0.6)^2$ = 0.36   = 36%

frequency of the homozygous recessive genotype (as already calculated)   = 16%

_____

100%

Genetic Drift

In a *small* population the Hardy-Weinberg law does not operate. Instead, there occurs a pattern of allelic frequency alteration called **genetic drift**. Change in allelic frequency due to simple chance is relatively likely in small populations. As a result, certain alleles may disappear while others become more prevalent. The variation in allelic frequency that accompanies genetic drift arises *by chance*, not according to any process of natural selection.

Please solve this problem:

- The **founder effect** is a form of genetic drift that results when a small population colonizes a new area. All of the following would apply in the founder effect EXCEPT:

    A. the gene frequencies of an isolated colony may differ substantially from those of the larger population from which the colony broke off.
    B. the population of the colony is sufficiently small for genetic drift to alter the gene pool.
    C. any differences in the colony's gene frequency from its original population are more likely to be adaptive than random.
    D. members of the colony may possess only a small portion of the available alleles of the gene pool of the population they left behind.

Problem solved:

C is correct. Genetic drift, of which the founder effect is one form, entails random changes in the allelic frequencies of populations. Choice A lists a common effect of genetic drift on a population, while choices B and D list conditions under which genetic drift may alter the gene pool.

Please solve this problem:

- Among the following, which will NOT alter the gene frequencies of a population?

    A. Genetic drift
    B. Natural selection
    C. Hardy-Weinberg equilibrium
    D. Mutation

Problem solved:

C is correct. The Hardy-Weinberg law establishes the stability of gene frequencies. When the Hardy-Weinberg law applies, the frequency with which a trait occurs in a population remains steady. A series of conditions must be met, however, in order for the Hardy-Weinberg law to take effect: large population, absence of mutations, absence of immigration or emigration, random reproduction, and the condition that any one gene has the same chance of reproducing as any other gene. Choices A, B, and D are incorrect because all can alter the gene frequencies of a population. Genetic drift produces random evolutionary changes in allele frequency; natural selection selects favorable alleles over unfavorable ones, leading to changes in the gene pool; and mutation entails direct changes in the nucleotide sequence of DNA, potentially producing new alleles.

TAXONOMIC ORGANIZATION

Taxonomy—the classification of organisms—is based upon the binomial system proposed by Carolus Linnaeus in the mid-eighteenth century. An organism is classified according to a hierarchical scheme and is given a two-part name based on its assumed evolutionary relationship to other organisms based on available data. The order of classification, from most comprehensive to most specific, is: kingdom, phylum, class, order, family, genus, and species.

The most exclusive unit of classification is the species. Closely related species comprise a **genus**; related genera comprise a **family**; related families comprise an **order**; related orders comprise a **class**; related classes make up a **phylum**; and related phyla comprise a **kingdom**. Among phyla, the chordates are identifiable by the presence at some point during development of (1) a dorsal nerve cord, (2) gill slits, and (3) a notochord. Of the chordates, vertebrates are recognized by possession of (a) a vertebral column, (b) a closed circulatory system, (c) a developed nervous system, and (d) a developed sensory apparatus.

Please solve this problem:

- Order the following groupings of *Homo sapiens* (humans) according to the binomial system of classification: Mammalia (Class), Hominidae (Family), Chordata (Phylum), Vertebrata (Subphylum), *Homo* (Genus), Primata (Order), *sapiens* (Species), Animalia (Kingdom).

Problem solved:

Kingdom	Animalia
Phylum	Chordata
Subphylum	Vertebrata
Class	Mammalia
Order	Primata
Family	Hominidae
Genus	*Homo*
Species	*Sapiens*

COEXISTENCE, ECOLOGICAL NICHE, AND ECOSYSTEM

Another form of classification pertains to the nature of the relationship a given member of one species may have with a member of another species. A prolonged intimate association between a member of one species and a member of another species is referred to as **symbiosis**. Symbiotic relationships are classified into three types: **mutualism**, **commensalism**, and **parasitism**. Each partner of a mutualistic relationship derives benefit from the association; in fact, two such individuals are frequently unable to survive independently of one another. Nitrogen-fixing bacteria and the legume root nodules they colonize constitute a mutualistic partnership: The plants receive nitrogen in a form that they can use, and the bacteria derive nutrition and shelter from the plant host.

Commensalism involves one partner that benefits from the symbiotic association and one partner that neither benefits nor is harmed by the association. Epiphytes, small "air plants" that use trees to anchor themselves, derives benefit. The tree to which the epiphyte attaches represents the partner that is unaffected by the association. Parasitism is a symbiotic relationship in which one organism benefits and the other is harmed. An example of parasitism is the association between tapeworms and humans. The tapeworm derives food from its human host to the detriment of the human.

The behaviors described allow a given organism or organisms to fill a particular niche within their ecosystem. As described above, the term *niche* encompasses all parameters of the "environment" of an organism; numerous niches are utilized by similar and different species in any given ecosystem. The term **ecosystem** is an equally complex concept: It characterizes a self-sustaining natural system, composed of both living and nonliving components as well as all of the interactions between them that help to mold it into a stable system.

Please solve this problem:

- Elucidate the benefits or costs to organisms belonging to the following symbiotic relationships: mutualism, parasitism, and commensalism.

Problem solved:

In mutualism, both organisms benefit from their intimate relationship; in parasitism, one organism benefits, while the other organism is harmed; in commensalism, one organism benefits, while the other organism neither benefits nor is harmed. All three relationships constitute forms of symbiosis, an intimate living arrangement between two organisms of different species.

32.2 MASTERY APPLIED: PRACTICE PASSAGE AND QUESTIONS

Passage

According to the principle of competitive exclusion, one species will always predominate over another if both are in competition for the same resource within the same community. The competition, states the theory, will cause the elimination of one of the two species from the community. To test the validity of the theory, two experiments were performed.

Experiment 1

At step 1, two species of bacteria, Species A and Species B, were cultured in separate flasks containing identical media. As shown in Figure 1, it was noted that the population of Species A showed a growth rate greater than that of Species B. At step 2, organisms belonging to both species were grown together in a single flask under the same conditions used in step 1. As shown in Figure 1, Species A survived and Species B died out.

Experiment 2

At step 1, two species of algae, Species C and Species D, were grown in separate flasks containing identical media. As measured by dry weight (Figure 2), the population of Species C grew more rapidly than did that of Species D. At step 2, Species C and D were grown together in a single flask under the same conditions used in step 1. The resulting data indicated that the population of Species D grew more rapidly than did that of Species C, the latter species eventually dying out (see Figure 2).

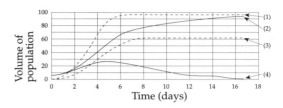

Key: (1) Species A (alone)
      (2) Species A (with Species B)
      (3) Species B (alone)
      (4) Species B (with Species A)

Figure 1

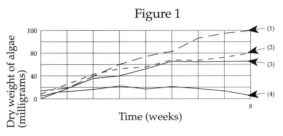

Key: (1) Species C (alone)
      (2) Species D (alone)
      (3) Species D (with Species C)
      (4) Species C (with Species D)

Figure 2

1. Organisms belonging to Species X are in competition for resource R. One organism belonging to the species acquires by mutation the ability to use resource S as a substitute for resource R. Which of the following choices best describes the situation?

   A. Competitive inhibition
   B. Hardy-Weinberg law
   C. Adaptive radiation
   D. Genetic drift

2. Among the following choices, which best describes the meaning of "fitness" in Darwinian terms?

   A. Ability to undergo random mutation
   B. Ability to escape predators
   C. Ability to adjust to changing environmental conditions
   D. Ability to reproduce

3. Among the following choices, which is best supported by the data derived from Experiment 1?

   A. Species A is more fit than Species B under the experimental conditions.
   B. Species A is more fit than Species B under all conditions.
   C. The period of Species A's presence on the earth is longer than that of Species B.
   D. If Species A and Species B lived in separate communities, Species B would become extinct before Species A.

4. Which of the following conclusions is contradicted by the data obtained in Experiments 1 and 2?

   A. Species A has an adverse effect on the reproductive capacity of Species B when they are cultured together.
   B. Species D has an adverse effect on the reproductive capacity of Species C when they are cultured together.
   C. If two species compete for the same resource, one will always outcompete the other.
   D. A species will better compete with another species if, when living in the absence of the other species, it shows greater population growth than does the other species.

5. With respect to Figure 1, which of the following choices most likely explains the apparent elimination, over time, of the gap between curves 1 and 2?

   A. Adaptation of Species A
   B. Evolution of Species A
   C. Mutation within Species A
   D. Elimination of Species B

6. Taken together, do the two experiments support the theory of competitive exclusion?

   A. Yes, because in each case the two competing species show different rates of population growth.
   B. Yes, because in each case one of the two competing species fails to survive.
   C. No, because the two experiments involve different species.
   D. No, because the two experiments do not necessarily involve the same growth medium or environments.

7. With reference to the first experiment, what was the difference after 10 days between the size of the population of Species B when grown alone and the population of Species B when grown together with Species A?

   A. 10 units
   B. 20 units
   C. 50 units
   D. 60 units

32.3 MASTERY VERIFIED: ANSWERS AND EXPLANATIONS

1. **C is correct.** Adaptive radiation generally refers to the situation in which a subpopulation of a species is able to occupy a new ecological niche. Through additional evolution, its progeny adapt themselves to the new niche and may ultimately generate a separate species. Competitive inhibition (choice A) refers to an enzyme-related phenomenon. The Hardy-Weinberg law accounts for the stability of gene frequencies in a large population that meets specific criteria (choice B). Genetic drift (choice D) refers to changes in a small population's gene pool through random processes.

2. **D is correct.** The measure of "fitness" in Darwinian terms is the organism's ability to survive for as long as is necessary to reproduce.

3. **A is correct.** Choice A is directly supported by data. Choice B is not refuted, but we have almost no evidence regarding this statement. We only know that Species A is more fit under one set of conditions; we have no evidence regarding any other possible set of circumstances. We have no evidence at all for either choice C or choice D.

4. **D is correct.** Choices A, B, and C are consistent with the data. While the data does not directly address reproductive capacity, it does not contradict the conclusions stated in choices A and B. It is also logically possible that the greater population growth of Species A in the first experiment and of Species D in the second experiment is attributable to such adverse influences. In choice C, it is true that in each experiment performed, one of the two species survived. The data does contradict the statement made in choice D, however, since in the second experiment, Species C showed greater population growth when grown alone, but died out when grown together with Species D.

5. **D is correct.** Examination of Figure 1 shows that the growth of Species A in the presence of Species B (curve 2) increases as the population of Species B decreases (curve 4). This logic suggests that the elimination of Species B gives Species A greater access to the resources for which Species B was competing.

6. **B is correct.** According to the passage, the theory of competitive exclusion states that if two species compete for the same resource, one must ultimately be eliminated. In both cases, one of the species did die out. In the first case, Species B died out; and in the second case, Species C died out. The statements that are made in choices A, C, and D are not relevant to the question.

7. **C is correct.** Curve 3 represents Species B's population growth when grown alone, and curve 4 represents Species B's population growth when Species B is grown together with Species A. At ten days, the population of Species B is sixty units when grown alone, and ten units when grown with Species A; 60 – 10 = 50 units.

CHAPTER 33

BONDING

33.1 MASTERY ACHIEVED

ORBITAL HYBRIDIZATION

As we mentioned in **Chapter 13**, the location of an atom's electrons is conventionally described in terms of atomic orbitals that represent spatial probabilities, and are labeled s, p, d, and f. This model, called the **atomic orbital theory**, describes the way in which electrons are arranged to build up atoms. Now let's look at how complex bonds are formed between atoms.

Consider the formation of beryllium chloride ($BeCl_2$):

$$Be + Cl_2 \rightarrow BeCl_2$$

Chlorine's atomic number is 17, and the configuration of its outer shell is $3s^2 3p^5$; it features one unpaired electron in the third p orbital of the third shell. Beryllium's atomic number is 4, and its electron configuration is $1s^2 2s^2$; it has no unpaired electrons. How does the beryllium atom form two bonds with an atom of chlorine?

The beryllium atom redistributes its electrons in the following manner: (1) one electron is "promoted" from a $2s$ orbital into an empty $2p$ orbital, leaving two unpaired electrons—one in the $2s$ orbital and one in the $2p$ orbital; (2) the $2s$ orbital and the $2p$ orbital then "hybridize" to form two sp orbitals, each of which contains an unpaired electron; (3) each of these two hybridized sp orbitals is able to donate an electron to a covalent bond.

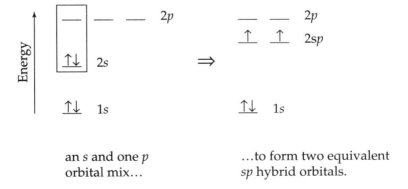

Orbital Energy Diagram for Be

This process is known as **orbital hybridization**. The hybridization just described is termed **sp hybridization** because it involves the combination of one s orbital and one p orbital.

Please solve this problem:

- The process of orbital hybridization facilitates:
    - **A.** the breaking of stable covalent bonds.
    - **B.** the conversion of ionic bonds to covalent bonds.
    - **C.** the generation of an increased number of unpaired electrons.
    - **D.** the pairing of otherwise unpaired electrons within a single atom.

Problem solved:

C is correct. As you now know, the process of orbital hybridization involves the movement of an electron from a subshell of relatively lower energy into a vacant orbital of relatively higher energy. This process leaves an unpaired electron in the lower energy orbital and creates an unpaired electron in a higher energy orbital, increasing the number of unpaired electrons that are capable of forming bonds.

Hybridization among one s orbital and two p orbitals is sp^2 **hybridization**. The formation of boron trifluoride (BF_3) illustrates this process.

Fluorine's atomic number is 9, and its electron configuration is $1s^2 2s^2 2p^5$; it has one unpaired electron in the third p orbital of its second shell, and shares it to form a covalent bond. Boron's atomic number is 5, so its electron configuration is $1s^2 2s^2 2p^1$; it carries one unpaired electron in its $2p$ orbital. To form three bonds, boron must reconfigure its electron distribution to create three unpaired electrons. One of its $2s$ electrons is moved to an empty p orbital to generate three sp^2 hybrid orbitals, each with one unpaired electron.

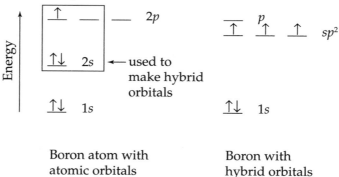

Boron atom with atomic orbitals

Boron with hybrid orbitals

On the MCAT, orbital hybridization arises in connection with carbon bonding. With an atomic number of 6, carbon has the electron configuration of $1s^2 2s^2 2p^2$; it carries two unpaired electrons in the p subshell.

Carbon–Carbon Bonding: Single, Double, and Triple Bonds

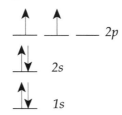

Carbon's electron configuration shows only two unpaired electrons in the outer shell. Superficial examination, then, would indicate that carbon has a capacity to form only two bonds. Yet, because of orbital hybridization, carbon can, in fact, form four bonds.

The carbon atom undergoes sp^3 **hybridization**: it forms four hybridized orbitals from one s orbital and three p orbitals. The atom promotes one of its paired $2s$ electrons into the vacant, third p orbital, leaving an unpaired electron in the s orbital and an unpaired electron in each of the three p orbitals. The s and the three p orbitals hybridize to form four equivalent sp^3 hybrid orbitals, each of which is capable of donating an electron to a covalent bond. The bonds thus formed are called **sigma (σ) bonds**.

orbital diagram for C

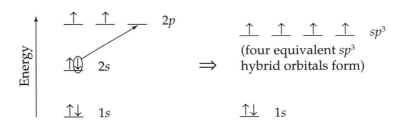

Please solve this problem:

- If an atom undergoes sp^3 hybridization, it will form:

  A. three orbitals equivalent in energy and in bonding properties.
  B. four orbitals equivalent in energy and in bonding properties.
  C. three orbitals that differ in energy and in bonding properties.
  D. three orbitals that differ in energy but not in bonding properties.

Problem solved:

B is correct. The definition of sp^3 hybridization is hybridization among one s orbital and three p orbitals, and the hybrid orbitals that are created are equivalent in *all* respects.

Please solve this problem:

- An investigator hypothesizes that although *sp*, *sp²*, and *sp³* hybridizations are observed, *sp⁴* and *sp⁵* hybridizations are not possible. Which of the following most plausibly justifies the hypothesis?

    A. No subshell carries more than three *p* orbitals.
    B. Such a predominance of *p* subshells would contravene the equivalence of hybrid orbitals.
    C. A *p* subshell may house as many as six electrons.
    D. Hybrid orbitals do not conform to any rules or laws that govern unhybridized orbitals.

Problem solved:

A is correct. The hypothesis is *plausible* because hybridization occurs among the orbitals that belong to the *s*, *p*, and *d* subshells. Hybridization occurs among *orbitals*, and since there are not more than three *p* orbitals per subshell, that would seem to be the maximum number of *p* orbitals available for hybridization.

Please solve this problem:

- With respect to hybrid orbitals, which of the following is FALSE?

    A. Hybrid oribitals increase the number of bonds in which an atom might participate.
    B. Hybrid orbitals are equivalent in their energy characteristics and bonding properties.
    C. Hybrid orbitals always produce double or triple bonding.
    D. Hybrid orbitals normally house one unpaired electron, capable of forming a covalent bond.

Problem solved:

C is correct. As just noted, *sp³* hybridization, as it occurs in the carbon atom, allows the carbon atom to form four single bonds, each of which is termed a sigma bond. Choice C, therefore, is false. Choices A, B, and D all make true statements.

As just explained, the carbon atom may undergo sp^3 hybridization to form four equivalent sp^3 orbitals and four single (sigma) bonds. Alternatively, the carbon atom may undergo a hybridization process in which one electron from an s orbital is moved to a p orbital to form three equivalent sp^2 orbitals and an unhybridized p orbital, each orbital housing one unpaired electron.

Formation of sp^2 hybrid orbitals in C

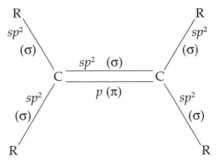

Each of the three sp^2 orbitals forms a sigma bond with another atom, at least one of which contains a p orbital. The unhybridized p orbital forms a second bond with the second carbon atom so that the first carbon atom, finally, is

(A) *singly* bonded to each of two other atoms and

(B) *doubly* bonded to a second atom.

Each of the two single bonds is a sigma (σ) bond attributable to an sp^2 orbital. The double bond is composed of (a) one sigma bond attributable to the third sp^2 orbital and (b) one **pi (π) bond**, attributable to the lone p orbital.

$$
\begin{array}{ccc}
R & & R \\
\diagdown sp^2 & & sp^2 \diagup \\
(\sigma) & & (\sigma) \\
& sp^2 \quad (\sigma) & \\
C & \rule{3cm}{0pt} & C \\
\diagup sp^2 & p\ (\pi) & sp^2 \diagdown \\
(\sigma) & & (\sigma) \\
R & & R \\
\end{array}
$$

The carbon atom may undergo not only (a) sp^3 hybridization (to form four single bonds) AND (b) sp^2 hybridization (to form two single bonds and a double bond), but also (c) sp hybridization, which produces the carbon–carbon **triple bond.**

Consider again carbon's electron configuration:

$$\uparrow \quad \uparrow \quad \underline{} \quad 2p$$

$$\uparrow\downarrow \quad 2s$$

$$\uparrow\downarrow \quad 1s$$

Suppose now that

(1) one electron from the 2s orbital moves to a p orbital,

(2) the s orbital hybridizes with one of the p orbitals to form two equivalent sp orbitals, and

(3) one electron remains in each of the two remaining p orbitals.

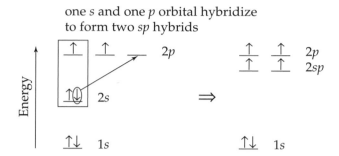

Having undergone sp hybridization, the atom can form two sigma bonds, one for each of the two sp orbitals, and two π bonds, one for each of the p orbitals.

The result is that the carbon atom forms:

(a) one sigma bond with one other atom (that may or may not be carbon);

(b) one sigma bond and two π bonds, which creates a carbon–carbon triple bond with a second similarly hybridized carbon atom.

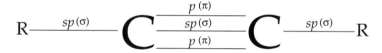

Please solve this problem:

- The carbon–carbon triple bond involves the overlap of:

   A. two hybrid sp^2 orbitals and one lobe of each of two p orbitals.
   B. two hybrid sp orbitals and both lobes of each of two p orbitals.
   C. two hybrid sp orbitals and one lobe of each of two p orbitals.
   D. three p orbitals.

Problem solved:

B is correct. The carbon–carbon triple bond involves hybridization that creates one sp hybrid orbital and reserves two p orbitals. The sp orbital of one carbon atom overlaps with the sp orbital of another to form a σ bond, and both lobes of the two p orbitals of one carbon atom overlap with two lobes of two p orbitals of the other to form two π bonds.

Hybridization and Geometry

For the MCAT, it is important to know that:

- sp^3 hybridization, with carbon bound to four atoms, produces a tetrahedral molecule:

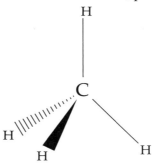

sp^3 hybridization produces
tetrahedral geometry

- sp^2 hybridization, with carbon singly bound to two atoms and doubly bound to a second atom, produces a planar molecule:

$$H \quad \quad H$$
$$\diagdown \quad \diagup$$
$$C = C$$
$$\diagup \quad \diagdown$$
$$H \quad \quad H$$

sp^2 hybridization produces
planar molecule

- sp hybridization, with carbon singly bound to one atom and triply bound to another atom, produces a linear molecule:

$$H \text{——} C \equiv C \text{——} H$$

sp hybridization produces
a linear molecule

POLAR BONDING AND DIPOLE MOMENT

As we mentioned in **Chapter 14**, the terms "polarity" and "polar bonds" generally refer to covalent bonds in which electrons are not shared equally. One of the atoms, the more electronegative, takes on a partial negative charge while the other takes on a partial positive charge. A **dipolar molecule** is a molecule whose polar bonds provide it with both a positive and negative end. If a molecule is dipolar, its centers of positive and negative charge do not coincide, and it has a **dipole moment**.

Generally, the elements with the greatest electronegativity are located in the upper right region of the periodic table, and those with the least electronegativity are in the lower left region. It is helpful to know that in terms of electronegativity:

$$F > O > N > Cl > Br > I > S > C \sim H$$

An organic molecule may contain polar bonds but have no dipole moment, meaning that the *molecule* itself is not then a dipole. Determining whether a particular molecule is a dipole requires an examination of its bonds, the relative electronegativities of its atoms and the spatial relationship of each bond to every other.

A molecule that is symmetrical and composed of a central carbon atom and two or more identical substituents will not form a dipole, even if the bonds between carbon and its substituents are polar. Consider, for example, the molecules carbon dioxide (CO_2) and carbon tetrachloride (CCl_4). Both are composed of polar covalent bonds, but because each is symmetrical and carries equivalent bonds symmetrically positioned in relation to the central carbon atom, it shows no net dipole moment.

Look at the structure of carbon dioxide:

$$O = C = O$$

Oxygen is more electronegative than carbon, and each oxygen atom tends to carry a negative charge, leaving the central carbon atom with a slightly positive charge. Because, however, the two negatively charged entities are equally distant from the carbon and arranged symmetrically around it, they "cancel" each other. The molecule is not a dipole, despite its polar bonds.

Carbon tetrachloride is tetrahedrally arranged: a central carbon atom is attached to four chlorine atoms.

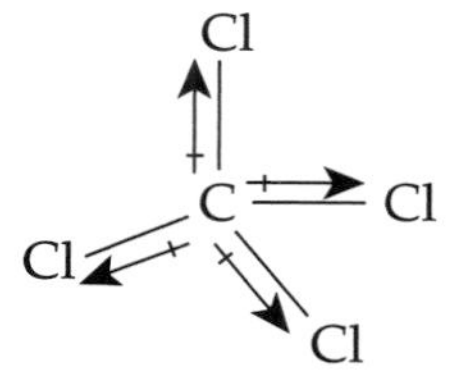

Carbon tetrachloride:
tetrahedral, dipole moment = 0

Chlorine is more electronegative than carbon, and so each bond is polar. But because the molecule is symmetrical and the polarity of all the bonds are equal, the overall dipole moment is zero.

If a molecule is not symmetrical, or if the central carbon is bound to atoms of differing electronegativities, centers of positive and negative charge will not coincide, and the molecule will show a dipole moment. Methyl chloride (CH_3Cl), for example, is tetrahedrally shaped and fulfills the criterion of symmetry. But chlorine is more electronegative than carbon, while carbon and hydrogen have similar electronegativity and are therefore nonpolar bonds. The center of positive charge lies below the central carbon atom in the diagram, but the center of negative charge lies somewhere *between* the central carbon atom and the chlorine atom:

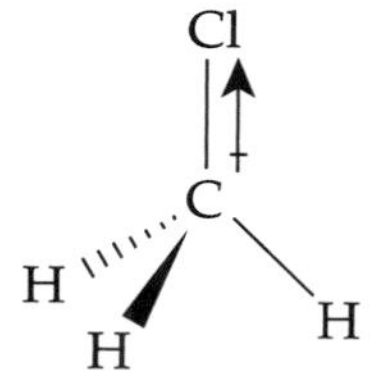

The molecule is therefore a dipole and shows a dipole moment.

Please solve this problem:

- An organic molecule will always show a dipole moment if

    A. some or all of its bonds are polar.
    B. some or all of its bonds are ionic.
    C. it is symmetrically oriented.
    D. its centers of positive and negative charge fail to coincide.

Problem solved:

D is correct. Remember, a molecule that contains polar bonds may or may not be a dipole, depending on whether its centers of negative and positive charge coincide. Even if a molecule is composed of polar bonds, it will not show a dipole moment if it is symmetrically arranged and all of its bonds are equivalent. Such is the case, for example, in the molecules CO_2, which is linearly arranged, and CCl_4, which is tetrahedrally arranged.

Please solve this problem:

- The bromomethane molecule pictured above is most likely:

    A. a dipole, because bromine is more electro-negative than carbon and hydrogen.
    B. a dipole, because the molecule contains four covalent bonds.
    C. not a dipole, because the molecule lacks double and triple bonds.
    D. not a dipole, because it involves no hybridized orbitals.

Problem solved:

A is correct. Bromine is more electronegative than carbon, and carbon is more electronegative than hydrogen. Although the molecule is somewhat symmetrically shaped, the centers of positive and negative charges do not coincide. The center of positive charge is near the carbon atom, and the center of negative charge is somewhere between the carbon and bromine atoms.

Please solve this problem:

$$N\equiv C\!-\!C\equiv N$$

- The molecule pictured above is most likely:
    - **A.** a dipole, because carbon is more electronegative than nitrogen.
    - **B.** a dipole, because nitrogen is more electronegative than carbon.
    - **C.** not a dipole, because the centers of positive and negative charges do not coincide.
    - **D.** not a dipole, because the molecule is linear and symmetrical in shape and composition.

Problem solved:

D is correct. Nitrogen is more electronegative than carbon. For each carbon–nitrogen triple bond, carbon carries a relative positive charge, and nitrogen carries a relative negative charge. However, the molecule is symmetrical in terms of shape and composition. The negative charges on the nitrogen atoms produce a center of negative charge midway between them. That, in turn, coincides with the center of positive charge that occurs midway between the two carbon atoms. The molecule, therefore, is not a dipole, even though it carries polar bonds.

Please solve this problem:

- The water molecule pictured above is most likely:
    - **A.** a dipole, because the O–H bonds are polar, and molecule is not symmetrically shaped.
    - **B.** a dipole, because hydrogen is more electronegative than oxygen.
    - **C.** not a dipole, because the centers of positive and negative charges coincide.
    - **D.** not a dipole, because the oxygen atom is bound to two other atoms, not four.

Problem solved:

A is correct. Although the water molecule's oxygen atom is bound to two hydrogen atoms, the molecule is bent, not linear. Combined with the polarity of the O–H bonds, the absence of radial symmetry means that centers of positive and negative charges fail to coincide. Note that choice D is incorrect because a central atom need not be bound to four atoms to eliminate a dipole moment. For example, carbon dioxide lacks a dipole moment even though carbon is bonded only to two oxygens. The molecule's linear shape causes positive and negative centers of charges to coincide.

HYDROGEN BONDING

If hydrogen is asymmetrically bound to an atom that has (a) relatively *high* electronegativity and (b) an unshared pair of electrons, there results a phenomenon called **hydrogen bonding**.

A hydrogen bond is not a true covalent bond. Rather, it is an attraction that occurs in a solution between (a) an unshared pair of electrons within a first molecule and (b) the partially positively charged hydrogen atom on an adjacent molecule of the same substance. For the MCAT, you should associate hydrogen bonding with molecules in which hydrogen is bound to nitrogen, fluorine, or oxygen. Hydrogen bonding arises, for example, in water, ammonia, and hydrogen fluoride. (As will be discussed in **Chapters 36** and **38**, it also arises in alcohols and carboxylic acids.)

Hydrogen bonding in (a) H_2O, (b) NH_3, and (c) HF

Hydrogen bonding raises the boiling point of a substance beyond what it would be in the absence of the hydrogen bonds. Without hydrogen bonding, for example, water would be a gas at room temperature. Moreover, because of hydrogen bonding, solid water (ice) forms a crystalline structure that makes it one of the few substances whose solid form is less dense than its liquid form.

Please solve this problem:

- Hydrogen bonding increases boiling point because it:

    A. promotes attraction among molecules in the liquid state.
    B. mimics the presence of an ionic solute.
    C. causes molecules to disperse more readily.
    D. increases vapor pressure.

Problem solved:

A is correct. Hydrogen bonding reflects the attraction between an unshared pair of electrons within one atom of a given molecule and the partially positively charged hydrogen atom of an adjacent molecule. For such molecules, escape from the liquid to the gas phase requires sufficient energy not only to produce a phase change but also to separate the adherent molecules. For this reason, hydrogen bonding increases boiling point. Note that choices C and D are clearly incorrect; the conditions they reflect would indicate a *decrease* in boiling point.

ELECTRON DELOCALIZATION AND RESONANCE STRUCTURES

Electron Delocalization

The **delocalization of electrons** increases a structure's stability. For example, the H_2 molecule is more stable than the H atom, partially because the covalent bond that joins two H atoms allows each of two electrons to move around *two* hydrogen nuclei instead of being confined to one. The O_2 molecule is more stable than the oxygen atom for the same reason; the covalent bond allows the valence electrons to move around two nuclei instead of one.

Resonance

The term **resonance** refers to a molecule or an ion with a configuration that cannot be accurately represented by a conventional diagram because one or more of its electrons is **delocalized**. Consider, for example, the carboxylate ion. It is formed by deprotonation of COOH, the carboxyl group of a carboxylic acid (**Chapter 38**).

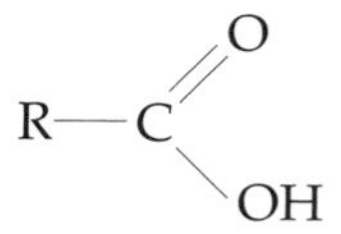

After losing a hydrogen ion, the carboxylate ion bears a negative charge and can be thought of as either this:

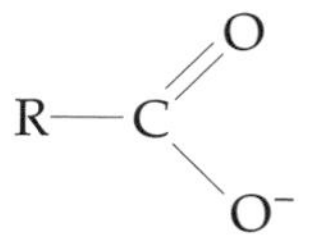

or this:

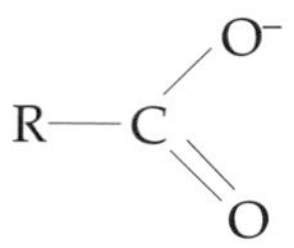

Although the carboxylate ion is sometimes said to resonate between the two forms shown above, no such resonance truly occurs. Instead, the carboxylate ion represents a **resonance hybrid** between the two structures, each of which is said to contribute to the true structure. The "extra" electron—which imparts the negative charge—is delocalized; it is not affiliated with either of the terminal oxygentoms alone, but is dispersed between the two oxygen atoms. It can also be represented like this:

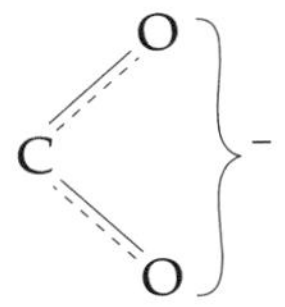

The nitrate anion (NO_3^-) has a resonance structure and is said to "resonate" among these three configurations:

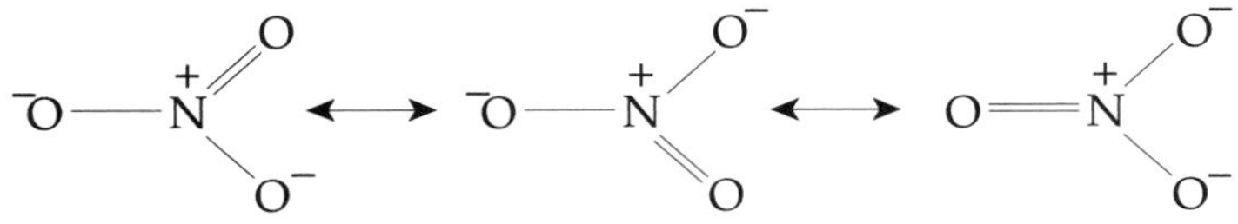

But in fact, none of the N–O bonds is a true double bond. Instead, each has a partial double-bond character, and the structure is better represented as:

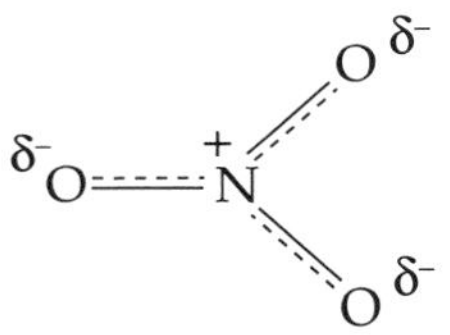

Here, as always, resonance denotes the delocalization of electrons. In the case of NO_3^-, the delocalized electrons are those in the double bond. They are not truly localized between the nitrogen atom and *one* of the oxygen atoms alone; they are "spread out" between the nitrogen atom and *all three* oxygen atoms.

The Significance of Resonance: Delocalization of Electrons and Stability

If one or more of the electrons associated with a molecule or an ion have relatively greater freedom to "roam" among separate nuclei, the entire species is stabilized.

Consider again a prototypical carboxylic acid. Its acidity—or its "willingness" to part with a hydrogen ion—depends partially on the stability of the anion that would follow from deprotonation.

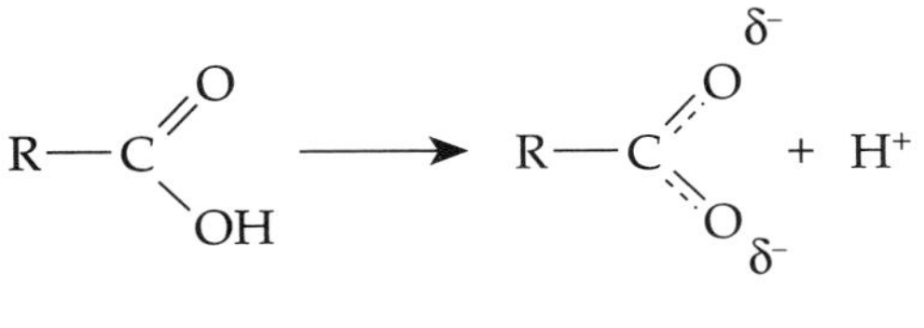

The carboxylate ion is particularly stable because it is a resonance structure.

Now consider a prototypical alcohol:

$$R—C—OH$$

The deprotonated anion R–C–O$^-$ does not exhibit resonance; it has no "opportunity" to delocalize its negative charge. The anion is less stable than the carboxylate ion, which is one of the reasons that alcohols are less acidic than carboxylic acids.

$$R—C—OH \longrightarrow R—C—O^- + H^+$$

Please solve this problem:

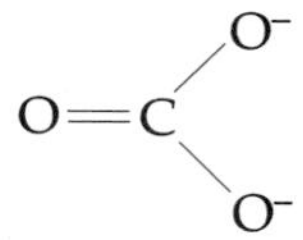

- The carbonate ion is often depicted as shown above. It has been discovered, however, that the ion's three carbon–oxygen bonds are of equal length and character. The most likely explanation is that the ion:

  A. represents a resonance structure in which positive charge is delocalized, and there is partial triple bond character between the central carbon atom and one of the oxygen atoms.
  B. rapidly alternates between two structures and does not truly carry at any one moment a full charge of –2.
  C. represents a resonance structure in which all carbon–oxygen bonds have partial double bond character and negative charge is delocalized among three oxygen atoms.
  D. does not represent a resonance structure.

Problem solved:

C is correct. A resonance structure depicts the delocalization of electrons, which may include those that participate in a bond, those that confer a negative charge, or both. In the case of the carbonate ion, resonance causes each of the three C—O bonds to bear partial double bond character, thereby delocalizing the associated bonding electrons. It also causes the three oxygen atoms to "share" the burden of the ion's negative charge. The ion may be depicted in these resonance forms:

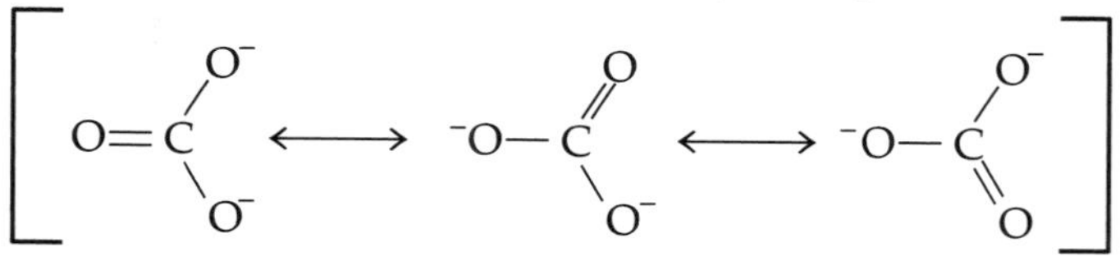

In truth, it exists as a single hybrid:

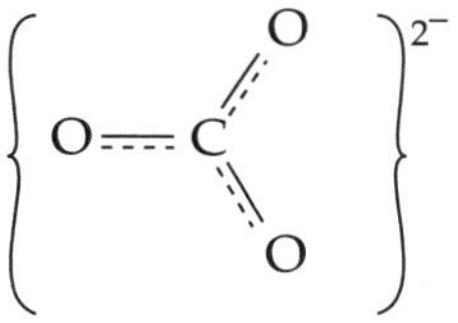

$$\left\{ O \text{---} C \begin{array}{c} O \\ \\ O \end{array} \right\}^{2-}$$

Please solve this problem:

$$CH_2 = CH - \overset{+}{C}H_2 \quad \longleftrightarrow \quad \overset{+}{C}H_2 - CH = CH_2$$

$$\qquad\qquad 1 \qquad\qquad\qquad\qquad\qquad 2$$

- The allyl carbocation is a hybrid of two structures, as shown above. Which of the following is true?

    A. Neither structure actually exists.
    B. Both structures exist but differ in stability.
    C. Both structures exist and are identical in their stability.
    D. A sample of allyl carbocation is composed 50 percent of one structure and 50 percent of the other.

Problem solved:

A is correct. As stated in the text, resonance molecules do not really alternate between two structures. Instead, the resonance structure represents a hybrid molecule that has, in part, the character of its contributing resonance forms. A resonance hybrid is roughly analogous to the hybrid created by the mating of a horse and donkey. The resulting mule is not a horse at one moment and a donkey at another. Rather, it is an entity unto itself, resembling a horse in some respects and a donkey in others.

33.2 MASTERY APPLIED: PRACTICE PASSAGE AND QUESTIONS

Passage

In order to perform their metabolic functions, organisms require a supply of free energy. In most biological systems, the immediate donor of free energy is adenosine triphosphate (ATP), which, when hydrolyzed, yields free energy, adenosine diphosphate (ADP), and inorganic phosphate, P_i.

The standard free energy of hydrolysis of ATP to form ADP and inorganic phos-phate is –7.3 kilocalorie/mole. This is low compared with the –2.2 kilocalorie/mole yielded in the hydrolysis of glycerol-3-phosphate.

$$ATP + H_2O \rightleftharpoons ADP + P_i$$

$$\Delta G° = -7.3 \text{ kcal/mol}$$

$$\text{glycerol-3-phosphate} + H_2O \rightleftharpoons \text{glycerol} + P_i$$

$$\Delta G° = -2.2 \text{ kcal/mol}$$

The relatively low standard free energy associated with ATP hydrolysis means that for the ATP molecule, phosphate group transfer potential is higher than it is for glycerol-3-phosphate. The relatively large phosphate group transfer potential for ATP reflects the difference between the standard free energy of the reactants (ATP and H_2O) and that of the products (ADP and inorganic phosphate). In part, the relative stability of the products is traceable to the resonance stabilization of inorganic phosphate shown in Figure 1 to the right.

For the molecules phosphoenolpyruvate, acetyl phosphate, and phosphocrea-tine (Figure 2), phosphate group transfer potential is higher than it is for ATP. Among the significant phosphorylated compounds in biological systems, ATP is associated with an intermediate phosphate group transfer potential. It is for that reason that ATP is well-suited to serve as a phosphate carrier and, therefore, as an immediate donor of free energy in metabolic processes. If phosphate group transfer potential were extremely high, ADP would not take on phosphate to form ATP. If it were extremely low, the ATP molecule would resist hydrolysis and would be unable to serve as a ready source of free energy.

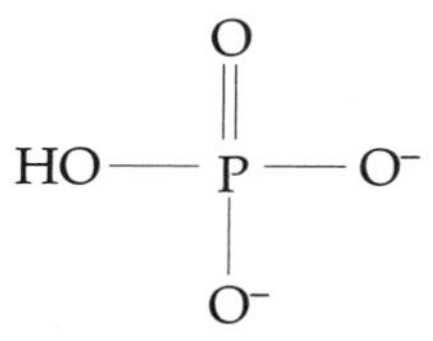

Figure 1

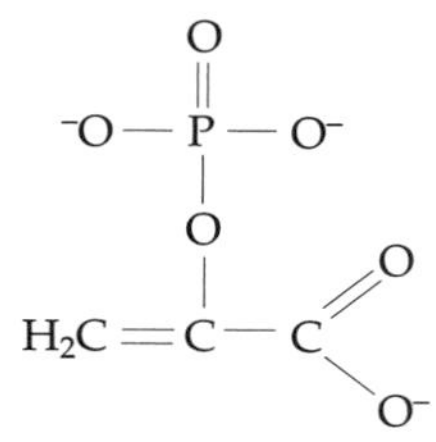

Phosphoenolpyruvate

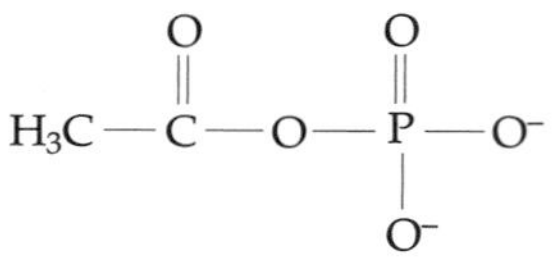

Acetyl phosphate

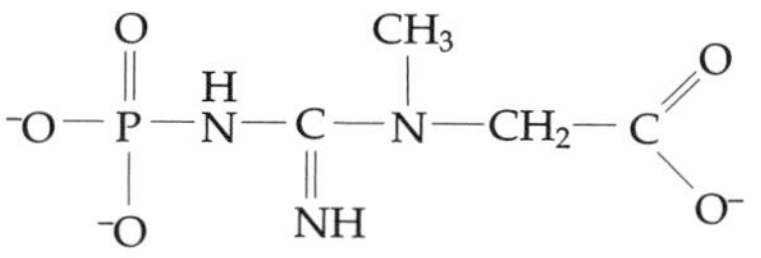

Phosphocreatine

Figure 2

Compound	ΔG° (kcal/mol)
Phosphoenolpyruvate	−14.8
Carbamoyl phosphate	−12.3
Acetyl phosphate	−10.3
Phosphocreatine	−10.3
Pyrophosphate	−8.0
ATP (to ADP)	−7.3
Glucose-1-phosphate	−5.0
Glucose-6-phosphate	−3.3
Glucose-3-phosphate	−2.2

Free energies of hydrolysis for some
biologically significant phosphorylated molecules

Table 1

1. In the molecule of acetyl phosphate
shown in Figure 2, the carbon atom that
is double bonded to oxygen:

    A. has undergone sp^2 hybridization.
    B. has undergone sp^3 hybridization.
    C. has formed no σ bonds.
    D. is in a higher energy state than un-
    bound atomic carbon.

2. Among the following choices, which
most likely contributes to the stability
of the dehydrogenated phosphocreatine
molecule shown in Figure 2?

    A. Repulsion between negative charge
    and positive charge
    B. Repulsion between negative charge
    and negative charge
    C. Low acidity of the carboxyl (COOH)
    group
    D. Electron delocalization within the
    carboxylate (COO⁻) moiety

3. Which among the following choices is
LEAST likely to represent a structure that
contributes to the inorganic phosphate
resonance structure?

4. Within the molecule acetyl phosphate,
shown in Figure 2, the single carbon–carbon bond is:

    A. dipolar ionic.
    B. nonpolar ionic.
    C. nonpolar covalent.
    D. polar covalent.

5. Which of the following molecules would show the greatest difference between its own standard free energy and that of the products that result from its hydrolysis into inorganic phosphate and the corresponding dephosphorylated molecule?

   A. Glucose-3-phosphate
   B. Phosphocreatine
   C. Carbamoyl phosphate
   D. Adenosine triphosphate

6. At physiologic pH, the ATP molecule is sufficiently deprotonated as to carry four negative charges. Which of the following choices, if added to the surrounding medium, would most likely DECREASE the molecule's phosphate group transfer potential?

   A. An inorganic base
   B. An inorganic acid
   C. An inorganic salt
   D. An organic nonpolar solute

7. A chemist considers the ramifications of hypothetical evolutionary trends in which organisms had not developed the capacity to synthesize ATP. Among the following compounds, which would be most thermodynamically suited to assume its role as immediate donor of phosphate?

   A. Glucose-6-phosphate
   B. Carbamoyl phosphate
   C. Phosphoenolpyruvate
   D. Pyrophosphate

33.3 MASTERY VERIFIED: ANSWERS AND EXPLANATIONS

1. **A is correct.** Although an unbound carbon atom has only two unpaired electrons in its outer shell, it can form up to four sigma bonds by hybridizing its orbitals. In this case three sigma bonds and one pi bond are formed from three sp^2 hybridized orbitals and one unhybridized p orbital.

2. **D is correct.** The carboxylate (COO⁻) moiety is a resonance structure; it represents a hybrid between two structures: each carbon–oxygen bond has a partial double bond character. The electrons that form the bond are highly delocalized; they move about the positively charged nuclei of two oxygen atoms and a carbon atom. The negative charge carried by the COO⁻ moiety is delocalized over the two oxygen atoms.

3. **A is correct.** Figure 1 shows one of the structures that contributes to the orthophosphate resonance structure. The other structures show delocalization of electrons by the movement of the double bond about the molecule and the dispersal of the molecule's two negative charges. Choice A shows the addition of a proton (hydrogen ion) to one of the oxygen atoms, which changes the molecule's constitution. The structure shown in choice A is not molecularly equivalent to the structure shown in Figure 1 or to those shown in choices B, C, and D.

4. **D is correct.** Ionic bonds arise only between atoms of markedly different electronegativities; they result in a true exchange of electrons. A polar covalent bond arises between atoms whose electronegativities are significantly different, but not so different as to produce an ionic bond. In a polar covalent bond, electrons are *shared unequally*: one atom carries a partial negative charge, and the other a partial positive charge. However, the MCAT test taker must be aware that a carbonyl carbon carries a partial positive charge due to the high electronegativity of oxygen. This partial positive charge makes the covalent bond between these two carbons somewhat polar.

5. **C is correct.** The substance that has the lowest standard free energy of hydrolysis will be the one for which the difference between the standard free energy of products and reactants is greatest. Among the molecules listed in choices A–D, carbamoyl phosphate shows the lowest standard free energy of hydrolysis: –12.3 kilocalorie/mol.

6. **B is correct.** The four negative charges associated with the ATP molecule at physiologic pH are attributable to deprotonation—loss of hydrogen ions. The addition of an inorganic or organic base would decrease the ambient concentration of hydrogen ions and (a) promote deprotonation and (b) increase the degree of negative charge. The addition of an inorganic acid would have the opposite effect. It would (a) increase ambient hydrogen ion concentration and (b) *re*protonate the ATP molecule.

   The ATP molecule's four negative charges repel one another and impair its stability, favoring its hydrolysis. Addition of an acid and the resulting reprotonation of the ATP molecule will reduce its number of negative charges and therefore stabilize it. If the ATP molecule's stability is increased, its tendency to be hydrolyzed and hence to transfer a phosphate group will be decreased.

   The addition of a base would have the opposite effect: by promoting deprotonation of the molecule, it would increase the degree of negative charge, destabilize the molecule, increase its tendency to undergo hydrolysis, and increase its phosphate group transfer potential. The addition of inorganic salt would depend on the K_{sp} for that salt and thus is not the best answer. A nonpolar solute would not affect the ATP molecule's stability.

7. **D is correct.** According to the passage's last paragraph, ATP is well-suited to its role as immediate donor of phosphate because it shows an intermediate value for standard free energy of hydrolysis. Among the biologically significant phosphorylated compounds, the best replacement would be another molecule that has a free energy of hydrolysis in the mid range. Choices A, B, and C are molecules whose standard free energies of hydrolysis are either extremely high or extremely low. Pyrophosphate, on the other hand, has the value of –8.0, which is relatively close to that of ATP and is in the mid range.

Chapter 34
STEREOCHEMISTRY

34.1 MASTERY ACHIEVED

Two molecules are said to be **isomers** if they have the same atomic content (and hence the same chemical formula) but differ in the way their atoms are bonded, connected, and arranged. Isomers are divided broadly into two categories: (1) **structural isomers** and (2) **stereoisomers**. In turn, there are two types of stereoisomers: (1) enantiomers, and (2) diastereomers. Diastereomers themselves are divided into two categories: (1) geometric (cis-trans) isomers and (2) configurational diastereomers epimers.

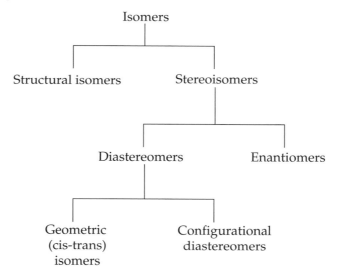

Two structural isomers represent two entirely different substances that happen to have identical chemical formulas.

Please solve this problem:

- Two structural isomers differ as to their:

    A. molecular weights.
    B. molecular structures.
    C. Both A and B
    D. Neither A nor B

Problem solved:

B is correct. By definition, all isomers of the same compound (structural isomers *and* stereo-isomers) contain the same atomic constituents; the number and types of atoms that compose the compounds are identical. Therefore, for any pair of structural isomers, molecular weight will always be equal. Two structural isomers differ, however, in the way in which the atoms are bonded to one another, as in the case of ethyl alcohol and dimethyl ether, shown above. Their molecular structures, therefore, differ.

Please solve this problem:

- Two substances are analyzed and found to have identical molecular formulas but different physical properties. An investigator postulates that the two substances represent a pair of structural isomers. Is the hypothesis plausible?

    A. Yes, because structural isomers can represent very different substances with different chemical properties.
    B. Yes, because structural isomers have different molecular weights and, therefore, different chemical properties.
    C. No, because a pair of structural isomers always shows a difference in chemical formula.
    D. No, because structural isomers show similar behaviors and properties.

Problem solved:

A is correct. Two molecules may have the same atomic content, but differ significantly in the way their constituent atoms are bonded to one another. Such molecules are structural isomers. The substances they represent are different (related, really, only by an accident of chemical "fate"— identical chemical formulas). Ordinarily, structural isomers differ markedly in their properties and behaviors.

Any pair of isomers that are *not* structural isomers are stereoisomers. Stereoisomers are isomers in which atoms are similarly bonded and connected, differing from each other only in the way the atoms are oriented in space. The rest of this chapter concerns stereoisomerism, much of which arises from the phenomenon of *chirality*.

CHIRALITY AND THE CHIRAL CENTER

Within any molecule, a chiral center refers to any central atom bonded to four different atoms or groups. (Often, chiral centers are labeled by an asterisk [*].) The prototypical chiral center conforms to this model:

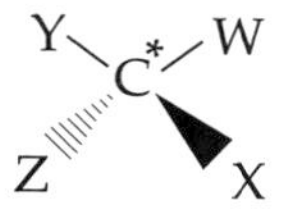

The letters W, X, Y, and Z refer to the four atoms or groups to which the chiral center (carbon in this case), is bound. Consider, for instance, a molecule of lactic acid, as shown below:

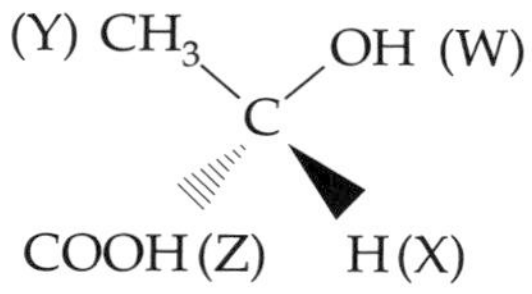

For the MCAT, chirality is significant in connection with molecules for which the chiral center is carbon.

CHIRAL MOLECULES AND ENANTIOMERISM

We have just discussed the chiral center. We now relate the chiral center to the chiral *molecule*. A molecule is chiral if it cannot be superimposed on the molecule that represents its mirror image. If for example, a pair of right-handed and left-handed gloves was molecules, each glove would be a chiral molecule.

If a molecule has only one chiral center, then that molecule is chiral. Examine, again, a molecule of lactic acid in its two enantiomeric forms:

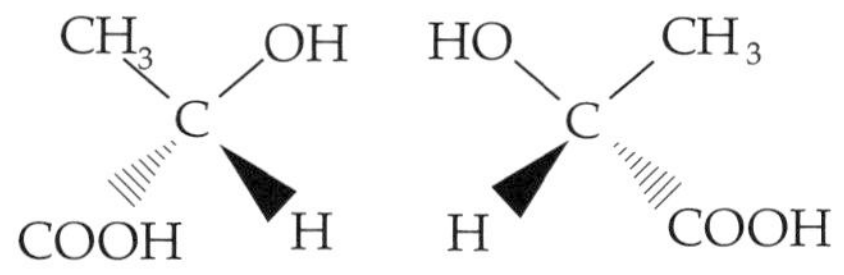

Lactic acid

In your mind's eye, try to superimpose the molecule on the left over the molecule on the right by sliding and turning the molecule on the left—*without lifting it from the plane of the page.* You'll find that you cannot do it. If the OH groups are superimposed on one another, the COOH and CH_3 groups will not coincide. If the COOH and CH_3 groups are superimposed on one another, the OH and H groups will not coincide. These two mirror image molecules cannot be superimposed on one another.

The two nonsuperimposable mirror-image molecules that follow from chirality are, of course, isomers. More specifically, they are stereoisomers and, more specifically still, they are enantiomers. A pair of enantiomers, then, is made up of two molecules that represent mirror images of each other but that cannot be superimposed on one another. Chirality gives rise to enantiomers, and enantiomers arise only from chirality.

Enantiomers behave as the same molecule for all intents and purposes, meaning all their physical properties, such as polarity, solubility, melting point, boiling point, etc. are identical. This makes the separation of enantiomers, or *resolution,* very difficult. The only property that differs for a pair of enantiomers is their optical activity, which will be addressed in a later section.

For the MCAT, know that:

- If a molecule is chiral, its mirror image is its enantiomer, and its enantiomer is its mirror image;

- Any molecule for which there is an enantiomer is chiral;

- A molecule that is not chiral is called a̲chiral; and

- Enantiomers have identical physical properties, except for their optical activity.

Please solve this problem:

- An investigator discovers a molecule that has only one chiral center. Is he justified in concluding that the molecule is not superimposable on its mirror image?

    A. Yes, because the presence of one or more chiral centers always indicates chirality.
    B. Yes, because the presence of only one chiral center always indicates chirality.
    C. No, because some chiral molecules are superimposable on their mirror image molecules.
    D. No, because in some cases, one member of an enantiomeric pair is superimposable on the other.

Problem solved:

B is correct. As explained in the text, any molecule with only one chiral center is definitely a chiral molecule. We cannot say that a molecule with one *or more* chiral centers is definitely chiral, which makes choice A wrong. (We will discuss molecules with more than one chiral center in connection with diastereomerism.) Choices C and D make false statements; no chiral molecule is superimposable on its mirror image. An enantiomeric pair is a pair of chiral molecules, meaning that neither member is superimposable on the other.

Absolute Configuration of Enantiomers: R and S

Every chiral center and its four bonded entities has an absolute configuration, designated either "R" or "S." For any pair of enantiomers, one member is designated R and the other is designated S. These designations of absolute configuration, R and S, are derived according to a convention, the first step of which requires that we assign a priority number to each substituent (atom or group) directly bonded to the chiral carbon.

Assign priority numbers according to this set of rules:

(1) If the chiral carbon is directly bonded to four different atoms (each of which might or might not be bonded to other atoms to form a group), then we assign priority numbers according to atomic number. The atom of highest atomic number takes priority number one, and the atom

of lowest atomic number takes priority number four. If two isotopes of the same element are attached to the chiral carbon, the one with the larger atomic weight gets the higher priority.

Consider, for example, the molecule below:

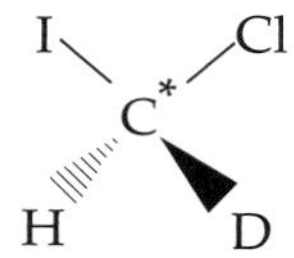

The central carbon is bonded to four different substituents: chlorine, hydrogen, iodine, and deuterium. In terms of atomic number,

$$I > Cl > D = H$$

Consequently, iodine is assigned priority number one and chlorine is assigned priority number two. Since deuterium, an isotope of hydrogen, has an atomic mass of 2 while hydrogen has an atomic mass of 1, D gets priority number three and H gets priority number four.

The central (chiral) carbon is bonded to hydrogen, chlorine, and two atoms of carbon. (The two atoms of carbon, in turn, are bonded to diverse atoms so that the central carbon is, nonetheless, bonded to four different substituents: Cl, CH_3CH_2, CH_3, and H—meaning that it is chiral.) Among the atoms of chlorine, carbon, and hydrogen, chlorine has the highest atomic number and takes priority one. Hydrogen has the lowest atomic number and takes priority four. Between the two carbons, the one with the bonded atom of highest number takes higher priority.

If two of the atoms directly bound to the central carbon are identical, then priority between them is assigned according to the atomic numbers of the atoms bonded *to* those identical atoms. This is referred to as finding the first point of difference. Consider, for instance, *sec*-Butyl chloride:

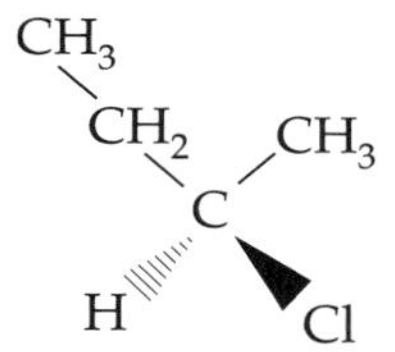

sec-butyl chloride

The methyl group (CH_3) carbon is bonded to three hydrogens, and the ethyl group (CH_3CH_2) carbon is bonded to two hydrogens and another carbon. Since carbon is of higher atomic number than hydrogen, the ethyl group is #2 while the methyl group is #3.

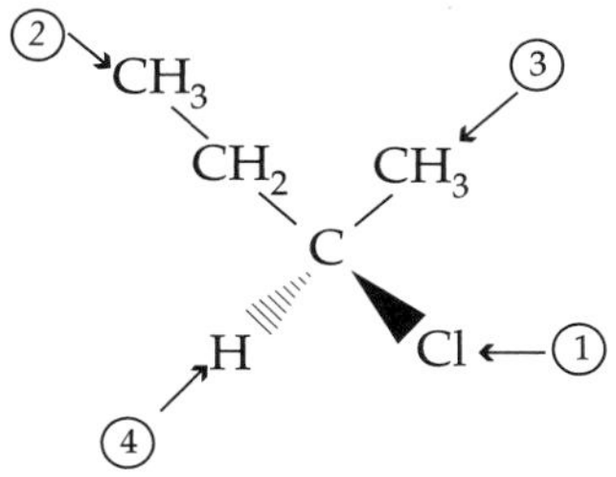

sec-butyl chloride

If the first point of difference is a difference in bond order, the higher bond order takes priority. Another way of saying this is that multiple bonds count multiple times. For example, consider the molecule below:

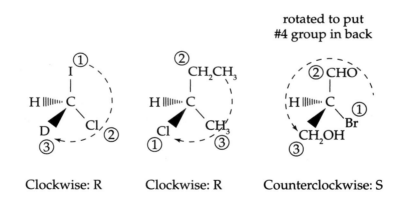

Based on the rules addressed so far, Br with the highest atomic number of the substituents attached to the chiral carbon gets priority one, while H with the smallest atomic number gets priority four. The other two substituents have C attached to the chiral center, and going out one more atom on those chains we reach the first point of difference. The top substituent, the aldehyde, has carbon in a double bond with oxygen, while the back substituent, the alcohol, has carbon in a single bond with oxygen. While both oxygen atoms have the same atomic number, treat the carbonyl carbon as though it is bonded to *two* oxygen atoms, while in the alcohol the carbon is only bonded to *one* oxygen atom. Therefore, the aldehyde gets priority two and the alcohol gets priority three.

Once priority numbers are assigned to the substituents,

(a) draw the molecule so that the substituent of lowest priority is pointed backward,

(b) ignore the substituent of lowest priority, and

(c) draw a curved arrow from substituent 1 to substituent 2 and then on to substituent 3.

If that curved arrow runs clockwise, then the enantiomer is designated R. If it runs counterclockwise, the enantiomer is designated S.

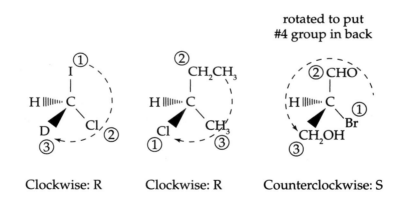

Please solve this problem:

- Draw and identify the R and S configurations of bromochloroiodomethane:

$$I \overset{\displaystyle Br}{\underset{\displaystyle H}{\overset{|}{\underset{|}{-C^*-}}}} Cl$$

Problem solved:

To identify the R and S configurations, we examine the flat projection and assign priority numbers. Each of the bonded entities is a single atom, and the order of priorities is easily ascertained from the periodic table. In terms of atomic number, the atoms are ordered from highest to lowest: I > Br > Cl > H. Each enantiomer is drawn so that the atom of lowest priority is pointed backward. For the resulting structures, we count one-two-three and note whether our progress is clockwise or counterclockwise. Clockwise progress denotes the R-enantiomer; counterclockwise progress denotes the S-enantiomer.

R-bromochloroiodomethane   s-bromochloroiodomethane

OPTICAL ACTIVITY AND RACEMIZATION

Chiral compounds are **optically active**, which means that they rotate the plane of polarized light. For any pair of enantiomers, one enantiomer rotates the plane of polarized light to the right, and is called the dextrorotatory (+) enantiomer. The other rotates the plane of polarized light to the left and is called the levorotatory (–) enantiomer. These molecules will rotate the light to the same extent (magnitude), just in opposite directions.

Consider again the compound bromochloroiodomethane, as drawn below (in Fischer projection):

$$I \overset{\displaystyle Br}{\underset{\displaystyle H}{\overset{|}{\underset{|}{-C-}}}} Cl$$

One of this molecule's enantiomers is the dextrorotatory (+) enantiomer, meaning that it rotates the plane of polarized light to the right, and the other is the levorotatory (–) enantiomer, which rotates the plane of polarized light to the left. To determine which enantiomer is (+) and which is (–), we subject each one to polarimeter. The polarimeter will indicate in which direction the plane of polarized light is rotated and thus identify the (+) and (–) enantiomers. *Other than evaluation via polarimetry, there exists no means of identifying the (+) and (–) enantiomers.*

Put otherwise, a molecule's absolute configuration—R or S—does NOT indicate the direction in which it rotates the plane of polarized light [sometimes called its "sign of rotation" (+) or (–)]. For one chiral molecule, the R-enantiomer might be dextrorotatory and the S-enantiomer levorotatory. For another chiral molecule, the S-enantiomer might be dextrorotatory, and the R-enantiomer levorotatory. Do not equate R and S absolute configurations with sign of rotation; there is no correlation.

The designations R and S refer to a pair of enantiomers. And if, for some chiral molecule (which, like those thus far discussed, has one and only one chiral center), we learn by polarimetry that the R-enantiomer is levorotatory (–), we can immediately conclude that the S-enantiomer is dextrorotatory (+). If for some other pair of enantiomers we learn via polarimetry that the S-enantiomer is levorotatory (–), we can immediately conclude that the R-enantiomer is dextrorotatory (+). But there is no way to determine which enantiomer is (+) and which is (–) except through polarimetry.

Please solve this problem:

- An investigator identifies the R-enantiomer of a particular enantiomeric pair. With no additional testing, which of the following may she justifiably conclude?

  A. The R-enantiomer rotates the plane of polarized light to the right.
  B. The R-enantiomer rotates the plane of polarized light to the left.
  C. Both A and B
  D. Neither A nor B

Problem solved:

D is correct. By convention, each member of an enantiomeric pair is assigned an absolute configuration of R or S, but these designations do not correlate with dextrorotation or levorotation. Because the investigator is dealing with a pair of enantiomers, she can conclude that one of them (R or S) rotates the plane of polarized light to the right and that the other rotates it to the left. However, she cannot know which enantiomer rotates in which direction except via polarimetry.

Please solve this problem:

- An investigator identifies the S-enantiomer of a particular enantiomeric pair and finds that it rotates the plane of polarized light to the right. With no additional testing, which of the following may she justifiably conclude?

  A. The R-enantiomer rotates the plane of polarized light to the right.
  B. The R-enantiomer rotates the plane of polarized light to the left.
  C. Both A and B
  D. Neither A nor B

Problem solved:

B is correct. Optical activity arises from chirality. Both members of any enantiomeric pair rotate the plane of polarized light, one to the left and the other to the right. In the absence of polarimetry, it cannot be determined which enantiomer—R or S—rotates the light in which direction. However, it is known that (a) each enantiomer rotates the light either to the right or the left and (b) the other enantiomer rotates it in the opposite direction.

Racemic Mixtures

A **racemic mixture** is any mixture of enantiomers in which dextrorotatory and levorotatory structures are present in equal concentrations. If for one chiral molecule with one chiral center, a fifty percent to fifty percent mixture of its two enantiomers is placed in a polarimeter, the polarimeter will show no rotation of polarized light because the enantiomers rotate light with equal magnitudes but opposite directions. Therefore, a racemic mixture does not rotate the plane of polarized light at all because the (+) rotation and the (−) rotation "cancel" each other.

Please solve this problem:

- A sample of *x*, a substance known to have a single chiral center, is subjected to polarimetry and causes no rotation of polarized light. Which of the following would explain the finding?

  A. The sample is a racemic mixture.
  B. The substance is not chiral.
  C. Both A and B
  D. Neither A nor B

Problem solved:

A is correct. We are told that the substance has a single chiral center, and that means that it is chiral. Choice B, therefore, is false, which means choice C is also wrong. A racemic mixture is one in which two enantiomers are represented in equal amounts. Although each enantiomer on its own would rotate the plane of polarized light in one direction or the other, the two together "cancel each other" and cause no rotation in either direction.

DIASTEREOMERS

The word *diastereomer* refers to isomers that are not enantiomers. Diastereomers are of two types (1) configurational diastereomers and (2) geometric diastereomers.

Configurational Diastereomers

Some molecules have more than one chiral center. Consider this illustration of 2,3-dichloropentane (in Fischer projection):

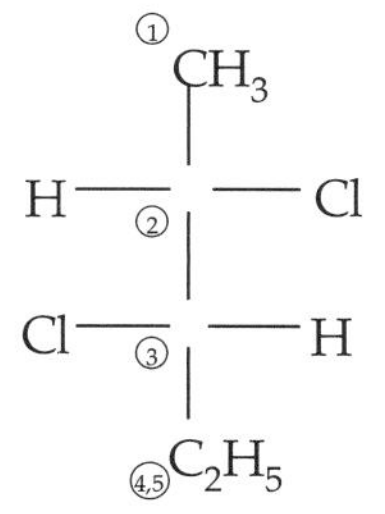

2,3-dichloropentane

Central carbons 2 and 3 each have four different substituents attached to them, making them both chiral.

For any molecule with n chiral centers, the maximum possible number of its stereoisomers (enantiomers plus diastereomers) is 2^n. For example, a molecule with one chiral center yields $2^1 = 2$ stereoisomers. A molecule with 2 chiral centers yields up to $2^2 = 4$ stereoisomers. A molecule with 3 chiral centers yields up to $2^3 = 8$ stereoisomers.

The molecule of 2,3-dichloropentane, shown above, has two chiral centers and gives rise to $2^2 = 4$ stereoisomers. The illustration above depicts one such stereoisomer. Let us now reverse the configuration at carbon 3 and identify another of its stereoisomers:

$$
\begin{array}{c}
\overset{①}{\text{CH}_3} \\
| \\
\text{H}-\overset{②}{\text{C}^*}-\text{Cl} \\
| \\
\text{H}-\overset{③}{\text{C}^*}-\text{Cl} \\
| \\
\underset{④⑤}{\text{C}_2\text{H}_5}
\end{array}
$$

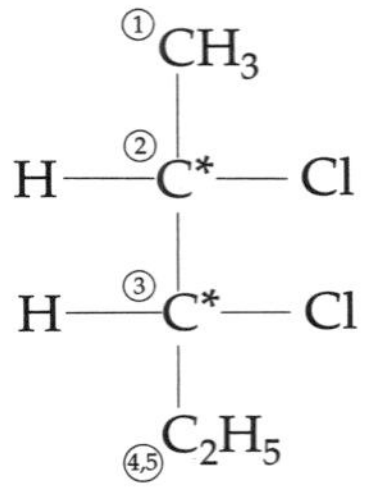

2,3-dichloropentane

The drawing just shown does *not* represent the mirror image of the previous drawing. By definition, therefore, it is not the enantiomer of the molecule originally drawn. It is, however, a stereoisomer of that molecule. More specifically, it is its diastereomer. Diastereomerism arises when a molecule has more than one chiral center and produces more than one stereoisomer, only one of which, naturally, can be its mirror image. The other two stereoisomers are its diastereomers and are enantiomers of each other.

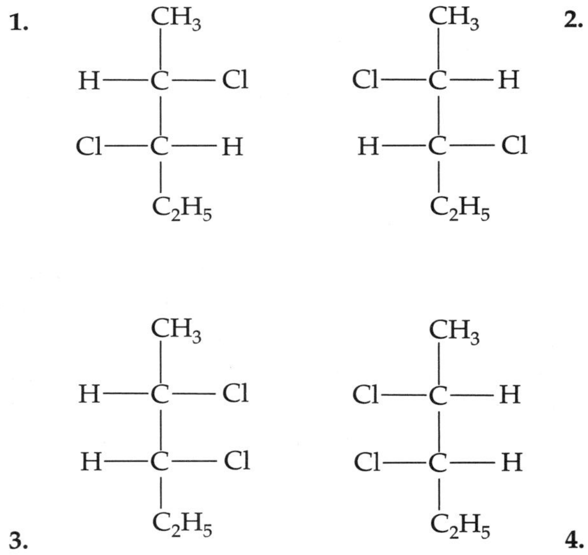

1.
$$
\begin{array}{c}
\text{CH}_3 \\
| \\
\text{H}-\text{C}-\text{Cl} \\
| \\
\text{Cl}-\text{C}-\text{H} \\
| \\
\text{C}_2\text{H}_5
\end{array}
$$

2.
$$
\begin{array}{c}
\text{CH}_3 \\
| \\
\text{Cl}-\text{C}-\text{H} \\
| \\
\text{H}-\text{C}-\text{Cl} \\
| \\
\text{C}_2\text{H}_5
\end{array}
$$

3.
$$
\begin{array}{c}
\text{CH}_3 \\
| \\
\text{H}-\text{C}-\text{Cl} \\
| \\
\text{H}-\text{C}-\text{Cl} \\
| \\
\text{C}_2\text{H}_5
\end{array}
$$

4.
$$
\begin{array}{c}
\text{CH}_3 \\
| \\
\text{Cl}-\text{C}-\text{H} \\
| \\
\text{Cl}-\text{C}-\text{H} \\
| \\
\text{C}_2\text{H}_5
\end{array}
$$

Stereoisomers of 2,3-dichloropentane

Examine the molecules immediately above and note that 2,3-dichloropentane exists as four stereoisomers. These four stereoisomers embody two pairs of enantiomers. Either member of such a pair constitutes the diastereomer of a member of the other pair. In the illustration above, molecules

1 and 2 are a pair of enantiomers. Molecules 3 and 4 are a pair of enantiomers. Molecules 1 and 3 are a pair of diastereomers and molecules 2 and 4 are a pair of diastereomers. *All four molecules are stereoisomers of 2,3-dichloropentane.*

Unlike enantiomers, diastereomers behave as different compounds, and all their physical properties are different. Therefore, diastereomers can often be easily separated based on these differing properties. In addition, the optical activity of diastereomers are different, but not in a predictable way. Whereas the optical activity of enantiomers is of equal magnitude but opposite sign, a pair of diastereomers may rotate light in the same or in opposite directions, or the magnitude of the rotations may be very similar or widely different. The most important thing to remember for the MCAT is that there is *no way to predict* what the optical activity of one diastereomer will be based on knowing the optical activity of another diastereomer.

Epimers

Epimers are a subclass of diastereomers in which only one stereocenter has two substituents switched. We say the chiral center has been inverted since switching the spatial orientation of two groups changes the R configuration to the S. For example, D-glucose has four stereocenters, and therefore has the potential of $2^4 = 16$ stereoisomers. Two such isomers are shown below, D-galactose and D-talose.

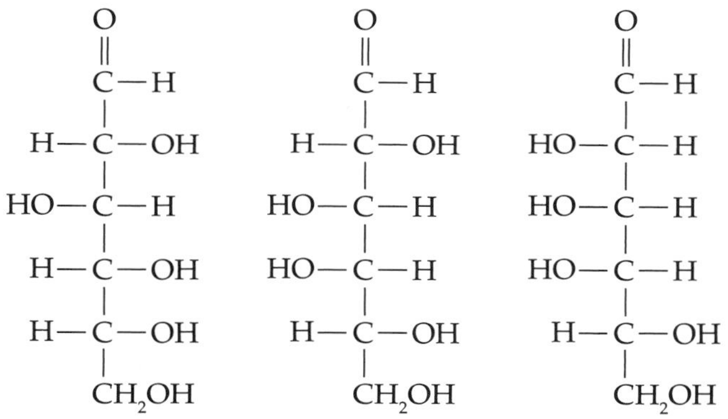

D-glucose   D-galactose   D-talose

Notice that when comparing glucose to galactose, the H and OH substituents at C-4 have switched positions, but otherwise all remaining chiral centers are untouched. Therefore, D-glucose and D-galactose are epimers (and also diastereomers, since they do not have a mirror image relationship). Similarly, D-galactose and D-talose differ only at C-2, and are also epimers and diastereomers. However, since D-glucose and D-talose differ at both C-2 and C-4, they are diastereomers, but NOT epimers. Remember, all epimers are diastereomers, but not all diastereomers are epimers.

Please solve this problem:

- A molecule with five chiral centers may have a maximum of how many stereoisomers?

A. 5
B. 10
C. 16
D. 32

Problem solved:

D is correct. If a molecule has n chiral centers, then it has 2^n potential stereoisomers. If a molecule has five chiral centers, it has up to $2^5 = 32$ stereoisomers.

Please solve this problem:

- A molecule with five chiral centers may have a maximum of how many pairs of enantiomers?

    A. 5
    B. 10
    C. 16
    D. 32

Problem solved:

C is correct. As just noted, a molecule with five chiral centers has up to thirty-two stereoisomers. Each stereoisomer has one enantiomer, and so the total of thirty-two stereoisomers represents sixteen pairs of enantiomers. Any member of one such pair is a diastereomer of any member of *another* such pair.

Please solve this problem:

- An investigator creates a substance that has three chiral centers. She isolates one of its stereoisomers, which she calls "stereoisomer W." Stereoisomer W may have a maximum of how many diastereomers?

    A. 4
    B. 6
    C. 7
    D. 12

Problem solved:

B is correct. The substance has three chiral centers and has, therefore, $2^3 = 8$ potential stereoisomers. Stereoisomer W is one of them, and like any of the eight stereoisomers, it has one enantiomer. The remaining six stereoisomers are its diastereomers.

Please solve this problem:

- An investigator discovers a substance containing four chiral centers. She isolates one of its stereoisomers, which she calls "stereoisomer X." How many diastereomers might stereoisomer X have?

    A. 14
    B. 15
    C. 16
    D. 32

Problem solved:

A is correct. The substance has four chiral centers and up to $2^4 = 16$ stereoisomers. Stereoisomer X is one of them, and like any of the sixteen stereoisomers, it has one enantiomer. The remaining fourteen stereoisomers are its diastereomers.

MESO COMPOUNDS

We know that any molecule with only one chiral center is a chiral molecule. It has an enantiomer, and it is optically active. We also know that a molecule might have more than one chiral center, a phenomenon that gives rise to diastereomers.

Some molecules with multiple chiral centers are chiral molecules (as in the case of 2,3-dichloropentane), but some are not. That is, any molecule with only one chiral center is a chiral molecule. A molecule with more than one chiral center might or might not be a chiral molecule, depending on whether or not it is a **meso compound**. If the molecule is a meso compound, it will *not* be chiral.

Consider this molecule of 2,3-dichlorobutane:

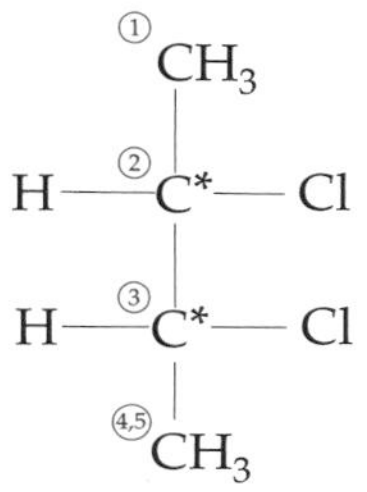

2,3-dichlorobutane

Note that the compound has two chiral centers, carbon 2 and carbon 3. Consider now, the molecule and its mirror image:

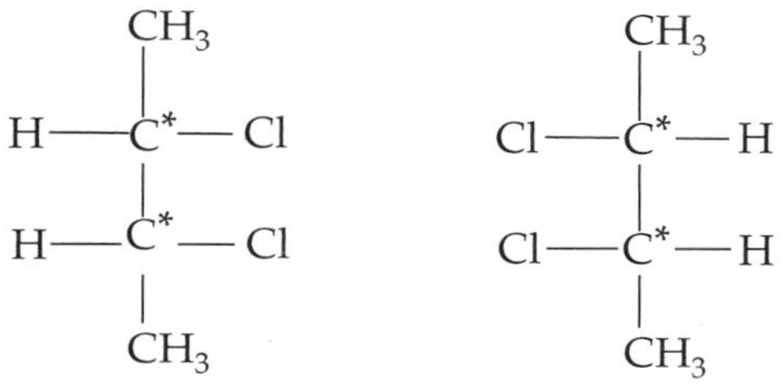

2,3-dichlorobutane and its Mirror Image

Note that the two mirror-image molecules are, in fact, superimposable on one another. If we take the molecule on the left and rotate it 180° counterclockwise, it is fully superimposable on the molecule to the right. These two molecules are, in fact, identical; they are not enantiomers. Each has a mirror image molecule superimposable on itself, so the molecule as a whole is not chiral, even though it features two chiral centers.

Look again at a molecule of 2,3-dichlorobutane, and notice that it features a plane of symmetry:

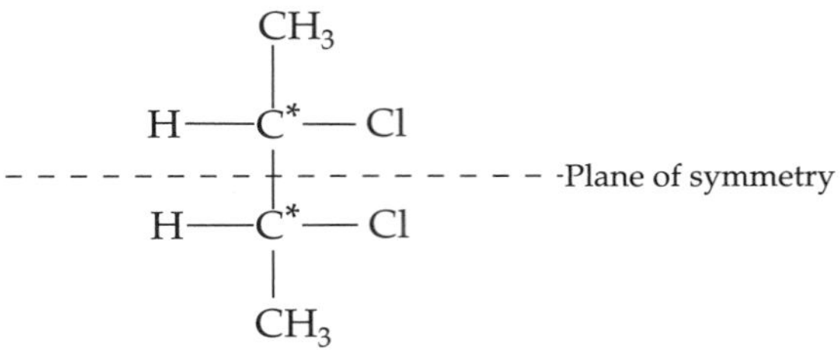

$$CH_3$$

$$H-\overset{*}{C}-Cl$$

- - - - - - - - - - - - - - - - -Plane of symmetry

$$H-\overset{*}{C}-Cl$$

$$CH_3$$

Across the plane of symmetry, each half of the molecule is the mirror image of the other. A meso compound is, in a sense, two mirror images bound within a single molecule. That phenomenon—the plane of symmetry within a molecule that has more than one chiral center—gives rise to meso compounds. Any molecule that has more than one chiral center but an intramolecular plane of symmetry, such that one part of the molecule is the mirror image of the other, is a meso compound. It is not chiral. Its own true mirror image is superimposable on itself and, like any other achiral molecule, it is not optically active.

Please solve this problem:

- An investigator identifies a chiral compound having two chiral centers and isolates three of its stereoisomers. Assuming this compound has four stereoisomers, which of the following may she justifiably conclude?

  A. All three stereoisomers rotate the plane of polarized light in the same direction.
  B. Two of the three stereoisomers rotate the plane of polarized light in one direction, and the third rotates it in the other direction.
  C. Both A and B
  D. Neither A nor B

Problem solved:

B is correct. We are told at the outset that the molecule *is chiral*. The four stereoisomers embody two pairs of enantiomers. Among the four stereoisomers, two are dextrorotatory and two are levorotatory. The investigator has isolated three of the four stereoisomers. That means that two of the three stereoisomers rotate polarized light in one direction (both to the right or both to the left), and the third rotates it in the other direction.

Please solve this problem:

- An experimenter identifies a chiral molecule with three chiral centers. He mixes two of its stereoisomers in equal concentrations, subjects the mixture to polarimetry, and notes a pronounced rotation to the left. Which of the following explains the finding?

  A. The sample is a racemic mixture.
  B. The two stereoisomers are diastereomers.
  C. Both A and B
  D. Neither A nor B

Problem solved:

B is correct. The substance has three chiral centers and gives rise, therefore, to as many as $2^3 = 8$ stereoisomers. These eight stereoisomers embody four pairs of enantiomers. Each pair, in turn, features a dextrorotatory enantiomer and a levorotatory enantiomer. The experimenter gathers a fifty percent to fifty percent mixture of two stereoisomers, and on performing polarimetry, notes leftward rotation. The mixture cannot be racemic because it rotates the plane of polarized light. Instead, it appears that the experimenter has mixed two diastereomers. Perhaps both are levorotatory. Perhaps one is levorotatory and one is dextrorotatory, with the levorotatory species creating more rotation than the dextrorotatory species so that net rotation is to the left.

Please solve this problem:

- Which of the following is true of a meso compound?

   A. It features a plane of symmetry.
   B. It is optically inactive.
   C. Both A and B
   D. Neither A nor B

Problem solved:

C is correct. A meso compound shows a plane of symmetry. One-half of a meso compound is the mirror image of the other half. A meso compound is optically inactive.

Please solve this problem:

- An experimenter identifies a molecule with two chiral centers. She subjects a sample of the substance to polarimetry and finds no rotation. Which of the following may she justifiably conclude?

   A. The molecule is a meso compound.
   B. She has prepared a racemic mixture.
   C. Either A or B
   D. Neither A nor B

Problem solved:

C is correct. The molecule has two chiral centers; it might be chiral, or it might be a meso compound. If it's chiral, however, its enantiomers might exist in equal proportions so as to produce a racemic mixture. It is possible that this investigator has gathered a racemic mixture. On the other hand, the molecule might be a meso compound. That is why choice C is correct.

Geometric (Cis-Trans) Diastereomers

Recall that "diastereomer" means stereoisomers that are not enantiomers. We have discussed configurational diastereomers, which arise because of multiple chiral centers within a chiral molecule. We will now discuss geometric diastereomers (which some authorities call, simply, "geometric isomers").

Geometric diastereomers arise not because of multiple chiral centers but because of **hindered rotation around double bonds**.

Examine these two drawings of 2-butene:

CIS   TRANS

Geometric Diastereomers of 2-butene

If the bond between the two carbons were single and not double, the two drawings would represent alternative ways of drawing identical molecules. Since the carbon bonds *are* double, however, and because rotation around double bonds is hindered, the two illustrations do not represent identical molecules.

Within a pair of geometric diastereomers, we can use the cis/trans naming system when each C of the double bond bears an H atom.

2-Butene, for example, conforms to this model. Each of the central carbons is bonded to a methyl group and a hydrogen atom. In such a case, distinguish the *cis*-diasteromer from the *trans*-diasteromer by remembering that:

(1) the *cis*-diasteromer is that in which the two Hs appear on the same side of the double bond, and

(2) the *trans*-diasteromer is that in which the two Hs appear on opposite sides of the double bond.

In other cases (should they arise on the MCAT), cis and trans are replaced with the E/Z naming system when three or more substituents on the double bond are not Hs. To name molecules as either E or Z:

(1) assign priority numbers one and two to each of the two substituents bound to each carbon of the double bond exactly as we do when distinguishing enantiomeric R and S configurations;

(2) determine whether the two highest priority substituents appear on the *same* side of the double bond or on *opposite* sides of the double bond.

If the two highest priority substituents appear on the same side of the double bond, then we have identified the Z diastereomer. If the two priority one ligands appear on opposite sides of the double bond, we have identified the E diastereomer.

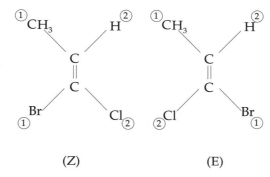

(Z)   (E)

34.2 MASTERY APPLIED: PRACTICE PASSAGE AND QUESTIONS

Passage

A neurological researcher is attempting to develop a pharmacologic agent effective in treating a degenerative disease of the cerebellum, called CDS. The disease impairs coordination of musculoskeletal movement. The researcher has isolated a substance that she calls X-TS and hypothesizes that it is effective in treating CDS. Dose-controlled studies suggest to her, however, that some samples of the substance are more effective than others. She then hypothesizes that the samples may produce different responses because they differ in their stereochemistry. Seeking to further assess and understand the matter, she conducts a pair of connected experiments.

Experiment 1

A group of six normal individuals are subjected to a neurologic performance test involving a variety of tasks that assess musculoskeletal coordination. For each patient, a score is noted and recorded on a scale of 1 to 100. A group of six patients afflicted with CDS are subjected to the same neurologic performance test, and their scores also are noted and recorded on a scale of 1 to 100. Results are shown below.

Normal

Patient	Score
1	88
2	84
3	71
4	80
5	79
6	80

Afflicted

Patient	Score
1	21
2	26
3	18
4	30
5	20
6	22

Table 1

Experiment 2

Six samples of X-TS, labeled 1 to 6, each equal in mass, are subjected to polarimetry. The degree to which each sample rotates the plane of polarized light is noted and recorded. A group of forty-two patients afflicted with CDS is divided into six groups of seven members each, and each patient is treated daily with 50 milligrams of chemical derived from one of the six samples. All members of a given group are treated with a chemical derived from the same sample. Group 1 patients are treated with substance from sample 1, group 2 patients with substance from sample 2, and so forth.

After administration of the agent for one week, all patients are subjected to the neurologic performance test applied in Experiment 1. For each of the six patient groups, average scores are recorded and noted. Results are shown in Table 2.

Group/Sample	Rotation*	Score
1	+6.2	29
2	+4.1	33
3	+0.1	43
4	−2.2	50
5	−4.8	65
6	−8.1	65

*(+): dextrorotatory
(−): levorotatory

Table 2

1. Among the following, polarimetry would best determine whether a chiral molecule is:

    I. the R- versus the S-isomer.
    II. the dextrorotatory versus the levorotatory isomer.
    III. the (+)- versus the (−)-isomer.

    A. I only
    B. I and II only
    C. II and III only
    D. I, II, and III

2. If an investigator subjects a sample of substance to polarimetry and finds no rotation of the plane of polarized light, is he justified in concluding that the substance is not chiral?

   A. Yes, because any molecule that rotates the plane of polarized light is chiral.

   B. Yes, because all chiral molecules rotate the plane of polarized light.

   C. No, because some chiral molecules do not rotate the plane of polarized light.

   D. No, because the sample may represent a racemic mixture.

3. The researcher described in the passage most likely performed polarimetry to determine if differences in therapeutic efficacy were due to differences in:

   A. cis versus trans configuration.

   B. stereoisomerism.

   C. molecular formula.

   D. molecular structure.

4. Among the following, the experimental data most strongly justify the conclusion that sample 6 is composed of:

   A. a nonracemic mixture.

   B. a levorotatory isomer only.

   C. a racemic mixture.

   D. achiral molecules.

5. In Experiment 2, which of the following served as a control?

   A. Averaging of neurologic performance scores

   B. Performance of Experiment 1

   C. Notation of both the degree of rotation and the neurologic test scores

   D. Use of unequal masses of sample X-TS

6. Among the following choices, which conclusion is most justified by the data derived from Experiments 1 and 2?

   A. X-TS is chemically analogous to an endogenously produced substance which, when absent, produces CDS.

   B. X-TS would be an ineffective treatment for CDS if the substance administered to the patient constituted a racemic mixture of (+)- and (−)-isomers.

   C. X-TS is ineffective for treating CDS unless composed of a purely levorotatory form of the isomer.

   D. A levorotatory form of X-TS effectively treats CDS, but benefit levels off after a certain degree of levorotation is attained in the sample.

34.3 MASTERY VERIFIED: ANSWERS AND EXPLANATIONS

1. **C is correct.** Polarimetry allows the investigator to determine whether a particular sample of chiral substance rotates polarized light to the right or to the left. The dextrorotatory (+) enantiomer rotates to the right, and the levorotatory (−) enantiomer rotates to the left. Statements II and III are accurate. Statement I is not. R and S refer to absolute configuration around a chiral center and are assigned according to convention unrelated to (+) and (−) designations.

2. **D is correct.** If a substance is subjected to polarimetry and does not rotate the plane of polarized light, then either its molecules are not chiral, or they are chiral but the examined sample is a racemic mixture of its dextrorotatory and levorotatory enantiomers.

3. **B is correct.** The polarimeter reveals optical activity. Optical activity refers to a substance's tendency to rotate the plane of polarized light, which closely relates to stereoisomerism and, more particularly, enantiomerism.

4. **A is correct.** The substance in sample 6 rotates the plane of polarized light to the left. Hence, it is composed of chiral molecules (since achiral molecules are not optically active). Choice D, therefore, is incorrect. Choice C is similarly incorrect; a racemic mixture has equal concentrations of opposing enantiomers and is therefore optically inactive. The investigator would not be justified, however, in concluding that sample 6 is composed *only* of levorotatory molecules (choice B). The sample might rotate the plane of polarized light to the left and still contain some dextrorotatory molecules as long as the levorotatory influence is predominant. The investigator can conclude that the mixture is nonracemic, since a racemic mixture is optically inactive.

5. **B is correct.** Data from Experiment 2 show a tendency for neurologic test scores to increase with increasing levorotation of the administered substance. The Experiment 2 data do not show, however, what test score a CDS patient might achieve in the absence of medication. In Experiment 1, afflicted patients underwent neurologic testing without having received medication. Their scores of 21, 26, 18, 20, and 22 yield an average of approximately 23. That suggests that in the absence of medication, the patients of Experiment 2 *would* have achieved average scores of about 23.

6. **D is correct.** The data show a correlation between extent of levorotation and neurologic performance. They strongly suggest that a levorotatory form of X-TS constitutes an effective treatment for CDS. Furthermore, the substances that produced levorotations of −4.8° and −8.1° yielded equal neurologic test performance. Since all samples were equal in mass when subjected to polarimetry, and all patients received 50 mg of medication per day, that finding suggests that levorotation in excess of −4.8° produces no added improvement in performance.

CHAPTER 35

HYDROCARBONS

35.1 MASTERY ACHIEVED

"**Hydrocarbon**" means a molecule composed *only* of hydrogen and carbon. Hydrocarbons are subdivided into **aliphatic** hydrocarbons and **aromatic** hydrocarbons. The aliphatic hydrocarbons, in turn, include the alkanes, alkenes, and alkynes (and, also, the aliphatic cyclic hydrocarbons).

```
                        Hydrocarbons
              ┌──────────────┴──────────────┐
           aromatic                       aliphatic
                              ┌──────┬──────┴──────┬──────┐
                           alkanes  alkenes     alkynes  cyclic
```

THE ALKANES

"Alkane" means a hydrocarbon composed of a chain of carbon atoms linked only by single bonds. Because each carbon is bound to the next one by a single bond, it is also bound to as many hydrogen atoms as are necessary to "saturate" its capacity to form four bonds. For that reason, each such carbon is said to be **saturated**, and alkanes are called **saturated hydrocarbons**. (Alkenes, to be discussed later, contain carbon–carbon double bonds, which constitute sites of *un*saturation.)

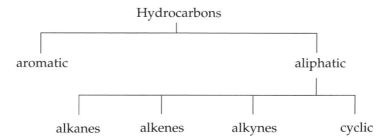

saturated hydrocarbon

unsaturated hydrocarbon

Naming the Alkanes

The alkanes are named with the suffix "-ane" preceded by a prefix (base name) that denotes the number of carbon atoms in the molecular chain, according to this table:

Number of carbons	Prefix
1	meth-
2	eth-
3	prop-
4	but-
5	pent-
6	hex-
7	hept-
8	oct-
9	non-
10	dec-

Table 35.1

Here are drawings of methane, ethane, propane, butane, and pentane:

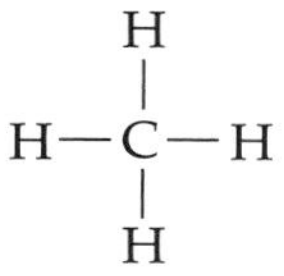

$$
\begin{array}{c}
H \\
| \\
H-C-H \\
| \\
H
\end{array}
$$

Methane

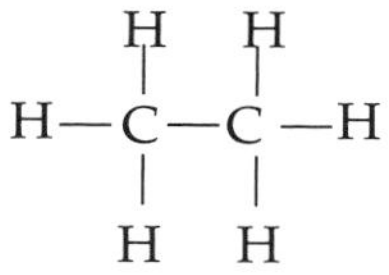

$$
\begin{array}{cc}
H & H \\
| & | \\
H-C-C-H \\
| & | \\
H & H
\end{array}
$$

Ethane

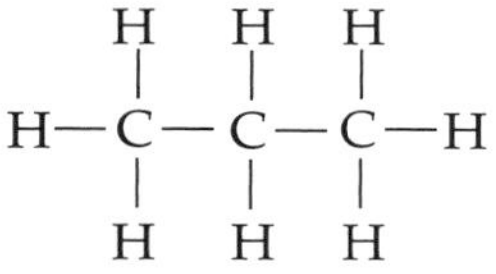

$$
\begin{array}{ccc}
H & H & H \\
| & | & | \\
H-C-C-C-H \\
| & | & | \\
H & H & H
\end{array}
$$

Propane

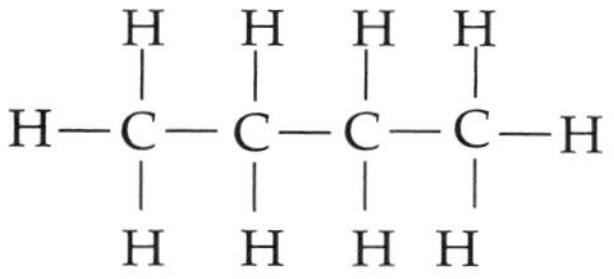

$$
\begin{array}{cccc}
H & H & H & H \\
| & | & | & | \\
H-C-C-C-C-H \\
| & | & | & | \\
H & H & H & H
\end{array}
$$

Butane

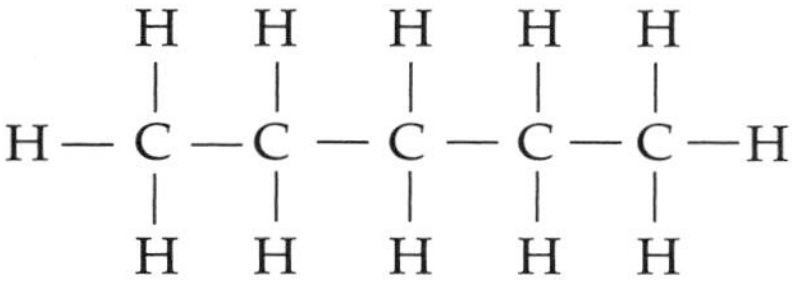

$$
\begin{array}{ccccc}
H & H & H & H & H \\
| & | & | & | & | \\
H-C-C-C-C-C-H \\
| & | & | & | & | \\
H & H & H & H & H
\end{array}
$$

Pentane

These illustrations depict unsubstituted hydrocarbons. "**Substituted hydrocarbon**" means a hydrocarbon in which one or more of the hydrogen atoms bound to a carbon atom is replaced by something else—a "substituent." The substituent might be something that derives from an alkane, in which case it is called an **alkyl group**. The substituted alkane that results is **branched**. Here, for instance is a branched alkane; the second carbon from the "right" has one hydrogen replaced by an alkyl group, more specifically, a methyl (CH_3) group.

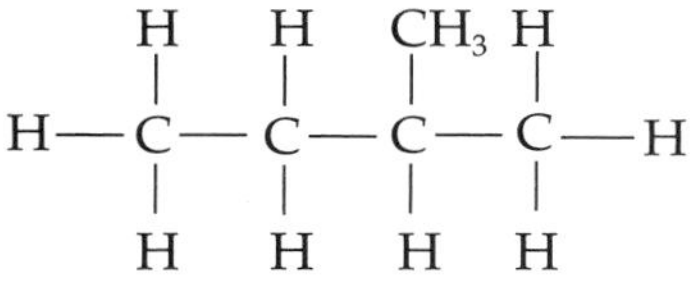

$$
\begin{array}{cccc}
H & H & CH_3 & H \\
| & | & | & | \\
H-C-C-C-C-H \\
| & | & | & | \\
H & H & H & H
\end{array}
$$

We can name this molecule according to these five steps:

1. Count the number of carbon atoms in the chain, proceeding in whatever direction yields the longest chain.

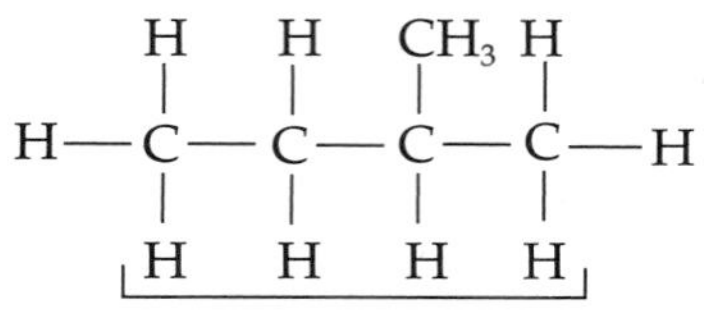

$$H-\underset{\underset{H}{|}}{\overset{\overset{H}{|}}{C}}-\underset{\underset{H}{|}}{\overset{\overset{H}{|}}{C}}-\underset{\underset{H}{|}}{\overset{\overset{CH_3}{|}}{C}}-\underset{\underset{H}{|}}{\overset{\overset{H}{|}}{C}}-H$$

chain length: 4

2. Name the compound, preliminarily, with the appropriate prefix.

$$H-\underset{\underset{H}{|}}{\overset{\overset{H}{|}}{C}}-\underset{\underset{H}{|}}{\overset{\overset{H}{|}}{C}}-\underset{\underset{H}{|}}{\overset{\overset{CH_3}{|}}{C}}-\underset{\underset{H}{|}}{\overset{\overset{H}{|}}{C}}-H$$

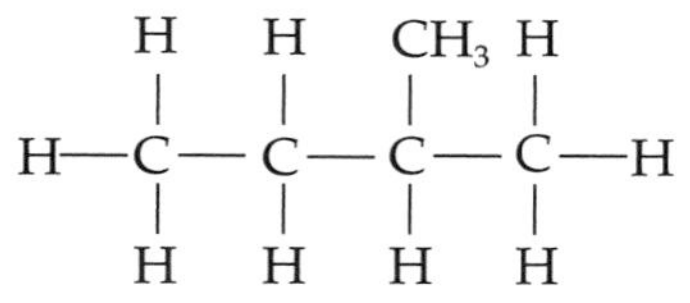

_____ butane

3. Look at the carbon that carries the substituent and ask yourself whether it is closer to the "left" or to the "right." If it is closer to the right, then number the carbons in the "main" chain starting at the right. If it's closer to the left, then number the carbons in the "main" chain starting at the left.

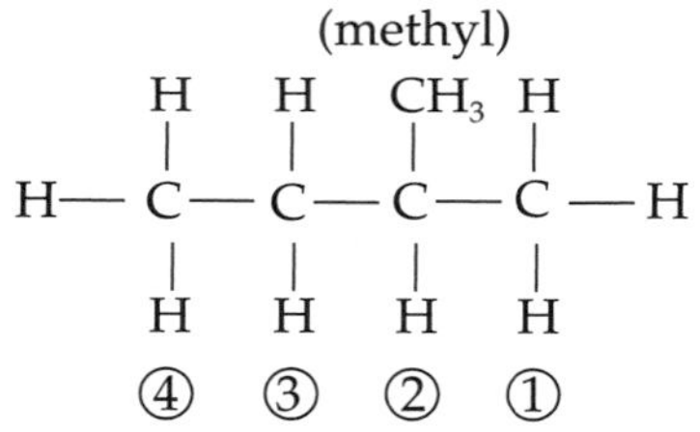

(methyl)

$$H-\underset{\underset{H}{|}}{\overset{\overset{H}{|}}{C}}-\underset{\underset{H}{|}}{\overset{\overset{H}{|}}{C}}-\underset{\underset{H}{|}}{\overset{\overset{CH_3}{|}}{C}}-\underset{\underset{H}{|}}{\overset{\overset{H}{|}}{C}}-H$$

④ ③ ② ①

_____ methyl butane

4. Look at the substituent, count the carbons in its chain, and name it with the appropriate prefix and the suffix "-yl."

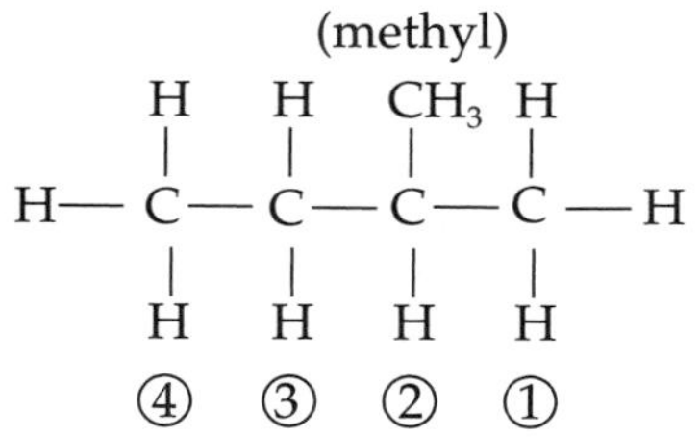

(methyl)

$$H-\underset{\underset{H}{|}}{\overset{\overset{H}{|}}{C}}-\underset{\underset{H}{|}}{\overset{\overset{H}{|}}{C}}-\underset{\underset{H}{|}}{\overset{\overset{CH_3}{|}}{C}}-\underset{\underset{H}{|}}{\overset{\overset{H}{|}}{C}}-H$$

④ ③ ② ①

_____ methyl butane

5. Add to the "front" of the name (a) the carbon number that bears the substituent, (b) a hyphen, and (c) the name of the substituent.

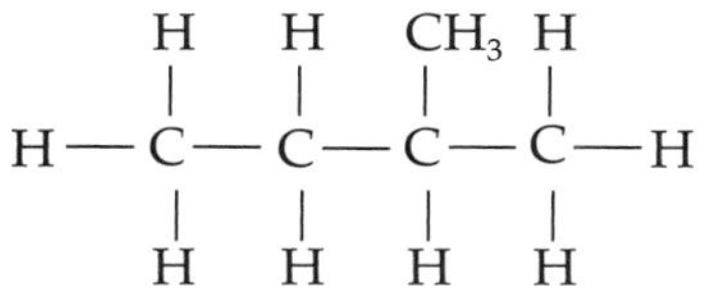

$$H \!-\! \underset{\underset{H}{|}}{\overset{\overset{H}{|}}{C}} \!-\! \underset{\underset{H}{|}}{\overset{\overset{H}{|}}{C}} \!-\! \underset{\underset{H}{|}}{\overset{\overset{CH_3}{|}}{C}} \!-\! \underset{\underset{H}{|}}{\overset{\overset{H}{|}}{C}} \!-\! H$$

2-methyl butane

Here is another substituted alkane, named according to the system just described.

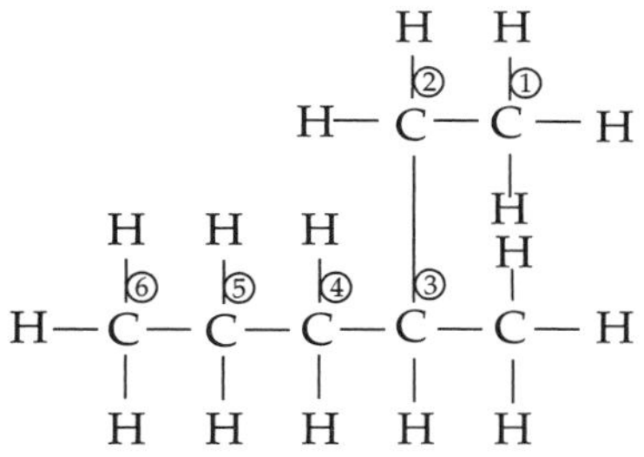

3-methyl hexane

If an alkane has more than one substituent, count the carbons from the end *nearest to the first branch point*, and elongate the "front" part of its name, like this:

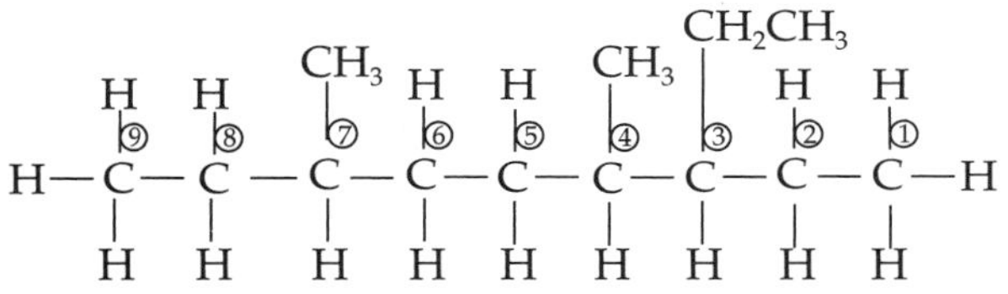

3-ethyl-4,7-dimethylnonane

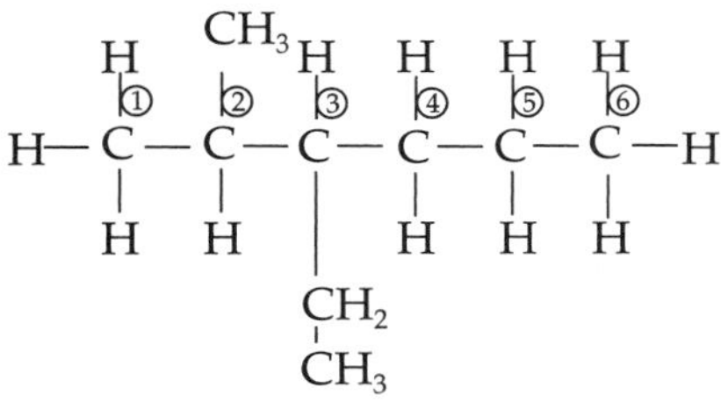

3-ethyl-2-methylhexane

The system just described is called the IUPAC system of nomenclature. Many three-carbon, four-carbon and five-carbon alkyl groups are known by certain common names not derived from the IUPAC system.

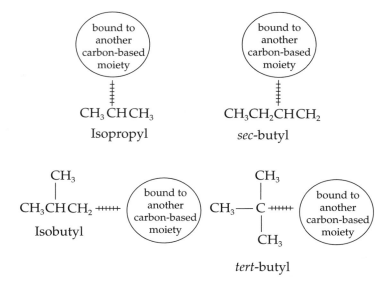

Physical Properties of the Alkanes

Alkanes are generally nonpolar. For that reason, they tend to be:

- insoluble in water (which is polar), and

- soluble in nonpolar solvents, like benzene, ether, and chloroform.

As for melting and boiling points, remember first that:

(1) alkane molecules are generally nonpolar,

(2) nonpolar molecules are held together primarily by van der Waal's forces,

(3) van der Waal's forces tend to increase with increasing molecular surface area, and

(4) when a nonpolar substance undergoes transition from one phase to another (solid to liquid, or liquid to gas), it must *overcome* the van der Waal's forces among its molecules.

These phenomena underlie the alkanes' trends as to melting and boiling points, and for the MCAT, *the underlying phenomena are as important as the trends themselves.*

Increasing molecular weight, by itself, tends to increase molecular surface area, thereby increasing van der Waal's forces. Increased molecular weight tends to increase melting and boiling points. At room temperature, alkanes with one, two, three, or four carbons in their "main" chains are gaseous. Those with five to sixteen carbons in their chain are liquids, and those with seventeen or more carbons are solids.

On the other hand, branching tends to reduce molecular surface area, which means that it also reduces (a) van der Waal's forces and (b) melting and boiling points. Pentane and 2-methylbutane, for instance, both contain five carbon atoms and twelve hydrogen atoms, which means their molecular weights are identical. Yet, 2-methylbutane has lower melting and boiling points.

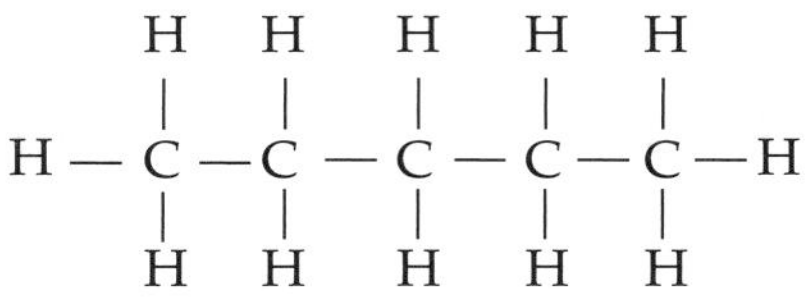

$$H—\underset{\underset{H}{|}}{\overset{\overset{H}{|}}{C}}—\underset{\underset{H}{|}}{\overset{\overset{H}{|}}{C}}—\underset{\underset{H}{|}}{\overset{\overset{H}{|}}{C}}—\underset{\underset{H}{|}}{\overset{\overset{H}{|}}{C}}—\underset{\underset{H}{|}}{\overset{\overset{H}{|}}{C}}—H$$

Pentane

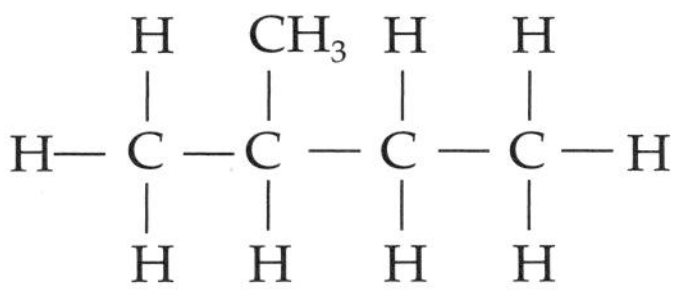

$$H—\underset{\underset{H}{|}}{\overset{\overset{H}{|}}{C}}—\underset{\underset{H}{|}}{\overset{\overset{CH_3}{|}}{C}}—\underset{\underset{H}{|}}{\overset{\overset{H}{|}}{C}}—\underset{\underset{H}{|}}{\overset{\overset{H}{|}}{C}}—H$$

2-methylbutane

Density follows the trends associated with melting and boiling. Higher molecular weight increases density, and branching reduces it.

For alkanes:

Associate	With	And
Higher molecular weight	Increased surface area	Increased melting point and boiling point
	which causes	
	Increased van der Waal's forces	Increased density
Increased branching	Decreased surface area	Decreased melting point and boiling point
	which causes	
	Decreased van der Waal's forces	Decreased density

Table 35.2

Please solve this problem:

- A researcher discovers that the boiling point of butane is 12 degrees higher than that of methylpropane. Among the following, the most likely explanation is that:

  A. melting point is lower for butane than for methylpropane.
  B. molecular weight is lower for butane than for methylpropane.
  C. van der Waal's forces are lower for butane than for methylpropane.
  D. molecular surface area is lower for methylpropane than for butane.

Problem solved:

D is correct. The two molecules butane and methylpropane have identical molecular weights, each consisting of four carbon atoms and ten hydrogen atoms. Choice B, therefore, is wrong. Butane is unbranched, and methylpropane is branched:

$$\begin{array}{ccccccc} & H & H & H & H & \\ & | & | & | & | & \\ H- & C & - C & - C & - C & -H \\ & | & | & | & | & \\ & H & H & H & H & \end{array}$$

Butane

$$\begin{array}{ccccc} & H & CH_3 & H & \\ & | & | & | & \\ H- & C & - C & - C & -H \\ & | & | & | & \\ & H & H & H & \end{array}$$

Methylpropane

Methylpropane's branched molecules have a smaller surface area and therefore experience lesser van der Waal's forces (which means choice C is wrong). The reduced van der Waal's forces would tend to make butane's melting point higher (not lower) than methylpropane's, which makes choice A wrong. The reduced van der Waal's forces (caused, in turn, by the smaller surface area) also explain why butane's boiling point is higher than **methylpropane's.** That's why choice D is correct.

Reactions of the Alkanes

HALOGENATION AND THE ALKYL FREE RADICAL

For the MCAT, **halogenation** represents the most important concept related to the reactions of alkanes. With X representing the halogen, and R representing the alkane and its terminal hydrogen atom, the reaction is generically characterized thus:

$$RH + X_2 \rightarrow RX + HX$$

The RX molecule is the halogenated alkane—the ultimate product of the reaction.

Halogenation of an alkane arises through a **chain reaction** that involves a **carbon free radical** intermediate. Like all chain reactions, this one embodies three steps: (1) initiation, (2) propagation (which makes for the "chain" of the chain reaction), and (3) termination.

Step 1: In the initiation step, the halogen gives rise to a halogen free radical reactant through a homolytic cleavage of the X-X bond using light or heat:

$$X_2 \rightarrow X\bullet + X\bullet$$

Step 2: In the propagation step,(a) the free radical reactant reacts with the alkane to produce a carbon free radical (R•) via abstraction of a hydrogen atom from the alkane:

$$X\bullet + R\text{-}H \rightarrow HX + R\bullet$$

and (b) the carbon free radical reacts with another molecule of halogen to produce a halogenated alkane and a new halogen free radical reactant:

$$R\bullet + X_2 \rightarrow RX + X\bullet$$

The RX molecule produced in the second part of the propagation step (2b) is the halogenated alkane, the ultimate product of the reaction. Yet, the reaction does not end there. The halogen free radical reactant (X•) combines with another molecule of alkane, and step 2(a) is repeated. Step 2(a) leads, once again, to step 2(b), which leads to step 2(a), and so forth, so that for every single halogen molecule that undergoes radical formation at the initiation step, *thousands* of alkyl halide molecules are formed. It is the repetition of steps 2(a) and 2(b), therefore, that constitute the "chain" of this chain reaction.

Step 3: In the termination step, the radicals are consumed, and the reaction is brought to an end.

$$X\bullet + X\bullet \rightarrow X\text{--}X$$

$$R\bullet + R\bullet \rightarrow R\text{--}R$$

$$R\bullet + X\bullet \rightarrow RX$$

SELECTIVITY OF RADICAL HALOGENATION

Radical halogenation reactions can be selective reactions such that only one halogenated product forms exclusively, or they can yield a complex mixture of several products in roughly equal amounts. When the new C-X bond forms, if the halogen only adds to one type of carbon in the compound, we call this a *regioselective* reaction (the X adds to one specific *region* of the molecule). Halogenations will be regioselective if bromine is used. The reason for the selectivity is due in part to the reactivity of the halogen, and in part the relative stabilities of the potential radicals that might form in the first propagation step of the chain reaction. The major product of the reaction will be that which follows from the most stable of the radicals produced.

In that regard, recall that within a carbon chain, a **primary** carbon atom (1°) is one that is bound to only one other carbon atom. A **secondary** carbon atom (2°) is one that is bound to two other carbon atoms, and a **tertiary** carbon atom (3°) is one that is bound to three other carbon atoms.

The energy required to abstract a hydrogen from a tertiary carbon is less than that required for abstraction from a secondary carbon, which is less than that required for abstraction from a primary carbon. In terms of stability, therefore, a tertiary carbon free radical is more stable than a secondary carbon free radical, which is more stable than a primary carbon free radical. Put otherwise, stability of carbon free radicals follows this ranking:

$$3° > 2° > 1°$$

Among the carbon free radicals that might be formed from a given alkane molecule, the *preference* will follow that same order:

$$3° > 2° > 1°$$

That means, ultimately, that among the different brominated alkanes that might result from the bromination reaction, the preference will be for bromination at the alkane molecule's most highly substituted carbon. If the molecule contains a tertiary carbon, that carbon will be the most favored site for bonding of the halogen.

Chlorination reactions are less selective since the halogen itself is more reactive. In this case, the relative stabilities of the intermediate radicals are not enough to predict the major product of the reaction. As a first order estimate, 1°: 2°: 3° radicals are likely to form with a 1:4:5 selectivity, respectively. This means that it is five times more likely that a 3° radical will form when compared with a 1° radical. Likewise, it is four times more likely that a 2° radical will form when compared with a 1° radical. While this may seem like a selective process, when compared with a 1:1600 ratio of 1°: 3° selectivity in the case of bromination, we see just how *unselective* chlorinations are.

Second, in order to predict the major product of a chlorination reaction, we must also consider how many possible ways there are to make a given radical intermediate.

Consider the products that might *theoretically* result from the halogenation of 2- methyl butane:

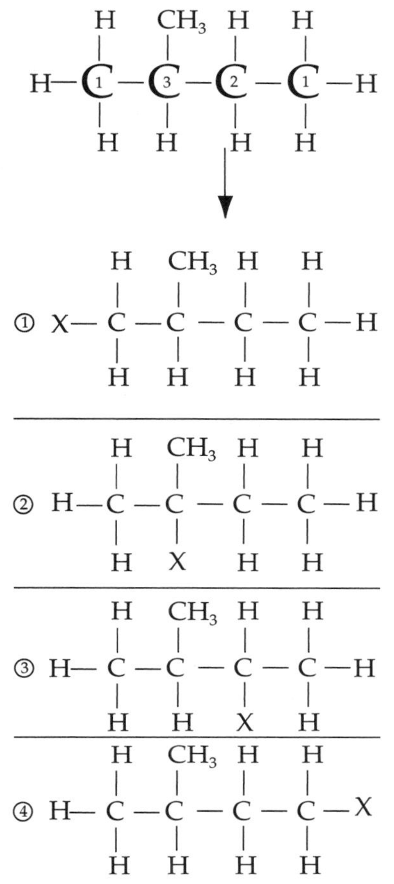

```
        H   CH₃  H    H
        |    |   |    |
  H ── C ── C ── C ── C ── H
       ①    ③   ②    ①
        |    |   |    |
        H    H   H    H
                 │
                 ▼

        H   CH₃  H    H
        |    |   |    |
① X ── C ── C ── C ── C ── H
        |    |   |    |
        H    H   H    H
────────────────────────────
        H   CH₃  H    H
        |    |   |    |
② H ── C ── C ── C ── C ── H
        |    |   |    |
        H    X   H    H
────────────────────────────
        H   CH₃  H    H
        |    |   |    |
③ H ── C ── C ── C ── C ── H
        |    |   |    |
        H    H   X    H
────────────────────────────
        H   CH₃  H    H
        |    |   |    |
④ H ── C ── C ── C ── C ── X
        |    |   |    |
        H    H   H    H
```

You might expect product 2 to be the major product since it is a tertiary compound. However, since there is only one 3° H in 2-methylbutane that can be abstracted by the chlorine radical, there is only one possible way to make 3° alkyl radical. To predict the ratio of products, we use the selectivity of 3° radical formation and multiply by the number of ways to make the given radical, and get $5 \times 1 = 5$. For comparison, in compound 3, we use the 2° selectivity factor of 4, but multiply by the 2 different Hs that can be removed to yield the 2° radical intermediate for $4 \times 2 = 8$. Therefore, we'd expect roughly fifty percent more of the secondary chloride to form compared to the tertiary product. Similar analyses for the remaining compounds will give a product distribution of compounds 1–4 of 6:5:8:3. As you can see, chlorinations give large mixtures of products, with no clear product being formed in great excess.

Please solve this problem:

- When liquid bromine is reacted with 2,2,3-trimethylpentane under ultraviolet light to produce the corresponding halogenated alkane, the major product will most likely be:

    A. 1-bromo-2,2,3-trimethylpentane.
    B. 2-bromo-2,2,3-trimethylpentane.
    C. 3-bromo-2,2,3-trimethylpentane.
    D. 4-bromo-2,2,3-trimethylpentane.

Problem solved:

C is correct.

$$
\underset{\underset{H}{|}}{\overset{\underset{H}{|①}}{H-\underset{1}{C}}}-\underset{\underset{CH_3}{|}}{\overset{\underset{CH_3}{|②}}{\underset{4}{C}}}-\underset{\underset{CH_3}{|}}{\overset{\underset{H}{|③}}{\underset{3}{C}}}-\underset{\underset{H}{|}}{\overset{\underset{H}{|④}}{\underset{2}{C}}}-\underset{\underset{H}{|}}{\overset{\underset{H}{|⑤}}{\underset{1}{C}}}-H
$$

2,2,3-trimethylpentane

The major bromination product will follow from the free radical that precedes it. 2,2,3-trimethylpentane is a five-carbon molecule in which carbons one and five are bound only to one other carbon, meaning that they are primary (1°). Carbon four is bound to two other carbons, meaning that it is secondary (2°). Carbon three is bound to three other carbons, meaning that it is tertiary (3°). Carbon two is fully substituted, being bound to four other carbons.

Among the free radicals that might follow from the attempted bromination of 2,2,3-trimethylpentane are (1) a primary radical at carbons one or five, (2) a secondary radical at carbon four, or (3) a tertiary radical at carbon three. Among these possibilities, the tertiary radical is most stable because, with regard to stability of free radicals, 3° > 2° > 1°. Consequently the pathway that produces the tertiary radical is most favored. The bromination product that follows from a tertiary radical would carry the bromine atom on the tertiary (number 3) carbon, giving 3-bromo-2,2,3-trimethylpentane.

$$
H-\underset{\underset{H}{|}}{\overset{\overset{H}{|}}{C}}-\underset{\underset{CH_3}{|}}{\overset{\overset{CH_3}{|}}{C}}-\underset{\underset{CH_3}{|}}{\overset{\overset{Br}{|}}{C}}-\underset{\underset{H}{|}}{\overset{\overset{H}{|}}{C}}-\underset{\underset{H}{|}}{\overset{\overset{H}{|}}{C}}-H
$$

3-bromo-2,2,3-trimethylpentane

COMBUSTION AND PYROLYSIS ("CRACKING")

Alkanes will burn, meaning that they undergo combustion (oxidation) in the presence of oxygen to produce water, carbon dioxide, and heat. The complete combustion of methane for example is depicted thus:

$$CH_4 + 2O_2 \longrightarrow CO_2 + 2H_2O + heat$$

Combustion of Methane

The burning of alkanes is important to modern civilization. It facilitates the operation of engines and the creation of household heat. (It also threatens to *destroy* our civilization because the carbon dioxide produced when alkanes are burned is a "greenhouse gas," meaning that it traps infrared light radiating outward from the earth and turns it to heat. The resultant trend toward "global warming," if not stemmed, may well produce cataclysmic upheaval of climactic conditions all over the earth.)

The pyrolysis ("cracking") of an alkane means exposing it to heat and thereby breaking it into (a) smaller alkanes, (b) alkenes, and (c) hydrogen:

$$\text{alkane} \longrightarrow H_2 + \text{smaller alkane} + \text{alkenes}$$

Cracking is critical to the production of gasoline from petroleum. The process involves carbon free radical intermediates, which are converted to the relatively smaller alkanes and alkenes produced in the process. Theories about the mechanisms of cracking need not be memorized; if the MCAT tests you on the subject, it will supply the necessary information.

THE ALKENES

"Alkene" means a hydrocarbon that contains a carbon-carbon double bond. Each of the doubly bonded carbons is bound only to three other atoms (the other doubly bound carbon and two additional atoms). The doubly bound carbon, therefore, is not "saturated" with single bonds. For that reason, a double bond is a **site of unsaturation**, and an alkene is an **unsaturated hydrocarbon**.

Naming the Alkenes

Naming the alkenes involves the same prefixes used for the alkanes, and the suffix "-ene" instead of "-ane." We number carbons by beginning at the molecular end closest to the double bond. Or, if the double bond is at the midpoint of the carbon chain, numbering begins at the end closest to the first branch point.

With the carbons thus numbered, the name shows, from left to right:

(1) the site and nature of branches,

(2) the site of the double bond,

(3) a prefix corresponding to the length of the (longest possible) carbon chain, and

(4) the alkene suffix ("-ene").

Sites of the branch points and double bond are located by counting carbons, beginning at the molecular end closest to the double bond. Or, if the double bond is at the midpoint of the carbon chain, counting begins at the end closest to the first branch point.

2-hexene

5-methyl-2-hexene

(As with the alkanes, many alkenes are still known by certain common names not derived from the IUPAC system.)

Cis-Trans (E–Z) Isomerism

In **Chapter 34**, we discussed cis-trans isomerism. Because rotation around a carbon–carbon double bond is hindered, any alkene can exist in cis or trans form if both of its doubly bound carbons are attached to two different substituents. If, on the other hand, either (or both) of the carbons has two identical substituents, cis and trans isomers do not exist. In such a case, two Fischer drawings that might *seem* to depict that cis and trans isomers represent, in fact, identical molecules.

$$
\begin{array}{cc}
\overset{W}{\underset{X}{>}}C = C\overset{Y}{\underset{Y}{<}} & \overset{X}{\underset{W}{>}}C = C\overset{Y}{\underset{Y}{<}}
\end{array}
$$

Identical compounds

$$
\begin{array}{cc}
\overset{W}{\underset{X}{>}}C = C\overset{Y}{\underset{Z}{<}} & \overset{X}{\underset{W}{>}}C = C\overset{Y}{\underset{Z}{<}}
\end{array}
$$

Cis-trans isomers

Reactions of the Alkenes

Alkenes undergo a wide variety of reactions. Most significant to the MCAT are the **electrophilic addition** reactions. In this context, "electrophilic addition" means a process in which the carbon-carbon double bond, acting as a nucleophile (Lewis base), donates electrons to an atom or ion, **the electrophile** that "seeks" electrons. The carbon-carbon double bond donates its π electrons to form a sigma bond with the electrophile (which acts as a Lewis acid).

$$
\overset{H}{\underset{H}{>}}C = C\overset{H}{\underset{H}{<}} + YZ \longrightarrow H-\overset{H}{\underset{Y}{C}}-\overset{H}{\underset{Z}{C}}-H
$$

The double bond disappears and leaves a product characterized by a chain of singly bonded carbons. The precise nature of the product depends on the added entity.

ELECTROPHILIC ADDITION OF A HYDROGEN HALIDE: CARBOCATION STABILITY AND MARKOVNIKOV'S RULE

A hydrogen halide adds to an alkene's double bond to form an alkyl halide. With "X" standing generically for a halide, the reaction is depicted like this:

$$
\overset{H}{\underset{H}{>}}C = C\overset{H}{\underset{H}{<}} + HX \longrightarrow H-\overset{H}{\underset{\mathbf{H}}{C}}-\overset{H}{\underset{\mathbf{X}}{C}}-H
$$

Consider the addition of hydrogen iodide to propene, an asymmetric alkene. Theoretically, the iodine atom might bond to either of the two carbon atoms involved in the double bond. The process allows, theoretically, for two competing products, one in which the iodine atom is bound to carbon two (isopropyl iodide) and another in which the iodine atom is bound to the terminal carbon (*n*-propyl iodide).

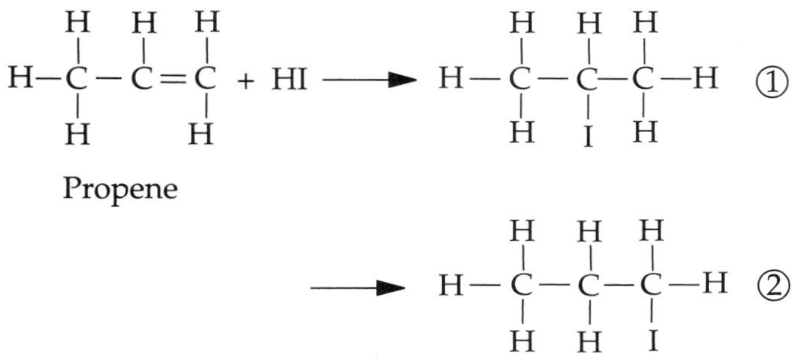

Propene

In most (but not all) circumstances, the reaction will produce, almost exclusively, the product in which the *electronegative atom binds to the carbon, which bears the lesser number of hydrogen atoms*. As is explained below, the reason for the predominance of that product pertains to the mechanism by which the reaction proceeds and the relative stability of competing carbocation intermediates.

Electrophilic addition to an alkene involves two steps, the first of which is the rate-determining step. In that first step, π electrons drawn from the carbon–carbon double bond attack the HX molecule's electropositive component to leave a **carbocation**.

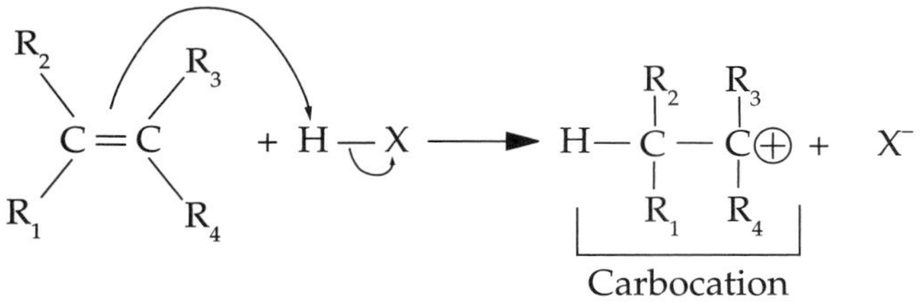

Carbocation

In the second step, the carbocation is consumed by the X^-,ion and the product is formed.

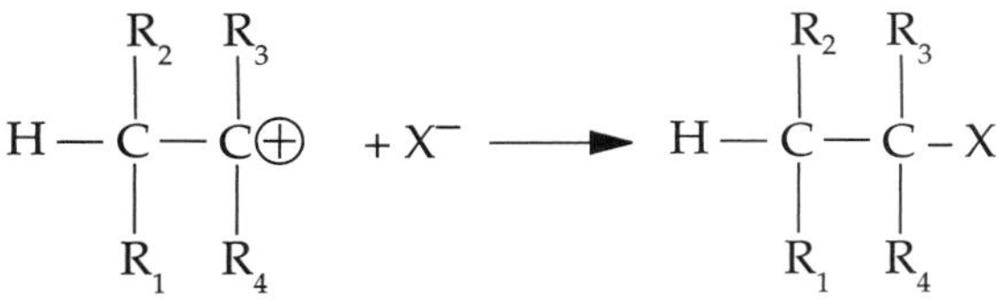

Step 1 is the rate-determining step, meaning that *the rate at which the carbocation intermediate is formed governs the rate at which the reaction occurs*. In terms of stability, carbocations (like carbon free radicals) follow this ranking:

$$3° > 2° > 1°$$

A carbocation in which a positive charge is carried on a tertiary carbon is more stable than one in which it is carried on a secondary carbon, which is more stable than one in which it is carried on a primary carbon.

Now, consider the addition of HCl to isobutene, and note that step 1 might theoretically lead to two carbocations:

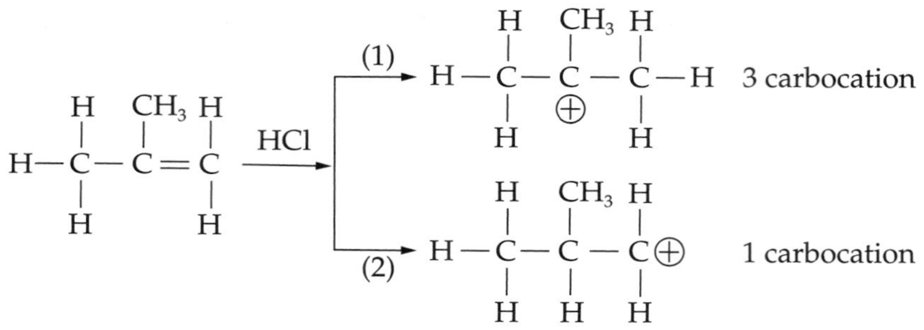

Between the two carbocations shown above, number one is more stable because the positive charge is born on the more highly substituted carbon—the carbon that bears the lesser number of hydrogen atoms. Between the two carbocations, one and two, number one will form more quickly than number two.

At step 2 of the reaction, the carbocation intermediate produces a product in which the chlorine atom is bound to the carbon that carried the positive charge. In terms of the final product, then, the chlorine atom binds preferentially (almost exclusively) to carbon 2, so that the preferred product is:

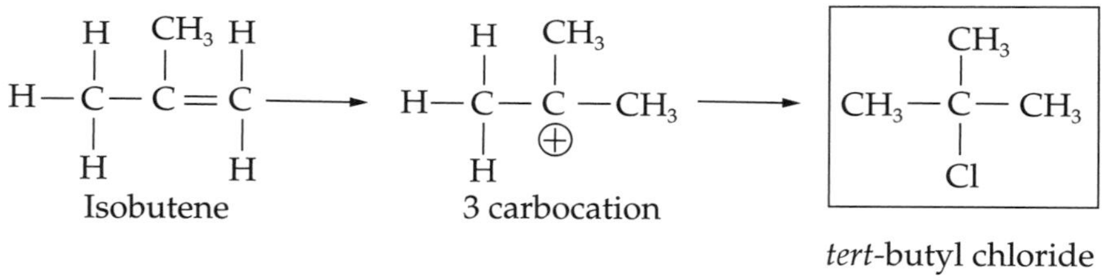

Electrophilic addition to an alkene normally follows the pattern just described; the electronegative species binds to that carbon, which is bound to the lesser number of hydrogens. That phenomenon is called **Markovnikov's addition** (a regioselective process), which follows from **Markovnikov's rule**: *Electrophilic addition to alkene molecule yields, preferentially, a product in which the electronegative species are bound to the more highly substituted of the two doubly bonded carbons.* Markovnikov's addition is *normally* the favored route of electrophilic addition to alkenes, and it follows from the fact that the intermediate carbocation of greater stability is that in which the positive charge is born on the more highly substituted carbon.

REARRANGEMENT OF THE CARBOCATION INTERMEDIATE: HYDRIDE AND METHYL SHIFTS

Consider the addition of HCl to 3-methyl-1-butene. Significant products include not only the 2-chloro-3-methylbutane, which follows from ordinary Markovnikov addition, but also 2-chloro-2-methylbutane, in which the chlorine atom is bound to a carbon atom that did not participate in the original carbon–carbon double bond.

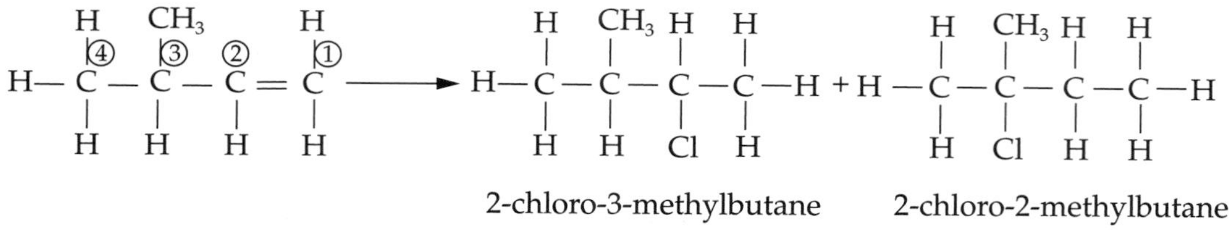

This additional product, not anticipated on the basis of ordinary Markovnikov addition, arises through **rearrangement** of the carbocation intermediate conceived thus:

(1) In the first step of the reaction, the alkene produces a 2° carbocation as anticipated.

$$H-\overset{\overset{\displaystyle H}{|}}{\underset{\underset{\displaystyle H}{|}}{C}}-\overset{\overset{\displaystyle CH_3}{|}}{\underset{\underset{\displaystyle H}{|}}{C}}-\overset{\overset{\displaystyle H}{|}}{C}=\overset{\overset{\displaystyle H}{|}}{\underset{\underset{\displaystyle H}{|}}{C}} \xrightarrow{H^+} H-\overset{\overset{\displaystyle H}{|}}{\underset{\underset{\displaystyle H}{|}}{C}}-\overset{\overset{\displaystyle CH_3}{|}}{\underset{\underset{\displaystyle H}{|}}{C}}-\overset{\overset{\displaystyle H}{|}}{\underset{\underset{\displaystyle \oplus}{}}{C}}-\overset{\overset{\displaystyle H}{|}}{\underset{\underset{\displaystyle H}{|}}{C}}-H$$

(2) Then, before the second step begins, most of these 2° carbocations rearrange themselves by undergoing a **hydride shift**: A hydrogen atom shifts position to form a more stable 3° carbocation.

Hydride shift

(3) The 3° carbocations thus formed create the product 2-chloro-2-methylbutane.

An analogous process, termed a **methyl shift,** also occurs. Consider, for example, the addition of hydroiodic acid to a molecule of 3,3-dimethyl-1-butene.

3-iodo-2,2-dimethylbutane

2-iodo-2,3-dimethylbutane

Significant products include not only 3-iodo-2,2-dimethylbutane, as is predicted from Markovnikov's rule, but also 2-iodo-2,3-dimethylbutane. By shifting a methyl group from carbon three, some of the 2° carbocations initially formed produce a 3° carbocation so that some of the final product follows from the 2° carbocation and some follows from the 3° carbocation:

$$CH_3 - \underset{\underset{\boxed{CH_3}}{\overset{CH_3}{|}}}{C} - \underset{\overset{\oplus}{\underset{}{|}}}{C} - CH_3 \longrightarrow CH_3 - \underset{\overset{CH_3}{|}}{C} - \underset{\overset{H}{|}}{C} - CH_3$$

2 carbocation

3-iodo-2,2-dimethylbutane

methyl shift

$$CH_3 - \underset{\overset{\oplus}{\underset{}{|}}}{\overset{CH_3}{C}} - \underset{\overset{H}{\underset{\boxed{CH_3}}{|}}}{C} - CH_3 \longrightarrow CH_3 - \underset{\overset{CH_3}{\underset{I}{|}}}{C} - \underset{\overset{H}{\underset{CH_3}{|}}}{C} - CH_3$$

3 carbocation   2-iodo-2,2-dimethylbutane

Please solve this problem:

- The electrophilic addition of hydrochloric acid to 4-methyl-3-heptene produces, primarily:

    A. 3-chloro-4-methyl-3-heptene.
    B. 4-chloro-4-methyl-3-heptene.
    C. 3-chloro-4-methylheptane.
    D. 4-chloro-4-methylheptane.

Problem solved:

D is correct. In an electrophilic addition of hydrogen halide to an alkene, the double bond is eliminated and an alkyl halide results. Choices A and B are wrong, therefore, because they describe alkenes, not alkanes. The process normally follows Markovnikov's rule and produces, preferentially, a product in which the halide atom is located at the more highly substituted of the doubly bonded carbons. Before the reaction occurs, carbon three is bound to one hydrogen atom and to two carbon atoms. Carbon four is bound to no hydrogen atoms and to three carbon atoms. Carbon four, therefore, is more highly substituted than carbon three.

$$H - \underset{\overset{H}{\underset{H}{|}}}{C} - \underset{\overset{H}{\underset{H}{|}}}{C} - \underset{\overset{H}{\underset{③}{|}}}{C} = \underset{\overset{CH_3}{\underset{④}{|}}}{C} - \underset{\overset{H}{\underset{H}{|}}}{C} - \underset{\overset{H}{\underset{H}{|}}}{C} - \underset{\overset{H}{\underset{H}{|}}}{C} - H$$

4-methyl-3-heptene

The chlorine atom will bond, preferentially, to carbon four, producing 4-chloro-4-methylheptane:

$$H - \underset{\overset{H}{\underset{H}{|}}}{C} - \underset{\overset{H}{\underset{H}{|}}}{C} - \underset{\overset{H}{\underset{H}{|}}}{C} - \underset{\overset{CH_3}{\underset{Cl}{|}}}{C} - \underset{\overset{H}{\underset{H}{|}}}{C} - \underset{\overset{H}{\underset{H}{|}}}{C} - \underset{\overset{H}{\underset{H}{|}}}{C} - H$$

4-chloro-4-methylheptane

ANTI-MARKOVNIKOV ADDITION IN THE PRESENCE OF PEROXIDES

When HBr adds to a double bond in the presence of *peroxides*, Markovnikov addition is not the norm. Electrophilic addition occurs according to a different mechanism—involving not a carbocation but a carbon free radical, and the new substituent appears at the *least* substituted carbon. That process is termed **anti-Markovnikov addition,** and is also a regioselective process:

propene → 1-bromopropane

Anti-Markovnikov addition
in the presence of peroxides:
addition occurs at the least
substituted carbon.

With respect to alkene electrophilic addition as it appears on the MCAT, you should know that:

- Normally, Markovnikov addition is the favored reaction, involving

(a) a carbocation in which positive charge is carried on the more highly substituted carbon and, consequently,

(b) a final product in which the electronegative species binds to that same carbon.

- In the presence of peroxides, addition of HBr to an alkene occurs in anti-Markovnikov fashion via a carbon free radical intermediate. The most favored product will be that in which addition occurs at the alkene molecule's *least* substituted carbon.

ADDITION OF WATER: HYDRATION

With an acid catalyst, water will add to an alkene's double bond to form an alcohol:

Alkene → Alcohol

The reaction proceeds through a carbocation intermediate whose formation here, as with the addition of hydrogen halide, is the rate-determining step. The reaction is favored by a stable carbocation and *follows Markovnikov's rule.*

Hydration of an alkene competes with the reverse process—dehydration of an alcohol. Equilibrium will lie toward hydration if the acid is relatively dilute and the temperature is low. Equilibrium will lie toward *de*hydration if the acid is relatively concentrated and temperature is relatively high.

Please solve this problem:

- When 3,3-dimethyl-1-butane undergoes acid catalyzed hydration, the chief product, 2,3-dimethyl-2-butanol, carries the OH group on neither of the carbons initially involved in the double bond:

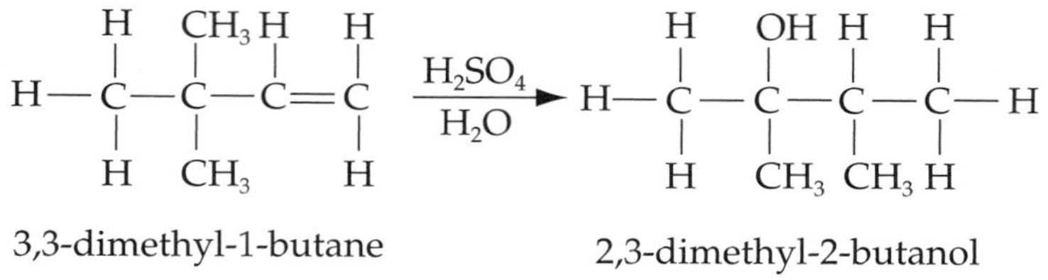

3,3-dimethyl-1-butane   2,3-dimethyl-2-butanol

The most likely explanation is that:

A. the carbocation initially formed rearranges to form a more highly substituted species.
B. the carbocation initially formed rearranges to form a less highly substituted species.
C. acid catalyzed hydration is anti-Markovnikov.
D. the OH group acts as an attacking electophile.

Problem solved:

A is correct. Choice D makes an incorrect statement. The OH group is a base and in this context, therefore, a nucleophile. It "wants" to donate electrons, not to acquire them. Choice C also makes a false statement; acid catalyzed hydration proceeds according to Markovnikov's rule. It is Critical to note for the MCAT that *reactions are favored, through rate increase, by factors that stabilize (reduce the energy state of) transition states or intermediates*. Acid catalyzed hydration of an alkene proceeds through a carbocation intermediate, and a carbocation is most stable when its charge is delocalized. Tertiary carbons delocalize charge better than secondary carbons, which delocalize charge better than primary carbons.

That means, first of all, that tertiary carbocations are more stable than secondary carbocations, which are more stable than primary carbocations. Carbocations, "wanting" to be as stable as possible, will actually rearrange to form more highly substituted intermediates not otherwise forseeable from the structure of the reactant. Choice B, therefore, makes a false statement. In this case, a secondary carbocation rearranges to form a tertiary carbocation, which is more highly substituted than the secondary carbocation. For that reason, the product carries its OH group on the tertiary carbon.

HYDROBORATION-OXIDATION

Addition of borane to an alkene double bond produces an organoborane, which, in turn, can undergo oxidation to form an alcohol. The transition state for the hydroboration reaction dictates a **syn addition** in which the hydrogen and boron add to the same side of the carbon–carbon double bond.

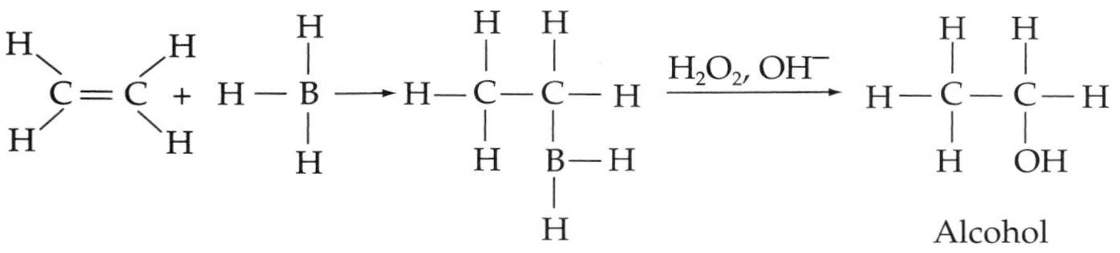

Alcohol

The ultimate product corresponds to that which would result from *anti-Markovnikov* addition of water. Given its "choice," the OH group in this reaction locates itself on the least substituted carbon. (The reaction is useful, therefore, because it allows for the production of alcohols not obtainable by acid-catalyzed hydration of alkenes.)

Please solve this problem:

- If a researcher wishes to obtain a primary alcohol from an alkene in which the first and second carbons are doubly bound, he would best resort to:

  A. acid catalyzed hydration, because addition is Markovnikov.
  B. acid catalyzed hydration, because addition is anti-Markovnikov.
  C. hydroboration and oxidation, because addition is Markovnikov.
  D. hydroboration and oxidation, because addition is anti-Markovnikov.

Problem solved:

D is correct. Choices B and C make false statements. In acid catalyzed hydration, addition is Markovnikov. In hydroboration-oxidation, addition is anti-Markovnikov. Choice A, therefore, makes a true statement but is not correct. If the researcher seeks a primary alcohol—the OH group being bound to a primary carbon—he wants not Markovnikov addition but anti-Markovnikov addition.

ADDITION OF HALOGENS (CHLORINE OR BROMINE)

In a solution of carbon tetrachloride, chlorine and bromine undergo an addition reaction with alkenes to form dihalides. The reaction proceeds according to these two steps:

Step 1: π electrons from the carbon-carbon double bond attack the halogen molecule to form a cyclic **halonium ion** intermediate and a halide ion.

Step 2: The halide ion makes a nucleophilic attack on the halonium ion to form the product.

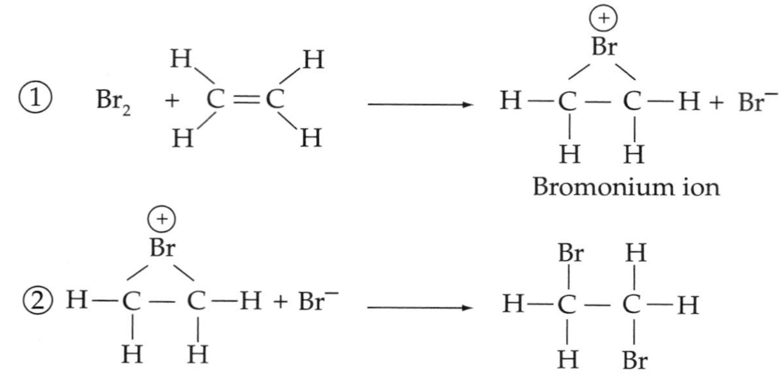

① Br$_2$ + (ethene) ⟶ Bromonium ion + Br$^-$

② Bromonium ion + Br$^-$ ⟶ (dibrominated product)

The halogen bridge that characterizes the halonium ion limits the halide ion to an attack on that face of the halonium ion opposite to the one that carries the bromine atom. That is, the two bromine atoms add, finally, to opposite sides of the carbon-carbon double bond, and the process is called **anti-addition** (as opposed to syn addition in which the two components of the added reagent add to the same side of the carbon-carbon double bond).

If halogenation of an alkene is conducted not in a carbon tetrachloride solution but in aqueous solution instead, the solvent molecules themselves react to produce a **halo alcohol**, also called a **halohydrin**.

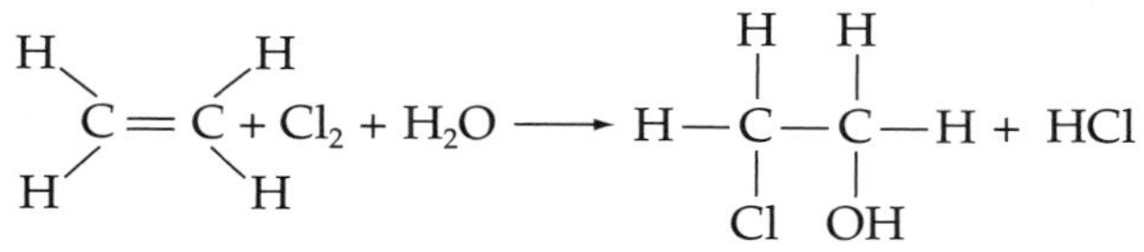

Halohydrin

Please solve this problem:

- In the second step of bromine addition to an alkene, the bromide ion acts as:

  A. a Lewis acid.
  B. a Lewis base.
  C. an electrophile.
  D. a rate-determining intermediate.

Problem solved:

B is correct. In the second step of the bromine addition, a bromide ion, "anxious" to share its unshared pair of electrons, combines with the positively charged bromonium ion to form the dibrominated product. It acts then as a nucleophile—a Lewis base (which makes choices A and C plainly wrong). It is the carbocation, not the bromide ion, that represents the rate-determining intermediate, and for that reason, choice D is wrong as well.

AROMATICITY AND SUBSTITUTION ON THE BENZENE RING

A molecule is **aromatic** if:

1. it has a planar, cyclic, conjugated structure in which all atoms of the ring have undergone sp^2 hybridization, and

2. it carries a **Huckel number** of π electrons.

A Huckel number is any number that conforms to the pattern $4n + 2$, where n is any integer. For $n = 0, 1, 2, 3, 4$, and 5, corresponding Huckel numbers are 2, 6, 10, 14, 18, and 22.

Benzene, the aromatic prototype, is a planar, cyclic structure with six π electrons.

Benzene
6π electrons

Other aromatic molecules include, for example, the cyclopropenal cation with *two* π electrons and the cyclopentadienyl anion with *six* π electrons. Aromatic compounds may also have N, O, or S in the ring in addition to C.

The phenomenon of a flat, planar ring with cyclic clouds of delocalized π electrons above and below the ring confers upon aromatic molecules a number of characteristic properties, including a *pronounced stability of the ring*, due to the delocalization of the π electrons. As a result, aromatic compounds are generally very unreactive.

Benzene

Benzene is the prototypical aromatic compound and, for the MCAT, aromaticity is addressed primarily in terms of benzene and its derivatives. Benzene is pictured in two resonance forms, or more realistically, as a hybrid between the two, with π electrons fully delocalized:

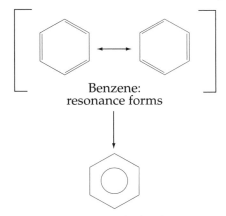

Benzene:
resonance forms

Benzene: hybrid

The benzene ring, like all aromatic rings is extraordinarily stable due, once again, to the delocalization of π electrons. For that reason, benzene tends not to undergo reactions in which the ring is disrupted but "prefers" instead reactions in which the ring is preserved. Consequently—and this is important for the MCAT—*benzene tends to undergo substitution rather than addition.*

Naming Substituted Benzene Rings

When one hydrogen atom of a benzene ring is replaced by another substituent (see details of the reactions below), the six carbon atoms that were once identical become different. The two positions of the ring adjacent, or 1,2 to the substituent, are referred to as *ortho* carbons, or the ortho positions, as shown in the structure of toluene below. The two positions of the ring that are 1,3 to the substituent are called the *meta* positions, and the carbon directly across the ring, or 1,4 to the substituent, is referred to as the *para* position.

Toluene

CH_3

ortho   ortho

meta   meta

para

Benzene Ring: Electrophilic Aromatic Substitution

The benzene ring (represented immediately below by "Ph" for aromatic ring) is suceptible to substitution by a variety of substituents. It undergoes, for example:

Halogenation: $PhH + Cl_2/AlCl_3$ or $Br_2/FeBr_3$ $\longrightarrow$ $Ph–Cl + HCl$

$Ph–Br + HBr$

Nitration: $PhH + HNO_3 + H_2SO_4$ $\longrightarrow$ $Ph–NO_2 + H_2O$

Alkylation: $PhH + RCl/AlCl_3$ $\longrightarrow$ $Ph–R + HCl$

Via **inductive effects**, a single substitution of a benzene ring raises or lowers the likelihood that the ring will undergo a *second substitution*. Because a second substitution (like the first one) involves π aromatic electrons acting as nucleophiles that attack the electrophilic substituent, a first substituent that *donates* electrons to the ring renders the ring relatively *more* susceptible to a second substitution. Similarly, a first substituent that *withdraws* electrons from the ring renders the ring relatively *less* susceptible to a second substitution.

In that regard, for the MCAT, it is important to know that:

- A group that donates (or "releases") electrons to the ring tends to increase the likelihood of additional substitution. It is said to activate the ring, and is termed a **ring activating group.** You can recognize most activating groups since they all have a lone pair of electrons on the atom directly attached to the ring.

- A group that withdraws electrons from the ring decreases the likelihood of additional substitution. It is said to **deactivate** the ring, and is termed a **ring deactivating group.** You can recognize most deactivating groups since they have a + or δ + charge on the atom directly attached to the ring.

A single benzene ring substituent affects not only the likelihood that a next substitution will occur, but also the *site* at which it will occur. Consider, again, for example, the toluene molecule shown above. If it is to undergo a second substitution, the second substituent might, theoretically, bind itself to any of the five unsubstituted carbons that remain on the ring. Three potential products then are in competition with one another.

The competing reactions that lead to the competing products proceed through carbocation intermediates. Certain ring substituents favor ortho and para substitution by reducing the activation energy and stabilizing the carbocation intermediate that leads to ortho and para substituted products. Other ring substituents favor meta substitution by rendering the activation energy tied to the meta substituted product more favorable than that tied to the ortho and para substituted product.

Depending on the nature of the first substituent, then (a methyl group in the case of toluene), a second substituent will be "directed" to a particular site on the ring—ortho, para, or meta. Hence, we say that substituents have not only activating and deactivating effects but also **directive effects.**

Specifically:

1. all electron-withdrawing groups *except the halogens* are meta directors;

2. all electron-donating groups *plus the halogens* are ortho, para directors.

Generally speaking, then, electron donating groups are (1) activators and (2) ortho, para directors. Electron withdrawing groups are (1) deactivators and (2) meta directors. Halogens are an exception. They are electron withdrawers. Like other withdrawing groups, they deactivate. But unlike other withdrawing groups, they are ortho, para directors.

Taken together, the relationships between a substituent's tendency to donate or withdraw electrons and its effects on activation and direction lead to the trends described in Table 35.3.

796 ■ CRACKING THE MCAT

Substituent	(De)Activity	Direction
OH	Activator	ortho, para
NR_2	Activator	ortho, para
OR	Activator	ortho, para
OCOR	Activator	ortho, para
NHCOR	Activator	ortho, para
R	Activator	ortho, para
Cl, Br, I	Deactivator	ortho, para
NR_3^+	Deactivator	meta
NO_2	Deactivator	meta
CN	Deactivator	meta
SO_3H	Deactivator	meta
COR	Deactivator	meta
COOH	Deactivator	meta
COOR	Deactivator	meta
$CONH_2$	Deactivator	meta

R = alkyl group

Table 35.3

Please solve this problem:

- The substitution of a nitro (NO_2) group on bromo-benzene will:

    A. proceed more readily than the substitution of a nitro group on benzene and will yield, primarily, 1-bromo-3-nitrobenzene.
    B. proceed less readily than the substitution of a nitro group on benzene and will yield, primarily, 1-bromo-3-nitrobenzene.
    C. proceed more readily than the substitution of a nitro group on benzene and will yield, primarily, 1-bromo-4-nitrobenzene.
    D. proceed less readily than the substitution of a nitro group on benzene and will yield, primarily, 1-bromo-4-nitrobenzene.

Problem solved:

D is correct. Bromobenzene is, of course, a molecule in which benzene has undergone a single substitution by a bromine atom. Bromine is an electron-withdrawing group and, like all electron-withdrawing groups, it *de*activates a benzene ring. Consequently, the tendency for bromobenzene to undergo a second substitution is less than the tendency for benzene itself to undergo an initial substitution. That means the substitution of an NO_2 group on bromobenzene will proceed less readily than the bromination of benzene itself. Choices A and C, therefore, are eliminated. The halogens, unlike all other ring deactivators are ortho, para directive. When 1-bromo-3-nitobenzene is formed from bromobenzene, the bromobenzene undergoes meta substitution. When 1-bromo-4-nitrobenzene is formed from bromobenzene, the bromobenzene undergoes para substitution, just as the bromine substituent would direct.

35.2 MASTERY APPLIED: PRACTICE PASSAGE AND QUESTIONS

Passage

The addition of a hydrogen halide to an unsymmetric alkene leads, potentially, to two products: (1) a compound in which the halide is situated on the more substituted carbon and (2) a compound in which the halide is located on the less substituted carbon. In the first case, the addition is said to represent Markovnikov's addition. The second case is said to represent anti-Markovnikov addition. If, in a given instance, the reaction leads exclusively or almost exclusively to only one of these two possible isomeric products, it is said to be *regiospecific*.

Benzene undergoes halogenation not by addition, but by a substitution, with the production of a halobenzene and a hydrogen halide. The reaction occurs according to Reaction 1, in which Ar represents the benzene ring and X represents the halide.

$$ArH + X_2 \rightarrow Ar\text{-}X + HX$$

Reaction 1

If the halogenated ring is made to undergo further substitution, competing isomeric products also form according to a preference, in which the ortho and para products predominate over the meta product.

Benzene undergoes a variety of substitution reactions, including, for example, Friedel Crafts acylation, which produces a ketone and a hydrogen halide according to Reaction 2:

$$ArH + RCOCl \xrightarrow{AlCl_3} Ar\text{-}COR + HCl$$

Reaction 2

The reaction is thought to proceed through a rate-determining step in which there is formed a carbocation intermediate called, more specifically, the acylium ion. The reaction requires, as a catalyst, a Lewis acid such as $AlCl_3$. Once bound to the benzene ring, the COR group, like a halogen, tends to withdraw electrons.

1. The electrophilic addition of hydrogen bromide to propene would most likely proceed according to:

   A. Markovnikov addition that is regio-specific.
   B. Markovnikov addition that is not regiospecifc.
   C. anti-Markovnikov addition that is regiospecific.
   D. anti-Markovnikov addition that is not regiospecific.

2. In an addition of HBr to 2-methyl-2-butene, only one of the potential products is formed in significant concentration. The relative predominance of the single product is most likely due to the fact that:

   A. a secondary carbocation is of greater stability than a primary carbocation.
   B. a tertiary carbocation is of greater stability than a secondary carbocation.
   C. addition occurs across the carbon–carbon double bond.
   D. addition occurs across one of the carbon–carbon single bonds.

3. A researcher finds that in the absence of peroxides, addition of HBr to 3-methyl-1-butene yields a mixture in which two alkyl bromides are present in significant concentrations. Among the following, the most likely explanation is:

   A. a predominance of anti-Markovnikov addition.
   B. a combination of Markovnikov and anti-Markovnikov addition.
   C. a carbocation rearrangement in which a bromine group shifts position.
   D. a carbocation rearrangement in which a hydrogen atom shifts position.

4. The benzene molecule tends not to undergo addition of halogens because:

   A. halogens donate electrons to the benzene ring.
   B. halogens withdraw electrons from the benzene ring.
   C. the benzene ring embodies delocalized π electrons.
   D. the benzene ring is nonaromatic.

5. If a benzene ring undergoes Reaction 2 and then is made to undergo a second substitution, the additional substituent will most likely locate itself on the:

   A. ipso carbon.
   B. ortho carbon.
   C. para carbon.
   D. meta carbon.

6. Among the following, $AlCl_3$ most likely facilitates the Friedel Crafts acylation by:

   A. activating the benzene ring through addition of a halide.
   B. deactivating the benzene ring through addition of a halide.
   C. reducing the energy necessary for formation of the acylium ion.
   D. increasing the energy necessary for formation of the acylium ion.

35.3 MASTERY VERIFIED: ANSWERS AND EXPLANATIONS

1. **A is correct.** Except in the presence of peroxides, electrophilic addition of a hydrogen bromide (and any hydrogen halide) to an alkene proceeds predominantly by Markovnikov's addition, so we can eliminate choices C and D. According to the passage, "regiospecific" refers to a reaction in which one of the potential isomeric products enjoys a preference that is nearly exclusive. Such is characteristic of the reaction in which a hydrogen halide is added to an alkene. The reaction yields, almost exclusively, the product that follows from Markovnikov addition, which, in this case, would be 2-bromopropane.

2. **B is correct.** Choice D makes a false statement. Choices A and C make true statements but do not explain the absence of one of the possible isomeric products. When a hydrogen halide is added to an alkene, the predominant product is that which follows from the more stable of the two potential carbocations initially formed from the alkene. (If structure of that carbocation permits rearrangement, then the reaction will lead to two products—one for the carbocation initially formed and one for the rearranged carbocation.) Theoretically, 2-methyl-2-butene might produce two carbocations, one of which is secondary and one of which is tertiary. Of these, the tertiary carbocation is the more stable because as to stability, carbocations follow the ranking: $3° > 2° > 1°$. Choice B, therefore, makes the true statement that explains this result. A tertiary carbocation is more stable than a secondary carbocation.

3. **D is correct.** Anti-Markovnikov addition will occur to a significant degree only in the presence of peroxides. That means that choices A and B are wrong. Yet, it is true that the carbocation that mediates addition of a halide to an alkene might rearrange itself, if structure permits, to form a more stable carbocation. The bromine atom becomes a part of the final product only after the carbocation is formed. It is not a part of the carbocation and so cannot be involved in the rearrangement. Choice C, therefore, is wrong. In this reaction, 3-methyl-1-butene forms, initially, a $2°$ carbocation:

By movement of a hydrogen atom (a hydride shift), some of these carbocations will rearrange themselves to form $3°$ carbocations:

The two carbocations, 2° and 3°, give rise to the two products:

$$\begin{array}{cccc} & H & CH_3\ H & H \\ & | & |\quad\ | & | \\ H\!-\!C\!-\!&C\!-\!\overset{\oplus}{C}\!-\!&C\!-\!H \\ & | & |\quad\ | & | \\ & H & H\qquad & H \end{array} \xrightarrow{\text{HBr}} \begin{array}{cccc} & H & CH_3\ H & H \\ & | & |\quad\ | & | \\ H\!-\!C\!-\!&C\!-\!C\!-\!&C\!-\!H \\ & | & |\quad\ | & | \\ & H & H\ \ Br & H \end{array}$$

$$\begin{array}{cccc} & H & CH_3\ H & H \\ & | & |\quad\ | & | \\ H\!-\!C\!-\!&\overset{\oplus}{C}\!-\!C\!-\!&C\!-\!H \\ & | & |\quad\ | & | \\ & H & H\qquad H \end{array} \xrightarrow{\text{HBr}} \begin{array}{cccc} & H & CH_3\ H & H \\ & | & |\quad\ | & | \\ H\!-\!C\!-\!&C\!-\!C\!-\!&C\!-\!H \\ & | & |\quad\ | & | \\ & H & Br\ \ H & H \end{array}$$

4. **C is correct.** Choices A and D make false statements. Benzene is an aromatic ring. When bound to the benzene ring, halogens withdraw electrons. Choice B makes a true statement, but it has no relevance to the fact that benzene molecule undergoes substitution and not addition. That fact pertains to the characteristics of benzene itself. Benzene and all aromatic molecules are characterized by high stability due to the delocalization of π electrons.

5. **D is correct.** Choice A is absurd because, by definition, the ipso carbon is that to which a first substituent is bound. Once a benzene molecule undergoes reaction 2, the COR group is bound, by definition, to the ipso carbon. We are told that the COR group *withdraws* electrons from the benzene ring. Groups that withdraw electrons tend to deactivate the benzene ring to further substitution. If further substitution is nonetheless achieved, electron-withdrawing groups—with the exception of the halogens—direct toward the meta position.

6. **C is correct.** Choices A and B are clearly wrong because addition of a halide would deactivate the ring, and deactivation of the ring would tend to *impair* the reaction, not facilitate it. You are asked to process information in the last paragraph of the passage and to *reason*. We are told that $AlCl_3$ serves as a catalyst, which means it serves to reduce activation energy. We are told also that the reaction is mediated by an acylium ion (a particular form of carbocation), the formation of which constitutes the rate-determining step. Among the choices, the most logical conclusion is that $AlCl_3$, acting as a catalyst, serves to reduce the energy necessary to formation of the intermediate.

Chapter 36

ALKYL HALIDES AND ALCOHOLS

36.1 MASTERY ACHIEVED

ALKYL HALIDES: SUBSTITUTION AND ELIMINATION REACTIONS

For the MCAT, two reactions of the alkyl halides are important to remember: (1) nucleophilic substitution and (2) elimination.

Nucleophilic Substitution

A variety of compounds undergo nucleophilic aliphatic substitution, but the alkyl halides serve as a good basis on which to study the process generically. "Nucleophilic substitution" means a reaction, conducted in a solvent, between an aliphatic compound (the substrate) and a **nucleophilic reagent**. The substrate:

(a) gives up a **leaving group**, and

(b) is "attacked" by a nucleophile, which substitutes for the leaving group.

$$R - W \ + \ Z \ \xrightarrow{\text{solvent}} \ R - Z \ + W$$

substrate   nucleophile   leaving group

The leaving group is a group that rather readily leaves a carbon atom and takes with it the electron pair it had shared *with* the carbon atom. The nucleophile is a species that has an unshared electron pair, which it brings *to* the carbon atom, thereby forming a covalent bond with it. The nucleophile might be negatively charged or neutral. The key to nucleophilicity is *the presence of an unshared electron pair*.

Here, for instance, is a reaction in which methyl bromide is the substrate, bromide ion the leaving group and hydroxide ion the nucleophile.

$$CH_3Br \ + \ OH^- \ \longrightarrow \ CH_3OH + Br^-$$

The bromine atom leaves the substrate, taking with it both electrons that it had shared with the carbon atom, to form a bromide ion. The hydroxide ion carries an unshared pair of electrons, *which makes it a "nucleophile."* The hydroxide ion approaches the carbon with its unshared pair of electrons, bonds to ("attacks") the carbon atom, thereby substituting itself for the bromide ion as the bromide leaves.

The reaction of methylbromide with hydroxide ion occurs because the bromine atom has a strong tendency to take the electron pair it shared with carbon and "leave." That means that bromide is a relatively good leaving group. It occurs also because the hydroxide ion has a relatively strong tendency to take its unshared electron pair and share it with the carbon atom, which makes hydroxide ion a relatively strong nucleophile.

THE S_N1 AND S_N2 REACTIONS

Nucleophilic aliphatic substitution occurs according to two mechanisms: (1) S_N1 and (2) S_N2.

THE S_N2 REACTION

The S_N2 mechanism occurs in one step. The nucleophile attacks the "back side" of the carbon atom as the leaving group leaves from the other side, creating a transition state in which the substrate is partially bound to the leaving group and partially bound to the nucleophile.

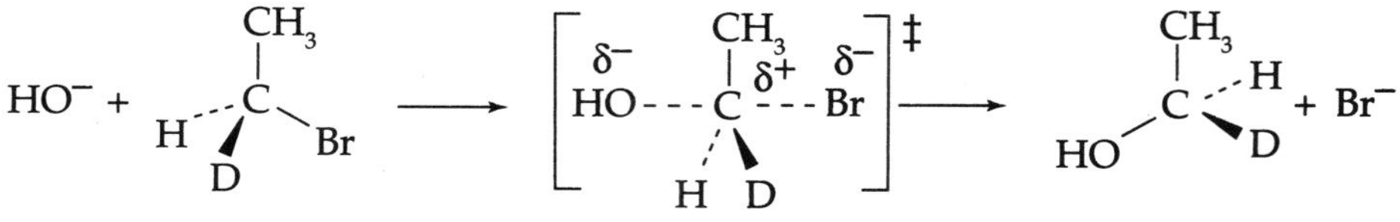

Because the single step of the S_N2 reaction involves both reactants, the substrate and the nucleophile, the reaction rate is dependent upon the concentration of both. It is *second order*:

$$rate = k[\text{substrate}][\text{nucleophile}]$$

For the reaction depicted above:

$$rate = k[\text{RBr}][\text{OH}^-]$$

In an S_N2 substitution, the nucleophile attacks the carbon on one side ("back-side attack") and the leaving group leaves from the other. The nucleophile ultimately finds itself not in the position that the leaving group had occupied, but rather on the *opposite* side. The product is opposite in geometry to the tetrahedron formed around that same carbon atom in the initial substrate. If the original substrate is chiral, the substituted product is also chiral, but it will have the opposite configuration. That is, S_N2 substitution is accompanied by **complete inversion of configuration**.

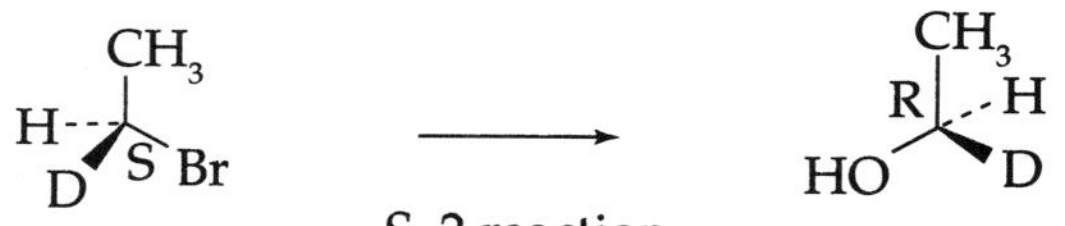

S_N2 reaction
inverts configuration

THE S_N1 REACTION

The S_N1 mechanism occurs in two steps:

Step 1: The leaving group leaves to form a carbocation.

Step 2: The nucleophile attacks the carbocation to form the substituted product.

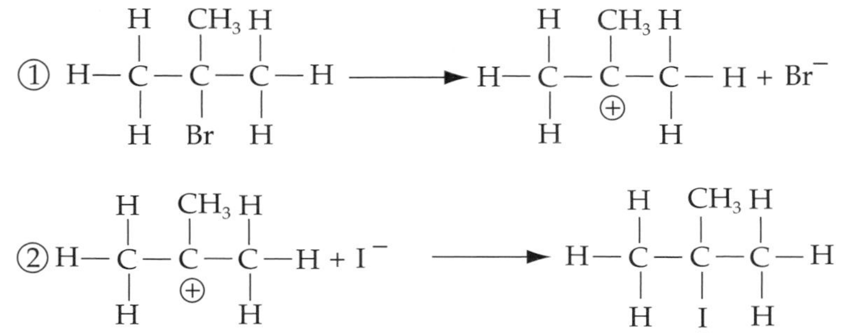

① $H-\underset{\underset{H}{|}}{\overset{\overset{H}{|}}{C}}-\underset{\underset{Br}{|}}{\overset{\overset{CH_3}{|}}{C}}-\underset{\underset{H}{|}}{\overset{\overset{H}{|}}{C}}-H \longrightarrow H-\underset{\underset{H}{|}}{\overset{\overset{H}{|}}{C}}-\overset{\overset{CH_3}{|}}{\underset{\oplus}{C}}-\underset{\underset{H}{|}}{\overset{\overset{H}{|}}{C}}-H + Br^-$

② $H-\underset{\underset{H}{|}}{\overset{\overset{H}{|}}{C}}-\overset{\overset{CH_3}{|}}{\underset{\oplus}{C}}-\underset{\underset{H}{|}}{\overset{\overset{H}{|}}{C}}-H + I^- \longrightarrow H-\underset{\underset{H}{|}}{\overset{\overset{H}{|}}{C}}-\underset{\underset{I}{|}}{\overset{\overset{CH_3}{|}}{C}}-\underset{\underset{H}{|}}{\overset{\overset{H}{|}}{C}}-H$

The slow step—the rate-determining step—is the first one, in which a bond is broken and a carbocation formed. Because this rate-determining step does not involve the nucleophile (I^- in the illustration above), *the rate is dependent only on the concentration of the substrate.* The S_N1 reaction, therefore, is *first order*:

$$\text{rate} = k[\text{substrate}]$$

For the reaction depicted above:

$$\text{rate} = k[(CH_3)_2CBrCH_3]$$

The carbocation intermediate is a planar, sp^2 - hybridized species, and is therefore achiral. When one enantiomer of a chiral molecule undergoes S_N1 substitution, it yields something close to a racemic mixture of enantiomeric products.

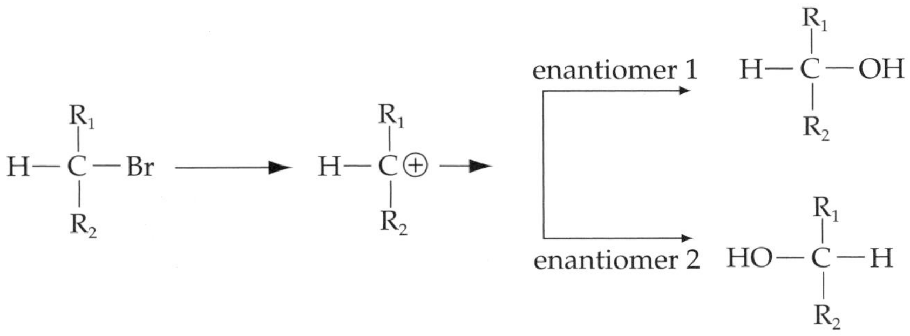

$H-\underset{\underset{R_2}{|}}{\overset{\overset{R_1}{|}}{C}}-Br \longrightarrow H-\overset{\overset{R_1}{|}}{\underset{\underset{R_2}{|}}{C}}\oplus \longrightarrow$ enantiomer 1 $\quad H-\underset{\underset{R_2}{|}}{\overset{\overset{R_1}{|}}{C}}-OH$

enantiomer 2 $\quad HO-\underset{\underset{R_2}{|}}{\overset{\overset{R_1}{|}}{C}}-H$

Finally, the carbocation intermediate may, as in the case of electrophilic addition, undergo rearrangement to form a more stable carbocation, which, in turn, affects the structure of the product.

EFFECTS OF SUBSTRATE, NUCLEOPHILE, SOLVENT, AND LEAVING GROUP

Reaction rates of the S_N1 and S_N2 reactions are affected, positively and negatively, by the nature of the substrate, nucleophile, solvent, and leaving group. Common to all such phenomena—and important for the MCAT—is the fundamental thermodynamic notion that the *universe tends toward lowest energy.* A species is more stable when it occupies a relatively lower energy state and less stable when it occupies a relatively higher energy state.

A reaction is favored by a circumstance that:

1. stabilizes and thus promotes the formation of the transition state, intermediate, and product(s), or

2. destabilizes or impairs the formation of the reactant(s).

A reaction is disfavored by a circumstance that:

1. destabilizes and thus impairs the formation of the transition state, intermediate, and product(s), or

2. stabilizes the reactant(s).

With that in mind, consider the effects on nucleophilic aliphatic substitution of substrate, leaving group, nucleophile, and solvent.

NATURE OF THE SUBSTRATE

Because S_N1 substitution proceeds via a carbocation intermediate, the reaction rate is enhanced by circumstances that *stabilize the intermediate*. We know that in terms of stability, carbocations (like carbon free radicals) follow this ranking:

$$3° > 2° > 1° > CH_3$$

The nature of the carbocation, in turn, relates to the structure of the substrate. Therefore, reactivity in S_N1 follows this hierarchy:

$$3° > 2° > 1° > CH_3$$

As already discussed, S_N2 substitution involves back-side attack. A secondary or tertiary carbon impedes back-side attack by "crowding" the nucleophile. In other words, secondary and tertiary carbons confront the S_N2 mechanism with **steric hindrance** that destabilizes (raises the energy of) the transition state. S_N2 reactions are favored when the substituted carbon is methyl or primary, but they are disfavored for secondary and tertiary carbons. Reactivity in S_N2, therefore follows this hierarchy:

$$CH_3 > 1° > 2° > 3°$$

NATURE OF THE LEAVING GROUP AND NUCLEOPHILE: RELEVANCE OF BASICITY

Nucleophilicity and leaving ability are, perhaps, "opposite sides of the same coin." They are opposing functions resulting from opposing phenomena—*the tendency and lack of tendency to share an electron pair to form a covalent bond*. A good leaving group is one that has a relatively weak tendency to share an electron pair, and thus a strong tendency to take the pair for itself. A strong nucleophile is a species that has a relatively strong tendency to share an electron pair and relatively weaker tendency to take the pair for itself.

We might look at the nucleophilic substitution as a contest between two Lewis bases—a weaker one (the leaving group) and a stronger one (the nucleophile). When a leaving group "decides" to leave, it "decides" that it will no longer donate an electron pair to the carbon atom. Rather it takes the pair away and departs. The nucleophile then "sees" an opportunity to donate *its* electron pair *to* the carbon atom and form a bond with the carbon atom. The nucleophile is acting as the stronger Lewis base and the leaving group as a weaker Lewis base.

LEAVING ABILITY AND BASICITY

Whether a particular species is a good leaving group is related to its basicity. In both the S_N2 and S_N1 reactions, therefore, the best leaving groups tend to be weaker bases or, put otherwise, conjugate bases of stronger acids. As for the halogens, then, leaving ability is enhanced as we move down the periodic table:

$$I^- > Br^- > Cl^- > F^-$$

For the MCAT, it is important to know how to explain the phenomenon in thermodynamic terms. In the S_N1 reaction, the carbocation intermediate is formed by departure of the leaving group. Any factor that promotes the departure tends also to promote formation of the intermediate and thus to favor the reaction. Weaker basicity promotes departure and thus favors leaving ability in the S_N1 reaction.

An S_N2 reaction involves a transition state in which the leaving group and the attacking nucleophile "share" the burden of bearing a negative charge. The best leaving group is one that best assists in delocalizing the charge. Greater ability to accommodate the negative charge makes for better leaving ability. Greater ability to accommodate negative charge corresponds to a tendency to "hold on to" the unshared electron pair and, therefore, to weaker basicity. Weaker basicity favors leaving ability in the S_N2 reaction, just as it does in the S_N1 reaction.

NUCLEOPHILICITY AND BASICITY

There is also a correlation between basicity and nucleophilicity, but the correlation is rough and imperfect. For the MCAT, it is important to know that between any two species, the stronger base *tends* to be a stronger nucleophile, and the weaker base *tends* to be a weaker nucleophile. It is generally true, for example, that among nucleophiles with the same attacking atom, the stronger base is the better nucleophile. Consider, for instance, nucleophiles in which oxygen is the attacking atom. In terms of nucleophilicity:

$$CH_3O^- \;>\; HO^- \;>\; CH_3CO_2^- \;>\; H_2O$$

Other factors, however, also affect nucleophilicity. They include, for example, molecular size, the nature of the atom to which the species is initially bound, and the solvent in which the reaction occurs. These factors are sufficiently important that, depending on the circumstance, a weaker base might be a stronger nucleophile than a stronger base.

Consequently, we *can* say that subject to other factors, stronger basicity *tends* to make for stronger nucleophiles and weaker basicity *tends* to make for better leaving groups.

But we *cannot* say that between two species, the stronger base is always the better nucleophile and the weaker base is the better leaving group.

NATURE OF THE SOLVENT

The effects of solvent on S_N2 reactions relates to *stability of the nucleophile*. **Protic solvents,** meaning those that contain –OH or NH groups, slow the S_N2 reaction by forming hydrogen bonds around the nucleophile. The hydrogen bonds *stabilize the nucleophile*, thereby making it less prone to react. Polar aprotic solvents raise the rate of S_N2 reactions by destabilizing the reactant. Such solvents tend to solvate metal cations while leaving nucleophilic anions "naked" and unsolvated. The naked anions have greater nucleophilicity and the S_N2 reaction rate is increased.

S_N1 reactions are favored by protic solvents and disfavored by nonpolar solvents. The reason pertains not to stability of the nucleophile but rather to *stability of the carbocation intermediate*. Polar solvents orient themselves so that their electron-rich ends face the carbocation's positive charge, adding to its stability. Nonpolar solvents have no such effect.

S_N1 AND S_N2 REACTIONS: COMPETITION AND COMPARISON

S_N1 and S_N2 represent competing mechanisms. Both have a tendency to occur, but one or the other will be favored, depending largely on the nature of the substrate. Thus, the two reactions exhibit opposite trends. For reasons already explained, reactivity in S_N1 relates to substrate according to this ranking:

$$3° > 2° > 1° > CH_3$$

Reactivity in S_N2 relates to substrate according to the opposite ranking:

$$CH_3 > 1° > 2° > 3°$$

S_N1 and S_N2 reactions exhibit nonidentical trends in relation to solvent. One or the other may be favored, depending on the solvent's nature. Polar solvents speed the S_N1 reaction. Nonpolar solvents slow it. Polar *aprotic* solvents speed the S_N2 reaction; protic solvents slow it.

Table 36.1 compares the S_N1 and S_N2 reactions in terms of mechanism, kinetics, reactivity, solvent effects, and stereochemistry.

	Mechanism	Kinetics	Reactivity	Stereochemistry	Solvent Effects
S_N1	2-step, with carbocation intermediate	first order	$3° > 2° > 1°$	tends to racemize	favored by polar, protic solvents; disfavored by nonpolar solvents;
S_N2	1-step, with back-side attack	second order	$CH_3 > 1° > 2° > 3°$	inverts configuration	favored by polar aprotic solvents; disfavored by protic solvents

Table 36.1

Please solve this problem:

- A researcher works with a pure sample of alkyl halide that rotates the plane of polarized light to the right. She subjects the substrate to a reaction in which the halide is replaced by an OH group according to an S_N2 mechanism. Will she be justified in concluding that the product will rotate the plane of polarized light to the left?

  A. Yes, because the OH group is a strong nucleophile.
  B. Yes, because the S_N2 mechanism inverts configuration around chiral carbons.
  C. No, because substrate and product are not enantiomers.
  D. No, because inversion of configuration means a change in the (+) versus (–) designations, not "R" and "S" designations.

Problem solved:

C is correct. Choice D is false. Inversion of configuration means a change in "R" and "S" designations, not in (+) versus (–) designations. Choice A is true, but irrelevant to the question. In choice B, everything after the word "yes" is true. The S_N2 mechanism *does* produce inversion of configuration—R to S or S to R. But this researcher has performed a substitution reaction. The substrate and product have different substituents on their chiral carbon. Substrate and product, therefore *do not represent a pair of enantiomers.*

Eliminations

In an elimination reaction, a small molecule, such as H_2O or HX, is removed from a larger molecule. During this process, two sigma bonds are broken and a new pi bond is formed. Examine, for instance, this reaction:

$$H-\overset{\overset{\displaystyle H}{|}}{\underset{\underset{\displaystyle H}{|}}{C}}-\overset{\overset{\displaystyle H}{|}}{\underset{\underset{\displaystyle Br}{|}}{C}}-\overset{\overset{\displaystyle H}{|}}{\underset{\underset{\displaystyle H}{|}}{C}}-H \ + \ KOH \ \xrightarrow[\text{heat}]{\text{alcohol}} \ H-\overset{\overset{\displaystyle H}{|}}{\underset{\underset{\displaystyle H}{|}}{C}}-\overset{\overset{\displaystyle H}{|}}{C}=\overset{\overset{\displaystyle H}{|}}{C}-H + KBr \ + \ H_2O$$

2-bromopropane   Propene

The 2-bromopropane molecule eliminates (a) a bromide ion from one carbon, and (b) a hydrogen ion from the adjacent carbon. There then forms between the two carbons a double bond.

Broadly, the elimination reaction involves these three events:

1. the halogen atom, acting again as a *leaving group*, leaves its carbon atom, taking with it the pair of electrons that bound it to the carbon atom;

2. the hydrogen atom is removed from the adjacent carbon atom by a base, leaving behind the pair of electrons that bound it to the carbon atom;

3. the electron pair left behind by the hydrogen atom is used to form a π bond between the two adjacent carbons, which then become doubly bound.

E1 AND E2 REACTIONS

Dehydrohalogenation occurs according to two mechanisms: **unimolecular elimination**, called **E1** and **bimolecular elimination**, called **E2**. Differences between the two mechanisms resemble the differences between S_N1 and S_N2 substitution.

E1 elimination has two steps:

Step 1: The alkyl halide loses a halide ion to form a carbocation intermediate.

Step 2: A weak base takes a proton from the intermediate to form the alkene.

$$① \ H-\overset{\overset{\displaystyle X}{|}}{\underset{\underset{\displaystyle H}{|}}{C}}-\overset{\overset{\displaystyle H}{|}}{\underset{\underset{\displaystyle H}{|}}{C}}-H \ \longrightarrow \ :X^- \ + \ H-\overset{\overset{\displaystyle \oplus}{|}}{\underset{\underset{\displaystyle H}{|}}{C}}-\overset{\overset{\displaystyle H}{|}}{\underset{\underset{\displaystyle H}{|}}{C}}-H$$

$$② \ H-\overset{\overset{\displaystyle \oplus}{|}}{\underset{\underset{\displaystyle H}{|}}{C}}-\overset{\overset{\displaystyle H}{|}}{\underset{\underset{\displaystyle H}{|}}{C}}-H \ + \ :B^- \ \longrightarrow \ \overset{\displaystyle H}{\underset{\displaystyle H}{}}C=C\overset{\displaystyle H}{\underset{\displaystyle H}{}} \ + \ HB$$

As in the case of S_N1 substitution, step 1 is the slow, rate-determining step. It does not involve the base, and is dependent therefore only on the concentration of alkyl halide. Its kinetics are first order:

$$\text{rate} = k[\text{alkyl halide}]$$

Reactivity in E1 is governed largely by stability of the carbocation intermediate, which means that it follows this familiar hierarchy:

$$3° > 2° > 1° > CH_3$$

Here, as in other reactions mediated by carbocations, the carbocation may undergo rearrangement to form more stable carbocations, which, in turn, affects the structure of the product. Due to carbocation rearrangement, the E1 reaction might produce "unanticipated" products in which the carbon skeleton may change and the double bond is located on a carbon different from the one that held the leaving group.

Separate from the stability (and potential rearrangement) of the carbocation intermediate is a competition that occurs at step 2, in which the base removes a hydrogen atom *from the* intermediate. Where the leaving group is not located on a terminal carbon, the base has a "choice" of removing the proton from either of the two adjacent carbons. It will choose, preferentially, to remove the proton from the more highly substituted carbon, and thus to yield an alkene in which the doubly bonded carbons carry the greater number of alkyl groups (and the fewest number of hydrogen atoms). The major product of E1 elimination reflects:

(a) Rearrangement of the carbocation formed at step 1 (if any is possible), followed by

(b) a preference, at step 2, to remove the hydrogen ion from a more highly substituted carbon.

(c) A preference for formation of the least sterically hindered product (for example, more E product than Z product).

E2 elimination occurs in one step. A strong base takes a hydrogen ion (proton) from a carbon atom and, at the same time, a halide ion is lost.

The single step involves both the base and the alkyl halide. Rate is dependent on the concentration of both, meaning that it is *second order*:

$$\text{rate} = k[\text{alkyl halide}][\text{base}]$$

A special requirement of the E2 reaction is that the abstracted H and the leaving group must be anti to each other in order for the reaction to proceed.

this is the only product that can form due to consraints on starting material conformation

Although the E2 reaction does not involve a carbocation intermediate, reactivity in E2 follows the same hierarchy as reactivity in E1:

$$3° > 2° > 1°$$

The reason relates to the stability of the alkene to be formed. A carbon-carbon double bond is more stable when the doubly bonded carbons are bound to greater numbers of alkyl groups (and fewer hydrogen atoms). The more substituted product will always form if a small base is used.

In an E2 reaction, the other important aspect is the size of the base. When a large, bulky base is used, the most easily accessible H is abstracted, resulting in formation of the least substituted double bond.

least hindered hydrogen

same reagent gives different product with larger base

Because reactivity in E1 and E2 follow the same hierarchy, $3° > 2° > 1°$, competition between the two mechanisms is not greatly affected by the degree of substitution at the halocarbon. Rather, it is affected chiefly by the concentration and strength of the base. The rate-determining step for the E1 reaction does not involve the base. The rate-determining step for the E2 reaction involves the base. Consequently, stronger base and/or greater concentration of base favors E2.

Please solve this problem:

- In unimolecular elimination of an alkyl halide, kinetics are first order because:

   A. the slower step involves only the alkyl halide and not the base.
   B. the slower step involves both the alkyl halide and the base.
   C. the faster step involves only the alkyl halide and not the base.
   D. the faster step involves both the alkyl halide and the base.

Problem solved:

A is correct. Reaction kinetics are a function of a reaction's rate-determining step—its slowest step. What is involved in the faster step, therefore, is largely irrelevant to kinetics. For that reason, choices C and D are wrong. In unimolecular elimination (E1), the slow step is the first one, in which a carbocation intermediate is formed. That is the step that governs kinetics, and it does not involve the base. Rather, it involves loss of a halide ion from the alkyl halide. Because the base plays no role in the rate-determining step, its concentration does not affect rate. Rate is dependent only on concentration of the alkyl halide, which is why kinetics are first order.

COMPETITION BETWEEN ELIMINATION AND SUBSTITUTION

We now know that alkyl halides undergo both elimination and substitution. The two processes cannot be separated on the basis of the second reagent—base or nucleophile—because nucleophiles *are* bases and bases *are* nucleophiles. Consequently, elimination and substitution compete. Tertiary substrates favor elimination over substitution; they yield elimination products almost exclusively. Primary and secondary substrates tend to give both elimination *and* substitution products. The elimination can be enhanced, however, through factors that favor the E2 process—a high concentration of strong base, heat and a solvent of low polarity.

ALCOHOLS

"Alcohol," generically designated R-OH, means an alkyl or substituted alkyl group (including an aryl group) bound to an OH group. An alcohol is designated primary, secondary, or tertiary depending on the corresponding status of the carbon to which the OH group is bound. An OH group bound to a primary carbon gives a **primary alcohol**, an OH group bound to a secondary carbon gives a **secondary alcohol**, and an OH group bound to a tertiary carbon gives a **tertiary alcohol**.

Naming the alcohols involves the same prefixes used for the alkanes, and the suffix "anol" instead of "ane." Carbons are numbered beginning at the molecular end closest to the OH group. Or, if the OH group is at the midpoint of the carbon chain, numbering begins at the end closest to the first branch point.

With the carbons thus numbered, the name shows, from left to right:

(1) the sites and nature of branches,

(2) the site of the OH group,

(3) a prefix corresponding to the length of the (longest possible) carbon chain, and

(4) the alcohol suffix ("anol").

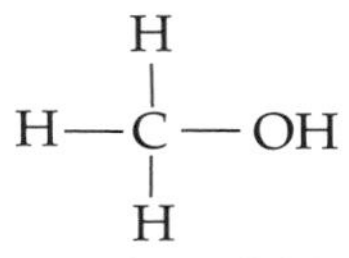

Methanol (1) 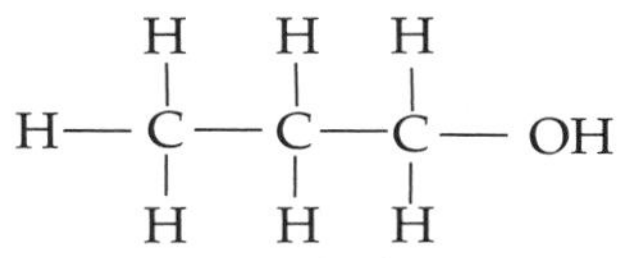   1-Propanol (1) 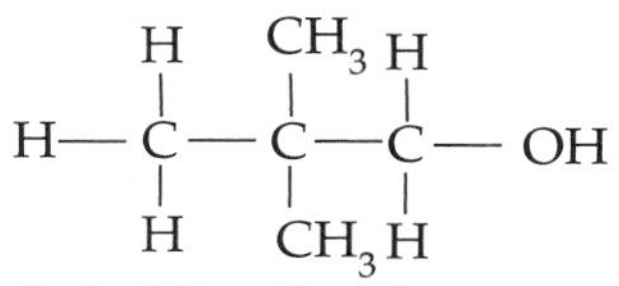   2, 2 - Dimethyl-1-propanol (1)

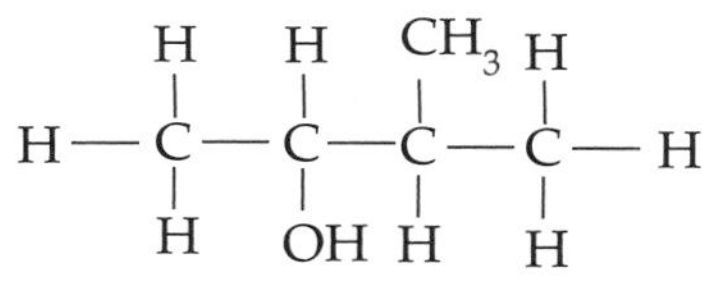

3-Methyl-2-butanol (2) 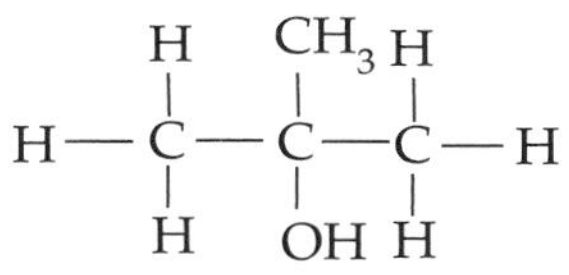   2-Methyl-2-propanol (3)

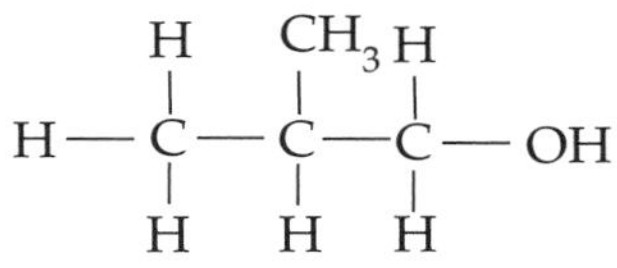

2-Methylpropanol (1)

"Phenol" means (1) a particular molecule—OH bound to a benzene ring, and (2) a class of substances derived *from* that substance, meaning a benzene ring with (a) an OH substituent and (b) one or more additional substituents.

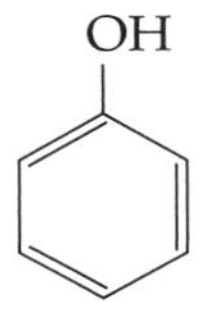

Phenol

For the MCAT, do not worry about naming the phenols (but do recognize phenol, the *substance*). Their names, if needed, will be supplied with diagrams of the structures.

Physical Properties of Alcohols: Boiling Point, Solubility, and Hydrogen Bonding

The boiling points of alcohols generally follow trends associated with the other hydrocarbons (see **Chapter 35**). Increasing molecular weight tends to increase boiling point, and increased branching tends to reduce boiling point. But when comparing an alcohol and a hydrocarbon of similar molecular weight, the *alcohol will have a much higher boiling point* because the hydroxyl group makes alcohol susceptible to *hydrogen bonding* (see **Chapter 33**). Unshared electrons on the oxygen atom of the OH group on one alcohol molecule hydrogen bonds to the hydrogen atom on the next.

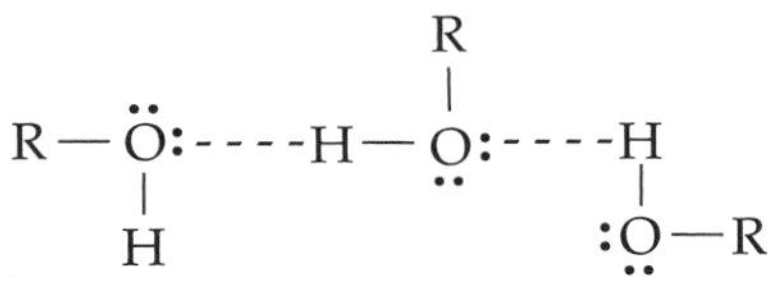

An alcohol molecule can form a hydrogen bond not only with another alcohol molecule, but also with a water molecule. For that reason, the small alcohols (five carbons or fewer for primary alcohols) are soluble in water (unlike hydrocarbons). As the carbon chain grows, and the OH group represents a smaller portion of the molecule, and water solubility decreases. A primary alcohol with five carbons or more tends to be insoluble in water.

ACIDITY AND BASICITY

Alcohols, like water, are weak acids and weak bases. The OH group can lose a proton to form an **alkoxide ion**, thereby acting as an acid, or acquire a proton to form an **oxonium ion**, thereby acting as a base.

It is the oxygen atom of the OH group that underlies both processes. On the one hand, oxygen is very electronegative. In the presence of base, it will give up a proton, "keeping" for "itself" the electron pair it had shared with the hydrogen atom. On the other hand, the oxygen atom has an unshared electron pair (which also explains the hydrogen bonding). In the presence of acid, the oxygen atom is "willing" to donate an electron pair to a proton and thereby bond it.

ACIDITY AND STABILIZATION OF THE ALKOXIDE ION

Acid strength is measured by K_a, and pK_a (see **Chapter 21**). Higher K_a corresponds with lower pK_a, both of which correspond with greater acidity. Water has a pK_a of about 15.7. In solution, methanol and ethanol are about as acidic as water. Acidity decreases (K_a decreases, pK_a increases) as alcohols get larger and acquire greater substitution by alkyl groups. Various substituents also reduce acidity; the reason relates to *stability of the alkoxide anion*, which in turn is affected by solvation effects and electron withdrawing effects.

Here, we again encounter this all-important MCAT theme (and an important theme in chemistry generally): The universe tends toward lowest energy. If some factor raises the energy of (destabilizes) a reactant, or lowers the energy of (stabilizes) a product, then it favors the reaction. If a factor lowers the energy of (stabilizes) a reactant, or raises the energy of (destabilizes) a product, then it disfavors the reaction.

Throughout **Chapter 34**, we probed the significance of this trend, noting, for example, that reactions mediated by carbocations and carbon free radicals were favored by factors that stabilized those intermediates. Resonance (the delocalization of electrons and/or charge) adds stability to the affected species by reducing its energy state. We noted, specifically, that S_N1 and S_N2 substitution might be favored or disfavored by ambient *solvent* because solvent, in turn, might stabilize an intermediate, stabilize a product, or destabilize a reactant. The acidity trends shown by alcohols derive from analogous phenomena related to thermodynamic stability of the alkoxide ion.

When an alcohol is deprotonated, the "product" is an alkoxide ion. The more readily the alkoxide ion is solvated by water molecules, the lower its energy state, the greater its stability, and the greater the tendency toward its formation. The small, simple alcohols create alkoxide ions that are "sterically accessible" to water as a solvent. Water has an "easy time" putting it into solution, thus stabilizing it. Larger, bulkier, highly substituted alcohols create large, bulky "sterically inaccessible" alkoxide ions. Water has a "difficult time" dissolving them. And for that reason, there arises the general trend that the smaller alcohols are more acidic than the larger, more highly substituted alcohols.

Electron withdrawal (an "inductive" effect) also modulates acidity of alcohols. The halides, for instance, withdraw electrons (which is why they deactivate the benzene ring). Electron withdrawal delocalizes the alkoxide ion's negative charge, "spreading it out" throughout the ion and thus adding to the ion's stability. A halide substituent, then, promotes the acidity of alcohols by delocalizing the charge carried by the alkoxide ion; it stabilizes the product of deprotonation.

Please solve this problem:

- Nonafluoro-*tert*-butyl alcohol has a pK_a of 5.4, whereas *tert*-butyl alcohol (2-methyl-2-ethanol) has a pK_a of 18. Among the following, the reason most likely is that:

$$CF_3 - \underset{\underset{CF_3}{|}}{\overset{\overset{CF_3}{|}}{C}} - OH \qquad CH_3 - \underset{\underset{CH_3}{|}}{\overset{\overset{CH_3}{|}}{C}} - OH$$

    Nonafluoro-*tert*-butyl alcohol   *tert*-butyl alcohol

  A. the fluorine atoms on nonafluoro-*tert*-butyl alcohol exert an electron-releasing effect that stabilizes the alkoxide ion.
  B. the fluorine atoms on nonafluoro-*tert*-butyl alcohol exert an electron-withdrawing effect that stabilizes the alkoxide ion.
  C. the methyl substituent on *tert*-butyl alcohol exerts an electron-releasing effect that stabilizes the alkoxide ion.
  D. the methyl substituent on *tert*-butyl alcohol exerts an electron-withdrawing effect that stabilizes the alkoxide ion.

Problem solved:

B is correct. Choices A and D make false statements. Fluorine is a halide, and halides withdraw electrons. Alkyl groups, like CH_3, release electrons. Choice C also makes a false statement in that an electron-releasing effect (which is characteristic of the methyl group) would tend to *destabilize* the alkoxide ion, since it would "aggravate" the effect of its negative charge by opposing its delocalization. Choice B is correct because fluorine atoms withdraw electrons, and the withdrawal of electrons would tend to delocalize the alkoxide ion's negative charge and thus stabilize the ion.

Preparation of Alcohols

Alcohols can be prepared by hydration of an alkene and by hydroboration-oxidation of an alkene, as discussed previously. They are prepared by other methods as well, including the following:

- Reduction of carbonyl compounds (aldehydes and ketones, which are generally discussed in **Chapter 37**). For this purpose, sodium borohydride ($NaBH_4$) and lithium aluminum hydride ($LiAlH_4$) are the most frequently used reducing agents. Reduction of an aldehyde produces a primary alcohol, and reduction of a ketone produces a secondary alcohol.

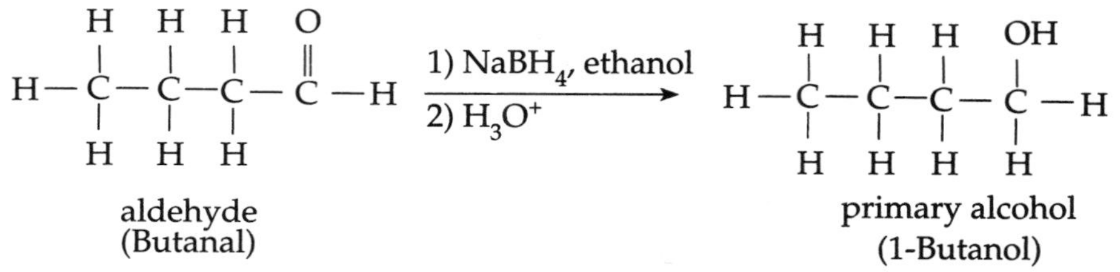

aldehyde
(Butanal)

primary alcohol
(1-Butanol)

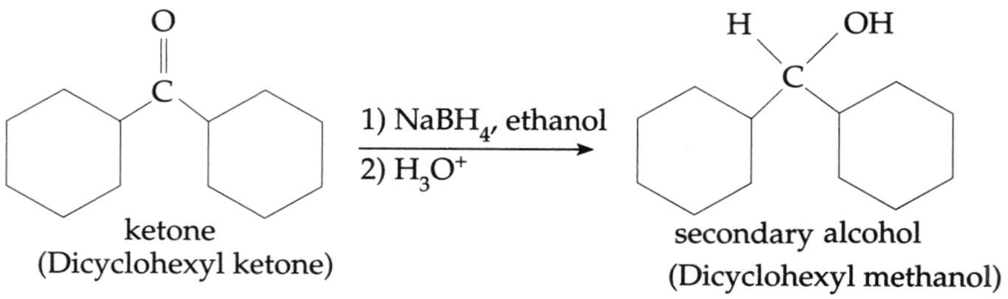

ketone
(Dicyclohexyl ketone)

secondary alcohol
(Dicyclohexyl methanol)

- Reduction of carboxylic acids (which is discussed generally in **Chapter 38**)

carboxylic acid

primary alcohol

- Reduction of esters

ester

primary alcohol

Grignard reagent, also called alkylmagnesium halide, means a molecule with general structure RMgX, where X is chlorine, bromine, or iodine. The Grignard reagent is highly reactive and useful in a wide variety of organic reactions, including the synthesis of an alcohol by reaction with an aldehyde or ketone. The Grignard reagent reacts with formaldehyde to give a primary alcohol, with aldehydes to give secondary alcohols, and with ketones to give tertiary alcohols.

Reactions of Alcohols

REACTION WITH HALIDES TO FORM ALKYL HALIDES: ACID CATALYZED SUBSTITUTION

In the presence of an acid catalyst, alcohols react with hydrogen halides (HCl, HBr, HI) to produce alkyl halides. Under non-acidic conditions, reaction with phosphorous tribromide (PBr$_3$) or thionyl chloride (SOCl$_2$) will accomplish the same transformation. The reaction involves substitution, with halide ultimately substituting itself for OH.

Recall that substitution calls first for a leaving group, and then, recognize that in relation to alcohols, OH$^-$ (a strong base and a strong nucleophile)- is a very *poor* leaving group. Seldom, if ever, will the OH group "leave," and for that reason, substitution of OH by a halide requires that the OH group first be converted to a *good* leaving group. The role of the acid catalyst is to protonate the OH group so that it becomes OH$_2^+$, which means that the ultimate group to be lost is water (a good leaving group).

Reaction of Alcohol with Hydrogen Halide: S_N1 and S_N2 Substitution

Tertiary and secondary alcohols react with hydrogen halides according to an S_N1 mechanism like that discussed earlier. The first step, however, is protonation of the OH group, which is then followed by formation of the carbocation and substitution of the halide ion—(the nucleophile).

(1) $\underset{R_2}{\overset{R_1}{C}}$—OH + HX $\rightleftharpoons$ (protonation) $\underset{R_2}{\overset{R_1}{C}}$—$\overset{+}{O}H_2$ + X$^-$

(2) $\underset{R_2}{\overset{R_1}{C}}$—$\overset{+}{O}H_2$ $\rightleftharpoons$ (carbocation formation) $\underset{R_2}{\overset{R_1}{C}}$ + H_2O

(3) $\underset{R_2}{\overset{R_1}{C}}$ + X$^-$ $\longrightarrow$ (nucleophilic attack) $\underset{R_2}{\overset{R_1}{C}}$—X

Reactivity in S_N1 follows a ranking consistent with the stability of carbocations. Tertiary alcohols are more reactive than secondary alcohols, which are more reactive than primary alcohols:

$$3° > 2° > 1°$$

In fact, primary alcohols will not react via the S_N1 mechanisms since 1° carbocations are too unstable. Since the S_N1 mechanism proceeds through a carbocation, the yield of product reflects carbocation rearrangement, as discussed previously.

Methyl alcohol (in which the alcoholic carbon is bound to three hydrogen atoms and to no carbon atoms) does not undergo S_N1 substitution, but rather undergoes substitution by an S_N2 mechanism like that discussed earlier. There is no carbocation intermediate, but rather a transition state in which both the halide ion (on "its way in") and the protonated OH group (on "its way out") are partially bound to the alcoholic carbon.

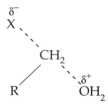

Primary alcohols also undergo the S_N2 mechanism, but because of steric hindrance greater than that which occurs with methanol, they are less reactive in S_N2 than methanol. Secondary and tertiary alcohols are even less reactive due to steric hindrance.

Tertiary and secondary alcohols readily undergo S_N1 substitution. Primary alcohols and methyl alcohol undergo S_N2 substitution rather readily.

DEHYDRATION OF ALCOHOLS: ACID CATALYZED ELIMINATION

Recall that elimination reactions use alkyl halides to produce alk<u>ene</u>s. Alcohols also undergo elimination to form alkenes, but unlike dehydrohalogenation of an alkyl halide, this process is *acid catalyzed*. The process resembles an E1 elimination. Once again, the acid catalyst serves to protonate the OH⁻ group so that water ultimately leaves the alcohol to form a carbocation. The carbocation then loses a proton to the conjugate base to form an alkene, with regeneration of the acid catalyst.

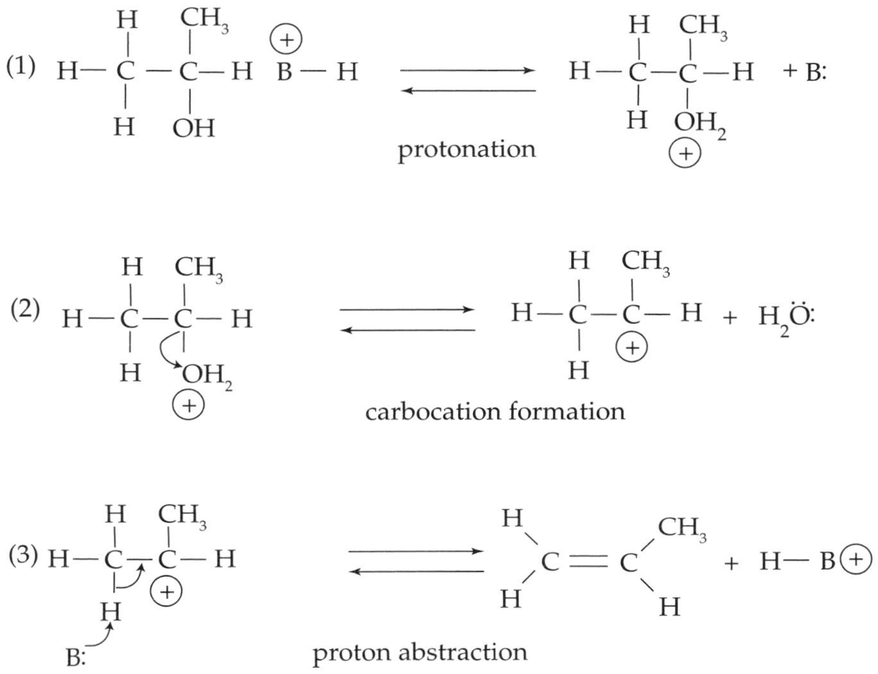

(1)

protonation

(2)

carbocation formation

(3)

proton abstraction

As expected with a carbocation intermediate, reactivity of alcohols to dehydration is:

$$3° > 2° > 1°$$

Where the carbocation's structure allows, rearrangement occurs. And, as in a true E1 elimination, there is, separately, a tendency for the proton to be abstracted from the more highly substituted carbon to form the more stable alkene.

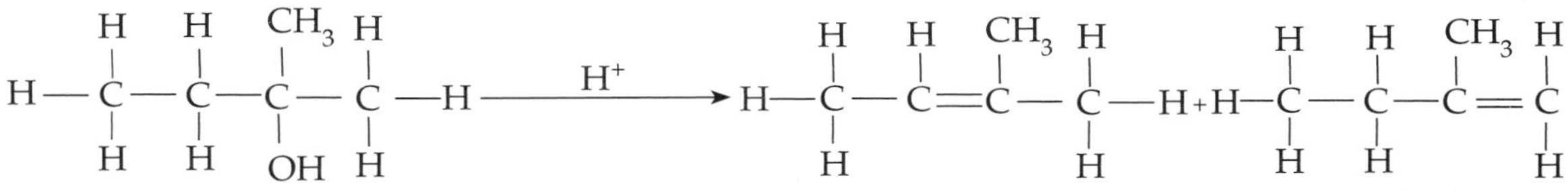

2-methyl-2-butanol → 2-methyl-2-butene (major product) + 2-methyl-1-butene (minor product)

OXIDATION OF PRIMARY AND SECONDARY ALCOHOLS TO FORM ALDEHYDES, KETONES, AND CARBOXYLIC ACIDS

When reacted with oxidizing agents, alcohols lose one or more of the hydrogens bound to the alcoholic carbon (the alpha hydrogens). How many hydrogen atoms the alcoholic carbon loses depends on (a) how many it carries to begin with and (b) the strength of the oxidizing agent.

Consider a primary alcohol. Reacted with a relatively mild oxidizing agent (like pyridinium chlorochromate), it loses one of its alpha hydrogens (and the H from the OH group) to form an aldehyde.

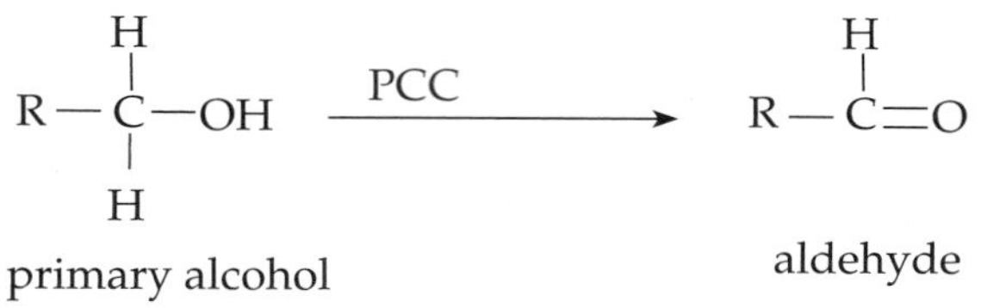

$$R - \overset{\overset{\displaystyle H}{|}}{\underset{\underset{\displaystyle H}{|}}{C}} - OH \xrightarrow{\text{PCC}} R - \overset{\overset{\displaystyle H}{|}}{C} = O$$

primary alcohol   aldehyde

Reacted with a stronger oxidizing agent (like potassium permanganate), a primary alcohol loses both of its alpha hydrogens to form a carboxylic acid and both of its alpha hydrogens to form a carboxylic acid.

$$R - \overset{\overset{\displaystyle H}{|}}{\underset{\underset{\displaystyle H}{|}}{C}} - OH \longrightarrow R - \overset{\overset{\displaystyle OH}{|}}{C} = O$$

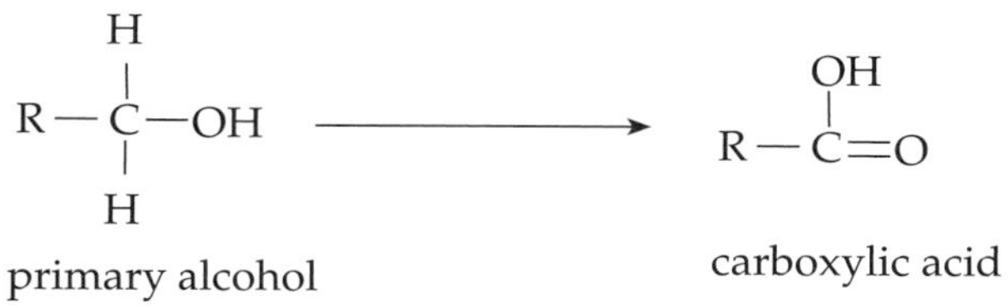

primary alcohol   carboxylic acid

A secondary alcohol has only one alpha hydrogen. Oxidation produces a ketone.

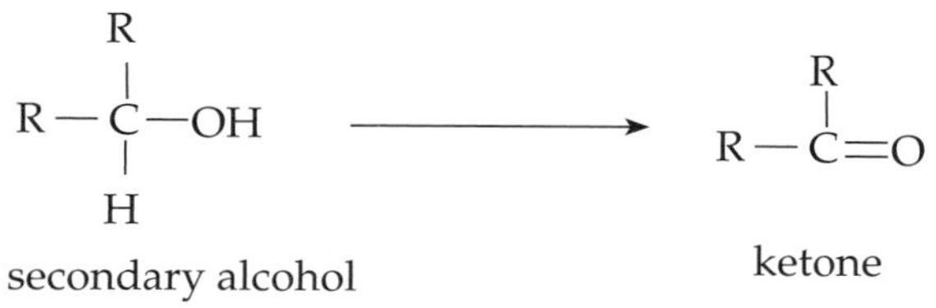

$$R - \overset{\overset{\displaystyle R}{|}}{\underset{\underset{\displaystyle H}{|}}{C}} - OH \longrightarrow R - \overset{\overset{\displaystyle R}{|}}{C} = O$$

secondary alcohol   ketone

A tertiary alcohol has no alpha hydrogens and thus does not undergo oxidation to form aldehydes, ketones, or carboxylic acids.

Please solve this problem:

• A researcher who wishes to produce an aldehyde from an alcohol should react:

A. a primary alcohol with a mild oxidizing agent.
B. a secondary alcohol with a strong oxidizing agent.
C. a tertiary alcohol with a mild oxidizing agent.
D. a tertiary alcohol with a strong oxidizing agent.

Problem solved:

A is correct. Choices B, C, and D are not viable. Tertiary alcohols will not undergo oxidation to produce aldehydes or ketones because they have no alpha hydrogens. Choice B is wrong because a secondary alcohol has its single alpha hydrogen on a nonterminal carbon, thus producing a ketone. A primary alcohol exposed to a mild oxidizing agent produces an aldehyde. Exposure to a stronger oxidizing agent causes loss of both alpha hydrogens to produce a carboxylic acid.

Please solve this problem:

- If reacted with the strong oxidizing agent $KMnO_4$, which of the following reactants would most likely produce a carboxylic acid?

A. 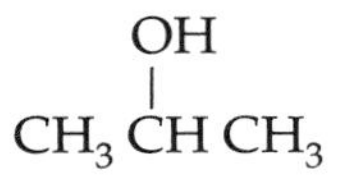 $$CH_3 \overset{\overset{\displaystyle OH}{|}}{CH} CH_3$$

B.  $$CH_3 \overset{\overset{\displaystyle OH}{|}}{CH} CH_2CH_3$$

C. 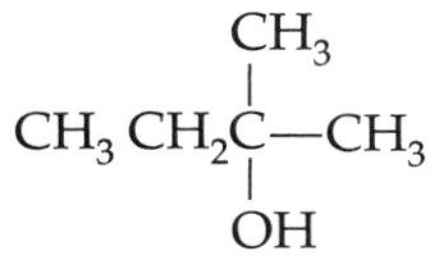 $$CH_3 CH_2\overset{\overset{\displaystyle CH_3}{|}}{\underset{\underset{\displaystyle OH}{|}}{C}}{-}CH_3$$

D. $CH_3 (CH_2)_8 CH_2OH$

Problem solved:

D is correct. Choices A and B show secondary alcohols, and choice C shows a tertiary alcohol. Choice D, however, shows a primary alcohol. Among primary, secondary, and tertiary alcohols, only a primary alcohol oxidizes to give a carboxylic acid because it has two alpha hydrogens. In the presence of a mild oxidizing agent, it loses one of them to produce an aldehyde. In the presence of a strong oxidizing agent, it loses both to produce a carboxylic acid. Choices A and B depict secondary alcohols, which oxidize to produce ketones only. Choice C depicts a tertiary alcohol, which does not react with oxidizing agents because it has no alpha hydrogens to lose.

36.2 MASTERY APPLIED: PRACTICE PASSAGE AND QUESTIONS

Passage

A chemistry student was given a sample of *tert*-butyl alcohol and asked by her professor to create an unsaturated hydrocarbon using a first order reaction. The product would later be used as a precursor in a complex synthesis. Attempting to satisfy the professor's request, the student combined the alcohol with concentrated HCl and placed the solution over heat. She heated the reactants for a short period of time at relatively low temperature. When the student analyzed the products, she found a small amount of alkene and a large amount of unknown product.

The student reported her results to the professor, who explained that the major product was most likely an alkyl halide produced by a reaction the student had not intended to conduct. The following week, the professor started with the same alcohol and used concentrated H_2SO_4. The professor heated the reactants for a long period of time at a high temperature. The resulting product consisted almost entirely of the desired unsaturated hydrocarbon.

The student then conducted a second series of reactions in which she first converted a primary alcohol to an alkyl halide and a tertiary alcohol to a sodium alkoxide compound. She then reacted the alkyl halide and the sodium alkoxide and studied the product.

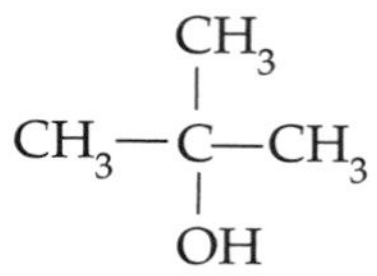

$$CH_3-\underset{\underset{OH}{|}}{\overset{\overset{CH_3}{|}}{C}}-CH_3$$

tert-Butyl alcohol

1. When the student conducted the reaction involving *tert*-butyl alcohol, she most likely hoped that the alkene would be produced by what kind of reaction?

   A S_N1 nucleophilic substitution
   B. S_N2 nucleophilic substitution
   C. Dehydration by an E1 mechanism
   D. Dehydration by an E2 mechanism

2. In the reaction in which the student produced the unwanted alkyl halide, the low pH produced by the concentrated HCl probably served to:

   A. convert the alcohol's OH group to a good leaving group.
   B. convert the alcohol's OH group into a good nucleophile.
   C. stabilize a positively charged reaction intermediate.
   D. stabilize a free radical reaction intermediate.

3. The professor most likely used H_2SO_4 instead of HCl in order:

   A. to supply the reaction medium with a strong nucleophile.
   B. not to supply the reaction medium with a strong nucleophile.
   C. to promote protonation of the OH group.
   D. not to promote protonation of the OH group.

4. If the professor had conducted his reaction using propanol instead of *tert*-butyl alcohol, would the reaction have occurred at a greater rate?

   A. Yes, because a primary carbocation is more stable than a tertiary carbocation.
   B. Yes, because the primary alcohol is more soluble in aqueous medium.
   C. No, because a primary alcohol is less reactive to dehydration than a tertiary alcohol.
   D. No, because a primary alcohol poses steric hindrance that impairs S_N1 substitution.

5. Among the following, the best solvent for the professor's reaction would be:

   A. a polar, nucleophilic substance.
   B. a polar non-nucleophilic substance.
   C. a nonpolar nucleophilic substance.
   D. a nonpolar, non-nucleophilic substance.

6. The major product of the professor's reaction was:

   A. butane.
   B. 2-methylpropane.
   C. 2-butene.
   D. 2-methylpropene.

36.3 MASTERY VERIFIED: ANSWERS AND EXPLANATIONS

1. **C is correct.** The passage tells us that the professor wished the student to produce an alkene from an alcohol. That requires elimination, not substitution, which makes choices A and B wrong. The reaction is to be first order, which means that it is dependent on the concentration of the alcohol only, not of the acid. E2 elimination, in which rate determination does not involve the formation of a carbocation, is second order. That makes choice D wrong. E1 elimination proceeds via a carbocation intermediate, and kinetics are first order.

2. **A is correct.** The production of the unwanted alkyl halide occurred by nucleophilic substitution, in which the OH group is lost and the halide, as nucleophile, replaces it. A substitution reaction between an alcohol and a hydrogen halide (the HCl in this case) first requires that the OH group be converted to a good leaving group. The acid medium protonates the OH group so that it becomes OH_2^+, with water as the ultimate leaving group. The acid medium does not serve to stabilize a carbocation intermediate, which makes choice C wrong. The OH group does not serve as a nucleophile, which makes choice B wrong. The reaction does not proceed via a free radical intermediate, which makes choice D wrong.

3. **B is correct.** Choice D is wrong because protonation of the alcohol is necessary to the dehydration/elimination reaction that the professor wishes to conduct. Choice C is wrong because protonation is achieved whether acidity is supplied by HCl or H_2SO_4. The student's reaction failed to produce significant quantities of alkene because an unwanted substitution reaction competed with the desired dehydration/elimination reaction. The substitution reaction occurred because chloride is a good nucleophile. The professor does *not* wish to supply the medium with a nucleophile, which makes choice A wrong. Rather, he wishes to avoid supplying it with a nucleophile so that substitution will not compete with elimination. The conjugate base of H_2SO_4 is not a good nucleophile and, instead, acts as a base, removing the proton from the intermediate carbocation.

4. **C is correct.** The professor's reaction is an E1 elimination/dehydration reaction. Choice D, therefore, is not only false but also irrelevant. Substitution is not at issue. The reactivity of alcohols to dehydration is $3° > 2° > 1°$ precisely because a tertiary carbocation is more stable than a secondary carbocation, which is more stable than a primary carbocation. Choice A, therefore, makes a false statement. The solubility, mentioned in choice B is not relevant to the question.

5. **B is correct.** The professor seeks to conduct a first order elimination reaction. For both first order elimination (and first order substitution), the best solvent is that which stabilizes the intermediate carbocation. Nonpolar solvents are not good ionizers and will not help to stabilize the carbocation. Choices C and D are therefore wrong. Choice A is wrong because the professor seeks to avoid nucleophilic substitution and to promote elimination. Consequently, he wishes to use a *non*-nucleophilic solvent.

6. **D is correct.** We are told that the professor wishes to produce an "unsaturated hydrocarbon" and that the professor did, in fact, produce that product. Unsaturation denotes the presence of double bonds, which means that the product cannot be an alkane. Choices A and B therefore are eliminated. Regarding choices C and D, note that all methyl groups of the carbocation intermediate are identical. Removal of a proton from any of them yields 2-methylpropene. That's why C is wrong and D is right.

CHAPTER 37

ALDEHYDES AND KETONES

37.1 MASTERY ACHIEVED

BASIC STRUCTURE OF ALDEHYDES AND KETONES

Carbonyl group means a carbon atom doubly bound to an oxygen atom. Any compound with a carbonyl group is a **carbonyl compound**. Carbonyl compounds can be divided into (1) carboxylic acids and their derivatives (**Chapter 38**) and (2) the **aldehydes** and **ketones**, discussed in this chapter.

In a ketone (R_2CHO), the carbonyl carbon is bound to two organic substituents. In an aldehyde, the carbonyl carbon is bound to one organic substituent and a hydrogen atom (RCHO). In one particular aldehyde, formaldehyde (IUPAC name: methanal), the carbonyl carbon is bound only to the oxygen atom and to two other hydrogen atoms; it is not bound to an organic substituent.

$$\begin{array}{ccc} R_1\!\!\diagdown & H\!\!\diagdown & H\!\!\diagdown \\ \quad\;\;\;C\!=\!O & \quad\;\;\;C\!=\!O & \quad\;\;\;C\!=\!O \\ R\!\!\diagup & R\!\!\diagup & H\!\!\diagup \\ \text{Ketone} & \text{Aldehyde} & \text{Formaldehyde} \end{array}$$

Please solve this problem:

- Among the three molecules shown below, which are aldehydes?

I.

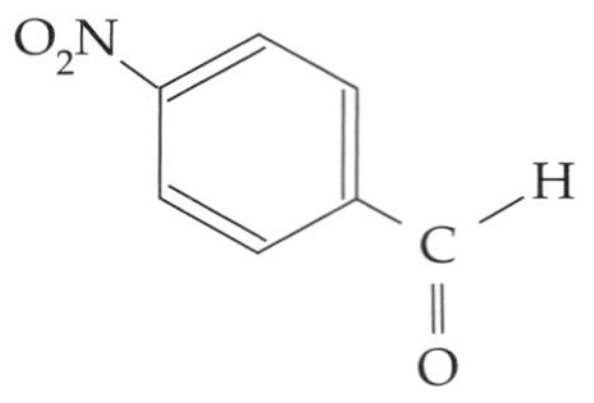

II.

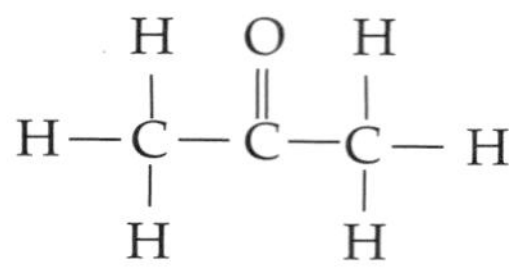

III.

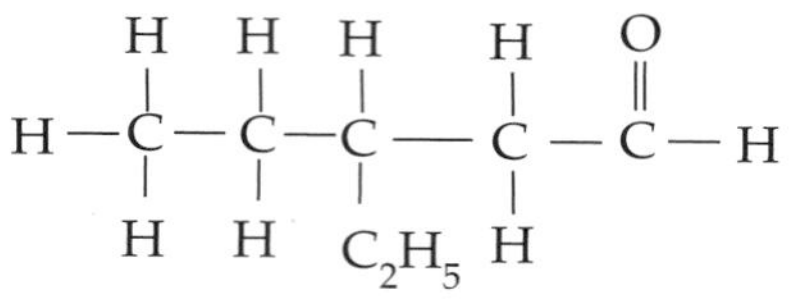

   A. I and II only
   B. II and III only
   C. I and III only
   D. I, II, and III

Problem solved:

   C is correct. Molecules I and III show that the carbonyl carbon is bound only to one organic group and to a hydrogen atom. That makes them aldehydes. Molecule II is a ketone; the carbonyl carbon is bound to two organic groups.

   The carbonyl carbon is sp^2 hybridized (see **Chapter 33**). It forms a sigma bond with each of the singly bonded atoms adjacent to it and, with the doubly bonded oxygen, a sigma bond and π bond. In aldehydes and ketones, the carbonyl carbon and its bonded atoms form a planar structure. The carbonyl bond is polar, with the strongly electronegative oxygen atom bearing a partial negative charge and the carbon atom bearing a partial positive charge.

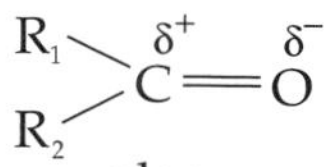

planar

NAMING THE ALDEHYDES AND KETONES

Naming Aldehydes

Giving IUPAC names to the aldehydes involves the same prefixes used for the alkanes and the suffix "-al" instead of "-ane." Carbons are numbered beginning at the carbonyl carbon. Substituents, as usual, are indicated by the name and the carbon to which they are attached. With the carbons thus numbered, the name shows, from left to right:

(1) the site and nature of substituents,

(2) a prefix corresponding to length of the (longest possible) carbon chain, and

(3) the aldehyde suffix ("-al").

As in the case of other compounds, certain common (non-IUPAC) names are widely in use, including "formaldehyde" for methanal, "acetaldehyde" for IUPAC ethanal, "propionaldehyde" for IUPAC propanal, and "n-butyraldehyde" for IUPAC butanal.

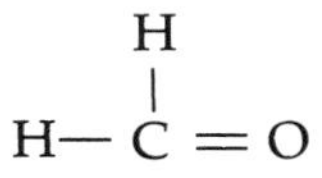

Formaldehyde
(Methanal)

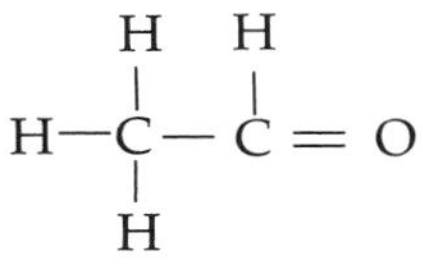

Acetaldehyde
(Ethanal)

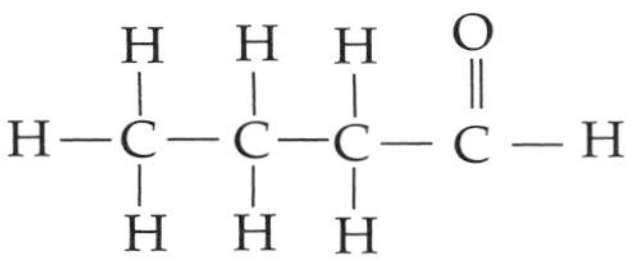

n– Butyraldehyde
(Butanal)

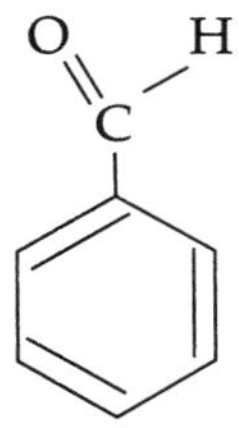

Benzaldehyde

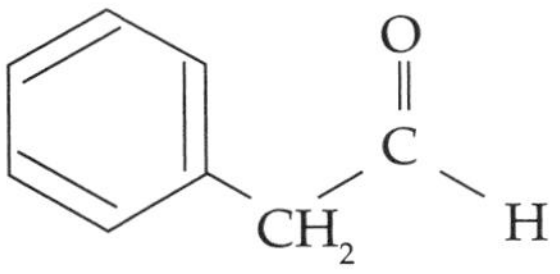

Phenylacetaldehyde
(Phenylethanal)

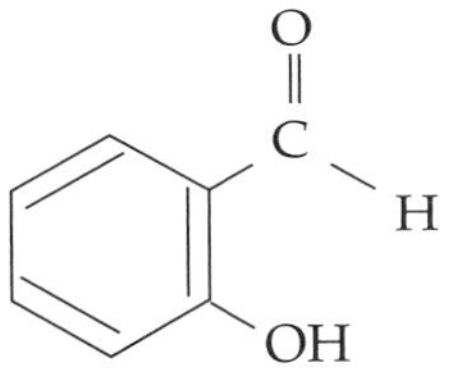

Salicylaldehyde
(o-Hydroxy benzaldehyde)

Naming Ketones

IUPAC names are given to the ketones by using the same familiar IUPAC prefixes followed by the suffix "-one." Carbons are numbered beginning at the end of the molecule closest to the carbonyl carbon.

With the carbons thus numbered, the name shows, from left to right:

(1) the site and nature of branches,

(2) the site of the carbonyl bond,

(3) a prefix corresponding to length of the (longest possible) carbon chain, and

(4) the ketone suffix ("-one").

Again, some ketones are known by certain common names derived from another system(s).

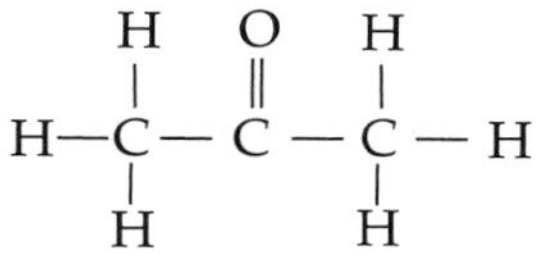

Acetone
(Propanone)

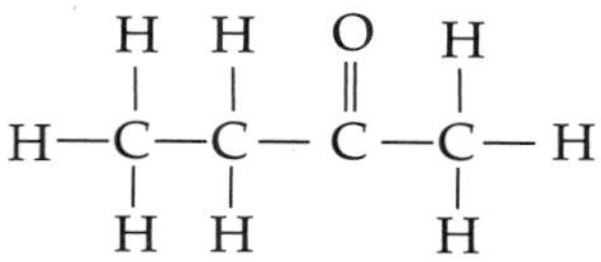

Ethyl methyl ketone
(Butanone)

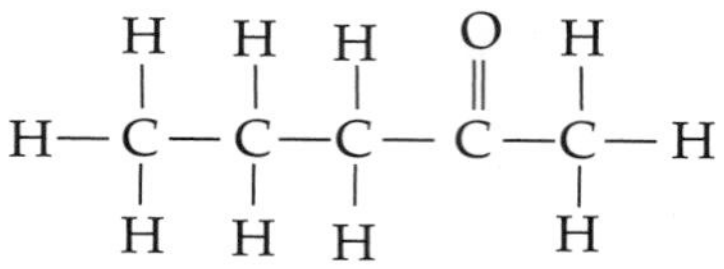

Methyl *n*– propyl ketone
(2–Pentanone)

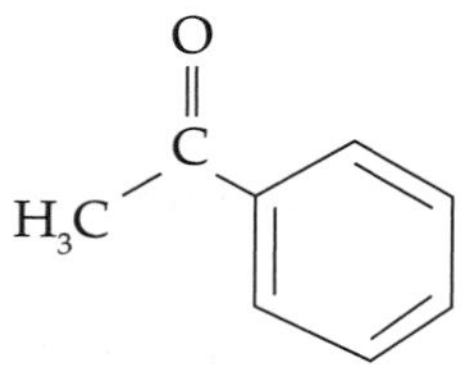

Acetophenone

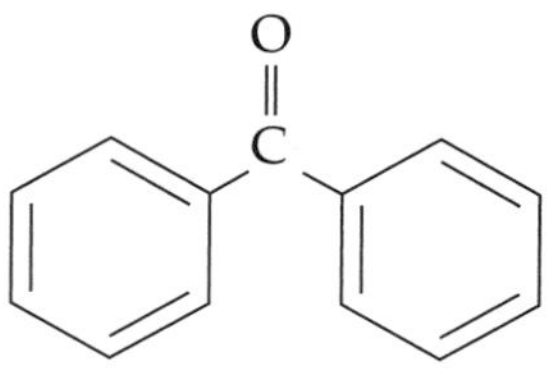

Benzophenone

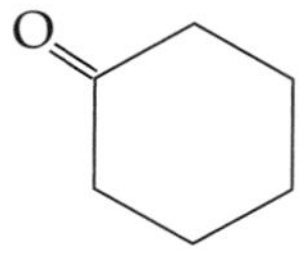

Cyclohexanone

PROPERTIES OF ALDEHYDES AND KETONES

The carbonyl bond is polar, with the strongly electronegative oxygen exerting a strong pull on the shared electrons. The oxygen atom is partially negative and the carbonyl carbon partially positive. Their boiling points exceed those of nonpolar compounds of similar weight. Yet, among aldehyde and ketone molecules themselves, there is no hydrogen bonding. (In these molecules, hydrogen is bound not to nitrogen, fluorine, or oxygen, but only to carbon.) For that reason, the boiling points of aldehydes and ketones are not as high as those of alcohols of similar molecular weight.

The doubly bound oxygen atom exhibits some hydrogen bonding with molecules of water, and for that reason, the smaller ("lower") aldehydes and ketones are water soluble. Water solubility is lost, however, when the molecule has six or more carbons.

Please solve this problem:

- The carbonyl carbon of an aldehyde or ketone tends to be partially:

   A. positively charged, because the carbonyl oxygen is strongly electronegative.
   B. positively charged, because of the inductive effects of surrounding alkyl groups.
   C. negatively charged, because of the polarity of the carbon-oxygen double bond.
   D. negatively charged, because of the relatively mobile π electrons.

Problem solved:

A is correct. The carbon-oxygen double bond is strongly polar due to the strong electronegativity of the oxygen atom. The polarity renders the boiling points of aldehydes and ketones higher than those of similarly weighted alkanes.

Please solve this problem:

- Aldehydes and ketones differ from alcohols of similar molecular weight in that:

    A. an alcohol's carbon chain cannot be substituted.
    B. alcohols undergo hydrogen bonding with water.
    C. alcohols have higher boiling points.
    D. alcohols have lower boiling points.

Problem solved:

C is correct. Alcohols have markedly higher boiling points than alkanes of similar molecular weight, and their boiling points are also higher than that of aldehydes and ketones of similar weight. The reason is that alcohols undergo hydrogen bonding with other molecules of alcohols and with molecules of water. Aldehyde and ketone molecules do not undergo hydrogen bonding among themselves, but they, too, experience hydrogen bonding with water. Thus, choice B is wrong. On alcohols, aldehydes, and ketones, the carbon chain can, of course, be substituted, which makes choice A wrong.

PREPARATION OF ALDEHYDES AND KETONES

Oxidation of Alcohols

As discussed in **Chapter 35**, aldehydes are formed from the oxidation of primary alcohols and ketones are formed from the oxidation of secondary alcohols.

Alkene Cleavage with Ozone (Ozonolysis)

Earlier, we discussed addition reactions in which the alkene double bond was converted to a single bond with a resulting molecule that had a carbon chain equivalent in size to the original alkene. We now discuss *cleavage* of an alkene into two smaller molecules, each of which is an aldehyde or ketone.

The reaction involves the addition of ozone (O_3) to form, first, a cyclic intermediate called a **molozonide**. The molozonide rearranges to become an **ozonide**, which when reduced with zinc in acetic acid, produces two carbonyl compounds—aldehyde or ketone.

alkene   aldehydes / ketones

If on one side of the alkene's double bond the carbon is bonded to two other carbons, then its "half" of the ozonolysis reaction will produce a ketone. If on one side of the double bond the carbon is bound only to one carbon, it will produce an aldehyde.

Please solve this problem:

- Treating an alkene double bond with ozone differs from treating it with addition of hydrogen halide in that:

  A. ozone adds a second double bond to the alkene to produce two sites of unsaturation.
  B. ozone produces two carbonyl compounds, and not a substituted alkane.
  C. ozone leaves the initial alkene carbon skeleton in tact and hydrogen halide does not.
  D. ozone treatment obeys the Markovnikov rule and hydrogen halide addition does not.

Problem solved:

B is correct. Ozonolysis refers to reaction of alkenes with ozone. The alkene is "split" into to aldehyde/ketone products. Choices A and C, therefore, are false. Addition of hydrogen halides to alkenes normally follows the Markovnikov rule, so choice D is false as well.

Preparation of Aryl Ketones by Friedel Crafts Acylation

Among the substitution reactions of aromatic rings is Friedel Crafts acylation, in which a benzene molecule reacts with an acid halide (catalyzed by a Lewis acid such as $AlCl_3$) to produce an aryl ketone (and hydrogen halide). The reaction is aromatic electrophilic substitution1. The electrophile is thought to be an **acylium ion,** which is, in fact, a kind of carbocation that is particularly *stable* because it has a resonance structure.

$$[\; R-\overset{\oplus}{C}=\underset{\cdot\cdot}{\overset{\cdot\cdot}{O}}: \quad\longleftrightarrow\quad R-C\equiv\overset{\oplus}{\underset{\cdot\cdot}{O}}:\;]$$

In the first step, the acid chloride gives up a chloride ion to the catalyst to form the acylium ion and $AlCl_4^-$. The aromatic ring then attacks the acylium ion to form a positively charged carbocation intermediate. Finally, in net effect, the carbocation gives up a proton that combines with a chloride ion (from $AlCl_4$) to regenerate the catalyst $AlCl_3$ and HCl.

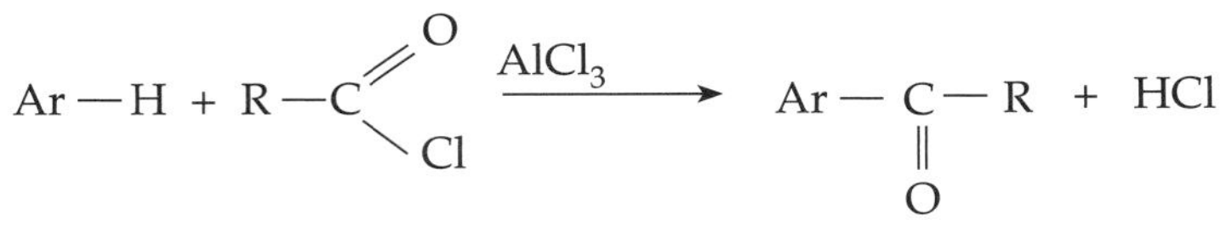

an acid chloride

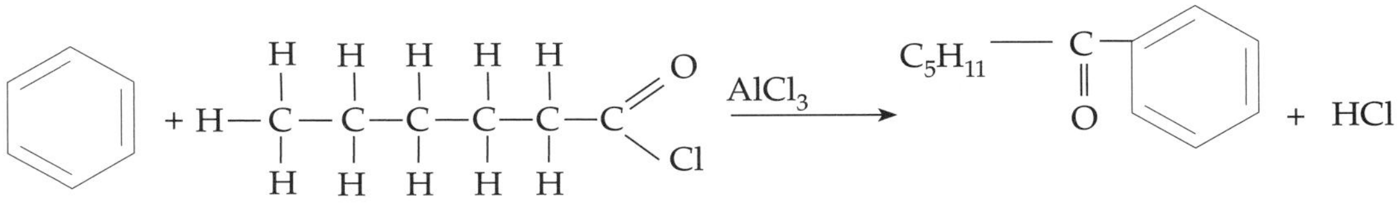

$C_6H_{11}OCl$

an acid chloride
(caproyl chloride)

n-hexyl phenyl ketone

Please solve this problem:

- In the production of ketones by Friedel Crafts acylation, the $AlCl_3$ (or other Lewis acid molecule):

  I. reacts directly with the benzene molecule.
  II. serves in carbocation (acylium ion) formation.
  III. is regenerated at the end of the reaction.

  A. I and II only
  B. I and III only
  C. II and III
  D. I, II, and III

Problem solved:

C is correct. In the Friedel Crafts acylation, the Lewis acid (often $AlCl_3$) acts as a catalyst. Like any catalyst, therefore, it is regenerated at the end of the reaction. That eliminates choice A. With $AlCl_3$ as the Lewis acid, the first step involves generating the acylium ion with the conversion of $AlCl_3$ to $AlCl_4^-$. Statement II, therefore is correct. In the second step, the benzene ring attacks the acylium ion; the acid catalyst is not involved. Statement I therefore is incorrect.

REACTIONS OF ALDEHYDES AND KETONES

Nucleophilic Addition in Aldehydes and Ketones

The polarity of the C–O double bond leaves the carbonyl carbon partially positive and susceptible, therefore, to nucleophilic attack. Furthermore, the planar structure surrounding the carbonyl carbon renders it susceptible to attack from "above" and "below." Aldehydes and ketones are characteristically susceptible, therefore, to nucleophilic addition.

For the MCAT, remember that:

Aldehydes and ketones are susceptible to nucleophilic addition because:

(a) the double C–O bond is polar, rendering the carbonyl carbon partially positive, and

(b) in and around the carbonyl carbon the molecule is planar.

Generally, in a nucleophilic attack on an aldehyde or ketone, the nucleophile attacks the carbonyl carbon, causing it to rehybridize from sp^2 to sp^3. The double bond between carbon and oxygen becomes a single bond, forming a tetrahedral alkoxide intermediate in which the oxygen atom carries a negative charge.

Please solve this problem:

- In rendering ketones susceptible to nucleophilic attack, which of the following factors is most important?

   A. Electronegativity of the carbonyl oxygen
   B. Acidity of alpha hydrogens
   C. Tetrahedral structure surrounding the carbonyl carbon
   D. Capacity for hydrogen bonding with water

Problem solved:

A is correct. The electronegativity of the carbonyl oxygen gives polarity to the carbonyl bond and makes the carbonyl carbon partially positive. This, together with the planar (*not* tetrahedral) structure surrounding the carbonyl carbon, renders the carbon highly susceptible to attack.

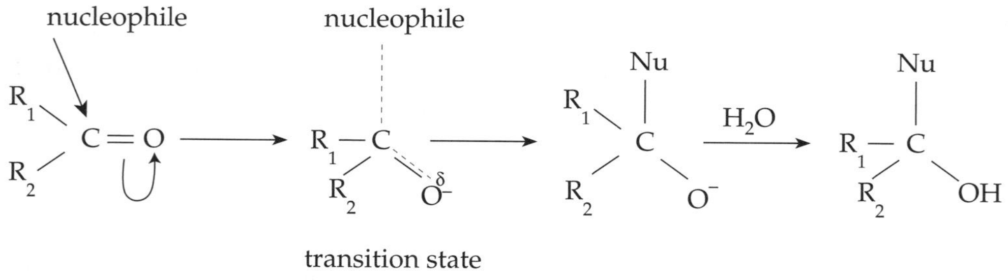

transition state

SUSCEPTIBILITY TO NUCLEOPHILIC ATTACK: ALDEHYDES VERSUS KETONES

Bear in mind the picture of the transition state just shown. Remember that in aldehydes, the carbonyl carbon is bound to a hydrogen atom and only *one* alkyl or aryl group. In ketones, the carbonyl carbon is bound to *two* alkyl or aryl groups.

Also remember that *aldehydes are generally more susceptible to nucleophilic addition than ketones* for these two reasons:

(1) the second alkyl or aryl group bound to the ketone has an electron donating effect and thus stabilizes the partial positive charge on the carbonyl carbon, making the ketone less reactive and less susceptible to nucleophilic attack;

(2) the second alkyl (or aryl) group bound to the ketone's carbonyl carbon presents some steric "crowding" that physically impedes attack by the nucleophile.

Please solve this problem:

- Between a ketone and an aldehyde, which is generally more susceptible to nucleophilic addition?

    A. Ketones, because the carbonyl carbon is destabilized by the two carbon atoms to which it is bound.
    B. Ketones, because the planar structure around the carbonyl carbon promotes nucleophilic attack.
    C. Aldehydes, because they contain fewer carbon-oxygen double bonds.
    D. Aldehydes, because the relative absence of steric hindrance facilitates the approach by the nucleophile.

Problem solved:

D is correct. Choices A and C are false statements. In a ketone, the carbonyl carbon is bound to two carbons, each of which represents an electron releasing group. The releasing groups stabilize the partial positive charge on the carbonyl group. As to choice C, aldehydes and ketones do not differ in the number of carbon-oxygen double bonds. Choice B makes a true statement, but does not answer the question. For both aldehydes *and* ketones the structure surrounding the carbonyl carbon is planar. Aldehydes are more susceptible (generally) to nucleophilic addition because of (a) relative lack of steric hinderance and (b) absence of a second alkyl, electron-releasing group.

Nucleophilic Addition of Alcohol

FORMATION OF HEMIACETALS AND HEMIKETALS

When aldehydes or ketones are dissolved in alcohol, a reversible reaction takes place, generally under acidic conditions, to form a hemiacetal.

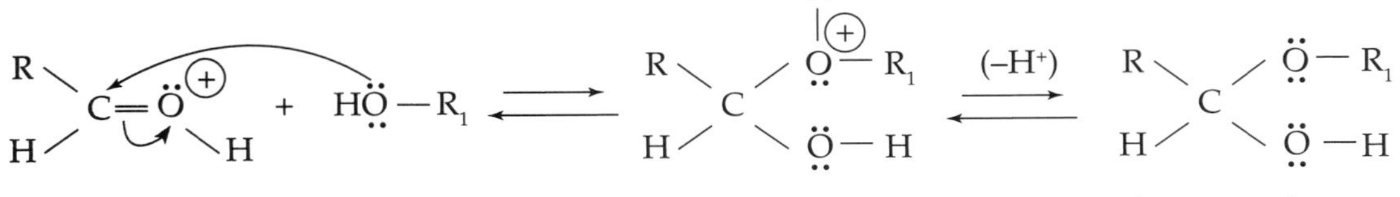

protonated aldehyde   alcohol   hemiacetal

The nucleophile is the alcohol, which attacks the carbonyl carbon. This reaction (like hydration) may be catalyzed with acid or base, with reaction mechanisms analogous to those that apply to acid and base catalyzed hydration. In the acid-catalyzed process, the carbonyl molecule is protonated and alcohol is the nucleophile. In the base-catalyzed reaction, alcohol loses a proton and alkoxide ion is the nucleophile.

Please solve this problem:

- Hydration of aldehydes and formation of hemiacetals have which of the following in common:

    A. the nucleophile is water.
    B. the nucleophile is OH⁻ ion.
    C. both may be catalyzed by acid or base.
    D. both may be catalyzed by acid, but neither is catalyzed by base.

Problem solved:

C is correct. Both reactions are subject to catalysis by (small amounts of) acid or base. The reactions also proceed by roughly analogous mechanisms. In the acid-catalyzed reaction, the aldehyde (or ketone) is protonated and neutral water or neutral alcohol act as nucleophiles. In the base-catalyzed reaction, OH⁻ or OR⁻ act as nucleophiles.

Please solve this problem:

- In a base-catalyzed reaction between an alcohol and an aldehyde:

    A. alcohol is the nucleophile.
    B. alkoxide ion is the nucleophile.
    C. the carbonyl molecule is protonated.
    D. a byproduct of the reaction is water.

Problem solved:

B is correct. Reaction of aldehyde (or ketone) with alcohol produces hemiacetals. In the base-catalyzed reaction, the alcohol is deprotonated, leaving an alkoxide ion to act as nucleophile. (In the acid-catalyzed reaction, the aldehyde or ketone is protonated, and the alcohol itself acts as the nucleophile.) Water is not eliminated since the $C = O$ of the substrate is attacked and there is no leaving group.

FORMATION OF ACETALS FROM HEMIACETALS

If a hemiacetal is reacted with a second molecule (or molar equivalent) of alcohol, an **acetal** results. In these compounds, the OH group of the hemi- species is replaced by an "OR" group so that the original carbonyl carbon is bound to two OR groups:

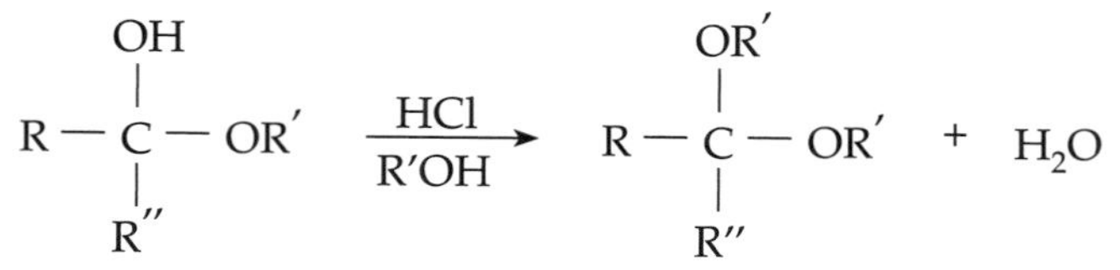

$$R - \underset{\underset{R''}{|}}{\overset{\overset{OH}{|}}{C}} - OR' \quad \xrightarrow[R'OH]{HCl} \quad R - \underset{\underset{R''}{|}}{\overset{\overset{OR'}{|}}{C}} - OR' \quad + \quad H_2O$$

The reaction involves these steps:

(1) acid-catalyzed loss of water from the hemiacetal to yield a positively charged oxonium intermediate,

(2) acid-catalyzed addition of a second alcohol molecule to the oxonium ion, plus loss of a proton to form the acetal.

In basic environments, acetals are stable, but in acidic environments, they are reconverted to the carbonyl molecules. In basic media, then, acetals serve to "protect" carbonyl groups while reactions are conducted on other components of the carbonyl molecule. That is, an aldehyde or ketone might first be converted to an acetal. In basic solution, some other desired reaction is carried out on another component of the molecule. The acetal components will not react. Afterward, the acetal is subjected to acid and reconverted to an aldehyde or ketone.

The equilibrium constant for formation of hemiacetals is very small (less than one). Reacting ketones with simple alcohols produces no significant yield of hemiacetals or acetals. If, however, a ketone is reacted not with a simple alcohol but with a diol in a benzene solvent, the yield is markedly increased. Benzene codistills with water, and removal of the water drives the equilibrium to the right (as any equilibrium is driven rightward by removal of one of the products).

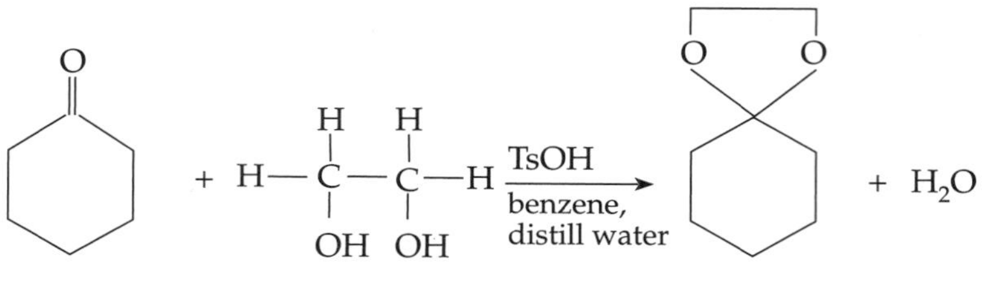

Cyclohexanone   1, 2–Ethanediol   Acyclic acetal

Please solve this problem:

- Formation of an acetal from a hemiacetal requires:

    A. addition of alcohol.
    B. addition of water.
    C. base catalysis.
    D. deprotonation of the hemiacetal.

Problem solved:

A is correct. Formation of acetal from hemiacetal is acid catalyzed (even though formation of the hemiacetal itself may be catalyzed by acid *or* base). The acid catalyst serves to protonate the hemiacetal (contrary to choice D) and thus convert the hydroxyl group into a good leaving group (water). Loss of water (contrary to choice B) yields the oxonium ion intermediate to which *alcohol is added,* as stated in choice A. On the alcohol molecule, one of oxygen's unshared electron pairs act as the immediate nucleophile.

Addition of Amines: Imine Formation

When ammonia (NH_3) and primary amines (RNH_2) are reacted with aldehydes or ketones, there results an imine molecule in which the carbonyl double bond is replaced by a double bond between carbon and nitrogen:

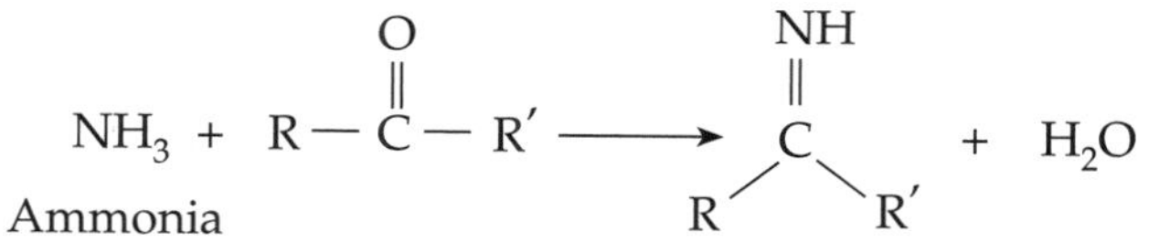

The reaction proceeds like this:

(1) Nucleophilic Addition of the Amine

(a) Nitrogen's lone electron pair nucleophically attacks the carbonyl carbon to form an intermediate that is dipolar and tetrahedral.

(b) A proton moves from nitrogen to oxygen and the intermediate is neutral.

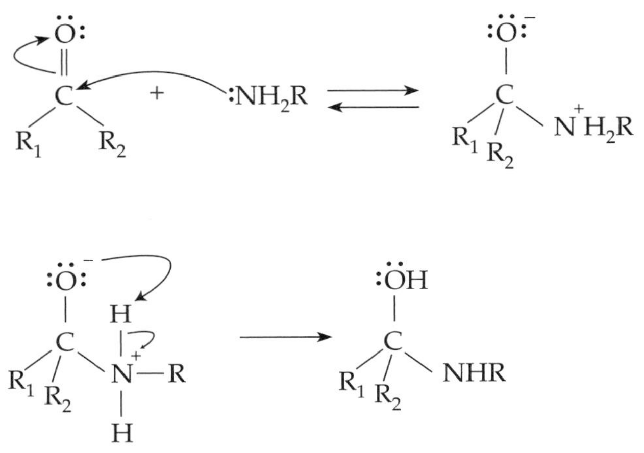

(2) Loss of water

(a) Acid catalyst protonates the OH group to create water as a good leaving group.

(b) Water is expelled, leaving a positively charged intermediate, with a double bond between carbon and nitrogen.

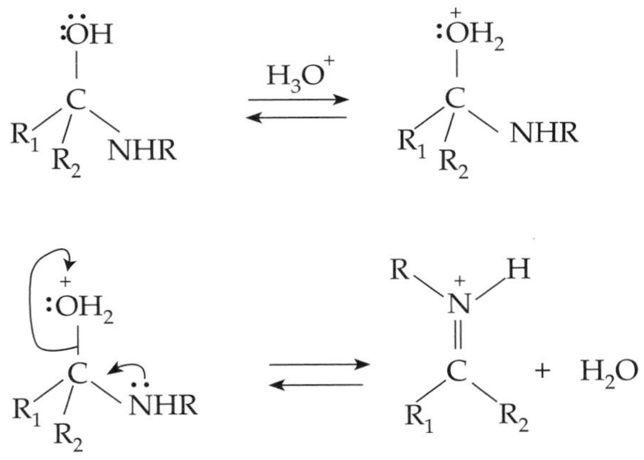

(3) Loss of proton

(a) the charged intermediate loses a proton to yield the neutral imine, with regeneration of the acid catalyst.

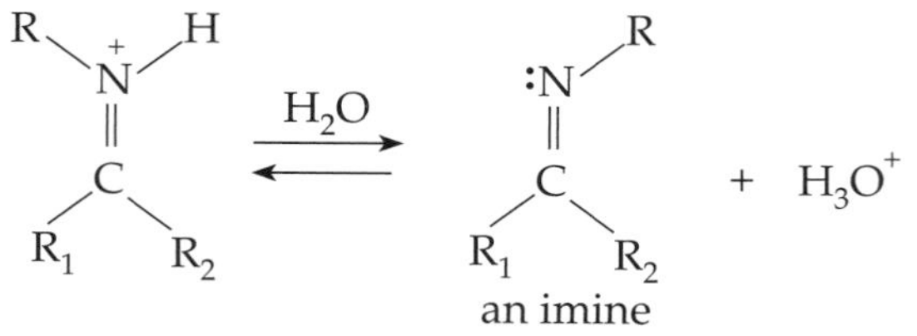

an imine

Although the reaction is acid catalyzed, a pH that is *too* low will cause protonation of the initial amine and prevent its addition to the carbonyl carbon. The reaction runs best at pH of about 5.

Please solve this problem:

- In the reaction of a primary amine and an aldehyde, the nucleophile is:

  A. the nitrogen atom of the amine molecule.
  B. the acid catalyst.
  C. the organic group of the amine molecule.
  D. a hydrogen atom of the amine molecule.

Problem solved:

A is correct. Choice B can be discarded; a catalyst is not a reactant. The nucleophilicity of an amine derives from the nitrogen atoms' unshared electron pair (the same feature that gives its basicityand that causes it to participate in hydrogen bonding).

The Enolate Ion, Aldol Reaction, and Aldol Condensation

In an aldehyde or ketone, the carbon immediately adjacent to the carbonyl carbon is called the **alpha carbon**. A hydrogen atom bonded to the alpha carbon is an **alpha hydrogen**. Among the important properties of aldehydes and ketones is the acidity of their alpha hydrogens. When an alpha carbon loses a proton, it forms an **enolate ion,** which is particularly stable because its charge is delocalized by resonance.

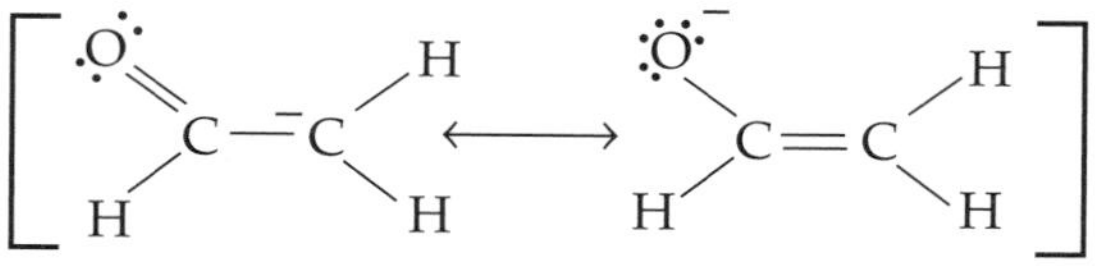

The enolate ion mediates many organic reactions, including the base-catalyzed **aldol reaction**. In the aldol reaction, two molecules of aldehyde react to form a dimer, with an enolate ion as intermediate. With acetaldehyde, for example, the reaction is:

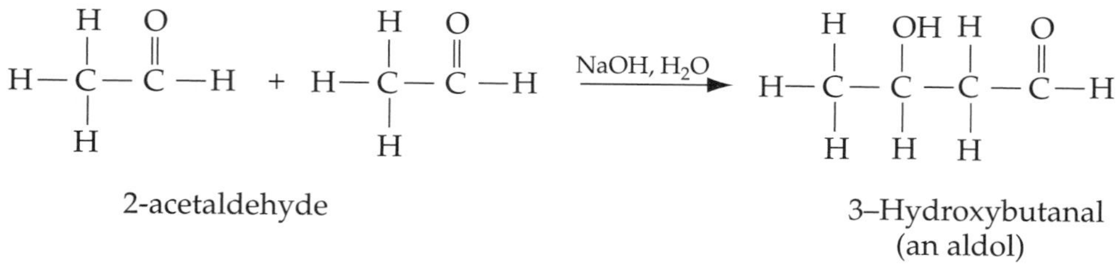

2-acetaldehyde

3–Hydroxybutanal
(an aldol)

The reaction is mediated by an enolate ion and occurs in these steps:

(1) Hydroxide ion abstracts an alpha hydrogen from the aldehyde to form the enolate ion.

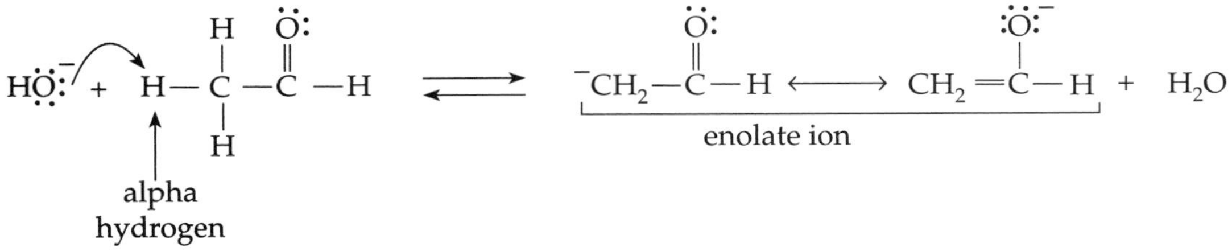

(2) The enolate ion acts as a nucleophile and attacks the carbonyl carbon on the *other* molecule of aldehyde to form an alkoxide ion.

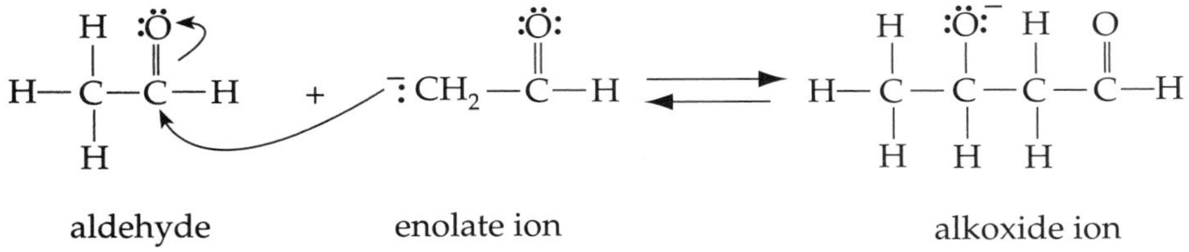

aldehyde   enolate ion   alkoxide ion

(3) The alkoxide ion takes a proton from water to generate the product, called an **aldol** (because it combines an <u>ald</u>ehyde with an alcoh<u>ol</u>).

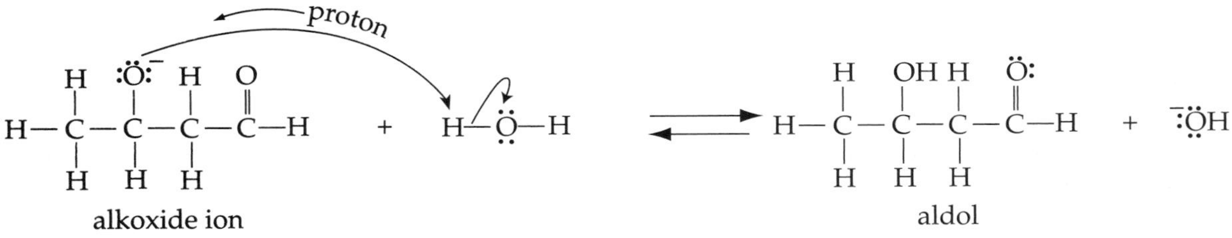

alkoxide ion   aldol

(Ketones may undergo the addition reaction just described, but the equilibrium lies heavily toward the original reactants, except under conditions where the product is removed from the medium as it is formed, thereby driving the equilibrium to the right. When a ketone is subjected to the reaction, the product is called a β-hydroxy ketone. And an aldol is sometimes called a β-hydroxy aldehyde.)

If the aldol (or β-hydroxy ketone) is heated, it undergoes dehydration to form an α, β– unsaturated enal (or **enone),** and this process is termed the **aldol condensation**.

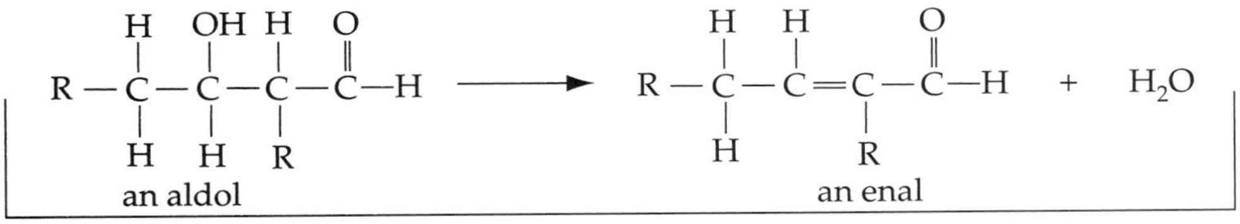

an aldol   an enal

aldol condensation

Please solve this problem:

• Consider two molecules of 2, 2-dimethyl-4-ethylbutanal.

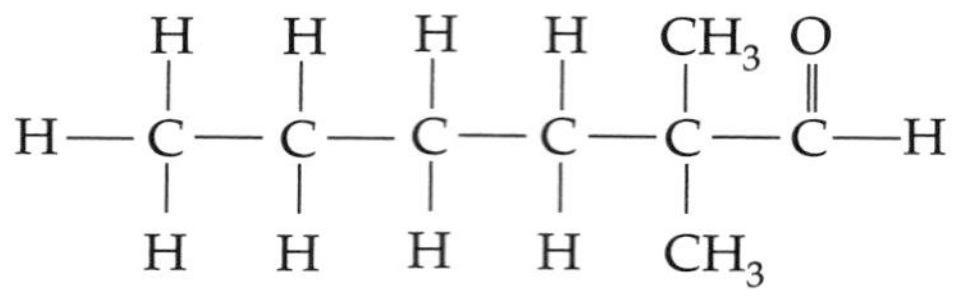

2, 2–dimethylhexanal

Will they undergo dimerization to form an aldol?

A. Yes, because the aldol reaction involves the carbonyl carbon only.
B. Yes, because the enolate ion is stabilized by resonance.
C. No, because the molecule contains no alpha hydrogen atoms.
D. No, because the molecule is sterically hindered next to the carbonyl carbon.

Problem solved:

C is correct. *The aldol reaction is mediated by the enolate ion.* It is, in fact, the nucleophile that attacks the "partner" aldehyde molecule. Enolate ion is formed by loss of a hydrogen atom from the alpha carbon (the carbon adjacent to the carbonyl carbon). The 2, 2-dimethylhexanal has no alpha hydrogens because the alpha carbon is bonded to four carbon atoms. For that reason, it cannot create an enolate ion, and the reaction cannot "get off the ground." Choice A makes a false statement because the alpha carbon as a donor of alpha hydrogens is involved in the reaction. Choice D is wrong because the aldehyde is only hindered from one side. The nucleophile can still attack from the side of the carbonyl with the hydrogen, and sterics will not effect the reaction. Choice B makes a true statement, but does not answer the question.

Conversion of Ketones or Aldehydes to Alkenes: The Wittig Reaction

If an aldehyde or a ketone is reacted with a phosphorous **ylide,** the carbonyl bond becomes a carbon–carbon double bond and the resulting product is an alkene.

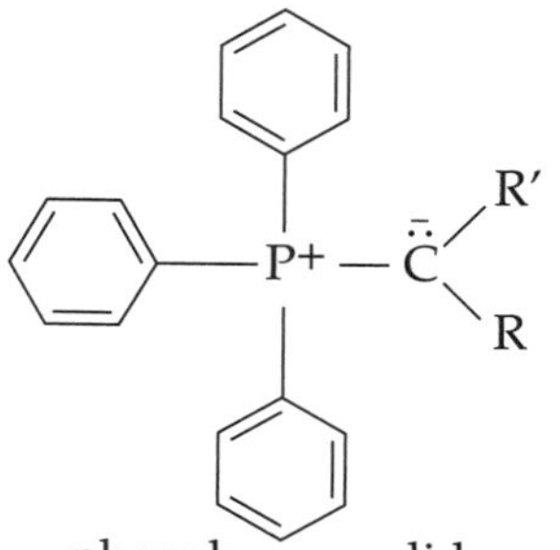

phosphorous ylide

In the ylide molecule, the triphenyl phosphorous component (often abbreviated Ph₃P) is bound to what we might call a "variable component"—a carbon atom that may, in turn, be bound to a variety of organic substituents. In the Wittig reaction, it is *that* carbon atom with its substituents that becomes doubly bonded to the carbonyl carbon and thus replaces the carbonyl oxygen.

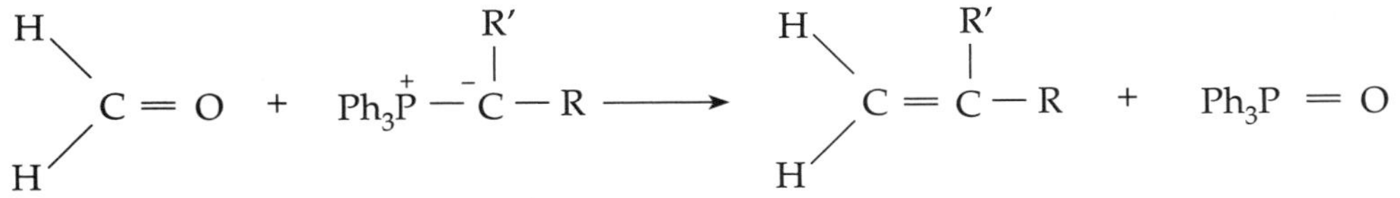

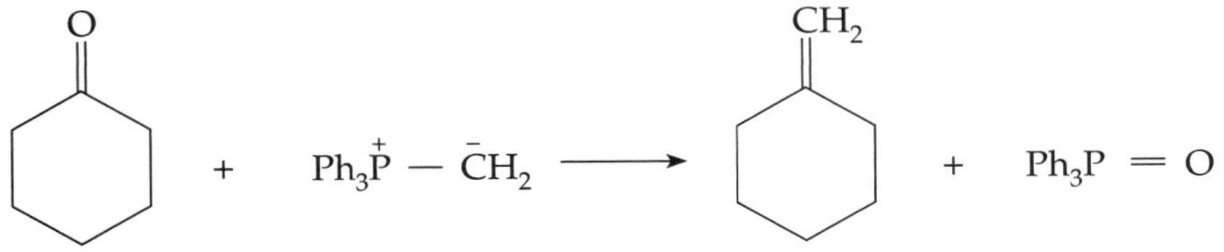

Cyclohexanone   Methylenecyclohexane

The reaction is useful because the carbon–carbon double bond will appear exactly where it did in the aldehyde or ketone precursor. If the chemist knows the structure of her starting carbonyl compound and the nature of the ylide molecule's "variable component" (as we call it here), then she can predict with virtual certainty the product of her reaction.

Please solve this problem:

- A Wittig reaction between 3-pentanone and Ph_3P^+—⁻ $CHCH_3$ will likely produce:

  A. 3-ethyl-2-pentene.
  B. 3-ethyl-3-pentene.
  C. 3-ethyl-5-heptene.
  D. 5-ethyl-3-heptene.

Problem solved:

A is correct. The alkyl portion of the ylide will replace the carbonyl oxygen, producing an alkene that on one side of its double bond will carry the two carbons derived from the ylide and on the other side the whole of the structure that had been bound to the carbonyl oxygen. The molecule will have seven carbons in all, two from the ylide and five from the ketone. Yet it will not be a heptene. It will be a pentene with an ethyl group substituted at carbon 3:

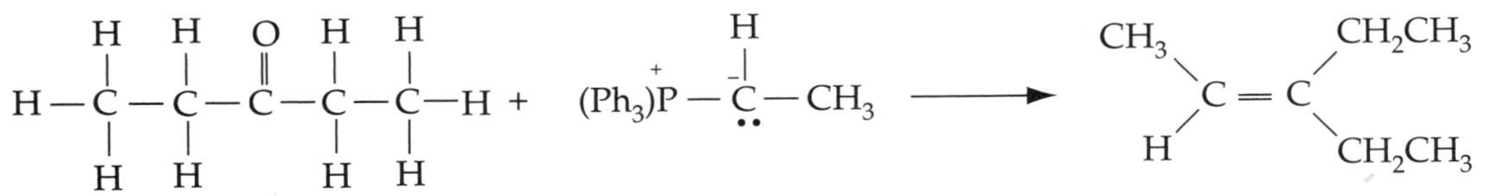

3-Pentanone   3–Ethyl–2–pentene

Oxidation of Aldehydes and Ketones

Aldehydes undergo oxidation rather readily to corresponding carboxylic acids (which are also carbonyl compounds). Ketones, however, to do not undergo oxidation because the carbonyl carbon is not bound to hydrogen, which must be abstracted during the oxidation reaction.

Benzaldehyde → (Na$_2$CR$_2$O$_7$) → Benzoic acid + Ag

Hexanal → (CrO$_3$, H$_3$O$^+$) → Hexanoic acid

Reduction of Aldehydes and Ketones

Aldehydes and ketones also undergo reduction to form alcohols, as discussed in **Chapter 36.**

37.2 MASTERY APPLIED: PRACTICE PASSAGE AND QUESTIONS

Passage

Within a laboratory working with cyclohexanones, Chemist 1 and Chemist 2 are assigned the task of converting 4-hydroxycyclohexanone to 4-cyanocyclohexanone, as summarized in Figure 1.

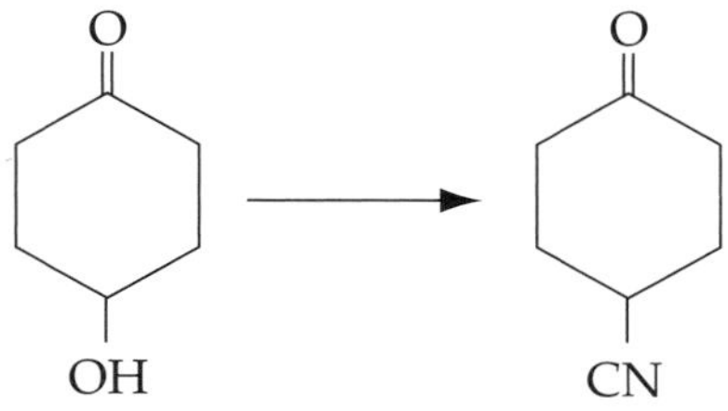

Figure 1

Chemist 3 is assigned the task of converting cyclohexanone to an imine derivative, as shown in Figure 2.

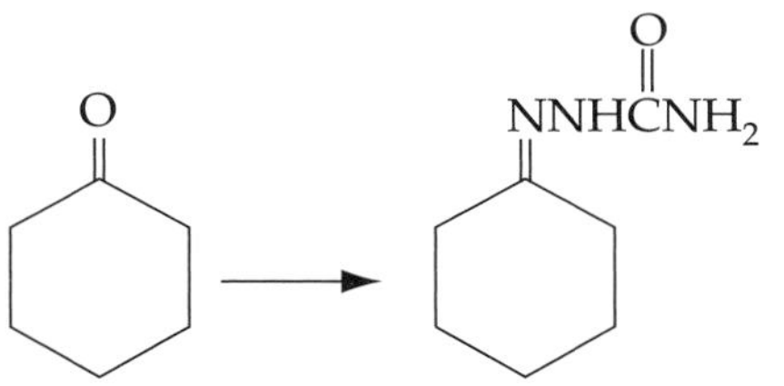

Figure 2

Chemists 1 and 2 have different approaches to completing their task, even though they seek the same outcome.

Chemist 1

Chemist 1 contemplates obtaining the desired product by first exposing the initial hydroxycyclohexanone to tosylchloride and then converting the product of that process to the desired cyanocyclohexanone, as shown in Figure 3.

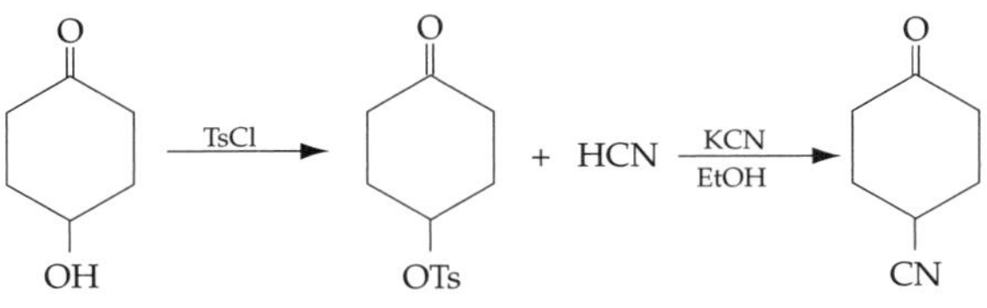

Figure 3

Chemist 2

Chemist 2 also contemplates the use of tosylchloride, but proposes first to react the initial cyclohexanone with the alcohol 1,2 ethanediol in a benzene solvent, knowing that benzene codistills with water. Chemist 2 then plans to expose the resulting product to tosylchloride, as shown in Figure 4, and to react the resulting tosylate with HCN and then to subject the product to acid.

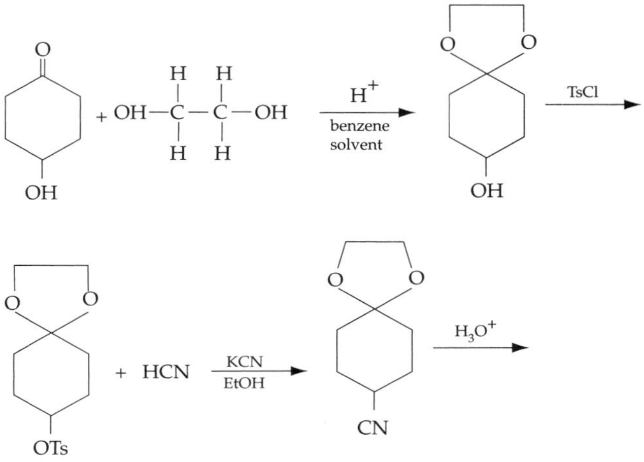

Figure 4

Chemist 2 then plans to reproduce step 2 of Chemist 1's proposed process to generate the desired cyanocyclohexanone.

Chemists 1 and 2 conducted their proposed processes. Chemist 2 produced the desired product in very significant quantity, but Chemist 1 obtained two products, only one of which was the desired one.

Chemist 3

Chemist 3 attempted, as shown in Figure 5, to react cyclohexanone with semicarbazide using an acid catalyst believed to be necessary. However, instead of obtaining the desired product, Chemist 3 found, on subsequent analysis, that the semicarbazide had been protonated, thus rendering it unable to react with the ketone.

Figure 5

1. Chemist 1 probably chose to treat the initial hydroxycyclohexanone with tosyl-chloride because:

   A. the tosyl substituent renders the carbonyl bond more polar.
   B. sulfonate ion is a weaker base than hydroxide ion.
   C. sulfonate ion is a stronger base than hydroxide ion.
   D. formation of the cyanohexanone involves a new carbon-carbon sigma bond.

2. Among the probable reasons that Chemist 1 obtained a product other than the one sought was that:

   A. cyanide ion is a stronger base than tosylate ion.
   B. cyanide ion is a weaker base than tosylate ion.
   C. cyanide ion is reactive with the carbonyl group.
   D. cyanide ion is unreactive with the carbonyl group.

3. Chemist 2 probably dissolved the hydroxycyclohexanone in acidic alcohol in order to:

   A. temporarily create a second OH group in place of the carbonyl oxygen.
   B. prepare the hydroxycyclohexanone molecule for aldol condensation.
   C. convert the hydroxycyclohexanone molecule to an aldehyde.
   D. convert the carbonyl group to an unreactive derivative.

4. The benzene solvent used by Chemist 2 was probably intended to:

   A. facilitate the removal of water from the reaction medium.
   B. facilitate the retention of water in the reaction medium.
   C. prevent protonation of the carbonyl oxygen by acid catalyst.
   D. stabilize the alcohol with which the ketone was reacted.

5. Which of the following, if done by Chemist 2, would most likely have prevented him from producing the desired product?

   A. Performing the reaction with alcohol in aqueous acid medium
   B. Performing the tosylation step in aqueous acid medium
   C. Leaving the tosylate substituent in place before reacting with HCN
   D. Hydrolyzing the product obtained after reaction with HCN

37.3 MASTERY VERIFIED: ANSWERS AND EXPLANATIONS

1. **B is correct.** Choices A and C make false statements. Choice D makes a true statement but is irrelevant to the question. As stated in the passage, both chemists wish to ultimately produce a product in which the OH group on the starting molecule is replaced by CN. Since OH⁻ is a strong base, and hence a strong nucleophile and poor leaving group, it must somehow be converted to a *better* leaving group. Instead of using the phrase "better leaving group," choice B speaks of a "weaker base." That is because leaving groups and nucleophiles *are* weak (Lewis) bases. Substitution of one for the other is a competition between a weaker one (the leaving group) and a stronger one (the nucleophile). Tosylate ion, the conjugate base of sulfonic acids, is a weaker base than OH⁻, and for that reason, it is used to replace OH as a better leaving group.

2. **C is correct.** Choices B and D make false statements. Cyanide ion is a stronger base/stronger nucleophile than tosylate, which is why tosylate is a good leaving group in the processes conducted by Chemists 1 and 2. Cyanide ion *does* react with carbonyl bonds (which, for instance, is how the cyanohydrins are formed). Displacement of the tosylate ion by HCN gave Chemist 1 the desired product, but also produced a reaction between CN and the carbonyl group that resulted in the unwanted product.

3. **D is correct.** Dissolving an aldehyde or ketone in alcohol (with an acid catalyst) converts it first to a hemiacetal or hemiketal, which, on further reaction with alcohol, converts it to an acetal or ketal. The acetal and ketal moieties are unreactive *in basic media* and thus allow for modification of other components of the molecule, followed, in *acid medium,* by regeneration of the original carbonyl group. If Chemist 2 (like Chemist 1) had failed first to react the starting molecule with alcohol, she would have left the carbonyl bond open to reaction with the cyanide ion and thus frustrated her reaction at its first step. Choices A, B, and C are senseless. Reacting the ketone with alcohol would neither convert the carbonyl oxygen to an OH group nor promote an aldol condensation. Neither would it convert a ketone to an aldehyde.

4. **A is correct.** Chemist 2 has undertaken to protect the carbonyl group by converting it to a ketal. Ketals do not form nearly so readily as acetals, the equilibrium between ketone and ketal tending to lie heavily to the left. One means of enhancing ketal production is by reacting the ketone not with a simple alcohol but with a diol (as Chemist 2 did) and by using benzene as a solvent. The benzene codistills with water and causes water to depart from the reaction medium. According to Le Chatalier's principle, removal of a product (water, in this case) drives equilibrium to the right. The benzene solvent, therefore, is intended ultimately to enhance the production of ketal. Choice B is incorrect. Choice C is, in this context, nonsensical. In acid-catalyzed formation of hemiacetal and hemiketal (which is followed by formation of the acetal or ketal), the acid functions first to protonate the carbonyl oxygen. That heightens the carbonyl carbon's susceptibility to nucleophilic attack by the lone pair of electrons situated on the alcohol's oxygen atom. Choice D is also nonsensical; benzene does not "stabilize" alcohol.

5. **B is correct.** The question requires that you understand the essential steps of protecting a carbonyl group by formation of an acetal or ketal. Reaction with the alcohol is acid catalyzed, which makes choice A wrong. The tosylate substituent serves as a leaving group and must be present in order that substitution by CN should occur. That makes choice C wrong. Once the desired reaction on the noncarbonyl portion of the molecule has occurred, hydrolysis is performed in order to regenerate the original carbonyl bond. That makes choice D wrong. Acetals and ketals protect carbonyl groups (or better, perhaps, "stand in for them" while the desired reaction is conducted) because they are unreactive in *basic medium*. In acid medium, the acetal or ketal will rehydrolyze before the desired reaction occurs, to form the original aldehyde or ketone. If, after forming the ketal, Chemist 2 had exposed the substance to an acid medium, he would likely have found himself "right back where he started."

CHAPTER 38

CARBOXYLIC ACIDS AND CARBOXYLIC ACID DERIVATIVES

38.1 MASTERY ACHIEVED

CARBOXYLIC ACIDS

The Carboxylic Group

"Carboxylic acid" means an organic molecule with a terminal **carboxyl group**:

$$R-C\underset{\displaystyle OH}{\overset{\displaystyle O}{}}$$

The carbon that carries the carboxyl group is the **acyl carbon**. Bound to the acyl carbon is an organic group, "big" or "little," aliphatic or aromatic. The compounds are generically designated RCOOH for aliphatic acids or ArCOOH for aromatic (benzoic) acids. Note that carboxylic acids, like ketones and aldehydes, are carbonyl compounds, since they contain the carbonyl group—a carbon doubly bound to oxygen. All carbonyl compounds can be divided into (1) aldehydes and ketones, as discussed in **Chapter 37**, and (2) carboxylic acids and their derivatives, as discussed in this chapter.

Carboxylic acid molecules can be large and complex. A single molecule might carry two or three carboxyl groups, in which case we speak of **dicarboxylic acids** $R(COOH)_2$ and **tricarboxylic acids** $R(COOH)_2$:

Malonic Acid (Propanedioic Acid)

Citric Acid (Tricarboxylic Acid)

Naming Carboxylic Acids

Naming the *open chain* carboxylic acids involves the same prefixes used for the alkanes and the suffix "oic acid" instead of "ane." We number carbons by beginning at the acyl carbon.

With the carbons thus numbered, the name shows, from left to right:

(1) the sites and nature of branches,

(2) a prefix corresponding to the length of the (longest possible) carbon chain, and

(3) the suffix "oic acid."

$$H-\underset{\underset{H}{|}}{\overset{\overset{H}{|}}{C}}-\underset{\underset{H}{|}}{\overset{\overset{H}{|}}{C}}-\overset{\overset{O}{\|}}{C}-OH \qquad : \qquad \text{Propanoic acid}$$

$$H-\underset{\underset{H}{|}}{\overset{\overset{H}{|}}{C}}-\underset{\underset{H}{|}}{\overset{\overset{CH_3}{|}}{C}}-\underset{\underset{H}{|}}{\overset{\overset{H}{|}}{C}}-\underset{\underset{H}{|}}{\overset{\overset{H}{|}}{C}}-\overset{\overset{O}{\|}}{C}-OH \qquad : \qquad \text{4-Methylpentanoic acid}$$

$$HO-\overset{\overset{O}{\|}}{C}-\underset{\underset{H}{|}}{\overset{\overset{H}{|}}{C}}-\underset{\underset{CH_2CH_3}{|}}{\overset{}{C}}-\underset{\underset{H}{|}}{\overset{\overset{H}{|}}{C}}-\underset{\underset{H}{|}}{\overset{\overset{H}{|}}{C}}-\underset{\underset{H}{|}}{\overset{\overset{CH_3}{|}}{C}}-\underset{\underset{H}{|}}{\overset{\overset{H}{|}}{C}}-\overset{\overset{O}{\|}}{C}-OH \quad : \qquad \text{3-Ethyl-6-methyloctanedioic acid}$$
(a <u>di</u>carboxylic acid)

Naming the ring-based carboxylic acids involves the whole phrase "carboxylic acid" (not the little "oic acid" shorthand). We number carbons on the ring beginning with the one to which the COOH group is attached. With the carbons thus numbered, the name shows, from left to right:

(1) the sites and nature of branches,

(2) the name of the ring structure, and

(3) the words "carboxylic acid."

ACYL GROUPS AND COMMON NAMES

3-Bromocyclohexanecarboxylic acid

"**Acyl group**" (RC=O) means a carbonyl group bound to some organic structure. An acyl group, therefore, is part and parcel of carboxylic acids, just as it is part of any carbonyl compound—aldehyde/ketone, carboxylic acid, and carboxylic acid derivative. Acyl groups vary, depending on the nature of "R" (which could be a hydrogen atom). And many acyl groups have "common names" not drawn from the IUPAC system, which create carboxylic acids with "common names" not drawn from the IUPAC system.

The acyl group HC=O, for example (where R is hydrogen) is the "formyl" group, and methanoic acid HCOOH is often called "formic acid." Table 38.1 lists a few carboxylic acids with their IUPAC names.

Carboxylic Acid	IUPAC Name
HCOOH	methanoic
CH_3COOH	ethanoic
CH_3CH_2COOH	propanoic
$CH_3(CH_2)_2COOH$	butanoic
$CH_3(CH_2)_3COOH$	pentanoic
$CH_3(CH_2)_4COOH$	hexanoic

Table 38.1

Physical Properties: Hydrogen Bonding, Boiling Point, and Solubility

The acyl carbon shares properties with the carbonyl carbon of aldehydes and ketones (see **Chapter 37**). It is sp^2 hybridized and has planar geometry. Unlike aldehydes and ketones, but *like* alcohols, carboxylic acid molecules form hydrogen bonds with one another. Boiling points for carboxylic acids, therefore, are much higher than they are for alkanes of similar molecular weight, and they are higher, even, than *alcohols* of similar molecular weight.

Two carboxylic acid molecules can, in fact, form *two* hydrogen bonds with one another because each has a carbonyl oxygen that can interact with an OH hydrogen. Hydrogen bonding between two carboxylic acid molecules produces a **cyclic dimer** and such is the arrangement in which carboxylic acid molecules normally "live together."

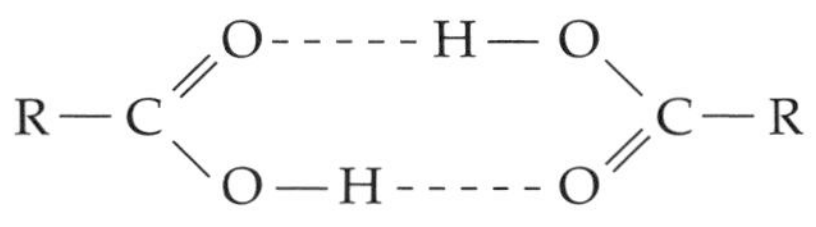

Please solve this problem:

- The characteristically high boiling points of carboxylic acids are due to:

    A. hydrogen bonding.
    B. resonance stabilization.
    C. nonpolarity of carbonyl and O-H bonds.
    D. unsaturation of carbon chains.

Problem solved:

A is correct. Hydrogen bonding tends to hold atoms together in the liquid state and to increase the energy required to move them into the gaseous state. As noted in the text, carboxylic acids may undergo hydrogen bonding at *two* sites. That phenomenon confers on them a higher boiling point than would otherwise be predicted on the basis of their molecular weight. Resonance stabilization (choice B) does not affect boiling point; it affects the stability of the carboxylate anion (to be discussed below). Choice C is false; the carbonyl and O-H bonds that compose the carboxylic groups are polar. Choice D refers to unsaturation of carbon chains, which is irrelevant to the question. The question concerns carboxylic aids generally. A carbon chain bond to the acyl carbon might be saturated or unsaturated.

Please solve this problem:

• Two carboxylic acid molecules hydrogen bond with one another, but two aldehyde molecules do not. The reason is that the aldehyde:

    A. is not truly a carbonyl compound.
    B. has no hydroxyl hydrogen.
    C. has a nonpolar carbonyl bond.
    D. does not have an acidic alpha hydrogen.

Problem solved:

B is correct. Choices A, C, and D make false statements. Aldehydes and ketones are carbonyl compounds, the carbonyl bond is polar, and the alpha hydrogens are acidic, which is how the all-important enolate ion is formed. For the MCAT, we associate hydrogen bonding with molecules in which hydrogen is bound to nitrogen, fluorine, or oxygen. The structure of aldehydes and ketone molecules offers no such situation, but the carboxylic acid (and alcohol) molecule does. In the carboxylic acid, the acyl carbon is doubly bound to one oxygen and singly bound to another, which, in turn, is bound to hydrogen. Hydrogen bonding between two carboxylic acid molecules occurs between the terminal hydrogen of one and the carbonyl carbon of the other. (Remember, on the other hand, that aldehydes and ketones *do* undergo hydrogen bonding with water molecules because the unshared electron pair on the carbonyl oxygen interacts with a hydrogen atom within the water molecule.)

Aliphatic carboxylic acids with fewer than five carbons on their aliphatic skeleton are soluble in water, and in this way resemble the alcohols. As with the alcohols, solubility is due to hydrogen bonding *with* water (see **Chapter 36**). Aliphatic acids larger than that and aromatic acids tend not to be soluble in water, but are soluble in less polar solvents such as ether and benzene. Once again, for the MCAT, relate the solubility of the smaller aliphatic carboxylic acids to hydrogen bonding with water, just as you do with alcohols.

Acidity of Carboxylic Acids

A carboxylic acid's acidity derives from its relative readiness to part with a proton. To a considerable degree, the carboxylic group owes that ability to the relative stability of the carboxylate anion $RCOO^-$, which is *stabilized by resonance*. The carboxylate ion's negative charge is delocalized, giving partial negative charge and partial double bond character to both oxygen atoms bound to the acyl carbon.

For the MCAT, it is important to know that the *stability of the carboxylate ion makes carboxylic acids more acidic than alcohol*s.

Please solve this problem:

- Between alcohols and carboxylic acids, which tend to be more acidic?

  A. Alcohols, due to solvation effects on the alkoxide ion.
  B. Alcohols, due to resonance stabilization of the oxonium ion.
  C. Carboxylic acids, due to polarity of the O-H bond.
  D. Carboxylic acids, due to delocalization of anionic charge.

Problem solved:

D is correct. Choice B makes a false and nonsensical statement. The oxonium ion is not a resonance structure and, moreover, it follows from the protonation of an alcohol, with alcohol acting as a *base*. Choices A and C embody truths, but do not answer the question. It is true that solvating effects tend to stabilize alkoxide ions and thus enhance the acidity of alcohols. It is also true that an O-H bond is polar. Neither of these facts, however, explains the difference in acidity between alcohols and carboxylic acids. Carboxylic acids are more acidic than alcohols because the carboxylate anion is stabilized by resonance. Choice D reflects that same statement, but instead of using the word "resonance," it refers to "delocalization" of negative (anionic) charge.

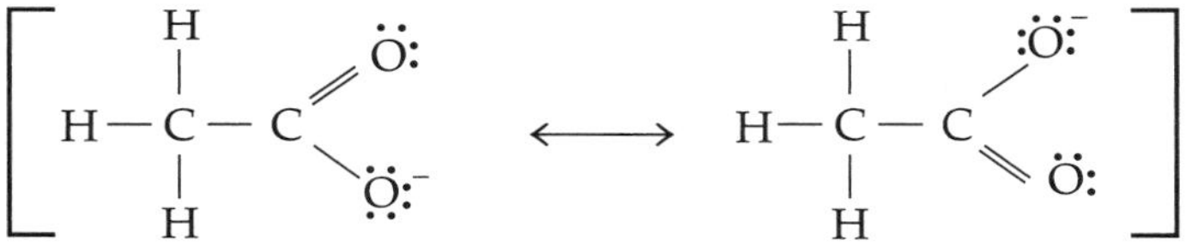

ACIDITY AS AFFECTED BY ALPHA CARBON SUBSTITUENTS

Factors that enhance the carboxylate anion's stability enhance the acidity of the corresponding protonated acid. Conversely, factors that tend to destabilize the anion tend to lessen the acidity of the corresponding acid. In this regard, **inductive effects** are significant.

Consider a molecule of 2-chloro-3-phenylpropanoic acid:

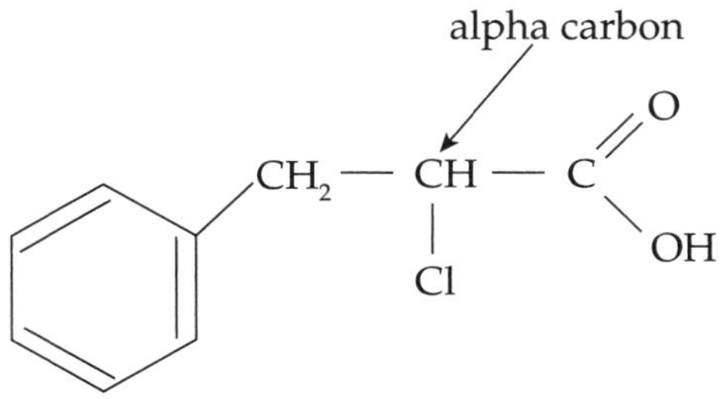

2-chloro-3-phenylpropanoic acid

Note that the carbon adjacent to the acyl carbon is called the **alpha carbon**. If a halogen atom is bound to the carboxylic acid's alpha carbon, the corresponding carboxylate ion is stabilized. This is because the halogen atom is electronegative and constitutes an electron withdrawing group. It tends to delocalize the anion's negative charge by partially "absorbing" it. It adds to the anion's stability thus increaseing the acidity of the corresponding acid. An electron-releasing group bound to the alpha carbon has the opposite effect. It destabilizes the anion and reduces acidity.

Consider this molecule of 2-methyl-3-phenylpropanoic acid in which we see bound to the alpha carbon not a chlorine atom, but a methyl group. Alkyl groups release/donate electrons (see Table 35.3, **Chapter 35**). They tend to destabilize the carboxylate ion and render the protonated precursor less acidic.

These phenomena apply whether we deal with aliphatic acids or aromatic acids. Whether the acid does or does not carry a benzene ring, the inductive effects of alpha carbon substitution are the same.

So, for the MCAT, remember that:

- alpha carbon substitution by an electron-withdrawing group tends to increase acidity;

- alpha carbon substitution by an electron-releasing group tends to decrease acidity.

Table 38.2 below reflects the trend.

Structure	pK_a (H_2O, 25°)
CH_3COOH	4.75
CH_3CH_2COOH	4.87
$(CH_3)_2CHCOOH$	4.84
$(CH_3)_3CCOOH$	5.03
$CH_3(CH_2)_{16}COOH$ (*stearic acid*)	4.89
$ClCH_2COOH$	2.85
$BrCH_2COOH$	2.96
ICH_2COOH	3.12
$CH_3CHCOOH$ $\quad\vert$ $\quad OH$	3.08

Table 38.2

Remember that halogens, in particular, are strong electron withdrawers and increase acidity. Remember also that alkyl groups (methyl, ethyl, propyl, etc.) are electron releasers/donators and decrease acidity. (For a reminder as to which groups release and withdraw electrons, consult Table 35.3, **Chapter 35**.)

Please solve this problem:

- Benzoic acid has a pKa of 4.19. When Benzoic acid undergoes substitution by a trifluoromethyl group, the product *p*-trifluoromethylbenzoic acid has a pKa of 3.6. The trifluoromethyl group is probably a ring:

  A. activator, since the reduced pKa suggests an electron withdrawing effect.
  B. activator, since the reduced pKa suggests an electron releasing effect.
  C. deactivator, since the reduced pKa suggests an electron withdrawing effect.
  D. deactivator, since the reduced pKa suggests an electron releasing effect.

Problem solved:

C is correct. We are dealing with a substituted benzoic acid, and we are told that the substituted acid is more acidic (lower pKa) than benzoic acid itself. Electron-releasing groups activate benzene rings and decrease their acidity. Choices B and D, therefore, are false. Electron-withdrawing groups (a) deactivate benzene rings and (b) delocalize the negative charge carried by the deprotonated benzoic acid. The delocalization of charge stabilizes the anion and increases acidity of the corresponding protonated acid. The trifluoromethyl substituent, therefore, must be an electron-withdrawing group, as stated in choice C.

Preparing Carboxylic Acids

OXIDATION OF ALCOHOLS, ALDEHYDES, AND ALKYLBENZENES

As discussed in **Chapter 36,** oxidation of primary alcohols with a strong oxidizing agent ($KMnO_4$ or CrO_3) will cause the alcohol to lose both its alpha hydrogens and produce a carboxylic acid. (A weaker oxidizing agent will produce an aldehyde, and secondary alcohols can be oxidized to ketones.) As discussed in **Chapter 37,** oxidation of aldehydes will produce carboxylic acids as well. **Tollens reagent** $Ag(NH_3)_2^+$ is best as an oxidizing agent because it minimizes side reactions.

$$RCH_2OH \xrightarrow[\substack{(2)\ H_3O^+}]{\substack{(1)\ KMnO_4,\ OH^- \\ heat}} RCO_2H$$

$$R\text{–}CHO \xrightarrow{CrO_3} RCO_2H$$

CARBOXYLATION OF GRIGNARD REAGENTS

The Grignard reagent is mentioned in **Chapter 36**. It is prepared by the reaction of organohalides (RX or ArX) with magnesium to produce an alkylmagensium halide or arylmagnesiumhalide, which *is* the Grignard reagent. It is represented with the shorthand RMgX (or ArMgX), where X is chlorine, bromine, or iodine. The Grignard reagent is sometimes called an "organometallic" compound because it involves a bond between carbon and a metal (magnesium).

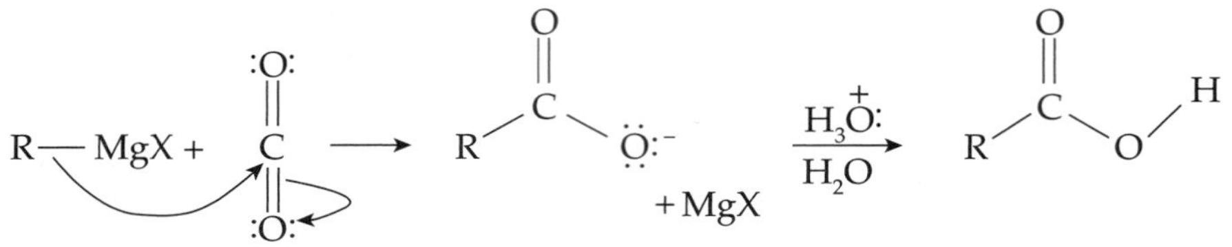

If a Grignard reagent is reacted with carbon dioxide, the result is a carboxylate ion (which, when protonated, produces a carboxylic acid).

Please solve this problem:

- Which of the following does NOT accurately characterize the Grignard reagent?

    A. Its reaction with carbon dioxide produces a carboxylic acid.
    B. Its organic component must not contain an aromatic ring.
    C. It has a metallic component.
    D. It may be prepared from an alkyl halide.

Problem solved:

B is correct. The Grignard reagent is prepared from an alkyl or aryl halide and magnesium (a metal). Its combination with carbon dioxide under appropriate conditions produces a carboxylic acid, that being the Grignard reaction. Choices A, C, and D, therefore, make *accurate* statements, and for this question, that makes them wrong. Because the progenitor of the Grignard reagent may be an alkyl or aryl halide, its organic component may contain an aromatic ring. Choice B, therefore, makes a false statement, and for this question, that makes it right.

Please solve this problem:

- Which of the following statements does NOT accurately characterize the formation of a carboxylic acid from a primary alcohol?

    A. It requires the presence of an organometallic compound.
    B. It requires the presence of an oxidizing agent.
    C. Both A and B
    D. Neither A nor B

Problem solved:

A is correct. The formation of a carboxylic acid from a primary alcohol is an oxidation reaction and requires the presence of a strong oxidizing agent, such as $KMnO_4$ or CrO_3. Choice B, therefore, makes an *accurate* statement and, for *this* question, is wrong. Choice A is an *inaccurate* statement, which makes it the *correct* answer to this question. "Organometallic compound" refers, in this context, to the Grignard reagent, which is not, of course, required for oxidation of an alcohol to a carboxylic acid.

Reactions of Carboxylic Acids

REDUCTION TO YIELD PRIMARY ALCOHOLS

With a powerful reducing agent like $LiAlH_4$ (which rapidly reduces all carbonyl groups) followed by treatment with acid (usually H_2SO_4), carboxylic acids can be reduced to primary alcohols. Hydride ion, a nucleophile, adds to the positively polarized acyl carbon to form an alkoxide ion, then an aldehyde, which on further reduction produces a carboxylic acid.

$$
H_3C - \overset{\overset{\displaystyle CH_3}{|}}{\underset{\underset{\displaystyle CH_3}{|}}{C}} - CH_2 - C \overset{\displaystyle O}{\underset{\displaystyle OH}{\big\backslash}}
\quad \xrightarrow[\text{2) } H_3O^+]{\text{1) } LiAlH_4, \text{ ether}} \quad
H_3C - \overset{\overset{\displaystyle CH_3}{|}}{\underset{\underset{\displaystyle CH_3}{|}}{C}} - CH_2CH_2OH
$$

3, 3 –Dimethylbutanoic acid   3, 3 –Dimethyl–1–butanol

3–Methoxybenzoic acid $\xrightarrow[\text{2) } H_3O^+]{\text{1) } LiAlH_4, \text{ ether}}$ 3–Methoxybenzyl alcohol

DECARBOXYLATION

"**Decarboxylation**" is the loss of a CO_2 molecule, meaning that the number of carbon atoms remaining on the product will be one less than the original.

$$
RCH_2\overset{\displaystyle O}{\overset{\|}{C}}OH \longrightarrow RCH_3 + CO_2
$$

Decarboxylation is slow, however, unless the carboxylic acid carries a second carbonyl group on the carbon that is "two doors down" from the acyl carbon. That carbon is the β carbon, and such acids are called β-keto acids. Decarboxylation of β-keto acids proceeds rather readily.

$$
R - \overset{\displaystyle O}{\overset{\|}{C}} - \overset{\overset{\displaystyle H}{|}}{\underset{\underset{\displaystyle H}{|}}{C}} - \overset{\displaystyle O}{\overset{\|}{C}} - OH \longrightarrow R - \overset{\displaystyle O}{\overset{\|}{C}} - \overset{\overset{\displaystyle H}{|}}{\underset{\underset{\displaystyle H}{|}}{C}} - H + CO_2
$$

For the MCAT, you should know the *reasons* for this.Decarboxylation of an already deprotonated acid (i.e., decarboxylation of the carboxylate ion) produces an enolate ion. The enolate ion is a *resonance stabilized intermediate*. It is much stabler than the ordinary RCH_2^- anion that would form without the second carbonyl group. Protonation of the enolate ion then yields the ultimate decarboxylated product.

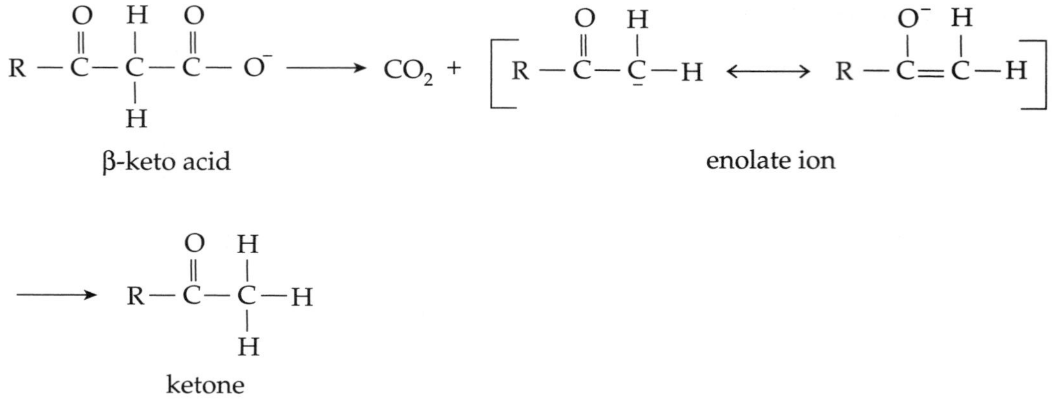

β-keto acid → CO_2 + enolate ion

ketone

Decarboxylation of the protonated acid itself proceeds through a six-membered cyclic transition structure, which, on loss of CO_2, forms a neutral enol that tautomerizes to a methyl ketone. This process, then, proceeds *without a negatively charged intermediate*. That favorable circumstance is also made possible because of the second carbonyl group of the β-keto acid.

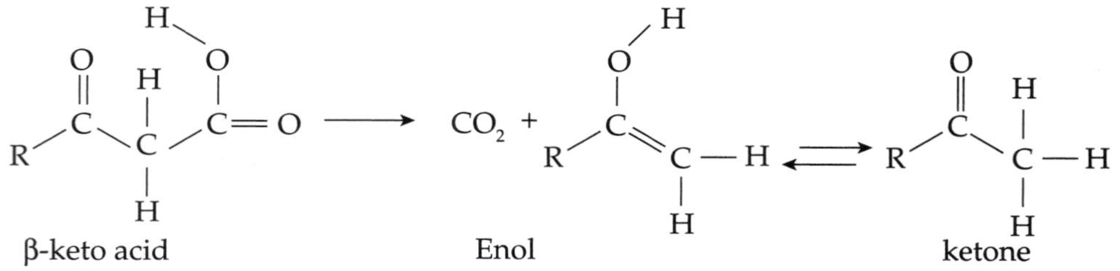

β-keto acid → CO_2 + Enol ⇌ ketone

Formation of Carboxylic Acid Derivatives

"**Carboxylic acid derivatives**" are categories of compounds generated from carboxylic acids. The derivatives have their own identities and, "in their own right," an independent significance to organic chemistry and the MCAT. Important *for the* MCAT are these carboxylic acid derivatives:

- acid chlorides,

- acid anhydrides,

- esters, and

- amides.

CARBOXYLIC ACIDS TO ACID CHLORIDES

Acid chlorides are prepared by reaction between a carboxylic acid and either PCl_3, PCl_5, or $SOCl_2$.

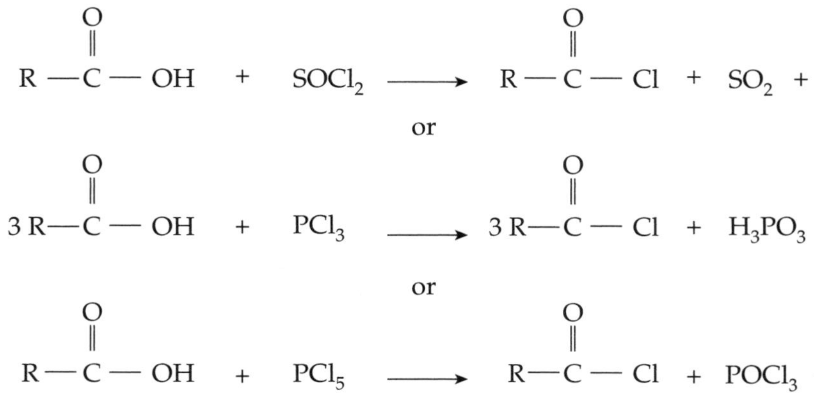

$$R-\overset{\overset{\displaystyle O}{\|}}{C}-OH \ + \ SOCl_2 \ \longrightarrow \ R-\overset{\overset{\displaystyle O}{\|}}{C}-Cl \ + \ SO_2 \ + \ HCl$$

or

$$3\,R-\overset{\overset{\displaystyle O}{\|}}{C}-OH \ + \ PCl_3 \ \longrightarrow \ 3\,R-\overset{\overset{\displaystyle O}{\|}}{C}-Cl \ + \ H_3PO_3$$

or

$$R-\overset{\overset{\displaystyle O}{\|}}{C}-OH \ + \ PCl_5 \ \longrightarrow \ R-\overset{\overset{\displaystyle O}{\|}}{C}-Cl \ + \ POCl_3 \ + \ HCl$$

CARBOXYLIC ACIDS TO ACID ANHYDRIDES

We might conceive of an acid anhydride as two carboxylic acids linked together with the loss of water (although that does not properly describe the *reaction* that produces them).

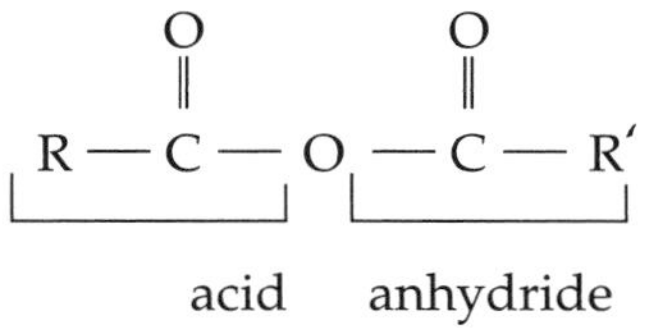

$$R-\overset{\overset{\displaystyle O}{\|}}{\underset{\underbrace{\qquad}_{\text{acid}}}{C}}-O-\overset{\overset{\displaystyle O}{\|}}{\underset{\underbrace{\qquad}_{\text{anhydride}}}{C}}-R'$$

With pyridine present in the solution, reaction between a carboxylic acid and an acid chloride (its derivative) yields an acid anhydride.

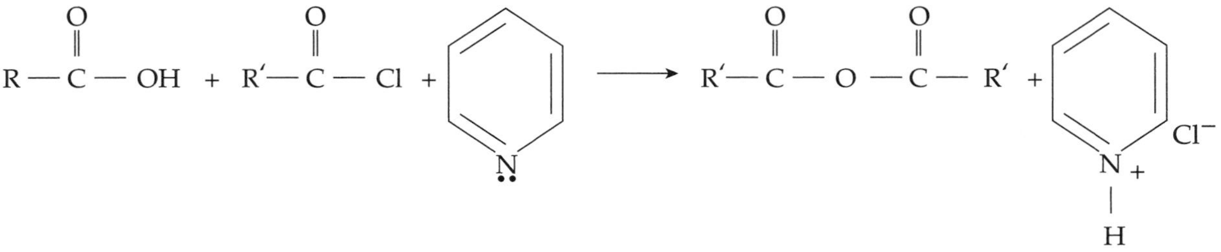

Dicarboxylic acids produce **cyclic anhydrides** on heating if the structure of the dicarboxylic acid is such that the resulting ring will have five or six members (meaning four or five carbon atoms plus the one oxygen atom).

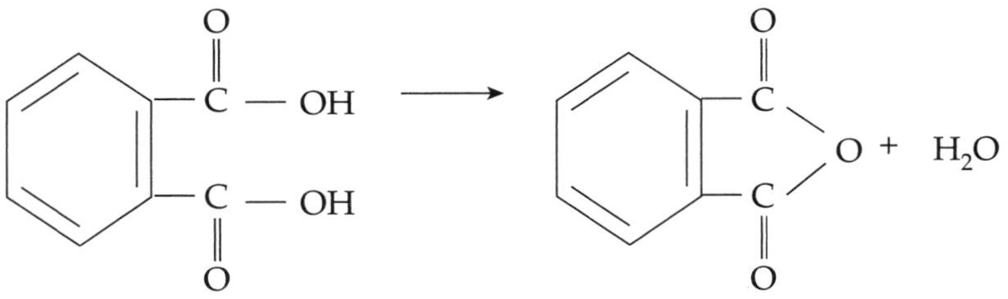

Phthalic acid
(a dicarcoboxylic acid)

Phthalic anhydride

CARBOXYLIC ACIDS TO ESTERS

"**Ester**" means a molecule in which the carboxylic acid's OH group is replaced by an OR group. Esters are formed in an acid-catalyzed reaction between carboxylic acid and alcohol.

$$R - \overset{\overset{\displaystyle O}{\|}}{C} - OH \;+\; R' - OH \;\underset{\longleftarrow}{\overset{H^+}{\longrightarrow}}\; R - \overset{\overset{\displaystyle O}{\|}}{C} - OR' \;+\; H_2O$$

Please solve this problem:

- A chemist attempting to synthesize an ester from an alcohol and a carboxylic acid is dissatisfied with the yield, noting that the reversibility of the reaction and its equilibrium point left her with less product than she wished to obtain. On repetition of the attempted synthesis, which of the following measures would most likely improve the yield?

  A. Reducing the quantity of carboxylic acid and increasing the quantity of alcohol
  B. Reducing the quantity of alcohol and increasing the quantity of carboxylic acid
  C. Adding water to the medium as the reaction proceeds
  D. Removing water from the medium as the reaction proceeds

Problem solved:

D is correct. This question, like many on the MCAT, seems to concern a highly specific topic—in this case, esterification. Yet, the question tests only your knowledge of equilibrium dynamics, a critical concept for the MCAT. Ester production involves water as a product. Among the truths that emerge from Le Chatelier's principle is this: Removal from the reaction medium of a product (which is analogous to removing a reactant of the reverse reaction) will drive the equilibrium to the right.

CARBOXYLIC ACIDS TO AMIDES

"**Amide**" means a molecule in which the carboxylic acid's OH group is replaced by NR_2, where R can either be hydrogen or an alkyl group.

$$R - \overset{\overset{\displaystyle O}{\|}}{C} - NR_2$$

Amides are produced by a reaction between a carboxylic acid and aqueous ammonia. The immediate product is not an amide but an ammonium salt because of the acid/base properties of the functional groups involved. Evaporation of water and application of heat will dehydrate the salt and produce the amide. Because this process is cumbersome, *amides are usually prepared from other carboxylic acid derivatives.*

Acid Chlorides to Amides

Carboxylic acids give rise rather readily to acid chlorides, and those in turn will produce amides by reaction with primary amines, secondary amines, or ammonia.

Acid Anhydrides to Amides

Carboxylic acids give rise rather readily to acyclic and cyclic anhydrides as explained above. Those derivatives in turn will produce amides by reaction with primary amines, secondary amines, or ammonia. Reaction of cyclic anhydrides, however, produce that which carries not only the characteristic amide $CONR_2$ moiety, but also a COOH moiety, making it both an amide and a carboxylic acid.

anhydride   amide/acid

If that product is dehydrated by heating, an **imide** results, which is characterized by a nitrogen atom bonded to one hydrogen atom and two carbonyl groups.

amide/acid   imide

Esters to Amides

Carboxylic acids rather readily produce esters as derivatives. If an ester is reacted with a primary amine, secondary amine, or ammonia, there results an amide. (The reaction with ammonia is called **ammonolysis**.)

$$R - \overset{\overset{\displaystyle O}{\|}}{C} - OR' \quad + \quad H - \overset{\overset{\displaystyle }{|}}{\underset{\underset{\displaystyle R'''}{|}}{N}} - R'' \quad \longrightarrow \quad R - \overset{\overset{\displaystyle O}{\|}}{C} - \overset{\overset{\displaystyle }{|}}{\underset{\underset{\displaystyle R'''}{|}}{N}} - R''$$

ester   2° amine   amide

CARBOXYLIC ACID DERIVATIVES

We have now introduced the carboxylic acid derivatives important to the MCAT: acid chlorides, acid anhydrides, esters, and amides. Each of these represents a significant category of compound, the chemistry of which is germane to the MCAT. Much of their chemistry concerns a nucleophilic addition by a weak base at the carbonyl carbon, followed by elimination of a leaving group. Together, the addition and elimination are called **acyl transfer**.

acyl transfer
(nucleophilic addition-elimination)

In **Chapter 37,** we discussed the carbonyl carbon of aldehydes and ketones, noting that its partial positivity and surrounding planar structure made it particularly susceptible to nucleophilic attack. Those factors apply also to the carbonyl carbon of carboxylic acid derivatives. For those same reasons, they are susceptible to nucleophilic attack.

In the case of aldehydes and ketones, the nucleophilic attack normally initiated a "full-blown" *addition* reaction in which (a) the carbonyl double bond was lost, (b) the (former) carbonyl carbon formed a fourth sigma bond, and (c) a tetrahedral product resulted. In the case of the acyl transfer characteristic of carboxylic acid derivatives, the initial nucleophilic attack does form a tetrahedral intermediate, which then undergoes an *elimination* so that (a) the carbonyl double bond regenerates and (b) a new substituent appears at the position "traditionally" occupied by an OH group on the corresponding carboxylic acid.

Acyl transfer is not a nucleophilic substitution reaction as we have seen them before. Yet it has in common with an $S_N 2$ substitution that one weak base must make a nucleophilic attack and that another must leave.

Many of the acyl transfer (and other) reactions of the carboxylic acid derivatives involve conversion from one derivative to another. It should be noted that the better the leaving group attached to the derivative, the more reactive the derivative is. The relative reactivity of the four important derivatives for the MCAT is therefore:

$$\underset{R \quad\quad Cl}{\overset{\overset{\displaystyle O}{\|}}{\diagup\diagdown}} \;>\; \underset{R \quad O \quad R^1}{\overset{\overset{\displaystyle O \quad\quad O}{\|\quad\quad\|}}{\diagup\diagdown\diagup\diagdown}} \;>\; \underset{R \quad\quad OR^1}{\overset{\overset{\displaystyle O}{\|}}{\diagup\diagdown}} \;>\; \underset{R \quad\quad NR^1_2}{\overset{\overset{\displaystyle O}{\|}}{\diagup\diagdown}}$$

Acid Chlorides

CONVERSION OF ACID CHLORIDES TO CARBOXYLIC ACIDS: AN ACYL TRANSFER

When an acid chloride reacts with water, the water's oxygen atom nucleophilically attacks the carbonyl carbon to form a tetrahedral intermediate. Subsequent loss of a chloride ion and proton regenerates the carbonyl bond and leaves an OH group where the chloride had been. The result then is the corresponding carboxylic acid.

$$
R - \overset{\overset{\displaystyle O}{\|}}{C} - Cl \quad + \quad \overset{\displaystyle O - H}{\underset{\displaystyle H}{|}} \quad \longrightarrow \quad R - \overset{\overset{\displaystyle O^-}{|}}{\underset{\underset{\displaystyle Cl}{|}}{C}} - \overset{+}{O} - H \ \underset{\displaystyle H}{}
$$

acid chloride

$$
\xrightarrow{H_2O} \quad R - \overset{\overset{\displaystyle O}{\|}}{C} - OH \quad + \quad Cl^- \quad + \quad H_3O^+
$$

carboxylic acid

CONVERSION OF ACID CHLORIDES TO ESTERS: AN ACYL TRANSFER

When an acid chloride reacts with an alcohol, the alcohol's oxygen atom nucleophilically attacks the carbonyl carbon to form a tetrahedral intermediate. Subsequent loss, once again, of a chloride ion and proton regenerates the carbonyl bond and leaves an OR group where the chloride had been. The result then is the corresponding ester.

$$
R - \overset{\overset{\displaystyle O}{\|}}{C} - Cl \quad + \quad R' - \overset{\displaystyle \cdot\cdot}{\underset{}{O}} - H \quad \longrightarrow \quad R - \overset{\overset{\displaystyle O}{\|}}{C} \diagdown_{O - R''} \quad + \quad HCl
$$

acid chloride   ester

Acid Anhydrides

ACID ANHYDRIDES TO ESTERS: AN ACYL TRANSFER

When an alcohol is reacted with an acid anhydride, the alcohol's oxygen atom nucleophilically attacks one of the carbonyl carbons to produce a tetrahedral intermediate. Then, *either*:

(1) a carboxylate ion is the leaving group, and thereafter abstracts a proton from the species it "leaves behind" to form a carboxylic acid and an ester:

carboxylic acid   ester

or (2) a carboxylic acid is the leaving group, which produces an ester:

leaving group   ester
(carboxylic acid)

For the MCAT, remember the simple *reason* for the dually available mechanism in this nucleophilic addition-elimination reaction and relate it to the rudiments of nucleophilic substitution: *both carboxylate ion and carboxylic acid are weak bases and, therefore, good leaving groups.*

Please solve this problem:

- In the formation of an ester from an acid anhydride, which of the following statements is most accurate?

    A. Alcohol acts as a weaker Lewis base than a carboxylate ion.
    B. Alcohol acts as a stronger Lewis base than a carboxylate ion.
    C. The reaction proceeds via a carbocation intermediate.
    D. The reaction proceeds via an S_N1 substitution mechanism.

Problem solved:

B is correct. Choices C and D are false. An S_N1 (unimolecular) substitution mechanism does involve a carbocation intermediate, but no such mechanism is at work in this reaction. This question asks that you exercise logical reasoning by applying familiar terms and concepts to situations in which you might not have heard them raised. This reaction is one of non-S_N1 nucleophilic substitution, which involves a kind of "contest" between two weak Lewis bases (see **Chapter 36**). The stronger of the two weak bases is the nucleophile and the weaker is the leaving group. In this case, alcohol arrives at the carbonyl carbon with a pair of electrons to donate. Faced with that "fact," the carboxylate ion takes its electron pair and leaves. In more scientific terms, we may say that by attacking and donating an electron pair to the carbonyl carbon, the alcohol acts as a Lewis base. By withdrawing its shared electron pair from the carbonyl carbon, the carboxylate ion acts as a *weaker* Lewis base. (The carboxylate ion does, of course, "pick up" a proton from the remaining intermediate to form a protonated carboxylic acid and leave behind the ester.)

Esters

ACID CATALYZED HYDROLYSIS: FORMATION OF CARBOXYLIC ACID

We know that acid catalyzed reaction of carboxylic acid and alcohol produces an ester . The reaction is reversible, meaning there also exists an acid catalyzed hydrolysis in which ester plus water produces carboxylic acid. Choosing one reaction over the other is really a matter of manipulating equilibrium.

Please solve this problem:

- If a chemist wishes to hydrolyze an ester to form a carboxylic acid and alcohol, then among the following, he would be best advised to:

    A. maintain the reaction medium at pH of 7.0.
    B. remove water as the reaction proceeds.
    C. use an excess of alcohol.
    D. use an excess of water.

Problem solved:

D is correct. This question asks only that you apply Le Chatelier's principle to a particular reaction. The formation of ester and water from carboxylic acid and alcohol, and the formation of carboxylic acid and alcohol from ester and water are two components of a reversible reaction. If the chemist wishes to hydrolyze the ester, he must (among those options available in the answer choices) choose that which will drive the equilibrium toward acid and alcohol. In that reaction, water is a reactant and alcohol is a product. Increasing the amount of available water will drive the equilibrium "away" from the water side and toward the acid/alcohol side. Choices B and C describe measures that would drive the equilibrium in the other direction. Choice A is wrong because the reaction is catalyzed by acid in both directions. A pH of 7.0 denotes the absence of an acid catalyst.

BASE PROMOTED HYDROLYSIS OF ESTERS: SOAP

If an ester is reacted with sodium hydroxide, the hydroxide ion will nucleophilically attack the acyl carbon to form a negatively charged tetrahedral intermediate, which then loses an alkoxide ion to form a carboxylic acid. The alkoxide ion abstracts a proton from the acid to form an alcohol and the sodium salt of the corresponding acid.

$$R-\overset{\overset{\textstyle O}{\|}}{C}-OR' \ + \ Na^+:\overset{..}{\underset{..}{O}}H \quad \longrightarrow \quad \longrightarrow \quad R-\overset{\overset{\textstyle O}{\|}}{C}-O^-Na^+ \ + \ R'OH$$

sodium carboxylate
(= soap, if R is long)

If the carboxylate portion of the salt is long (twelve to eighteen carbon atoms) the salt is, in fact, a **soap** (although hydrolysis of esters is not the usual process of manufacture. Soaps are usually manufactured by hydrolysis of triglycerides to yield glycerol and salts of the three related carboxylic acids). The soap molecule has a polar "head" (the carboxylate terminus) and a long nonpolar "tail." The soap molecule is not itself a water-soluble entity. When added to water, individual soap molecules are not dissolved as are true water-soluble substances. Rather, the molecules (hundreds of them, perhaps) coalesce to form a spherical **micelle** in which the outward directed polar heads are solvated by water and dissolve in the inward-directed nonpolar tails, "hide" from the water, and meet at the center. At the nonpolar center, solvation occurs between nonpolar, water-insoluble "dirt" (like oil), while the polar heads remain "dissolved" in water. By this mechanism, a mixture of soap and water removes unwanted nonpolar substances from wherever they are unwanted.

ESTERS TO OTHER ESTERS: TRANSESTERIFICATION

If an ester RCOOR' is reacted with an alcohol R"OH, with appropriate manipulation of equilibrium, the OR" group will replace the OR' group, creating a new ester RCOOR" and new alcohol, R'OH.

$$R-\overset{\overset{\textstyle O}{\|}}{C}-OR' \ + \ R''OH \ \rightleftarrows \ R-\overset{\overset{\textstyle O}{\|}}{C}-OR'' \ + \ R'-O-H$$

ESTERS TO ALCOHOLS: REDUCTION

In **Chapter 36,** we noted that the reduction of an ester will produce two primary alcohols, ROH and R'OH. Recall that an ester is a carboxylic acid in which the OH group has been replaced by an OR group (RCOOH → RCOOR'). In the two primary alcohols that result from reduction of an ester, one of the two R groups represents the carbon chain (or aryl group) of the corresponding carboxylic acid, and the other represents the group (R') of the "OR" bound to the carbonyl carbon.

$$R - \overset{\overset{\displaystyle O}{\|}}{C} - OR' \quad \xrightarrow[\text{2) } H_3O^+]{\text{1) LiAlH}_4, \text{ ether}} \quad R - \overset{\overset{\displaystyle H}{|}}{\underset{\underset{\displaystyle H}{|}}{C}} - OH \quad + \quad R' - OH$$

ester   1° alcohol   1° alcohol

AMIDES

AMIDES TO CARBOXYLIC ACIDS: HYDROLYSIS

An amide will undergo acid or base catalyzed hydrolysis to yield a carboxylic acid and an amine.

In the acid catalyzed reaction, a hydronium ion protonates the amide. Water nucleophilically attacks the carbonyl carbon. A positively charged tetrahedral intermediate results. Loss of a proton and ammonia generate the carboxylic acid and NH_4^+ (reflecting, in principle, regeneration of the acid catalyst, since $NH_4^+ + H_2O \rightarrow NH_3 + H_3O^+$):

$$R - \overset{\overset{\displaystyle O}{\|}}{C} - OH \quad + \quad NH_4^+ \quad (\; \underset{\longleftarrow}{\overset{H_2O}{\longrightarrow}} \; NH_3 \quad + \quad H_3O^+)$$

carboxylic acid

In the base catalyzed process (with plenty of OH^- running around "loose" in the solution), hydroxide ion nucleophilically attacks the carbonyl carbon to form a negatively charged tetrahedral intermediate. Another OH^- ion deprotonates the OH group to produce a tetrahedral intermediate with a double negative charge. Loss of NH_2^- and its immediate protonation leaves the carboxylate ion and ammonia. (These two deprotonated species reflect the basic solution in which the reaction occurred.)

$$\underset{\longleftarrow}{\rightleftharpoons} \quad R - \overset{\overset{\displaystyle O}{\|}}{C} - O^- \quad + \quad NH_3$$

Please solve this problem:

- The production of a primary alcohol from a carboxylic acid requires:

    A. a reducing agent.
    B. potassium permanganate.
    C. Both A and B
    D. Neither A nor B

Problem solved:

A is correct. Production of an alcohol from carboxylic acid is a reduction reaction, which means that potassium permanganate, a strong oxidizing agent, would be most "unwelcome." Choices B and C, therefore, are wrong. A reducing agent *is* necessary.

The essence of the reaction is nucleophilic addition by a hydride ion to the carbonyl carbon. There then forms an aldehyde, and, on further reduction, an alcohol.

38.2 MASTERY APPLIED: PRACTICE PASSAGE AND QUESTIONS

Commonly used analgesic (pain-killing) agents include acetylsalicylic acid (aspirin), indomethacin, ibuprofen, and acetaminophen. The structure of each of these compounds is shown in Figure 1.

Acetylsalicylic acid is a derivative of salicylic acid, which is synthesized according to the Kolbe reaction, in which a phenol salt is treated with carbon dioxide. This results in the phenyl ring losing a hydrogen atom, which is then replaced by a carbonyl group, as shown in Figure 2. Aspirin is synthesized by reacting salicylic acid with the compound shown in Figure 3.

Aspirin, indomethacin, and ibuprofen have analgesic and anti-inflammatory properties. Therefore, they are often prescribed for pain that is due to inflammation, as in the case of arthritis. The anti-inflammatory effects are chiefly due to their inhibition of prostaglandin synthesis.

In some patients, acetylsalicylic acid, indomethacin, and ibuprofen cause gastric disturbance. In such patients, prolonged use may lead to a gastric ulcer. Some authorities believe that acetylsalicylic acid and indomethacin tend to cause such effects more frequently than ibuprofen. Acetaminophen tends not to produce such effects at all.

An investigator wishes to find an explanation for the adverse gastric effects of acetylsalicylic acid, indomethacin, and ibuprofen, and to explore the reasons for which acetaminophen seems to not produce such unwanted effects.

Experiment

From one hundred patients diagnosed with osteoarthritis, four groups of twenty-five are assembled and identified as Groups 1, 2, 3, and 4. Each group is treated daily with one of the analgesic agents described above: group 1 with aspirin, group 2 with indomethacin, group 3 with ibuprofen, and group 4 with acetaminophen. All subjects are evaluated biweekly for reports of pain relief and objective manifestations of reduced inflammation at previously inflamed joints. Results are shown in Table 1.

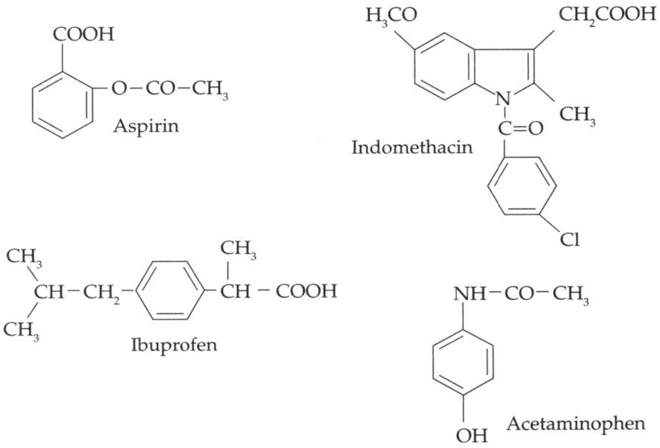

Figure 1

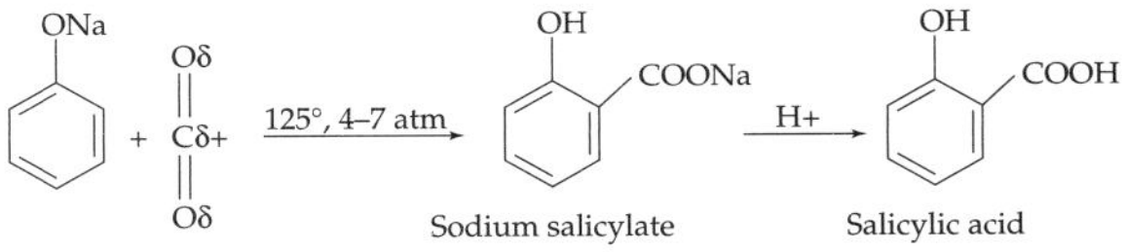

Figure 2

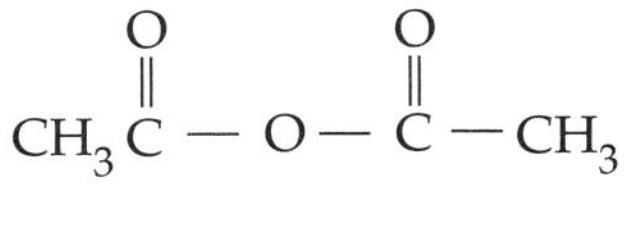

Figure 3

Group	Pain Relief	Reduced Inflammation
1	++	+
2	++	+
3	++	+
4	+	O

Key: ++ very significant   + significant
      O not significant

Table 1

1. The reaction in which aspirin is formed from salicylic acid most closely resembles:

   A. the conversion of an ester to a carboxylic acid.
   B. the conversion of a carboxylic acid to a primary alcohol.
   C. the conversion of a primary alcohol to an acid anhydride.
   D. the conversion of an acid anhydride to an ester.

2. Figure 1 and Table 1 indicate that acetaminophen differs from aspirin in that:

   I. it has no significant analgesic effect.
   II. it has no significant anti-inflammatory effect.
   III. it is not a carboxylic acid.

   A. I only
   B. I and II only
   C. II and III only
   D. I, II, and III

3. If, with respect to salicylic acid as depicted in Figure 2, it is found that the carboxyl group is more acidic than the hydroxyl group, the finding is most likely explained by the fact that:

   A. the carboxyl anion is stabilized by charge delocalization.
   B. the carboxyl anion is destabilized by charge delocalization.
   C. oxygen is highly electronegative.
   D. the aromatic ring is a resonance structure.

4. An investigator finds that the Kolbe intermediate that is the immediate precursor to salicylic acid, as depicted in Figure 2, has some analgesic effect, but that the effect is less than that of salicylic acid or aspirin. She tentatively hypothesizes that the analgesic effect is negatively correlated with higher pKa. Is the hypothesis plausible?

   A. No, because the precursor to salicylic acid is not acidic.
   B. No, because the data in Table 1 are inconsistent with the hypothesis that analgesic effect is related to acidity.
   C. Yes, because sodium salicylate and acetaminophen are likely to have lower pKa values than the other analgesics under investigation.
   D. Yes, because neither acetaminophen nor sodium salicylate is a carboxylic acid.

5. With respect to the four medications under study, information provided in Figure 1 and Table 1 give support to which of the following conclusions?

   I. Gastric disturbance is associated with acidity.
   II. Acidity is essential to anti-inflammatory effects.
   III. Anti-inflammatory effects and analgesia are unrelated.

   A. I only
   B. I and II only
   C. II and III only
   D. I and III only

6. If the investigator wished to determine whether acetaminophen is a relatively less effective pain reliever due to its failure to reduce inflammation, which of the following experimental procedures would be most advisable?

   A. Treat one group of osteoarthritic patients with acetaminophen alone, treat another group with acetaminophen and an anti-inflammatory that has no independent analgesic properties, and determine whether pain relief approximates that which is observed with the other three medications under study.
   B. Administer acetaminophen to two groups of patients, each with separate painful conditions that do not relate to inflammation, and determine whether the two groups differ as to the degree of pain relief they experience.
   C. Select four different animal species with four different forms of arthritis, treat each species with one of the four agents under study, and determine whether the acidic agents provide greater relief than acetaminophen.
   D. Prepare isomeric forms of the acidic agents under study and determine whether in some isomeric conformations the analgesic properties are preserved while the anti-inflammatory properties are lost.

38.2 MASTERY VERIFIED: ANSWERS AND EXPLANATIONS

1. **C is correct.** The passage tells us that aspirin is formed when salicylic acid is reacted with the compound shown in Figure 3. That compound is an acid anhydride. Salicylic acid is, of course, a carboxylic acid, but it carries an OH group so that in structural concept, it has the character also of a phenol. When an alcohol (or phenol) is reacted with an acid anhydride, an acyl transfer occurs and produces an ester. The aspirin molecule, acetylsalicylic acid, as shown in Figure 1 has an ester moiety where salicylic acid held the OH group. If we swallow hard and shut our eyes to the ring's COOH group, the process then resembles the reaction of an acid anhydride with an alcohol/phenol to produce an ester.

2. **C is correct.** Table 1 shows that patients treated with aspirin had a marked reduction in pain, and that those treated with acetaminophen had some significant reduction in their pain. Statement I, therefore, does not describe a difference between the two drugs. Table 1 also shows that aspirin produces a marked anti-inflammatory effect, but that acetaminophen does not. Therefore, statement II is accurate. Figure 1 shows that aspirin is a carboxylic acid (bearing a COOH group) but that acetaminophen is not. Statement III, therefore, is accurate. Since statements II and III are accurate and I is not, choice C is correct.

3. **A is correct.** The question asks only that you understand this vital principle: *The carboxyl anion RCOO⁻ has particular stability because it is a resonance structure.* Resonance is one means of producing charge delocalization. The negative charge with which the ion is "burdened" is shared between the two oxygen atoms bound to the carbonyl carbon (with the consequence that there is partial double bond character between the carbon atom and each of the oxygen atoms). Choice B is incorrect. Choice C is a true statement; oxygen *is* electronegative. That fact, however, would tend to promote the acidity of the OH group and would not explain the finding that the OH group showed less acidity than the COOH group. Choice D also makes a true statement: The aromatic ring is a resonance structure. But that fact does not enhance acidity of an aromatic carboxylic acid.

4. **D is correct.** Figure 1 demonstrates that acetaminophen is not a carboxylic acid; it does not conform to the prototypical structures RCOOH or ArCOOH. Sodium salicylate is a salt, not a carboxylic acid. It conforms to the structure ArCOONa, not ArCOOH. Choice A makes a correct statement, but is not relevant to the question. The fact that sodium salicylate's precursor is not an acid does not bear on the investigator's hypothesis. Choice B is incorrect. The data in Table 1 are consistent with the investigator's hypothesis. Among the medications tested, acetaminophen is the only one that is not an acid, and it shows the least degree of analgesic effect. Choice C is incorrect as well. Acetaminophen and sodium salicylate are not acids. They most likely have higher pKa values than the other substances under study.

5. **B is correct.** According to the passage, the only group of patients to be free of gastric disturbance was the one treated with acetaminophen, which, as shown in Figure 1, is the only one of the four tested agents that is not an acid. Statement I, therefore, represents a correct response. That same group of patients is the only group to show no significant reduction in inflammation. Statement II also reflects a correct response. Statement III is not justifiable. Acetaminophen seems to produce no anti-inflammatory effects and shows less analgesic effect than the other three agents. The data do not support the conclusion that the anti-inflammatory effects and analgesia are unrelated.

6. **A is correct.** This question requires you to apply logical reasoning in connection with experimental science. The question does not draw on any substantive knowledge concerning carboxylic acids. The investigator has observed (Table 1) that acetaminophen produces a smaller degree of pain relief than aspirin, indomethacin, and ibuprofen. She has noted also that acetaminophen is the only one of the four agents that does not produce anti-inflammatory effects. She postulates that the additional pain relief produced by the other three drugs might be a direct consequence of the fact that they have a separate anti-inflammatory effect.

In order to test her hypothesis, the researcher would like to administer an agent that is identical to acetaminophen except that it has an independent anti-inflammatory property If such an agent produces the level of pain relief associated with the other three agents, she will have support for her hypothesis. If it does not, she will not. In order to simulate an agent that is identical to acetaminophen but has a separate anti-inflammatory effect, the investigator might administer acetaminophen together with an anti-inflammatory agent that does not itself have an independent analgesic effect. She could then assess the level of pain relief it affords, precisely as described in choice A. Choices B, C, and D do not describe any processes logically connected to the investigator's objective. Unfortunately, answer choices like these attract students who assume that two experimental groups are better than one, that animal experiments are more "science-like" than others, or that creation of isomers is more in the nature of "real organic chemistry."

CHAPTER 39

AMINES, AMINO ACIDS, AND PROTEINS

39.1 MASTERY ACHIEVED

AMINES

"Amine" means a molecule in which nitrogen is bound to one, two, or three organic groups. Amines are derivatives of ammonia, NH_3, in which nitrogen is bound to three hydrogen atoms.

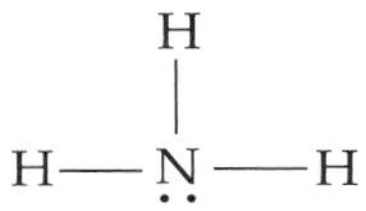

$$H - \underset{\underset{H}{|}}{\overset{\overset{H}{|}}{\underset{\bullet\bullet}{N}}} - H$$

Ammonia

Generically, amines are characterized as:

- RNH_2 or **primary amines**, meaning that the nitrogen atom is bound to *one* organic group and two hydrogen atoms;

- R_2NH, or **secondary amines**, meaning that the nitrogen atom is bound to *two* organic groups and one hydrogen atom; and

- R_3N, or **tertiary amines**, meaning that the nitrogen atom is bound to *three* organic groups and no hydrogen atoms.

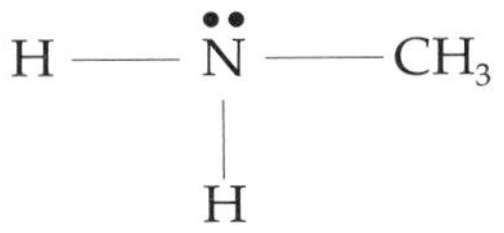

$$H - \overset{\bullet\bullet}{\underset{\underset{H}{|}}{N}} - CH_3 \qquad C_2H_5 - \overset{\bullet\bullet}{\underset{\underset{H}{|}}{N}} - CH_3$$

1° Amine 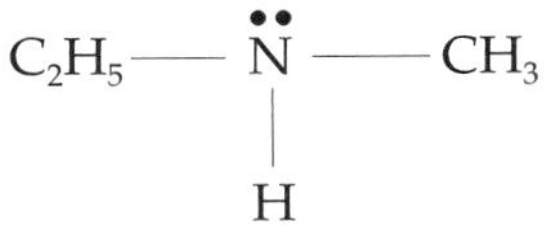   2° Amine

$$C_2H_5 - \overset{\bullet\bullet}{\underset{\underset{C_2H_5}{|}}{N}} - \text{(phenyl)}$$

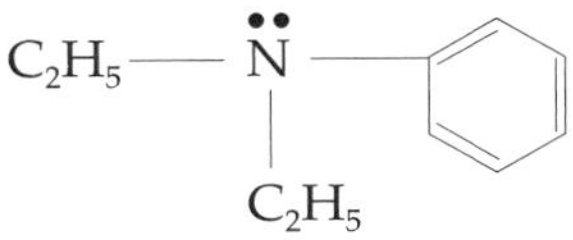

3° Amine

"Quarternary ammonium salt" refers to a nitrogen atom bound to four groups (and no hydrogen atoms) meaning that it will carry a positive charge (and thus be associated with a compensating anion).

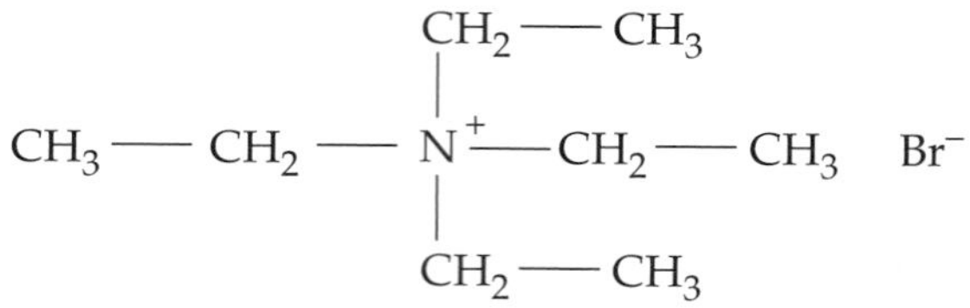

$$CH_2 \text{---} CH_3$$
$$|$$
$$CH_3 \text{---} CH_2 \text{---} \overset{+}{N} \text{---} CH_2 \text{---} CH_3 \quad Br^-$$
$$|$$
$$CH_2 \text{---} CH_3$$

Tetraethyl ammonium bromide
(quaternary ammonium salt)

"Amino group" means the substituent NH_2 which appears in a primary amine. It may be bound to an aromatic ring or other nonaromatic cyclic structure, giving primary amines like these (in which the "R" groups happen to be cyclohexane and benzene):

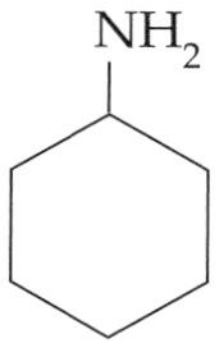

$$NH_2 \qquad\qquad\qquad NH_2$$

Cyclohexylamine

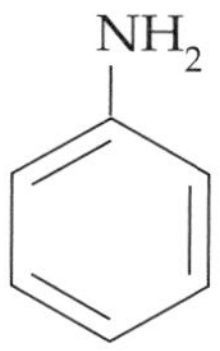

Aniline
(an aromatic amine)

The amino group may also sit as a substituent on noncyclic molecules of familiar categories, like alcohols, and carboxylic acids (in which case the molecular name normally characterizes the amino group *as* a substituent).

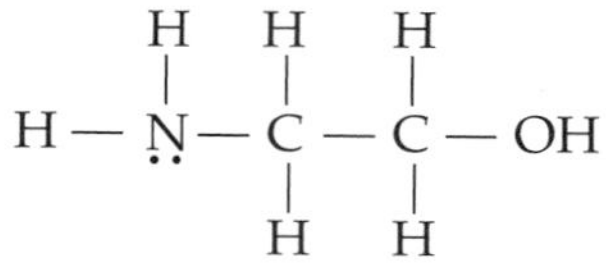

$$\begin{array}{ccc} H & H & H \\ | & | & | \\ H \text{---} \underset{\cdot\cdot}{N} \text{---} C & \text{---} C & \text{---} OH \\ & | & | \\ & H & H \end{array}$$

2–Aminoethanol

$$\begin{array}{cccc} H & H & H & O \\ | & | & | & \| \\ H \text{---} \underset{\cdot\cdot}{N} \text{---} C & \text{---} C & \text{---} C & \text{---} OH \\ & | & | & \\ & H & H & \end{array}$$

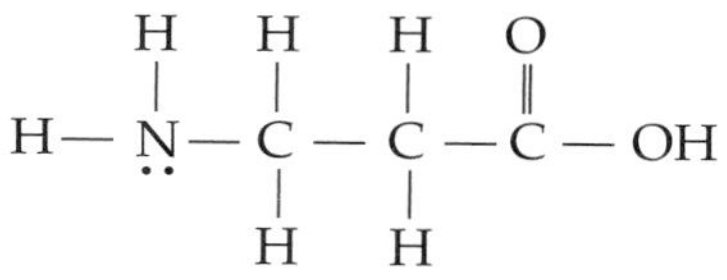

3–Aminopropanoic acid

"Cyclic Amine" (to be distinguished from cyclohexylamine and benzylamine as shown above) are molecules in which a nitrogen atom is integrated within a cyclic structure:

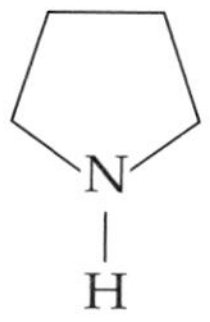

Pyrrolidine

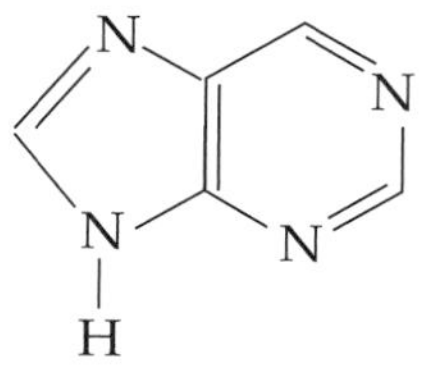

Purine

Cyclic amines

Naming Primary Amines

By and large, we name *primary amines* by identifying the longest continuous carbon chain, beginning at the end closest to the amino group. With the carbons thus numbered, the name describes from left to right:

(1) the sites and nature of branches,

(2) the site of the amino group,

(3) a prefix corresponding to length of the longest continuous carbon chain, and

(4) the amine suffix ("-amine").

Ethylamine
(1 amine)

2– Methyl-1-propylamine
(1 amine)

2– Methyl-2-propylamine
(1 amine)

Physical Properties: Boiling Points, Water Solubility, and Hydrogen Bonding

Amines are polar molecules because nitrogen has a higher electronegativity than hydrogen and most other alkyl or aryl substituents. The polarity, together with an unshared electron pair on the nitrogen atom, means, among other things, that primary and secondary amine molecules exhibit hydrogen bonding among themselves. Tertiary amines do not because they bear no hydrogen atoms bound directly to the nitrogen atom (see **Chapter 33**).

```
        H                                    R
        |                                    |
   R — N — H                            H — N — R
       ··    H                              ··    R
             |                                    |
        H — N — R                            H — N — R
        ··                                   ··
        |                                         ··
   R — N — H                             R — N — H
        ··                                    |
                                              R
```

Amines have boiling points higher than alkanes of similar molecular weight, but not as high as alcohols. Tertiary amine molecules, which do not form hydrogen bonds among themselves, have lower boiling points than primary and secondary amines of similar molecular weight.

All three classes of amines, however—primary, secondary, and tertiary—can form hydrogen bonds with water. For that reason, all of the relatively "small" amines are water soluble. Among primary amines, for example, water solubility begins to wane when the parent alkyl compound (longest carbon chain) is six carbons or longer.

```
        ·O·                          R
       /    \                        |
      H      H ---------- :N — R
                                     |
                                     R


        ·O·                          H
       /    \                        |
      H      H ---------- :N — R
                                     |
                                     R


        ·O·                          H
       /    \                        |
      H      H ---------- :N — H
                                     |
                                     R
```

Basicity of Amines

An ammonia (NH_3) molecule is, of course, a base.

$$NH_3 \; + \; H_2O \; \rightleftharpoons \; NH_4^+ \; + \; OH^-$$

Amines are bases, too. They are derivatives of ammonia, in which one or more of ammonia's three hydrogen atoms are replaced by substituents. Those substituents have inductive effects that raise or lower the amine's basicity (analogous, in this way, to inductive effects on the acidity of alcohols as described in **Chapter 36**).

Please solve this problem:

- Do two molecules of the same tertiary amine exhibit hydrogen bonding between themselves?

  A. Yes, because the molecules are polar.
  B. Yes, because the molecules are nonpolar.
  C. No, because the molecules have no hydrogen atoms bound to their central nitrogen atoms.
  D. No, because the only molecule to exhibit hydrogen bonding with a second, identical molecule is water.

Problem solved:

C is correct. Hydrogen bonding occurs between a molecule that bears a partially positive hydrogen atom and an unshared electron pair that belongs to some other molecule. The process occurs between two molecules of ammonia, two molecules of a primary amine, and two molecules of a secondary amine. Each of those molecules has at least one hydrogen atom that can interact with the unshared electron pair on the nitrogen atom of a second identical molecule. A tertiary amine, on the other hand, is one in which all three hydrogen atoms associated with ammonia are replaced by alkyl or aryl substituents. The resulting molecule has no hydrogen atoms to its central nitrogen atom and so cannot exhibit hydrogen bonding. Choice A reflects, in part, a true statement. A tertiary amine is polar, but that does not mean it undergoes hydrogen bonding. Choice B reflects a false statement because it characterizes an amine as nonpolar. Choice D is also incorrect. While one water molecule undergoes hydrogen bonding with a second water molecule, the word "only" falsifies the choice. Two identical molecules of alcohol will hydrogen bond as will two molecules of carboxylic acid.

Please solve this problem:

- What will most likely be the effect of adding an amine to water?

  A. Reduce pH
  B. Increase pOH
  C. Both A and B
  D. Neither A nor B

Problem solved:

D is correct. Like ammonia itself, amines are basic. The fact that their nitrogen atom carries a lone pair of electrons allows them easily to donate an electron pair. In aqueous solution, therefore, an amine molecule has a tendency to take up a proton, thereby decreasing the solution's hydrogen ion concentration (increasing pH) and increasing the solution's hydroxide ion (OH^-) concentration (decreasing pOH). Choices A and B are both false.

Please solve this problem:

- Between compound 1 and compound 2, shown below, in an aqueous solution, the more basic is:

Compound 1   Compound 2

- **A.** compound 1, because its benzene ring carries only one substituent.
- **B.** compound 1, because an aromatic ring exhibits resonance stabilization.
- **C.** compound 1, because on compound 2, the substituent meta to the amino inductively reduces the N's ability to donate its electrons.
- **D.** compound 2, because in aqueous solution a primary amine is more basic than a secondary amine.

Problem solved:

C is correct. After the word "because," choices A, B, and D are all true statements. None of these choices, however, correctly answers the question. It is true that compound 1 carries only one substituent, but that does not make it more basic than compound 2. An aromatic ring does exhibit resonance stabilization, but that does not make compound 1 more basic than compound 2. In aqueous solution, a primary amine is more basic than a secondary amine because of the dual hydrogen bonding available to the primary amine. But compound 2 is not a secondary amine, so the statement made in choice D is irrelevant. Choice C is correct because the NO_2 substituent (meta to the NH_2 group) is an electron withdrawer. That makes the N less nucleophilic and renders compound 2 less basic than compound 1.

Please solve this problem:

- A primary amine bearing an ethyl group is likely to be:

- **A.** more acidic than hydrochloric acid.
- **B.** more acidic than acetic acid.
- **C.** more basic than ammonia.
- **D.** more basic than sodium hydroxide.

Problem solved:

C is correct. Ammonia is a weak base and, in an aqueous solution, does not ionize completely. Sodium hydroxide, on the other hand, is a strong base. In an aqueous solution, it does ionize completely. An amine in which a single hydrogen atom is replaced by an alkyl group (ethyl in this case) is also a weak base, but tends to be more basic than ammonia (because of the alkyl group's electron releasing effect). Choice A suggests that an amine is a strong acid, and choice B raises the possibility that an amine is a weak acid. But these statements are false. Choice D suggests that an amine is a strong base. That too is false.

AMINO ACIDS

For the MCAT, the most important ammonia derivative is the alpha amino acid, generically depicted like this:

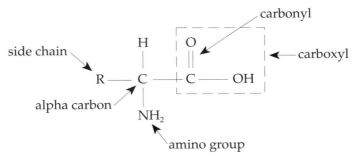

The NH_2 moiety is, of course, the amino group. The COOH moiety is the carboxyl group (see **Chapter 38**). Note in the picture above that the amino group is located on the carbon "next door" to the carboxyl carbon. That "next door" carbon is the **alpha carbon**, and the location of the amino group on the alpha carbon makes for an alpha amino acid. Alpha amino acids are the amino acids of importance to the MCAT (and, generally, to biological systems). The R group represents the **side chain** and is the molecule's variable portion; it makes each amino acid distinct from every other.

Chirality of Amino Acids

Chirality, the chiral center, and the associated phenomena of stereoisomers are addressed in **Chapter 34**. For most biologically significant amino acids, the alpha carbon is chiral; that is, it bears four different substituents: (1) the side chain (R), (2) the amino group, (3) the carboxyl (COOH) group, and (4) a hydrogen atom.

The amino acid glycine is an exception. Its side chain is a lone hydrogen atom. Its alpha carbon, therefore, carries two hydrogen atoms (plus a carboxyl and amino group).

$$H_2N - \overset{\overset{\displaystyle H}{|}}{\underset{\underset{\displaystyle H}{|}}{C}} - C \overset{\displaystyle O}{\underset{\displaystyle OH}{<}}$$

Glycine

Since there are two Hs attached, glycine's alpha carbon is not chiral.

Please solve this problem:

- Most biologically significant amino acids exhibit:

    A. enantiomerism.
    B. chirality.
    C. Both A and B
    D. Neither A nor B

Problem solved:

C is correct. The text notes that for most biologically significant amino acids, the alpha carbon is chiral, and the molecule itself as chiral as well. All chiral molecules exhibit enantiomerism; that is, none is superimposable on the molecule that represents its mirror image (see **Chapter 34**). Choices A and B both make accurate statements.

Please solve this problem:

- An amino acid in which the amino group is bound to the carbon atom two spaces removed from the carboxyl carbon is not truly:

    A. an acid.
    B. an alpha amino acid.
    C. covalently bound.
    D. a derivative of ammonia.

Problem solved:

B is correct. Choices A, C, and D make false statements. All amino acids are acids due to the presence of the COOH group. All are covalently bound, and all are derivatives of ammonia. The term "alpha amino acid" that appears in choice B applies to every amino acid in which the amino group (NH_2) is bound to the alpha carbon. If the amino group is bound elsewhere, then the amino acid is not an alpha amino acid. Most amino acids of biological (and MCAT) importance are alpha amino acids.

Please solve this problem:

- Each alpha amino acid is given its own identity by:

    A. placement of the carboxyl group relative to the amino group.
    B. variability of the R group.
    C. the presence or absence of a hydrogen atom bound to the alpha carbon.
    D. the orientation of the N-H bonds within the amino group.

Problem solved:

B is correct. In alpha amino acids, the alpha carbon carries an amino group (NH_2), a hydrogen atom, and a carboxyl group (COOH). Amino acids differ from one another as to the fourth substituent bound to the alpha carbon. That substituent is known, generically, as the R group and affords each amino acid its own identity. For glycine, the R group is a single hydrogen atom. For the amino acid serine, on the other hand, the R group is CH_2OH. For threonine, it is CH_3CHOH, and for valine it is $CH(CH_3)_2$.

Please solve this problem:

- Most alpha amino acids do NOT:

    A. exhibit stereoisomerism.
    B. tend to generate a carboxylate anion in a basic environment.
    C. exist as dextrorotatory and levorotatory isomers.
    D. show optical inactivity.

Problem solved:

D is correct. Choices A, B, and C make true statements and so, for this question, are incorrect. As noted in the text, most biologically significant amino acids are alpha amino acids, and most of these are chiral. Chiral molecules exist as enantiomers. For any pair of enantiomers one member is the (+) isomer and the other is the (–) isomer. Both are optically active. Choice D, which refers to optical inactivity, is false, and for this question, that makes choice d correct.

Configuration of Amino Acids as "L" and "D"

By convention we often draw amino acids by Fischer projection, with the carboxyl group attached to the "top" of the alpha carbon and the R group attached at the "bottom." That means the amino group and hydrogen atom must be on right and left or left and right sides, respectively. When we draw the amino group to the left, then (according to conventions surrounding the Fischer projection and certain understandings relating to the structural relationship between amino acids and glyceraldehyde) we have drawn what is called an **L-amino acid** as opposed to a **D-amino acid** (in which the amino group appears on the right).

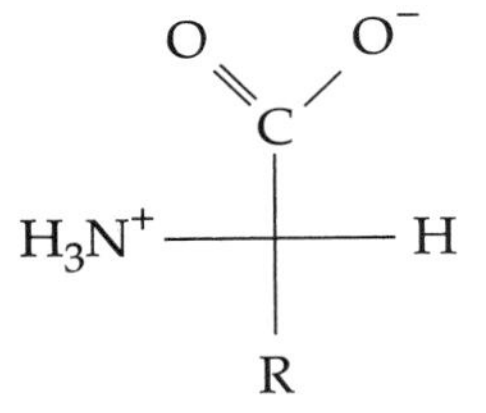

L–amino acid 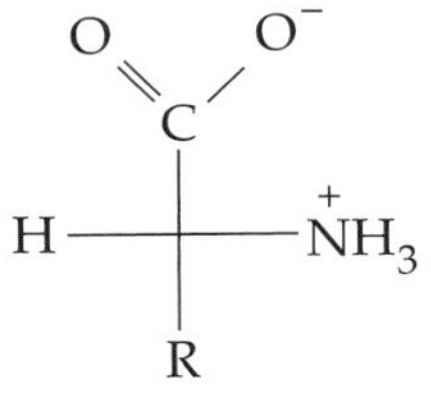   D–amino acid

Now, the designations "L" and "D" do **NOT** mean (–) and (+) or "S" and "R." They represent yet another classification of stereoconfiguration whose conceptual origin is not relevant to the MCAT.

But the following *is* relevant to the MCAT:

(1) All animal amino acids are of the "L" type.

(2) When you see an amino acid depicted by standard Fischer projection, with the amino group on the left and the hydrogen atom on the right, you're looking at an "L" amino acid.

(3) The designation "L" amino acid does *not* mean that the molecule is levorotatory. By itself, it means nothing about the direction in which it rotates polarized light (just as the "R" and "S" designations by themselves mean nothing about the direction of polarized light rotation).

Classification of Amino Acids as Neutral, Basic, and Acidic

We classify amino acids in terms of common characteristics associated with side chains. As already noted, every amino acid carries one carboxyl group and one amino group bound to the alpha carbon. But it is also possible that the side chain itself (also bound to the alpha carbon) might carry *its own* carboxyl group or basic group. Look, for example, at this amino acid, called aspartic acid:

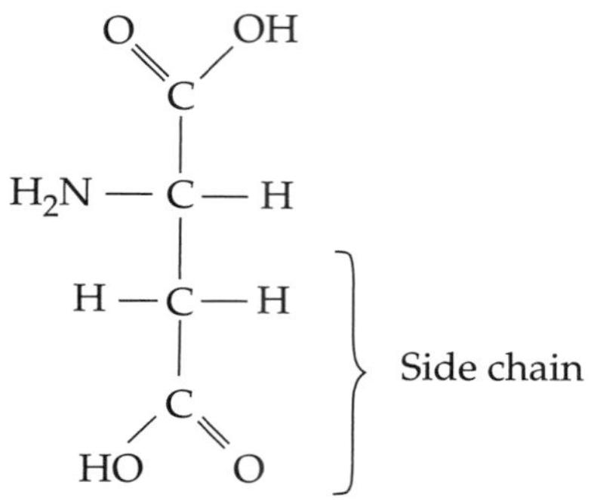

Aspartic acid

It has the "usual" carboxyl group on the alpha carbon and also has a carboxyl group on its side chain. Because of the "extra" carboxyl group, the one located on the side chain, we say that aspartic acid is an **acidic amino acid.**

Look, now at lysine:

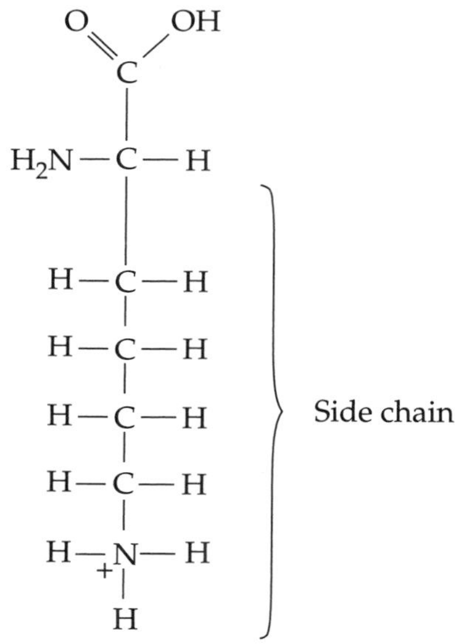

Lysine

It has the "usual" amino group on the alpha carbon and also an "extra" amino group on its side chain. Because of this "extra" amino group (a basic group), we say that lysine is a **basic amino acid.**

Amino acids whose side chains have neither an "extra" acidic or basic group are said to be **neutral amino acids.** (The two amino acids asparagine and glutamine have on their side chains an amino group *bound to a carbonyl carbon.* These two amino acids are not "basic" amino acids despite the appearance of the amino group. They are neutral amino acids.)

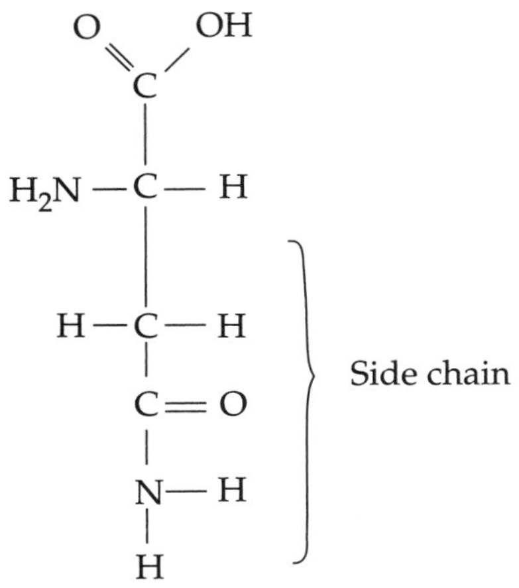

Asparagine

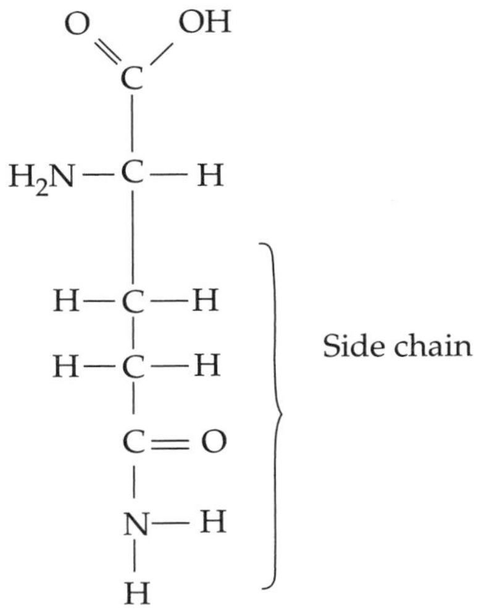

Glutamine

THE SULFUR SIDE CHAINS

Three amino acids normally encountered in biological systems contain sulfur in their side chains. They are methionine, cysteine, and cystine. Cystine is formed when two molecules of cysteine are linked by a **disulfide bridge.** All three of these sulfur-containing amino acids belong to the "neutral" category.

The L-amino acids most significant to animal systems are listed as follows, and they might find their way on to the MCAT in some context or other. There is no reason to offer a formalized "table" describing names and structures. It will burden you with a feeling that you must memorize its contents when, in fact, you shouldn't. In the name of "completeness," however we'll give you the list.

- The neutral L alpha amino acids are: glycine, alanine, valine, leucine, isoleucine, phenylalanine, asparagine, glutamine, tryptophan, proline, serine, threonine, tyrosine, hydroxyproline, cysteine, cystine, and methionine.

- The acidic species are aspartic acid and glutamic acid.

- The basic ones are lysine, arginine, and histidine.

Now *do not* memorize that, but know that there are "acidic" and "basic" amino acids, meaning, respectively, those whose side chains carry a carboxyl group or a basic group (which might or might not be another amino group).

Please solve this problem:

- If an amino acid carries a carboxyl group on its side chain, it belongs to what category of amino acids?

  A. Basic
  B. Acidic
  C. Polar
  D. Nonpolar

Problem solved:

B is correct. All amino acids carry one carboxyl group, which is why they're called "acids." Some amino acids have a second carboxyl group on their side chains. Those are *acidic* amino acids.

Please solve this problem:

- Which of the following amino acids contains sulfur in its side chain?

    A. Cysteine
    B. Cystine
    C. Both A and B
    D. Neither A nor B

Problem solved:

C is correct. Cystine and cysteine both contain sulfur in their side chains. Cyst<u>ine</u> is composed of two cyst<u>eine</u> molecules, linked by a disulfide bridge, as illustrated in the text.

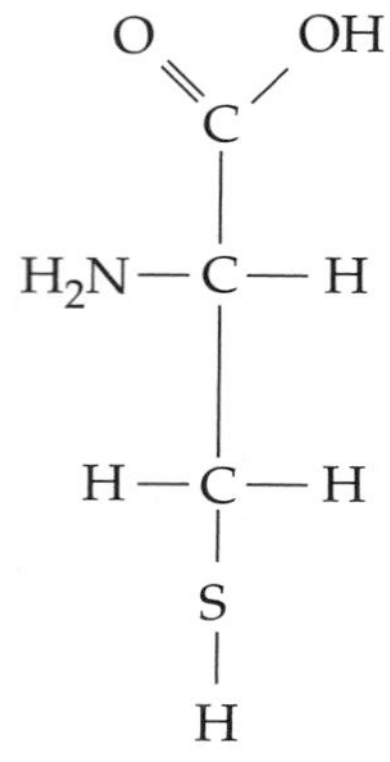

Cysteine

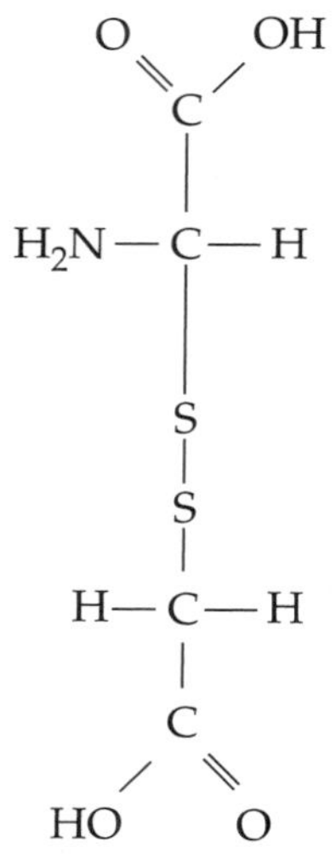

Cystine

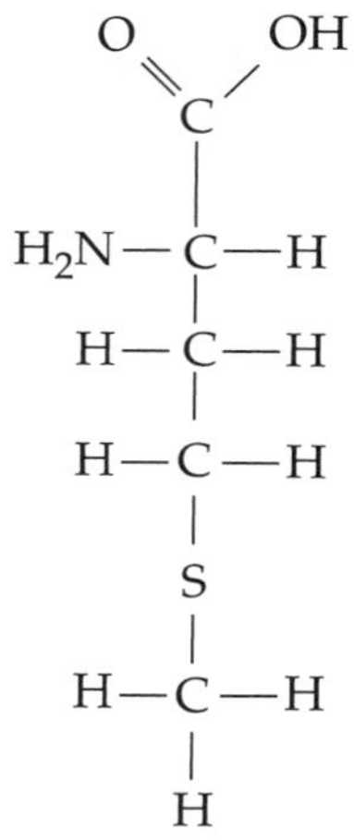

Methionine

Amino Acids as Zwitterions: Dipolarity and Isoelectric Point

You now know that an amino acid drawn in "pure" "pristine" form carries both an acidic COOH group and a basic NH_2 group. A basic medium (high pH) tends to strip the COOH group of a proton and turn it into a negatively charged carboxylate moiety. An acidic medium tends to force a proton onto the NH_2 group and create a positively charged NH_3^+ group.

Different amino acids differ as to just *how* acidic they are at their COOH "end" and just *how* basic they are at their NH_2 end. And, for every amino acid, there is *some* "compromise" pH, called **isoelectric point,** at which the COOH group is deprotonated, turning it to COO^-, and the NH_2 group is protonated, turning it to NH_3^+. When an amino acid sits in a medium whose pH is equal to its **isoelectric point,** it is negatively charged at its carboxylate "end" and positively charged at its amino "end." In that circumstance, we say the amino acid exists as a **zwitterion,** also called **dipolar ion,** meaning, simply, that it is positively charged at one spot and negatively charged at another.

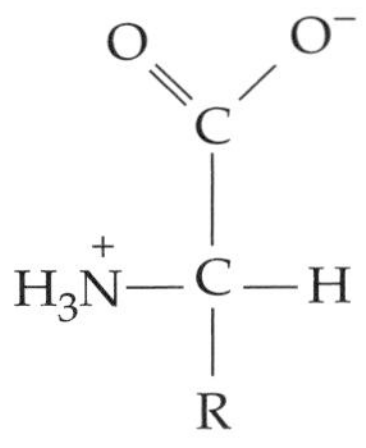

O=C—O⁻

H₃N⁺—C—H

R

Zwitterion / dipolar ion

Now, think about Le Chatelier's principle, especially as it affects acid/base dynamics (see **Chapter 16**). When an amino acid "sits" in a pH *below* (more acidic than) its isoelectric point, the COO⁻ carboxylate ion tends to "keep" its proton and the NH₂ group acquires one. The resulting species carries COOH and NH₃⁺, thus bearing a net positive charge. Conversely, when an amino acid "sits" in a pH *above* (less acidic than) its isoelectric point, the NH₂ remains unprotonated and COOH deprotonates. The molecule carries NH₂ and COO⁻, thus bearing a net *negative* charge.

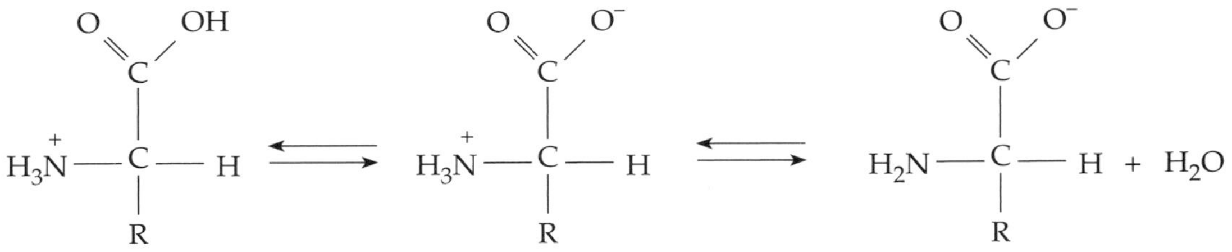

| low pH: net positive charge | Isoelectric point | high pH: net negative charge |

Please solve this problem:

- At very low pH, valine is likely to bear:

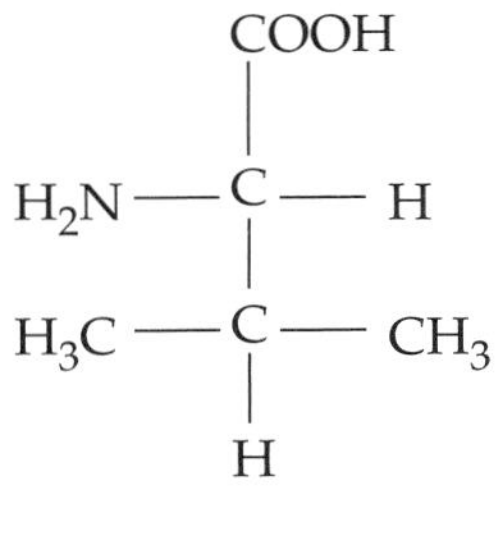

COOH

H₂N—C—H

H₃C—C—CH₃

H

Valine

A. a net positive charge.
B. a net negative charge.
C. no net charge.
D. a net double negative charge.

Problem solved:

A is correct. Valine is a "neutral" amino acid, meaning it carries no "extra" carboxyl group or basic group on its side chain. But, like any other ordinary amino acid, it has carboxyl and amino groups bound to its alpha carbon. At its isoelectric point, valine exists almost exclusively in zwitterion/dipolar ion form, having undergone what we might consider an internal acid-base interaction—the proton from the COOH group having been lost and used to protonate the NH_2 group. In a very acidic medium, proton concentration is high. The COOH group will not lose a proton, but the amino group will acquire one to become NH_3^+. The molecule will bear a net positive charge.

Please solve this problem:

- At very basic pH, far above its isoelectric point, is phenylalanine likely to carry a net positive charge?

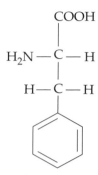

Phenylalanine

A. Yes, because phenylalanine is an acidic amino acid.
B. Yes, because phenylalanine is a basic amino acid.
C. No, because phenylalanine contains an aromatic component.
D. No, because the molecule will likely carry an unprotonated alpha amino group.

Problem solved:

D is correct. Choices A and B make false statements. Phenylalanine carries no "extra" carboxyl or basic group on its side chain. After the word "no," choice C makes a true statement that does not, however, explain the answer. In a pH far above its isoelectric point, phenylalanine, as any other amino acid, will carry a carboxylate anion (COO^-) and, just as choice C states, an unprotonated amino (NH_2) group. The molecule's net charge will be *negative*, not positive.

Please solve this problem:

- At its isoelectric point, is the amino acid glycine likely to carry a net charge?

A. Yes, because for glycine, the side chain is composed of only a single hydrogen atom.
B. Yes, because the isoelectric point is that point at which any amino acid carries its characteristic net charge, positive or negative.
C. No, because acidic and amino groups will be deprotonated and protonated, respectively.
D. No, because net charge will be carried only on those amino acids containing acidic or basic groups on their side chains.

Problem solved:

C is correct. Choices B and D are false. The isoelectric point has no meaning such as that suggested by choice B. And, contrary to choice D, isoelectric points are not by any means limited to acidic and basic amino acids. Any "ordinary" amino acid has an isoelectric point. After the word "yes" (which is wrong), choice A makes a true statement that is wholly irrelevant to the question. At its isoelectric point, glycine, as any other amino acid, will carry no net charge because the isoelectric point is that pH at which the carboxyl group is in its deprototaned anionic (COO^-) form, and the amino group is in its protonated cationic NH_3^+ form. For any amino acid, the isoelectric point is that pH that is not so acidic as to leave the carboxyl group protonated, and not so basic as to leave the amino group unprotonated. Rather, it's the pH that is "just right" for zwitterion formation.

AMINO ACIDS AS AMPHOTERIC SPECIES

Since an amino acid is an acid and a base (depending on ambient pH), it can, depending on environment and reaction medium, react as either. That fact groups amino acids among chemistry's amphoteric species, which react as acids *or* bases.

Relative Acidity of Carboxyl and Amino Groups

At a pH well below its isoelectric point, an amino acid carries a positive charge on its amino group and a proton on its carboxyl group. If ambient pH is raised (by the addition of base, for example), both the carboxyl group and the protonated amino group will tend to <u>de</u>protonate so that the carboxyl group acquires a negative charge ($COOH \rightarrow COO^-$) and the amino group becomes neutral. ($NH_3^+ \rightarrow NH_2$). This has already been established. But now, for the MCAT, know this: *For any alpha amino acid, the carboxyl group is more acidic than the protonated amino group.* Suppose an amino acid is "sitting around" in solution, with both its carboxyl and amino groups protonated:

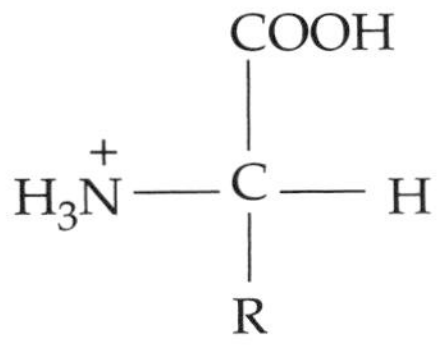

$$H_3\overset{+}{N} - \underset{\underset{R}{|}}{\overset{\overset{COOH}{|}}{C}} - H$$

Now suppose pH is raised (acidity is reduced) bit by bit. The carboxyl group will deprotonate before the amino group does. Why? Because, as was just stated, the protonated carboxyl group is more acidic than the protonated amino group, meaning that between the two groups, the carboxyl group is more "ready and willing" to give up its proton. Conversely, if an amino acid is "sitting around" in solution with both carboxyl and amino groups *de*protonated, and pH is lowered (acidity is <u>in</u>creased) bit by bit, the amino group will acquire a proton before the carboxyl group. Why? For the same reason as before. The carboxyl group, being more acidic then the amino group is also less basic than the amino group as well. Between the two groups, the amino group will accept a proton before the carboxylate group.

Please solve this problem:

- For a given alpha amino acid, X, the isoelectric point is 5.6. At pH 5.0, both the carboxyl group and the amino group are protonated, and the species carries a net positive charge. The pH is raised slowly until, finally, it carries a net *negative* charge. During the period in which pH increases:

    A. the carboxyl group will deprotonate first, and the ammonium group will deprotonate thereafter.
    B. the ammonium group will deprotonate first, and the carboxyl group will deprotonate thereafter.
    C. the carboxyl and ammonium groups will protonate simultaneously, as soon as pH reaches the isoelectric point.
    D. neither the ammonium group nor the carboxyl group will deprotonate, and negative charge will result from loss of a proton derived from the hydrogen atom independently bound to the alpha carbon.

Problem solved:

A is correct. Choices B, C, and D make false statements. The ammonium group is less acidic than the carboxyl group and will deprotonate *after* the carboxyl group. For that same reason, the two groups will not deprotonate simultaneously. Both the carboxyl group and the ammonium group *will* deprotonate—in that order—which makes choice D wrong as well. We are told that the molecule begins with a net positive charge, meaning that both carboxyl and ammonium groups are protonated. We are also told that pH will be raised sufficiently to provide the molecule with a net *negative* charge, which means that both the COOH and NH_3^+ group must <u>de</u>protonate. Choice A is right for the same reasons that choices B, C, and D are wrong. *The carboxyl group is more acidic than the ammonium group.* As pH is raised, it first will deprotonate, and the ammonium group will do so thereafter. (Regarding choice C, it is true that pH will have to pass through the isoelectric point, a point at which the COOH group will have deprotonated and the ammonium group will not yet have done so, giving the molecule, at *that* time, a net charge of zero.)

Please solve this problem:

- For a given alpha amino acid, X, the isoelectric point is 5.2. At pH 5.8, both the carboxyl group and the amino group are deprotonated and the species carries a net negative charge. The pH is then lowered slowly until, finally, the species carries a net *positive charge*. During the period in which pH falls:

   A. the carboxylate group will protonate first, and the amino group will protonate thereafter.

   B. the amino group will protonate first, and the carboxylate group will protonate thereafter.

   C. the amino and carboxyl groups will protonate simultaneously, as soon as pH reaches the isoelectric point.

   D. neither the amino group nor the carboxyl group will deprotonate, and positive charge will result from loss of a hydride ion derived from the hydrogen atom independently bound to the alpha carbon.

Problem solved:

B is correct. This question is the "flip side" of the previous one. We begin with an alpha amino acid carrying a net negative charge. Why? Because pH is above the isoelectric point, meaning that both carboxyl and amino groups are deprotonated. (It is the deprotonated carboxyl group that creates the negative charge. The deprotonated amino group, NH_2, is neutral.) As pH is to be lowered (acidity <u>in</u>creased), the amino group being the more basic of the two functional groups, first acquires a proton after which the carboxylate group acquires a proton.

FORMATION OF PROTEINS FROM AMINO ACIDS

Two alpha amino acids may join by formation of a **peptide bond,** through a **dehydration synthesis,** in which the OH group from the carboxyl terminus of one molecule and a hydrogen ion from the amino group of the other are removed to form a molecule of water. A peptide bond results between the carbonyl carbon of the first amino acid and the amino nitrogen of the second.

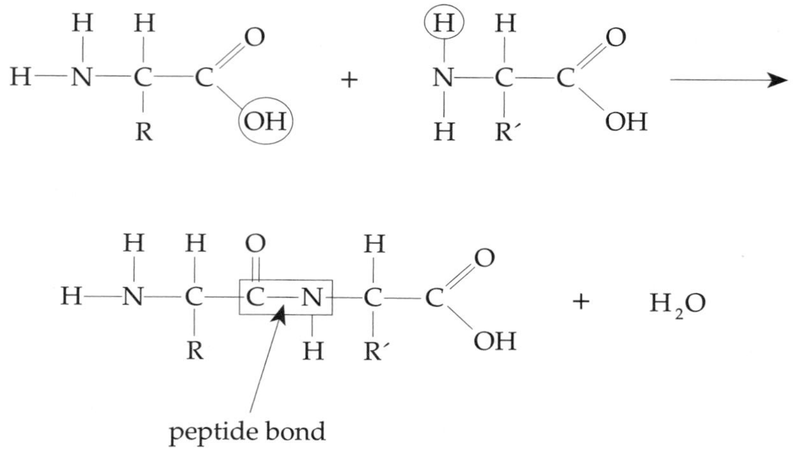

Two amino acids thus linked are a dipeptide. The **dipeptide** might, in turn, form additional peptide bonds with other amino acids to produce a long chain of peptides called a polypeptide. (A *long* polypeptide, or combination of polypeptides bound together by cross-links, is a protein.) The amino acid constituents of a polypeptide are sometimes called **amino acid residues,** which means, simply, amino acid constituent.

Hydrolysis breaks peptide bonds, and might be pictured as a reversal of dehydration synthesis. In the hydrolytic process, a molecule of water is interposed within a peptide bond. The OH moiety bonds to the carbonyl carbon of one amino acid and the hydrogen ion bonds to the nitrogen atom of another.

Please solve this problem:

- The formation of a protein from its constituent amino acids involves:

    A. multiple episodes of hydrolysis.
    B. dehydration synthesis.
    C. Both A and B
    D. Neither A nor B

Problem solved:

B is correct. As noted in the text, the binding of two amino acids to make a dipeptide involves a dehydration synthesis in which a molecule of water is removed, and the nitrogen terminus of one amino acid is bound to the carbonyl carbon of another. The manufacture of a protein (one or more polypeptides) involves repetition of the process. Choice A describes hydrolysis, the process through which peptide bonds are *broken,* not formed.

PROTEINS

Structure

"Protein" means a long polypeptide or combination of polypeptides bound together by cross-links. "Protein" and "polypeptide," therefore, are not quite synonymous because some proteins, as just stated, comprise more than one polypeptide.

Proteins are conceived in terms of their primary structure, secondary structure, tertiary structure, and quarternary structure.

PRIMARY AND SECONDARY STRUCTURES

Primary structure refers to the sequence of amino acids that make up the protein. To describe a protein's primary structure is to list, in sequence, the amino acids that compose it. Amino acids in primary structure are by convention listed from the N-terminus (the end of the protein with a free -NH$_2$ group) to the C-terminus (the end of a free -COOH group). **Secondary structure** refers to *local*, segmental conformations of the protein's "backbone" of NH and CO groups. (The regular repeating peptide bond sequence does not include the side chain.) Secondary structure most often involves the **alpha helix,** or a **β-pleated sheet.**

The alpha helix is a right-handed spiral, five angstroms wide. Each turn of the helix embodies 3.6 amino acids, each amino acid being 1.5 angstroms from the next. For the MCAT, these *numbers* are not important. Rather, you should be familiar with the general conformation of a helix as a form of secondary structure. On each amino acid within the alpha helix, the oxygen of the alpha carboxyl group makes a hydrogen bond to a proton bonded to a nitrogen atom four residues away.

The β-pleated sheet is a second form of secondary structure. Polypeptide chains align themselves in parallel. Hydrogen bonds form between NH and CO groups on amino acid residues relatively far apart from one another, and/or between separate polypeptide chains. The side chains ("R" component) extend above or below the plane of the sheet.

In a **parallel β-pleated sheet,** adjacent polypeptide chains run in the same direction (N to C and N to C), and in an **anti-parallel β-pleated,** adjacent polypeptide chains run in opposite directions (N to C vs. C to N).

β-pleated sheet shown in flat projection

TERTIARY AND QUARTERNARY STRUCTURES

Tertiary structure refers to the way in which interactions between (a) side chains distant from one another and (b) solvent cause the protein molecule to fold. Normally (with the universe, as always tending toward lowest energy) the folding characteristic of tertiary structure will cause nonpolar ("hydrophobic") side chains to "hide" in the interior of the structure, away from the aqueous solvent, with the polar ("hydrophilic") side chains exposing themselves at the surface, in contact *with* the aqueous solvent and curling in *three dimensions*. The result, frequently, is a **globular protein**:

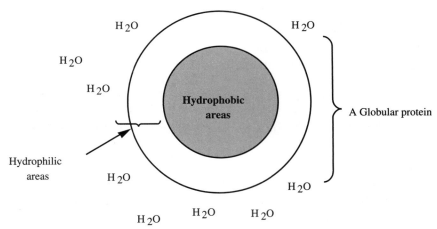

A common occurrence in tertiary structure is the formation of disulfide bonds between two cysteine residues that are in close spatial proximity. These bonds are not required for tertiary struture, but often help to stabilize the three-dimensional structure.

Quarternary structure refers only to proteins composed of more than one polypeptide chain. To refer to such a protein's quarternary structure is to refer to the way its several polypeptide chains form bonds and cross-links between and among its separate polypeptides.

Please solve this problem:

- A biochemist subjects a protein to a degradation process discovers both the identity of the amino acids that compose it and the sequence in which they are arranged. He has thus discovered the protein's:

    A. primary structure.
    B. secondary structure.
    C. tertiary structure.
    D. quarternary structure.

Problem solved:

A is correct. The question asks only that you understand the meaning of the term "primary structure" as it relates to a protein. It refers to the identity and sequence of the amino acids that compose it.

Please solve this problem:

- A biochemist works with protein Y that is composed of several polypeptide chains. He studies and ascertains the manner in which the several polypeptides are folded and linked. He has thus discovered the protein's:

  A. primary structure.
  B. secondary structure.
  C. tertiary structure.
  D. quarternary structure.

Problem solved:

D is correct. The question asks only that you understand the meaning of the term "quarternary structure" as it relates to a protein. The phrase refers only to proteins composed of more than one polypeptide chain and, more particularly, to the way the separate chains are folded and linked.

Please solve this problem:

- A biochemist subjects a protein to study, wishing to determine whether its conformation is in the nature of an alpha helix or β-pleated sheet. She is thus attempting to ascertain:

  A. the primary structure of the protein.
  B. the secondary structure of the protein.
  C. the tertiary structure of the protein.
  D. the quarternary structure of the protein.

Problem solved:

B is correct. The question asks only that you be familiar with the notion of "secondary structure" as it relates to proteins. The two most common forms of secondary structure are the alpha helix and β-pleated sheet, as described in the text.

Please solve this problem:

- In terms of a protein's secondary structure, hydrogen bonding between CO and NH groups occurs in the case of the:

  A. alpha helix.
  B. β-pleated sheet.
  C. Both A and B
  D. Neither A nor B

Problem solved:

C is correct. As stated in the text, on each amino acid within the alpha helix, the oxygen of the alpha carboxyl group makes a hydrogen bond to a proton attached to a nitrogen atom four residues away. As for the β-pleated sheet, the text explains that hydrogen bonds form between NH and CO groups on amino acid residues relatively far apart from one another and/or between separate polypeptide chains. Choices A and B, therefore, both make true statements.

39.2 MASTERY APPLIED: PRACTICE PASSAGE AND QUESTIONS

Adult human hemoglobin, a protein, is the basis of oxygen transport in erythrocytes. It is made up of four polypeptide chains, which may be thought of as existing in pairs; two chains are of the alpha type and two are of the beta type. (One percent to three percent of adult hemoglobin also features a third type of polypeptide termed the delta chain, which, in that small proportion of molecules, replaces the beta chains.) Alpha chains contain 141 amino acid residues, and beta chains contain 146. Chains are linked together by noncovalent forces.

Fetal hemoglobin is distinct from adult hemoglobin. It consists of two zeta chains and two epsilon chains. As fetal development proceeds, zeta chains are gradually replaced by alpha chains, and epsilon chains are gradually replaced by beta chains, to form adult hemoglobin. The time of the replacements is depicted in Figure 1.

The sequence of amino acids in the polypeptide chains of the hemoglobin molecule varies among different species. Hemoglobin, therefore, does not represent a single substance, but rather a class of substances. The hemoglobin molecule is highly folded and coiled and, in particular, the amino acid constituents in the internal aspects of the molecule vary considerably across species. Yet, in most species, residues located on the internal aspect of the molecule are nonpolar. On the surface of most hemoglobin molecules, the amino acid constituents do not show particular patterns of in terms of acidity or basicity.

Notwithstanding the variations just described, however, certain positions of the hemoblogins that have undergo laboratory study show commonality as to the amino acid residues that occupy them. Some of the relevant observations in this regard are listed in Table 1. Research suggests that the invariance of these amino acid residues

at the applicable locations means that the particular constituents play a critical role in hemoglobin's central physiologic purpose of oxygen delivery to the tissues.

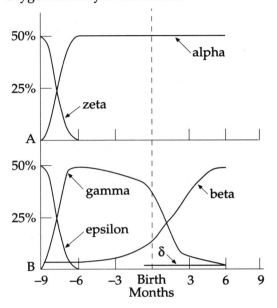

Figure 1

Invariant amino acid residues in hemoglobins	
Position	Amino Acid
F8	Histidine
E7	Histidine
CD1	Phenylalanine
F4	Leucine
B6	Glycine
C2	Proline
HC2	Tyosine
C4	Threonine
H10	Lysine

Table 1

1. Which of the following facts would be LEAST applicable to a particular hemoglobin, called Hemoglobin R, with a complex quarternary structure?

    A. The molecule's polypeptide chains are of different types.
    B. The molecule's various polypeptide chains bear noncovalent links.
    C. At certain sites, the molecule's amino acid constituents show great similarity to those of another hemoglobin called hemoglogin S.
    D. The molecule is composed of an extraordinarily long single polypeptide chain, with hydrogen bonds among and between various amino acid residues.

2. Alpha and beta hemoglobin chains differ in that:

    I. they show different primary structures.
    II. one is present in early fetal hemoglobin and the other is not.
    III. one is composed of amino acids and the other is not.

    A. I only
    B. II only
    C. I and II only
    D. II and III only

3. If an investigator wishes to ascertain the composition of the zeta chain of fetal hemoglobin, which of the following would be the most appropriate initial procedure?

    A. Isolate the chain and perform dehydration synthesis.
    B. Isolate the chain and perform direct ammonolysis.
    C. Isolate the chain and perform the Edman degradation.
    D. Isolate the chain and perform the Strecker synthesis.

4. An investigator hypothesizes that the internal aspects of a particular globular hemoglobin molecule must be composed entirely of nonpolar amino acids in order for the molecule as a whole to remain in solution while coursing through the blood. Among the following statements, which represents the most reasonable challenge to the hypothesis?

    A. Polar amino acids are relatively soluble in water.
    B. Protein solubility in water depends largely on molecular surface composition.
    C. Nonpolar amino acids are relatively insoluble in water.
    D. Water itself is a polar molecule with a capacity for hydrogen bonding.

5. If one amino acid is isolated from a zeta chain and noted to be a neutral amino acid, then that amino acid would NOT:

    A. carry both negatively and positively charged components at its isoelectric point.
    B. carry an amino group on its side chain.
    C. have a carboxyl group that is more acidic than its charged alpha amino group.
    D. carry a net positive charge at pH far below the isoelectric point.

6. According to Figure 1, the replacement of an epsilon chain by a beta chain during and after fetal development has, as an intermediate event:

    A. overproduction of epsilon chains.
    B. elimination of all alpha chains.
    C. conversion of epsilon chains to beta chains.
    D. replacement of the epsilon chain by a gamma chain.

39.3 MASTERY VERIFIED: ANSWERS AND EXPLANATIONS

1. **D is correct.** Quarternary structure applies only to a protein with more than one polypeptide chain. Choices A, B, and C are consistent with that condition. Choice D does refer to bonding between amino residues, but it describes a molecule with a *single chain*. A single chained protein has no quarternary structure. Rather, the hydrogen bonding to which the choice refers pertains to its *secondary structure*—usually an alpha helix or β-pleated sheet.

2. **A is correct.** Statements II and III are false. Early fetal hemoglobin lacks *both* alpha and beta chains, having zeta and epsilon chains instead. Statement II would be accurate only if fetal hemoglobin carried either alpha or beta chains, but it carries neither. Statement III is virtually nonsensical. Hemoglobin is composed of polypeptides, which are composed of amino acids. Statement I, on the other hand refers to a difference in primary structure, which meansthat the particular amino residues that compose a polypeptide chain in a particular order. It is enough to know, as the passage states, that the alpha chain contains 141 residues and the beta chain contains 146 residues. *That alone* means that the chains differ in their primary structure.

3. **C is correct.** Choices A, B, and D are inappropriate. Dehydration synthesis is a process in which peptide bonds are formed, not broken. Choices B and D refer to processes through which amino acids (not proteins) are formed (not degraded). As noted in the text, the Edman degradation is an orderly process of hydrolysis in which peptide bonds are sequentially broken so that each amino acid residue can be removed from a polypeptide and identified. Since the investigator wishes to ascertain the identity and sequence of the residues that compose the zeta chain, she should first perform the Edman degradation.

4. **B is correct.** This investigator posits that the presence of polar amino acids at the molecule's interior will preclude water solubility. We are looking for a statement that best challenges his thinking. Whether or not a globular protein is soluble in water depends on the nature of its exterior—the component that comes in contact *with* the solvent. What sits on the interior has no particular effect on solubility. Choices A, C, and D all make true statements that do not, however, pose a challenge to the investigator's hypothesis. Polar amino acids are relatively soluble in water, as choice A indicates, but that is not to say that polar amino acids could not also be found on a protein molecule's *in*terior. Their presence there would not disturb the solubility. Choice C is wrong for that same reason. While it is true that nonpolar amino acids are relatively insoluble in water and that in globular proteins they tend to "hide" within the molecular interior, any polar amino acids that "joined" them there would not significantly affect interactions between the solvent and the molecule's *ex*terior. And, as choice D states, water is a polar molecule. Again, however, the presence of polar amino acids at the protein's interior won't "bother" the water. Choice B makes the statement that challenges the investigator's hypothesis—the very statement that makes choices A, C, and D incorrect. Water solubility of a globular protein is governed by the nature of the protein molecule's *ex*terior. The *in*terior, whether its contents be polar or nonpolar is not terribly important to the matter of water solubility.

5. **B is correct.** Choices A, C, and D all make true statements, which means that for *this* question, they are wrong. All neutral amino acids carry both a positive and a negative charge at their isoelectric point because at the isoelectric pH (characteristic of a given amino acid), the COOH group is deprotonated, to give the negatively charged COO- carboxylate anion, and the amino group is protonated to give the positively charged NH_3^+ moiety. For all amino acids, generally, the carboxyl group is more acidic than the protonated alpha amino group, and all neutral amino acids are positively charged at extremely low pH. A "neutral amino acid" is one that carries on its side chain neither a carboxyl group nor an extra amino (or other basic) group. As for choice D, all amino acids are positively charged at pH values far below their isoelectric points. The COOH group is protonated (and uncharged). The amino group is protonated and positively charged. The definition of "neutral" amino acid is one that on its side chain carries neither an additional carboxyl group nor an additional amino (or other basic) group. By definition, therefore, a neutral amino acid does not carry an amino group on its side chain, and that's why choice B is correct.

6. **D is correct.** Examine Figure 1 (see **Chapter 2**). Some students are intimidated by graphs, charts, and illustrations, and the MCAT *writers* want them to be. Many are designed so that you'll "take one look and run." But note that as to this question, for example, the upper graph of Figure 1 is wholly irrelevant because it concerns the development of alpha chains whereas the question concerns the development of beta chains. So we ignore the upper graph and look at the lower one. Now, then, a graph is a graph. Look at the curve that represents the epsilon chain. It falls very low at the six month mark before birth. As it falls, the curve marked "gamma" rises. So, as the epsilon chains disappear, gamma chains appear. Then, at birth, the gamma curve begins to fall sharply, and the beta curve begins to rise significantly. So the whole thing is pretty simple: Epsilon chains are replaced first by gamma chains, that exchange being complete at about the sixth month before birth. Then the gamma chains are replaced by beta chains, that exchange being complete at about six months after birth. According to choice D, the replacement of epsilon chains by beta chains has as an intermediate event, the replacement of epsilon chains by gamma chains. That's exactly what the lower graph of Figure 1 shows.

CHAPTER 40

CARBOHYDRATES

40.1 MASTERY ACHIEVED

MEANING OF "CARBOHYDRATE" AND "SUGAR": "COMPLEX" VERSUS "SIMPLE"

"Carbohydrate" means a "hydrate" of carbon. In other words, for each C atom in the molecule, there is an equivalent of water. Therefore carbohydrates have the general formula $C_n(H_2O)_n$, or $C_nH_{2n}O_n$.

Additionally, a carbohydrate is:

(1) an aldehyde or ketone with OH group attached to each carbon atom of its carbon chain,

or

(2) a compound which, on hydrolysis, yields such a molecule.

In "fancier" terms, we say that a carbohydrate is a "polyhydroxylated aldehyde" or "ketone" or any molecule that may be hydrolyzed *to* a polyhydroxylated aldehyde or ketone (Regarding the structure of aldehydes and ketones, see **Chapter 37**).

"Sugar" and "carbohydrate" mean the same thing. A sugar is a carbohydrate; a carbohydrate is a sugar.

"Simple carbohydrate" or "simple sugar" means a carbohydrate that answers to number (1) above: a polyhydroxylated aldehyde or ketone. "Complex carbohydrate" or "complex sugar" means a carbohydrate that answers to number (2) above: a compound that, on hydrolysis, produces a simple carbohydrate. The simple carbohydrates are also called **monosaccharides**.

MONOSACCHARIDES

Since monosaccharides are polyhydroxylated aldehydes and polyhydroxylated ketones, all can be divided broadly into (1) *aldoses* and (2) *ketoses* depending on whether or not the carbonyl group is terminal.

Please solve this problem:

- Consider the three carbohydrate molecules—X, Y, and Z—and then determine which of the following statements are true.

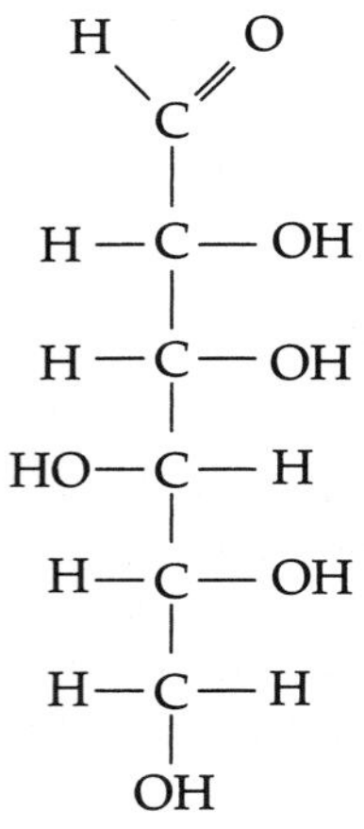

Molecule X 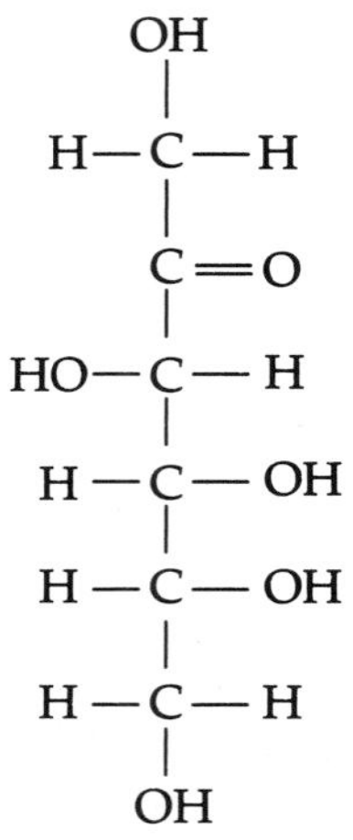   Molecule Y 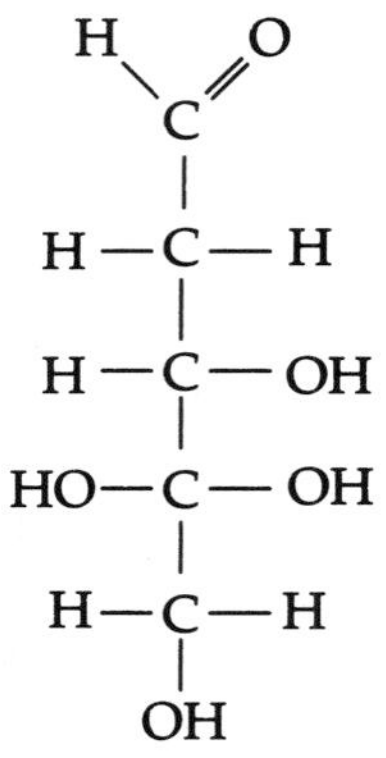   Molecule Z

I. Molecule X is a ketose
II. Molecule Y is a ketose
III. Molecule Z is an aldose

A. I only
B. I and II only
C. II and III only
D. I, II and III

Problem solved:

C is correct. Statement I is false. Molecule X carries a carbonyl group on its terminal carbon, meaning it conforms to the generic formula RCHO and so has the essential feature of an aldehyde. It is an <u>al</u>dose, not a ketose. That means choices A, B, and D are wrong, which, on that basis alone, allows you correctly to select choice C. Molecule Y is a ketose, conforming to the generic formula R_2CO; the carbonyl group does not appear on the terminal carbon and so is bound to two organic groups. Molecule Z is an aldose for the same reason that molecule X is an aldose. Statements II and III are true. Statement I is not.

Stereochemistry of Monosaccharides: "(+)," "(−)," "D," "L"

The simplest monosaccharides are:

(1) glyceraldehyde, an aldose, which is sometimes called an aldotriose because it carries three carbon atoms, and

(2) dihydroxyacetone, a ketose, sometimes called a ketotriose because it carries three carbon atoms.

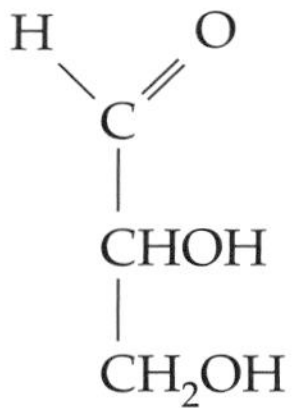

Glyceraldehyde
(an aldotriose)

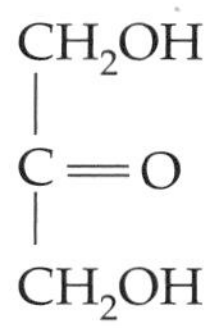

Dihydroxyacetone
(a ketotriose)

Glyceraldehyde contains a chiral center; dihydroxyacetone does not. Since glyceraldehyde has a single chiral center, it exists as two enantiomers: (+) glyceraldehyde, which rotates the plane of polarized light to the right, and (−) glyceraldehyde, which rotates the plane of polarized light to the left (see **Chapter 34**). Although, the absolute configuration designations "R" and "S" have no generic correspondence to the designations (+) and (−), it happens that in the case of glyceraldehydes, the "R" enantiomer is (+) and the S enantiomer is (−).

All monosaccharides also carry the designation "D" or "L." It is important for the MCAT that you know how to distinguish a "D sugar" from an "L sugar." Look at glyceraldehyde's two enantiomers drawn in Fischer projection, and look especially at the chiral carbon.

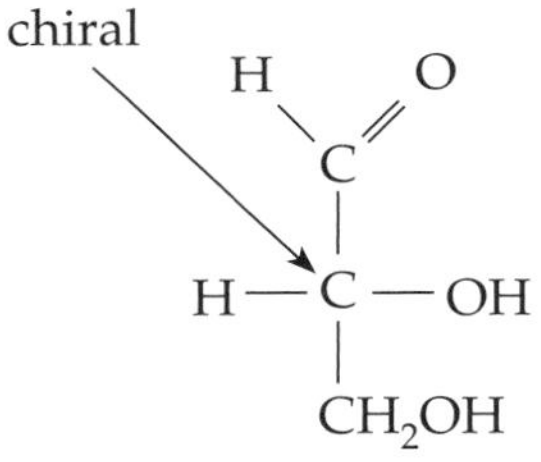

D (+) Glyceraldehyde 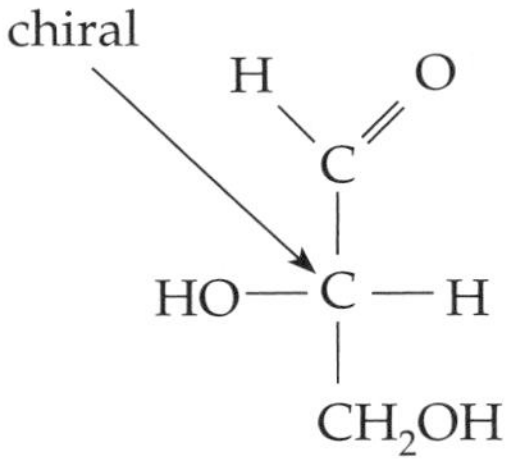   L (−) Glyceraldehyde

At the chiral carbon of the (+) enantiomer, the H atom is to the left, with the OH group to the right. In the (−) enantiomers, that situation is reversed; the H atom is on the right with the OH group at the left. By convention (the origins of which are unimportant for the MCAT):

(1) (+) glyceraldehyde, in which the OH appears on the right, is also called D-glyceraldehyde;

(2) (−) glyceraldehydes, in which the OH appears on the left, is also called L-glyceraldehyde;

AND

(3) *every monosaccharide is designated "D" or "L" depending on whether its highest numbered chiral center has an orientation analogous to that of D-glyceraldehyde or L-glyceraldehyde.*

Before we continue, be sure to know that just as "R" and "S" do not generically correspond to (+) or (–) (see **Chapter 34**), neither to "D" or "L" correspond to (+) or (–). When we say that a given carbohydrate is "L," we mean that absolute configuration around the chiral carbon farthest from the carbonyl carbon is of the S type, *but that does not tell us that the molecule rotates the plane of polarized light to the right or the left.* When we say that a given carbohydrate is "D," we mean that absolute configuration around the chiral carbon farthest from the carbonyl carbon is of the R type, but neither does that tell us that the molecule rotates the plane of polarized light to the right or the left. A given L sugar might rotate the plane of polarized light to the right or left, and the only test for *that* is polarimetry. Similarly, a particular D carbohydrate might rotate the plane of polarized light to the right or left, and the only test for that is polarimetry.

With that settled, look at the monosaccharides ribose, glucose, and fructose in the Fischer drawing:

| Ribose | Glucose | Fructose |

In each case, look at the highest numbered chiral carbon (the *chiral* carbon farthest from the carbonyl carbon). Compare the orientation of H and OH on *that* carbon to their orientation around the chiral carbon of R- and L-glyceraldehyde. For all three molecules, the H is on the left and OH is on the right. That means we're looking at D-ribose, D-glucose, and D-fructose. In nature, most monosaccharides, including glyceraldehyde, glucose, and fructose, occur in their D forms. When speaking of monosaccharides, we sometimes say "D-sugars are natural sugars," and it is the D sugars that are of biological importance.

Please solve this problem:

- Examine this depiction of the monosaccharide xylose in Fischer projection.

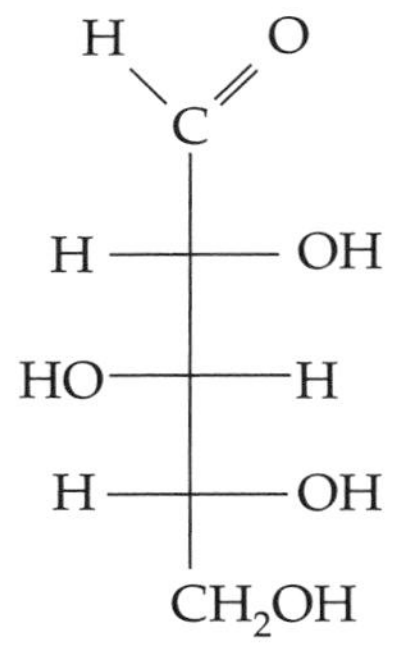

$$
\begin{array}{c}
\text{H}\diagdown\diagup\text{O} \\
\text{C} \\
| \\
\text{H} \rule{1.2cm}{0.4pt} \text{OH} \\
\text{HO} \rule{1.2cm}{0.4pt} \text{H} \\
\text{H} \rule{1.2cm}{0.4pt} \text{OH} \\
| \\
\text{CH}_2\text{OH}
\end{array}
$$

Xylose

It is:

A. a D-ketosugar.
B. a D-aldosugar.
C. an L-aldosugar.
D. an L-ketosugar.

Problem solved:

B is correct. The xylose molecule shows a carbonyl (C–O double bond) at the terminal carbon, meaning that it is an aldose, not a ketose. Choices A and D, therefore, are wrong. Whether the molecule belongs to the "D" or "L" category depends on the orientation of H and OH around the chiral carbon farthest from carbon 1, which, in this case, is carbon 4. (Carbon 5, of course, is not chiral; it is bound to two H atoms and so does not carry four different substituents.) On that highest-numbered chiral carbon, the OH group is to the right. This is the "D" form of the molecule, making choice C wrong and choice B correct.

Please solve this problem:

- A student is shown this depiction of the monosaccharide gulose in Fischer projections:

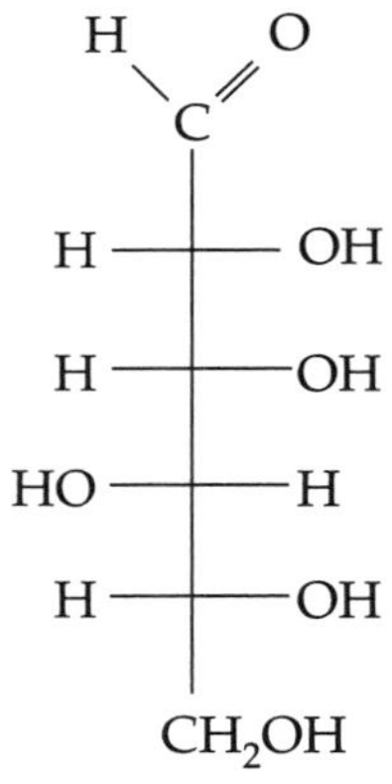

Gulose

On the basis of the depiction, is the student justified in concluding that it represents a dextrorotatory isomer?

A. Yes, because on carbon 5, the OH group sits on the right.
B. Yes, because gulose is a ketose and not an aldose.
C. No, because gulose is an aldose and not a ketose.
D. No, because "L" and "D" are not equivalent to "(−)" and "(+)."

Problem solved:

D is correct. Knowing that a sugar is "L" or "D" does not tell us in what direction it rotates the plane of polarized light. So choices A and B are wrong. Choice C makes a true statement except for the word *because*. That gulose is an aldose has nothing do with the answer to this question. Choice D is right because as emphasized in the text, just as "R" and "S" do not generically correspond to (+) or (−), neither to "D" or "L" correspond to (+) or (−).

The number of stereoisomers for a monosaccharide molecule with x carbons is $2x^{-2}$. Glyceraldehyde, we said, has one chiral center, and it has $2^1 = 2$ stereoisomers, each of which is an enantiomer of the other. A four-carbon sugar ("tetatrose") has $2^2 = 4$ stereoisomers meaning, also, that it has two *pairs* of D and L enantiomers. Do not memorize their names for the MCAT, but see that the four tetroses are D- and L-erythrose and D- and L-threose.

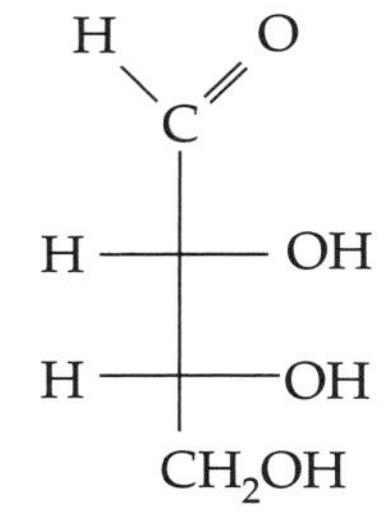

$$\begin{array}{c}
H\diagdown C\diagup\!\!\diagup O \\
H\!-\!\!-OH \\
H\!-\!\!-OH \\
CH_2OH
\end{array}$$

D–Erythrose

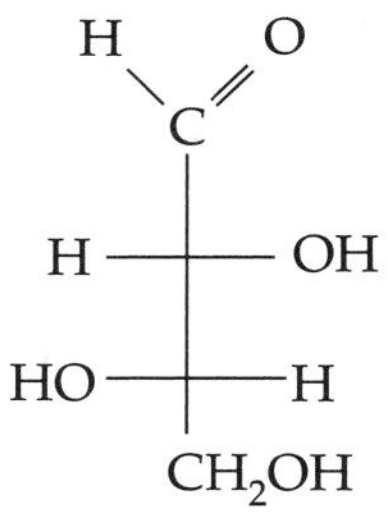

$$\begin{array}{c}
H\diagdown C\diagup\!\!\diagup O \\
H\!-\!\!-OH \\
HO\!-\!\!-H \\
CH_2OH
\end{array}$$

L–Erythrose

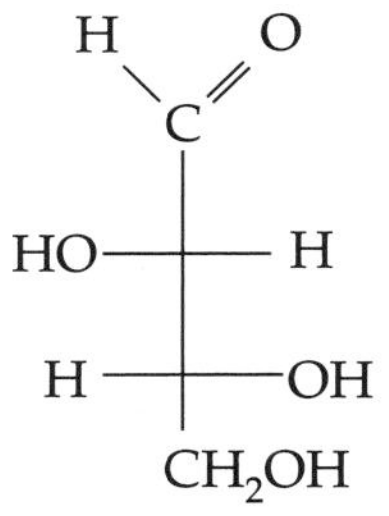

$$\begin{array}{c}
H\diagdown C\diagup\!\!\diagup O \\
HO\!-\!\!-H \\
H\!-\!\!-OH \\
CH_2OH
\end{array}$$

D–Threose

$$\begin{array}{c}
H\diagdown C\diagup\!\!\diagup O \\
HO\!-\!\!-H \\
HO\!-\!\!-H \\
CH_2OH
\end{array}$$

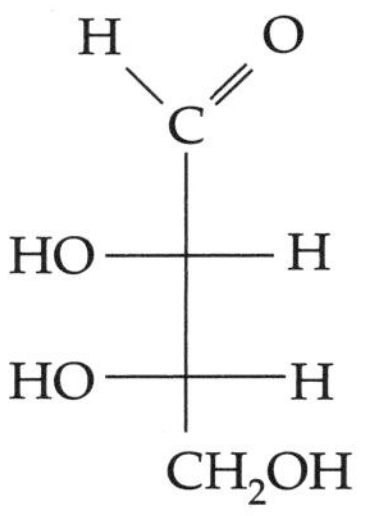

L–Threose

The D-tetroses are the ones of biological importance. A five-carbon sugar (pentose) has $2^3 = 8$ stereoisomers, meaning that it has four pairs of D and L enantiomers, the D enantiomers being the ones of biological importance. Again, do not memorize names and structures, but see that a six-carbon sugar (hexose) has $2^4 = 16$ steroisomers, meaning that it has eight pairs of D and L enantiomers. Again, the D enantiomers are the ones of biological importance and, particularly, D-glucose is of *greatest* biological importance.

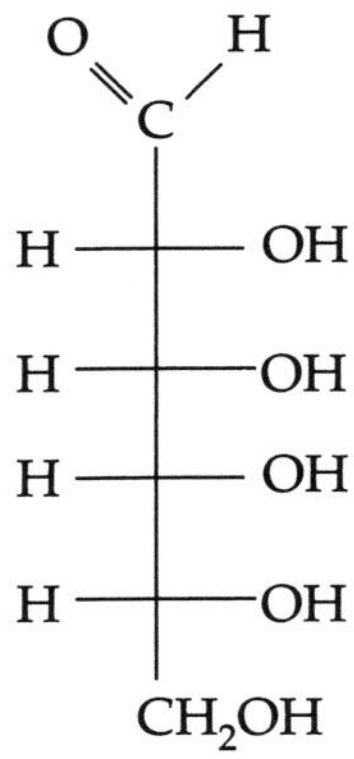

D–Allose

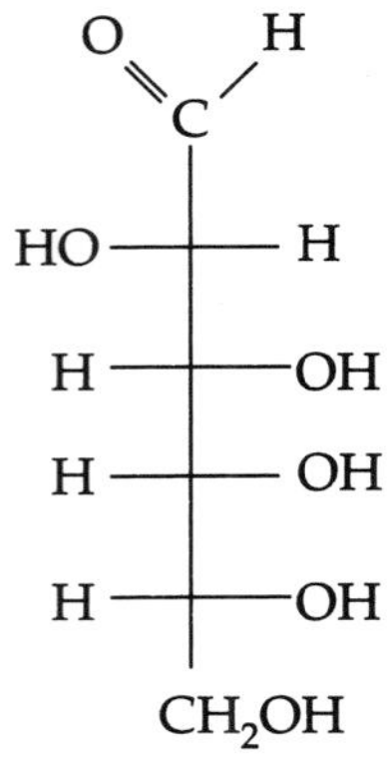

D–Altrose

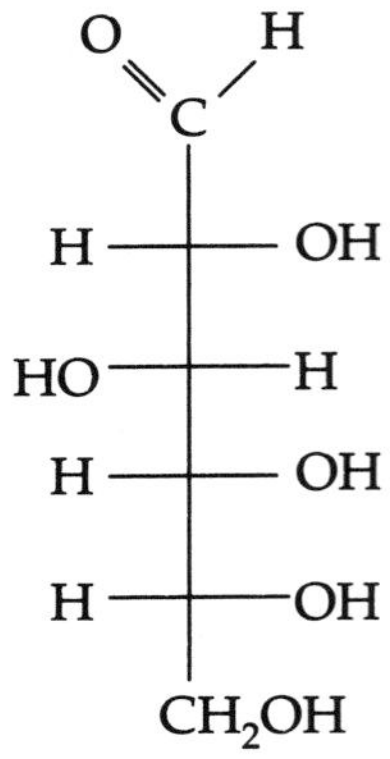

D–Glucose

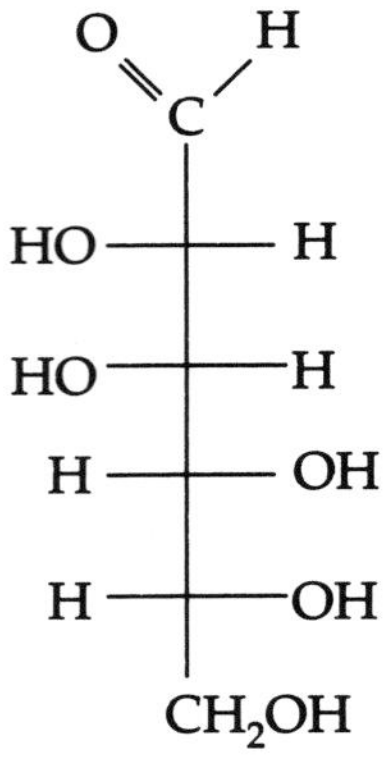

D–Mannose

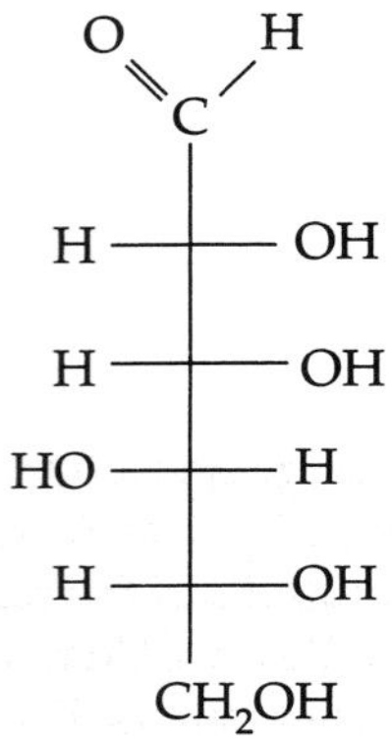

D–Gulose

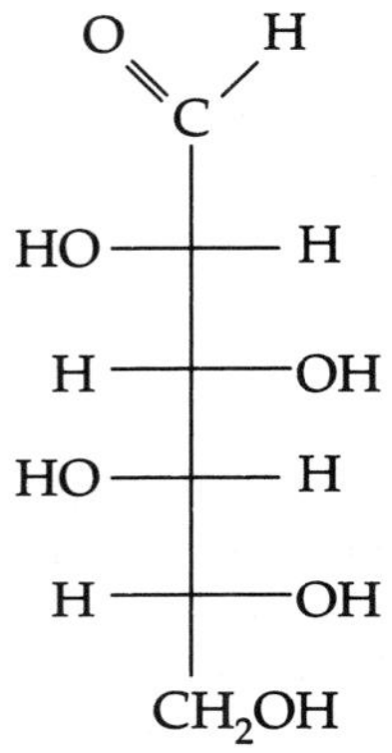

D–Idose

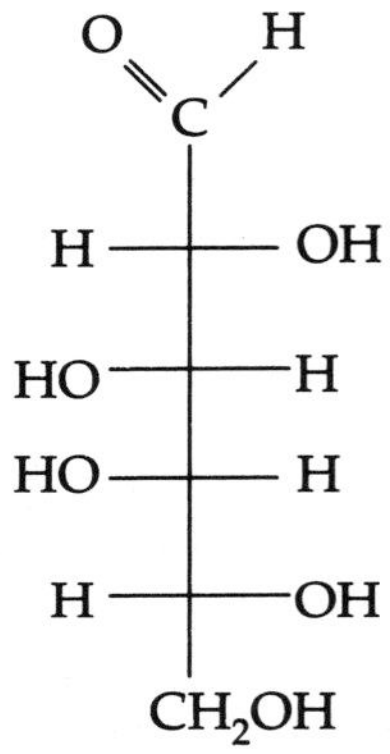

D–Galactose

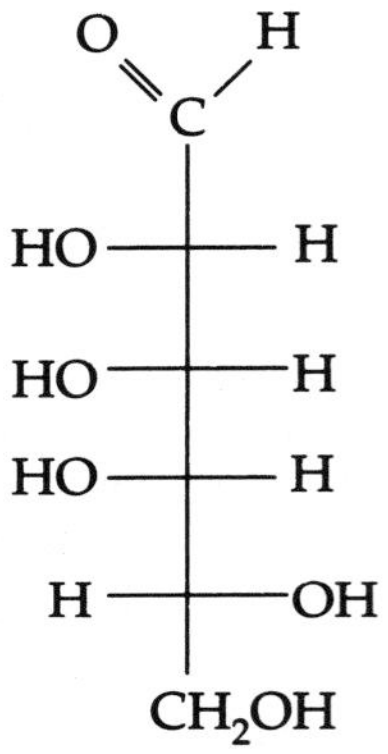

D–Talose

Please solve this problem:

- The molecules D-galactose and D-mannose are:

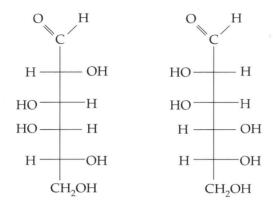

D–Galactose   D–Manose

    A. enantiomeric ketohexoses.
    B. diastereomeric ketohexoses.
    C. diastereomeric aldohexoses.
    D. enantiomeric aldohexoses.

Problem solved:

C is correct. The Fischer projections just presented show that the hexoses mannose and galactose have carbonyl bonds at their terminal carbons. They are aldoses, not ketoses. Choices A and B, therefore, are wrong. The two molecules do not represent D and L configurations of the same molecule, so they are not enantiomers. That makes choice d wrong as well. Review **Chapter 34**, and recall that there are two types of stereoisomers: (1) enantiomers and (2) diastereomers. Diastereomers (also of two types, geometric and nongeometric) are stereoisomers that are not enantiomers. So choice C is right. These two hexoses are aldoses, and each is a diastereomer of the other.

Cyclic Monosaccharides: Anomers

Recall **Chapter 37** where we discuss the formation of hemiacetals and hemiketals. By chemistry born of those same phenomena, monosaccharides can exist either in an **open chain form** (as depicted in the Fischer drawings we have been examining) or in a **ring form**. In an aldohexose such as glucose, ring structures follow from the nucleophilic attack by an OH group at carbon 5 on the carbonyl carbon (carbon 1). The resulting six-membered ring, in which oxygen is a member of the ring, is called a pyranose, and in the case of glucose, it is sometimes called glucopyranose. The former carbonyl carbon becomes part of hemiacetal, and is referred to as the **anomeric** carbon.

The carbon chain in a sugar is numbered from the end closest to the most oxidized carbon. In this case, the aldehyde is C-1, and therefore the anomeric C in the ring forms is C-1.

A <u>keto</u>hexose, such as fructose, will form a five-membered ring, called a **furanose**, in which, once again, oxygen is a member of the ring. In a ketose, the most oxidized carbon is not a terminal atom, so the anomeric carbon is not C-1 on the cyclic form.

When the open chain aldose and pentose formed the cyclic pyranose and furanose, as just discussed, the carbonyl carbon acquired chirality. It became tetrasubstituted, and a new chiral carbon was "born." The former carbonyl carbon, now chiral, is called the **anomeric carbon**, and the two diastereomers resulting *from* its formation are **anomers** of one another. Anomers are designated alpha or beta, depending on the placement in a conventional **Hayworth projection** of the OH group at the anomeric carbon. In an alpha anomer, the OH group at the anomeric carbon points downward. In the beta anomer, it points upward. Here, for instance are the alpha and beta anomers of D-glucose:

α-glucose   β-glucose

Ring structures are sometimes drawn in **chair form**, as shown for D-glucose:

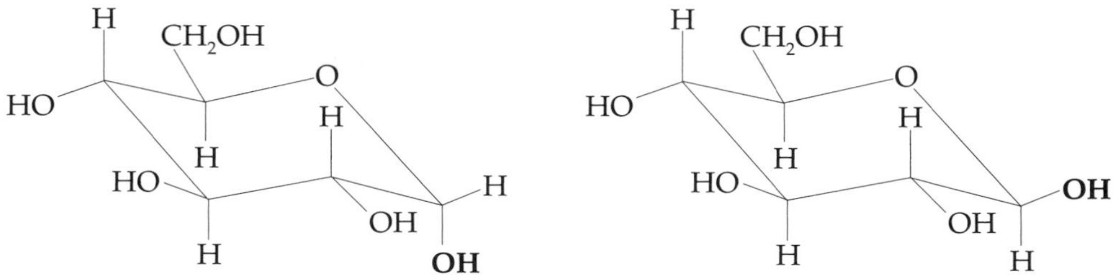

Note that the ring closures shown above are equilibria. Both the alpha and beta anomers rapidly interconvert with the straight chain form of the sugar in solution. The cyclic form of the sugar is the thermodynamically favored form, and the process by which the alpha and beta forms of cyclic sugars interconvert through this double equilibrium is known as **mutarotation**.

Disaccharides and Polysaccharides

Disaccharides and polysaccharides are composed of two or more monosaccharides joined by a special form of ether linkage, called a **glycosidic linkage**, which might, in turn, be an α- or β-glycosidic linkage. An α- or β-glycosidic linkage is normally characterized with two numbers, representing the two carbons between which the linkage actually forms. Here, for example, the disaccharide maltose arises from an α-1,4-glycosidic linkage between two molecules of glucose:

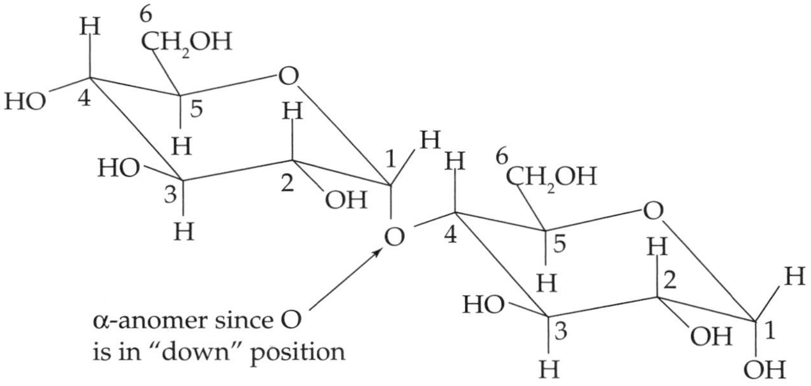

α-anomer since O is in "down" position

Here is the disaccharide cellobiose formed by β-1,4 glycosidic linkage between two molecules of glucose:

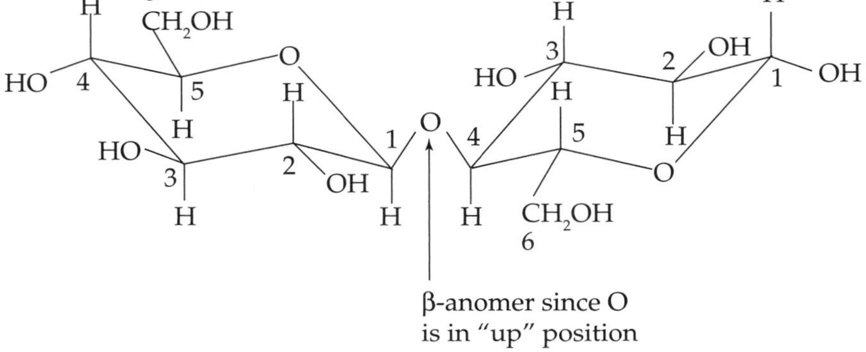

β-anomer since O is in "up" position

Here is the disaccharide sucrose (table sugar) formed by an α-1, 2-glycoside linkage between one molecule of glucose and one molecule of fructose. The linkage is made between the anomeric carbons of each molecule:

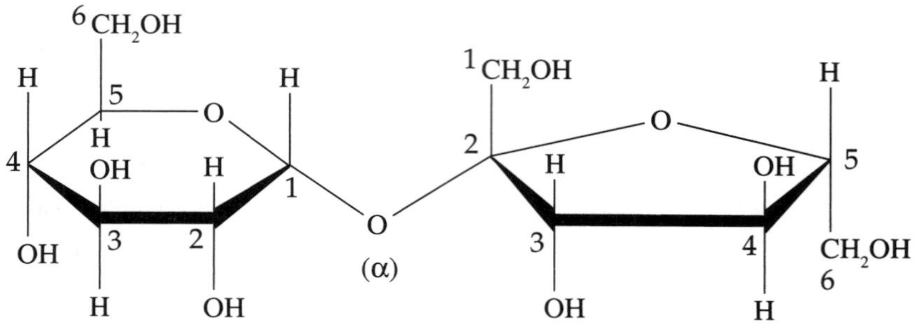

$^6CH_2OH$

$^1CH_2OH$

(glucose) (fructose)

Sucrose

STARCH, GLYCOGEN, AND CELLULOSE

Starch is a polysaccharide comprising more than 1,000 units of D-glucose joined by α-1,4-glycosidic linkages. It is found in plants (rice and potatoes, for example). On heating, starch yields two isolable fractions: (1) **amylose**, the less prevalent, and (2) **amylopectin**, the more prevalent. The difference between the fractions amylose and amylopectin is this: In amylopectin, branching occurs at various points between carbon 6 of one glucose molecule and carbon 1 of another. Here, for instance, are two units of an amylose molecule (of which in the true molecule there would be more than 1,000):

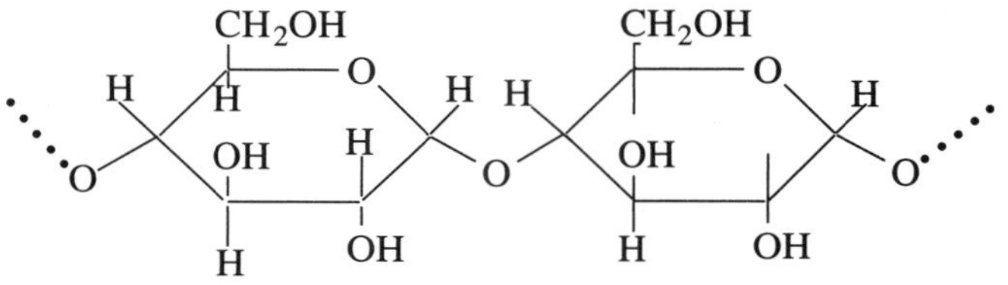

And here is a relatively short segment of an amylopectin molecule, showing one of its characteristic branch points:

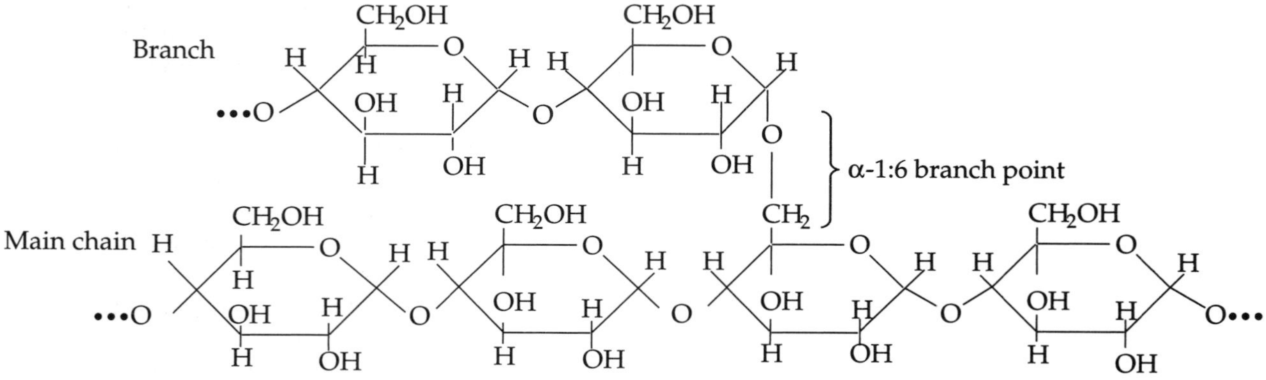

Branch

α-1:6 branch point

Main chain

Starch is biologically significant as (1) the form in which plants *store* carbohydrate for nutrition and (2) a source from which animal *derive* carbohydrate nutrition, converting it then to the storage form of carbohydrate: **glycogen**. Animals eat starch by a series of enzymatic hydrolytic processes; they "take it apart" into its glucose and fructose subunits and use the resulting monosaccharides to form glycogen, which they then use as a storage form of nutritional energy.

To say that plants and animals "store energy" in the form of starch and glycogen, respectively, is to say that glycogen serves as a ready source of *glucose* that individual cells use to generate ATP via processes described in **Chapter 28**.

Glycogen resembles amylopectin. It is a polymer of D-glucose units joined by α-1,4-glycosidic linkages. It differs from amylopectin in that (1) the polymers are shorter, comprising perhaps twelve to fourteen glucose units and (2) it is more highly branched than amylopectin. Since glycogen serves a purpose for animals analogous to that which starch serves for plants, there exists the (dying) term "animal starch," which means, simply, glycogen. When the alpha 1-6 branching is accounted for, the entire glycogen unit might comprise 100,000 glucose units (even though the α 1-4 polymers themselves are shorter than those of amylopectin).

Benedict's Test for Reducing Sugars

A common test used in sugar chemistry is the **Benedict's test**. Benedict's reagent is comprised of a basic solution containing Cu^{2+} ions. In the presence of a reducing sugar (one that contains an aldehyde or ketone), the copper ions are reduced, thereby gaining an electron to form Cu^+ while the carbonyl in the sugar itself is oxidized to a carboxylic acid. A positive test for the reaction is indicated by the formation of the red precipitate Cu_2O.

All monosaccharides are reducing sugars since these molecules exist in equilibrium between their cyclic forms (containing a hemiacetal) and straight chain forms (containing an aldehyde or ketone). Many disaccharides also give positive tests with Benedict's reagent. The glycosidic linkage of a sugar like cellobiose can no longer open up to yield the aldehyde of the first glucose molecule, but the second sugar ring CAN still open to yield an aldehyde and react with copper ions. Therefore, cellobiose is a reducing sugar. Note, however, that sucrose will give a negative test with Benedict's reagent since the anomeric carbons of both glucose and fructose are a part of the glycosidic linkage. Therefore, there are no hemiacetals in sucrose to ring open, and sucrose is not a reducing sugar. Polysaccharides like starch will give negative Benedict's tests.

Please solve this problem:

- Among the following, amylopectin most closely resembles:

  A. glucopyranose.
  B. fructofuranose.
  C. mannose.
  D. glycogen.

Problem solved:

D is correct. Amylopectin is a polysaccharide that represents a fractional component of starch (the more prevalent fraction). Choices A, B, and C are wrong because they all describe monosaccharides. Glucopyranose and fructofuranose are the ring forms of glucose and fructose, respectively; a hemiacetal in the case of glucose and hemiketal in the case of fructose. Mannose, too, is a monosaccharide. Glycogen is a polysaccharide — a long polymer of D-glucose units joined by α-1,4-glycosidic linkages. The polymer is highly branched by linkages between a carbon 1 of one glucose unit and a carbon 6 of another. That same description applies to amylopectin except that in amylopectin, (a) the branching is less extensive and (b) the polymer is longer.

Please solve this problem:

- Starch serves largely to store nutritional energy in:

  A. plants.
  B. animals.
  C. both.
  D. neither.

Problem solved:

A is correct. Animals *eat* starch (plenty of it) as a source of nutrition, but they do not ordinarily maintain starch in their bodies as a storage form of carbohydrate. Rather, by a series of hydrolytic enzymatic processes, they break it into its glucose subunits and use them to form glycogen, the carbohydrate that they use to store energy.

Cellulose is a polysaccharide. Like starch, it is an unbranched polymer of D-glucose units joined by 1,4 glycosidic linkages. The linkages, however, are not alpha, but *beta*.

Cellulose tends to serve in plants not as nutritional storage, but rather as a key component of physical structure. It is the essence, for instance, of wood and cotton. Animals do eat cellulose. Humans lack the enzymes to hydrolyze it into its component monosaccharide units, and so we say that it is "indigestible," which is by no means to say that it is bad. Cellulose is the "fiber" referred to in high-fiber diets, and there is ample evidence to suggest that for many purposes, diets high in cellulose are good for humans, notwithstanding its indigestibility. Its passage through the digestive tract appears, for instance, to reduce the incidence of colon cancer.

40.2 MASTERY APPLIED: PRACTICE PASSAGE AND QUESTIONS

Two diastereomeric aldoses that differ only as to the configuration about carbon 2 (the carbon adjacent to the carbonyl carbon) are termed *epimers*. D-mannose and D-galactose, for example, are epimers of D-glucose. One manner of determining that two aldoses are in fact epimers is by osazone formation.

Aldoses, like most aldehydes, will react with phenylhydrazine to form phenylhydrazones. With excess phenylhydrazine, the phenylhydrazone forms an osazone. Two epimers of the same aldose will yield identical osazones, shown as Process 1.

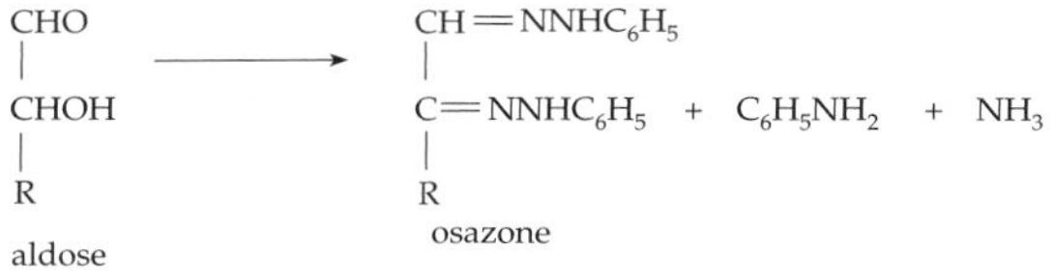

Process 1

The conversion of glucose to fructose is an important component of the glycolytic pathway and is thought to proceed through an enolization reaction, the course of which is summarized below as Process 2.

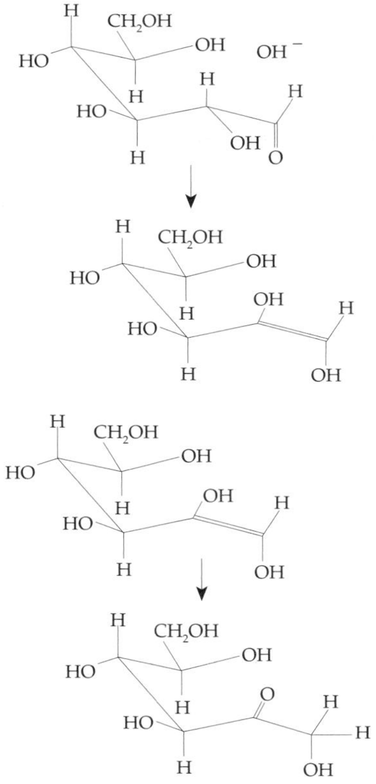

Process 2

Glucose may produce a different product according to a different process, the course of which is summarized below as Process 3.

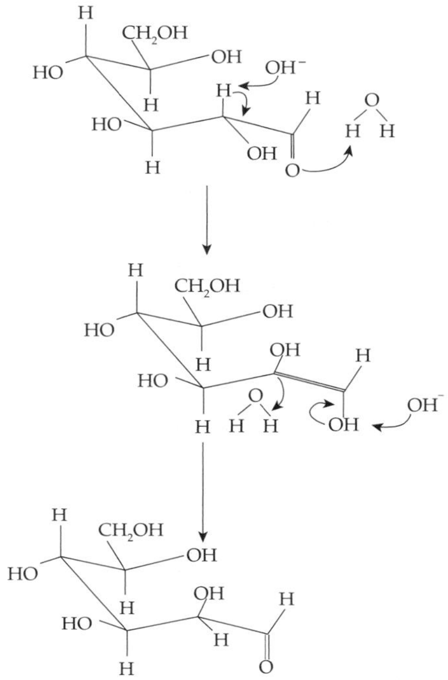

Process 3

1. The product of the third pathway represented in the passage is:

    A. D-mannose.
    B. D-galactose.
    C. L-glucose.
    D. L-sucrose.

2. The relationship between D-mannose and D-galactose is:

    A. anomeric.
    B. epimeric.
    C. enantiomeric.
    D. diastereomeric.

3. D-Fructose and D-glucose are:

   A. enantiomeric.
   B. diastereomeric.
   C. geometric isomers.
   D. structural isomers.

4. D-Fructose and D-mannose are:

   A. enantiomeric.
   B. diastereomeric.
   C. geometric isomers.
   D. structural isomers.

5. When glucose is placed into a solution containing dilute NaOH, the reaction produces 70 percent glucose, 20 percent fructose, 1 percent mannose, and the remainder goes to decomposition products. In the body, the conversion of glucose to fructose is nearly quantitative. Which of the following choices offers the best explanation for this discrepancy?

   A. Biological systems are more efficient than man-made systems.
   B. In the body, the fructose produced is consumed; in the experiment, it is not.
   C. The body does not contain pure glucose in dilute alkali, as the experiment did.
   D. At the location of glycolysis within the body the base concentration is much higher than in the experiment.

40.3 MASTERY VERIFIED: ANSWERS AND EXPLANATIONS

1. **A is correct.** We know from the passage that glucose is epimeric with mannose at carbon 2. The product of the third pathway differs from glucose only at carbon 2. It must, therefore, be D-mannose.

2. **D is correct.** From the passage, we know that D-mannose differs from D-glucose at carbon 2 and that D-galactose differs from D-glucose at carbon 4. Therefore, D-mannose and D-galactose must differ from one another at both carbon 2 and carbon 4. The difference in these two chiral centers makes these two molecules diastereomeric.

3. **D is correct.** D-Fructose and D-glucose have the same chemical formula ($C_6H_{12}O_6$), so they are isomers of one another. D-fructose is a ketohexose; D-glucose is an aldohexose. Since one contains a ketone group and the other contains an aldehyde group, they cannot be more than structural isomers.

4. **D is correct.** D-fructose and D-mannose have the same chemical formula ($C_6H_{12}O_6$), so they are isomers of one another. D-fructose is a ketohexose, D-mannose is an aldohexose. Since one contains a ketone group and the other contains an aldehyde group, they cannot be more than structural isomers.

5. **B is correct.** As fructose is produced during glycolysis it is also consumed. Based on Le Chatelier's principle, this will drive the equilibrium of the interconversion of glucose to fructose to the product side, causing the production of more fructose.

CHAPTER 41

SEPARATION AND IDENTIFICATION OF ORGANIC COMPOUNDS

41.1 MASTERY ACHIEVED

SEPARATION AND PURIFICATION TECHNIQUES

General Principles

Separations rely upon the differences in the physical properties of the substances to be separated. Several of these properties have been covered elsewhere: solubility (**Chapter 18**), boiling point (**Chapter 20**), melting point (**Chapter 20**), acid/base properties (**Chapter 21**), and bonding properties (**Chapter 14**).

Extraction

Extraction is the process of removing a solute from one solvent through the use of a second solvent that is insoluble in the first solvent. The efficacy of extraction is controlled by the immiscibility of the two solvents and the solute's higher affinity for (solubility in) the second solvent.

The solubility characteristics and intermolecular forces of a substance are used to determine which components of a solution can be differentially extracted (and with which solvents). Most often, the properties involved in the choice of an extraction solvent are polarity and acid/base properties.

Remember the rule of thumb that "like dissolves like," meaning that polar compounds will dissolve in polar solvents (like water), and nonpolar compounds will dissolve in nonpolar solvents, which are usually the organic solvents in the extraction process.

Another good rule to watch for on the MCAT is that organic molecules with five or fewer carbon atoms and one or more polar functional groups will be more soluble in the aqueous layer of an extraction. Molecules with six or more carbon atoms with only one or two polar groups are more likely to be soluble in the organic layer. Essentially, you're looking to see which part of the molecule is more predominant, the polar or nonpolar sections. For example, sugar molecules that are six carbons long are highly soluble in water because each carbon has a polar functional group attached.

The final thing to remember is that regardless of the size of the molecule and its hydrophobic, or nonpolar portion, if you can generate a charge on the molecule by taking advantage of the acid/base properties of one or more functional groups, the compound will preferentially dissolve in the aqueous layer. There are three functional groups that can be altered in this way: the amine, the carboxylic acid, and the phenol.

Amines are basic, as previously described, and when treated with an acid will accept a proton to form a positively charged aminium ion.

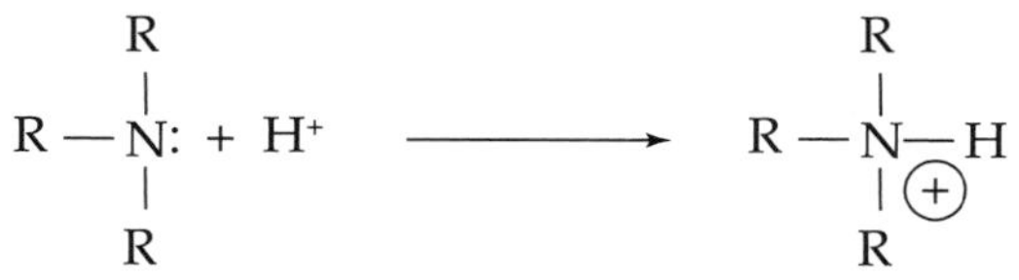

$$R-\underset{\underset{R}{|}}{\overset{\overset{R}{|}}{N}}: \;+\; H^+ \;\longrightarrow\; R-\underset{\underset{R}{|}}{\overset{\overset{R}{|}}{N}}\!-\!H \;\;\oplus$$

an amine,
soluble in organic
layer when R
groups are large.

an aminium ion,
soluble in H_2O,
regardless of
R group size.

Carboxylic acids and phenols are acidic, and when treated with a base will lose a proton to form negatively charged carboxylate and phenolate ions, respectively.

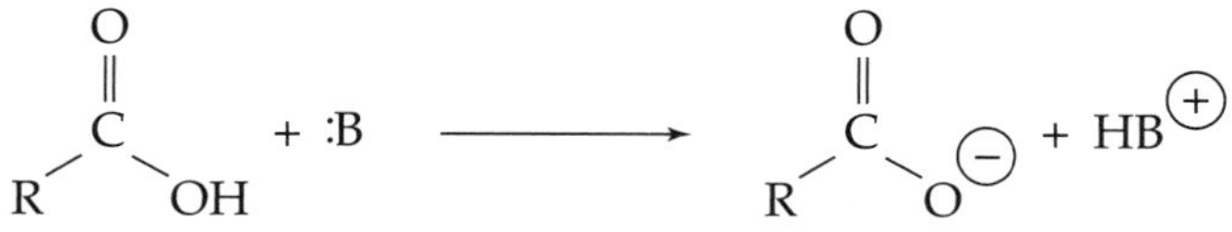

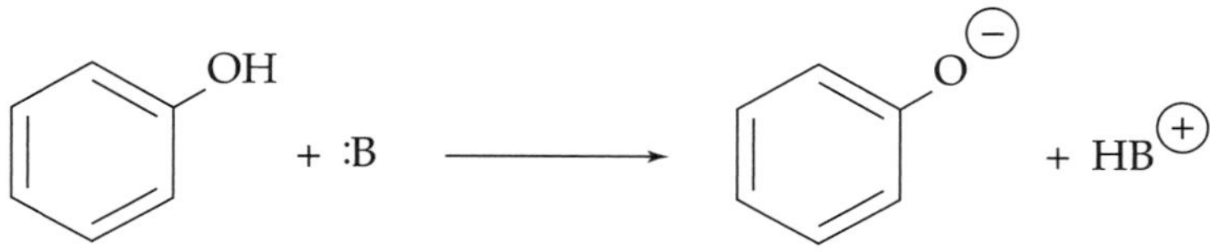

$$\underset{R}{\overset{O}{\overset{\|}{C}}}\!-\!OH \;+\; :B \;\longrightarrow\; \underset{R}{\overset{O}{\overset{\|}{C}}}\!-\!O^{\ominus} \;+\; HB^{\oplus}$$

Acidic forms can be
soluble in organic
solvents when R is large.

Conjugate bases
preferentially dissolve
in aqueous layer.

Since carboxylic acids and phenols have very different acidities, they can be sequentially removed from the organic layer if treated with first a weak base, like $NaHCO_3$, to remove the stronger acid (the COOH), followed by a strong base, like NaOH, to remove the weaker acid (the phenol). The order of base addition is important, since a strong base like hydroxide will deprotonate both the carboxylic acid and the phenol. If both are in their charged form, both will dissolve in the water layer so will still not be separated.

Let's look at a sample extraction scheme in which we attempt to separate four organic molecules: benzoic acid, phenol, aniline, and benzyl alcohol. All four molecules have at least six carbon atoms, and no more than one functional group. Therefore, they should all be more soluble in diethyl ether (a common organic solvent used for extractions) than water.

| benzoic acid (1) | phenol (2) | aniline (3) | benzylalcohol (4) |

To separate out the amine first, add an aqueous solution of HCl. By protonating the NH_2 group, the aniline will wash into the water layer, leaving the remaining compounds in the ether layer and allowing for separation. Next, wash the ether with an aqueous solution of $NaHCO_3$. This will wash the benzoic acid into the second water layer, leaving the two alcohols in the ether. Finally, wash with an aqueous solution of NaOH, which will deprotonate the phenol, leaving the alkyl alcohol untouched since it is not nearly as acidic. The phenol will wash into the final water layer, and the benzyl alcohol will remain in the ether layer.

Please solve this problem:

- Extraction separates substances based on the principle of:

  A. polarity.
  B. solubility.
  C. molecular weight.
  D. acid/base properties.

Problem solved:

B is correct. Choices A and D are properties that must be considered in the selection of an extraction solvent, not the principles on which extraction is based.

Recrystallization

Recrystallization is a technique for isolating one solid substance from a mixture containing other solids, other liquids, or both. Recrystallization is an inefficient process. Significant amounts of the desired material are often lost in the process of recrystallization.

Recrystallization differs from simple precipitation in two important ways. First, recrystallization is a slow process that may require several hours and sometimes days, while precipitation is a rapid process that takes only seconds. Recrystallization, on the other hand, increases the purity of the desired substance by eliminating impurities. Precipitation increases the amount of impurities in the desired substance (in solid phase), since precipitation occurs around nucleation sites, which are generally impurities in the mixture.

Recrystallization solvents are often difficult to select. Such a solvent should possess a low affinity for the substance to be recrystallized at low temperatures, but a much higher affinity for the substance at higher temperatures. In other words, the solubility of the substance to be recrystallized should approach zero at low temperatures, but should be fairly high at higher temperatures. Additionally, the melting point of the recrystallized material must exceed the boiling point of the recrystallization solvent. When a recrystallant is allowed to melt within a recrystallization solvent, the end result is an oil rather than the desired solid product. A final quality of the recrystallization solvent is a high vapor pressure at low temperatures. This solvent volatility makes for the easy removal of the solvent from the crystals once they have formed.

A recrystallization solvent will usually exhibit a higher affinity for impurity molecules than for the desired substance, particularly at low temperatures. The lower the percentage of impurities present in the initial mixture, the higher the probability of a successful recrystallization.

Please solve this problem:

- Among the following, the best recrystallization solvent would have:

  A. a boiling point higher than the melting point of the recrystallant.

  B. a boiling point lower than the melting point of the recrystallant.

  C. a boiling point higher than the boiling point of the recrystallant.

  D. a boiling point lower than the boiling point of the recrystallant.

Problem solved:

B is correct. In order to avoid "boiling out," the boiling point of the recrystallization solvent must be lower than the melting point of the solute to be recrystallized. While choice D must also be true, it is not sufficient to solve the problem.

Distillation

Distillation is a separation method based on boiling point differences. Two important distillation techniques are **simple distillation** and **fractional distillation**.

A simple distillation is a one-step process in which the mixture is heated to the boiling point of the liquid for which recovery is sought. The liquid is then allowed to vaporize and then condense into a separate flask (the receiving flask). Simple distillations are best for purifying solvents from high boiling point liquids or solid impurities since this method separates compounds effectively only when the difference in boiling points of the components in the mixture are greater than 30°C.

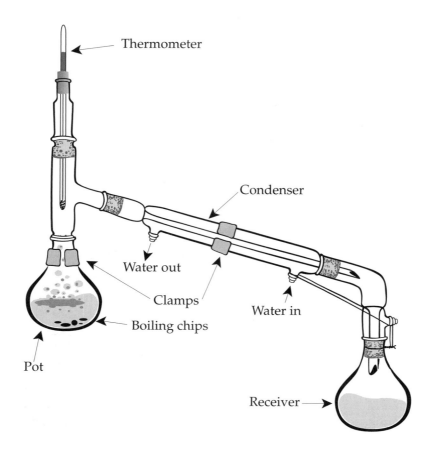

Apparatus for Simple Distillation

Figure 41.1

When the boiling points differ by less than 30°C, a fractional distillation becomes necessary.

A fractional distillation is a series of simple distillations carried out in a single apparatus. A fractional distillation requires the addition of a fractionating column between the distilling flask and the condenser.

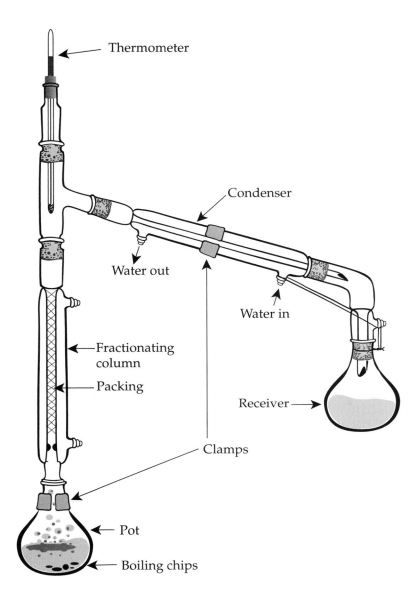

Apparatus for Fractional Distillation

Figure 41.2

In a fractionating column, several distillation steps occur prior to the distillate reaching the condenser. As long as the temperature is controlled, the lower boiling point liquid will vaporize faster and can be collected in a relatively pure form in the first "fractions" that reach the receiver. The higher boiling point liquid will then be collected in later fractions after the temperature is increased.

Chromatography

Chromatography is a separation technique that takes advantage of a *stationary phase* (usually a polar substance) that differentially adsorbs substances from a *mobile phase* (solvent). The many types of chromatography are based upon common underlying principles. The three most important types for the MCAT are thin-layer chromatography, column chromatography, and gas chromatography.

Thin-layer chromatography (TLC) is essentially a small-scale column chromatography. In TLC, a stationary phase is adsorbed to a glass plate prior to the experiment. The stationary phase is typically a polar substance, such as silica (SiO_2). A small amount of the mixture to be separated is applied approximately one inch from the end of the plate. The plate is then placed into chambers containing small volumes of the solvent that will act as the mobile phase. The depth of the mobile phase must be such that the mobile phase does not wash the applied solvent off the plate.

The container with the plate and mobile phase is then closed and left undisturbed while the mobile phase advances up the plate via a "wicking" action. As the solvent advances, it carries with it those materials that are not tightly bound to the polar stationary phase. The substances in the mixture will interact differently with the stationary and mobile phases such that the least polar molecule (having the lowest affinity for the polar stationary phase) will move the farthest distance with the mobile phase. Polar molecules will interact strongly with the stationary phase, and therefore, will move lesser distances.

An important measurement during TLC separations is the R_f value. This is a simple ratio of the distance the compound travels up the plate compared to the distance the solvent travels. As such, R_f values are always less than 1. Since nonpolar molecules do not interact as strongly with the plate and therefore travel farther with the solvent, they have high R_f values. In contrast, polar compounds that stick strongly to the polar plate do not travel as far with the solvent, and therefore have low R_f values. The figure below indicates that a mixture of compounds A and B can be separated based on their polarities using TLC.

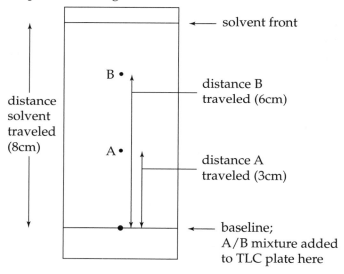

Developed TLC plate showing
separation of compounds
A and B.

$$R_f \text{ for A} = \frac{3}{8} = 0.38$$

$$R_f \text{ for B} = \frac{6}{8} = 0.75$$

Figure 41.3

It should be apparent that compound B is less polar than compound A due to the differences in their R_f values.

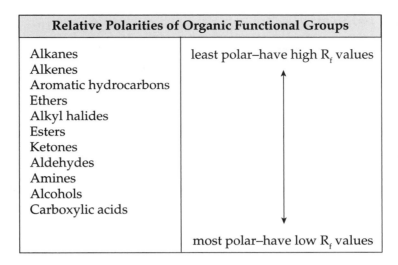

Table 41.1

In **column chromatography**, the stationary phase is packed into a vertical column through which the mixture is eluted by the mobile phase. In **gas chromatography,** the mixture is vaporized and eluted through a liquid stationary phase by a carrier gas (mobile phase).

Solvent (mobile phase) selection is based on the polarity of the substances in the mixture and the expected solubilities of the substances in the mixture. Preferably, all mixture components will be soluble in the mobile phase. Table 41.1 lists the common organic functional groups from least to most polar.

Please solve this problem:

- Thin-layer chromatography (TLC) separates substances based on the principle of:

  A. polarity.
  B. solubility.
  C. molecular weight.
  D. acid/base properties.

Problem solved:

A is correct. In TLC, substances are adsorbed by a polar stationary phase and eluted by a mobile phase.

Electrophoresis

Electrophoresis is similar to chromatography except in the means of separation. Whereas chromatography separates components of a mixture based on differences in polarity, electrophoresis separates mixture components based on electric charge. One end of a plate is supplied with a positive charge, the other with a negative charge. Solutes move along the plate, toward one pole or the other, based on the laws of electrostatics. Since amino acids and proteins have different charge characteristics at differing pHs, electrophoresis is used extensively as a separation method for these compounds.

Please solve this problem:

- Electrophoresis separates substances based on the principle of:

    A. polarity.
    B. molecular weight.
    C. acid/base properties.
    D. electric charge.

Problem solved:

D is correct. In electrophoresis, substances are adsorbed by a stationary phase through which an electric field is established. Substances migrate toward either the positive or the negative end of the stationary phase-coated plate, based on their charge characteristics. Choice C is a consideration when determining electric charge, but acid/base reactions are not the sole determinants of charge in a molecule. Choice D is the better answer.

SPECTROSCOPIC METHODS

General Principles

Spectroscopy deals with a material's absorption or emission of energy in a defined portion of the electromagnetic spectrum. Four spectroscopic methods are outlined in the following sections: mass spectroscopy, ultraviolet (UV) spectroscopy, infrared (IR) spectroscopy, and nuclear magnetic resonance (NMR) spectroscopy. All of these techniques, except mass spectroscopy, are absorption spectroscopies. These spectroscopies are used, either together or separately, to determine the identities of unknown chemical substances.

Mass Spectroscopy

Mass spectroscopy is employed to determine the molecular weight of a substance. In this spectroscopic method, the substance to be analyzed is placed in a chamber where it is bombarded by a stream of high-energy electrons. The substance is broken into smaller pieces by this bombardment. Some of the small pieces take a positive charge and some remain neutral—depending on the particular bond cleavage processes. Once these particles are formed, they are subjected to a magnetic field that serves to filter out the neutral molecules, leaving only the positively charged ions. These positively charged ions are then dispersed based on their mass-to-charge ratio (m/z) and focused on a detector. The result is a mass spectrum—a pattern of peaks corresponding to structural features of the sample substance.

The mass spectrum provides information about the initial molecular weight of the substance and gives insight into the structure of the molecule, since certain peaks are indicative of certain structures.

The mass spectrum of methyl bromide (CH_3Br) is given in Figure 41.4.

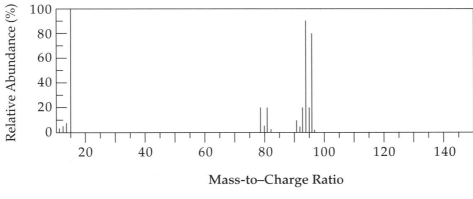

Figure 41.4

For the MCAT, it is less important to be an expert at determining structures from mass spectral than it is to understand the underlying principles of the technique.

Please solve this problem:

- In a typical mass spectrometer, the particles that are detected are:

  A. neutral molecules.
  B. positive ions.
  C. negative ions.
  D. all of the above.

Problem solved:

B is correct. Although a mass spectrometer may be set up to record either positive ions or negative ions, the typical experiment records positive ions. Neutral molecules are not detected in either experimental design.

Ultraviolet (UV) Spectroscopy

In **ultraviolet spectroscopy**, a sample is irradiated with a continuous source of UV radiation of varying wavelengths. The energy associated with the UV portion of the electromagnetic spectrum coincides with the difference in energy levels between molecular orbitals. When a molecule is subjected to a UV wavelength that "matches" the difference in energy between an occupied molecular orbital and an unoccupied molecular orbital, this UV radiation is absorbed—causing an electron to move from the ground state (occupied orbital) to an excited state (the previously unoccupied orbital).

In UV spectroscopy, the sample is placed between the UV source and a detector. If no radiation is absorbed, the amount of UV radiation emitted by the source is the amount of radiation detected at the detector. However, when UV energy is absorbed by the sample, these two amounts differ. It is the difference that allows for the "construction" of a UV spectrum.

The important concept for the MCAT, in relation to UV spectroscopy, is that double bonds absorb UV radiation. Isolated double bonds absorb weakly, while conjugated double bonds and aromatic systems absorb strongly in the UV energy region.

Please solve this problem:

- All the following are expected to be UV active (i.e., produce peaks in the UV spectrum) EXCEPT:

  A. 1,2-dichloroethylene.
  B. 1-propyne.
  C. cyclopentadiene.
  D. 1,3-dibromoethane.

Problem solved:

D is correct. The three compounds in choices A, B, and C each contain at least one site of unsaturation other than a ring (a double bond or a triple bond). 1,3-Dibromoethane is a saturated compound, and therefore, it is expected to be UV inactive.

Infrared (IR) Spectroscopy

Infrared spectroscopy involves the absorption of energy in the IR region of the electromagnetic spectrum. Energy in this region coincides with vibrational modes within a molecule—such as the bond stretching and the bond angle bending that occurs in all molecules at temperatures above absolute zero. Vibrational frequencies are highly indicative of functional groups within a sample. Therefore, the primary use of IR spectroscopy is the identification of functional groups within a sample.

IR spectral units are most often reported in wave numbers. A wave number is the reciprocal of the wavelength. The range of IR wave numbers is from approximately 625 centimeters^{-1} to 4000 centimeters^{-1}. The IR spectrum of N-cyclohexylformamide is provided in Figure 41.5.

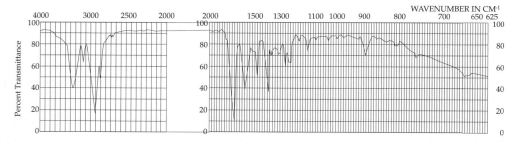

Figure 41.5

The structure of this compound is:

On the MCAT, questions about IR may ask about the types of bonds shown in Table 41.2. Each of the IR bands produced by the stretching or bending of bonds represents the characteristic absorption ranges of the corresponding functional group. While there are many other stretches that might appear in a spectrum, only the ones in the table are likely to appear on the MCAT, so you should be familiar with these wave numbers.

	Bond Type	Stretch (cm⁻¹)
1	C = 0	1690 – 1720
2	O – H	3600 – 3200
3	C = C	~1650
4	C ≡ C C ≡ N	2250 – 2100
5	C – H alkane	2960 – 2850

Table 41.2

Please solve this problem:

- The reaction between methanol and propanoyl chloride to form methyl propanoate could best be followed by:

  A. the appearance of an IR peak at 3,400 cm⁻¹ and the appearance of an IR peak at 1,740 cm⁻¹.
  B. the disappearance of an IR peak at 3,400 cm⁻¹ and the appearance of an IR peak at 1,740 cm⁻¹.
  C. the appearance of an IR peak at 3,400 cm⁻¹ and the disappearance of an IR peak at 1,740 cm⁻¹.
  D. the disappearance of an IR peak at 3,400 cm⁻¹ and the disappearance of an IR peak at 1,740 cm⁻¹.

Problem solved:

B is correct. The IR peak at 3,400 cm⁻¹ coincides with the stretching wave number of the hydroxyl group of methanol. The peak at 1,740 cm⁻¹ coincides with the stretching wave number of the carbonyl group of an ester.

To solve this problem, we must first recognize that one peak referred to in all four choices is an OH stretch and the other is in the carbonyl range. Next, we must recognize that as the ester forms a new C=0 stretch, the OH bond of the alcohol should disappear. Choices A and D can be eliminated since we'd expect one functional group to be changed into another, not two new groups to form or two groups to go away.

To decide between choices B and C, we must remember that an OH stretch has a high wave number.

Nuclear Magnetic Resonance (NMR) Spectroscopy

Nuclear Magnetic Resonance (NMR) Spectroscopy provides a detailed "blueprint" of an organic molecule's carbon-hydrogen framework. It relies on the fact that both protons and carbon nuclei (although not all atomic nuclei) behave as though they were rapidly rotating (spinning) around an axis. The spin, together with the positive charge (produced by nuclear protons), makes them much like little magnets that, in turn, affect and are affected by nearby magnetic fields.

In the absence of an external magnetic field, the magnetic vectors of the nuclei in a molecule are randomly oriented and "cancel each other out." When a large external magnetic field is applied to a chemical sample, the individual nuclei within the sample will align either with the field or in opposition to the field. Nuclei that align with the field are termed **low energy spin state nuclei**. Nuclei that align opposite the field are called **high-energy spin state nuclei**. The application of radio waves causes nuclei in the low spin state to absorb this radiation and "flip" into the high spin state. The absorption of this spin flip energy is measured and recorded as an NMR spectrum.

Not all nuclei show activity under NMR. In order for a nucleus to be NMR active, it must have an odd mass number or an even mass number and an odd atomic number. Two common isotopes used in organic chemistry are ^{1}H and ^{13}C. The proton (^{1}H) NMR spectrum of p-ethoxybenzaldehyde is given in Figure 41.6, and the carbon-13 (^{13}C) NMR spectrum of 3-methyl-2-butanone is given in Figure 41.7.

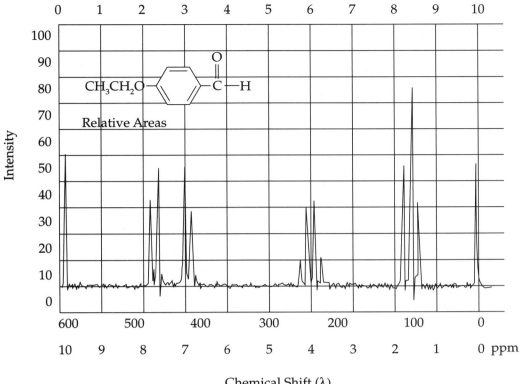

Chemical Shift (λ)

Figure 41.6

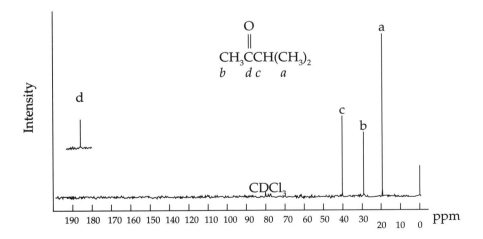

Chemical Shift

Figure 41.7

Carbon-13 NMR is presented on the MCAT in determining the number of different carbons appearing in a molecule (since each different carbon will give rise to a peak at a distinct chemical shift). It is not necessary to memorize the relative shift values of various carbons. It is important to remember, however, that a molecule that possesses symmetry may have several carbons represented by a single peak. For example, 2,2-dimethyl propane {$(CH_3)_4C$} will give rise to only two carbon-13 NMR peaks—one from the central carbon and one from the other four equivalent methyl carbons.

The relative scale used in NMR is the chemical shift, measured in ppm (part per million). A chemical shift of 1 ppm coincides with a change in the applied rf frequency of 1 part per million. The standard for organic chemistry is tetramethylsilane (TMS): The chemical shift of this substance is set as 0 ppm, and all peaks are measured and recorded relative to TMS.

Progressing from left to right along an NMR spectrum, the energy that is absorbed to cause the spin flip increases because of a phenomenon called **shielding**, produced by the electron density that surrounds the nucleus. Nuclei with a low chemical shift (upfield) are said to be shielded, while nuclei with a high chemical shift (downfield) are said to be **deshielded**. As a proton becomes more deshielded, it moves to the left on the NMR spectrum (higher ppm, downfield). The more shielded a proton becomes, the farther to the right it will appear on the NMR spectrum (lower ppm, upfield). Characteristic NMR shift values for protons in different environments are provided in Figure 41.8.

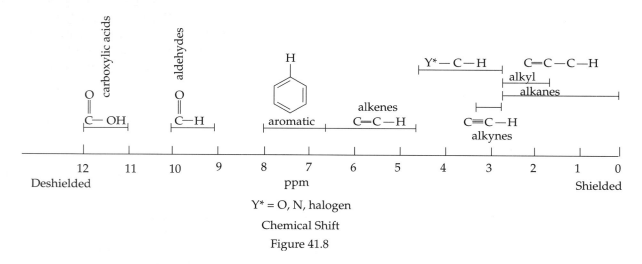

Y* = O, N, halogen

Chemical Shift

Figure 41.8

For a proton NMR spectrum, the area under each peak gives the relative abundance of the protons contributing to that peak. Therefore, in the NMR spectrum of chloroethane ($ClCH_2CH_3$), we expect to see two peaks—one with an integration area of two, the other with an integration area of three. Integration areas are extremely useful for the determination of the total number of hydrogens in a molecule (or contributing to a single peak). However, care must be exercised in that integration areas are *relative* areas, not absolute areas. Therefore, a molecule with symmetry may appear to have fewer hydrogens than it actually does. Consider the NMR spectrum of propane ($CH_3CH_2CH_3$). The two methyl groups are equivalent. Thus, they cause a single peak, with an integration area of three. The methylene group causes a second peak, with an integration area of one. (The ratio 3:1 represents 6:2.)

A final consideration in the interpretation of proton NMR spectra is a phenomenon known as spin-spin splitting (or spin-spin coupling), symbolized *J*. It is important to recognize that a particular nucleus "feels" not only the field applied by our instrument, but also the fields of the nearby protons. The *sum* of the applied fields and those produced by neighboring protons will differ slightly from the applied field and produce the peak patterns that we ultimately observe. Although this phenomenon might create severely confounding complications, for the MCAT, you need concern yourself only with coupling that occurs between the nearest neighboring hydrogens, which we call $J_{1,3}$ **coupling**.

$J_{1,3}$ coupling occurs when two nonequivalent protons are separated from one another (within the same molecule) by two other atoms. For example, if the hydrogens H_A and H_B are chemically nonequivalent, they will experience $J_{1,3}$ coupling; whereas, H_C and H_D will not couple (*insofar as the MCAT is concerned*).

$$
\begin{array}{ccc}
& \text{OH} & \text{Br} \\
& | & | \\
H_A-\!\!\!& C-\!\!\!\!\!-\!\!\!\!\!-C &-H_B \\
& | & | \\
& H_A & H_B
\end{array}
\qquad
\begin{array}{ccccc}
& \text{OH} & \text{H} & \text{Br} \\
& | & | & | \\
H_C-\!\!\!& C-\!\!\!\!\!-\!\!\!\!\!-C-\!\!\!\!\!-\!\!\!\!\!-C &-H_D \\
& | & | & | \\
& H_C & \text{H} & H_D
\end{array}
$$

One peak arises for each nonequivalent proton in the NMR spectrum. When the proton giving rise to one of these peaks is split by a neighboring nonequivalent proton, the peak is split into (n + 1) peaks, where n equals the number of protons that are splitting the proton. Consider, again, the NMR spectrum of propane ($CH_3CH_2CH_3$). As we saw earlier, the two methyl groups are equivalent. Thus, they cause a single peak, with an integration area of 3. The methylene group causes a second peak, with a relative integration area of one. Labeling these two types of hydrogen as H_E and H_F, we see:

$$
\begin{array}{ccccc}
& H_E & H_F & H_E \\
& | & | & | \\
H_E-\!\!\!& C-\!\!\!\!\!-\!\!\!\!\!-C-\!\!\!\!\!-\!\!\!\!\!-C &-H_E \\
& | & | & | \\
& H_E & H_F & H_E
\end{array}
$$

From the above discussion, we can see that the H_E's on the left are split by the two H_F's, as are the 2 H_E's on the right. This causes the methyl peak to be split into three (n + 1, where n = 2) peaks—or a triplet. Likewise, we can see that the H_F's are split by all six H_E's. This causes the methylene peak to be split into seven (n + 1, where n = 6) peaks—or a septet.

What if the hydrogens on the left and right carbons are not equivalent? Consider the NMR spectrum of 1-chloropropane:

$$
\begin{array}{ccccc}
& H_X & H_Y & H_Z \\
& | & | & | \\
\text{Cl}-\!\!\!& C-\!\!\!\!\!-\!\!\!\!\!-C-\!\!\!\!\!-\!\!\!\!\!-C &-H_Z \\
& | & | & | \\
& H_X & H_Y & H_Z
\end{array}
$$

Here, we expect peaks at three distinct chemical shifts (H_X, H_Y, and H_Z). The peak for H_X will be a triplet (split by the two H_Y's). The peak for H_Z will also be a triplet (split by the two H_Y's). The peak for H_Y will be split into a triplet by the two H_X's, each of which, in turn, is split into a quartet by the three H_Z's. The resultant peak is not a sextet, but a quartet of triplets—*twelve peaks*.

In all likelihood, not all of the twelve peaks will be visible in the NMR spectrum. Some will be lost in the baseline or will overlap. In cases where surrounding protons are not equivalent but are somewhat similar, the instrument may "see" them as equivalent. If that were so in this case, a sextet would appear. Oftentimes signals with 5 or more lines are referred to as multiplets.

NMR splitting for:		Type
H_x		Triplet
H_z		Triplet
H_y		Quartet of triplets (multiplet)

Table 41.3

Please solve this problem:

- The proton NMR spectrum of 1-bromo-4-chlorobutane (shown below) will show which of the following sets of peaks (assuming that all the theoretically observable peaks can actually be seen)?

$$Br-CH_2-CH_2-CH_2-CH_2-Cl$$

A. one triplet and one multiplet (of 9 peaks)
B. two triplets and two multiplets (of 9 peaks each)
C. one triplet and two multiplets (of 9 peaks each)
D. two triplets and one multiplet (of 9 peaks)

Problem solved:

B is correct. The molecule is asymmetric, which means it confronts us with four nonequivalent sets of protons, one on each carbon. Consequently, we will observe four signals in the spectrum. That means, immediately, that choices A, C, and D are wrong. Now, consider choice B. Here's the molecule at issue:

$$Br-CH_2-CH_2-CH_2CH_2-Cl$$
$$a \quad b \quad c \quad d$$

Protons H_b and H_a sit on adjacent carbons. Protons H_b will split protons H_a into a triplet according to the $n + 1$ rule. Similarly, protons H_c will split protons H_d into a triplet. The absorption for protons H_b will be split into a triplet by protons H_c, and each peak of that triplet will be split into a triplet by the protons of group H_a (which are not equivalent to H_c). That will produce a multiple of nine peaks: $(n + 1) \times (n + 1)$ for H_b. Exactly the same thing will happen for the absorption of protons in group H_c except that this absorption is split into a triplet by protons H_b and further split into a triplet of triplets by H_d $(n + 1) \times (n + 1)$. Since the protons in groups a and d are adjacent to atoms of high (but differing) electronegativity, the triplets they produce will appear at slightly different positions in the spectrum (and to the left of the multiples for H_b and H_c, which are farther from the electronegative atoms). The answer is easily arrived at by quick and simple elimination of choices A, C, and D. Yet, sufficient details are provided so that you may become tangled in their "knots" and spend much time *verifying* the correctness of choice B.

41.2 MASTERY APPLIED: PRACTICE PASSAGE AND QUESTIONS

Passage

A wide variety of techniques can be used to separate and identify compounds. Most of these techniques are based on differences in physical properties. Procedures differ in their specific mode of action, each of which may separate or help to identify a compound based on a different characteristic of the unknown sample. Extraction separates solutions by drawing into aqueous solution chemicals that are acidic, basic, or highly polar and at low molecular weight. A series of extractions are used in a solution with many components. Distillation is based on differences in boiling points. This technique can be used only when the vapor pressures are far enough apart to allow one substance to be completely removed without boiling out the others simultaneously. Frequently, a technique is used that involves purification and separation through a process of solvation. This procedure is known as recrystallization. When dealing with substances of significantly different polarity, thin layer chromatography (TLC) can reveal different elution distances as a result of differences in polarity of the unknown components of the solution. A similar technique is electrophoresis. This procedure is commonly used in genetic sequencing. DNA is broken down, and its components are drawn through a gel based on the attraction of opposite charges. Different negatively charged nucleotides arrive at a positively charged plate at varying times, revealing the nucleotide sequence of the sample. Other methods of identification include methods of spectroscopy. Proton nuclear magnetic resonance and infrared spectroscopy are the most common. The former identifies compounds based on differing magnetic environments of protons, while the latter compares absorption frequencies of electromagnetic energy.

1. Which of the following techniques would be best for distinguishing compounds of differing dipole moments within a solution?

   A. Electrophoresis
   B. Extraction
   C. Thin layer chromatography
   D. Distillation

2. In the process of recrystallization, why must the desired solute, relative to the solvent, have high solubility at high temperatures and low solubility at low temperatures?

   A. The desired solute must be in the liquid phase at high temperatures, otherwise it would melt.
   B. The solubility must be high at high temperatures to allow the desired solute to pass into solution and ultimately be purified, but low at low temperature so that the purified solute can recrystallize upon cooling.
   C. The solubility must be high at high temperatures so impurities will remain in their solid form to be removed by filtration.
   D. The solubility must be high at high temperatures and low at low temperatures so that the solute can pass into solution and the two compounds can be boiled off and recondensed at different times.

3. Why would a chemist NOT run an IR on an unknown most likely to be identified as hexane?

   A. An IR would not be effective because all the protons in hexane have the same magnetic environments.
   B. An IR would not be effective because there are no stretching frequencies between carbon and hydrogen in hexane.
   C. An IR would not be effective because it typically distinguishes compounds based on functional groups.
   D. An IR would not be effective because hexane would not absorb electromagnetic energy.

4. Which of the following describes the proton NMR pattern seen for 2-chloropropane?

   A. Two singlets
   B. A doublet and a septet
   C. A singlet and a septet
   D. A doublet and a sextet

5. An extraction is performed in which a substance is separated out with the addition of sodium bicarbonate. Which of the following would *definitely* be removed by the extraction?

   A. Methane
   B. A phenol
   C. An ether
   D. Acetic acid

6. Immediately following the extraction described in the previous question, a second extraction is performed in which an amine is removed after passing into the aqueous phase. What compound was used to extract the amine?

   A. Diethyl ether
   B. $NaHCO_3$
   C. HCl
   D. NaOH

7. Which of the following procedures breaks up compounds by bombarding them with high-energy electrons to yield information regarding mass/charge ratio?

   A. NMR
   B. Mass spectroscopy
   C. IR
   D. Electrophoresis

41.3 MASTERY VERIFIED: ANSWERS AND EXPLANATIONS

1. **C is correct.** To speak of dipole moments is to imply polarity. Thin layer chromatography uses polarity to differentiate between components of a solution. More polar substances tend to remain in the stationary phase while less polar substances will elute further in the mobile phase. Distillation involves boiling points and extraction involves solubility. Electrophoresis requires charge, which is not necessary for polarity.

2. **B is correct.** The basis of recrystallization is that a substance can be purified when heated and solvated, and will *recrystallize* upon cooling. Choice A implies that melting point is the critical factor, which it is not. Although filtration (choice C) may occur at some point in the process, it does not explain why the solvent requires certain characteristics. Choice D implies that boiling point is the determining factor in choosing a solvent. While boiling point may be a factor, it does not explain why solubility must change at different temperatures.

3. **C is correct.** Infrared spectroscopy is based on absorption frequencies of functional groups with different dipole moments. Hexane has no functional groups. Choice A describes NMR. Choices B and D are incorrect; C-H stretches do exist for hexane, and electromagnetic energy would be absorbed.

4. **B is correct.** The single proton on the central carbon would be split by six neighboring carbons (three from each attached methyl group). The two methyl groups would be split by the single proton on the central carbon. According to the $n + 1$ rule, there would be a doublet and a septet.

5. **D is correct.** Extraction removes substances by separating them from an ether solution to an aqueous solution. The components that react with, or are soluble in, the added compounds will pass into aqueous solution. In this case, a base, sodium bicarbonate, will interact with an acid. The only definite acid among the answers is acetic acid. Although phenols are acidic, $NaHCO_3$ is not a strong enough base to deprotonate it.

6. **C is correct.** Again, the same principles apply as in question five. This is simply the opposite situation. Here, we are extracting an amine, which is a base. The most likely compound added would be an acid, which would react with the base and pass into aqueous solution. The only acid given is HCl.

7. **B is correct.** NMR involves magnetic environments. Electrophoresis is a separation and identification technique based on movement of charged particles. Infrared spectroscopy involves absorption frequencies of various bonds within a molecule. Mass spectroscopy is the only process that yields information regarding mass/charge ratio.

CHAPTER 42

MASTERING VERBAL REASONING

The MCAT verbal reasoning section contains several reading passages, each followed by 4 to 7 questions. The test taker is allowed sixty minutes to read the passages and answer the questions. Students vary widely as to the degree to which they find this portion of the examination challenging; it has proven especially challenging for those test takers whose native language is not English. Nonetheless, the verbal reasoning portion of the MCAT is susceptible to *strategy*.

To begin, students should not make the *passage* the central focus of their effort. They must remember that the test is scored by the number of answers marked *correct*. If students are able to apply a strategy that allows them to maximize the number of correct answers they select, they should do so, even if it means they do not truly comprehend the passage in its entirety. The test taker who performs most successfully on the MCAT verbal reasoning section is the one who recognizes that the passages are in a sense "secondary" to the task and who approaches the task strategically.

Most students who sit for the MCAT exam have developed good study habits in secondary school and college, and most have produced high cumulative grade-point averages throughout their undergraduate years. For this sort of student, the suggestion that passages laden with fact, theory, and information represent obstacles to their success on this exam will probably be very difficult to accept. Good students do not usually look to avoid reading, learning, or understanding. Certainly, successful medical students will not wish to shortchange their professors, future patients, or themselves by seeking "shortcuts" around the challenging reading assignments that characterize the study of medicine.

However, in medical school, you are not obliged to read under the same time restrictions that apply to the MCAT. The tasks on this section of the MCAT are unlike the academic challenges met in college or medical school. You should not, therefore, be averse to approaching the MCAT's verbal reasoning section with our shortcuts and strategies. Our recommendation that you do so is based on our wish to see you achieve a high score. *We make no such recommendation in respect of medical school itself*, nor indeed in respect of any serious scholarly endeavor.

42.1 PASSAGES AND QUESTIONS OVERVIEW

Like all multiple-choice questions, verbal reasoning questions feature (1) a *stem* (the portion that precedes the answer choices) and (2) answer choices.

Passages might concern almost any topic. Each usually presents 1 to 2 passages addressing a natural science topic. The remaining passages concern the social sciences, history, public policy, the humanities, literature, philosophy, religion, or a writer's personal account of her own experience or perspective.

SCIENCE PASSAGES

Passages that concern technology or the natural sciences often feature substantial amounts of factual information, conceptual distinctions, and technical explanations. For example, consider this passage segment:

Excerpt 42A

The "knot problem," as it has been called, relates largely to the difficulties associated with classifying knots. In mathematical terms, a knot is any closed curve in three-dimensional space that never passes more than once through the same point of space and that may be thought of as starting at a point S and ultimately returning to S.

Any two knots belong to the same knot class if a continuous deformation of space carries one of them into the position initially held by the other. If a knot should belong to the same class as a circle, it is *considered* unknotted. The reason pertains to cognitive convenience. Just as it is conceptually helpful to view a straight line as one particular species of curve, so is it mentally useful to consider an unknotted curve as one subtype of knot.

Curves with a reasonable degree of regularity are ordinarily conceived of as threads, twisted and tangled in such a manner as to have their ends sealed to each other. According to this conception, the "knot problem," in some minds, asks for a description of the conditions under which the process of stretching, shrinking, and bending will allow one twisted…

For passages concerning science or technology, many (but not all) questions require you to recognize a statement that paraphrases technical information provided by the author. Consider the following simulated MCAT question:

1. According to the passage, a knot is characterized by a curve whose beginning point:

   A. represents a spot on an arbitrary circle.
   B. generates a curve with a reasonable degree of regularity.
   C. coincides with the point of its own ending.
   D. fails to approximate its own end point.

C is correct. This choice paraphrases the end of the last sentence of the first paragraph: "a knot… may be thought of as starting at point S and ultimately returning to S."

However, some of the questions associated with natural science passages require not only a direct and immediate understanding of the text, but also (1) extrapolation, (2) abstraction, and/or (3) application of the text to a seemingly unrelated subject. Consider the "knot" passage and read this simulated MCAT question:

2. When celestial navigators work their calculations, they find it practical to envision the earth as the center of an orbit through which the sun moves. This manner of thought most closely parallels which of the following views described in the passage?

   A. A knot cannot conveniently be conceived as embodying a straight line.
   B. The "knot problem" is not susceptible to any single solution but is instead understandable from a variety of perspectives.
   C. A knot never passes through the same point twice.
   D. A knot belonging to the same class as a circle is considered "unknotted."

D is correct. This question asks you to use abstraction and application to find an analogy between the information in the question stem and a view expressed in the passage. The stem describes using a view that contradicts reality (that the sun moves around the earth), in order to calculate orbits. In the part of the passage cited in choice D, the author states that it is "mentally useful" to consider a certain type of unknotted curve to be a knot, that is, to conceive of a knot that is not a knot (a contradiction of reality).

HUMANITIES AND SOCIAL SCIENCE PASSAGES

Humanities and social science passages *sometimes* ask the student to recognize statements that paraphrase the text. More often, they call for some kind of extrapolation and abstraction. At times, they call for an understanding of the author's tone or attitude. Frequently, they require the student to understand the sense of a word or phrase that appears in the passage.

Consider this simulated MCAT passage segment and the questions that follow it:

Excerpt 42B

In ancient times, the spiritual life of an individual remained tethered to a vibrant, intricate, and vivid natural world. Humans required a means by which their own actions might achieve control and mastery over "reality." Despite great diversity and variation among the myriad ancient civilizations that developed and declined during the ages, this objective reality retained certain unchanging elements. For example, virtually all cultures confronted the need to protect themselves from dangerous and nihilistic external powers. Common throughout antiquity was the strategic use of animism and anthropomorphism to constrain climactic, cosmological, and natural phenomena within familiar and readily understood paradigms.

By conjuring forces imagined more dark and more brutal even than the "real" phenomena beyond human influence—which nearly always appeared antithetical to the goals and aspirations of individuals and societies—

"magic" provided a systematic method for acquiring supernatural leverage. As human theology matured, the dark forces lost cultural favor, and communities appointed priests to petition benevolent potencies for protection against menace and destruction.

Cultural history gradually transformed these benevolent potencies into deities of creation and gods of healing, and the ancient Greek hierarchy, for example, bestowed upon them a more exalted position than it accorded the evil powers. If a community faced a period of cultural waning, however, and passed through a crisis of confidence, foreign cabals and alien sects of tremendous variety would become prominent and popular. Despite governmental sanctions, these exotic cults offered novel perspectives and esoteric rituals for a population dissatisfied with displaced traditions and dissipated spiritual conceptions.

1. According to the passage, early human cultures resorted to animism and anthropomorphism because:

   A. sorcery threatened to disrupt their communities.
   B. animal sacrifice relieved stress on scarce food resources.
   C. priests became involved in tribal political struggles.
   D. simple models of reality mollified their sense of vulnerability.

2. As used in the second paragraph, the word "dark" most nearly means:

   A. unenlightened.
   B. invisible.
   C. threatening.
   D. benighted.

Both of these questions ask you, in some form, to find the answer that is best supported by information in the passage. The answer to question 1 is choice D, which corresponds to the claim in the last two sentences in paragraph 1 that most cultures used "familiar and readily understood paradigms" to "protect themselves from dangerous and nihilistic external powers." Question 2 asks for the meaning of the word "dark" in the context of the passage. The word "threatening" in the correct answer, choice C, best captures the meaning of "dark" in the second paragraph; "dark forces" are contrasted here with "benevolent potencies."

As further illustration, consider this passage segment and the questions that follow it:

Excerpt 42C

Playwrights of the naturalist school believed in representationalism rather than expressionism as the most appropriate mode for dramaturgy. This belief translated in practice to constraining their dialogues and actions to forms they observed in everyday life. Such a strategy proved facile for writers whose interests delved no more deeply than the superficial interactions of human affairs: Ordinary discussions of jobs and meals and mating mishaps required no expressionistic elaboration to articulate the pauses and silences that punctuate normal human discourse.

The more significant playwrights, however, wished to explore weightier themes relating to the entire experience of the human condition, but not at the expense of their artistic commitment to naturalistic dialogue. Out of this dilemma evolved the recourse to "symbolism," through which many of our most accomplished playwrights—Chekhov, Ibsen, and Strindberg, for instance—enlisted visual metaphors to convey a substantial portion of the dramaturgical gist. Thus, by restricting their dialogue to the patterns and rhythms of normal conversation, the naturalists uncovered a wealth of theatrical representation in the visual dimension.

1. Which of the following statements, if true, most weakens the author's argument in the second paragraph?

   A. Some playwrights who rejected expressionism confined themselves to depictions of superficial matters.
   B. Expressionist playwrights attempted to explore weighty themes that expressed the human condition.
   C. The way in which Chekhov and Ibsen staged and presented their plays was visually indistinguishable from the staging of the most expressionist plays.
   D. Ibsen and Strindberg rejected dialogue devices that stylized the ordinary tempos and syntax of conversation.

2. Suppose a naturalist playwright wants an audience to perceive that a particular character is experiencing grief over the loss of a loved person or object. Among the following, the playwright would LEAST likely attempt to achieve that goal by:

   A. creating dialogue in which the character describes the grief he feels and the reasons why he feels it.
   B. conveying the character's sense of grief through a conversation that concerns ordinary daily affairs.
   C. introducing a symbolic representation of grief.
   D. conveying the concept of grief through visual imagery.

Each of these questions requires more complex reasoning on your part than do the questions attached to Excerpt 42B. Question 1 asks you to find an answer choice that provides new information that most weakens or undermines the author's claims in the passage. The correct answer, choice C, attacks the author's argument that these naturalist playwrights distinguished themselves by a greater use of visual symbolism or metaphor. Question 2 gives you new information in the question stem itself that you need to apply to the passage in order to find the answer that is least consistent with the description of naturalism in the passage. The correct answer, choice A, is inconsistent with the author's description of naturalist playwrights' reliance on natural dialogue and visual imagery to convey their message.

PERSONAL EXPERIENCE PASSAGES

For passages that describe a personal experience some questions might require the reader to search the passage for factual details. Other questions will ask the reader to abstract, extrapolate, or interpret information given in the passage. Consider this excerpt from a simulated MCAT passage and the questions that follow:

Excerpt 42D

In my adolescence and adulthood, I went through experiences that I could only describe as supernatural interventions, such episodes varying from visual manifestations and audible voices to the feeling that animals conceived a special—and extraordinary—communicability with me. On one occasion, I even received physical, serendipitous manna falling from the providential skies. Raised in an agnostic tradition by loving parents who never openly professed a belief in a divine being, I did not know exactly how to incorporate my formative understanding of the world and the human condition with these undeniably odd perceptions and unworldly contacts.

Did all these episodes occur under the direction of a beneficent God? I yearned for the certainty that some of my friends declared, friends who had devoted their childhood Saturdays and Sundays to religious services; absent that, I considered the likelihood of the Oz explanation—that some human agency possessing a vast, secret, futuristic technology could transmit graphic holograms and microradiowaved sounds to my brain. Somehow, it seemed more plausible than the possibility that a divine being would take the time and the interest to communicate with and watch out for me especially. Nonetheless, the Oz explanation was terribly frightening, too, and I knew better than to speak openly of it outside private and trusted circles. After all, people were diagnosed as schizophrenic—and stowed away in locked hospital wards—just for talking about such ideas!

1. Based on this passage, the author's feelings about himself are best characterized as demonstrating:

    A. self-hatred and obsession.
    B. conceit and narcissism.
    C. humility and self-doubt.
    D. apathy and self-destruction.

2. Suppose a person believes that his misfortunes are the result of evil spirits that have placed themselves within his body. Given the discussion of the "Oz explanation," the author would most likely advise this person to:

    A. consider his observations as serendipitous, but not truly providential.
    B. exercise caution when choosing the people in whom he confides his belief.
    C. seek psychotherapy in order that he better understand his feelings and impulses.
    D. pray to a divine power for relief.

Question 1 requires you to describe how the author feels about himself, based on the information in, and wording of, the passage. Choice C is correct because it best matches up with the passage's description of the author's search for meaning and understanding of both the world and his "undeniably odd perceptions," and of the author's reluctance to openly express his ideas. Question 2 is more complex; it provides new information in the question stem that is analogous to the "Oz explanation" described in the passage, and then asks how the author would respond. Choice B is correct because it best matches the author's own reaction to this "frightening" idea.

Mastery Verified: Answers

<u>42 A</u>   <u>42 C</u>
1. C   1. C
2. D   2. A

<u>42 B</u>   <u>42 D</u>
1. D   1. C
2. C   2. B

QUESTION TYPES

Now that you have an overview of the types of passages that appear in the verbal section and have seen some of the kinds of questions that are often asked about those types of passages, let's take a more general look at verbal reasoning question types. Questions in the verbal section fall into one of three categories: Specific, General, and Complex.

Specific Questions

Specific questions ask you to find the answer that is best supported by the passage text. They may ask you to simply retrieve information about a particular subject or issue. These often have wording like, "According to the passage…" or "The author states…" Question 1 for Excerpt 42A and question 1 for Excerpt 42B are examples of this question type. The correct answer will usually paraphrase information given in the passage. Look out for wrong answers that "sound like" the passage, and that may even have some of the same vocabulary, but that have a different meaning.

Another type of Specific question asks you to make an inference based on passage information. They may be worded as: "Which of the following can be inferred from the passage," "Which of the following is best supported by the passage," "The passage suggests which of the following," or "With which of the following statements would the author be most likely to agree?" These questions may or may not give you a reference within the question stem to specific content in the passage. While finding the answer to these questions may require you to extrapolate from the information in the passage, you are still looking for the answer choice that is most closely based on the passage text and only that text. Look out for wrong answers that require you to use your own opinion or outside knowledge, or that go too far beyond the scope or strength of the author's claims.

A third type of Specific question asks what the author means by a particular word or phrase, as in question 2 for Excerpt 42B. Again, you are looking for an answer choice that best matches, and logically fits into, the relevant part of the text. Therefore, look out for wrong answers that may be a common definition of a relevant word, but that don't accurately match up with what the author means to communicate with that word or phrase.

General Questions

General questions, while still asking you to find an answer that is best supported by the passage, require you to keep the scope of the question task in mind; they are asking you to find an answer that sums up the passage as a whole. They usually include a phrase like "main idea" or "primary purpose." General questions may also ask you for the overall tone of the passage or attitude of the author. Look for a correct answer that captures the overall theme of the passage rather than just one chunk of it.

Complex Questions

Complex questions still require you to actively use the passage, but they also entail some level of abstraction or application of new information.

The most common of these are questions that provide new information in the question stem, as in question 2 for Excerpt 42A and question 2 for Excerpt 42D. The question might ask how the author would respond, or how that new information would strengthen or weaken the passage. Regardless, make sure that you summarize the point or theme of the new information, and how it relates to the passage, before evaluating the choices.

Another common type of Complex question asks what choice would most strengthen (or support) or weaken (or undermine) the passage, and gives you new information in each answer choice to apply to the passage text. It is crucial when answering these questions to recognize that, unlike Specific questions, they are not asking you to find an answer that is best supported by what you already know from the passage. The four choices are, by definition, true statements, and your task is to find the choice that most supports or detracts from the author's argument. When answering strengthen and weaken questions, keep close track of what direction the correct answer needs to take: with or against the passage.

A rarer form of Complex question asks you to make an analogy to something in the passage. Question 2 for Excerpt 42A is an example of this question type. These questions require both abstraction and application. You must figure out the underlying logic of the relevant part of the passage, and then find the new information in the correct answer that best matches up with that logic. When answering an analogy question, be sure to think beyond the surface content of the passage; define the logic of the relevant section before evaluating the answer choices.

Finally, other Complex questions will ask you to describe the logic of the passage in some form. They might ask you why the author makes a particular statement (for example, "The author mentions Ibsen in order to...") or if, or how well, one of the author's claims is supported (for example, "The author's claim that exotic cults may arise in times of cultural waning is supported..."). While these questions do not require you to apply new information, they do require some level of abstraction. You will need to define how different parts of the passage logically relate to each other, or in some cases, evaluate the strength or validity of the author's claims.

Question Formats

Most of these question types can also show up in two alternative formats.

1. EXCEPT/LEAST/NOT

These questions usually ask, in some form, what is not supported by the passage. For example, it may say, "The author would agree with all of the following statements EXCEPT," "Which of the following is NOT supported by the passage," or "Which of the following statements is LEAST supported by the passage." When addressing these questions, keep close track of the question task in order to eliminate the three choices that ARE supported and to find the exception that is not.

2. Roman numeral

These questions give you three statements labeled with Roman numerals, and different numerals or combinations of numerals in each answer choice. For example:

Which of the following statements is/are supported by the passage?

I.

II.

III.

A. I only

B. I and II only

C. II and III only

D. I, II, and III

When answering these questions, if you are sure a numeral is supported by the passage, eliminate all choices that do not include it. If you are sure a statement in a numeral is not supported, eliminate all choices that do include it. If you are down to two or three choices, compare them to each other, and look most closely at the numerals that are in one choice but not another.

42.2 THE RIGHT ANSWER: UNMASKING DISGUISES

In many verbal reasoning questions, the correct answer takes a statement made in the passage and restates it using different words. One primary "skill" that this MCAT section evaluates is your ability to recognize textual meaning "dressed up" in verbal disguise. For example:

The Phrase	By and Large Conveys the same Meaning As the Phrase
a convincingly communicated insight	a perception articulated with persuasion
the philosophy underlying her position	the modes and patterns of thought on which a viewpoint is founded
The intricate dynamic by which these phenomena may affect one another continue to elude those who study and attempt to understand them.	Investigators remain puzzled by the complex relations among these varied things and events and the impact each may have on others.

Consider this sentence:

> In accordance with the nature of health care work and the character of those who enter the field, most dedicated health care professionals, regardless of ethnicity or gender, are known to derive substantial gratification when their therapeutic efforts lead to positive patient outcomes.

Based on this one sentence, choose the one most appropriate answer to the following question:

1. Which of the following assertions best reflects the author's belief about the way medical workers feel regarding patient care?

   A. Doctors and nurses largely prefer to recommend medical treatments rather than surgical measures.
   B. Interns and residents enjoy emergency room rotations more than they do other hospital duties.
   C. Dedicated healers find substantial gratification from positive outcomes.
   D. Sensitive physicians don't discuss their patients' private records.

C is clearly correct (and most students can see that). The statements made in options A, B, and D are not nonsensical or erroneous per se, but they reflect ideas not expressed in the passage.

When a verbal reasoning question asks for the characterizations of an author's belief or position, the correct answer will usually not reproduce, precisely, the author's own words. Rather, it will in most cases restate the author's meaning in *paraphrase*. The correct answer might not, therefore, "leap out." Be "wise" to the questioners' tendency to *paraphrase,* and search for an answer that conveys the author's meaning in different words. Consider again this sentence, and then the question that follows it:

> In accordance with the nature of health care work and the character of those who enter the field, most dedicated health care professionals, regardless of ethnicity or gender, are known to derive substantial gratification when their therapeutic efforts lead to positive patient outcomes.

> Which of the following assertions best reflects the author's belief about the way medical workers feel regarding patient care?

> A. Doctors and nurses largely prefer to recommend medical treatments rather than surgical measures.
> B. Interns and residents enjoy emergency room rotations more than they do other hospital duties.
> C. Devoted caregivers garner meaningful satisfaction from successful therapeutic interventions.
> D. Sensitive physicians don't discuss their patients' private records.

C remains the correct answer, even though the statement is reworded. Test takers who understand that verbal disguise is a principal device used by the MCAT writers are less often deceived by paraphrase.

Master a few simple techniques that will help you penetrate disguises. Three brief samples of MCAT-like paraphrases are offered below. Remember to do the following:

- Read the selection.

- Carefully consider the meaning of the text.

- Think about each answer choice while bearing the meaning of the text in mind.

- Decide which one best reflects a *disguised* version of the author's meaning.

Example 1

> The realities of life lend themselves to a myriad interpretations, and not infrequently one's personal orientation and attitude colors one's subjective experience. Life is not so much what it is—but rather, what it seems.
>
> According to the passage, one's subjective experience of life:
>
> A. is appropriate subject matter for literature and art.
> B. depends on an individual's perspective and disposition.
> C. varies according to the season of the year.
> D. depends on parental teachings and values.

The author's meaning is that the way a person perceives the hazards and vicissitudes that characterize the human condition can affect the way he or she thinks and feels about life. The author believes that two different people might experience an identical phenomenon, and because of the difference in the way they view things, their respective sense of what had happened to them might be remarkably distinct. Mindful of that, the student should analyze each answer option and identify the one that represents the author's message—in disguise.

Choice A means that an individual's life experiences provide good material for artistic representation. Although this sounds like a sensible statement, it is not anything like the statement conveyed by the passage. Choice B means approximately the same thing as the text, only presented to the test taker in paraphrase:

"colors"
is disguised as
"depends on"

"perspective"
is disguised as
"orientation"

"attitude"
is disguised as
"disposition"

Option C refers to the idea that people's sense of their experiences can change with the seasons. The passage says nothing close to that in meaning. Option D indicates that an individual's experience of life may be greatly determined by his or her formative upbringing. This idea is certainly not a silly one, however, it is not directly related to the author's message; the passage text doesn't tell us that a person's upbringing shapes that person's personal orientation or attitude. Option B is the only one of the four suggested options that is similar enough to the author's meaning: It is the only answer that represents the author's meaning in disguise.

Example 2

> Powerful politicians and important states persons have arisen from origins tremendously diverse in terms of the social, economic and educational conditions of their respective lives. The student of history must conclude from this observation that political greatness stems from individual traits of personality and inner character.

> The text implies that successful political careers are due to:

> **A.** the ability of individuals to educate themselves.
> **B.** a lack of sophistication on the part of the voting public.
> **C.** strategic intervention at crucial historical moments.
> **D.** human characteristics unrelated to cultural or pecuniary circumstance.

To begin with, the author's text conveys the view that regardless of an individual's background, history has demonstrated that he or she can achieve political success given the right combination of personal attributes.

Option A states that a politician's success depends on his or her level of self-education. While this notion seems intriguing, it is not what was said in the passage. Option B implies that only in the context of a population that is uneducated, uninterested, uninformed, or easily misled can politicians achieve success. Although historians might enjoy debating this idea, it is not in the least similar to the author's message. Option C focuses on a particular aspect of a politician's activities, the ability to anticipate political trends and manage crises adroitly. Again, the assertion appears coherent and logical; the author, however, does not mention it. Option D, on the other hand, very closely approximates the significance of the text, by presenting the author's idea in disguise:

"individual traits of personality and inner character"
is disguised as
"human characteristics"

"social, economic and educational conditions"
is disguised as
"cultural or pecuniary circumstance"

Hence, D is the correct answer.

Example 3

> People's willingness to believe in tales of extraterrestrial visitations and flying saucer abductions reveals a fundamental dearth of fulfillment in their daily experience: thus, the invention of extraordinary activities and involvements to convince themselves of their own importance.

> The author contends that experiences of extraterrestrial contacts derives from:

> **A.** the intellectual desire to integrate new astronomical findings with daily experience.
> **B.** the moral need to believe in deliverance from human problems.
> **C.** an underlying lack of satisfaction with their lives.
> **D.** a basic conviction that technologies on other planets are more advanced than those on Earth.

The author asserts that in order to compensate for the ordinariness and tedium of their everyday lives, some people profess to have been visited by or witness to manifestations of creatures from outer space. Option A states that stories of space alien exploits stem from a wish to incorporate daily life with recent scientific discoveries. Nothing like this sentiment appears in the passage. Option B refers to a spiritual hunger for salvation from the dilemmas of mortal humanity as the motive behind reports of extraterrestrial phenomena. Although as a psychological thesis this notion may prove feasible, it reflects nothing of what this author wrote. Option C concerns a basic dissatisfaction with daily routine and circumstance as the cause of people's accounts of extraterrestrial activity. On reflection, that is quite similar to the author's meaning:

"fundamental dearth of fulfillment"
is disguised as

"underlying lack of satisfaction" "in their daily experience"
is disguised as
"with their lives"

Option D cites a suspicion that extraterrestrial civilizations have invented far more sophisticated technologies than humans on Earth have developed as the reason for descriptions of alien sightings. The author did not refer to such a concept. Option C is the only one of the four that paraphrases the author's original text. It is correct.

Most correct answers appear, to some extent, "in disguise" in order to make it more challenging for you to find them. However, occasionally a right answer to a Specific question will quote the passage almost word for word. Even if the question asks what can be inferred or what is suggested, if the answer choice corresponds to the question stem and directly and accurately quotes the passage, it is still a correct answer.

CHAPTER 43

VERBAL REASONING DISTRACTORS

43.1 DISCARDING WRONG ANSWERS

Your fundamental approach to evaluating the answer choices should be Process of Elimination, or POE. Approach the answers critically; rather than looking for and immediately choosing the answer that "sounds good," eliminate down to the credited response by striking out the incorrect choices. The "least wrong" answer is the credited response, but it is not always the answer that looks the best at first glance.

Incorrect answers are called "Distractors" because that is what they do--they distract you away from the correct answer and lure you into bad decisions. Question writers know what test takers will be thinking and looking for, and what kinds of logical mistakes people tend to make. These test writers are also highly skilled at creating wrong answers that "look good" but still have some, at times quite subtle, fatal flaw. Distractors may be so artfully composed as to derail even those who read with great diligence and comprehension.

One way to maximize your verbal reasoning score is to understand how Distractors are designed, and to actively search them out and strike them out as you take the test. This will improve not only your accuracy but also your speed. More quickly recognizing and eliminating wrong answers gets you to the right answer faster.

There are three overall categories of Distractors, with several subtypes within each category. The categories and subtypes are not mutually exclusive; one answer choice may embody a variety of Distractors.

43.2 DISTRACTOR CATEGORY 1: DECOYS

Decoys are wrong answers that are written to sound and look just like correct answers. Test writers use them very much like hunters do. Hunters put out a lure that sounds or looks just like a member of the animal's own species; the prey is so excited to find a friend that it overlooks the differences and falls right into the trap. Here are some types of decoys you will see on the test.

1. MANGLERS

This is the most common type of decoy. Manglers use words or phrases from the passage, but mangle or distort the meaning of the text by taking those words out of context. For example, consider this sentence and the following question:

"Whenever Alice was feeling lonely, it always seemed to rain."

1. Which of the following assertions best reflects the author's description of Alice?

   A. Every time it rained, Alice felt lonely.
   B. Alice thought the rain always sounded lonely.
   C. Rain seemed to fall whenever Alice found herself in a lonesome mood.
   D. Lonely as she was, Alice liked the rain.

Each of answer choices A, B, and D includes words from the original sentence. However, each one also changes or mangles the meaning of the original text. Only choice C accurately captures its meaning.

Test takers who rely too much on their memory, or who only glance back at the passage without reading the relevant text carefully, often fall for this trap.

2. RIGHT ANSWER, WRONG QUESTION

These Distractors are statements that are in fact supported by the passage, but that do not directly respond to the passage content referred to by the question stem. Or, they may answer the wrong question type, such as an answer that strengthens the passage when the question asked you to weaken it, or a choice that is the main point of only one paragraph of the passage when the question asked for the primary purpose of the passage as a whole. For example, take a look at the following passage excerpt and the question that follows. Note that two of the answer choices have already been eliminated, so that you can focus on this particular Distractor as compared to the correct answer.

Excerpt 43A

Keeping in focus the multitudes of children who enter school under the tyranny of totalitarian values and authoritarian compulsion, or, inversely, who are surrounded by an uncaring, dysfunctional, or disrupted familial structure, it becomes incumbent upon educators to discover methodologies to overcome the social and political suppression of such individuals' intrinsic intellectual capacities. As more than one authority has emphasized, absent the development of cognitive aptitudes, a child in school might readily assume the form of a robot, with inflexible behavioral and ethical restrictions and the absolute impossibility of liberty.

1. The author most likely believes that some children fail to learn well because before beginning school:

   A. —
   B. —
   C. they readily assume the form of robots.
   D. they have lived in broken homes.

A test taker who has lost track of the question stem might select choice C because it repeats part of the last sentence of the paragraph. However, the question asks what is true of students before beginning school, while choice C describes what may happen to students in school. The correct answer is choice D, which captures the meaning of the author when she indicates that students coming from "dysfunctional, or disrupted familial structure[s]" may have inadequately developed cognitive abilities.

To avoid falling for this kind of trap, keep track of the question stem as you compare answer choices back to the passage text. If you are between two answers, or if you are struggling with a question, reread the stem to remind yourself of what your task actually is.

3. HALF RIGHT, HALF WRONG

These Distractors have one part that is beautifully supported by the passage, but another part that is not. The part that is supported may even be "better" on its own, that is, more obviously supported by the passage, than the correct answer, but there is still that other part that is definitively wrong. The test writers hope that you will get so distracted and attracted by the good stuff that you overlook the bad. Remember, if one piece is wrong, so is the entire choice. Test takers who fail to read and carefully consider all parts of each answer choice often fall for this trap.

Take a look at the following passage excerpt and the question that follows:

Excerpt 43B

For participating student teachers, the program expects students to benefit personally and professionally from exposure to a "hands-on" learning environment. Students learn to identify more and less successful strategies and techniques of classroom teaching as well as to articulate the challenges and concerns specific to the teaching of foreign languages to elementary school students. The maintenance of a teaching portfolio, including all lesson plans and teaching materials, will provide the basis from which students will prepare a written self-assessment of their experience, identifying areas of achievement, need for improvement, and need for growth.

1. According to the passage, a teaching portfolio:

 A. gives student teachers a basis on which they can prepare a written self-assessment of their experience, but may also import too much rigidity into their lesson plans.

 B. —

 C. provides a basis on which student teachers can evaluate their own performance and identify ways in which they can improve in the future.

 D. —

A test taker who is overly impatient may select choice A, because the first half almost directly quotes the passage text. However, the second part of choice A makes a claim that is not supported by the passage. The correct answer, choice C, is somewhat disguised because it paraphrases rather than quotes the passage, but its meaning as a whole matches up with the author's meaning in the text. When you are down to two answers that are similar in some ways but different in others, focus on the parts that are different (going back to the passage to see which one is fully supported and which one is not) to narrow it down to the correct choice.

4. REVERSALS/OPPOSITE

These Distractors either state the exact opposite of the passage, or reverse a relationship described in the passage. They sound good because they reproduce or reflect claims made in the passage, but they flip the meaning around, often by inserting (or removing) a negative word to create an opposite, or by putting the claims into the wrong relationship with each other.

A version of this Distractor that often appears is an answer choice that has the wrong attitude. For example, the passage expresses a positive opinion, but the answer choice has a negative tone, or vice versa.

Take a look at the following passage excerpt and the choices that follow; here you have all four answer choices to evaluate.

Excerpt 43C

Until such time as the Soviet Union developed significant air delivery systems for their nuclear weapons, the United States military discerned no necessity to build a large strategic air capability. Because of the lessons learned at Pearl Harbor, the readiness doctrines put into practice after World War II rendered U.S. air forces virtually beyond the reach of a surprise assault. Military strategists needed only to consider the pace and extent of a Soviet land invasion of Western Europe to plan an appropriate response. It was not so much the magnitude of the U.S. air delivery system, but rather its uniqueness, that produced the desired strategic effect known as "deterrence."

However, once the Soviets mounted a nuclear air capability of their own, the issue of relative strength became crucial. Not only did the United States require a capability to deliver retaliatory atomic weapons by air at a moment's notice, but such capability had to be of sufficient strength to absorb a sneak first strike. In this regard, during the first three years of the decade, the government undertook a decisive program to bolster the deterrent force by intensive thermonuclear research and development, steep increases in the production of delivery systems, and a determined organizational effort to prepare for any contingent second-strike scenario.

1. The author suggests which of the following to be true about United States military strategy?

   A. The creation of a significant United States strategic air capacity led the Soviet Union to further develop its nuclear air delivery capability.
   B. Between 1950 and 1953, the United States cut budgetary appropriations for nuclear strategic military production.
   C. The United States failed to reverse historical American vulnerability to attack after World War II.
   D. The United States authorized the creation of an enlarged atomic strike capacity during the 1950's.

Let's take a look at each answer choice. Choice A reverses the causal relationship put forth in the passage. According to the first paragraph, the development by the Soviet Union of "significant air delivery systems for their nuclear weapons" led the United States to begin to "build a large strategic air capability," not the other way around. Choices B and C indicate the opposite of the author's claims. In paragraph 2, the author states that during the 1950's "the [U.S.] government undertook a decisive program to bolster the deterrent force by intensive thermonuclear research and development." Therefore, choice B is incorrect; there is evidence that budgets would have increased, not decreased. As for choice C, the author states in the first paragraph that "the readiness doctrines put into practice after World War II rendered U.S. air forces virtually beyond the reach of a surprise assault." Therefore, choice C also contradicts the passage. Finally choice D, the correct answer, is directly supported by the second half of the second paragraph.

Note that choice D and choice B are essentially opposites of each other. When you compare choices to each other, look for this relationship between them. When you have two answers that are opposites or reversals of each other, often (but not always) one of those two is the correct answer.

43.3 DISTRACTOR CATEGORY 2: EXTREMES

These Distractors are based on material that would make for a correct answer, but take the strength of the language either too far, or not far enough.

1. TOO EXTREME

For any question that asks you to find the answer that is best supported by the passage, look out for overly extreme or absolute language. This may appear in the form of absolute wording, such as "always," "never," "must," or "only." Choices worded in this way can be correct if they are supported by equally strong language in the passage. However, they are wrong more often than not.

The test writers have figured out that test takers have learned to look out for these words. Therefore, although there are still many answers that are wrong because they are too extreme, they now more often appear in the form of extreme statements that do not include these common words. For example, an answer choice may state, "Physicians are required to divulge relevant information to their patients about possible treatment options." This is a somewhat disguised way of saying that physicians must always do so. If the passage allows for any exceptions to this rule, this choice is incorrect.

One common variation of this Distractor relates to tone or attitude. If the author takes a neutral position, any answer that suggests a positive or negative tone is incorrect (you might also think of this as an Opposite Distractor). Or, the author may express "qualified criticism," while the wrong answer states that the author offers "severe condemnation."

Therefore, always evaluate the strength of the claim being made in each answer choice, and actively look out for Distractors that go too far past what can be supported by the passage text.

2. Too MODERATE

On the other hand, for questions that ask you to strengthen or weaken the passage, extreme or strong language can be a good thing. For these questions, answers are often wrong because they do not go far enough. Take a look at the question and two answer choices below.

> 1. Which of the following claims, if true, would most strengthen the author's argument as it is stated in the passage?
>
>   A. An individual's self-image cannot possibly be improved by self-hypnotic techniques.
>   B. Sometimes self-hypnosis is ineffective in improving people's self-image.
>   C. —
>   D. —

If you are down to a choice between A and B, and if one of them is the correct answer, it essentially has to be choice A regardless of what the original text says. If choice B would strengthen the passage, choice A, which states the same idea but in stronger terms, would have to strengthen it even more. This is another reason to keep close track of the question type. Strong language or claims that would be suspicious for a Specific or General question would be promising for a strengthen or weaken question, and moderate language that probably does not go far enough to "most strengthen" or "most weaken" may be just right for a Specific or General question.

3. MORAL JUDGMENT OR RECOMMENDATION

A variation of Extreme Distractors is an answer that makes a moral judgment or recommendation that is not supported by the passage. That is, the attitude expressed in the answer choice is too extreme to be supported by an essentially neutral text.

For example, imagine a passage that states that burning coal causes pollution. Unless the author takes the next step and claims that this is illegitimate, unhealthy, unnecessary, or that it should be limited in some way, an answer choice that states "We should burn less coal," or, "Alternatives to burning coal should be used" is incorrect (even though they seem to make perfect sense in a real-world context). Be careful not to use your own opinion when selecting answers.

43.4 DISTRACTOR CATEGORY 3: OUT OF SCOPE

These Distractors embody statements that either go too far beyond the scope of the passage, or, that do not fit with the scope of the question task.

1. OUTSIDE KNOWLEDGE/COMMON SENSE

These choices present you with a statement either that you know to be factually true or that sounds reasonable or corresponds to a common belief, but that is not directly supported by the passage. One advantage of the nature of the verbal reasoning section is that it is an open-book test: everything you need to know is given to you in the passage text. However, that advantage brings with it a responsibility to use ONLY that passage text. No matter how "true" a statement may be in the real world, if it isn't based on the passage, it is not the credited response.

2. CRYSTAL BALL

Crystal Ball Distractors predict the future or, what would follow from what is described in the passage, in a way that goes beyond the temporal scope of the text. They are similar to Outside Knowledge/Common Sense Distractors in that they often sound extremely reasonable. However, in the same way, if the passage does not say what happened next or what will happen in the future, you cannot use your own speculations to answer the question.

For examples of both Outside Knowledge/Common Sense and Crystal Ball Distractors, take a look at the following paragraph and question.

Excerpt 43D

Insomnia, a sleep disorder characterized by inadequate or non-restful sleep under conditions that should allow normal sleep, is a virtually universal experience for adults at some time in their lives. Because the condition is so ubiquitous, pharmaceutical companies, having identified insomnia as a major potential revenue source, are devoting significant resources to developing effective cures or treatments for the disorder.

1. With which of the following statements would the author be most likely to agree?

   A. Insomnia occurs in conditions that are generally conducive to good sleep.
   B. Long-term insomnia has deleterious effects on sufferers' capacity to focus and concentrate on difficult tasks.
   C. More effective medications to treat sleeplessness will be available in the future.
   D. Many of those who suffer from insomnia would use medications that effectively treated the condition as long as those medications were safe and relatively inexpensive.

Choice A is correct. Insomnia is defined as a condition that occurs "under conditions that should allow normal sleep." This answer choice paraphrases that piece of information ("conducive" is not too strong; it means "lends itself to," not "guarantees"). Therefore, you can infer that the author would agree with this statement. Note that although the wording of the question task is fairly vague, it is a Specific, not a General question. Therefore, the fact that choice A does not sum up the overall idea of the paragraph is not a problem; the answer choice has an appropriate scope.

Choice B is an Outside Knowledge/Common Sense trap. This statement is in fact true in real life; plenty of research has demonstrated it. However, there is no evidence for it in the passage. Choice C is a Crystal Ball trap. One would think that all those resources being expended by pharmaceutical companies would pay off sometime in the future, but again, we don't know that from the passage text alone. Finally, choice D is another Outside Knowledge/Common Sense Distractor. Sleep medication is a huge market already, and, it seems reasonable that many insomniacs would use an effective, safe, and inexpensive treatment. And yet, we don't have any evidence from the passage to directly support that inference.

Both of these Distractor types can be very seductive, especially when the correct answer is a dull, unexciting paraphrase of the passage (as in choice A above). It feels like you should be doing more work to find the answer, or, that the correct answer can't be more or less stated in the passage. However, don't make it harder on yourself than it has to be. For any question that asks you in some form to retrieve or infer from the passage, the closer to the passage the answer choice is, the better.

3. Not the Issue

In a sense, this is a catch-all category for "the passage doesn't say that." Often there is at least one wrong answer that is so far outside the scope of the passage that it seems that only a person who had never even glanced at the passage text would choose it. However, don't feel stupid if you fall for one of these. It often means that you are thinking too creatively, too far "outside the box," putting a lot of effort into imagining multiple connections between the passage and that answer choice in order to try to make it fit.

Other choices in this category are more subtle, however. For example, the answer may draw a comparison between two things that are in fact mentioned, but not compared to each other in the text. Or, it may take one thing that is mentioned, and state a connection between that thing and something else that is never mentioned. Or, it may broaden the scope beyond the precise issue of the passage. If a passage is limited to discussing a particular Japanese poet, for example, an answer choice that encompasses all of Japanese poetry is most likely too broad to fit with the scope of the text (especially on a Specific or General question).

Wrong answers that fall into the category of Not the Issue often fall into other categories as well. For example, two things may be compared in the passage and yet contrasted in the wrong answer; the choice is Not the Issue because it is a Reversal or the Opposite of what the passage says. Or, the incorrect choice may take a neutral statement from the passage and infer that the author does in fact have a positive or negative opinion; it is Not the Issue because it is Too Extreme or the Opposite.

Take a look at the next two paragraphs and the questions that follow.

Excerpt 43E

Although not considered a mystic herself, Sor Juana, Mexico's finest colonial poet, created verse comparable in greatness to that of the Peninsular mystic poets. The illegitimate daughter of a Spanish colonizer and his Creole lover, Juana Inés Asbaje melded her multicultural origins in her artistic consciousness.

In one of her most famous works, *The Divine Narcissus*, she identifies Christian leitmotifs in the pre-Colombian sacrifice and eating sacrament of the Mexican God of Corn. In suggesting that long before the arrival of the Spanish conquistadors and their Catholic missionaries, the indigenous people's ancient theology had developed such modern sophistication as rituals of divine communion, Sor Juana offended the sensibilities of the ecclesiastical authorities. The girl who educated herself in childhood and adolescence through the resources of her grandfather's extensive book collection, swimming from her earliest years against the tides of tradition and prejudice, became the adult woman eventually chastised and condemned as a heretic for her verse and polemics.

1. The author most likely describes *The Divine Narcissus* in order to:

   A. illustrate the innovative quality of Creole poetry.
   B. give an example of the rhyme scheme most commonly employed in Sor Juana's poetry.
   C. give an example of magical realism.
   D. illustrate how Sor Juana combined Old World and New World themes.

2. Which of the following statements, if true, would most *undermine* the author's argument regarding the source of Sor Juana's unique poetic vision?

   A. Mexican poetry rarely employs themes and images drawn from indigenous non-Christian religious traditions.
   B. Sor Juana was brought up by an indigenous family in a small rural village, never knowing her biological parents.
   C. Sor Juana had no formal musical training.
   D. Few colonial Mexican poets were publicly condemned by the Catholic Church.

The first question asks why the author describes *The Divine Narcissus*, a description that comes in the second paragraph. Choice A characterizes Sor Juana's work as "Creole poetry," a genre or category that is never mentioned in the passage. You could also say that this choice is Half Right, Half Wrong. The author does suggest that Sor Juana was innovative by calling her "original" and a "pioneer." However, if one part of the choice is wrong, the answer must be eliminated. As for choice B, while the author does mention the poet's "beautiful rhymes," her rhyme scheme is never mentioned or described. Choice C has no connection to the passage as the author never mentions magical realism.

Choice D is correct. When you go back to the passage to reread the relevant section and to answer in your own words, you should notice that the discussion of *The Divine Narcissus* that begins at the start of the second paragraph continues the idea from the end of the first paragraph that Sor Juana inherited "the diverse attitudes of her Old World father and New World mother" and "integrated them in her original vision." The second paragraph discusses how the work in question combined Christian (New World) and pre-Columbian (Old World) images and themes.

The second question asks what statement, if taken to be true, would most undermine the author's argument. Identifying Not the Issue answers on weaken and strengthen questions requires careful attention, since even the correct answer will bring in new information that is not already provided by the passage text. However, that new information does need to be directly relevant to the appropriate part of the author's argument. Choice A is too broad in scope. The fact that Mexican poetry in general rarely uses such themes tells you nothing about whether or not Sor Juana did so and why. Choice B, however, is directly relevant to and inconsistent with the author's claim that her "original vision" came from a combination of attitudes inherited from her father and mother. If Sor Juana had no contact with her parents, it is unlikely that her parents' attitudes had a formative influence on her poetry. At this point, you would leave in choice B as a possibility, but go on to evaluate choices C and D.

Choice C raises an issue, musical training, that is never mentioned in the passage. Finally, choice D is "not the issue" in two ways. First, like choice A, it is too broad; what is true of colonial Mexican poets as a whole does not necessarily apply to Sor Juana. Secondly, the issue in the question stem is the source of Sor Juana's poetic vision, not the reaction of the Catholic Church to her poetry. In the end, then, you are left with choice B as the statement that most weakens the relevant part of the passage.

4. TOO NARROW

This is a Distractor connected in particular to General questions. The scope of this question task requires that the correct answer sum up, or at least implicitly include, all of the major themes of the passage (or at least more of those themes than any other choice that may also be consistent with the passage text). As an example, take the two paragraphs of the Sor Juana passage (above) as constituting an entire passage. Take a look at the main point question below, and the two answer choices that follow.

1. Which of the following best expresses the main point of the passage?

   A. —
   B. Sor Juana suggested in her poetry that ancient indigenous theology was in many ways just as sophisticated as Catholicism.
   C. —
   D. Sor Juana was a pioneer in how she combined Old and New World themes, and in so doing challenged the commonly accepted beliefs of her time.

Choice B is certainly supported by information in the second paragraph. However, this is just one point made by the author. Choice D better captures the theme of the passage as a whole. Notice that the claim in choice B (about one unique aspect of Sor Juana's work) supports the larger claim represented in choice D; this was one way in which she challenged commonly accepted beliefs. If on a General question you are down to two choices that are both supported by the passage, and if one of them provides evidence in support of the other, the broader answer will be the credited response.

43.5 DRILL: IDENTIFYING DISTRACTORS

Below you will find a passage and a question. Following the question are ten answer choices that are either correct or Distractors. For each wrong answer, identify what type of Distractor it is and write it down. If you think that it falls into two or more Distractor categories, identify them all (although when taking a real test, once you have found one thing wrong with a choice, strike it out and move on rather than searching for additional mistakes in that choice). Answers follow at the end of the drill.

Excerpt 43F

The recent and remarkable "by reserved appointment only" exhibition at New York's Museum of Modern Art demonstrated the dynamic and nurturing relationship between two great artists of the twentieth century. Although many critics find profound and substantial differences between the portfolios of Matisse and Picasso, these two painters throughout their lives feasted on each other's work to energize their own production and stimulate the evolution of their respective visions.

The distorted forms and perspectives portrayed by Picasso reveal an artistic sensibility apparently haunted by disturbingly radical perceptions... [and] therefore outside and beyond the experience of most humans. Alternatively, one might suppose, the enormous acclaim accorded this Spanish painter results precisely from his ability to expose universal feelings and insights through superb technique and audacious craftsmanship; ... [and the] secret of his brilliance shrieks out in the uncompromisable honesty of his brush and the unyielding frankness of his canvas. As is evident in the self-portrait that concludes the exhibit, Picasso's intense renditions impossibly melded objective reality with subjective sensation through a panhistorical and transdimensional lens of overlapping shadows and mutating shades to forge and generate an acute and exquisite intercultural metamorphosis.

In contrast, Matisse's self-portrait—hung side-by-side with the Picasso—depicts an awe-struck artist basking in the glory of a resplendent cosmos streaming through a studio window flung open wide. Matisse's

964 ■ Cracking the MCAT

unabashed childlike willingness to embrace and express sensual perception as a natural and unequivocal purity, and to process that apparently immaculate perfection through an artistic instrument at once passionate and chaste, simultaneously sensuous and reverent, stands in stark antithesis—and as polar complement—to his colleague's riotous and complex collage.

The author of the passage would most likely agree that:

1. Picasso's stature in the art world derives from his unwillingness to combine his personal perceptions with external truths.
2. Picasso's work exhibited a childlike honesty, while Matisse's embodied an intercultural metamorphosis.
3. artists working in different genres and styles often benefit from sharing inspiration and insight with each other.
4. Matisse and Picasso differed in their use of color.
5. Picasso's objective consideration of panhistorical trends lent itself to sensationalistic portrayals of cultural trends.
6. Picasso's portrayals were fundamentally based on and limited to perceptions far beyond the experience of most people.
7. Picasso commented on violence in the world through doing violence to form and shape.
8. Matisse' self-portrait, when seen in comparison with Picasso's, is more awe-inspiring due to Matisse's greater willingness to embrace the purity of sensual perception.
9. Matisse opened himself to the experience of natural phenomena, as most clearly seen in his work representing the constellations.
10. the work of Picasso differed from that of Matisse in its level of complexity and synthesis of different elements or themes.

Answers and Analysis

1. Incorrect. This is a "Decoy: Opposite" Distractor. Picasso did in fact combine personal perception with external truth, according to the second paragraph.

2. Incorrect. This is a "Decoy: Reversal" Distractor. It mixes up what is true of Picasso with what is true of Matisse.

3. Incorrect. This can be labeled either "Extremes: Too Extreme" or "Not the Issue: Too Broad." We only know about Picasso and Matisse, not about artists in general.

4. Incorrect. You might have labeled this either as a "Decoy: Half Right, Half Wrong" Distractor, or as "Out if Scope: Not the Issue." Yes, the two artists differed, but the passage never discusses either's use of color.

5. Incorrect. This is a "Decoy: Mangler" Distractor. Many of these words appear in the passage, but the meaning of this statement does not correspond to the text (for example, the reference to sensationalistic portrayal of cultural trends).

6. Incorrect. This is an "Extremes: Too Extreme" Distractor (although you might also have labeled it as a "Decoy: Opposite"). While the author indicates in the beginning of paragraph 2 that some might agree with this statement, the author goes on to express a different opinion. That is, that Picasso exposed "universal truths and insights." Therefore, while it is possible that the author would agree that some of Picasso's perspectives are "subjective" and perhaps beyond the experience of others, Picasso's work is not limited to such perspectives.

7. Incorrect. This is an "Out of Scope: Outside Knowledge" trap. While Picasso did in fact paint some works that have been interpreted in this way (for example, *Guernica*), there is no mention of this in the passage.

8. Incorrect. This choice uses words from the passage out of context, and therefore falls into the "Decoy: Mangler" category. It also suggests that the author believes that Matisse's self-portrait was better (more awe-inspiring) than Picasso's, which puts it in the "Extremes: Too Extreme" and "Judgment" (here, an artistic rather than moral judgment) categories.

9. Incorrect. This choice is a "Decoy: Half Right Half, Wrong" trap. The second part (which also interprets the word "cosmos" in the passage out of context and therefore mangles it) is not supported by the passage.

10. Correct. This choice, in somewhat disguised form, corresponds to the author's description in paragraph 2 of Picasso's use of a "panhistorical and transdimensional lens...to forge and generate an acute and exquisite intercultural metamorphosis," and to the statement at the end of the passage that Picasso's "riotous and complex collage" stood in antithesis to Matisse's work.

CHAPTER 44

SYSTEMATIC IDENTIFICATION OF CORRECT ANSWERS

The fact that MCAT verbal reasoning passages seem difficult has less to do with your abilities than with the conditions under which you are tested. A medical student who wishes to learn basic medical science, for example, ought not to read one short fragment from one subject—say, physiology—and two minutes later leap to a brief clipping from a second—say, microbiology. To be sure, the medical sciences are fundamentally and profoundly interrelated, but one cannot comprehend the whole without a preliminary understanding of its parts. Rushed, disconnected readings with no unifying direction will never afford a medical student the sort of detailed understanding that only hours of organized, focused study can provide.

But the MCAT is *not* medical school. The MCAT assesses your ability first to immerse yourself for a few minutes in disconnected parcels of unrelated text, and then to select the particular shred of minutiae that yields a correct answer. Medical school (and all serious learning) calls for slow, meticulous reading with no limits set on the reader's time and attention. The MCAT's verbal reasoning passages, on the other hand, require that students operate under artificial time constraints, processing many bits of information, each clamoring for attention, with limited clues to help you decide which ones matter.

Raising your MCAT verbal reasoning score requires systematic efficiency. Building on **Chapters 42 and 43**, *this* chapter presents a five-step process that will help you strategically process the passage, read the questions, and select your answers.

44.1 MAPPING THE PASSAGE

To begin with, remember this: A typical passage is 600 to 900 words long. Many of its paragraphs, words, and sentences do *not* give rise to questions. Whole bodies of text filled with names, dates, and data may be entirely unrelated to the relatively few questions that follow the passage. *Attempting at the outset to understand the whole passage in detail is counterproductive.* Your purpose is to score points in the time allowed—not to waste time in an attempt to understand arcane material unrelated to the questions you must answer.

Your first step is to read the passage relatively quickly and create a map of each paragraph's main idea. Don't read too closely or try to understand too thoroughly. Read each paragraph quickly. Skim it. Sift it. Jot down a few words on your scratch paper that remind you of its central topic. Once you have read through the entire passage, define its main point or bottom line, including the author's tone. For sure, this is no way for a serious medical student to read—once he or she is *in* medical school. But it *is* the way to approach an MCAT verbal reasoning passage. Minutes later, when you begin to answer questions, you'll read *certain portions* of the passage closely, for detail. The questions and your map will direct you to those parts of the passage that require your careful attention. But your *first* reading should be quick and sketchy—not for deep understanding, but for a map.

Develop a "sifting mentality." Ask yourself, "What is each paragraph and the passage as a whole about?" You should answer those questions in as few words as possible.

Please read and map these several paragraphs from a humanities passage.

Excerpt 44A

Within the four decades between 1494 and 1530, the Italian Renaissance achieved its artistic pinnacle and suffered its spiritual, social, and political collapse. One could not remain alive and cognizant during that swiftly passing span of years and emerge unchanged by the influences and events that defined it: Notions regarding Humanity's rightful place in the Universe, and conceptions of the community's relationship with the individual and the proper role and prerogatives of each, underwent radical modification. The moral essence of the period evolved through a four-stage process, each stage being embodied by one great cultural authority of the era.

Fascinated by Nature's anarchy, the Renaissance individual came to understand the inevitable vengeance of unleashed Cosmic license: The sheer hazard of fortune dangled over one's life like the sword of Damocles. Destiny's permutations lay beyond the reach and outside the control of the individual. Such a spiritual predicament provoked the quest for faith, and four seers arose in turn who whispered private terrors and bequeathed revelatory prophecies each to the next. One wishes to confer upon them the title of lawgivers because history tells us that like parched horses mustering toward water, their peers and contemporaries rallied to the ideas promulgated, and the causes championed, by this quartet of greatness.

In retrospect, the four definitive Renaissance figures—Savonarola, Machiavelli, Castiglione, and Aretino—loom larger than life over the cultural evolutions they influenced. In their lives, these progressions become highlighted, foreshadowed, and manifest. Locating the precise center of life, respectively, in the spirit, intellect, culture, and instinct, each one encountered the core truth of earthly existence in harmony with his personal essence—be it in theology, politics, gentility, or sensuality. The tours of status and leverage conducted by their respective oracles counterbalance one another like coherent and sensible sequels.

Savonarola's spartan humility, Machiavelli's resourceful expediency, Castiglione's courtly congeniality, and Aretino's primitive hedonism: Each represents an eternal response to life, respectively, that of one who dreads life, who assents to it, who settles with it, and who surrenders to it. As the centuries have barreled by, their perspectives on human experience and their perceptions of the human condition—the beliefs and understandings which informed and directed their lives—have today achieved the stature of truisms. If the cocoon of time, however, has metamorphosed their vital truths into well-learned platitudes, these are platitudes essentially undulled by the fleeting years; and for being basic, they are no less primary.

Paragraph 1:

The paragraph discusses the individual and social changes that occurred during four decades of the Italian Renaissance. On your scratch paper, you might write:

4 decades>>radical changes

Paragraph 2:

This second paragraph describes the sense of existential dread that apparently afflicted people during this period, and the consequent search for faith and spiritual authority, which elevated four Renaissance figures. On your scratch paper, you might write:

spiritual terrors>>4 seers

Paragraph 3:

This paragraph focuses on the individual authorities of interest to the author, and identifies each one's intellectual propensity. On your scratch paper, you might write:

intellectual essence of the 4

Paragraph 4:

The excerpt's final paragraph further elaborates on the attitudes and orientations of the four individuals, and observes that their teachings have endured through the centuries to become commonplace wisdom in our own times. On your scratch paper, you might write:

their perceptions>> valuable truisms

Bottom Line:

The passage as a whole discusses how these four figures, in reaction to their time period and their own individual perspectives, defined basic truths that continue to be valid. On your scratch paper, then, you might write: *4 Renaissance thinkers provided different, valuable perspectives on life.*

You can learn to map a typical MCAT-like passage in approximately two to four minutes. **Chapter 45** will help you practice these skills.

44.2 ADDITIONAL TECHNIQUES

PREVIEWING THE QUESTIONS

Many test-takers find it useful to preview the question stems before reading the passage for the first time. Previewing the questions for references to passage content has several potential benefits. First, it helps you decide what is more or less important as you read the passage. If you find that you get bogged down in irrelevant details, or that you are reading every part of the passage closely and with equal attention, previewing may help you move through the passage more quickly and effectively. Second, it gives you some context for understanding what you are reading, and the main themes of the passage may "stick" better the first time through. If you find yourself having little or no idea what you just read when you reach the end of the passage, previewing may help you to focus. Third, it allows you to find and highlight references in the passage that you will need to revisit as you answer the questions. Given that there are no line references and only occasional paragraph references on the test, some test takers find that they must spend inordinate amounts of time hunting down relevant information as they answer the questions. Try previewing the questions so that you can incorporate the location of question topics into your mapping of the passage.

An effective preview focuses on only the question stems, not the answer choices, and only references to passage content, not question types. It should take you only 15 to 20 seconds once you practice it, time that you may well get back later, when you are able to answer the questions more efficiently.

HIGHLIGHTING

One of your CBT tools is a highlighting function. You can highlight only in the passage text, not in the question stems or answer choices. Highlighting serves two main functions. First, it helps you focus your attention while reading the passage on the things that will help you understand the main points of the paragraphs and the Bottom Line of the passage. Second, as part of your map, it gives you a trail of breadcrumbs to follow as you go back to the passage in order to answer the questions. To serve either of these functions, however, your highlighting must be concise and purposeful. Rather than highlighting large chunks of text or everything that "seems important," highlight only words and phrases that indicate the logic of the passage (such as the "directional arrows" discussed in the next section) or that correspond to question topics you have seen in your preview.

SCRATCH PAPER

You will be given scratch paper or a whiteboard at the testing center. Use it to jot down the main points and Bottom Line of the passage when necessary (especially on harder, more complex passages). You can also use it to translate difficult questions and answer choices, and to organize your evaluation of the answer choices on Roman numeral and EXCEPT/LEAST/NOT questions. Finally, use it to keep track of any passages that you decide to skip over your first time through the section and come back to later.

44.3 DIRECTIONAL ARROWS

While mapping a passage, look for and highlight words or phrases that signal direction. That is, a logical connection between different parts of, or statements in, the passage. Certain words indicate that a point just made might be confirmed, shifted, conditioned, reversed, undercut, or otherwise modified. For example, words like, "therefore," "hence," and "thus" signal that a conclusion will be drawn.

Look at the twenty words and phrases listed below. Each is a directional arrow. As you read through the list, think about what each word or phrase might tell you about the part of the passage in which it appears.

accordingly
but
consequently
conversely
despite
hence
however
in this connection
in spite of
ironically
nonetheless
notwithstanding
on the contrary
on the other hand
rather
regardless
still
therefore
unfortunately
yet

While making your map, look for words and phrases like these. Make note of and highlight them. When you return to the passage to read closely *some* of its text, these words will help you understand it and answer questions.

Consider the last sentence of Excerpt 44A:

If the cocoon of time, however, has metamorphosed
their vital truths into well-learned platitudes, these are
platitudes essentially undulled by the fleeting years; and
for being basic, they are no less primary.

"However" is a signal. How does it help you? It helps you see the author's point which is this: The insights described in the passage might be platitudes. Nonetheless, they are as valid now as they were when first set forth.

44.4 SETTLING ON CORRECT ANSWERS

After mapping the passage, including highlighting key words and phrases, defining the main point of each paragraph, and articulating the Bottom Line of the passage as a whole, you are ready to answer the questions by following these steps.

1. Read the question word for word (no skimming here!). Even though you may have already previewed the question, don't rely on your preview to give you an adequate understanding of exactly what the question is asking.

2. Translate the question. Identify the question type, and define exactly what that question is asking you to do with or to the passage.

3. Go back to the passage. If the question includes a specific reference to the passage text, go back to the passage before you read the answer choices. Find the reference and read above and below it. A good guideline is at least five lines above and below. However, you should start reading where the author begins discussing that issue, and keep reading until the author moves on to the next issue. Do not rely on your memory of your first quick read-through of the passage. If there is no passage reference, move on to step 5.

4. Answer the question in your own words. Your answer should be based very closely on the passage text and on the question task. Define what the correct answer needs to do. If it is a general question, you have already done this by defining the Bottom Line of the passage.

5. Evaluate the answer choices using process of elimination. Read each choice word for word and look for what is wrong with each answer choice. Keep the Bottom Line of the passage in mind, even on Specific and Complex questions. On your first pass through the choices, strike out an answer if you can define what is wrong with it. If it looks good, or even if you don't like it but don't know why, leave it in until you have read all four. Never select an answer until you have read all four choices word for word. In many cases you will be down to two choices after your first pass through the answers. In this situation, reread the question and then compare the choices to each other, looking for relevant differences. Go back to the passage if necessary. In the end, there may be no perfect answer; simply choose the "least wrong" option.

As you evaluate the choices, especially when you are down to two answers, look out for common Distractors. Is an answer too extreme to be supported by the passage? Is it focused on the wrong issue in the passage? Does it have the wrong scope (such as being too narrow to answer a general question)? Does it include words from the passage, but mangle its meaning? Is it the exact opposite of what the passage says? Is it half right but half wrong? Use your knowledge of common types of wrong answers to avoid the traps set for you by the test writers. Also keep in mind that the correct answer may be disguised by using different wording with the same meaning as the relevant part or parts of the passage.

If you have been through the answers several times and followed this process carefully but are still stuck between two or more choices, make your best educated guess between the options that remain and move on. No single question is worth a huge percentage of your time.

44.5 SPECIAL CONSIDERATION: AUTHOR'S ATTITUDE

Occasionally, an MCAT question will ask the student to characterize the author's attitude, feeling, or state of mind. Sometimes, the options are limited to single adjectives:

1. Regarding … etc., etc., etc., … the author's attitude was:

   A. disapproving.
   B. incredulous.
   C. open-minded.
   D. intrigued.

2. In this passage, the author's basic feeling was one of:

   A. security.
   B. relief.
   C. confidence.
   D. anticipation.

Consider this excerpt from a simulated MCAT passage:

Excerpt 44B

> Having concluded that I would probably never come to comprehend fully the nature of the force—or forces?—responsible for these strange visitations in my life, I at last found in my imagination a metaphor that made sense to me, for some reason, and afforded me a measure of tranquillity. Lately, I'd been struck with the idea that somehow, for some mysterious motive, a window had been shown to me. Whether this window opened onto another dimension, another world, a top-secret governmental apparatus, the angelic operations of the divine, or the diabolic enterprise of the demon, I did not know, could not know, might never know, it seemed. I looked to my *only hope* and took from it a positive feeling. I had to decide that whatever the source and motive of these powers clearly beyond my knowledge and well beyond my control, I'd best not ignore them, and intending my moral relativist's level best, would do my best to understand their purpose and their meaning.

The author's decision as to how best to deal with her perceptions and experiences left her feeling:

A. knowledgeable.
B. empty.
C. hopeful.
D. exuberant.

Because you only have single words to go by, distractors on these questions can be particularly confusing. To clarify it, convert the question into a true/false statement:

TRUE OR FALSE: The author was left feeling _____.

Make four sentences by filling in the blank with each answer option. One sentence will better match the tone of the relevant part of the passage than the other three. That sentence reveals the correct answer.

Apply the technique to the question above:

TRUE OR FALSE: The author was left feeling <u>knowledgeable.</u>

TRUE OR FALSE: The author was left feeling <u>empty.</u>

TRUE OR FALSE: The author was left feeling <u>hopeful.</u>

TRUE OR FALSE: The author was left feeling <u>exuberant.</u>

So, true or false? The author is feeling knowledgeable. False: Choice A contradicts the passage. The author writes, "... I did not know, could not know, might never know, it seemed." So, is the author feeling empty because of her lack of certainty? False: she says that she "looked to my only hope and took from it a positive feeling," and she vows to "do my best to understand [the] purpose and... meaning" of the mysterious powers that may be at work. Is she hopeful? True: those same lines clearly express hopefulness. Finally (because you should always give all four choices careful consideration) is she feeling exuberant? False: this choice takes the positive tone of the passage too far. This leaves you with choice C as the best expression of the author's tone.

Defining the author's tone should always be part of your passage map: the tone of each paragraph and of the passage as a whole. Make sure to actively use your map when answering these questions.

Use the social sciences passage below to practice the technique for author's attitude questions:

Excerpt 44C

Over the past decade, the line between news and entertainment has become increasingly blurred. When Norman Lear's "All In The Family" opened its hugely successful tenure as a prime-time situation comedy in the early seventies, it pioneered the entertainment vehicle as a forum for discussion of the critical social issues of the day, questions that until that time had remained entirely within the province of the news divisions. Around the same time, television news underwent a quantum evolution: From something akin to a prudent parrot of government propaganda, it developed almost overnight into a powerful, nonpartisan, independently thinking entity devoted to an honest, objective exploration of government, society, and the world.

A decade after Watergate, however, the media's objectivity began to blur its focus in the intoxicating ether of the freewheeling eighties. Where once a noble quest for truth and reason had defined the goal, the new programmers, driven by a lust for economic supremacy, now fixated and obsessed on the bottom line. Profitability became the primary organizational principle, and ratings represented the golden gate to profits. Whatever excited, entertained, titillated, or sold—these fields of straw became the fecund yellow ground for journalists of the electronic media!

In these two paragraphs, the author's attitude in reference to the post-Watergate media is most accurately described as:

A. critical.
B. approving.
C. congratulatory.
D. apathetic.

Construct four TRUE/FALSE statements, one for each answer option.

About the media, the author remarked that after Watergate:

- "... the media's objectivity began to blur..."

- "Whatever excited, entertained, titillated, or sold—these fields of straw became the fecund yellow ground for journalists of the electronic media."

TRUE OR FALSE: This person was being ironic.

TRUE OR FALSE: This person was being approving.

TRUE OR FALSE: This person was being congratulatory.

TRUE OR FALSE: This person was being apathetic.

Surely, choice D sounds false. The author's tone in discussing the subject does not lack concern or energy. Some might argue that in the first paragraph of this excerpt, the author enthusiastically applauds the media's coming-of-age:

- "... pioneered the entertainment vehicle as a forum for discussion of the critical social issues of the day..."

- "... television news underwent a quantum evolution... into a powerful, nonpartisan, independently thinking entity devoted to an honest, objective exploration..."

Accordingly, distractors B and C might tempt some test takers with some justification. Nonetheless, the final paragraph which discusses changes in the decade following Watergate casts those earlier observations into shadow. The correct answer is A; "critical" is supported by the negative tone of the second paragraph.

CHAPTER 45

NINE PRACTICE
VERBAL REASONING PASSAGES

45.1 PASSAGE I

Passage and Questions

In the first decade of the twenty-first century, America continues to confront a broad agenda of perplexing policy questions. Not only must we continue to deal successfully with the realities of advanced technology, surging international expertise, and international productivity, we must also design effective strategies to remedy the difficult social problems emerging from current domestic demographic trends. Because meeting these diverse national challenges will require citizens to be equipped with advanced knowledge and superior skills, the need for higher education and professional training becomes greater than perhaps at any other period in our history.

In times of economic cutbacks and downsizing, however, when real wages for most Americans continue to shrink even as the national economy grows, voters are wary of proposals to increase—or even maintain—current levels of government spending. They equate increased spending with increased taxation. Yet recent studies show that over the long run, increased financial support for education combined with increased access for all citizens to the nation's colleges and universities will offer advantages to all taxpayers, regardless of economic status.

Even among those who advocate cutting the higher-education budget, few would question the immediate practical benefits of post-secondary schooling to the individual student, or "consumer" of learning. Data derived from the latter part of the twentieth century show, for example, that increases in individual earnings relate directly to educational achievement: The higher the level of education completed, the higher the income. According to White House data, the mean earnings of a college graduate in 1992 reached almost $40,000, 25% higher than those of persons who started college but did not finish, and more than 60% above that of individuals with no schooling at all beyond high school. This last group, in turn, earned 25% more than those who did not finish high school.

A similar correspondence occurs with unemployment statistics: As years of schooling increase, the probability of joblessness diminishes. Thus, the 1993 unemployment rate for those who completed college was only 3.5%, less than half the 7.2% for high school graduates with no college at all. Experiencing a joblessness rate just about midway between those levels, at 5.7%, as might be expected, were people with some college credits still short of graduation. High school dropouts, meanwhile, again suffered most, with a 12.6% rate of unemployment, almost double that of high school graduates.

The more education one acquires, then, the more likely he or she is to find work, and at a higher salary. Of course, as salaries increase, so do taxes. An individual who attains a higher degree of education also generally achieves a higher tax bracket. What might be less apparent, although critical for determining policy, is that taking federal income tax revenues as a whole, the percentage paid by college graduates is considerably out of proportion with their numbers in the population.

A recent issue of the "Post-secondary Education Opportunity" research newsletter reported government statistics demonstrating that as of 1991, college graduates headed 23% of U.S. households that together accounted for 43.2% of annual IRS revenues. (Conversely, 54.9% of U.S. households that year were headed by individuals with no college at all, and they paid only 33.9% of all federal income taxes. Heads of households with some college credit who did not attain a diploma made up the rest.)

These analyses further indicate that between 1970 and 1991, as the percentage of college-educated citizens increased among the population, so did the size of the middle class, and with it, the tax base of higher-wage earners. As one well-known Chicago business leader testified before the National Commission on Responsibilities for Financing Post-secondary Education (NCRFPE), "It seems to me that the social costs of no education or miseducation may very well exceed the finite costs of a sound, competitive education.... I think we might demonstrate that a strategic investment in education is a relative bargain."

1. The author's statement that voters are wary of increased government expenditure on education suggests that such wariness:

    I. represents concern over increased taxation.

    II. arises from their hesitancy to bear financial responsibility for the associated cost.

    III. reflects their belief that college education no longer serves any significant needs of the society at large.

  A. I only
  B. I and II only
  C. I and III only
  D. I, II, and III

2. What evidence does the author introduce to support her assertion that few people would question the immediate practical benefits of post-secondary schooling to the individual student?

    I. Students who continue education beyond high school enjoy a better economic status than those who do not.

    II. Most Americans experience a reduction in real wages even though the nation's economy is expanding.

    III. Increases in salary correspond to increases in taxation.

  A. I only
  B. I and II only
  C. I and III only
  D. I, II, and III

3. Which of the following, if true, would best strengthen the author's view that America needs to promote higher education and professional training?

  A. Large numbers of American college students are foreign born and tend to return to their native countries after graduation.

  B. American colleges have become increasingly dependent on charitable donations from their alumni and other philanthropic donors.

  C. Most graduates of American colleges do not pursue post-graduate or professional training.

  D. Foreign nations that invest in education consistently demonstrate increased economic growth and greater per capita income.

4. According to the passage, which of the following statements most accurately describes the relevance of technological advances to education?

  A. Rapid technological advances have no place in determining public education policy.

  B. Rapid technological advances have made it more difficult for students to make effective use of higher education.

  C. Rapid technological advances should make universal access to higher education a national objective.

  D. Rapid technological advances should make universal access to higher education a luxury generally reserved for the wealthy.

5. Analyses in the newsletter "Post-secondary Education Opportunity" suggested that between 1970 and 1991:

   A. the percentage of college-educated citizens decreased among the population.
   B. the tax base of higher wage earners decreased among the population.
   C. the tax base of higher wage earners increased among the population.
   D. the size of the upper class increased among the population.

6. According to the passage, "current domestic demographic trends" will cause the society to experience:

   A. greater barriers to opportunity because of international competition.
   B. greater and more challenging social problems.
   C. social problems that are more easily remedied.
   D. the elimination of most educational barriers to opportunity.

7. The author's general attitude about the nation's future would best be described as:

   A. cynical.
   B. optimistic.
   C. concerned.
   D. apathetic.

Passsage I: Answers and Explanations

1. **B is correct.** The relevant text is in paragraph 2, which concerns, generally, the reluctance of some citizens to favor increased expenditure for education. The paragraph's chief message is that (1) improved educational resources carry a cost, presumably in the form of taxation, and (2) that many citizens are resistant to increased taxation. Statements I and II reflect both those propositions. Statement III is not embodied in paragraph 2 and is *contradicted* by paragraph 3, in which the author states that even those who resist increased expenditure nonetheless acknowledge the practical benefit that would be associated with improved educational resources.

2. **A is correct.** The pertinent text is in paragraph 3 whose principal point is that education yields practical benefits. Among the data offered to support the point is that "This last group," meaning those whose education ends at high school graduation, "earned 25 percent more than those who did not finish high school." Statement II represents the right answer to the wrong question. It embodies a statement genuinely made in the passage (in paragraph 2), but it does not logically follow the stem. Statement III has the same problem. The author does state (in paragraph 5) that increased earnings produce increased taxation. She does not, however, offer that proposition as evidence that few would question the practical benefits of education for the student.

3. **D is correct.** The question asks you to strengthen the author's claim. There is a meaningful, logical connection between the propositions that (1) America will reap economic gain by investing in education and (2) other countries have reaped the gain by making that investment. Choice A weakens rather than strengthens. Choice B is out of scope or not the issue. Increased reliance on charitable donations has no impact on the author's argument about promotion of higher education. Choice C is also out of scope. The author's argument does not depend on a certain level of post-graduate or professional education; the issue in the passage is "higher education" as a whole.

4. **C is correct.** The relevant text is in the first paragraph. The author cites technological advance (among other matters) as a challenge that increases the need for higher education. The words "access" and "universal" tend to *disguise* the statement, but the statement closely reflects the author's meaning. Choice A is contrary to the author's view, as expressed in paragraph 1. Choice B is a decoy. The passage addresses a problem, choice B seems to describe a problem, and superficial examination gives B a "ring" of plausibility. Yet the author makes no such statement in the passage. Choice D sounds good, in part because it may correspond to some people's opinion. However, it is outside of the scope of the passage.

5. **C is correct.** The question directs us to paragraphs 6 and 7, where the author refers to the newsletter and its analyses. In paragraph 7, she states that according to the newsletter analyses, the middle class has grown, and the tax base of higher wage earners has increased. Choice A contradicts the author's statement in the last paragraph that between 1970 and 1991 "the percentage of college-educated citizens increased among the population…" Choice B is a reversal; it presents the word "decreased" where it should present the word *increased* (as is correctly presented in choice C). Choice D is out of scope. The author refers to the increased size of the *middle* class and the increased *tax base* of higher wage earners.

6. **B is correct.** The relevant text is in paragraph 1. The author refers to a number of phenomena, including technological advance, surging international expertise and productivity, and *current domestic trends*. All of these, the author writes, will produce a society with "diverse national challenges." The phrase "greater and more challenging social problems," as set forth in choice B, reflects the author's thinking with some *disguise*. Choices A and D take words out of context. They resort to words and concepts within the passage like "opportunity" and "international," but combine them in a way that does not reflect the author's thinking or respond to the question stem. Choice C is contrary to the message set forth in paragraph 1.

7. **C is correct.** The question requires that we get a "feel" for the author's attitude and tone. The author describes a problem and urges that it be solved; she is *concerned*. She is not apathetic for that would suggest a *lack* of concern. She is worried, but not cynical. Neither is she particularly hopeful or optimistic.

45.2 PASSAGE II

Passage and Questions

The question of how forager honeybees communicate to their hivemates the exact location of new food sources has perplexed naturalists at least since Aristotle observed the phenomenon in the fourth century B.C. Only in this century have scientists determined that several characteristics of honeybee dances vary precisely according to the geographic relation between the nest and the food source. Even more recently, experimenters have demonstrated that honeybee communication occurs along a multisensory pathway, of which some sensory channels appear to be more crucial than others.

After locating a new food source, a forager bee returns to the hive and initiates an intricate series of movements, including wiggles of the bee's body as well as brief looping figure-eights over a circumscribed area of the comb. Other bees observe this dance, and some observers follow the forager in her movements, as though learning the dance steps by rote imitation. In 1943, Karl von Frisch established an exact correlation between the dancing bee's spatial orientation as she looped in eights—straight up or angled to the left or right—and the sun's relation to the new food source. Furthermore, von Frisch concluded that the rate at which the dance leader beats her wings supplies specific information about the hive-to-source distance. During the first half of this century, investigators believed that the visual spectacle of the forager bee's dance provided all the signals necessary to inform the dance observers about the food location and to recruit them to it.

Despite the elegance of von Frisch's correlations, however, a nagging conundrum remained: Given the darkness of the interior hive, how could the bees see the dance movements? Researchers Wolfgang Kirchner, William Towne, and Alex Michelsen measured minute changes in air currents close to the forager dance leader's body, and later determined that dance observers detect these changes in air flow as low-frequency sound through Johnson's organ, a bilateral cluster of nerve cells on the second joint of each antenna. By virtue of these vibratory sonic signals—the dancesong, so to say—honeybees can learn and follow the route to a new food site.

Other experiments added interesting details to the process of honeybee dance communication, indicating that it rests on multisensory mechanisms. At certain points during the dance, for example, the dance attenders will press against the honeycomb with their thoraxes, producing a quick squeaking noise. When the dance leader hears this sound, she pauses in her movements to distribute a bit of the food she has found as samples to her hivemates. On the basis of these observations, Kirchner and Michelsen concluded that taste and odor also play a role in identifying a new food source to the hive. Later investigations showed, however, that bees with congenitally or surgically shortened wings, who could not emit sonic signals in the dance, were not able to recruit nestmates to the food source, even though dance observers who were not given taste and odor samples did learn new locations based on the dancesong alone.

Without the dance, forager bees cannot inform their hivemates how to find food; without food, workers in the nest cannot provide sustenance for the queen; without sustenance, the queen—and so, the hive—cannot survive. In describing his view of the rhythmic vitality of the universe, the groundbreaking English psychologist Havelock Ellis wrote: "Dancing . . . is no mere translation or abstraction from life; it is life itself." However accurate that perception may be in general, it is absolutely true for honeybees.

1. Which of the following best describes the principal subject of the passage?

   A. Research techniques concerning communicative methods among honeybees
   B. The maintenance of social structure among honeybees
   C. The role of the honeybee's dance as a nonvisual form of communication
   D. An elucidation of the way in which honeybees communicate regarding the location of food

2. The fact that forager bees must perform a dance to direct their hivemates to a food source is used to support the author's point that:

   A. the queen cannot survive without well-nourished workers.
   B. honeybees perceive dance as changes in air flow.
   C. for the honeybee, dance is equivalent to life itself.
   D. honeybee communication occurs along a multisensory pathway.

3. In relation to the passage, the word "elegance" (paragraph 3) means:

   A. precision.
   B. tastefulness.
   C. gracefulness.
   D. propriety.

4. As described in the passage, the fact that bees with shortened wings are unable to communicate effectively most strongly suggests that:

   A. taste and odor signals are more important to communication than is the dancesong.
   B. the dancesong is more important to communication than are taste and odor signals.
   C. normal wings are not necessary to the emission of sonic signals.
   D. communication among honeybees is a multisensory phenomenon.

5. If the author were to write a critical assessment of researchers who have studied honeybee communication, he would most likely regard Karl von Frisch with:

   A. disapproval because he did not address the issues with appropriate scientific thoroughness.
   B. indifference because he added only slightly to that which Aristotle had reported in the fourth century B.C.
   C. respect because his work was refined and scientific even though it left certain questions unanswered.
   D. awe because he correctly theorized that the dancesong was effective primarily as a visual signal.

6. The honeybee is traditionally described as a "social organism." If the author were to take note of that description in the passage, he would most likely do so in order to:

   A. prove that for many species, the procurement of food requires interaction among individual members.
   B. illustrate the fact that the dancesong is ineffective without auditory and visual components.
   C. emphasize that the honeybee depends on communication for its survival.
   D. establish that honeybees live according to a hierarchy that includes a queen and foragers.

7. The author suggests that a forager bee communicates information about each of the following EXCEPT:

   A. the color of the flower at which food is located.
   B. the odor given off by food.
   C. the distance between a food source and the hive.
   D. the direction of a food source from the hive.

Passage II: Answers and Explanations

1. **D is correct.** Roughly, the passage is about the honeybees' dancesong, which is the means through which they communicate regarding the location of food. Knowing that, you should look among the choices for a phrase of like meaning. Choice D does not mention the dancesong explicitly, but among the other choices, it most closely mirrors the bottom line. Choices A and B pertain to subjects on which the author does touch but they are both too narrow to be the principal subject of the passage. Choice C is also too narrow; it refers to the *role* of the honeybees' dancesong, which is not the author's chief topic. The author discusses the dancesong in general—its role, the way in which it has been studied and understood, and the way in which it operates.

2. **C is correct.** The question *stem* refers to the subject of the last paragraph. Choices A, C, and D point to paragraph 5, choice B to paragraph 3. To select among the four, the student must ask: "which among the four choices reflects a point that the author supports by noting that the dancesong is essential to the location of food?" At the beginning of paragraph 5, we read that without the dancesong, the bees "cannot inform their hivemates how to find food…." The remainder of the paragraph builds from that observation toward the conclusion that, for the honeybee, *dance is life itself*. While choices A, B, and D each represent a statement made in the passage, none relates to the issue of the question (that is, they are the right answers to the wrong questions).

3. **A is correct.** The stem clearly directs you to the beginning of paragraph 3, where the word *elegance* appears. You must "read around" the word and determine which among the answer choices best restates its meaning in context. If the correct answer is not immediately evident, substitute the word tied to each answer choice into the sentence and determine whether it makes sense. "Despite the *precision* of von Frisch's correlations…" is sensible and meaningful within the surrounding context. In paragraph 2 the author describes certain correlations and findings put forth by von Frisch, and they might be called precise. "Despite the *tastefulness* of von Frisch's correlations…" and "Despite the *gracefulness* of von Frisch's correlations…" create no sensible meaning. "Despite the *propriety* of von Frisch's correlations…" is not meaningless, but it is not well-aligned with the author's meaning. The author intends to focus on the fact that von Frisch's experiments showed care, subtlety, refinement, and attention to detail.

4. **B is correct.** The stem points to paragraph 4, where the author writes of bees with surgically shortened wings. Closely reading the surrounding text, we learn that taste and odor signals play a role in communication regarding food source. We learn further that bees with surgically shortened wings cannot emit sonic signals and thus lose their ability to communicate effectively, even if their "audience" is given taste and odor signals. On the other hand, in the absence of taste and odor signals, a honeybee does communicate if its wings emit appropriate sonic signals. The point? The dancesong is more important to communication than are taste and odor signals. Choices A and C both state the opposite of what the passage suggests. Choice D is the right answer to the wrong question. The author does characterize honeybee communication as a multisensory phenomenon (in paragraphs 1 and 4), but that fact bears no logical relationship to the question stem.

5. **C is correct.** The question points to paragraphs 2 and 3. In paragraph 2, the author describes von Frisch's work, and in paragraph 3, he calls the correlations "elegant." The author's attitude toward von Frisch is *positive*, which eliminates A and B, leaving us to choose between C and D. In the first sentence of paragraph 3, the author describes von Frisch's correlations as elegant, but notes that a "nagging conundrum remained…." Choice C expresses that same message in disguise. The words *refined* and *scientific* roughly reflect the meaning of *elegance*. The phrase "it left certain questions unanswered" roughly reflects the "nagging conundrum"

that "remained." Choice D is inconsistent with the passage. It refers to "visual signal," a concept that does appear in the passage (in paragraph 2). Yet choice D distorts the author's meaning. Paragraph 3 teaches us that those who thought the dancesong to operate as a visual signal were <u>in</u>correct. Researchers who followed von Frisch demonstrated that it operated primarily as a *sonic* signal.

6. **C is correct.** The question asks you to apply new information to the passage. Consider the new information and ask yourself which of the answer choices best relates to it in the context of the passage. Choice C connects the new information in the question stem to the author's claim in the last paragraph of the passage. Choice A is too broad for the scope of the author's argument. This passage is just about bees, not other species. Choice B is the right answer to the wrong question. It is relevant to the passage, but not to the new information in the question stem. Choice D is seductive, but it is too specific to one aspect of social behavior, hierarchy, that is only suggested in passing in paragraph 5. In contrast to choice D, choice C focuses on an issue that is (a) an important issue in the passage and (b) directly relevant to the new information in the question stem.

7. **A is correct.** Notice the word *EXCEPT*, and search among the answer options for the one form of information that the passage does NOT associate with honeybee communication regarding food source. Ask:
For choice A, "Does the passage indicate that honeybee communication carries information regarding *flower color*?" Answer: **no. A is correct.**
For choice B, "Does the passage indicate that honeybee communication carries information regarding *odor*?" Answer: yes, in paragraph 4
For choice C, "Does the passage indicate that honeybee communication carries information regarding *distance*?" Answer: yes, in paragraph 2
For choice D, "Does the passage indicate that honeybee communication carries information regarding *direction*?" Answer: yes, in paragraph 2. The phrase "sun's relation to the new food source" concerns direction.

45.3 PASSAGE III

Passage and Questions

Perhaps the most salient artistic revelation generated by the Impressionist aesthetic is the inclusion of *movement* as a crucial element of human perception and experience. Impressionist painters, for example, sought to portray on their canvases more than the mere form and beauty of the world before them. They needed to convey the transient quality of reality's composition and of the artist's individual observations of reality. In the world of literature, the Symbolist writers adopted the Impressionist commitment to transience by disdaining narrative exactitude and precision in favor of suggestion and inference.

Wholesale transformations in the structure and function of social, economic, and political relationships impelled artists to abandon ideas of permanence and to recognize the ever-changing nature of the universe. The painters spurned a photographic imitation of reality as too static, and thereby untrue to human life. They developed new strategies of color and stroke to depict a vision of volume and shape actively shifting moment by moment, techniques that reached their zenith, perhaps, in the Pointillist school. Meanwhile, the Symbolist poets and novelists delved into the worlds of dream, fantasy, and myth for their visions, implying that the inner lens of the human spirit provided a truer representation of human perceptions than a narrower, journalistic focus on events.

Where graphic artists forfeited realism to seize on perception, and writers surrendered verbatim description to immerse themselves in stream-of-consciousness and inner monologue, musical artists sacrificed the formalistic restrictions and formulaic preconceptions of traditional techniques to emphasize and exalt sensation and feeling. Among the greatest of the Impressionist composers stands Claude-Achille Debussy, who affirmed that in his music, he wanted "to reproduce what I hear" in the world. His emphasis on the subjective sensation of his hearing over the aural, physical, and mathematical structures of sound drove him to shed inhibitions, to revere spontaneity,

and to reclaim freedom. In part, his objective was to prevent his listeners from responding to his music on an intellectual plane, and so he purposefully ruptured their conventional expectations by rejecting cliché and arbitrary limitations, aiming instead to liberate his audience with compositions that reproduced the textures and immediacy of improvisation.

To achieve his ambitious artistic goals, and in accordance with Impressionist priorities, Debussy engineered a thorough expurgation of major-minor key progressions, so rigid and inflexible in their rules and relationships; he explored and exploited the pentatonic scales for innovative approaches to harmony, while the seemingly haphazard meanderings of his melodies drew heavily on the eastern musical forms: arabesques, and even whole-tone scales, so alien and incongruous to the western ear. Perhaps even more importantly, Debussy ushered in a new ascendancy for harmony, whose role until his era had always been decidedly subservient to melody. Now harmony acquired an identity and a dimension all its own, no longer regimented and subjugated by a strictly controlled melodic tyranny, but free, willful, and expressive of its own truth, its own sensations, constantly shifting the resonant background through and against which his melody wove.

Debussy's third great Impressionistic contribution consisted of the revolutionary principles of orchestration he introduced. Where earlier composers had conventionally divided their musicians into distinctly compartmentalized and segregated sections—woodwind, brass, percussion, and string—Debussy conceived of his orchestra not by category, but instrument by instrument. Each musician played a crucial and independent part, the flow and ebb of each instrument's timbre providing essential, if fleeting, detail within the elusive whole, producing an overall effect of multilayered sensation and pointillist evanescence looming, dissipating, and emerging yet again within a multicolored matrix of continual flux and movement.

1. The central thesis of the passage is that:
   A. Impressionism evolved first in painting, and only later in the other arts.
   B. Impressionism was limited primarily to the avant-garde artists.
   C. Impressionism became popular in several art forms to communicate visions of change and movement.
   D. Impressionism represents the zenith of visionary artistic movements.

2. As used in the passage, the term "freedom" (paragraph 3) refers to Debussy's wish to:
   A. separate his work from the restrictions imposed on the graphic arts and literature.
   B. create music that did not necessarily adhere to preexisting conventions of form and technique.
   C. teach his audiences that their lives should not be ruled by their intellects.
   D. mark the distinction between perception on the one hand and sensation and feeling on the other.

3. The author implies that the Symbolist writers differed from their predecessors in that they:
   A. preoccupied themselves with fact and exactitude.
   B. invested their writings with allusion and subtlety.
   C. rejected stream-of-consciousness techniques.
   D. believed that mythical imagery was better suited to painting than to writing.

4. According to the passage, Impressionism had which of the following effects on painters, writers, and composers?
   A. It gave them their first united vision of the human condition.
   B. It caused them to lose the approval of artists of earlier schools.
   C. It inspired them to depict reality as dynamic rather than stationary.
   D. It helped them to appreciate the essential similarities among their art forms.

5. The passage indicates that Debussy made use of the pentatonic scales primarily in order to:

   A. construct melodies that pleased his own ears.
   B. avoid the melodic chaos that had previously characterized his music.
   C. reveal himself to the artistic community as a composer with ambitious objectives.
   D. create music that was not constrained by the major-minor key relationships of his day.

6. The author mentions the Pointillist school in the second paragraph in order to illustrate:

   A. the Impressionists' tendency to have their paintings depict movement.
   B. the Impressionists' general disdain for photography.
   C. the analogy between Symbolist writing and Impressionistic painting.
   D. the interdependency of color and shape.

7. According to the author, which of the following contributed most directly to the development of Impressionism?

   A. The recognition by artists that truth could not be depicted by any one art form
   B. The rapid emergence of photographic technologies
   C. Significant changes in the society and its underpinnings
   D. The unwillingness of most people to value their own perceptions and sensations

Passage III: Answers and Explanations

1. **C is correct.** Overall, the passage is about Impressionism, its focus on motion and change, and the way it affected a variety of art forms. Choice C best captures that idea. Choice A is seductive; a student who fails to keep his or her mind on the stem and the passage might choose A simply because the author first describes Impressionist painters and then other kinds of artists. However, the passage does not suggest that Impressionism appeared first among painters. Choice D is too extreme. Although the author does seem to regard Impressionism favorably and to believe that Impressionist artists were innovative, he or she doesn't compare it in this way to other artistic movements. Furthermore, choice D is a mangler, taking words out of context. More than once, the author uses the word *vision* in connection with Impressionism, and in paragraph 2, the author notes that the Pointillist school constituted the "zenith" of certain techniques associated with Impressionism. Choice B is out of scope, setting forth a statement not made in the passage.

2. **B is correct.** The word *freedom* appears near the end of paragraph 3; Impressionistic composers like Debussy "sacrificed the formalistic restrictions and formulaic preconceptions of traditional techniques." Debussy rejected "arbitrary limitations" imposed by convention and so "ruptured" "conventional expectations." Choice B consolidates such statements *in disguise*. Choice A draws a contrast that isn't supported. The passage refers to a rejection of restrictions, to the graphic arts, and to literature. Nowhere, however, does it suggest that Impressionist composers sought to separate their work from restrictions imposed on other kinds of artists. Choice D takes words out of context, making inappropriate use of the words *perception*, *sensation*, and *feeling*, all of which do appear in the passage, but not in order to draw this contrast. Choice C is out of scope. In paragraph 3, the author refers to "intellect," but nowhere speaks of lives being *ruled* by intellect. Yet the student who loses sight of the stem might think "it sounds good—people should not let intellect *rule* their lives. Emotion is important as well." Attractive or not, that idea does not respond to the stem, and is not supported by the passage.

3. **B is correct.** The author discusses Symbolist writers at the end of paragraph 1, stating that they disdained "narrative exactitude and precision in favor of suggestion and inference." Choice B paraphrases this statement. Choices A and C borrow words from the passage but express a meaning opposite to the author's. Choice D contradicts the passage as well; according to the second paragraph, these writers used mythical imagery.

4. **C is correct.** The stem concerns Impressionism and its effect on painters, writers, and composers (all three). Throughout the passage we learn that Impressionist artists rejected arbitrary limitations, narrative exactitude, and mathematical precision, and somehow invested their art with movement. With its use of the words *stationary* and *dynamic*, choice C summarizes such statements *in disguise*. Choices A and B are out of scope. The passage does not go so far as to say that Impressionism provided the first united vision of humanity, and there is no discussion of how earlier schools reacted. Choice D is half right, but half wrong. Impressionism did represent a similarity between art forms, but the author does not suggest that it had the effect of helping artists to recognize essential similarities.

5. **D is correct.** The relevant text appears at the beginning of paragraph 4, where we learn that Debussy made an "expurgation of major-minor key progressions." As a part of that process, he "explored and exploited the pentatonic scales." Choice D summarizes those statements in disguise. Choices A, B, and C are out of scope, and take words out of context. They misuse, respectively (a) the reference to Debussy's wish to "reproduce what I hear," (b) the appearance of the word *haphazard* in paragraph 4, and (c) the use of the phrase "ambitious goals" at the beginning of paragraph 4.

6. **A is correct.** In paragraph 3, the author describes the Pointillist school as the "zenith" of "new strategies" that depicted "volume and shape actively shifting moment by moment." Choice A summarizes that statement *in disguise*. Choices B and C are right answers to the wrong questions. It is true that (a) impressionist painters did not wish their art to resemble photography and (b) the author analogizes Symbolist writing to impressionism. However, neither of those truths pertains to the author's mention of the Pointillist School. Choice D has the same problem. The author does discuss how Impressionist painters used "color and stroke to depict a vision of volume and shape" (paragraph 2). However, this is mentioned as an aspect of the Pointillist School; the Pointillists are not mentioned in order to illustrate how color and shape relate to each other.

7. **C is correct.** The relevant text is in paragraph 2. "Wholesale transformations in the structure and function of social, economic, and political relationships…" inspired Impressionism. Choice C reflects that message *in disguise*. Choice A tries to play on your outside knowledge or opinion. The student who loses sight of the stem and passage might be drawn to the open-minded attitude expressed in choice A. Choices B and D take words out of context, playing on the author's reference to photography in paragraph 2 (but, no such causal relationship is suggested) and the repeated appearance of the words "perception" and "sensation" throughout the passage (but no such unwillingness is mentioned).

45.4 PASSAGE IV

Passage and Questions

Among the many issues Norman Mailer seems to probe in *The Executioner's Song* is the question of personal courage: Was Gary Gilmore's decision a courageous one? Does it require great human courage to choose death over a life of infinite, daily psychological tortures? Of course, with life imprisonment, Gilmore would always have had the possibility to escape. Or was his choice, Mailer wants to ask, a convict's last-ditch attempt to snub his nose at a system that had, in his own eyes, abused and belittled him all his life? Was Gilmore, unloved by a "rounder" of a father, acting out childhood frustrations by demanding recognition from a substitute paternal authority—the judicial and penal system, equally insensitive and uncaring as his father—by pretending to be just as tough and callous as his real father had been? Or was his unflinching confrontation with the unknown, with death, Gilmore's attempt to convert himself from villain to anti-hero?

After all, Gilmore was, for all his viciousness, in other respects merely human: Were the choice available, he certainly would have chosen escape over execution. Moreover, Gilmore, an individual of unusual intelligence and artistic ability, might have made as productive and creative a life as possible within prison even without escape. Mailer seems to say, however, that in the end, Gilmore decided on a mean, vengeful, and perhaps cowardly final course: execution at the hands of a state firing squad—a death empty, insignificant, pitiful, and ultimately sordid.

Nonetheless, Gilmore assumes his burden, what he recognizes as his responsibility, and through the donation of his organs to the living, he seeks to rectify his existential debt to the species; Mailer, however, does not quite permit the reader to feel that even this last act of sacrifice and charity can make amends for Gilmore's cruelty or balance the scales for the lives he destroyed. And Gilmore, himself, is aware of that ultimate imbalance, for it forms a part of his final knowledge:

"'Vern, there's no use talking about the situation. I killed those men, and they're dead. I can't bring them back, or I would.'"

In the Mailerian orchestration, though, Gilmore's persona crescendos to an ecclesiastical dimension: martyred to a death of his own choosing, his twentieth-century "church" is the established American media—television, magazines, newspapers, films, and novels. His "disciples" are reporters, producers, actors, authors, editors, and publishers—and in particular, one Lawrence Schiller (together with his gnomelike collaborator, Barry Farrell), a reporter/producer who figures largely in the second part of the novel as collator of Gilmore's inner life and marshall of his conscience. The "bible" for this church of the latter-day American sinner, is, perhaps, Mailer's novel itself, *The Executioner's Song*.

As readers of this gospel, we are present at the failure of Gary Gilmore's life and at the futility of his death; and as citizens acquiescent to his execution by the state, we learn his awful rage and pride by heart. For with his bound demand that the state end his life, Gilmore makes lifetakers of us all: In the flicker of the rifles' smokey fire, and the instant of the flashbulb's glittery glare, as readers—as Americans—we cannot but bear witness to his squalid, cruel truth.

The best we can do, perhaps, in our deepest holds of mercy, is find redemption in his epic song. According to this gospel, we cannot, like Gilmore on parole, expect to be handed the good life as our due, simply for the asking nor are we permitted, like Nicole, to rest content on survival by the pure charity of state welfare. Rather, like Schiller and Farrell, and the thousand others who populate this novel in Salt Lake City, Denver, New York, Washington, Los Angeles, and points beyond, we must find the courage to strive and reason, plan and persevere, tread a careful line between enlightened self-interest and service to humankind, and wrest from a pressured, predatory environment—both human and natural—our good works, and our good name.

For nourishment in our human condition, our human life, Mailer seems to say, we find love: love for our fellow human, for our family, for our sexual partners, for ourselves. That nourishment provides our spiritual necessities and enables us to accept our choices, our lives, ourselves. And in that acceptance, in that discovery and sharing of self, and in the discovery of that sharing, we are transcendent, we are communed, and we are redeemed.

In this novel, above all, the gift of life is ours: ours to possess, ours to create, ours to take and to give. All the price already paid for life on this planet—all the frustration, the loneliness, the ambivalence, and the rigor of human life—notwithstanding, we remain indebted, we can never reimburse the value of this gift; we are in the red, we owe. And what we owe is love.

1. Given the views set forth in the passage, the phrases "paying a debt to society," "life is a matter of give and take," and "you have to give something back," are best interpreted to mean:
   A. daily life requires ongoing payment and repayment.
   B. the privilege of life comes with an obligation.
   C. human existence carries a price that few can afford to pay.
   D. human existence carries a price that many would rather not pay.

2. As described in the passage, Mailer's views regarding Gilmore's wish to be executed might be most relevant to:
   A. a psychology professor discussing the effects on children of indifferent and unloving parents.
   B. a philosopher of ethics studying the issue of legalized suicide.
   C. a sociological economist considering the social costs and benefits of capital punishment.
   D. a political candidate who argues in favor of capital punishment as a deterrent to crime.

3. Based only on Mailer's views, as they are described in the passage, a convicted murderer who proclaims "I demand to die for my crime" may be attempting to achieve all of the following EXCEPT to:
   A. transform himself into an anti-hero.
   B. receive from society recognition withheld by his parents.
   C. restore the balance of right and wrong by sacrificing his own life.
   D. show contempt for a society he believed to be uncaring.

4. According to the author, Mailer's depiction of Gilmore's public image analogizes:
   I. a convicted criminal to a self-sacrificing hero.
   II. news reporters to martyrs.
   III. informational sources to a religious institution.
   A. I only
   B. II only
   C. I and II only
   D. I and III only

5. Based on the information in the passage, one might correctly conclude that Gilmore had:

   A. innate abilities that gave him the potential for a productive life.
   B. the capacity to become a charismatic religious figure.
   C. no chance for a successful life from the day he was born.
   D. no experience of love from another human being.

6. According to the passage, Mailer believes that the pressures of human life require that we:

   A. sacrifice the interests of others in order to preserve our own good names.
   B. take from the public sector the support to which we are entitled.
   C. carefully balance our own interests against the well-being of others.
   D. sacrifice spiritual nourishment in favor of practical necessities.

7. According to the passage, the "existential debt" (paragraph 3) that Gilmore attempts to repay is owed to:

   A. himself as a spiritual being.
   B. other people in general.
   C. the surviving family members of his victims.
   D. his own family members.

Passage IV: Answers and Explanations

1. **B is correct.** Each of the statements to which the stem refers lends itself to the author's conclusion that life carries an obligation—the obligation to love. Choice A sounds good, but is too specific to "daily life" and "repayment." Choice C is half right, but half wrong; the passage does not suggest that "few can afford to pay," and Choice D has the same problem. We don't know that many prefer not to "pay."

2. **A is correct.** The question seems to go beyond the passage, yet it refers us to a particular portion of its text. Mailer's views regarding Gilmore's wish to be executed are discussed in the second part of the first paragraph. Focusing solely on that, as the question directs us to do, it is not terribly difficult to dismiss C and D as out of scope. Choice B is a mangler. Although the passage does allude to Gilmore's voluntary choice of death as a possible means of avoiding "a life of infinite, daily...tortures," and although he did require and enlist professional assistance in carrying out his wish, the legal issues involved in the Gilmore case—and especially as discussed in the passage—relate to capital punishment, not legalized suicide. The paragraph does refer to the effects of an indifferent and loving parent on Gilmore's mental processes, which through process of elimination leaves Choice A as the "least wrong" answer.

3. **C is correct.** The stem prominently presents the word "EXCEPT." Therefore, you need to find the answer choice that does NOT apply. Choices A, B, and D all find support in paragraph 1, which concerns Gilmore's motivation for choosing death ("wanting" to die for his crime). The paragraph describes a speculation that Gilmore may want to convert himself from villain to anti-hero (choice A), "demand attention from a substitute paternal authority" (choice B), or "snub his nose" at a society that had not cared for him (choice D). Only choice C *lacks* support. The passage does refer to Gilmore's possible wish to donate organs as a means of righting his wrongs. That reference, however, does not logically follow the stem. The stem asks about a murderer's demand that he die for his crime, not his wish to donate organs.

4. **D is correct.** The applicable text is in paragraph 4. There, the author refers to an "ecclesiastic" crescendo, analogizing various aspects of the Gilmore case to participants in a church-related episode. Reading closely, we learn that the "church" is the media (statement III), the "disciples" (not martyrs) are reporters, and the criminal is a "martyred" figure (statement I). Note that statements I and III reflect the text in disguise. The phrase "self-sacrificing hero" stands for a martyred figure, "informational sources" stands for news media, and "religious institution" stands for church. Statement II does not represent a comparison made in the passage, however, according to the author, Mailer would analogize news reporters to disciples, not martyrs.

5. **A is correct.** The answer is found in paragraph 2 which states that, "...Gilmore, an individual of unusual intelligence and artistic ability, might have made as productive and creative a life as possible...." Choice B takes words out of context, misusing the passage's reference to religion. Choice C is precisely contrary to the author's statements and represents a flip. Choice D is a tempting seducer, but it is too extreme. The author does state that Gilmore was unloved by his father, but he does not indicate that Gilmore's life was entirely devoid of love.

6. **C is correct.** The relevant text is in paragraph 6. Reading it carefully, we learn that "...we must...tread a careful line between enlightened self-interest and service to humankind...." Choice C makes a similar statement *in disguise*.

7. **B is correct.** In paragraph 3, the author refers to Gilmore's "existential debt to the species." "The species" means Gilmore's own species--human beings. Choice B restates the text *in disguise*. Choice A misrepresents the author's reference to "spiritual" necessities, and choices C and D misuse references to Gilmore's own family and to the "lives" that Gilmore "destroyed." Choice A contradicts the passage, which states in paragraph 7 that we must balance self-interest against service to others. Choice B is also inconsistent. The author argues in favor of spiritual nourishment in paragraph 9.

45.5 PASSAGE V

Passage and Questions

It is difficult to specify at precisely what point in their evolution human beings began to experience a spiritual dimension to their existence. The archaeological record makes clear, however, that modern religious practice developed out of what we, today, generally regard as a more "primitive" system of belief and ritual. Early humans relied on magical rites to maintain their healthy and correct relationship with an animistic universe of spirits and natural forces.

As magic grew influential, amulets played an important part in the mediation between the daily life and physical needs of human beings, and the influences on their general welfare that seemed emergent from an altogether different level of reality obviously beyond their control. Through the proper use of the appropriate amulet, the tribe might assure themselves of reproductive fertility; the necessary incantation focused through the correct amulet might induce the unknown powers to provide food and drink, whether through hunting, gathering, or pillaging; similarly, the magic of amulets could bestow upon the tribe and their descendants cunning and endurance in conflicts with other tribes or in the face of natural disasters.

As magic practice evolved, so did animistic theory, such that these powerful, otherworldly forces acquired personification in the form of deities. Amulets became the concrete media through which the deities' made their magical power accessible to humans. The amulet was not viewed simply as a one-way conduit from the gods to humans; rather, amulets also enabled the deities to function, as though their own survival depended on a human agency and complicity in their magic. The men and women who claimed to understand the significance and use of amulets gradually developed into a class of priests, who eventually came to represent themselves as especially gifted by the deities to bestow divine magic—and the benefits that flowed from it—on their tribesfolk.

Although the advent of monotheism included an official forbiddance of their use, many sects and priests permitted amulets to their congregants as an expedience to help minify disruptions in the continuity of their spiritual practices, particularly as the fundamental theological concepts regarding relationships between the human and the divine underwent significant transformation. Even the official prohibitions against the traditions of magic, however, often served to stimulate the popularity of the sanctioned objects. It should be remembered, too, that great craftsmanship had developed in the manufacture of amulets, and the distribution, barter, and sale of these items was not unimportant to the economy of the time.

The fact that amulets occupied a crucial and necessary place in ancient Egyptian and Babylonian religions appears beyond doubt. In the turbulent period between the end of the Sixth Dynasty and the emergence of Thebes as a world power, large areas of ancient civilization came under the sway of the Mideast potentate Khati. Khati, who ruled some three thousand years before the birth of Jesus Christ, set down religious teachings that survive today in a St. Petersburg papyrus. According to this tract, Ra, the sun god, whom the Egyptians considered the Creator of humankind, invented magic and provided amulets for the advantage and profit of his followers. "For...[the]...pleasure of the flocks and herds of God," Khati wrote, "Ra made heaven and earth...and dissipated the darkness of the primeval ocean...[and] made the breezes of life for their nostrils"; and "He gave them the gift of magic...a weapon for resisting the force of unwanted occurrences and the terrors of the night and day."

1. The author's primary thesis is that:

   A. amulets led primitive societies into sorcery and devil worship.

   B. amulets allowed early humans to channel their need to influence forces beyond their control.

   C. amulets acquired magical power by virtue of their association with Nature deities.

   D. amulets acquired magical power by virtue of their association with the caste of priests.

2. About which of the following does the author express uncertainty?

   I. The ways in which amulets played a role in daily life

   II. The fact that amulets were vital to ancient religions

   III. The time at which spirituality became a part of human culture

   A. I only

   B. III only

   C. I and III only

   D. II and III only

3. The author states that otherworldly forces acquired "personification." In the context of the passage, that word refers to:

   A. the practice of incantation by tribesfolk.

   B. the emergence of priests.

   C. the magical powers associated with inanimate objects.

   D. early conceptions of gods and spirits.

4. The author seems to believe that the "sanctioned" objects continued in use partly because of:

   A. their measurable ability to bestow benefits on believers.

   B. political pressure.

   C. economic interests.

   D. disrespect for priests.

5. The author claims that official prohibitions against the traditions of magic stimulated the popularity of amulets. Which of the following, if true, would most *weaken* the claim?

   A. Tribespeople of the time did not dare defy the official dictates of their priests.

   B. The artisans who produced amulets did not actually believe their products had magical properties.

   C. Some early monotheistic leaders believed in the use of amulets.

   D. The prevailing economy did not depend on production of amulets or the trade they produced.

6. Some people today carry charms that they believe will bring them good luck. Such practices suggest that:

   A. modern society promotes a belief in chance over a belief in animism.

   B. modern society rejects the belief that amulets mediate connections with deities.

   C. some people have rejected modern religion and prefer more primitive systems of belief and ritual.

   D. the human impulse to rely on amulets persists even in modern times.

Passage V: Answers and Explanations

1. **B is correct.** Overall, the passage is about amulets and the way humans at one time thought they could rely on them to control their circumstances. Choice B best captures this idea. Choice A is out of scope; for example, there is no discussion of devil worship in the passage. Choice C is supported, but too narrow to be the primary thesis. Choice D is misrepresents the author's discussion of priests. Priests, the author states, arose from those men and women who claimed a special knowledge of how to use amulets. Furthermore, even if it were supported, it would be too narrow.

2. **B is correct.** Read the passage's very first sentence. There the author reveals uncertainty regarding the time at which spirituality became a part of human culture. Nowhere does the author express uncertainty as to (1) the fact that amulets played an important role in early religions and (2) the ways in which amulets functioned in the daily lives of those who relied on them.

3. **D is correct.** The word appears in paragraph 3. There, the author all but answers the question for us, writing that "…these powerful otherworldly forces acquired personification in the form of deities." Choice D substitutes the words "gods and spirits" for deities. Choices A and B are not relevant to the question stem. Choice C is tempting, but it is also the right answer to the wrong question. "Personification" doesn't refer to the magical powers of the amulets, but to the dieties who expressed that power.

4. **C is correct.** The phrase "sanctioned" objects appears in paragraph 4. At the end of that paragraph, the author observes that barter and sale of amulets was "not unimportant" to the economy. Choice A misrepresents the author's opinion. There is no evidence that he or she believes that amulets had actual or measurable powers. Choices B and D are out of scope. There is no evidence of disrespect for priests, or for the existence of political pressure.

5. **A is correct.** In paragraph 4, the author notes that priests' prohibition against the use of amulets sometimes stimulated their use. If it were true that tribespeople did not dare defy their priests, then it could scarcely be true that they made use of amulets when priests had prohibited it. Choice B is out of scope. The author's argument about the relationship between prohibition and popularity of amulets does not rest on an assumption that the artisans believed the amulets had magical powers; the issue is what people in general believed. Choice C is not strong or extreme enough to weaken the passage. The fact that some monotheistic leaders believed in amulets does not invalidate the claim that the "advent of monotheism" as a whole "included an official forbiddance of [amulets'] use" (paragraph 4). Finally, choice D is the right answer to the wrong question. While this statement is in fact inconsistent with the second part of the author's argument about the continued popularity of amulets (see end of paragraph 4), the question asks about the first part of that argument, dealing with the prohibitions themselves stimulating popularity.

6. **D is correct.** The question asks you to apply new information in the context of the passage. The passage indicates that human beings have a deep-rooted tradition of relying on symbolic objects for their well-being. To carry a good-luck charm is, perhaps, to follow that tradition. Choice A is both too extreme and not the issue. The new information in the question stem is not enough to tell us what modern society promotes. Furthermore, nothing in the passage or in the question stem tells us that carrying an amulet reflects a belief in chance over animism. Choice B is goes in the wrong direction. The new information suggests some belief in the power of good luck charms or amulets, while choice B tells us that people do not believe in one type of power amulets might have. Choice C is too extreme. The fact that people carry good luck charms is not enough to suggest that they have rejected modern religion as a whole.

45.6 PASSAGE VI

Passage and Questions

The Humanist Alliance for Curricular Integration and Awareness (HACIA) is an independent administrative entity that monitors foreign policy trends and developments with a special focus on related academic issues. Our primary concern is for foreign literature and language departments in our public universities, where budgetary constraints and state admission requirements often leave administrators overloaded—if not overwhelmed—with their own daily paper process. Our purpose is to call attention to certain recent American foreign policy ramifications and evaluate their potential implications for current and prospective curricular planning. We must emphasize that in no way do we seek to impinge on individual or institutional independence and autonomy: Our goal is simply to provide formative perspectives to an understaffed and overburdened academy for appropriate consideration and planning.

Our world is changing and growing at such a dizzying pace these days that even the cartographers are having trouble drawing all their "P's" and "Q's" in the proper places. New challenges present themselves everyday for the political scientist, the historian, the cultural studies experts, and the mathematicians and natural scientists. Not only do nations around the globe transform and redirect themselves before our very eyes, but here at home, new openness in cultural diversity and interdependent sensitivities demand our good-faith perception and efforts.

Among these global changes is the historic new initiative in North American relations. Now, Canada and Mexico have joined together with the United States to form the North American Free Trade Agreement (NAFTA). The Canadians, of course, have always been vital economic and strategic partners in our best endeavors. For the first time, however, the Mexicans are receiving formal recognition for being friendly, supportive, and constructive allies in our economic, political, and intellectual purposes.

This new relationship with Mexico behooves us to examine most carefully our own cultural assumptions and biases. We all love those dear romantic images of beautiful Old Mexico: the soulful señoritas, the strolling mariachis, and the poor but simple sombreroed campesinos dancing and drinking late into the night (when not lounging idly but menacingly in a cantina doorway), with their quaintly casual notions of social responsibility and charmingly ambiguous interpretations of personal punctuality. Unfortunately, all too many of our academic textbooks, on both the secondary and university levels, misinform their readers and convey those pictures of stereotypical Mexico as though they were the reality of modern Mexico, a nation of nearly 70 million inhabitants and enormous natural resources.

Modern Mexico has about as much to do with strolling mariachis and simple campesinos as today's America has to do with dance hall girls and drunken cowboys: Sure, their contemporary equivalents are still here with us today, but no one in his or her right mind would dream of portraying, and much less defining, the United States based on those anachronistic cultural stereotypes. Disgracefully, when it comes to Mexico, even at some of our finest universities, students are brainwashed with those unfortunate, outdated, and culturally and intellectually irrelevant images.

Modern Mexico, our nearest neighbor to the south, boasts an educationally sophisticated and numerically growing citizenry; a developing, cosmopolitan technology; a vast consumer market; and a diligent, energetic labor force within an exponentially expanding economy and a culturally advanced and intellectually fertile society. If we are to prepare our students adequately for the challenges and opportunities they will face in the coming century, we must impart to them a truthful image of the world they will live in: To continue to do otherwise would be both intellectually corrupt and professionally irresponsible. Anachronistic and irrelevant stereotypes will not do the job. We owe our students our best efforts at illuminating the truth about these real concerns, so that their futures in a competitive and interrelated global environment will be absolutely the brightest they can be.

Accordingly, and because present prognostications point to a significantly increased demand for studious individuals with a solid preparation in Latin American culture—and specifically in that of our closest neighbor—we would urge college and university Spanish departments, at a *minimum*, to do nothing to discourage their undergraduate or graduate students from exploring and studying the Latin American and Mexican literatures.

1. The author's belief that the world is changing rapidly, expressed in the second paragraph, is supported by:

    A. textbook references to global transformations.
    B. testimony from foreign language department administrators.
    C. statements regarding the tasks of those who study social and natural sciences.
    D. an economic analysis of NAFTA.

2. It is probably the author's view that a principal purpose of studying foreign language and literature is to afford students:

    A. an appreciation of traditional images of foreign countries.
    B. an understanding of their own culture in relation to others.
    C. a knowledge of international relations.
    D. a view of foreign countries based on modern realities.

3. According to the passage, which of the following characterizes modern Mexico?

    I. It has a rapidly expanding economy.
    II. It has a growing population.
    III. It is actively developing its technological resources.

    A. I only
    B. II only
    C. II and III only
    D. I, II, and III

4. Given the information in the passage, if the HACIA is successful in achieving its goals, which of the following changes would most likely be effected in foreign literature and language departments of public universities?

   A. They would be less occupied with their own paperwork.
   B. They would be better prepared to plan their curricula.
   C. They would experience a reduction in budgetary pressures.
   D. They would be pressured to conform to HACIA guidelines.

5. The author indicates that the scholastic pursuit of foreign languages and cultures is relatively unenlightening when it:

   A. relies on conventional notions of foreign civilizations.
   B. differentiates between romantic images and reality.
   C. includes a consideration of geopolitical developments.
   D. emphasizes the achievements of foreign civilizations.

6. Suppose an economic study indicates that Mexico presently significantly lags behind the other North American nations in the implementation of computer technologies. Such findings, if made, would most *challenge* the assertion that:

   A. many students who study Mexican literature and culture are misinformed.
   B. the relationships created by NAFTA are new and innovative.
   C. Mexico is prepared to serve as a partner in modern economic enterprise.
   D. United States relations with Canada are invariably advantageous.

Passage VI: Answers and Explanations

1. **C is correct.** In paragraph 2, the author states that the world is changing rapidly. In support of that statement, the author writes that political scientists, historians, cultural studies experts, mathematicians, and natural scientists face new challenges. Choice C reflects such references, in disguise. Choice A is incorrect, as the textbook references come up later in the passage in a different context. As for Choice B, while foreign language department administrators are mentioned in the first paragraph, no testimony is cited, and the issue in that section of the passage is budgetary constraints, not rapid change. Choice D is attractive because the author's reference to NAFTA does support the point that the world is changing rapidly. But the author provides no *economic analysis* of NAFTA. Those two words make choice D incorrect.

2. **D is correct.** Toward the end of paragraph 4, the author bemoans the way in which high school and university courses depict Mexican culture. The depiction, says the author, is outdated. From this you can infer that the author would want such study to reflect modern realities.

3. **D is correct.** Modern Mexico is described in paragraph 6. The author tells us that it boasts a "numerically growing citizenry" (statement II), a "developing, cosmopolitan technology" (statement III), and a "vast consumer market" with a "diligent, energetic labor force" (statement I). All three statements apply.

4. **B is correct.** The relevant information is in paragraph 1, where the author discusses HACIA. The last three sentences describe its purpose, which is to identify American foreign policy trends that might have an impact on curricular planning. Choice B reflects HACIA's purpose as just described. Choices A and C don't respond to the issue of the question stem. The author does note that foreign language and literature departments now experience budgetary constraints and burdensome paperwork. These concerns, however, do not underlie HACIA's purpose. Choice D contradicts the passage. The author writes that HACIA does *not* wish to intrude on institutional autonomy.

5. **A is correct.** The pertinent text is found in paragraphs 4 and 5. There, the author sharply criticizes educational institutions and textbooks for depicting Mexico in anachronistic stereotypical terms. Although the text refers particularly to Mexico, extrapolation indicates that the author would deem the study of any foreign language or culture unenlightening when it rests on conventional images and stereotypes. Choice A correctly characterizes this view. Choice B takes words out of context, misusing the author's reference to romantic images and thus distorting the meaning. Choices C and D are inconsistent with the author's position. The passage has a positive, not a negative tone towards recognizing the achievements of other nations, and towards understanding geopolitical realities.

6. **C is correct.** The question asks you to find the assertion made in the passage that is most inconsistent with the new information in the question stem. The author characterizes Mexico as a modern, dynamic society, with technologies and sophistication that qualify it as a partner in modern economic activity. If a nation were shown to be lagging behind modern computer technologies, that nation would be less well-qualified as a partner. Choice A is not the issue of the information in the question stem, and is also the right answer to the wrong question. The author does believe that today's textbooks misinform their readers regarding the nature of Mexican culture, but this belief is unrelated to the question stem. Choice B is wrong for the same reasons. Choice D is too extreme. The author does not go so far as to assert (in paragraph 3) that relations with Canada are always beneficial.

45.7 PASSAGE VII

Passage and Questions

In June 1963, five months before President Kennedy was shot and the world seemed to change forever for most Americans (certainly for those too young to know the horrors of World War II), I supervised production at Manhattan Braid and Lace Producers as an assistant foreman. Our factory was located on Tenth Avenue, close to the West Side piers. I ran the machines and repaired them when necessary; I drew designs for textile patterns in lace and nylon from those blueprints; I built intricate arrays of chains and crosslinks that wove the cotton into delicate filigrees; and I made sure the beams spun straight and the knitters tended to their tasks. Many brides around the world came with their betrothed to trade their blessed altar vows dressed and fancied in our lace; and when they raised their shining faces and puckered newlywed lips for that first, unforgettable matrimonial kiss, the veils their grooms lifted proved the tender care in our looms.

The textile field boomed in the early sixties due mostly to overseas expansion and escalating foreign competition in Europe and Asia. And while that pleased retailers and consumers, who could get product in the market at lower cost, it turned out hard on American textile workers. The American share of the business was draining down. Italy and Hong Kong began to take over. Put simply, the prospects in New York textile manufacture, which a scant decade earlier had seemed incandescent, now dimmed significantly.

About that time New York City was slowly coming to the conclusion that if it was to provide effective law enforcement, safe streets, and a livable social milieu for its decent, hard-working, law-abiding citizens, it would need to enhance the rewards and compensations offered to those charged with ensuring public safety and civil order. There was talk then of raising the annual wages of peace officers—transit police, corrections officers, and city cops—up to ten thousand dollars, with retirement pensions after twenty years at half retirement-grade pay!

Now don't get me wrong: I liked being assistant foreman on the looms. We had some great times! As the machines hummed and buzzed and clanked and rang, we workers would compose original songs, and down there by the docks, as we fed our looms, by God, we used to sing! Out loud! Like a Broadway chorus!

Every day at breathless pace
We spin the nylon and the lace
We twirl the links and knit the loops
So every handsome groom who swoops

His bride from earth's to heaven's charms
Yet holds her close within his arms
Will gaze upon her white veiled face
And feel the love of pure embrace

But Manhattan Braid and Lace Producers paid me only seven thousand dollars a year, and that with considerable overtime, and they could promise only fifty dollars a month as pension to employees who survived in the company to sixty-five. Thirty-four years old, married, and father of two, I felt the push of present and future responsibilities.

In June, I sat for the Civil Service exam for peace officers, along with seven or eight thousand others. I did not know then that it would be a full year before openings became available. Nor did I know for certain to which force the City might assign me, or if, indeed, I'd be assigned, or accepted, at all. In those days, wherever the need first arose, be it transit, corrections, or NYPD, was where they sent the rookies. I did believe that I had at least one edge over most of the other applicants. In Korea, nine years earlier, I'd served with the United States Army Combat Engineers and Signal Forces, and with the Airborne Special Forces. My experience under fire, behind enemy lines, and performing difficult, dangerous, and sensitive missions, might well prove attractive to my prospective employers.

1. The author decided to leave his factory job for a position with the police force because he:

   A. was concerned about job stability.
   B. was weary of factory work.
   C. felt the lure of adventure.
   D. felt the need for better compensation.

2. In the context of the passage, the word *incandescent* (paragraph 2) means:

   A. intensely hot.
   B. filamentous.
   C. bright.
   D. fluorescent.

3. Which of the following statements, if true, would most *weaken* the author's claim that the textile boom of the 1960s pleased retailers?

   A. The decreased activity in the American textile industry occurred only in New York, not in other U.S. cities.
   B. The textile industry was not responsible for the majority of economic growth in either Italy or Hong Kong.
   C. Intense competition among wholesalers was limited primarily to domestic producers.
   D. Instead of creating competition among wholesalers, the boom created noncompetitive monopolies and oligopolies.

4. In giving advice to a gathering of young people about to enter the labor force, the author would most likely counsel them to:

   A. decide what they love to do, and follow their dream aggressively.
   B. choose a career path and remain open and ready to adapt their goals to new realities.
   C. derive a good living wage from part-time jobs in diverse fields, recognizing that any one industry may flounder.
   D. devote some time to the national military because soldiering is always salable.

5. A recent analysis of U.S. employment trends reported that "the labor market is a dog-eat-dog world" and that "lifetime job security is a benefit much in demand among today's workers." If the author had cited these statements, he would probably have done so in order to:

   A. support the notion that employees should work together harmoniously.
   B. illustrate his idea that employment is analogous to battle.
   C. emphasize his implication that people should be realistic about job expectations.
   D. explain why an industry might at one time flourish and later falter.

Passage VII: Answers and Explanations

1. **D is correct.** The pertinent text is in paragraphs 2, 3, and 4. In those paragraphs, we learn that New York's textile industry experienced downturn and that the writer felt the need to better his income by becoming a police officer. Choices A and C make common sense, but they are not supported by the passage. Choice B contradicts the passage. The writer speaks fondly of textile work, and he seems never to have grown weary of it.

2. **C is correct.** Reread the appropriate text. The author writes that "…the prospects in New York textile manufacture…had seemed incandescent" but now "dimmed." Incandescence is contrasted with dimness. It is sensible to conclude, therefore, that it means "bright." Choices A, B, and D all correspond to outside knowledge (things that in real life could be connected to incandescence), but they do not connect to the context and meaning of the passage.

3. **D is correct.** The relevant text is in the second sentence of paragraph 2. Retailers were pleased because foreign competition, apparently, caused wholesalers to reduce their costs. If that were *not* true, retailers would not have been pleased. Choice D reflects that observation. Choices A, B, and C all have similar problems: none of them are relevant to the issue of the question stem. For choice A, the author only specifically mentions the decline in New York in the passage. So, if the decline were limited to New York, this would not be inconsistent with the author's claim. Furthermore, it wouldn't affect the author's argument about the impact on retailers' costs. For choice B, the main cause of economic growth in Italy and Hong Kong is not an issue in the passage. As for choice C, the issue in the passage is lower costs for retailers. The fact that most intense competition occurred among domestic producers has no direct impact on the author's argument about their costs.

4. **B is correct.** The question calls for (1) an understanding of the passage's main idea and (2) application of the new information in the question stem. The writer reports that he chose and liked one occupation but decided to leave it in response to altered economic circumstance. He seems, moreover, to believe that he did the right thing. Choice B reflects the writer's experience and point of view. Choice A is inconsistent with the writer's experience of changing his profession. Choice C is out of scope; the author does not recommend or choose himself holding many jobs at once. Choice D is too extreme. The writer refers to his service in the military as an experience that might have helped him secure work on the police force. Nowhere does he state or imply that soldiering is *always* marketable.

5. **C is correct.** The question calls for (1) a general comprehension of the author's point of view and (2) application of new information from the question stem. Choice C, of the four options, has the closest connection to both the new information and the passage text. In particular, it reflects the author's own "realistic" decision to give up a job he enjoyed in order to better meet his responsibilities. Choice A is unresponsive to both the stem and the passage text. Choice B does not reflect the author's view; the tone is too negative. Choice D does not respond to the stem; it relates to an industry, not to individual workers.

45.8 PASSAGE VIII

Passage and Questions

For many Native American societies, religious ideology and ritual expressed the intimacy their peoples experienced between humankind and nature. Their spiritual instincts led them closer to an awareness of the wholeness of Creation, of the intact chain of life from the simplest forms to the most highly evolved. In fact, they achieved this awareness much earlier than did the Judeo-Christian-Muslim traditions.

Centuries before Charles Darwin dared to risk the wrath of organized, institutional religion by declaring or implying a direct lineage from paramecium to humans, Native American peoples acknowledged their connection to their animal ancestors, and also to more fundamental forces of Nature.

Whereas the Bible and the Koran assign to God the creation of human beings in the story of Adam and Eve, the doctrines of the Wisconsin Menomini, for instance, which probably predate both Bible and Koran, teach that at the Great River's Mouth, the Earth gave birth to two bears. These bears, distinguished from each other by gender, transmogrified into the first man and woman. A brief analysis of this ancient Menomini revelation demonstrates its intuition of profound insights that western societies only began to understand in relatively modern times.

In the Menomini creation, water provides the fount of land-based life, just as biologists today believe that the atoms of hydrogen and oxygen in water furnish the essential elements without which organic compounds—and the life forms they generate and sustain—will not form. Also, the story affirms that fecundated by the virile fluids at the river mouth, the Earth itself—which today we recognize as a great carbon/nitrogen reservoir—serves as the uterus of animal creation. Still more striking, perhaps, the Menomini intuited that human life owed its origin ultimately to animal and elemental forebears.

Several Native American origin testaments did not limit themselves to the physical process itself, but included an important moral dimension as well. Some indigenous societies in the northwest United States, for example, blame the development of community evils, such as disease, famine, discord, or infertility, on the excessive selfishness of one or more of its members. This belief roots in a vision of the beginnings in which chaos reigns supreme throughout the created universe until the hero figure initiates prosperity and order by the purposeful sharing of resources and assets with the less fortunate. Without generosity as a founding principle, the lesson says, no individual can prosperously organize a commonwealth; and to maintain a healthy society, leaders must distribute tribal wealth fairly.

Moral edification, however, did not always eradicate selfishness (or, for that matter, other human traits deemed undesirable for the tribal well-being) from the community. In such cases, the community needed a reference to guide them in dealing with moral offenses. Thus, the possibility of individual redemption found expression in certain creation doctrines of the Native Americans, often through the metaphor of a dual creation.

The Iroquois, for example, teach that creation results from the efforts of not one, but two primordial hero-spirits, one of whom engenders the noble elements of human character, while the other begets the negative traits. Frequently, the two spirits are related, oftentimes brothers, and their opposite intentions inevitably lead to personal conflict with each other. Some Iroquois teach, for example, that in this struggle, the good brother triumphs and threatens to destroy his evil twin. The evil brother can escape certain death only by vowing to endow humans with the knowledge of medicine and guide them in the arts of healing. Such creation metaphors allow for the existence of human sin, moral conflict, and ultimate redemption through a personal commitment to life activity beneficial to self and community.

1. According to the passage, an analysis of Native American religions in terms of Western scientific thought indicates that:

   A. some Native American beliefs were similar to those reflected in modern Western science.
   B. some Native American peoples intuitively incorporated modern Western scientific methods into their religious rituals.
   C. many Native American peoples developed theories that were more sophisticated than the teachings of Western science.
   D. many Native American religions were directly influenced by Western scientific thought.

2. Suppose it is discovered that a particular Native American group attributes drought and epidemic disease to the wrath of supernatural beings. How would this discovery affect the claim, as made in the passage, that Native American accounts of creation embody a moral dimension?

   A. It would prove the claim to be valid.
   B. It would tend to weaken the claim if the god had been angered arbitrarily.
   C. It would tend to weaken the claim only if the god had been angered by the selfish behavior of a human being.
   D. It would tend to weaken the claim only if the god had been conceived by primordial heroic figures.

3. Suppose a researcher theorizes that the Menomini account of human creation was not created until the twentieth century. What effect would the theory have on the author's view of Menomini teachings as they relate to Darwinian thought?

   A. It would confirm the author's claim that the Menomini believed intuitively that humans had animal forbears.
   B. It would support the author's claim that the Menomini's ideas foreshadowed those later promulgated by Darwin.
   C. It would undermine the author's claim that the Menomini belief that humans had animal ancestors pre-existed Darwin's theories of human origins.
   D. It would refute the author's claim that the Menomini believed in a lineal connection between animals and humans.

4. As used in the passage, the word *virile* (paragraph 4) probably refers most specifically to:

   A. power.
   B. speed.
   C. richness.
   D. fertility.

5. As evidence that Native American accounts of creation were not limited to physical phenomena, the author describes a cause-and-effect relationship between:

   A. generosity and order.
   B. heroism and chaos.
   C. animals and humans.
   D. animals and elements.

6. Among the following, the passage's overall description of Native American religious belief might be most relevant to:

   A. a religious philosopher who contends that all human beings have a basic tendency toward goodness.
   B. a sociologist who postulates that unconnected peoples reach similar conclusions about their own beginnings.
   C. a biologist who hypothesizes that Darwin's theories leave some evolutionary phenomena unexplained.
   D. a poet analogizing the conflicts between siblings to those among members of a social community.

7. In the context of the passage, the reference to Adam and Eve serves to:

   A. emphasize the difference between those theories of creation that depend on dieties and those that do not.
   B. highlight the similarities among Judeo-Christian-Muslim teachings.
   C. contradict the view that any one religious belief is superior to another.
   D. support the view that Native American thought was, in some sense, ahead of Western thought.

Passage VIII: Answers and Explanations

1. **A is correct.** The question asks, generally, about the relationship between Native American religions and Western scientific thought. In paragraphs 1 and 2, the author writes that in their view of creation, Native Americans acknowledged a link to their animal ancestors. That means their beliefs were similar to those of modern Western science. Choice B is inconsistent with a main theme in the passage, that many Native American beliefs pre-existed similar Judeo-Christian-Muslim or "scientific" beliefs. Choice C is too extreme; the author argues for an equivalent level of sophistication, or, that the cultures had similar ideas, not for a more advanced level of thought. Choice D, like choice B, is inconsistent with the author's argument in the passage; the author indicates that many ideas in Western scientific thought already existed in Native American religion.

2. **B is correct.** The author's discussion of a "moral dimension" appears in paragraph 5. There, we read that according to some Native American religions, disaster might befall a community because one or more of its members exhibits selfishness. That claim runs counter to—would be *weakened* by—a finding that the community attributed drought and disease not to selfish behavior but to deities who are arbitrarily angry—for no reason. Choice A is too extreme. There is no reference in the new information in the question stem that would directly support, much less prove, the author's claim about morality. Choice C represents a flip; it is precisely opposite to a correct statement. If the God had been angered by human selfishness, the claim would be *strengthened*. Choice D is out of scope of the question. Primordial heroic figures are not directly relevant to the authors discussions of morality.

3. **C is correct.** The new information in the question suggests that the Menomini idea that humans came from a "direct lineage" beginning with paramecium (see paragraph 2) came after, not before, Darwin's ideas, which contradicts the author's claim in the beginning of paragraph 2. Choice A is out of scope. The issue of who came up with certain ideas first has no impact on the author's description of what the Menomini in fact believed. Choice B is the opposite; it would weaken rather than support that claim. Choice D is too extreme. This new information would have no impact on the author's argument about what the Menomini believed; the issue in the new information is the relative timing of the origin of those and other beliefs.

4. **D is correct.** In paragraph 4, the author describes the Menomini view of creation and refers to the "virile" fluids at the river mouth. According to the Menomini, the fluids gave rise to life. The virility is intended to imply fertility; note the analogy between Earth and a uterus. Choice A is tempting, but "power" is too vague: power to do what? For choice B, the speed or rapidity of the generation of life forms is not the issue in the passage. Choice C is seductive, but, if you were thinking that "richness" may suggest the idea of fertility, choice D is still more directly supported by the passage.

5. **A is correct.** The relevant information is in paragraph 5, where the author first notes that "Native American origin testaments did not limit themselves to the physical..." The paragraph describes how, according to some Native Americans, a hero invested the world with order by sharing of resources (generosity). Choice A, therefore, correctly characterizes the text *in disguise.* Choice B is the opposite; pargraph 5 suggests a relationship between heroism and order, not chaos. Choices C and D represent relationships that exist in the passage (although the relationship between animals and humans is not a causal one), but neither

responds to the question stem, which asks specifically about the issue of creation as not limited to physical phenomena.

6. **B is correct.** One of the passage's chief themes is that Native American religious doctrine resembles the teachings of modern Western religion and science. In particular, the author focuses on creation (beginnings of life). Choice B, therefore, correctly characterizes the passage's central theme and, among the choices, properly identifies the professional to whom it would be most relevant. Choices A, C, and D all use words from the passage out of context. Choice A is inconsistent with the passage, which discusses the view that good and bad coexist. Choice C has leaving phenomena unexplained as its theme, while the religious beliefs discussed in the passage serve an explanatory function. As far as Choice D, the religious beliefs descibed embody the idea of redemption and reconciliation, rather than ongoing conflict (paragraph 7).

7. **D is correct.** The author mentions Adam and Eve at the beginning of paragraph 3. She goes on to describe the Menomini view of creation, which (1) recognizes two primal figures of opposite sex and (2) "probably predates" the Bible. The author thus points out that Native American religious doctrine was, in its way, ahead of Western teaching. Choices A and B are manglers, each borrowing words and phrases from the text and reproducing them in distorted context. Choice C is seductive because it expresses an attractive (to many) point of view, but it has no direct connection to the reference to Adam and Eve.

45.9 PASSAGE IX

Passage and Questions

Most people who have paid even minimal attention to health insurance issues are familiar with the concept of cost-shifting by healthcare providers. In hospitals, for example, patients with good insurance coverage—whose policies reimburse providers fully and adequately for the realistic costs of healthcare—wind up underwriting care for indigent, uninsured, or underinsured patients. This sort of cost-shifting is fairly self-evident: One person's insurance may reimburse the hospital and doctors, say, five thousand dollars for a hernia reduction, while Medicaid might cover only a fraction of that expense for an indigent patient. Obviously, the average cost for a hernia reduction at that hospital lies somewhere between those two figures.

However, there is another sort of insurance cost-shifting that has received very little, if any, attention, although it stands to reason that such account juggling must occur within the industry: Huge insurance conglomerates, and re-insurers, beset with tremendous losses from natural and human-made disasters—earthquakes, floods, wildfires, hurricanes, oil spills, riots, etc.—outrageously balance their profit margins by raising revenues from the one, guaranteed source with little or no clout to dispute price increases or seek redress: ordinary citizens, whose budgetary struggles to make everyday ends meet, must include the ever-rising monthly health insurance premiums for themselves and their families.

In this light, the so-called "healthcare crisis" becomes refocused as an "insurance industry crisis." Accordingly, the brunt of legislative remedies ought to be aimed at reforming the financial structure of the insurance industry, not that of a healthcare system which, until now, has been the envy of the world. Modest suggestions along these lines include prohibiting insurance companies and re-insurers doing business in the United States from mixing their revenues from health insurance premiums with other kinds of insurance receipts or payouts. This way, healthcare users will not be paying huge rate increases to provide relief to victims of earthquakes, floods, and hurricanes, or to reimburse merchants burned out of business in a wildfire or civil riot, or to fund multimillion-dollar judgments awarded by juries as penalties for corporate negligence.

Also too often ignored in the public debate is a second element crucial to the drive to improve healthcare. The media has devoted far too little discussion exploring the enormous expenditure of clinicians' time and office resources devoted to conflict with "utilization review" personnel of the insurance companies. Do Americans really want to require their trained, experienced, licensed physicians to partake of this costly and profligate procedure? Can there be any method more inefficient and potentially hazardous than to allow insurance personnel, buttressed only by a computer printout of actuarial statistics, to demand disputatious justification for—much less to overrule—an expert physician's clinical observations, clinical reasoning and clinical determinations?

It must be said, of course, that this sort of "review" very closely mirrors the educational process by which physicians are trained, first in medical school and later in hospital residencies, except that in the professional training experience, the "reviewers" are not insurance company personnel—they are experienced, expert physicians themselves, as they must be, to shoulder such a serious responsibility as maintaining the standards and quality of sound clinical practice. Their experience has taught them certain medical truths not included in the curriculum of insurance accountants and database personnel: that each clinical case can be decided only on the facts and observations in the specific clinical situation, not on some formulaic basis of statistics and probabilities.

The logic of the insurance utilization review process, however, would seem to call into question the very need for professors of medicine altogether: Why not simply let a medical student, an intern, or a resident read textbooks, examine patients, and phone in their findings and tentative diagnoses to insurance company clerks? Then let insurance company pharmacists, not highly trained clinical specialists, prescribe the most appropriate—read "cost-effective"—treatment. After all, that's the way things are beginning to work in the real world of daily practice!

1. One expert in public health has proclaimed that "HMOs exert moderate pressure on primary care physicians to limit referrals. In contrast, in a PPS, the highly trained specialist must withhold certain treatments until obtaining approval from utilization reviewers." This expert would most likely:

A. endorse legislation eliminating government regulation of health insurance policies.
B. favor a one-payer healthcare system in the U.S.
C. reject the belief that either HMOs or PPSs interfere with patients' access to physicians and care.
D. conclude that both HMOs and PPSs interfere with the physician/patient interaction, but PPSs to a greater extent.

2. The author of the passage would likely favor federal legislation that:

A. requires people to choose regional physician groups from whom they would receive all healthcare.
B. restricts patients' rights to appeal an insurance company decision affecting their healthcare.
C. denies insurance companies the final power to decide that they will or will not reimburse the cost of a particular treatment.
D. limits the number of yearly specialist referrals for each patient.

3. The author believes that shifting insurance losses from home insurance policies and corporate liability settlements to health insurance premiums probably results in:

I. unjustifiably high health insurance costs.
II. inadequate healthcare for those who are underinsured.
III. unfair burdens to patients with relatively better health insurance.

A. I only
B. II only
C. II and III only
D. I, II, and III

4. Which of the following points is/are presented in the passage to argue that utilization review procedures are potentially problematic?

I. Utilization review personnel rely on statistical models rather than a specific clinical situation to approve or deny recommended treatment.
II. Patient outcomes under utilization review procedures are significantly worse than in their absence.
III. Utilization review procedures consume physician's time that could be more valuably used attending to patients.

A. I only
B. I and II only
C. I and III only
D. I, II, and III

5. Which of the following findings, if true, would best support the author's contention that health insurance pricing policies are unfair?

   A. Many Americans cannot afford health insurance.

   B. The increase in the cost of health insurance is far greater than the rise in actual healthcare claims paid by insurance companies.

   C. Most Americans believe that if you maintain good nutritional and life style habits you will maintain good health.

   D. Insurance company revenue from non–health insurance policies is greater than expenditures in those areas.

6. According to the passage, which of the following is likely to be true about the relationship between utilization review procedures and physicians' attendance to patients' needs?

   A. The more review required, the less attendance to patients' needs.

   B. The more review required, the greater attendance to patients' needs.

   C. The less review required, the less attendance to patients' needs.

   D. The passage does not indicate any connection between utilization review requirements and attendance to patients' needs.

Passage IX: Answers and Explanations

1. **D is correct.** The question asks you to evaluate new information in the context of the passage. The "expert" proclaims that (1) HMOs exert *moderate* pressure on primary care physicians but that (2) PPSs actually forbid specialists to administer certain treatment without permission. According to the expert, therefore, the HMOs impose some interference with physician/patient interaction and the PPSs create greater interference. Choices A and B have little to do with the passage and nothing to do with the stem. Choice C contradicts the sense of the stem; both situations represent some level of interference.

2. **C is correct.** A reading of paragraphs 4, 5, and 6 reveals the author's attitude. He generally opposes the interference by insurance companies with the physician's medical decision making. Choice C corresponds to this view. Choice A doesn't have any direct connection to issues raised in the passage. Choices B and D are contrary to the author's views, as they would both potentially impede good care.

3. **A is correct.** The relevant information is set forth in paragraph 2. According to the author, insurance companies raise the cost of health insurance in order to compensate for the claims they pay on other forms of insurance. He characterizes the practice as outrageous. Statement I therefore clearly applies. Statement II relies on outside knowledge. The passage itself does not indicate that the underinsured receive inadequate care. Statement III is the right answer to the wrong question. It loosely refers to the cost-shifting described in the *first paragraph*. It is, however, unresponsive to the stem, which concerns the cost-shifting described in the *second paragraph* (which, at the beginning of paragraph 2, the author describes as "another sort" of cost-shifting).

4. **C is correct.** In paragraph 4, the author begins his criticism of utilization review. He asks, rhetorically, whether the system should require trained, experienced physicians to partake of this costly and profligate (wasteful, extravagant) procedure (statement III). He refers to the inefficiency and danger that arise when insurance personnel make decisions on the basis of actuarial statistics, overruling the physician's determinations based on clinical reasoning (statement I). However, Statement II is unsupported. The author never cites data on actual patient outcomes.

5. **B is correct.** This question asks you to find new information in the correct answer that strengthens the author's claim. A reading of the second paragraph indicates that the author opposes the sort of cost-shifting under which insurance companies raise healthcare premiums in order to cover claims paid on other forms of insurance. The author's view would be supported and confirmed if it were shown that the increase in health insurance premiums exceeds insurance claims paid for healthcare. Choices A and C make what many believe to be true statements, but they are unrelated to the passage or stem. Choice D is the opposite of whate we need. A finding that non–health insurance policies generated more revenue than they cost in claims would tend to deflate, not support, the author's arguments.

6. **A is correct.** In criticizing utilization review at paragraphs 4, 5, and 6, the author expresses a view that utilization review generally impairs the quality of healthcare (disguised in choice A as "patient needs") by (1) consuming physicians' time and (2) allowing insurance personnel to make decisions that properly belong to physicians. He believes that utilization review promotes a lesser attendance to patient needs. Choices B and C are reversals; note that they both suggest the opposite of Choice A. Choice D ignores the thrust of paragraphs 4, 5, and 6; a connection is in fact indicated in the passage.

CHAPTER 46

UNDERSTANDING THE MCAT ESSAY

46.1 THE ESSAY QUESTION

The third portion of the MCAT requires you to write two essays, each within thirty minutes. Both essays are scored. Taken together, the two scores generate a single score, reported as a letter J–T, where J is low and T is high. Each essay problem provides you with a short statement, the *prompt*, and an instruction to comment on the prompt. This chapter will show you (a) how the exercises are designed and (b) how to approach them systematically. Chapter 47 sets forth six sets of simulated MCAT essay problems together with sample answers that would likely receive high scores.

THE PROMPT

As noted, each essay exercise provides you first with a *prompt*. The prompt is a quasi-philosophical statement concerning some aspect of human thought or activity. It might, for example, concern politics, history, art, literature, education, or human relationships.

Following are five simulated prompts, each of which might serve as the basis for an MCAT essay exercise.

1. No person should obey a law that violates his or her own conscience.

2. Education is ultimately the study of one's own ignorance.

3. Achievements are valuable only to the extent that they are lasting.

4. War is waged not by governments but by people.

5. No two people can form a relationship unless they first trust each other.

THE INSTRUCTIONS

You are instructed to read the statement and then to write a unified essay in which you perform three "tasks." You are to (1) explain the statement's meaning, (2) describe a situation to which the statement does not apply, and (3) discuss the factors that affect the statement's validity.

46.2 ESSAY GRADES AND GRADING

The test taker writes two essays. Each is evaluated and scored by two graders, one human and one computer grading program, each of whom assigns it a raw score on a 1 to 6 scale. If the two graders' scores differ by more than one point, the essay is passed to a third "supervisory" grader. In the end, all of the raw scores for both essays are combined and averaged into a single reported score on the J–T scale.

The essay portion does not allow for the same kind of "objective" grading as the multiple choice sections of the test. If a multiple-choice question carries option "D" as the keyed answer, there is little room for dispute as to whether you did or did not select it. Your response to a multiple-choice question is evaluated by a machine on the basis of the oval you fill in with your pencil, while the essay is evaluated at least in part by a human being. And no matter how fair-minded, diligent, detailed, and meticulous the reader may be, there is always room for reasonable dispute as to the correctness of an evaluation.

Moreover, AAMC policy requires that essays be read and graded "holistically." Readers are instructed *not* to evaluate an essay in terms of any set of enumerated criteria. Rather they are instructed to view the essay as a "whole" and to award a grade *without* separately considering such matters as clarity, word choice, or sentence structure. Indeed, the human graders are encouraged to read and evaluate each essay in less than two minutes. Therefore, the grade an essay receives is going to depend on the *impression* it gives its reader.

46.3 APPROACHING THE MCAT ESSAY SYSTEMATICALLY

Remembering that the essay will be read quickly and holistically, you should be sure to (a) address all three of the tasks assigned to you and (b) make it absolutely clear that you have done so. No matter how solid your response to one of the tasks might be, an essay that ignores or significantly slights one or more of the tasks will not get a high score. The three tasks are of equal importance, and therefore each should get more or less equal attention in your response.

Before you begin to write, spend at least five minutes brainstorming and outlining your essay. Define what examples you will be using, and what criteria you will discuss in the third task. Don't, if at all possible, make it up as you go along. Have a clear direction from the start, so that you can in fact write a "unified" and logically coherent essay.

Address the tasks in the order in which they appear in the question, so that the grader can easily follow the logic of your response and how it relates to each task. Three paragraphs, one per task, are sufficient; this is not your standard five-paragraph essay. The simplest and most straightforward approach is to write a three paragraph essay, with one paragraph devoted to each task. Do not combine discussion of more than one task within a paragraph. When you move on to the next task, begin that new paragraph with a clear transition to alert the reader that you are moving on to the next part of the question.

The basic nature of the three tasks is very consistent from question to question. However, always carefully read the entire paragraph underneath the bold-face prompt statement, so that you can be sure to directly respond to any unexpected twists in the wording.

Let's first consider a sample prompt in order to get an overview of what those three tasks entail. Later in this chapter we will go through each task in more detail.

No person should obey a law that violates his or her own conscience.

Write a unified essay in which you perform the following tasks. Explain what the above statement means. Describe a specific situation in which one should obey a law that violates his or her own conscience. Discuss what you think determines whether or not a person should obey a law that violates his or her own conscience.

The question will always appear in this format: a prompt statement in bold, and a paragraph underneath that sets out the tasks. The first sentence, "Write a unified essay in which you perform the following tasks," is always the same. Take the word "unified" seriously; all parts of your essay need to be logically consistent with each other, and all need to be closely focused on the question, exactly as it is worded. Be careful to directly address the exact wording of the question throughout your essay. Essays that stray, either in part or as a whole, will not get a high score.

First task: The second sentence defines your first task: "Explain what the above statement means." This task essentially asks you to interpret the statement, including defining terms when necessary, and to explain when and why this statement would be true. Therefore, for this question, the first part of your essay should explain what "violating his or her own conscience" might mean, how it relates to obedience to the law, and when and why this statement would be true. Even though the question does not ask for an example here, providing one can only clarify and improve your argument, and make the third task easier to address.

Second task: The third sentence gives you the second task: "Describe a specific situation in which one should obey a law that violates his or her own conscience." Remember that the essay must be logically unified and consistent. Therefore, this task is not in fact asking you to contradict an argument for the statement that you made in the first part of the essay. Answering these questions should not be like writing "pro" and "con" positions in a debate. By the nature of the question as a whole, the prompt statement is sometimes true, but in other situations it is false. Therefore, the second task is asking you to consider certain contexts or situations in which one should follow the law even if it goes against his or her conscience.

Your response to the first two tasks, then, when taken together, should present a contrast between situations in which the prompt statement is true, and other situations in which it is false.

Third task: The last sentence lays out the third task. It asks you to explain what factors or conditions would determine when following one's own conscience would justify violating a law, and when it would not. This paragraph should give a rule or set of criteria that could be used to determine whether or not a violation of a law, based on conscience, would be justified.

Now, let's take a look at each task in more detail, using the prompt below:

Education is ultimately the study of one's own ignorance.

Write a unified essay in which you perform the following tasks. Explain what the above statement means. Describe a specific situation in which education might not be the study of one's own ignorance. Discuss what you think determines whether or not education is ultimately the study of one's own ignorance.

TASK 1: DESCRIBING THE STATEMENT'S MEANING

> "In many cases, it can be said that education consists of discovering what we do not know."

After your introductory sentence, go on to elaborate further on the core idea of the prompt statement. This may involve defining key terms, either explicitly or implicitly. For example,

> "While education always involves gaining new knowledge in some form, certain kinds of education are founded on the idea that our existing knowledge is incomplete, insufficient, or inaccurate, and it is only by identifying these gaps or lapses in our current knowledge that we can progress."

A good way of elaborating on an idea is to give an example. Here, you might say,

> "For example, in the area of theoretical science, such as astrophysics, while undergraduate and graduate education certainly involves learning what has already been discovered and theorized, the basic assumption is that we have not yet found the truth. Education in these fields then has as its basic goal to equip students who will move on to higher levels within the field to push the boundaries, and to come up with new and better ways of envisioning and describing reality. In astrophysics, "string theory" was one such innovative way of depicting the structure of the universe; now this theory has fallen out of favor as astrophysicists seek a better, more predictive model. The assumption that education means discovering what we do not know more than what we do know means that these fields are always in flux, with the basic tenets being taught changing, sometimes radically, from decade to decade."

TASK 2: THE ANTITHESIS TO THE STATEMENT

After addressing the first task, signal to the reader, at the beginning of a new paragraph, that you are moving on to the second task. This transition can be as simple as placing the word "however" in front of a paraphrase of the second task statement. For our prompt, that might be,

> "However, other forms of education should not be seen as a study of what we do not know. Instead, they have as their goal imparting to students a certain body of knowledge that remains fairly consistent and agreed upon over long periods of time."

This second task explicitly requires you to give an example. Make sure to (a) explain the relevance of your example to the terms of the prompt, and (b) choose an example that clearly contrasts with your discussion and example from the first task, and (c) make that contrast clear. For our prompt, the part of rest of the second paragraph might read,

> "One such area would be mathematics. Except at the very highest levels of the field, where academics may in fact try to push the theoretical boundaries outwards, education in

math essentially entails mastering a set body of knowledge, rules, and procedures. Even new proofs in upper level math do not involve creating new visions of how numbers relate to each other, but rather a new application of existing knowledge. Mathematics cannot exist unless everyone is working by the same basic agreed-upon rules. Education in math, then, consists of filling in gaps in our knowledge, but with the assumption that by doing so we are constantly reducing our level of ignorance, rather than coming to new realizations of what we do not know or understand."

TASK 3: DETERMINING FACTORS

The third task asks you to explain what determines whether the prompt statement is true or false. It may be tempting to choose sides at this point; for example, to write, "Since we can always learn more, education of any kind is really a study of our own ignorance." Resist this temptation. If you argue that one side or the other is always true, (a) you are not really answering the question they are asking you, and (b) you will contradict something that you argued earlier in either the first or second task. Remember that, by the nature of these questions, the prompt statement is sometimes true and yet sometimes false. Your goal in the third task is to lay out the conditions or factors that would make it either true or false in any particular situation or context.

A good way of leading into the task is to paraphrase the task statement and introduce your criteria. (This should happen at the earliest at the beginning of the third paragraph; an essay should never be shorter then three paragraphs, one paragraph her task.) For our sample prompt, you might write:

> "What determines whether or not education is fundamentally a study of our own ignorance is the nature of the field."

Then go on to elaborate on your criteria. You can refer back to points you have already made, including your examples, but your response to the third task should not simply repeat what you have already said. Remember that this is not a standard "five paragraph essay" where the first paragraph or introduction tells the reader what you are going to say, and the last paragraph or conclusion sums up what you have just said. Make sure that your argument in the third task is consistent with the contrast you have drawn in and between the first two tasks. At the end of the paragraph, have a simple concluding statement to wrap it up.

Keep in mind that the last paragraph is the last thing that the grader sees; it is human nature to be most strongly affected by what you have read most recently. Therefore, manage your time carefully, so that you can give the third task sufficient attention.

The rest of your essay on our sample prompt might read as follows.

"Education in fields of study that try to describe and predict reality will always be based on the assumption that we are fundamentally ignorant, that our current understanding is flawed, and that we need to come up with new models of reality. This does not only apply to the natural sciences. The history of the social sciences, for example political science or economics, is defined by a succession of theoretical schools and models, each purporting to better describe reality than the model that came before. In fact, an innovation in political science that has come in the last few decades is the application of economic theory to political science, in particular "game theory." This way of envisioning and predicting political behavior is quite different from earlier models, and only came into being because political scientists assumed that those earlier models could not give us a full understanding. Education in these fields, then, must involve the assumption that our knowledge is never complete. On the other hand, education in fields that involve application of existing rules and models assume that we have all the knowledge necessary to proceed. This is especially true not only of mathematics, but of technical or vocational education. Computer programmers for example, just like math students, can't be taught effectively unless both teacher and student assume that our knowledge is complete, accurate, and sufficient, and that success in that form of education comes from fully absorbing, understanding, and being able to implement a defined set of rules or body of knowledge. So, we can see that education in different fields varies not only in content but in basic assumptions regarding our capacity to achieve complete knowledge."

46.4 EXPLOITING YOUR RESOURCES

You should use every tool at your disposal to enhance the reader's impression of your essay. If you have a flair for writing you should exploit it. Consider these two phrases:

1. "In order to make a relationship that will exist for an extended period of time…"

2. "In order to forge an enduring relationship…"

The second phrase is better than the first. The word *forge* is more expressive than *make*, and the word *enduring* is more precise than the phrase "that will exist for an extended period of time."

Consider these two sentences:

1. No one can fully predict that which will happen in his or her life and one's life is generally accompanied by the appearance, at times, of difficulty and problems that are unforeseen.

2. Life is full of surprises; vicissitude is its frequent visitor.

The second sentence is better than the first because it is tight, terse, and engaging. Its words are sophisticated but not pretentious, and it features only ten words, not thirty.

If in writing your essays, you meaningfully cite a well-regarded authority, you can only improve the impression left by your argument. Relevant references to Confucius, the Bible, William Shakespeare, Thomas Moore, Abraham Lincoln, Thurgood Marshall, John Fitzgerald Kennedy, or Martin Luther King, Jr., for example, may well improve your score. Consider, for example, these paragraphs:

1. In a great many cases, wars are fought in order to protect and defend special interests of only a minority of a country's citizens. The interests of the majority of the people are not taken into account. In all probability, the peoples that find themselves at war have very little dispute with one another. To a considerable degree, they share common goals and objectives and would profit more from cooperation than from fighting.

2. War generally serves the interest not of the many but of the few. In the most vital of their needs, warring populations have more commonality than difference. As President Kennedy proclaimed, "We all inhabit this small planet; we all breathe the same air; we all cherish our children's futures and, finally, we are all mortal."

The second paragraph is better than the first. It employs a relatively tight, engaging style and cites the words of a highly regarded figure. If you can work an authoritative quotation into your essay, you should do so.

46.5 LENGTH AND APPEARANCE

Aim to write approximately 500 to 600 words for each essay. An essay that is substantially shorter than 500 to 600 words gives the appearance of a writer who (a) fails to take the assignment seriously or (b) has little thought to share. Similarly, an essay that is far longer but not well-organized or, that is repetitious, suggests that the author has not carefully designed his essay, but rather has written aimlessly.

It is difficult to construct a *well-ordered* essay in thirty minutes, particularly if the topic is not of your own choosing. You'll give the *appearance* of organization, however, if you avoid long paragraphs and and skip a line at the beginning of each one.

CHAPTER 47

SIX ESSAY EXERCISES

47.1 ESSAY EXERCISE I

Consider this statement:

Without suffering, human beings can experience no real joy.

Write a unified essay in which you perform the following tasks. Explain what you think the above statement means. Describe a specific situation in which human beings can experience joy without suffering. Discuss what you think determines whether human beings can or cannot experience joy without suffering.

Good Response:

It is often said that youth is wasted on the young. If only we could enjoy the physical vitality and mental acuity of youth after already experiencing the physical pains and mental deterioration that comes with old age, we could truly revel in a healthy body and quick mind. In many ways, we can only truly experience joy once we ourselves have gone through a period of physical and/or mental suffering. True joy is not simply comfort or pleasure, but a higher level and more deeply intense experience. People who have undergone the anguish of a near-death event such as a plane crash, or who have survived a prolonged and painful illness, often say that they emerge from that experience with a new appreciation of life; even everyday sensations have a new depth and meaning. One thing that we often take for granted is freedom of movement. Those who have been imprisoned for many years, such a POW released from captivity, often feel that even everyday decisions and actions that we normally take for granted, such as running an errand to the local grocery store, have a new meaning. If you have never been deprived of basic freedoms, it is almost impossible to really appreciate the joy of everyday existence.

However, this only applies to our own suffering, not to that of others. We can in fact take great joy in the well-being or successes of those we care about without having seen them undergo suffering, or having undergone our own suffering at the sight of their misfortunes. This is the opposite of "schadenfreude," or taking pleasure in the misery of others; in many cases, we take great pleasure in the happiness of others, for its own sake, rather than needing the contrast of pain to fully appreciate pleasure. In a trivial sense, this happens when sports figures become national heroes. When Michael Phelps swam in the Olympics, millions took vicarious pleasure in his success and felt, however momentarily, almost a pure form of joy when he won his seventh medal. We have this strange phenomenon of rabid fandom, such that we identify ourselves with an individual or a team, and live with them through their victories. We don't need to see them fail in order to intensely experience their victories. It may seem strange to call this joy, but perhaps because the relationship of a fan to a sports hero is so abstract, joy can come through unmediated by sorrow. Much more profound, however, is the relationship between a parent and child. Parents do not need to see their child suffer in order to feel deep joy when that child is happy. We don't need the contrast of suffering in this case in order to feel the opposite extreme. If anything, if a child suffers, the fear that her experience of pain will affect her for the rest of her life tempers our happiness even when the suffering is over.

Therefore, what determines whether or not we must experience suffering in order to feel real joy is whether the joy comes from our own experiences or from the experiences of others. Without contrast, we cannot always put things in real perspective. In some cases, to experience the highest emotions, we must have experienced the lowest. However, one of the most admirable human emotions is our ability to take pleasure in the well-being of others. Perhaps this is because our own experiences are muddled with so many conflicting and unclear sensations, we need a stark contrast to put our positive emotions into relief. However, there is a certain purity in our love for others. Without the inner turmoil of our own thoughts and feelings to sort out, we don't need that contrast but can experience joy more directly, using only our capacity to step outside of ourselves and our own experiences to feel joy at the successes of those we idolize on one hand, or that we love and care about on the other.

47.2 ESSAY EXERCISE II

Consider this statement:

One who has no committed belief has no meaningful purpose in life.

Write a unified essay in which you perform the following tasks. Explain what you think the above statement means. Describe a specific situation in which a person may have a meaningful purpose in life without a committed belief. Discuss what you think determines whether a person can have a meaningful purpose in life without having a committed belief.

Good Response:

This statement means that one who does not adhere firmly to a guiding principle or set of principles will find no objective of any true significance in life. The statement indicates that to have substance, a person's ambition must be rooted in a fundamental conviction that the person holds strongly. Furthermore, in the absence of such conviction, a person's life will be devoid of vital goals.

In order to describe a specific situation in which the statement does not apply, it is necessary to examine the meaning of the words contained in the statement. Without a lucid comprehension of "committed belief" and "meaningful purpose," it is impossible to evaluate the essence of the statement.

A "committed belief" may mean to some people a conviction that is absolute and inflexible, regardless of the situational ethics that may be involved. Thus, the injunction "Thou shalt not kill" is primary in Western law and religion. Nevertheless, a state legislator, a governor, an attorney general, a judge, a jury, and an executioner who support, sign, endorse, sentence, enforce, and enact a death penalty for a capital crime may believe that in doing so, they are not violating their commitment to the First Commandment. Moreover, they all may assure themselves that they are, each in his or her respective roles, fulfilling an important purpose.

The concept of "meaningful purpose" might also vary according to an individual's perception of it. An activity that may seem trivial and shallow to some may offer significance and purpose to another. In certain cases, it may be that activity itself, devoid of conviction or import, can offer a meaning and an objective to an individual who would otherwise face the gloom and exasperation of inertia.

On the other hand, it may well be true that some individuals who feel no deep or abiding convictions may find their ambitions in life hollow and superficial. A writer, for example, may find little or no significance in completing a "hack" assignment merely for money. Indeed, the task, even though well remunerated, may present itself as pure drudgery. That same writer, though, might be willing and eager to spend hours upon hours creating a work whose themes have special and vital relevance to his or her life, but which no one is willing to buy.

The truth of this statement, then, varies with the situation to which it is applied, and the interpretation by which it is understood. In some circumstances, a committed belief endows an otherwise empty existence with profoundly significant goals. In other situations, genuine purpose can be found even in the absence of such conviction.

47.3 ESSAY EXERCISE III

Consider this statement:

Human nature ultimately overcomes tyrannical government.

Write a unified essay in which you perform the following tasks. Explain what you think the above statement means. Describe a specific situation in which human nature does not overcome tyrannical government. Discuss what you think determines whether human nature does or does not overcome tyrannical government.

Good Response:

The meaning of this statement is that regardless of the oppressive nature of any given governmental regime, the will, intelligence, and humanity of its subjects will ultimately succeed in overcoming it and installing a more representative form of rule. Human beings will not tolerate despotism forever, and eventually their resentment of and resistance to arbitrary and unreasonable limitations on their personal freedoms will lead them to oppose actively such unconscionable restrictions. As Robert Frost once wrote, "Something there is that doesn't love a wall, and wants it down."

Nevertheless, there may be some specific situations in which the idea expressed by this statement does not hold true. There are some societies that have never known anything other than autocratic rule. In these nations, whether by force of habit or lack of awareness of any other political tradition, the people have suffered through centuries of one form of dictatorship or another.

Witness Russia, for example. Prior to the establishment of a repressive Communist regime in the 1920s, that country suffered under generations of harsh, authoritarian rule by the czars. Even since the overthrow of the communists, Russian society has experienced great difficulty establishing a truly democratic system. Instead of representative rule through legislators elected by popular will, the country is apparently currently run by cartels of organized crime, corrupt military officials, and former party apparatchiks. Instead of rule by constitutional law, the system functions on the basis of terror, bribery, cultism, and personal whim. Tyranny by any other name will smell as rank.

Circumstances that determine whether the statement will hold true include the level of education of the people, the degree to which the people have access to a means of political control, and even, perhaps, the genetic makeup of the population. A citizenry with little or no education in history, political and social science, or philosophy, will have less basis upon which to formulate a popular movement against authority than one whose educational horizons are broad and diverse. Similarly, people who have no effective access either to military weapons, mass media outlets, or the secular or religious educational podiums, will have little ability to establish an effective political organization. It may also be true that the "human nature" of some humans is genetically different from that of other humans, and that part of the difference may be expressed in a predisposition to accept illegitimate authority or, conversely, in a willfulness to personal liberty and social freedom.

The more recent course of human history, by and large, and certainly in the western countries, has been one of evolution from societies run by minority, central authority, with little or no regard for individual rights, to systems in which the preservation and extension of individual freedom constitutes an important social priority. In societies where, whether by governmental edict, social tradition, or plain ignorance, the people have historically been denied open communication and interchange with the rest of the world, the human push toward liberty has been more easily constrained. However, wherever a citizenry has available to them the means of education and/or military clout, tyranny will not long be tolerated.

47.4 ESSAY EXERCISE IV

Consider this statement:

It is more difficult to relate to people one knows well than to those one knows casually.

Write a unified essay in which you perform the following tasks. Explain what you think the above statement means. Describe a specific situation in which it is easier to relate to people one knows well than to those one knows casually. Discuss what you think determines whether it is more difficult to relate to people one knows well than to those one knows casually.

Good Response:

This statement means that it is easier for a person to be open and honest with strangers than to be so with close friends. Indeed, we often keep our most guarded secrets from those who know us best. Conversely, the very fact of distance between two people can sometimes unlock the gates of intimacy.

There are specific situations in which this dictum might not apply. The circumstance of being arrested for an alleged crime represents one such situation. Confronted with the apparatus of the criminal justice system, an individual would probably relate more easily to a friend or family member than to a stranger. Thus, whereas an agent of the police or the district attorney's office might encounter only silence and suspicion from an accused suspect, a family member or trusted friend might be able to engage the individual in frank conversation. In a context where a person feels threatened and powerless, and must reach out to others for assistance, it is usually to those familiar and trusted, rather than to those unknown, that he or she will relate more readily.

In more everyday settings, however, when dealing with people we know well, numerous factors enter into our consideration and play much less of a role in our relations with casual acquaintances. For one thing, we know a lot more about our close friends than we do about casual acquaintances. Because we understand the issues that our friends are sensitive about or proud of, we might tailor our conversations and relations with them in the light of that understanding. With casual acquaintances, on the other hand, we might brazenly stumble around the conversational turf like bulls in a china shop, not realizing the value to the acquaintance's life of certain issues, or even what those issues might be.

By the same token, if we do unintentionally step on the toes of a close friend, we regret it more deeply than if we offend a casual acquaintance. The emotional stakes are higher when friends, rather than acquaintances, are involved. Even though close friends might be more willing than casual acquaintances to forgive an offense, we still feel the remorse more deeply if it's a friend we've wounded.

Nonetheless, and seemingly paradoxically, we might be more willing to open up to a casual acquaintance—such as a therapist we've met for the first time or a stranger at a party—than to a close friend or colleague from the office. With people we know well, there is often a tendency to project our best self forward, to hide our faults and minimize our weaknesses, so that in our everyday dealings, we will not feel at a disadvantage. In the company of people we know less well, in relation with whom we have little or nothing to lose, and whose opinions mean less to us than do those of our friends, we often feel more able to "let our hair down" and let it "all hang out."

The applicability of the statement, then, depends on the context in which it is considered. In extreme situations of threat or terror, we would probably feel more comfortable relating to people we know well. In other circumstances, though, under certain conditions, it might be easier to relate to casual acquaintances.

47.5 ESSAY EXERCISE V

Consider this statement:

No work constitutes art unless it appeals to some person other than its creator.

Write a unified essay in which you perform the following tasks. Explain what you think the above statement means. Describe a specific situation in which a work might constitute art even though it appeals only to its creator. Discuss what you think determines whether a creation can constitute art if it appeals to no one other than its creator.

Good Response:

This statement means that in order for any creative endeavor to be called art, it must, on some level, stimulate in a positive way the aesthetic senses of at least one person other than the one who created it. If someone writes a book, choreographs a dance, stages a play, or paints a portrait, and the finished product does not excite or tantalize or stir a single other human being, the author of the work has not produced art. By the same measure, even if a creative work engages or interests no more than one person other than its maker, it has, indeed, earned the name of art.

A specific situation to which this statement might not pertain would be a particular work created intentionally to repel the aesthetic senses of its audience. That is, if an artist conceived a project whose objective was to create a feeling of disgust or repulsion or apathy in the audience, and if, in the presentation of the work the artist successfully achieved that objective, then one might fairly say that the work in question was, indeed, art. In such a circumstance, the artist, by creation and/or performance of a purely artificial construct, would have stirred in the audience a genuine human emotion. Thus, even if the emotion generated in the audience was a wholly negative one, and even if the piece could not be said to have "appealed" to anyone, the artist, through the art, would have accomplished his or her artistic purpose.

Normally, one supposes, if a particular work does not appeal to anyone, then it will not serve as a vehicle for communication of its creator's perceptions, values, or vision. If a creative work refuses in this way to communicate to its audience, perhaps it cannot, justly, be called art. If a tree falls in the forest, and there's no one near to hear it, does it make a sound? If an artist, for example, intending to portray all the furious beauty and dazzling energy of life, puts brush to canvas, and if everyone who views the finished product can see only a muddy chaos of meaningless lines and senseless forms, then perhaps the painter has only filled the empty space with paint and has not made art. If there is absolutely no appeal to an audience, and there is absolutely no communication, then perhaps there is no art either.

Therefore, the statement's aptness depends on the context in which it is proposed. Certain works of art, whose very purpose might be to alienate or confuse or repel its audience, might achieve their objectives through the very act of negating their own aesthetic appeal. More generally, however, if a creative work finds no audience, and thus communicates nothing and entertains no one, perhaps it surrenders the right to the title of art.

47.6 ESSAY EXERCISE VI

Consider this statement:

Intelligence and skill are not nearly as valuable as stability and persistence.

Write a unified essay in which you perform the following tasks. Explain what you think the above statement means. Describe a specific situation in which intelligence and skill are more valuable than stability and persistence. Discuss what you think determines whether intelligence and skill are as valuable as stability and persistence.

Good Response:

This statement means that the traits of evenness of temperament and "stick-to-it-iveness" of habit are more important to a successful life than are brilliance of mind and technique. Like the famous fable of the tortoise and the hare, the slow and steady often appear more effective than the meteoric and inconsistent. As someone once said, "Inspiration is ninety-nine percent hard work."

This statement might not apply in the specific situation of someone who is a true genius, and whose endeavors are overly constrained in an educational and social system designed for the average. Albert Einstein, it is widely reported, failed his high school mathematics courses. The material was not too difficult for him to master, it was simply too boring. He preferred not to waste his time or intellectual energy on concepts he deemed elemental and tedious. Because he could not bring himself to squander his hours doing the simple algebra exercises or learning the trigonometry tables, he failed the course.

Nevertheless, later years proved his genius despite his high school transcripts. Would the world have been better off had Einstein not possessed the genius of intellect that led him to his revolutionary insights, and had he, instead, been an individual of ordinary mental ability and mathematical skill who diligently completed every high school homework assignment? There might be honest debate on that question, but surely his genius and ability are more valuable, in the general sense, than the more stable persistence, however admirable, of his classmates.

On the other hand, it must be acknowledged that a person equipped with all the intelligence and skill in the world will never accomplish anything until and unless he or she sets a goal and then sets out to pursue it. A very intelligent person might imagine a revolutionary design for, say, a spaceship; without the pluck and tenacity necessary to transform the imaginative act into a form that can be understood by engineers and technicians, the design will never be brought to fruition. A writer, blessed with insight and skill, can not even begin to express his or her vision and ideas if he or she is unwilling to sit down at the computer, or blank sheet of paper and put the words down for others to read.

It goes without saying that individuals of average intelligence and only moderate abilities make important contributions day in and day out, and they do so by virtue of steadiness of habit and perseverance of labor. The basketball player who plays twenty minutes every game, scoring ten points with five rebounds, can be counted on for a consistent, nightly contribution to the team effort. The superstar, conversely, who might possess sufficient skill to score fifty points on a given night, but whose unstable temperament causes him or her to lose control and be ejected from the game, might prove less valuable to the team's success in the long run.

The truth of the statement, therefore, greatly depends on the situation to which it is applied. Intelligence and skill count for a great deal and, in some cases, may be more important than steadiness and consistency. In many contexts, though, stability and persistence will prove to be the more valuable characteristics.

INDEX

circulation (heart), 597
citric acid cycle (Krebs cycle), 571
classical dominance, 702, 706
classifications of nature, 725
cleavage, 533
cleavage furrow, 515
closed system, 309
clycolysis, 567
cocci, 545
cochlea, 687
cochlear nerve, 687
coding strand, 473
co-dominance, 705-706
codon, 488
coenzymes, 564
cofactors, 564
collecting duct, 636
colligative property, 338
collisions, 116, 351
collisions in two dimensions, 118
colon, 618
column chromatography, 925
combined gas law, 354
combustion, 782
commensalism, 725-726
common bile duct, 617
compact bone, 619-620
competitive inhibition, 566
complete inversion of configuration, 804
compression, 204
COMT (catechol-O-methyl transferase), 674
concave mirror, 225
concentrated solution, 331
concentration, 418
concentration cell, 425
concomitant reduction, 413
condensing, 370
condensing formula, 374
conduction, 141
cones, 688
configurational diastereomers, 759, 765
conformation of mirror images, 227
conjugate acid-base pairs, 391
conjugation, 546
consensus sequences, 476
conservation of linear momentum, 115
conservation of mechanical energy, 106
conservative forces, 102
contact catalyst, 290
contact charge, 141
contractile, 605
contraction of heart, 605
control sequences, 485
converging lenses, 230

convex mirror, 225
coordinates, 18
core electrons, 244
core enzyme, 475
core of nucleic acid, 548
core shell, 244
cornea, 688
corona radiata, 528
corpus callosum, 677
corpus luteum, 654
cortisol, 650-651
cosine (cos), 22
coulomb, 147
Coulomb's forces, 147
Coulomb's law, 147
coupled processes, 576
coupling, 933
covalent bonds, 261
crests, 204
cretinism, 652
crista, 687
cristae, 445
critical angle, 224
critical point, 382
crossbridges, 623
crossing over, 515, 707
CSF cerebrospinal fluid, 677
current, 174
current (I), 415
curvilinear graphs, 18
cusps, 600
cycle, 200
cyclic amine, 874
cyclic anhydrides, 857
cystolic NADH, 579
Cytochrome Carrier System, 575
cytockeleton, 446
cytokinesis, 510
cytoplasm, 433
cytoplasmic division, 510
cytosine, 458

D

Dalton's law of partial pressures, 360
Darwin, Charles, 718
Darwinian Fitness, 718
daughter chromosome, 513
de Broglie hypothesis, 252
decarboxylation, 855
decibel (dB), 207
decomposition reaction, 276
defibrinated plasma, 608
degenerate, 500
degenerate orbitals, 247

superior vena cava, 599, 603
supersaturated solution, 331
suppresser cells, 611
surface tension, 594
surfactant, 594
surroundings (surr), 309
symbiosis, 725
sympathetic nervous system, 683
sympatric speciation, 721
syn addition, 790
synapse, 673
synapsis, 515
synaptic cleft, 673
synaptic terminals, 663
synaptic vesicles, 663
synaptonemal membrane, 515
synovial fluid, 621
synovial joints, 621
synthesis phase, 510
synthesis reaction, 275
system (sys), 309
systemic circulation, 598

T

T tubules, 626
tactile, 686
tactile receptors, 686
tail fiber, 548
tangent (tan), 22
target cells, 645
taste receptors, 686
TATA box, 485
taxonomic organization, 725
taxonomy, 725
telophase, 512
temperature, 309, 349, 418
template, 465
template recognition, 475
tendons, 621
tensile strain, 128
tensile stress, 128
tension, 72
terminals, 173
termination, 475
termination phase, 491, 495
terminator, 482
tertiary alcohol, 812
tertiary amines, 873
tertiary carbon atom, 779
tertiary structure, 892
tesla (T), 189
testcross, 704
testes, 522

testis, 657
testosterone, 657
tetrads, 515
tetrahedral molecule, 737
thalamus, 678
thermodynamics, 309
thermoreceptors, 686
thermoregulators, 598
thick filaments, 623
thin filaments, 623
thin lens equation, 227
thin lenses, 230
thin-layer chromatography, 924
third law of thermodynamics, 319
thoracic duct, 610
thorax, 589
threshold, 624, 666
thymine (T), 458
thymus, 610
thyroid, 651
thyroid-stimulating hormone (TSH), 658
thyroxine, 651
tight junctions, 443
tissues, 539
titration, 399
titration of a weak acid, 401
T-lymphocytes (T cells), 610-611
tolerant anaerobes, 556
Tollens reagent, 853
torque, 87
torr, 351
total internal reflection, 224
trachea, 591-592
traits, 700, 702
trajctory, 50
transcription, 473, 488-498
transcription bubble, 481
transcription factors, 486
transcription unit, 476-502
transduction, 546
transesterification, 864
transfer of energy, 104
transformation, 546
transformed cell, 546
transition metals, 251
transition state (ts), 286, 320
translation, 488, 498
translational equilibrium, 90
transmembrane proteins, 434
transuranium elements, 251
transverse waves, 199
tricarboxylic acid cycle, 571
tricarboxylic acids, 847
tricuspid valve, 600
triiodothyronine, 651

NOTES

NOTES

NOTES

NOTES

NOTES

NOTES

NOTES

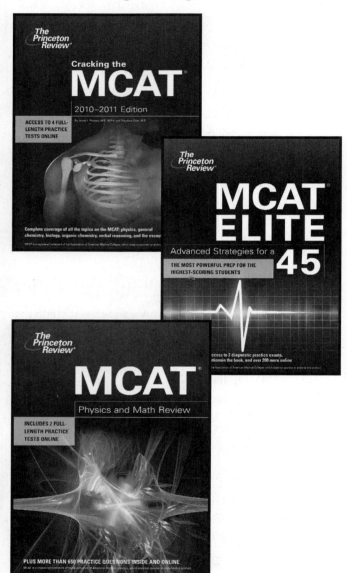

PHYSICS

KINEMATICS

Displacement (d) : The change in position that goes in a straight-line path from the initial position to the final; it is independent of the path taken (SI unit: m)

Distance: The length of the particular path

Average velocity: $v = \dfrac{\Delta d}{\Delta t}$ (SI units: m/s)

Average speed: $\dfrac{distance}{\Delta t}$

Acceleration: The rate of change of an object's velocity; it is a vector quantity if acceleration is constant (uniform): $a = \dfrac{\Delta v}{\Delta t}$ (SI units: m/s²)

Linear motion

$v = v_0 + at$

$\quad = v_0 t + \dfrac{1}{2} at^2$

$v^2 = v_0^2 + 2a\mathbf{d}$

$v_{avg} = \left(\dfrac{v_0 + v}{2}\right)$

$\mathbf{d} = vt = \left(\dfrac{v_0 + v}{2}\right)t$

- When solving for time, there will be two values for t; when the projectile is initially launched and when it impacts the ground.
- To find max height, remember that the vertical velocity of the projectile is 0 at the highest point of the path.

Projectile motion

- vertical component of velocity: $v\sin\theta$
- horizontal component of velocity: $v\cos\theta$
- v_x is constant $(d_x = v_x t)$

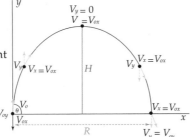

WORK, ENERGY, AND MOMENTUM

Work: For a constant force F acting on an object that moves through a displacement d, the work is $W = Fd\cos\theta$ where θ is the angle between F and d. (For a force perpendicular to the displacement, $W = 0$). [SI unit: Joule = N·m]

Power: The rate at which work is performed, and is found by:

$$P = \dfrac{W}{t} \text{ (SI unit: Watt = J/s)}$$
$$\text{or } P = Fv\cos\theta$$

Kinetic energy: The energy associated with moving objects. It is found by: $KE = \dfrac{1}{2}mv^2$ (SI unit: J)

Potential energy: The energy associated with a body's position. Gravitational potential energy of an object is due to the force of gravity acting on it, and it is expressed as: $PE = mgh$ (SI unit: J)

Total mechanic energy: $E = PE + KE$
Mechanic energy is conserved when the sum of kinetic and potential energies remains constant.

Work-energy theorem: Relates the work performed by all forces acting on a body in a particular time interval to the change in kinetic energy at that time. The expression is: $W_{TOTAL} = \Delta KE$

Conservation of energy: When there are not any nonconservative forces (such as friction) acting on a system, the total mechanical energy remains constant: $\Delta E = \Delta KE + \Delta PE = 0$

Work, Power, and Energy are scalars.

Momentum: A vector quantity. It's given by: $\mathbf{p} = mv$

Impulse: A vector quantity. It's given by: $J = F_{av}\cdot\Delta t$

Impulse-momentum theorem: $J = \Delta p$

Conservation of momentum: When there are no net external forces acting on a system of objects (e.g., during a collision), total momentum is conserved: $\mathbf{P}_{TOTAL\,before} = \mathbf{P}_{TOTAL\,after}$

Elastic collision: A collision where KE is conserved.

Inelastic collision: A collision where KE is not conserved.

Perfectly inelastic collision: A collision where the objects stick and move together.

NEWTON'S LAWS

Newton's first law (law of inertia): A body in a state of motion or at rest will remain in that state unless acted upon by a net force.

Newton's second law: When a net force is applied to a body of mass m, the body will be accelerated in the same direction as the force applied to the mass. This is expressed by the formula $\mathbf{F}_{net} = m\mathbf{a}$ (SI unit: Newton (N) = kg·m/s²)

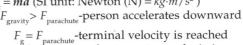

$F_{gravity} > F_{parachute}$ -person accelerates downward

$F_g = F_{parachute}$ -terminal velocity is reached (person travels at constant velocity)

Newton's third law: If a body A exerts a force on body B, then B will exert a force back onto A that is equal in magnitude, but opposite in direction. This can be expressed as $\mathbf{F}_{b\,on\,a} = -\mathbf{F}_{a\,on\,b}$

Newton's law of gravitation: All forms of matter experience an attractive force to other forms of matter in the universe. The magnitude of force is represented by: $F_g = \dfrac{Gm_1 m_2}{r^2}$.

- **Mass (m):** a scalar quantity that measures a body's inertia (SI unit: kg)
- **Weight (W):** the vector quantity that measures a body's gravitational attraction to the earth ($W = mg$) (SI unit: N)

FRICTIONAL FORCES

Static friction (f_s) is the force that must be overcome to set an object in motion. It has the formula: $0 \le f_s \le \mu_s N$

Kinetic friction (fk) opposes the motion of objects moving relative to each other. It has the formula: $f_k = \mu_k N$

Uniform circular motion:

F_c is the force needed to keep an object moving in a circular motion.

$$a_c = \frac{v^2}{r}$$

$$F_c = \frac{mv^2}{r}$$

CENTER OF MASS AND TORQUE

Center of mass: the location where a system of objects would balance: $x_{cm} = \dfrac{m_1 x_1 + m_2 x_2 + \ldots}{m_1 + m_2 + \ldots}$

Torque: for a force acting on an object at a distance r from its pivot point, $\tau = rF\sin\theta$, where θ is the angle between F and r. (SI units: $N \cdot m$)

Alternate formula: $\tau = \ell F$ where ℓ is the lever arm.

Static equilibrium: For objects in static equilibrium, $F_{net} = 0$ and $\tau_{net} = 0$

FLUIDS

Density $(\rho) = \dfrac{m}{V}$ where V is volume [SI units: kg/m³]

Specific gravity $= \dfrac{\rho_{substance}}{\rho_{water}}$ [no units]

$$\rho_{water} = 10^3 \, kg/m^3$$

Weight (W) $= \rho g V$

Pressure: a scalar quantity defined as force per unit area:

$$P = \frac{F}{A} \quad \text{[SI Units: Pascal = N/m²]}$$

- **Standard atmospheric pressure:** $P_o \approx 10^5 \, Pa$
- **Absolute pressure** in a static fluid due to gravity a distance d below the surface is given by:

  $P = P_0 + \rho g d$, where P_o is the pressure at the surface.
- **Gauge pressure:** $p_{gauge} = \rho g d$

Buoyant force: the upward force exerted by a fluid on object totally or partially submerged.

$$F_b = \rho_{fluid} \, g V_{submerged}$$

Floating objects: the fraction of a floating object that is submerged in a fluid is equal to $\dfrac{\rho_{object}}{\rho_{fluid}}$

Flow rate: $f = Av$ [SI unit: m³/s]

Continuity equation: $A_1 V_1 = A_2 V_2$

Bernoulli's equation: $P + \dfrac{1}{2}\rho v^2 + \rho g h =$

Pascal's principle A change in the pressure applied to an enclosed fluid is transmitted undiminished to every portion of the fluid and to the walls of the containing vessel.

$$\Delta P = \frac{F_1}{A_1} = \frac{F_2}{A_2} \quad \text{and} \quad W = F_1 d_1 = F_2 d_2$$

ELECTROSTATICS

Coulomb's law

$$F = \frac{kq_1 q_2}{r^2}$$

[SI units: Newtons]

Opposite charges attract; like charges repel.

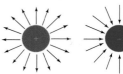

Electric field

$$E = \frac{F}{q} = \frac{kq}{r^2}$$

[SI units: N/C or V/m]

field lines

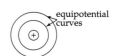

- A positive point charge will move in the same direction as the electric field vector; a negative charge will move in the opposite direction.

Potential difference (voltage)

Voltage $(V) = \Delta\phi$

[SI units: Volt = J/C]

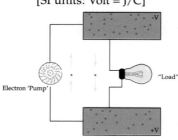

Electron 'Pump'

"Load"

- When two oppositely charged parallel plates are separated by a distance d, a nearly uniform electric field is created, and a potential difference exists between the plates, given by $V = Ed$.

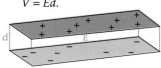

Electric potential energy (PE)

The electric potential energy stored by two point charges:

$$PE = \frac{kq_1 q_2}{r}$$

The work done by the electrostatic force is equal to $-\Delta PE$.

The work done against the electrostatic force is equal to ΔPE.

Electric potential (ϕ)

$$\phi = \frac{PE}{q} = \frac{kq}{r} \quad \text{[SI unit: V = J/c]}$$

equipotential curves

Work done by the electrostatic force $= -q\Delta\phi$

Work done against the electrostatic force $= +q\Delta\phi$

DC AND AC CIRCUITS

DIRECT CURRENT

Current: the flow of electric charge. Current is given by:

$$I = \frac{\Delta q}{\Delta t} \text{ [SI units: Amp (A) = C/s]}$$

(The direction of current is the direction positive charge would flow, or from high to low potential.)

Ohm's law and resistance

$V = IR$ (can be applied to entire circuit or individual resistors)

Resistance: opposition to the flow of charge. $R = \frac{\rho L}{A}$ (Resistance increases with increasing temperatures with most conductors.)

[SI Units: Ohm (Ω)]

CIRCUIT LAWS

Kirchoff's laws:

1. At any junction within a circuit, the sum of current flowing into that point must equal the current leaving.
2. The sum of voltage sources equals the sum of voltage drops around a closed circuit loop.

Alternating current

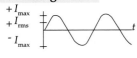

$$V_{ms} = \frac{V_{max}}{\sqrt{2}}$$

$$I_{ms} = \frac{V_{max}}{\sqrt{2}}$$

$$P_{avg} = I_{rms}V_{rms}$$

Series circuits

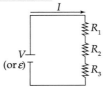

$$R_{eq} = R_1 + R_2 + R_3 + ...$$
$$I = I_1 = I_2 = I_3 = ...$$
$$V = V_1 + V_2 + V_3 + ...$$

Parallel circuits

$1/R_{eq} = 1/R_1 + 1/R_2 + 1/R_3$
$I = I_1 + I_2 + I_3 + ...$
$V = V_1 = V_2 = V_3 = ...$

Power dissipated by resistors

$$P = IV = \frac{V^2}{R} = I^2R$$

(Can be applied to entire circuit or individual resistors)

CAPACITORS

Capacitance: the ability to store charge per unit voltage. It is given by: $C = \frac{Q}{V}$. [SI unit: Farad(F) = c/V]

Energy stored by capacitors: $P_E = \frac{1}{2}QV = \frac{1}{2}CV^2 = \frac{1}{2}Q^2/C$

Adding a dielectric always increases the capacitance.

Capacitors in parallel add
$C_{eq} = C_1 + C_2 + C_3$

$$C = \kappa\frac{\varepsilon_0 A}{d}$$

Capacitors in series add as reciprocals.

$$\frac{1}{C_{eq}} = \frac{1}{C_1} + \frac{1}{C_2} + \frac{1}{C_3} ...$$

MAGNETISM

The magnetic field (B): Magnetic fields are created by permanent magnets and moving charges.

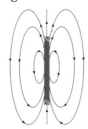

Magnetic field lines depict the direction a compass needle would point if placed in the field from the North Pole to the South Pole.

[SI Units = Tesla (T) $=N\cdot s/m\cdot c$]

Force on a moving charge

A charge moving in a magnetic field experiences a force exerted on it.

$F_B = qvB\sin\theta$ where θ is the angle between **V** and **B**

The magnetic force is zero when charges move parallel or antiparallel to the magnetic field.

Right-hand rule for finding direction of force

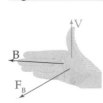

Note that the right-hand rule gives the direction of magnetic force on a positive charge. The direction of force on a negative charge is simply the opposite direction of the force on a positive charge (or you may use a left-hand rule).

The magnetic force never does work and never changes the speed of a particle.

A charged particle moving perpendicular to a uniform magnetic field will travel in a circle: $qVB = \frac{mv^2}{r}$

Force on a current-carrying wire

$F_B = ILB\sin\theta$ where θ is the angle between the current and **B**.

Right-hand rule for direction of B field produced by current-carrying wires

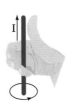

- Right thumb points in the direction of current flow.
- Wrap your fingers around the wire as if you were grabbing it with your palm.
- The direction that the fingers curl is the direction of the magnetic field.

Special cases

Center of Wire Loop

$$B = \frac{\mu_0 i}{2r}$$

Around a Straight Wire

$$B = \frac{\mu_0 i}{2\pi r}$$

PHYSICS

PERIODIC MOTION

Period: T is the time it takes to complete one cycle.

Frequency: $f = \dfrac{1}{T}$ [SI unit: Hertz (Hz)=1/s]

Angular frequency: $w = 2\pi f = \dfrac{2\pi}{T}$ [SI unit: radian]

Simple harmonic motion is periodic motion where the period (and frequency) are independent of amplitude.

Mass spring: $F_s = -kx, PE = \dfrac{1}{2}kx^2, f = \dfrac{1}{2}\pi\sqrt{\dfrac{k}{m}}$

Pendulum: only simple harmonic for small angles, $f = \dfrac{1}{2}\pi\sqrt{\dfrac{g}{L}}$

at equilibrium	at amplitude
V is max	$V = 0$
$a = 0$	a is max
KE is max	$KE = 0$
$PE = 0$	PE is max

WAVES

Wavelength: λ is the distance between corresponding points on consecutive pulses.

$v = f\lambda$ (1) V is the same for all waves (of the same angle) in the same medium; (2) f is constant when a wave passes into a new medium.

Waves in a string: $v = \sqrt{\dfrac{tension}{mass / length}}$

Wave superposition

(add amplitudes)

in phase — constructive interference

(substract amplitudes)

= destructive interference

180° out of phase

RESONANCE

String attached at each end: $\lambda_n = \dfrac{2L}{n}(n = 1,2,...)$

Open pipe: $\lambda_n = \dfrac{2L}{n}(n = 1,2,...)$ **Closed pipe:** $\lambda_n = \dfrac{4L}{n}(1,3,5...)$

SOUND

Sound propagates through a deformable medium by the oscillation of particles along the direction of the wave's motion.

Intensity (I) $= P/A$ [SI units: W/m²]

Sound level $= 10 \log (l/l_o)$ [unit = decibel = dB]

Adding 10 dB corresponds to multiplying the intensity by 10. Subtracting 10 dB corresponds to dividing the intensity by 10.

Beats occur when two waves that have slightly different frequencies are superimposed: $f_{beat} = |f_1 - f_2|$

Doppler effect

When a source and a detector move relative to one another, the perceived frequency of the sound received differs from the actual frequency emitted even though the source velocity and frequency is unchanged.

$$f' = f\dfrac{(v \pm v_D)}{(v \pm v_S)}$$

LIGHT AND OPTICS

Light is an Electromagnetic (EM) Wave. EM Waves do not need a medium.

Speed of light in a vacuum: $c = 3 \times 10^8$ m/s

Diffraction: Light bends around corners and spreads out when passing through a small slit.

Refraction

$$n = \dfrac{c}{v} \quad \text{(speed of light} = 3 \times 10^8 \text{ m/s)}$$

Snell's law: $n_1 \sin\theta_1 = n_2 \sin\theta_2$ when $n_2 > n_1$, light bends toward normal, when $n_2 > n_1$, light bends away from normal.

Spherical Mirrors and Lenses

Mirror / lens equation: $\dfrac{1}{o} + \dfrac{1}{c} = \dfrac{1}{f}$

- o is always positive.
- i is positive for real images and negative for virtual images.

Magnification equation: $m = \dfrac{-i}{o}$

- m is positive for upright images and negative for inverted images.
- All real images are inverted; all virtual images are upright.

Spherical mirrors

- Real images are formed on the same side of the object.
- Virtual images are formed on the side opposite the object.

Concave mirrors

- $f = r/2$ (positive)
- If $0 > f$, a real image is formed.
- If $0 < f$, a virtual image is formed.

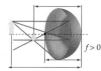

$f > 0$

Convex mirrors

- $f = -r/2$ (negative)
- Only virtual images are formed.

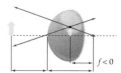

$f < 0$

Thin spherical lenses

- Real images are formed on the side opposite the object.
- Virtual images are formed on the same side as the object.

Converging (convex) lenses

- f is positive.
- If $0 > f$, a real image is formed.
- If $0 < f$, a virtual image is formed.

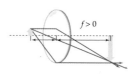

$f > 0$

Diverging (concave) lenses

- f is negative.
- Only virtual images are formed.

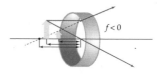

$f < 0$

GENERAL CHEMISTRY

ATOMIC STRUCTURE

Atomic weight: The weight in grams of one mole (mol) of a given element and is expressed in terms of g/mol.

$$\underset{\substack{\text{atomic number}\\(3\text{ of protons})}}{\overset{\substack{\text{mass number}\\(\text{protons + neutrons})}}{{}_Z^A}} X \text{—— element}$$

A **mole** is a unit used to count particles and is represented by **Avogadro's number**: 6.022×10^{23} particles

$$\text{Moles} = \frac{\text{grams}}{\text{atomic or molecular weight}}$$

Isotopes: For a given element, multiple species of atoms with the same number of protons (same atomic number) but different numbers of neutrons (different mass numbers).

Planck's quantum theory: Energy emitted as electromagnetic radiation from matter exists in discrete bundles called quanta.

The Bohr atom: Electrons reside in discreet energy levels around the nucleus. Electrons can absorb energy and move to higher levels of energy or shed energy as photons and settle to lower energy states.

Quantum numbers:

#	Character	Symbol	Value
1st	Shell	n	N
2nd	Subshell	l	From zero to n-1
3rd	Orbital	m_ℓ	Between 1 and -1
4th	Spin	m_s	$\frac{1}{2}$ or $\frac{1}{2}$

Principal quantum number (n): The larger the integer value of n, the higher the energy level and radius of the electron's orbit. The maximum number of electrons in energy level n is $2n^2$.

Azimuthal quantum number (l) refers to subshells, or sublevels. The four subshells corresponding to l = 0, 1, 2, and 3 are known as s, p, d and f, respectively. The maximum number of electrons that can exist within a subshell is given by the equation $\frac{4}{+2}$.

Magnetic quantum number (m_ℓ): This specifies the particular orbital within a subshell where an electron is highly likely to be found at a given point in time.

Spin quantum number (m_s): The spin of a particle is its intrinsic angular momentum and is characteristic of a particle, like its charge.

ELECTRONIC CONFIGURATION

Electrons are filled in order, from left to right, along the periodic table. The shell in which electrons fall is dictated by their block, and their row. For s and p electrons, n = # of row, for d electrons, n = row # - 1, and for f electrons n = row # - 2.

Hund's rule: Within a given subshell, orbitals are filled with that there are a maximum number of half-filled orbitals with parallel spins.

Valence electrons: Electrons of an atom that are in its outer energy shell or that are available for bonding.

KINETICS AND EQUILIBRIUM

Experimental determination of rate law: The values of k, x, and y in the rate law equation (rate = $k\,[A]^x\,[B]^y$) must be determined experimentally for a given reaction at a given temperature. The rate is usually measured as a function of the initial concentrations of the reactants, A and B.

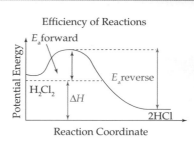

Efficiency of Reactions

The following factors affect reaction rates: reactant concentrations, temperature, medium, catalysts.

Catalysts are unique substances that increase reaction rate without being consumed; they do this by lowering the activation energy.

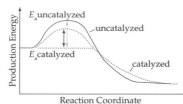

The rate determining step (RDS) is always the slowest step in a multistep reaction, and can be used to determine the rate law. If the RDS is $A + 2B \rightarrow C$, then rate = $k[A][B]^2$.

Law of mass action $a\,A + b\,B \rightleftharpoons c\,C + d\,D$

$$K_c = \frac{[C]^c [D]^d}{[A]^a [B]^b}$$

K_c is the equilibrium constant. (c stands for concentration.)

Properties of the Equilibrium Constant
Pure solids/liquids don't appear in expression.

- If K_{eq} is characteristic of a given system at a given temperature.
- If $K_{eq} \gg 1$, an equilibrium mixture of reactants and products will contain very little of the reactants compared to the products.
- If $K_{eq} \ll 1$, an equilibrium mixture of reactants and products will contain very little of the products compared to the reactants.

- If K_{eq} is close to 1, an equilibrium mixture of products and reactants will contain approximately equal amounts of the two.

Reaction quotient (Q): Once a reaction commences, the standard state conditions no longer hold. For the reaction,

$$a\,A + b\,B \rightleftharpoons c\,C + d\,D \qquad Q = \frac{[C]^c[D]^d}{[A]^a[B]^b}$$

A + B $\rightleftharpoons$ C + heat	
Will Shift to the Right	**Will Shift to the Left**
1. if more A or B added	1. if more C added
2. if C taken away	2. if A or B taken away
3. if pressure applied or volume reduced (assuming A, B, and C are gases)	3. if pressure reduced or volume increased (assuming A, B, and C are gases)
4. if temperature reduced	4. if temperature increased

$$\Delta G° = -RT\ln K_c$$

BONDING AND CHEMICAL INTERACTIONS

Formal charges

$$\text{Formal Charge} = \text{Valence electrons} - \frac{1}{2}N_{bonding} - N_{nonbonding}$$

INTERMOLECULAR FORCES

Hydrogen bonding: The partial positive charge of the hydrogen atom interacts with the partial negative charge located on the electronegative atoms (F, O, N) of nearby molecules.

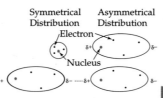

Dipole-dipole interactions: Polar molecules orient themselves such that the positive region of one molecule is close to the negative region of another molecule.

Dispersion forces: The bonding electrons in covalent bonds may appear to be equally shared between two atoms, but at any point in time they will be located randomly throughout the orbital. This permits unequal sharing of electrons, causing rapid polarization and counterpolarization of the electron clouds of neighboring molecules, inducing the formation of more dipoles.

Symmetrical Distribution   Asymmetrical Distribution
Electron
Nucleus

ACIDS AND BASES

Arrhenius definition: An acid is a species that produces H^+ (a proton) in an aqueous solution, and a base is a species that produces OH^- (a hydrogen ion).

Bronsted-Lowry definition: An acid is a species that donates protons, while a base is a species that accepts protons.

Lewis definition: An acid is an electron-pair acceptor, and a base is an electron-pair donor.

Properties of Acids and Bases

$$pH = -\log[H^+]$$
$$pH = -\log[OH^-]$$
$$H_2O(l) \rightleftharpoons H^+(aq) + OH^-(aq)$$
$$K_w = [H^+][OH^-] = 10^{-14}$$
$$pH + pOH = 14$$

Weak Acids and Bases

$$HA(aq) + H_2O(l) \rightleftharpoons H_3O^+(aq) + A^-(aq)$$
$$K_a = \frac{[H_3O^+][A^-]}{[HA]}$$
$$K_b = \frac{[B^+][OH^-]}{[BOH]}$$

Henderson-Hasselbalch equation is used to estimate the pH of a solution in the buffer region where the concentrations of the species and its conjugate are present in approximately equal concentrations.

$$pH = pK_a + \log\frac{[\text{conjugate base}]}{[\text{weak acid}]}$$

$$pOH = pK_b + \log\frac{[\text{conjugate acid}]}{[\text{weak base}]}$$

Neutralization: Acids and bases may react with each other, forming a salt and (often, but not always) water in a neutralization reaction.

$$HA + BOH \longrightarrow BA + H_2O$$

Titration and Buffers

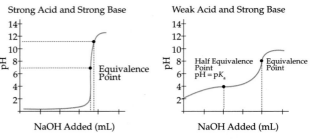

Titration is a procedure used to determine the molarity of an acid or base by reacting a known volume of solution of an unknown concentration with a known volume of a solution of a known concentration.

THE GAS PHASE

1 atm = 760 mm Hg = 760 torr

Do not confuse STP with standard conditions—the two standards involve different temperatures and are used for different purposes. STP (0°C or 273 K) is generally used for gas law calculations; standard conditions (25°C or 298 K) is used when measuring standard enthalpy, entropy, Gibbs free energy, and voltage.

Boyle's law

$$PV = k \text{ or } P_1V_1 = P_2V_2$$

Law of Charles and Gay-Lussac

$$\frac{V}{T} = k \text{ or } \frac{V_1}{T_1} = \frac{V_2}{T_2}$$

Avogadro's principle

$$\frac{n}{V} = k \quad \text{or} \quad \frac{n_1}{V_1} = \frac{n_2}{V_2}$$

Ideal gas law

$$PV = nRT$$

SOLUTIONS

UNITS OF CONCENTRATION

Percent composition by mass: $= \dfrac{\text{Mass of solute}}{\text{Mass of solution}} \times 100 \ (\%)$

Mole fraction: $\dfrac{\text{\# of mol of compound}}{\text{total \# of moles in system}}$

Molarity: $\dfrac{\text{\# of mol of solute}}{\text{liter of solution}}$

Molality: $\dfrac{\text{\# of mol of solute}}{\text{kg of solvent}}$

Normality: $\dfrac{\text{\# of gram equivalent weights of solute}}{\text{liter of solution}}$

PHASES AND PHASE CHANGES

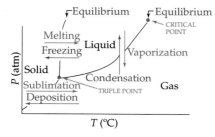

Colligative properties: These are physical properties derived solely from the number of particles present, not the nature of those particles. These properties are usually associated with dilute solutions.

Freezing point depression $\Delta T_f = K_f im$

Boiling point elevation $\Delta T_b = K_b im$

Osmotic pressure $\Pi = IMRT$

Van 't Hoff factor (i): the number of particles a given substance will form in solution. For binary salts (e.g., NaCl) $i = 2$.

Vapor-pressure lowering (Raoult's law) $P_A = X_A P^\circ_A \ ; \ P_B = X_B P^\circ_B$

Solutions that obey Raoult's law are called ideal solutions.

GRAHAM'S LAW OF DIFFUSION AND EFFUSION
Diffusion occurs when gas molecules diffuse through a mixture.

Effusion is the flow of gas particles under pressure from one compartment to another through a small opening. Both diffusion and effusion have the same formula.

$$\frac{r_1}{r_2} = \left(\frac{M_{w2}}{M_{w1}}\right)^{\frac{1}{2}}$$

REDOX REACTIONS AND ELECTROCHEMISTRY

Oxidation: loss of electrons

Reduction: gain of electrons

Oxidizing agent: causes another atom to undergo oxidation, and is itself reduced.

Reducing agent: causes another atom to be reduced, and is itself oxidized.

Galvanic cell: Electrons flow from an oxidation reaction at the anode to a reduction reaction at the cathode via spontaneous reactions at each respective electrode. The sum of the oxidation potential at the anodes and the reduction potential at the cathode is positive.

Electrolytic cell: Electrons flow from an oxidation reaction at the anode to a reduction reaction at the cathode, but electron flow must be forced by an external power source. The sum of the oxidation potential at the anode and the reduction potential at the cathode is negative.

THERMOCHEMISTRY

Constant-volume and constant-pressure calorimetry: used to indicate conditions under which the heat changes are measured.

$q = mc\Delta T$, where q is the heat absorbed or released in a given process, m is the mass, c is the specific heat, and ΔT is the change in temperature.

States and state functions are described by the macroscopic properties of the system. These are properties whose magnitude depends only on the initial and final states of the system, and not on the path of the change.

Enthalpy (H) is used to express heat changes at constant pressure.

Standard heat of formation (ΔH°_f): the enthalpy change that would occur if one mole of a compound were formed directly from its elements in their standard states.

Standard heat of reaction (ΔH°_{rxn}): the hypothetical enthalpy change that would occur if the reaction were carried out under standard conditions.

$\Delta H^\circ_{rxn} = $ (sum of ΔH°_{rxn} of products) – (sum of ΔH°_{rxn} of reactants)

Hess's law states that enthalpies of reactions are additive.

The reverse of any reaction has an enthalpy of the same magnitude as that of the forward reaction, but its sign is opposite.

Bond dissociation energy: an average of the energy required to break a particular type of bond in one mole of gaseous molecules.

Entropy (S): the measure of the disorder, or randomness, of a system.

$$\Delta S \ \text{universe} = \Delta S \ \text{system} + \Delta S \ \text{surroundings}$$

Gibbs free energy (G) combines the two factors which affect the spontaneity of a reaction—changes in enthalpy, ΔH , and changes in entropy, ΔS .

$$\Delta G = \Delta H - T\Delta S$$

If ΔG is negative, then rxn is spontaneous

If ΔG is positive, then rxn is not spontaneous

If ΔG is zero, the system is in a state of equilibrium; thus $\Delta G = 0$ and $\Delta H = T\Delta S$

GENERAL CHEMISTRY

ΔH	ΔS	Outcome
−	+	Spontaneous at all temps
+	−	Nonspontaneous at all temps
+	+	Spontaneous only at high temps
−	−	Spontaneous only at low temps

NUCLEAR CHEMISTRY

Unstable nuclei decay, becoming new stable nuclei through the emission of a number of different particles (α, β, γ, etc). In any nuclear chemistry reaction the total mass and total atomic number in the reactants must equal the total mass and atomic number of the products.

Summary of Radioactive Decay		
$\boxed{N\downarrow \ Z\downarrow}$	Alpha Decay	Decreases the number of neutrons and protons in large nucleus Substracts 4 from the mass number Substracts 2 from the atomic number $$^{A}_{Z}X \xrightarrow{\alpha} {}^{A-4}_{Z-2}Y + {}^{4}_{2}\alpha$$
$\boxed{N\downarrow \ Z\uparrow}$	Beta⁻ Decay	Decreases the number of neutrons, increases the number of protons Adds 1 to the atomic number $$^{A}_{Z}X \xrightarrow{\beta^-} {}^{A}_{Z+1}Y + {}^{0}_{-1}e^-$$
$\boxed{N\uparrow \ Z\downarrow}$	Beta⁺ Decay	Increases the number of neutrons, decreases the number of protons Substracts 1 from the atomic number $$^{A}_{Z}X \xrightarrow{\beta^+} {}^{A}_{Z-1}Y + {}^{0}_{+1}e^+$$
$\boxed{N\uparrow \ Z\downarrow}$	Electron Capture	Increases the number of neutrons, decreases the number of protons Substracts 1 from the atomic number $$^{A}_{Z}X + {}^{0}_{+1}e^- \xrightarrow{EC} {}^{A}_{Z-1}Y$$
	Gamma Decay	Brings an excited nucleus to a lower energy state Doesn't change mass number or atomic number $$^{A}_{Z}X^* \xrightarrow{\gamma} {}^{A}_{Z}X + \gamma$$

Half life: the amount of time it takes a sample of radioactive material to decay to half its original mass.

MOLECULAR GEOMETRY AND SHAPE

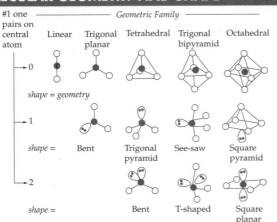

ATOMIC AND NUCLEAR PHENOMENA

BLACKBODY RADIATION
A **blackbody** is an object that absorbs all incident electromagnetic radiation upon it and emits energy that is characteristic to the system itself.

Wien's displacement law: $\lambda_{peak}T = $ constant

Stefan-Boltzmann law: $E_{total} = \sigma T^4$

Photoelectric effect

$$E = hf = \frac{hc}{\lambda}$$
$$K = hf - W$$

Box: K is the maximum kinetic energy of ejected electron; W is the minimum energy required to eject an electron.

NUCLEAR BINDING ENERGY
Mass defect: the difference between the sum of the masses of nucleons in the nucleus and the mass of the nucleus. The mass defect results from the conversion of matter to energy, embodied by $E=mc^2$. This energy is the **binding energy** that holds nucleons within the nucleus.

EXPONENTIAL DECAY

Half life

$$n = n_0 e^{-\lambda t}$$

Alpha decay

$$^{238}_{92}U \rightarrow {}^{234}_{90}Th + {}^{4}_{2}He$$

Beta minus decay

$$^{137}_{55}Cs \rightarrow {}^{137}_{56}Ba + {}^{0}_{-1}e^- + v_-$$

Beta plus decay

$$^{22}_{11}Cs \rightarrow {}^{22}_{10}Ne + {}^{0}_{-1}e^+ + v$$

THERMODYNAMICS

Specific heat

$Q = mc\Delta T$
- can only be used to find Q when the object does not change phase
- $Q > 0$ means heat is gained, $Q < 0$ Means heat is lost [SI unit: Joules or calories]

Heat of transformation: the quantity of heat required to change the **phase** of 1 kg of a substance.

$Q = mL$ (phase changes are isothermal processes)

System work

- When the piston expands, work is done by the system ($W > 0$).
- When the piston compresses the gas, work is done on the system ($W < 0$).
- The area under a P vs. V curve is the amount of work done in a system.

First law of thermodynamics: $\Delta U = Q - W$

Process	First Law Becomes
Constant Volume ($W = 0$)	$\Delta U = Q$
Closed Cycle ($\Delta U = 0$)	$Q = W$

Second law of thermodynamics: In any thermodynamic process that moves from one state of equilibrium to another, the entropy of the system and environment together will either increase or remain unchanged.

BIOLOGY

THE CELL

The plasma membrane
- Phospholipid bilayer with cholesterol and embedded proteins
- Exterior hydrophilic phosphoric acid region
- Interior hydrophobic fatty acid region

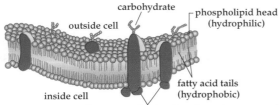

carbohydrate — phospholipid head (hydrophilic)

outside cell

fatty acid tails (hydrophobic)

inside cell

transmembrane proteins (carrier, channel or receptor)

ORGANELLES
- **Ribosome:** protein synthesis via translation
- **Nucleus:** houses the genome in chromosomes
- **Mitochondria:** cell respiration and energy production
- **Rough ER and Golgi:** protein trafficking and modification
- **Lysosome:** autophagy and degradation
- **Peroxisome:** degradation and detoxification

HOMEOSTASIS

HORMONAL REGULATION
Aldosterone
- stimulates Na^+ reabsorption and K^+ secretion, increasing water reabsorption, blood volume and blood pressure
- steroid hormone secreted from adrenal cortex
- is regulated by renin-angiotensin system

ADH
- increases collecting duct's permeability to water to increase water reabsorption
- peptide hormone secreted from posterior pituitary when [solutes] is high in the blood

The liver's roles in homeostasis
1. gluconeogenesis
2. processing of nitrogenous wastes (urea)
3. detoxification of wastes/chemicals/drugs
4. storage of iron and vitamin B12
5. synthesis of bile and blood proteins
6. beta-oxidation of fatty acids to ketones
7. interconversion of carbs, fat, and amino acids

ENZYMES AND CELL RESPIRATION

REGULATION

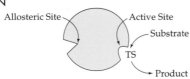

Allosteric Site

Active Site

Substrate

TS

Product

- **Allosteric:** binding of an effector molecule at allosteric site to enhance or inhibit enzyme function
- **Feedback inhibition:** end product inhibits an initial enzyme pathway
- **Reversible inhibition:** competitive inhibitors bind to active site; noncompetitive inhibitors to the allosteric site

GLUCOSE CATABOLISM
Glycolysis occurs in the cell cytoplasm:

$$C_6H_{12}O_6 + 2ADP + 2P_i + 2NAD^+ \rightarrow 2Pyruvate + 2ATP + 2NADH + 2H^+ + 2H_2O.$$

Fermentation occurs in anaerobic conditions. Pyruvate is converted into lactic acid (in muscle) or ethanol (in yeast).

Respiration occurs in aerobic conditions
- **Pyruvate decarboxylation:** Pyruvate converted to Acetyl-CoA in the mitochondrial matrix.
- **Citric acid cycle:** Acetyl-CoA enters, reduced electron carriers (NADH, $FADH_2$) and CO_2 exit.
- **Electron transport chain:** NADH and $FADH_2$ are oxidized, electrons are passed from carrier to carrier, a proton gradient is generated across the inner mitochondrial membrane
- **Oxidative phosphorylation:** Proton gradient provides energy for ATP synthase to phosphorylate ADP into ATP.

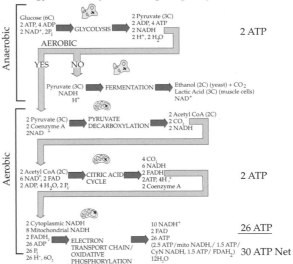

MUSCULOSKELETAL SYSTEM

Sarcomere
- Contractile unit of the fibers in a skeletal muscle
- Contains thin actin and thick myosin filaments

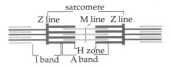

sarcomere

Z line   M line   Z line

I band   A band   H zone

CONTRACTION
- ACh release from a neuron leads to action potential
- Ca^{2+} in the sarcoplasm increases
- Actin released from troponin/tropomyosin regulation
- Myosin and actin interact and cause muscle contraction
- Sarcomeres, H zone and I band shorten

BIOLOGY

Bone formation and remodelling
- Osteoblasts: builds bone
- Osteoclasts: breaks down bone

REPRODUCTION

Cell division

- G_1: cell growth, organelle and protein synthesis, metabolism
- S: DNA replication
- G_2: same as G_1
- M: the cell divides in two
- Mitosis = PMAT
- Meiosis = PMAT $\times$ 2

SEXUAL REPRODUCTION

Meiosis I
- Replicated homologous chromosomes (each has two chromatids) pair up to form a tetrad in prophase I.
- Crossing over leads to genetic recombination I prophase I.
- Recombined homologous chromosomes are separated into haploid daughter cells.

Meiosis II
- Similar to mitosis.
- Recombined sister chromatids are separated into haploid daughter cells that have a single copy of one set of chromosomes, 23 in humans.

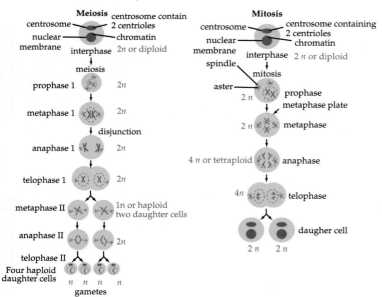

In humans
- Spermatogenesis in males (making sperm in the seminiferous tubules of the testes) and oogenesis (making ova in the ovaries) in females are examples of meiosis.

FOUR STAGES OF EARLY DEVELOPMENT

Cleavage: mitotic divisions of the zygote to form the morula

Implantation: blastocyst (trophoblast and inner cell mass) implants into the uterus wall

Gastrulation: ectoderm, endoderm, and mesoderm form

Neurulation: germ layers develop a nervous system

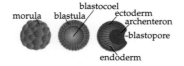

CIRCULATION

Blood typing: Antigens are located on the surface of red blood cells.

Blood Type	RBC antigen	Antibodies	Donates to:	Receives from:
A	A	Anti-B	A, AB	A, O
B	B	Anti-A	B, AB	B, O
AB	A, B	None	AB only	All
O	None	Anti-A, B	All	O

Blood cells with Rh factor are Rh+ and produce no antibody. Rh- lack antigen and produce an antibody.

IMMUNE SYSTEM

The body distinguishes between "self" and "nonself."

HUMORAL IMMUNITY (SPECIFIC DEFENSE)

B lymphocytes

Memory cells
Remember antigen, speed up secondary response

Plasma cells
Make and release antibodies (IgG, IgA, IgM, IgD, IgE), which induce antigen phagocytosis

- **Active immunity:** Antibodies are produced during an immune response.
- **Passive immunity:** Antibodies produced by one organism are transferred to another organism.

CELL-MEDIATED IMMUNITY

T lymphocytes

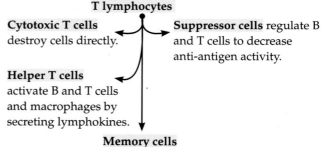

Cytotoxic T cells destroy cells directly.

Suppressor cells regulate B and T cells to decrease anti-antigen activity.

Helper T cells activate B and T cells and macrophages by secreting lymphokines.

Memory cells

Nonspecific immune response includes skin, passages lined with cilia, macrophages, acidic stomach and vagina, inflammatory response, and interferons (proteins that help prevent the spread of a virus).

Lymphatic system
- Lymph vessels meet at the thoracic duct in the upper chest and neck, draining into veins of the cardiovascular system.
- Vessels carry **lymph** (excess interstitial fluid) and **lacteals** collect fats by absorbing chylomicrons in the small intestine.
- **Lymph nodes** are swellings along the vessels with phagocytic cells (leukocytes) that remove foreign particles from lymph.

ENDOCRINE SYSTEM

Direct hormones directly stimulate organs; tropic hormones stimulate other glands. Mechanisms of hormone action: **Peptides (P)** act via binding a receptor on the PM and inducing second messengers. **Steroids (S)** diffuse across the plasma membrane and act via hormone/receptor binding to DNA. **Amino acid derivatives (aa)** may do either.

Hormone	Source	Action	Action
Follicle-stimulating (FSH)	Anterior Pituitary	P	Stimulates follicle maturation; spermatogenesis
Luteinizing (LH)	Anterior Pituitary	P	Stimulates ovulation; testosterone synthesis
Adrenocorticotropic (ACTH)	Anterior Pituitary	P	Stimulates adrenal cortex to make and secrete glucocorticoids
Thyroid-stimulating (TSH)	Anterior Pituitary	P	Stimulates the thyroid to produce hormones
Prolactin	Anterior Pituitary	P	Stimulates milk production and secretion
Growth hormone	Anterior Pituitary	P	Stimulates bone and muscle growth/lipolysis
Oxytocin	Hypothalamus; stored in posterior pituitary	P	Stimulates uterine contractions during labor, milk secretion during lactation
Vasopressin (ADH)	Hypothalamus; stored in posterior pituitary	P	Stimulates water reabsorption in kidneys
Thyroid hormones (T4 ,T3)	Thyroid	aa	Stimulate metabolic activity
Calcitonin	Thyroid	P	Decreases blood calcium level
Parathyroid hormone	Parathyroid	P	Increases the blood calcium level
Cortisol	Adrenal cortex	S	Increase blood glucose level and decrease protein synthesis
Aldosterone	Adrenal cortex	S	Increase sodium reabsorption and potassium secretion in kidneys
Epinephrine	Adrenal medulla	aa	Increases blood glucose level and heart rate
Glucagon	Pancreas	P	Stimulates conversion of glycogen to glucose in the liver, increases blood glucose
Insulin	Pancreas	P	Lowers blood glucose, increases glycogen stores
Somatostatin	Pancreas	P	Suppresses secretion of glucagons and insulin
Testosterone	Testes	S	Maintains male secondary sexual characteristics
Estrogen	Ovary/Placenta	S	Maintains female secondary sex characteristics
Progesterone	Ovary/Placenta	S	Promotes growth/maintenance of endometrium

DIGESTION

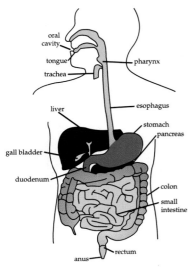

Carbohydrate Digestion

Enzyme	Site of Production	Site of Function	Hydrolysis Reaction
Salivary amylase (ptyalin)	Salivary glands	Mouth	Starch → maltose
Pancreatic amylase	Pancrease	Small Intestine	Starch → maltose
Maltase	Intestinal glands	Small Intestine	Maltose → 2 glucoses
Sucrase	Intestinal glands	Small Intestine	Sucrose → glucose, fructose
Lactase	Intestinal glands	Small Intestine	Lactose → glucose, galactose

Protein Digestion

Enzyme	Production Site	Function Site	Function
Pepsin	Gastric glands (chief cells)	Stomach	Hydrolyzes specific peptide bonds
Trypsin	Pancreas	Small Intestine	Hydrolyzes specific peptide bonds, activates other zymogen proteases
Chymotrypsin	Pancreas	Small Intestine	Hydrolyzes specific peptide bonds
Carboxypeptidase	Pancreas	Small Intestine	Hydrolyzes terminal peptide bond at carboxyl
Aminopeptidase	Intestinal glands	Small Intestine	Hydrolyzes terminal peptide bond at amino
Dipeptidases	Intestinal glands	Small Intestine	Hydrolyzes pairs of amino acids
Enterokinase	Intestinal glands	Small Intestine	Convets trypsinogen to trypsin

Nucleic acid

- Basic unit: nucleotide (sugar, nitrogenous base, phosphate).
- Sugar in DNA is deoxyribose; sugar in RNA is ribose.
- 2 types of bases: double-ringed purines (adenine, guanine) and single-ringed pyrimidines (cytosine, thymine, uracil).
- DNA double helix; antiparallel strands joined by hydrogen bonding between base pairs (A=T, G ≡ C).
- RNA is usually single-stranded: A pairs with U, not T.

Transcript Regulation in Prokaryotes

Operon: An operator and promoter control transcription of one or many structural genes.

- Operator: binding site of repressor protein
- Promoter: binding site of RNA polymerase
- Generates polycistronic transcripts that are translated by polyribosomes
- Inducible systems need an inducer for transcription to occur; common in catabolic processes
- Repressive systems need a corepressor to inhibit transcription; common in biosynthetic pathways

MUTATIONS

Point: One nucleotide is substituted by another; they are silent if the amino acid sequence doesn't change.

Frameshift: Insertions or deletions shift reading frame; protein can be unaffected (common effect if insert or delete a multiple of 3 nucleotides), nonfunctional, a different length or is not formed.

Viruses

- Acellular structures of double or single-stranded DNA or RNA in a protein coat
- Lytic cycle: virus kills the host
- Lysogenic cycle: virus enters host genome

DNA Replication

- **Semiconservative:** Each new helix has an intact strand from the parent helix and a newly synthesized strand.

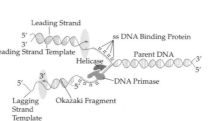

- Key enzymes are helicase (unwinds the DNA), primase (lays down RNA primer), and DNA polymerases (sythesize DNA).

EUKARYOTIC PROTEIN SYNTHESIS

- **Transcription:** RNA polymerase synthesizes hnRNA using DNA, "antisense strand" as a template.
- **Post-transcriptional processing:** Introns are cut out of hnRNA, exons spliced to form mRNA; mRNA is 5' and 3' capped and exported out of the nucleus.

- **Translation** occurs on ribosomes in the cytoplasm.

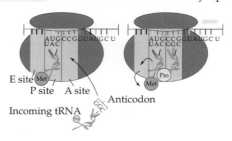

Post-translational modifications: (i.e., disulfide bonds) made before the polypeptide becomes a functional protein.

Law of independent assortment: Alleles of unlinked genes assort independently in meiosis.

- If both parents are *Rr*, the alleles separate to give a genotypic ratio of 1:2:1 and a phenotypic ration of 3:1.
- For two traits: *AbBb* parents will produce *AB*, *Ab*, *aB*, and *ab* gametes.
- The phenotypic ratio for an *AaBb* × *AaBb* cross is 9:3:3:1.

Statistical calculations

- The probability of producing a genotype that requires multiple events to occur equals the *product* of the probability of each event.
- The probability of producing a genotype that can be the result of multiple events equals the *sum* of each probability.

Genetic mapping

- Crossing over during meiosis I can unlink genes (Prophase I).
- Genes are most likely unlinked when far apart.
- One map unit is 1% recombinant frequency.

Given recombination frequencies

X and Y: 8%

X and Z: 12%

Y and Z: 4%

INHERITED DISORDERS IN PEDIGREES

- **Autosomal recessive:** skips generations
- **Autosomal dominant:** appears every generation
- **X-linked (sex-linked):** no male-to-male transmission, and more males affected; can be recessive (red/green colorblindness or hemophilia) or dominant.

ORGANIC CHEMISTRY

NOMENCLATURE

- Find the longest carbon chain containing the principle functional group (highest priority groups are generally more oxidized).
- Number the carbon chain so that the principle functional group gets the lowest number (1).
- Proceed to number the chain so that the lowest set of numbers is obtained for the substituents.
- Name the substituents and assign each a number.

Complete the name by listing substituents in alphabetical order, place commas between numbers and dashes between numbers and words.

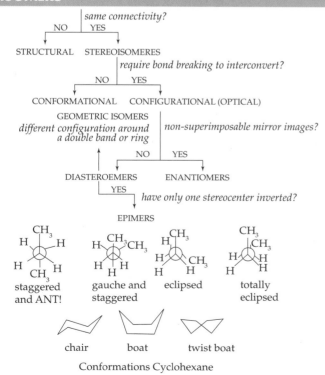

Functional Group	Suffix
Carboxylic Acid	-oic acid
Ester	-oate
Acyl halide	-oyl halide
Amide	-amide
Nitrile/ Cyanide	-nitrile
Aldehyde	-al
Alkene	-ene

Functional Group	Suffix
Ketone	-one
Thiol	-thiol
Alcohol	-ol
Amine	-amine
Imine	-imine
Ether	-ether
Alkyne	-yne

R/S CONFIGURATION

For chiral centers, assign priority to each substituent:
- Highest priority to group with highest atomic number, then atomic weight.
- Go to first point of difference on chains.
- Count multiple bonds as higher priority.
- With #4 group in back of molecule a clockwise connection of groups $1 \to 2 \to 3$ is R; a counterclockwise connection is S.

Amines & Nitrogen Containing Compounds

Amide   Imine   Enamine

$RC \equiv N$
Nitrile

BONDING

Bond order	Single	Double	Triple
Bond type	Sigma	Sigma	Sigma
		pi	2 pi
Hybridization	sp^3	sp^2	sp
Angles	109.5°	120°	180°
Example	C-C	C=C	C ≡ C

ISOMERS

same connectivity?
NO   YES

STRUCTURAL   STEREOISOMERES

require bond breaking to interconvert?
NO   YES

CONFORMATIONAL   CONFIGURATIONAL (OPTICAL)

GEOMETRIC ISOMERS
different configuration around a double band or ring

non-superimposable mirror images?
NO   YES

DIASTEROEMERS   ENANTIOMERS
YES

have only one stereocenter inverted?

EPIMERS

staggered and ANT!   gauche and staggered   eclipsed   totally eclipsed

chair   boat   twist boat

Conformations Cyclohexane

STABILIZATION

Induction: electron deficient group
Radicals and carbocations are more stable when substituted.

$$\oplus CH_3 < CH_3\overset{\oplus}{C}H_2 < CH_3\overset{\oplus}{C}HCH_3 < CH_3 - \overset{\oplus}{\underset{CH_3}{\overset{CH_3}{C}}}$$

Electron rich groups (carbanions) are more stable when less substituted, or when adjacent to electron withdrawing groups.

$$\ominus CH_3 > CH_3\overset{\ominus}{C}H_2 > CH_3\overset{\ominus}{C}HCH_3 > CH_3 - \overset{\ominus}{\underset{CH_3}{\overset{CH_3}{C}}}$$

$$CF_3\overset{\ominus}{C}H_2 > CH_3\overset{\ominus}{C}H_2$$

Resonance: Compounds can be stabilized through delocalization of π electrons and charge.

More resonance structures generally leads to more stability.

Charge must be adjacent to π bond for resonance to occur.

(No resonance allowed)

ORGANIC CHEMISTRY

REACTIVITY

Leaving groups (weak bases best) $I^- > Br^- > Cl^- > F^-$

Nucleophilicity and basicity

$$CH_3^- > NH_2^- > RO^- > HO^- > RCO_2^- > ROH > H_2O$$

Nucleophicity size $I^- > Br^- > Cl^-$

ALKANES

REACTIONS
Free radical halogenation

- initiation
- propagation
- termination

Combustion

$$C_3H_8 + 5O_2 \rightarrow 3CO_2 + 4H_2O + heat$$

ALKYL HALIDES
Synthesis

tosyl chloride

REACTIONS
Substitutions

S_N1	S_N2
2 steps, rearrangements possible	1 step, backside attack
3° > 2° > 1° > methyl	Methyl > 1° > 2° > 3°
Racemic products	Optically active and inverted products
Rate = $k[RX]$	Rate = $k[Nu][RX]$
Strong nucleophile not required	Favored with strong nucleophile
Favored in polar protic solvents	Favored in polar aprotic solvents

Eliminations

E1	E2
2 steps, rearrangements possible	1 step, antiperiplanar H and LG
3° > 2° > 1°	3° > 2° > 1°
Zaitser (most substituted) product forms; trans > cis	Stereochemistry of double bond determined by starting conformation
Rate = k [substrate]	Rate = k [substrate][base]
Favored with heat and weak base	Favored with heat and strong base; small base gives most substituted DB; bulky base gives least substituted DB

ALKENES

Electrophilic addition of HX (Markovnikov)

Free radical addition (anti-Markovnikov)

most stable radical

Electrophilic addition of X$_2$

Anti-addition

Electrophilic addition of H$_2$O (Markovnikov)

Hydroboration (anti-Markovnikov, *syn* orientation)

Catalytic reduction

Oxidation with KMnO$_4$

Oxidation with O$_3$

ALKYNES

Reduction with Lindlar's catalyst or Na in liquid ammonia

cis-2-butene

trans-2-butene

ALCOHOLS

- Higher boiling points than alkanes
- Weakly acidic hydroxyl hydrogen

Synthesis

- Addition of water to double bonds
- S_N1 and S_N2 reactions
- Reduction of carboxylic acids, aldehydes, ketones and esters
  - Aldehydes and ketones with $NaBH_4$
  - Esters and carboxylic acids with $LiAlH_4$

REACTIONS

E1 dehydration reactions in strongly acidic solutions

Hoffman Product

Zaitsev Product

Oxidation

- PCC takes a primary alcohol to an aldehyde.

- CrO_3, $KMnO_4$ and dichromate salts will convert secondary alcohols and ketones and primary alcohols to carboxylic acids.

- Tertiary alcohols cannot be oxidized without breaking a carbon to carbon bond.

ALDEHYDES AND KETONES

The dipole moment of carbonyl compounds causes an elevation of boiling point, but not as high as alcohols since there is no hydrogen bonding.

Synthesis

- Oxidation of primary or secondary alcohols
- Ozonolysis of alkenes

Nucleophilic addition to a cart

Commonly used $Nu^- = RMgBr$, ROH, RNH_2

When $Nu^- = H^-$, this reaction is a reduction.

Aldol condensation

An **aldehyde** acts both as nucleophile (enolate) and electrophile (keto form).

Reactions of enolates (Michael additions)

Oxidation and reduction

CARBOXYLIC ACIDS

Carboxylic acids have pK_a's of around 5 due to resonance stabilization of the conjugate base. Electronegative atoms increase acidity with inductive effects. Boiling point is higher than alcohols because of the ability to form two hydrogen bonds.

Synthesis

Oxidation of primary alcohols with $KMnO_4$

Organometallic reagents with CO_2 (Grignard)

Reactions

Formation of soap by reacting carboxylic acids with NaOH; arrange in micelles

nonpolar tail   polar head

Reduction to alcohols

CARBOXYLIC ACID DERIVATIVES

All derivatives go through additional-elimination mechanisms when they are interconverted.

All derivatives can be synthesized from an appropriate nucleophile and a more reactive derivative.

Relative reactivity of derivatives

ORGANIC CHEMISTRY

Amides Amine + acid chloride, anhydride, or ester

Esters

Alcohol + acid chloride or anhydride

Synthesis via condensation of carboxylic acids and alcohols (acid catalyzed)

Anhydride

Carboxylate + acid halide

Synthesis via reaction of carboxylic acid with an acid chloride

Acid halide can only be synthesized from acid directly.

$$RCOOH + SOCl_2 \longrightarrow$$

Acid halide formation

$$+ SOCl_2 \longrightarrow$$

AMINO ACIDS, PEPTIDES, AND PROTEINS

Amino acids have four substituents: amine group, carboxyl group, hydrogen, and R group. Amino acids are **amphoteric**, meaning they can act as either acids or bases and often take the form of **zwitterions** (dipolar ions).

amino acid   zwitterion

PROTEIN STRUCTURE
Primary: sequence of amino acids

Secondary: α-helix, β-pleated sheet

Tertiary: hydrophobic/hydrophilic interactions, disulfide bridges

Quaternary: arrangement of polypeptides

Henderson-Hasselbalch equation

$$pH = pK_a + \log [\text{conj. base}] / [\text{acid}]$$

SUGARS

CHO
—OH
CH_2OH
(D) Sugar
OH on Right

CHO
HO—H
CH_2OH
(L) Sugar
OH on Left

Furanose ring = 5 atoms

Pyranose ring = 6 atoms

α- anomer   β- anomer

OH group down   OH group up

LAB TECHNIQUES

Extractions: separates based on solubility.
- NH_2 extracted with HCl
- COOH extracted with $NaHCO_3$
- PhOH extracted with NaOH

Chromatography separates based on polarity.

High polarity = low R_f values

Low polarity = high R_f values

Gas chromatography separates based on boiling point.

High boiling point comes off column late

Low boiling point comes off column early

Distillation separates based on boiling point.

Simple-solvents with very different bps

Fractional-solvents with similar bps

Spectroscopy: IR

Functional group	Wave number
C = O	1720 cm⁻¹
C = C	1650 cm⁻¹
O-H	3200-3600 cm⁻¹
C≡C, C≡N	2100-2260 cm⁻¹

'H NMR–spectrum tells four things about structure.

1. # of nonequivalent Hs = # signals
2. # of Hs in each signal = integration
3. # of nonequivalent neighboring Hs = splitting pattern

   (follows $n + 1$ rule where n = # neighboring Hs)

4. chemical environment of Hs = chemical shift

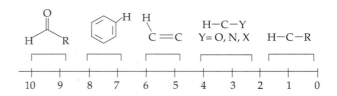